PENGUIN CLASSICS

GRUNDRISSE

KARL MARX was born in Trier in 1818 of a German-Jewish family converted to Christianity. As a student in Bonn and Berlin he was influenced by Hegel's dialectic, but he later reacted against idealist philosophy and began to develop his theory of historical materialism. He related the state of society to its economic foundations and mode of production, and recommended armed revolution on the part of the proletariat. In Paris in 1844 Marx met Friedrich Engels, with whom he formed a life-long partnership. Together they prepared the *Manifesto of the Communist Party* (1848) as a statement of the Communist League's policy. In 1848 Marx returned to Germany and took an active part in the unsuccessful democratic revolution. The following year he arrived in England as a refugee and lived in London until his death in 1883. Helped financially by Engels, Marx and his family nevertheless lived in great poverty. After years of research (mostly carried out in the British Museum), he published in 1867 the first volume of his great work, *Capital*. From 1864 to 1872 Marx played a leading role in the International Working Men's Association, and his last years saw the development of the first mass workers' parties founded on avowedly Marxist principles. Besides the two posthumous volumes of *Capital* compiled by Engels, Karl Marx's other writings include *The German Ideology, The Poverty of Philosophy, The Civil War in France, Grundrisse: Foundations of the Critique of Political Economy, The Revolutions of 1848, Surveys from Exile, The First International and After* and *Theories of Surplus-Value.*

KARL MARX

Grundrisse

Foundations of the
Critique of Political Economy
(Rough Draft)

Translated with a Foreword
by Martin Nicolaus

Penguin Books
in association with *New Left Review*

PENGUIN BOOKS

Published by the Penguin Group
Penguin Books Ltd, 27 Wrights Lane, London W8 5TZ, England
Penguin Books USA Inc., 375 Hudson Street, New York, New York 10014, USA
Penguin Books Australia Ltd, Ringwood, Victoria, Australia
Penguin Books Canada Ltd, 10 Alcorn Avenue, Toronto, Ontario, Canada M4V 3B2
Penguin Books (NZ) Ltd, 182–190 Wairau Road, Auckland 10, New Zealand

Penguin Books Ltd, Registered Offices: Harmondsworth, Middlesex, England

New Left Review, 7 Carlisle Street, London W1
Grundrisse der Kritik der Politischen Ökonomie (*Rohentwurf*) first published 1939
This translation published in Pelican Books 1973
Reprinted in Penguin Books 1993
10 9 8 7 6 5 4 3

Printed in Great Britain by Antony Rowe Ltd, Chippenham, Wiltshire
Set in Monotype Times

Contents

Foreword

This is a series of seven notebooks rough-drafted by Marx, chiefly for purposes of self-clarification, during the winter of 1857–8. The manuscript became lost in circumstances still unknown and was first effectively published, in the German original, in 1953.[1] Among the many of Marx's works which first appeared in print in the twentieth century, the *Grundrisse* represents unquestionably the most significant new development, comparable in importance only to the *Theories of Surplus Value* and the *Economic-Philosophical Manuscripts of 1844* ('Paris Manuscripts'). Marx considered these workbooks to contain the first scientific elaboration of the theoretical foundations of communism. Besides their great biographical and historical value, they add much new material, and stand as the only outline of Marx's full political-economic project. The manuscripts display the key elements in Marx's development and overthrow of the Hegelian philosophy. They cast a fresh light on the inner logic of *Capital*, and are a sourcebook of inestimable value for the study of Marx's method of inquiry. The *Grundrisse* challenges and puts to the test every serious interpretation of Marx yet conceived.

1. A limited edition was published by Foreign Language Publishers in Moscow in two volumes, 1939 and 1941 respectively, under the editorship of the Marx–Engels–Lenin Institute, Moscow. The first volume contained the Introduction and the seven notebooks (hereafter MELI) translated here. The second added fragments from Marx's 1851 notebooks of excerpts from Ricardo, the fragment 'Bastiat and Carey' (also included in this translation), and miscellaneous related material; also extensive annotations and sources. A photo-offset reprint of the two volumes bound in one, minus illustrations and facsimiles, was issued by Dietz Verlag, Berlin (E.), in 1953, and is the basis of the present translation. It is referred to hereafter as *Grundrisse* (MELI). Rosdolsky states that only three or four copies of the 1939–41 edition ever reached 'the western world'. (R. Rosdolsky, *Zur Entstehungsgeschichte des Marxschen Kapital. Der Rohentwurf des Kapital, 1857–8*, 2 vols., Frankfurt and Vienna, 1968, p. 7n.)

I

In Marx's life, the *Grundrisse* stands midway between the *Manifesto of the Communist Party* (1848) and the publication of the first volume of *Capital* in 1867. It was the onset of the economic crisis of 1857 which stimulated Marx to sum up and set on paper the economic studies of a decade and a half, but this was only the trigger. The force originated in the revolutions of 1848–50, or more precisely in the defeat of these revolutions.

In a series of insurrections and civil wars in virtually every nation-state, kingdom and principality of continental Europe, the 'spectre' of communism, to which the *Manifesto* gave speech, made its first appearance as a cohesive body on the political stage, was everywhere bloodily crushed, and became a ghostly presence again, bottled up in fragile little magazines edited and read by refugees in foreign-speaking ghettoes of London and New York. As the clearest and most determined voices of the 'left wing' of the democratic-radical forces, and as leading spokesmen of the most advanced workers' organization, the League of Communists, Marx and Engels were notorious to the governments of Prussia, France and Belgium. Officially expelled and banished, with arrest warrants out for them, Marx and Engels moved to London and, for the first couple of years, like the whole German exile community, kept their coats on, awaiting the break that would signal a new revolution. As the forces of reaction began to settle in for a long reign, however, it was the exiles who broke first. After the defeat of the workers' insurrection in Paris, in July 1850, Marx and Engels advanced the thesis that revolution had become impossible in the immediately foreseeable future, that a rapid return could not be counted on, and that the tasks of the League of Communists must be reset accordingly to give first priority to the work of education, study and development of revolutionary theory. It fell like cold water on the flames of exile fantasy. Although Marx and Engels won the League's London central committee over to their position by a slim majority – and thus remained its *de jure* London representatives – the great majority of the exiles stood against them, even the workers. 'I want at most twelve people in our circle, as few as possible,' Marx stated, and, under taunts of being counter-revolutionaries, anti-proletarians and impractical literati – taunts which they later repaid with compound interest – Marx and Engels withdrew from organizational and practical political activity; Engels to Manchester to earn a living, Marx to the British Museum to begin his economic studies anew from the beginning.[2] There they remained for more than a decade. Throughout the period of reaction which fastened itself upon Europe in the 1850s, the German public heard next to nothing from Marx or Engels. The League dissolved in 1852.

It was Marx's second withdrawal from the political stage into his study. But while in the first period (1843-7) Marx's concerns had been various – to learn to speak competently on questions of material interest, to become familiar with the French theories of socialism and communism, to battle a 'storm of doubts' regarding the Hegelian philosophy – now a single focus is apparent from the beginning.[3] Marx's and Engels's summary and analysis of the character of the 1848 revolutions, and the causes of its defeat, bring out the nature of this aim. Two major classes composed the revolutionary camp, the working class and the lower-middle class or petite bourgeoisie. Owing to the political inexperience of the working class and the illusions and limitations of its leaders, the latter class had held the initiative and leadership of the revolutionary movement as a whole. This was the outstanding cause of defeat. 'In each of the provisional governments which were formed in all the rebellious regions,' wrote Engels, who had fought in the civil war in southern Germany, 'the majority was representative of this part of the people, and its performance may therefore rightly be taken as the measure of what the German petty bourgeoisie is capable of – as we shall see, of nothing else but to ruin every movement which confides itself into its hands.'[4] It was a lesson paid for in blood. Worse was the political decay that flourished after the working-class uprising was crushed by the army. A new politics arose, calling itself 'Social-Democracy', in which '... the social demands of the proletariat had their revolutionary point broken off and were given a democratic bent, the democratic appeals of the petty bourgeoisie [were] stripped of their merely political form, their socialist point brought out'.[5] The weaker it became, the more did the entire small bourgeoisie take to calling itself 'socialist' and 'red', and to stamping its every demand, every measure, speech and banality with this imprint,

2. *Marx-Engels Werke* (hereafter *MEW*) VIII, pp. 591, 598-9.
3. See *Preface to the Critique of Political Economy, MEW* XIII, p. 8.
4. *Revolution and Counterrevolution in Germany, MEW* VIII, p. 99.
5. *Eighteenth Brumaire, MEW* VIII, p. 141.

whose nub and essence was that the workers '. . . should remain wage workers as before, only the democratic petty bourgeois wish better wages and a more secure existence for them, and hope to achieve this by having the state supply jobs for part of them, and through welfare measures; in short, they hope to bribe the workers with more or less hidden doles and, by making their condition momentarily bearable, to break their revolutionary power.'[6] The defeat of this influence, next time, and the elevation of the working class to the position of leadership of the revolutionary camp as a whole, next time, was the overriding aim of Marx's studies.

Marx chose as his principal theoretical antagonists in the *Grundrisse* two figures who stood as giants in their respective arenas. These were David Ricardo, the British political economist, and Pierre Joseph Proudhon, a Frenchman and self-proclaimed socialist.

Ricardo had been dead for some thirty-five years already, but his repute had risen despite the numerous errors his critics were able to prove against him. He had been the able teacher and theoretical champion of the British manufacturers and industrialists during their troubled adolescence in the first decades of the century, when this class had been hard-pressed by the economic and political power of the British landed aristocracy. The immediate issue had been the price of grain. The landlords combined to drive the price higher, and to prevent the importation of cheap grain from abroad; and as grain was the staple of the working-class diet, in the form of bread, its high price necessitated a rise of wages. This in turn, Ricardo argued, inexorably depressed the industrialist's profit, to the advantage of the landowners' rent. A struggle of several decades was required before the industrial capitalists succeeded, in 1843–4, in breaking the landlord's control of Parliament and repealing the prohibitive duties against the import of grain. This was a posthumous victory for Ricardo, who had died a wealthy stockbroker in 1823; and the ensuing upswing in the affairs of British industry carried the name of Ricardo, as its prophet, to the rank of pre-eminence among British economists.

Proudhon (1809–65) was nearly a decade Marx's senior, and had been amongst his political mentors in the mid-forties. The son of a cooper and himself a worker, Proudhon was entirely self-educated; he starved in garrets to buy books. In 1845, Marx had

6. *MEW* VII, p. 247.

described a work of Proudhon's as 'a scientific manifesto of the French proletariat, [which] has therefore a wholly different significance from the literary artifice of one or another Critical Critic',[7] and he always retained a certain respect for the man's genuine personal devotion to the workers' cause, despite Proudhon's associations with, and support of, political charlatans and careerists of every description. Yet, already a decade before beginning the *Grundrisse*, Marx had reached the conclusion that Proudhon's *ideas*, however striking their formulation ('Property is theft', for example), represented on balance merely a cosmetic alteration of unscientific, non-revolutionary notions, which were liable, as such, to become a drag upon the political advance of the class. Marx had begun his critique of Proudhon's theories in *The Poverty of Philosophy* (1847); but the onset of the 1848 revolutions, from which Proudhon emerged as the head of a growing movement, had left Marx no leisure to bring this critique to a conclusion. At the time of the *Grundrisse*, Proudhon was undoubtedly the leading spkesman of socialism in all France, if not the world.

During the fifties, Marx lived in misery. His only source of income during the decade was the writing of articles for the New York *Tribune* and for the *New American Cyclopedia*. He was paid worse than a penny-a-liner, and haphazardly, always late. The family lived in one of the poorest districts of London. Creditors and landlord's agents hounded the door. Some days Marx could not go out because his shoes and overcoat were at the pawnbrokers'. Constant illness, his family's or his own, compounded the cycle of debt. 'Never has anyone written about "money in general" amidst such total lack of money in particular,' he once wrote.[8] It was Engels, diverting funds under a pretext from his family's cotton firm, who pulled the Marx family through, time after time.

The course of Marx's economic studies from 1850 to 1857 is still incompletely known. Between September 1850 and August 1853, he filled twenty-four notebooks with reading notes on the subjects of commodities, money, capital, wage labour, landed property, international trade, the history of technology and inventions, credit, population theory, the economic history of

7. *Holy Family, MEW* II, p. 43.

8. Letter, *MEW* XXIX, p. 385. He adds, 'Most writers on this subject were profoundly at peace with the subject of their researches.'

states, the history of customs and manners, literature, the world market, colonialism and other matters. During March–April 1851, he wrote a manuscript entitled 'Das vollendete Geldsystem' ('The Money System as a Whole'), of unknown size, which is extant but has not been published.[9] His notebooks of excerpts from Ricardo (April–May 1851) show that he had pinpointed the source of surplus value in the production process, but had not yet worked out the ramifications for the theory of value and wages.[10] He was distracted from economic study during much of 1853 by a trial of members of the League of Communists taking place in Germany; he wrote a pamphlet attacking the prosecution, which cost him his German publisher for his projected work on economics.[11] From about November 1854 to January 1855, he drafted a manuscript on the different theories of the rate of exchange, which is described as 'extraordinarily rich in content'; bearing the title 'Geldwesen, Kreditwesen, Krisen' ('Money System, Credit System, Crises'), it also, like the 1851 text on the money system, is extant but has not been published.[12] During 1855 and much of 1856, he took time from his economic studies to collaborate on Ernest Jones's Chartist *People's Paper*; and much journalism and domestic misery made other inroads. With the onset of the economic crisis, he began working late into the night to pull together his economic studies. In the last week of August 1857 he began the present 'Introduction', finishing about mid-September. Sometime in October he began the first notebook; by mid-March the next year the whole work was finished except for a few pages added at the end of May.

9. Described as 'unpublished manuscript of *c.* March–April 1851', in Index of Sources, *Grundrisse* (MELI), p. 1073.
10. For example, the following phrases: 'The surplus does not consist in this exchange, although it realizes itself in it. It consists of the fact that for this product, which costs 20 work days, the worker gets the product of only 10 work days etc. As the productive power of labour increases, the value of wages decreases proportionately.' This is beyond Ricardo's theory of profit, but still inside his theory of value and of wages. In *Grundrisse* (MELI), supplementary materials, p. 829.
11. Letter, *MEW* VIII, p. 560.
12. Described as 'unpublished manuscript from end of 1854/early 1855' in Index of Sources, *Grundrisse* (MELI), p. 1073. An editorial footnote on p. 1044, ibid., further describes this text as 'extraordinarily rich in content, its factual material critically sifted and evaluated', and estimates November 1854–January 1855 as dates. Evidently these manuscripts (see note 9 above) are in the possession of the Marx–Engels–Lenin Institute, Moscow.

II

The manuscript consists of a core, composed of the two main chapters 'On Money' and 'On Capital'; and of two more or less auxiliary essays, namely the 'Introduction' and the fragment on Bastiat and Carey.

The relation of these latter two pieces to the main text is problematic. Chronologically, the unfinished piece on Bastiat and Carey comes first of all. It was written in July 1857, even before the Introduction; but whether it was intended as an independent essay or as a preliminary to the *Grundrisse* we do not know. It has something of both qualities, and may usefully be read as an alternative introduction to the main text, or may be looked at in the course of the discussion on p. 755 of the Chapter on Capital, where Marx intended to 'bring in something from it'; or, finally, it may stand brilliantly as a separate essay.

Problems of a different sort attend the Introduction. This appears in a notebook outside the series of seven which begins with the Chapter on Money, and several weeks passed in the interval between writings. There is no immediately obvious continuity between the Introduction and the first chapter. Nevertheless, there can be no question here (unlike the case of 'Bastiat and Carey') that the Introduction and the main text form an organic whole from the bibliographic, or textual, viewpoints. The difficulties lie deeper. They are: to what extent did Marx himself, on later review, consider this Introduction a valid starting point at all; and to what extent did he, in the course of writing the main body of the text, come to regard some of the views expressed in the Introduction as inadequate? The fact is that when Marx, in 1859, set about readying the Chapter on Money for publication, intending to follow suit with the Chapter on Capital, he chose to drop this Introduction altogether and to write a different one in its place. These questions, and the possible reasons for Marx's decision, will be considered in the third section of this Foreword.

The division of the core of the text into just two chapters (the second several times longer than the first) is filled with significance. It implies at the outset that money and capital, though connected, are distinct entities deserving of separate treatment; a point which not every economist would concede. As Marx develops his argument in detail, it becomes apparent that these two categories, which lend their names to the main chapters, also play a role as arch-antagonists within the work as a whole. 'Money' comes to signify not merely some scrap of paper or metal, but rather an entire system of social relationships based on certain rules and laws, and involving a certain type of politics, culture, even personality; while 'Capital', for its part, is shown to be, likewise, a system of social relations, but based on altogether opposite laws, and driving towards an antithetical politics, culture, etc.; so that, in simplified terms, capitalist economy as a whole may be seen to be both impelled onwards and undermined by the inner tensions between these, its joint constituent forces.

Let us pursue the argument in more detail.

The structure of the argument in the Chapter on Money is at first difficult to follow. This is due partly to repeated digressions, interesting in themselves, on the history of currency and the metallurgy etc. of gold and silver, which chop up the continuity. It is due chiefly to the presence of cross-purposes. As Marx writes in a letter, he intended both to summarize the results of his economic studies, i.e. to advance a systematic theory of his own, and at the same time to get out a pamphlet on the ongoing economic crisis.[13] The chapter begins with the latter purpose apparently uppermost; moves gradually, but in fits and starts, towards the exposition of the systematic theory; and when the critique does encounter the theoretical exposition, it is at a point – the distinction between price and value – which presupposes that a great deal of earlier development has been grasped. When later, on reviewing the manuscript, Marx complained that everything was jumbled up together in it, he probably had this chapter foremost in mind.

The beginning addresses a proposal for bank 'reform' by a leading Proudhonist, Darimon. There is a drain of gold from France. This produces a scarcity of 'money' domestically. Interest rates go up. 'The people' – small businessmen, farmers – cannot afford to borrow. Industry is paralysed. Solution: go off the gold standard, let the banks supply credit as demanded, bring interest rates to zero. This is the content of the Proudhonist slogan 'Free Credit'. After ripping through Darimon's analysis of the causes of the gold drain, pointing out the difference between money and credit, Marx loses little time showing the ordinariness of the inspiration behind the proposal. Marx shreds Darimon's

13. Marx to Engels, 18 December 1857, *MEW* XXIX, p. 232.

'radical' and 'socialist' mask; the proposal is a bourgeois dream – the dream of printing-press alchemy – combined with poor bourgeois economics. At the time of Marx's writing, Darimon was one of the most fiery and renowned radicals in France; a few years later he went over to the Bonapartist regime, was decorated, and died a reactionary.

The second phase of the Proudhonists' plan brings Marx to his major theoretical questions. The plan is to replace the present money system with all its evils, establishing a currency based on labour time instead. This scheme for 'labour money' was a favourite among utopian socialists of the nineteenth century. Marx is able to show that the same notion presented by the Proudhonists as a hot new item had actually been dreamed up fifty years before by two English political economists named Bray and Gray (see also p. 805). The labour-money scheme has no significant life today, and Marx's refutation of it – the most systematic in any of his published writings – would be of little interest as well, except that he brings out its general presuppositions and in the process raises his own. Marx agrees with the labour-money proponents that the value of any commodity is determined by the labour time it cost to produce. What they forget, however, is that this is true only on the *average* (p. 137) and not necessarily, only rarely, in particular. Money serves the function – this is one of its functions – of averaging the particulars out to form a common measure or standard. To do that, money requires to be different from each of the particulars individually. If one tries to remove the means of averaging different particular labour times, but still hold to the determination of value by labour time, the result is that one man's hour-chit equals another's two-hour chit or another's half-hour chit etc.; so that the face value of the notes becomes merely imaginary, and the circulation of this 'currency' must break down in chaos and confusion (p. 139). Either there must be a money based on non-particular, non-individual labour time – regardless of whether this money takes the shape of gold, silver, paper or whatever – or else the determination of value by labour time must be given up altogether, not as a theory but in practice. The only way to retain the determination of value by labour time, and yet operate with labour money, would be for the 'bank' which issues the labour money also to become the universal buyer and seller of all commodities – 'the papacy of production' (p. 156). Alternatively, if the determination of value by labour time no longer stands, then the need for money of any sort falls away, and there is no longer a ground on which the demand for labour money can be raised (p. 172).

To expose the foundations of the labour-money scheme, Marx has taken a 'detour' (p. 136) from the immediate polemical purpose, for the 'delusions on which the time-chit rests ... allow us an insight into the depths of the secret which links Proudhon's theory of circulation with his general theory', this 'secret' being his theory of the determination of value. As the chapter progresses, the 'detour' becomes the main road. What remains hidden in Proudhon is brought into the open in the *Grundrisse*. The determination of value is the major question to which the work as a whole addresses itself. It forms the spine in the skeleton of the argument through both chapters. The bulk of the content is the examination of this question in its various aspects, at various levels of abstraction and with different degrees of simplicity or complexity. Not only Proudhon and his socialism, but also his secret theoretical soul-mate Ricardo along with the whole classical school of bourgeois political economy are hauled over the coals on this question. In the course of the Chapter on Money, the theory of value is developed in relation to the different functions of money identified by political economy (for instance medium of circulation, measure and standard of value, store of value etc.), and these in turn are brought into relation to form the system of simple circulation.

The more narrowly technical aspects of the theory of money and circulation are of relatively less interest, and are not so well developed in this manuscript as in later works which Marx prepared for publication, e.g. the *Critique of Political Economy* and *Capital*. Marx's terminology in places is not quite untangled from and clear of the Ricardian lexicon; this will be the case occasionally also in the second chapter.[14] There are elements of the theory of money here, such as the notion of its role as 'symbol', which ap-

14. In particular, in the second chapter, the difference between the polarities fixed capital *v.* circulating capital, on one side, and constant capital *v.* variable capital, are not as sharply worked out as they later become in *Capital,* e.g. Vol. II, pp. 213–14, 218–19 (International Publishers edn). This lack of ultimate precision must be considered in weighing the passages in the *Grundrisse* on machinery, e.g. pp. 704–6, which are formulated in terms of 'fixed capital'; when machinery is considered, instead, as constant capital, then its effect on the rate of profit enters directly into the calculation and acts as a limit on the development. Compare Rosdolsky, Vol. II, pp. 418–25.

pear imprecisely formulated from the standpoint of later published writings.[15] As Marx himself notes, the manner of presentation suffers from idealist defects. (This point will be considered
again.) Consequently, those particular aspects of Marx's theory of
value and money which join the questions usually raised under that
heading in economics textbooks are best studied from works
Marx prepared for publication after the *Grundrisse*. The relative
strength of the present manuscript lies in areas into which economics books normally do not venture. Marx does not 'discover'
any new functions of money. His contribution is, rather, to uncover
the social, political, legal and other presuppositions of the stock
definitions of money carried in political economy texts, that is, to
treat value and money as social relations; it is, secondly, to treat
the different functions of money in interconnection, exposing the
contradictions between them and within them; and, finally, to
treat this set of social relations in historical perspective, as having
had an origin and implying an end.

Marx's exposition of money and value as social relations, with
legal and psychological ramifications in a particular historic
context, makes up some of the most immediately rewarding passages in the *Grundrisse* (e.g. pp. 156–65, 171–3, 196–8, 221–6,
233–5, 238).

Accordingly, the system of simple circulation Marx constructs
in the Chapter on Money is more than a mechanism for the conversion of commodities into money and vice versa. (It is also a
mechanism for blocking this conversion under given circumstances.) It contains elements both from the economic foundation
of capitalist society and from its superstructure. It has a particular
law of appropriation: everyone owns the product of his labour. It
has a class structure of a peculiar sort: everyone is a proprietor
and a worker at the same time. Money, here, is both a social bond,
a social *thing* connecting unsocial individuals; and it is, when
angered, an alien tyrant whipping up the waters of the world
market.

(The exposition continues into the first pages of the Chapter on
Capital.)

The relations among the individuals in this sphere are those of
liberty and equality. Equality, because the exchange of commodities is based, on the average, on the law of equivalence; the
products exchanged are the embodiment of equal amounts of

15. Cf. Rosdolsky, I, pp. 142–3.

labour time. Liberty, because the partners in exchange presume and recognize each other as proprietors, and none takes from the other by force. Entry and exit into exchange are freely chosen. Individual A and individual B are distinguishable only as buyer and seller; in an instant they exchange these roles, drop even this difference and become a single kind of being.

What is the reality of this sphere?

As a whole, complete with all its parts, it has no historical basis. In one respect, it points to the earliest stage in capitalist history, when artisans and free peasants – each proprietor and worker in one person – prevailed. But at that time neither the law of equivalent exchange nor the action of the world market were developed nearly to the degree also presupposed in the sphere of simple circulation.

Nor is this sphere developed capitalist economy as a whole. It abstracts the law of équivalent exchange and the world market from developed capitalism, but the absence of classes disqualifies it as an image of developed capitalism *in toto*.

The sphere of exchange Marx has constructed possesses the double presence of an optical illusion. Each side of it is true in a way, but only if the other side is blocked out of view; and the whole, as a real whole, is impossible, which is exactly Marx's point.

The sphere of circulation is, firstly, one side of capitalist production relations as a whole, in their developed form. It has a real existence as that part of the whole system within which equivalents are exchanged for equivalents, equals are equals, and persons are free proprietors. This is the market-place, the realm – let us assume – of free competition. Here lies 'the productive, real basis of all *equality* and *freedom*' for individual proprietors. 'As pure ideas', equality and liberty 'are merely idealized expressions' of the relations prevailing in the sphere of exchange. The legal, political, social relations which frame the liberty and equality of individual proprietors are merely a superstructure upon the market-place (p. 245). Here, at the point where commodities are purchased by the final consumer, the king, the millionaire and the proletarian are formal equals; each must wait his turn in line at the cash register in the food market, first come first served (p. 251). The class differences between them are extinguished beneath the single common role of 'buyer' or 'consumer'. On the opposite side of the counter, commodities present themselves as stemming from 'the producer', a role in which worker and capitalist are combined into a single being; and it is easy to 'show' that 'producer' and 'consumer' are one and the same.

On the other hand, where is the historical reference point of this sphere, when conceived as a *whole* society? Only in the most primitive stages of capitalist production, which is not even fully capitalist yet, but still has one foot in the guilds and yeomanry of the Middle Ages. Any attempt, therefore, to portray the sphere of circulation as the whole of a society, to reduce the whole to this part, has as its real presupposition a regression to this primitive stage of production, in which, moreover, the law of equivalent exchange together with its superstructure of bourgeois liberty and equality are but insignificantly developed.

The contradictions within this mental construct are the contradictions within the ideology of radical bourgeois democracy, as typified to the highest degree and with the most socialist coloration, in Marx's time, by the Proudhonists. They wish to make bourgeois liberty and bourgeois equality more perfect, to realize them fully and completely, and to that end rail and rant about the tyranny of money and the venality of the market-place, not knowing that this very market-place is the real foundation of the bourgeois liberty and equality they wish to perfect. The opponents of the bourgeois radicals among the bourgeoisie, namely the political economists, have a sounder understanding of this particular question to the extent that they understand what are the real relations between bourgeois freedom and the market-place. Thus Marx.

However (as he writes upon returning to the topic later on), the political economists themselves err fundamentally when they assume that the individuals are set free in and by the market-place. 'It is not the individuals who are set free by free competition; it is, rather, capital which is set free' (p. 650).

'The analysis of what free competition really is, is the only rational reply to the middle-class prophets who laud it to the skies or to the socialists who damn it to hell' (p. 652).

And what is it actually? To begin with, 'in present bourgeois society as a whole, this positing of prices and their circulation etc., appears as *the surface process, beneath which, in the depths, entirely different processes go on, in which this apparent individual equality and liberty disappear*' (p. 247 – my italics).

At this point in the text, the argument commences a strategic

dive from the surface into the depths, from the exchange process
to the 'entirely different processes' taking place at the point of
production. We depart here, for some two hundred pages or
more, from the simple, limited world of money and of its circulation – where everything equals everything else – to enter into
the world of Capital, where opposite laws hold sway.

The movement of the argument touches ground and gains its
basic orientation for the remainder of its way in a short section
beginning on p. 266. The question here is no longer what happens
in the process of the exchange of commodities generally, but
rather, more particularly, what takes place when the commodity
being exchanged is '*labour*'. This is crucial. Here the *two* processes
become visible. Firstly, there is the ordinary exchange process;
the worker sells the capitalist 'labour', like any commodity, in
exchange for which the capitalist gives him its price, a certain sum
of money, that is, wages. As in any other exchange of commodities,
the buyer gives the seller the money-equivalent of the commodity's
exchange value, and obtains from the seller the commodity's use
value, i.e. the physical qualities, the object itself. It is a rule in
political economy that, once this exchange is completed, the commodity has left the province. What the buyer does with the use
value of the commodity he has purchased is his private affair and
has no economic relevance; if I buy a loaf of bread and take a
notion to paper the wall with its slices instead of eating it, that is
my business and the political economist, at least, will ask no
questions. With the purchase of 'labour', the matter is different,
not perhaps for political economy, but for Marx. The use value
of the commodity 'labour' within the capitalist production process
is not a non-economic affair, because the use value of 'labour' for
its buyer, the capitalist, is precisely *to create exchange values*, commodities, products to be sold. The capitalist's consumption of the
'labour' he has bought makes up the second process; and this is
'qualitatively different from exchange, and only by misuse could it
have been called any sort of exchange at all. It stands directly opposite exchange; essentially different category' (p. 275).

This directly opposite process is the process of exploitation, or
the extraction of surplus product from the worker's labour time.
This process is the source of capitalist accumulation.

Along with the discovery of the 'essentially different category'
comes an important new formulation. In common with Adam
Smith, Ricardo, and most of the remainder of political economy,

Marx had heretofore referred to the commodity which the worker sells the capitalist as '*labour*'. Now this turns out to be inadequate. Unlike other commodities, this particular one 'is not materialized in a product, does not exist apart from him [the worker] at all, thus exists not really, but only in potentiality, as his capacity [*Fähigkeit*]'; and therefore ought properly to be called not 'labour' but rather '*labour power*' or '*labour capacity*'. (pp. 281, 282, 293, 359.) This appears to be the first usage, in Marx's published work, of the new terminology which later becomes standard. (This question is discussed in more detail in the fourth section of this Foreword.)

After clearing some preliminaries, the argument arrives at the question proper, where does surplus value come from? It cannot come from the exchange process, since there, on the average and on the whole, equal values are exchanged; and surplus value is the direct opposite of equivalence. 'The capitalist must obtain more value than he has given', otherwise no surplus value, no capitalist, no capitalism as a system. He gets the surplus because the value of the worker's wages, expressed in hours of labour time, is smaller than the number of hours the worker works for the capitalists in 'exchange' for his wages. If the commodity the worker sells the capitalist were an inanimate object, there could be no surplus value; 'but because it exists not as a thing, but as the capacity of a living being.', a surplus value can be extracted from 'it', day after day, as long as the worker is alive and able-bodied (pp. 321–6).

'It is clear, therefore, that the worker cannot become *rich* in this exchange, since, in exchange for his labouring capacity as a fixed, available magnitude, he surrenders its *creative power*, like Esau his birthright for a mess of pottage. Rather, he necessarily impoverishes himself, as we shall see further on, because the creative power of his labour establishes itself as the power of capital, as an *alien power* confronting him ... Thus all the progress of civilization, or in other words every increase in the *powers of social production*, ... in the *productive powers of labour itself* – such as results from science, inventions, division and combination of labour, improved means of communication, creation of the world market, machinery etc. – enriches not the worker, but rather *capital*; hence it only magnifies again the power dominating over labour; increases only the productive power of capital. Since capital is the antithesis of the worker, this merely increases the *objective power* standing over labour' (pp. 307–8).

For the next seventy pages or so of the text, the concept of exploitation, which has thus been grounded both in and against the classical theory of value, is given the dimensions of quantity and measure. Marx proceeds to divide the working day into the two portions well known from *Capital*, that is, the hours of necessary labour during which the worker produces commodities equal in value to his entire wages for the day, and the hours of surplus labour, productive of values in excess of the day's wage, and forming the capitalist's 'gross profit' or surplus value, later shared out among the industrial capitalist (profit), the banker (interest) and the landlord (rent).

We pass rapidly over the appearance, in some cases the first appearance, of the categories absolute vs relative surplus value, constant and variable capital and others, noting the demolition of Ricardo's theory of profit and the rise of the distinction between profit and surplus value (pp. 373–86), to arrive at the next strategic turning point. (Actually, the distinction between profit and surplus value is itself a major breakthrough, but is fully developed only towards the end of the manuscripts (pp. 745–64).) Marx's exposition has been following the production process on the shop floor, in the depths of bourgeois society. The process leads to the loading dock and from there to the next crucial point: the re-entry into circulation. The argument returns, therefore, to the subject matter first raised in the Chapter on Money, but with vital, transforming differences.

The Chapter on Money analysed the process through which equal amounts of labour time are, on average, exchanged. This is expressed as the law of equivalence. The Chapter on Capital, up to this point, has traced the opposite process, the exploitation process, where the overriding law (for the capitalist) is the extraction of an equivalent-plus, a super-equivalent. Now the two opposite processes encounter each other. 'The surplus value ... requires a surplus equivalent' (p. 405). The contradictions beneath the surface, touched on as possibilities in the Chapter on Money, now rise to the surface and determine the further course of the argument. Marx's investigation of the confrontation between the process of equivalent exchange and the opposite process, of accumulation, occupies the greater part of the remaining four hundred or so pages of the manuscript; and, as always, the social, political, historical, legal and even social-psychological aspects of the underlying fundamental question are brought out.

This must serve as an introduction to the structure of the argument. The confrontation between the two processes is mapped out on pp. 401–58. Some of the most interesting territory lies there and beyond. To pursue the argument further into these questions, for instance the theory of overproduction crises, the reproduction schemes, questions regarding the law of value and related matters, would require extensive commentary. One such work of commentary, Rosdolsky's, confined chiefly to the economic side, amounts to two volumes by itself.[16] All that follows in the remaining four hundred pages of the *Grundrisse* is built on the basic elements here outlined.

In the process of the further investigation, Marx is led to set on paper a number of striking passages which have justifiably added to the renown of these manuscripts. Here, for example, is an excerpt from one of these, which is part of the analysis of the tendential fall in the rate of profit, which in turn follows from the argument already outlined. Marx happens, in this passage, to write in English; he says: 'Hence the highest development of productive power together with the greatest expansion of existing wealth will coincide with depreciation of capital, degradation of the labourer, and a most straitened exhaustion of his vital powers. These contradictions lead to explosions, cataclysms, crises, in which by momentaneous suspension of labour and annihilation of a great portion of capital the latter is violently reduced to the point where it can go on ... Yet, these regularly recurring catastrophes lead to their repetition on a higher scale, and finally to

16. Rosdolsky's second volume is of interest, in particulai, in regard to the portions of the *Grundrisse* after p. 401. The value of Rosdolsky's commentary lies in the relations he traces between certain of the themes of the *Grundrisse*, (and *Capital*), particularly the question of realization, and the widespread and many-sided debates which occurred internationally, on these questions, during 1890–1925. The work constitutes a retrospective on this 'golden age' of political-economic Marxist theory, and is one possible introduction to it, certainly the most comprehensive (if debatable) one written. It is to be regretted that the terms in which this debate was cast remain also those of Rosdolsky's commentary; in particular, the virtual exclusion of the question of method (and of Hegel) from the debates of this epoch leads Rosdolsky likewise to confine himself to a few, valuable and insightful remarks. Rosdolsky's death interrupted his work, leaving it in an excessively quotation-ridden state, lacking overall perspective. He reviews virtually the entire literature, assigning praise here and blame there (for reasons whose theoretical grounds remain inarticulate and appear often quite arbitrary) without himself taking the science a single step further.

its violent overthrow' (p. 750). In such passages the co-author of the *Manifesto of the Communist Party* again clearly distinguishes his position from the opinion which believes in a gradual, smooth, peaceful path of capitalist development and a gradual, smooth, peaceful transition to socialism. These passages are, for us, a reminder that Marx's theoretical labours were not concerned with economics for the sake of economics, philosophy for the sake of philosophy, or criticism for its own sake; but rather that the aim of this work was to prepare, to educate the next generation of leaders of the working class in the objective preconditions, possibility and necessity of the historic task.

III

Marx did not provide his seven notebooks with a comprehensive title. The name by which the manuscript is known today is a composite of various references in Marx's correspondence; it was chosen by the 1939 editors at the Marx–Engels–Lenin Institute.

It is tempting to quarrel a little with their editorial judgement here, because in a letter to Lassalle (22 February 1858), Marx appears very clearly to have had a different title in mind, namely *'Critique of the Economic Categories'*. How very fitting, in some respects, this title would be! Still, there are excellent grounds also for preferring the present name. Pre-eminent among these is the continuity thereby established with Marx's *Critique of Political Economy* of 1859, a work which is chiefly a re-draft of the first *Grundrisse* chapter, and whose title is 'authentic' beyond question. However, the exact wording of the title is ultimately an insignificant question. Once a book is launched, it seems to acquire a life of its own, and one name may serve it as well as another. The important point is not this title or that, but rather the *absence* of a title, originally.

The lack of a title signals, at the outset, the unfinished quality of the manuscript. As the 1939 editors are careful to point out in a parenthetical appendage to 'their' title, we have here a *rough draft*. The reader of this translation will discover this quality immediately, in the form, for example, of missing elements of grammar, of difficult, sometimes awkward, obscure and even altogether inaccurate formulations, endless sentences and paragraphs, irritating digressions and reiterations, etc. It is a text which proclaims on nearly every page its unripeness for print. Not that there is a lack of beauty, of strength and of Marx's characteristic lucidity! On the contrary. But roughness and difficulty are the overriding qualities. It is a demanding text to read and a hazardous one to quote, since the context, the grammar and the very vocabulary raise doubts as to what Marx 'really' meant in a given passage. Let the quoter, the excerptor, beware. Beneath these choppy waters are reefs to sink many a hasty cargo of interpretation.

These deficiencies of form, however, bring with them a powerful compensation. The beauty of first drafts generally, and of this one in particular, is that one may see, by their evidence, something of *how* their author *worked out* in his mind the ideas which later take the form of ready-made, polished, quotable conclusions.

In every science there is a difference between the method of working and the method of presentation. It is the difference of form between the laboratory and the lecture hall. Very little about the physical world, say, would be widely understood if the only 'presentation' of results came in the form of a film or diary displaying the scientist working. Conversely, relatively less would be understood about the scientific method of working if the only source of knowledge about it were papers presenting results.[17]

In this respect, the *Grundrisse* is unique. No other published text from this period of Marx's life allows so direct an inquiry into his most important achievement and legacy, namely his *method of working*. The manuscript 'comes like a veritable revelation'; it 'introduces us, so to speak, into Marx's economic laboratory and lays bare all the refinements, all the complex bypaths of his methodology' (Rosdolsky). The *Grundrisse* is the record of Marx's mind at work, grappling with fundamental problems of theory. This is the manuscript's most valuable distinguishing characteristic.

To trace out every 'refinement' and 'bypath' in Marx's method, as laid bare in the *Grundrisse*, is of course an impossible task within the scope of this Foreword. It is indispensable, however, to outline the most important of the major avenues.

On 16 January 1858, while Marx was somewhere in the fourth notebook (pp. 373–479), he reported on its progress to Engels in

17. See the Afterword to the second German edition of Vol. I of *Capital*: 'Of course the method of presentation must differ in form from that of inquiry . . .' (International Publishers ed.), p. 19.

Manchester: 'I am getting some nice developments. E.g. I have overthrown the entire doctrine of profit as previously conceived. In the *method* of working [*Methode* des Bearbeitens] it was of great service to me that by mere accident . . . I leafed through Hegel's *Logic* again.'[18]

The new theory of profit worked out in the *Grundrisse* (pp. 373–86, 745–64) and later presented in *Capital* is one of Marx's most important theoretical and political break-throughs. On its basis, Marx is able to demonstrate that it is not the rate of profit as commonly understood which measures the degree to which the worker is exploited, but that it is rather the quite different, tendentially inversely directional rate of surplus value (p. 374). The rate of profit, Marx shows, actually *falsifies* the rate of exploitation, and falsifies it to a higher degree as capitalism develops (p. 762). This is of fundamental importance for Marx's theory of wages, of strategy towards trade unionism and social-democracy, and much else.

Nor are the 'services' rendered by Hegel's *Logic* confined to the specific question of the profit rate. The whole of the *Grundrisse* testifies to their presence. Though he did not know of the *Grundrisse*, V. I. Lenin perceived the influence of Hegel on Marx's political economy as a whole, upon restudying the first volume of *Capital*. 'It is impossible completely to understand Marx's *Capital*,' he wrote, in his *Philosophical Notebooks*, '. . . without having thoroughly studied the *whole* of Hegel's *Logic*.'

In short, the question of Hegel can hardly be avoided when studying the *Grundrisse*. What, then, was Hegel; and what were the strengths and weaknesses of his *Logic* as regards Marx's method of working? These are the questions which confront any serious reader of the *Grundrisse*, and require at least the kernel of an answer.

G. W. F. Hegel (1770–1831) was one of the great thinkers and scholars of all time. He was accomplished in mathematics, natural science, history, law, political theory, philosophy, aesthetics and theology, and conversed as an equal with the foremost specialists of his time in these fields. He was also an extremely contradictory phenomenon as a philosopher.

The dramatist Brecht has one of his characters say about Hegel that 'he had the stuff to be one of the greatest humorists among philosophers, like Socrates, who had a similar method. But he had

18. Marx to Engels, *MEW* XXIX, p. 260.

the bad luck it seems to become a civil servant in Prussia and so he sold himself to the state.'[19] That is to say, Hegel's philosophy was at once dialectical, subversive as was Socrates', and idealist, mystical like a priest's.

The idealist side of his philosophy was that he denied the *reality* of what the senses perceive. He recognized that there are senses and that they do perceive something, and he correctly pointed out that these perceptions *by themselves* can grasp only the appearance of things, not their truth. The truth can be worked out only through the criticism and reconstruction of sense-perceptions by logical reasoning. From this correct principle, Hegel drew the false conclusion that *only* the logical concepts worked up by the mind have any *reality*. Arguing that the senses only perceive appearances, and appearances are false, he leaped to the conclusion that therefore appearances are unreal. 'Only the true is real', is one of his fundamental pronouncements.[20] Then he went further. Not wishing to give the impression that only the concepts within his own personal mind were real, he evicted 'mind' from its bodily laboratory altogether, endowed it effectively with capital letters, and asserted that 'The Mind' by itself, outside and independently of anyone's head, was the summation and totality of absolute truth. Thus the path of sense perception which transmits what moves outside the head to the brain inside, became for him a pointless and disruptive detour. It was only a natural step from there to the thesis that this 'objective' but immaterial 'Subject' *governed* the development of the world, had always done so, and that it was pleased thus to unfold and reveal itself over the course of the centuries. From this to God was no step at all; it left Hegel towards the end a philosopher–pope bestowing benediction, as popes must, on the temporal emperor; here alone, in the Prussian military bureaucratic Junker autocracy, had the Absolute Mind fully revealed itself, not only to philosophy but also to the senses. To forestall any doubts of his pious earnest, he inserted into his scriptures innumerable passages reeking of the vilest sycophancy; behaved accordingly; and was buried with state honours.

The other extreme of the contradiction that was Hegel is his work on dialectics. Dialectics has a very long history. (The term comes from the Greek '*dia*', meaning split in two, opposed,

19. Brecht, *Flüchtlingsgespräche*, Suhrkamp (Frankfurt), 1961, p. 108.

20. Hegel, *Werke*, Suhrkamp (Frankfurt), 1969; *Logic* II (Vol. 6, pp. 462–3); *Enzyklopädie* (Vol. 8, p. 47); and elsewhere.

clashing; and '*logos*', reason; hence 'to reason by splitting in two'.) Among the early Greek philosophers, who were also among the earliest natural scientists, were some whose special interest was in the phenomena of change, motion, process. Seeing, for example, an arrow in flight or a bird winging across a river, they would reason in this way: in its motion, the thing is changed from being here to being there. Since 'here' and 'there' exclude each other, they reasoned that motion is the transformation of one state of things into the opposite state; or, since motion includes both the beginning and its opposite, the end, that motion is the unity of these opposites; or, in sum, that motion is contradiction. Since there were other philosophers who asserted that *everything* is motion, it is easy to see why dialectics could become an important tendency within philosophy from very early on, even though constant warring among the different schools, the backwardness of social and scientific development, the regimes' fear of the subversive consequences (as in the case of Socrates), and the commercial distortion of dialectics as casuistry and double talk placed a severe limit on what could be achieved.[21]

One of Hegel's great merits was to have reviewed and gathered together in systematic form the previous history of dialectics from many civilizations of the world – Asia, the Middle East, as well as Greece and the remainder of Europe. He showed that dialectics had played a role in the thinking of virtually all great figures in philosophy, even – though in lifeless form – in that of his predecessor and antagonist, Immanuel Kant. Hegel's even greater merit was to have brought the dialectic to a new, higher level by founding his entire system of logic upon dialectic principles as he understood them. This method of logic is expounded most extensively in his book by that name.

Hegel asked, 'what is it to have a concept of a thing?' To have a 'concept' (*Begriff*) means, firstly, to 'grasp' or 'grip' the thing mentally (as in forceps, biceps), to get hold of it, to hold it still.[22]

21. Hegel, *Werke* XVIII (*Geschichte der Philosophie* I), pp. 305, 325; see also Lenin, *Philosophical Notebooks* (*Collected Works* XXXVIII, pp. 254–60).

22. Hegel characterizes '*Begreifen*' ('to grasp') as *appropriation* (*Logic* II, *Werke* VI, p. 255). See Lenin's commentary: 'We cannot imagine, express, measure, depict movement, without interrupting continuity, without simplifying, coarsening, dismembering, strangling that which is living. The representation of movement by means of thought always makes coarse, kills – and not only by means of thought, but also by sense-perception, and not only

But what if the thing is in motion, and this motion is part or all of its truth? Marx expresses this difficulty in this way: 'The *fixed* presuppositions themselves become fluid in the further course of development. But only by holding them fast at the beginning is their development possible without confounding everything' (p. 817).

This difficulty is not confined to a special separate branch of philosophy devoted to the study of changes, nor to a special department of political economy devoted to the question of development. The whole is in motion, the totality of it develops, it all had a beginning and implies an end.

'When we consider bourgeois society in the long view and as a whole, then the final result of the process of social production always appears as the society itself, i.e. the human being itself in its social relations. Everything that has a fixed form, such as the product etc., appears as merely a moment, a vanishing moment, in this movement. The direct production process itself here appears only as a moment. The conditions and objectifications of the process are themselves equally moments of it, and its only subjects are the individuals, but individuals in mutual relationships, which they equally reproduce and produce anew . . . in which they renew themselves even as they renew the world of wealth they create' (p. 712).

Because movement is the only constant, Marx, like Hegel, uses the term 'moment' to refer to what in a system at rest would be called 'element' or 'factor'. In Marx the term carries the senses both of 'period of time' and of 'force of a moving mass'. He much improves on Hegel's use; Hegel's usage was more mechanical, and time was absent from it.[23]

'Capital is not a simple relation, but a *process*, in whose various

---

of movement, but *every* concept. And in that lies the *essence* of dialectics. And precisely *this essence* is expressed by the formula: the unity, identity of opposites.' *Philosophical Notebooks* (*Collected Works* XXXVIII, p. 259–60).

23. Hegel takes 'moment' from Newton; despite his general disdain for 'mechanics', he derives the sense of this rather central concept from the action of the lever. *Logic* I (*Werke* V), pp. 114, 301. On the absence of time in Hegel, see Lenin's remarks on the *Logic*, op. cit., p. 228 (*Collected Works*, XXXVIII). Marx's investigation of the problem of time (production time, circulation time etc.) is an endeavour profoundly contrary to Hegel's method, and marks the most directly tangible contrast between the two methods. This element which does not exist for Hegel at all is, for Marx, the 'ultimate question to which all economy reduces itself' (*Grundrisse*, pp. 172–3, 711–12).

moments it is always capital' (p. 258). '*Money . . . as capital, has lost its rigidity, and from a tangible thing has become a process*' (p. 263).

In short, for Marx, as for Hegel, the problem of grasping a thing is firstly the problem of grasping that it is in motion. This step of logic is rendered more difficult by the fact that in the ordinary course of events it is by no means obvious that this is so. Only when things suddenly crack and break apart does it become obvious that there was a dynamic within them all the time; but ordinarily, things present an appearance of rest. This surface of calm over unceasing restlessness Hegel called *Dasein*, or presence; and when the senses are brought into the relation, it becomes the appearance of things. Hegel wittily defined this presence as 'having the form of the one-sided, immediate unity' of the opposites beneath its surface.[24]

This 'presence' or appearance of one-sided immediate unity, of surface rest and harmony, was useful to Marx in working out the main lines of the sphere of simple circulation, and its relation to the remainder. The market-place is the most public, the most apparent, the most present set of relations of capitalist society; and the ideology abstracted from it is a complex not only of this appearance, but also of the further steps, semblance and illusion. The market-place is where the forms of liberty and equality present themselves; where the distinction between buyer and seller vanishes into their unity. 'It is impossible to find any trace of distinction, not to speak of contradiction, between them; not even a difference' (p. 241).

This presence is neither accidental nor irrelevant. It is only the surface, and displays only the 'one-sided immediate unity' of the process beneath, but it is an objective 'moment' of the whole and must be included in its concept. This presence is a *determinate* one; it is something, has specific qualities, and moreover may be quantified and measured. The ideas which people may form about this presence may be pure delusion and fantasy, because they do not get past its one-sided unity with itself. Nevertheless, as surface, this presence is also a *limit* (boundary, barrier), because it opposes itself from the outset to the thing's infinite expansion. The law of equivalent exchange, that is, the law of value, is such a limit to the expansion of capital, a limit which forms an objective part of the surface process of capitalism. It is a limit as quantity (mass of ex-

24. *Logic* I (*Werke* V), p. 113.

change values in money form, ultimately wages); as measure (labour time as measure of value); and as quality (requirement to labour at all in order to create wealth); on this question, the *Grundrisse* contains numerous passages (for example pp. 270, 324–5, 334–5, 405–23 etc.). To treat this surface process therefore as merely an empty formality, as only nominally important, is to fail in grasping the whole; this is an error of, for instance, Ricardo on the question of money (pp. 331–3).

However, to remain on the surface and become enraptured by 'the immediacy of its being' is to fall into 'pure illusion'. Circulation – the surface – '*is the phenomenon of a process taking place behind it*' (p. 255). To get a grasp on the whole requires penetrating into its essence; from Money to Capital. Here, behind the 'no trespassing' signs, barbed-wire fences, armed patrols and guard dogs, *contradiction* ceases to be a mere reflection and may be studied at the source. In Hegel's view, *negation* is the creative force. Here, the harder the worker negates himself, or is negated by capital, the more wealth does he create. (Numerous passages, for instance p. 308.) For Hegel, negation creates its opposite, 'position' (to posit); and negation therefore not only gives a thing its specific character in itself (*Ansich*) but, as position, gives it its character *for-others*.[25] Here in the essence of capital, as the worker negates himself, not only does he *posit* surplus value *for others*, but he also creates and re-creates the relations of wage labour in themselves, himself as wage-slave and capital as capital. As for the worker and the capitalist, taken individually, they figure in the process only as 'wage labour' and 'capital' *for-themselves* (p. 303), as any qualities or relations they may otherwise have are suppressed by, or irrelevant to, the production process. The production process as a whole tends to limitlessness in itself, first to absolute negation of the worker, then to infinite sharpening of the relative contradiction; it pushes and drives against all boundaries. If the society as a whole is to be grasped in motion, in process, it is first and foremost essential to comprehend the dynamics of the direct production process, because – as Hegel said – the energy, the drive of the whole has its source in its underlying contradiction.[26]

Now to consider what is included in the concept so far. Two processes, one the surface process, resulting in one-sided immediate identity, and lacking the motive power for its own re-

25. *Logic* I, pp. 116, 130–31.   26. *Logic* II (*Werke* VI), pp. 275–6.

generation. The other, beneath the surface, a process of raging contradiction. One process an identity, the other the opposite of identity; so that, in the most abstract formulation – Hegel's – the whole is 'the identity of identity and non-identity'.[27] In this whole, the non-identity, the contradiction is the overriding moment; it stamps its character upon the other and defines the nature of the whole. That is, to name the whole 'the market system' or 'free exchange' or 'free enterprise' etc. is to claim that the surface process determines the nature of the whole. In fact, the surface is the barrier to its nature, and in the course of development this barrier becomes an ever more painful confinement. At a certain point occurs what Hegel and Marx call the *Umschlag* – the abrupt, leap-like inversion or overthrow, in which the previous barrier, the identity, law of equivalence etc. is negated, the underlying contradiction is *suspended*, and the whole is transformed into its opposite, with identities and contradictions of a different order and on a higher level. A word about *suspension*. It translates – Marx himself uses it to translate (p. 750) – Hegel and Marx's term *Aufhebung*. Hegel took delight in the word, as it expresses in ordinary language precisely two opposite senses at once: 'it means as much as to preserve, to *sustain* and at the same time as much as to let cease, *to make an end*'.[28] The English 'suspend' has precisely the same contradictory senses; as for instance in commerce it means to stop (payment) while in music the sense is to continue, sustain (a note), and in bureaucratic administration (as in school systems) it means both at once. Hegel was particularly at pains to point out the difference between suspension and annihilation; that which is suspended has not become nothing, but continues on as 'a result, which has come out of a being; hence it still has in itself the determinateness out of which it comes . . . '

If one considers not only the extensive use of Hegelian terminology in the *Grundrisse*, not only the many passages which reflect self-consciously on Hegel's method and the use of the method, but also the basic structure of the argument in the *Grundrisse*, it becomes evident that the services rendered Marx by his study of the *Logic* were very great indeed. The terminology is the least and the most fleeting of these services; not infrequently Marx employs a term of Hegel's to express precisely the opposite relation to that in Hegel's usage, and before *Capital* found its way

27. *Logic* I, p. 74; *Logic* II, pp. 40–42.   28. *Logic* I, p. 114.

into print Marx discarded most of this lexicon as baggage which had served for its journey but outlasted its day.[29] The usefulness of Hegel lay in providing guide-lines for what to do in order to grasp a moving, developing totality with the mind:

'The exact development of the concept of capital is necessary, since it is the fundamental concept of modern economics, just as capital itself, whose abstract, reflected image [*Gegenbild*] is its concept, is the foundation of bourgeois society. The sharp formulation of the basic presuppositions of the relation must bring out all the contradictions of bourgeois production, as well as the boundary where it drives beyond itself' (p. 331).

This method, whose essence is to grasp wholes as contradictions, is the greatest of the lessons Marx learned from Hegel.

However, the method of Hegel had at the same time its own limitations. It could not have been otherwise, because G. W. F. Hegel was one person, not two. With him idealism and the dialectic formed a unity, penetrated each other; just as his most absolutist benedictions on the state seem to imply, beneath their surface, the contradiction of what they say, so does there hang a shroud of mysticism over the leaping soul of his dialectic.

Marx's critique of Hegel is a process in two major logical phases. The first of these major phases required getting a grip on the entire realm of the 'independent objective Mind' which Hegel had sent floating into the heavens and returning it to its native residence in the mortal human body. At once Hegel's 'subject' and Hegel's 'object' will be found to have been upside down, and are now right side up again. It becomes clear now that the real history of the world is not the product of a *sui generis* 'Mind', but rather that this 'Mind' and all its relations are a product of the human head; and, moreover, of a human head anchored in real history, both driven and limited by particular, changing social-economic modes of existence; finally, a human head integrated into a sensual, material and social body which, by its conduct, can and does alter its history, and therefore alters also the sources and conditions of thought. This major phase in the overthrow of the Hegelian

29. '. . . just as I was working at the first volume of *Capital*, it was the good pleasure of the peevish, arrogant, mediocre epigones who now talk large in cultured Germany, to treat Hegel . . . as a "dead dog". I therefore openly avowed myself the pupil of that mighty thinker, and even here and there, in the chapter on the theory of value, coquetted with the mode of expression peculiar to him' (*Capital* I, International Publishers edn, pp. 19–20). But in the remainder of the work the mode of expression is peculiarly Marx's own.

philosophy was accomplished in the early 1840s by both Feuerbach and Marx to different degrees; is brilliantly recapitulated in the Introduction preceding the *Grundrisse* (pp. 101–2); and is summarized in Marx's 1873 Preface to Vol. I of *Capital* as 'standing Hegel on his feet again'.[30]

Feuerbach had called the clashings of the categories and concepts in Hegel's absolute 'Mind' a 'war of the Gods'.[31] This raises the question: once this heavenly battlefield is brought down to earth and its immaterial antagonists are given body, in what way must the *rules* of their warfare, the tactics and strategy of their conflict, be altered to be true to life? The elementary structure of the idealist dialectic, the basic processes of its motion, are nothing but a projection, into the world of ideas, of the actual clashes and transformations taking place in history; *but* in that projection, in that idealization, something essentially present in the dialectic of material history must have become covered up, spirited from view. This second major phase in the overthrow of the Hegelian system Marx formulates as 'stripping off the mystical shell from the rational core'.[32] This is the critique of Hegel's *dialectic method*, therefore a critique of his theory of contradiction, hence a critique of the fundamental processes of the Hegelian *concept*, of Hegel's basic grasp of movement.

Of course, such a large and complex subject as Marx's critique of Hegel's dialectic cannot be fully, adequately treated in the scope of this Foreword. The *Grundrisse* will put almost everything previously written on this topic to a severe test, and consign most of it to the dustbin. At the same time, the manuscript contains enough material to fuel perhaps several generations of additional philosophical treatises. The intention here is not to pre-empt these, but rather solely to draw attention to a couple of especially striking points which are, in any case, unavoidable for a proper appreciation of Marx's Introduction and of its relation to the main text. These two aspects, which show in particularly sharp relief some important differences between Hegel's and Marx's concept of the dialectic method, may be summarized as, firstly,

---

30. *Capital* I, p. 20.   31. *Holy Family, MEW* II, p. 98.

32. 'It must be turned right side up again, if you would discover the rational kernel within the mystical shell' (*Capital* I, p. 20). Note that Marx does *not* say that to turn Hegel's dialectic right side up again is *sufficient* to have the materialist dialectic; this first step only *permits* the second step (the discovery) to proceed.

the question of where to begin; and secondly, the question whether the contradictions within any unity are identical immediately and necessarily, or rather, indirectly and conditionally.

Hegel begins his *Logic* with the most general and universal abstraction in philosophy, pure, indeterminate *being*, being in general, which he asserted to be the most elementary reality. For Marx, the materialist, this 'being-in-general' is a figment of the philosophic mind, a category which has 'reality' only in the imagination of the fabricator. He therefore begins the Introduction which precedes the *Grundrisse* with a category of material life, of political economy, namely 'material production', and hastens to add that, of course, material production *in society* is the only real form of its existence (p. 83). As Hegel then proceeds to show that pure 'being' is *identical* to 'nothing', cannot be conceived without its opposite, so does Marx in the Introduction proceed to the opposite of material production, namely consumption, without which production cannot be conceived. However, even before the examination of this identity of the opposites (production and consumption) begins (pp. 90–94), the beginning just begun is already called into question. 'Material production' is shown to be a category which abstracts from historical development, rather than explaining it. ' *Production in general* is an abstraction, but a rational abstraction in so far as it really brings out and fixes the common element and thus saves us repetition. Still, this *general* category, this common element sifted out by comparison, is itself segmented many times over and splits into different determinations . . . The determinations valid for production as such must be sorted out precisely so that in their unity . . . their essential difference is not forgotten' (p. 85). In sum, 'production in general' is a category with which 'no real historical stage of production can be grasped' (p. 88).

In other words, the mere substitution of a 'materialist' category (e.g. material production) for an idealist one (e.g. pure, indeterminate being) leaves Marx still dissatisfied. It turns out that to begin with social production in general, and to proceed then to its direct opposite, consumption in general, is not so significant a forward step as it might seem. It replaces one unhistorical abstraction with another, and ultimately progresses no further than the 'prosaic economists' themselves, who also begin their works with recitations of precisely such generalities.

The several pages in the Introduction which treat the 'identities between production and consumption' are at one and the same time an earnest imitation of this standard textbook opening, and a mocking parody of it. The initial proposition, 'production is immediately identical with consumption', echoes Hegel's 'Being is immediately identical with Nothing'; and, by comparison to what is ordinarily extracted from this proposition, Marx's treatment is immortal. But it is, in the main, a display of *idealist* dialectics, which testifies to the enormous superiority of idealist dialectics over mechanistic or empiricist materialism.[33] It is important not to overlook Marx's mocking remarks about these 'identities' both at the outset and afterwards; '. . . as if the task were the dialectic balancing of concepts, and not the grasping of real relations' (p. 90). And, having duly spun out these identities in triplicate *à la* Hegel (p. 93), Marx concludes drily, 'Thereupon nothing simpler for a Hegelian than to posit production and consumption as identical. And this has been done not only by socialist belletrists [an allusion to Proudhon], but by prosaic economists themselves . . .' (p. 93).

The question of the proper beginning further preoccupies Marx throughout the section of the Introduction titled 'The Method of Political Economy' (pp. 100–108). At the outset here, Marx describes two journeys, or paths, which political-economic inquiry has taken. The first takes 'living wholes' as its point of departure, for instance a given nation-state, France, England etc., and finishes 'by discovering through analysis a small number of determinant, abstract, general relations such as division of labour, money, value etc.' (p. 100). The other journey moves in the reverse direction, beginning with the simple, abstract, general relations, and arriving at the 'living wholes' at the end. 'The latter,' Marx concludes, 'is obviously the scientifically correct method.'[34]

It seems here as if the doubts Marx had earlier encountered about the propriety of beginning with the category 'material production' – surely as simple, general and abstract a relation as one could wish – were now laid to rest. Immediately, however, a fresh doubt arises from a different quarter: 'But do not these

33. See Lenin, *Philosophical Notebooks* (*Collected Works* XXXVIII, p. 276).

34. In a sense, Hegel's *Logic* is concerned with little else but this question of the two journeys. The metaphor, the outlines, even the formulation of the concrete as a concentrate of many abstractions are from that work, see *Logic* II, pp. 276, 296, 326, 360. It is Hegel, too, who insisted that the latter is the scientifically correct method.

simpler categories also have an independent historical or natural existence predating the more concrete ones?' (p. 102). In other words, if one begins with a category such as 'material production', must one not therefore begin with neolithic man and his flint tools, and then, step by step, wind one's way laboriously up to the intended subject proper, namely material production in the capitalist form of society? Marx's profound reflections on this question – these pages contain the basic principles of Marxist historiography – lead him to the conclusion that this would be an error. The proper beginning is not with the dawn of history, but rather with that category which occupies a predominant position within the particular social formation being studied (p. 107–8). It would seem to follow, though Marx does not so state it, that the proper beginning for the critique of the bourgeois economic categories (and system) would be not 'material production in general' but rather 'capital', or at least 'production for exchange value'; for these are the categories which rule this historic society.

The question of the proper beginning remains unsettled in Marx's Introduction. What he says about it in the summary paragraph (p. 108) is inconclusive: 'The order obviously has to be (1) the general, abstract determinants which obtain in more or less all forms of society, but in the above-explained sense.' This, however, is a manifest impossibility, since the 'above-explained sense' is precisely that *not* the categories obtaining in more or less all societies, but rather those which dominate a particular society in distinction to other societies, ought to form the starting point. This formulation does not solve the problem. The halting, provisional and in a sense purely accidental start made by the Chapter on Money – Darimon's bank schemes – testifies to this lingering difficulty.

To find the proper beginning – the starting point where the mystical Hegel, the 'prosaic economists' and Marx's own doubts are left behind – one must turn to the very last page of the *Grundrisse*'s seventh notebook (p. 881), a section Marx subtitled '(1) Value', with the note, 'to be brought forward'. This short fragment is an initial attempt to recapitulate the content of the whole manuscript in systematic, cohesive form. Its beginning is this: 'The first category in which bourgeois wealth presents itself is that of the *commodity*. The commodity itself appears as unity of two aspects [namely use value and exchange value] . . .'.

It is this category, the commodity, which forms the starting point also of Marx's *Critique of Political Economy* (1859) and of *Capital* I (1867). It is a beginning which is at once concrete, material, almost tangible, as well as historically specific (to capitalist production); and it contains within it (is the unity of) a key antithesis (use value *v.* exchange value) whose development involves all the other contradictions of this mode of production. Unlike Hegel's *Logic*, and unlike Marx's own initial attempts earlier, this beginning begins not with a pure, indeterminate, eternal and universal abstraction, but rather with a compound, determinate, delimited and concrete whole – 'a concentration of many determinations, hence unity of the diverse' (p. 101). In a word, this 'impure' beginning with which the *Grundrisse* ends is superior *as dialectics* to the previous starts, because it *contains* contradiction from the outset, in embryo; whereas the 'pure'(indeterminate, eternal, absolute and universal) beginning starts, falsely, by *excluding* an opposite (else it would not be pure!), and hence has to pull its antithesis in by the hairs, out of 'nothing', by magic, which procedure then becomes the bad precedent for all subsequent developments and transformations. Only a materialist beginning, that is, a beginning with the concrete, the determinate, and hence (as Hegel himself maintained) the contradictory in-itself, can therefore be a truly dialectical beginning, and can alone realize the powers latent in the method which Hegel both perfected and mystified.

That the start of the *Grundrisse* Introduction had been a false one, Marx acknowledged about a year and a half later, in 1859, after he had twice rewritten the Chapter on Money to ready it for print. The notion that the path of investigation must proceed from simple, general, abstract relations towards complex particular wholes no longer appeared to him, then, as 'obviously the scientifically correct procedure'. In his justly famous 'Preface' to the *Critique of Political Economy*, written to replace the *Grundrisse* Introduction, he writes as follows:

'I am suppressing a general Introduction which I had thrown on paper, because on closer consideration [*bei näherem Nachdenken*] any anticipation of yet-to-be-proved results seems to me a distraction, and the reader who wishes to follow me at all must resolve to climb from the particular up to the general.'[35]

Now to the second point announced above, in which an

35. *MEW* XIII, p. 7.

essential difference between the dialectic method in idealist *v.* in materialist hands shows itself, namely the question of the immediacy of identities. The issue here is this: given that every unity (identity, totality, whole; it does not matter here) is composed of contradictory poles or aspects, are we to understand that the unity of these opposites is absolute, immediate and unconditional, or is it rather the case that the opposites require an intermediary in order to form a unity, and that the effectiveness of this intermediary (and hence the maintenance of the whole) is dependent on certain conditions which may or may not be present?

In lieu of a lengthy philosophical discussion of this question, which would be required to get to the bottom of it, we may proceed to show something of its economic and political significance by contrasting certain passages from the *Grundrisse* Introduction with others in the body of the text.

If one compares the 'identities' between production and consumption 'demonstrated' on pp. 90–94 with the corresponding point in the body of the *Grundrisse* notebooks, one will see in sharp relief the direction in which Marx's ironical remarks about 'immediate identities leaving immediate dualities intact' in the Introduction are driving. The most strategic point for making the comparison is at the moment when the capitalist production process is completed and its results, the commodities, are about to re-enter circulation with destination, consumption. Here the question of their identity as opposites is posed not 'in general', throughout history, but for capitalism in particular. *Is* the unity of production and consumption (realization) an *immediate* one? Just the opposite:

'The main point here – where we are concerned with the general concept [*Begriff*] of capital – is that it is this *unity of production and realization*, not *immediately* [*unmittelbar*] but only as a *process*, which is linked to certain conditions . . .' (p. 407).

In several pages in the entire (logical) subsection of the text which treats the question of the unity of capitalist production and capitalist consumption (pp. 401–58), Marx explicitly attacks the notion that 'production is immediately identical with consumption', and shows that this notion, in the greatest of hands – for instance Ricardo's – may lead to profound insights, but not to a grasp of the totality in process, and ultimately results, in lesser hands, in childishness and absurdity (pp. 410–14). '*First of all, there is a limit, not inherent to production generally, but to produc-*

tion founded on capital' (p. 415 – Marx's italics). This is the materialist formulation of the identity of opposites, which denies the immediacy and absoluteness, the *inevitability* of this identity, and affirms in its place that this identity is a process taking place in space and time, requiring a material means, inherently limited and conditional in nature.

The study in detail of the materialist dialectic in the *Grundrisse* would have to be a study of Marx's *mediations*.[36] There is a rich material for such an investigation, not only in the *Grundrisse* but in the volumes of *Capital* as well.

It may be argued by defenders of Hegel that he too speaks of mediations, and that there are lines of continuity between Hegel's chapter on mediation and Marx's on money. This is the case; and that chapter is one of Hegel's most materialist ones.[37] But in the

36. There have been many attempts to grasp the essential difference between Hegel's dialectic and Marx's. The clearest and most precise, and the one fully corroborated in all essentials by the *Grundrisse*, is that given by Lenin in his article-fragment 'On the Question of Dialectics' and in scattered remarks throughout the *Philosophical Notebooks*; see e.g. *Collected Works* XXXVIII, pp. 359–63, 266, 283, 292, 301, 319–20. The *Grundrisse* had not, of course, been discovered at the time Lenin was writing. Rosdolsky correctly points to the essence of the matter in one short paragraph (Vol. II, p. 669), regrettably without any further development. Lukács, in *History and Class Consciousness*, rightly makes much of the importance of 'mediation' in Marx's work, without however appearing to see that in this lies not only Marx's affinity to Hegel, but rather, even more, Marx's opposition to Hegel; Lukács remains too much a Hegelian to see this. Korsch's attempt (in *Marxismus und Philosophie*, pp. 130–33) is inadequate owing to its failure to pose the question: what is dialectics? He employs the term endlessly but uncritically, often as bludgeon, and hits himself on the head with it more soundly than his opponents. Marcuse's formulation (in *Reason and Revolution*) correctly lays stress on the historical nature of the dialectic in Marx, but does not move beyond this broad generality. The most recent attempt, Althusser's (in *Contradiction et surdétermination*), is itself in need of being stood on its feet; for his 'over-determination' is either a purely quantitative matter (the 'greatest sum, the accumulation of contradictions'), in which case there is little to be said for it, or else it is a roundabout, upside-down formulation of the conditionality, the mediatedness of contradiction. On the central question, what is rational and what is mystical in Hegel's *Begriff*, Althusser remains ultimately ambiguous. Neither the *Grundrisse* nor Lenin's *Philosophical Notebooks* are considered in this seminal essay.

37. Inspiration for Marx's theory of money may be found in Hegel's chapter on Measure (*Logic* I, pp. 387–442) as well as in the pages on Teleology (*Logic* II, pp. 436–61). The clash of Hegel's idealism (the Absolute Concept) with his dialectic is particularly graphic in the latter section, which contains at one and the same time some of Hegel's most directly materialist passages as well as some of his grossest, most undialectical idealism, as for example in the 'vanishing of the mediation' (pp. 458–9).

basic structure of Hegel's argument, the mediations are either subjective or absolute, or, usually, both at the same time. To return to the beginning: where does Hegel indicate the *conditions* on which the identity of Being and Nothing depends? What moment of their contradiction contains the possibility of their non-identity? What basis is given for a potential breakdown in the mediating movement of Becoming? None whatever; there is no such basis, no such possibility; the identity and the mediation are unconditional and absolute. Now compare Marx's starting point in the *Critique of Political Economy* or in *Capital*: the commodity. This is the unity (identity) of two opposites: use value, exchange value. Can one conceive of this identity breaking down? Are grounds given on which the mediating movement (money, exchange) may fail to take place? Certainly. The entire work is addressed precisely to the historic, economic, political etc. conditions on which this initial identity depends; more: the main purpose of the work is to demonstrate that the contradictions within this identity necessarily lead to the suspension of these same conditions and hence to the break-up of commodity production, and to the rise of a system of production founded on use values. For Marx, the identity of opposites is conditional; but their non-identity, their struggle, antagonism and break-up are inevitabilities. Just the opposite in Hegel. It is the difference between a conciliatory, harmonizing 'dialectic' (ultimately no dialectic at all), and a revolutionary, subversive method.

Nor are the outcomes the same. Hegel concludes with simple self-identical Being, Being-at-rest, Being-without-nothing; while the outcome, for Marx, is a new Becoming, conditional on the absence of social antagonism.

To conclude by returning to the particular question raised at the outset – in what way may Hegel's *Logic* have served Marx in overthrowing the Ricardian doctrine of profit? The reader interested in pursuing the matter further will find the necessary clues on pp. 557 ff., where it is shown that the identity of the opposites, wages and profits (or, as moderns would say, their inverse correlation), is neither absolute nor immediate, as Ricardo had thought; but depends, rather, on certain fluctuating intermediaries and on ever-changing external conditions.

Thus the *form* of the text appears as a series of obstacles only at first approach. On second effort the barriers vanish to offer a perspective unequalled by any published work of Marx's.

To read the *Grundrisse* as the record of a mind working is to become aware that Marx had to wage a battle against classical political economy and at the same time forge his armaments; and the converse is also true, that he had to battle against the mystical method of inevitable identities, and required to grasp the essence of capital as a means of doing so. The *unity* of the structure and the method is *visible* in the *Grundrisse* on the surface; and this is its ultimately most important distinguishing characteristic.

However, the unity of method and structure, of materialist dialectics and political-economic theses, is no more direct and immediate in the *Grundrisse* than anywhere else in the world. To grasp this unity requires reading the work as a process, a struggle with leaps and setbacks, in cognizance of origins and ends. Especially is this true of Marx's Introduction. It is a very great and important essay. It reflects in its every line the struggle of Marx against Hegel, Ricardo and Proudhon. From it, Marx carried off the most important objective of all, namely the basic principles of writing history dialectically; but he did not then and there complete his victory in all details, not even in some very important ones. The *suspension* of Hegel and of Ricardo – the demolition of what was metaphysical, mystical in their doctrines, the preservation of the rational cores – is a struggle with which Marx is occupied throughout the pages of the seven workbooks. The rational core therefore still bears, as Hegel put it, some aspects of the being from which it came. Marx recognized these birth-stains in his manuscript even as he was writing it. He criticizes himself expressly for the 'idealist manner of presentation' shown by phrases such as 'product becomes commodity; commodity, exchange value; exchange value, money' (p. 15). Such phrases – and they occur elsewhere as well – stem from Hegel's *Logic*, where 'Becoming' is the 'mediation' that never fails; the Mind need only 'posit' it, think it, and the contradictories are one. These phrases are for Marx a shorthand indicating to himself that the real conditions and intermediations of the transformation are to be considered in detail later. For Marx the absolute is itself conditional. Only when the barriers to human productivity imposed by capitalist relations are broken and cast off do the conditions exist, he says, when one may speak of humanity entering 'the absolute movement of becoming' (p. 488).

In reading the *Grundrisse*, the process and conditions of *its* becoming must never be forgotten, or else the perspectives it opens will once again turn into barriers.

There is a wealth of method more in the *Grundrisse* and in Hegel's great *Logic* than has even been touched on here. Many strands of the very complex relation of Hegel to Marx have been treated as secondary or omitted for the sake of brevity.

Much earlier than 1857–8, in his first known manuscripts on Hegel, Marx had announced the intention to make a critical review of the *Logic*, and had pointed, abstractly, to defects in the dialectic method as Hegel presented and used it.[38] The *Grundrisse* shows the first known attempt self-consciously to change, and to apply the method, at the same time, to major problems of theory.

In the letter to Engels on the *Logic* quoted earlier, Marx wrote that he would very much like, 'if the time ever comes again for such work', to set on paper in plain language 'what is *rational* in the method Hegel discovered but at the same time mystified'. 'That time' never came; and Marx nowhere elaborates on his remark in the 1873 *Preface* regarding the mystical shell and the rational core.

Since the time of the *Grundrisse*, and despite its long absence, the knowledge of materialist dialectics has developed, spread and grown.[39] The materialist dialectic is not exempt from its own

38. Cf. *MEW* I, pp. 203–333, especially pp. 292–5; *MEW Ergänzungsband* I, pp. 568–88. All the elements of Marx's particular character as materialist *and* as dialectician are present here, but the announced intent of focusing and systematizing the many points of difference with Hegel's *Logic* is not carried out.

39. Lenin's *Philosophical Notebooks* contain the essence of all the later development, and are indispensable reading on the question. Bukharin's *Historical Materialism* contains some perceptions, but is as a whole a regression to the pre-Hegelian level of dialectics, proximating Kant. Stalin's *Dialectical and Historical Materialism* condenses Lenin's 'sixteen points' (in the *Philosophical Notebooks*, pp. 221–3) into four points, and is a useful first introduction, particularly for pedagogic purposes. A real development from Lenin occurs in Mao Tse-tung's *On Contradiction* and *On Practice*. These essays are at one and the same time strictly orthodox in the Marxist sense and highly original. Written in 1937, they remain today the classic exposition of materialist dialectics as a whole, the standard against which all other writings must be measured, and which will probably remain unequalled for a very long time. An understanding of these essays is a highly useful preparation for tackling the *Grundrisse*.

laws. It is not carved in tablets. If Marx is right about the course of development then there will be a time in the far-distant future when materialist dialectics will be so universal an acquisition of the human race that its study and mastery will require no special effort, and its application in life will be as unremarkable as breathing.

IV

A number of interrelated *transformations* occur in the course of the *Grundrisse*. The transformation of the Hegelian method has already been considered. There are others.

It was pointed out earlier that, in the *Grundrisse*, Marx begins for the first time to substitute the concept 'labour power' or 'labour capacity' for the classical political-economic concept of 'labour'. What is the significance of this shift?

The determination of value by average labour time – the labour theory of value – was one of the greatest achievements of classical bourgeois political economy. Elsewhere Marx shows that this conception of value had as its presupposition the bourgeois *revolutionary* principle that all persons are created equal; the principle that 'all kinds of labour are equal and equivalent, because and so far as they are human labour in general, cannot be deciphered, until the notion of human equality has already acquired the fixity of a popular prejudice'.[40] However, the bourgeois economists themselves encountered an irreducible sticking-point within their own theory when they began to pose the question – which must inevitably present itself – what is the value of *labour*? This question is at the core of the theory, and without an answer to it the theory itself becomes a mere tautology: 'the value of labour is the value of labour'. Classical economics sensed the difficulty but got itself into an insoluble dilemma attempting to avoid it. Two answers are possible within this framework. One may answer that the 'value of labour' is expressed by the worker's wages. The consequence is ruinous for the founding premise of the theory; for, since the value created by the worker is higher than the worker's wages, this is only another way of saying that 'the value of labour' (as output) is greater than 'the value of labour' (as wages), or that there is some source of value other than labour, which shatters the premise.

40. *Capital* I (International Publishers edn), p. 60.

By this path one is led to the 'factors of production' notion, according to which 'land, labour and capital' link arms 'jointly' to create 'value'; but this, fundamentally, is only a mystical way of giving up the inquiry into value altogether. The other alternative answer within the classical framework is to say that 'value of labour' is expressed in the value of the worker's output, value of the product. This highlights the discrepancy between the value of output and the amount of wages, and strongly suggests that the worker is not paid 'the value of his labour', but is in fact cheated of its value. Because Ricardo leaned in the direction of this alternative, he was accused of radicalism; in fact he was merely a captive of the theory's limitations. Apart from the direct political implications, either of the two possible ways round the dilemma resulted in poor political economy. The accumulation and growth of exchange value, both relatively (in the hands of the capitalist class) and absolutely (aggregate of the whole society) cannot be explained within this framework, but must be brought in through arbitrary, *deus-ex-machina* postulations. The central proposition of the labour theory of value thus acquired the character of an immediate identity of opposites: the 'value of labour' is and is not 'the value of labour' at one and the same time. Classical political economy got around this inherent mysticism only by surreptitiously employing now one, now the opposite determination as the convenience of argument dictated. Eventually, as the development of capitalist economy led the bourgeoisie to suppress its own revolutionary principle, that all men are created equal, and to propagate in its place the opposite notion, political economy gave up inquiring into value altogether, in the objective sense, and its theoretical basis became a kind of astrology of prices.

Marx's approach to the dilemma is to show that it rests on an erroneous conception of the commodity-form. Classical political economy assumed that things are by nature commodities, which is only another way of saying that nature decreed the bourgeois mode of production. It easily fell therefore into the error of asserting that commodities are, by nature, *things*. This is a serviceable assumption for many applications, but, when applied to the commodity 'labour', it only reveals the capitalist prejudice that workers are so many objects to be used, manipulated and cast away when worn out. As political economy, however, the notion that 'labour' is a *thing* leads inevitably to nonsense once it is asked what is that thing's value. Marx points out that 'it did not exist as a thing, but as the capacity of a living being' (p. 323), and he therewith not only restates 'what side he is on', but also unlocks the mystery of accumulation. The commodity which the worker sells the capitalist is not an inanimate object, but a power inseparable from the worker's own bodily existence. On this basis, the question 'what is the value of labour?' appears as badly posed to begin with, like asking the colour of a logarithm. *Labour* is the *activity* of the worker. It *creates* all value, and is itself invaluable; its only measure is time. The commodity the worker sells the capitalist is his power to labour, or, yet more accurately, the *'right of disposition'* over his (or her) labour power (pp. 284, 293), that is, the right to determine how this power will be used. The sale of disposition over labour power is therefore not only a 'purely economic' but also a political act. During the period of work, the worker does not have the right of self-determination, but becomes an unfree person, little distinguishable from a slave. With this concept of what it is the worker sells the capitalist, the term 'political economy' acquires its full meaning. Marx's reasoning is explicitly both political and economic not only at the conclusion of the argument, as a consequence of the premises – or as an afterthought, as in so many modern 'political economies' – but also in the fundamental premise itself, from the very beginning.) Marx's thinking preserves the revolutionary foundation *implicit in* the labour theory of value, namely the principle of general human equality, and shows that in its bourgeois form this principle amounts for the worker to the very opposite of human liberty. With the conception of 'labour power', Marx resolves the inherent contradiction of the classical theory of value; he preserves what is sound in it, namely the determination of value by working time, and on this foundation proceeds to solve the problems of the theory of accumulation which the bourgeois theory could not even face squarely. By thus preserving what was sound and revolutionary in the theory, and bursting through the bourgeois limitations contained in it, Marx turned the old theory into its opposite; from a legitimation of bourgeois rule into the theory of communist parties explaining how the capitalist class grows wealthy from the workers' labour, and showing how this system must lead to ruin; and leading the struggles to overthrow it.

Despite its length, a quotation from Engels's preface to an 1891 reprint of Marx's 1849 pamphlet *Wage Labour and Capital* will help to cast the significance of the shift from 'labour' to 'labour power' into perspective. Engels writes:

'In the forties Marx had not yet brought his critique of political economy to conclusion. This happened only towards the end of the fifties. Thus those of his writings published before the first instalment of *Critique of Political Economy* (1859) diverge in individual points from those composed since 1859, contain expressions and whole sentences which, from the standpoint of the later writings, appear off-centre and even incorrect ... I am certain of acting in his spirit when, *for this edition*, I undertake the few alterations and additions which are required ...

'My alterations all revolve around one point. According to the original, what the worker sells the capitalist in exchange for wages is his *labour*; according to the present text, his labour *power*. And for this change I owe an explanation. Explanation to the workers, so that they may see that this is not merely a case of squabbling over words, but rather one of the most important points of political economy. Explanation to the bourgeois, so that they may convince themselves how powerfully the uneducated workers – to whom the most difficult economic developments can easily be made comprehensible – are superior to our snotty "educated gentlemen", for whom such complicated questions remain insoluble all their lives long.'[41]

Engels then proceeds to give, in five pages, one of the best short explanations of the difference between the old labour theory of value and Marx's labour theory of surplus value. Competent modern editions of the pamphlet *Wage Labour and Capital* give the text as revised by Engels, indicating with footnotes where Engels made changes.

Because he had not yet worked out the theory of surplus value, much of Marx's earlier economic writing, pre-*Grundrisse*, was less than clear on the question of the workers' material conditions under capitalism. The sharpening of the gap between the relative conditions of the two major classes – relative impoverishment – is a constant theme in his writing from beginning to end. The ambiguity, earlier, lay in the question of absolute impoverishment, or whether the wages of employed workers necessarily drop down to and below the level required for bare animal survival. The original

41. *MEW* VI, p. 593.

text of *Wage Labour and Capital* was essentially unclear on this question; but an 1847 manuscript *On Wages* published posthumously reflects Marx's thinking at the time in more detail.[42] The manuscript admits wage fluctuations over the short term, both up and down, due to 'changing fashions, seasons and states of commerce', but argues that a downward ratchet effect was operative, preventing wages, once they had fallen, from ever rising again to their full previous level; so that, over the longer term, 'the minimum ... sinks ever closer to the absolutely lowest level' and '. . . the quantity of commodities the worker obtains in exchange becomes ever smaller'. Marx then still stood, on this question, on the same level as Ricardo, and held, like Ricardo, that there was a strict 'inverse relation between profit and wages'.[43] From this it follows that every increase in capitalist profit presupposes a drop in wages; hence capitalist accumulation is possible only by killing off the working class through starvation. This one-sided view is corrected in the *Grundrisse* with the overthrow of Ricardo's theory of profit. The immediate inverse identity of profit and wages holds only in the short run, and only if the intensity of exploitation (for example speed of production) is held constant. Over the somewhat longer term, specifically during the upward phase of the economic cycle, however, both wages and profits may show an absolute increase at the same time; and during such periods the worker may either take the risk of accumulating a small fund of savings for the next crisis, or may broaden the sphere of his consumption to take a small part in 'higher, even cultural satisfactions, . . . [for instance] agitation for his own interests, newspaper subscriptions, attending lectures, educating his children, developing his taste etc.,' constituting the worker's 'only share of civilization which distinguishes him from the slave' (p. 287). During such periods of prosperity, the relation of capital and labour reveals a side which 'is an essential civilizing moment, and on which the historic justification, but also the contemporary power of capital rests' (p. 287). It is furthermore theoretically possible, quite apart from the question of the economic cycle, for one fraction of the working class (but not the whole) to receive, via the mechanisms of the distribution of profit among the different capitalists, 'an extremely small share of' the surplus value produced by themselves in the form of 'surplus wages' (p. 438). This is one side of the matter. However,

42. *MEW* VI, p. 535.   43. *MEW* VI, pp. 543, 544, 554.

there is also at the same time the other side. Firstly, the course of capitalist development proceeds in cycles of 'prosperity' alternating with crises, during which latter there is 'suspension of labour' (unemployment), 'degradation of the labourer' and a most straitened exhaustion of his vital powers' (p. 750) (Marx's English; that is, an absolute reduction in real wages combined with speed-up). Furthermore, quite apart from, but modulated by, crises, there is, with the advance of capitalist accumulation, also an increase in the percentage of the working class as a whole which exists as a surplus population, that is, surplus relative to the employment capital makes available. A portion of this surplus labour power is held to reserve for periods of capitalist accumulation; another portion is maintained out of state revenue as perpetual paupers; a fragment becomes lumpen (pp. 608–10). The whole of this surplus population – surplus relative to the needs of capitalist accumulation – grows larger as capital approaches its inherent limits and barriers (p. 608). Finally, the periodic crises of overproduction repeat themselves 'on a higher scale', with increasing severity (p. 750). Thus, in sum, the long-run historic tendency towards relative impoverishment is accompanied by the long-run historic tendency towards absolute impoverishment of an increasing proportion of the working class; and the experience of the remainder of the working class as a whole is one of periods of absolute improvement accompanied by growing insecurity, and broken by increasingly sharp crises during which absolute impoverishment is the general fate.

Thus the theory emerging from the *Grundrisse* – and later elaborated, in most points, in *Capital* – is not a single-element or single-trend formula. It corresponds much more accurately to the real experience of working-class life, in which the level of real wages at any one time makes up only one of the elements of the material condition as a whole. The theory worked out in the *Grundrisse* is also politically superior to the old one in that the relevance of labour unions receives a theoretical foundation; with the previous single-element linear absolute-impoverishment thesis, it is difficult to see what use such organizations would be economically. A similar theory, the so-called 'iron law of wages', was employed by Weitling and later Lassalle in Germany to attempt to prevent workers from combining into unions on precisely these grounds; in England, the Owenite 'Citizen' Weston based himself on such a theory of wages to argue to the same effect.[44] Marx's overthrow of the Ricardian doctrine of profit in the *Grundrisse,* and the consequent ramifications for his theory of wages, are the key elements which allowed him later to defeat the Weitling–Lassalle–Weston tendencies theoretically and organizationally within the First International.

(The difference between surplus value and profit also leads Marx to an elementary formulation of exploitative trade relations (p. 872).)

A brief word here only about the theory of *alienation*; brief not because it lacks interest, quite the contrary – it is one of the most fascinating portions of the work – but because to comment at all would mean to comment fairly extensively.

The earlier writings, notably *Economic-Philosophical Manuscripts of 1844* ('Paris Manuscripts') were less than altogether unambiguous on the question whether 'alienation' was to be conceived as a universal, eternal human condition, or whether it was rooted in the particular historical mode of capitalist production and hence transitory. This state of less than total consistency and clarity variously 'grounded' itself in, and expressed itself as, identification of the concept 'alienation' with the concept 'objectification'. Since objectification – that is, making things – is inseparable from any human society more advanced than gathering berries, the identification of the two terms could wilfully be interpreted as Marx's 'vision' of alienation forever. In the *Grundrisse* the issue is met squarely and altogether consistently. To quote only a brief excerpt from one passage among many: 'The bourgeois economists are so much cooped up within the notions belonging to a specific historic stage of social development that the necessity of the *objectification* of the powers of social labour appears to them as inseparable from their *alienation vis-à-vis* living labour' (p.832).

Accordingly, alienation is conceived of as fundamentally a particular relation of *property*, namely involuntary sale (surrender of ownership) to a hostile Other; see for example p. 455. The term thus re-acquires much of the original juridical and economic meaning; see for example Steuart's use of it, cited on p. 779.

It follows that the historical phase in which alienation is the

44. A good account of these different trends, and of Marx's position towards them, may be found in W. Z. Foster, *History of the Three Internationals* (International Publishers, 1955), pp. 44–72.

predominant form of objectification must be judged not merely a lamentable disaster, but rather also at the same time a definite forward step, a progressive stage, which creates the presuppositions of its abolition. This progressive side of the relation must be stressed against the romantic critique (see for example pp. 162, 515, 831).

Finally, instead of 'species-being', the *Grundrisse* speaks of two very broadly and generally defined types of human individuality. The first is the 'private individual', meaning the individual as private proprietor, both as owner of the means of production and as 'owner' of the commodity, labour power; the individual within the exchange-value relation. The abolition of the relations of private property is the abolition of the conditions which produce and reproduce this kind of individual. The place of this type is taken by the *social individual*, the individual of classless society, a personality type which is not less, but rather more, developed as an individual because of its direct social nature. As opposed to the empty, impoverished, restricted individuality of capitalist society, the new human being displays an all-sided, full, rich development of needs and capacities, and is universal in character and development (pp. 161–2, 172–3, 325, 487–8, 540–42, 611, 652, 706, 708, 712, 749, 831–2).

A word must also be said here, in passing, about the justly famous passages on machinery and automation (pp. 670–711), which have been so often quoted. Marx here points out, among other things (and, incidentally, this insight is already in Hegel), that with the advance of the division of labour and the growing scale of capitalist production, the role of the worker in the industrial process has a tendency to be transformed from active to passive, from master to cog, and even from participant to observer, as the system of machinery becomes more automatic. Do these passages imply, as some writers have thought, that manual, industrial work, and hence the class which does it, will therefore, under capitalism, disappear, to be replaced, perhaps, by a 'new vanguard' of engineers and technicians?[45] Such a reading of these passages would be altogether false. It would ignore Marx's unambiguous statements, in many other passages, that there are counter-tendencies which prevent mechanization

45. This, for example, is the misinterpretation projected into the *Grundrisse* by C. Oglesby, ed., *New Left Reader* (New York, 1969), p. 84.

and automation from advancing beyond a certain limited point, under capitalism; such a counter-tendency, for example, is the decline in the rate of profit which results from increased investment in machinery relative to living labour. Even in the very same passage on machinery, Marx adds, significantly, that (under capitalism) 'the most developed machinery thus forces the worker to work longer than the savage does, or than he himself did with the simplest, crudest tools' (pp. 708–9). Neither here nor anywhere else in Marx's work is there a prediction that manual industrial labour will be abolished in capitalist society; indeed, the weight of Marx's argument carries in the contrary direction.

One could go on. Marx's theory of the sphere of circulation, together with the theory of production, provides, implicitly, the basis for a theory of forms of the state, for example, roughly, the former as basis for the shell of democracy, the latter the basis of capitalist dictatorship. Marx as much as states that a theory of state forms is implicit in the work, in a letter to Kugelmann.[46] But it would need to be developed.

Since Marx's time the theory of value – law of value – has become a question of dispute in countries where a socialist revolution occurred. An enormous amount of material in the *Grundrisse* bears on this question.

The famous 1859 *Preface* speaks of the contradiction between the forces of production and the relations of production. Relatively little is said in *Capital* about this question. The *Grundrisse* is one long extended commentary upon it; inversely, the 1859 formulation is a summary, in a word, of the *Grundrisse*.

One could go on and on. The *Grundrisse* is like an anticipation, on paper, of the rich, all-sided individuality Marx was talking about. Each time one returns to it, one finds something new.

V

Marx valued highly the material contained in his seven workbooks. As he said in his letter to Engels already quoted, he had 'some nice developments' indeed. His evaluation of the new theory of profit he had worked out – 'in every respect the most important law of modern political economy, and the most essential for

46. *MEW* XXX, p. 639.

understanding the most difficult relations' (p. 748) – forms a part of this judgement. In a letter to Lassalle, he terms it 'the result of fifteen years of research, thus of the best period of my life'. Even more strongly (Marx was sparing to the utmost with the adjective 'scientific'), in the same letter: '. . . the first scientific representation of an important view of social relations'.[47] The tone of achievement, of overview and summing-up, appearing in his 1859 *Preface to the Critique of Political Economy*, is a reflection of Marx's estimate of the worth of these notebooks. By Marx's standards of self-evaluation – he was very modest – this ranks very high. It is even unique; not, however, because Marx never achieved anything greater, but because the more he did, the more he saw yet to be done, and measured his achievements against the latter standard. Late in life, asked about his 'complete works', he is said to have remarked, 'they would first have to be written'.

The *form* of the manuscript was another question altogether. It was partly a question of the internal order of the subject matter. '. . . The reading of my manuscript', Marx wrote to Engels, 'will cost me nearly a week. The devil is that in the manuscript (it would be a fat volume in print) everything is jumbled up together like beets and cabbages, much that is designed only for much later parts.'[48] As for the writing style, Marx found it 'dull, wooden', smacking of an ailing liver.[49] It was not merely a question of writing style, however; before long, the form of the manuscript also became an important political question. These moments of content, form of presentation (in the larger sense) and writing style (form in the narrower sense) make up a complex struggle with which Marx was occupied for much of the time during the following decade. This story is an important part of the *Grundrisse*.

The early part of the manuscripts contains several plans. The first of these, in the Introduction (p. 108) begins with '(1) the general, abstract determinants which obtain in more or less all forms of society . . .' and proceeds to sketch four additional sections covering capital, wage labour, landed property, the state, international trade, the world market and crises together with related subjects. A second plan, towards the end of the Chapter on Money, omits the 'general, abstract determinants'; possibly Marx had already at this point decided not to use the introduction. Otherwise the content of this plan is substantially the same as the first (p. 228). Two additional plans give further details (pp. 264,

47. *MEW* XXIX, p. 566.   48. ibid., p. 330.   49. ibid., p. 566.

275–81). In a letter written at the end of February, before completion of the manuscript, Marx describes the project as a whole as
consisting of six books:[50]

1. Capital
2. Landed Property
3. Wage Labour
4. The State
5. International Trade
6. World Market

In a letter to Engels at the beginning of April, Marx repeats precisely this plan of six books.[51] The same plan is mentioned repeatedly in correspondence thereafter, and there is no evidence
that Marx ever decided that the logic of this plan was unsound.[52]
Indeed, the sixth book, on the world market, is mentioned in the
third volume of *Capital*, together with the credit system, as subjects which 'do not come within the scope of this work [that is
Capital] and belong to its eventual continuation'.[53]

The whole opus composed of these six books was to bear the
comprehensive title *Critique of Political Economy*, and was to
appear in a series of instalments with a German publisher.

The present manuscript is the basic outline of this entire opus.
The plans for the further books contained in the *Grundrisse* are
the only known comprehensive view of the intended contents of
this project, including the only plans for the projected fourth book
on the state (pp. 109, 264). Only the still unpublished 1854/5
manuscript on the exchange rate and crises, held in Moscow, is
likely to add to the contents of the *Grundrisse* and *Capital* in
regard to the fifth and sixth of the projected works, on international trade and the world market.

However, Marx did not at any point intend to make each of the
six books of about equal size. In a letter written even before the

50. *MEW* XXIX, p. 549.   51. ibid., p. 312.
52. Engels's statement paraphrased in McLellan, that 'what Marx intended
to say on the subject is said there, somehow or other', clearly refers only to the
second volume of *Capital*, not to Marx's political-economic work as a whole.
See *Capital* II (International Publishers edn), p. 4; compare McLellan,
Marx's Grundrisse (Macmillan, London, 1971), p. 9. See also Rosdolsky, I,
pp. 24–78, who (because he leaves Hegel and the question of method aside)
unfortunately does not distinguish between '*Aufbauplan*' (roughly, blueprint)
and the inner construction, that is, the logic of the content itself.
53. *Capital* III (International Publishers edn), p. 110.

completion of the seven workbooks, he said, 'It is by no means my intention to work out evenly all six of the books into which I divide the whole, but rather, in the last three, to give mostly only the basic strokes; whereas in the first three, which contain the basic developments proper, elaboration of details is not always avoidable.'[54]

Unevenness becomes the keynote of the further development. By the end of 1862, Book I ('Capital') has grown into a manuscript of such proportions that Marx announces the intention of publishing it independently under that title, with 'Critique of Political Economy' only as subtitle.[55] However, even within this first book, the divisions and subdivisions undergo a highly disproportionate development.

The first book of the six (the one on capital) was to consist – according to a plan in a letter to Engels (2 April 1858) – of four sections:[56]

(a) capital in general
(b) competition
(c) credit
(d) 'share capital, as the most complete form (turning over into communism), together with all its contradictions'

The first of these four sections ('capital in general') was in turn subdivided into three parts, namely 1. Value, 2. Money, 3. Capital. The major part of the *Grundrisse* is composed of exactly this latter content; the first two subdivisions being combined in the Chapter on Money, the third subdivision being the Chapter on Capital. Thus while on one scale the *Grundrisse* is the Olympian overview of the whole, on another scale it is one fourth of one sixth of the entire opus as originally projected. The first three volumes of *Capital*, however, are themselves, in subject matter, no more than this first of the four projected parts of the original design of the book on capital.

The determinant elements in the disproportionate nature of the further development were two. The first was lack of time and money. Marx was repeatedly kept from working by illness, by slanderous public attacks on him on the part of a Bonapartist agent (during much of 1860–61), by desperate lack of money, and by the demands of political activity in London. The second and

54. *MEW* XXIX, p. 554.   55. *MEW* XXX, p. 630.
56. *MEW* XXIX, p. 312.

probably major factor was the political content of the work and the problem of reaching the proper audience, or, in short, the problem of finding the correct *method of presentation*.

Marx rewrote the contents of the Chapter on Money in the *Grundrisse* twice during 1858. With each of the revisions, more of the polemical content disappeared; the explicit critique of Darimon and the Proudhonists goes out, except for a mild remark or two; the passages on capitalism as a transitory historical mode of production vanish; about all that remains is some acerbic criticism of Ricardo. Most of the Hegelian language, interestingly enough, remained. The tone was what Marx in a letter called 'strictly scientific, i.e. not liable to police censorship'; for all printed material in Germany then, as in Tsarist Russia during Lenin's time, had to be police-inspected.[57] Marx sent the manuscript off in February 1859, writing, 'I hope to win a scientific victory for our Party. It will now have to show, however, whether it is numerous enough to buy enough copies to satisfy the publisher's "scruples".'[58]

Marx had originally intended to include the Chapter on Capital in this first instalment of the *Critique of Political Economy*, but then changed his mind. 'You will see,' he wrote to Lassalle before the publication of the *Critique*, 'that the first part does not yet contain the main chapter, namely the third one on *capital*. I held this advisable on *political* grounds, because the actual battle begins with III, and it seemed advisable not to throw a fright into people right at the outset.'[59]

The reaction to the publication of the first instalment of the *Critique* (containing value and money) was anything but fright. It was dead silence.

'You are mistaken,' – to Lassalle – 'if you think I had expected praise and recognition from the German press, or cared. I expected attacks or criticism, anything except to be totally ignored, which must also hurt sales significantly. At various times these people cursed out my communism so copiously that one would expect them to unload their wisdom now on its theoretical foundation. After all, there are some professional economics journals in Germany.'[60]

But these, of course, were journals of the bourgeoisie. Despite or perhaps because of the unpolemical, 'strictly-scientific' manner

57. *MEW* XXIX, p. 551.　　58. ibid., p. 573.
59. ibid., p. 586.　　60. ibid., p. 618.

of presentation, the work was met with a conspiracy of silence at this level.

The German press in the United States, on the other hand, discussed the work widely. But here the other side of the work's style hindered its acceptance: 'I am only afraid that for the working-class public there [in the U.S.] it is on too theoretical a level.'[61] Much later, in 1862, Marx puts it more bluntly. 'The manner of presentation, admittedly, was very non-popular.'[62]

Even the 'Party-friends' – the informal network of veterans of 1848 who kept in touch – in Germany were no help. To Marx personally, they gushed praise; but lifted not a finger to circulate the work.[63]

The work had fallen between chairs.

The question of the proper method of presentation of the content of the Chapter on Money was different from that of the content of the Chapter on Capital. In the former, the subject matter was itself abstract and nothing was said explicitly about exploitation, the contradiction of labour and capital, etc. As Engels put it, Marx's exposition of the value-form is the '*An-sich* of the whole bourgeois garbage', that is, the revolutionary implications are there in themselves, like a fish-hook in an innocuous-looking worm.[64] It requires the second chapter, however, to set the hook. Here the point is no longer '*an-sich*' but 'for-others'. The problem is: which others? To write with the expectation of reviews in professional journals might well have some usefulness under the circumstances of censorship in the case of the first chapter; but to expect, especially after the conspiracy of silence, that the *openly* revolutionary chapter would be more hospitably received – unthinkable.

The political content of the chapter dictated that it be written in such a way as to be directly accessible to a working-class readership.

By this, Marx understood something different from actual 'popularization'. '*Scientific* attempts to revolutionize a science can never be truly popular.'[65] But *more* popularly written than the *Critique of Political Economy*, definitely. And this required not thinning out the material, but rather an enormous additional labour of research to pack the entire argument in concrete significant detail.

61. ibid., p. 618.   62. *MEW* XXX, p. 640.   63. ibid., p. 640.
64. *MEW* XXXI, p. 308.   65. *MEW* XXX, p. 640.

Between August 1861 and July 1863, Marx rewrote the entire Chapter on Capital, plus the manuscript later published as Vol. 4 of *Capital* ('Theories of Surplus Value'); the whole making twenty-three notebooks totalling 1,472 quarto pages.

Between 1863 and 1865, virtually all of this, except the history of the theory, is rewritten again, with new material added; Vols. 2 and 3 of *Capital* are chiefly based on this manuscript.

Between 1865 and 1867, further research and rewriting prior to the publication of Vol. I of *Capital*.

'It is becoming much more popular and *the method is much more hidden* than in Part I' (to Engels, December 1861).[66] At the same time, Marx works on the theory of ground rent, and on a reproduction table. The point was to present a work in which the most complex problems of political economy were taken up and resolved in the most rigorous manner – and to present it in a form accessible to readers without university education.

'In this last draft, the thing, it seems to me, is taking a tolerably popular form, discounting a few unavoidable M–C and C–Ms' (to Engels, August 1863).[67]

'The form will be a little different, more popular to some degree. By no means out of inner drive on my part, but firstly this second part has a direct revolutionary task, and then, too, the relations I depict are more concrete.'[68]

In 1862, Marx gave up the earlier plan to publish the *Critique* in the form of a series. He also dropped the projected outline of the 'book on capital' communicated to Engels in April 1858. That is, instead of the plan to divide this book into (a) capital in general, (b) competition, (c) credit and (d) share capital, Marx decided to stay with the original subdivisions of the Chapter on Capital in the *Grundrisse*, that is, production process, circulation of capital, and the unity of the two, or division of surplus value into profit, interest, rent; these to form a volume each, respectively, with a fourth volume to be added on the history of theories of surplus value.[69] Dropped, in effect, were the projected volumes on competition, credit and share capital; these became chapters and fragments of chapters in the three volumes of *Capital* which eventually appeared. It is improbable that Marx had made any serious steps towards the execution of the projected volumes on competition, credit and share capital, beyond the material con-

66. *MEW* XXX, p. 207 (emphasis added).   67. ibid., p. 368.
68. ibid., p. 565.   69. *MEW* XXX, p. 640; XXXI, p. 132.

tained in the *Grundrisse*. The abandonment of this plan and the return to the original plan of the second chapter of the *Grundrisse* therefore did not signify scrapping any material already accumulated, or altering a structure already built. When Marx speaks in his letters of the period of having had to 'turn everything upside down', he is referring not to the work already achieved in his manuscripts – of having to scrap this and start again – but rather that in his work he had to overthrow virtually all of previous political economy.[70] On the contrary, the decision to let the questions of competition, credit and share capital remain as chapters rather than as independent volumes flows consistently from his announced intention, at the beginning, of developing the whole opus unevenly, concentrating on the 'basic development' and leaving the derivative questions to be dealt with in brief, broad outlines only. This is made clear in Marx's letter to Kugelmann announcing the dropping of the further volumes, concentrating instead on the first, 'capital in general'. He writes 'This volume contains what the English call "the principles of political economy". It is the quintessence (together with the first part [value, money]), and the development of what follows (with the exception perhaps of the relation of the different forms of the state to the different economic structures of society) could easily be accomplished by others on the basis of it.'[71]

The important questions in regard to the transformation between the *Grundrisse* and *Capital* are not questions of this volume or that, this chapter or another. Marx undertook changes in the chapters of the first volume of *Capital* even between the first and the second German editions. The point, rather, is the *inner structure* of the argument, the inner logic and method of the whole. Marx had long been aware of the dialectic between this and the method of presentation. Directly after completing the *Grundrisse* manuscript, Marx took time to read a work by Lassalle, just published, which attempted to reconstruct the system of Heraclitus's philosophy on the basis of the scattered fragments extant. After expressing regrets that Lassalle had employed the Hegelian method in the orthodox Hegelian way, without any '*critical* indications of your relation to the Hegelian dialectic', Marx adds tactfully that 'the difficulties you had to overcome in your work

70. *MEW* XXX, p. 368; also p. 280. Rosdolsky's reading is the correct one (I, p. 42n.).

71. *MEW* XXX, p. 640.

are all the more clear to me as about 18 years ago I wrote a similar work on a much easier philosopher, Epicurus – namely the presentation of the total system on the basis of fragments ... Even with philosophers who gave their work a systematic form, e.g. Spinoza, the real inner structure [*innere Bau*] of his system, is after all, wholly different from the form in which he consciously presented it.'[72]

This is the case also of *Capital*, particularly of the first volume, the only one Marx personally prepared for publication. The *inner* structure is *identical* in the main lines to the *Grundrisse*, except that in the *Grundrisse* the structure lies on the surface, like a scaffolding, while in *Capital* it is built *in*; and this inner structure is nothing other than the materialist dialectic method. In the *Grundrisse* the method is visible; in *Capital* it is deliberately, consciously hidden, for the sake of more graphic, concrete, vivid and *therefore* more materialist-dialectical presentation. This is precisely the sense of a famous aphorism of Lenin's, that 'it is impossible completely to understand Marx's *Capital*, and especially its first chapter, without having thoroughly studied and understood the *whole* of Hegel's *Logic*. Consequently, half a century later none of the Marxists understood Marx!!'[73] What is not visible in, cannot be understood directly from, *Capital* is the *method of working* by which the whole was built.

The question whether, now that the *Grundrisse* is published – Lenin did not know of it when he wrote this aphorism – it is any longer necessary to read Hegel's *Logic* in order completely to understand *Capital* – this question is ultimately a practical one. Theoretically speaking, perhaps the best is to read the *Grundrisse* as preparation for reading the *Logic* and then to read *Capital*, for it will be difficult completely to understand the relevance of the *Logic* for *Capital* without reading the whole of the *Grundrisse* first. Sound theoretical arguments can also be made for reading in reverse order, or in several cycles, etc. etc. But, as Marx put it in the *Grundrisse*, in all theoretical questions the 'real subject ... must always be kept in mind as the presupposition' (pp. 101–2); and it would be a misreading of Lenin's intent to argue that, in

72. *MEW* XXIX, p. 561. See Lenin, *Collected Works* XXXVIII, p. 319; 'If Marx did not leave behind him a "*Logic*" (with a capital letter), he did leave the *logic* of *Capital*, and this ought to be utilized to the full in the question [of dialectics].'

73. Lenin, *Collected Works* XXXVIII, p. 180.

order to understand the 4,000 pages of the whole of *Capital* one absolutely must first read the 800 pages of the *Grundrisse* and the 1,000 pages of the *Logic*! This is a project for a long term in prison; meanwhile, much can be gained from *Wages, Price and Profit* and *On Contradiction*.[74]

The fact that much content in the *Grundrisse* is not carried over into *Capital* – particularly the directly, outspokenly 'revolutionary' passages – is due precisely to the requirements of the method of presentation employed in *Capital*. Very little is stated in the latter work, especially its first volume, which is not embedded in several layers of historical illustration and documentation. The point on which the effect of the work crucially depended was its acceptance by the most conscious elements among the working class, *directly*, without requiring to be filtered down through professional economics journals of the bourgeoisie. To achieve this effect, the presentation had above all to be *concrete*. Unfortunately there were in 1867 no examples in history of a successful proletarian revolution to employ as illustration and documentation for the 'revolutionary passages'. It would have come across, to the public, as evidence of the author's eccentricity; and hence the prediction that 'the integument must burst asunder' is advanced prudently and only once. Had the 1917 revolution already taken place, *Capital* would have had a far greater latitude of form.

The *Grundrisse* and *Capital I* have opposite virtues of form. The latter is the model of the method of presentation, the former the record of the method of working. To imitate the *Grundrisse* as a 'style' of presentation would be an absurd affectation. The fact that one can read the *Grundrisse* at all today, and understand it, is due solely to Marx's labours in working its basic concept *out*, in *presenting* the content in a form accessible to a public in a position to act on it. In 1858, not a single person in the world understood the *Grundrisse* except Marx, and even he had his troubles with it. It was an altogether unique and in every sense *strange* product of

74. In May 1865, Marx was asked by the General Council of the First International to present a refutation of Weston's views. He was at first dubious about the possibility of getting to the bottom of the question in so short a time. 'You can't compress a course of Political Economy into one hour. But we shall do our best.' (Letter to Engels, 20 May 1865, *MEW* XXXI, p. 123.) The result was the text later published as *Wages, Price and Profit*, which is indeed a whole course of political economy compressed into an eighty-page pamphlet.

the intellect, and must have appeared like the reflections of some man from a distant planet. Emerging from a rat hole of an apartment in a London slum, a bearded foreigner in worn clothing makes his way to the British Museum; writes articles all day for a newspaper in far-off New York; reads obscure treatises no one else has read; pores over a ton of government Blue Books ignored by all; returns to the slum, works deep into the night, piling up notebooks in an illegible script. Hegel? Adam Smith? Ricardo? Proudhon? Who knew or cared? If Marx had died in mid-1858 (it was not so distant a possibility) these seven winter workbooks might well have remained a book of as many seals. Instead, he emerged in 1863 as the only man in London – where working-class leaders from all over the world were in exile or visiting – who could precisely articulate the grounds for the general working-class feeling that the emancipation of wage-slaves required the abolition of slavery in its chattel form;[75] the only man in 1864 who could formulate the elementary principles of unity for the first effective international association of workers;[76] the only man within that association who could refute the narrow reformism of the trade-union leaders *and* the doctrinaire anti-unionism of the utopians and anarchists, all in one coherent systematic argument.[77] Amidst the enormous welter of sects, tendencies, utopias, schemes and hare-brained notions which rose to the surface of the early working-class movement like froth in a storm, there was only one person who had the basic outlines of the entire historical movement firmly and clearly in mind; who had a *concept* of the whole, of its contradictions and limits, and of the road to its overthrow. If we are able to understand the *Grundrisse* at all today, it is because

75. Black labour in the U.S. South supplied the bulk of the raw cotton for the English textile industry. When the Union blockade of the Confederacy cut off these supplies, the result was widespread unemployment and misery among workers in England. In early 1862, seizing upon the 'Trent' affair, English cotton-owners launched an agitation to bring Britain into the war on the Confederate side, to break the Union blockade. Despite their immediate material suffering, the workers in England replied with a peace-agitation of their own which in a short time made the holding of public meetings in favour of intervention impossible. See for example *Marx and Engels on the U.S. Civil War* (International Publishers), or *Documents of the First International*, Vol. I (Lawrence & Wishart).

76. See Foster, *History of the Three Internationals*, pp. 44–72, for an account of Marx's role.

77. These conclusions are drawn and their ramifications stated in the final chapter of *Wages, Price and Profit*.

Marx began and others have continued to demonstrate the actuality of its concept in practice, and because history itself has leaped
ahead. Much that could be expressed in 1857 only in the form of a
hopelessly abstract abstraction has become today so concrete
and familiar as almost to become a commonplace. 'Cataclysms,
crises'? The crisis of 1857 was the first world-wide overproduction
crisis in history. Since then there have been plenty of them,
and we are now entering perhaps the greatest and last. 'Restriction of capitalist production by the law of value'? In the U.S.A.
14 million people, a number equal to the combined populations
of New York, Chicago and Los Angeles, depend on welfare payments for survival as paupers; Capital knows no way to strike a
surplus value from their labour power.[78] 'Abolition of the individual as private proprietor, rise of the social individual'? One has
only to consider the youth of Vietnam and China to see budding
embodiments of this, in 1857, utopian-seeming generality. What is
remarkable about all this development is not so much that it has
developed, but that Marx was able more than a century ago to
grasp its outlines. This is a tribute not to his 'genius' – that is a
nonsense term – but to his *method of work*.

These seven workbooks have been available in the German
original for twenty years now, or more than thirty if one counts
the wartime Moscow edition. Why, after all this time, does the
call now arise (indeed, a small clamour) for an English translation?
Surely a main impetus comes from the series of shocks which the
imperial Anglo-American pragmatism, so long complacent, has
newly suffered from outside and within. In a word, the times have
once more turned 'dialectical'; and so these texts out of a London
winter, long ago, are coming home.

M.N.
San Francisco
1 May 1972

78. Data from *Wall Street Journal*, 27 March 1972, p. 1. This is of course
only one of the ways in which the restriction of production by exchange-value
shows itself. For a broader survey, though not cast in these specific terms, see
Lenin's *Imperialism*.

Note on the Translation

The translation aims at a tight fit to the original, including the roughness of grammar etc. To attempt to 'polish' this text would have been to tamper with an essential part of its significance. On the few occasions where an explanatory word had to be inserted, this is indicated in square brackets. The 1939 editors inserted some additions and corrections of their own; where these are carried in the translation, they are similarly bracketed. Special problems are footnoted. The translation gives a 'smoother' reading than the original in only one significant respect: passages where Marx switched between German, French and English in mid-sentence are given entirely in English.

The 1939 editors chose to switch some passages out of the main text into footnotes, without so noting in each specific case. Consequently, some of the footnotes which appear here as 'Marx's' are actually Marx's own, others represent the material switched by the editors. There is no way of distinguishing them. This would require checking with the handwritten manuscript in Moscow.

The text of the Introduction given in the 1939/53 edition of the *Grundrisse* differs in minor particulars from that later published in Vol. XIII of the *Marx-Engels Werke*; the latter is based on a new study of the handwritten text (Marx's script is virtually a cipher) and succeeds in clarifying a few obscure turns of phrase; it also divides the text into additional paragraphs, which is, to say the least, surprising. Older versions of Marx's Introduction and of the fragment on Bastiat and Carey (pp. 883–93), based on texts edited and published by Kautsky, contained a number of substantial inaccuracies and must be regarded as having been superseded by the 1939/53 and the *Werke* editions, on which the present translation is based.

Our paragraphing follows the 1939/53 edition, which follows the handwriting. However, virtually all the subtitles are taken by the 1939/53 editors from Marx's 'Index to the seven notebooks' and his 'References to my notebooks' – compiled by Marx for his own use in 1858–9 – and inserted in the text at what appeared the appropriate points. This convenience in reading is retained in the translation; however, all such headings not found in the original seven notebooks are here given in roman type. A very few additional such headings were composed by the 1939 editors; these appear in brackets. Notebook headings and chapter titles are Marx's own. Subheadings in italics are also Marx's.

Marx often translated the English text of the writers he quoted into German in such a way as to bring out what for him were the vital points of the writer's thought. For this reason, Marx's own German version has been re-translated into English, hence the slight verbal and stylistic divergences from the original English texts.

*

My thanks go to the persons who helped with problems of translation, in particular B.B. in Frankfurt/Main and F.G. in Padua; and to friends and comrades in San Francisco who read and made criticisms of portions of the translation and the Foreword, or who gave moral and material support during the work.

Special thanks are due to Ben Fowkes for his work in preparing the editorial footnotes to the translation, the Analytical Contents List, the bibliographical and chronological notes at the end of the book, and the index.

Grundrisse

Analytical Contents List[1]

1. In February 1859 Marx made a list of the contents of all his notebooks, except Notebook I. This list is printed in *Grundrisse* (MELI), pp. 951–67. In compiling the present table of contents, we have used Marx's list wherever possible.

THE CHAPTER ON CAPITAL
(Notebooks II pp. 8–28, III, IV, V, VI and VII)

SECTION ONE: THE PRODUCTION PROCESS OF CAPITAL

Introduction

Late August – Mid-September 1857

1. Production, Consumption, Distribution, Exchange (Circulation)

(1) PRODUCTION

Independent Individuals. Eighteenth-century Ideas

The object before us, to begin with, *material production*.

Individuals producing in society – hence socially determined individual production – is, of course, the point of departure. The individual and isolated hunter and fisherman, with whom Smith and Ricardo begin, belongs among the unimaginative conceits of the eighteenth-century Robinsonades,[1] which in no way express merely a reaction against over-sophistication and a return to a misunderstood natural life, as cultural historians imagine. As little as Rousseau's *contrat social*, which brings naturally independent, autonomous subjects into relation and connection by contract, rests on such naturalism. This is the semblance, the merely aesthetic semblance, of the Robinsonades, great and small. It is, rather, the anticipation of 'civil society', in preparation since the sixteenth century and making giant strides towards maturity in the eighteenth. In this society of free competition, the individual appears detached from the natural bonds etc. which in earlier historical periods make him the accessory of a definite and limited human conglomerate. Smith and Ricardo still stand with both feet on the shoulders of the eighteenth-century prophets, in whose imaginations this eighteenth-century individual – the product on one side of the dissolution of the feudal forms of society, on the other side of the new forces of production developed since the sixteenth century – appears as an ideal, whose existence they project into the past. Not as a historic result but as history's point of departure. As the Natural Individual appropriate to their notion of human nature, not arising historically, but posited by nature. This illusion has been common to each new epoch to this day.

1. Utopias on the lines of Defoe's *Robinson Crusoe*.

Steuart[2] avoided this simple-mindedness because as an aristocrat, and in antithesis to the eighteenth century, he had in some respects a more historical footing.

The more deeply we go back into history, the more does the individual, and hence also the producing individual, appear as dependent, as belonging to a greater whole: in a still quite natural way in the family and in the family expanded into the clan [*Stamm*]; then later in the various forms of communal society arising out of the antitheses and fusions of the clans. Only in the eighteenth century, in 'civil society', do the various forms of social connectedness confront the individual as a mere means towards his private purposes, as external necessity. But the epoch which produces this standpoint, that of the isolated individual, is also precisely that of the hitherto most developed social (from this standpoint, general) relations. The human being is in the most literal sense a ζῶον πολιτιχόν,[3] not merely a gregarious animal, but an animal which can individuate itself only in the midst of society. Production by an isolated individual outside society – a rare exception which may well occur when a civilized person in whom the social forces are already dynamically present is cast by accident into the wilderness – is as much of an absurdity as is the development of language without individuals living *together* and talking to each other. There is no point in dwelling on this any longer. The point could go entirely unmentioned if this twaddle, which had sense and reason for the eighteenth-century characters, had not been earnestly pulled back into the centre of the most modern economics by Bastiat,[4] Carey,[5] Proudhon etc. Of course it is a convenience for Proudhon et al. to be able to give a historico-philosophic account of the

2. Sir James Steuart (1712–80), 'the rational exponent of the Monetary and Mercantile System' (Marx), an adherent of the Stuart cause who went into exile in 1745 and pursued economic studies on the Continent. Author of *An Inquiry into the Principles of Political Economy*, London, 1767 (2 vols), Dublin, 1770 (3 vols – the edition used by Marx).

3. A political animal.

4. Frédéric Bastiat (1801–50), French economist, and 'modern bagman of Free Trade' (Marx). A believer in *laissez-faire* and the natural harmony of interests between labour and capital; a fierce opponent of socialism in theory and in practice (as deputy in the Constituent and Legislative Assemblies of 1848 to 1851).

5. Henry Charles Carey (1793–1879), American economist, opponent of Ricardian pessimism ('Carey, who does not understand Ricardo' – Marx), believed in state intervention to establish harmony between the interests of labour and of capital, and in the tendency of real wages to rise.

source of an economic relation, of whose historic origins he is ignorant, by inventing the myth that Adam or Prometheus stumbled on the idea ready-made, and then it was adopted, etc. Nothing is more dry and boring than the fantasies of a *locus communis.*[6]

Eternalization of historic relations of production. – Production and distribution in general. – Property

Whenever we speak of production, then, what is meant is always production at a definite stage of social development – production by social individuals. It might seem, therefore, that in order to talk about production at all we must either pursue the process of historic development through its different phases, or declare beforehand that we are dealing with a specific historic epoch such as e.g. modern bourgeois production, which is indeed our particular theme. However, all epochs of production have certain common traits, common characteristics. *Production in general* is an abstraction, but a rational abstraction in so far as it really brings out and fixes the common element and thus saves us repetition. Still, this *general* category, this common element sifted out by comparison, is itself segmented many times over and splits into different determinations. Some determinations belong to all epochs, others only to a few. [Some] determinations will be shared by the most modern epoch and the most ancient. No production will be thinkable without them; however, even though the most developed languages have laws and characteristics in common with the least developed, nevertheless, just those things which determine their development, i.e. the elements which are not general and common, must be separated out from the determinations valid for production as such, so that in their unity – which arises already from the identity of the subject, humanity, and of the object, nature – their essential difference is not forgotten. The whole profundity of those modern economists who demonstrate the eternity and harmoniousness of the existing social relations lies in this forgetting. For example. No production possible without an instrument of production, even if this instrument is only the hand. No production without stored-up, past labour, even if it is only the facility

6. Of a commonplace (mind). Marx refers here to Bastiat's *Harmonies économiques*, Paris, 1851, pp. 16–19, and Carey's *Principles of Political Economy*, Pt I, Philadelphia, 1837, pp. 7–8.

gathered together and concentrated in the hand of the savage by repeated practice. Capital is, among other things, also an instrument of production, also objectified, past labour. Therefore capital is a general, eternal relation of nature; that is, if I leave out just the specific quality which alone makes 'instrument of production' and 'stored-up labour' into capital. The entire history of production relations thus appears to Carey, for example, as a malicious forgery perpetrated by governments.

If there is no production in general, then there is also no general production. Production is always a *particular* branch of production – e.g. agriculture, cattle-raising, manufactures etc. – or it is a *totality*. But political economy is not technology. The relation of the general characteristics of production at a given stage of social development to the particular forms of production to be developed elsewhere (later). Lastly, production also is not only a` particular production. Rather, it is always a certain social body, a social subject, which is active in a greater or sparser totality of branches of production. Nor does the relationship between scientific presentation and the real movement belong here yet. Production in general. Particular branches of production. Totality of production.

It is the fashion to preface a work of economics with a general part – and precisely this part figures under the title 'production' (see for example J. St. Mill)[7] – treating of the *general preconditions* of all production. This general part consists or is alleged to consist of (1) the conditions without which production is not possible. I.e. in fact, to indicate nothing more than the essential moments of all production. But, as we will see, this reduces itself in fact to a few very simple characteristics, which are hammered out into flat tautologies; (2) the conditions which promote production to a greater or lesser degree, such as e.g. Adam Smith's progressive and stagnant state of society. While this is of value in his work as an insight, to elevate it to scientific significance would require investigations into the periodization of *degrees of productivity* in the development of individual peoples – an investigation which lies outside the proper boundaries of the theme, but, in so far as it does belong there, must be brought in as part of the development of competition, accumulation etc. In the usual formulation, the

7. John Stuart Mill (1806–73), English political theorist and economist; radical in politics, confusedly and eclectically Ricardian in economics. His *Principles of Political Economy*, London, 1848, begin in Bk I, Ch. 1, with the analysis of production.

answer amounts to the general statement that an industrial people reaches the peak of its production at the moment when it arrives at its historical peak generally. In fact. The industrial peak of a people when its main concern is not yet gain, but rather to gain. Thus the Yankees over the English. Or, also, that e.g. certain races, locations, climates, natural conditions such as harbours, soil fertility etc. are more advantageous to production than others. This too amounts to the tautology that wealth is more easily created where its elements are subjectively and objectively present to a greater degree.

But none of all this is the economists' real concern in this general part. The aim is, rather, to present production – see e.g. Mill – as distinct from distribution etc., as encased in eternal natural laws independent of history, at which opportunity *bourgeois* relations are then quietly smuggled in as the inviolable natural laws on which society in the abstract is founded. This is the more or less conscious purpose of the whole proceeding. In distribution, by contrast, humanity has allegedly permitted itself to be considerably more arbitrary. Quite apart from this crude tearing-apart of production and distribution and of their real relationship, it must be apparent from the outset that, no matter how differently distribution may have been arranged in different stages of social development, it must be possible here also, just as with production, to single out common characteristics, and just as possible to confound or to extinguish all historic differences under *general human* laws. For example, the slave, the serf and the wage labourer all receive a quantity of food which makes it possible for them to exist as slaves, as serfs, as wage labourers. The conqueror who lives from tribute, or the official who lives from taxes, or the landed proprietor and his rent, or the monk and his alms, or the Levite and his tithe, all receive a quota of social production, which is determined by other laws than that of the slave's, etc. The two main points which all economists cite under this rubric are: (1) property; (2) its protection by courts, police, etc. To this a very short answer may be given:

to 1. All production is appropriation of nature on the part of an individual within and through a specific form of society. In this sense it is a tautology to say that property (appropriation) is a precondition of production. But it is altogether ridiculous to leap from that to a specific form of property, e.g. private property. (Which further and equally presupposes an antithetical form, *non-property*.) History rather shows common property (e.g. in India, among the Slavs, the early Celts, etc.) to be the more[8] original form, a form which long continues to play a significant role in the shape of communal property. The question whether wealth develops better in this or another form of property is still quite beside the point here. But that there can be no production and hence no society where some form of property does not exist is a tautology. An appropriation which does not make something into property is a *contradictio in subjecto*.

to 2. Protection of acquisitions etc. When these trivialities are reduced to their real content, they tell more than their preachers know. Namely that every form of production creates its own legal relations, form of government, etc. In bringing things which are organically related into an accidental relation, into a merely reflective connection, they display their crudity and lack of conceptual understanding. All the bourgeois economists are aware of is that production can be carried on better under the modern police than e.g. on the principle of might makes right. They forget only that this principle is also a legal relation, and that the right of the stronger prevails in their 'constitutional republics' as well, only in another form.

When the social conditions corresponding to a specific stage of production are only just arising, or when they are already dying out, there are, naturally, disturbances in production, although to different degrees and with different effects.

To summarize: There are characteristics which all stages of production have in common, and which are established as general ones by the mind; but the so-called *general preconditions* of all production are nothing more than these abstract moments with which no real historical stage of production can be grasped.

(2) THE GENERAL RELATION OF PRODUCTION TO DISTRIBUTION, EXCHANGE, CONSUMPTION

Before going further in the analysis of production, it is necessary to focus on the various categories which the economists line up next to it.

The obvious, trite notion: in production the members of society appropriate (create, shape) the products of nature in accord with human needs; distribution determines the proportion in which the

8. *MEW* XIII omits 'more'.

individual shares in the product; exchange delivers the particular products into which the individual desires to convert the portion which distribution has assigned to him; and finally, in consumption, the products become objects of gratification, of individual appropriation. Production creates the objects which correspond to the given needs; distribution divides them up according to social laws; exchange further parcels out the already divided shares in accord with individual needs; and finally, in consumption, the product steps outside this social movement and becomes a direct object and servant of individual need, and satisfies it in being consumed. Thus production appears as the point of departure, consumption as the conclusion, distribution and exchange as the middle, which is however itself twofold, since distribution is determined by society and exchange by individuals. The person objectifies himself in production, the thing subjectifies itself in the person[9]; in distribution, society mediates between production and consumption in the form of general, dominant determinants; in exchange the two are mediated by the chance characteristics of the individual.

Distribution determines the relation in which products fall to individuals (the amount); exchange determines the production[10] in which the individual demands the portion allotted to him by distribution.

Thus production, distribution, exchange and consumption form a regular syllogism; production is the generality, distribution and exchange the particularity, and consumption the singularity in which the whole is joined together. This is admittedly a coherence, but a shallow one. Production is determined by general natural laws, distribution by social accident, and the latter may therefore promote production to a greater or lesser extent; exchange stands between the two as formal social movement; and the concluding act, consumption, which is conceived not only as a terminal point but also as an end-in-itself, actually belongs outside economics except in so far as it reacts in turn upon the point of departure and initiates the whole process anew.

The opponents of the political economists – whether inside or outside its realm – who accuse them of barbarically tearing apart things which belong together, stand either on the same ground as they, or beneath them. Nothing is more common than the re-

9. *MEW* XIII substitutes 'in consumption'.
10. *MEW* XIII substitutes 'products'.

proach that the political economists view production too much as an end in itself, that distribution is just as important. This accusation is based precisely on the economic notion that the spheres of distribution and of production are independent, autonomous neighbours. Or that these moments were not grasped in their unity. As if this rupture had made its way not from reality into the textbooks, but rather from the textbooks into reality, and as if the task were the dialectic balancing of concepts, and not the grasping of real relations!

[Consumption and Production]

(a₁) Production is also immediately consumption. Twofold consumption, subjective and objective: the individual not only develops his abilities in production, but also expends them, uses them up in the act of production, just as natural procreation is a consumption of life forces. Secondly: consumption of the means of production, which become worn out through use, and are partly (e.g. in combustion) dissolved into their elements again. Likewise, consumption of the raw material, which loses its natural form and composition by being used up. The act of production is therefore in all its moments also an act of consumption. But the economists admit this. Production as directly identical with consumption, and consumption as directly coincident with production, is termed by them *productive consumption*. This identity of production and consumption amounts to Spinoza's thesis: *determinatio est negatio*.[11]

But this definition of productive consumption is advanced only for the purpose of separating consumption as identical with production from consumption proper, which is conceived rather as the destructive antithesis to production. Let us therefore examine consumption proper.

Consumption is also immediately production, just as in nature the consumption of the elements and chemical substances is the production of the plant. It is clear that in taking in food, for example, which is a form of consumption, the human being produces his own body. But this is also true of every kind of con-

11. 'Determination is negation', i.e., given the undifferentiated self-identity of the universal world substance, to attempt to introduce particular determinations is to negate this self-identity. (Spinoza, *Letters*, No. 50, to J. Jelles, 2 June 1674.)

sumption which in one way or another produces human beings in some particular aspect. Consumptive production. But, says economics, this production which is identical with consumption is secondary, it is derived from the destruction of the prior product. In the former, the producer objectified himself, in the latter, the object he created personifies itself. Hence this consumptive production – even though it is an immediate unity of production and consumption – is essentially different from production proper. The immediate unity in which production coincides with consumption and consumption with production leaves their immediate duality intact.

Production, then, is also immediately consumption, consumption is also immediately production. Each is immediately its opposite. But at the same time a mediating movement takes place between the two. Production mediates consumption; it creates the latter's material; without it, consumption would lack an object. But consumption also mediates production, in that it alone creates for the products the subject for whom they are products. The product only obtains its 'last finish'[12] in consumption. A railway on which no trains run, hence which is not used up, not consumed, is a railway only δυνάμει,[13] and not in reality. Without production, no consumption; but also, without consumption, no production; since production would then be purposeless. Consumption produces production in a double way, (1) because a product becomes a real product only by being consumed. For example, a garment becomes a real garment only in the act of being worn; a house where no one lives is in fact not a real house; thus the product, unlike a mere natural object, proves itself to be, *becomes*, a product only through consumption. Only by decomposing the product does consumption give the product the finishing touch; for the product is production not as[14] objectified activity, but rather only as object for the active subject; (2) because consumption creates the need for *new* production, that is it creates the ideal, internally impelling cause for production, which is its presupposition. Consumption creates the motive for production; it also creates the object which is active in production as its determinant aim. If it is clear that production

12. In English in the original.
13. 'Potentially'. Cf. Aristotle, *Metaphysics* Bk VIII, Ch. 6, 2.
14. The manuscript has: 'for the product is production not only as . . .'. *MEW* XIII substitutes: 'for the product is a product not as . . .'.

offers consumption its external object, it is therefore equally clear that consumption *ideally posits* the object of production as an internal image, as a need, as drive and as purpose. It creates the objects of production in a still subjective form. No production without a need. But consumption reproduces the need.

Production, for its part, correspondingly (1) furnishes the material and the object for consumption.[15] Consumption without an object is not consumption; therefore, in this respect, production creates, produces consumption. (2) But the object is not the only thing which production creates for consumption. Production also gives consumption its specificity, its character, its finish. Just as consumption gave the product its finish as product, so does production give finish to consumption. *Firstly*, the object is not an object in general, but a specific object which must be consumed in a specific manner, to be mediated in its turn by production itself. Hunger is hunger, but the hunger gratified by cooked meat eaten with a knife and fork is a different hunger from that which bolts down raw meat with the aid of hand, nail and tooth. Production thus produces not only the object but also the manner of consumption, not only objectively but also subjectively. Production thus creates the consumer. (3) Production not only supplies a material for the need, but it also supplies a need for the material. As soon as consumption emerges from its initial state of natural crudity and immediacy – and, if it remained at that stage, this would be because production itself had been arrested there – it becomes itself mediated as a drive by the object. The need which consumption feels for the object is created by the perception of it. The object of art – like every other product – creates a public which is sensitive to art and enjoys beauty. Production thus not only creates an object for the subject, but also a subject for the object. Thus production produces consumption (1) by creating the material for it; (2) by determining the manner of consumption; and (3) by creating the products, initially posited by it as objects, in the form of a need felt by the consumer. It thus produces the object of consumption, the manner of consumption and the motive of consumption. Consumption likewise produces the producer's *inclination* by beckoning to him as an aim-determining need.

The identities between consumption and production thus appear threefold:

15. The manuscript has 'for production'.

(1) *Immediate identity:* Production is consumption, consumption is production. Consumptive production. Productive consumption. The political economists call both productive consumption. But then make a further distinction. The first figures as reproduction, the second as productive consumption. All investigations into the first concern productive or unproductive labour; investigations into the second concern productive or non-productive consumption.

(2) [In the sense] that one appears as a means for the other, is mediated by the other: this is expressed as their mutual dependence; a movement which relates them to one another, makes them appear indispensable to one another, but still leaves them external to each other. Production creates the material, as external object, for consumption; consumption creates the need, as internal object, as aim, for production. Without production no consumption; without consumption no production. [This identity] figures in economics in many different forms.

(3) Not only is production immediately consumption and consumption immediately production, not only is production a means for consumption and consumption the aim of production, i.e. each supplies the other with its object (production supplying the external object of consumption, consumption the conceived object of production); but also, each of them, apart from being immediately the other, and apart from mediating the other, in addition to this creates the other in completing itself, and creates itself as the other. Consumption accomplishes the act of production only in completing the product as product by dissolving it, by consuming its independently material form, by raising the inclination developed in the first act of production, through the need for repetition, to its finished form; it is thus not only the concluding act in which the product becomes product, but also that in which the producer becomes producer. On the other side, production produces consumption by creating the specific manner of consumption; and, further, by creating the stimulus of consumption, the ability to consume, as a need. This last identity, as determined under (3), [is] frequently cited in economics in the relation of demand and supply, of objects and needs, of socially created and natural needs.

Thereupon, nothing simpler for a Hegelian than to posit production and consumption as identical. And this has been done not only by socialist belletrists but by prosaic economists themselves, e.g. Say[16]; in the form that when one looks at an entire people, its production is its consumption. Or, indeed, at humanity in the abstract. Storch[17] demonstrated Say's error, namely that e.g. a people does not consume its entire product, but also creates means of production, etc., fixed capital, etc. To regard society as one single subject is, in addition, to look at it wrongly; speculatively. With a single subject, production and consumption appear as moments of a single act. The important thing to emphasize here is only that, whether production and consumption are viewed as the activity of one or of many individuals, they appear in any case as moments of one process, in which production is the real point of departure and hence also the predominant moment. Consumption as urgency, as need, is itself an intrinsic moment of productive activity. But the latter is the point of departure for realization and hence also its predominant moment; it is the act through which the whole process again runs its course. The individual produces an object and, by consuming it, returns to himself, but returns as a productive and self-reproducing individual. Consumption thus appears as a moment of production.

In society, however, the producer's relation to the product, once the latter is finished, is an external one, and its return to the subject depends on his relations to other individuals. He does not come into possession of it directly. Nor is its immediate appropriation his purpose when he produces in society. *Distribution* steps between the producers and the products, hence between production and consumption, to determine in accordance with social laws what the producer's share will be in the world of products.

Now, does distribution stand at the side of and outside production as an autonomous sphere?

Distribution and production

(b₁) When one examines the usual works of economics, it is immediately striking that everything in them is posited doubly.

16. Jean-Baptiste Say (1767–1832), 'the inane Say', who 'superficially condensed political economy into a textbook' (Marx), a businessman who popularized and vulgarized the doctrines of Adam Smith in his *Traité d'économie politique*, Paris, 1803.

17. Heinrich Friedrich Storch (1766–1835), Professor of Political Economy in the Russian Academy of Sciences at St Petersburg. Say issued Storch's

For example, ground rent, wages, interest and profit figure under distribution, while land, labour and capital figure under production as agents of production. In the case of capital, now, it is evident from the outset that it is posited doubly, (1) as agent of production, (2) as source of income, as a determinant of specific forms of distribution. Interest and profit thus also figure as such in production, in so far as they are forms in which capital increases, grows, hence moments of its own production. Interest and profit as forms of distribution presuppose capital as agent of production. They are modes of distribution whose presupposition is capital as agent of production. They are, likewise, modes of reproduction of capital.

The category of wages, similarly, is the same as that which is examined under a different heading as wage labour: the characteristic which labour here possesses as an agent of production appears as a characteristic of distribution. If labour were not specified as wage labour, then the manner in which it shares in the products would not appear as wages; as, for example, under slavery. Finally, to take at once the most developed form of distribution, ground rent, by means of which landed property shares in the product, presupposes large-scale landed property (actually, large-scale agriculture) as agent of production, and not merely land as such, just as wages do not merely presuppose labour as such. The relations and modes of distribution thus appear merely as the obverse of the agents of production. An individual who participates in production in the form of wage labour shares in the products, in the results of production, in the form of wages. The structure [*Gliederung*] of distribution is completely determined by the structure of production. Distribution is itself a product of production, not only in its object, in that only the results of production can be distributed, but also in its form, in that the specific kind of participation in production determines the specific forms of distribution, i.e. the pattern of participation in distribution. It is altogether an illusion to posit land in production, ground rend in distribution, etc.

Thus, economists such as Ricardo, who are the most frequently accused of focusing on production alone, have defined distribution as the exclusive object of economics, because they instinc-

---

work *Cours d'économie politique* with critical notes in 1823; he attacked Say's interpretation of his views in *Considérations sur la nature du revenu national*, Paris, 1824, pp. 144–59.

tively conceived the forms of distribution as the most specific expression into which the agents of production of a given society are cast.

To the single individual, of course, distribution appears as a social law which determines his position within the system of production within which he produces, and which therefore precedes production. The individual comes into the world possessing neither capital nor land. Social distribution assigns him at birth to wage labour. But this situation of being assigned is itself a consequence of the existence of capital and landed property as independent agents of production.

As regards whole societies, distribution seems to precede production and to determine it in yet another respect, almost as if it were a pre-economic fact. A conquering people divides the land among the conquerors, thus imposes a certain distribution and form of property in land, and thus determines production. Or it enslaves the conquered and so makes slave labour the foundation of production. Or a people rises in revolution and smashes the great landed estates into small parcels, and hence, by this new distribution, gives production a new character. Or a system of laws assigns property in land to certain families in perpetuity, or distributes labour [as] a hereditary privilege and thus confines it within certain castes. In all these cases, and they are all historical, it seems that distribution is not structured and determined by production, but rather the opposite, production by distribution.

In the shallowest conception, distribution appears as the distribution of products, and hence as further removed from and quasi-independent of production. But before distribution can be the distribution of products, it is: (1) the distribution of the instruments of production, and (2), which is a further specification of the same relation, the distribution of the members of the society among the different kinds of production. (Subsumption of the individuals under specific relations of production.) The distribution of products is evidently only a result of this distribution, which is comprised within the process of production itself and determines the structure of production. To examine production while disregarding this internal distribution within it is obviously an empty abstraction; while conversely, the distribution of products follows by itself from this distribution which forms an original moment of production. Ricardo, whose concern was to grasp the specific social structure of modern production, and who is the economist of production *par excellence*, declares for precisely that reason that *not* production but distribution is the proper study of modern economics.[18] This again shows the ineptitude of those economists who portray production as an eternal truth while banishing history to the realm of distribution.

The question of the relation between this production-determining distribution, and production, belongs evidently within production itself. If it is said that, since production must begin with a certain distribution of the instruments of production, it follows that distribution at least in this sense precedes and forms the presupposition of production, then the reply must be that production does indeed have its determinants and preconditions, which form its moments. At the very beginning these may appear as spontaneous, natural. But by the process of production itself they are transformed from natural into historic determinants, and if they appear to one epoch as natural presuppositions of production, they were its historic product for another. Within production itself they are constantly being changed. The application of machinery, for example, changed the distribution of instruments of production as well as of products. Modern large-scale landed property is itself the product of modern commerce and of modern industry, as well as of the application of the latter to agriculture.

The questions raised above all reduce themselves in the last instance to the role played by general-historical relations in production, and their relation to the movement of history generally. The question evidently belongs within the treatment and investigation of production itself.

Still, in the trivial form in which they are raised above, they can be dealt with equally briefly. In all cases of conquest, three things are possible. The conquering people subjugates the conquered under its own mode of production (e.g. the English in Ireland in this century, and partly in India); or it leaves the old mode intact and contents itself with a tribute (e.g. Turks and Romans); or a reciprocal interaction takes place whereby something new, a synthesis, arises (the Germanic conquests, in part). In all cases, the mode of production, whether that of the conquering people, that of the conquered, or that emerging from the fusion of both, is decisive for the new distribution which arises.

18. David Ricardo, *On the Principles of Political Economy and Taxation*, 3rd edn, London, 1821, preface, p.v.

Although the latter appears as a presupposition of the new period of production, it is thus itself in turn a product of production, not only of historical production generally, but of the specific historic mode of production.

The Mongols, with their devastations in Russia, e.g., were acting in accordance with their production, cattle-raising, for which vast uninhabited spaces are a chief precondition. The Germanic barbarians, who lived in isolation on the land and for whom agriculture with bondsmen was the traditional production, could impose these conditions on the Roman provinces all the more easily as the concentration of landed property which had taken place there had already entirely overthrown the earlier agricultural relations.

It is a received opinion that in certain periods people lived from pillage alone. But, for pillage to be possible, there must be something to be pillaged, hence production. And the mode of pillage is itself in turn determined by the mode of production. A stock-jobbing nation, for example, cannot be pillaged in the same manner as a nation of cow-herds.

To steal a slave is to steal the instrument of production directly. But then the production of the country for which the slave is stolen must be structured to allow of slave labour, or (as in the southern part of America etc.) a mode of production corresponding to the slave must be created.

Laws may perpetuate an instrument of production, e.g. land, in certain families. These laws achieve economic significance only when large-scale landed property is in harmony with the society's production, as e.g. in England. In France, small-scale agriculture survived despite the great landed estates, hence the latter were smashed by the revolution. But can laws perpetuate the small-scale allotment? Despite these laws, ownership is again becoming concentrated. The influence of laws in stabilizing relations of distribution, and hence their effect on production, requires to be determined in each specific instance.

(c₁) Exchange, Finally, and Circulation

Exchange and production

Circulation itself [is] merely a specific moment of exchange, or [it is] also exchange regarded in its totality.

In so far as *exchange* is merely a moment mediating between production with its production-determined distribution on one side and consumption on the other, but in so far as the latter itself appears as a moment of production, to that extent is exchange obviously also included as a moment within the latter.

It is clear, firstly, that the exchange of activities and abilities which takes place within production itself belongs directly to production and essentially constitutes it. The same holds, secondly, for the exchange of products, in so far as that exchange is the means of finishing the product and making it fit for direct consumption. To that extent, exchange is an act comprised within production itself. Thirdly, the so-called exchange between dealers and dealers is by its very organization entirely determined by production, as well as being itself a producing activity. Exchange appears as independent of and indifferent to production only in the final phase where the product is exchanged directly for consumption. But (1) there is no exchange without division of labour, whether the latter is spontaneous, natural, or already a product of historic development; (2) private exchange presupposes private production; (3) the intensity of exchange, as well as its extension and its manner, are determined by the development and structure of production. For example. Exchange between town and country; exchange in the country, in the town etc. Exchange in all its moments thus appears as either directly comprised in production or determined by it.

The conclusion we reach is not that production, distribution, exchange and consumption are identical, but that they all form the members of a totality, distinctions within a unity. Production predominates not only over itself, in the antithetical definition of production, but over the other moments as well. The process always returns to production to begin anew. That exchange and consumption cannot be predominant is self-evident. Likewise, distribution as distribution of products; while as distribution of the agents of production it is itself a moment of production. A definite production thus determines a definite consumption, distribution and exchange as well as *definite relations between these different moments*. Admittedly, however, *in its one-sided form*, production is itself determined by the other moments. For example if the market, i.e. the sphere of exchange, expands, then production grows in quantity and the divisions between its different branches become deeper. A change in distribution

changes production, e.g. concentration of capital, different distribution of the population between town and country, etc. Finally,
the needs of consumption determine production. Mutual interaction takes place between the different moments. This the case
with every organic whole.

(3) THE METHOD OF POLITICAL ECONOMY

When we consider a given country politico-economically, we
begin with its population, its distribution among classes, town,
country, the coast, the different branches of production, export
and import, annual production and consumption, commodity
prices etc.

It seems to be correct to begin with the real and the concrete,
with the real precondition, thus to begin, in economics, with e.g.
the population, which is the foundation and the subject of the
entire social act of production. However, on closer examination
this proves false. The population is an abstraction if I leave out,
for example, the classes of which it is composed. These classes in
turn are an empty phrase if I am not familiar with the elements
on which they rest. E.g. wage labour, capital, etc. These latter in
turn presuppose exchange, division of labour, prices, etc. For
example, capital is nothing without wage labour, without value,
money, price etc. Thus, if I were to begin with the population, this
would be a chaotic conception [*Vorstellung*] of the whole, and I
would then, by means of further determination, move analytically
towards ever more simple concepts [*Begriff*], from the imagined
concrete towards ever thinner abstractions until I had arrived at
the simplest determinations. From there the journey would have
to be retraced until I had finally arrived at the population again,
but this time not as the chaotic conception of a whole, but as a
rich totality of many determinations and relations. The former is
the path historically followed by economics at the time of its
origins. The economists of the seventeenth century, e.g., always
begin with the living whole, with population, nation, state, several
states, etc.; but they always conclude by discovering through
analysis a small number of determinant, abstract, general relations
such as division of labour, money, value, etc. As soon as these
individual moments had been more or less firmly established and
abstracted, there began the economic systems, which ascended
from the simple relations, such as labour, division of labour, need,

exchange value, to the level of the state, exchange between nations and the world market. The latter is obviously the scientifically correct method. The concrete is concrete because it is the concentration of many determinations, hence unity of the diverse. It appears in the process of thinking, therefore, as a process of concentration, as a result, not as a point of departure, even though it is the point of departure in reality and hence also the point of departure for observation [*Anschauung*] and conception. Along the first path the full conception was evaporated to yield an abstract determination; along the second, the abstract determinations lead towards a reproduction of the concrete by way of thought. In this way Hegel fell into the illusion of conceiving the real as the product of thought concentrating itself, probing its own depths, and unfolding itself out of itself, by itself, whereas the method of rising from the abstract to the concrete is only the way in which thought appropriates the concrete, reproduces it as the concrete in the mind. But this is by no means the process by which the concrete itself comes into being. For example, the simplest economic category, say e.g. exchange value, presupposes population, moreover a population producing in specific relations; as well as a certain kind of family, or commune, or state, etc. It can never exist other than as an abstract, one-sided relation within an already given, concrete, living whole. As a category, by contrast, exchange value leads an antediluvian existence. Therefore, to the kind of consciousness – and this is characteristic of the philosophical consciousness – for which conceptual thinking is the real human being, and for which the conceptual world as such is thus the only reality, the movement of the categories appears as the real act of production – which only, unfortunately, receives a jolt from the outside – whose product is the world; and – but this is again a tautology – this is correct in so far as the concrete totality is a totality of thoughts, concrete in thought, in fact a product of thinking and comprehending; but not in any way a product of the concept which thinks and generates itself outside or above observation and conception; a product, rather, of the working-up of observation and conception into concepts. The totality as it appears in the head, as a totality of thoughts, is a product of a thinking head, which appropriates the world in the only way it can, a way different from the artistic, religious, practical and mental appropriation of this world. The real subject retains its autonomous existence outside the head just as before; namely as long as the head's conduct is merely speculative, merely theoretical. Hence, in the theoretical method, too, the subject, society, must always be kept in mind as the presupposition.

But do not these simpler categories also have an independent historical or natural existence predating the more concrete ones? That depends. Hegel, for example, correctly begins the Philosophy of Right with possession, this being the subject's simplest juridical relation. But there is no possession preceding the family or master–servant relations, which are far more concrete relations. However, it would be correct to say that there are families or clan groups which still merely *possess*, but have no *property*. The simple category therefore appears in relation to property as a relation of simple families or clan groups. In the higher society it appears as the simpler relation of a developed organization. But the concrete substratum of which possession is a relation is always presupposed. One can imagine an individual savage as possessing something. But in that case possession is not a juridical relation. It is incorrect that possession develops historically into the family. Possession, rather, always presupposes this 'more concrete juridical category'. There would still always remain this much, however, namely that the simple categories are the expressions of relations within which the less developed concrete may have already realized itself before having posited the more many-sided connection or relation which is mentally expressed in the more concrete category; while the more developed concrete preserves the same category as a subordinate relation. Money may exist, and did exist historically, before capital existed, before banks existed, before wage labour existed, etc. Thus in this respect it may be said that the simpler category can express the dominant relations of a less developed whole, or else those sub-ordinate relations of a more developed whole which already had a historic existence before this whole developed in the direction expressed by a more concrete category. To that extent the path of abstract thought, rising from the simple to the combined, would correspond to the real historical process.

It may be said on the other hand that there are very developed but nevertheless historically less mature forms of society, in which the highest forms of economy, e.g. cooperation, a developed division of labour, etc., are found, even though there is no kind of money, e.g. Peru. Among the Slav communities also, money and the exchange which determines it play little or no role within the individual communities, but only on their boundaries, in traffic with others; it is simply wrong to place exchange at the centre of communal society as the original, constituent element. It originally appears, rather, in the connection of the different communities with one another, not in the relations between the different members of a single community. Further, although money everywhere plays a role from very early on, it is nevertheless a predominant element, in antiquity, only within the confines of certain one-sidedly developed nations, trading nations. And even in the most advanced parts of the ancient world, among the Greeks and Romans, the full development of money, which is presupposed in modern bourgeois society, appears only in the period of their dissolution. This very simple category, then, makes a historic appearance in its full intensity only in the most developed conditions of society. By no means does it wade its way through all economic relations. For example, in the Roman Empire, at its highest point of development, the foundation remained taxes and payments in kind. The money system actually completely developed there only in the army. And it never took over the whole of labour. Thus, although the simpler category may have existed historically before the more concrete, it can achieve its full (intensive and extensive) development precisely in a combined form of society, while the more concrete category was more fully developed in a less developed form of society.

Labour seems a quite simple category. The conception of labour in this general form – as labour as such – is also immeasurably old. Nevertheless, when it is economically conceived in this simplicity, 'labour' is as modern a category as are the relations which create this simple abstraction. The Monetary System,[19] for example, still locates wealth altogether objectively, as an external thing, in money. Compared with this standpoint, the commercial, or manufacture, system took a great step forward by locating the

19. Marx considered that the Monetary System, as defined here, covered economists from the sixteenth century to the Physiocrats. However, within the Monetary System there arose what he calls here the 'commercial, or manufacture system' but elsewhere the Mercantile System (known to economics textbooks as Mercantilism). He distinguishes between the two systems on pp. 327–8, but his normal practice is to link them together, since 'the Mercantile System is merely a variant of the Monetary System' (*A Contribution to the Critique of Political Economy,* London, 1971, p. 158).

source of wealth not in the object but in a subjective activity – in commercial and manufacturing activity – even though it still always conceives this activity within narrow boundaries, as money-making. In contrast to this system, that of the Physiocrats posits a certain kind of labour – agriculture – as the creator of wealth, and the object itself no longer appears in a monetary disguise, but as the product in general, as the general result of labour. This product, as befits the narrowness of the activity, still always remains a naturally determined product – the product of agriculture, the product of the earth *par excellence*.

It was an immense step forward for Adam Smith to throw out every limiting specification of wealth-creating activity – not only manufacturing, or commercial or agricultural labour, but one as well as the others, labour in general. With the abstract universality of wealth-creating activity we now have the universality of the object defined as wealth, the product as such or again labour as such, but labour as past, objectified labour. How difficult and great was this transition may be seen from how Adam Smith himself from time to time still falls back into the Physiocratic system. Now, it might seem that all that had been achieved thereby was to discover the abstract expression for the simplest and most ancient relation in which human beings – in whatever form of society – play the role of producers. This is correct in one respect. Not in another. Indifference towards any specific kind of labour presupposes a very developed totality of real kinds of labour, of which no single one is any longer predominant. As a rule, the most general abstractions arise only in the midst of the richest possible concrete development, where one thing appears as common to many, to all. Then it ceases to be thinkable in a particular form alone. On the other side, this abstraction of labour as such is not merely the mental product of a concrete totality of labours. Indifference towards specific labours corresponds to a form of society in which individuals can with ease transfer from one labour to another, and where the specific kind is a matter of chance for them, hence of indifference. Not only the category, labour, but labour in reality has here become the means of creating wealth in general, and has ceased to be organically linked with particular individuals in any specific form. Such a state of affairs is at its most developed in the most modern form of existence of bourgeois society – in the United States. Here, then, for the first time, the point of departure of modern economics, namely the abstraction of the category 'labour', 'labour as such', labour pure and simple, becomes true in practice. The simplest abstraction, then, which modern economics places at the head of its discussions, and which expresses an immeasurably ancient relation valid in all forms of society, nevertheless achieves practical truth as an abstraction only as a category of the most modern society. One could say that this indifference towards particular kinds of labour, which is a historic product in the United States, appears e.g. among the Russians as a spontaneous inclination. But there is a devil of a difference between barbarians who are fit by nature to be used for anything, and civilized people who apply themselves to everything. And then in practice the Russian indifference to the specific character of labour corresponds to being embedded by tradition within a very specific kind of labour, from which only external influences can jar them loose.

This example of labour shows strikingly how even the most abstract categories, despite their validity – precisely because of their abstractness – for all epochs, are nevertheless, in the specific character of this abstraction, themselves likewise a product of historic relations, and possess their full validity only for and within these relations.

Bourgeois society is the most developed and the most complex historic organization of production. The categories which express its relations, the comprehension of its structure, thereby also allows insights into the structure and the relations of production of all the vanished social formations out of whose ruins and elements it built itself up, whose partly still unconquered remnants are carried along within it, whose mere nuances have developed explicit significance within it, etc. Human anatomy contains a key to the anatomy of the ape. The intimations of higher development among the subordinate animal species, however, can be understood only after the higher development is already known. The bourgeois economy thus supplies the key to the ancient, etc. But not at all in the manner of those economists who smudge over all historical differences and see bourgeois relations in all forms of society. One can understand tribute, tithe, etc., if one is acquainted with ground rent. But one must not identify them. Further, since bourgeois society is itself only a contradictory form of development, relations derived from earlier forms will often be found within it only in an entirely stunted form, or even travestied. For example, communal property. Although it is true, therefore, that the categories of bourgeois economics possess a truth for all other forms of society, this is to be taken only with a grain of salt. They can contain them in a developed, or stunted, or caricatured form etc., but always with an essential difference. The so-called historical presentation of development is founded, as a rule, on the fact that the latest form regards the previous ones as steps leading up to itself, and, since it is only rarely and only under quite specific conditions able to criticize itself – leaving aside, of course, the historical periods which appear to themselves as times of decadence – it always conceives them one-sidedly. The Christian religion was able to be of assistance in reaching an objective understanding of earlier mythologies only when its own self-criticism had been accomplished to a certain degree, so to speak, δυνάμει.[20] Likewise, bourgeois economics arrived at an understanding of feudal, ancient, oriental economics only after the self-criticism of bourgeois society had begun. In so far as the bourgeois economy did not mythologically identify itself altogether with the past, its critique of the previous economies, notably of feudalism, with which it was still engaged in direct struggle, resembled the critique which Christianity levelled against paganism, or also that of Protestantism against Catholicism.

In the succession of the economic categories, as in any other historical, social science, it must not be forgotten that their subject – here, modern bourgeois society – is always what is given, in the head as well as in reality, and that these categories therefore express the forms of being, the characteristics of existence, and often only individual sides of this specific society, this subject, and that therefore this society by no means begins only at the point where one can speak of it *as such*; this holds *for science as well*. This is to be kept in mind because it will shortly be decisive for the order and sequence of the categories. For example, nothing seems more natural than to begin with ground rent, with landed property, since this is bound up with the earth, the source of all production and of all being, and with the first form of production of all more or less settled societies – agriculture. But nothing would be more erroneous. In all forms of society there is one specific kind of production which predominates over the rest,

20. See p. 91, n.13.

whose relations thus assign rank and influence to the others. It is a general illumination which bathes all the other colours and modifies their particularity. It is a particular ether which determines the specific gravity of every being which has materialized within it. For example, with pastoral peoples (mere hunting and fishing peoples lie outside the point where real development begins). Certain forms of tillage occur among them, sporadic ones. Landed property is determined by this. It is held in common, and retains this form to a greater or lesser degree according to the greater or lesser degree of attachment displayed by these peoples to their tradition, e.g. the communal property of the Slavs. Among peoples with a settled agriculture – this settling already a great step – where this predominates, as in antiquity and in the feudal order, even industry, together with its organization and the forms of property corresponding to it, has a more or less landed-proprietary character; is either completely dependent on it, as among the earlier Romans, or, as in the Middle Ages, imitates, within the city and its relations, the organization of the land. In the Middle Ages, capital itself – apart from pure money-capital – in the form of the traditional artisans' tools etc., has this landed-proprietary character. In bourgeois society it is the opposite. Agriculture more and more becomes merely a branch of industry, and is entirely dominated by capital. Ground rent likewise. In all forms where landed property rules, the natural relation still predominant. In those where capital rules, the social, historically created element. Ground rent cannot be understood without capital. But capital can certainly be understood without ground rent. Capital is the all-dominating economic power of bourgeois society. It must form the starting-point as well as the finishing-point, and must be dealt with before landed property. After both have been examined in particular, their interrelation must be examined.

It would therefore be unfeasible and wrong to let the economic categories follow one another in the same sequence as that in which they were historically decisive. Their sequence is determined, rather, by their relation to one another in modern bourgeois society, which is precisely the opposite of that which seems to be their natural order or which corresponds to historical development. The point is not the historic position of the economic relations in the succession of different forms of society. Even less is it their sequence 'in the idea' (Proudhon)[21] (a muddy notion of historic movement). Rather, their order within modern bourgeois society.

The purity (abstract specificity) in which the trading peoples – Phoenicians, Carthaginians – appear in the old world is determined precisely by the predominance of the agricultural peoples. Capital, as trading-capital or as money-capital, appears in this abstraction precisely where capital is not yet the predominant element of societies. Lombards, Jews take up the same position towards the agricultural societies of the Middle Ages.

As a further example of the divergent positions which the same category can occupy in different social stages: one of the latest forms of bourgeois society, *joint-stock companies*. These also appear, however, at its beginning, in the great, privileged monopoly trading companies.

The concept of national wealth creeps into the work of the economists of the seventeenth century – continuing partly with those of the eighteenth – in the form of the notion that wealth is created only to enrich the state, and that its power is proportionate to this wealth. This was the still unconsciously hypocritical form in which wealth and the production of wealth proclaimed themselves as the purpose of modern states, and regarded these states henceforth only as means for the production of wealth.

The order obviously has to be (1) the general, abstract determinants which obtain in more or less all forms of society, but in the above-explained sense. (2) The categories which make up the inner structure of bourgeois society and on which the fundamental classes rest. Capital, wage labour, landed property. Their interrelation. Town and country. The three great social classes. Exchange between them. Circulation. Credit system (private). (3) Concentration of bourgeois society in the form of the state. Viewed in relation to itself. The 'unproductive' classes. Taxes. State debt. Public credit. The population. The colonies. Emigration. (4) The international relation of production. International division of labour. International exchange. Export and import. Rate of exchange. (5) The world market and crises.[22]

21. Pierre Joseph Proudhon, *Système des contradictions économiques ou philosophie de la misère*, Paris, 1846, Vol. I, p. 146.
22. See p. 54, n.53.

(4) PRODUCTION. MEANS OF PRODUCTION AND RELATIONS OF PRODUCTION. RELATIONS OF PRODUCTION AND RELATIONS OF CIRCULATION. FORMS OF THE STATE AND FORMS OF CONSCIOUSNESS IN RELATION TO RELATIONS OF PRODUCTION AND CIRCULATION. LEGAL RELATIONS. FAMILY RELATIONS.

Notabene in regard to points to be mentioned here and not to be forgotten:

(1) *War* developed earlier than peace; the way in which certain economic relations such as wage labour, machinery etc. develop earlier, owing to war and in the armies etc., than in the interior of bourgeois society. The relation of productive force and relations of exchange also especially vivid in the army.

(2) *Relation of previous ideal historiography to the real. Namely of the so-called cultural histories,* which are only histories of religions and of states. (On that occasion something can also be said about the various kinds of previous historiography. The so-called objective. Subjective (moral among others). The philosophical.)

(3) *Secondary and tertiary* matters; in general, *derivative, inherited,* not original relations of production. Influence here of international relations.

(4) *Accusations about the materialism of this conception. Relation to naturalistic materialism.*

(5) *Dialectic of the concepts productive force (means of production) and relation of production,* a dialectic whose boundaries are to be determined, and which does not suspend the real difference.

(6) *The uneven development of material production relative to e.g. artistic development.* In general, the concept of progress not to be conceived in the usual abstractness. Modern art etc. This disproportion not as important or so difficult to grasp as within practical-social relations themselves. E.g. the relation of education. Relation of the *United States* to Europe. But the really difficult point to discuss here is how relations of production develop unevenly as legal relations. Thus e.g. the relation of Roman private law (this less the case with criminal and public law) to modern production.

(7) *This conception appears as necessary development.* But legitimation of chance. How. (Of freedom also, among other things.) (Influence of means of communication. World history has not always existed; history as world history a result.)

(8) *The point of departure obviously from the natural charac-teristic*; subjectively and objectively. Tribes, races etc.

(1) In the case of the arts, it is well known that certain periods of their flowering are out of all proportion to the general develop-ment of society, hence also to the material foundation, the skeletal structure as it were, of its organization. For example, the Greeks compared to the moderns or also Shakespeare. It is even recog-nized that certain forms of art, e.g. the epic, can no longer be produced in their world epoch-making, classical stature as soon as the production of art, as such, begins; that is, that certain signi-ficant forms within the realm of the arts are possible only at an undeveloped stage of artistic development. If this is the case with the relation between different kinds of art within the realm of the arts, it is already less puzzling that it is the case in the relation of the entire realm to the general development of society. The difficulty consists only in the general formulation of these contra-dictions. As soon as they have been specified, they are already clarified.

Let us take e.g. the relation of Greek art and then of Shakespeare to the present time. It is well known that Greek mythology is not only the arsenal of Greek art but also its foundation. Is the view of nature and of social relations on which the Greek imagination and hence Greek [mythology] is based possible with self-acting mule spindles and railways and locomotives and electrical telegraphs? What chance has Vulcan against Roberts & Co., Jupiter against the lightning-rod and Hermes against the Crédit Mobilier? All mytho-logy overcomes and dominates and shapes the forces of nature in the imagination and by the imagination; it therefore vanishes with the advent of real mastery over them. What becomes of Fama alongside Printing House Square? Greek art presupposes Greek mythology, i.e. nature and the social forms already reworked in an unconsciously artistic way by the popular imagination. This is its material. Not any mythology whatever, i.e. not an arbitrarily chosen unconsciously artistic reworking of nature (here meaning everything objective, hence including society). Egyptian mythology could never have been the foundation or the womb of Greek art. But, in any case, a *mythology*. Hence, in no way a social develop-ment which excludes all mythological, all mythologizing relations to nature; which therefore demands of the artist an imagination not dependent on mythology.

From another side: is Achilles possible with powder and lead? Or the *Iliad* with the printing press, not to mention the printing machine? Do not the song and the saga and the muse necessarily come to an end with the printer's bar, hence do not the necessary conditions of epic poetry vanish?

But the difficulty lies not in understanding that the Greek arts and epic are bound up with certain forms of social development. The difficulty is that they still afford us artistic pleasure and that in a certain respect they count as a norm and as an unattainable model.

A man cannot become a child again, or he becomes childish. But does he not find joy in the child's naïveté, and must he himself not strive to reproduce its truth at a higher stage? Does not the true character of each epoch come alive in the nature of its children? Why should not the historic childhood of humanity, its most beautiful unfolding, as a stage never to return, exercise an eternal charm? There are unruly children and precocious children. Many of the old peoples belong in this category. The Greeks were normal children. The charm of their art for us is not in contradiction to the undeveloped stage of society on which it grew. [It] is its result, rather, and is inextricably bound up, rather, with the fact that the unripe social conditions under which it arose, and could alone arise, can never return.

NOTEBOOK I

October 1857

The Chapter on Money

Alfred Darimon, *De la réforme des banques,* Paris, 1856.[1]

'The root of the evil is the predominance which opinion obstinately assigns to the role of the precious metals in circulation and exchange.' (pp. 1, 2.)[2]

Begins with the measures which the Banque de France adopted in October 1855 to 'stem the progressive diminution of its reserves'. (p. 2.) Wants to give us a statistical tableau of the condition of this bank during the six months preceding its October measures. To this end, compares its bullion assets during these three months and the '*fluctuations du portefeuille*', i.e. the quantity of discounts extended by the bank (commercial papers, *bills of exchange* in its portfolio). The figure which expresses the value of the securities held by the bank, 'represents', according to Darimon, 'the greater or lesser need felt by the public for its services, *or, which amounts to the same thing, the requirements of circulation*'. (p. 2.) Amounts to the same thing? Not at all. If the mass of bills presented for discount were identical with the 'requirements of circulation', of *monetary turnover* in the proper sense, then the turnover of banknotes would have to be determined by the quantity of discounted bills of exchange. But this movement is on the average not only not parallel, but often an inverse one. The quantity of discounted bills and the fluctuations in this quantity express the requirements of credit, whereas the quantity of money in circulation is determined by quite different influences. In order to reach any conclusions about circulation at all, Darimon would

1. Alfred Darimon (1819–1902), a follower of Proudhon. He edited Proudhonist newspapers in 1848, wrote on financial questions in the 1850s and was a democratic opponent of Napoleon III until 1864 when he went over to the Bonapartists.

2. In French in the original. Throughout this edition, passages in French, Italian and Spanish have been translated in the main body of the text; English has been left; Greek and Latin have been left in the text and translated in the notes.

above all have had to present a column showing the amount of notes in circulation next to the column on bullion assets and the column on discounted bills. In order to discuss the requirements of circulation, it did not require a very great mental leap to look first of all at the fluctuations in circulation proper. The omission of this necessary link in the equation immediately betrays the bungling of the dilettante, and the intentional muddling together of the requirements of credit with those of monetary circulation – a confusion on which rests in fact the whole secret of Proudhonist wisdom. (A mortality chart listing illnesses on one side and deaths on the other, but forgetting births.) The two columns (see p. 3) given by Darimon, i.e. the bank's metallic assets from April to September on the one side, the movement of its portfolio on the other, express nothing but the tautological fact, which requires no display of statistical illustration, that the bank's portfolio filled up with bills of exchange and its vaults emptied of metal in proportion as bills of exchange were presented to it for the purpose of withdrawing metal. And the table which Darimon offers to prove this tautology does not even demonstrate it in a pure form. It shows, rather, that the metallic assets of the bank declined by about 144 million between 12 April and 13 September 1855, while its portfolio holdings increased by about 101 million. The decline in bullion thus exceeded the rise in discounted commercial papers by 43 million. The identity of both movements is wrecked against this net imbalance at the end of six months. A more detailed comparison of the figures shows us additional incongruities.

Metal in bank	*Paper discounted by bank*
12 April – 432,614,799 fr.	12 April – 322,904,313
10 May – 420,914,028	10 May – 310,744,925

In other words: between 12 April and 10 May, the metal assets decline by 11,700,769, while the amount of securities increases by 12,159,388; i.e. the increase of securities exceeds the decline of metal by about half a million (458,619 fr.).[3] The opposite finding, but on a far more surprising scale, appears when we we compare the months of May and June:

3. Should read: '. . . while the amount of securities decreases by 12,159,388; i.e. the decline of securities exceeds the decline of metal . . .'. The correction of these and similar errors would in no way touch the substance of Marx's conclusions concerning Darimon's statistical ideas.

Metal in bank	*Paper discounted by bank*
10 May – 420,914,028	10 May – 310,744,925
14 June – 407,769,813	14 June – 310,369,439

That is, between 10 May and 14 June the metal assets of the bank declined by 13,144,225 fr. Did its securities increase to the same degree? On the contrary, they fell during the same period by 375,486 fr. Here, in other words, we no longer have a merely quantitative disproportion between the decline on one side and the rise on the other. Even the inverse relation of both movements has disappeared. An enormous decline on one side is accompanied by a relatively weak decline on the other.

Metal in bank	*Paper discounted by bank*
14 June – 407,769,813	14 June – 310,369,439
12 July – 314,629,614	12 July – 381,699,256

Comparison of the months June and July shows a decline of metal assets by 93,140,199 and an increase of securities by 71,329,817; i.e. the decline in metal assets is 21,810,382 greater than the increase of the portfolio.

Metal in bank	*Paper discounted by bank*
12 July – 314,629,614	12 July – 381,699,256
9 August – 338,784,444	9 August – 458,689,605

Here we see an increase on both sides; metal assets by 24,154,830, and on the portfolio side the much more significant 76,990,349.

Metal in bank	[*Paper discounted by bank*]
9 August – 338,784,444	9 August – 458,689,605
13 Sept. – 288,645,333	[13 Sept.] – 431,390,562

The decline in metal assets of 50,139,111 fr. is here accompanied by a decline in securities of 27,299,043 fr. (Despite the restrictive measures adopted by the Banque de France, its reserves again declined by 24 million in December 1855.)

What's sauce for the gander is sauce for the goose. The conclusions that emerge from a sequential comparison of the six-month period have the same claim to validity as those which emerge from Mr Darimon's comparison of the beginning of the series with its end. And what does the comparison show? Conclusions which reciprocally devour each other. Twice, the portfolio increases more rapidly than the metal assets decrease (April–May, June–July). Twice the metal assets and the portfolio both decline, but the former more rapidly than the latter (May–June, August–September). Finally, during one period both metal assets and the portfolio increase, but the latter more rapidly than the former. Decrease on one side, increase on the other; decrease on both sides; increase on both sides; in short, everything except a lawful regularity, above all no inverse correlation, not even an interaction, since a decline in portfolio cannot be the cause of a decline in metal assets, and an increase in portfolio cannot be the cause of an increase in metal assets. An inverse relation and an interaction are not even demonstrated by the isolated comparison which Darimon sets up between the first and last months. Since the increase in portfolio by 101 million does not cover the decrease in metal assets, 144 million, then the possibility remains open that there is no causal link whatever between the increase on one side and the decrease on the other. Instead of providing a solution, the statistical illustration threw up a quantity of intersecting questions; instead of one puzzle, a bushelful. These puzzles, it is true, would disappear the moment Mr Darimon presented columns on circulation of banknotes and on deposits next to his columns on metal assets and portfolio (discounted paper). An increase in portfolio more rapid than a decrease in metal would then be explained by a simultaneous increase in metallic deposits or by the fact that a portion of the banknotes issued in exchange for discounted paper was not converted into metal but remained instead in circulation, or, finally, that the issued banknotes immediately returned in the form of deposits or in repayment of due bills, without entering into circulation. A decrease in metal assets accompanied by a lesser decrease in portfolio could be explained by the withdrawal of deposits from the bank or the presentation of banknotes for conversion into metal, thus adversely affecting the bank's discounts through the agency of the owners of the withdrawn deposits or of the metallized notes. Finally, a lesser decline in metal assets accompanied by a lesser decline in portfolio could be explained on the same grounds (we entirely leave out of consideration the possibility of an outflow of metal to replace silver currency inside the country, since Darimon does not bring it into the field of his observations). But a table whose columns would have explained one another reciprocally in this manner would have proved what was not supposed to be proved, namely that the fulfilment by the bank of increasing commercial needs does not necessarily entail an increase in the turnover of its notes, that the increase or decrease of this turnover does not correspond to the increase or decrease of its metallic assets, that the bank does not control the quantity of the means of circulation, etc. – a lot of conclusions which did not fit in with Mr Darimon's intent. In his hasty effort to present in the most lurid colours his preconceived opinion that the metal basis of the bank, represented by its metallic assets, stands in contradiction to the requirements of circulation, which, in his view, are represented by the bank's portfolio, he tears two columns of figures out of their necessary context with the result that this isolation deprives the figures of all meaning or, at the most, leads them to testify against him. We have dwelt on this *fact* in some detail in order to make clear with one example what the entire worth of the statistical and positive illustrations of the Proudhonists amounts to. Economic facts do not furnish them with the test of their theories; rather, they furnish the proof of their lack of mastery of the facts, in order to be able to play with them. Their manner of playing with the facts shows, rather, the genesis of their theoretical abstractions.

Let us pursue Darimon further.

When the Bank of France saw its metal assets diminished by 144 million and its portfolio increased by 101 million, it adopted, on 4 and 18 October 1855, a set of measures to defend its vaults against its portfolio. It raised its discount rate successively from 4 to 5 and from 5 to 6% and reduced the time of payment of bills presented for discount from 90 to 75 days. In other words: it raised the terms on which it made its metal available to commerce. What does this demonstrate? 'That a bank', says Darimon, 'organized on present principles, i.e. on the rule of gold and silver, withdraws its services from the public precisely at the moment when the public most needs them.' Did Mr Darimon require his figures to prove that supply increases the cost of its services to the same degree as demand makes claims upon them (and exceeds them)? And do not the gentlemen who represent the 'public' *vis-à-vis* the bank follow the same 'agreeable customs of life'? The philanthropic grain merchants who present their bills to the bank in order to receive notes, in order to exchange the notes for the bank's gold, in order to exchange the bank's gold for another country's grain, in order to exchange the grain of another country for the money of the French public – were they perhaps motivated by the idea that, since the public then had the greatest need of grain, it was therefore their duty to let them have grain on easier terms, or did they not rather rush to the bank in order to exploit the increase of grain prices, the misery of the public and the disproportion between its supply and its demand? And the bank should be made an exception to these general economic laws? *Quelle idée!* But perhaps the present organization of the banks has as its consequence that gold must be piled up in great quantity so that the means of purchase, which, in case of insufficient grain, could have the greatest utility for the nation, should be condemned to lie fallow; in short, so that capital, instead of passing through the necessary transformation of production, becomes the unproductive and lazy basis of circulation. In this case the problem would be, then, that the unproductive stock of metal still stands above its necessary minimum within the present system of bank organization, because hoarding of the gold and silver in circulation has not yet been restricted to its economic limits. It is a question of something more or something less, but on the same foundation. But then the question would have been deflated from the socialist heights down to the practical bourgeois plains where we find it promenading among the majority of the English bourgeois opponents of the Bank of England. What a come-down! Or is the issue not a greater or lesser saving of metal by means of banknotes and other bank arrangements, but a departure from the metal basis altogether? But then the statistical fable is worthless again, as is its moral. If, for any reason whatever, the bank must send precious metals to other countries in case of need, then it must first accumulate them, and if the other country is to accept these metals in exchange for its commodities, then the predominance of the metals must first have been secured.

The causes of the precious metals' flight from the bank, according to Darimon, were crop failures and the consequent need to import grain from abroad. He forgets the failure of the silk harvest and the need to purchase it in vast quantities from China. Darimon further cites the numerous great undertakings coinciding with the last months of the industrial exhibition in Paris. Again he forgets the great speculations and ventures abroad launched by the Crédit Mobilier and its rivals for the purpose of showing, as Isaac

Péreire[4] says, that French capital is as distinguished among capitals by its cosmopolitan nature as is the French language among languages. Plus the unproductive expenditures entailed by the Crimean War: borrowings of 750 million. That is, on one side, a great and unexpected collapse in two of the most important branches of French production! On the other, an unusual employment of French capital in foreign markets for undertakings which by no means immediately paid their way and which in part will perhaps never cover their costs of production! In order to balance the decrease of domestic production by means of imports, on the one side, and the increase of industrial undertakings abroad on the other side, what would have been required were not symbols of circulation which facilitate the exchange of equivalents, but these equivalents themselves; not money but capital. The losses in French domestic production, in any case, were not an equivalent for the employment of French capital abroad. Now suppose that the Bank of France did not rest on a metallic base, and that other countries were willing to accept the French currency or its capital in any form, not only in the specific form of the precious metals. Would the bank not have been equally forced to raise the terms of its discounting precisely at the moment when its 'public' clamoured most eagerly for its services? The notes with which it discounts the bills of exchange of this public are at present nothing more than drafts on gold and silver. In our hypothetical case, they would be drafts on the nation's stock of products and on its directly employable labour force: the former is limited, the latter can be increased only within very positive limits and in certain amounts of time. The printing press, on the other hand, is inexhaustible and works like a stroke of magic. At the same time, while the crop failures in grain and silk enormously diminish the directly exchangeable wealth of the nation, the foreign railway and mining enterprises freeze the same exchangeable wealth in a form which creates no direct equivalent and therefore devours it, for the moment, without replacement! Thus, the directly exchangeable wealth of the nation (i.e. the wealth which can be circulated and is acceptable abroad) absolutely diminished! On the other side, an unlimited increase in bank drafts. Direct consequence: increase in the price of products, raw materials and labour. On the other side,

4. Isaac Péreire (1806–80), French banker and railway king who, together with his brother Émile, founded the Crédit Mobilier in 1852. A close associate of Napoleon III.

decrease in price of bank drafts. The bank would not have increased the wealth of the nation through a stroke of magic, but would merely have undertaken a very ordinary operation to devalue its own paper. With this devaluation, a sudden paralysis of production! But no, says the Proudhonist. Our new organization of the banks would not be satisfied with the negative accomplishment of abolishing the metal basis and leaving everything else the way it was. It would also create entirely new conditions of production and circulation, and hence its intervention would take place under entirely new preconditions. Did not the introduction of our present banks, in its day, revolutionize the conditions of production? Would large-scale modern industry have become possible without this new financial institution, without the concentration of credit which it created, without the state revenues which it created in antithesis to ground rent, without finance in antithesis to landed property, without the moneyed interest in antithesis to the landed interest; without these things could there have been stock companies etc., and the thousand forms of circulating paper which are as much the preconditions as the product of modern commerce and modern industry?

We have here reached the fundamental question, which is no longer related to the point of departure. The general question would be this: Can the existing relations of production and the relations of distribution which correspond to them be revolutionized by a change in the instrument of circulation, in the organization of circulation? Further question: Can such a transformation of circulation be undertaken without touching the existing relations of production and the social relations which rest on them? If every such transformation of circulation presupposes changes in other conditions of production and social upheavals, there would naturally follow from this the collapse of the doctrine which proposes tricks of circulation as a way of, on the one hand, avoiding the violent character of these social changes, and, on the other, of making these changes appear to be not a presupposition but a gradual result of the transformations in circulation. An error in this fundamental premise would suffice to prove that a similar misunderstanding has occurred in relation to the inner connections between the relations of production, of distribution and of circulation. The above-mentioned historical case cannot of course decide the matter, because modern credit institutions were as much an effect as a cause of the concentration of capital, since they only form a moment of the latter, and since concentration of wealth is accelerated by a scarcity of circulation (as in ancient Rome) as much as by an increase in the facility of circulation. It should further be examined, or rather it would be part of the general question, whether the different civilized forms of money – metallic, paper, credit money, labour money (the last-named as the socialist form) – can accomplish what is demanded of them without suspending the very relation of production which is expressed in the category money, and whether it is not a self-contradictory demand to wish to get around essential determinants of a relation by means of formal modifications? Various forms of money may correspond better to social production in various stages; one form may remedy evils against which another is powerless; but none of them, as long as they remain forms of money, and as long as money remains an essential relation of production, is capable of overcoming the contradictions inherent in the money relation, and can instead only hope to reproduce these contradictions in one or another form. One form of wage labour may correct the abuses of another, but no form of wage labour can correct the abuse of wage labour itself. One lever may overcome the inertia of an immobile object better than another. All of them require inertia to act at all as levers. This general question about the relation of circulation to the other relations of production can naturally be raised only at the end. But, from the outset, it is suspect that Proudhon and his associates never even raise the question in its pure form, but merely engage in occasional declamations about it. Whenever it is touched on, we shall pay close attention.

This much is evident right at the beginning of Darimon, namely that he completely identifies *monetary turnover* with *credit*, which is economically wrong. (The notion of *crédit gratuit*, incidentally, is only a hypocritical, philistine and anxiety-ridden form of the saying: property is theft. Instead of the workers *taking* the capitalists' capital, the capitalists are supposed to be compelled to *give* it to them.) This too we shall have to return to.

In the question under discussion now, Darimon got no further than the point that banks, which deal in credit, like merchants who deal in commodities or workers who deal in labour, sell at a higher price when demand rises in relation to supply, i.e. they make their services more difficult for the public to obtain at the very moment the public has the greatest need for them. We saw that the bank has to act in this way whether the notes it issues are convertible or inconvertible.

The behaviour of the Bank of France in October 1855 gave rise to an 'immense clamour' (p. 4) and to a 'great debate' between it and the spokesmen of the public. Darimon summarizes, or pretends to summarize, this debate. We will follow him here only occasionally, since his synopsis displays the weak sides of both opponents, revealed in their constant desultory irrelevances. Groping about in extrinsic arguments. Each of the antagonists is at every moment dropping his weapon in order to search for another. Neither gets to the point of striking any actual blows, not only because they are constantly changing the weapons with which they are supposed to hit each other, but also because they hardly meet on one terrain before they take rapid flight to another.

(The discount rate in France had not been raised to 6% since 1806: for 50 years the time of payment for commercial bills of exchange had stood firm at 90 days.)

The weakness of the bank's defending arguments, as presented by Darimon, and his own misconceptions, emerge for example from the following passage in his fictitious dialogue:

Says the bank's opponent: 'By virtue of your monopoly you are the dispenser and regulator of credit. When you take up an attitude of severity, the discounters not only imitate you but they further exaggerate your rigour ... Your measures have brought business to a standstill.' (p. 5.)

The bank replies, and indeed 'humbly': ' "What would you have me do?" the bank humbly said ... "To defend myself against the foreigner, I have to defend myself against our citizens ... Above all I must prevent the outflow of the currency, without which I am nothing and can do nothing." ' (p. 5.)

The bank's script is ridiculous. It is made to sidetrack the question, to turn it into a rhetorical generality, in order to be able to answer it with a rhetorical generality. In this dialogue the bank is made to share Darimon's illusion that its monopoly really allows it to regulate credit. In fact the power of the bank begins only where the private 'discounters' stop, hence at a moment when its power is already extraordinarily limited. Suppose that during easy conditions on the money market, when everybody else is discounting at $2\frac{1}{2}\%$, the bank holds at 5%; instead of imitating it, the discounters will discount all its business away before its very eyes. Nowhere is this more vividly demonstrated than in the history of the Bank of England since the law of 1844, which made it into a real rival of the private bankers in the business of discounting, etc. In order to secure for itself a share, and a growing share, of the discount business during the periods of easiness on the money market, the Bank of England was constantly forced to reduce its rates not only to the level adopted by the private bankers but often below it. Its 'regulation of credit' is thus to be taken with a grain of salt; Darimon, however, makes his superstitious faith in its absolute control of the money market and of credit into his point of departure.

Instead of analysing critically the determinants of the bank's real power over the money market, he immediately grabs on to the phrase that cash is everything for the bank and that it has to prevent its outflow from the country. A professor of the Collège de France (Chevalier)[5] replies: 'Gold and silver are commodities like any other . . . The only purpose of the bank's metallic reserves is to make purchases abroad in moments of emergency.' The bank rejoins: 'Metallic money is not a commodity like any other; it is an instrument of exchange, and by virtue of this title it holds the privilege of prescribing laws for all the other commodities.' Now Darimon leaps between the combatants: 'Thus the privilege held by gold and silver, that of being the only authentic instrument of circulation and exchange, is responsible not only for the present crisis, but for the periodic commercial crises as well.' In order to control all the undesirable features of crises 'it would be enough that gold and silver were made commodities like any other, or, precisely expressed, that all commodities were made instruments of exchange on an equal footing (*au même titre*) with gold and silver; that products were truly exchanged for products'. (pp. 5–7.)

Shallowness with which the disputed question is presented here. If the bank issues drafts on money (notes) and promissory notes on capital repayable in gold (or silver) (deposits), then it is self-evident that it can watch and endure the decrease of its metal reserves only up to a certain point without reacting. That has nothing to do with the theory of metallic money. We will return to Darimon's theory of crises later.

In the chapter 'Short History of the Crises of Circulation', Mr

5. Michel Chevalier (1806–79), follower of Saint-Simon up to 1833; later Bonapartist. From 1850 he was Professor of Political Economy at the Collège de France, and a supporter in the 1850s of Bonaparte's move towards free trade.

Darimon omits the English crisis of 1809–11 and confines himself to noting the appointment of the Bullion Committee in 1810; and for 1811 he again leaves out the crisis itself (which began in 1809), and merely mentions the adoption by the House of Commons of the resolution that 'the depreciation of notes relative to bullion stems not from a depreciation of paper money but from an increase in the price of bullion', together with Ricardo's pamphlet which maintains the opposite thesis, the conclusion of which is supposed to read: 'A currency is in its most perfect state when it consists wholly of paper money.' (pp. 22, 23.)[6] The crises of 1809 and 1811 were important here because the bank at that time issued inconvertible notes, meaning that the crises did not stem from the convertibility of notes into gold (metal) and hence could not be restrained by the abolition of convertibility. Like a nimble tailor, Darimon skips over these facts which contradict his theory of crises. He clutches on to Ricardo's aphorism, which had nothing to do with the real subject of discussion in the pamphlet, namely the depreciation of banknotes. He is unaware that Ricardo's theory of money is as completely refuted as its false assumptions that the bank controls the quantity of notes in circulation, and that the quantity of means of circulation determines prices, whereas on the contrary prices determine the quantity of means of circulation etc. In Ricardo's time all detailed studies of the phenomena of monetary circulation were still lacking. This by the way.

Gold and silver are commodities like the others. Gold and silver are not commodities like the others: as general instruments of exchange they are the privileged commodities and degrade the other commodities by virtue of this privilege. This is the last analysis to which Darimon reduces the antagonism. His final judgement is: abolish the privilege of gold and silver, degrade them to the rank of all other commodities. Then you no longer have the specific evils of gold and silver money, or of notes convertible into gold and silver. You abolish all evils. Or, better, elevate all commodities to the monopoly position now held by gold and silver. Let the pope remain, but make everybody pope. Abolish money by making every commodity money and by equipping it with the specific attributes of money. The question here arises whether this problem does not already pronounce its own nonsensicality, and whether the impossibility of the solution

6. Ricardo's pamphlet, *Proposals for an Economical and Secure Currency*, London, 1816.

is not already contained in the premises of the question. Frequently the only possible answer is a critique of the question and the only solution is to negate the question. The real question is: does not the bourgeois system of exchange itself necessitate a specific instrument of exchange? Does it not necessarily create a specific equivalent for all values? One form of this instrument of exchange or of this equivalent may be handier, more fitting, may entail fewer inconveniences than another. But the inconveniences which arise from the existence of every specific instrument of exchange, of any specific but general equivalent, must necessarily reproduce themselves in every form, however differently. Darimon naturally skips over this question with enthusiasm. Abolish money and don't abolish money! Abolish the exclusive privilege possessed by gold and silver in virtue of their exclusive monetary role, but turn all commodities to money, i.e. give them all together equally a quality which no longer exists once its exclusiveness is gone.

The bullion drains do in fact bring to the surface a contradiction which Darimon formulates superficially and distorts as well. It is evident that gold and silver are not commodities like the others, and that modern economics is horrified to see itself suddenly and temporarily thrown back again and again to the prejudices of the Mercantile System. The English economists attempt to overcome the difficulty by means of a distinction. What is demanded in moments of such monetary crises, they say, is not gold and silver as money, not gold and silver as coin, but gold and silver as capital. They forget to add: yes, capital, but capital in the specific form of gold and silver. Why else is there an outflow of precisely these commodities, while most of the others depreciate owing to lack of outflow, if capital were exportable in every form?

Let us take specific examples: drain as a result of domestic harvest failures in a chief food crop (e.g. grain), crop failure abroad and hence increased prices in one of the main imported consumer goods (e.g. tea); drain because of a crop failure in decisive industrial raw materials (cotton, wool, silk, flax etc.); drain because of excessive imports (caused by speculation, war etc.). The replacement of a sudden or chronic shortage (grain, tea, cotton, flax, etc.) in the case of a domestic crop failure deprives the nation doubly. A part of its invested capital or labour is not reproduced – real loss of production. A part of that capital which has been reproduced has to be shifted to fill this gap; and this part, moreover, does not stand in a simple arithmetical relation to the loss, because the deficient product rises and must rise on the world market as a result of the decreased supply and the increased demand. It is necessary to analyse precisely how such crises would look if money were disregarded, and what determinants money introduces into the given relations. (*Grain crop failures* and *excess imports* the most important cases. The impact of war is self-evident, since economically it is exactly the same as if the nation were to drop a part of its capital into the ocean.)

Case of a grain crop failure: Seen in comparison to other nations, it is clear that the nation's capital (not only its real wealth) has diminished, just as clear as that a peasant who burns his loaves and has to buy bread at the baker's is impoverished to the extent of the price of his purchase. In reference to the domestic situation, the rise in grain prices, as far as value enters into the question, seems to leave everything as it was. Except for the fact that the lesser quantity of grain multiplied by the increased price, in real crop failures, never = the normal quantity multiplied by the lesser price. Suppose that the entire English wheat crop were 1 quarter, and that this 1 quarter fetched the same price as 30 million quarters previously. Then, leaving aside the fact that it lacks the means to reproduce either life or wheat, and if we postulate that the working day necessary to produce 1 quarter $= A$, then the nation would exchange $A \times 30$ million working days (cost of production) for $1 \times A$ working days (product); the productive force of its capital would have diminished by millions and the sum of all values in the land would have diminished, since every working day would have depreciated by a factor of 30 million. Every unit of capital would then represent only 1/30,000,000 of its earlier value, of its equivalent in production costs, even though in this given case the nominal value of the nation's capital would not have diminished (apart from the depreciation of land and soil), since the decrease in value of all other products would have been exactly compensated by the increase in value of the 1 quarter of wheat. The increase in the wheat price by a factor of $A \times 30$ million would be the expression of an equivalent depreciation of all other products. This distinction between domestic and foreign, incidentally, is altogether illusory. The relation between the nation which suffers a crop failure and another nation where the former makes purchases is like that between every individual of the nation and the farmer or grain merchant. The surplus sum which it must expend in purchasing grain is a direct subtraction from its capital, from its disposable means.

So as not to obscure the question with unessential influences, it must be postulated that the nation has free trade in grain. Even if the imported grain were as cheap as the domestically produced grain, the nation would still be poorer to the amount of capital not reproduced by the farmers. However, on the above assumption of free trade, the nation always imports as much foreign grain as is possible at the normal price. The increase of imports thus presupposes a rise in the price.

The rise in the grain price is = to the fall in the price of all other commodities. The increased cost of production (represented by the price) at which the quarter of wheat is obtained is = to the decreased productivity of capital in all other forms. The surplus used to purchase grain must correspond to a deficit in the purchase of all other products and hence already a decline in their prices. With or without metallic money, or money of any other kind, the nation would find itself in a crisis not confined to grain, but extending to all other branches of production, not only because their productivity would have positively diminished and the price of their production depreciated as compared to their value, which is determined by the normal cost of production, but also because all contracts, obligations etc. rest on the average prices of products. For example, x bushels of grain have to be supplied to service the state's indebtedness, but the cost of producing these x bushels has increased by a given factor. Quite apart from the role of money the nation would thus find itself in a general crisis. If we abstract not only from money but from exchange value as well, then products would have depreciated and the nation's productivity diminished while all its economic relations are based on the average productivity of its labour.

A crisis caused by a failure in the grain crop is therefore not at all created by the drain of bullion, although it can be aggravated by obstacles set up to impede this drain.

In any case, we cannot agree with Proudhon either when he says that the crisis stems from the fact that the precious metals alone possess an authentic value in contrast to the other commodities; for the rise in the grain price first of all means only that more gold and silver have to be given in exchange for a certain quantity of grain, i.e. that the price of gold and silver has declined relative to the price of grain. Thus gold and silver participate with all other commodities in the depreciation relative to grain, and no privilege protects them from this. The depreciation of gold and silver relative to grain is identical with the rise of the grain price (not quite correct. The quarter of grain rises from 50s. to 100s., i.e. by 100%, but cotton goods fall by 80. Silver has declined by 50 relative to grain; cotton goods (owing to declining demand etc.) have declined by 80% relative to it. That is to say, the prices of other commodities fall to a greater extent than those of grain rise. But the opposite also occurs. For example in recent years, when grain temporarily rose by 100%, it never entered the heads of the industrial products to decline in the same proportion in which gold had declined relative to grain. This circumstance does not immediately affect the general thesis). Neither can it be said that gold possesses a privilege because its quantity is precisely and authentically defined in the coin form. One thaler (silver) remains under all circumstances one thaler. But a bushel of wheat is also always a bushel, and a yard of linen a yard.

The depreciation of most commodities (labour included) and the resultant crisis, in the case of an important crop mishap, cannot therefore be crudely ascribed to the export of gold, because depreciation and crisis would equally take place if no gold whatever were exported and no grain imported. The crisis reduces itself simply to the law of supply and demand, which, as is known, acts far more sharply and energetically within the sphere of primary needs – seen on a national scale – than in all other spheres. Exports of gold are not the cause of the grain crisis, but the grain crisis is the cause of gold exports.

Gold and silver in themselves can be said to intervene in the crisis and to aggravate its symptoms in only two ways: (1) When the export of gold is made more difficult by the metal reserve requirements to which the banks are bound; when the measures which the banks therefore undertake against the export of gold react disadvantageously on domestic circulation; (2) When the export of gold becomes necessary because foreign nations will accept capital only in the form of gold and not otherwise.

Difficulty No. 2 can remain even if difficulty No. 1 is removed. The Bank of England experienced this precisely during the period when it was legally empowered to issue inconvertible notes.[7] These

7. A reference to the period during which the Bank Restriction Act was in operation (1797–1819).

notes declined in relation to gold bullion, but the mint price of gold likewise declined in relation to its bullion price. In relation to the note, gold had become a special kind of commodity. It can be said that the note still remained dependent on gold only to the extent that it nominally represented a certain quantity of gold for which it could not in fact be exchanged. Gold remained its denomination, although it was no longer legally exchangeable for this quantity of gold at the bank.

There can be hardly a doubt (?) (this is to be examined later and does not directly belong with the subject under discussion) that as long as paper money retains its denomination in gold (i.e. so long as a £5 note for example is the paper representative of 5 sovereigns), the convertibility of the note into gold remains its economic law, whether this law also exists *politically* or not. The Bank of England's notes continued during the years 1799–1819 to state that they represented the value of a given quantity of gold. How can this assertion be put to the test other than by the fact that the note indeed commands so-and-so-much bullion? From the moment when bullion to the value of 5 sovereigns could no longer be had for a £5 note, the note was depreciated even though it was inconvertible. The equivalence of the note with an amount of gold equal to its face-value immediately entered into contradiction with the factual non-equivalence between banknotes and gold. The point in dispute among the English who want to keep gold as the denomination of notes is not in fact the convertibility of the note into gold – which is only the practical equivalence of what the face of the note expresses theoretically – but rather the question how this convertibility is to be secured, whether through limits imposed by law on the bank or whether the bank is to be left to its own devices. The advocates of the latter course assert that this convertibility is achieved on the average by a bank of issue which lends against bills of exchange and whose notes thus have an assured reflux, and charge that their opponents despite everything never achieved better than this average measure of security. The latter is a fact. The average, by the way, is not to be despised, and calculations on the basis of averages have to form the basis for banks just as well as for all insurance companies etc. In this regard the Scottish banks are above all, and rightly, held up as a model. The strict bullionists say for their part that they take convertibility as a serious matter, that the bank's obligation to convert notes keeps the notes convertible, that the necessity of this convertibility is given by the denomination of the notes themselves, that this forms a barrier against over-issue, and that their opponents are pseudo-defenders of inconvertibility. Between these two sides, various shadings, a mass of little 'species'.[8] The defenders of inconvertibility, finally, the determined anti-bullionists, are, without knowing it, just as much pseudo-defenders of convertibility as their opponents are of inconvertibility, because they retain the denomination of the note and hence make the practical equation between a note of a given denomination and a given quantity of gold the measure of their notes' full value. Prussia has paper money of forced currency. (A reflux is secured by the obligation to pay a portion of taxes in paper.) These paper thalers are not drafts on silver; no bank will legally convert them. They are not issued by a commercial bank against bills of exchange but by the government to meet its expenses. But their denomination is that of silver. A paper thaler proclaims that it represents the same value as a silver thaler. If confidence in the government were to be thoroughly shaken, or if this paper money were issued in greater proportions than required by circulation, then the paper thaler would in practice cease to be equal to the silver thaler and would be depreciated because it had fallen beneath the value proclaimed on its face. It would even depreciate if neither of the above conditions obtained but if a special need for silver, e.g. for exports, gave silver a privileged position *vis-à-vis* the paper thaler. Convertibility into gold and silver is therefore the practical measure of the value of every paper currency denominated in gold or silver, whether this paper is legally convertible or not. Nominal value runs alongside its body as a mere shadow; whether the two balance can be shown only by actual convertibility (exchangeability). A fall of real value beneath nominal value is depreciation. Convertibility is when the two really run alongside each other and change places with each other. The convertibility of inconvertible notes shows itself not in the bank's stock of bullion but in the everyday exchange between paper and the metal whose denomination the paper carries. In practice, the convertibility of convertible notes is already endangered when this is no longer confirmed by everyday routine exchange in all parts of the country, but has to be established specifically by large-scale operations on the part of the bank. In the Scottish countryside paper money is even preferred to metal

8. A play on the two meanings of the French word '*espèces*': (1) sorts; (2) specie.

money. Before 1845, when the English law of 1844[9] was forced upon it, Scotland naturally took part in all English social crises, and experienced some crises to a higher degree because the clearing of the land proceeded more ruthlessly there. Nevertheless, Scotland never experienced a real monetary crisis (the fact that a few banks, exceptions, collapsed because they had made careless loans is irrelevant here); no depreciation of notes, no complaints and no inquiries into the sufficiency or insufficiency of the currency in circulation etc. Scotland is important here because it shows on the one hand how the monetary system can be completely regulated on the present basis – all the evils Darimon bewails can be abolished – without departing from the present social basis; while at the same time its contradictions, its antagonisms, the class contradiction etc. have reached an even higher degree than in any other country in the world. It is characteristic that both Darimon and the patron who introduces his book – Émile Girardin,[10] who complements his practical swindles with theoretical utopianism – do not find the antithesis of the monopoly banks of France and England in Scotland, but rather look for it in the United States, where the banking system, owing to the need to obtain a charter from the individual State, is only nominally free, where the prevailing system is not free competition among banks but a federation of monopoly banks. The Scottish banking and monetary system was indeed the most perilous reef for the illusions of the circulation artists. Gold or silver money (except where coins of both kinds are legal tender) are not said to depreciate no matter how often their value changes relative to other commodities. Why not? Because they form their own denomination; because their title is not a title to a value, i.e. they are not measured in a third commodity, but merely express fractional parts of their own substance, 1 sovereign = so much gold of a given weight. Gold is therefore nominally undepreciable, not because it alone expresses *an authentic value*, but because as money it does *not* express *value at all*, but merely expresses a given quantity of its

9. The Currency Act of 1844, which stringently limited the number of banknotes the country banks could issue, and also limited the fiduciary issue of the Bank of England to £14,000,000; any further issue had to be backed by coin or bullion.

10. Émile de Girardin (1806–81), French journalist, who edited *La Presse* from 1830 to 1857 and wrote the introduction to Darimon's book. A politician entirely lacking in scruples, he was a moderate republican in 1848, a Montagnard deputy to the Legislative Assembly in 1850 and a Bonapartist in 1852.

own substance, merely carries its own quantitative definition on its forehead. (To be examined more closely later: whether this characteristic mark of gold and silver money is in the last analysis an intrinsic property of all money.) Deceived by this nominal un-depreciability of metallic money, Darimon and consorts see only the one aspect which surfaces during crises: the appreciation of gold and silver in relation to nearly all other commodities; they do not see the other side, the *depreciation* of gold and silver or of *money* in relation to all other commodities (labour perhaps, not always, excluded) in periods of so-called *prosperity*, periods of a temporary general rise of prices. Since this depreciation of metallic money (and of all kinds of money which rest on it) always precedes its appreciation, they ought to have formulated the problem the other way round: how to prevent the periodic depreciation of money (in their language, to abolish the privileges of commodities in relation to money). In this last formulation the problem would have reduced itself to: how to overcome the rise and fall of prices. The way to do this: abolish prices. And how? By doing away with exchange value. But this problem arises: exchange corresponds to the bourgeois organization of society. Hence one last problem: to revolutionize bourgeois society economically. It would then have been self-evident from the outset that the evil of bourgeois society is not to be remedied by 'transforming' the banks or by founding a rational 'money system'.

Convertibility, therefore – legal or not – remains a requirement of every kind of money whose title makes it a value-symbol, i.e. which equates it as a quantity with a third commodity. The equation already includes the antithesis, the possibility of non-equivalence; convertibility includes its opposite, inconvertibility; appreciation includes depreciation, δυνάμει,[11] as Aristotle would say. Suppose for example that the sovereign were not only called a sovereign, which is a mere honorific for the xth fraction of an ounce of gold (accounting name), in the same way that a metre is the name for a certain length, but were called, say, *x hours of labour time*. $\frac{1}{x}$ ounce of gold is in fact nothing more than $\frac{1}{x}$ hours of labour time materialized, objectified. But gold is labour time accumulated in the past, labour time defined. Its title would make a given quantity of labour as such into its standard. The pound of gold would have to be convertible into x hours of labour time,

11. See p. 91, n. 13.

would have to be able to purchase it at any given moment: as soon as it could buy a greater or a lesser amount, it would be appreciated or depreciated; in the latter case its convertibility would have ceased. What determines value is not the amount of labour time incorporated in products, but rather the amount of labour time necessary at a given moment. Take the pound of gold itself: let it be the product of 20 hours' labour time. Suppose that for some reason it later requires only 10 hours to produce a pound of gold. The pound of gold whose title advises that it = 20 hours' labour time would now merely = 10 hours' labour time, since 20 hours' labour time = 2 pounds of gold. 10 hours of labour are in practice exchanged for 1 pound of gold; hence 1 pound of gold cannot any longer be exchanged for 20 hours of labour time. Gold money with the plebeian title *x hours of labour* would be exposed to greater fluctuations than any other sort of money and particularly more than the present gold money, because gold cannot rise or fall in relation to gold (it is equal to itself), while the labour time accumulated in a given quantity of gold, in contrast, must constantly rise or fall in relation to present, living labour time. In order to maintain its convertibility, the productivity of labour time would have to be kept stationary. Moreover, in view of the general economic law that the costs of production constantly decline, that living labour becomes constantly more productive, hence that the labour time objectified in products constantly depreciates, the inevitable fate of this golden labour money would be constant depreciation. In order to control this evil, it might be said that the title of labour time should go not to gold but, as Weitling proposed, with Englishmen ahead of him and French after, Proudhon & Co. among them, to paper money, to a mere symbol of value. The labour time incorporated in the paper itself would then have as little relevance as the paper value of banknotes. The former would be merely the representation of hours of labour, as the latter is of gold or silver. If the hour of labour became more productive, then the chit of paper which represents it would rise in buying power, and vice versa, exactly as a £5 note at present buys more or less depending on whether the relative value of gold in comparison to other commodities rises or falls. According to the same law which would subject golden labour money to a constant depreciation, paper labour money would enjoy a constant appreciation. And that is precisely what we are after; the worker would reap the joys of the rising productivity of his labour, instead of creating proportionately more alien wealth and devaluing himself as at present. Thus the socialists. But, unfortunately, there arise some small scruples. First of all: if we once presuppose money, even if it is only time-chits, then we must also presuppose the accumulation of this money, as well as contracts, obligations, fixed burdens etc., which are entered into in the form of this money. The accumulated chits would constantly appreciate together with the newly issued ones, and thus on the one hand the rising productivity of labour would go to the benefit of non-workers, and on the other hand the previously contracted burdens would keep step with the rising yield of labour. The rise and fall in the value of gold or silver would be quite irrelevant if the world could be started afresh at each new moment and if, hence, previous obligations to pay a certain quantity of gold did not survive the fluctuations in the value of gold. The same holds, here, with the time-chit and hourly productivity.

The point to be examined here is the convertibility of the time-chit. We reach the same goal if we make a detour. Although it is still too early, a few observations can be made about the delusions on which the time-chit rests, which allow us an insight into the depths of the secret which links Proudhon's theory of circulation with his general theory – his theory of the determination of value. We find the same link e.g. in Bray[12] and Gray.[13] Whatever basis in truth it may happen to have will be examined later[14] (but first, incidentally: seen only as drafts on gold, banknotes should not be issued in amounts exceeding the quantity of gold which they pretend to replace, or they depreciate. Three drafts of £15 which I issue to three different creditors on the same £15 in gold are in fact only drafts on $\frac{£15}{3} = £5$ each. Each of these notes would have depreciated to $33\frac{1}{3}$ per cent from the outset.)

The *value* (the real exchange value) of all commodities (labour

<hr>

12. John Francis Bray (1809–95), economic pamphleteer and political activist in the England of the 1830s. In 1837 he became treasurer of the Leeds Working Men's Association. He advocated utopian socialist ideas in the pamphlet *Labour's Wrongs and Labour's Remedy*, Leeds, 1839, and was described by Marx as an 'English Communist' (*The Poverty of Philosophy*, Moscow, 1966, p. 60).

13. John Gray (1799–1850), economic pamphleteer and utopian socialist, author of *The Social System*, Edinburgh, 1831, and *Lectures on the Nature and Use of Money*, Edinburgh, 1848.

14. See below, pp. 153–60.

included) is determined by their cost of production, in other words by the labour time required to produce them. Their *price* is this exchange value of theirs, expressed in money. The replacement of metal money (and of paper or fiat money denominated in metal money) by labour money denominated in labour time would therefore equate the *real value* (exchange value) of commodities with their *nominal value, price, money value*. Equation of *real value and nominal value, of value and price*. But such is by no means the case. The value of commodities as determined by labour time is only their *average value*. This average appears as an external abstraction if it is calculated out as the average figure of an epoch, e.g. 1 lb. of coffee = 1s. if the average price of coffee is taken over 25 years; but it is very real if it is at the same time recognized as the driving force and the moving principle of the oscillations which commodity prices run through during a given epoch. This reality is not merely of theoretical importance: it forms the basis of mercantile speculation, whose calculus of probabilities depends both on the median price averages which figure as the centre of oscillation, and on the average peaks and average troughs of oscillation above or below this centre. The *market value* is always different, is always below or above this average value of a commodity. Market value equates itself with real value by means of its constant oscillations, never by means of an equation with real value as if the latter were a third party, but rather by means of constant non-equation of itself (as Hegel would say, not by way of abstract identity, but by constant negation of the negation, i.e. of itself as negation of real value).[15] In my pamphlet against Proudhon I showed that real value itself – independently of its rule over the oscillations of the market price (seen apart from its role as the *law* of these oscillations) – in turn negates itself and constantly posits the real value of commodities in contradiction with its own character, that it constantly depreciates or appreciates the real value of already produced commodities; this is not the place to discuss it in greater detail.[16] *Price* therefore is distinguished from *value* not only as the nominal from the real; not only by way of the denomination in gold and silver, but because the latter appears as the law of the motions which the former runs through. But the two are constantly different and never balance out, or balance only coincidentally and exceptionally. The price of a commodity constantly stands above

15. Hegel, *Science of Logic*, tr. A. V. Miller, London, 1969, p. 416.
16. Cf. Marx, *The Poverty of Philosophy*, pp. 52–68.

or below the value of the commodity, and the value of the commodity itself exists only in this up-and-down movement of commodity prices. Supply and demand constantly determine the prices
of commodities; never balance, or only coincidentally; but the
cost of production, for its part, determines the oscillations of
supply and demand. The gold or silver in which the price of a
commodity, its market value, is expressed is itself a certain
quantity of accumulated labour, a certain measure of materialized
labour time. On the assumption that the production costs of a
commodity and the production costs of gold and silver remain
constant, the rise or fall of its market price means nothing more
than that a commodity, $= x$ labour time, constantly commands $>$
or $< x$ labour time on the market, that it stands above or beneath
its average value as determined by labour time. The first basic
illusion of the time-chitters consists in this, that by annulling the
nominal difference between real value and market value, between
exchange value and price -- that is, by expressing value in units
of labour time itself instead of in a given objectification of labour
time, say gold and silver -- that in so doing they also remove the
real difference and contradiction between price and value. Given
this illusory assumption it is self-evident that the mere introduction
of the time-chit does away with all crises, all faults of bourgeois
production. The money price of commodities $=$ their real value;
demand $=$ supply; production $=$ consumption; money is simultaneously abolished and preserved; the labour time of which the
commodity is the product, which is materialized in the commodity, would need only to be measured in order to create a corresponding mirror-image in the form of a value-symbol, money,
time-chits. In this way every commodity would be directly transformed into money; and gold and silver, for their part, would be
demoted to the rank of all other commodities.

It is not necessary to elaborate that the contradiction between
exchange value and price -- the average price and the prices of
which it is the average -- that the difference between magnitudes
and average magnitudes is not overcome merely by suppressing the
difference in name, e.g. by saying, instead of: 1 lb. bread costs 8d.,
1 lb. bread $= \dfrac{1}{x}$ hours of labour. Inversely, if 8d. $= \dfrac{1}{x}$ hours of
labour, and if the labour time which is materialized in one pound
of bread is greater or less than $\dfrac{1}{x}$ hours of labour, then, because

the measure of value would be at the same time the element in which the price is expressed, the difference between price and value, which is hidden in the gold price or silver price, would never be glaringly visible. An infinite equation would result. $\frac{1}{x}$ hours of labour (as contained in 8d. or represented by a chit) $> <$ than $\frac{1}{x}$ hours of labour (as contained in the pound of bread).

The time-chit, representing *average labour time*, would never correspond to or be convertible into *actual labour time*; i.e. the amount of labour time objectified in a commodity would never command a quantity of labour time equal to itself, and vice versa, but would command, rather, either more or less, just as at present every oscillation of market values expresses itself in a rise or fall of the gold or silver prices of commodities.

The constant depreciation of commodities – over longer periods – in relation to time-chits, which we mentioned earlier, arises out of the law of the rising productivity of labour time, out of the disturbances within relative value itself which are created by its own inherent principle, namely labour time. This inconvertibility of the time-chits which we are now discussing is nothing more than another expression for the inconvertibility between real value and market value, between exchange value and price. In contrast to all other commodities, the time-chit would represent an ideal labour time which would be exchanged sometimes against more and sometimes against less of the actual variety, and which would achieve a separate existence of its own in the time-chit, an existence corresponding to this non-equivalence. The general equivalent, medium of circulation and measure of commodities would again confront the commodities in an individual form, following its own laws, alienated, i.e. equipped with all the properties of money as it exists at present but unable to perform the same services. The medium with which commodities – these objectified quantities of labour time – are compared would not be a third commodity but would be rather their own measure of value, labour time itself; as a result, the confusion would reach a new height altogether. Commodity A, the objectification of 3 hours' labour time, is = 2 labour-hour-chits; commodity B, the objectification, similarly, of 3 hours' labour, is = 4 labour-hour-chits. This contradiction is in practice expressed in money prices, but in a veiled form. The difference between price and value, between the commodity measured by the labour time whose product it is, and the product of the labour time against which it is exchanged, this difference calls for a third commodity to act as a measure in which the real exchange value of commodities is expressed. *Because price is not equal to value, therefore the value-determining element – labour time – cannot be the element in which prices are expressed, because labour time would then have to express itself simultaneously as the determining and the non-determining element, as the equivalent and non-equivalent of itself.* Because labour time as the measure of value exists only as an ideal, it cannot serve as the matter of price-comparisons. (Here at the same time it becomes clear how and why the value relation obtains a separate material existence in the form of money. This to be developed further.) The difference between price and value calls for values to be measured as prices on a different standard from their own. Price as distinct from value is necessarily money price. It can here be seen that the *nominal* difference between price and value is conditioned by their *real* difference.

Commodity A = 1s. (i.e. $= \frac{1}{x}$ silver); commodity B = 2s. (i.e. $\frac{2}{x}$ silver). Hence commodity B = double the value of commodity A. The value relation between A and B is expressed by means of the proportion in which they are exchanged for a quantity of a third commodity, namely silver; they are not exchanged for a value-relation.

Every commodity (product or instrument of production) is = the objectification of a given amount of labour time. Their value, the relation in which they are exchanged against other commodities, or other commodities against them, is = to the quantity of labour time realized in them. If a commodity e.g. = 1 hour of labour time, then it exchanges with all other commodities which are the product of 1 hour of labour time. (This whole reasoning on the presupposition that exchange value = market value; real value = price.) The value of the commodity is different from the commodity itself. The commodity is a value (exchange value) only within exchange (real or imagined); value is not only the exchangeability of the commodity in general, but its specific exchangeability. Value is at the same time the exponent of the relation in which the commodity is exchanged with other commodities, as well as the exponent of the relation in which it has already been exchanged with other commodities (materialized labour time) in production; it is their quantitatively determined exchangeability. Two commodities, e.g. a yard of cotton and a measure of oil, considered as cotton and as oil, are different by nature, have different properties, are measured by different measures, are incommensurable. Considered as values, all commodities are qualitatively equal and differ only quantitatively, hence can be measured against each other and substituted for one another (are mutually exchangeable, mutually convertible) in certain quantitative relations. Value is their social relation, their economic quality. A book which possesses a certain value and a loaf of bread possessing the same value are exchanged for one another, are the same value but in a different material. As a value, a commodity is an equivalent for all other commodities in a given relation. As a value, the commodity is an equivalent; as an equivalent, all its natural properties are extinguished; it no longer takes up a special, qualitative relationship towards the other commodities; but is rather the general measure as well as the general representative, the general medium of exchange of all other commodities. As value, it is *money*. But because the commodity, or rather the product or the instrument of production, is different from its value, its existence as value is different from its existence as product. Its property of being a value not only can but must achieve an existence different from its natural one. Why? Because commodities as values are different from one another only quantitatively; therefore each commodity must be qualitatively different from its own value. Its value must therefore have an existence which is qualitatively distinguishable from it, and in actual exchange this separability must become a real separation, because the natural distinctness of commodities must come into contradiction with their economic equivalence, and because both can exist together only if the commodity achieves a double existence, not only a natural but also a purely economic existence, in which latter it is a mere symbol, a cipher for a relation of production, a mere symbol for its own value. As a value, every commodity is equally divisible; in its natural existence this is not the case. As a value it remains the same no matter how many metamorphoses and forms of existence it goes through; in reality, commodities are exchanged only because they are not the same and correspond to different systems of needs. As a value, the commodity is general; as a real commodity it is particular. As a value it is always exchangeable; in real exchange it is exchangeable only if it fulfils particular conditions. As a value, the measure of its exchange-ability is determined by itself; exchange value expresses precisely the relation in which it replaces other commodities; in real exchange it is exchangeable only in quantities which are linked with its natural properties and which correspond to the needs of the participants in exchange. (In short, all properties which may be cited as the special qualities of money are properties of the commodity as exchange value, of the product as value as distinct from the value as product.) (The exchange value of a commodity, as a separate form of existence accompanying the commodity itself, is *money*; the form in which all commodities equate, compare, measure themselves; into which all commodities dissolve themselves; that which dissolves itself into all commodities; the universal equivalent.) Every moment, in calculating, accounting etc., that we transform commodities into value symbols, we fix them as mere exchange values, making abstraction from the matter they are composed of and all their natural qualities. On paper, in the head, this metamorphosis proceeds by means of mere abstraction; but in the real exchange process a real *mediation* is required, a means to accomplish this abstraction. In its natural existence, with its natural properties, in natural identity with itself, the commodity is neither constantly exchangeable nor exchangeable against *every other commodity*; this it is only as something different from itself, something distinct from itself, as exchange value. We must first transpose the commodity into itself as exchange value in order then to be able to compare this exchange value with other exchange values and to exchange it. In the crudest barter, when two commodities are exchanged for one another, each is first equated with a symbol which expresses their exchange value, e.g. among certain Negroes on the West African coast, $= x$ bars. One commodity is $= 1$ bar; the other $= 2$ bars. They are exchanged in this relation. The commodities are first transformed into bars in the head and in speech before they are exchanged for one another. They are appraised before being exchanged, and in order to appraise them they must be brought into a given numerical relation to one another. In order to bring them into such a numerical relation, in order to make them commensurable, they must obtain the same denomination (unit). (The bar has a merely imaginary existence, just as, in general, a relation can obtain a particular embodiment and become individualized only by means of abstraction.) In order to cover the excess of one value over another in exchange, in order to liquidate the balance, the crudest barter, just as with international trade today, requires payment in money.

Products (or activities) are exchanged only as commodities; commodities in exchange exist only as values; only as values are they comparable. In order to determine what amount of bread I need in order to exchange it for a yard of linen, I first equate the yard of linen with its exchange value, i.e. $= \frac{1}{x}$ hours of labour time. Similarly, I equate the pound of bread with its exchange value, $= \frac{1}{x}$ or $\frac{2}{x}$ etc. hours of labour time. I equate each of the commodities with a third; i.e. not with themselves. This third, which differs from them both, exists initially only in the head, as a conception, since it expresses a relation; just as, in general, relations can be established as existing only by being *thought*, as distinct from the subjects which are in these relations with each other. In becoming an exchange value, a product (or activity) is not only transformed into a definite quantitative relation, a relative number – that is, a number which expresses the quantity of other commodities which equal it, which are its equivalent, or the relation in which it is their equivalent – but it must also at the same time be transformed qualitatively, be transposed into another element, so that both commodities become magnitudes of the same kind, of the same unit, i.e. commensurable. The commodity first has to be transposed into labour time, into something qualitatively different from itself (qualitatively different (1) because it is not labour time as labour time, but materialized labour time; labour time not in the form of motion, but at rest; not in the form of the process, but of the result; (2) because it is not the objectification of labour time in general, which exists only as a conception (it is only a conception of labour separated from its quality, subject merely to quantitative variations), but rather the specific result of a specific, of a naturally specified, kind of labour which differs qualitatively from other kinds), in order then to be compared as a specific amount of labour time, as a certain magnitude of labour, with other amounts of labour time, other magnitudes of labour. For the purpose of merely making a comparison – an appraisal of products – of determining their value ideally, it suffices to make this transformation in the head (a transformation in which the product exists merely as the expression of quantitative relations of production). This abstraction will do for comparing commodities; but in actual exchange this abstraction in turn must be objectified, must be symbolized, realized in a symbol. This necessity enters into force for the following reasons: (1) As we have already said, both the commodities to be exchanged are transformed in the head into common relations of magnitude, into exchange values, and are thus reciprocally compared. But if they are then to be exchanged in reality, their natural properties enter into contradiction with their character as exchange values and as mere denominated numbers. They are not divisible at will etc. (2) In the real exchange process, particular commodities are always exchanged against particular commodities, and the exchangeability of commodities, as well as the relation in which they are exchangeable, depends on conditions of place and time, etc. But the transformation of the commodity into exchange value does not equate it to any other particular commodity, but expresses it as equivalent, expresses its exchangeability relation, *vis-à-vis* all other commodities. This comparison, which the head accomplishes in one stroke, can be achieved in reality only in a delimited sphere determined by needs, and only in successive steps. (For example, I exchange an income of 100 thalers as my needs would have it one after another against a whole range of commodities whose sum = the exchange value of 100 thalers.) Thus, in order to realize the commodity as exchange value in one stroke, and in order to give it the general influence of an exchange value, it is not enough to exchange it for one particular commodity. It must be exchanged against a third thing which is not in turn itself a particular commodity, but is the symbol of the commodity as commodity, of the commodity's exchange value itself; *which thus represents, say, labour time as such*, say a piece of paper or of leather, which represents a fractional part of labour time. (Such a symbol presupposes general recognition; it can only be a social symbol; it expresses, indeed, nothing more than a social relation.) This symbol represents the fractional parts of labour time; it represents exchange value in such fractional parts as are capable of expressing all relations between exchange values by means of simple arithmetical combination; this symbol, this material sign of exchange value, is a product of exchange itself, and not the execution of an idea conceived *a priori*. (In fact the commodity which is required as medium of exchange becomes transformed into money, into a symbol, only little by little; as soon as this has happened, it can in turn be replaced by a symbol of itself. It then becomes the conscious sign of exchange value.)

The process, then, is simply this: The product becomes a commodity, *i.e. a mere moment of exchange*. The commodity is transformed into exchange value. In order to equate it with itself as an exchange value, it is exchanged for a symbol which represents it as exchange value as such. As such a symbolized exchange value, it can then in turn be exchanged in definite relations for every other commodity. Because the product becomes a commodity, and the commodity becomes an exchange value, it obtains, at first only in the head, a double existence. This doubling in the idea proceeds (and must proceed) to the point where the commodity appears double in real exchange: as a natural product on one side, as exchange value on the other. I.e. the commodity's exchange value obtains a material existence separate from the commodity.

The definition of a product as exchange value thus necessarily implies that exchange value obtains a separate existence, in isolation from the product. The exchange value which is separated from commodities and exists alongside them as itself a commodity, this is – *money*. In the form of *money*, all properties of the commodity as exchange value appear as an object distinct from it, as a form of social existence separated from the natural existence of the commodity. (This to be further shown by enumerating the usual properties of money.) (The material in which this symbol is expressed is by no means a matter of indifference, even though it manifests itself in many different historical forms. In the development of society, not only the symbol but likewise the material corresponding to the symbol are worked out – a material from which society later tries to disentangle itself; if a symbol is not to be arbitrary, certain conditions are demanded of the material in which it is represented. The symbols for words, for example the alphabet etc., have an analogous history.) Thus, the exchange value of a product creates money alongside the product. Now, just as it is impossible to suspend the complications and contradictions which arise from the existence of money alongside the particular commodities merely by altering the form of money (although difficulties characteristic of a lower form of money may be avoided by moving to a higher form), so also is it impossible to abolish money itself as long as exchange value remains the social form of products. It is necessary to see this clearly in order to avoid setting impossible tasks, and in order to know the limits within which monetary reforms and transformations of circulation are able to give a new shape to the relations of production and to the social relations which rest on the latter.

The properties of money as (1) measure of commodity exchange; (2) medium of exchange; (3) representative of commodities (hence object of contracts); (4) general commodity alongside the particular commodities, all simply follow from its character as exchange value separated from commodities themselves and objectified. (By virtue of its property as the general commodity in relation to all others, as the embodiment of the exchange value of the other commodities, money at the same time becomes the realized and always realizable form of capital; the form of capital's appearance which is always valid – a property which emerges in bullion drains; hence capital appears in history initially only in the money form; this explains, finally, the link between money and the rate of interest, and its influence on the latter.)

To the degree that production is shaped in such a way that every producer becomes dependent on the exchange value of his commodity, i.e. as the product increasingly becomes an exchange value in reality, and exchange value becomes the immediate object of production – to the same degree must *money relations* develop, together with the contradictions immanent in the *money relation*, in the relation of the product to itself as money. The need for exchange and for the transformation of the product into a pure exchange value progresses in step with the division of labour, i.e. with the increasingly social character of production. But as the latter grows, so grows the power of *money*, i.e. the exchange relation establishes itself as a power external to and independent of the producers. What originally appeared as a means to promote production becomes a relation alien to the producers. As the producers become more dependent on exchange, exchange appears to become more independent of them, and the gap between the product as product and the product as exchange value appears to widen. Money does not create these antitheses and contradictions; it is, rather, the development of these contradictions and antitheses which creates the seemingly transcendental power of money. (To be further developed, the influence of the transformation of all relations into money relations: taxes in kind into money taxes, rent in kind into money rent, military service into mercenary troops, all personal services in general into money services, of patriarchal, slave, serf and guild labour into pure wage labour.)

The product becomes a commodity; the commodity becomes

exchange value; the exchange value of the commodity is its immanent money-property; this, its money-property, separates itself from it in the form of money, and achieves a general social existence separated from all particular commodities and their natural mode of existence; the relation of the product to itself as exchange value becomes its relation to money, existing alongside it; or, becomes the relation of all products to money, external to them all. Just as the real exchange of products creates their exchange value, so does their exchange value create money.

The next question to confront us is this: are there not contradictions, inherent in this relation itself, which are wrapped up in the existence of money alongside commodities?

Firstly: The simple fact that the commodity exists doubly, in one aspect as a specific product whose natural form of existence ideally contains (latently contains) its exchange value, and in the other aspect as manifest exchange value (money), in which all connection with the natural form of the product is stripped away again – this double, *differentiated* existence must develop into a *difference*, and the difference into *antithesis* and *contradiction*. The same contradiction between the particular nature of the commodity as product and its general nature as exchange value, which created the necessity of positing it doubly, as this particular commodity on one side and as money on the other – this contradiction between the commodity's particular natural qualities and its general social qualities contains from the beginning the possibility that these two separated forms in which the commodity exists are not convertible into one another. The exchangeability of the commodity exists as a thing beside it, as money, as something different from the commodity, something no longer directly identical with it. As soon as money has become an external thing alongside the commodity, the exchangeability of the commodity for money becomes bound up with external conditions which may or may not be present; it is abandoned to the mercy of external conditions. The commodity is demanded in exchange because of its natural properties, because of the needs for which it is the desired object. Money, by contrast, is demanded only because of its exchange value, as exchange value. Hence, whether or not the commodity is transposable into money, whether or not it can be exchanged for money, whether its exchange value can be posited for it – this depends on circumstances which initially have nothing to do with it as exchange value and are independent of that. The transposability of the commodity depends on the natural properties of the product; that of money coincides with its existence as symbolized exchange value. There thus arises the possibility that the commodity, in its specific form as product, can no longer be exchanged for, equated with, its general form as money.

By existing outside the commodity as money, the exchangeability of the commodity has become something different from and alien to the commodity, with which it first has to be brought into equation, to which it is therefore at the beginning unequal; while the equation itself becomes dependent on external conditions, hence a matter of chance.

Secondly: Just as the exchange value of the commodity leads a double existence, as the particular commodity and as money, so does the act of exchange split into two mutually independent acts: exchange of commodities for money, exchange of money for commodities; purchase and sale. Since these have now achieved a spatially and temporally separate and mutually indifferent form of existence, their immediate identity ceases. They may correspond or not; they may balance or not; they may enter into disproportion with one another. They will of course always attempt to equalize one another; but in the place of the earlier immediate equality there now stands the constant movement of equalization, which evidently presupposes constant non-equivalence. It is now entirely possible that consonance may be reached only by passing through the most extreme dissonance.

Thirdly: With the separation of purchase and sale, with the splitting of exchange into two spatially and temporally independent acts, there further emerges another, new relation.

Just as exchange itself splits apart into two mutually independent acts, so does the overall movement of exchange itself become separate from the exchangers, the producers of commodities. Exchange for the sake of exchange separates off from exchange for the sake of commodities. A mercantile estate[17] steps between the producers; an estate which only buys in order to sell and only sells so as to buy again, and whose aim in this operation is not the possession of commodities as products but merely the obtaining of exchange values as such, of money. (A mercantile estate can take shape even with mere barter. But since only the overflow of production on both sides is at its disposal, its influence on produc-

17. *Kaufmannsstand*: This refers above all to the merchants of the sixteenth and seventeenth centuries, who formed an 'estate' rather than a 'class'.

tion, and its importance as a whole, remain completely secondary.)
The rise of exchange (commerce) as an independent function torn
away from the exchangers corresponds to the rise of exchange
value as an independent entity, as money, torn away from products.
Exchange value was the measure of commodity exchange; but its
aim was the direct possession of the exchanged commodity, its
consumption (regardless of whether this consumption consists of
serving to satisfy needs directly, i.e. serving as product, or of serving in turn as a tool of production). The purpose of commerce is
not consumption, directly, but the gaining of money, of exchange
values. This doubling of exchange – exchange for the sake of consumption and exchange for exchange – gives rise to a new disproportion. In his exchange, the merchant is guided merely by the
difference between the purchase and sale of commodities; but the
consumer who buys a commodity must replace its exchange value
once and for all. Circulation, i.e. exchange within the mercantile
estate, and the point at which circulation ends, i.e. exchange
between the mercantile estate and the consumers – as much as they
must ultimately condition one another – are determined by quite
different laws and motives, and can enter into the most acute
contradiction with one another. The possibility of commercial
crises is already contained in this separation. But since production
works directly for commerce and only indirectly for consumption,
it must not only create but also and equally be seized by this incongruency between commerce and exchange for consumption.
(The relations of demand and supply become entirely inverted.)
(The money business then in turn separates from commerce
proper.)

Aphorisms. (All commodities are perishable money; money is
the imperishable commodity. With the development of the division
of labour, the immediate product ceases to be a medium of exchange. The need arises for a general medium of exchange, i.e. a
medium of exchange independent of the specific production of each
individual. Money implies the separation between the value of
things and their substance. Money is originally the representative
of all values; in practice this situation is inverted, and all real products and labours become the representatives of money. In direct
barter, every article cannot be exchanged for every other; a specific
activity can be exchanged only for certain specific products.
Money can overcome the difficulties inherent in barter only by

generalizing them, making them universal. It is absolutely necessary that forcibly separated elements which essentially belong together manifest themselves by way of forcible eruption as the *separation* of things which belong together in essence. The unity is brought about *by force*. As soon as the antagonistic split leads to eruptions, the economists point to the *essential unity* and abstract from the alienation. Their apologetic wisdom consists in forgetting their own definitions at every decisive moment. The product as direct medium of exchange is (1) still directly bound to its natural quality, hence limited in every way by the latter; it can, for example, deteriorate etc.; (2) connected with the immediate need which another may have or not have at the time, or which he may have for his own product. When the product becomes subordinated to labour and labour to exchange, then a moment enters in which both are separated from their owner. Whether, after this separation, they return to him again in another shape becomes a matter of *chance*. When money enters into exchange, I am forced to exchange my product for exchange value in general or for the general capacity to exchange, hence my product becomes dependent on the state of general commerce and is torn out of its local, natural and individual boundaries. For exactly that reason it can cease to be a product.)

Fourthly: Just as exchange value, in the form of money, takes its place as the *general commodity* alongside all particular commodities, so does exchange value as money therefore at the same time take its place as a *particular commodity* (since it has a particular existence) alongside all other commodities. An incongruency arises not only because money, which exists only in exchange, confronts the particular exchangeability of commodities as their general exchangeability, and directly extinguishes it, while, nevertheless, the two are supposed to be always convertible into one another; but also because money comes into contradiction with itself and with its characteristic by virtue of being itself a *particular* commodity (even if only a symbol) and of being subject, therefore, to particular conditions of exchange in its exchange with other commodities, conditions which contradict its general unconditional exchangeability. (Not to speak of money as fixed in the substance of a particular product, etc.) Besides its existence in the commodity, exchange value achieved an existence of its own in money, was separated from its substance exactly because the natural characteristic of this substance contradicted its general characteristic as exchange value. Every commodity is equal (and comparable) to every other as exchange value (*qualitatively*: each now merely represents a *quantitative* plus or minus of exchange value). For that reason, this equality, this unity of the commodity is distinct from its natural differentiation; and appears in money therefore as their common element as well as a third thing which confronts them both. But on one side, exchange value naturally remains at the same time an inherent quality of commodities while it simultaneously exists outside them; on the other side, when money no longer exists as a property of commodities, as a common element within them, but as an individual entity apart from them, then money itself becomes a *particular* commodity alongside the other commodities. (Determinable by demand and supply; splits into different kinds of money, etc.) It becomes a commodity like other commodities, and at the same time it is not a commodity like other commodities. Despite its general character it is one exchangeable entity among other exchangeable entities. It is not only the general exchange value, but at the same time a particular exchange value alongside other particular exchange values. Here a new source of contradictions which make themselves felt in practice. (The particular nature of money emerges again in the separation of the money business from commerce proper.)

We see, then, how it is an inherent property of money to fulfil its purposes by simultaneously negating them; to achieve independence from commodities; to be a means which becomes an end; to realize the exchange value of commodities by separating them from it; to facilitate exchange by splitting it; to overcome the difficulties of the direct exchange of commodities by generalizing them; to make exchange independent of the producers in the same measure as the producers become dependent on exchange.

(It will be necessary later, before this question is dropped, to correct the idealist manner of the presentation, which makes it seem as if it were merely a matter of conceptual determinations and of the dialectic of these concepts. Above all in the case of the phrase: product (or activity) becomes commodity; commodity, exchange value; exchange value, money.)

(*Economist*. 24 January 1857. The following passage to be borne in mind on the subject of banks:

'So far as the mercantile classes share, which they now do very generally, in the profits of banks – and may to a still greater extent by the wider diffusion of joint-stock banks, the abolition of all corporate privileges, and the extension of perfect freedom to the business of banking – they have been enriched by the increased rates of money. In truth, the mercantile classes by the extent of their deposits, are virtually their own bankers; and so far as that is the case, the rate of discount must be to them of little importance. All banking and other reserves must of course be the results of continual industry, and of savings laid by out of profits; and consequently, taking the mercantile and industrious classes as a whole, they must be their own bankers, and it requires only that the principles of free trade should be extended to all businesses, to equalize or naturalize for them the advantages and disadvantages of all the fluctuations in the money market.')

All contradictions of the *monetary system* and of the exchange of products under the monetary system are the development of the relation of products as *exchange values*, of their definition as *exchange value* or as *value* pure and simple.

(*Morning Star*. 12 February 1857. 'The pressure of money during last year, and the high rate of discount which was adopted in consequence, has been very beneficial to the profit account of the Bank of France. Its dividend has gone on increasing: 118 fr. in 1852, 154 fr. in 1853, 194 fr. in 1854, 200 fr. in 1855, 272 fr. in 1856.')

Also to be noted, the following passage: The English silver coins issued at a price higher than the value of the silver they contain. A pound silver of an intrinsic value of 60–62s. (£3 on an average in gold) was coined into 66s. The Mint pays the 'market price of the day, from 5s. to 5s. 2d. the ounce, and issues at the rate of 5s. 6d. the ounce. There are two reasons which prevent any practical inconvenience resulting from this arrangement:' (*of silver tokens*, not of intrinsic value) 'first, the coin can only be procured at the Mint, and at that price; as home circulation, then, it cannot be depreciated, and it cannot be sent abroad because it circulates here for more than its intrinsic value; and secondly, as it is a legal tender only up to 40s., it never interferes with the gold coins, nor affects their value.' Gives France the advice to do the same: to issue subordinate coins of silver tokens, not of intrinsic value, and limit[ing] the amount to which they should be a legal tender. But at the same time: in fixing the quality of the coin, to take a larger margin between the intrinsic and the nominal value than we have in England, because the increasing value of silver in relation to gold may very probably, before long, rise up to our present Mint price, when we may be obliged again to alter it. Our silver coin is now little more than 5% below the intrinsic value: a short time since it was 10%. (*Economist*. 24 January 1857.)

Now, it might be thought that the issue of time-chits overcomes all these difficulties. (The existence of the time-chit naturally already presupposes conditions which are not directly given in the examination of the relations of exchange value and money, and which can and do exist without the time-chit: public credit, bank etc.; but all this not to be touched on further here, since the time-chit men of course regard it as the ultimate product of the 'series', which, even if it corresponds most to the 'pure' concept of money, 'appears' last in reality.) To begin with: If the preconditions under which the price of commodities = their exchange value are fulfilled and given; balance of demand and supply; balance of production and consumption; and what this amounts to in the last analysis, *proportionate production* (the so-called relations of distribution are themselves relations of production), then the money question becomes entirely secondary, in particular the question whether the tickets should be blue or green, paper or tin, or whatever other form social accounting should take. In that case it is totally meaningless to keep up the pretence that an investigation is being made of the real relations of money.

The bank (any bank) issues the time-chits.[18] A commodity, A = the exchange value x, i.e. = x hours of labour time, is exchanged for a quantity of money representing x labour time. The bank would at the same time have to purchase the commodity, i.e. exchange it for its representative in monetary form, just as e.g. the Bank of England today has to give notes for gold. The commodity, the substantial and therefore accidental existence of exchange value, is exchanged for the symbolic existence of exchange value as exchange value. There is then no difficulty in transposing it from the form of the commodity into the form of money. The labour time contained in it only needs to be authentically verified (which, by the way, is not as easy as assaying the purity and weight of gold and silver) and thereby immediately creates its *counter-value*, its monetary existence. No matter how we may turn and twist the

18. The following two paragraphs are directed specifically against the scheme outlined by John Gray in *The Social System*, pp. 62–86.

matter, in the last instance it amounts to this: the bank which issues the time-chits buys commodities at their costs of production, buys all commodities, and moreover this purchase costs the bank nothing more than the production of snippets of paper, and the bank gives the seller, in place of the exchange value which he possesses in a definite and substantial form, the symbolic exchange value of the commodity, in other words a draft on all other commodities to the amount of the same exchange value. Exchange value as such can of course exist only symbolically, although in order for it to be employed as a thing and not merely as a formal notion, this symbol must possess an objective existence; it is not merely an ideal notion, but is actually presented to the mind in an objective mode. (A measure can be held in the hand; exchange value measures, but it exchanges only when the measure passes from one hand to the other.) So the bank gives money for the commodity; money which is an exact draft on the exchange value of the commodity, i.e. of all commodities of the same value; the bank buys. The bank is the general buyer, the buyer of not only this or that commodity, but all commodities. For its purpose is to bring about the transposition of every commodity into its symbolic existence as exchange value. But if it is the general buyer, then it also has to be the general seller; not only the dock where all wares are deposited, not only the general warehouse, but also the owner of the commodities, in the same sense as every merchant. I have exchanged my commodity A for the time-chit B, which represents the commodity's exchange value; but I have done this only so that I can then further metamorphose this B into any real commodity C, D, E etc., as it suits me. Now, can this money circulate outside the bank? Can it take any other route than that between the owner of the chit and the bank? How is the convertibility of this chit secured? Only two cases are possible. Either all owners of commodities (be these products or labour) desire to sell their commodities at their exchange value, or some want to and some do not. If they all want to sell at their exchange value, then they will not await the chance arrival or non-arrival of a buyer, but go immediately to the bank, unload their commodities on to it, and obtain their exchange value symbol, money, for them: they redeem them for its money. In this case the bank is simultaneously the general buyer and the general seller in one person. Or the opposite takes place. In this case, the bank chit is mere paper which claims to be the generally recognized symbol of exchange value, but has in fact no value. For this symbol has to have the property of not merely representing, but *being*, exchange value in actual exchange. In the latter case the bank chit would not be money, or it would be money only by convention between the bank and its clients, but not on the open market. It would be the same as a meal ticket good for a dozen meals which I obtain from a restaurant, or a theatre pass good for a dozen evenings, both of which represent money, but only in this particular restaurant or this particular theatre. The bank chit would have ceased to meet the qualifications of money, since it would not circulate among the general public, but only between the bank and its clients. We thus have to drop the latter supposition.

The bank would thus be the general buyer and seller. Instead of notes it could also issue cheques, and instead of that it could also keep simple bank accounts. Depending on the sum of commodity values which X had deposited with the bank, X would have that sum in the form of other commodities to his credit. A second attribute of the bank would be necessary: it would need the power to establish the exchange value of all commodities, i.e. the labour time materialized in them, in an authentic manner. But its functions could not end there. It would have to determine the labour time in which commodities could be produced, with the average means of production available in a given industry, i.e. the time in which they would have to be produced. But that also would not be sufficient. It would not only have to determine the time in which a certain quantity of products had to be produced, and place the producers in conditions which made their labour equally productive (i.e. it would have to balance and to arrange the distribution of the means of labour), but it would also have to determine the amounts of labour time to be employed in the different branches of production. The latter would be necessary because, in order to realize exchange value and make the bank's currency really convertible, social production in general would have to be stabilized and arranged so that the needs of the partners in exchange were always satisfied. Nor is this all. The biggest exchange process is not that between commodities, but that between commodities and labour. (More on this presently.) The workers would not be selling their labour to the bank, but they would receive the exchange value for the entire product of their labour, etc. Precisely seen, then, the bank would be not only the general buyer and seller, but also the general producer. In fact either it would be a despotic ruler of production and trustee of distribution, or it would indeed be nothing more than a board which keeps the books and accounts for a society producing in common. The common ownership of the means of production is presupposed, etc., etc. The Saint-Simonians made their bank into the papacy of production.

The dissolution of all products and activities into exchange values presupposes the dissolution of all fixed personal (historic) relations of dependence in production, as well as the all-sided dependence of the producers on one another. Each individual's production is dependent on the production of all others; and the transformation of his product into the necessaries of his own life is [similarly] dependent on the consumption of all others. Prices are old; exchange also; but the increasing determination of the former by costs of production, as well as the increasing dominance of the latter over all relations of production, only develop fully, and continue to develop ever more completely, in bourgeois society, the society of free competition. What Adam Smith, in the true eighteenth-century manner, puts in the prehistoric period, the period preceding history, is rather a product of history.

This reciprocal dependence is expressed in the constant necessity for exchange, and in exchange value as the all-sided mediation. The economists express this as follows: Each pursues his private interest and only his private interest; and thereby serves the private interests of all, the general interest, without willing or knowing it. The real point is not that each individual's pursuit of his private interest promotes the totality of private interests, the general interest. One could just as well deduce from this abstract phrase that each individual reciprocally blocks the assertion of the others' interests, so that, instead of a general affirmation, this war of all against all produces a general negation. The point is rather that private interest is itself already a socially determined interest, which can be achieved only within the conditions laid down by society and with the means provided by society; hence it is bound to the reproduction of these conditions and means. It is the interest of private persons; but its content, as well as the form and means of its realization, is given by social conditions independent of all.

The reciprocal and all-sided dependence of individuals who are indifferent to one another forms their social connection. This social bond is expressed in *exchange value*, by means of which alone each individual's own activity or his product becomes an activity and a product for him; he must produce a general product – *exchange value*, or, the latter isolated for itself and individualized, *money*. On the other side, the power which each individual exercises over the activity of others or over social wealth exists in him as the owner of *exchange values*, of *money*. The individual carries his social power, as well as his bond with society, in his pocket. Activity, regardless of its individual manifestation, and the product of activity, regardless of its particular make-up, are always *exchange value*, and exchange value is a generality, in which all individuality and peculiarity are negated and extinguished. This indeed is a condition very different from that in which the individual or the individual member of a family or clan (later, community) directly and naturally reproduces himself, or in which his productive activity and his share in production are bound to a specific form of labour and of product, which determine his relation to others in just that specific way.

The social character of activity, as well as the social form of the product, and the share of individuals in production here appear as something alien and objective, confronting the individuals, not as their relation to one another, but as their subordination to relations which subsist independently of them and which arise out of collisions between mutually indifferent individuals. The general exchange of activities and products, which has become a vital condition for each individual – their mutual interconnection – here appears as something alien to them, autonomous, as a thing. In exchange value, the social connection between persons is transformed into a social relation between things; personal capacity into objective wealth. The less social power the medium of exchange possesses (and at this stage it is still closely bound to the nature of the direct product of labour and the direct needs of the partners in exchange) the greater must be the power of the community which binds the individuals together, the patriarchal relation, the community of antiquity, feudalism and the guild system. (See my Notebook XII, 34 B.)[19] Each individual possesses

19. This note refers to an unknown manuscript by Marx, which must be older than his work of 1851 on 'The Completed Money System'. Possibly it refers to one of the missing parts of the manuscript of 1845–7 on the 'Critique of Politics and Political Economy', fragments of which are reprinted in *Marx-Engels Gesamtausgabe* (*MEGA*) 1/3, pp. 33–172, 437–583 and 592–6. The 1851 manuscript, 'The Completed Money System', is not extant in full, and remains unpublished. [MELI note.]

social power in the form of a thing. Rob the thing of this social power and you must give it to persons to exercise over persons. Relations of personal dependence (entirely spontaneous at the outset) are the first social forms, in which human productive capacity develops only to a slight extent and at isolated points. Personal independence founded on *objective* [*sachlicher*] dependence is the second great form, in which a system of general social metabolism, of universal relations, of all-round needs and universal capacities is formed for the first time. Free individuality, based on the universal development of individuals and on their subordination of their communal, social productivity as their social wealth, is the third stage. The second stage creates the conditions for the third. Patriarchal as well as ancient conditions (feudal, also) thus disintegrate with the development of commerce, of luxury, of *money*, of *exchange value*, while modern society arises and grows in the same measure.

Exchange and division of labour reciprocally condition one another. Since everyone works for himself but his product is nothing for him, each must of course exchange, not only in order to take part in the general productive capacity but also in order to transform his own product into his own subsistence. (See my 'Remarks on Economics', p. V (13, 14).)[20] Exchange, when mediated by exchange value and money, presupposes the all-round dependence of the producers on one another, together with the total isolation of their private interests from one another, as well as a division of social labour whose unity and mutual complementarity exist in the form of a natural relation, as it were, external to the individuals and independent of them. The pressure of general demand and supply on one another mediates the connection of mutually indifferent persons.

The very necessity of first transforming individual products or activities into *exchange value*, into *money*, so that they obtain and demonstrate their social *power* in this *objective* [*sachlichen*] form, proves two things: (1) That individuals now produce only for society and in society; (2) that production is not *directly* social, is not 'the offspring of association', which distributes labour internally. Individuals are subsumed under social production; social production exists outside them as their fate; but social production is not subsumed under individuals, manageable by them as their common wealth. There can therefore be nothing more erroneous

20. See p. 157, n. 19.

and absurd than to postulate the control by the united individuals of their total production, on the basis of *exchange value*, of *money*, as was done above in the case of the time-chit bank. The *private exchange* of all products of labour, all activities and all wealth stands in antithesis not only to a distribution based on a natural or political super- and subordination of individuals to one another (to which *exchange* proper only runs parallel or, by and large, does not so much take a grip on the life of entire communities as, rather, insert itself between different communities; it by no means exercises general domination over all relations of production and distribution) (regardless of the character of this super- and subordination: patriarchal, ancient or feudal) but also to free exchange among individuals who are associated on the basis of common appropriation and control of the means of production. (The latter form of association is not arbitrary; it presupposes the development of material and cultural conditions which are not to be examined any further at this point.) Just as the division of labour creates agglomeration, combination, cooperation, the antithesis of private interests, class interests, competition, concentration of capital, monopoly, stock companies – so many antithetical forms of the unity which itself brings the antithesis to the fore – so does private exchange create world trade, private independence creates complete dependence on the so-called world market, and the fragmented acts of exchange create a banking and credit system whose books, at least keep a record of the balance between debit and credit in private exchange. Although the private interests within each nation divide it into as many nations as it has 'full-grown individuals', and although the interests of exporters and of importers are antithetical here, etc. etc., national trade does obtain the *semblance* of existence in the form of the rate of exchange. Nobody will take this as a ground for believing that a *reform of the money market* can abolish the *foundations* of internal or external private trade. But within bourgeois society, the society that rests on *exchange value*, there arise relations of circulation as well as of production which are so many mines to explode it. (A mass of antithetical forms of the social unity, whose antithetical character can never be abolished through quiet metamorphosis. On the other hand, if we did not find concealed in society as it is the material conditions of production and the corresponding relations of exchange prerequisite for a classless society, then all attempts to explode it would be quixotic.)

We have seen that, although exchange value is = to the relative labour time materialized in products, money, for its part, is = to the exchange value of commodities, separated from their substance; and that in this exchange value or money relation are contained the contradictions between commodities and their exchange value, between commodities as exchange values and money. We saw that a bank which directly creates the mirror image of the commodity in the form of labour-money is a utopia. Thus, although money owes its existence only to the tendency of exchange value to separate itself from the substance of commodities and to take on a pure form, nevertheless commodities cannot be directly transformed into money; i.e. the authentic certificate of the amount of labour time realized in the commodity cannot serve the commodity as its price in the world of exchange values. How is this?

(In one of the forms of money – in so far as it is *medium* of exchange (not *measure* of exchange value) – it is clear to the economists that the existence of money presupposes the objectification [*Versachlichung*] of the social bond; in so far, that is, as money appears in the form of *collateral* which one individual must leave with another in order to obtain a commodity from him. Here the economists themselves say that people place in a thing (money) the faith which they do not place in each other. But why do they have faith in the thing? Obviously only because that thing is an *objectified relation* between persons; because it is objectified exchange value, and exchange value is nothing more than a mutual relation between people's productive activities. Every other collateral may serve the holder directly in that function: money serves him only as the 'dead pledge of society',[21] but it serves as such only because of its social (symbolic) property; and it can have a social property only because individuals have alienated their own social relationship from themselves so that it takes the form of a thing.)

In the *lists of current prices*, where all values are measured in money, it seems as though this independence from persons of the social character of things is, by the activity of commerce, on this basis of alienation where the relations of production and distribution stand opposed to the individual, to all individuals, at the same time subordinated to the individual again. Since, 'if you please', the autonomization of the world market (in which the activity of each individual is included), increases with the develop-

21. Aristotle, *Nicomachean Ethics*, Bk V, Ch. 5, para. 14.

ment of monetary relations (exchange value) and vice versa, since the general bond and all-round interdependence in production and consumption increase together with the independence and indifference of the consumers and producers to one another; since this contradiction leads to crises, etc., hence, together with the development of this alienation, and on the same basis, efforts are made to overcome it: institutions emerge whereby each individual can acquire information about the activity of all others and attempt to adjust his own accordingly, e.g. lists of current prices, rates of exchange, interconnections between those active in commerce through the mails, telegraphs etc. (the means of communication of course grow at the same time). (This means that, although the total supply and demand are independent of the actions of each individual, everyone attempts to inform himself about them, and this knowledge then reacts back in practice on the total supply and demand. Although on the given standpoint, alienation is not overcome by these means, nevertheless relations and connections are introduced thereby which include the possibility of suspending the old standpoint.) (The possibility of general statistics, etc.) (This is to be developed, incidentally, under the categories '*Prices, Demand and Supply*'. To be further noted here only that a comprehensive view over the whole of commerce and production in so far as lists of current prices in fact provide it, furnishes indeed the best proof of the way in which their own exchange and their own production confront individuals as an *objective* relation which is *independent* of them. In the case of the *world market*, the *connection of the individual* with all, but at the same time also the *independence of this connection from the individual*, have developed to such a high level that the formation of the world market already at the same time contains the conditions for going beyond it.) *Comparison* in place of real communality and generality.

(It has been said and may be said that this is precisely the beauty and the greatness of it: this spontaneous interconnection, this material and mental metabolism which is independent of the knowing and willing of individuals, and which presupposes their reciprocal independence and indifference. And, certainly, this objective connection is preferable to the lack of any connection, or to a merely local connection resting on blood ties, or on primeval, natural or master–servant relations. Equally certain is it that individuals cannot gain mastery over their own social interconnections before they have created them. But it is an insipid notion to conceive of this merely *objective bond* as a spontaneous, natural attribute inherent in individuals and inseparable from their nature (in antithesis to their conscious knowing and willing). This bond is their product. It is a historic product. It belongs to a specific phase of their development. The alien and independent character in which it presently exists *vis-à-vis* individuals proves only that the latter are still engaged in the creation of the conditions of their social life, and that they have not yet begun, on the basis of these conditions, to live it. It is the bond natural to individuals within specific and limited relations of production. Universally developed individuals, whose social relations, as their own communal [*gemeinschaftlich*] relations, are hence also subordinated to their own communal control, are no product of nature, but of history. The degree and the universality of the development of wealth where *this* individuality becomes possible supposes production on the basis of exchange values as a prior condition, whose universality produces not only the alienation of the individual from himself and from others, but also the universality and the comprehensiveness of his relations and capacities. In earlier stages of development the single individual seems to be developed more fully, because he has not yet worked out his relationships in their fullness, or erected them as independent social powers and relations opposite himself. It is as ridiculous to yearn for a return to that original fullness[22] as it is to believe that with this complete emptiness history has come to a standstill. The bourgeois viewpoint has never advanced beyond this antithesis between itself and this romantic viewpoint, and therefore the latter will accompany it as legitimate antithesis up to its blessed end.)

(The relation of the individual to science may be taken as an example here.)

(To compare money with blood – the term circulation gave occasion for this – is about as correct as Menenius Agrippa's comparison between the patricians and the stomach.)[23] (To compare money with language is not less erroneous. Language does not

22. This is directed against the doctrines of the Romantic reaction, as put forward by such people as Adam Müller (*Die Elemente der Staatskunst*, Berlin, 1809) and Thomas Carlyle (*Chartism*, London, 1840).

23. Menenius Agrippa (*c.* 530–493 B.C.) was a Roman patrician who is said to have persuaded the plebeians to return to Rome by comparing the patricians to the stomach and the plebeians to the limbs without which the stomach could not survive.

transform ideas, so that the peculiarity of ideas is dissolved and their social character runs alongside them as a separate entity, like prices alongside commodities. Ideas do not exist separately from language. Ideas which have first to be translated out of their mother tongue into a foreign language in order to circulate, in order to become exchangeable, offer a somewhat better analogy; but the analogy then lies not in language, but in the foreignness of language.)

(The exchangeability of all products, activities and relations with a third, *objective* entity which can be re-exchanged for every-thing *without distinction* – that is, the development of exchange values (and of money relations) is identical with universal venality, corruption. Universal prostitution appears as a necessary phase in the development of the social character of personal talents, cap-acities, abilities, activities. More politely expressed: the universal relation of utility and use. The equation of the incompatible, as Shakespeare nicely defined money.[24] Greed as such impossible with-out money; all other kinds of accumulation and of mania for ac-cumulation appear as primitive, restricted by needs on the one hand and by the restricted nature of products on the other (*sacra auri fames*[25]).)

(The development of the money system obviously presupposes other, prior developments.)

When we look at social relations which create an undeveloped system of exchange, of exchange values and of money, or which correspond to an undeveloped degree of these, then it is clear from the outset that the individuals in such a society, although their relations appear to be more personal, enter into connection with one another only as individuals imprisoned within a certain de-finition, as feudal lord and vassal, landlord and serf, etc., or as members of a caste etc. or as members of an estate etc. In the money relation, in the developed system of exchange (and this semblance seduces the democrats), the ties of personal dependence, of distinctions of blood, education, etc. are in fact exploded, ripped up (at least, personal ties all appear as *personal* relations); and individuals *seem* independent (this is an independence which is at bottom merely an illusion, and it is more correctly called indif-ference), free to collide with one another and to engage in ex-

24. '. . . Thou visible God!/That solder'st close impossibilities,/And mak'st them kiss! . . .' (*Timon of Athens*, Act 4, Scene 3).

25. 'that accursed hunger for gold' (Virgil, *Aeneid*, Bk 3, line 57).

change within this freedom; but they appear thus only for someone who abstracts from the *conditions*, the *conditions of existence* within which these individuals enter into contact (and these conditions, in turn, are independent of the individuals and, although created by society, appear as if they were *natural conditions*, not controllable by individuals). The definedness of individuals, which in the former case appears as a personal restriction of the individual by another, appears in the latter case as developed into an objective restriction of the individual by relations independent of him and sufficient unto themselves. (Since the single individual cannot strip away his personal definition, but may very well overcome and master external relations, his freedom *seems* to be greater in case 2. A closer examination of these external relations, these conditions, shows, however, that it is impossible for the individuals of a class etc. to overcome them *en masse* without destroying them. A particular individual may by chance get on top of these relations, but the mass of those under their rule cannot, since their mere existence expresses subordination, the necessary subordination of the mass of individuals.) These external relations are very far from being an abolition of 'relations of dependence'; they are rather the dissolution of these relations into a general form; they are merely the elaboration and emergence of the general *foundation* of the relations of personal dependence. Here also individuals come into connection with one another only in determined ways. These *objective* dependency relations also appear, in antithesis to those of *personal* dependence (the objective dependency relation is nothing more than social relations which have become independent and now enter into opposition to the seemingly independent individuals; i.e. the reciprocal relations of production separated from and autonomous of individuals) in such a way that individuals are now ruled by *abstractions*, whereas earlier they depended on one another. The abstraction, or idea, however, is nothing more than the theoretical expression of those material relations which are their lord and master. Relations can be expressed, of course, only in ideas, and thus philosophers have determined the reign of ideas to be the peculiarity of the new age, and have identified the creation of free individuality with the overthrow of this reign. This error was all the more easily committed, from the ideological stand-point, as this reign exercised by the relations (this objective dependency, which, incidentally, turns into certain definite relations of personal dependency, but stripped of all illusions) appears within the consciousness of individuals as the reign of ideas, and because the belief in the permanence of these ideas, i.e. of these objective relations of dependency, is of course consolidated, nourished and inculcated by the ruling classes by all means available.

(As regards the illusion of the 'purely personal relations' in feudal times, etc., it is of course not to be forgotten for a moment (1) that these relations, in a certain phase, also took on an objective character within their own sphere, as for example the development of landed proprietorship out of purely military relations of subordination; but (2) the objective relation on which they founder has still a limited, primitive character and therefore *seems* personal, while, in the modern world, personal relations flow purely out of relations of production and exchange.)

The product becomes a commodity. The commodity becomes exchange value. The exchange value of the commodity acquires an existence of its own alongside the commodity; i.e. the commodity – in the form in which (1) it is exchangeable with all other commodities, (2) it has hence become a commodity in general, and its natural specificity is extinguished, and (3) the measure of its exchangeability (i.e. the given relation within which it is equivalent to other commodities) has been determined – this commodity is the commodity as money, and, to be precise, not as money in general, but as a *certain definite sum of money*, for, in order to represent exchange value in all its variety, money has to be countable, quantitatively divisible.

Money – the common form into which all commodities as exchange values are transformed, i.e. the universal commodity – must itself exist as a *particular* commodity alongside the others, since what is required is not only that they can be measured against it in the head, but that they can be changed and exchanged for it in the actual exchange process. The contradiction which thereby enters, to be developed elsewhere. Money does not arise by convention, any more than the state does. It arises out of exchange, and arises naturally out of exchange; it is a product of the same. At the beginning, that commodity will serve as money – i.e. it will be exchanged not for the purpose of satisfying a need, not for consumption, but in order to be re-exchanged for other commodities – which is most frequently exchanged and circulated as an object of consumption, and which is therefore most certain to be exchangeable again for other commodities, i.e. which represents

within the given social organization wealth κατ᾽ ἐξοχήν,[26] which
is the object of the most general demand and supply, and which
possesses a particular use value. Thus salt, hides, cattle, slaves.
In practice such a commodity corresponds more closely to itself as
exchange value than do other commodities (a pity that the difference between *denrée* and *marchandise* cannot be neatly reproduced in German). It is the particular usefulness of the commodity, whether as a particular object of consumption (hides),
or as a direct instrument of production (slaves), which stamps it as
money in these cases. In the course of further development precisely the opposite will occur, i.e. that commodity which has the
least utility as an object of consumption or instrument of production
will best serve the needs of *exchange as such*. In the former case,
the commodity becomes money because of its particular use value;
in the latter case it acquires its particular use value from its
serviceability as money. The precious metals last, they do not alter,
they can be divided and then combined together again, they can
be transported relatively easily owing to the compression of great
exchange value in little space – for all these reasons they are
especially suitable in the latter stage. At the same time, they form
the natural transition from the first form of money. At somewhat
higher levels of production and exchange, the instrument of production takes *precedence* over products; and the *metals* (prior to
that, stones) are the first and most indispensable instruments of
production. Both are still combined in the case of *copper*, which
played so large a role as money in antiquity; here is the particular
use value as an instrument of production together with other attributes which do not flow out of the use value of the commodity
but correspond to its function as exchange value (including medium
of exchange). The *precious* metals then split off from the remainder by virtue of being inoxidizable, of standard quality etc., and
they correspond better, then, to the higher stage, in that their direct
utility for consumption and production recedes while, because of
their rarity, they better represent value purely based on exchange.
From the outset they represent superfluity, the form in which
wealth originates. Also, metals preferably exchanged for metals
rather than for other commodities.

The first form of money corresponds to a low stage of exchange
and of barter, in which money still appears more in its quality of
measure rather than as a real *instrument of exchange*. At this stage,

26. *par excellence.*

the measure can still be purely imaginary (although the bar in use among Negroes includes iron) (sea shells etc., however, correspond more to the series of which gold and silver form the culmination).

From the fact that the commodity develops into general exchange value, it follows that exchange value becomes a specific commodity: it can do so only because a specific commodity obtains the privilege of representing, symbolizing, the exchange value of all other commodities, i.e. of becoming *money*. It arises from the essence of exchange value itself that a specific commodity appears as the money-subject, despite the monetary properties possessed by every commodity. In the course of development, the exchange value of money can again exist separately from its matter, its substance, as in the case of paper money, without therefore giving up the privilege of this specific commodity, because the separated form of existence of exchange value must necessarily continue to take its denomination from the specific commodity.

It is because the commodity is exchange value that it is exchangeable for money, is posited = to money. The proportion of its equivalence with money, i.e. the specificity of its exchange value, is *presupposed* before its transposition into money. The proportion in which a particular commodity is exchanged for money, i.e. the quantity of money into which a given quantity of a commodity is transposable, is determined by the amount of labour time objectified in the commodity. The commodity is an exchange value because it is the realization of a *specific* amount of labour time; money not only measures the amount of labour time which the commodity represents, but also contains its general, conceptually adequate, exchangeable form. Money is the physical medium into which exchange values are dipped, and in which they obtain the form corresponding to their general character. Adam Smith says that labour (labour time) is the original money with which all commodities are purchased.[27] As regards the act of production, this always remains true (as well as in the determination of relative values). In production, every commodity is continuously exchanged for labour time. The necessity of a money other than labour time arises precisely because the quantity of labour time must not be expressed in its immediate, particular product, but in a mediated, general product; in its particular product, as a product equal to and convertible into all other products of an equal labour time;

27. Adam Smith, *An Inquiry into the Nature and Causes of the Wealth of Nations*, new edition, London, 1843, Vol. I, pp. 100–101.

of the labour time not in a particular commodity, but in all commodities at once, and hence in a particular commodity which represents all the others. Labour time cannot directly be money (a demand which is the same, in other words, as demanding that every commodity should simply be its own money), precisely because in fact labour time always exists only in the form of particular commodities (as an object): being a general object, it can exist only symbolically, and hence only as a particular commodity which plays the role of money. Labour time does not exist in the form of a general object of exchange which is independent of and separate (in isolation) from the particular natural characteristics of commodities. But it would have to exist in that form if it were directly to fulfil the demands placed on money. The objectification of the general, social character of labour (and hence of the labour time contained in exchange value) is precisely what makes the product of labour time into exchange value; this is what gives the commodity the attributes of money, which, however, in turn imply the existence of an independent and external money-subject.

A particular expenditure of labour time becomes objectified in a definite, particular commodity with particular properties and a particular relationship to needs; but, in the form of exchange value, labour time is required to become objectified in a commodity which expresses no more than its quota or quantity, which is indifferent to its own natural properties, and which can therefore be metamorphosed into – i.e. exchanged for – every other commodity which objectifies the same labour time. The object should have this character of generality, which contradicts its natural particularity. This contradiction can be overcome only by objectifying it: i.e. by positing the commodity in a double form, first in its natural, immediate form, then in its mediated form, as money. The latter is possible only because a particular commodity becomes, as it were, the general substance of exchange values, or because the exchange values of commodities become identified with a particular commodity different from all others. That is, because the commodity first has to be exchanged for this general commodity, this symbolic general product or general objectification of labour time, before it can function as exchange value and be exchanged for, metamorphosed into, any other commodities at will and regardless of their material properties. Money is labour time in the form of a general object, or the objectification of general labour time, labour time as a *general commodity*. Thus, it may seem a very simple matter that labour time should be able to serve directly as money (i.e. be able to furnish the element in which exchange values are realized as such), because it regulates exchange values and indeed is not only the inherent measure of exchange values but their substance as well (for, as exchange values, commodities have no other substance, no natural attributes). However, this appearance of simplicity is deceptive. The truth is that the exchange-value relation – of commodities as mutually equal and equivalent objectifications of labour time – comprises contradictions which find their objective expression in a *money which is distinct from* labour time.

In Adam Smith this contradiction still appears as a set of parallels. Along with the particular product of labour (labour time as a particular object), the worker also has to produce a quantity of the general commodity (of labour time as general object). The two determinants of exchange value appear to Smith as existing externally, *alongside* one another. The interior of the commodity as a whole does not yet appear as having been seized and penetrated by contradiction. This corresponds to the stage of production which Smith found in existence at that time, in which the worker still directly owned a portion of his subsistence in the form of the product; where neither his entire activity nor his entire product had become dependent on exchange; i.e. where subsistence agriculture (or something similar, as Steuart calls it)[28] still predominated to a great extent, together with patriarchal industry (hand weaving, domestic spinning, linked closely with agriculture). Still it was only the excess which was exchanged within a large area of the nation. Exchange value and determination by labour time not yet fully developed on a national scale.

(*Incidental remark*: It is less true of gold and silver than of any other commodities that their consumption can grow only in inverse proportion to their costs of production. Their consumption grows, rather, in proportion with the growth of general wealth, since their use specifically represents wealth, excess, luxury, because they themselves *represent* wealth in general. Apart from their use as money, silver and gold are consumed more in proportion as wealth in general increases. When, therefore, their supply suddenly increases, even if their costs of production or their value does not proportionately decrease, they find a rapidly expanding market which retards their depreciation. A number of problems which appear inexplicable to the economists – who generally make con-

28. Steuart, *An Inquiry*, Vol. I, p. 88.

sumption of gold and silver dependent solely on the decrease in their costs of production – in regard to the *California–Australia* case,[29] where they go around in circles, are thereby clarified. This is precisely linked with their property as money, as representation of wealth.)

(The contrast between gold and silver, as eternal commodities, and the others, which are not, is to be found in Petty,[30] but is already present in Xenophon, *On Revenues*, in reference to marble and silver. 'οὐ μόνον δὲ κρατεῖ τοῖς ἐπ' ἐνιαυτὸν θάλλουσί τε καὶ γηράσκουσιν, ἀλλὰ καὶ ἀίδια ἀγαθὰ ἔχει ἡ χώρα. πέφυκε μὲν γὰρ λίθος ἐν αὐτῇ ἄφθονος, etc. (namely marble) ἔστι δὲ καὶ γῆ, ἡ σπειρομένη μὲν οὐ φέρει καρπόν, ὀρυττομένη δὲ πολλαπλασίους τρέφει ἢ ἐι σῖτον ἔφερε.')[31] (Important to note that exchange between different tribes or peoples – and this, not private exchange, is its first form – begins when an uncivilized tribe sells (or is cheated out of) an excess product which is not the product of its labour, but the natural product of the ground and of the area which it occupies.)

(Develop the ordinary economic contradictions arising from the fact that money has to be symbolized in a particular commodity, and then develop those that arise from this commodity itself (gold, etc.) This No. II.[32] Then determine the relation between the quantity of gold and silver and commodity prices, and whether the exchange takes place in reality or only in the mind, since all commodities have to be exchanged for money in order to be determined as *prices*. This No. III.[33] It is clear that, merely *measured* in gold or silver, the quantity of these metals has no influence on the prices of commodities; the difficulty enters with actual exchange, where the metals actually serve as instruments of exchange; the relations of demand and supply etc. But it is obviously as a measure that its value as an instrument of circulation is affected.)

29. The discovery of gold in California and Australia in the 1850s.

30. Sir William Petty (1623–87), the 'founder of political economy' (Marx, *Theories of Surplus Value*, p. 1) and an advocate of the labour theory of value. Author of *A Treatise of Taxes*, London, 1667, and *Several Essays in Political Arithmetick*, London, 1699.

31. 'And the pre-eminence of the land (Attica) is not only in the things that bloom and wither annually: she has other good things that last for ever. Nature has put in her abundance of stone etc. .... Again, there is land that yields no fruit if sown, and yet, when quarried, feeds many times the number it could support if it grew corn' (Xenophon, *On Revenues*, Ch. 1, printed in Xenophon, *Scripta minora*, London, 1925, pp. 193–4).

32. See pp. 171–87.   33. See pp. 187–95.

Labour time itself exists as such only subjectively, only in the form of activity. In so far as it is exchangeable (itself a commodity) as such, it is defined and differentiated not only quantitatively but also qualitatively, and is by no means general, self-equivalent labour time; rather, labour time as subject corresponds as little to the general labour time which determines exchange values as the particular commodities and products correspond to it as object.

A. Smith's thesis, that the worker has to produce a general commodity alongside his particular commodity, in other words that he has to give a part of his products the form of money, more generally that he has to convert into money all that part of his commodity which is to serve not as use value for himself but as exchange value – this statement means, subjectively expressed, nothing more than that the worker's particular labour time cannot be directly exchanged for every other particular labour time, but rather that this, its general exchangeability, has first to be mediated, that it has first to take on an objective form, a form different from itself, in order to attain this general exchangeability.

The labour of the individual looked at in the act of production itself, is the money with which he directly buys the product, the object of his particular activity; but it is a *particular* money, which buys precisely only this *specific* product. In order to be *general money* directly, it would have to be not a *particular*, but *general* labour from the outset; i.e. it would have to be *posited* from the outset as a link in *general production*. But on this presupposition it would not be exchange which gave labour its general character; but rather its presupposed communal character would determine the distribution of products. The communal character of production would make the product into a communal, general product from the outset. The exchange which originally takes place in production – which would not be an exchange of exchange values but of activities, determined by communal needs and communal purposes – would from the outset include the participation of the individual in the communal world of products. On the basis of exchange values, labour is *posited* as general only through *exchange*. But on this foundation it would be *posited* as such before exchange; i.e. the exchange of products would in no way be the *medium* by which the participation of the individual in general production is mediated. Mediation must, of course, take place. In the first case, which proceeds from the independent production of individuals – no matter how much these independent productions determine and modify each other *post festum* through their interrelations – mediation takes place through the exchange of commodities, through exchange value and through money; all these are expressions of one and the same relation. In the second case, the *presupposition is itself mediated*; i.e. a communal production, communality, is presupposed as the basis of production. The labour of the individual is posited from the outset as social labour. Thus, whatever the particular material form of the product he creates or helps to create, what he has bought with his labour is not a specific and particular product, but rather a specific share of the communal production. He therefore has no particular product to exchange. His product is *not an exchange value*. The product does not first have to be transposed into a particular form in order to attain a general character for the individual. Instead of a division of labour, such as is necessarily created with the exchange of exchange values, there would take place an organization of labour whose consequence would be the participation of the individual in communal consumption. In the first case the social character of production is *posited* only *post festum* with the elevation of products to exchange values and the exchange of these exchange values. In the second case *the social character of production* is presupposed, and participation in the world of products, in consumption, is not mediated by the exchange of mutually independent labours or products of labour. It is mediated, rather, by the social conditions of production within which the individual is active. Those who want to make the labour of the individual directly into *money* (i.e. his product as well), into *realized exchange value*, want therefore to determine that labour *directly* as general labour, i.e. to negate precisely the conditions under which it must be made into money and exchange values, and under which it depends on private exchange. This demand can be satisfied only under conditions where it can no longer be raised. Labour on the basis of exchange values presupposes, precisely, that neither the labour of the individual nor his product are *directly* general; that the product attains this form only by passing through an *objective mediation*, by means of a form of *money* distinct from itself.

On the basis of communal production, the determination of time remains, of course, essential. The less time the society requires to produce wheat, cattle etc., the more time it wins for other production, material or mental. Just as in the case of an individual, the multiplicity of its development, its enjoyment and its activity depends on economization of time. Economy of time, to this all economy ultimately reduces itself. Society likewise has to distribute its time in a purposeful way, in order to achieve a production adequate to its overall needs; just as the individual has to distribute his time correctly in order to achieve knowledge in proper proportions or in order to satisfy the various demands on his activity. Thus, economy of time, along with the planned distribution of labour time among the various branches of production, remains the first economic law on the basis of communal production. It becomes law, there, to an even higher degree. However, this is essentially different from a measurement of exchange values (labour or products) by labour time. The labour of individuals in the same *branch of work*, and the various kinds of work, are different from one another not only quantitatively but also qualitatively. What does a solely *quantitative* difference between things presuppose? The identity of their *qualities*. Hence, the quantitative measure of labours presupposes the equivalence, the identity of their quality.

(Strabo, Book XI. On the Albanians of the Caucasus: 'καὶ οἱ ἄνθρωποι κάλλει καὶ μεγέθει διαφέροντες, ἁπλοῖ δὲ καὶ οὐ καπηλικοί· οὐδὲ γὰρ νομίσματι τὰ πολλὰ χρῶνται, οὐδὲ ἀριθμὸν ἴσασι μείζω τῶν ἑκατόν, ἀλλὰ φορτίοις τὰς ἀμοιβὰς ποιοῦνται.' It says there further: 'ἄπειροι δ'εἰσὶ καὶ μέτρων τῶν ἐπ' ἀκριβὲς καὶ σταθμῶν.')[34]

Money appears as *measure* (in Homer, e.g. oxen) earlier than as *medium of exchange*, because in barter each commodity is still its own medium of exchange. But it cannot be its own measure or its own standard of comparison.

(2)[35] This much proceeds from what has been developed so far: A particular product (commodity) (material) must become the subject of money, which exists as the attribute of every exchange value. The subject in which this symbol is represented is not a matter of indifference, since the demands placed on the representing subject are contained in the conditions – conceptual determinations, characteristic relations – of that which is to be re-

34. 'The inhabitants of this country are unusually handsome and large. And they are frank in their dealings, and not mercenary; for they do not in general use coined money, nor do they know any number greater than one hundred, but carry on business by means of barter . . . They are also unacquainted with accurate measures and weights' (Strabo, *Geography*, Bk XI, Ch. 4, section 4, London, 1917; Loeb edn, Vol. V, pp. 226–7).

35. There is no heading (1) in the original text.

presented. The study of the precious metals as subjects of the
money relations, as incarnations of the latter, is therefore by no
means a matter lying outside the realm of political economy, as
Proudhon believes, any more than the physical composition of
paint, and of marble, lie outside the realm of painting and sculp-
ture. The attributes possessed by the commodity as exchange
value, attributes for which its natural qualities are not adequate,
express the demands made upon those commodities which κατ'
ἐξοχήν[36] are the material of money. These demands, at the level to
which we have up to now confined ourselves, are most completely
satisfied by the precious metals. Metals as such [enjoy] preference
over other commodities as instruments of production, and among
the metals the one which is first found in its physical fullness and
purity – gold; then copper, then silver and iron. The precious
metals take preference over others in realizing *metal*, as Hegel
would say.[37]

The precious metals uniform in their physical qualities, so that
equal quantities of them should be so far identical as to present no
ground for preferring this one to the others. Not the case, for
example, with equal numbers of cattle and equal quantities of grain.

(a) Gold and silver in relation to the other metals

The other metals oxidize when exposed to air; the precious metals
(mercury, silver, gold, platinum) are unaffected by the air.

Aurum (Au). Specific gravity = 19·5; melting point: 1,200° C.
'Glittering gold is the most magnificent of all metals, and was
therefore referred to in antiquity as the sun or the king of metals.
Widely distributed, never in great quantities, and is hence also
more precious than the other metals. Found generally in pure
metallic state, partly in larger pieces, partly in the form of smaller
granules fused with other minerals. As the latter decompose, there
arises gold-bearing sand, carried by many rivers, from which gold,
owing to its greater specific gravity, can be washed out. Enormous
malleability of gold; one grain can be drawn to make a 500-foot
long wire, and can be hammered into leaves barely 1/200,000 of an
inch thick. Gold resists all acids, only chlorine in a free state dissolves it (*aqua regia*, a mixture of nitric and hydrochloric acids).
To gild.'

36. *par excellence.*
37. Hegel, *Philosophy of Nature*, Glockner edn, Vol. IX, pp. 413–24.

Argentum (Ag). Specific gravity = 10. Melting point = 1,000° C. Bright appearance; the friendliest of metals, very white and malleable; can be beautifully worked up and drawn in very thin wires. Silver found as unalloyed solid; frequently also combined with lead in silvery lead ores.

So much for *chemical* properties of gold and silver. (Divisibility and fusibility, uniformity of pure gold and silver etc. well known.)

Mineralogical:

Gold. It is surely noteworthy that the more precious the metals are, the more isolated is their occurrence; they are found separately from the more commonly prevalent bodies, they are higher natures far from the common herd. Thus we find gold, as a rule, in unalloyed metallic state, as a crystal in various die-shaped forms, or in the greatest variety of shapes; irregular pieces and nuggets, sand and dust, in which form it is found fused into many kinds of stone, e.g. granite: and it finds its way into the sand of rivers and the gravel of floodlands as a result of the disintegration of this stone. Since the specific gravity of gold in this state goes up to 19·4, even the tiniest pieces can be extracted by stirring gold-bearing sand in water. The heavier, metallic elements settle first and can thus, as the saying goes, be washed out. Most frequently found in the company of gold is silver, and one encounters natural combinations of both metals, containing from 0·16 to 38·7 per cent silver; which naturally entails differences in colour and weight.

Silver. With the great variety of its minerals, appears as one of the more prevalent metals, both as unalloyed metal and combined with other metals or with arsenic and sulphur. (Silver chloride, silver bromide, carbonic silver oxide, bismuth–silver ore, Sternbergite, polybasite, etc.)

The chief *chemical* properties are: *all precious metals*: do not oxidize on contact with air; of gold (and platinum): are not dissolved by acids, except in chlorine. Do not oxidize, thus remain pure, free of rust; they present themselves as that which they are. Resistance to oxygen – *imperishability* (so highly lauded by the gold and silver fanatics of antiquity).

Physical properties: *Specific gravity*, i.e. a great deal of weight in a small space, especially important for means of circulation. Gold 19·5, silver 10. *Brilliance*. Gleam of gold, whiteness of silver, magnificence, *malleability*; hence so serviceable for jewellery, ornamentation, and for the addition of splendour to other objects. The *white* shade of silver (which reflects all light rays in their original composition); red-yellow of gold (which absorbs all colours of a mixed beam and reflects back only the red). *Difficult to melt*.

Geological properties: Found (gold especially) as an unalloyed solid, separate from other bodies; isolated, individualized. Individual presentation, independent of the elemental.

About the two other precious metals: (1) *Platinum* lacks the colour: grey on grey (soot of metals); too rare; unknown in antiquity; discovered only after the discovery of America; also discovered in the Urals in the nineteenth century; soluble only in chlorine; always solid; specific gravity $= 21$; the strongest fire does not melt it; more of scientific value. (2) *Mercury*: found in liquid form; evaporates; vapours poisonous; can be combined with other liquids (amalgams). (Specific gravity $= 13 \cdot 5$, boiling point $= 360°$ C.) Thus neither platinum, nor much less mercury, are suitable as money.

One of the *geological* properties is common to all the precious metals: *rarity*. Rarity (apart from supply and demand) is an element of value only in so far as its opposite, the non-rare as such, the negation of rarity, the elemental, has no value because it does not appear as the result of production. In the original definition of value, that which is most independent of conscious, voluntary production is the most valuable, assuming the existence of demand. Common pebbles have no value, relatively speaking, because they are to be had *without production* (even if the latter consists only of searching). For something to become an object of exchange, to have exchange value, it must not be available to everyone without the mediation of exchange; it must not appear in such an elemental form as to be common property. To this extent, rarity is an element of exchange value and hence this property of the precious metal is of importance, even apart from its further relation to supply and demand.

When we look at the advantages of the metals as such as instruments of production, then gold has to its credit that it is at bottom the *first metal to be discovered as metal*. For a double reason. *First*, because more than the others, it presents itself in nature as the most metallic, the most distinct and distinguishable metal; *second*, because in its preparation nature has done the work otherwise left to artifice, and for its first discovery only rough labour is necessary, but neither science nor developed instruments of production.

'Certain it is that gold must take its place as *the earliest metal known*, and in the first record of man's progress it is indicated as a standard of man's position' (because in the form of excess, the first form in which wealth appears. The first form of value is *use value*, the everyday quality that expresses the relation of the individual to nature; the second, exchange value ALONGSIDE use value, its command over other people's use values, its social connectedness: exchange value is itself originally a value for use on Sundays only, going beyond immediate physical necessity.)

Very early discovery of gold by man: 'Gold differs remarkably from the other metals, with a very few exceptions, in the fact that it is found in nature in its metallic state. Iron and copper, tin, lead and silver are ordinarily discovered in chemical combinations with oxygen, sulphur, arsenic, or carbon; and the few exceptional occurrences of these metals in an uncombined, or, as it was formerly called, virgin state, are to be cited rather as mineralogical curiosities than as common productions. Gold is, however, always found native or metallic ... Therefore, as a metallic mass, curious by its yellow colour, it would attract the eye of the most uneducated man, whereas the other substances likely to lie in his path would offer no features of attraction to his scarcely awakened powers of observation. Again gold, from the circumstance of its having been formed in those rocks which are most exposed to atmospheric action, is found in the *débris* of the mountains. By the disintegrating influences of the atmosphere, of changes of temperature, of the action of water, and particularly by the effects of ice, fragments of rock are continually broken off. These are borne by floods into the valleys and rolled into pebbles by the constant action of flowing water. Amongst these, pebbles, or particles, of gold are discovered. The summer heats, by drying up the waters, rendered those beds which had formed river channels and the courses of winter torrents paths for the journeys of migratory man; and here we can imagine the early discovery of gold.'

'Gold most frequently occurs pure, or, at all events, so nearly so that its metallic nature can be at once recognized, in rivers as well as in quartz veins.'

'The specific gravity of quartz, and of most other heavy compact rocks is about $2\frac{1}{2}$, whilst the specific gravity of gold is 18 or 19. Gold, therefore, is somewhere about seven times as heavy as any rock or stone with which it is likely to be associated. A current of water accordingly having sufficient strength to bear along sand or pebbles of quartz or any other rock, might not be able to move the fragments of gold associated with them. Moving water, therefore, has done for the auriferous rocks formerly, just what the miner would do now, break it, namely, up, into fragments, sweep away the lighter particles, and leave the gold behind it. Rivers are, indeed, great natural *cradles*, sweeping off all the lighter and finer particles at once, the heavier ones either sticking against natural impediments, or being left whenever the current slackens its force or velocity.' (See *Gold* (*Lectures on*). London, 1852.) (pp. 12 and 13.)[38]

'In all probability, from tradition and early history, the *discovery of gold in the sand and gravel of streams would appear to have been the first step in the recognition of metals*, and in almost all, perhaps in all, the countries of Europe, Africa and Asia, greater or smaller quantities of gold have from very early times been washed by simple contrivances from auriferous deposits. Occasionally, the success of gold-streams has been great enough to produce a pulse of excitement which has vibrated for a while through a district, but has been hushed down again. In 760 the poor people turned out in numbers to wash gold from the river sands south of Prague, and three men were able in the day to extract a mark ($\frac{1}{2}$ lb.) of gold; and so great was the consequent rush to the "diggings" that in the next year the country was visited by famine. We read of a recurrence of similar events several times within the next few centuries, although here, as elsewhere, the general attraction to surface-spread riches has subsided into regular and systematic mining.'

'Two classes of deposits in which gold is found, the *lodes or veins*, which intersect the solid rock in a direction more or less perpendicular to the horizon; and the *drift beds* or '*streams*', in which the gold mingled with gravel, sand, or clay, has been deposited by the mechanical action of water, upon the surface of those rocks, which are penetrated to unknown depths by the lodes. To the former class belongs more specially the art of *mining*; to the latter the simple operations of *digging*. Gold mining, properly so

38. See *Government School of Mines and Science Applied to the Arts. Lectures on Gold for the Instruction of Emigrants about to Proceed to Australia.* Delivered at the Museum of Practical Geology, London, 1852. Marx's page-reference is incorrect. The last sentence comes from p. 12, but the rest of the paragraph is from p. 10. The two preceding paragraphs come from pp. 171–2 and p. 8 of this work, and the two following ones from pp. 93–5 and 95–7 respectively.

called, is, like other mining, an art requiring the employment of capital, and of a skill only to be acquired by years of experience. There is no art practised by civilized men which requires for its full development the application of so many sciences and collateral arts. But although so essential to the miner, scarcely any of these are necessary to the gold-washer or streamer, who must trust chiefly to the strength of his arm, or the buoyancy of his health. The apparatus which he employs must necessarily be simple, so as to be conveyed from place to place, to be easily repaired if injured, and not to require any of those niceties of manipulation which would cause him to lose time in the acquiring of small quantities.'

Difference betwęen the drift-deposits of gold, best exemplified at the present day in Siberia, California and Australia; and the fine sands annually brought down by rivers, some of which are also found to contain gold in workable quantities. The latter are of course found literally at the surface, the former may be met with under a cover of from 1 to 70 feet in thickness, consisting of soil, peat, sand, gravel, etc. The modes of working the two must be identical in principle. For the stream-worker nature has pulled down the highest, proudest and richest parts of the lodes, and so triturated and washed up the materials, that the streamer has the heaviest part of the work already done for him: whilst the miner, who attacks the poorer, but more lasting, deep-going lodes, must aid himself with all the resources of the nicest art.

Gold has justly been considered the noblest of metals from various physical and chemical properties. It is unchangeable in air and does not rust. (Its unchangeability consists precisely in its resistance against the oxygen in the atmosphere.) Of a bright reddish yellow colour when in a coherent state, and very dense. Highly malleable. Requires a strong heat to melt it. Specific gravity.

Thus three modes of its production: (1) In the river sand. Simple finding on the surface. *Washing.* (2) In river beds and floodlands. *Digging.* (3) *Mining.* Its production requires, hence, no development of the productive forces. Nature does most of the work in that regard.

(The *roots* of the words for gold, silver, etc. (see Grimm);[39] here we find a number of general concepts of *brilliance*, soon to be

39. Jacob Grimm, *Geschichte der deutschen Sprache*, Vol. I, Leipzig, 1848, pp. 13–14.

transferred to the words, proximate to *colour*. Silver white; gold yellow; brass and gold, brass and iron exchange names. Among the Germans bronze in use before iron. Direct affinity between *aes* (bronze) and *aurum* (gold).)

Copper (*brass, bronze*: tin and copper) and gold in use before silver and iron.

'Gold in use long before silver, because it is found pure or only lightly admixed with silver; obtained by simple washing. Silver is found in general in veins threaded through the hardest rocks in primitive terrain: its extraction requires complicated labour and machines. In southern America, veins of gold are not exploited, only gold in the form of dust and nuggets in alluvial terrain. In Herodotus's time, similarly. The most ancient monuments of Greece, Asia, Northern Europe and the New World prove that the use of gold for utensils and for ornamentation is possible in a semi-barbarian condition; while the use of silver for the same purposes by itself already denotes a fairly advanced state of society.' See Dureau de la Malle, Notebook. (2.)[40]

Copper as main instrument of war and peace (ibid. 2) (as *money* in Italy ibid.).

(b) Fluctuations in the value-relation between the different metals

If the use of metals as the substance of money, as well as their comparative uses, their earlier or later appearance, are to be examined at all, then it is necessary to look also at the *fluctuations in their relative value*. (Letronne, Böckh, Jacob.)[41] (That part of the question which is linked to the question of the mass of circulating metals as such, and its relation to prices, is to be looked at later, as a historical appendix to the chapter on the relation between money and prices.)

The successive fluctuations between gold, silver and copper in

40. A reference to Marx's own excerpt-book, No. XIV (1851), p. 2 of which contains the excerpt mentioned, from pp. 48–9 of Dureau de la Malle, *Économie politique des Romains*, Paris, 1840, Vol. I. In general pp. 180–84 are based on excerpts from Dureau de la Malle's work.

41. J.-A. Letronne, *Considérations générales sur l'évaluation des monnaies grecques et romaines, et sur la valeur de l'or et de l'argent avant la découverte de l'Amérique*, Paris, 1817; W. Jacob, *An Historical Inquiry into the Production and Consumption of the Precious Metals*, London, 1831; A. Böckh, *The Public Economy of Athens*, London, 1842.

various epochs had to depend first of all on the nature of the sites where they are found, and on their greater or lesser purity. Then, on political changes, such as the invasion of Asia and of a part of Africa by the Persians and the Macedonians; later the conquest of parts of three continents by the Romans (*orbis Romanus*, etc.). Dependent, therefore, on their relative purity and their location.

The value relation between the different metals can be determined without recourse to prices – by means of the simple *quantitative* ratio in which one exchanges for the other. We can employ this form, in general, when we are comparing only a few commodities which have the same measure; e.g. so many quarters of rye, barley, oats for so many quarters of wheat. This method employed in barter, where little of anything is exchanged and where even fewer commodities enter the traffic, and where, hence, no money is required.

Among an *Arab* people neighbouring on Sabaea, according to Strabo, pure gold was so abundant that 10 lb. of it were given for 1 lb. of iron, and 2 lb. were given for 1 lb. silver. A wealth of gold in the Bactrian region (Bactara, etc., in short, Turkestan) and in the part of Asia situated between the Paropamisus (Hindu-kush) and the Imaus (Mustagh Mountains), i.e. in the *Desertum arenosum auro abondans*[42] (Desert of Cobi): according to Dureau de la Malle it is probable, therefore, that from the fifteenth to the sixth century B.C. the ratio of gold to silver was 6:1 or 8:1, the same which existed in China and Japan until the beginning of the nineteenth century; Herodotus puts it at 13:1 for Persia under Darius Hystaspes. According to the code of Manou, written between 1300 and 600 B.C., gold to silver $= 2\frac{1}{2}:1$. Silver mines must nearly always be established in primitive terrain; that is where the deposits lie, and only lesser veins are found in easier ground. Instead of in alluvial sand and gravel, silver is ordinarily embedded in the most compact and hard rocks, such as quartz, etc. This metal is more common in regions which are cold, either from latitude or from elevation, while gold generally frequents warm countries. In contrast to gold, silver is only very rarely found in a pure state (usually combined with arsenic or sulphur) (muriatic acid, nitric saltpetre). As far as the quantity of deposits is concerned (prior to the discovery of Australia and California), Humboldt in 1811 estimates the proportion of gold to silver in America at 1:46, and

42. 'Sandy desert rich in gold'.

in Europe (including Asiatic Russia) at 1:40. The mineralogists of the Académie des Sciences estimate in our time (1842) that the ratio is 1:52; despite that, the lb. of gold is only worth 15 lb. of silver; thus their value relation = 15:1.

Copper. Specific gravity = 8·9. Beautiful dawn-red colour; fairly hard; requires very high temperatures to melt. Not infrequently encountered pure; frequently combined with oxygen or sulphur. Deposits found in primordial, ancient terrain. However, found more frequently close to the surface, at no great depth, agglomerated in masses of pure metal, sometimes of a considerable weight. Used in peace and war before iron. (Gold relates to silver as the substance of money in the same way as copper to iron as instrument of labour in historical development.) Circulates in great quantity in Italy under the Romans during the first to the fifth centuries. One can determine *a priori* a people's degree of civilization if one knows no more than the metal, gold, copper, silver or iron, which it uses for weapons, tools or ornamentation. Hesiod, in his poem on agriculture: 'χαλκῷ δ'εἰργάζοντο μέλας δ'οὐκ ἔσκε σίδηρος'.[43]

Lucretius: '*Et prior aeris erat quam ferri cognitus usus.*'[44] Jacob cites ancient copper mines in Nubia and Siberia (see Dureau I, 58); Herodotus says that the Massagetians had only bronze, but no iron. To judge by the collection known as the Oxford Marbles, iron unknown before 1431 B.C. In Homer, iron rare; however, very common use of bronze (an alloy of copper, zinc and tin) which Greek and Roman society used for a very long period, even for the fabrication of axes and razors. Italy fairly wealthy in native copper; thus copper money formed, if not the only currency, at least the normal currency, the monetary unit of central Italy, up to 247 B.C. The Greek colonies in southern Italy received silver directly from Greece and Asia, or via Tyre and Carthage; and used it for money starting in the fifth and sixth centuries. The Romans, it seems, possessed silver money prior to the expulsion of the Kings, but, Pliny says, '*interdictum id vetere consulto patrum, Italiae parci*' (i.e the silver mines) '*jubentium.*'[45] They feared the consequences

43. 'Of bronze were their implements; there was no black iron' (Hesiod, *Works and Days*, line 151; Leob edn, London, 1914, p. 12).

44. 'The use of bronze was known before iron' (Lucretius, *De rerum natura*, Bk V, line 1,287).

45. 'Mining is prohibited by an old resolution of the Senate forbidding the exploitation of Italy' (Pliny, *Historia naturalis*, Bk III, Ch. 20, section 138).

of a convenient means of circulation – opulence, increase of slaves, accumulation, concentration of land ownership. Among the Etruscans, too, copper money before gold.

Garnier is wrong when he says (see Notebook III, p. 28), 'The material destined for accumulation was naturally sought for and selected from the realm of the minerals.'[46] On the contrary, accumulation began after metal money was found (whether as money proper or only as preferred medium of exchange by weight). This point to be discussed especially in regard to gold. Reitemeier is right (see Notebook III, p. 34): 'Gold, silver and copper were used by the ancients as implements for hacking and breaking, despite their relative softness, before the advent of iron and before they were used as money.'[47] (Improvement of implements when men learned to temper copper and thus make it hard enough to defy solid rock. A very much hardened copper was used to make the chisels and hammers used for mastering rock. Finally, iron was discovered.) Jacob says: 'In patriarchal times' (see Notebook IV, p. 3), 'when the metals used for making weapons, such as (1) brass and (2) iron, were rare and enormously expensive compared with the common food and clothing then used, then, although coined money made of the precious metals was still unknown, yet gold and silver had acquired the faculty of being more easily and conveniently exchanged for the other metals than corn and cattle.'[48]

'Besides, in order to obtain the pure or nearly pure gold found in the immense alluvial lands situated between the Hindu-kush chains and the Himalaya, only a simple washing operation was required. In those times the population in these countries of Asia was abundant, and hence labour was cheap. Silver was relatively more expensive owing to the (technical) difficulties of obtaining it. The opposite tendency set in in Asia and in Greece after the death of Alexander. The gold-bearing sands became exhausted; the price of slaves and of manpower rose; and, since mechanics and geometry had made immense progress from Euclid to Archimedes, it was possible to exploit with profit the rich veins of silver mined in Asia, in Thrace and in Spain; and, silver being 52 times more

46. G. Garnier, *Histoire de la monnaie depuis les temps de la plus haute antiquité jusqu'au règne de Charlemagne*, Paris, 1819, Vol. I, p. 7.

47. J. F. Reitemeier, *Geschichte des Bergbaues und Hüttenwesens bey den alten Völkern*, Göttingen, 1785, pp. 14, 15–16, 32.

48. Jacob, *An Historical Inquiry*, Vol. I, p. 142.

abundant than gold, the value ratio between them necessarily changed, so that the *livre* of gold, which at the time of Xenophon, 350 B.C., was exchanged for 10 *livres* of silver, came to be worth 18 *livres* of the latter metal in the year A.D. 422.'[49] Thus, it rose from 10:1 to 18:1.

At the end of the fifth century A.D. an extraordinary diminution in the quantity of precious metals; a halt in mining. In the Middle Ages up to the end of the fifteenth century a relatively significant portion of money in gold coins. (The diminution affected, most of all, silver, which had previously circulated most widely.) Ratio in the fifteenth century = 10:1, in the eighteenth century 14:1 on the continent, in England = 15:1. In most of Asia, silver more as a commodity in trade; especially in China, where copper money (Tehen, a composition of copper, zinc and lead) coin of the realm; in China, gold (and silver) by weight as a commodity to balance foreign trade.

Large fluctuations in Rome between the value of copper and silver (in coins). Up to Servius, metal in bullion form, *aes rude*, for trade. The monetary unit, the copper *as* = 1 pound of copper. In the time of Servius, silver to copper = 279:1; until the beginning of the Punic war = 400:1; during the First Punic War = 140:1; Second Punic War = 112:1.

Gold very expensive in Rome at first, whereas silver from Carthage (and Spain); gold used only in ingots until 547. Gold to silver in trade = 13·71:1, in coins = 17·4:1, under Caesar = 12:1 (at the outbreak of the civil war, after the plunder of the *aerarium*[50] by Caesar, only 8:1); under Honorius and Arcadius (397) fixed at = 14·4:1; under Honorius and Theodosius the Younger (422) = 18:1. First silver coin in Rome minted 485; first gold coin: 547. As soon as, after the Second Punic War, the *as* was reduced to 1 ounce, it became small change; the *sesterce* (silver) the monetary unit, and all large payments made in silver. (In everyday commerce copper (later iron) remained the chief metal. Under the Emperors of the Orient and Occident, the *solidus* (*aureus*), i.e. gold, was the monetary standard.)

Thus, in antiquity, taking the average:

First: *Relative increase in value of silver as compared with gold*. Apart from special phenomena (Arabs) where gold cheaper than silver and still cheaper than iron, in Asia from the fifteenth to the

49. Dureau de la Malle, *Économie politique des Romains*, Vol. I, pp. 62–3.
50. The treasury.

sixth centuries B.C., gold to silver = 6:1 or 8:1 (the latter ratio in China and Japan until the beginning of the nineteenth century). In the Manou Code itself = $2\frac{1}{2}$:1. This lower ratio arises from the same causes which promote the discovery of gold as the first metal. Gold in those days chiefly from Asia and Egypt. This period corresponds to that of *copper* money in Italian history. In general, copper as main instrument of peace and war corresponds to the pre-eminence of gold among the precious metals. Even in Xenophon's time, gold to silver = 10:1.

Secondly: after the death of Alexander, relative rise in the value of gold compared to silver, with the exhaustion of the gold-bearing sand, progress in technology and civilization; and hence establishment of silver mines; now the influence of the quantitatively greater prevalence of silver over gold in the earth's crust. But especially the Carthaginians, the exploitation of Spain, which necessarily had to revolutionize the relation of silver to gold in somewhat the same way as the discovery of American silver at the end of the fifteenth century. Ratio in Caesar's time = 17:1; later 14:1; finally, after A.D. 422 = 18:1. (The decline of gold under Caesar for accidental reasons.) The decline of silver relative to gold corresponds to iron being the chief instrument of production in war and peace. While in the first period, influx of gold from the East, in the second, influx of silver from the cooler West.

Thirdly in the Middle Ages: Again the ratio as in the time of Xenophon, 10:1. (In some places = 12:1?)

Fourthly, after the discovery of America: Again about the ratio as in the time of Honorius and Arcadius (397); 14 to 15:1. Although since about 1815–44 an increase in the production of gold, gold was at a premium (e.g. in France). It is probable that the discovery of California and Australia

fifthly, will reintroduce the ratio of the Roman Imperium, 18:1, if not greater. The relative depreciation of silver due to progress in the production of precious metals, in antiquity as well as after, [proceeds] from East to West, until California and Australia reverse this. In the short run, great fluctuations; but when one looks at the main differences, these repeat themselves in a remarkable fashion.

In antiquity, copper three or four times as expensive as today. (Garnier.)

(c) Now to be examined, the sources of gold and silver and their connection with historical development.

(d) *Money as coin*. Briefly the historical aspect of coins. Depreciation and appreciation, etc.

Circulation, or the *turnover of money*, corresponds to an opposite *circulation, or turnover, of commodities*. A commodity possessed by A passes into the hands of B, while B's money passes into the hands of A, etc. The circulation of money, like that of commodities, begins at an infinity of different points, and to an infinity of different points it returns. Departures from a single centre to the different points on the periphery and the return from all points of the periphery to a single centre do not take place in the circulatory process at the stage here being examined, i.e. its *direct* stage; they belong, rather, in a circulatory system *mediated* by a banking system. This first, spontaneous and natural circulation does consist, however, of a mass of turnovers. Circulation proper, nevertheless, begins only where gold and silver cease to be commodities; between countries which export precious metals and those which import them, no circulation in this sense takes place, but mere simple exchange, since gold and silver function here not as money but as commodities. Where money plays the role of mediating the exchange of commodities (that means here their circulation) and is hence a means of exchange, it is an *instrument of circulation*, a *vehicle of circulation*; but wherever, in this process, it is itself circulated, where it changes hands along its own lines of motion, there it itself has a *circulation, monetary circulation, monetary turnover*. The aim is to find out to what extent this circulation is determined by particular laws. This much is clear from the outset: if money is a vehicle of circulation for the commodity, then the commodity is likewise a vehicle for the circulation of money. If money circulates commodities, then commodities circulate money. The circulation of commodities and the circulation of money thus determine one another. As regards monetary turnover, three things merit attention: (1) the form of the movement itself; the line which it describes (its concept); (2) the quantity of money circulating; (3) the rate at which it completes its motion, its velocity of circulation. This can happen only in connection with the circulation of commodities. This much is clear from the outset, that there are moments in the circulation of commodities which are entirely independent of the circulation of money, and which either directly determine the latter, or which are determined along with monetary circulation by a third factor, as in the case of, e.g., the velocity. The overall character of the mode of production will determine them both, and will determine the circulation of commodities more directly. The mass of persons engaged in exchange (population): their distribution between the town and the country; the absolute quantity of commodities, of products and agencies of production; the relative mass of commodities which enter into circulation; the development of the means of communication and transport, in the double sense of determining not only the sphere of those who are in exchange, in contact, but also the speed with which the raw material reaches the producer and the product the consumer; finally the development of industry, which concentrates different branches of production, e.g. spinning, weaving, dyeing, etc., and hence makes superfluous a series of intermediate exchanges. The circulation of commodities is the original precondition of the circulation of money. To what extent the latter then reacts back on the circulation of commodities remains to be seen.

The first task is firmly to establish the *general concept of circulation or of turnover.*

But first let us note that what is circulated by money is exchange value, hence *prices.* Hence, as regards the circulation of commodities, it is not only their mass but, equally, their prices which must be considered. A large quantity of commodities at a low exchange value (price) obviously requires less money for its circulation than a smaller quantity at double the price. Thus, actually, the concept of price has to be developed *before* that of circulation. Circulation is the positing of prices, it is the process in which commodities are transformed into prices: their realization as prices. Money has a dual character: it is (1) *measure,* or element in which the commodity is realized as exchange value, and (2) *means of exchange,* instrument of circulation, and in each of these aspects it acts in quite opposite directions. Money only circulates commodities which have already been *ideally* transformed into money, not only in the head of the individual but in the conception held by society (directly, the conception held by the participants in the process of buying and selling). This ideal transformation into money is by no means determined by the same laws as the real transformation. Their interrelation is to be examined.

(a) An essential characteristic of circulation is that it circulates exchange values (products or labour), and, in particular, exchange values in the form of *prices.* Thus, not every form of commodity exchange, e.g. barter, payment in kind, feudal services, etc., constitutes circulation. To get circulation, two things are required above all: *Firstly*: the precondition that commodities are prices; *Secondly*: not isolated acts of exchange, but a circle of exchange, a totality of the same, in constant flux, proceeding more or less over the entire surface of society; a system of acts of exchange. The commodity is specified as an exchange value. As an exchange value, it functions in a given proportion (relative to the labour time contained in it) as equivalent for all other values (commodities); but it does not directly correspond to this, its function. As an exchange value it differs from itself as a natural, material thing. A mediation is required to posit it as an exchange value. Money presents the exchange value of the commodity to the commodity as something different from itself. The commodity which is posited as money is, at the outset, the commodity as pure exchange value, or, the commodity as pure exchange value is money. But at the same time, money now exists outside and alongside the commodity; its exchange value, the exchange value of all commodities, has achieved an existence independent of the commodity, an existence based in an autonomous material of its own, in a particular commodity. The exchange value of the commodity expresses the totality of the quantitative relations in which all other commodities can be exchanged for it, determined by the unequal quantities of the same which can be produced in the same labour time. Money then exists as the exchange value of all commodities alongside and outside them. It is the universal material into which they must be dipped, in which they become gilded and silver-plated, in order to win their independent existence as exchange values. They must be translated into money, expressed in money. Money becomes the general denomination of exchange values, of commodities as exchange values. Exchange value expressed as money, i.e. equated with money, is *price*. After money has been posited as independent in relation to exchange values, then the exchange values are posited in their particularity in relation to their subject, money. But every exchange value is a particular quantity; a quantitatively specific exchange value. As such, it is = a particular quantity of money. This particularity is given, in the general law, by the amount of labour time contained in a given exchange value. Thus an exchange value which is the product of, say, one day is expressed in a quantity of gold or silver which = one day of labour time, which is the product of one day of labour. The general measure of exchange values now becomes the measure which exists between each exchange value and the money to which it is *equated*. (Gold and silver are determined, in the first place, by their cost of production in the country of production. 'In the mining countries all prices ultimately depend on the costs of production of the precious metals; ... the remuneration paid to the miner, ... affords the scale, on which the remuneration of all other producers is calculated. The gold value and silver value of all commodities exempt from monopoly depends in a country without mines on the gold and silver which can be obtained by exporting the result of a given quantity of labour, the current rate of profit, and, in each individual case, the amount of wages, which have been paid, and the time for which they have been advanced.' (Senior.)[51] In other words: on the quantity of gold and silver which is directly or indirectly obtained from the mining countries in exchange for a given quantity of labour (exportable products). Money is in the first instance that which expresses the relation of equality between all exchange values: in money, they all have the same name.)

Exchange value, posited in the character of money, is price. Exchange value is expressed in price as a specific quantity of money. Money as price shows first of all the *identity* of all exchange values; secondly, it shows the unit of which they all contain a given number, so that the equation with money expresses the quantitative specificity of exchange values, their quantitative relation to one another. Money is here posited, thus, as the *measure* of exchange values; and prices as exchange values measured in money. The fact that money is the measure of prices, and hence that exchange values are compared with one another on this standard, is an aspect of the situation which is self-evident. But what is more important for the analysis is that *in price, exchange value is compared with money*. After money has been posited as independent exchange value, separated from commodities, then the individual commodity, the particular exchange value, is again *equated* to money, i.e. it is posited as equal to a given quantity of money, expressed as money, translated into money. By being equated to money, they again become related to one another as they were, conceptually, as exchange values: they balance and equate themselves with one another in given proportions. The particular exchange value, the commodity, becomes expressed as, subsumed

51. Nassau Senior, *Three Lectures on the Cost of Obtaining Money*, London, 1830, p. 15.

under, posited in the character of the independent exchange value, of money. How this happens (i.e. how the quantitative relation between the quantitatively defined exchange value and a given quantity of money is found), above. But, since money has an independent existence apart from commodities, the price of the commodity appears as an *external* relation of exchange values or commodities to money; the commodity *is not price*, in the way in which its social substance stamped it as exchange value; this quality is not *immediately* coextensive with it; but is mediated by the commodity's comparison with money; the commodity *is* exchange value, but it *has* a price. Exchange value was in immediate identity with it, it was its immediate quality, from which it just as immediately split, so that on one side we found the commodity, on the other (as money) its exchange value; but now, as *price*, the commodity relates to money on one side as something existing outside itself, and secondly, it is *ideally* posited as money itself, since money has a reality different from it. The price is a property of the commodity, a quality in which it is *presented* as money. It is no longer an immediate but a reflected quality of it. Alongside real money, there now exists the commodity as ideally posited money.

This next characteristic, a characteristic of money *as measure* as well as of the commodity as *price*, is most easily shown by means of the distinction between *real money* and *accounting money*. As measure, money always serves as accounting money, and, as price, the commodity is always transformed only ideally into money.

'The appraisal of the commodity by the seller, the offer made by the buyer, the calculations, obligations, rents, inventories, etc., in short, everything which leads up to and precedes the material act of payment, must be expressed in accounting money. Real money intervenes only in order to realize payments and to balance (liquidate) the accounts. If I must pay 24 *livres* 12 *sous*, then accounting money presents 24 units of one sort and 12 of another, while in reality I shall pay in the form of two material pieces: a gold coin worth 24 *livres* and a silver coin worth 12 *sous*. The total mass of real money has necessary limits in the requirements of circulation. Accounting money is an ideal measure, which has no limits other than those of the imagination. Employed to *express every sort of wealth if considered from the aspect of its exchange value alone*; thus, national wealth, the income of the state and of individuals; the accounting values, regardless of the form in which these values may exist, regulated in one and the same form; so that there is not a single article in the mass of consumable objects which is not several times transformed into money by the mind, while, compared to this mass, the total sum of effective money is, at the most = 1:10.' (Garnier.)[52] (This last ratio is poor. 1:many millions is more correct. But this entirely unmeasurable.)

Thus, just as originally money expressed exchange value, so does the commodity as price, as ideally posited, mentally realized exchange value, now express a sum of money: money in a definite proportion. As prices, all commodities in their different forms are representatives of money, whereas earlier it was money, as the independent form of exchange value, which was the representative of all commodities. After money is posited as a commodity in reality, the commodity is posited as money in the mind.

It is clear so far, then, that in this ideal transformation of commodities into money, or in the positing of commodities as *prices*, the quantity of really available money is altogether a matter of indifference, for two reasons: *Firstly*: the ideal transformation of commodities into money is *prima facie* independent of and unrestricted by the mass of real money. Not a single piece of money is required in this process, just as little as a measuring rod (say, a yardstick) really needs to be employed before, for example, the ideal quantity of yards can be expressed. If, for example, the entire national wealth of England is appraised in terms of money, i.e. expressed as a price, everyone knows that there is not enough money in the world to realize this price. Money is needed here only as a category, as a mental relation. *Secondly*: because money functions as a unit, that is, the commodity is expressed in such a way that it contains a definite sum of equal parts of money, is measured by it, it follows that the measure between both [is] the general measure of exchange values – costs of production or labour time. Thus if $\frac{1}{3}$ of an ounce of gold is the product of 1 working day, and the commodity x is the product of 3 working days, then the commodity x = 1 oz. or £3 17s. 4d. With the measurement of money and of the commodity, the original measure of exchange values enters again. Instead of being expressed in 3 working days, the commodity is expressed in the quantity of gold or silver which is the product of 3 working days. The quantity of really available money obviously has no bearing on this proportion.

(*Error by James Mill*: overlooks that their cost of production

52. Garnier, *Histoire de la monnaie*, Vol. I, pp. 72, 73, 77, 78.

and not their quantity determines the value of the precious metals, as well as the prices of commodities measured in metallic value.)[53]

('Commodities in exchange are their own reciprocal measure . . . But this process would require as many reference points as there are commodities in circulation. If a commodity were exchanged only for one, and not for two commodities, then it would not serve as term of comparison . . . Hence the necessity of a common term of comparison . . . This term can be purely ideal . . . The determination of measure is fundamental, more important than that of wages . . . In the trade between Russia and China silver is used to evaluate all commodities, but nevertheless this commerce is done by means of barter.' (Storch.)[54] 'The operation of measuring with money is similar to the employment of weights in the comparison of material quantities. The same name for the two units whose function is to count the weight as well as the value of each thing. *Measures of weight and measures of value the same names.* An *étalon* of invariable weight was easily found. In the case of money, the question was again the *value* of a pound of silver, which = its cost of production.' (Sismondi.)[55] Not only the same names. Gold and silver were originally measured by weight. Thus, the *as* = 1 pound of copper among the Romans.)

'Sheep and oxen, not gold and silver, *money* in Homer and Hesiod, as measure of value. Barter on the Trojan battlefield.' (Jacob.) (Similarly, *slaves* in the Middle Ages. ibid.)[56]

Money can be posited in the character of measure and in that of the general element of exchange values, without being realized in its further qualities; hence also before it has taken on the form of metal money. In simple barter. However, presupposed in that case that little exchange of any kind takes place; that commodities are not developed as exchange values and hence not as *prices*. ('A common standard in the price of anything presupposes its frequent and familiar alienation. This not the case in simple states of society. In non-industrial countries many things without definite price . . . Sale alone can determine prices, and frequent sale alone

53. Marx discusses James Mill's theory more fully later on; see pp. 867–70.

54. Storch, *Cours d'économie politique*, Vol. I, pp. 81, 83, 84, 87, 88.

55. J.-C.-L. Simonde de Sismondi (1773–1842), Swiss political economist and historian, who held that the value of a product was determined by the quantity of labour needed to produce it, not by its cost. He was the father of the romantic-reactionary opposition to capitalism. The reference here is to *Études sur l'économie politique*, Vol. II, Brussels, 1838, pp. 264–5.

56. Jacob, *An Historical Inquiry*, Vol. I, pp. 109, 351.

can fix a standard. The frequent sale of articles of first necessity depends on the relation between town and country' etc.)[57]

A developed determination of prices presupposes that the individual does not directly produce his means of subsistence, but that his direct product is an *exchange value*, and hence must first be mediated by a social process, in order to become the *means of life* for the individual. Between the full development of this foundation of industrial society and the patriarchal condition, many intermediate stages, endless nuances. This much appears from (a). If the cost of production of the precious metals rises, then all commodity prices fall; if the cost of production of the precious metals falls, then all commodity prices rise. This is the general law, which, as we shall see, is modified in particular cases.

(b) If exchange values are *ideally* transformed into money by means of prices, then, in the act of exchange, in purchase and sale, they are *really* transformed into money, exchanged for money, in order then to be again exchanged as money for a commodity. A particular exchange value must first be exchanged for exchange value in general before it can then be in turn exchanged for particulars. The commodity is realized as an exchange value only through this mediating movement, in which money plays the part of middleman. Money thus circulates in the opposite direction from commodities. It appears as the middleman in commodity exchange, as the medium of exchange. It is the wheel of circulation, the instrument of circulation for the turnover of commodities; but, as such, it also has a circulation of its own – *monetary turnover, monetary circulation*. The price of the commodity is realized only when it is exchanged for real money, or in its real exchange for money.

This is what emerges from the foregoing. Commodities are really exchanged for money, transformed into real money, after they have been ideally transformed into money beforehand – i.e. have obtained the *attribute of price* as *prices*. *Prices*, therefore, are the *precondition* of monetary circulation, regardless of how much their realization appears to be a result of the latter. The circumstances which make the *prices* of commodities rise above or fall below their average value because their exchange value does so are to be developed in the section on exchange value, and precede the process of the actual *realization* of the prices of commodities

57. Steuart, *An Inquiry*, Vol. I, pp. 395–6.

through money; they thus appear, at first, as completely independent of it. The relations of numbers to one another obviously remain the same when I change them into decimal fractions. This is only giving them *another name*. In order really to circulate commodities, what is required is *instruments of transport*, and transport cannot be performed by money. If I have bought 1,000 lb. of iron for the amount of £x, then the ownership of the iron has passed into my hand. My £x have done their duty as means of exchange and have circulated, along with the title of ownership. The seller, inversely, has realized the price of iron, iron as exchange value. But in order then to bring the iron from him to me, money itself is useless; that requires wagons, horses, roads, etc. The real circulation of commodities through time and space is not accomplished by money. Money only realizes their *price* and thereby transfers the title to the commodity into the hands of the buyer, to him who has proffered means of exchange. What money circulates is not commodities but their titles of ownership; and what is realized in the opposite direction in this circulation, whether by purchase or sale, is again not the commodities, but their prices. The quantity of money which is, then, required for circulation is determined initially by the level of the prices of the commodities thrown into circulation. The sum total of these prices, however, is determined *firstly*: by the prices of the individual commodities; *secondly*: by the quantity of commodities at given prices which enter into circulation. For example, in order to circulate a quarter of wheat at 60s., twice as many s. are required as would be to circulate it at 30s. And if 5,000 of these quarters at 60s. are to be circulated, then 300,000 s. are required, while in order to circulate 200 such quarters only 12,000s. are needed. Thus, the amount of money required is dependent on the level of commodity prices and on the quantity of commodities at specified prices.

Thirdly, however, the quantity of money required for circulation depends not only on the sum total of prices to be realized, but on the rapidity with which money circulates, completes the task of this realization. If 1 thaler in one hour makes 10 purchases at 1 thaler each, if it is exchanged 10 times, then it performs quite the same task that 10 thalers would do if they made only 1 purchase per hour. Velocity is the negative moment; it substitutes for quantity; by its means, a single coin is multiplied.

The circumstances which determine the mass of commodity prices to be realized, on the one hand, and the velocity of circulation of money, on the other hand, are to be examined later. This much is clear, that prices are not high or low because much or little money circulates, but that much or little money circulates because prices are high or low; and, further, that the velocity of the circulating money does not depend on its quantity, but that the quantity of the circulating medium depends on its velocity (heavy payments are not counted but weighed; through this the time necessary is shortened).

Still, as already mentioned, the circulation of money does not begin from a single centre, nor does it return to a single centre from all points of the periphery (as with the *banks of issue* and partly with state issues); but from an infinite number of points, and returns to an infinite number (this return itself, and the time required to achieve it, a matter of chance). The velocity of the circulating medium can therefore substitute for the quantity of the circulating medium only up to a certain point. (Manufacturers and farmers pay, for example, the worker; he pays the grocer, etc.; from there the money returns to the manufacturers and farmers.) The same quantity of money can effectuate a series of payments only *successively*, regardless of the speed. But a certain mass of payments must be made *simultaneously*. Circulation takes its point of departure at one and the same time from many points. A definite quantity of money is therefore necessary for circulation, a sum which will always be engaged in circulation, and which is determined by the sum total which starts from the simultaneous points of departure in circulation, and by the velocity with which it runs its course (returns). No matter how many ebbs and floods this quantity of the circulating medium is exposed to, an average level nevertheless comes into existence; since the permanent changes are always very gradual, take place only over longer periods, and are constantly paralysed by a mass of secondary circumstances, as we shall see.

(To (a). '*Measure*, used as attribute of money, means *indicator of value*' ... Ridiculous, that 'prices must fall, because commodities are judged as being worth so many ounces of gold, and the amount of gold is diminished in this country ... The efficiency of gold as an indicator of value is unaffected by its quantity being greater or smaller in any particular country. If the employment of banking expedients were to succeed in reducing the paper and metal circulation in this country by half, the relative value of money and commodities would remain the same.' Example of Peru in the sixteenth century and transmission from France to England. Hubbard, VIII, 45.)[58] ('On the African coast neither gold nor silver the measure of value; instead of them, an ideal standard, an imaginary *bar.*') (Jacob, V, 15.)[59]

In its quality of being a measure, money is indifferent to its quantity, or, the existing quantity of money makes no difference. Its quantity is measured in its quality as medium of exchange, as instrument of circulation. Whether these two qualities of money can enter into contradiction with one another – to be looked at later.

(The concept of *forced, involuntary circulation* (see Steuart)[60] does not belong here yet.)

To have *circulation*, what is essential is that exchange appear as a process, a fluid whole of purchases and sales. Its first presupposition is the circulation of commodities themselves, as a natural, many-sided circulation of those commodities. The precondition of commodity circulation is that they be produced as *exchange values*, not as *immediate use values*, but as mediated through exchange value. Appropriation through and by means of divestiture [*Entäusserung*] and alienation [*Veräusserung*] is the fundamental condition. Circulation as the realization of exchange values implies: (1) that my product is a product only in so far as it is for others; hence suspended singularity, generality; (2) that it is a product for me only in so far as it has been alienated, become for others; (3) that it is for the other only in so far as he himself alienates his product; which already implies (4) that production is not an end in itself for me, but a means. Circulation is the movement in which the general alienation appears as general appropriation and general appropriation as general alienation. As much, then, as the whole of this movement appears as a social process, and as much as the individual moments of this movement arise from the conscious will and particular purposes of individuals, so much does the totality of the process appear as an objective interrelation, which arises spontaneously from nature; arising, it is true, from the mutual influence of conscious individuals on one another, but neither located in their consciousness, nor subsumed under them

58. J. G. Hubbard (1805–89), English financier, a director of the Bank of England in 1838, later a Conservative M.P. *The Currency and the Country*, London, 1843, pp. 44–6. Marx's reference (VIII, 45) is to his own excerpt-book.

59. Jacob, *An Historical Inquiry*, Vol. II, p. 326.

60. Steuart, *An Inquiry*, Vol. II, p. 389.

as a whole. Their own collisions with one another produce an *alien* social power standing above them, produce their mutual interaction as a process and power independent of them. Circulation, because a totality of the social process, is also the first form in which the social relation appears as something independent of the individuals, but not only as, say, in a coin or in exchange value, but extending to the whole of the social movement itself. The social relation of individuals to one another as a power over the individuals which has become autonomous, whether conceived as a natural force, as chance or in whatever other form, is a necessary result of the fact that the point of departure is not the free social individual. Circulation as the first totality among the economic categories is well suited to bring this to light.

At first sight, circulation appears as a *simply infinite* process.[61] The commodity is exchanged for money, money is exchanged for the commodity, and this is repeated endlessly. This constant renewal of the same process does indeed form an important moment of circulation. But, viewed more precisely, it reveals other phenomena as well; the phenomena of completion, or, the return of the point of departure into itself. The commodity is exchanged for money; money is exchanged for the commodity. In this way, commodity is exchanged for commodity, except that this exchange is a mediated one. The purchaser becomes a seller again and the seller becomes purchaser again. In this way, each is posited in the double and the antithetical aspect, and hence in the living unity of both aspects. It is entirely wrong, therefore, to do as the economists do, namely, as soon as the contradictions in the monetary system emerge into view, to focus only on the end results without the process which mediates them; only on the unity without the distinction, the affirmation without the negation. The commodity is exchanged in circulation for a commodity: at the same time, and equally, it is not exchanged for a commodity, in as much as it is exchanged for money. The acts of purchase and sale, in other words, appear as two mutually indifferent acts, separated in time and place. When it is said that he who sells also buys in as much as he buys money, and that he who buys also sells in as much as he sells money, then it is precisely the distinction which is overlooked, the specific distinction between commodity and

61. Marx may also be alluding to Hegel's concept of *schlechte Unendlichkeit* ('bad' or 'spurious' infinity), an infinity of connections merely piled on top of one another (*Science of Logic*, Glockner edn, Vol. IV, pp. 165–83).

money. After the economists have most splendidly shown that barter, in which both acts coincide, does not suffice for a more developed form of society and mode of production, they then suddenly look at the kind of barter which is mediated by money as if it were not so mediated, and overlook the *specific* character of this transaction. After they have shown us that money is necessary in addition to and distinct from commodities, they assert all at once that there is no distinction between money and commodities. They take refuge in this abstraction because in the real development of money there are contradictions which are unpleasant for the apologetics of bourgeois common sense, and must hence be covered up. In so far as purchase and sale, the two essential moments of circulation, are indifferent to one another and separated in place and time, they by no means need to coincide. Their indifference can develop into the fortification and apparent independence of the one against the other. But in so far as they are both essential moments of a single whole, there must come a moment when the independent form is violently broken and when the inner unity is established externally through a violent explosion. Thus already in the quality of money as a medium, in the splitting of exchange into two acts, there lies the germ of crises, or at least their possibility, which cannot be realized, except where the fundamental preconditions of classically developed, conceptually adequate circulation are present.

It has further been seen that, in circulation, money only realizes prices. The price appears at first as an ideal aspect of the commodity; but the sum of money exchanged for a commodity is its realized price, its real price. The price appears therefore as *external to* and *independent of* the commodity, as well as existing in it ideally. If the commodity cannot be realized in money, it ceases to be capable of circulating, and its price becomes merely imaginary; just as originally the product which has become transformed into exchange value, if it is not really exchanged, ceases to be a product. (The rise and fall of prices not the question here.) From viewpoint (a) *price* appeared as an *aspect of the commodity*; but from (b) *money* appears as *the price outside the commodity*. The commodity requires not simply demand, but demand which can pay in money. Thus, if its price cannot be realized, if it cannot be transformed into money, the commodity appears as *devalued, depriced*. The exchange value expressed in its price must be sacrificed as soon as this specific transformation into money is necessary. Hence the complaints by Boisguillebert,[62] e.g. that money is the hangman of all things, the moloch to whom everything must be sacrificed, the despot of commodities. In the period of the rising absolute monarchy with its transformation of all taxes into money taxes, money indeed appears as the moloch to whom real wealth is sacrificed. Thus it appears also in every monetary panic. From having been a servant of commerce, says Boisguillebert, money became its despot.[63] But, in fact, already the determination of prices in themselves contains what is counterposed to money in exchange; that money no longer represents the commodity, but the commodity, money. Lamentations about commerce in money as illegitimate commerce are to be found among several writers, who form the transition from the feudal to the modern period; the same later among socialists.

(α) The further the division of labour develops, the more does the product cease to be a medium of exchange. The necessity of a general medium of exchange arises, a medium independent of the specific production of each and every one. When production is oriented towards immediate subsistence, not *every* article can be exchanged for *every* other one, and a specific activity can be exchanged only for *specific* products. The more specialized, manifold and interdependent the products become, the greater the necessity for a general medium of exchange. At the beginning, the product of labour, or labour itself, is the general medium of exchange. But this ceases more and more to be general medium of exchange as it becomes more specialized. A fairly developed division of labour presupposes that the needs of each person have become very many-sided and his product has become very one-sided. The *need for exchange* and the *unmediated medium of exchange* develop in inverse proportion. Hence the necessity for a *general medium of exchange*, where the specific product and the specific labour must be exchanged for *exchangeability*. The exchange value of a thing is nothing other than the quantitatively specific expression of its capacity for serving as *medium of exchange*. In money the *medium of exchange* becomes a thing, or, the exchange value of the thing

62. Pierre le Pesant Boisguillebert (1646–1714). French judge and precursor of the Physiocrats who opposed Mercantilism, upheld free competition, and denounced the misery of the French agricultural population, which, under Louis XIV, earned him exile to the Auvergne.

63. Boisguillebert, *Dissertation sur la nature des richesses, de l'argent, et des tributs*, printed in *Économistes Financiers du XVIIIe siècle*, ed. E. Daire, Paris, 1843, pp. 395 and 417.

achieves an independent existence apart from the thing. Since the commodity is a medium of exchange of limited potency compared with money, it can cease to be a medium of exchange as against money.

(β) The splitting of exchange into purchase and sale makes it possible for me to buy without selling (stockpiling of commodities) or to sell without buying (accumulation of money). It makes speculation possible. It turns exchange into a special business; i.e. it founds the *merchant estate*.[64] This separation of the two elements has made possible a mass of transactions in between the definitive exchange of commodities, and it enables a mass of persons to exploit this divorce. It has made possible a mass of *pseudo-transactions*. Sometimes it becomes evident that what appeared to be an essentially divided act is in reality an essentially unified one; then again, sometimes, that what was thought to be an essentially unified act is in reality essentially divided. At moments when purchasing and selling assert themselves as essentially different acts, a general depreciation of all commodities takes place. At moments where it turns out that money is only a medium of exchange, a depreciation of money comes about. General fall or rise of prices.

Money provides the possibility of an absolute division of labour, because of independence of labour from its specific product, from the immediate use value of its product for it. The general rise of prices in times of speculation cannot be ascribed to a general rise in its *exchange value* or its *cost of production*; for if the *exchange value or the cost of production* of gold were to rise in step with that of all other commodities, then their exchange values expressed in money, i.e. their *prices*, would remain the same. Nor can it be ascribed to a decline in the production price of gold. (Credit is not yet on the agenda here.) But since money is not only a general commodity, but *also* a particular, and since, as a particular, it comes under the laws of supply and demand, it follows that the general demand for particular commodities as against money must bring it down.

We see that it is in the nature of money to solve the contradictions of direct barter as well as of exchange value only by positing them as general contradictions. Whether or not a *particular medium of exchange* was exchanged for another particular was a matter of coincidence; now, however, the commodity must be exchanged for the *general medium of exchange*, against which its

64. See p. 148, n. 17.

particularity stands in a still greater contradiction. In order to secure the exchangeability of the commodity, exchangeability itself is set up in opposition to it as an independent commodity. (It was a means, becomes an end.) The question was, whether a particular commodity encounters another particular one. But money suspends the act of exchange itself in two mutually indifferent acts.

(Before the questions regarding circulation, its strength, weakness, etc., and notably the disputed point regarding the quantity of money in circulation and prices, are further developed, money should be looked at from the point of view of its third characteristic.[65])

One moment of circulation is that the commodity exchanges itself through money for another commodity. But there is, equally, the other moment, not only that commodity exchanges for money and money for commodity, but equally that money exchanges for commodity and commodity for money; hence that money is mediated with itself by the commodity, and appears as the unity which joins itself with itself in its circular course. Then it appears no longer as the medium, but as the aim of circulation (as e.g. with the merchant estate) (in commerce generally). If circulation is looked at not as a constant alternation, but as a series of circular motions which it describes within itself, then this circular path appears as a double one: Commodity–Money–Money–Commodity; and in the other direction Money–Commodity–Commodity–Money; i.e. if I sell in order to buy, then I can also buy in order to sell. In the former case money only a means to obtain the commodity, and the commodity the aim; in the second case the commodity only a means to obtain money, and money the aim. This is the simple result when the moments of circulation are brought together. Looking at it as mere circulation, the point at which I intervene in order to declare it the point of departure has to be a matter of indifference.

Now, a specific distinction does enter between a commodity in circulation and money in circulation. The commodity is thrown out of circulation at a certain point and fulfils its definitive function only when it is definitively withdrawn from circulation, consumed, whether in the act of production or in consumption proper.

65. See above, p. 146; money is '(3) representative of commodities (hence object of contracts)', and see below section c, 'money as material representative of wealth', p. 203.

The function of money, by contrast, is to remain in circulation as its vehicle, to resume its circular course always anew like a *perpetuum mobile*.

Nevertheless, this second function is also a part of circulation, equally with the first. Now one can say: to exchange commodity for commodity makes sense, since commodities, although they are equivalent as prices, are qualitatively different, and their exchange ultimately satisfies qualitatively different needs. By contrast, exchanging money for money makes no sense, unless, that is, a quantitative difference arises, less money is exchanged for more, sold at a higher price than purchased, and with the category of profit we have as yet nothing to do. The circle Money–Commodity–Commodity–Money, which we drew from the analysis of circulation, would then appear to be merely an arbitrary and senseless abstraction, roughly as if one wanted to describe the life cycle as Death–Life–Death; although even in the latter case it could not be denied that the constant decomposition of what has been individualized back into the elemental is just as much a moment of the process of nature as the constant individualization of the elemental. Similarly in the act of circulation, the constant monetarization of commodities, just as much as the constant transformation of money into commodities. In the real process of buying in order to sell, admittedly, the motive is the profit made thereby, and the ultimate aim is to exchange less money, by way of the commodity, for more money, since there is no qualitative difference (here we disregard special kinds of metal money as well as special kinds of coins) between money and money. All that given, it cannot be denied that the operation may come to grief and that hence the exchange of money for money without quantitative difference frequently takes place in reality and, hence, can take place. But before this process, on which commerce rests and which therefore, owing to its extension, forms a chief phenomenon of circulation, is possible at all, the circular path Money–Commodity–Commodity–Money must be recognized as a particular form of circulation. This form is specifically different from that in which money appears as a mere medium of exchange for commodities; as the middle term; as a minor premise of the syllogism. Along with its quantitative aspect, visible in commerce, it must be separated out in its purely qualitative form, in its specific movement. *Secondly*: it already implies that money functions neither only as measure, nor only as medium of exchange, nor only as both; but has yet a third quality. It appears here *firstly* as an end in itself, whose sole realization is served by commodity trade and exchange. *Secondly*, since the cycle concludes with it at that point, it steps *outside* it, just as the commodity, having been exchanged for its equivalent through money, is thrown out of circulation. It is very true that money, in so far as it serves only as an agent of circulation, constantly remains enclosed in its cycle. But it appears here, also, that it is still something more than this instrument of circulation, that it also has an independent existence outside circulation, and that in this new character it can be withdrawn from circulation just as the commodity must constantly be definitively withdrawn. We must then observe money in its third quality, in which both of the former are included, i.e. that of serving as measure as well as the general medium of exchange and hence the realization of commodity prices.

(c) Money as material representative of wealth (accumulation of money; before that, money as the general material of contracts, etc.)

It is in the nature of circulation that every point appears simultaneously as a starting-point and as a conclusion, and, more precisely, that it appears to be the one in so far as it appears to be the other. The specific form M–C–C–M therefore just as correct as the other, which appears the more original, C–M–M–C. The difficulty is that the other commodity is qualitatively different; not so the other money. It can differ only quantitatively. – Regarded as *measure* the material substance of money is essential, although its availability and even more its quantity, the *amount* of the portion of gold or silver which serves as *unit*, are entirely irrelevant for it in this quality, and it is employed in general only as an imaginary, non-existent unit. In this quality it is needed as a unit and not as an amount. If I say a pound of cotton is worth 8d., then I am saying that 1 pound of cotton = $\frac{1}{116}$ oz. of gold (the ounce at £3 17s. 7d.) (931d.). This expresses at the same time its particularity as exchange value as against all other commodities, as equivalent of all other commodities, which contain the ounce of gold this or that many times, since they are all in the same way compared to the ounce of gold. This original relation of the pound of cotton with gold, by means of which the quantity of gold contained in an ounce of cotton is determined, is fixed by the quantity of labour time realized in one and the other, the real common substance of exchange values. This is to be presupposed from the chapter dealing with exchange value as such. The difficulty of finding this equation is not as great as it may appear. For example, labour which directly produces gold directly reveals a certain quantity of gold to be the product of, say, one working day. Competition equates the other working days with that one, *modificandis modificatis*. Directly or indirectly. In a word, in the direct production of gold, a definite quantity of gold directly appears as product and hence as the value, the equivalent, of a definite amount of labour time. One has therefore only to determine the amount of labour time realized in the various commodities, and to equate them to the labour time which directly produces gold, in order to state how much gold is contained in a given commodity. The determination of all commodities as prices – as measured exchange values – is a process which takes place only gradually, which presupposes frequent exchange and hence frequent comparison of commodities as exchange values; but as soon as the existence of commodities as prices has become a precondition – a precondition which is itself a product of the social process, a result of the process of social production – then the determination of new prices appears simple, since the elements of production cost are themselves already present in the form of prices, and are hence simply to be added. (*Frequent alienation, sale, frequent sale,* Steuart.[66] Rather, all this must have continuity so that prices achieve a certain regularity.) However, the point we wanted to get at here is this: in so far as gold is to be established as the unit of measurement, the relation of gold to commodities is determined by barter, direct, unmediated exchange; like the relation of all other commodities to one another. With barter, however, the product is exchange value only *in itself*; it is its first phenomenal form; but the product is not yet posited as exchange value. Firstly, this character does not yet dominate production as a whole, but concerns only its superfluity and is hence itself more or less *superfluous* (like exchange itself); an accidental enlargement of the sphere of satisfactions, enjoyments (relations to new objects). It therefore takes place at only a few points (originally at the borders of the natural communities, in their contact with strangers), is restricted to a narrow sphere, and forms something which passes production by, is auxiliary to it; dies out just as much by chance as it arises. The

66. Steuart, *An Inquiry*, Vol. I, pp. 395–6.

form of barter in which the overflow of one's own production is exchanged by chance for that of others' is only the *first occurrence* of the product as exchange value in general, and is determined by accidental needs, whims, etc. But if it should happen to continue, to become a continuing act which contains within itself the means of its renewal, then little by little, from the outside and likewise by chance, regulation of reciprocal exchange arises by means of regulation of reciprocal production, and thé costs of production, which ultimately resolve into labour time, would thus become the measure of exchange. This shows how exchange comes about, and the exchange value of the commodity. But the circumstances under which a relation occurs for the first time by no means show us that relation either in its purity or in its totality. A product posited as exchange value is in its essence no longer a simple thing; it is posited in a quality differing from its natural quality; it is posited as a *relation*, more precisely as a relation in general, not to one commodity but to every commodity, to every possible product. It expresses, therefore, a general relation; the product which relates to itself as the realization of a *specific quantity* of labour in general, of social labour time, and is therefore the equivalent of every other product in the proportion expressed in its exchange value. Exchange value presupposes social labour as the substance of all products, quite apart from their natural make-up. Nothing can express a relation without relating to one particular thing, and there can be no general relation unless it relates to a general thing. Since labour is motion, time is its natural measure. Barter in its crudest form presupposes labour as substance and labour time as measure of commodities; this then emerges as soon as it becomes regularized, continuous, as soon as it contains within itself the reciprocal requirements for its renewal. – A commodity is *exchange value* only if it is expressed in another, i.e. as a relation. A bushel of wheat is worth so many bushels of rye; in this case wheat is exchange value in as much as it is expressed in rye, and rye is exchange value in as much as it is expressed in wheat. If each of the two is related only to itself, it is not exchange value. Now, in the relation in which money appears as measure, it itself is not expressed as a relation, not as exchange value, but as a natural quantity of a certain material, a natural weight-fraction of gold or silver. In general, the commodity in which the exchange value of another is expressed, is never expressed as exchange value, never as relation, but rather as a definite quantity of its natural make-up.

If 1 bushel of wheat is worth 3 bushels of rye, then only the bushel
of wheat is expressed as a value, not the bushel of rye. Of course,
the other is also posited *in itself*; the 1 bushel of rye is then $= \frac{1}{3}$
bushel of wheat; but this is not *posited*, but merely a second relation, which is admittedly directly present in the first. If one commodity is expressed in another, then it is posited as a relation, and
the other as simple quantity of a certain material. 3 bushels of rye
are in themselves no value; rather, rye filling up a certain volume,
measured by a standard of volume. The same is true of money as
measure, as the unit in which the exchange values of other commodities are measured. It is a specific weight of the natural substance by which it is represented, gold, silver, etc. If 1 bushel of
wheat has the price of 77s. 7d., then it is expressed as something
else, to which it is equal, as 1 ounce of gold, as relation, as exchange value. But 1 ounce of gold is in itself no exchange value; it
is not expressed as exchange value; but as a specific quantity of
itself, of its natural substance, gold. If 1 bushel of wheat has the
price of 77s. 7d. or of 1 ounce of gold, then this can be a greater or
lesser value, since 1 ounce of gold will rise or fall in relation to the
quantity of labour required for its production. But for the determination of its price as such, this is irrelevant; for its price of 77s.
7d. exactly expresses the relation in which it is equivalent to all
other commodities, in which it can buy them. The specificity of
price determination, whether the bushel is 77 or 1,780s., is a different matter altogether from the determination of price as such,
i.e. the positing of wheat as price. It has a price, regardless of
whether it costs 100 or 1s. The price expresses its exchange value
only in a unit common to all commodities; presupposes therefore
that this exchange value is already regulated by other relations. To
be sure, the fact that 1 bushel of wheat has the price of 1 ounce of
gold – since gold and wheat as natural objects have no relation
with one another, are *as such* not a measure for one another,
are *irrelevant* to one another – this fact is found out by bringing
the ounce of gold itself into relation with the amount of labour
time necessary for its production, and thus bringing both wheat
and gold in relation to a third entity, labour, and equating them
through this relation; by comparing them both, therefore, as
exchange values. But this shows us only how the price of wheat is
found, the quantity of gold to which it is equal. In this relation
itself, where gold appears as the price of wheat, it is itself not in
turn posited as a relation, as exchange value, but as a certain

quantity of a natural material. In exchange value, commodities (products) are posited as relations to their social substance, to labour; but as prices, they are expressed as quantities of other products of various natural make-ups. Now, it can admittedly be said that the price of money is also posited as 1 bushel of wheat, 3 bushels of rye and all the other quantities of different commodities, whose price is 1 ounce of gold. But then, in order to express the price of money, the whole sphere of commodities would have to be listed, each in the quantity which equals 1 ounce of gold. Money would then have as many prices as there are commodities whose price it itself expresses. The chief quality of price, *unity*, would disappear. No commodity expresses the price of money, because none expresses its relation to all other commodities, its general exchange value. But it is the specific characteristic of price that exchange value must be expressed in its generality and at the same time in a specific commodity. But even this is irrelevant. In so far as money appears as a material in which the price of all commodities is expressed and measured, to that extent is money itself posited as a particular amount of gold, silver, etc., in short, of its natural matter; a simple amount of a certain material, not itself as exchange value, as relation. In the same way, every commodity which expresses the price of another is itself not *posited* as exchange value, but as a simple amount of itself. In its quality as unit of exchange value, as their measure, their common point of comparison, money is essentially a natural material, gold, silver; since, as the price of the commodity, it is not an exchange value, not a relation, but a certain weight of gold, silver; e.g. a pound with its subdivisions, and thus money appears originally as pound, *aes grave*. This is precisely what distinguishes price from exchange value, and we have seen that exchange value necessarily drives towards price formation. Hence the nonsensicality of those who want to make labour time as such into money, i.e. who want to posit and then not posit the distinction between price and exchange value. Money as measure, as element of price determination, as measuring unit of exchange values thus presents the following phenomena: (1) it is required only as an imagined unit once the exchange value of an ounce of gold compared to any one commodity has been determined; its actual presence is superfluous, along with, even more so, its available quantity: as an indicator (an indicator of value) the amount in which it exists in a country is irrelevant; required only as accounting unit; (2) while it thus only needs to be posited ideally, and, indeed, in the form of the price of a commodity is only ideally posited *in* it; at the same time, as a simple amount of the natural substance in which it is represented, as a given weight of gold, silver, etc. which is accepted as unit, it also yields the point of comparison, the unit, the measure. Exchange values (commodities) are transformed by the mind into certain weights of gold or silver, and are ideally posited as being = to this imagined quantity of gold etc.; as expressing it.

But when we now go over to the second quality of money, money as medium of exchange and realizer of prices, then we have found that in this case it must be present in a certain *quantity*; that the given weight of gold and silver which has been posited as a unit is required in a given quantity in order to be adequate to this function. If the sum of prices to be realized, which depends on the price of a particular commodity multiplied by its quantity, is given on one side, and the velocity of monetary circulation on the other, then a certain quantity of the circulating medium is required. When we now examine the original form more closely, the direct form in which circulation presents itself, C–M–M–C, then we see that money appears here as a pure medium of exchange. The commodity is exchanged for a commodity, and money appears merely as the medium of this exchange. The price of the first commodity is realized with money, in order to realize the price of the second commodity with the money, and thus to obtain it in exchange for the first. After the price of the first commodity is realized, the aim of the person who now has its price in money is not to obtain the price of the second commodity, but rather to pay its price in order to obtain the commodity. At bottom, therefore, money served him to exchange the first commodity for the second. As mere medium of exchange, money has no other purpose. The man who has sold his commodity and got money wants to buy another commodity, and the man from whom he buys it needs the money in order to buy another commodity etc. Now, in this function, as pure medium of circulation, the specific role of money consists only of this circulation, which it brings about owing to the fact that its quantity, its amount, was fixed beforehand. The number of times in which it is itself contained in the commodities as a unit is determined beforehand by their prices, and as medium of circulation it appears merely as a multiple of this predetermined unit. In so far as it realizes the price of commodities, the commodity is exchanged for its real equivalent in gold and silver; its exchange value is really exchanged for another commodity, money; but in so far as this process takes place only in order to transform this money back into a commodity, i.e. in order to exchange the first commodity for the second, then money appears only fleetingly, or, its substance consists only in this constant appearance as disappearance, as this vehicle of mediation. Money as medium of circulation is *only* medium of circulation. The only attribute which is essential to it in order to serve in this capacity is the attribute of quantity, of amount, in which it circulates. (Since the amount is co-determined by the velocity, the latter does not require special mention here.) In so far as it realizes the price, its material existence as gold and silver is essential; but in so far as this realization is only fleeting and destined to suspend itself, this is *irrelevant*. It is only a *semblance*, as if the point were to exchange the commodity for gold or silver as particular commodities: a semblance which disappears as soon as the process is ended, as soon as gold and silver have again been exchanged for a commodity, and the commodity, hence, exchanged for another. The character of gold and silver as mere media of circulation, or the character of the medium of circulation as gold and silver, is therefore irrelevant to their make-up as particular natural commodities. Suppose the total price of circulating commodities = 1,200 thalers. Their measure is then 1 thaler = x weight of silver. Now let 100 thalers be necessary to circulate these commodities in 6 hours; i.e. every thaler pays the price of 100 thalers in 6 hours. Now, what is essential is that 100 thalers be present, the amount of 100 of the metallic unit which measures the sum total of commodity prices; 100 of these units. That these units consist of silver is irrelevant to the process itself. This is already visible in the fact that a single thaler represents in the cycle of circulation a mass of silver 100 times greater than is contained in it in reality, even though in each particular transaction it only represents the silver weight of 1 thaler. In circulation as a whole, the 1 thaler thus represents 100 thalers, a weight of silver a hundred times greater than it really contains. It is in truth only a *symbol* for the weight of silver contained in 100 thalers. It realizes a price which is 100 times greater than it realizes in reality as a quantity of silver. Let the pound sterling be = $\frac{1}{3}$ ounce of gold (it is not as much as that). In so far as the price of a commodity at £1 is paid, i.e. its price of £1 is realized, it is exchanged for £1, to that extent it is of decisive importance that the £1 really contain $\frac{1}{3}$ ounce of gold. If it were a counterfeit £, alloyed with non-precious metals, a £ only in appearance, then indeed the price of the commodity would not be realized; in order to realize it, it would have to be paid for in as great a quantity of the non-precious metal as equals $\frac{1}{3}$ of an ounce of gold. Looking at this moment of circulation in isolation, it is thus essential that the unit of money should really represent a given quantity of gold or silver. But when we take circulation as a totality, as a self-enclosed process, C–M–M–C, then the matter stands differently. In the first case the realization of price would be only apparent: in reality only a *part* of its price would be realized. The price posited in it ideally would not be posited in reality. The commodity which is ideally equated to a given weight of gold would in actual exchange not bring in as much gold as that. But if a fake £ were to circulate in the place of a real one, it would render absolutely the same service in circulation as a whole as if it were genuine. If a commodity, A, with the price of £1, is exchanged for 1 fake £, and if this fake pound is again exchanged for commodity B, price £1, then the fake pound has done absolutely the same service as if it had been genuine. The genuine pound is, therefore, in this process, nothing more than a *symbol*, in so far as the moment in which it realizes prices is left out, and we look only at the totality of the process, in which it serves only as medium of exchange and in which the realization of prices is only a *semblance*, a fleeting mediation. Here the gold pound serves only to allow commodity A to be exchanged for commodity B, both having the same price. The real realization of the price of commodity A is, here, the commodity B, and the real realization of the price of B is the commodity A or C or D, which amounts to the same as far as the form of the relation is concerned, for which the particular content of the commodity is entirely irrelevant. Commodities with identical prices are exchanged. Instead of exchanging commodity A directly for commodity B, the price of commodity A is exchanged for the price of commodity B and the price of commodity B for commodity A. Money thus represents to the commodity only the latter's price. Commodities are exchanged for one another at their prices. The price of the commodity expresses about it, ideally, that it is an amount of a certain natural unit (weight units) of gold or silver, of the material in which money is embodied. In the form of money, or its realized price, the commodity now confronts a real amount of this unit. But in so far as the realization of the price is not the final act, and the point is not to possess the price of commodities as price, but as the price of another commodity, to that extent the material of money is irrelevant, e.g. gold and silver. Money becomes a subject as instrument of circulation, as medium of exchange, and the natural material in which it presents itself appears as an accident whose significance disappears in the act of exchange itself; because it is not in this material that the commodity exchanged for money is supposed to be realized, but rather in the material of another commodity. For now, apart from the moments that, in circulation, (1) money realizes prices, (2) money circulates titles of ownership; we have (3), additionally, that by means of it something takes place which could not happen otherwise, namely that the exchange value of the commodity is expressed in every other commodity. If 1 yard of linen costs 2s. and 1 lb. of sugar 1s., then the yard of linen is realized, by means of the 2s., in 2 lb. of sugar, while the sugar is converted into the material of its exchange value, into the material in which its exchange value is realized. As a mere medium of circulation, in its role in the constant flow of the circulatory process, money is neither the measure of prices, because it is already posited as such in the prices themselves; nor is it the means for the realization of prices, for it exists as such in one single moment of circulation, but disappears as such in the totality of its moments; but is, rather, the mere *representative* of the price in relation to all other commodities, and serves only as a means to the end that all commodities are to be exchanged at equivalent prices. It is exchanged for one commodity because it is the general representative of its exchange value; and, as such, as the *representative* of every other commodity of equal exchange value, it is the general representative; and that is, as such, what it is in circulation itself. It *represents* the price of the one commodity as against all other commodities, or the price of all commodities as against the one commodity. In this relation it is not only the *representative* of commodity prices, but the *symbol* of itself; i.e. in the act of circulation itself, its material, gold and silver, is irrelevant. It *is* the price; it is a given quantity of gold or silver; but in so far as this reality of the price is here only fleeting, a reality destined constantly to disappear, to be suspended, not to count as a definitive realization, but always only as an intermediate, mediating realization; in so far as the point here is not the realization of the price at all, but rather the realization of the exchange value of one particular commodity in the material of another commodity, to that extent its own material is irrelevant; it is ephemeral as a realization of the price, since this itself disappears; it exists, therefore, in so far as it remains in this constant movement, only as a representative of exchange value, which becomes real only if the real exchange value constantly steps into the place of its representative, constantly changes places with it, constantly exchanges itself for it. Hence, in this process, its reality is not that it is the price, but that it *represents* it, is its representative – the materially present representative of the price, thus of itself, and, as such, of the exchange value of commodities. As medium of exchange, it realizes the prices of commodities only in order to posit the exchange value of the one commodity in the other, as its unit; i.e. in order to realize its exchange value in the other commodity; i.e. to posit the other commodity as the material of its exchange value.

Only within circulation, then, is it such a material symbol; taken out of circulation, it again becomes a realized price; but within the process, as we have seen, the quantity, the amount of these material symbols of the monetary unit is the essential attribute. Hence, while the material substance of money, its material substratum of a given quantity of gold or silver, is irrelevant within circulation, where money appears as something existing in opposition to commodities, and where, by contrast, its amount is the essential aspect, since it is there only a *symbol* for a given amount of this unit; in its role as measure, however, where it was introduced only ideally, its material substratum was essential, but its quantity and even its existence as such were irrelevant. From this it follows that money as gold and silver, in so far as *only* its role as means of exchange and circulation is concerned, can be replaced by any other *symbol* which expresses a given quantity of its unit, and that in this way symbolic money can replace the real, because material money as mere medium of exchange is itself symbolic.

It is these contradictory functions of money, as measure, as realization of prices and as mere medium of exchange, which explain the otherwise inexplicable phenomenon that the *debasement* of metallic money, of gold, silver, through admixture of inferior metals, causes a depreciation of money and a rise in prices; because in this case the measure of prices [is] no longer the cost of production of the ounce of gold, say, but rather of an ounce consisting of $\frac{2}{3}$ copper etc. (The debasement of the coinage, in so far as it consists merely of falsifying or changing the names of the fractional weight units of the precious metal, e.g. if the eighth part of an ounce were to be called a sovereign, makes absolutely no difference in the measure and changes only its name. If, earlier, ¼ of the ounce was called 1 sovereign, and now it is ⅛, then the price of 1 sovereign now expresses merely ⅛ of an ounce of gold; thus (about) 2 sovereigns are necessary to express the same price which was earlier expressed by 1 sovereign); or in the case of a mere falsification of the name of the fractional parts of the precious metal, the measure remains the same, but the fractional part [is] expressed in twice as many francs etc. as before; on the other hand, if the substratum of money, gold, silver, is entirely suspended and replaced by paper bearing the symbol of given quantities of real money, in the quantity required by circulation, then the paper circulates at the full gold and silver value. In the first case, because the medium of circulation is at the same time the material of money as measure, and the material in which prices are definitively realized; in the second case, because money only in its role as medium of circulation.

Example of the clumsy confusion between the contradictory functions of money: 'Price is exactly determined by the quantity of money there is to buy it with. All the commodities in the world can fetch no more than all the money in the world.' First, the determination of prices has nothing to do with actual sale; money, in sale, serves only as measure. Secondly, all commodities (in circulation) can fetch a thousand times more money as is in the world, if every piece of money were to circulate a thousand times. (The passage is quoted from the *London Weekly Dispatch*, 8 November 1857.)

Since the total sum of prices to be realized in circulation changes with the prices of the commodities and with the quantity of them thrown into circulation; and since, on the other side, the velocity of the medium of circulation is determined by circumstances independent of itself, it follows from this that the quantity of media of circulation must be capable of changing, or expanding and contracting – *contraction and expansion of circulation*.

In its role as mere medium of circulation, it can be said about money that it ceases to be a commodity (*particular* commodity), when its material is irrelevant and it meets only the needs of circulation itself, and no other direct need: gold and silver cease to be commodities as soon as they circulate as money. It can be said about it, on the other hand, that it is now *merely* a commodity (*general* commodity), the commodity in its pure form, indifferent to its natural particularity and hence indifferent to all direct needs, without natural relation to a particular need as such. The followers of the Monetary System, even partly of the protectionist system (see e.g. Ferrier, p. 2),[67] have clung only to the first aspect, while the modern economists cling to the second; e.g. Say, who says that money should be treated like a 'particular' commodity, a commodity like any other.[68] As medium of exchange, money appears in the role of necessary mediator between production and consumption. In the developed money system, one produces only in order to exchange, or, one produces only by exchanging. Strike out money, and one would thereby either be thrown back to a lower stage of production (corresponding to that of auxiliary barter), or one would proceed to a higher stage, in which exchange value would no longer be the principal aspect of the commodity, because social labour, whose representative it is, would no longer appear merely as socially mediated private labour.

The question whether money as medium of exchange is productive or not productive is solved just as easily. According to Adam Smith, money not productive.[69] Of course, Ferrier says e.g.: 'It creates values, because they would not exist without it.' One has to look not only at 'its *value* as metal, but equally its *property* as money'. A. Smith is correct, in so far as it is not the instrument of any particular branch of production; Ferrier is right too because it is an essential aspect of the mode of production resting on exchange value that product and agency of production should be posited in the character of money, and because this characteristic presupposes a money distinct from products; and because the money relation is itself a relation of production if production is looked at in its totality.

When C–M–M–C is dissected into its two moments, although the *prices* of the commodities are presupposed (and this makes the major difference), circulation splits into two acts of direct barter.

C–M: the exchange value of the commodity is expressed in another particular commodity, in the material of money, like that

67. F.-L.-A. Ferrier, *Du gouvernement considéré dans ses rapports avec le commerce*, Paris, 1805, p. 35. Ferrier (1777–1861) was a high French customs official who both operated and wrote in favour of Napoleon I's protective system.

68. Louis Say (1774–1840), brother of Jean-Baptiste Say, issued a number of economic pamphlets criticizing the latter's opinions. The reference here is to *Principales Causes de la richesse ou de la misère des peuples et des particuliers*, Paris, 1818, pp. 31–2.

69. Adam Smith, *Wealth of Nations*, Vol. II, Bk 2, pp. 270–77.

of money in the commodity; similarly with M–C. To this extent, A. Smith is right when he says that money as medium of exchange is only a more complicated kind of barter. But when we look at the whole of the process, and not at both as equivalent acts, realization of the commodity in money and of money in the commodity, then A. Smith's opponents are correct when they say that he misunderstood the nature of money and that monetary circulation suppresses barter; that money serves only to balance the accounts of the 'arithmetical division' arising from the division of labour. These 'arithmetical figures' no more need to be of gold and silver than do the measures of length. (See Solly, p. 20.)[70]

Commodities change from being *marchandises* to being *denrées*, they enter consumption; money as medium of circulation does not; at no point does it cease to be commodity, *as long as* it remains within the role of medium of circulation.

We now pass on to the third function of money, which initially results from the second form of circulation:

M–C–C–M; in which money appears not only as *medium*, nor as *measure*, but as end-in-itself, and hence steps outside circulation just like a particular commodity which ceases to circulate for the time being and changes from *marchandise* to *denrée*.

But first it must be noted that, once the quality of money as an intrinsic relation of production generally founded on exchange value is presupposed, it is possible to demonstrate that in some particular cases it does service as an instrument of production. 'The utility of gold and silver rests on this, that they replace labour.' (Lauderdale, p. 11.)[71] Without money, a mass of swaps would be necessary before one obtained the desired article in exchange. Furthermore, in each particular exchange one would have to undertake an investigation into the relative value of commodities. Money spares us the first task in its role as instrument of exchange (instrument of commerce); the second task, as measure of value and representative of all commodities (idem, loc. cit.). The opposite assertion, that money is *not* productive, amounts

70. Edward Solly, *The Present Distress in Relation to the Theory of Money*, London, 1830, p. 5.

71. James Maitland, Earl of Lauderdale (1759–1839), Whig, then Tory, politician, author of economic works attacking Smith's distinction between productive and unproductive labour. Marx refers here to the French translation of one of his books, entitled *Recherches sur la nature et l'origine de la richesse publique, et sur les moyens et les causes qui concourent à son accroissement*, Paris, 1808, p. 140.

only to saying that, apart from the functions in which it is productive, as measure, instrument of circulation and representative of value, it is *unproductive*; that its quantity is productive only in so far as it is necessary to fulfil these preconditions. That it becomes not only *unproductive*, but *faux frais de production*, the moment when more of it is employed than necessary for its productive aspect – this is a truth which holds for every other instrument of production or exchange; for the machine as well as the means of transportation. But if by this it is meant that money exchanges only real wealth which already exists, then this is false, since labour, as well, is exchanged for it and bought with it, i.e. productive activity itself, *potential* wealth.

The *third attribute* of money, in its complete development, presupposes the first two and constitutes their unity. Money, then, has an independent existence outside circulation; it has stepped outside it. As a *particular* commodity it can be transformed out of its form of money into that of luxury articles, gold and silver jewellery (as long as craftsmanship is still very simple, as e.g. in the old English period, a constant transformation of silver money into plate and vice versa. See Taylor)[72]; or, as money, it can be *accumulated* to form a *treasure*. When money in its independent existence is derived from circulation, it appears in itself as a result of circulation; by way of circulation, it closes the circle with itself. This aspect already latently contains its quality as *capital*. It is negated only as medium of exchange. Still, since it can be historically posited as measure before it appears as medium of exchange, and can appear as medium of exchange before it is posited as measure – in the latter case it would exist merely as preferred *commodity* – it can therefore also appear historically in the third function before it is posited in the two prior ones. But gold and silver can be accumulated *as money* only if they are already present in one of the other two roles, and it can appear in a developed form of the third role only if the two earlier ones are already developed. Otherwise, accumulating it is nothing more than the accumulation of gold and silver, not of money.

(As an especially interesting example, go into the *accumulation of copper money* in the earlier periods of the Roman republic.)

Since money as *universal material representative of wealth*

72. James Taylor, *A View to the Money System of England, from the Conquest; with Proposals for Establishing a Secure and Equitable Credit Currency*, London, 1828, pp. 18–19.

emerges from circulation, and is as such itself a *product of circulation*, both of exchange at a higher potentiality, and a *particular* form of exchange, it stands therefore in the third function, as well, in connection with circulation; it stands independent of circulation, but this independence is only its own process. It derives from it just as it returns to it again. Cut off from all relation to it, it would not be money, but merely a simple natural object, gold or silver. In this character it is just as much its precondition as its result. Its independence is not the end of all relatedness to circulation, but rather a *negative* relation to it. This comes from its independence as a result of M–C–C–M. In the case of money as *capital*, money itself is posited (1) as precondition of circulation as well as its result; (2) as having independence only in the form of a *negative* relation, but always a relation to circulation; (3) as itself an *instrument of production*, since circulation no longer appears in its primitive simplicity, as quantitative exchange, but as a process of production, as a real metabolism. And thus money is itself stamped as a particular moment of this process of production. Production is not only concerned with simple determination of prices, i.e. with translation of the exchange values of commodities into a common unit, but with the creation of exchange values, hence also with the creation of the *particularity* of prices. Not merely with positing the form, but also the content. Therefore, while in simple circulation, money appears generally as productive, since circulation in general is itself a moment of the system of production, nevertheless this quality still only exists *for us*, and is not yet *posited* in money. (4) As capital, money thus also appears posited as a relation to itself mediated by circulation – in the *relation* of *interest and capital*. But here we are not as yet concerned with these aspects; rather, we have to look simply at money in the third role, in the form in which it emerged as something *independent* from circulation, more properly, from both its earlier aspects.

('An increase of money only an increase in the *means of counting*.' Sismondi.[73] This correct only in so far as defined as mere medium of exchange. In the other property it is also an increase in the *means of paying*.)

'Commerce separated the shadow from the body, and introduced the possibility of owning them separately.' (Sismondi.)[74] Thus, money is now exchange value become independent (it never puts in more than a fleeting appearance as such, as *medium of exchange*)

73. Sismondi, *Études*, Vol. II, p. 278.   74. ibid., p. 300.

in its general form. It possesses, it is true, a particular body or substance, gold and silver, and precisely this gives it its independence; for what only exists as an aspect or relation of something else is not independent. On the other side, with this bodily independence, as gold and silver, it represents not only the exchange value of one commodity as against another, but rather exchange value as against all commodities; and although it possesses a substance of its own, it appears at the same time, in its particular existence as gold and silver, as the general exchange value of all commodities. On one side, it is possessed as their exchange value; they stand on the other side as only so many particular substances of exchange value, so that it can either transform itself into every one of these substances through exchange, or it can remain indifferent to them, aloof from their particularity and peculiarity. They are therefore merely accidental existences. It is the '*précis de toutes les choses*',[75] in which their particular character is erased; it is general wealth in the form of a concise compendium, as opposed to its diffusion and fragmentation in the world of commodities. While wealth in the form of the particular commodity appears as one of the moments of the same, or the commodity as one of the moments of wealth; in the form of gold and silver general wealth itself appears as concentrated in a particular substance. Every particular commodity, in so far as it is exchange value, has a price, expresses a certain quantity of money in a merely imperfect form, since it has to be thrown into circulation in order to be realized, and since it remains a matter of chance, due to its particularity, whether or not it is realized. However, in so far as it is realized not as price, but in its natural property, it is a moment of wealth by way of its relation to a particular need which it satisfies; and, in this relation, [it] expresses (1) only the wealth of uses [*Gebrauchsreichtum*], (2) only a quite particular facet of this wealth. Money, by contrast, apart from its particular usefulness as a valuable commodity, is (1) the realized price; (2) satisfies every need, in so far as it can be exchanged for the desired object of every need, regardless of any particularity. The commodity possesses this property only through the mediation of money. Money possesses it directly in relation to all commodities, hence in relation to the whole world of wealth, to wealth as such. With money, general wealth is not only a form, but at the same time the content itself. The concept of wealth, so to speak, is realized, *individualized* in a particular object.

75. 'The epitome of all things' (Boisguillebert, *Dissertation*, p. 399).

NOTEBOOK II

c. November 1857

The Chapter on Money (continuation)

(Superfluity, accumulation)

In the particular commodity, in so far as it is a price, wealth is posited only as an ideal form, not yet realized; and in so far as it has a particular use value, it represents merely a quite singular facet of wealth. In money, by contrast, the price is realized; and its substance is wealth itself considered in its totality in abstraction from its particular modes of existence. Exchange value forms the substance of money, and exchange value is wealth. Money is therefore, on another side, also the embodied form of wealth, in contrast to all the substances of which wealth consists. Thus, while on one side the form and the content of wealth are identical in money, considered for itself, on the other side, in contrast to all the other commodities, money is the general form of wealth, while the totality of these particularities form its substance. Thus, in the first role, money is wealth itself; in the other, it is the *general material representative of wealth*. This totality exists in money itself as the comprehensive representation of commodities. Thus, wealth (exchange value as totality às well as as abstraction) exists, individualized as such, to the exclusion of all other commodities, as a singular, tangible object, in gold and silver. Money is therefore the god among commodities.

Since it is an individuated, tangible object, money may be randomly searched for, found, stolen, discovered; and thus general wealth may be tangibly brought into the possession of a particular individual. From its servile role, in which it appears as mere medium of circulation, it suddenly changes into the lord and god of the world of commodities. It represents the divine existence of commodities, while they represent its earthly form. Before it is replaced by exchange value, every form of natural wealth presupposes an essential relation between the individual and the objects, in which the individual in one of his aspects objectifies [*vergegenständlicht*] himself in the thing, so that his possession of the thing appears at the same time as a certain development of his individuality: wealth in sheep, the development of the individual as shepherd, wealth in grain his development as agriculturist, etc. *Money, however, as the individual* of general wealth, as something emerging from circulation and representing a general quality, as a *merely social result*, does not at all presuppose an individual relation to its owner; possession of it is not the development of any particular essential aspect of his individuality; but rather possession of what lacks individuality, since this social [relation] exists at the same time as a sensuous, external object which can be mechanically seized, and lost in the same manner. Its relation to the individual thus appears as a purely accidental one; while this relation to a thing having no connection with his individuality gives him, at the same time, by virtue of the thing's character, a general power over society, over the whole world of gratifications, labours, etc. It is exactly as if, for example, the chance discovery of a stone gave me mastery over all the sciences, regardless of my individuality. The possession of money places me in exactly the same relationship towards wealth (social) as the philosophers' stone would towards the sciences.

Money is therefore not only *an* object, but is *the* object of greed [*Bereicherungssucht*]. It is essentially *auri sacra fames*.[1] Greed as such, as a particular form of the drive, i.e. as distinct from the craving for a particular kind of wealth, e.g. for clothes, weapons, jewels, women, wine etc., is possible only when general wealth, wealth as such, has become individualized in a particular thing, i.e. as soon as money is posited in its third quality. Money is therefore not only the object but also the fountainhead of greed. The mania for possessions is possible without money; but greed itself is the product of a definite social development, not *natural*, as opposed to *historical*. Hence the wailing of the ancients about money as the source of all evil. Hedonism [*Genussucht*] in its general form and miserliness [*Geiz*] are the two particular forms of monetary greed. Hedonism in the abstract presupposes an object which possesses all pleasures in potentiality. Abstract hedonism realizes that function of money in which it is the *material representative of wealth*; miserliness, in so far as it is only the general form of wealth as against its particular substances, the commodities. In order to maintain it as such, it must sacrifice all relationship to the objects of particular needs, must abstain, in order to satisfy the need of greed for

1. See p. 163, n. 25.

money as such. Monetary greed, or mania for wealth, necessarily brings with it the decline and fall of the ancient communities [*Gemeinwesen*]. Hence it is the antithesis to them. It is itself the community [*Gemeinwesen*],[2] and can tolerate none other standing above it. But this presupposes the full development of exchange values, hence a corresponding organization of society. In antiquity, exchange value was not the *nexus rerum*; it appears as such only among the mercantile peoples, who had, however, no more than a carrying trade and did not, themselves, produce. At least this was the case with the Phoenicians, Carthaginians, etc. But this is a peripheral matter. They could live just as well in the interstices of the ancient world, as the Jews in Poland or in the Middle Ages. Rather, this world itself was the precondition for such trading peoples. That is why they fall apart every time they come into serious conflict with the ancient communities. Only with the Romans, Greeks etc. does money appear unhampered in both of its first two functions, as measure and as medium of circulation, and not very far developed in either. But as soon as either their trade etc. develops, or, as in the case of the Romans, conquest brings them money in vast quantities – in short, suddenly, and at a certain stage of their economic development, money necessarily appears in its third role, and the further it develops in that role, the more the decay of their community advances. In order to function productively, money in its third role, as we have seen, must be not only the precondition but equally the result of circulation, and, as its precondition, also a moment of it, something posited by it. Among the Romans, who amassed money by stealing it from the whole world, this was not the case. It is inherent in the simple character of money itself that it can exist as a developed moment of production only where and when *wage labour* exists; that in this case, far from subverting the social formation, it is rather a condition for its development and a driving-wheel for the development of all forces of production, material and mental. A particular individual may even today come into money by chance, and the possession of this money can undermine him just as it undermined the communities of antiquity. But the dissolution of this individual within modern society is in itself only the enrichment of the productive section of society. The owner of money, in the ancient sense, is dissolved by the industrial process, which he serves

2. The term *Gemeinwesen* also carries the nuances 'common essence', 'common system' and 'common being'.

whether he wants and knows it or not. It is a dissolution which affects only his person. *As material representative of general wealth*, as *individualized exchange value*, money must be the *direct* object, aim and product of general labour, the labour of all individuals. Labour must directly produce exchange value, i.e. money. It must therefore be *wage labour*. Greed, as the urge of all, in so far as everyone wants to make money, is only created by general wealth. Only in this way can the general mania for money become the wellspring of general, self-reproducing wealth. When labour is wage labour, and its direct aim is money, then general wealth is *posited* as its aim and object. (*In this regard, talk about the context of the military system of antiquity when it became a mercenary system.*) Money as aim here becomes the means of general industriousness. General wealth is produced in order to seize hold of its representative. In this way the real sources of wealth are opened up. When the aim of labour is not a particular product standing in a particular relation to the particular needs of the individual, but money, wealth in its general form, then, firstly, the individual's industriousness knows no bounds; it is indifferent to its particularity, and takes on every form which serves the purpose; it is ingenious in the creation of new objects for a social need, etc. It is clear, therefore, that when wage labour is the foundation, money does not have a dissolving effect, but acts productively; whereas the ancient community as such is already in contradiction with wage labour as the general foundation. General industriousness is possible only where every act of labour produces general wealth, not a particular form of it; where therefore the individual's reward, too, is money. Otherwise, only particular forms of industry are possible. Exchange value as direct product of labour is money as direct product of labour. Direct labour which produces exchange value as such is therefore wage labour. Where money is not itself the community [*Gemeinwesen*], it must dissolve the community. In antiquity, one could buy labour, a slave, directly; but the slave could not buy money with his labour. The increase of money could make slaves more expensive, but could not make their labour more productive. *Negro slavery* – a purely industrial slavery – which is, besides, incompatible with the development of bourgeois society and disappears with it, *presupposes* wage labour, and if other, free states with wage labour did not exist alongside it, if, instead, the Negro states were isolated, then all social conditions there would immediately turn into pre-civilized forms.

Money as individualized exchange value and hence as wealth incarnate was what the alchemists sought; it figures in this role within the Monetary (Mercantilist) System. The period which precedes the development of modern industrial society opens with general greed for money on the part of individuals as well as of states. The real development of the sources of wealth takes place as it were behind their backs, as a means of gaining possession of the representatives of wealth. Wherever it does not arise out of circulation – as in Spain – but has to be discovered physically, the nation is impoverished, whereas the nations which have to work in order to get it from the Spaniards develop the sources of wealth and really become rich. This is why the search for and discovery of gold in new continents, countries, plays so great a role in the history of revaluation, because by its means colonization is improvised and made to flourish as if in a hothouse. The hunt for gold in all countries leads to its discovery; to the formation of new states; initially to the spread of commodities, which produce new needs, and draw distant continents into the metabolism of circulation, i.e. exchange. Thus, in this respect, as the general representative of wealth and as individualized exchange value, it was doubly a means for expanding the universality of wealth, and for drawing the dimensions of exchange over the whole world; for creating the true *generality* [*Allgemeinheit*] of exchange value in substance and in extension. But it is inherent in the attribute in which it here becomes developed that the illusion about its nature, i.e. the fixed insistence on one of its aspects, in the abstract, and the blindness towards the contradictions contained within it, gives it a really magical significance behind the backs of individuals. In fact, it is because of this self-contradictory and hence illusory aspect, because of this abstraction, that it becomes such an enormous instrument in the real development of the forces of social production.

It is the elementary precondition of bourgeois society that labour should directly produce exchange value, i.e. money; and, similarly, that money should directly purchase labour, and therefore the labourer, but only in so far as he alienates [*veräussert*] his activity in the exchange. *Wage labour* on one side, *capital* on the other, are therefore only other forms of developed exchange value and of money (as the incarnation of exchange value). Money thereby directly and simultaneously becomes the *real community* [*Gemeinwesen*], since it is the general substance of survival for all, and at the same time the social product of all. But as we have seen, in money the community [*Gemeinwesen*] is at the same time a mere abstraction, a mere external, accidental thing for the individual, and at the same time merely a means for his satisfaction as an isolated individual. The community of antiquity presupposes a quite different relation to, and on the part of, the individual. The development of money in its third role therefore smashes this community. All production is an objectification [*Vergegenständlichung*] of the individual. In money (exchange value), however, the individual is not objectified in his natural quality, but in a social quality (relation) which is, at the same time, external to him.

Money *posited* in the form of the medium of circulation is *coin* [*Münze*]. As coin, it has lost its use value as such; its use value is identical with its quality as medium of circulation. For example, it has to be melted down before it can serve as money as such. It has to be demonetized. That is why the coin is also only a *symbol* whose material is irrelevant. But, as coin, it also loses its universal character, and adopts a national, local one. It decomposes into coin of different kinds, according to the material of which it consists, gold, copper, silver, etc. It acquires a political title, and talks, as it were, a different language in different countries. Finally, within a single country it acquires different denominations, etc. Money in its third quality, as something which *autonomously* arises out of and stands against circulation, therefore still negates its character as coin. It reappears as gold and silver, whether it is melted down or whether it is valued only according to its gold and silver weight-content. It also loses its national character again, and serves as medium of exchange between the nations, as universal medium of exchange, no longer as a *symbol*, but rather as a definite amount of gold and silver. In the most developed international system of exchange, therefore, gold and silver reappear in exactly the same form in which they already played a role in primitive barter. Gold and silver, like exchange itself originally, appear, as already noted, not within the sphere of a social community, but where it ends, on its boundary; on the few points of its contact with alien communities. Gold (or silver) now appears posited as the *commodity* as such, the universal commodity, which obtains its character as commodity in all places. Only in this way is it the material representative of *general* wealth. In the Mercantilist System, therefore, gold and silver count as the measure of the power of the different communities. 'As soon as the precious metals become objects of commerce, an universal equivalent for everything, they also become the measure of power between nations. Hence the Mercantilist System.' (Steuart.)[3] No matter how much the modern economists imagine themselves beyond Mercantilism, in periods of general crisis gold and silver still appear in precisely this role, in 1857 as much as in 1600. In this character, gold and silver play an important role in the creation of the world market. Thus the circulation of American silver from the West to the East; the metallic band between America and Europe on one side, with Asia on the other side, since the beginning of the modern epoch. With the original communities this trade in gold and silver was only a peripheral concern, connected with excess production, like exchange as a whole. But in developed trade it is posited as a moment essentially interconnected with production etc. as a whole. It no longer appears for the purpose of exchanging the excess production but to balance it out as part of the total process of international commodity exchange. It is coin, now, only as *world coin*. But, as such, its formal character as medium of circulation is essentially irrelevant, while its material is everything. As a form, in this function, gold and silver remain the universally acceptable *commodity*, the commodity as such.

(In this first section, where exchange values, money, prices are looked at, commodities always appear as already present. The determination of forms is simple. We know that they express aspects of social production, but the latter itself is the precondition. However, they are *not posited* in this character [of being aspects of social production]. And thus, in fact, the first exchange appears as exchange of the superfluous only, and it does not seize hold of and determine the whole of production. It is the *available* overflow of an overall production which lies outside the world of exchange values. This still presents itself even on the surface of developed society as the directly available world of commodities. But by itself, it points beyond itself towards the economic relations which are posited *as relations of production*. The internal structure of production therefore forms the second section; the concentration of the whole in the state the third; the international relation the fourth; the world market the conclusion, in which production is posited as a totality together with all its moments, but within which, at the same time, all contradictions come into play. The world market then, again, forms the presupposition of the whole

3. Steuart, *An Inquiry*, Vol. I, p. 327.

as well as its substratum. Crises are then the general intimation which points beyond the presupposition, and the urge which drives towards the adoption of a new historic form.) 'The quantity of goods and the quantity of money may remain the same, and price may rise or fall notwithstanding' (namely through greater expenditure, e.g. by the moneyed capitalists, landowners, state officials etc. Malthus, X, 43).[4]

Money, as we have seen, in the form in which it independently steps outside of and against circulation, is the negation (negative unity) of its character as medium of circulation and measure.* We have developed, so far:

Firstly. Money is the negation of the medium of circulation as such, of the *coin*. But it also contains the latter at the same time as an aspect, negatively, since it can always be transformed into coin; positively, as *world coin*, but, as such, its formal character is irrelevant, and it is essentially a commodity as such, the omnipresent commodity, not determined by location. This indifference is expressed in a double way: *Firstly because* it is now money only as gold and as silver, not as *symbol*, not in the form of the coin. For that reason the *face* which the state impresses on money as coin has no value; only its metal content has value. Even in domestic commerce it has a merely temporary, local value, 'because it is no more useful to him who owns it than to him who owns the commodity to be bought'. The more domestic commerce is conditioned on all sides by foreign commerce, the more, therefore,

*In so far as money is a medium of circulation, 'the quantity of it which circulates can never be employed individually; it must always circulate'. (Storch.) The individual can employ money only by divesting himself of it, by positing it as *being for others*, in its social function. This, as Storch correctly remarks, is a reason why the material of money 'should not be indispensable to human existence', in the manner of such things as hides, salt, etc., which serve for money among some peoples. For the quantity that is in circulation is lost to consumption. Hence, firstly, metals enjoy preference over other commodities as money, and secondly, the precious metals enjoy preference over those which serve as instruments of production. It is characteristic of the economists that Storch expresses this in the following manner: the material of money should 'have direct value, but on the basis of an *artificial need*'. Artificial need is what the economist calls, firstly, the needs which arise out of the *social* existence of the individual; secondly, those which do not flow from his naked existence as a natural object. This shows the inner, desperate poverty which forms the basis of bourgeois wealth and of its science.

4. T. R. Malthus, *Principles of Political Economy*, London, 1836, p. 391.

does the value of this face vanish: it does not exist in private exchange, but appears only as tax. *Then*: in their capacity as *general* commodity, as world coin, the return of gold and silver to their point of departure, and, more generally, circulation as such, are not necessary. *Example*: Asia and Europe. Hence the wailings of the upholders of the Monetary System, that money disappears among the heathen without flowing back again. (See Misselden about 1600.)[5] The more external circulation is conditioned and enveloped by internal, the more does the world coin as such come into circulation (rotation). This higher stage is as yet no concern of ours and is not contained in the simple relation which we are considering here.

Secondly: Money is the negation of itself as mere realization of the prices of commodities, where the particular commodity always remains what is essential. It becomes, rather, the price realized in itself and, as such, the *material representative of wealth* as well as the *general form of wealth* in relation to all commodities, as merely particular substances of it; but

Thirdly: Money is also negated in the aspect in which it is merely the *measure* of exchange values. As the general form of wealth and as its material representative, it is no longer the ideal measure of other things, of exchange values. For it is itself the adequate [*adäquat*] reality of exchange value, and this it is in its metallic being. Here the character of measure has to be posited in it. It is its own unit; and the measure of its value, the measure of itself as wealth, as exchange value, is the quantity of itself which it represents. The multiple of an amount of itself which serves as unit. As measure, its amount was irrelevant; as medium of circulation, its materiality, the matter of the unit, was irrelevant: as money in this third role, the amount of itself as of a definite quantity of material is essential. If its quality as general wealth is given, then there is no difference within it, other than the quantitative. It represents a greater or lesser amount of general wealth according to whether its given unit is possessed in a greater or lesser quantity. If it is general wealth, then one is the richer the more of it one possesses, and the only important process, for the individual as well as the nation, is to pile it up [*Anhäufen*]. In keeping with this role, it was seen as that which steps outside circulation.

5. Edward Misselden (seventeenth-century Mercantilist writer, active in the Merchant Adventurers' Company, d. 1654), *Free Trade, or the Meanes to Make Trade Flourish*, London, 1622, pp. 19–24.

Now this withdrawing of money from circulation, and *storing it up*, appears as the essential object [*Gegenstand*] of the drive to wealth and as the essential process of becoming wealthy. In gold and silver, I possess general wealth in its tangible form, and the more of it I pile up, the more general wealth do I appropriate. If gold and silver represent general wealth, then, as specific quantities, they represent it only to a degree which is definite, but which is capable of indefinite expansion. This accumulation[6] of gold and silver, which presents itself as their repeated withdrawal from circulation, is at the same time the act of bringing general wealth into safety and away from circulation, in which it is constantly lost in exchange for some particular wealth which ultimately disappears in consumption.

Among all the peoples of antiquity, the piling-up of gold and silver appears at first as a priestly and royal privilege, since the god and king of commodities pertains only to gods and kings. Only they deserve to possess wealth as such. This accumulation, then, occurs on one side merely to display overabundance, i.e. wealth as an extraordinary thing, for use on Sundays only; to provide gifts for temples and their gods; to finance public works of art; finally as *security* in case of extreme necessity, to buy arms etc. Later in antiquity, this accumulation becomes political. The *state treasury*, as reserve fund, and the temple are the original banks in which this holy of holies is preserved. Heaping-up and accumulating attain their ultimate development in the modern banks, but here with a further-developed character. On the other side, among private individuals, accumulation takes place for the purpose of bringing wealth into safety from the caprices of the external world in a tangible form in which it can be *buried* etc., in short, in which it enters into a wholly *secret* relation to the individual. This, still on a large historical scale, in Asia. Repeats itself in every panic, war etc. in bourgeois society, which then falls back into barbaric conditions. Like the accumulation of gold etc. as ornament and ostentation among semi-barbarians. But a very large and constantly growing part of it withdrawn from circulation as an object of luxury in the most developed bourgeois society. (See Jacob etc.)[7] As representative of general wealth, it is precisely its

6. German: *Akkumulation*. But Marx presumably intended this word to have the sense *Anhäufung* (piling-up), as on p. 229, rather than the more technical economic sense he usually gives to the word.

7. Jacob, *An Historical Inquiry*, Vol. II, pp. 271–323.

retention without abandoning it to circulation and employing it for particular needs, which is proof of the wealth of individuals; and to the degree that money develops in its various roles, i.e. that wealth as such becomes the general measure of the worth of individuals, [there develops] the drive to display it, hence the display of gold and silver as representatives of wealth; in the same way, Herr v. Rothschild displays as his proper emblem, I think, two banknotes of £100,000 each, mounted in a frame. The barbarian display of gold etc. is only a more naïve form of this modern one, since it takes place with less regard to gold as money. Here still the simple *glitter*. There a premeditated point. The point being that it is *not* used as money; here the form antithetical to circulation is what is important.

The accumulation of all other commodities is less ancient than that of gold and silver: (1) because of their perishability. Metals as such represent the enduring, relative to the other commodities; they are also accumulated by preference because of their greater rarity and their exceptional character as the instruments of production *par excellence*. The precious metals, because not oxidized by the air, are again more durable than the other metals. What other commodities lose is their form; but this form is what gives them their exchange value, while their use value consists in overcoming this form, in consuming it. With money, on the other hand, its substance, its materiality, is itself its form, in which it represents wealth. If money appears as the general commodity in all places, so also does it in all times. It maintains itself as wealth at all times. Its specific durability. It is the treasure which neither rust nor moths eat up. All commodities are only transitory money; money is the permanent commodity. Money is the omnipresent commodity; the commodity is only local money. But accumulation is essentially a process which takes place in time. In this connection, Petty says:

'The great and ultimate effect of trade is not wealth as such, but preferably an overabundance of silver, gold and jewels, which are not *perishable*, nor as *fickle* as other commodities, but are wealth in all times and all places. A superfluity of wine, grain, poultry, meat etc. is wealth, but *hic et nunc* . . . Therefore the production of those commodities and the effects of that trade which endow a land with gold and silver are advantageous above others.' (p. 3.) 'If taxes take money from one who eats or drinks it up, and give it to one who employs it in improving the land, in fisheries, in the working of mines, in manufactures or even in clothing, then for the community there is always an advantage; for even clothes are not as perishable as meals; if in the furnishing of houses, even more; in the building of houses yet more; in the improvement of land, working·of mines, fisheries, more again; the most of all, when employed so as to bring gold and silver into the country, for these things alone *do not pass away*, but are prized at all times and in all places as wealth.' (p. 5.)[8] Thus a writer of the seventeenth century. One sees how the piling-up of gold and silver gained its true stimulus with the conception of it as the material representative and general form of wealth. The cult of money has its asceticism, its self-denial, its self-sacrifice – economy and frugality, contempt for mundane, temporal and fleeting pleasures; the chase after the *eternal* treasure. Hence the connection between English Puritanism, or also Dutch Protestantism, and money-making. A writer of the beginning of the seventeenth century (Misselden) expresses the matter quite unselfconsciously as follows:

'The natural material of commerce is the commodity, the artificial is money. Although money by nature and in time comes after the commodity, it has become, in present custom, the most important thing.' He compares this to the two sons of old Jacob: Jacob placed his right hand on the younger and his left on the older son. (p. 24.) 'We consume among us too great an excess of wines from Spain, France, the Rhine, the Levant, the Islands: raisins from Spain, currants from the Levant, cambrics from Hainault and the Netherlands, the silkenware of Italy, the sugar and tobacco of the West Indies, the spices of East India; all this is not necessary for us, but is paid for in *hard* money . . . If less of the foreign and more of the domestic product were sold, then the difference would have to come to us in the form of gold and silver, as treasure.' (loc. cit.)[9] The modern economists naturally make merry at the expense of this sort of notion in the general section of books on economics. But when one considers the anxiety involved in the doctrine of money in particular, and the feverish fear with which, in practice, the inflow and outflow of gold and silver are watched in times of crisis, then it is evident that the aspect of money which the followers of the Monetary and Mercantilist System conceived in an artless one-sidedness is still to be taken seriously, not only in the mind, but as a real economic category.

8. Petty, *Political Arithmetick*, pp. 178–9.
9. Misselden, *Free Trade*, pp. 7, 12–13.

The antithesis between the real needs of production and this supremacy of money is presented most forcibly in Boisguillebert. (See the striking passages in my Notebook.)[10]

(2) The accumulation of other commodities, their perishability apart, essentially different in two ways from the accumulation of gold and silver, which are here identical with money. First, the accumulation of other commodities does not have the character of accumulating wealth in general, but of accumulating particular wealth, and it is therefore itself a particular act of production; here simple accumulation will not do. To accumulate grain requires special stores etc. Accumulating sheep does not make one into a shepherd; to accumulate slaves or land requires relations of domination and subordination etc. All this, then, requires acts and relations distinct from simple accumulation, from increase of wealth as such. On the other hand, in order then to realize the accumulated commodity in the form of general wealth, to appropriate wealth in all its particular forms, I have to engage in trade with the particular commodity I have accumulated, I have to be a grain merchant, cattle merchant, etc. Money as the *general* representative of wealth absolves me of this.

The accumulation of gold and silver, of money, is the first historic appearance of the gathering-together of capital and the first great means thereto; but, as such, it is not yet accumulation of capital. For that, the re-entry of what has been accumulated into circulation would itself have to be posited as the moment and the means of accumulation.

Money in its final, completed character now appears in all directions as a contradiction, a contradiction which dissolves itself, drives towards its own dissolution. As the *general form of wealth*, the whole world of real riches stands opposite it. It is their pure abstraction – hence, fixated as such, a mere conceit. Where wealth as such seems to appear in an entirely material, tangible form, its existence is only in my head, it is a pure fantasy. Midas. On the other side, as *material representative of general wealth*, it is realized only by being thrown back into circulation, to disappear in exchange for the singular, particular modes of wealth. It remains in circulation, as medium of circulation; but for the accumulating

10. The notes on Boisguillebert are in an unnumbered excerpt-book compiled in June and July 1845 and printed in *MEGA*, 1/3, pp. 568–79. Marx discussed Boisguillebert's polemic against the power of money in *A Contribution to the Critique of Political Economy*, London, 1971, pp. 54–5 and 124–6.

individual, it is lost, and this disappearance is the only possible way to secure it as wealth. To dissolve the things accumulated in individual gratifications is to realize them. The money may then be again stored up by other individuals, but then the same process begins anew. I can really posit its being for myself only by giving it up as mere being for others. If I want to cling to it, it evaporates in my hand to become a mere phantom of real wealth. Further: [the notion that] to accumulate it is to increase it, [since] its own quantity is the measure of its value, turns out again to be false. If the other riches do not [also] accumulate, then it loses its value in the measure in which it is accumulated. What appears as its increase is in fact its decrease. Its independence is a mere semblance; its independence of circulation exists only in view of circulation, exists as dependence on it. It pretends to be the general commodity, but because of its natural particularity it is again a particular commodity, whose value depends both on demand and supply, and on variations in its specific costs of production. And since it is incarnated in gold and silver, it becomes one-sided in every real form; so that when the one appears as money, the other appears as particular commodity, and vice versa, and in this way each appears in both aspects. As absolutely secure wealth, entirely independent of my individuality, it is at the same time, because it is something completely external to me, the absolutely insecure, which can be separated from me by any accident. Similarly, it has entirely contradictory qualities as measure, as medium of circulation, and as money as such. Finally, in the last-mentioned character, it also contradicts itself because it must represent value as such; but represents in fact only a constant amount of fluctuating value. It therefore suspends itself as *completed* exchange value.

As mere measure it already contains its own negation as medium of circulation; as medium of circulation and measure, as money. To negate it in the last quality is therefore at the same time to negate it in the two earlier ones. If negated as the mere *general form of wealth*, it must then realize itself in the particular substances of real wealth; but in the process of proving itself really to be the *material representative* of the totality of wealth, it must at the same time preserve itself as the general form. Its very entry into circulation must be a moment of its staying at home [*Beisichbleiben*], and its staying at home must be an entry into circulation. That is to say that as realized exchange value it must be simultaneously posited as the process in which exchange value is realized. This is at the same time the negation of itself as a purely objective form, as a form of wealth external and accidental to individuals. It must appear, rather, as the production of wealth; and wealth must appear as the result of the mutual relations among individuals in production. Exchange value is now characterized, therefore, no longer simply as a thing for which circulation is only an external movement, or which appears individually in a particular material: [but rather] as relation to itself through the process of circulation. On the other side, circulation itself is no longer [qualified] merely as the simple process of exchanging commodities for money and money for commodities, merely as the mediating movement by which the prices of the various commodities are realized, are equated as exchange values, with both [commodities and money] appearing as external to circulation: the presupposed exchange value, the ultimate withdrawal of the commodity into consumption, hence the destruction of exchange value, on one side, and the withdrawal of the money, its achievement of independence *vis-à-vis* its substance, which is again another form of its destruction [on the other]. [Rather,] exchange value itself, and now no longer exchange value in general, but measured exchange value, has to appear as a presupposition posited by circulation itself, and, as posited by it, its presupposition. The process of circulation must also and equally appear as the process of the production of exchange values. It is thus, on one side, the regression of exchange value into labour, on the other side, that of money into exchange value, which is now posited, however, in a more profound character. With circulation, the determined price is presupposed, and circulation as money posits it only formally. The *determinateness* of exchange value itself, or the measure of price, must now itself appear as an act of circulation. Posited in this way, exchange value is *capital*, and circulation is posited at the same time as an act of production.

To be brought forward: In circulation, as it appears as money circulation, the simultaneity of both poles of exchange is always presupposed. But a difference of time may appear between the existence of the commodities to be exchanged. It may lie in the nature of reciprocal services that a service is performed today, but the service required in return can be performed only after a year etc. 'In the majority of contracts,' says Senior, 'only one of the contracting parties has the thing available and lends it; and if exchange is to take place, one party has to cede it immediately on the condition of receiving the equivalent only in a later period. Since, however, the value of all things changes in a given space of time, the means of payment employed is that thing whose value varies least, and which maintains a given average capacity to buy things for the longest time. Thus money becomes *the expression or the representative* of value.'[11] According to this there would be no connection at all between the latter quality of money and the former. But this is wrong. Only when money is posited as the autonomous representative of value do contracts cease to be valued e.g. in quantities of grain or in services to be performed. (The latter was current e.g. in feudalism.) It is merely a notion held by Mr Senior that money has a 'longer average capacity' to maintain its value. The fact is that it is employed as the general material of contracts (*general commodity of contracts*, says Bailey)[12] because it is the *general commodity*, the *representative of general wealth* (says Storch),[13] because it is *exchange value become independent*. Money has to be already very developed in its two earlier functions before it can appear generally in this role. Now it turns out in fact that, although the quantity of money remains uniformly the same, its value changes: that, in general, as a specific amount, it is subject to the mutability of all values. Here its nature as a particular commodity comes to the fore against its general character. To money as measure, this change is irrelevant, for 'in a changing medium, two different relations to the same thing can always be expressed, just as well as in a constant medium'.[14] As medium of circulation it is also irrelevant, since its quantity as such is set by the measure.

11. Nassau Senior, *Principes fondamentaux de l'économie politique, tirés de leçons édites et inédites,* Paris, 1836, pp. 116–17. (This is the translation by J. Arrivabene of Senior's *Outline of the Science of Political Economy,* London, 1836). Senior himself (1790–1864) was an English political economist, a member of numerous mid-nineteenth-century government commissions, Professor of Political Economy in Oxford from 1847 to 1852, and noted for his two theories, that the profit of capital is the product of the last hour of the working day, and that the accumulation of capital results from the abstinence of the capitalist from consumption.

12. Samuel Bailey (1791–1870, successful Sheffield businessman, 'coarse practical bourgeois' (Marx), and author of several economic pamphlets against Ricardo's theory of value), *Money and its Vicissitudes in Value; as They Affect National Industry and Pecuniary Contracts; with a Postscript on Joint-Stock Banks,* published anonymously, London, 1837, p. 3.

13. Storch, *Cours d'économie politique,* Vol. II, p. 135.

14. Bailey, *Money and its Vicissitudes,* pp. 9–11.

But as *money* in the form in which it appears in contracts, this is essential, just as, in general, its contradictions come to the fore in this role.

In separate sections, to be brought forward:

(1) *Money as coin.* This very summarily about coinage. (2) Historically the sources of gold and silver. Discoveries etc. The history of their production. (3) Causes of the variations in the value of the precious metals and hence of metallic money; effects of this variation on industry and the different classes. (4) *Above all:* quantity of circulation in relation to rise and fall of prices. (Sixteenth century. Nineteenth century.) Along the way, to be seen also how it is affected as measure by rising quantity etc. (5) About circulation: velocity, necessary amount, effect of circulation; more, less developed etc. (6) Solvent effect of money.

(*This to be brought forward.*) (Herein the specific economic investigations.)

(The specific gravity of gold and silver, to contain much weight in a relatively small volume, as compared with other metals, repeats itself in the world of values so that it contains much value (labour time) in relatively small volume. The labour time, exchange value realized in it, is the specific weight of the commodity. This makes the precious metals particularly suited for service in circulation (since one can carry a significant amount of value in the pocket) and for accumulation, since one can secure and stockpile a great amount of value in a small space. Gold does not turn into something else in the process, like iron, lead etc. Remains what it is.)

'If Spain had never owned the mines of Mexico and Peru, it would never have had need of the grain of Poland.' (Ravenstone.)[15]

'*Illi unum consilium habent et virtutem et potestatem suam bestiae tradent ... Et ne quis posset emere aut vendere, nisi qui habet characterem aut nomen bestiae, aut numerum nominis ejus.*' (*Apocalypse. Vulgate.*)[16] 'The correlative quantities of commodities which are given for one another, constitute the price of

15. Piercy Ravenstone, *Thoughts on the Funding System and its Effects* London, 1824, p. 20.

16. 'These have one mind, and shall give their power and strength unto the beast' (Revelation xvii, 13); 'And that no man might buy or sell, save that he had the mark, or the name of the beast, or the number of his name' (Revelation xiii, 17).

the commodity.' (Storch.) 'Price is the degree of exchangeable value.' (loc cit.)[17]

As we have seen, in simple circulation as such (exchange value in its movement), the action of the individuals on one another is, in its content, only a reciprocal, self-interested satisfaction of their needs; in its form, [it is] exchange among equals (equivalents). Property, too, is still posited here only as the appropriation of the product of labour by labour, and of the product of alien labour by one's own labour, in so far as the product of one's own labour is bought by alien labour. Property in alien labour is mediated by the equivalent of one's own labour. This form of property – quite like freedom and equality – is posited in this simple relation. In the further development of exchange value this will be transformed, and it will ultimately be shown that private property in the product of one's own labour is identical with the separation of labour and property, so that labour will create alien property and property will command alien labour.

17. Storch, *Cours d'économie politique*, Vol. I, pp. 72–3.

The Chapter on Capital[18]

'From the beginnings of civilization, men have fixed the exchange value of the products of their labour not by comparison with the *products offered in exchange*, but by comparison with a product they preferred.' (Ganilh, 13,9.)[19]

Simple exchange. Relations between exchangers. *Harmonies of equality, freedom, etc.* (*Bastiat, Proudhon*)

The special difficulty in grasping money in its fully developed character as money – a difficulty which political economy attempts to evade by forgetting now one, now another aspect, and by appealing to one aspect when confronted with another – is that a social relation, a definite relation between individuals, here appears as a metal, a stone, as a purely physical, external thing which can be found, as such, in nature, and which is indistinguishable in form from its natural existence. Gold and silver, in and of themselves, are not money. Nature does not produce money, any more than it produces a rate of exchange or a banker. In Peru and Mexico gold and silver did not serve as money, although it does appear here as jewellery, and there is a developed system of production. To be money is not a natural attribute of gold and silver, and is therefore quite unknown to the physicist, chemist etc. as such. But money is directly gold and silver. Regarded as a measure, money still predominates in its formal quality; even more so as coin, where this appears externally on its face impression; but in its third aspect, i.e. in its perfection, where to be measure and coinage appear as functions of money alone, there all formal character has vanished, or directly coincides with its metallic existence. It is not at all apparent on its face that its character of being money is merely the result of social processes; it *is* money. This is all the more difficult since its immediate use value for the living individual stands in no relation whatever to this role, and because, in general, the memory of use value, as distinct from exchange value, has

18. The first few pages of the Chapter on Capital (pp. 239–50) were entitled by Marx 'Chapter on Money as Capital'.
19. Charles Ganilh (1758–1836; French neo-Mercantilist economist, an advocate of the Napoleonic Continental System), *Des systèmes d'économie politique, de leurs inconvéniences, de leurs avantages, et de la doctrine la plus favorable aux progrès de la richesse des nations*, Paris, 1809, Vol. II, pp. 64–5.

become entirely extinguished in this incarnation of pure exchange value. Thus the fundamental contradiction contained in exchange value, and in the social mode of production corresponding to it, here emerges in all its purity. We have already criticized the attempts made to overcome this contradiction by depriving money of its metallic form, by positing it outwardly, as well, as something *posited* by society, as the expression of a social relation, whose ultimate form would be that of labour-money. It must by now have become entirely clear that this is a piece of foolishness as long as exchange value is retained as the basis, and that, moreover, the illusion that metallic money allegedly falsifies exchange arises out of total ignorance of its nature. It is equally clear, on the other side, that to the degree to which opposition against the ruling relations of production grows, and these latter themselves push ever more forcibly to cast off their old skin – to that degree, polemics are directed against metallic money or money in general, as the most striking, most contradictory and hardest phenomenon which is presented by the system in a palpable form. One or another kind of artful tinkering with money is then supposed to overcome the contradictions of which money is merely the perceptible appearance. Equally clear that some revolutionary operations can be performed with money, in so far as an attack on it seems to leave everything else as it was, and only to rectify it. Then one strikes a blow at the sack, intending the donkey. However, as long as the donkey does not feel the blows on the sack, one hits in fact only the sack and not the donkey. As soon as he feels it, one strikes the donkey and not the sack. As long as these operations are directed against money as such, they are merely an attack on consequences whose causes remain unaffected; i.e. disturbance of the productive process, whose solid basis then also has the power, by means of a more or less violent reaction, to define and to dominate these as mere passing *disturbances*.

On the other hand, it is in the character of the money relation – as far as it is developed in its purity to this point, and without regard to more highly developed relations of production – that all inherent contradictions of bourgeois society appear extinguished in money relations as conceived in a simple form; and bourgeois democracy even more than the bourgeois economists takes refuge in this aspect (the latter are at least consistent enough to regress to even simpler aspects of exchange value and exchange) in order to construct apologetics for the existing economic relations. Indeed, in so far as the commodity or labour is conceived of only as exchange value, and the relation in which the various commodities are brought into connection with one another is conceived as the exchange of these exchange values with one another, as their equation, then the individuals, the subjects between whom this process goes on, are simply and only conceived of as exchangers. As far as the formal character is concerned, there is absolutely no distinction between them, and this is the economic character, the aspect in which they stand towards one another in the exchange relation; it is the indicator of their social function or social relation towards one another. Each of the subjects is an exchanger; i.e. each has the same social relation towards the other that the other has towards him. As subjects of exchange, their relation is therefore that of *equality*. It is impossible to find any trace of distinction, not to speak of contradiction, between them; not even a difference. Furthermore, the commodities which they exchange are, as exchange values, equivalent, or at least count as such (the most that could happen would be a subjective error in the reciprocal appraisal of values, and if one individual, say, cheated the other, this would *happen not because of the nature of the social function in which they confront one another*, for this is *the same*, in this they are *equal*; but only because of natural cleverness, persuasiveness etc., in short only the purely individual superiority of one individual over another. The difference would be one of natural origin, irrelevant to the nature of the relation as such, and it may be said in anticipation of further development, the difference is even lessened and robbed of its original force by competition etc.). As regards the pure form, the economic side of this relation – the content, outside this form, here still falls entirely outside economics, or is posited as a natural content distinct from the economic, a content about which it may be said that it is still entirely separated from the economic relation because it still directly coincides with it – then only three moments emerge as formally distinct: the subjects of the relation, *the exchangers* (posited in the same character); the objects of their exchange, exchange values, *equivalents*, which not only are equal but are expressly supposed to be equal, and are posited as equal; and finally the act of exchange itself, the mediation by which the subjects are posited as exchangers, equals, and their objects as equivalents, equal. The equivalents are the objectification [*Vergegenständlichung*] of one subject for another; i.e. they themselves are of equal worth, and assert themselves in the act of exchange as equally worthy, and at the same time as mutually indifferent. The subjects in exchange exist for one another only through these equivalents, as of equal worth, and prove themselves to be such through the exchange of the objectivity in which the one exists for the other. Since they only exist for one another in exchange in this way, as equally worthy persons, possessors of equivalent things, who thereby prove their equivalence, they are, as equals, at the same time also indifferent to one another; whatever other individual distinction there may be does not concern them; they are indifferent to all their other individual peculiarities. Now, as regards the content outside the act of exchange (an act which constitutes the positing as well as the proving of the exchange values and of the subjects as exchangers), this content, which falls outside the specifically economic form, can only be: (1) The natural particularity of the commodity being exchanged. (2) The particular natural need of the exchangers, or, both together, the different use values of the commodities being exchanged. The content of the exchange, which lies altogether outside its economic character, far from endangering the social equality of individuals, rather makes their natural difference into the basis of their social equality. If individual A had the same need as individual B, and if both had realized their labour in the same object, then no relation whatever would be present between them; considering only their production, they would not be different individuals at all. Both have the need to breathe; for both the air exists as atmosphere; this brings them into no social contact; as breathing individuals they relate to one another only as natural bodies, not as persons. Only the differences between their needs and between their production gives rise to exchange and to their social equation in exchange; these natural differences are therefore the precondition of their social equality in the act of exchange, and of this relation in general, in which they relate to one another as productive. Regarded from the standpoint of the natural difference between them, individual A exists as the owner of a use value for B, and B as owner of a use value for A. In this respect, their natural difference again puts them reciprocally into the relation of equality. In this respect, however, they are not indifferent to one another, but integrate with one another, have need of one another; so that individual B, as objectified in the commodity, is a need of individual A, and vice versa; so that they stand not only in an equal, but also in a social, relation to one another. This is not all. The fact that this need on the part of one can be satisfied by the product of the other, and vice versa, and that the one is capable of producing the object of the need of the other, and that each confronts the other as owner of the object of the other's need, this proves that each of them reaches beyond his own particular need etc., as a *human being*, and that they relate to one another as human beings; that their common species-being [*Gattungswesen*] is acknowledged by all. It does not happen elsewhere – that elephants produce for tigers, or animals for other animals. For example. A hive of bees comprises at bottom only one bee, and they all produce the same thing. Further. In so far as these natural differences among individuals and among their commodities (products, labour etc. are not as yet different here, but exist only in the form of commodities, or, as Mr Bastiat prefers, following Say, *services*[20]; Bastiat fancies that, by reducing the economic character of exchange value to its natural content, commodity or service, and thereby showing himself incapable of grasping the economic relation of exchange value as such, he has progressed a great step beyond the classical economists of the English school, who are capable of grasping the relations of production in their specificity, as such, in their pure form) form the motive for the integration of these individuals, for their social interrelation as exchangers, in which they are *stipulated* for each other as, and *prove* themselves to be, equals, there enters, in addition to the quality of equality, that of *freedom*. Although individual A feels a need for the commodity of individual B, he does not appropriate it by force, nor vice versa, but rather they recognize one another reciprocally as proprietors, as persons whose will penetrates their commodities. Accordingly, the juridical moment of the Person enters here, as well as that of freedom, in so far as it is contained in the former. No one seizes hold of another's property by force. Each divests himself of his property voluntarily. But this is not all: individual A serves the need of individual B by means of the commodity *a* only in so far as and because individual B serves the need of individual A by means of the commodity *b*, and vice versa. Each serves the other in order to serve himself; each makes use of the other, reciprocally, as his means. Now both things are contained in the consciousness of the two individuals: (1) that each arrives at his end only in so far as he serves the other as means; (2) that each becomes

20. Say, *Traité d'économie politique*, Vol. II, pp. 480–82.

means for the other (being for another) [*Sein für andres*] only as end in himself (being for self) [*Sein für sich*][21]; (3) that the reciprocity in which each is at the same time means and end, and attains his end only in so far as he becomes a means, and becomes a means only in so far as he posits himself as end, that each thus posits himself as being for another, in so far as he is being for self, and the other as being for him, in so far as he is being for himself – that this reciprocity is a necessary fact, presupposed as natural precondition of exchange, but that, as such, it is irrelevant to each of the two subjects in exchange, and that this reciprocity interests him only in so far as it satisfies his interest to the exclusion of, without reference to, that of the other. That is, the common interest which appears as the motive of the act as a whole is recognized as a fact by both sides; but, as such, it is not the motive, but rather proceeds, as it were, behind the back of these self-reflected particular interests, behind the back of one individual's interest in opposition to that of the other. In this last respect, the individual can at most have the consoling awareness that the satisfaction of his antithetical individual interest is precisely the realization of the suspended antithesis, of the social, general interest. Out of the act of exchange itself, the individual, each one of them, is reflected in himself as its exclusive and dominant (determinant) subject. With that, then, the complete freedom of the individual is posited: voluntary transaction; no force on either side; positing of the self as means, or as serving, only as means, in order to posit the self as end in itself, as dominant and primary [*übergreifend*]; finally, the self-seeking interest which brings nothing of a higher order to realization; the other is also recognized and acknowledged as one who likewise realizes his self-seeking interest, so that both know that the common interest exists only in the duality, many-sidedness, and autonomous development of the exchanges between self-seeking

21. *Sein für andres* is a basic concept of Hegel's logic, described in the *Science of Logic* (p. 119 of the translation by A. V. Miller, London, 1969) as 'a negation of the simple relation of being to itself which is supposed to be determinate being'. However, it is paired, not with *Sein für sich*, but with *Sein in sich* (being in itself, described as 'something returned into itself out of the being for other'). In any case, it is difficult to detect any relation between Marx's use of *Sein für andres* and Hegel's use. The situation is different with the concept of *Sein für sich*, since Hegel described being for self in the *Lesser Logic* (p. 179 of the translation by W. Wallace, Oxford, 1892) in the following way: 'Being for self is a self-subsistent, the One', and added 'The readiest instance of being for self is found in the "I".' This comes close to Marx's 'each individual . . . as an end in himself'.

interests. The general interest is precisely the generality of self-seeking interests. Therefore, when the economic form, exchange, posits the all-sided equality of its subjects, then the content, the individual as well as the objective material which drives towards the exchange, is *freedom*. Equality and freedom are thus not only respected in exchange based on exchange values but, also, the exchange of exchange values is the productive, real basis of all *equality* and *freedom*. As pure ideas they are merely the idealized expressions of this basis; as developed in juridical, political, social relations, they are merely this basis to a higher power. And so it has been in history. Equality and freedom as developed to this extent are exactly the opposite of the freedom and equality in the world of antiquity, where developed exchange value was not their basis, but where, rather, the development of that basis destroyed them. Equality and freedom presuppose relations of production as yet unrealized in the ancient world and in the Middle Ages. Direct forced labour is the foundation of the ancient world; the community rests on this as its foundation; labour itself as a 'privilege', as still particularized, not yet generally producing exchange values, is the basis of the world of the Middle Ages. Labour is neither forced labour; nor, as in the second case, does it take place with respect to a common, higher unit (the guild).

Now, it is admittedly correct that the [relation between those] engaged in exchange, in so far as their motives are concerned, i.e. as regards natural motives falling outside the economic process, does also rest on a certain compulsion; but this is, on one side, itself only the other's indifference to my need as such, to my natural individuality, hence his equality with me and his freedom, which are at the same time the precondition of my own; on the other side, if I am determined, forced, by my needs, it is only my own nature, this totality of needs and drives, which exerts a force upon me; it is nothing alien (or, my *interest* posited in a general, reflected form). But it is, after all, precisely in this way that I exercise compulsion over the other and drive him into the exchange system.

In Roman law, the *servus* is therefore correctly defined as one who may not enter into exchange for the purpose of acquiring anything for himself (see the *Institutes*).[22] It is, consequently, equally clear that although this legal system corresponds to a social

22. *Institutes*, Bk II, Title IX, para. 3 'A slave, who is in the power of another person, can have nothing of his own' (*The Institutes of Justinian*, tr. J. B. Moyle, Oxford, 1906, p. 58).

state in which exchange was by no means developed, nevertheless, in so far as it was developed in a limited sphere, it was able to develop the *attributes of the juridical person, precisely of the individual engaged in exchange*, and thus anticipate (in its basic aspects) the legal relations of industrial society, and in particular the right which rising bourgeois society had necessarily to assert against medieval society. But the development of this right itself coincides completely with the dissolution of the Roman community.

Since money is only the realization of exchange value, and since the system of exchange values has realized itself only in a developed money system, or inversely, the money system can indeed only be the realization of this system of freedom and equality. As measure, money only gives the equivalent its specific expression, makes it into an equivalent in form, as well. A distinction of form does, it is true, arise within circulation: the two exchangers appear in the different roles of buyer and seller; exchange value appears once in its general form, in the form of money, then again in its particular form, in the natural commodity, now with a price; but, first of all, these forms alternate; circulation itself creates not a disequation, but only an equation, a suspension of the merely negated difference. The inequality is only a purely formal one. Finally, even equality now posits itself tangibly, in money as medium of circulation, where it appears now in one hand, now in another, and is·indifferent to this appearance. Each appears towards the other as an owner of money, and, as regards the process of exchange, as money itself. Thus indifference and equal worthiness are expressly contained in the form of the thing. The particular natural difference which was contained in the commodity is extinguished, and constantly becomes extinguished by circulation. A worker who buys commodities for 3s. appears to the seller in the same function, in the same equality – in the form of 3s. – as the king who does the same. All distinction between them is extinguished. The seller *qua* seller appears only as owner of a commodity of the price of 3s., so that both are completely equal; only that the 3s. exist here in the form of silver, there again in the form of sugar, etc. In the third form of money, a distinguishing quality might seem to enter between the subjects of the process. But in so far as money here appears as the material, as the general commodity of contracts, all distinction between the contracting parties is, rather, extinguished. In so far as money, the general form of wealth, becomes the object of accumulation, the subject here appears to withdraw it from circulation only to the extent that he does not withdraw commodities of an equal price from circulation. Thus, if one individual accumulates and the other does not, then none does it at the expense of the other. One enjoys real wealth, the other takes possession of wealth in its general form. If one grows impoverished and the other grows wealthier, then this is of their own free will and does not in any way arise from the economic relation, the economic connection as such, in which they are placed in relation to one another. Even inheritance and similar legal relations, which perpetuate such inequalities, do not prejudice this natural freedom and equality. If individual A's relation is not in contradiction to this system originally, then such a contradiction can surely not arise from the fact that individual B steps into the place of individual A, thus perpetuating him. This is, rather, the perpetuation of the social relation beyond one man's natural lifespan: its reinforcement against the chance influences of nature, whose effects as such would in fact be a suspension of individual freedom. Moreover, since the individual in this relation is merely the individuation of money, therefore he is, as such, just as immortal as money, and his representation by heirs is the logical extension of this role.

If this way of conceiving the matter is not advanced in its historic context, but is instead raised as a refutation of the more developed economic relations in which individuals relate to one another no longer merely as exchangers or as buyers and sellers, but in specific relations, no longer all of the same character; then it is the same as if it were asserted that there is no difference, to say nothing of antithesis and contradiction, between natural bodies, because all of them, when looked at from e.g. the point of view of their weight, have weight, and are therefore equal; or are equal because all of them occupy three dimensions. Exchange value itself is here similarly seized upon in its simple character, as the antithesis to its more developed, contradictory forms. In the course of science, it is just these abstract attributes which appear as the earliest and sparsest; they appear in part historically in this fashion, too; the more developed as the more recent. In present bourgeois society as a whole, this positing of prices and their circulation etc. appears as the surface process, beneath which, however, in the depths, entirely different processes go on, in which this apparent individual equality and liberty disappear. It is forgotten, on one side, that the *presupposition* of exchange value, as the objective basis of the whole of the system of production, already in itself implies compulsion over the individual, since his immediate product is not a product for him, but only *becomes* such in the social process, and since it *must* take on this general but nevertheless external form; and that the individual has an existence only as a producer of exchange value, hence that the whole negation of his natural existence is already implied; that he is therefore entirely determined by society; that this further pre-supposes a division of labour etc., in which the individual is already posited in relations other than that of mere *exchanger*, etc. That therefore this presupposition by no means arises either out of the individual's will or out of the immediate nature of the indi-vidual, but that it is, rather, *historical*, and posits the individual as already *determined* by society. It is forgotten, on the other side, that these higher forms, in which exchange, or the relations of produc-tion which realize themselves in it, are now posited, do not by any means stand still in this simple form where the highest distinction which occurs is a formal and hence irrelevant one. What is over-looked, finally, is that already the simple forms of exchange value and of money latently contain the opposition between labour and capital etc. Thus, what all this wisdom comes down to is the attempt to stick fast at the simplest economic relations, which, conceived by themselves, are pure abstractions; but these re-lations are, in reality, mediated by the deepest antithesis, and represent only one side, in which the full expression of the anti-theses is obscured.

What this reveals, on the other side, is the foolishness of those socialists (namely the French, who want to depict socialism as the realization of the ideals of *bourgeois* society articulated by the French revolution) who demonstrate that exchange and exchange value etc. are *originally* (in time) or *essentially* (in their adequate form) a system of universal freedom and equality, but that they have been perverted by money, capital, etc.[23] Or, also, that history has so far failed in every attempt to implement them in their true manner, but that they have now, like Proudhon, discovered e.g. the real Jacob, and intend now to supply the genuine history of these relations in place of the fake. The proper reply to them is: that exchange value or, more precisely, the money system is in fact the system of equality and freedom, and that the disturbances

23. See Marx's critique of Proudhon's doctrine of exchange value in *Poverty of Philosophy*, pp. 37–8.

which they encounter in the further development of the system are disturbances inherent in it, are merely the realization of *equality and freedom*, which prove to be inequality and unfreedom. It is just as pious as it is stupid to wish that exchange value would not develop into capital, nor labour which produces exchange value into wage labour. What divides these gentlemen from the bourgeois apologists is, on one side, their sensitivity to the contradictions included in the system; on the other, the utopian inability to grasp the necessary difference between the real and the ideal form of bourgeois society, which is the cause of their desire to undertake the superfluous business of realizing the ideal expression again, which is in fact only the inverted projection [*Lichtbild*] of this reality. And now, indeed, in opposition to these socialists there is the stale argumentation of the degenerate economics of most recent times (whose classical representative as regards insipidness, affectation of dialectics, puffy arrogance, effete, complacent platitudinousness and complete inability to grasp historic processes is *Frederick Bastiat*, because the American, Carey, at least brings out the specific American relations as against the European), *which demonstrates* that economic relations everywhere express *the same* simple determinants, and hence that they everywhere express the equality and freedom of the simple exchange of exchange values; this point entirely reduces itself to an infantile abstraction. For example, the relation between capital and interest is reduced to the exchange of exchange values. Thus, after first taking from the empirical world the fact that exchange value exists not only in this simple form but also in the essentially different form of capital, capital is then in turn reduced again to the simple concept of exchange value; and interest, which, to crown all, expresses a specific relation of capital as such, is similarly torn out of this specificity and equated with exchange value; the whole relation in its specific character is reduced to an abstraction and everything reduced to the undeveloped relation of commodity exchange. In so far as I abstract from what distinguishes a concrete from its abstract, it is of course the abstract, and does not differ from it at all. *According to this, all economic categories are only so many names for what is always the same relation, and this crude inability to grasp the real distinctions is then supposed to represent pure common sense as such. The 'economic harmonies' of Mr Bastiat amount* au fond *to the assertion that there exists only one single economic relation which takes on different names, or that any differences which occur, occur*

only in name. The reduction is not even formally scientific to the
minimal extent that everything is reduced to a real economic
relation by dropping the difference that development makes;
rather, sometimes one and sometimes another side is dropped in
order to bring out now one, now another side of the identity. For
example, the wage for labour is payment for a service done by one
individual for another. (The economic form as such is dropped
here, as noted above.) Profit is also payment for a service done by
one individual for another. Hence wages and profit are identical,
and it is, in the first place, an error of language to call one payment wages, the other profit. But let us now look at profit and
interest. With profit, the payment of the service is exposed to chance
fluctuations; with interest, it is fixed. Thus, since, with wages, payment is relatively speaking exposed to chance fluctuations, while
with profit, in contrast to labour, it is fixed, it follows that the
relation between interest and profit is the same as that between
wages and profit, which, as we have seen, is the exchange of equivalents for one another. The opponents[24] then take this twaddle
(which goes back from the economic relations where the contradiction is expressed to those where it is only latent and obscured)
literally, and demonstrate that e.g. with capital and interest there
is not a simple exchange, since capital is not replaced by an equivalent, but that the owner of capital, rather, having consumed the
equivalent 20 times over in the form of interest, still has it in the
form of capital and can exchange it for 20 more equivalents.
Hence the unedifying debate in which one side asserts that there is
no difference between developed and undeveloped exchange value,
and the other asserts that there is, unfortunately, a difference, but,
by rights, there ought not to be.

Capital. Sum of values. – Landed property and capital. –
Capital comes from circulation. Content exchange value. –
Merchant capital, money capital, and money interest. –
Circulation presupposes another process. Motion between
presupposed extremes

Money as capital is an aspect of money which goes beyond its
simple character as money. It can be regarded as a higher realiza-

24. The socialist opponents of Bastiat, in particular Proudhon. This passage
is in fact a critique of the discussion between Bastiat and Proudhon, printed
as F. Bastiat et P.-J. Proudhon, *Gratuité du crédit*, Paris, 1850, pp. 1–20, 32–47
and 285–6.

tion; as it can be said that man is a developed ape. However, in this way the lower form is posited as the primary subject, over the higher. In any case, *money as capital* is distinct from *money as money*. The new aspect is to be developed. On the other hand, *capital as money* seems to be a regression of capital to a lower form. But it is only the positing of capital in a particular form which already existed prior to it, as non-capital, and which makes up one of its presuppositions. Money recurs in all later relations; but then it does not function as mere money. If, as here, the initial task is to follow it up to its totality as money-market, then the rest of the development is presupposed and has to be brought in occasionally. Thus we give here the general character of capital before we proceed to its particularity as money.

If I state, like for example Say, that capital is a *sum of values*,[25] then I state nothing more than that *capital* = *exchange value*. Every sum of values is an exchange value, and every exchange value is a sum of values. I cannot get from exchange value to capital by means of mere addition. In the pure accumulation of money, as we have seen, the relation of capitalizing [*Kapitalisieren*] is not yet posited.

In so-called retail trade, in the daily traffic of bourgeois life as it proceeds directly between producers and consumers, in petty commerce, where the aim on one side is to exchange the commodity for money and on the other to exchange money for commodity, for the satisfaction of individual needs – in this movement, which proceeds on the surface of the bourgeois world, there and there alone does the motion of exchange values, their circulation, proceed in its pure form. A worker who buys a loaf of bread and a millionaire who does the same appear in this act only as simple buyers, just as, in respect to them, the grocer appears only as seller. All other aspects are here extinguished. The *content* of these purchases, like their *extent*, here appears as completely irrelevant compared with the formal aspect.

As in the theory the concept of value precedes that of capital, but requires for its pure development a mode of production founded on capital, so the same thing takes place in practice. The economists therefore necessarily sometimes consider capital as the creator of values, as their source, while at other times they presuppose values for the formation of capital, and portray it as itself only a sum of values in a particular function. The existence

25. Say, *Traité d'économie politique*, Vol. II, pp. 428–30 and 478–80.

of value in its purity and generality presupposes a mode of production in which the individual product has ceased to exist for the producer in general and even more for the individual worker, and where nothing exists unless it is realized through circulation. For the person who creates an infinitesimal part of a yard of cotton, the fact that this is value, exchange value, is not a formal matter. If he had not created an exchange value, money, he would have created nothing at all. This determination of value, then, presupposes a given historic stage of the mode of social production and is itself something given with that mode, hence a historic relation.

At the same time, individual moments of value-determination develop in earlier stages of the historic process of social production and appear as its result.

Hence, within the system of bourgeois society, capital follows immediately after money. *In history, other systems come before*, and they form the material basis of a less complete development of value. Just as exchange value here plays only an accompanying role to use value, it is not capital but the relation of landed property which appears as its real basis. Modern landed property, on the other hand, cannot be understood at all, because it cannot exist, without capital as its presupposition, and it indeed appears historically as a transformation of the preceding historic shape of landed property by capital so as to correspond to capital. It is, therefore, precisely in the development of landed property that the gradual victory and formation of capital can be studied, which is why Ricardo, the economist of the modern age, with great historical insight, examined the relations of capital, wage labour and ground rent within the sphere of landed property, so as to establish their specific form. The relation between the industrial capitalist and the proprietor of land appears to be a relation lying outside that of landed property. But, as a relation between the modern farmer and the landowner, it appears posited as an immanent relation of landed property itself; and the [latter],[26] as now existing merely in its relation to capital. The history of landed property, which would demonstrate the gradual transformation of the feudal landlord into the landowner, of the hereditary, semi-tributary and often unfree tenant for life into the modern farmer, and of the resident serfs, bondsmen and villeins who belonged to the property

26. The German text has here 'the other', but since the reference back is to 'landed property itself' this has been replaced with 'the latter'.

into agricultural day-labourers, would indeed be the history of the formation of modern capital. It would include within it the connection with urban capital, trade, etc. But we are dealing here with developed bourgeois society, which is already moving on its own foundation.

Capital comes initially from circulation, and, moreover, its point of departure is money. We have seen that money which enters into circulation and at the same time returns from it to itself is the last requirement, in which money suspends itself. It is at the same time the first concept of capital, and the first form in which it appears. Money has negated itself as something which merely dissolves in circulation; but it has also equally negated itself as something which takes up an independent attitude towards circulation. This negation, as a single whole, in its positive aspects, contains the first elements of capital. Money is the first form in which capital as such appears. M–C–C–M; that money is exchanged for commodity and the commodity for money; *this movement of buying in order to sell, which makes up the formal aspect of commerce, of capital as merchant capital*, is found in the earliest conditions of economic development; it is the first movement in which exchange value as such forms the content – is not only the form but also its own content. This motion can take place within peoples, or between peoples for whose production exchange value has by no means yet become the presupposition. The movement only seizes upon the surplus of their directly useful production, and proceeds only on its margin. Like the Jews within old Polish society or within medieval society in general, entire trading peoples, as in antiquity (and, later on, the Lombards), can take up this position between peoples whose mode of production is not yet determined by exchange value as the fundamental presupposition. Commercial capital is only circulating capital, and circulating capital is the first form of capital; in which it has *as yet by no means become the foundation of production*. A more developed form is *money capital* and *money interest*, usury, whose independent appearance belongs in the same way to an earlier stage. Finally, the form C–M–M–C, in which money and circulation in general appear as mere means for the *circulating commodity*, which for its part again steps outside circulation and directly satisfies a need, this is itself the presupposition of that original appearance of merchant capital. The presuppositions appear distributed among different peoples; or, within society, commercial capital as such appears only as determined by this purely consumption-directed circulation. On the other side, the *circulating commodity*, the commodity which realizes itself only by taking on the form of another commodity, which steps outside circulation and serves immediate needs, is similarly [the][27] first form of capital, which is essentially *commodity capital*.

On the other side it is equally clear that the simple movement of exchange values, such as is present in pure circulation, can never realize capital. It can lead to the withdrawal and stockpiling of money, but as soon as money steps back into circulation, it dissolves itself in a series of exchange processes with commodities which are consumed, hence it is lost as soon as its purchasing power is exhausted. Similarly, the commodity which has exchanged itself for another commodity through the medium of money steps outside circulation in order to be consumed, destroyed. But if it is given independence from circulation, as money, it then merely represents the non-substantial general form of wealth. Since equivalents are exchanged for one another, the form of wealth which is fixed as money disappears as soon as it is exchanged for the commodity; and the use value present in the commodity, as soon as it is exchanged for money. All that can happen in the simple act of exchange is that each can be lost in its role for the other as soon as it realizes itself in it. None can maintain itself in its role by going over into the other. For this reason the sophistry of the bourgeois economists, who embellish capital by reducing it in argument to pure exchange, has been countered by its inversion, the equally sophistical, but, in relation to them, legitimate demand that capital be *really* reduced to pure exchange, whereby it would disappear as a power and be destroyed, whether in the form of money or of the commodity.*

The repetition of the process from either of the points, money or commodity, is not posited within the conditions of exchange itself. The act can be repeated only until it is completed, i.e. until the amount of the exchange value is exchanged away. It cannot ignite itself anew through its own resources. *Circulation therefore does not carry within itself the principle of self-renewal. The moments of*

_____

*Just as exchange value, i.e. all relations of commodities as exchange values, appears in money to be a thing, so do all aspects of the activity which creates exchange values, labour, appear in *capital*.

_____

27. The German reads 'as', the sense seems to require 'the'.

the latter are presupposed to it, not posited by it. Commodities constantly have to be thrown into it anew from the outside, like fuel into a fire. Otherwise it flickers out in indifference. It would die out with money, as the indifferent result which, in so far as it no longer stood in any connection with commodities, prices or circulation, would have ceased to be money, to express a relation of production; only its metallic existence would be left over, while its economic existence would be destroyed. Circulation, therefore, which appears as that which is immediately present on the surface of bourgeois society, exists only in so far as it is constantly mediated. Looked at in itself, it is the mediation of presupposed extremes. But it does not posit these extremes. Thus, it has to be mediated not only in each of its moments, but as a whole of mediation, as a total process itself. Its immediate being is therefore pure semblance. *It is the phenomenon of a process taking place behind it.* It is now negated in every one of its moments: as a commodity – as money – and as a relation of the two, as simple exchange and circulation of both. While, originally, the act of social production appeared as the positing of exchange values and this, in its later development, as circulation – as completely developed reciprocal movement of exchange values – now, circulation itself returns back into the activity which posits or produces exchange values. It returns into it as into its ground.[28] It is commodities (whether in their particular form, or in the general form of money) which form the presupposition of circulation; they are the realization of a definite labour time and, as such, values; their presupposition, therefore, is both the production of commodities by labour and their production as exchange values. This is their point of departure, and through its own motion it goes back into exchange-value-creating production as its result. We have therefore reached the point of departure again, *production* which posits, creates exchange values; but this time, *production which presupposes circulation as a developed moment* and which appears as a constant process, which posits circulation and constantly returns from it into itself in order to posit it anew. The movement which creates exchange value thus appears here in a much more complex form, since it is no longer only the movement of presupposed exchange values, or the movement which posits them formally as prices, but which creates, brings them forth at the same time as presupposi-

28. Cf. Hegel, *Science of Logic* (tr. A. V. Miller), p. 71: 'That into which the movement returns as into its *ground* is (also) *result*.'

tions. Production itself is here no longer present in advance of its products, i.e. presupposed; it rather appears as simultaneously bringing forth these results; but it does not bring them forth, as in the first stage, as merely leading into circulation, but as simultaneously presupposing circulation, the developed process of circulation. (Circulation consists at bottom only of the formal process of positing exchange value, sometimes in the role of the commodity, at other times in the role of money.)

Transition from circulation to capitalist production. – Capital objectified labour etc. – Sum of values for production of values

This movement appears in different forms, not only historically, as leading towards value-producing labour, but also within the system of bourgeois production itself, i.e. production for exchange value. With semi-barbarian or completely barbarian peoples, there is at first interposition by trading peoples, or else tribes whose production is different by nature enter into contact and exchange their superfluous products. The former case is a more classical form. Let us therefore dwell on it. The exchange of the overflow is a traffic which posits exchange and exchange value. But it extends only to the overflow and plays an accessory role to production itself. But if the trading peoples who solicit exchange appear repeatedly (the Lombards, Normans etc. play this role towards nearly all European peoples), and if an ongoing commerce develops, although the producing people still engages only in so-called *passive* trade, since the impulse for the activity of positing exchange values comes from the outside and not from the inner structure of its production, then the surplus of production must no longer be something accidental, occasionally present, but must be constantly repeated; and in this way domestic production itself takes on a tendency towards circulation, towards the positing of exchange values. At first the effect is of a more physical kind. The sphere of needs is expanded; the aim is the satisfaction of the new needs, and hence greater regularity and an increase of production. The organization of domestic production itself is already modified by circulation and exchange value; but it has not yet been completely invaded by them, either over the surface or in depth. This is what is called the *civilizing influence* of external trade. The degree to which the movement towards the establishment of exchange value then attacks the whole of production depends partly on the intensity of this external influence, and partly on the degree of development attained by the elements of domestic production – division of labour etc. In England, for example, the import of Netherlands commodities in the sixteenth century and at the beginning of the seventeenth century gave to the surplus of wool which England had to provide in exchange, an essential, decisive role. In order then to produce more wool, cultivated land was transformed into sheep-walks, the system of small tenant-farmers was broken up etc., clearing of estates took place etc. Agriculture thus lost the character of labour for use value, and the exchange of its overflow lost the character of relative indifference in respect to the inner construction of production. At certain points, agriculture itself became purely determined by circulation, transformed into production for exchange value. Not only was the mode of production altered thereby, but also all the old relations of population and of production, the economic relations which corresponded to it, were dissolved. Thus, here was a circulation which presupposed a production in which only the overflow was created as exchange value; but it turned into a production which took place only in connection with circulation, a production which posited exchange values as its exclusive content.

On the other hand, in modern production, where exchange value and developed circulation are presupposed, it is prices which determine production on one side, and production which determines prices on the other.

When it is said that capital 'is accumulated (realized) labour (properly, *objectified* [*vergegenständlichte*] labour), which serves as the means for new labour (production)',[29] then this refers to the simple material of capital, without regard to the formal character without which it is not capital. This means nothing more than that capital is – an instrument of production, for, in the broadest sense, every object, including those furnished purely by nature, e.g. a stone, must first be appropriated by some sort of activity before it can function as an instrument, as means of production. According to this, capital would have existed in all forms of society, and is something altogether unhistorical. Hence every limb of the body is capital, since each of them not only has to be developed through activity, labour, but also nourished, reproduced, in order to be active as an organ. The arm, and especially the hand, are then

29. Adam Smith, *Wealth of Nations*, Vol. II, pp. 355–6.

capital. Capital would be only a new name for a thing as old as the human race, since every form of labour, including the least developed, hunting, fishing, etc., presupposes that the product of prior labour is used as means for direct, living labour. A further characteristic contained in the above definition is that the material stuff of products is entirely abstracted away, and that antecedent labour itself is regarded as its only content (matter); in the same way, abstraction is made from the particular, special purpose for which the making of this product is in its turn intended to serve as means, and merely production in general is posited as purpose. All these things only seemed a work of abstraction, which is equally valid in all social conditions and which merely leads the analysis further and formulates it more abstractly (generally) than is the usual custom. If, then, the specific form of capital is abstracted away, and only the content is emphasized, *as which it is a necessary moment of all labour, then of course nothing is easier than to demonstrate that capital is a necessary condition for all human production.* The proof of this proceeds precisely by abstraction from the specific aspects which make it the moment of a specifically developed *historic* stage of human production. The catch is that if all capital is objectified labour which serves as means for new production, it is not the case that all objectified labour which serves as means for new production is capital. *Capital is conceived as a thing, not as a relation.*

If it is said on the other hand that capital is a sum of values used for the production of values, then this means: capital is self-reproducing exchange value. But, formally, exchange value reproduces itself even in simple circulation. This explanation, it is true, does contain the form wherein exchange value is the point of departure, but the connection with the content (which, with capital, is not, as in the case of simple exchange value, *irrelevant*) is dropped. If it is said that capital is exchange value which produces profit, or at least has the intention of producing a profit, then capital is already presupposed in its explanation, for profit is a specific relation of capital to itself. Capital is not a simple relation, but a *process*, in whose various moments it is always capital. This process therefore to be developed. Already in *accumulated* labour, something has sneaked in, because, in its essential characteristic, it should be merely *objectified* labour, in which, however, a certain amount of labour is accumulated. But accumulated labour already comprises a quantity of objects in which labour is realized.

'At the beginning everyone was content, since exchange extended only to objects which had no value for each exchanger: no significance was assigned to objects other than those which were without value for each exchanger; no significance was assigned to them, and each was satisfied to receive a useful thing in exchange for a thing without utility. But after the division of labour had made every one into a merchant and society into a commercial society, no one wanted to give up his products except in return for their equivalents; it thus became necessary, in order to determine this equivalent, to know the *value* of the thing received.' (Ganilh, 12, b.)[30] This means in other words that exchange did not stand still with the formal positing of exchange values, but necessarily advanced towards the subjection of production itself to exchange value.

(1) Circulation, and exchange value deriving from circulation, the presupposition of capital

To develop the concept of capital it is necessary to begin not with labour but with value, and, precisely, with exchange value in an already developed movement of circulation. It is just as impossible to make the transition directly from labour to capital as it is to go from the different human races directly to the banker, or from nature to the steam engine. We have seen that in money, as such, exchange value has already obtained a form independent of circulation, but only a negative, transitory or, when fixated, an illusory form. It exists only in connection with circulation and as the possibility of entering into it; but it loses this character as soon as it realizes itself, and falls back on its two earlier roles, as measure of exchange value and as medium of exchange. As soon as money is posited as an exchange value which not only becomes independent of circulation, but which also maintains itself through it, then it is no longer money, for this as such does not go beyond the negative aspect, but is *capital*. That money is the first form in which exchange value proceeds to the character of capital, and that, hence, the first *form* in which capital *appears* is confused with capital itself, or is regarded as sole adequate form of capital – this is a historic fact which, far from contradicting our development, rather confirms it. The first quality of capital is, then, this: that exchange value deriving

30. The reference is to Marx's own excerpt-book; the quotation is from Ganilh, *Des systèmes d'économie politique*, Vol. II, pp. 11–12.

from circulation and presupposing circulation preserves itself within it and by means of it; does not lose itself by entering into it; that circulation is not the movement of its disappearance, but rather the movement of its real self-positing [*Sichsetzen*] as exchange value, its self-realization as exchange value.[31] It cannot be said that exchange value as such is realized in simple circulation. It is always realized only in the moment of its disappearance. If the commodity is exchanged via money for another commodity, then its value-character disappears in the moment in which it realizes itself, and it steps outside the relation, becomes irrelevant to it, merely the direct object of a need. If money is exchanged for a commodity, then even the disappearance of the form of exchange is posited; the form is posited as a merely formal mediation for the purpose of gaining possession of the natural material of the commodity. If a commodity is exchanged for money, then the form of exchange value, exchange value posited as exchange value, money, persists only as long as it stays outside exchange, withdraws from it, is hence a purely illusory realization, purely ideal in this form, in which the independence of exchange value leads a tangible existence. If, finally, money is exchanged for money – the fourth form in which circulation can be analysed, but at bottom only the third form expressed in the form of exchange – then not even a formal difference appears between the things distinguished; a distinction without a difference; not only does exchange value disappear, but also the formal movement of its disappearance. At bottom, these four specific forms of simple circulation are reducible to two, which, it is true, coincide in themselves; the distinction consists in the different placing of the emphasis, the accent; which of the two moments – money and commodity – forms the point of departure. Namely, money for the commodity: i.e. the exchange value of the commodity disappears in favour of its material content (substance); or commodity for money, i.e. its content (substance) disappears in favour of its form as exchange value. In the first case, the form of exchange value is extinguished; in the second, its substance; in both, therefore, its realization is its disappearance. Only with *capital* is exchange value posited as exchange value in such a way that it preserves itself in circulation; i.e. it neither becomes substanceless, nor constantly realizes itself in other substances or a totality of them; nor loses its specific form, but rather preserves its identity with itself in each of the different substances. It there-

31. Cf. Hegel, *Science of Logic*, pp. 106–8, 129–31.

fore always remains money and always commodity. It is in every moment both of the moments which disappear into one another in circulation. But it is this only because it itself is a constantly self-renewing circular course of exchanges. In this relation, too, its circulation is distinct from that of simple exchange values as such. Simple circulation is in fact circulation only from the standpoint of the observer, or *in itself*, not posited as such. It is not always the same exchange value – precisely because its substance is a particular commodity – which first becomes money and then a commodity again; rather, it is always different commodities, different exchange values which confront money. Circulation, the circular path, consists merely of the simple repetition or alternation of the role of commodity and money, and not of the identity of the real point of departure and the point of return. Therefore, in characterizing simple circulation as such, where money alone is the persistent moment, the term mere *money circulation, money turnover* has been applied.

'Capital values are self-perpetuating.' (Say, 14.)[32] 'Capital – permanent' ('self-multiplying' does not belong here as yet) 'value which no longer decayed; this value tears itself loose from the commodity which created it; like a metaphysical, insubstantial quality, it always remained in the possession of the same *cultivateur*' (here irrelevant; say *owner*) 'for whom it cloaked itself in different forms.' (Sismondi, VI.)[33]

The immortality which money strove to achieve by setting itself negatively against circulation, by withdrawing from it, is achieved by capital, which preserves itself precisely by abandoning itself to circulation. Capital, as exchange value existing prior to circulation, or as presupposing and preserving itself in circulation, not only is in every moment ideally both of the two moments contained in simple circulation, but alternately takes the form of the one and of the other, though no longer merely by passing out of the one into the other, as in simple circulation, but rather by being in each of these roles at the same time a relation to its opposite, i.e. containing it ideally within itself. Capital becomes commodity and money alternately; but (1) *it is itself the alternation of both these roles*; (2) it becomes commodity; but not this or the other com-

32. The reference is to Marx's own excerpt-book; the quotation is from Say, *Traité d'économie politique*, Vol. II, p. 185.

33. Sismondi, *Nouveaux Principes d'économie politique*, Paris, 1827, Vol. I, p. 89.

modity, rather a *totality of commodities*. It is not indifferent to
the substance, but to the particular form; appears in this respect as
a constant metamorphosis of this substance; in so far as it is then
posited as a particular content of exchange value, this particularity
itself is a totality of particularity; hence indifferent not to particularity as such, but to the single or individuated particularity.
The identity, the form of generality [*Allgemeinheit*], which it obtains is that of being exchange value and, as such, money. It is still
therefore posited as money, in fact it exchanges itself as commodity
for money. But posited as money, i.e. as this contradictory form of
the generality of exchange value, there is posited in it at the same
time that it must not, as in simple exchange, lose this generality,
but must rather lose the attribute antithetical to generality, or
adopt it only fleetingly; therefore it exchanges itself again for the
commodity, but as a commodity which itself, in its particularity,
expresses the generality of exchange value, and hence constantly
changes its particular form.

If we speak here of capital, this is still merely a word. The only
aspect in which capital is here posited as distinct from direct exchange value and from money is *that of exchange value which preserves and perpetuates itself in and through circulation*. We have so
far examined only one side, that of its self-preservation in and
through circulation. The other equally important side is that exchange value is *presupposed*, but no longer as simple exchange
value, such as it exists as a merely ideal quality of the commodity
before it enters into circulation, or as, rather, a merely intended
quality, since it becomes exchange value only for a vanishing
moment in circulation; nor as exchange value as it exists as a
moment in circulation, as money; it exists here, rather, as money,
as objectified exchange value, but with the addition of the relation
just described. What distinguishes the second from the first is that
it (1) exists in the form of objectivity; (2) arises out of circulation,
hence presupposes it, but at the same time proceeds from itself as
presupposition of circulation.

There are two sides in which the result of simple circulation
can be expressed:

The simply negative: The commodities thrown into circulation
have achieved their purpose; they are exchanged for one another;
each becomes an object of a need and is consumed. With that,
circulation comes to an end. Nothing remains other than money as

simple residue. As such a residue, however, it has ceased to be money, loses its characteristic form. It collapses into its material, which is left over as the inorganic ashes of the process as a whole.

The positively negative: Money is negated not as objectified, independent exchange value – not only as vanishing in circulation – but rather the *antithetical* independence, the merely abstract generality in which it has firmly settled, is negated; but

thirdly: Exchange value as the presupposition and simultaneously the result of circulation, just as it is assumed as having emerged from circulation, must emerge from it again. If this happens in a merely formal manner, it would simply become money again; if it emerges as a real commodity, as in simple circulation, then it would become a simple object of need, consumed as such, and again lose its quality as form. For this emergence to become real, it must likewise become the object of a need and, as such, be consumed, but it must be consumed by labour, and thereby reproduce itself anew.

Differently expressed: Exchange value, as regards its content, was originally an objectified amount of labour or labour time; as such it passed through circulation, in its objectification, until it became money, tangible money. It must now again posit the point of departure of circulation, which lay outside circulation, was presupposed to it, and for which circulation appeared as an external, penetrating and internally transforming movement; this point was labour; but [it must do so] now no longer as a simple equivalent or as a simple objectification of labour, but rather as objectified exchange value, now become independent, which yields itself to labour, becomes its material, only so as to renew itself and to begin circulating again by itself. And with that it is no longer a simple positing of equivalents, a preservation of its identity, as in circulation; but rather *multiplication* of itself. Exchange value posits itself as exchange value only by realizing itself; i.e. increasing its value. *Money* (as returned to itself from circulation), *as capital, has lost its rigidity, and from a tangible thing has become a process*. But at the same time, labour has changed its relation to its objectivity; it, too, has returned to itself. But the nature of the return is this, that the labour objectified in the exchange value posits living labour as a means of reproducing it, whereas, originally, exchange value appeared merely as a product of labour.

Exchange value emerging from circulation, a presupposition
of circulation, preserving and multiplying itself in it by
means of labour

⟨[34] I. (1) General concept of capital. – (2) Particularity of capital:
circulating capital, fixed capital. (Capital as the necessaries of life,
as raw material, as instrument of labour.) (3) Capital as money. II.
(1) *Quantity of capital. Accumulation.* (2) *Capital measured by itself. Profit. Interest. Value of capital*: i.e. capital as distinct from
itself as interest and profit. (3) *The circulation of capitals.* (α) Exchange of capital and capital. Exchange of capital with revenue.
Capital and *prices.* (β) *Competition of capitals.* (γ) *Concentration
of capitals.* III. Capital as credit. IV. Capital as share capital. V.
Capital as money market. VI. Capital as source of wealth. The capitalist. After capital, landed property would be dealt with. After
that, wage labour. All three presupposed, the *movement of prices*,
as circulation now defined in its inner totality. On the other side,
the three classes, as production posited in its three basic forms and
presuppositions of circulation. Then the *state*. (State and bourgeois society. – Taxes, or the existence of the unproductive classes.
– The state debt. – Population. – The state externally: colonies.
External trade. Rate of exchange. Money as international coin. –
Finally the world market. Encroachment of bourgeois society over
the state. Crises. Dissolution of the mode of production and form
of society based on exchange value. Real positing of individual
labour as social and vice versa.)⟩

Product and capital. Value and capital. Proudhon

(Nothing is more erroneous than the manner in which economists
as well as socialists regard *society* in relation to economic conditions. Proudhon, for example, replies to Bastiat by saying (XVI,
29): '*For society*, the difference between capital and product does
not exist. This difference is entirely *subjective*, and related to
individuals.'[35] Thus he calls subjective precisely what is social;
and he calls society a subjective abstraction. The difference between product and capital is exactly this, that the product expresses, as capital, a particular relation belonging to a historic
form of society. This so-called contemplation from the standpoint

34. Marx used brackets (shown here by ⟨ and ⟩) to indicate a digression.
35. Bastiat et Proudhon, *Gratuité du crédit*, p. 250.

of society means nothing more than the overlooking of the *differences* which express the *social relation* (relation of bourgeois society). Society does not consist of individuals, but expresses the sum of interrelations, the relations within which these individuals stand. As if someone were to say: Seen from the perspective of society, there are no slaves and no citizens: both are human beings. Rather, they are that outside society. To be a slave, to be a citizen, are social characteristics, relations between human beings A and B. Human being A, as such, is not a slave. He is a slave in and through society. What Mr Proudhon here says about capital and product means, for him, that from the viewpoint of society there is no difference between capitalists and workers; a difference which exists precisely only from the standpoint of society.)

(For Proudhon in his polemic against Bastiat, '*Gratuité du crédit*', everything comes down to his own wish to reduce the exchange between capital and labour to the simple exchange of commodities as exchange values, to the moments of simple circulation, i.e. he abstracts from just the specific difference on which everything depends. He says: 'At a given moment, every product becomes capital, because everything which is consumed is at a given moment consumed reproductively.' This very false, but never mind. 'What is it that makes the motion of the product suddenly transform itself into that of capital? It is the *idea of value*. That means that the product, in order to become capital, needs to have passed through an authentic evaluation, to have been bought or sold, its price debated and fixed by a sort of legal convention. E.g. leather, coming from the slaughterhouse, is the product of the butcher. Is this leather bought by the tanner? The latter then immediately carries it or carries its value into his exploitation fund [*fonds d'exploitation*]. By means of the tanner's labour, this capital becomes product again etc.'[36] Every capital is here '*a constituted value*'. Money is the '*most perfect value*',[37] constituted value to the highest power. This means, then: (1) Product becomes capital by becoming value. Or capital is just nothing more than simple value. There is no difference between them. Thus he says commodity (the natural side of the same, expressed as product) at one time, value another time, alternatively, or rather, since he presupposes the act of buying and selling, price. (2) Since money

36. ibid., pp. 177–80.
37. Constituted value is '*valeur faite*'; most perfect value is '*valeur la plus parfaite*', ibid., p. 183.

appears as the perfected form of value such as it is in simple circulation, therefore money is also the true *constituted value*.)

Capital and labour. Exchange value and use value for exchange value. – Money and its use value (labour) in this relation, capital. Self-multiplication of value is its only movement. – The phrase that no capitalist will employ his capital without drawing a gain from it. – Capital, as regards substance, objectified labour. Its antithesis, living, productive (i.e. value-preserving and value-increasing) labour. – Productive labour and labour as performance of a service. – Productive and unproductive labour. A. Smith etc. – Thief in Lauderdale's sense and productive labour

The transition from simple exchange value and its circulation to capital can also be expressed in this way: Within circulation, exchange value appears double: once as commodity, again as money. If it is in one aspect, it is not in the other. This holds for every particular commodity. But the wholeness of circulation, regarded in itself, lies in the fact that the same exchange value, exchange value as subject, posits itself once as commodity, another time as money, and that it is just this movement of positing itself in this dual character and of preserving itself in each of them as its opposite, in the commodity as money and in money as commodity. This in itself is present in simple circulation, but is not posited in it. Exchange value posited as the unity of commodity and money is *capital*, and this positing itself appears as the circulation of capital. (Which is, however, a spiral, an expanding curve, not a simple circle.)

Let us analyse first the simple aspects contained in the relation of capital and labour, in order by this means to arrive at the inner connection not only of these aspects, but also of their further development from the earlier ones.

The first presupposition is that capital stands on one side and labour on the other, both as independent forms relative to each other; both hence also alien to one another. The labour which stands opposite capital is *alien* [*fremde*] labour, and the capital which stands opposite labour is *alien* capital. The extremes which stand opposite one another are *specifically* different. In the first positing of simple exchange value, labour was structured in such a way that the product was not a direct use value for the labourer, not a direct means of subsistence. This was the general condition for the creation of an exchange value and of exchange in general. Otherwise the worker would have produced only a product – a direct use value for himself – but not an exchange value. This exchange value, however, was materialized in a product which had, as such, a use value for others, and, as such, was the object of their needs. The use value which the worker has to offer to the capitalist, which he has to offer to others in general, is not materialized in a product, does not exist apart from him at all, thus exists not really, but only in potentiality, as his capacity. It becomes a reality only when it has been solicited by capital, is set in motion, since activity without object is nothing, or, at the most, mental activity, which is not the question at issue here. As soon as it has obtained motion from capital, this use value exists as the worker's specific, productive activity; it is his vitality itself, directed toward a specific purpose and hence expressing itself in a specific form.

In the relation of capital and labour, exchange value and use value are brought into relation; the one side (capital) initially stands opposite the other side as *exchange value*,* and the other

* Is not *value* to be conceived as the unity of use value and exchange value? In and for itself, is value as such the general form, in opposition to use value and exchange value as *particular* forms of it? Does this have significance in economics? Use value presupposed even in simple exchange or barter. But here, where exchange takes place only for the reciprocal use of the commodity, the use value, i.e. the content, the natural particularity of the commodity has as such no standing as an economic form. Its form, rather, is exchange value. The content apart from this form is irrelevant; is not a content of the relation as a social relation. But does this content as such not develop into a system of needs and production? Does not use value as such enter into the form itself, as a determinant of the form itself, e.g. in the relation of capital and labour? the different forms of labour? – agriculture, industry etc. – ground rent? – effect of the seasons on raw product prices? etc. If *only* exchange value as such plays a role in economics, then how could elements later enter which relate purely to use value, such as, right away, in the case of capital as raw material etc.? How is it that the physical composition of the soil suddenly drops out of the sky in Ricardo?[38] The word *ware* [commodity] (German *Güter* [goods] perhaps as *denrée* [good] as distinct from *marchandise* [commodity]?) contains the connection. The price appears as a merely formal aspect in it. This is not in the slightest contradicted by the fact that exchange value is the predominant aspect. But of course use does not come to a halt because it is determined *only* by exchange; although of course it obtains its direction thereby. In any case, this is to be examined with exactitude in the examination of value, and not, as Ricardo does, to be entirely abstracted from, nor like the dull Say, who puffs himself up with the mere presupposition of the

38. For Ricardo's discussion of the effect of difficulties of cultivation on rent, see *On the Principles of Political Economy*, pp. 55–75.

(labour), stands opposite capital, as use value. In simple circulation, each of the commodities can alternately be regarded in one or the other role. In both cases, when it counts as commodity as such, it steps outside circulation as object of a need and falls entirely outside the economic relation. In so far as the commodity becomes fixed as exchange value – money – it tends towards the same formlessness, but as falling within the economic relation. In any case, the commodities are of interest in the exchange-value relation (simple circulation) only in so far as they have exchange value; on the other side their exchange value is of only passing interest, in that it suspends the one-sidedness – the usefulness, use value, existing only for the specific individual, hence existing *directly* for him – but not this use value itself; rather, it posits and mediates it as use value for others etc. But to the degree that exchange value as such becomes fixed in money, use value no longer confronts it as anything but abstract chaos; and, through just this separation from its substance, it collapses into itself and tends away from the sphere of simple exchange value, whose highest movement is simple circulation, and whose highest perfection is money. But within the sphere itself, the distinctness exists in fact only as a superficial difference, a purely formal distinction. Money itself in its highest fixedness is itself a commodity again, and distinguishes itself from the others only in that it expresses exchange value more *perfectly*; but, as currency, and precisely for that reason, it loses its *exchange value* as intrinsic quality, and becomes *mere* use value, although admittedly use value for determining the prices etc. of commodities. The aspects still immediately coincide

word 'utility'.[39] Above all it will and must become clear in the development of the individual sections to what extent use value exists not only as presupposed matter, outside economics and its forms, but to what extent it enters into it. Proudhon's nonsense, see the 'Misère'.[40] This much is certain: in exchange we have (in circulation) the commodity – use value – as price; that it is, apart from its price, a commodity, an object of need, goes without saying. The two aspects in no way enter into relation with each other, except in so far as the particular use value appears as the natural limit of the commodity and hence posits money, i.e. its exchange value, simultaneously as an existence apart from itself, in money, but only formally. Money itself is a commodity, has a use value for its substance.

39. Say, *Traité d'économie politique*, Vol. I, pp. 2–6.

40. The 'Misère': Proudhon's *Système des contradictions économiques, ou philosophie de la misère*. His doctrine of exchange value is put forward in Vol. I, pp. 39–50.

and just as immediately they separate. Where they relate to one another independently, *positively*, as in the case of the commodity which becomes an object of consumption, it ceases to be a moment of the economic process; where negatively, as in the case of money, it becomes *madness*; madness, however, as a moment of economics and as a determinant of the practical life of peoples.

We have seen earlier that it cannot be said that exchange value is realized in simple circulation.[41] This is so, however, because use value does not stand as such opposite exchange value, as something defined as use value by exchange value; while inversely use value as such does not stand in a connection with exchange value, but becomes a specific exchange value only because the common element of use values – labour time – is applied to it as an external yardstick. Their unity still immediately splits, and their difference still immediately coincides. It must now be posited that use value as such becomes what it becomes through exchange value, and that exchange value mediates itself through use value. In money circulation, all we had was the different forms of exchange value (price of the commodity – money) or only different use values (commodity – C), for which money, exchange value, is merely a vanishing mediation. A real connection of exchange value and use value did not take place. The commodity as such – its particularity – is for that reason an irrelevant, merely accidental, and in general imaginary content, which falls outside the relation of economic forms; or, the latter is a merely superficial form, a formal quality: the real substance lies outside its realm and stands in no relation at all to the substance as such; therefore if this formal quality as such becomes fixed in money, then it transforms itself on the sly into an irrelevant natural product, a metal, in which every trace of a connection, whether with the individual or with intercourse between individuals, is extinguished. Metal as such of course expresses no social relations; the coin form is extinguished in it as well; the last sign of life of its social significance.

Posited as a side of the relation, exchange value, which stands opposite use value itself, confronts it as money, but the money which confronts it in this way is no longer money in its character as such, but money as *capital*. The *use value* or commodity which confronts capital or the posited *exchange value* is no longer the commodity such as it appeared in opposition to money, where its specific form was as irrelevant as its content, and which appeared

41. See above, pp. 260–61.

only as a completely undefined substance. First, as use value for capital, i.e. therefore as an object in exchange with which capital does not lose its value-quality, as for example does money when it is exchanged for a particular commodity. The only utility whatsoever which an object can have for capital can be to preserve or increase it. We have already seen, in the case of money, how value, having become independent as such – or the general form of wealth – is capable of no other motion than a quantitative one; to increase itself. It is according to its concept the quintessence of all use values; but, since it is always only a definite amount of money (here, capital), its quantitative limit is in contradiction with its quality. It is therefore inherent in its nature constantly to drive beyond its own barrier. (As consumption-oriented wealth, e.g. in imperial Rome, it therefore appears as limitless waste, which logically attempts to raise consumption to an imaginary boundlessness, by gulping down salad of pearls etc.) Already for that reason, value which insists on itself as value preserves itself through increase; and it preserves itself precisely only by constantly driving beyond its quantitative barrier, which contradicts its character as form, its inner generality. Thus, growing wealthy is an end in itself. The goal-determining activity of capital can only be that of growing wealthier, i.e. of magnification, of increasing itself. A specific sum of money (and money always exists for its owner in a specific quantity, always as a specific sum of money) (this is to be developed as early as in the money chapter) can entirely suffice for a specific consumption, in which it ceases to be money. But as a representative of general wealth, it cannot do so. As a quantitatively specific sum, a limited sum, it is only a limited representative of general wealth, or representative of a limited wealth, which goes as far, and no further than, its exchange value, and is precisely measured in it. It thus does not by any means have the capacity which according to its general concept it ought to have, namely the capacity of buying all pleasures, all commodities, the totality of the material substances of wealth; it is not a '*précis de toutes les choses*'[42] etc. Fixed as wealth, as the general form of wealth, as value which counts as value, it is therefore the constant drive to go beyond its quantitative limit: an endless process. Its own animation consists exclusively in that; it *preserves* itself as a self-validated exchange value distinct from a use value only by *constantly multiplying* itself. (It is damned difficult for Messrs the

42. See p. 218, n. 75.

economists to make the theoretical transition from the self-preservation of value in capital to its multiplication; and this in its fundamental character, not only as an accident or result. See e.g. Storch, how he brings this fundamental character in with an adverb, 'properly'.[43] Admittedly, the economists try to introduce this into the relation of capital as an essential aspect, but if this is not done in the brutal form of defining capital as that which brings profit, where the increase of capital itself is already posited as a special *economic* form, profit, then it happens only surreptitiously, and very feebly, as we shall later show in a brief review of all that the economists have contributed towards determining the concept of capital. Drivel to the effect that nobody would employ his capital without drawing a gain from it [44] amounts either to the absurdity that the good capitalists will remain capitalists even *without* employing their capital; or to a very banal form of saying that gainful investment is inherent in the concept of capital. Very well. In that case it would just have to be demonstrated.) – Money as a sum of money is measured by its quantity. This measuredness contradicts its character, which must be oriented towards the measureless. Everything which has been said here about money holds even more for capital, in which money actually develops in its completed character for the first time. The only use value, i.e. usefulness, which can stand opposite capital as such is that which increases, multiplies and hence preserves it as capital.

Secondly. Capital is by definition money, but not merely money in the simple form of gold and silver, nor merely as money in opposition to circulation, but in the form of all substances – commodities. To that degree, therefore, it does not, as capital, stand in opposition to use value, but exists apart from money precisely only in use values. These, its substances themselves, are thus now transitory ones, which would have no exchange value if they had no use value; but which lose their value as use values and are dissolved by the simple metabolism of nature if they are not actually used, and which disappear even more certainly if they are actually used. In this regard, the opposite of capital cannot itself be a particular commodity, for as such it would form no opposition to capital, since the substance of capital is itself use value; it is not this commodity or that commodity, but all commodities. The communal substance of all commodities, i.e. their substance not

43. Storch, *Cours d'économie politique*, Vol. I, p. 154.
44. As in Adam Smith, *Wealth of Nations*, Vol. I, pp. 131–2.

as material stuff, as physical character, but their communal substance as *commodities* and hence *exchange values*, is this, that they
are *objectified labour*.* The only thing distinct from *objectified*
labour is *non-objectified* labour, labour which is still objectifying
itself, *labour* as subjectivity. Or, *objectified* labour, i.e. labour
which is *present in space*, can also be opposed, as *past labour*, to
labour which is *present in time*. If it is to be present in time, alive,
then it can be present only as the *living subject*, in which it exists
as capacity, as possibility; hence as *worker*. The only *use value*,
therefore, which can form the opposite pole to capital is *labour*
(*to be exact, value-creating, productive labour*. This marginal
remark is an anticipation; must first be developed, by and by.
Labour as mere performance of services for the satisfaction of
immediate needs has nothing whatever to do with capital, since
that is not capital's concern. If a capitalist hires a woodcutter to
chop wood to roast his mutton over, then not only does the woodcutter relate to the capitalist, but also the capitalist to the woodcutter, in the relation of simple exchange. The woodcutter gives
him his service, a use value, which does not increase capital;
rather, capital consumes itself in it; and the capitalist gives him
another commodity for it in the form of money. The same relation
holds for all services which workers exchange directly for the
money of other persons, and which are consumed by these persons.
This is consumption of revenue, which, as such, always falls
within simple circulation; it is not consumption of capital. Since
one of the contracting parties does not confront the other as a
capitalist, this performance of a service cannot fall under the
category of productive labour. From whore to pope, there is a
mass of such rabble. But the honest and 'working' lumpenproletariat belongs here as well; e.g. the great mob of porters etc.
who render service in seaport cities etc. He who represents money
in this relation demands the service only for its use value, which
immediately vanishes for him; but the porter demands money, and
since the party with money is concerned with the commodity and

---

*But only this economic (social) substance of use values, i.e. of their
economic character as content as distinct from their form (but this form
value, because specific amount of this *labour*), comes into question when searching for an antithesis to capital. As far as their natural differences are concerned, none of them excludes capital from entering into them and making
their bodies its own, so long as none excludes the character of exchange value
and of the commodity.

the party with the commodity, with money, it follows that they represent to one another no more than the two sides of simple circulation; goes without saying that the porter, as the party concerned with money, hence directly with the general form of wealth, tries to enrich himself at the expense of his improvised friend, thus injuring the latter's self-esteem, all the more so because he, a hard calculator, has need of the service not *qua capitalist* but as a result of his ordinary human frailty. A. Smith was *essentially* correct with his *productive* and *unproductive* labour, correct from the standpoint of bourgeois economy.[45] What the other economists advance against it is either horse-piss (for instance Storch, Senior even lousier etc.),[46] namely that every action after all acts upon something, thus confusion of the product in its natural and in its economic sense; so that the pickpocket becomes a productive worker too, since he indirectly produces books on criminal law (this reasoning at least as correct as calling a judge a productive worker because he protects *from* theft). Or the modern economists have turned themselves into such sycophants of the bourgeois that they want to demonstrate to the latter that it is productive labour when somebody picks the lice out of his hair, or strokes his tail, because for example the latter activity will make his fat head – blockhead – clearer the next day in the office. It is therefore quite correct – but also characteristic – that for the consistent economists the workers in e.g. luxury shops are productive, although the characters who consume such objects are expressly castigated as unproductive wastrels. The fact is that these workers, indeed, are productive, as far as they increase the capital of their master; unproductive as to the material result of their labour. In fact, of course, this 'productive' worker cares as much about the crappy shit he has to make as does the capitalist himself who employs him, and who also couldn't give a damn for the junk. But, looked at more precisely, it turns out in fact that the true definition of a productive worker consists in this: A person who needs and demands exactly as much as, and no more than, is required to enable him to gain the greatest possible benefit for his capitalist. All this nonsense. Digression. But return in more detail to the productive and unproductive).

45. Adam Smith, *Wealth of Nations*, Vol. II, pp. 355–85.

46. Storch's views in *Considérations*, pp. 38–50; Senior's in *Principes fondamentaux*, pp. 284–308.

The two different processes in the exchange of capital with labour.
(Here the use value of that which is exchanged for capital
belongs to the specific economic form etc.)

The *use value* which confronts capital as posited exchange value
is *labour*. Capital exchanges itself, or exists in this role, only in
connection with *not-capital*, the negation of capital, without which
it is not capital; the real *not-capital* is *labour*.

If we consider the exchange between capital and labour, then
we find that it splits into two processes which are not only formally
but also qualitatively different, and even contradictory:

(1) The worker sells his commodity, labour, which has a
use value, and, as commodity, also a *price*, like all other commodities, for a specific sum of exchange values, specific sum of money,
which capital concedes to him.

(2) The capitalist obtains labour itself, labour as value-
positing activity, as productive labour; i.e. he obtains the
productive force which maintains and multiplies capital, and
which thereby becomes the productive force, the reproductive
force of capital, a force belonging to capital itself.

The separation of these two processes is so obvious that they
can take place at different times, and need by no means coincide.
The first process can be and usually, to a certain extent, is completed before the second even begins. The completion of the
second act presupposes the completion of the product. The payment of wages cannot wait for that. We will even find it an
essential aspect of the relation, that it does not wait for that.

In simple exchange, circulation, this double process does not
take place. If commodity A is exchanged for money B, and the
latter then for the commodity C, which is destined to be consumed – the original object of the exchange, for A – then the
using-up of commodity C, its consumption, falls entirely outside
circulation; is irrelevant to the form of the relation; lies beyond
circulation itself, and is of purely physical interest, expressing no
more than the relation of the individual A in his natural quality
to an object of his individual need. What he does with commodity
C is a question which belongs outside the economic relation.
Here, by contrast, *the use value of that which is exchanged for*
money appears as a particular economic relation, and the *specific*
utilization of that which is exchanged for money forms the ultimate
aim of both processes. Therefore, this is already a distinction of

form between the exchange of capital and labour, and simple exchange – two different processes.

If we now further inquire how the exchange between capital and labour is different in content from simple exchange (circulation), then we find that this difference does not arise out of an external connection or equation; but rather that, in the totality of the latter process, the second form distinguishes itself from the first, in that this equation is itself comprised within it. The difference between the second act and the first – note that the particular process of the appropriation of labour by capital is the second act – is exactly the difference between the exchange of capital and labour, and exchange between commodities as it is mediated by money. *In the exchange between capital and labour, the first act is an exchange, falls entirely within ordinary circulation; the second is a process qualitatively different from exchange, and only by misuse* could it have been called *any sort of exchange at all.* It stands directly opposite exchange; essentially different category.

Capital and modern landed property. – Wakefield

⟨*Capital.* I. *Generality:* (1) (a) Emergence of capital out of money. (b) Capital and labour (mediating itself through *alien* labour). (c) The elements of capital, dissected according to their relation to labour (Product. Raw material. Instrument of labour.) (2) *Particularization of capital:* (a) Capital circulant, capital fixe. Turnover of capital. (3) *The singularity of capital:* Capital and profit. Capital and interest. Capital as *value*, distinct from itself as interest and profit. II. *Particularity:* (1) Accumulation of capitals. (2) Competition of capitals. (3) Concentration of capitals (quantitative distinction of capital as at same time qualitative, as *measure* of its size and influence). III. *Singularity:* (1) Capital as credit. (2) Capital as stock-capital. (3) Capital as money market. In the money market, capital is posited in its totality; there it *determines prices, gives work, regulates production,* in a word, is the *source of production*; but capital, not only as something which produces itself (positing prices materially in industry etc., developing forces of production), but at the same time as a creator of values, has to posit a value or form of wealth specifically distinct from capital. This is *ground rent.* This is the only value created by capital which is distinct from itself, from its own production. By its nature as well as historically, capital is the *creator* of modern landed property, of ground rent; just as its action therefore appears also as the dissolution of the old form of property in land. The new arises through the action of capital upon the old. Capital is this – in one regard – as creator of modern agriculture. The inner construction of modern society, or, capital in the totality of its relations, is therefore posited in the economic relations of modern landed property, which appears as a process: ground rent–capital–wage labour (the form of the circle can also be put in another way: as wage labour–capital–ground rent; but capital must always appear as the active middle). The question is now, how does the transition from landed property to wage labour come about? (The transition from wage labour to capital arises by itself, since the latter is here brought back into its active foundation.) Historically, this transition is beyond dispute. It is already given in the fact that landed property is the product of capital. We therefore always find that, wherever landed property is transformed into money rent through the reaction of capital on the older forms of landed property (the same thing takes place in another way where the modern farmer is created) and where, therefore, at the same time agriculture, driven by capital, trans- forms itself into industrial agronomy, there the cottiers, serfs, bondsmen, tenants for life, cottagers etc. become day labourers, wage labourers, i.e. that *wage labour* in its totality is initially created by the action of capital on landed property, and then, as soon as the latter has been produced as a form, by the proprietor of the land himself. This latter himself then 'clears', as Steuart says,[47] the land of its excess mouths, tears the children of the earth from the breast on which they were raised, and thus trans- forms labour on the soil itself, which appears by its nature as the direct wellspring of subsistence, into a mediated source of sub- sistence, a source purely dependent on social relations. (The reciprocal dependence has first to be produced in its pure form before it is possible to think of a real social communality [*Gemein- schaftlichkeit*]. All relations as posited by society, not as deter- mined by nature.) Only in this way is the application of science possible for the first time, and the development of the full force of production. There can therefore be no doubt that *wage labour* in its *classic form*, as something permeating the entire expanse of society, which has replaced the very earth as the ground on which

47. Steuart, *An Inquiry*, Vol. I, p. 45.

society stands, is initially created only by modern landed property, i.e. by landed property as a value created by capital itself. This is why landed property leads back to wage labour. In one regard, it is nothing more than the extension of wage labour, from the cities to the countryside, i.e. wage labour distributed over the entire surface of society. The ancient proprietor of land, if he is rich, needs no capitalist in order to become the modern proprietor of land. He needs only to transform his workers into wage workers and to produce for profit instead of for revenue. Then the modern farmer and the modern landowner are presupposed in his person. This change in the form in which he obtains his revenue or in the form in which the worker is paid is not, however, a formal distinction, but presupposes *a total restructuring of the mode of production* (agriculture) itself; it therefore presupposes conditions which rest on a certain development of industry, of trade, and of science, in short of the forces of production. Just as, in general, production resting on capital and wage labour differs from other modes of production not merely formally, but equally presupposes a total revolution and development of material production. Although capital can develop itself completely as commercial capital (only not as much quantitatively), without this transformation of landed property, it cannot do so as industrial capital. Even the development of manufactures presupposes the beginning of a dissolution of the old economic relations of landed property. On the other hand, only with the development of modern industry to a high degree does this dissolution at individual points acquire its totality and extent; but this development itself proceeds more rapidly to the degree that modern agriculture and the form of property, the economic relations corresponding to it, have developed. Thus England in this respect the model country for the other continental countries. Likewise: if the first form of industry, large-scale manufacture, already presupposes dissolution of landed property, then the latter is in turn conditioned by the subordinate development of capital in its primitive (medieval) forms which has taken place in the cities, and at the same time by the effect of the flowering of manufacture and trade in other countries (thus the influence of Holland on England in the sixteenth and the first half of the seventeenth century). These countries themselves had already undergone the process, agriculture had been sacrificed to cattle-raising, and grain was obtained from countries which were left behind, such as Poland etc., by import

(Holland again). It must be kept in mind that the new forces of production and relations of production do not develop out of *nothing*, nor drop from the sky, nor from the womb of the self-positing Idea; but from within and in antithesis to the existing development of production and the inherited, traditional relations of property. While in the completed bourgeois system every economic relation presupposes every other in its bourgeois economic form, and everything posited is thus also a presupposition, this is the case with every organic system. This organic system itself, as a totality, has its presuppositions, and its development to its totality consists precisely in subordinating all elements of society to itself, or in creating out of it the organs which it still lacks. This is historically how it becomes a totality. The process of becoming this totality forms a moment of its process, of its development. – On the other hand, if within one society the modern relations of production, i.e. capital, are developed to its totality, and this society then seizes hold of a new territory, as e.g. the colonies, then it finds, or rather its representative, the capitalist, finds, that his capital ceases to be capital without wage labour, and that one of the presuppositions of the latter is not only landed property in general, but modern landed property; landed property which, as capitalized rent, is expensive, and which, as such, excludes the direct use of the soil by individuals. Hence Wakefield's theory of colonies, followed in practice by the English government in Australia.[48] Landed property is here artificially made more expensive in order to transform the workers into wage workers, to make capital act as capital, and thus to make the new colony *productive*; to develop wealth in it, instead of using it, as in America, for the momentary deliverance of the wage labourers. Wakefield's theory is infinitely important for a correct understanding of modern landed property. – Capital, when it creates landed property, therefore goes back to the production of wage labour as its general creative basis. Capital arises out of circulation and posits labour as wage labour; takes form in this way; and, developed as a whole, it posits landed property as its precondition as well as its opposite. It turns out, however, that it has thereby

48. Edward Gibbon Wakefield (1796–1862) was an English diplomat and economist, who put forward his views on the colonies in *A View of the Art of Colonization, with Present Reference to the British Empire,* London, 1849. He proposed that the government should reserve land in the colonies and put a higher price on it than prevailed in the open market.

only created wage labour as its general presupposition. The latter must then be examined by itself. On the other hand, modern landed property itself appears most powerfully in the process of clearing the estates and the transformation of the rural labourers into wage labourers. Thus a double transition to wage labour. This on the positive side. Negatively, after capital has posited landed property and hence arrived at its double purpose: (1) industrial agriculture and thereby development of the forces of production on the land; (2) wage labour, thereby general domination of capital over the countryside; it then regards the existence of landed property itself as a merely transitional development, which is required as an action of capital on the old relations of landed property, and a *product of their decomposition*; but which, as such – once this purpose achieved – is merely a limitation on profit, not a necessary requirement for production. It thus endeavours to dissolve landed property as private property and to transfer it to the state. This the negative side. Thus to transform the entire domestic society into capitalists and wage labourers. When capital has reached this point, then wage labour itself reaches the point where, on one side, it endeavours to remove the landowner as an excrescence, to simplify the relation, to lessen the burden of taxes etc., in the same form as the bourgeois; on the other hand, in order to escape wage labour and to become an independent producer – for immediate consumption – it demands the breaking-up of large landed property. Landed property is thus negated from two sides; the negation from the side of capital is only a change of form, towards its undivided rule. (Ground rent as the universal state rent (state tax), so that bourgeois society reproduces the medieval system in a new way, but as the latter's total negation.) The negation from the side of wage labour is only concealed negation of capital, hence of itself as well. It must now be regarded as independent in respect to capital. Thus the transition double: (1) *Positive transition* from modern landed property, or from capital through the mediation of modern landed property, to general wage labour; (2) *negative transition:* negation of landed property by capital, i.e. thus negation of autonomous value by capital, i.e. precisely negation of capital by itself. But its negation is *wage labour*. Then negation of landed property and, through its mediation, of capital, on the part of wage labour, i.e. on the part of wage labour which wants to posit itself as independent.⟩

⟨The *market*, which appears as an abstract quality at the

beginning of economics, takes on total shapes. First, the *money market*. This includes the discount market; in general, the loan market; hence money trade, bullion market. As *money-lending market* it appears in the banks, for instance the discount at which they discount: loan market, billbrokers etc.; but then also as the market in all *interest-bearing bills*: state funds and the share market. The latter separate off into larger groups (first the *shares of money institutions* themselves; bank shares; joint-stock bank shares; *shares* in the means of communication (*railway shares* the most important; *canal* shares; steam navigation shares, telegraph shares, omnibus shares); *shares of general industrial enterprises* (*mining shares* the chief ones). Then in the supply of common elements (*gas* shares, water-supply shares). *Miscellaneous* shares of a thousand kinds. For the *storage of commodities* (dock shares etc.). *Miscellaneous* in infinite variety, such as enterprises in industry or trading companies founded on shares. Finally, as security for the whole, *insurance shares* of all kinds.) Now, just as the market by and large is divided into home market and foreign market, so the internal market itself again divides into the market of home shares, national funds etc. and foreign funds, foreign shares etc. This development actually belongs properly under the world market, which is not only the internal market in relation to all foreign markets existing outside it, but at the same time the internal market of all foreign markets as, in turn, components of the home market. *The concentration of the money market* in a chief location within a country, while the other markets are more distributed according to the division of labour; although here, too, great concentration in the capital city, if the latter is at the same time a port of export. – The various markets other than the money market are, firstly, as different as are products and branches of production themselves. The chief markets in these various products arise in centres which are such either in respect of import or export, or because they are either themselves centres of a given production, or are the direct supply points of such centres. But these markets proceed from this simple difference to a more or less organic separation into large groups, which themselves necessarily divide up according to the basic elements of capital itself: product market and raw-material market. The instrument of production as such does not form a separate market; it exists as such chiefly, first, in the raw materials themselves which are sold as means of production; then, however, in particular in the metals, since these exclude all thought of direct consumption, and then the products, such as coal, oil, chemicals, which are destined to disappear as auxiliary means of production. Likewise dyes, wood, drugs etc. Hence:

I. *Products.* (1) *Grain market* with its various subdivisions. E.g. seed market: rice, sago, potatoes etc. This very important economically; at the same time market for production and for direct consumption. (2) *Colonial-produce market.* Coffee, tea, cocoa, sugar; spices (pepper, tobacco, pimento, cinnamon, cassia lignea, cloves, ginger, mace, nutmegs, etc.). (3) *Fruits.* Almonds, currants, figs, plums, prunes, raisins, oranges, lemons etc. *Molasses* (for production etc.). (4) *Provisions.* Butter; cheese; bacon; hams; lard; pork; beef (smoked), fish etc. (5) *Spirits.* Wine, rum, beer etc. II. *Raw Materials.* (1) *Raw materials for mechanical industry.* Flax; hemp; cotton; silk; wool; hides; leather; gutta-percha etc. (2) *Raw materials for chemical industry.* Potash, saltpetre; turpentine; nitrate of soda etc. III. *Raw materials which at the same time instruments of production. Metals* (copper, iron, tin, zinc, lead, steel etc.), *wood.* Lumber. Timber. Dye-woods. Specialized wood for shipbuilding etc. *Accessory means of production and raw materials.* Drugs and dyes. (Cochineal, indigo etc. Tar. Tallow. Oil. Coals etc.) Of course, every product must go to market, but really great markets, as distinct from retail trade, are formed only by the great consumption goods (economically important are only the grain market, the tea, the sugar, the coffee market (wine market to some extent, and market in spirits generally), or those which are raw materials of industry: wool, silk, wood, metal market etc.) To be seen at what point the abstract category of the market has to be brought in.⟩

Exchange between capital and labour. Piecework wages. –
Value of labour power. – Share of the wage labourer in general
wealth determined only quantitatively. – The worker's equivalent,
money. Thus confronts capital as equal. – But aim of his
exchange satisfaction of his need. Money for him only
medium of circulation. – *Savings, self-denial as means of the*
worker's enrichment. – Valuelessness and devaluation of the
worker a condition of capital

The exchange between the worker and the capitalist is a simple exchange; each obtains an equivalent; the one obtains money,

the other a commodity whose *price* is exactly equal to the money
paid for it; what the capitalist obtains from this simple exchange
is a use value: disposition over alien labour. From the worker's
side – and service is the exchange in which he appears as seller –
it is evident that the use which the buyer makes of the purchased
commodity is as irrelevant to the specific form of the relation here
as it is in the case of any other commodity, of any other use value.
What the worker sells is the disposition over his labour, which
is a specific one, specific skill etc.

What the capitalist does with his labour is completely irrelevant,
although of course he can use it only in accord with its specific
characteristics, and his disposition is restricted to a *specific*
labour and is *restricted in time* (so much labour time). The piecework system of payment, it is true, introduces the semblance that
the worker obtains a specified share of the product. But this is
only another form of measuring time (instead of saying, you will
work for 12 hours, what is said is, you get so much per piece;
i.e. we measure the time you have worked by the number of
products); it is here, in the examination of the general relation,
altogether beside the point. If the capitalist were to content himself with merely the capacity of disposing, without actually
making the worker work, e.g. in order to have his labour as a
reserve, or to deprive his competitor of this capacity of disposing
(like e.g. theatre directors who buy singers for a season not in
order to have them sing, but so that they do not sing in a competitor's theatre), then the exchange has taken place in full. True,
the worker receives money, hence exchange value, the general
form of wealth, in one or another quantity; and the more or less
he receives, the greater or the lesser is the share in the general
wealth he thus obtains. How this more or less is determined, how
the quantity of money he receives is measured, is of so little
relevance to the general relation that it cannot be developed
out of the latter. In general terms, the exchange value of his
commodity cannot be determined by the manner in which its
buyer uses it, but only by the amount of objectified labour contained in it; hence, here, by the amount of labour required to
reproduce the worker himself. For the use value which he offers
exists only as an ability, a capacity [*Vermögen*] of his bodily
existence; has no existence apart from that. The labour objectified
in that use value is the objectified labour necessary bodily to
maintain not only the general substance in which his labour

power exists, i.e. the worker himself, but also that required to modify this general substance so as to develop its particular capacity. This, in general terms, is the measure of the amount of value, the sum of money, which he obtains in exchange. The further development, where wages are measured, like all other commodities, by the labour time necessary to produce the worker as such, is not yet to the point here. Within circulation, if I exchange a commodity for money, buy a commodity for it and satisfy my need, then the act is at an end. Thus it is with the worker. But he has the possibility of beginning it again from the beginning, because his life is the source in which his own use value constantly rekindles itself up to a certain time, when it is worn out, and constantly confronts capital again in order to begin the same exchange anew. Like every individual subject within circulation, the worker is the owner of a use value; he exchanges this for money, for the general form of wealth, but only in order to exchange this again for commodities, considered as the objects of his immediate consumption, as the means of satisfying his needs. Since he exchanges his use value for the general form of wealth, he becomes co-participant in general wealth up to the limit of his equivalent – a quantitative limit which, of course, turns into a qualitative one, as in every exchange. But he is neither bound to particular objects, nor to a particular manner of satisfaction. The sphere of his consumption is not qualitatively restricted, only quantitatively. This distinguishes him from the slave, serf etc. Consumption certainly reacts on production itself; but this reaction concerns the worker in his exchange as little as it does any other seller of a commodity; rather, as regards mere circulation – and we have as yet no other developed relation before us – it falls outside the economic relation. This much, however, can even now be mentioned in passing, namely that the relative restriction on the sphere of the workers' consumption (which is only quantitative, not qualitative, or rather, only qualitative as posited through the quantitative) gives them as consumers (in the further development of capital the relation between consumption and production must, in general, be more closely examined) an entirely different importance as agents of production from that which they possessed e.g. in antiquity or in the Middle Ages, or now possess in Asia. But, as noted, this does not belong here yet. Similarly, because the worker receives the equivalent in the form of money, the form of general wealth, he is in this exchange an equal *vis-à-vis* the capitalist, like every other party in exchange; at least, so he *seems*. In fact this equality is already disturbed because the worker's relation to the capitalist as a use value, in the form specifically distinct from exchange value, in opposition to value posited as value, is a presupposition of this seemingly simple exchange; because, thus, he already stands in an economically different relation – outside that of exchange, in which the nature of the use value, the particular use value of the commodity is, as such, irrelevant. This semblance exists, nevertheless, as an illusion on his part and to a certain degree on the other side, and thus essentially modifies his relation by comparison to that of workers in other social modes of production. But what is essential is that the purpose of the exchange for him is the satisfaction of his need. The object of his exchange is a direct object of need, not exchange value as such. He does obtain money, it is true, but only in its role as coin; i.e. only as a self-suspending and vanishing mediation. What he obtains from the exchange is therefore not exchange value, not wealth, but a means of subsistence, objects for the preservation of his life, the satisfaction of his needs in general, physical, social etc. It is a specific equivalent in means of subsistence, in objectified labour, measured by the cost of production of his labour. What he gives up is his power to dispose of the latter. On the other side, it is true that even within simple circulation the coin may grow into money, and that in so far as he receives coin in exchange, he can therefore transform it into money by stockpiling it, etc., withdrawing it from circulation; fixes it as general form of wealth, instead of as vanishing medium of exchange. In this respect it could thus be said that, in the exchange between capital and labour, the worker's object – hence, for him, the product of the exchange – is not the means of subsistence, but wealth; not a particular use value, but rather exchange value as such. Accordingly the worker could make exchange value into his own *product* only in the same way in which wealth in general can *appear* solely as *product of simple circulation* in which equivalents are exchanged, namely by sacrificing substantial satisfaction to obtain the *form* of wealth, i.e. through *self-denial*, saving, cutting corners in his consumption so as to withdraw less from circulation than he puts *goods* into it. This is the only possible form of enriching oneself which is posited by circulation itself. Self-denial could then also appear in the more active form, which is not posited in simple circulation, of denying himself more and more rest, and in general denying himself any existence other than his existence as worker, and being as far as possible a worker only; hence more frequently renewing the act of exchange, or extending it quantitatively, hence through *industriousness*.[49] Hence still today the demand for industriousness and also for *saving, self-denial*, is made not upon the capitalists but on the workers, and namely by the capitalists. Society today makes the paradoxical demand that he for whom the object of exchange is subsistence should deny himself, not he for whom it is wealth. The illusion that the capitalists in fact practised 'self-denial'[50] – and became capitalists thereby – a demand and a notion which only made any sense at all in the early period when capital was emerging from feudal etc. relations – has been abandoned by all modern economists of sound judgement. The workers are supposed to save, and much bustle is made with savings banks etc. (As regards the latter, even the economists admit that their proper purpose is not wealth, either, but merely a more purposeful distribution of expenditure, so that in their old age, or in case of illness, crises etc., they do not become a burden on the poorhouses, on the state, or on the proceeds of begging (in a word, so that they become a burden on the working class itself and not on the capitalists, vegetating out of the latter's pockets), i.e. so that they save for the capitalists; and reduce the costs of production for them.) Still, no economist will deny that if the workers *generally*, that is, as *workers* (what the individual worker does or can do, as distinct from his genus, can only exist just as *exception*, not as *rule*, because it is not inherent in the character of the relation itself), that is, if they acted according to this demand as a *rule* (apart from the damage they would do to general consumption – the loss would be enormous – and hence also to production, thus also to the amount and volume of the exchanges which they could make with capital, hence to themselves as workers) then the worker would be employing means which absolutely contradict their purpose, and which would directly degrade him to the level of the Irish, the level of wage labour where the most animal minimum of needs and subsistence appears to him as the sole object and purpose of his exchange with capital. If he

49. Cf. Adam Smith, *Wealth of Nations*, Vol. I, pp. 104–5.
50. A reference to the abstinence theory advanced by Nassau Senior (*Principes fondamentaux*, pp. 307–8).

adopted wealth as his purpose, instead of making his purpose use value, he would then, therefore, not only come to no riches, but would moreover lose use value in the bargain. For, as a rule, the maximum of industriousness, of labour, and the minimum of consumption – and this is the maximum of his self-denial and of his moneymaking – could lead to nothing else than that he would receive for his maximum of labour a minimum of wages. By his exertions he would only have diminished the general *level* of the production costs of his own labour and therefore its general price. Only as an exception does the worker succeed through will power, physical strength and endurance, greed etc., in transforming his coin into money, as an exception from his class and from the general conditions of his existence. If all or the majority are too industrious (to the degree that industriousness in modern industry is in fact left to their own personal choice, which is not the case in the most important and most developed branches of production), then they increase not the value of their commodity, but only its quantity; that is, the demands which would be placed on it as use value. If they all save, then a general reduction of wages will bring them back to earth again; for general savings would show the capitalist that their wages are in general too high, that they receive more than its equivalent for their commodity, the capacity of disposing of their own labour; since it is precisely the essence of simple exchange – and they stand in this relation towards him – that no one throws more into circulation than he withdraws; but also that no one can withdraw more than he has thrown in. An individual worker can be *industrious* above the average, more than he has to be in order to live as a worker, only because another lies below the average, is lazier; he can save only because and if another wastes. The most he can achieve on the average with his self-denial is to be able better to endure the fluctuations of prices – high and low, their cycle – that is, he can only distribute his consumption better, but never attain wealth. And that is actually what the capitalists demand. The workers should save enough at the times when business is good to be able more or less to live in the bad times, to endure short time or the lowering of wages. (The wage would then fall even lower.) That is, the demand that they should always hold to a minimum of life's pleasures and make crises easier to bear for the capitalists etc. Maintain themselves as pure labouring machines and as far as possible pay their own wear and tear. Quite apart from the sheer brutalization to which this would lead – and such a brutalization itself would make it impossible even to strive for wealth in general form, as money, stockpiled money – (and the worker's participation in the higher, even cultural satisfactions, the agitation for his own interests, newspaper subscriptions, attending lectures, educating his children, developing his taste etc., his only share of civilization which distinguishes him from the slave, is economically only possible by widening the sphere of his pleasures at the times when business is good, where saving is to a certain degree possible), [apart from this,] he would, if he saved his money in a properly ascetic manner and thus heaped up premiums for the lumpenproletariat, pickpockets etc., who would increase in proportion with the demand, he could conserve savings – if they surpass the piggy-bank amounts of the official savings banks, which pay him a minimum of interest, so that the capitalists can strike high interest rates out of his savings, or the state eats them up, thereby merely increasing the power of his enemies and his own dependence – conserve his savings and make them fruitful only by putting them into banks etc., so that, afterwards, in times of crisis he loses his deposits, after having in times of prosperity foregone all life's pleasures in order to increase the power of capital; thus has saved in every way *for* capital, not for himself.

Incidentally – in so far as the whole thing is not a hypocritical phrase of bourgeois 'philanthropy', which consists in fobbing the worker off with 'pious wishes' – each capitalist does demand that his workers should save, but only *his own*, because they stand towards him as workers; but by no means the remaining *world of workers*, for these stand towards him as consumers. In spite of all 'pious' speeches he therefore searches for means to spur them on to consumption, to give his wares new charms, to inspire them with new needs by constant chatter etc. It is precisely this side of the relation of capital and labour which is an essential civilizing moment, and on which the historic justification, but also the contemporary power of capital rests. (This relation between production and consumption to be developed only under capital and profit etc.) (Or, then again, under accumulation and competition of capitals.) These are nevertheless all exoteric observations, relevant here only in so far as they show the demands of hypocritical bourgeois philanthropy to be self-contradictory and thus to prove precisely what they were supposed to refute, namely that in the exchange between the worker and capital, the worker finds himself in the relation of simple circulation, hence obtains not wealth but only subsistence, use values for immediate consumption. That this demand contradicts the relation itself emerges from the simple reflection (the recently and complacently advanced demand that the workers should be given a certain share in profits[51] is to be dealt with in the section *wage labour*; other than as a *special bonus* which can achieve its purpose only as an exception from the rule, and which is in fact, in noteworthy practice, restricted to the buying-up of individual overlookers etc. in the interests of the employer *against* the interests of their class; or to travelling salesmen etc., in short, no longer *simple workers*, hence also not to the simple relation; or else it is a special way of cheating the workers and of *deducting a part of their wages* in the more precarious form of a profit depending on the state of the business) that, if the worker's savings are not to remain merely the product of circulation – saved up money, which can be realized only by being converted sooner or later into the substantial content of wealth, pleasures etc. – then the saved-up money would itself have to become capital, i.e. buy labour, relate to labour as use value. It thus presupposes labour which is not capital, and presupposes that labour has become its opposite – not-labour. In order to become capital, it itself presupposes labour as not-capital as against capital; hence it presupposes the establishment at another point of the contradiction it is supposed to overcome. If, then, in the original relation itself, the object and the *product* of the worker's exchange – as product of mere exchange, it can be no other – were not use value, subsistence, satisfaction of direct needs, withdrawal from circulation of the equivalent put into it in order to be destroyed by consumption – then labour would confront capital not as labour, not as not-capital, but as capital. But capital, too, cannot confront capital if capital does not confront labour, since capital is only capital as not-labour; in this contradictory relation. Thus the concept and the relation of capital itself would be destroyed. That there are situations in which property-owners who themselves work engage in exchange with one another is certainly not denied. But such conditions are not those of the society in which capital as such exists in developed form; they are destroyed at all points, therefore, by its development. As capital it can posit itself only by positing labour as not-capital, as pure use value. (As a slave, the

51. As in Charles Babbage, *Traité sur l'économie des machines et des manufactures*. Traduit de l'anglais sur la troisième édition, Paris, 1833, pp. 329–51.

worker has *exchange value*, a *value*; as a free wage-worker he has *no value*; it is rather his power of disposing of his labour, effected by exchange with him, which has value. It is not he who stands towards the capitalist as exchange value, but the capitalist towards him. His *valuelessness* and *devaluation* is the presupposition of capital and the precondition of *free* labour in general. Linguet regards it as a step backwards;[52] he forgets that the worker is thereby formally posited as a person who is something for himself *apart from his* labour, and who alienates his life-expression only as a means towards his own life. So long as the worker as such has *exchange value, industrial capital* as such cannot exist, hence nor can developed capital in general. Towards the latter, labour must exist as *pure use value*, which is offered as a commodity by its possessor himself in exchange for it, for its *exchange value*, which of course becomes real in the worker's hand only in its role as general medium of exchange; otherwise vanishes.) Well. The worker, then, finds himself only in the relation of simple circulation, of simple exchange, and obtains only *coin* for his use value; subsistence; but mediated. This form of mediation is, as we saw, essential to and characteristic of the relation. That it can proceed to the transformation of the coin into money – savings – proves precisely only that his relation is that of simple circulation; he can save more or less; but beyond that he cannot get; he can realize what he has saved only by momentarily expanding the sphere of his pleasures. It is of importance – and penetrates into the character of the relation itself – that, because money is the product of his exchange, general wealth drives him forward as an illusion; makes him industrious. At the same time, this not only formally opens up a field of arbitrariness in the realiz . . .[53]

52. Simon Linguet, (1736–94) was a French lawyer and historian, a conservative critic of the Enlightenment and of the economics of the Physiocrats, an opponent of the French Revolution. He was guillotined during the Terror. The reference here is to his book *Théorie des lois civiles, ou principes fondamentaux de la société*, published anonymously in London, 1767, Vol. II, pp. 462–8.

53. The manuscript breaks off here, and the following page (page 29) is missing. Marx noted its contents as follows: 'Capital a merely objective power *vis-à-vis* the worker. Without personal value. Distinction from the performance of service. Purpose of the worker in the exchange with capital – consumption. Must always begin again anew. *Labour* as the *capital* of the *worker*' (*Grundrisse* (MELI), p. 953).

NOTEBOOK III

29 November –
c. mid-December 1857

The Chapter on Capital (continuation)

(Labour power as capital!) *– Wages not productive*

[1] ... processes of the same subject; thus e.g. the substance of the eye, the capital of vision etc. Such belletristic phrases, which relate everything to everything else by means of some analogy, may even appear profound the first time they are expressed, all the more so if they identify the most disparate things. Repeated, however, and then repeated with outright complacency as statements of scientific value, they are purely and simply ridiculous. Good only for belletristic sophomores and empty chatterboxes who defile all the sciences with their liquorice-sweet filth. The fact that labour is a constant new source of exchange for the worker as long as he is capable of working – meaning not exchange in general, but exchange with capital – is inherent in the nature of the concept itself, namely that he only sells a temporary disposition over his labouring capacity,[2] hence can always begin the exchange anew as soon as he has taken in the quantity of substances required in order to reproduce the externalization of his life [*Lebensäusserung*]. Instead of aiming their amazement in this direction – and considering the worker to owe a debt to capital for the fact that he is alive at all, and can repeat certain life processes every day as soon as he has eaten and slept enough – these whitewashing sycophants of bourgeois economics should rather have fixed their attention on the fact that, after constantly repeated labour, he always has *only* his

1. This is the continuation from the missing final page of the previous notebook. The first seven pages of the present (third) notebook are taken up by the section 'Bastiat and Carey' (see pp. 883–93), which was written in July 1857. The present text begins, then, on the eighth page of the third notebook, which carries the date '*29th, 30th November, December*' in Marx's hand. See *Grundrisse* (MELI), pp. 200 n., 842 n.

2. Cf. Hegel, *Philosophy of Right*, para. 67: 'I can give to someone else the use of my abilities for a restricted period ... but by alienating the whole of my time I would be making the substance of my being into another's property.'

living, direct labour itself to exchange. The repetition itself is in fact only apparent. *What he exchanges for capital is his entire labouring capacity, which he spends, say, in 20 years.* Instead of paying him for it in a lump sum, capital pays him in small doses, as he places it at capital's disposal, say weekly. This alters absolutely nothing in the nature of the thing and gives no grounds whatsoever for concluding that – because the worker has to sleep 10–12 hours before he becomes capable of repeating his labour and his exchange with capital – labour forms *his capital*.[3] What this argument in fact conceives as capital is the limit, the interruption of his labour, since he is not a perpetuum mobile. The struggle for the ten hours' bill etc. proves that the capitalist likes nothing better than for him *to squander his dosages of vital force as much as possible, without interruption.* We now come to the second process, which forms the relation between capital and labour *after* this exchange. We want to add here only that the economists themselves express the above statement by saying that *wages* are *not productive.* For them, of course, to be productive means to be productive of wealth. Now, since wages are the product of the exchange between worker and capital – and the only product posited *in* this act itself – they therefore admit that the worker produces *no wealth* in this exchange, neither for the capitalist, because for the latter the payment of money for a use value – and this *payment* forms the only function of capital in this relation – is a sacrifice of wealth, not creation of the same, which is why he tries to pay the smallest amount possible; nor for the worker, because it brings him only subsistence, the satisfaction of individual needs, more or less – *never* the general form of wealth, never wealth. Nor can it do so, since the content of the commodity which he sells rises in no way above the general laws of circulation: [his aim is] to obtain for the value which he throws into circulation its equivalent, through the coin, in another use value, which he consumes. Such an operation, of course, can never bring wealth, but has to bring back him who undertakes it exactly to the point at which he began. This does not exclude, as we saw, but rather includes, the fact that the sphere of his immediate gratifications is capable of a certain contraction or expansion. On the other side, if the capitalist – who is not yet posited as capitalist at all in this exchange, but only as *money* – were to repeat this act again and again, his money would soon be eaten up by the worker, who would have wasted it in a

3. As in P. Gaskell, *Artisans and Machinery*, London, 1836, pp. 261–2.

series of other gratifications, mended trousers, polished boots – in short, services received. In any case, the repetition of this operation would be precisely limited by the circumference of his money-bag. They would no more enrich him than does the expenditure of money for other use values for his beloved person, which, as is well known, do not – pay him, but cost him.

The exchange between capital and labour belongs within simple circulation, does not enrich the worker. – Separation of labour and property the precondition of this exchange. – Labour as object absolute poverty, labour as subject general possibility of wealth. – Labour without particular specificity confronts capital

It may seem peculiar, in this relation between labour and capital, and already in this first relation of exchange between the two, that the worker here buys the exchange value and the capitalist the use value, in that labour confronts capital not as *a* use value, but as *the* use value pure and simple, but that the capitalist should obtain wealth, and the worker merely a use value which ends with consumption. ⟨In so far as this concerns the capitalist, to be developed only with the second process.⟩ This appears as a dialectic which produces precisely the opposite of what was to be expected. However, regarded more precisely, it becomes clear that the worker who exchanges his commodity goes through the form C–M–M–C in the exchange process. If the point of departure in circulation is the commodity, use value, as the principle of exchange, then we necessarily arrive back at the commodity, since money appears only as coin and, as medium of exchange, is only a vanishing mediation; while the commodity as such, after having described its circle, is consumed as the direct object of need. On the other hand, capital represents M–C–C–M, the antithetical moment.

Separation of property from labour appears as the necessary law of this exchange between capital and labour. Labour posited as *not-capital* as such is: (1) *not-objectified labour* [*nicht-vergegenständlichte Arbeit*]*, conceived negatively* (itself still objective; the not-objective itself in objective form). As such it is not-raw-material, not-instrument of labour, not-raw-product: labour separated from all means and objects of labour, from its entire objectivity. This living labour, existing as an *abstraction* from these moments of its actual reality (also, not-value); this complete denudation, purely subjective existence of labour, stripped of all objectivity. Labour as *absolute poverty*: poverty not as shortage, but as total exclusion of objective wealth. Or also as the existing *not-value*, and hence purely objective use value, existing without mediation, this objectivity can only be an objectivity not separated from the person: only an objectivity coinciding with his immediate bodily existence. Since the objectivity is purely immediate, it is just as much direct not-objectivity. In other words, not an objectivity which falls outside the immediate presence [*Dasein*] of the individual himself. (2) *Not-objectified labour, not-value,* conceived *positively*, or as a negativity in relation to itself, is the not-*objectified*, hence non-objective, i.e. subjective existence of labour itself. Labour not as an object, but as activity; not as itself *value*, but as the *living source* of value. [Namely, it is] general wealth (in contrast to capital in which it exists objectively, as reality) as the *general possibility* of the same, which proves itself as such in action. Thus, it is not at all contradictory, or, rather, the in-every-way mutually contradictory statements that labour is *absolute poverty as object*, on one side, and is, on the other side, the *general possibility* of wealth as subject and as activity, are reciprocally determined and follow from the essence of labour, such as it is *presupposed* by capital as its contradiction and as its contradictory being, and such as it, in turn, presupposes capital.

The last point to which attention is still to be drawn in the relation of labour to capital is this, that as *the* use value which confronts money posited as capital, labour is not this or another labour, but *labour pure and simple*, abstract labour; absolutely indifferent to its particular *specificity* [*Bestimmtheit*], but capable of all specificities. Of course, the particularity of labour must correspond to the particular substance of which a given capital consists; but since capital *as such* is indifferent to every particularity of its substance, and exists not only as the totality of the same but also as the abstraction from all its particularities, the labour which confronts it likewise subjectively has the same totality and abstraction in itself. For example, in guild and craft labour, where capital itself still has a limited form, and is still entirely immersed in a particular substance, hence is not yet *capital as such*, labour, too, appears as still immersed in its particular specificity: not in the totality and abstraction of labour *as such*, in which it confronts capital. That is to say that labour is of course in each single case a specific labour, but capital can come into relation with every *specific* labour; it confronts the *totality* of all labours δυνάμει,[4] and the particular one it confronts at a given time is an accidental matter. On the other side, the worker himself is absolutely indifferent to the specificity of his labour; it has no interest for him as such, but only in as much as it is in fact *labour* and, as such, a use value for capital. It is therefore his economic character that he is the carrier of labour as such – i.e. of labour as *use value* for capital; he is a worker, in opposition to the capitalist. This is not the character of the craftsmen and guild-members etc., whose economic character lies precisely in the *specificity* of their labour and in their relation to a *specific master*, etc. This economic relation – the character which capitalist and worker have as the extremes of a single relation of production – therefore develops more purely and adequately in proportion as labour loses all the characteristics of art; as its particular skill becomes something more and more abstract and irrelevant, and as it becomes more and more a *purely abstract activity*, a purely mechanical activity, hence indifferent to its particular form; a merely *formal* activity, or, what is the same, a merely *material* [*stofflich*] activity, activity pure and simple, regardless of its form. Here it can be seen once again that the particular specificity of the relation of production, of the category – here, capital and labour – becomes real only with the development of a particular *material mode of production* and of a particular stage in the development of the industrial *productive forces*. (This point in general to be particularly developed in connection with this relation, later; since it is here already *posited* in the relation itself, while, in the case of the abstract concepts, exchange value, circulation, money, it still lies more in our subjective reflection.)

Labour process absorbed into capital. (*Capital and capitalist*)

(2) We now come to the second side of the process. The exchange between capital or capitalist and the worker is now finished, in so far as we are dealing with the process of *exchange* as such. We now proceed to the relation of capital to labour as capital's use value. Labour is not only the *use value* which confronts capital, but, rather, it is *the use value* of capital itself. As the not-being of values in so far as they are objectified, labour is their being in so far as they are not-objectified; it is their ideal being; the possibility of values,

4. Potentially.

and, as activity, the positing of value. As against capital, labour is the merely abstract form, the mere possibility of value-positing activity, which exists only as a capacity, as a resource in the bodiliness of the worker. But when it is made into a real activity through contact with capital – it cannot do this by itself, since it is without object – then it becomes a really value-positing, productive activity. In relation with capital, this activity can in general consist only of the reproduction of itself – of the preservation and increase of itself as the *real* and *effective* value, not of the merely intended value, as with money as such. Through the exchange with the worker, capital has appropriated labour itself; labour has become one of its moments, which now acts as a fructifying vitality upon its merely existent and hence dead objectivity. Capital is money (exchange value posited for itself), but no longer is it money as existing in a particular substance and hence excluded from other substances of exchange value and existing alongside them, but rather money as obtaining its ideal character from all substances, from the exchange values of every form and mode of objectified labour. Now, in so far as capital, money existing in all particular forms of objectified labour, enters into the process with not-objectified, but rather living labour, labour existing as process and as action, it is initially this qualitative difference of the substance in which it exists from the form in which it now *also* exists as labour. It is the process of this differentiation and of its suspension, in which capital itself becomes a process. Labour is the yeast thrown into it, which starts it fermenting. On the one side, the objectivity in which it exists has to be worked on, i.e. consumed by labour; on the other side, the mere subjectivity of labour as a mere form has to be suspended, and labour has to be objectified in the material of capital. The relation of capital, in its content, to labour, of objectified labour to living labour – in this relation, where capital appears as passive towards labour, it is its passive being, as a particular substance, which enters into relation with the forming activity of labour – can, in general, be nothing more than the relation of labour to its objectivity, its material – which is to be analysed already in the first chapter, which has to precede exchange value and treat of production in general – and in connection with labour as activity, the material, the objectified labour, has only two relations, that of the *raw material*, i.e. of the formless matter, the mere material for the form-positing, purposive activity of labour, and that of the *instrument of labour*, the objective means which subjective activity inserts between itself as an object, as its conductor. The concept of the *product*, which the economists introduce here, does not yet belong here at all as an aspect *distinct* from raw material and instrument of labour. It appears as *result*, not as *presupposition* of the process between the passive content of capital and labour as activity. As a *presupposition*, the product is not a distinct relation of the object to labour; distinct from raw material and instrument of labour, since raw material and instrument of labour, as substance of values, are themselves already *objectified* labour, *products*. The substance of value is not at all the particular natural substance, but rather objectified labour. This latter itself appears again in connection with *living labour* as *raw material* and *instrument of labour*. As regards the pure act of production in itself, it may seem that the instrument of labour and the raw material are found freely in nature, so that they need merely to be *appropriated*, i.e. made into the object and means of labour, which is not itself a labour process. Thus, in contrast to them, the *product* appears as something qualitatively different, and is a product not only as a result of labour with an instrument on a material, but rather as the first *objectification of labour* alongside them. But, as components of capital, raw material and instrument of labour are themselves already objectified labour, hence *product*. This does not yet exhaust the relation. For, e.g. in the kind of production in which no exchange value, no capital at all exists, the product of labour can become the means and the object of new labour. For example, in agricultural production purely for use value. The hunter's bow, the fisherman's net, in short the simplest conditions, already presuppose a product which ceases to count as product and becomes *raw material* or more specifically *instrument of production*, for this [is] actually the first specific form in which the product appears as the means of reproduction. This link therefore by no means exhausts the relation in which *raw material* and *instrument of labour* appear as moments of capital itself. The economists, incidentally, introduce the *product* as third element of the substance of capital in another connection entirely, as well. This is the product in so far as its character is to step outside both the process of production and circulation, and to become immediate object of individual consumption; *approvisionnement*, as Cherbuliez calls it.[5] That is, the products presupposed so that the worker lives

5. Antoine Cherbuliez (1797–1869, Swiss lawyer and economist, follower of Sismondi, although he added some elements of Ricardian theory), *Richesse ou*

as a worker and is capable of living during production, before a new product is created. That the capitalist possesses this capacity is posited in the fact that every element of capital is money, and, as such, can be transformed from its general form of wealth into the material of wealth, object of consumption. The economists' *approvisionnement* thus applies only to the workers; i.e. it is money expressed in the form of articles of consumption, use values, which they obtain from the capitalist in the act of exchange between the two of them. But this belongs within the first act. The extent to which this first relates to the second is not yet the question here. The only diremption posited by the process of production itself is the original diremption, that posited by the difference between objective labour and living labour itself, i.e. that between *raw material* and *instrument of labour*. It is quite consistent of the economists to confuse these two aspects with each other, because they must bring the two moments in the relation between capital and labour into confusion and cannot allow themselves to grasp their specific difference.

Thus: the raw material is consumed by being changed, formed by labour, and the instrument of labour is consumed by being used up in this process, worn out. On the other hand, labour also is consumed by being employed, set into motion, and a certain amount of the worker's muscular force etc. is thus expended, so that he exhausts himself. But labour is not only consumed, but also at the same time fixed, converted from the form of activity into the form of the object; materialized; as a modification of the object, it modifies its own form and changes from activity to being. The end of the process is the *product*, in which the raw material appears as bound up with labour, and in which the instrument of labour has, likewise, transposed itself from a mere possibility into a reality, by having become a real conductor of labour, but thereby also having been consumed in its static form through its mechanical or chemical relation to the material of labour. All three moments of the process, the material, the instrument, and labour, coincide in the neutral result – the *product*. The moments of the process of production which have been consumed to form the product are simultaneously reproduced in it. The whole process therefore appears as *productive consumption*, i.e. as consumption which terminates

---

pauvreté: Exposition des causes et des effets de la distribution actuelle des richesses sociales, Paris, 1841, p. 16.

neither in a *void*, nor in the mere subjectification of the objective, but which is, rather, again posited as an *object*. This consumption is not simply a consumption of the material, but rather consumption of consumption itself; in the suspension of the material it is the suspension of this suspension and hence the *positing* of the same.[6] This *form-giving* activity consumes the object and consumes itself, but it consumes the given form of the object only in order to posit it in a new objective form, and it consumes itself only in its subjective form as activity. It consumes the objective character of the object – the indifference towards the form – and the subjective character of activity; forms the one, materializes the other. But as *product*, the result of the production process is *use value*.

If we now regard the result so far obtained, we find:

Firstly: The appropriation, absorption of labour by capital – money, i.e. the act of buying the capacity of disposing over the worker, here appears only as a means to bring this process about, not as one of its moments – brings capital into ferment, and makes it into a process, *process of production*, in whose totality it relates to itself not only as objectified by living labour, but also, because objectified, [as] mere *object* of labour.

Secondly: Within simple circulation, the substance of the commodity and of money was itself indifferent to the formal character, i.e. to the extent that commodity and money remained moments of circulation. As for the substance of the commodity, it fell outside the economic relation as an object of consumption (of need); money, in so far as its form achieved independence, was still related to circulation, but only negatively, and was only this negative relation. Fixed for itself, it similarly became extinguished in dead materiality, and ceased to be money. Both commodity and money were expressions of exchange value, and differed only as general and particular exchange value. This difference itself was again merely a nominal one, since not only were the two roles switched in real circulation, but also, if we consider each of them by itself, money itself was a particular commodity, and the commodity as price was itself general money. The difference was only formal. Each of them was posited in the one role only in so far as and because it was not posited in the other. Now however, in the

6. Cf. Hegel, *Science of Logic*, p. 753: 'The third relation, mechanism . . . is a sublating (*aufheben*) of the means, of the object already posited as sublated, and is therefore a second sublating and a reflection-into-self.'

process of production, capital distinguishes itself as form from itself as substance. It is both aspects at once, and at the same time the relation of both to one another. But:

Thirdly: It still only appeared as this relation *in itself*. The relation is not *posited* yet, or it is posited initially only in the character of one of its two moments, the *material* moment, which divides internally into material (raw material and instrument) and form (labour), and which, as a relation between both of them, as a real process, is itself only a material relation again – a relation of the two material elements which form the content of capital as distinct from its formal relation as capital. If we now consider the aspect of capital in which it originally appears in distinction from labour, then it is merely a passive presence in the process, a merely objective being, in which the formal character which makes it capital – i.e. a social relation existing as being-for-itself [*für sich seiendes*] – is completely extinguished. It enters the process only as content – as objectified labour in general; but the fact that it is objectified labour is completely irrelevant to labour – and the relation of labour to it forms the process; it enters into the process, is worked on, rather, only as object, not as *objectified labour*. Cotton which becomes cotton yarn, or cotton yarn which becomes cloth, or cloth which becomes the material for printing and dyeing, exist for labour only as available cotton, yarn, cloth. They themselves do not enter into any process as products of labour, as objectified labour, but only as material existences with certain natural properties. *How* these were posited in them makes no difference to the relation of living labour towards them; they exist for it only in so far as they exist as distinct from it, i.e. as material for labour. This [is the case], in so far as the point of departure is capital in its objective form, presupposed to labour. On another side, in so far as labour itself has become one of capital's objective elements through the exchange with the worker, labour's distinction from the objective elements of capital is itself a merely objective one; the latter in the form of rest, the former in the form of activity. The relation is the material relation between one of capital's elements and the other; but not *its own* relation to both. It therefore appears on one side as a merely *passive object*, in which all formal character is extinguished; it appears on the other side only as a simple *production process* into which capital as such, as distinct from its substance, does not enter. It does not even appear in the substance appropriate to itself – as objectified labour, for this is the substance of exchange value – but rather only in the natural form-of-being [*Daseinsform*] of this substance, in which all relation to exchange value, to objectified labour, and to labour itself as the use value of capital – and hence all relation to capital itself – is extinguished. Regarded from this side, the process of capital coincides with the simple process of production as such, in which its character as capital is quite as extinguished in the form of the process, as money was extinguished as money in the form of value. To the extent to which we have examined the process so far, capital in its being-for-itself, i.e. the capitalist, does not enter at all. It is not the capitalist who is consumed by labour as raw material and instrument of labour. And it is not the capitalist who does this consuming but rather labour. Thus the process of the production of capital does not appear as the process of the production of capital, but as the process of production in general, and capital's *distinction from labour* appears only in the material character of *raw material* and *instrument of labour*. It is this aspect – which is not only an arbitrary abstraction, but rather an abstraction which takes place within the process itself – on which the economists seize in order to represent capital as a necessary element of every production process. Of course, they do this only by forgetting to pay attention to its conduct as capital during this process.

This is the occasion to draw attention to a moment which here, for the first time, not only arises from the standpoint of the observer, but is posited in the economic relation itself. In the first act, in the exchange between capital and labour, labour as such, existing *for itself*, necessarily appeared as *the worker*. Similarly here in the second process: capital as such is posited as a value existing for itself, as egotistic value, so to speak (something to which money could only aspire). But capital in its being-for-itself is the *capitalist*. Of course, socialists sometimes say, we need capital, but not the capitalist.[7] Then capital appears as a pure thing, not as a relation of production which, reflected in itself, is precisely the capitalist. I may well separate capital from a given individual capitalist, and it can be transferred to another. But, in losing capital, he loses the quality of being a capitalist. Thus capital is indeed separable from an individual capitalist, but not from *the* capitalist, who, as such, confronts *the* worker. Thus also the individual worker can cease to be the being-for-itself [*Fürsichsein*] of labour;

7. For example John Gray, *The Social System*, p. 36, and J. F. Bray, *Labour's Wrongs*, pp. 157–76.

he may inherit or steal money etc. But then he ceases to be a
worker. As a worker he is nothing more than labour in its being-
for-itself. (This to be further developed later.)[8]

Production process *as content of capital. Productive and .
unproductive labour (productive labour – that which produces
capital). – The worker relates to his labour as exchange value,
the capitalist as use value etc. – He divests himself* [entäussert
sich] *of labour as the wealth-producing power. (Capital
appropriates it as such.) Transformation of labour into capital
etc. Sismondi, Cherbuliez, Say, Ricardo, Proudhon etc.*

Nothing can emerge at the end of the process which did not appear
as a presupposition and precondition at the beginning. But, on the
other hand, everything also has to come out. Thus, if at the end of
the process of production, which was begun with the presuppositions of capital, capital appears to have vanished as a formal
relation, then this can have taken place only because the invisible
threads which draw it through the process have been overlooked.
Let us therefore consider this side.

The first result, then, is this:

(α) Capital becomes the process of production through the incorporation of labour into capital; initially however, it becomes
the *material* process of production; the process of production in
general, so that the process of the production of capital is not distinct from the material process of production as such. Its formal
character is completely extinguished. Because capital has exchanged a part of its objective being for labour, its objective being
is itself internally divided into object and labour; the connection
between them forms the production process, or, more precisely,'
the *labour process*. With that, the *labour process posited prior to
value, as point of departure* – which, owing to its abstractness, its
pure materiality, is common to all forms of production – here reappears *again within capital*, as a process which proceeds within its
substance and forms its content.

(It will be seen that even within the production process itself this
extinguishing of the formal character is merely a semblance.)[9]

In so far as capital is value, but appears as a process initially in
the form of the simple production process, the production process
posited in no particular *economic* form, but rather, the production

process pure and simple, to that extent – depending on which particular aspect of the simple production process (which, as such, as we saw, by no means presupposes capital, but is common to all modes of production) is fixed on – it can be said that capital becomes product, or that it is instrument of labour or raw material for labour. Further, if it is conceived in one of the aspects which confronts labour as material or as mere means, then it is correct to say that capital is not productive,* because it is then regarded merely as the object, the material which confronts labour; as merely passive. The correct thing, however, is that it appears not as one of these aspects, nor as a difference within one of these aspects, nor as mere result (product), but rather as the simple production process itself; that this latter now appears as the self-propelling *content* of capital.

(β) Now to look at the side of the form-character, such as it preserves and modifies itself in the production process.

As *use value*, labour exists only *for capital*, and is itself the use value of capital, i.e. the mediating activity by means of which it *realizes* [*verwertet*] itself. Capital, as that which reproduces and increases its value, is autonomous exchange value (money), as a process, as the *process of realization*. Therefore, labour does not exist as a use value for the worker; *for* him it is therefore not a *power productive of wealth*, [and] not a means or the activity of gaining wealth. He brings it as a use value into the exchange with

---

* What is *productive labour* and what is *not*, a point very much disputed back and forth since Adam Smith made this distinction,[10] has to emerge from the dissection of the various aspects of capital itself. *Productive labour* is only that which produces *capital*. Is it not crazy, asks e.g. (or at least something similar) Mr Senior, that the piano maker is a *productive worker*, but not the *piano player*, although obviously the piano would be absurd without the piano player?[11] But this is exactly the case. The piano maker reproduces *capital*; the pianist only exchanges his labour for revenue. But doesn't the pianist produce music and satisfy our musical ear, does he not even to a certain extent produce the latter? He does indeed: his labour produces something; but that does not make it *productive labour* in the *economic sense*; no more than the labour of the madman who produces delusions is productive. *Labour becomes productive only by producing its own opposite.* Other economists therefore allow the so-called unproductive worker to be productive indirectly. For example, the pianist stimulates production; partly by giving a more decisive, lively tone to our individuality, and also in the ordinary sense of awakening a new need for the satisfaction of which additional energy becomes expended in direct

---

10. Adam Smith, *Wealth of Nations,* Vol. II, pp. 355–85.
11. Senior, *Principes fondamentaux,* pp. 197–206.

capital, which then confronts him not as capital but rather as *money*. In relation to the worker, it is capital as capital only in the consumption of labour, which initially falls outside this exchange and is independent of it. A *use value* for capital, labour is a *mere exchange value* for the worker; available *exchange value*. It is posited as such in the act of exchange with capital, through its sale for money. The use value of a thing does not concern its seller as such, but only its buyer. The property of saltpetre, that it can be used to make gunpowder, does not determine the price of saltpetre; rather, this price is determined by the cost of production of saltpetre, by the amount of labour objectified in it. The value of use values which enter circulation as prices is not the product of circulation, although it realizes itself only in circulation; rather, it is *presupposed* to it, and is realized only through exchange for money. Similarly, the labour which the worker sells as a *use value* to capital is, for the worker, his *exchange value,* which he wants to realize, but which is already *determined* prior to this act of exchange and presupposed to it as a condition, and is determined like the value of every other commodity by supply and demand; or, in general, which is our only concern here, by the cost of production, the amount of objectified labour, by means of which the labouring capacity of the worker has been produced and which he therefore obtains for it, as its equivalent. The exchange value of labour, the realization of which takes place in the process of exchange with the capitalist, is therefore *presupposed*, predeter-

---

material production. This already admits that only such labour is productive as produces capital; hence that labour which does not do this, regardless of how *useful* it may be – it may just as well be harmful – is not productive for capitalization, is hence unproductive labour. Other economists say that the difference between productive and unproductive applies not to production but to consumption. Quite the contrary. The producer of tobacco is productive, although the consumption of tobacco is unproductive. Production for unproductive consumption is quite as productive as that for productive consumption; always assuming that it produces or reproduces capital. '*Productive labourer he that directly augments his master's wealth,*' Malthus therefore says, quite correctly (IX,40)[12]; correct at least in one aspect. The expression is too abstract, since in this formulation it holds also for the slave. The master's wealth, in relation to the worker, is the form of wealth itself in its relation to labour, namely capital. Productive labourer he that directly augments capital.

---

12. Malthus, *Principles of Political Economy*, p. 47, footnote by the editor, William Otter, Bp of Chichester.

mined, and only undergoes the formal modification which every only ideally posited price takes on when it is realized. It is not determined by the use value of labour. It has a use value for the worker himself only in so far as it ıs *exchange value,* not in so far as it produces exchange values. It has exchange value for capital only in so far as it is use value. It is a use value, as distinct from exchange value, not for the worker himself, but only for capital. The worker therefore sells labour as a simple, predetermined exchange value, determined by a previous process – he sells labour itself as *objectified labour*; i.e. he sells labour only in so far as it already objectifies a definite amount of labour, hence in so far as its equivalent is already measured, given; capital buys it as living labour, as the general productive force of wealth; activity which increases wealth. It is clear, therefore, that the worker cannot become *rich* in this exchange, since, in exchange for his labour capacity as a fixed, available magnitude, he surrenders its *creative power*, like Esau his birthright for a mess of pottage. Rather, he necessarily impoverishes himself, as we shall see further on, because the creative power of his labour establishes itself as the power of capital, as an *alien power* confronting him. He *divests* himself [*entäussert sich*] of labour as the force productive of wealth; capital appropriates it, as such. The separation between labour and property in the product of labour, between labour and wealth, is thus posited in this act of exchange itself. What appears paradoxical as *result* is already contained in the presupposition. The economists have expressed this more or less empirically. Thus the productivity of his labour, his labour in general, in so far as it is not a *capacity* but a motion, *real* labour, *comes* to confront the worker as an *alien power*; capital, inversely, realizes itself through the *appropriation of alien labour.* (At least the possibility of realization is thereby posited; as result of the exchange between labour and capital. The relation is realized only in the act of production itself, where capital really consumes the alien labour.) Just as labour, as a *presupposed* exchange value, is exchanged for an equivalent in money, so the latter is again exchanged for an equivalent in *commodities*, which are consumed. In this process of exchange, labour is not productive; it becomes so only for capital; it can take out of circulation only what it has thrown into it, a *predetermined* amount of commodities, which is as little its own product as it is its own value. Sismondi says that the workers exchange their labour for grain, which they consume, while their

labour 'has become *capital* for its master'. (Sismondi, VI.)[13]
'Giving their labour in exchange, the workers *transform* it into
capital.' (id., VIII.)[14] By selling his labour to the capitalist, the
worker obtains a right only to the *price of labour*, not to the
product of this labour, nor to the value which *his labour has added
to it*. (Cherbuliez XXVIII.) '*Sale of labour = renunciation of all
fruits of labour*.' (loc. cit.)[15] Thus all the progress of civilization, or in
other words every increase in the *powers of social production*
[*gesellschaftliche Produktivkräfte*], if you like, in the *productive
powers of labour itself* – such as results from science, inventions,
division and combination of labour, improved means of communication, creation of the world market, machinery etc. – enriches not the worker but rather *capital*; hence it only magnifies
again the power dominating over labour; increases only the productive power of capital. Since capital is the antithesis of the
worker, this merely increases the *objective power* standing over
labour. The *transformation of labour* (as living, purposive activity)
into *capital* is, *in itself*, the result of the exchange between capital
and labour, in so far as it gives the capitalist the title of ownership
to the product of labour (and command over the same). *This
transformation* is *posited* only in the *production process* itself. Thus,
the question whether capital is productive or not is absurd. Labour
itself is *productive only* if absorbed into capital, where capital
forms the basis of production, and where the capitalist is therefore
in command of production. The productivity of labour becomes
the productive force of capital just as the general exchange value
of commodities fixes itself in money. Labour, such as it exists *for
itself* in the worker in opposition to capital, that is, labour in its
immediate being, separated from capital, is *not productive*. Nor
does it ever become *productive* as an activity of the worker so long
as it merely enters the simple, only formally transforming process
of circulation. Therefore, those who demonstrate that the productive force ascribed to capital is a *displacement*, a *transposition
of the productive force* of labour,[16] forget precisely that capital
itself is essentially this *displacement, this transposition*, and that
wage labour as such presupposes capital, so that, from its standpoint as well, capital is this *transubstantiation*; the necessary process of positing its own powers as *alien* to the worker. Therefore,
the demand that wage labour be continued but capital suspended

13. Sismondi, *Nouveaux Principes*, Vol. I, p. 90.   14. ibid., p. 105.
15. Cherbuliez, *Richesse ou pauvreté*, pp. 58, 64.   16. See p. 303, n. 7.

is self-contradictory, self-dissolving. Others say, even economists, e.g. Ricardo, Sismondi etc., that *only labour* is productive, not capital.[17] But then they do not conceive[18] capital in its *specific character as form*, as a *relation of production* reflected into itself, but think only about its material substance, raw material etc. But these material elements do not make capital into capital. Then, however, they recall that capital is also in another respect a *value*, that is, something *immaterial*, something indifferent to its material consistency. Thus, Say: '*Capital is always an immaterial essence*, because it is not material which makes capital, but the *value* of this material, a value which has nothing corporeal about it.' (Say, 21.)[19] Or: Sismondi: 'Capital is a commercial *idea*.' (Sismondi, LX.)[20] But then they recall that capital is a different economic quality as well, other than *value*, since otherwise it would not be possible to speak of capital *as distinct from value* at all, and, if all capitals were value, all values as such would still not be capital. Then they take refuge again in its material form within the production process, e.g. when Ricardo explains that capital is 'accumulated labour employed in the production of new labour',[21] i.e. merely as *instrument of labour* or *material for labour*. In this sense Say even speaks of the '*productive service of capital*',[22] on which remuneration is supposed to be based, as if the instrument of labour as such were entitled to thanks from the worker, and as if it were not precisely because of him that it is posited as instrument of labour, as *productive*. This presupposes the autonomy of the instrument of labour, i.e. of its *social* character, i.e. its character as capital, in order to derive the privileges of capital from it. Proudhon's phrase '*le capital vaut, le travail produit*'[23] means absolutely nothing more than: capital is value, and, since nothing further is here said about capital other than that it is value, that value is value (the subject

17. In Ricardo: *On the Principles of Political Economy*, pp. 320–37. In Sismondi: *Études*, Vol. I, p. 22.

18. The MELI edition gives *lassen* (let, leave) rather than *fassen* (grasp, conceive, formulate); this is almost certainly either a misprint (the first of two on that page) or a misreading.

19. Say, *Traité d'économie politique*, Vol. II, p. 429 n.

20. Sismondi, *Études*, Vol. II, p. 273.

21. This is Adam Smith's phrase, not Ricardo's (Smith, *Wealth of Nations*, Vol. II, p. 355).

22. Say, *Traité d'économie politique*, Vol. II, p. 425.

23. 'Capital has value, labour produces.' Proudhon, *Système des contradictions économiques*, Vol. I, p. 61.

of the judgement is here only another name for the predicate)[24];
and labour produces, is productive labour, i.e. labour is labour,
since it is precisely nothing apart from '*produire*'.[25] It must be
obvious that these identical judgements do not contain any particularly deep wisdom, and that above all, they cannot express a
relation in which value and labour enter into connection, in which
they connect and divide in relation to one another, and where they
do not lie side by side in mutual indifference. Already the fact that
it is *labour* which confronts capital as subject, i.e. the worker only
in his character as *labour*, and not *he himself*, should open the eyes.
This alone, disregarding capital, already contains a relation, a
relation of the worker to his own activity, which is by no means the
'*natural*' one, but which itself already contains a specific *economic*
character.

To the extent that we are considering it here, as a relation distinct from that of value and money, capital is *capital in general*, i.e.
the incarnation of the qualities which distinguish value as capital
from value as pure value or as money. Value, money, circulation
etc., prices etc. are presupposed, as is labour etc. But we are still
concerned neither with a *particular* form of capital, nor with an
individual capital as distinct from other individual capitals etc. We
are present at the process of its becoming. This dialectical process
of its becoming is only the ideal expression of the real movement
through which capital comes into being. The later relations are to
be regarded as developments coming out of this germ. But it is
necessary to establish the specific form in which it is posited at
a *certain* point. Otherwise confusion arises.

Realization process [Verwertungsprozess]. – (*Costs of production.*)
– (*Surplus value not explicable by exchange*. Ramsay. Ricardo.)
Capitalist cannot live from his wage *etc.* (Faux frais de production.)[26] – *Mere self-preservation, non-multiplication of value
contradicts the essence of capital*

Hitherto, capital has been regarded from its material side as a
simple production process. But, from the side of its formal speci-

24. Cf. Hegel, *Science of Logic*, p. 633: 'In the judgement the subject is
determined by the predicate . . . the predicate is determined in the subject.'

25. 'The act of producing'.

26. Incidental 'false' expenses of production: the category into which the
political economists from Adam Smith onwards relegated the cost of maintaining necessary but unproductive workers, e.g. soldiers, doctors etc.

ficity, this process is a *process of self-realization*. Self-realization includes preservation of the prior value, as well as its multiplication.

Value enters as subject. Labour is purposeful activity, and the material side therefore presupposes that the instrument of labour has really been used as means to an end in the production process, and that the raw material has obtained a higher use value as product than it had before, whether this is due to chemical alteration or mechanical modification. However, this side alone, as impinging merely on the use value, still belongs in the simple production process. It is not the point here – this is, rather, understood, presupposed – that a higher use value has been created (this in itself is very relative; when grain is transformed into spirits, the higher use value is itself already posited in respect of circulation); no higher use value has yet been created for the individual, the producer. This, in any case, is accidental, and does not affect the relation as such; rather, a higher use value *for others*. The point is, [rather,] that a *higher exchange value* be created. In the case of simple circulation, the process ended for the individual commodity by its being consumed as use value. With that, it left circulation; lost its exchange value, its economic form-character [*Formbestimmung*] in general. Capital has consumed its material with labour and its labour with material; it has consumed itself as use value, but only as *use value for itself*, as capital. Its consumption as use value therefore in this case falls within circulation itself, or rather it itself posits the *beginning of circulation* or its end, as one prefers. The consumption of the use value itself here falls within the economic process, because the use value here is itself determined by exchange value. In no moment of the production process does capital cease to be capital or value to be value, and, as such, *exchange value*. Nothing is more ridiculous than to say, as does Mr Proudhon, that capital changes from a product into an exchange value by means of the act of exchange, i.e. by re-entering simple circulation.[27] We would then be thrown back to the beginning, to direct barter even, where we observe the origin of exchange value out of the product. Already its presupposition as self-preserving exchange value comprises the possibility that capital can and does re-enter into circulation as a commodity at the end of the production process, after its consumption as use value. However, in so far as the product now again becomes commodity,

27. Bastiat et Proudhon, *Gratuité du crédit*, p. 180.

and as commodity, exchange value, and obtains a price and is realized as such in money, to that extent it is a simple commodity, exchange value as such, and, as such, its fate within circulation may be to be realized in money, or it may equally be that it does not realize itself in money; i.e. that its exchange value becomes money or not. Thus its exchange value has become much more problematic – before, it was posited ideally – than the fact that it came into existence. What is more, its being *really* posited as a higher exchange value in circulation cannot originate out of circulation itself, in which, in its simple character, only equivalents are exchanged. Therefore, it if comes out of circulation as a higher exchange value, it must have entered into it as such.

Capital as a form consists not of objects of labour and labour, but rather of *values*, and, still more precisely, of *prices*. The fact that its value-elements have various substances in common during the production process does not affect their character as values; they are not changed thereby. If, out of the form of unrest – of the process – at the end of the process, they again condense themselves into a resting, objective form, in the product, then this, too, is merely a change of the material [*Stoffwechsel*] in relation to value, and does not alter the latter.[28] True, the substances as such have been destroyed, but they have not been made into nothing, but rather into a substance with another form. Earlier, they appeared as elemental, indifferent preconditions of the product. Now they are the product. The value of the product can therefore only = the sum of the values which were materialized in the specific material elements of the process, i.e. raw material, instrument of labour (including the merely instrumental commodities), and labour itself. The raw material has been entirely used up, labour has been entirely used up, the instrument has been only partly used up, hence continues to possess a part of the value of the capital in its specific mode of existence as present prior to the process. This part therefore does not come under view here at all, since it has suffered no modification. The different modes in which the values existed were a pure semblance; value itself formed the constantly self-identical essence within their disappearance. Regarded as a value, the product has in this respect not become

28. Cf. Hegel, *Science of Logic*, pp. 717–18; 'The action passes over into *rest*. It shows itself to be a merely *superficial*, transient alteration in the self-enclosed indifferent totality of the object. This return constitutes the *product* of the mechanical process.'

product, but rather remained identical, unchanged value, which merely exists in a different mode, which is, however, irrelevant to it and which can be exchanged for money. The value of the product is = to the value of the raw material + the value of the part of the instrument of labour which has been destroyed, i.e. transferred to the product, and which is suspended in its original form, + the value of labour. Or, the price of the product is equal to these costs of production, i.e. = to the sum of the prices of the commodities consumed in the production process. That means, in other words, nothing more than that the production process in its material aspect has been irrelevant to value; that value therefore has remained identical with itself and has merely taken on another mode of existence, become materialized in another substance and form. (The form of the substance is irrelevant to the economic *form*, to value as such.) If capital was originally = to 100 thalers, then afterwards, as before, it remains equal to 100 thalers, although the 100 thalers existed in the production price as 50 thalers of cotton, 40 thalers of wages + 10 thalers of spinning machine, and now exist as cotton yarn to the price of 100 thalers. This reproduction of the 100 thalers is a simple retention of self-equivalence [*Sichselbstgleichbleiben*], except that it is mediated through the material production process. The latter must therefore proceed to the product, for otherwise cotton loses its value, instrument of labour used up for nothing, wages paid in vain. The only stipulation for the self-preservation of value is that the production process really be a total process, i.e. continue to the point where a product exists. The completeness [*Totalität*] of the production process, i.e. the fact that it proceeds to the product, is here in fact the precondition of the self-preservation, the self-equivalent retention of value; but this is already contained in the first precondition, that capital really becomes use value, a real production process; is therefore *presupposed* at this point. On the other hand, the production process is a production process for capital *only* to the extent that it preserves itself in this process as value, i.e. as product. The statement that the necessary price = the sum of the prices of the costs of production is therefore purely analytical. It is the presupposition of the production of capital itself. First capital is posited as 100 thalers, as simple value; then it is posited in this process as a sum of prices of specific value-elements of itself, elements specified by the price of production itself. The price of capital, its value expressed in money, = the price of its product. That means the value of capital as the result of the production process is the same as it was as the presupposition of the process. However, during the process it does not retain the simplicity it had at the beginning, and which it takes on once again at the end, as the result; rather, it decomposes into the initially quite irrelevant quantitative elements of value of labour (wage), value of the instrument of labour, and value of the raw material. No further relation has been posited, other than that the simple value decomposes quantitatively to form the price of production, as a number of values which recombine in their simplicity in the product, but which exists now as a *sum*. But the sum is = to the original unity. Otherwise, as regards value, and apart from the quantitative subdivision, there is not the least difference in the relation between the distinct amounts of value. The original capital was 100 thalers; the product is 100 thalers, but now 100 thalers as the sum of 50 + 40 + 10 thalers. I could just as well have regarded the original 100 thalers as a sum of 50 + 40 + 10 thalers, but equally as a sum of 60 + 30 + 10 thalers, etc. The fact that they now appear as the sum of specific amounts of units is posited because each of the different material elements into which capital decomposed in the production process represents a part of its value, but a specific part.

It will be seen later that these amounts into which the original unity is decomposed themselves have certain relations with one another, but this does not concern us here yet. In so far as any movement in the value itself is posited during the production process, it is the purely formal one which consists of the following simple act: that value exists first as a unity, a specific amount of units, which are themselves regarded as a unity, a whole: capital in the amount of 100 thalers; secondly, that this unity is divided during the production process into 50 thalers, 40 thalers and 10 thalers, a division which is essential to the extent that material, instrument and labour are required in specific quantities, but which here appears, in regard to the 100 thalers themselves, merely as an irrelevant decomposition of the same unity into different amounts; finally, that the 100 thalers reappear as a sum in the product. The only process, as regards value, [is] that it sometimes appears as a whole, unity; then as a division of this unity into certain amounts; finally, as sum. The 100 thalers which appear at the end as a sum are just as much a sum and in fact exactly the same sum as that which appeared at the outset as a unity. The character of being a sum, of being added up, arose only out of the subdivision which took place in the act of production; but does not exist in the product as such. The statement thus says nothing more than that the price of the product = the price of the costs of production, or that the value of capital = the value of the product, that the value of the capital has preserved itself in the act of production, and now appears as a sum. With this mere identity of capital, or, reproduction of its value throughout the production process, we would have come no further than we were at the beginning. What was there at the outset as presupposition is now there as result, and in unchanged form. It is clear that it is not in fact this to which the economists refer when they speak of the determination of price by the cost of production. Otherwise, a value greater than that originally present could never be created; no greater exchange value, although perhaps a greater use value, which is quite beside the point here. We are dealing with the *use value of capital* as such, not with the use of value of a commodity.

When one says that the cost of production or the necessary price of a commodity is = to 110, then one is calculating in the following way: Original capital = 100 (e.g. raw material = 50; labour = 40; instrument = 10) + 5% interest + 5% profit. Thus the production cost = 110, not = 100; the production cost is thus greater than the cost of production. Now, it is no help at all to flee from exchange value to the use value of the commodity, as some economists love to do. Whether the use value is greater or lesser is not, as such, determined by the exchange value. Commodities often fall beneath their prices of production, although they indisputably have obtained a higher use value than they had in the period *prior* to production. It is equally useless to seek refuge in circulation. I produce at 100, but I sell at 110. 'Profit is not made by exchanging. Had it not existed before, neither could it after that transaction.' (Ramsay, IX, 88.)[29] This signifies the attempt to explain the augmentation of value with the aid of simple circulation, despite the fact that the latter *expressly* posits value as an equivalent only. It is clear even empirically that if everyone sold for 10% too much, this is the same as if they all sold at the cost of production. The surplus value [*Mehrwert*] would then be purely nominal, artificial, a convention, an empty phrase.

29. Sir George Ramsay (1800–1871, philosopher and political economist, the first to distinguish between constant and variable capital), *An Essay on the Distribution of Wealth*, Edinburgh, 1836, p. 184.

And, since money is itself a commodity, a product, it also would be sold for 10% too much, i.e. the seller who received 110 thalers would in fact receive only 100. (Consult Ricardo on foreign trade, which he conceives as simple circulation, and says, therefore: 'foreign trade can never increase the amount of exchange value in a country'. (Ricardo, 39, 40.)[30] The grounds he cites for this conclusion are absolutely the same as those which 'prove' that exchange as such, simple circulation, i.e. commerce in general, in so far as it is conceived as such, can never increase *exchange values*, never create *exchange value*.) The statement that the price = the cost of production would otherwise have to read, also: the price of a commodity is always greater than its cost of production. In addition to the simple division and re-addition, the production process also adds the formal element to value, namely that its elements now appear as *production costs*, i.e. precisely that the elements of the production process are not preserved in their material character, but rather as *values*, while the mode of existence which these had *before* the production process is consumed.

It is clear, on another side, that if the act of production is merely the reproduction of the value of capital, then it would have undergone a merely material but not an economic change, and such a simple preservation of its value contradicts its concept [*Begriff*]. True, it would not remain outside circulation, as in the case of autonomous money, but would, rather, take on the form of different commodities; however, it would do so for nothing; this would be a purposeless process, since it would ultimately represent only the same sum of money, and would only have run the risk of suffering some damage in the act of production – [moreover, it is a process] which can fail, and in which money surrenders its immortal form. Well then. The production process is now at an end. The product, too, is realized in money again, and has again taken on the original form of the 100 thalers. But the capitalist has to eat and drink, too; he cannot live from this change into the form of money. Thus, a part of the 100 thalers would have to be exchanged not as capital, but as coin for commodities as use values, and be consumed in this form. The 100 thalers would have become 90, and since he always ultimately reproduces capital in the form of money, more precisely, in the quantity of money with which he began production, at the end the

30. Ricardo, *On the Principles of Political Economy*, p. 131.

100 thalers would be eaten up and the capital would have disappeared. But the capitalist is paid for the *labour* of throwing the 100 thalers into the production process as capital, instead of eating them up. But with what is he to be paid? And does not his labour appear as absolutely useless, since capital includes the wage; so that the workers could live from the simple reproduction of the cost of production, which the capitalist cannot do? He would thus appear among the *faux frais de production*.[31] But, whatever his merits may be, reproduction would be possible without him, since, in the production process, the workers only transfer the value which they take out, hence have no need for the entire relation of capital in order to begin it always anew; and secondly, there would then be no fund out of which to pay him what he deserves, since the price of the commodity = the cost of production. But, if his labour were defined as a particular labour alongside and apart from that of the workers, e.g. that of the labour of superintendence etc.,[32] then he would, like them, receive a certain wage, would thus fall into the same category as they, and would by no means relate to labour as a capitalist; and he would never get rich, but receive merely an exchange value which he would have to consume via circulation. The existence of capital *vis-à-vis* labour requires that capital in its being-for-itself, the capitalist, should exist and be able to live as *not-worker*. It is equally clear, on the other side, that capital, even as conventionally defined, would *not* retain its value if it could retain nothing but its *value*. *The risks of production have to be compensated.* Capital has to preserve itself through the fluctuations of prices. The constantly ongoing devaluation of capital, resulting from the increase in the force of production, has to be compensated, etc. The economists therefore state flatly that if no gain, no profit were to be made, everyone would eat up his money instead of throwing it into production and employing it as capital. In short, if this *not-realization* [*Nichtverwerten*], i.e. the non-multiplication of the value of capital, is presupposed, then what is presupposed is that capital is not a real element of production, that it is not a *specific relation of production*; then a condition is presupposed in which the production costs do not have the form of capital and where capital is not posited as the condition of production.

It is easy to understand how labour can increase use value; the

31. See p. 310, n. 26.
32. As in Carey, *Principles of Political Economy*, Pt I, p. 338.

difficulty is, how it can create exchange values greater than those with which it began.

Suppose that the exchange value which capital pays the worker were an exact equivalent for the value which labour creates in the production process. In that case, an increase in the exchange value of the product would be impossible. Everything which labour as such had brought into the production process, in addition to the already present value of the raw material and of the instrument of labour, would have been paid to the worker. In so far as the value of the product is a surplus over and above the value of raw material and instrument, that value would go to the worker; except that the capitalist would pay him this value in his wages, and that the worker pays it back to the capitalist in the product.

Capital enters the cost of production as capital.
Interest-bearing capital. Proudhon

⟨Interest on borrowed capital makes tangible the truth that what is meant by *the cost of production* – even by economists who make this assertion – is not the sum of values which enter into production. For the industrial capitalist, interest is among his direct expenses, his *real* costs of production. But interest itself already presupposes that capital emerges from production as surplus value, since interest is itself only *one form* of this surplus value. Therefore, since, from the standpoint of the borrower, interest already enters into his *direct production costs*, it is apparent that capital enters as such into the cost of production, but that capital as such is not the mere addition of its value-components. – As interest, capital itself appears again in the character of a *commodity*, but a commodity *specifically* distinct from all other commodities; *capital as such* – not as a mere sum of exchange values – enters into circulation and becomes a *commodity*. Here, the character of the commodity is itself present as an *economic, specific* determinant, not irrelevant as in simple circulation, nor directly related to labour as its opposite, as its use value, as with industrial capital; [but, rather,] capital as it exists in its further aspects, after emerging from circulation and production. The commodity as capital, or capital as *commodity*, is therefore not exchanged for an equivalent in circulation; by entering into circulation, it *obtains its being-for-itself*; it obtains its original relation to its owner, even when it passes into the possession of another. It is therefore merely *loaned*. For its owner, its use value as such is its *realization* [*Verwertung*]; money as money, not as medium of circulation; its *use value as capital*. The demand raised by Mr Proudhon, that capital should not be loaned out and should bear no interest, but should be sold like a commodity for its equivalent,[33] amounts at bottom to no more than the demand that exchange value should never become capital, but always remain simple exchange value; that *capital* should *not exist as capital*. This demand, combined with the other, that wage labour should remain the general basis of production, reveals a happy confusion with regard to the simplest economic concepts. Hence the miserable role he plays in the polemic with Bastiat, about which, later. His chatter about considerations of fairness and right only amounts to this, that he wants to use the relation of property or of law corresponding to simple exchange as the measuring-rod for the relation of property and law at a higher stage of exchange value. Which is why Bastiat himself, unconsciously, stresses those moments of simple circulation which drive in the direction of capital. – Capital itself as commodity is *money as capital* or *capital as money*.⟩

⟨The third moment to be developed in the formation of the concept of capital is *original accumulation* [*ursprüngliche Akkumulation*] as against labour, hence the still objectless labour *vis-à-vis* accumulation. The *first moment* took its point of departure from value, as it arose out of and presupposed circulation. This was the *simple concept* of capital; money on the direct path to becoming capital; the *second moment* proceeded from capital as the presupposition and result of production; the *third moment* posits capital as a *specific unity* of circulation and production. (Relation between capital and labour, capitalist and worker itself [posited] as a result of the production process.) A distinction is to be drawn between the accumulation of capitals, which presupposes capitals, the relation of capital as *present* [*daseiend*], which also presupposes its relations to labour, prices (fixed capital and circulating capital), interest and profit.[34] But in order to come into being, capital presupposes a certain accumulation; which is

33. Bastiat et Proudhon, *Gratuité du crédit*, pp. 65–74. For Marx's later discussions of the polemic between Bastiat and Proudhon, see pp. 640–41, 754–8, 843–5.

34. 'A distinction is to be drawn between this, on one side, and the accumulation of capitals, on the other; the latter presupposes its relations to

already contained in the independent antithesis between objectified and living labour; in the independent survival of this antithesis. This accumulation, necessary for capital to come into being, which is therefore already included in its concept as presupposition – as a moment – is to be distinguished essentially from the accumulation of capital which has already become capital, where there must already be *capitals*.⟩

⟨We have already seen so far that capital presupposes: (1) the production process in general, such as is common to all social conditions, that is, without historic character, *human*, if you like; (2) *circulation* which is already a specific *historic* product in each of its moments, and even more so in its totality; (3) *capital* as a *specific* unity of the two. Now, the extent to which the production process in general comes to be modified historically as soon as it becomes merely an element of capital has to be found out in the course of developing it; just as the simple conception of the specific characteristics of capital must yield its general historic presuppositions.⟩

⟨Everything else is empty chatter. Only at the end, and as a result of the whole development, can it become clear which aspects belong in the first section, 'Production in General', and which into the first section of the second section, 'Exchange Value in General'. We already saw, for example, that the distinction between use value and exchange value belongs within economics itself, and that use value does not lie dead as a simple presupposition, which is what Ricardo makes it do.[35] The chapter on production objectively ends with the product as result; that on circulation begins with the *commodity*, which is itself again a *use value* and an *exchange value* (hence, also, distinct from both, a *value*), circulation as the unity of both – which is, however, merely formal and hence collapses into the commodity as mere object of consumption, extra-economic, and exchange value as independent money.⟩

---

labour, prices (fixed capital and circulating capital), interest and profit.' Our reconstruction is based on a comparison with the passage on p. 310 where a distinction is drawn between 'capital in the process of its becoming' and 'the later relations' or 'the specific form in which capital is posited at a *certain* point'. Marx is repeating this distinction here, but in a different manner.

35. Ricardo, *On the Principles of Political Economy*, pp. 1–3.

Surplus value. Surplus labour time. – Bastiat on wages.
Value of labour. How determined? – Self-realization is
self-preservation of capital. Capitalist may not live merely from
his labour etc. Conditions for the self-realization of capital.
Surplus labour time etc. – To the extent that capital is
productive (as creator of surplus labour etc.), this only
historic-transitory. – The free blacks in Jamaica. –
Wealth which has gained autonomy requires slave labour or
wage labour (forced labour in both cases)

The surplus value which capital has at the end of the production
process – a surplus value which, as a higher price of the product,
is realized only in circulation, but, like all prices, is realized in it
by already being ideally *presupposed* to it, determined before they
enter into it – signifies, expressed in accord with the general
concept of exchange value, that the labour time objectified in the
product – or amount of labour (expressed passively, the magnitude of labour appears as an amount of space; but expressed in
motion, it is measurable only in time) – is greater than that which
was present in the original components of capital. This in turn is
possible only if the labour objectified in the price of labour is
smaller than the living labour time purchased with it. The labour
time objectified in capital appears, as we have seen,[36] as a sum
consisting of three parts: (a) the labour time objectified in the raw
material; (b) the labour time objectified in the instrument of
labour; (c) the labour time objectified in the price of labour. Now,
parts (a) and (b) remain unchanged as components of capital;
while they may change their form, their modes of material existence, in the process, they remain unchanged as values. Only in
(c) does capital exchange one thing for something qualitatively
different; a given amount of objectified labour for an amount of
living labour. If living labour reproduced only the labour time
objectified in the labour price, this also would be merely formal,
and, as regards value, the only change which would have taken
place would have been that from one mode to another mode of
the existence of the same value, just as, in regard to the value of
the material of labour and the instrument, only a change of its
mode of material existence has taken place. If the capitalist has
paid the worker a price = one working day, and the worker's
working day adds only one working day to the raw material and

36. See above, pp. 297–303.

the instrument, then the capitalist would merely have exchanged exchange value in one form for exchange value in another. He would not have acted as capital. At the same time, the worker would not have remained within the simple exchange process; he would in fact have obtained the product of his labour in payment, except that the capitalist would have done him the favour of paying him the price of the product in advance of its realization [*Realisation*]. The capitalist would have advanced him credit, and free of charge at that, *pour le roi de Prusse*.[37] *Voilà tout*. No matter that for the worker the exchange between capital and labour, whose result is the price of labour, is a simple exchange; as far as the capitalist is concerned, it has to be a not-exchange. He has to obtain more value than he gives. Looked at from the capitalists' side, the exchange must be only *apparent*; i.e. must belong to an economic category other than exchange, or capital as capital and labour as labour in opposition to it would be impossible. They would be exchanged for one another only as identical exchange values existing in different material modes. – Thus the economists take refuge in this simple process in order to construct a legitimation, an apology for capital by explaining it with the aid of the very process which makes its existence impossible. In order to demonstrate it, they demonstrate it away. You pay me for my labour, you exchange it for its product and deduct from my pay the value of the raw material and instrument which you have furnished. That means we are *partners* who bring different elements into the process of production and exchange according to their values. Thus the product is transformed into money, and the money is divided in such a way that you, the capitalist, obtain the price of your raw material and your instrument, while I, the worker, obtain the price which my labour added to them. The benefit for you is that you now possess raw material and instrument in a form in which they are capable of being consumed (circulated); for me, that my labour has realized itself [*sich verwertet*]. Of course, you would soon be in the situation of having eaten up all your capital in the form of money, whereas I, as worker, would enter into the possession of both.

What the worker exchanges with capital is his labour itself (the capacity of disposing over it); he *divests himself of it* [*entäussert sie*]. What he obtains as price is the *value* of this divestiture

37. The expression in full is '*travailler pour le roi de Prusse*' ('to work for the king of Prussia'), i.e. to work for the purposes of another without recompense.

[*Entäusserung*]. He exchanges value-positing activity for a pre-determined value, regardless of the result of his activity.* Now how is its value determined? By the objectified labour contained in his commodity. This commodity exists in his vitality. In order to maintain this from one day to the next – we are not yet dealing with the working class, i.e. the replacement for wear and tear so that it can maintain itself as a class, since the worker here confronts capital as a *worker*, i.e. as a presupposed perennial subject [*Subjekt*], and not yet as a mortal individual of the working species – he has to consume a certain quantity of food, to replace his used-up blood etc. He receives no more than an equivalent. Thus tomorrow, after the completed exchange – and only after he has formally completed the exchange does he execute it in the process of production – his labouring capacity exists in the same mode as before: he has received an exact equivalent, because the price which he has obtained leaves him in possession of the same exchange value he had before. Capital has paid him the amount of objectified labour contained in his vital forces. Capital has consumed it, and because it did not exist as a thing, but as the capacity of a living being, the worker can, owing to the *specific* nature of his commodity – the specific nature of the life process – resume the exchange anew. Since we are dealing here not with any *particularly* qualified labour but with labour in general, simple labour, we are here not yet concerned with the fact that there is more labour objectified in his immediate existence than is con-

*One of Mr Bastiat's tremendous profundities is that *wage labour* is an inessential, only formal form, a form of association, which, *as such*, has nothing to do with the economic relation of labour and capital. If, he says, the workers were rich enough to be able to await the completion and sale of the product, then wages, wage labour, would not hinder them from making as advantageous a contract with their capitalist as their capitalist makes with another capitalist. Thus the evil lies not in the wage form, but in conditions independent of it. That these conditions are themselves the *wage condition* naturally does not occur to him. If the workers were capitalists at the same time, then indeed they would relate to non-working capital not as working workers, but as working capitalists – i.e. not in the form of wage-labourers. That is why wages and profit are *essentially* the same for him as *profit* and *interest*. This he calls the *harmony of economic relations*, namely that only *seemingly* economic relations exist, but in fact, in essence, there exists only one relation, that of simple exchange. The *essential* forms therefore appear to him as *lacking content*, i.e. not as real forms.[38]

38. See below, pp. 883–5.

tained in his mere vitality – i.e. the labour time necessary to pay for the products necessary to maintain his vitality – namely the values he has consumed in order to produce a specific *labouring capacity*, a special *skill* – and the value of these shows itself in the costs necessary to produce a similar labouring skill.

If one day's work were necessary in order to keep one worker alive for one day, then capital would not exist, because the working day would then exchange for its own product, so that capital could not realize itself and hence could not maintain itself as capital. The self-preservation of capital is its self-realization. If capital also had to work in order to live, then it would not maintain itself as capital but as labour. Property in raw materials and instruments of labour would be merely *nominal*; economically they would belong to the worker as much as to the capitalist, since they would create *value* for the capitalist only in so far as he himself were a worker. He would relate to them therefore not as capital, but as simple material and means of labour, like the worker himself does in the production process. If, however, only half a working day is necessary in order to keep one worker alive one whole day, then the surplus value of the product is self-evident, because the capitalist has paid the price of only half a working day but has obtained a whole day objectified in the product; thus has exchanged *nothing* for the second half of the work day. The only thing which can make him into a capitalist is not exchange, but rather a process through which he obtains *objectified labour time*, i.e. *value*, without exchange. Half the working day costs capital *nothing*; it thus obtains a value for which it has given no equivalent. And the multiplication of values can take place only if a value in excess of the equivalent has been obtained, hence *created*.

Surplus value in general is value in excess of the equivalent. The equivalent, by definition, is only the identity of value with itself. Hence surplus value can never sprout out of the equivalent; nor can it do so originally out of circulation; it has to arise from the production process of capital itself. The matter can also be expressed in this way: if the worker needs only half a working day in order to live a whole day, then, in order to keep alive as a worker, he needs to work only half a day. The second half of the labour day is forced labour; surplus-labour. What appears as surplus value on capital's side appears identically on the worker's side as surplus labour in excess of his requirements as worker, hence in excess of his immediate requirements for keeping himself alive. The great historic quality of capital is to *create* this *surplus labour*, superfluous labour from the standpoint of mere use value, mere subsistence; and its historic destiny [*Bestimmung*] is fulfilled as soon as, on one side, there has been such a development of needs that surplus labour above and beyond necessity has itself become a general need arising out of individual needs themselves – and, on the other side, when the severe discipline of capital, acting on succeeding generations [*Geschlechter*], has developed general industriousness as the general property of the new species [*Geschlecht*] – and, finally, when the development of the productive powers of labour, which capital incessantly whips onward with its unlimited mania for wealth, and of the sole conditions in which this mania can be realized, have flourished to the stage where the possession and preservation of general wealth require a lesser labour time of society as a whole, and where the labouring society relates scientifically to the process of its progressive reproduction, its reproduction in a constantly greater abundance; hence where labour in which a human being does what a thing could do has ceased. Accordingly, capital and labour relate to each other here like money and commodity; the former is the general form of wealth, the other only the substance destined for immediate consumption. Capital's ceaseless striving towards the general form of wealth drives labour beyond the limits of its natural paltriness [*Naturbedürftigkeit*], and thus creates the material elements for the development of the rich individuality which is as all-sided in its production as in its consumption, and whose labour also therefore appears no longer as labour, but as the full development of activity itself, in which natural necessity in its direct form has disappeared; because a historically created need has taken the place of the natural one. This is why *capital is productive; i.e. an essential relation for the development of the social productive forces*. It ceases to exist as such only where the development of these productive forces themselves encounters its barrier in capital itself.

The Times of November 1857 contains an utterly delightful cry of outrage on the part of a West-Indian plantation owner. This advocate analyses with great moral indignation – as a plea for the re-introduction of Negro slavery – how the *Quashees* (the free blacks of Jamaica) content themselves with producing only what is strictly necessary for their own consumption, and, alongside this 'use value', regard loafing (indulgence and idleness) as the real luxury good; how they do not care a damn for the sugar and the fixed capital invested in the plantations, but rather observe the planters' impending bankruptcy with an ironic grin of malicious pleasure, and even exploit their acquired Christianity as an embellishment for this mood of malicious glee and indolence.[39] They have ceased to be slaves, but not in order to become wage labourers, but, instead, self-sustaining peasants working for their own consumption. As far as they are concerned, capital does not exist as capital, because autonomous wealth as such can exist only either on the basis of *direct* forced labour, slavery, or *indirect* forced labour, *wage labour*. Wealth confronts direct forced labour not as capital, but rather as *relation of domination* [*Herrschaftsverhältnis*]; thus, the relation of domination is the only thing which is reproduced on this basis, for which wealth itself has value only as gratification, not as wealth itself, and which can therefore never create *general industriousness*. (We shall return to this relation of slavery and wage labour.)[40]

Surplus value. *Ricardo. Physiocrats. A. Smith. Ricardo*

The difficulty of grasping the creation of value shows itself (1) in those modern English economists who accuse Ricardo of not having understood the surplus, the *surplus value* (see *Malthus on value*, who at least tries to proceed scientifically),[41] whereas, among all the economists, Ricardo alone understood it, as is demonstrated by his polemic against A. Smith's confusion of the determination of value by wages and by the labour time objectified in the commodity. The newcomers are just plain simpletons. However, Ricardo himself often gets into confusion, because, although he well understands that the creation of surplus value is the presupposition of capital, he often goes astray in conceiving the multiplication of values on any basis other than the investment of *additional objectified labour time* in the same product, in other words, on any basis other than when production becomes

39. *The Times*, London, Saturday, 21 November 1857, No. 22,844, p. 9. 'Negroes and the Slave Trade. To the Editor of *The Times*. By Expertus', Marx's English in this sentence has been changed to conform to modern usage.

40. See below, pp. 419–20, 464–9, 471–514, 547–8.

41. This is a generalized reference to Malthus's numerous discussions of value, e.g. in *Principles of Political Economy*, London, 1836, pp. 50–135, *The Measure of Value*, London, 1823, and *Definitions in Political Economy*, London, 1827, pp. 23–36.

more difficult. Hence the absolute antithesis in his thinking between *value* and *wealth.* Hence the one-sidedness of his theory of ground rent; his erroneous theory of international trade, which is supposed to produce only use value (which he calls wealth), not exchange value.[42] The only avenue for the increase of values as such, apart from the *growing difficulty of production* (theory of rent), remains population growth (the natural increase among workers resulting from the growth of capital), although he himself never plainly summarized this relation. The basic mistake, that he never investigates where actually the distinction between the determination of value by wages and that by objectified labour comes from. Money and exchange itself (circulation) therefore appear only as purely formal elements in his economics; and although, according to him, economics is concerned *only* with exchange value, profit etc. appears there *only* as a percentage share of the product, which happens just as much on the basis of slavery. He never investigated the form of the mediation.

(2) *The Physiocrats.* Here the difficulty of grasping capital, the self-realization of value, hence the surplus value created by capital in the act of production, presents itself in tangible form, and this was necessarily so among the fathers of modern economics, just as was the case with the creation of surplus value in Ricardo, which he conceives in the form of rent, during the final classical conclusion of this economics. It is at bottom the question of the concept of capital and of wage labour, and therefore the fundamental question which presents itself at the threshold of the system of modern society. The Monetary System had understood the autonomy of value only in the form in which it arose from simple circulation – *money*; it therefore made this *abstract form* of wealth into the exclusive object [*Objekt*] of nations which were just then entering into the period in which the *gaining of wealth as such* appeared as the aim of society itself. Then came the Mercantile System, an epoch where industrial capital and hence wage labour arose in manufactures, and developed in antithesis to and at the expense of non-industrial wealth, of feudal landed property. [The Mercantilists] already have faint notions of money as capital, but actually again only in the form of money, of the

42. Ricardo's polemic against Smith, in *On the Principles of Political Economy*, pp. 4–12; Ricardo on the effect on value of difficulties of production, pp. 60–67; the essential difference between value and wealth, p. 320; the theory of ground rent, pp. 53–75; the theory of international trade, pp. 131–61.

circulation of *mercantile* capital, of capital which *transforms* itself into *money*. Industrial capital has value for them, even the highest value – as a means, not as wealth itself in its productive process – because it creates mercantile capital and the latter, via circulation, becomes money. Labour in manufactures – i.e. at bottom industrial labour, but agricultural labour was and appeared to them, in antithesis, as chiefly productive of use values; raw products, processed, are more valuable, because in a clearer form, likewise more suitable for circulation, commerce; creating more money for the mercantile form (in this regard the historic view of wealth of non-agricultural peoples such as Holland, for example, in antithesis to that of the agricultural, feudal; agriculture did not appear at all in industrial form, but in feudal, hence as source of feudal, not of bourgeois wealth). Thus one form of wage labour, the industrial, and one form of capital, the industrial, were recognized as sources of wealth, but only in so far as they produced money. Exchange value itself therefore not yet conceived in the form of capital. Now the *Physiocrats*. They distinguish between capital and money, and conceive it in its general form as autonomous exchange value which preserves and increases itself in and through production. They also therefore examine the relation for itself, not merely as a moment of simple circulation, but rather as its presupposition which constantly rises out of it to become its presupposition again. They are therefore the fathers of modern economics. They also understand that the creation of surplus value by wage labour is the self-realization [*Selbstverwertung*], i.e. the realization [*Verwirklichung*] of capital. But how does labour act as a means to produce a surplus value out of capital, i.e. already-present value? Here they let the form drop altogether and only look at the simple production process. Hence only that labour can be productive which takes place in the kind of field where the natural force of the instrument of labour tangibly permits the labourer to produce more value than he consumes. Surplus value therefore does not arise from labour as such, but rather from the natural forces which labour uses and conducts – agriculture. This is therefore the only *productive labour*, for they have come so far that [they consider that] *only labour which creates surplus value is productive* (that surplus value has to express itself in a material product is a crude view which still occurs in A. Smith.[43] Actors are productive

43. Adam Smith, *Wealth of Nations*, Vol. II, p. 356.

workers, not in so far as they produce a play, but in so far as they increase their employer's wealth. But what sort of labour takes place, hence in what form labour materializes itself, is absolutely irrelevant for *this relation*. It is not irrelevant, again, from later points of view); but this surplus value surreptitiously transforms itself into a quantity of use value coming out of production, larger than that which is consumed in it. This multiplication of use values, the excess of the product above that which has to serve as a means for new production – of which a part can therefore be consumed unproductively – appears tangibly only in the relation between the natural seed and its product. Only a part of the harvest has to be directly returned to the soil as seed; products found in nature, the elements air, water, earth, light, and added substances such as fertilizer, then re-create the seed again in multiplied quantity as grain etc. In short, human labour has only to conduct the chemical processes (in agriculture), and in part also to promote them mechanically, or promote the reproduction of life itself (cattle-raising) in order to obtain the surplus, i.e. to transform the identical natural substances from a useless into a valuable form. An over-abundance of agricultural products (grain, cattle, raw materials) is therefore the true form of general wealth. From the economic viewpoint, therefore, *rent* is the only form of wealth. Thus it is that the first prophets of capital conceive only the not-capitalists, the *feudal landed proprietors*, as the representatives of *bourgeois* wealth. The consequence, the levy of all taxes on rent, is then, however, entirely to the advantage of bourgeois capital. The bourgeois glorify feudalism in theory – many a feudal figure, like the elder Mirabeau[44] has been duped by this – only in order to ruin it in actual practice. All other values merely represent raw material + labour; labour itself represents grain or other products of the soil, which labour consumes; hence the factory worker etc. adds no more to the raw material than he consumes in raw materials. Therefore, his labour as well as his employer create no additional wealth – wealth being the surplus above the commodities consumed in production – but merely give it forms more pleasant and useful for consumption. At that time the utilization of natural energy in industry had not developed, nor

44. Victor, Marquis de Mirabeau (1715–89), was an eccentric French aristocrat converted by Quesnay to the cause of Physiocracy in the 1750s, who subsequently wrote two of the main Physiocratic works, the *Théorie de l'impôt* (1760) and the *Philosophie rurale* (1763).

the division of labour etc. which increases the natural force of labour itself. This was the case, however, in A. Smith's time. With him, therefore, labour in principle the source of value, likewise of wealth, but actually labour too posits surplus value only in so far as in the division of labour the surplus appears as just as much a gift of nature, a natural force of society, as the soil with the Physiocrats. Hence the weight A. Smith lays on the division of labour. *Capital*, on the other hand, appears to him – because, although he defines labour as productive of value, he conceives it as use value, as productivity for-itself [*für sich seiend*], as *human* natural force in general (this distinguishes him from the Physiocrats), but not as wage labour, not in its *specific* character as form in antithesis to capital – not as that which contains wage labour as its internal contradiction from its origin, but rather in the form in which it emerges from circulation, as money, and is therefore created out of circulation, by *saving*. Thus capital does not originally realize itself – precisely because the appropriation of alien labour [*fremde Arbeit*] is not itself included in its concept. Capital appears only *afterwards*, after already having been presupposed as *capital* – a vicious circle – as *command over alien labour*. Thus, according to A. Smith, labour should actually have its own product for wages, wages should be = to the product, hence labour should not be wage labour and capital not capital. Therefore, in order to introduce profit and rent as original elements of the cost of production, i.e. in order to get a surplus value out of the capitalist production process, he presupposes them, in the clumsiest fashion. The capitalist does not want to give the use of his capital for nothing; the landowner, similarly, does not want to give land and soil over to production for nothing. They want something in return. This is the way in which they are introduced, with their demands, as historical facts, but not explained. Wages are actually the *only economically* justifiable, because necessary, element of production costs. Profit and rent are only *deductions* from wages, arbitrarily wrested by force in the historical process by capital and landed property, and justified *by law*, not economically. But on the other side, since he [Adam Smith] then confronts labour with the means and materials of production in the form of landed property and capital, as independent entities, he has essentially posited labour as wage labour. Therefore contradictions. Hence his vacillation in the determination of value; the placing of profit and ground rent on the same level; erroneous views about the influence of wages on prices etc. Now Ricardo (see 1).[45] With him, however, wage labour and capital are again conceived as a natural, not as a historically specific social form [*Gesellschaftsform*] for the creation of wealth as use value; i.e. their form as such, precisely because it is natural, is *irrelevant*, and is not conceived in its *specific* relation to the form of wealth, just as wealth itself, in its exchange-value form, appears as a merely formal mediation of its material composition; thus the specific character of bourgeois wealth is not grasped – precisely because it appears there as the adequate form of wealth as such, and thus, although *exchange value* is the point of departure, the *specific economic forms of exchange* themselves play no role at all in his economics. Instead, he always speaks about distribution of the general product of labour and of the soil among the three classes, as if the form of wealth based on *exchange value* were concerned only with *use value*, and as if exchange value were merely a ceremonial form, which vanishes in Ricardo just as money as medium of circulation vanishes in exchange. Therefore, in order to bring out the true laws of economics, he likes to refer to this relation of money as a merely formal one. Hence also his weakness in the doctrine of money proper.

The exact development of the concept of capital [is] necessary, since it [is] the fundamental concept of modern economics, just as capital itself, whose abstract, reflected image [is] its concept [*dessen abstraktes Gegenbild sein Begriff*], [is] the foundation of bourgeois society. The sharp formulation of the basic presuppositions of the relation must bring out all the contradictions of bourgeois production, as well as the boundary where it drives beyond itself.

⟨It is important to note that wealth as such, i.e. bourgeois wealth, is always expressed to the highest power as exchange value, where it is posited as *mediator*, as the mediation of the extremes of exchange value and use value themselves. This intermediary situation [*Mitte*] always appears as the *economic* relation in its completeness, because it comprises the opposed poles, and ultimately always appears as a one-sidedly higher power *vis-à-vis* the extremes themselves; because the movement, or the relation, which *originally* appears as mediatory between the extremes necessarily develops dialectically to where it appears as mediation with itself, as the subject [*Subjekt*] for whom the extremes are merely its

45. A reference back to the brief discussion of Ricardo on pp. 326–7.

moments, whose autonomous presupposition it suspends in order to posit itself, through their suspension, as that which alone is autonomous. Thus, in the religious sphere, Christ, the mediator between God and humanity – a mere instrument of circulation between the two – becomes their unity, God-man, and, as such, becomes more important than God; the saints more important than Christ; the popes more important than the saints. Where it is posited as middle link, exchange value is always the total economic expression, itself one-sided against the extremes; e.g. money in simple circulation; capital itself as mediator between production and circulation. Within capital itself, one form of it in turn takes up the position of use value against the other as exchange value. Thus e.g. does industrial capital appear as producer as against the merchant, who appears as circulation. Thus the former represents the material [*stofflich*], the latter the formal side, i.e. wealth as wealth. At the same time, mercantile capital is itself in turn the mediator between production (industrial capital) and circulation (the consuming public) or between exchange value and use value, where both sides are posited alternately, production as money and circulation as use value (consuming public) or the former as use value (product) and the latter as exchange value (money). Similarly within commerce itself: the wholesaler as mediator between manufacturer and retailer, or between manufacturer and agriculturalist, or between different manufacturers; he is the same mediator at a higher level. And in turn, in the same way, the commodity brokers as against the wholesalers. Then the banker as against the industrialists and merchants; the joint-stock company as against simple production; the financier as mediator between the state and bourgeois society, on the highest level. *Wealth as such* presents itself more distinctly and broadly the further it is removed from direct production and is itself mediated between poles, each of which, considered for itself, is already posited as economic form. Money becomes an end rather than a means; and the higher form of mediation, as capital, everywhere posits the lower as itself, in turn, labour, as merely a source of surplus value. For example, the bill-broker, banker etc. as against the manufacturers and farmers, which are posited in relation to him in the role of labour (of use value); while he posits himself toward them as capital, extraction of surplus value; the wildest form of this, the financier.⟩

Capital is *direct unity* of product and money or, better, of production and circulation. Thus it itself is again something *im-*

mediate, and its development consists of positing and suspending itself as this unity – which is posited as a specific and therefore simple relation. The unity at first appears in capital as something *simple*.

⟨Ricardo's reasoning is simply this: products are exchanged for one another – hence capital for capital – according to the amounts of objectified labour contained in them. A day's work is always exchanged for a day's work. This is presupposition. Exchange itself can therefore be entirely left out. The product – capital posited as product – is exchange value *in itself*, to which exchange merely adds form; formal form with him. The only question is now in what *proportions* this product is divided up and distributed. Whether these *proportions* are regarded as specific quotas of the presupposed exchange value, or of its content, material wealth, [is] the same thing. Moreover, since exchange as such is merely circulation – money as circulation – it is better to abstract from it altogether, and to examine only the proportions of material wealth which have been distributed within the production process or because of it to the various factors. In the *exchange* form, all value etc. is merely *nominal*; it is real only in the form of the *proportion*. Exchange as a whole, to the extent that it creates no greater *material* variety, is *nominal*. Since a full day's work is always exchanged for a full day's work, the sum of *values* remains the same – the growth in the forces of production affects only the content of wealth, not its form. An increase of values can arise, therefore, only out of an increasing difficulty in production – and this can take place only where the forces of nature no longer afford an equal service to equal quantities of human labour, i.e. where the fertility of the natural elements decreases – in agriculture. The decline of profits is therefore caused by rent.[46] Firstly the false presupposition that a *full day's work* is always worked in all social conditions; etc. etc. (see above[47]).⟩

Surplus value and productive force. Relation when these increase. – Result. – Productive force of labour is productive force of capital. – In proportion as necessary labour is already diminished, the realization of capital becomes more difficult

We have seen: The worker needs to work only e.g. half a working day in order to live a whole one; and hence to be able to begin the

46. Ricardo, *On the Principles of Political Economy*, pp. 120–25.
47. pp. 326–7.

same process again the next day. Only half a day's work is objectified in his labouring capacity – to the extent that it exists in him as someone *alive*, or as a *living* instrument of labour. The worker's entire living day (day of life) is the static result, the objectification of half a day's work. By appropriating the entire day's work and then consuming it in the production process with the materials of which his capital consists, but by giving in exchange only the labour objectified in the worker – i.e. half a day's work – the capitalist creates the surplus value of his capital; in this case, half a day of objectified labour. Now suppose that the productive powers of labour double, i.e. that the same labour creates double the *use value* in the same time. (For the moment, use value is defined in the present relation as only that which the worker consumes in order to stay alive as a worker; the quantity of the means of life for which, through the mediation of money, he exchanges the labour objectified in his living labouring capacity.) The worker would then have to work only $\frac{1}{4}$ day in order to live a full day; the capitalist then needs to give the worker only $\frac{1}{4}$ day's objectified labour in exchange, in order to increase his surplus value in the production process from $\frac{1}{2}$ to $\frac{3}{4}$; so that he would gain $\frac{3}{4}$ day's objectified labour instead of $\frac{1}{2}$. At the end of the production process, the value of the capital would have risen by $\frac{3}{4}$ instead of by $\frac{2}{4}$. Thus the capitalist would have to make the workers work only $\frac{3}{4}$ day, in order to add the same surplus value – that of $\frac{1}{2}$ or $\frac{2}{4}$ objectified labour – to his capital. However, as representative of the general form of wealth – money – capital is the endless and limitless drive to go beyond its limiting barrier. Every boundary [*Grenze*] is and has to be a barrier [*Schranke*] for it.[48] Else it would cease to be capital – money as self-reproductive. If ever it perceived a certain boundary not as a barrier, but became comfortable within it as a boundary, it would itself have declined from exchange value to use value, from the general form of wealth to a specific, substantial mode of the same. Capital as such creates a specific surplus value because it cannot create an infinite one all at once; but it is the constant movement to create more of the same. The quantitative boundary of the surplus value appears to it as a

48. Cf. Hegel, *Science of Logic*, pp. 131–7, especially p. 132: 'Something's own boundary posited by it as a negative which is at the same time essential, is not merely boundary as such but barrier.' Also, p. 135: 'The sentient creature, in the limitation of hunger, thirst, etc., is the drive to go beyond its limiting barrier, and it does overcome it.'

mere natural barrier, as a necessity which it constantly tries to violate and beyond which it constantly seeks to go.* Therefore (quite apart from the factors entering in later, competition, prices etc.) the capitalist will make the worker work not only $\frac{3}{4}$ day, because the $\frac{3}{4}$ day bring him the *same surplus value* as the whole day did before, but rather he will make him work the full day; and the increase in the productive force which allows the worker to work for $\frac{1}{4}$ day and live a whole day now expresses itself simply in that he now has to work $\frac{3}{4}$ day for capital, whereas before he worked for it only $\frac{2}{4}$ day. The increased productive force of his labour, to the extent that it is a shortening of the time required to replace the labour objectified in him (for use value, subsistence), appears as a lengthening of the time he labours for the realization of capital (for exchange value). From the worker's standpoint, he now has to do a surplus labour of $\frac{3}{4}$ day in order to live a full day, while before he only had to do a surplus labour of $\frac{2}{4}$ day. The increase, the doubling of the productive force, has increased his surplus labour by $\frac{1}{4}$ [day]. One remark here: the productive force has doubled, the surplus labour the worker has to do has not doubled, but has only grown by $\frac{1}{4}$ [day]; nor has capital's surplus value doubled; but it, too, has grown by only $\frac{1}{4}$ [day]. This shows, then, that surplus labour (from the worker's standpoint) or surplus value (from capital's standpoint) does not grow in the same numerical proportion as the productive force. Why? The doubling in the productive force is the reduction of necessary labour (for the worker) by $\frac{1}{4}$ [day], hence also the [increase of the] production of surplus value by $\frac{1}{4}$, because the original relation was posited as $\frac{1}{2}$. If the worker had to work, originally, $\frac{2}{3}$ day in order to live one full day, then the surplus value would have been $\frac{1}{3}$, and the surplus labour the same. The doubling in the productive force of labour would then have enabled the worker to restrict his necessary labour to half of $\frac{2}{3}$ or $\frac{2}{3 \times 2}$, $\frac{2}{6}$ or $\frac{1}{3}$ day, and the capitalist would have gained $\frac{1}{3}$ [day] of value. But the total surplus labour would have become $\frac{2}{3}$ [day]. The

*The barrier appears as an accident which has to be conquered. This is apparent on even the most superficial inspection. If capital increases from 100 to 1,000, then 1,000 is now the point of departure, from which the increase has to begin; the tenfold multiplication, by 1,000%, counts for nothing; profit and interest themselves become capital in turn. *What appeared as surplus value now appears as simple presupposition etc.*, as included in *its simple composition.*

doubling of the productive force, which resulted in $\frac{1}{4}$ [day] surplus value and surplus labour in the first example, would now result in $\frac{1}{3}$ [day] surplus value or surplus labour. The multiplier of the productive force – the number by which it is multiplied – is therefore not the multiplier of surplus labour or of surplus value; but rather, if the original relation of the labour objectified in the labour price was $\frac{1}{2}$ of the labour objectified in 1 working day, which always appears as the limit,* then the doubling is equal to the division of $\frac{1}{2}$ by 2 (in the original relation), i.e. $\frac{1}{4}$. If the original relation was $\frac{2}{3}$, then the doubling equals the division of $\frac{2}{3}$ by $2 = \frac{2}{6}$ or $\frac{1}{3}$. The multiplier of the productive force is thus never the multiplier but always the divisor of the original relation, not the multiplier of its numerator but of its denominator. If it were the former, then the multiplication of the productive force would correspond to the multiplication of the surplus value. Instead, the surplus value is always equal to the division of the original relation by the multiplier of the productive force. If the original relation was $\frac{8}{9}$, i.e. the worker needs $\frac{8}{9}$ of a working day to live, so that capital gains only $\frac{1}{9}$ in its exchange with living labour, if surplus labour equals $\frac{1}{9}$, then the worker can now live from half of $\frac{8}{9}$ of a working day, i.e. with $\frac{8}{18} = \frac{4}{9}$ (whether we divide the numerator or multiply the denominator the same thing), and the capitalist, who orders a full day's work, would have a total surplus value of $\frac{4}{9}$ working day; subtracting the original surplus value of $\frac{1}{9}$ from this leaves $\frac{3}{9}$ or $\frac{1}{3}$. The doubling of the productive force therefore = here an increase in surplus value or surplus time by $\frac{1}{3}$. This is simply because the surplus value is always equal to the relation between the whole working day and that part of the working day necessary to keep the worker alive. The unit in which surplus value is calculated is always a fraction, i.e. the given part of a day which exactly represents the price of labour. If that is $= \frac{1}{2}$, then the increase in the productive force = the reduction of necessary labour to $\frac{1}{4}$; if it is $= \frac{1}{3}$, then reduction of

---

*Messrs the manufacturers have, however, also prolonged it into the night, *ten hours' bill*. See the report of Leonard Horner.[49] The working day itself does not recognize daylight as a limit; it can be lengthened *deep into the night*; this belongs to the chapter on *wages*.

---

49. Leonard Horner (1785–1864) was originally a geologist, and from 1833 to 1860 Chief Factory Inspector in Lancashire. His many reports on factory conditions there were an important source for Marx in the writing of *Capital*; the reference here would be to one of Horner's reports on the breaches of the Ten Hours' Act committed by manufacturers during the 1850s.

necessary labour to $\frac{1}{6}$; hence in the first, the total surplus value $=$ $\frac{3}{4}$; in the second $=\frac{5}{6}$; the relative surplus value, i.e. relative to that present before, in the first case $=\frac{1}{4}$, in the second $=\frac{2}{6}$ or $\frac{1}{3}$. Therefore the value of capital does not grow in the same proportion as the productive force increases, but in the proportion in which the increase in the productive force, the multiplier of productive force, divides the fraction of the working day which expresses the part of the day belonging to the worker. The extent to which the productive force of labour increases the value of capital thus depends on the original relation between the portion of labour objectified in the worker and his living labour. This portion is always expressed as a fractional part of the whole working day, $\frac{1}{3}$, $\frac{2}{3}$, etc. The increase in productive force, i.e. its multiplication by a given amount, is equal to a division of the numerator or the multiplication of the denominator of this fraction by the same amount. Thus the largeness or smallness of the increase of value depends not only on the number which expresses the multiplication of the productive force, but equally on the previously given relation which makes up the part of the work day belonging to the price of labour. If this relation is $\frac{1}{3}$, then the doubling of the productive force of the working day $=$ a reduction of the same to $\frac{1}{6}$; if it is $\frac{2}{3}$, then reduction to $\frac{2}{6}$. The objectified labour contained in the price of labour is always equal to a fractional part of the whole day; always arithmetically expressed as a fraction; always a relation between numbers, never a simple number. If the productive force doubles, multiplies by 2, then the worker has to work only $\frac{1}{2}$ of the previous time in order to get the price of labour out of it; but how much labour time he still needs for this purpose depends on the first, given relation, namely on the time which was required before the increase in productive force. The multiplier of the productive force is the divisor of this original fraction. Value or surplus labour therefore does not increase in the same numerical relation as productive force. If the original relation is $\frac{1}{2}$ and the productive force is doubled, then the *necessary* (for the worker) labour time reduces itself to $\frac{1}{4}$ and the surplus value grows by only $\frac{1}{4}$. If the productive force is quadrupled, then the original relation becomes $\frac{1}{8}$ and the value grows by only $\frac{1}{8}$. The value can never be equal to the entire working day; i.e. a certain part of the working day must always be exchanged for the labour objectified in the worker. Surplus value in general is only the relation of living labour to that objectified in the worker; *one member of the relation must therefore always remain.* A certain relation between increase in productive force and increase of value is already given in the fact that the relation is constant as a relation, although its factors vary. We see therefore, on one side, that relative surplus value is exactly equal to relative surplus labour; if the working day was $\frac{1}{2}$ and the productive force doubles, then the part belonging to the worker, *necessary labour*, reduces itself to $\frac{1}{4}$ and the new value is also exactly $\frac{1}{4}$; but the total value is now $\frac{3}{4}$. While surplus value rose by $\frac{1}{4}$, i.e. in the relation of $1:4$, the total surplus value $= \frac{3}{4} = 3:4$. Now if we assume that $\frac{1}{4}$ was the original *necessary* working day, and a doubling in productive force took place, then necessary labour is reduced to $\frac{1}{8}$ and surplus labour or surplus value exactly $= \frac{1}{8} = 1:8$. The total surplus value by contrast $= 7:8$. In the first example the original total surplus value $= 1:2$ ($\frac{1}{2}$) and then rose to $3:4$; in the second case the original total surplus value was $\frac{3}{4}$ and has now risen to $7:8$ ($\frac{7}{8}$). In the first case it has grown from $\frac{1}{2}$ or $\frac{2}{4}$ to $\frac{3}{4}$; in the second from $\frac{3}{4}$ or $\frac{6}{8}$ to $\frac{7}{8}$; in the first case by $\frac{1}{4}$, in the second by $\frac{1}{8}$; i.e. in the first case it rose twice as much as in the second: but in the first case the total surplus value is only $\frac{3}{4}$ or $\frac{6}{8}$, while it is $\frac{7}{8}$ in the second, i.e. $\frac{1}{8}$ more.

Let *necessary labour* be $\frac{1}{16}$, then total surplus value $= \frac{15}{16}$; which was $\frac{5}{8} = \frac{10}{16}$ in the previous relation; thus the total surplus value presupposed is by $\frac{5}{16}$ higher than in the previous case.[50] Now let the productive force double, then necessary labour $= \frac{1}{32}$; which was previously $= \frac{2}{32}$ ($\frac{1}{16}$); hence surplus time has risen by $\frac{1}{32}$, surplus value by the same proportion. As regards the total surplus value, which was $\frac{16}{16}$ or $\frac{30}{32}$, this is now $\frac{31}{32}$. Compared to the earlier relation (where *necessary* labour was $\frac{1}{4}$ or $\frac{8}{32}$), the total surplus value is now $\frac{31}{32}$, whereas it was only $\frac{30}{32}$ earlier, hence grew by $\frac{1}{32}$. But regarded relatively, the doubling of production increased it in the first case by $\frac{1}{8}$ or $\frac{4}{32}$, while it has now increased by only $\frac{1}{32}$, i.e. by $\frac{3}{32}$ less.

If *necessary labour* had already been reduced to $1/1,000$, then the total surplus value would be $= 999/1,000$. Now if the productive force increased a thousandfold, then *necessary labour* would decline to $1/1,000,000$ working day and the total surplus value would amount to $999,999/1,000,000$ of a working day; whereas before this increase in productive force it amounted to only $999/1,000$ or $999,000/1,000,000$; it would thus have grown by $999/1,000,000 =$

50. This is a slip of the pen on Marx's part. The 'previous relation' was $\frac{5}{8} = \frac{14}{16}$, not $\frac{5}{8} = \frac{10}{16}$. Therefore the total surplus value was higher by $\frac{1}{16}$ not $\frac{5}{16}$.

$\frac{1}{11}$ $\left(\text{with the addition of } \frac{1}{11 + \frac{1}{999}}\right)$,[51] i.e. the thousandfold increase in productive force would have increased the total surplus by not even $\frac{1}{11}$, i.e. not even by $\frac{3}{33}$, whereas in the previous case it rose by $\frac{1}{32}$ owing to a mere doubling of the productive force. If necessary labour falls from 1/1,000 to 1/1,000,000, then it falls by exactly 999/1,000,000 (for 1/1,000 = 1,000/1,000,000), i.e. by the surplus value.

If we summarize this, we find:

Firstly: The increase in the productive force of living labour increases the *value* of capital (or diminishes the value of the worker) not because it increases the quantity of products or use values created by the same labour – the productive force of labour is its natural force – but rather because it diminishes *necessary* labour, hence, in the same relation as it diminishes the former, it creates *surplus labour* or, what amounts to the same thing, surplus value; because the surplus value which capital obtains through the production process consists only of the excess of surplus labour over *necessary labour*. The increase in productive force can increase surplus labour – i.e. the excess of labour objectified in capital as product over the labour objectified in the exchange value of the working day – only to the extent that it diminishes the relation of *necessary labour* to *surplus labour,* and only in the proportion in which it diminishes this relation. Surplus value is exactly equal to surplus labour; the increase of the one [is] exactly measured by the diminution of *necessary labour*.

Secondly: The surplus value of capital does not increase as does the multiplier of the productive force, i.e. the amount to which the productive force (posited as unity, as multiplicand) increases; but by the surplus of the fraction of the living work day which originally represents necessary labour, in excess over this same fraction divided by the multiplier of the productive force. Thus if *necessary labour* $= \frac{1}{4}$ of the living work day and the productive force doubles, then the value of capital does not double, but grows by $\frac{1}{8}$; which is equal to $\frac{1}{4}$ or $\frac{2}{8}$ (the original fraction of the work day which represents necessary labour) $- \frac{1}{4}$ divided by 2, or $= \frac{2}{8}$ minus $\frac{1}{8} = \frac{1}{8}$. (That value doubles itself can also be expressed, it grows $\frac{4}{2}$ [-fold] or $\frac{16}{8}$ [-fold]. Its growth would relate to that of the productive force

51. This should read $\frac{999}{1,000,000} = \frac{1}{1,001 + \frac{1}{999}}$.

by 1:16. (That is it!)[52] If the fraction was 1/1,000 and the productive force increases a thousandfold, then the value of capital does not grow a thousandfold, but rather by far less than $\frac{1}{11}$; it grows by 1/1,000 − 1/1,000,000, i.e. by 1,000/1,000,000 − 1/1,000,000 = 999/1,000,000.)

Thus the *absolute sum* by which capital increases its value through a given increase of the productive force depends on the *given fractional part* of the working day, on the fractional part of the working day which represents *necessary labour*, and which therefore expresses the original relation of necessary labour to the living work day. The increase in productive force in a given relation can therefore increase the value of capital differently e.g. in the *different countries*. A general increase of productive force in a given relation can increase the value of capital differently in the different branches of industry, and will do so, depending on the different relation of *necessary labour* to the living work day in these branches. This relation would naturally be the same in all branches of business in a system of free competition, if labour were simple labour everywhere, hence *necessary labour* the same. (If it represented the same amount of objectified labour.)

Thirdly: The larger the surplus value of capital *before the increase of productive force*, the larger the amount of presupposed surplus labour or surplus value of capital; or, the smaller the fractional part of the working day which forms the equivalent of the worker, which expresses necessary labour, the smaller is the increase in surplus value which capital obtains from the increase of productive force. Its surplus value rises, but in an ever smaller relation to the development of the productive force. Thus the more developed capital already is, the more surplus labour it has created, the more terribly must it develop the productive force in order to realize itself in only smaller proportion, i.e. to add surplus value – because its barrier always remains the relation between the fractional part of the day which expresses *necessary labour*, and the entire working day. It can move only within these boundaries. The smaller already the fractional part falling to *necessary labour*, the greater the *surplus labour*, the less can any increase in productive force perceptibly diminish necessary labour; since the denominator has grown enormously. The self-realization of capital becomes more difficult to the extent that it has already been realized. The increase of productive

52. In English in the original.

force would become irrelevant to capital; realization itself would become irrelevant, because its proportions have become minimal, and it would have ceased to be capital. If necessary labour were 1/1,000 and the productive force tripled, then it would fall to only 1/3,000 or surplus labour would have increased by only 2/3,000. But this happens not because wages have increased or the share of labour in the product, but because it has *already* fallen so low, regarded in its relation to the product of labour or to the living work day.*

(All these statements correct only in this abstraction for the relation from the present standpoint. Additional relations will enter which modify them significantly. The whole, to the extent that it proceeds entirely in generalities, *actually already belongs in the doctrine of profit*.)

So much in general for the time being: the development of the productive force of labour – first the positing of surplus labour – is a necessary condition for the growth of value or the realization of capital. As the infinite urge to wealth, it strives consistently towards infinite increase of the productive forces of labour and calls them into being. But on the other hand, every increase in the productive force of labour – leaving aside the fact that it increases the use values for the capitalist – is an increase in the productive force of capital and, from the present standpoint, is a productive force of labour only in so far as it is a productive force of capital.

Concerning increases in the value of capital

This much is already clear, can at least be mentioned in anticipation: the increase in the productive force does not in and by itself increase prices. For example the bushel of wheat. If a half of a working day objectifies itself in one bushel of wheat, and if this is the worker's price, then the surplus labour can only produce 2 bushels of wheat. Thus 2 bushels of wheat [is] the value of one working day, and if that = 26s. in money, = 26s. Each bushel = 13s. Now if the productive force doubles, then the bushel of wheat no more than = $\frac{1}{4}$ working day; = $6\frac{1}{2}$s. With the productive force, the price of this fractional part of the commodity fell. But the total

---

*The labour objectified in the worker here shows itself as a fraction *of his own living work day*; for that is the same as [the proportion] in which the objectified labour which he obtains from capital as wages stands to the entire working day.

price remained; but now a surplus of $\frac{3}{4}$ working day. Every fourth = 1 bushel wheat = $6\frac{1}{2}$s. Thus the total product = 26s. = 4 bushels. Same as before. The value of the capital increased from 13s. to $19\frac{1}{2}$s. The value of labour diminished from 13s. to $6\frac{1}{2}$s.; material production rose from 2 bushels to 4. Now $19\frac{1}{2}$.[53] Now, if the force of production were to double also in gold production, so that, if 13s. were the product of half a working day and this half a day were the *necessary labour* before; now $\frac{1}{4}$ [working day] produces 52s. or $52-13 = 39$s. more. 1 bushel of wheat now = 13s.; the same fractional price afterwards as before; but the total product = 52s.; before only = 26s. On the other hand, the 52s. would now buy 4 bushels, while the 26, earlier, bought only 2.

Well. First of all it is clear that if capital has already raised surplus labour to the point where the entire living work day is consumed in the production process (and we here assume the working day to be the natural amount of labour time which the worker is able to put at the disposal of capital; this is always only for a *specific time*, i.e. *specific labour time*), then an increase in the productive force cannot increase labour time, nor, therefore, objectified labour time. The product objectifies one working day, whether *the necessary time of labour* is represented by 6 or 3 hours, by $\frac{1}{2}$ or $\frac{1}{4}$ of the working day. The surplus value of capital has grown; i.e. its value relative to the worker – for if it was only = $\frac{2}{4}$ before, it is now = to $\frac{3}{4}$ of objectified labour time; but its value increased not because the *absolute* but because the *relative amount of labour* grew; i.e. the total amount of labour did not grow; the working day is as long before as after; hence no absolute increase in surplus time (surplus labour time); rather the *amount of necessary labour decreased*, and that is how relative surplus labour increased. The worker in fact worked a whole day before, but only $\frac{1}{2}$ day of surplus time; afterwards, as before, he works the whole day, but $\frac{3}{4}$ of a day of surplus time. To that extent, therefore, the price (presupposing this as its gold and silver value), or the exchange value of capital, has not increased with the doubling of the productive force. This therefore concerns the *rate of profit*, not the price of the product or the value of the capital, which became a commodity again in the product. But in fact the absolute values also increase in this manner, because that part of wealth which is posited as capital – as self-realizing value – also increases. (*Accumu-*

53. This seems to refer back to the value of the capital rather than the material production (the latter would still be 26s.).

lation of capitals.) Take our earlier example. Let *capital* = 100 thalers, and let it decompose in the production process into the following parts: 50 thalers cotton, 40 thalers wages, 10 thalers instrument. Assume at the same time, in order to simplify the arithmetic, that the entire instrument of labour is consumed in one act of production (and this is quite beside the point here, so far), so that its entire value would reappear in the form of the product. Suppose in this case that the 40 thalers which go to labour express a labour time objectified in living labouring capacity of, say, 4 hours, giving capital 8 hours. Presupposing the instrument and the raw material, the total product would amount to 100 thalers, if the worker works only 4 hours, i.e. if the raw material and the instrument were his property and he worked for 4 hours only. He would increase the 60 thalers by 40, which he could consume, since firstly he replaces the 60 thalers in raw material and instrument required for production, and then adds a surplus value of 40 thalers as reproduction of his own living labour capacity or of the time objectified in him. He could repeat the work again and again, since he would have reproduced the value of the raw material and of the instrument as well as of the labouring capacity; the latter by constantly increasing the value of the former by 4 hours of objectified labour. But now let him receive the 40 thalers in wages only by working 8 hours, so that he would add to the material and instrument of labour, which now confront him as capital, a surplus value of 80 thalers; while the former surplus value of 40 thalers, which he added, is only exactly the value of his labour. He would thus add a surplus value exactly = to the surplus labour or surplus time.* The value of capital would thus have increased from 100 thalers to 140.†

* It is not in the least necessary at this point to assume that the material and instrument also has to increase along with surplus labour or surplus time. How surplus labour by itself increases the raw material, see Babbage, e.g. the working of gold wire etc.[54]

† Assume further that raw material doubles and the instrument of labour (for the sake of simpler arithmetic) increases by one-half. Then capital costs would amount to 100 thalers cotton, 20 thalers instrument, i.e. 120 thalers; for labour, now as then, 40 thalers; altogether 160 thalers. If a surplus labour of 4 hours increases 100 thalers by 40%, then it increases 160 thalers by 64 thalers. Hence the total product = 224 thalers. We here have presupposed,

54. Babbage, *Traité sur l'économie des machines et des manufactures*, pp. 218–19.

Now, capital regarded as simple exchange value would be absolutely greater, 140 thalers instead of 100; but in fact, a new value would merely have been created, i.e. a value which is not merely necessary to replace the 60 thalers in advances for the materials and the instrument of labour and the 40 thalers for labour, a new value of 40 thalers. The values in circulation would have been increased by 80 thalers, by 40 thalers of additional objectified labour time.

Now assume the same presupposition. 100 thalers capital; specifically, 50 for cotton, 40 for labour, 10 for instrument of production; let the surplus labour time remain as before, i.e. 4 hours, and the total labour time 8 hours. Thus in all cases the product only = 8 hours labour time = 140 thalers. Now suppose the productive force of labour doubles; i.e. 2 hours would be enough for the worker to realize raw materials and instrument to the extent required to maintain his labouring capacity. If 40 thalers were an objectified labour time of 4 hours, then 20 thalers would be the objectified labour time of 2 hours. These 20 thalers now express the same use value as the 40 thalers before. The exchange value of labouring capacity has diminished by half, because half of the original labour time creates the same use value, while the exchange value of the use value is measured purely by the labour time objectified in it. But the capitalist makes the workers work 8 hours now as before, and his product therefore represents now as before a labour time of 8 hours = 80 thalers of labour time, while the value of raw material and material remain the same, namely 60 thalers; altogether, as before, 140 thalers. (In order to live, the worker himself would have had to add to the 60 thalers of raw material and instrument a value of no more than 20 thalers, he would thus have created a value of only 80 thalers. The total value of his product would have diminished, by the doubling of production, from 100 to 80, by 20 thalers, i.e. by $\frac{1}{5}$ of 100 = 20%.) But the surplus time or surplus value for capital is now 6 hours instead of 4, or 60 thalers instead of 40. Its increment is 2 hours, 20 thalers. His accounts would now show the following: for raw material, 50;

---

further, that the rate of profit does not vary with the size of capital; and material and instrument of labour are not regarded as being themselves realizations, capitalizations of surplus labour; as we saw, the greater the already posited surplus time, i.e. the size of capital as such, the more is it presupposed that an *absolute increase of labour time* is impossible, and that a relative increase, resulting from an increase in the productive force, declines in geometric proportion.

for labour, 20; for instrument, 10; costs = 80 thalers. Gain = 60 thalers. Now as before he would sell the product for 140 thalers, but would show a gain of 60 thalers instead of 40 as before. On one side, therefore, he throws only the same exchange value into circulation as before, 140 thalers. But the surplus value of his capital has grown by 20 thalers. Accordingly, only the share he gets of the 140 thalers [is] the rate of his profit. The worker in fact worked 2 hours more for him free of charge, i.e. 6 hours instead of 4, and this is the same for him as if he had worked 10 hours instead of 8 in the earlier relation, had increased his *absolute labour time*. But indeed a *new value* has arisen also; namely 20 additional thalers are posited as *autonomous* value, as objectified labour which has become free, unbound from the task of serving only in exchange for earlier labour power [*Arbeitskraft*]. This can present itself in two ways. Either the 20 thalers set as much additional labour into motion as becomes *capital* and creates larger exchange value: make more objectified labour into the point of departure for the new production process; or the capitalist exchanges the 20 thalers as money for commodities other than those which he needs in its production as industrial capital; all commodities other than labour and money themselves thus are exchanged for 20 more thalers, for 2 more hours of objectified labour time. Their *exchange value* has thus increased by just this *liberated sum*. In fact, 140 thalers are 140 thalers, as the very 'perceptive' French publisher of the Physiocrats remarks against Boisguillebert.[55] But it is false that these 140 thalers only represent more use value; they represent a greater amount of *independent exchange value*, of *money*, of *latent capital*; i.e. of wealth posited as *wealth*. The economists themselves admit this later when they allow the accumulation of capitals to accumulate not only the mass of use values, but that of *exchange values* too; for, according to Ricardo himself, the element of the accumulation of capitals is posited just as completely with relative surplus labour as with absolute – impossible any other way.[56] On the other side, it is already implicit in the thesis best developed by Ricardo, that these excess 20 thalers, which are created purely by the increase in pro-

55. The 'perceptive' publisher was the editor of Eugène Daire (1798–1847), who issued the works of the Physiocrats during the 1840s. The comments on Boisguillebert are in *Économistes financiers du XVIIIe siècle*, Paris, 1843, p. 419, notes 1 and 2.

56. Ricardo, *On the Principles of Political Economy*, pp. 88–92.

ductive force, can become capital again. Earlier, only 40 of the 140 thalers (leaving capital's consumption aside for now) could become new capital; 100 do not become capital but remain capital; now 60 [can], i.e. the present capital is greater by an exchange value of 20 thalers. Thus, exchange value, *wealth as such*, has increased, although the total sum of the same has *not* directly increased. Why has it increased? Because that part of the total sum has increased which was not a mere medium of circulation, but money; or which was not merely equivalent, but *exchange value for-itself* [*für sich seiend*]. Either the liberated 20 thalers were accumulated as money, i.e. added to the stock of exchange values in general (abstract) exchange value form; or they all circulated, and then the prices of the commodities bought with them rise; they all represent more money, as well as, since the production cost of gold has not fallen (rather, risen relative to the commodity produced by the more productive capital), more objectified labour (because of this, the excess production, which at first only appeared on the side of the one producing capital, now appears on the side of the others, which produce the more expensive commodities); or the 20 thalers are directly used up as capital by the originally circulating capital. Thus a new capital of 20 thalers is posited – a sum of self-preserving and self-realizing wealth. Capital has risen by the exchange value of 20 thalers. (Circulation actually does not yet concern us here, since we are here dealing with capital in general, and circulation can only mediate between capital in the form of money and capital in its form as capital; the first capital may realize money as such, i.e. exchange it for commodities, consume more than before; but in the hand of the producer of these commodities this money becomes capital. Thus it becomes capital directly in the hands of the first capital, or, via a detour, [in those] of another capital. But the other capital is always in turn capital as such; and we are concerned here with *capital as such*, [let us] say the capital of the whole society. The differentiation etc. of capitals does not concern us yet.) In general, these 20 thalers can appear only in a double form. As money, so that capital again exists in the character of money which has not yet become capital – its point of departure; the abstract-autonomous form of exchange value or of general wealth; or itself in turn as capital, as a new domination of objectified labour over living labour.* (Every increase in the mass

* In the example given, the productive force has doubled, risen by 100%, the value of capital has risen by 20%.

of capital employed can increase the *productive force* not only at an arithmetical but at a geometrical rate; although it can increase profit at the same time – as increase of productive force – only at a much lower rate. The influence of the increase of capital on the increase of productive force is thus infinitely greater than that of the increase of the productive force on the growth of capital.) As general wealth, materialized in the form of money (of the thing, in its mere abstractness), or of *new* living labour. The capitalist consumes, say, 20 of the 140 thalers as use values for himself, through the mediation of money as means of circulation. Thus, in the first presupposition, he could begin the process of self-realization only with a larger capital, a larger use value of 120 (as against 100). After the doubling in the productive forces, he can do it with 140 thalers without restricting his consumption. A larger part of the exchange values solidifies as exchange value, instead of vanishing in use value (whether it solidifies as such, through production, directly or indirectly). To create a larger capital means to create a larger exchange value; although exchange value in its *direct form* as simple exchange value has not been increased by the growth of productivity, it has in its intensified form as *capital*. This larger capital of 140 thalers represents, absolutely, more objectified labour than the earlier capital of 120 thalers. It therefore also, at least relatively, sets more living labour into motion and therefore also ultimately reproduces more simple exchange value. The capital of 120 thalers at 40% produced a product or simple exchange value of 60 thalers at 40%; the capital of 140 thalers a simple exchange value of 64 thalers. Here, then, the increase in exchange value in the form of capital is still posited directly as an increase in exchange value in its simple form. It is of the highest importance to remember this. It is not enough to say, like Ricardo, that exchange value does not increase; i.e. the abstract form of wealth; but only exchange value as capital.[57] In saying this he is looking only at the original production process. But if relative surplus labour increases – and capital therefore increases absolutely – then there is necessarily also an increase within circulation also of *relative exchange value existing as exchange value*, money as such, and therefore, through the mediation of the production process, *absolute exchange value*. In other words, of this same amount of exchange value – or money – and the product of the realization process appears in this simple form – the product is surplus value only relative to

57. Ricardo, *On the Principles of Political Economy*, pp. 327–8.

capital, to value such as it existed before the production process; for itself, regarded as an independent existence, it is merely *quantitatively defined exchange value* – a part has become liberated, which does not exist as equivalent for already present exchange values or for already present labour time. If it is exchanged for those already present, it gives them not an equivalent but more than an equivalent, and thus liberates a part of the exchange value on their side. In a static state, this liberated exchange value by which society has become richer can only be money, in which case only the abstract form of wealth has increased; [is] in motion: [it] can realize itself only in *new* living labour (whether labour which had been dormant is set into motion, or *new workers* are created (population [growth] is accelerated) or again a new circle of exchange values, of exchange values in circulation, is expanded, which can occur on the production side if the liberated exchange value opens up a *new branch of production*, i.e. a new object of exchange, objectified labour in the form of a new use value; or the same is achieved when objectified labour is put in the sphere of circulation in a new country, by an expansion of trade). The latter must then be created.

The form in which Ricardo attempts to clarify the matter for himself (and he is very unclear in this regard) says at bottom nothing more than that he just introduces a certain relation, instead of saying, simply, that out of the same sum of simple exchange values a smaller part posits itself in the form of simple exchange value (equivalent) and a larger part in the form of money (money as the original, antediluvian form out of which capital always arises anew; money in its character as money, not as coin etc.); that therefore the part posited *as* exchange value for-itself, i.e. as *value*, increases, i.e. *wealth in the form of wealth* (whereas he comes to just the mistaken conclusion that it increases only in the form of *material, physical* wealth as use value). The origin of *wealth as such*, in so far as it arises not from *rent*, i.e., according to him, not from the *increase* in productive force, but rather from the *decrease of the same*, is therefore *totally incomprehensible* to him, and he entangles himself in the wildest contradictions. Let us take the form of the matter.[58] Capital 1,000 sets 50 workers into motion; or 50 living work days; through a doubling of the productive force, it could set 100 working days into motion. But these latter do not exist in the

58. Ricardo, *On the Principles of Political Economy*, pp. 29–35.

presupposition, and are introduced arbitrarily, because otherwise
– unless *more real working days* are introduced – he does not
grasp the increase in exchange value which arises from increased
productivity. At the same time, the *growth of population* is never
developed by him as an *element in the increase* of exchange values;
never clearly and definitely stated. Let the presupposition be
capital 1,000 and workers 50. The correct deduction, which he
himself *also draws* (see Notebook)[59]: capital 500 with 25 workers
can produce the same use value as before; the other 500 with the
other 25 workers establish a new business and likewise produce
an exchange value of 500. The profit remains the same, since it
arises not from the exchange of 500 for 500, but from the proportions in which profit and wages originally divide in the 500, and
since exchange deals in equivalents, which can no more increase
value than *external trade* can, which Ricardo explicitly demonstrates. Since the exchange of equivalents just means nothing
more than that the value in the hands of *A* before the exchange
with *B* still exists in his hands after the exchange with *B*. The
total value or wealth has remained the same. Use value, however,
or the *material of wealth*, has doubled. Now, there is absolutely
no reason here why *wealth* should grow *as wealth, exchange
value as such* – as far as the *increase in the productive forces* is
concerned. If the productive forces again double in both branches,
then capital A can again divide into two of 250 with $12\frac{1}{2}$ working
days each, capital B can do the same.[60] There are now four
capitals with the same total exchange value of £1,000, consuming
50 living work days as before,* producing four times as much
use value as before the doubling of consumption value. Ricardo
is too classical to commit absurdities, like those who claim to

*It is *at bottom false to say* that living labour consumes capital; capital
(objectified labour) consumes the living in the production process.

---

59. This refers to Marx's notebooks of excerpts from the works of Ricardo,
with Marx's critical commentary. A section of one of the excerpt-books in
this series is published in *Grundrisse* (MELI), pp. 787–839. Marx wrote these
notebooks, which contain, additionally, excerpts from ten works by other
authors, as well as from various volumes of *The Economist*, in early 1851. See
Grundrisse (MELI), p. 782 n.

60. The following sentence appears in the upper margin of this page of the
manuscript, without indication of the place in the text where it might be
inserted: '(*Money* for itself has to be termed neither use value nor exchange
value, but *value*.)'

improve on him, who derive the larger value after the increase in productive force from one party selling at a higher price within circulation. As soon as the capital of 500 has become commodity, simple exchange value, instead of exchanging it for 500, he exchanges it for 550 (at 10%), but then the other party obviously only gets 450 in exchange value instead of 500 and the total sum remains 1,000 as before. This happens often enough in commerce, but explains the profit made by one capital only by the loss of the other capital, and not *the* profit of *capital*; and without this presupposition there can be profit neither on one nor on the other side. Ricardo's process can therefore go on without any other limit than the *increase of the productive force* (and this is again physical, located outside the *economic relation* itself) possible with a capital of 1,000 and 50 workers. See the following passage: 'Capital is that part of the wealth of a country which is employed with a view to future production, *and may be increased in the same manner as wealth.*'[61] (*Wealth* for him the abundance of use values; and, seen from the standpoint of simple exchange, the identical objectified labour can express itself in limitless use values and constantly remain *the same exchange value*, as long as it remains the same amount of objectified labour, for its *equivalent* is measured not by the mass of use value in which it exists, but rather by its own amount.) 'An *additional capital* will be equally efficacious in the formation of future wealth, whether it be obtained from improvements of skill or machinery, or from using more revenue productively; for wealth' (use value) 'always depends on the *quantity* of commodities produced' (also somewhat on their variety, it seems), 'without regard to the facility with which the instruments employed in production may have been produced' (i.e. the labour time objectified in them). 'A certain quantity of clothes and provisions will maintain and employ the same number of men; but they will be of twice the value' (*exchange value*) 'if 200 have been employed on their production.' If, owing to an increase in the productive force, 100 produce as much in use values as 200 earlier, then: 'of the 200, half are let go, so that the remaining 100 produce as much as the 200 did before. Thus a half of the capital can be withdrawn from this branch of business; as much capital has become free as labour. And since one half of the capital now does quite the same service as did the whole, two capitals have now been formed etc.' (cf. 39, 40 ibid.

61. Ricardo, *On the Principles of Political Economy*, pp. 327–8.

on national trade,[62] to which we must return). Ricardo does not speak here about the working day; [the fact] that, if the capitalist earlier exchanged half of an objectified working day for the worker's entire living work day, [he] thus at bottom gains only half a living work day, since he gives the other half in objectified form to the worker, and obtains it from him in the living form, i.e. pays the worker a half of the working day, instead of in the form of simultaneous working days, i.e. of different workers; this does not alter the matter, only its expression. Each one of these working days furnishes so much more surplus time. If the capitalist, before, had *the* working day as limit, he now has 50 working days etc. As has been said, this form does not posit an increase in exchange values with an increase in the number of capitals through productivity, and, according to Ricardo, it would also be possible for the population to fall from, say, 10,000,000 to 10,000, without a decrease in exchange values or the quantity of use values (see conclusion of his book).[63] We are the last to deny that *capital* contains contradictions. Our purpose, rather, is to develop them fully. But Ricardo *does not develop them*, but rather shifts them off by considering the value in exchange as indifferent for the formation of wealth. That is to say, he contends that in a society based upon the value of exchange, and wealth resulting from such value, the contradictions to which this form of wealth is driven with the development of productive powers etc. do not exist, and that a progress of value is not necessary in such a society to secure the progress of wealth, consequently that value as the form of wealth does not at all affect that wealth itself and its development, i.e. he regards exchange value as merely *formal*. Then, however, he remembers (1) that the capitalists are concerned with value, (2) that, historically, with the progress of the productive forces (of international trade too, he *should have* noted), there is a growth in *wealth as such*, i.e. the sum of values. Now, how to explain this? Capitals accumulate faster than the population; thus wages rise; thus population; thus grain prices; thus the difficulty of production and hence the *exchange values*. The latter are then finally reached by a detour. We will here entirely omit the moment of rent, since we are not

62. A reference to Marx's own excerpt-book VIII. Ricardo's doctrine of *foreign* trade (*On the Principles of Political Economy*, pp. 131–8) is covered in *Grundrisse* (MELI), pp. 808–11.

63. Ricardo, *On the Principles of Political Economy*, pp. 416–17.

yet concerned with increased difficulty of production but rather with its opposite, with increase in the productive forces. With the accumulation of capitals, wages rise unless population grows simultaneously; the worker marries, production is spurred on or his children live better, do not die before their time etc. In short, the population grows. Its growth, however, gives rise to competition among the workers, and thereby forces the worker to sell his labour power to the capitalist at its *value* again, or momentarily even below it. Now the accumulated capital, which has meanwhile grown up more slowly, again has the surplus which it earlier spent in the form of wages, i.e. as coin, in order to buy the use value of labour, available to it in the form of money, in order to realize it as capital in living labour, and, since it now also disposes over a greater amount of working days, its *exchange value* grows in turn. (Even this not really developed in Ricardo, but mixed up with the theory of rent; since the surplus which capital earlier lost in the form of wages is now lost to it in the form of rent, owing to the growth of population.) But even the growth of population is not really comprehensible in his theory. At no time has he shown that there is an *inherent* relation between the whole of the labour objectified in capital and the living work day (whether the latter is represented as one working day of 50 × 12 hours, or as 12 hours of labour by 50 workers, is the same thing as far as the relation goes), and that this inherent relation is just the *relation between the fractional part of the living work day*, or that between the equivalent of the objectified labour with which the worker is paid, and the living working day; where the whole is the day itself, and the inherent relation is the variable relation (the day itself is a constant) between the *fractional part of the necessary hours of labour* and the *hours of surplus labour*. And, just because he has not developed this relation, he has also not developed [the point] (which did not concern us up to now, since we were concerned with *capital as such* and introduced the development of the productive forces as an external relation) that the development of the productive forces itself presupposes both the increase of capital and the increase of simultaneous working days, which, however, within the given barrier of a capital that sets one working day into motion (even if it be a day of 50 × 12 hours, 600 hours), is itself the barrier to the development of its productive force. The wage covers not only the worker, but also his reproduction; so that when this specimen of the working class dies, another replaces it; after the 50 workers are dead, 50 new ones are there to replace them. The 50 workers themselves – as living labour capacities – represent not only the costs of their own production, but also the costs which had to be paid to their parents above and beyond their wages as individuals, in order to replace themselves with 50 new individuals. Thus the population progresses even without a rise in wages. But now, why does it not progress rapidly enough? and why does it need a special stimulus? Surely only because the aim of capital is not served merely by obtaining more 'wealth' in the Ricardian sense, but because it wants more *value*, to command more objectified labour. But indeed, according to him, it can command the latter only if wages fall; i.e. if more living work days are exchanged for the same capital with objectified labour, and hence a greater value is created. In order to make wages fall, he presupposes increase of population. And in order to prove increase of population here, he presupposes that the demand for working days increases, in other words, that capital can buy more *objectified labour* (objectified in labouring capacity), hence that its *value* has grown. Originally, however, he proceeded from just the contrary presupposition, and took the detour only *because* that is where he began. If £1,000 was able to buy 500 working days, and the productive force increases, then either it can proceed to employ the 500 in the same branch of work, or it can divide up and employ 250 in one branch of work, 250 in another, so that this capital splits into 2 capitals of 500 each. But it can never command more than 500 working days, since otherwise, according to Ricardo, not only the use values it produces but also their *exchange value* must have multiplied itself, the *objectified labour time* over which it exercises command. Thus, given his presupposition, an increased demand for labour cannot take place. But if it does take place, then capital's *exchange value* has grown. Compare *Malthus on value*, who *senses* the contradictions, but falls flat when he himself tries to develop them.[64]

64. See p. 326, n. 41.

Labour does not reproduce the value of the material in which, and of the instrument with which, it works. It preserves their value simply by relating to them in the labour process as to their objective conditions. This animating and preserving force costs capital nothing; *appears, rather, as its own force etc.*

We have always spoken only about the two elements of capital, the two parts of the living work day, of which one represents wages, the other profit; one, necessary labour, the other, surplus labour. But what about the other two parts of capital, which are realized in the material of labour and the instrument of labour? As far as the simple production process is concerned, labour presupposes the existence of an instrument which facilitates the work, and of a material in which it presents itself, which it forms. This form gives it its use value. This use value becomes exchange value through exchange, to the extent that it contains objectified labour. But are they, as components of capital, values which labour must replace? Thus in the above example (and such objections [were] heaped on Ricardo; that he regarded profit and wages only as components of production costs, not the machine and the material), it seems that if the capital is 100, divided 50 for cotton, 40 for wages, 10 for instrument; and if the wages, of 40 thalers, = 4 hours of objectified labour, and capital orders a working day of 8 hours, then the worker who has to reproduce 40 thalers for wages, 40 thalers surplus time (profit), 10 thalers instrument, 50 thalers cotton = 140 thalers, reproduces only 80 thalers. For 40 thalers are the product of half a working day; 40 are the other, surplus half. But the value of the two other component parts of capital is 60 thalers. Since the worker's real product is 80 thalers, he can reproduce only 80, not 140. He would have, instead, decreased the value of the 60; since 40 of the 80 [is] replacement for his wages; and the remaining 40 of surplus labour [is] smaller by 20 than 60. Instead of a profit of 40, the capitalist would have a loss of 20 on the part of his original capital consisting of instrument and material. How is the worker supposed to create still another 60 on top of the 80 thalers of value, since one half of his working day, as his wages show, creates only 40 thalers out of the instrument and the material; the other half only the same; and he disposes of only one working day, cannot work two days in one? Suppose the 50 thalers in material = x lb. of cotton yarn; the 10 thalers in instrument = spindle. Now, first, as regards the *use value*, it is clear that if the cotton did not already have the form of yarn and wood and iron the form of the spindle, then the worker could produce no *fabric*, no higher use value. For him himself, the 50 thalers and the 10 thalers in the production process are *nothing but yarn and spindle, not exchange values*. His labour has given them a higher use value, and added objectified labour to the amount of 80 thalers to them, i.e. 40 thalers to reproduce his wages, 40 surplus time. The use value – the fabric – contains one additional working day, half of which, however, replaces only that part of capital for which the disposition over the labouring capacity has been exchanged. The worker has not created the objectified labour contained in yarn and spindle, which form a part of the value of the product; for him they were and remain material to which he gave another form and into which he incorporated new labour. The only condition is that he should not waste them, and this he did not do, in so far as his product has use value, and a higher use value than before. It now contains objectified labour in two parts – his working day, and that already contained in his material, yarn and spindle, independent of him and before him. The previously objectified labour was the condition of *his* labour; it was necessary to make his labour what it is, costs him no labour. Suppose they were not already presupposed as components of capital, as *values*, and had cost *him* nothing. Then the value of the product, if he worked a whole day, would be 80, if a half day, 40 thalers. It would just = one objectified working day. Indeed, they cost him nothing in production; however, this does not destroy the labour time objectified in them, which remains and merely obtains another form. If, in addition to the fabric, the worker also had to create the yarn and the spindle in the same working day, then the process would be in fact impossible. The fact, therefore, that they call for his labour neither as use values in their original form, nor as exchange values, but are *on hand*, makes it possible for the addition of a working day by him to create a product of a value higher than one working day. He succeeds in this, however, to the extent that he does not have to create this additional part, but rather *finds it on hand* as material, as presupposition. It can therefore only be said that he reproduces these values in so far as *without* labour they would rot, be useless; but *without them, labour* would be equally useless. In so far as the worker reproduces these values, he does so not by giving them a higher exchange value, or entering into any process with their exchange value at all, but merely by subordinating them to the simple production process, merely by *working*. But this costs him no additional labour time *besides* what he needs for their processing and higher realization. It is a situation into which capital has put him so that he may work. He reproduces the values only by giving them a higher value, and this giving of a higher value is = his working day. Otherwise he lets them be as they are. That their old value is preserved happens because a new one is added to them, not that the old is itself *reproduced*, created. In so far as they are products of previous labour, a product of previous labour, a sum of previously objectified labour remains an element of his *product*, so that the product contains, in addition to its new value, the old as well. He therefore in fact produces in this product only the day's work which he adds to it, and the preservation of the old value costs him absolutely nothing apart from what it costs him to add the new. For him it is only a material, and remains that no matter how it changes its form; therefore [it is] something present *independently* of his labour. That this material, which remains that, since it only obtains a different form, itself already contains labour time is the business of capital, not his own; similarly, it is *independent* of his labour and continues on *after* it, just as it existed before it. This so-called reproduction costs him no labour time, but is rather the condition of his labour time, since it is nothing more than positing the substance on hand as the material of his labour, relating to it as material. He therefore replaces the old labour time by the *act* of working itself, not by the addition of special labour time for this purpose. He replaces it simply by the addition of the *new*, by means of which the old is preserved in the product and becomes an element of a new product. Thus the worker in his working day does not replace the raw material and the instrument in so far as they are values. *The capitalist thus obtains this preservation of the old value just as free of charge as he obtains surplus labour*. But he obtains it free of charge, because it costs the worker nothing, and is, instead, the result of the fact that the material and the instrument of labour are already in his hands as *presupposition*, and the worker cannot *work*, therefore, without making this already objectified labour, now in the hands of capital, into the material of his own labour, thereby also preserving the labour objectified in this material. The capitalist, then, pays the worker nothing for the fact that the yarn and the spindle – their value – reappear, as far as their value is concerned, in the fabric, and are thus preserved. This preservation takes place simply by the addition of new labour, which adds a higher value. What arises from the original relation between capital and labour, then, is that the same service which living labour as living labour performs for objectified labour costs capital nothing, just as it costs the worker nothing, but merely expresses the relation that the material and the instrument of labour confront the worker as capital, as presuppositions *independent* of him. The preservation of the old value is not a separate act from the addition of the new, but happens by itself; appears as a natural result of the same. But the fact that this preservation costs capital nothing and costs the worker nothing either is already posited in the relation of *capital and labour*, which in itself is already the former's profit and the latter's wage.

The individual capitalist may imagine (and for his accounts it serves as well) that, if he owns a capital of 100 thalers, 50 thalers in cotton, 40 thalers to buy labour with, 10 thalers in instrument, plus a profit of 10% counted as part of his production costs, then labour has to replace his 50 thalers of cotton, 40 thalers subsistence, 10 thalers instrument plus 10% of 50, of 40 and of 10; so that in his imagination, labour creates 55 thalers of raw material, 44 thalers subsistence and 11 thalers instrument for him, together = 110. But this is a peculiar notion for economists, even though it has been advanced with great pomp as an innovation against Ricardo. If the worker's working day = 10 hours, and if he can create 40 thalers in 8 hours, i.e. can create his wage, or, what is the same, can maintain and replace his labour capacity, then he needs $\frac{4}{5}$ of a day in order to replace his wages for capital, and he gives capital $\frac{1}{5}$ in surplus labour, or 10 thalers. In exchange for the 40 thalers in wages, for 8 hours of objectified labour, therefore, capital obtains 10 hours of living labour, and this excess constitutes the entirety of its profit. The total objectified labour which the worker has created, then, is 50 thalers, and, regardless of the costs of the instrument and of the raw materials, more he cannot add, for his day cannot objectify itself in more labour than that; now, the fact that he adds these 50 thalers – 10 hours of labour (of which only 8 replace the wage) – to the 60 thalers contained in raw material and instrument – and thereby has simultaneously preserved the raw material and the instrument – they are preserved just by coming into contact again with living labour, and being used as instrument and as material – this costs him no labour (and he would have no time available in which to do this), nor does the capitalist pay him for it. Like every other natural or social power of labour unless it is the product of previous labour, or of such previous labour as does not need to be repeated (e.g. the historical development of the worker etc.), this natural animating power of labour – namely that, by using the material and instrument, it preserves them in one or another form, including the labour objectified in them, their exchange value – becomes a *power of capital*, not of labour. Hence not paid for by capital. As little as the worker is paid for the fact that he can think etc.

We have seen the original presupposition of the coming into being of *capital* is the existence of *money as money*, i.e. as money which has withdrawn from circulation and asserts itself *negatively* towards it, i.e. *value* which has become independent from and *against* circulation – i.e. the commodity for which the character of exchange value is not merely a formal, vanishing character, [which it possesses only] before being exchanged for another use value and finally disappearing as an object of consumption. On the other side, *money* (in its third, adequate form) – as value which no longer enters circulation as equivalent, but is not yet potentiated as capital, i.e. value independent of and relating *negatively* against circulation – is at the same time the result of capital's product, in so far as that product is not merely its own *reproduction* (but this reproduction is merely formal, since, of the three parts of its value, only one is really consumed and hence reproduced, namely that which replaces wages; profit, on the other hand, is not reproduction but addition of value, surplus value). Just as money at first appeared as the presupposition, the cause of capital, so it now appears as its effect. In the first movement, money arose out of simple circulation; in the second it arises from the production process of capital. In the first, it *makes a transition to* capital; in the second it appears as a presupposition of capital posited by capital itself; and is therefore already posited as capital *in itself* [*an sich*], already contains the ideal relation towards capital. It does not simply make a transition to capital, but rather, as *money*, its potential to be transformed into capital is already posited in it.

Absolute surplus labour time. Relative. – It is not the quantity
of living labour, but rather its quality *as labour which
simultaneously preserves the labour time already contained in the
material etc. – The change of form and substance in the direct
production process. – The preservation of the previous stage of
production by the subsequent one is contained in the simple
production process etc. – Preservation of the old use value by new
labour etc. – Process of production and process of realization.
The* quantity *of objectified labour is preserved because contact
with living labour preserves its quality as use value for new
labour. – In the real production process, the separation of labour
from its objective conditions of existence is suspended. But in
this process labour already incorporated in capital etc. Appears
as capital's power of self-preservation. Eternalization of value*

The increase of values is therefore the result of the self-realization
of capital; [regardless of] whether this self-realization is the result
of *absolute* surplus time or of *relative*, i.e. of a real increase in
absolute labour time or of an increase in relative surplus labour,
i.e. of a decrease in the fractional part of the working day which is
required as labour time necessary to preserve the labouring
capacity, as *necessary labour* in general.

Living labour time reproduces nothing more than that part of
objectified labour time (of capital) which appears as an equivalent
for the power of disposition over living labour capacity, and
which, therefore, as an equivalent, must replace the labour time
objectified in this labouring capacity, i.e. replace the production
costs of the living labour capacities, in other words, must keep
the workers alive as workers. What it produces in addition to that
is not reproduction but rather new creation, and, more specifically,
creation of new values, because it is the objectification of new
labour time in a use value. That the labour time contained in the
raw material and instrument is preserved at the same time is a
result *not of the quantity of labour*, but of its *quality* of being labour
as such; and there is no special payment for this, its general
quality, for the fact that *labour, as labour, is labour* – leaving
aside all special qualifications, all specific kinds of labour –
because capital has bought *this quality* as part of its exchange
with the worker.

But the equivalent for this quality (for the specific use value of
labour) is measured simply by the *quantity* of labour time which

has produced it. Initially the worker's use of the instrument as an instrument, and his shaping of the raw material, adds to the value of the raw material and of the instrument as much new form as is = to the labour time contained in his own wage; what he adds additionally is surplus labour time, surplus value. For their part, the raw materials and the instrument are preserved not in their form but in their substance, through the simple relation of being used as instrument and being posited as the raw material of labour, the simple process of coming into contact with labour, being posited as its means and object and therefore as objectification of living labour, moments of labour itself; and, viewed economically, their substance is objectified labour time. By being posited as a material mode of existence – means and end [*Objekt*] – of living labour, objectified labour time ceases to exist in a one-sided, objective form, in which, as a mere thing, it is at the prey of processes of chemical decay etc. There is an indifference on the part of the substance [*Stoff*] towards the form, which develops out of merely objectified labour time, in whose objective existence labour has become merely the vanished, *external form* of its natural substance, existing merely in the external form of the substantial [*das Stoffliche*] (e.g. the form of the table for wood, or the form of the cylinder for iron)[65]; no immanent law of reproduction maintains this form in the way in which the tree, for example, maintains its form as a tree (wood maintains itself in the specific form of the tree because this form is a form of the wood; while the form of the table is accidental for wood, and not the intrinsic form of its substance); it exists only as a form external to the substance, or it exists only as a substance [*stofflich*]. The dissolution to which its substance is prey therefore dissolves the form as well. However, when they are posited as conditions of living labour, they are themselves reanimated. Objectified labour ceases to exist in a dead state as an external, indifferent form on the substance, because it is itself again posited as a moment of living labour; as a relation of living labour to itself in an objective material, as the *objectivity* of living labour (as means and end [*Objekt*]) (the *objective* conditions of living labour). The transformation of the material by living labour, by the realization of living labour in the material – a transformation which, as purpose, determines labour and is its purposeful activation (a trans-

65. Cf. Hegel, *Science of Logic*, pp. 450–56, e.g. p. 451: 'Matter is that which is indifferent to form.'

formation which does not only posit the form as external to the inanimate object, as a mere vanishing image of its material consistency) – thus preserves the material in a definite form, and subjugates the transformation of the material to the purpose of labour. Labour is the living, form-giving fire; it is the transitoriness of things, their temporality, as their formation by living time. In the simple production process – leaving aside the realization process – the transitoriness of the forms of things is used to posit their usefulness. When cotton becomes yarn, yarn becomes fabric, fabric becomes printed etc. or dyed etc. fabric, and this becomes, say, a garment, then (1) the substance of cotton has preserved itself in all these forms. (The chemical process, regulated by labour, has everywhere consisted of an exchange of (natural) equivalents etc.); (2) in each of these subsequent processes, the material has obtained a more useful form, a form making it more appropriate to consumption; until it has obtained at the end the form in which it can directly become an object of consumption, when, therefore, the consumption of the material and the suspension of its form satisfies a human need, and its transformation is the same as its use. The substance of cotton preserves itself in all of these processes; it becomes extinct in one form of use value in order to *make way for a higher one, until the object is in being as an object of direct consumption.* But when cotton is posited, say, as twist, then it is posited in a specific relation to a further kind of labour. If this labour were not to take place, then not only has the form been posited in it uselessly, i.e. the previous labour is not reaffirmed by new labour, but the material is also spoiled, because, in the form of twist, it has a use value only in so far as it is worked on further: it is a use value only in respect of the use which further labour makes of it; is use value only in so far as its form as twist is suspended in the form of fabric; while cotton in its existence as cotton is capable of an infinite number of useful employments. Thus, without further labour, the use value of cotton and twist, material and form, would be botched; it would be destroyed instead of produced. Material as well as form, substance like form, are preserved by further labour – preserved as use value, until they obtain the form of use value as such, whose use is consumption. It is therefore already a part of the simple production process that the earlier stage of production is preserved by the later, and that positing the higher use value preserves the old, or, the old use value is transformed only to the extent that it is raised to a higher use value. It is living labour which preserves the use value of the incomplete product of labour by making it the material of further labour. It preserves it, however, i.e. protects it from uselessness and decay, only by working it in a purposeful way, by making it the object of new living labour. *This preservation of the old use value* is not a process taking place separately from the increase or the completion of the use value by new labour; it takes place, rather, entirely in this new labour of raising the use value. When the labour of weaving transforms yarn into fabric, i.e. treats yarn as the raw material of weaving (a particular form of living labour) (and twist has a use value only if it is woven into fabric), it thereby preserves the use value which cotton had as such, as well as that which cotton had obtained specifically as yarn. It preserves the product of labour by making it into the raw material of new labour; but what happens is not that it (1) adds new labour and (2) besides that, by means of additional labour, preserves the use value of the raw material. *It preserves the utility of cotton as yarn by weaving the yarn into fabric.* (All this belongs already in the first chapter *on production in general.*) *Preserves it by weaving it.* This preservation of labour as product – of the use value of the product of labour by its becoming the raw material of new labour, being again posited as material objectivity of purposeful living labour – is given with the simple production process. As regards use value, labour has the property of preserving the existing use value by raising it, and it raises it by making it into the object of new labour as defined by an ultimate aim; by changing it in turn from the form of its indifferent consistency into that of objective material, the body of labour. (*The same holds for the instrument.* A spindle maintains itself as a use value only by being used up for spinning. If it is not, the specific form which is here posited in iron and wood would be spoiled for use, together with the labour which posited it and the material in which it did the positing. The use value of wood and iron, and of their form as well, are preserved only by being posited as a means of living labour, as an objective moment of the existence of labour's vitality. As an instrument of labour, it is their destiny [*Bestimmung*] to be used up, but used up in the process of spinning. The increased productivity which it lends to labour creates more use values and thereby replaces the use value eaten up in the consumption of the instrument. This appears most clearly in agriculture, because there the instrument appears most easily, because most anciently, as a use value, directly as a means of life – in contrast to exchange value. If the hoe allows the tiller to grow twice as much grain as before, then he has to spend less time on the production of the hoe itself; he has enough food to make a new hoe.) Now, in the realization process, the value components of capital – the one in the form of the material, the other in the form of instrument – confront the worker, i.e. living labour (for the labourer exists in the process only as such) not as values, but rather as simple moments of the production process; as use values for labour, as the objective conditions of its efficacity, or as its objective moments. It lies in the nature of labour itself to preserve them by using the instrument as instrument and by giving the raw material a higher form of use value. But, as components of capital, the use values thus obtained from labour are exchange values; as such, determined by the costs of production contained in them, the amount of labour objectified in them. (Use value is concerned only with the *quality* of the labour already objectified.) The quantity of *objectified labour* is preserved in that its *quality* is preserved as *use value for further labour*, through the contact with living labour. The use value of cotton, as well as its use value as yarn, are preserved by being woven; by existing as one of the objective moments (together with the spinning wheel) in the weaving process. *The quantity of labour time contained in the cotton and the cotton yarn are therefore also preserved thereby. The preservation of the quality of previous labour in the simple production process, – hence of its material* as well – becomes, in the realization process, the preservation of the quantity of labour already objectified. *For capital*, this preservation is the preservation of the amount of objectified labour *by* the production process; for *living labour* itself, it is merely the preservation of the already present use value. Living labour *adds a new amount of labour*; however, it is not this *quantitative addition* which preserves the amount of already objectified labour, but rather its *quality as living labour*, the fact that it relates as labour to the use values in which the previous labour exists. But living labour is not paid for this quality, which it possesses as living labour – if it were not living labour, it would not be bought at all – rather, it is paid for the *amount of labour* contained in itself. What is paid for is only the *price* of its use value, like that of all other commodities. It does not receive payment for its specific quality of adding new amounts of labour to the amounts of labour already objectified, and at the same time preserving labour which is already objectified as objectified labour; and this quality does not cost the worker anything either, since it is a natural property of his labouring capacity. Within the production process, the separation of labour from its objective moments of existence – instruments and material – is *suspended*. *The existence of capital and of wage labour rests on this separation. Capital does not pay for the suspension of this separation which proceeds in the real production process* – for otherwise work could not go on at all. (Nor does this suspension take place in the process of exchange with the worker; but rather *in the process of work itself, during production*. But, as *ongoing labour*, it is itself already incorporated in capital, and a moment of the same. This preserving force of labour therefore appears as the self-preserving force of capital. The worker has merely added new labour; as for previous labour – owing to the existence of capital – this has an eternal existence as value, quite independent of its material existence. This is how the matter appears to capital and to the worker.) If it had to pay for this quality also, then it would just cease to be capital. This is part of the material role which labour plays by its nature in the production process; of its use value. But as use value, labour belongs to the capitalist; it belongs to the worker merely as exchange value. Its living quality of preserving objectified labour time by using it as the objective condition of living labour in the production process is none of the worker's business. *This appropriation, by means of which living labour makes instrument and material in the production process* into the body of its soul and thereby resurrects them from the dead, does indeed stand in antithesis to the fact that labour itself is objectless, is a reality only in the immediate vitality of the worker – and that the instrument and material, in capital, exist as beings-for-themselves [*für sich selbst seiende*]. (Return to this.) The process of the realization of capital proceeds by means of and within the simple production process, by putting living labour into its natural relation with its moments of material being. But to the extent that labour steps into this relation, this relation exists not for itself, but for capital; labour itself has become already a moment of capital.

Capitalist obtains surplus labour free of charge together with the
maintenance of the value of material and instrument. Labour,
by adding a new value to the old one, at the same time maintains,
eternizes [sic] the latter. – The preservation of values in the
product costs capital nothing. – By means of the appropriation
of ongoing labour, the capitalist already possesses a claim to (and,
respectively) appropriation of future labour

We see therefore that the capitalist, by means of the exchange
process with the worker – by indeed paying the worker an equivalent
for the costs of production contained in his labour capacity, i.e.
giving him the means of maintaining his labour capacity, but appropriating living labour for himself – obtains two things free of
charge, first the surplus labour which increases the value of his
capital; but at the same time, secondly, the quality of living labour
which maintains the previous labour materialized in the component parts of capital and thus preserves the previously existing
value of capital. But this preservation does not take place as a
result of an *increase in the amount of labour objectified* by living
labour, a creation of value, but simply as a result of its existence as
living *labour* in the proper relation with material and instrument,
i.e. through its *quality* as living labour. As such a quality, it is itself
a moment of the simple production process and does not cost the
capitalist anything, any more than yarn and spindle do, apart from
their price, for having also become moments of the production
process.

When e.g. in times of stagnations of trade etc. the mills are shut
down, then it can indeed be seen that the machinery rusts away
and that the yarn is useless ballast and rots, as soon as their connection with living labour ceases. If the capitalist employs labour
only in order to create surplus value – to create value in addition
to that already present – then it can be seen as soon as he orders
work to stop that his already present capital, as well, becomes devalued; that living labour hence not only adds new value, but, by
the very act of adding a new value to the old one, maintains,
eternizes it. (This shows clearly the absurdity of the charge against
Ricardo, that he conceives *only* profits and wages as necessary
components of the cost of production, and not also the part of
capital contained in raw materials and instrument. To the extent
that the value which they represent is merely preserved, there are
no new production costs. But as far as these present values them-

selves are concerned, they all dissolve again into objectified labour
– necessary labour and surplus labour – wages and profit. The
purely natural material in which *no* human labour is objectified,
to the extent that it is merely a material that exists independently
of labour, has no *value*, since only objectified labour is value; as
little value as is possessed by the common elements as such.) The
maintenance of present capital by the labour which realizes it
therefore costs capital nothing and hence does not belong among
the production costs; although the present values are preserved in
the product and equivalents have therefore to be given for them in
exchange. But the *maintenance of these values* in the product costs
capital nothing and cannot therefore be cited among the costs of
production. Nor are they replaced by labour, since they are not consumed, except in so far as they are consumed apart from and outside labour, i.e. as labour *consumes* (suspends) their *transitoriness*.
Only the wage is really consumed.

Let us return once more to our example. 100 thalers capital, i.e.
50 thalers raw material, 40 thalers labour, 10 thalers instrument of
production. Let the worker require 4 hours in order to create the
fraction of production necessary for his maintenance, the 40
thalers representing the means of his life. Let his working day be 8
hours. The capitalist then obtains a surplus of 4 hours free of
charge; his surplus value equals 4 objectified hours, 40 thalers;
hence his product $= 50 + 10$ (preserved, not reproduced values;
remained *constant, unchanged* as values) $+ 40$ thalers (wages, reproduced, because consumed in the form of wage) $+ 40$ thalers of
surplus value. *Sum*: 140 thalers. Of these 140, 40 are excess. The
capitalist had to live during production and before he began to
produce; say 20 thalers. He had to own the latter apart from his
capital of 100 thalers; hence equivalents for them had to be present
in circulation. (How these arose does not concern us here.) Capital
presupposes circulation as a constant magnitude. These equivalents now present again. Thus consumes 20 thalers of his gain.
These enter into simple circulation. The 100 thalers also enter
into simple circulation, but only in order to be transformed
again into the conditions of new production, 50 thalers of raw
material, 40 subsistence for workers, 10 instrument. There remains a surplus value, an addition as such, newly created, of 20
thalers. This is *money*, posited as a negatively independent value
against circulation. It cannot enter into circulation as a mere
equivalent, in order to exchange for objects of mere consumption,

since circulation is presupposed as constant. But the independent, illusory existence of money is suspended; it now only exists in order to be realized, i.e. to become capital. In order to become that, however, it would again have to be exchanged for the moments of the production process, subsistence for workers, raw material and instrument; all these dissolve into objectified labour, can only be posited by living labour. *Money*, then, in so far as it now already *in itself* exists as capital, is therefore simply *a claim on future* (new) labour. It exists, objectively, merely as *money*. Surplus value, the new growth of *objectified labour*, to the extent that it exists for itself, is *money*; but now, it is money which *in itself* is already capital; and, as such, it is a *claim on new labour*. Here capital already no longer enters into relation with ongoing labour, but with future labour. And it no longer appears dissolved into its simple elements in the production process, but as money; no longer, however, as money which is merely the abstract form of general wealth, but as a claim on the real possibility of general wealth – labour capacity, and more precisely, *labour capacity in the process of becoming* [*das werdende Arbeitsvermögen*]. As a claim, its material existence as money is irrelevant, and can be replaced by any other title. Like the creditor of the state, every capitalist with his newly gained value possesses a claim on future labour, and, by means of the appropriation of ongoing labour has already at the same time appropriated future labour. (This side of capital to be developed to this point. But already here its property of existing as value separately from its substance can be seen. This already lays the basis for credit.) To stockpile it in the form of money is therefore by no means the same as materially to stockpile the material conditions of labour. This is rather a stockpiling of property titles to labour. Posits future labour as *wage labour*, as use value for capital. No *equivalent* on hand for the newly created value; its possibility only in new labour.

In this example, then, an absolute surplus labour time of 4 hours created, added to the old values, to the world of available wealth, a new value of 20 thalers money, and money already in connection with its form as capital (already as *posited possibility* of capital, not as before, becoming the possibility of capital as such only by ceasing to be money as such).

Now if the productive force doubles, so that instead of 4 hours the worker has to put in only 2 hours of *necessary labour*, and if the capitalist makes him work 8 hours as before, then the accounts are as follows: 50 thalers material, 20 wages, 10 instrument of labour, 60 surplus value (6 hours, 4 before). New growth of absolute surplus value: 2 hours or 20 thalers. *Sum*: 140 thalers (in the product).

A total of 140 thalers as before; but now 60 of them are surplus value; of which 40 for absolute increase in surplus time as before, 20 for relative. But the simple exchange value only contains 140 thalers as before. Now, is it only the use values which have increased, or has a new value been created? Before, capital had to begin again with 100 in order to realize itself anew at 40%. What happens to the 20 of surplus value? Before, the capitalist ate up 20 of them; he was left with a value of 20. Now he eats up 20 and is left with 40. On another side, the capital entering into production remained 100; now it has become 80. What is gained in value on one side in one form is lost as value on the other side in another form. The first capital re-enters into the production process; again produces a surplus value (capitalist's consumption deducted) of 20. At the end of this second operation, a newly created value is present without equivalent. 20 thalers together with the first 40. Now let us take the second capital.

Material, 50; wages (2 hours), 20; instrument, 10. But in the 2 hours he produces a value of 8, i.e. 80 thalers (of which 20 for costs of production). Remainder, 60, since 20 reproduce the wage (disappear as wage). $60 + 60 = 120$. At the end of this second operation, 20 thalers for consumption; remainder surplus value 20; together with the first operation, 60. In the third operation with the first capital, 60; with the second, 80; in the fourth operation with the first capital 80, with the second, 100. The first capital has increased as *value* in proportion as its exchange value, as productive capital, has decreased.

Suppose both capitals together with their surplus can be used as capital; i.e. their surplus exchanged for new labour. We then get the following calculation (leaving consumption aside): the *first* capital produces 40%, the second 60%. 40% of 140 is 56; 60% of 140 (i.e. capital, 80; surplus value, 60) is 84. The total product in the first case $140 + 56 = 196$; in the second $140 + 84 = 224$. In the second case absolute surplus value 28 higher than in the first. The first capital has 40 thalers with which to buy new labour time; the value of the hour of labour was presupposed at 10 thalers; therefore, his 40 thalers buy 4 new hours of labour, which produce 80 for him (of which 40 go to replace the wages of 8 hours of labour). At the end it was $140 + 80$ (i.e. reproduction of the capital of 100:

surplus value of 40, or reproduction of 140; or, in the first case, 100 thalers reproduce themselves as 140; the second 40, since they are spent only to buy new labour, hence do not *simply* replace value – impossible presupposition, by the way) which produce 80. $140 + 80 = 220$. The second capital of 140; the 80 produce 40; or the 80 thalers reproduce themselves as 120; the remaining 60, however, reproduce themselves (since they are spent *purely* for the purchase of *labour*, and do not therefore simply replace any value, but reproduce out of themselves and posit the surplus) as 180; then $120 + 120 = 240$. (Produced 40 thalers more than the first capital, exactly the surplus time of two hours, for the first is a surplus time of 2 hours as assumed in the first case). Thus the result is a greater exchange value, because more labour objectified; 2 hours more surplus labour.

Something else should be noted here as well: 140 thalers at 40% yield 56; capital and interest together $= 140 + 56 = 196$; but we have obtained 220; according to which the interest on 140 would be not 56 but 84; which would be 60% on 140 ($140:84 = 100:x$; $x = 8,400/140 = 60$). Similarly in the second case: 140 at 60% $=$ 84; capital and interest $= 140 + 84 = 224$; but we obtain 240; according to which the interest on the 140 is not 84 but 100; ($140 + 100 = 240$); i.e., %, ($140:100 = 100:x$; $x = 10,000/140$); [$x = 71\frac{3}{7}$%]. Now where does this come from? (In the first case 60% instead of 40; in the second $71\frac{3}{7}$ instead of 60%.) In the first case, where it was 60 instead of 40, hence 20% too much came out; in the second case $71\frac{3}{7}$ instead of 60, i.e. $11\frac{3}{7}$ too much. Why, then, firstly the difference between the two cases and secondly the difference in each case?

In the first case, the original capital was $100 = 60$ (material and instrument of labour) plus 40 in labour; $\frac{2}{5}$ labour, $\frac{3}{5}$ (material). The first $\frac{3}{5}$ bring no interest at all; the last $\frac{2}{5}$ bring 100%. But computed on the basis of the whole capital, the increase is only 40%; $\frac{2}{5}$ of $100 = 40$. But the 100% on the latter amount to only 40% on the whole 100; i.e. an increase of $\frac{2}{5}$ in the whole. Now, if only $\frac{2}{5}$ of the newly arrived capital of 40 had increased by 100%, then this would yield an increase of the whole by 16 [thalers]. $40 + 16 = 56$. This together with the $140 = 196$; which is then actually 40% on 156, capital and interest reckoned together. 40 increased by 100%, doubled, is 80; $\frac{2}{5}$ of 40 increased by 100% is 16.[66] 40 of the 80 replace capital. Gain of 40.

66. This should be 32, not 16, since $\frac{2}{5}$ of 40 is itself already 16.

The account then: $100c + 40$ interest $+ 40c + 40i = 220$; or, capital of 140 with an interest of 80; but if we had calculated $100c + 40i + 40c + 16i = 196$; or, capital of 140 with interest of 56.

An interest of 24 on a capital of 40 is too much; but $24 = \frac{3}{5}$ of 40 ($3 \times 8 = 24$); i.e. in addition to the capital, only $\frac{3}{5}$ of the capital grew by 100%; the whole capital therefore by only $\frac{2}{5}$, i.e. 16%.[67] The interest computation on 40 is 24% too high (by 100% on $\frac{3}{5}$ of the capital); 24 on 24 is 100% on 3×8 ($\frac{3}{5}$ of 40). But on the whole amount of 140, it is 60% instead of 40; i.e. 24 too much out of 40, 24 out of 40 = 60%. Thus we figured 60% too much on a capital of 40 ($60 = \frac{3}{5}$ of 100). But we figured 24 too high on 140 (and this is the difference between 220 and 196); this is first $\frac{1}{5}$ of 100 then $\frac{1}{12}$ of 100 too much; $\frac{1}{5}$ of $100 = 20\%$; $\frac{1}{12}$ of $100 = 8\frac{4}{12}\%$ or $8\frac{1}{3}\%$; thus altogether $28\frac{1}{3}\%$ too high. Thus on the whole not 60%, as on 40, but only $28\frac{1}{3}\%$ too much; which makes a difference of $31\frac{2}{3}$, depending on whether we figure 24 too many on the 40 [or on] the capital of 140. Similarly in the other example.

In the first 80 which produce 120, $50 + 10$ was simply replaced, but 20 reproduced itself threefold: 60 (20 reproduction, 40 surplus).

Hours of labour

If 20 posit 60, making up triple the value, then
    60   180.

67. This should be 40%. In these passages, the use of the term 'interest' (*Zins*) is, strictly speaking, incorrect; it should read 'surplus value'. Similarly, in some passages further on, the terminology does not correspond in every case with Marx's later usage.

NOTEBOOK IV

Mid-December 1857 –
22 January 1858

The Chapter on Capital (continuation)

Confusion of profit and surplus value. Carey's erroneous calculation. – The capitalist, who does not pay *the worker for the* preservation *of the old value, then demands remuneration for giving the worker permission to preserve the old capital. – Surplus value and profit etc. – Difference between consumption of the instrument and of wages. The former consumed in the production process, the latter outside it. – Increase of surplus value and decrease in rate of profit. (Bastiat)*

This highly irksome calculation will not delay us further. The point is simply this: if, as in our first example, material and instrument amount to $\frac{3}{5}$ (60 out of 100), and wages $\frac{2}{5}$ (40), and if the capital yielded a gain of 40%, then it equals 140 at the end (this 40% gain equal to the fact that the capitalist made the workers put out 12 hours of labour, where 6 were necessary, hence gained 100% on the necessary labour time). Now if the 40 thalers which were gained go to work again as capital with the same presuppositions – and at the present point, the presuppositions have not changed yet – then of the 40 thalers $\frac{3}{5}$ i.e. 24 thalers have to be used for material and instrument, and $\frac{2}{5}$ for labour; so that the only thing that doubles is the wage of 16 which becomes 32, 16 for reproduction, 16 surplus labour; so that altogether at the end of production $40 + 16 = 56$ or 40%. Thus the entire capital of 40 would have produced 196 under the same conditions. It should not be assumed, as happens in most of the economics books, that the 40 thalers are spent purely for wages, to buy living labour, and thus yield 80 thalers at the end of production.

⟨If it is said: a capital of 100 yields 10% in one period, 5% in another, then nothing is more mistaken than to conclude, as do Carey and consorts, that the share of capital in production was $\frac{1}{10}$ and that of labour $\frac{9}{10}$ in the first case; in the second case, the share of capital only $\frac{1}{20}$ and that of labour $\frac{19}{20}$; i.e. that the share of labour rises as the rate of profit falls.[1] From the viewpoint of capital – and capital has no awareness whatever of the nature of its process of realization, and has an interest in having an awareness of it only in times of *crisis* – a profit of 10% on a capital of 100 looks like a profit on each of its value components – material, instrument, wages – equally and indifferently, as if this capital were simply a sum of 100 thalers of value which had, as such, increased by 10%. But the question is, in fact: (1) what was the relation between the component parts of capital and (2) how much surplus labour did it buy with the wage – with the hours of labour objectified in the wage? If I know the total size of a capital, the relation of its value components to one another (in practice, I would also have to know what part of the instrument of production is used up in the process, i.e. actually enters into it), and if I know the profit, then I know how much surplus labour has been created. If $\frac{3}{5}$ of the capital consisted of material (which for the sake of convenience we here suppose to be entirely consumed productively as material of production), i.e. 60 thalers, and wages 40, and if the profit on the 100 thalers is 10, then the labour bought for 40 thalers of objectified labour time has created 50 thalers of objectified labour in the production process, hence has worked a surplus labour time or created a surplus value of 25% $= \frac{1}{4}$ of the necessary labour time. Then if the worker works a day of 12 hours, he has worked 3 hours of surplus time, and the labour time necessary to maintain him alive for one day was 9 hours of labour. The new value created in production may only be 10 thalers, but, according to the real rate, these 10 thalers are to be reckoned on the base of the 40, not of the 100. The 60 thalers of value have created no value whatever; the working day has. Thus the worker has increased the part of capital spent for labour capacity by 25%, not by 10%. The total capital has grown by 10%. 10 is 25% of 40; it is only 10% of 100. Thus the profit rate on capital in no way expresses the rate at which living labour increases objective labour; for this increase is merely $=$ to the surplus with which the worker reproduces his wage, i.e. $=$ to the time which he works over and above that which he would have to work in order to reproduce his wages. If the worker in the above example were not a worker for a capitalist, and if he related to the use values contained in the 100 thalers not as to capital but simply as to the objective conditions of his labour, then, before beginning

1. Carey, *Principles of Political Economy*, pp. 15–16, 27–48.

the production process anew, he would possess 40 thalers in subsistence, which he would consume during the working day, and 60 thalers in instrument and material. He would work only $\frac{3}{4}$ of a day, 9 hours, and at the end of the day his product would be not 110 thalers but 100, which he would again exchange in the above proportions, beginning the process again and again. But he would also work 3 hours less; i.e. he would save 25% surplus labour = 25% surplus value out of the exchange which he undertakes between 40 thalers in subsistence and his labour time; and if at some time he worked 3 hours extra, because the material and the instrument were there on hand, then it would not occur to him to say that he had created a new value of 10%, but rather one of 25%, because he could buy one fourth additional subsistence, 50 thalers' worth instead of 40; and, since he is concerned with use values, these items of subsistence by themselves would be of value for him. This illusion that the new value is derived not from the exchange of 9 hours of labour time as objectified in 40 thalers for 12 hours of living labour, i.e. a surplus value of 25% on this part, but that it comes from an even 10% increase in the total capital – 10% of 60 is 6 and of 40 is 4 – this illusion is the basis of the notorious Dr Price's *compound interest calculation*,[2] which led the heaven-born Pitt to his *sinking fund* idiocy.[3] The identity of surplus gain with surplus labour time – absolute and relative – sets a qualitative limit on the accumulation of capital, namely the *working day*, the amount of time out of 24 hours during which labouring capacity can be active, the degree to which the productive forces are developed, and the population, which expresses the number of simultaneous working days etc. If, on the other side, surplus value is defined merely as interest – i.e. as the relation in which capital increases itself by means of some imaginary sleight of hand, then the limit is merely quantitative, and there is then absolutely no reason why capital cannot every other day convert the interest into capital and thus yield interest on its interest in infinite geometrical progression. Practice has shown the economists that Price's interest-multiplication is impossible; but they have never discovered the blunder contained in it.

2. Dr Richard Price (1723–91; Nonconformist minister and writer on political and financial subjects), *An Appeal to the Public on the Subject of the National Debt*, London, 1772, p. 19. See below, pp. 842–3.

3. In 1786 William Pitt the Younger established a sinking fund of £1,000,000 in accordance with Dr Price's proposals.

Of the 110 thalers which emerge at the end of production, 60 thalers (material and instrument), in so far as they are values, have remained absolutely unchanged. The worker took nothing away from them and added nothing to them. Of course, from the standpoint of the capitalist, the fact that the worker maintains the value of objectified labour by the very fact of his labour being living labour appears as if the worker still had to pay the capitalist to get permission to enter into the proper relation with the objectified moments, the objective conditions, of labour. Now, as regards the remaining 50 thalers, 40 of them represent not only preservation but *actual reproduction*, since capital has divested itself of them [*von sich entäussert*] in the form of wages and the worker has consumed them; 10 thalers represent production above and beyond reproduction, i.e. ¼ surplus labour (of 3 hours). Only these 50 thalers are a product of the production process. Therefore, if the worker, as is wrongly asserted, divided the product with the capitalist so that the former's share were $\frac{9}{10}$, then he would have to get not 40 thalers (and he has obtained them in advance, in exchange for which he has reproduced them and paid them back in their entirety, as well as maintaining the already existing values for the capitalist free of charge), which is only $\frac{8}{10}$; but rather 45, which would leave capital only 5. Then, having begun the production process with 100 thalers, the capitalist would have at the end only 65 thalers as product. But the worker obtains none of the 40 thalers he has reproduced, nor any of the 10 thalers of surplus value. If the 40 thalers which have been reproduced are to serve for the purchase of further living labour, then, as far as the relation is concerned, all that can be said is that an objectified labour of 9 hours (40 thalers) buys living labour for 12 hours (50 thalers) and thus yields a surplus value of 25% of the real product (partly reproduced as wage fund, partly newly produced as surplus value) in the realization process.

Just now the original capital of 100 was: $50 - 10 - 40$.[4] Produced surplus gain of 10 thalers (25% surplus time). *Altogether* 110 thalers.

Now suppose it were: $60 - 20 - 20$. The result would be 110 thalers, so says the ordinary economist, and the even more ordinary capitalist says that 10% has been produced in equal proportions by all parts of the capital. Again, 80 thalers of capital would merely be preserved; no change taken place in its value. Only the

4. 50: material of labour; 10: instrument of labour; 40: wages of labour.

20 thalers would have turned into 30; i.e. surplus labour would have increased by 50%, not by 25% as before.

Take the third case: 100: 70 – 20 – 10. Result 110.

Then the invariable value, 90. The new product 20; hence surplus value or surplus time 100%. Here we have three cases in which the profit on the whole capital is always 10, but in the first case the new value created was 25% above the objectified labour spent to buy living labour, in the second case 50%, in the third: 100%.⟩

The devil take this wrong arithmetic.[5] But never mind. *Commençons de nouveau.*

In the first case we had:

Invariable value	*Wage labour*	*Surplus value*	*Total*
60	40	10	110

We continue to presuppose a working day = 12 hours. (We could also assume a growing working day, e.g. x hours before, but now $x + b$ hours, while productive force remains constant; or both factors variable.)

	Hours	*Thalers*	
If the worker produces in	12	50	
then in	1	$4\frac{1}{6}$	
then in	$9\frac{3}{5}$	40 ⎫	in 12 hours 50 thalers
then in	$2\frac{2}{5}$	10 ⎭	

The worker's necessary labour then amounts to $9\frac{3}{5}$ hours (40 thalers); hence surplus labour $2\frac{2}{5}$ hours (value of 10 thalers). $2\frac{2}{5}$ hours is $\frac{1}{5}$ of the working day. The worker's surplus labour amounts to $\frac{1}{5}$ of the day, i.e. = the value of 10 thalers. Now if we look at these $2\frac{2}{5}$ hours as a percentage which capital has gained above the labour time objectified in $9\frac{3}{5}$ hours, then $2\frac{2}{5} : 9\frac{3}{5} = \frac{12}{5} : \frac{48}{5}$, i.e. = 12:48 = 1:4. Thus $\frac{1}{4}$ of the capital = 25% of it. Likewise, 10 thalers: 40 thalers = 1:4 = 25%. Now, summarizing the whole result:[6]

5. The numerical examples above and below contained occasional, always trivial, errors of arithmetic. The corrections, as indicated by MELI, have been implicitly substituted here, unless noted.

6. In the following table the quantity of value is always expressed in thalers.

No. I

Original capital: 100	Constant value: 60	Value reproduced for wages: 40	Surplus value from production: 10	Total sum: 110	Surplus time and value: 2⅖ hours or 10. (2⅖ of labour)	% of objectified labour exchanged: 25%

(It might be said that the *instrument of labour*, its value, has to be not only replaced but reproduced; since it is in fact used up, consumed in production. This to be looked at under *fixed capital*. In actuality the value of the instrument is transposed to that of the material; to the extent that it is objectified labour, it only changes its form. If in the above example the value of the material was 50 and that of the instrument 10, then now, with the instrument used up by 5, the value of the material is 55 and that of the instrument 5; if it disappears altogether, then that of the material has reached 60. This is an element of the simple production process. Unlike wages, the instrument has not been consumed *outside the production process*.)

Now to the second presupposition:

Original capital: 100	Constant value: 80	Value reproduced for wages: 20	Surplus value from production: 10	Total sum: 110

If the worker produces 30 thalers in 12 hours, then in 1 hour 2¼ thalers, in 8 hours 20 thalers, in 4 hours 10 thalers. 10 thalers are 50% of 20 thalers; as are 4 hours out of 8 hours; the surplus value = 4 hours, ⅓ of a day, or 10 thalers surplus value.

Thus:

No. II

Original capital: 100	Constant value: 80	Value reproduced for wages: 20 8 hours	Surplus value from production: 10	Total sum: 110	Surplus time and value: 4 hours or 10. 2 working days	% on capital: 50%

In the first case, like the second, the profit on a total capital of $100 = 10\%$, but in the first case the real surplus value which capital obtains from the production process is 25%, in the second, 50%.

The conditions presupposed in No. II are in themselves as possible as those in No. I. But brought into connection with one another, those of No. II are absurd. Material and instrument have been raised from 60 to 80, the productivity of labour has fallen from $4\frac{1}{6}$ thalers per hour to $2\frac{3}{4}$, and surplus value increased by 100%. (Suppose, however, that the increased expenditure for wages expresses more working days in the first case, fewer in the second, and then the presupposition is correct.) It is in itself irrelevant that necessary wages, i.e. the value of labour expressed in thalers, have fallen. Whether the value of an hour of labour is expressed in 2 thalers or in 4, in both cases the product of 12 hours of labour is exchanged (in circulation) for 12 hours of labour, and in both cases surplus labour appears as surplus value. The absurdity of the presupposition comes from the fact (1) that we have posited 12 hours as the minimum working time; and hence cannot introduce additional or fewer working days; (2) the more we make capital increase on one side, the more we not only make *necessary* labour decline, but have also to decrease its *value*, although the value is the same. In the second case, the price would, rather, have to rise. The fact that the worker can live from less work, i.e. that he produces more in the same number of hours, would have to be shown not in a decrease in the thalers for necessary labour, but in the number of necessary hours. If he gets, as e.g. in the first case, $4\frac{1}{6}$ thalers, but if the use value of this value, which has to be *constant* in order to express *value* (not price), had multiplied, then he no longer needs $9\frac{2}{8}$ but only 4 hours for the reproduction of his living labouring capacity, and this would have to express itself in the surplus over the value. But the way we have set up the presuppositions, our 'invariable value' is variable, while the 10% are invariable, here a constant addition to reproductive labour, although it expresses different percentage parts of the same. In the first case the invariable value is smaller than in the second case, but the total product of labour is larger; since, if one part of 100 is smaller, the other has to be larger; and, since absolute labour time is fixed at the identical amount, and since further the total product of labour becomes smaller, in proportion as 'invariable value' becomes larger, and larger as the latter becomes smaller, we therefore obtain less product (absolutely) from the same labour time in proportion as more capital is employed. Now, this would be quite correct, since, if out of a given sum such as 100 more is spent as 'invariable value', less can be spent for labour time, and thus, *relative* to total capital, less new overall value can be created; but then, if capital is to make a profit, one cannot hold *labour time* constant, as is done here, or, if one holds it constant, the *value of the working hour* cannot become smaller, as it does here; which is impossible if 'invariable value' becomes larger and *surplus value* becomes *larger*; the *number* of working hours would have to become smaller. But that is what we have assumed in the example. We assume in the first case that 50 thalers are produced in 12 hours of labour; in the second case, only 30 thalers. In the first, we make the worker work $9\frac{3}{5}$ hours; in the second only 6, although he produces less per hour. It's absurd. But, understood differently, is there not after all something correct in these figures? Does not absolute new value decrease despite an increase in the relative, as soon as relatively more material and instrument than labour is introduced into the component parts of capital? Relative to a given capital, less living labour is employed; hence, even if the excess of this living labour above its costs is greater, and therefore the percentage of wages rises, i.e. the percentage relative to capital actually consumed, then the absolute new value does not necessarily become relatively smaller than in the case of a capital which employs less material and instrument (and this is the main point of the change in invariable value, i.e. value unchanged as value in the production process) and relatively more living labour; precisely because relatively more living labour is employed? An increase in the productive force then corresponds to the increase in the instrument, since the surplus value of the instrument does not keep pace, as in the previous mode of production, with its use value, its productive force, and since any increase in productive force creates more surplus value, although by no means in the same numerical proportion. The increase in the productive forces, which has to express itself in an enlargement of the value of the instrument – the space it takes up in capital expenditure – necessarily brings with it an increase in the material, since more material has to be worked in order to produce more product. (The increase in the productive force can, however, also relate to quality; but if that is given, only to quantity; or to quantity if quality is given; or to both.) Now, although there is less (necessary) labour in relation to surplus labour, and absolutely less living labour in relation to capital, is it not possible for its surplus value to rise, although in relation to the capital as a whole it declines, i.e. the so-called rate of profit declines? Take for example a capital of 100. Let material be 30 at first. 30 for instrument. (Together, invariable value of 60.) Wages 40 (4 working days). Profit 10%. Here profit is 25% on wages and 10% on capital as a whole. Now let material become 40 and instrument 40. Let productivity double, so that only 2 working days necessary $= 20$. Now posit that the absolute profit be smaller than 10; i.e. the profit on total capital. Is it not possible for profit on labour employed to be more than 25%, i.e. in the given case, more than merely a fourth of 20? In fact, a third of 20 is $6\frac{2}{3}$; i.e. less than 10, but $33\frac{1}{3}$% of labour employed, while in the previous case it was only 25%. In this case, we would end up with only $106\frac{2}{3}$, while in the previous case we would have had 110, but still, with the same capital (100) the surplus labour, surplus gain relative to labour employed, would be greater than in the first case; but since 50% less labour was employed, in absolute terms, than in the first case, while the profit on labour employed was only $8\frac{1}{3}$ more than in the first case, it follows that the absolute quantity which results has to be smaller, and the same applies to the profit on total capital. For $20 \times 33\frac{1}{3}$ is smaller than 40×25. This whole instance is improbable and cannot count as a general example in economics; for an increase in the instrument and an increase in the material worked are both presupposed, while not only the relative but the absolute number of workers has declined. (Of course, when two factors $=$ a third, one has to grow smaller as the other grows larger.) But an increase in the value of the instrument in relation to capital as a whole, and an increase in the value of the material, all in all presuppose a division of labour, hence at least an absolute increase in the number of workers, if not an increase relative to capital as a whole. However, take the case of the lithographing machine, which everyone can use to make lithographs without special skill; suppose the value of the instrument immediately upon its invention to be greater than that which 4 workers absorbed before these handy things were invented; it now requires only 2 workers (here, as with many instrument-like machines, no further division of labour takes place; instead, the qualitative division disappears); let the instruments originally have a value of only 40, but let 4 working days be necessary (necessary, here, for the capitalist to make a profit). (There are machines, e.g.

forced air heating ducts, where labour as such disappears altogether except at a single point; the duct is open at one point, and carries heat to the others; no workers are required at all. This the case generally (see Babbage)[7] with energy transmission, where, previously, energy had to be carried in material form by numbers of workers, here firemen, from one point to another – where the transmission from one room to another, which has now become a physical process, appeared as the labour of numbers of workers.) Now, if he uses this lithographing machine as a source of income, as capital, and not as use value, then the material must necessarily increase, since he can put out more lithographs in the same amount of time, which is precisely where this greater profit comes from. Let this lithographer then employ an instrument to the amount of 40, material 40, 2 working days (20) which [give] him $33\frac{1}{3}\%$, i.e. $6\frac{2}{3}$ out of an objectified labour time of 20; then his capital, like the other's, consists of 100, only yields $6\frac{2}{3}\%$, but he gains $33\frac{1}{3}$ on labour employed, while the other gains 10 on capital, but only 25% on labour. The value obtained from labour employed may be smaller, but the profits on the whole capital are greater if the other elements of capital are relatively smaller. Despite this, the business at $6\frac{2}{3}\%$ on the total capital and $33\frac{1}{3}\%$ on labour could become more profitable than the earlier one based on 25% on labour and 10% profit on the total capital. Suppose e.g. that grain prices etc. rose so that the maintenance of the worker rose by 25% in value. The 4 working days would now cost the first lithographer 50 instead of 40. His instruments and material would remain the same: 60 thalers. He would then have to lay out a capital of 110. With this capital, his profit on the 50 thalers for 4 working days would be 12 (25%). Hence 12 thalers on 110 (i.e. $9\frac{1}{6}\%$ on the total capital of 110). The other lithographer: machine 40, material 40; but the 2 working days will cost him 25% more than 20, i.e. 25. He would thus have to lay out 105; his surplus value on labour $33\frac{1}{3}\%$, i.e. $\frac{1}{3}$, is $8\frac{1}{3}$. He would gain then, $8\frac{1}{3}$ on 105; $13\frac{1}{8}\%$. Then suppose a 10-year cycle with 5 bad and 5 good harvests at the above average proportions; then the first lithographer would gain 50 thalers of interest on the second during the first 5 years; in the last 5 $45\frac{5}{8}$; altogether $95\frac{5}{8}$ thalers; average interest over the 10 years $9\frac{7}{12}$ thalers. The other capitalist would have gained $31\frac{1}{3}$ in the first 5 years, $65\frac{5}{8}$ in the last; $96\frac{2}{2}\frac{3}{4}$ altogether; a 10-year average of $9\frac{84}{120}$. Since No. II uses up more material at the same price, he sells

7. C. Babbage, *Traité sur l'économie des machines et des manufactures*, p. 29.

cheaper. It could be said in reply that he sells dearer because he uses up more instrument; especially because he uses up more of the value of the machine in proportion as he uses up more material; however, it is in practice not true that machines wear out and have to be replaced more rapidly as they work more material. But all this is beside the point. Let the relation between the value of the machine and that of the material be constant in both cases.

This example attains significance only if we assume a smaller capital which employs more labour and less material and machinery, but yields a higher percentage on the total capital; and a larger capital employing more machinery and more material, as many working days in absolute numbers but relatively fewer, and a smaller percentage on the whole, because less on labour, being more productive, division of labour used, etc. It also has to be postulated (which was not done above) that the use value of the machine significantly greater than its value; i.e. that its devaluation in the service of production is not proportional to its increasing effect on production.

Thus, as above, a press (first, hand-operated printing press; second, self-acting printing press).

Capital I, 100, uses 30 in material; 30 for the manual press; 4 working days = 40 thalers; gain 10%; hence 25% on living labour ($\frac{1}{4}$ surplus time).

Capital II, 200, uses 100 in materials, 60 in press, 4 working days (40 thalers); gain on the 4 working days $13\frac{1}{3}$ thalers = 1 working day and $\frac{1}{3}$, compared to only 1 working day in the first case; total sum: $213\frac{1}{3}$. I.e. $6\frac{2}{3}$%, compared to 10% in the first case. Nevertheless, the surplus value on the labour which has been employed is $13\frac{1}{3}$ in this second case, as against 10 in the first; in the first, 4 days create 1 surplus day in 4 working days; in the second, 4 days create $1\frac{1}{3}$ surplus days. But the rate of profit on the total capital is $\frac{1}{3}$ or $33\frac{1}{3}$% smaller than in the first; the total amount of the gain is $\frac{1}{3}$ greater. Now let us suppose that the 30 and the 100 in material are sheets of book paper, and that the instruments wear out in the same space of time, say 10 years or $\frac{1}{10}$ per year. Then No. I has to replace $\frac{1}{10}$ of 30 in material, i.e. 3; No. II, $\frac{1}{10}$ of 60, i.e. 6. The material does not enter further into annual production (which may be regarded as 4 working days of 3 months each) on either side, see above.

Capital I sells 30 sheets at 30 for materials + 3 for instrument + 50 (objectified labour time) (production time) = 83.

Capital II sells 100 sheets at 100, material, $+$ 6, instrument, $+$ 53⅓ $=$ 159⅓.

Capital I sells 30 sheets for 83 thalers, 1 sheet at $\frac{83}{30}$ thalers $=$ 2 thalers, 23 silver groschen.

Capital II sells 100 sheets for 159 thalers, 10 silver groschen; 1 sheet at $\dfrac{159 \text{ thalers } 10 \text{ silver groschen}}{100}$ i.e. 1 thaler, 17 silver groschen, 8 pfennigs.

It is clear then that Capital I is done for, because its selling price is infinitely too high. Now, although in the first case the profit on total capital was 10% and in the second case only 6⅔%, the first capital only took in 25% on labour time, while the second takes – 33⅓%. With Capital I, necessary labour is greater relative to the total capital; and hence surplus labour, while smaller in absolute terms than with Capital II, shows up as a higher rate of profit on the smaller total capital. 4 working days at 60 are greater than 4 at 160; in the first, 1 working day corresponds to a capital of 15; in the second, 1 working day corresponds to 40. But with the second capital, labour is more productive (which is given both in the *greater* amount of machinery, hence the greater amount of space that it takes up among the value components of capital; and in the greater amount of material in which a working day, which consists of a greater proportion of surplus time and hence uses more material in the same time, is expressed). It creates more surplus time (relative surplus time, i.e. determined by the development of the force of production). In the first case, surplus time is ¼, in the second, ⅓. It therefore creates more use values and a higher exchange value in the same amount of time; but the latter not in proportion with the former, since, as we saw, exchange value does not rise in the same numerical proportion as the productivity of labour. The fractional price is therefore smaller than the total production price – i.e. the fractional price multiplied by the amount of fractional prices produced is greater. Now, if we had assumed an *absolutely greater* number of working days than in No. I, although a relatively smaller number, then the matter would have been even more striking. The profit of the larger capital, working with more machinery, therefore appears smaller than that of the smaller capital working with relatively or absolutely more living labour, precisely because the *higher profit on living labour* appears as smaller, when calculated on the basis of a total capital in which living labour makes up a lesser proportion

of the whole, than the *lower profit on living labour* which makes up
a larger proportion of the smaller total capital. But the fact that
No. II can employ more material, and that a larger proportion of
the total value is in the instrument, is only the expression of the
productivity of labour.

This, then, is the unfortunate Bastiat's famous riddle; he had
firmly convinced himself – to which Mr Proudhon had no
answer – that because the rate of profit of the larger and more productive total capital is smaller, it follows that the worker's share
has grown larger, whereas precisely the *opposite* is the case; his
surplus labour has grown larger.[8]

Nor does Ricardo seem to have understood the matter, for
otherwise he would not have tried to explain the periodic decline
of profit merely by the rise in wages caused by the rise in grain
prices (and hence of rent).[9] But at bottom, surplus value – in so far
as it is indeed the foundation of profit, but still distinct from profit
commonly so-called – has never been developed. The unfortunate
Bastiat would have said in the above case that in the first example
the profit was 10 % (i.e. $\frac{1}{10}$), in the second only $6\frac{1}{4}$ %, i.e. $\frac{1}{16}$ (leaving
out the percentage), so that the worker receives $\frac{9}{10}$ in the first
case, $\frac{15}{16}$ in the second. The relation is correct in neither of the two
cases, nor is their relation to one another correct. Now, as far as
the further relation of the new value of capital to capital as *indifferent total value* is concerned (and this is how capital as such
appeared to us at the beginning, before we moved on into the production process, and it must again appear to us in this way at the
end of the process), this is to be developed partly under the rubric
of *profit*, where the new value obtains a new character, and partly
under the heading of *accumulation*. We are here initially concerned
only with developing the nature of surplus value as the equivalent
of the absolute or relative labour time mobilized by capital above
and beyond necessary labour time.

The consumption, in the production process, of the element of
value consisting of the instrument cannot in the least [serve to] distinguish the instrument of labour from the material – here, where
all that is to be explained is the creation of surplus value, self-
realization. This is because this consumption is part of the simple
production process itself, hence the value of the consumed instrument (whether it be the *simple use value* of the instrument it-

8. Bastiat et Proudhon, *Gratuité du crédit*, pp. 127–32, 135–7, 288.
9. Ricardo, *On the Principles of Political Economy*, pp. 117–19.

self, or the exchange value, if production has already progressed to where there is a division of labour and where at least the surplus is exchanged) has to be recovered again in the value (exchange value) or the use value of the product – so that the process can begin anew. The instrument loses its use value in the same proportion as it helps to raise the exchange value of the raw material and serves as a means of labour. This point must, indeed, be examined, because the distinction between the invariable value, the part of capital which is preserved; that which is reproduced (*reproduced* for capital; from the standpoint of the real production of labour – *produced*); and that which is newly produced, is of essential importance.

Multiplication of simultaneous working days. (Accumulation of capital.) – *Growth of the constant part of capital in relation to the variable part spent on wages = growth of the productivity of labour. – Proportion in which capital has to increase in order to employ the same number of workers if productivity rises*

It is now time to finish with the question of the value resulting from the growth of the productive forces. We have seen: this creates a *surplus value* (not merely a greater use value) just as in the case of an absolute increase in surplus labour. If a certain limit is given, say e.g. that the worker needs only half a day in order to produce his subsistence for a *whole* day – and if the natural limit has been reached – then an increase of absolute labour time is possible only if more workers are employed *at the same time*, so that the real working day is simultaneously multiplied instead of only lengthened (in the given conditions, the individual worker can work no more than 12 hours; if a surplus time of 24 hours is to be gained, then there have to be 2 workers). Capital in this case, before entering the self-realization process, has to buy 6 additional hours of labour in the act of exchange with the worker, i.e. has to lay out a greater part of itself; at the same time it has to lay out more for material, on the average (beside the fact that the extra worker has to be *available*, i.e. that the working population has to have grown). Hence the possibility of this further realization process depends here on a previous accumulation of capital (as regards its material existence). If, however, productivity increases, and hence relative surplus time – at the present point we can still regard capital as always directly engaged in the production of subsistence, raw materials etc. – then less expenditure is necessary for wages and the growth in the material is created by the realization process itself. But this question belongs, rather, with the *accumulation* of capitals.

We now come to the point where we last broke off.[10] An increase in productivity increases the *surplus value*, although it does not increase the absolute amount of exchange values. It increases values because it creates a new *value as value*, i.e. a value which is not merely an equivalent destined for exchange, but which asserts itself as such; in a word, more money. The question is: does it ultimately also increase the amount of exchange values? This is, at bottom, admitted; for even Ricardo admits that along with the accumulation of capitals there is an increase in savings, hence a growth in the exchange values produced. The growth of savings means nothing more than the growth of independent values – of money. But Ricardo's demonstration contradicts his own assertion.

Our old example. 100 thalers capital; 60 thalers in constant value; 40 in wages; produces 80; hence product = 140.* Let these 40 in surplus value be absolute labour time.

Now suppose that productivity doubles: then, if a wage of 40 gives 8 hours of necessary labour, the worker could now produce a whole day of living labour in 4 hours. Surplus time would then

---

* Here we see again that the surplus value on the whole of the capital = to half of the newly produced value, since a half of the latter = to necessary labour. The relation between this surplus value, which is always equal to surplus time, i.e. = to the worker's total product minus the part which forms his wage, depends (1) on the relation between the constant part of capital and the productive part; (2) between necessary labour time and surplus time. In the above case, the relation of surplus time to necessary time is 100%; gives 40% on a capital of 100; hence (3) it depends further, not only on the relation given above in (2), but also on the absolute magnitude of necessary labour. If, in a capital of 100, the constant part were 80, then the part exchanged for necessary labour would be = 20, and if this created 100% surplus time, the profit on capital would be 20%. But if the capital were 200 with the same relation between the constant and the variable part (i.e. $\frac{4}{5}$ to $\frac{1}{5}$), then the total would be 280, which is 40 out of 100. In this case the absolute amount of profit would rise from 40 to 80, but the relation would remain at 40%. However, if out of the 200 the constant element were 120 and the quantity of necessary labour 80, but the latter increased by only 10%, i.e. 8, then the total sum would be = 208, i.e. a profit of 4%; if it increased by only 5, then the total 205, i.e. $2\frac{1}{2}$%.

---

10. This is a continuation of the critique of Ricardo, broken off on p. 353.

increase by $\frac{1}{3}$ ($\frac{2}{3}$ of a day to produce a whole day before, now $\frac{1}{3}$). $\frac{2}{3}$ of the product of the working day would be surplus value, and if the hour of necessary labour = 5 thalers ($5 \times 8 = 40$), then he would now need only $5 \times 4 = 20$ thalers. For capital, then, a surplus gain of 20, i.e. 60 instead of 40. At the end, 140, of which $60 =$ the constant value, $20 =$ the wage and $60 =$ the surplus gain; together, 140. The capitalist can then begin production anew with 80 thalers of capital:

Let capitalist A on the same stage of old production invest his capital of 140 in new production. Following the original proportions, he needs $\frac{3}{5}$ for the invariable part of capital, i.e. $3 \times \frac{140}{5} = 3 \times 28 = 84$, leaving 56 for necessary labour. Before, he spent 40 on labour, now 56; $\frac{2}{5}$ of 40 additionally. Then at the end, his capital $= 84 + 56 + 56 = 196$.

Capitalist B on the higher stage of production would similarly employ his 140 thalers for new production. If out of a capital of 80 he needs 60 for invariable value and only 20 for labour, then out of a capital of 60 he needs 45 for invariable value and 15 for labour; thus the total would be $= 60 + 20 + 20 = 100$ in the first and, secondly, $45 + 15 + 15 = 75$. Thus his total yield is 175, while that of the first $= 196$. An increase in the productivity of labour means nothing more than that the same capital creates the same value with less labour, or that less labour creates the same product with more capital. That less necessary labour produces more surplus labour. The necessary labour is smaller in relation to capital; for the process of its realization this is obviously the same as: capital is larger in relation to the necessary labour which it sets into motion; for the same capital sets more surplus labour in motion, hence less necessary labour.*

*If it is postulated, as in our case, that the capital remains the same, i.e. that both begin again with 140 thalers, then in the case of the more productive capital, a larger part has to go to capital (i.e. to its invariable part), while with the less productive capital, a larger part to labour. The first capital of 140 thus sets into motion a necessary labour of 56, and this necessary labour presupposes an invariable part of 84 out of the total capital. The second sets labour in the amount of $20 + 15 = 35$ into motion, and an invariable capital of $60 + 45 = 105$ (it further follows from what was developed earlier that an increase in the force of production does not proportionately increase value). − In the first case, as already shown above, the absolute new value is greater than in the second, because the mass of labour employed is greater in relation to the invariable part; while in the second the former is smaller, precisely because labour is more productive. However (1) the difference between the new value of 60 in one case and 40 in the other means that the first cannot begin

It is sometimes said about machinery, therefore, that it *saves labour*; however, as Lauderdale correctly remarked, the mere *saving* of labour is not the characteristic thing;[12] for, with the help of machinery, human labour performs actions and creates things which without it would be absolutely impossible of accomplishment. The latter concerns the use value of machinery. What is characteristic is the *saving* of necessary labour and the creating of *surplus labour*. The higher productivity of labour is expressed in the fact that capital has to buy a smaller amount of necessary labour in order to create the same value and a greater quantity of use values, or that less necessary labour creates the same exchange value, realizes more material and a greater mass of use values. Thus, *if the total value of the capital remains the same*, an increase in the productive force means that the constant part of capital (consisting of machinery and material) grows relative to the variable, i.e. to the part of capital which is exchanged for living labour and forms the wage fund. This means at the same time that a smaller quantity of labour sets a larger quantity of capital in motion. If the *total value of capital* entering into the production process increases, then the wage fund (this variable part of capital) must decrease *relatively*, compared to the relation if the productivity of labour, i.e. the relation of necessary to surplus labour, had remained the same. Now let us assume in the above case that the capital of 100 is agricultural capital. Then, 40 thalers for seeds, fertilizer etc.; 20 thalers instrument of labour, and 40 thalers wage labour, at the old level of production. (Let these 40 thalers = 4 days of necessary labour.) At the old production level, these create a total of 140. Now let fertility double, owing to improvement either in the instrument or in the fertilizer

---

production anew with the same capital as the second; for a part of the new value on both sides has to enter into circulation as an equivalent so that the capitalist can live, and live from his capital. If both of them eat up 20 thalers then the first begins anew with a capital of 120, the other also with 120 etc. See above. Return to this whole matter again[11]; but the question of the relation between the new value created by the increased force of production and the new value created by absolute increases in labour belongs in the chapter on *accumulation and profit*.

---

11. See below, pp. 765–71.
12. Lauderdale, *Recherches sur la nature et l'origine de la richesse publique*, p. 137.

etc. In this case the product has to = 140 thalers (given that the instrument is entirely consumed). Let fertility double, so that the price of the necessary working day falls by half; so that only 4 necessary half days of work (i.e. 2 whole ones) are necessary in order to produce 8. 2 working days to produce 8 is the same as when $\frac{1}{4}$ of each working day (3 hours) is required for necessary labour. Now, instead of 40 thalers, the farmer has to spend only 20 for labour. Thus at the end of the process the component parts of capital have changed; from the original 40 for seed etc., which now have double the use value; 20 for instrument and 20 for labour (2 whole working days). Before the relation of the constant part of capital to the variable = 60:40 = 3:2; now 80:20 = 4:1. Looking at the whole capital, necessary labour was = $\frac{2}{5}$; now $\frac{1}{5}$. Now, if the farmer wants to continue to use labour in the old relation, then by how much would his capital have to increase? Or – in order to avoid the *nefarious presupposition* that he continued to operate with a constant capital of 60 and a wage fund of 40 – after a doubling of productive force, which introduces false relations*; because it presupposes that, despite the doubled force of production, capital continued to operate with the same component parts, to employ the same quantity of necessary labour without spending more for raw material and instrument of labour†; then, therefore, productivity doubles, so that he now needs to spend only 20 thalers on labour, whereas he needed 40 before. (If it is given that 4 whole working days were necessary, each = 10 thalers, in order to create a surplus of 4 whole working days, and if this surplus is provided for him by the transformation of 40 thalers of cotton into yarn, then he now needs only 2 whole working days in order to create the same value, i.e. that of 8 working days; the value of the yarn expressed a surplus time of 4 working days before, now of 6. Or, each of the workers needed 6 hours of necessary labour time before in order to create 12; *now* 3. Necessary labour time was 12 × 4 = 48, or 4 days. In each of these days, the surplus time was = $\frac{1}{2}$ day (6 hours). It

---

*Although in the case e.g. of the farmer this is quite correct, if the seasons bring a doubling of fertility, and correct for every industrialist if the force of production doubles not in his branch, but in the branch whose output he uses; i.e. if e.g. raw cotton cost 50% less and grain (i.e. wages) and the instrument likewise; he would then continue as before to spend 40 thalers for raw cotton, but in twice the quantity, 20 for machinery, 40 for labour.

†Suppose cotton alone doubled in productivity, the machine remains the same, then – this to be examined further.

now amounts to only $12 \times 2 = 24$ or 2 days; 3 hours per day. In order to bring forth the surplus value, each of the 4 workers would have to work 6×2 hours; i.e. 1 day; now he needs to work only 3×2 hours; i.e. $\frac{1}{2}$ day. Now, whether 4 work $\frac{1}{2}$ a day or 2 a whole (1) day is the same. The capitalist could dismiss 2 workers. He would even have to dismiss them, since a certain quantity of cotton is only enough to make a certain quantity of yarn; thus he cannot order 4 whole days of work any more, but only 4 half days. But if the worker has to work 12 hours in order to obtain 3 hours, i.e. his *necessary* wage, then, if he works 6 hours, he will obtain only $1\frac{1}{2}$ hours of exchange value. But if he can live for 12 hours with 3 hours of necessary labour, then with $1\frac{1}{2}$ he can live only 6 hours. Thus if all 4 workers were to be employed, each of the 4 could live only half a day; i.e. the same capital cannot keep all 4 alive as *workers*, but only 2. The capitalist could pay 4 out of the old fund for 4 half days of work; then he would pay 2 too many and would make the workers a present of the productive force; since he can use only 4 half days of living labour; such 'possibilities' neither occur in practice, nor can we deal with them here, where we are concerned with the relation of capital as such.) Now 20 thalers of the capital of 100 are not directly employed in production. The capitalist uses 40 thalers of raw material, 20 for instrument, together 60 as before, but now only 20 thalers for labour (2 working days). Of the whole capital of 80 he uses $\frac{3}{4}$ (60) for the constant part and only $\frac{1}{4}$ for labour. Then if he employs the remaining 20 in the same way, $\frac{3}{4}$ for constant capital, $\frac{1}{4}$ for labour; then 15 for the first, 5 for the second. Now since 1 working day $= 10$ thalers (given), 5 would be only $= 6$ hours $= \frac{1}{2}$ working day. With the new value of 20, gained through productivity, capital could buy only $\frac{1}{2}$ a working day more, if it continues to realize itself in the same proportion. It would have to grow three-fold (namely, 60) (together with the $20 = 80$) in order to employ the 2 dismissed workers for the previous 2 full working days. In the new relation, the capital uses $\frac{3}{4}$ in constant capital in order to employ $\frac{1}{4}$ as wage fund.

Thus if 20 is the whole capital, $\frac{3}{4}$ i.e. 15 constant and $\frac{1}{4}$ labour (i.e. 5) $= \frac{1}{2}$ a working day.

With a whole capital of 4×20, hence $4 \times 15 = 60$ constant, hence $4 \times 5 = 20$ wages $= \frac{4}{2}$ working days $= 2$ working days.

Therefore, if the productive force of labour doubles, so that a capital of 60 thalers in raw materials and instrument now needs only 20 thalers in labour (2 working days) for its realization, whereas it needed 100 before, then the total capital of 100 would have to grow to 160, or the capital of 80 now being dealt with would have to double in order to retain all the labour put out of work. But the doubling of productive force creates a new capital of only 20 thalers $= \frac{1}{2}$ of the labour time employed earlier; and this is only enough to employ $\frac{1}{2}$ a working day additionally. Before the doubling of the productive force, the capital was 100 and employed 4 working days (on the supposition that $\frac{2}{5} =$ wage fund of 40); now, when the wage fund has fallen to $\frac{1}{5}$ of 100, to $20 = 2$ working days (but to $\frac{1}{4}$ of 80, the capital newly entering into the realization process), it would have to rise to 160, by 60%, in ordeɪ still to be able to employ 4 working days as before. It can only employ $\frac{1}{2}$ a new working day with the 20 thalers drawn from the increase in the productive force, if the whole old capital continues operating. Before, it employed with 100, $\frac{16}{4}$ (4 days) working days; it could now employ only $\frac{5}{4}$. Therefore, when the force of production doubles, capital does not need to double in order to set the same necessary labour into motion, 4 working days; i.e. it does not need to rise to 200, but needs to rise only by double the whole, minus the part deducted from the wage fund. $(100 - 20 = 80) \times 2 = 160$. (By contrast, the first capital, before the increase in productive force, which divided 100 as 60 constant 40 wages (4 working days), in order to employ two additional days, would need to grow from 100 to only 150; i.e. $\frac{3}{5}$ constant capital (30) and $\frac{2}{5}$ wage fund (20). If it is given that the working day doubles in both cases, then the second would amount to 250 at the end, the first only 160.) Of the part of capital which is withdrawn from the wage fund owing to the increase in the force of production, one part has to be transformed again into raw material and instrument, another part is exchanged for living labour; this can take place only in the proportions between the different parts which are posited by the new productivity. It can no longer take place in the old proportion, for the relation of the wage fund to the constant fund has decreased. If the capital of 100 first used $\frac{2}{5}$ for wage fund (40) and, owing to a doubling of productive force, then used only $\frac{1}{5}$ (20), then $\frac{1}{5}$ of the capital has become free (20 thalers); and the employed part, 80, uses only $\frac{1}{4}$ as wage fund. Thus, of the 20, similarly, only 5 thalers ($\frac{1}{2}$ working day). The whole capital of 100 therefore now employs $2\frac{1}{2}$ working days; or, it would have to grow to 160 in order to employ 4 again.

If the original capital had been 1,000, divided in the same way: $\frac{3}{5}$ constant capital, $\frac{2}{5}$ wage fund, then 600 + 400 (let 400 equal 40 working days; each working day = 10 thalers). Now double the productive force of labour, i.e. only 20 working days required for the same product (= 200 thalers), then the capital necessary to begin production anew would be = 800; that is 600 + 200; 200 thalers would have been set free. Employed in the same relation, then $\frac{3}{4}$ for constant capital = 150 and $\frac{1}{4}$ wages = 50. Thus, if the 1,000 thalers are employed in their entirety, then now 750 constant + 250 wage fund = 1,000 thalers. But 250 wage fund would be = 25 working days (i.e. the new fund can employ labour time only in the new relation, i.e. at $\frac{1}{4}$; in order to employ the entire labour time as before, it would have to *quadruple*). The liberated capital of 200 would employ a wage fund of 50 = 5 working days ($\frac{1}{4}$ of the liberated labour time). (The part of the labour fund disconnected from capital is itself employed as capital at only $\frac{1}{4}$ for labour fund; i.e. precisely in the relation in which that part of the new capital which is labour fund stands to the total sum of the capital.) Thus in order to employ 20 working days (4 × 5 working days), this fund would have to grow from 50 to 4 × 50 = 200; i.e. the liberated part would have to grow from 200 to 600, i.e. triple; so that the entire new capital would amount to 800. Then the total capital, 1,600; of this, 1,200 constant part and 400 labour fund. Thus if a capital of 1,000 originally contained a labour fund of 400 (40 working days), and if, owing to a doubling of productive force, it now needs to employ a labour fund of only 200 in order to buy *necessary* labour, i.e. only $\frac{1}{2}$ of the previous labour; then the capital would have to grow by 600 in order to employ all the previous labour in its entirety (in order to gain the same amount of surplus time). It would have to be able to employ twice the labour fund, i.e. 2 × 200 = 400; but, since the relation of the labour fund to the total capital is now = $\frac{1}{4}$, this requires a total capital of 4 × 400 = 1,600.*

*The total capital which would be necessary in order to employ the old labour time is therefore = *to the old labour fund multiplied by the denominator* of the fraction which now expresses the relation of the labour fund to the new total capital. If the doubling of productive force has reduced the latter to $\frac{1}{4}$, then multiplied by 4; if to $\frac{1}{3}$, then multiplied by 3. If the productive force has doubled, then necessary labour, and thereby the labour fund, is reduced to $\frac{1}{2}$ of its earlier value; but this makes up $\frac{1}{4}$ relative to the new total capital of 800 or $\frac{1}{5}$ relative to the old total capital of 1,000. *Or the new total capital is* = 2 ×

Or, which is the same thing, it is $= 2 \times$ *the new capital* which owing to the new productive force replaces the old in production (*800* $\times$ 2) (thus if the productive force had quadrupled, quintupled etc. $= 4 \times, 5 \times$ *the new capital* etc. If the force of production has doubled, then *necessary labour* is reduced to $\frac{1}{2}$; likewise the labour fund. Thus if it amounted, as in the above case of the old capital of 1,000, to 400, i.e. $\frac{2}{5}$ of the total capital, then, afterwards, $\frac{1}{5}$ or 200. This relation, by which it is reduced, is the liberated part of the labour fund $= \frac{1}{5}$ of the old capital $= 200$. $\frac{1}{5}$ of the old $= \frac{1}{4}$ of the new. The new capital is $=$ to the old $+ \frac{1}{3}$ of the same. These trivia more closely later etc.)

Given the same original relations between the parts of the capital and the same increase in the productive force, the largeness or smallness of the capital is completely irrelevant for the general theses. Quite another question is whether, when capital grows *larger*, the relations remain the same (but this belongs under accumulation). But, given this, we see how an increase in the force of production changes the relations between the component parts of capital. If in both cases $\frac{3}{5}$ was originally constant and $\frac{2}{5}$ labour fund, then doubling the productive force acts in the same way on a capital of 100 as on one of 1,000. (The word *labour fund* is here used only for convenience's sake; we have not yet developed capital in this *specificity* [*Bestimmtheit*]. So far two parts; the one exchanged for commodities (material and instrument), the other for labour capacity.) (The *new capital*, i.e. the part of the old capital which represents its *function*, is $=$ the old minus the liberated part of the labour fund; this liberated part, however, $=$ the fraction which used to express necessary labour (or, same thing, the labour fund) divided by the multiplier of the productive force. Thus, if the old capital $= 1,000$ and the fraction expressing necessary labour or the labour fund $= \frac{2}{5}$, and if the force of pro-

---

the old capital minus the liberated part of the *labour fund*; $(1,000 - 200) \times 2 = 800 \times 2 = 1,600$. The new total capital expresses the total sum of constant and variable capital required in order to employ half of the old labour time ($\frac{1}{3}, \frac{1}{4} \frac{1}{x}$ etc., depending on whether the force of production increased $3 \times$, $4 \times, x \times$); $2 \times$ then the capital required to employ all of it (or $3 \times, 4 \times, x \times$ etc., depending on the relation in which the productive force has grown). The original relation of the parts of capital must here always be given (*technologically*); on this depends, e.g., in what ratios the multiplication of productive force expresses itself as a division of *necessary labour*.

duction doubles, then the new capital which represents the
function of the old = 800, i.e. $\frac{2}{3}$ of the old capital = 400; this
divided by 2, the multiplier of productive force, = $\frac{2}{10}$ = $\frac{1}{5}$ = 200.
Then the new capital = 800 and the liberated part of the labour
fund = 200.)

We have seen that under these conditions a capital of 100
thalers has to grow to 160, and a capital of 1,000 to 1,600, in
order to retain the same labour time (of 4 or 40 working days)
etc.; both have to grow by 60%, i.e. $\frac{3}{5}$ of themselves (of the old
capital), in order to be able to re-employ the liberated labour
time (in the first case 20 thalers, in the second 200) of $\frac{1}{5}$ – the
liberated labour fund – as such.

Percentage of total capital can express very different relations. –
Capital (*like property*) *rests on* productivity of labour

⟨*Notabene*. We saw above that identical percentages of the total
capital can express very different relations in which capital creates
its surplus value, i.e. posits surplus labour, relative or absolute.[13]
If the relation between the invariable value-part of capital and the
variable part (that exchanged for labour) such that the latter = $\frac{1}{2}$
the total capital (i.e. capital 100 = 50 (constant) + 50 (variable),
then the part exchanged for labour would have to increase by
only 50% in order to yield 25% on the capital; i.e. 50 + 50 (+ 25)
= 125; while in the above example 75 + 25 (+ 25) = 125; i.e.
the part exchanged for living labour increases by 100% in order
to yield 25% on the capital. Here we see that, if the relations
remain the same, the same percentage on the total capital holds
no matter how big or small it may be; i.e. if the relation of the
labour fund to the total capital remains the same; thus, above, $\frac{1}{4}$.
Thus: 100 yields 125, 80 yields 100, 1,000 yields 1,250, 800 yields
1,000, 1,600 yields 2,000 etc., always = 25%. If capitals whose
component parts are in different relations, including therefore
their forces of production, nevertheless yield the same percentages
on total capital, then the real surplus value has to be very different
in the different branches.⟩

⟨Thus the example is correct, the productive force compared
under the same conditions with the same capital *before* the rise
in productive force. Let a capital of 100 employ constant value 50,
labour fund = 50. Let the fund increase by 50%, i.e. $\frac{1}{2}$; then the

13. See above, pp. 373–8.

total product = 125. Let the labour fund of 50 thalers employ 10 working days, pay 5 thalers per day. Since the new value is $\frac{1}{2}$, the surplus time has to be = 5 working days; i.e. the worker who needed to work only 10 working days in order to live for 15 has to work 15 for the capitalist in order to live for 15; and his surplus labour of 5 days constitutes capital's surplus value. Expressed in hours, if the work day = 12 hours, then surplus labour = 6 per day. Thus in 10 days or 120 hours, the worker works 60 hours = 5 days too many. But now with the doubling of productivity, relations within the 100 thalers would be 75 and 25, i.e. the same capital now needs to employ only 5 workers in order to create the same value of 125; the 5 working days then = 10; doubled; i.e. 5 working days are paid, 10 produced. The worker would need to work only 5 days in order to live 10 (before the increase in productive force he had to work 10 to live 15; thus, if he worked 5, he could live only $7\frac{1}{2}$); but he has to work 10 for the capitalist in order to live 10; the latter thus makes a profit of 5 days; 1 day per day; or, expressed in days, the worker had to work $\frac{1}{2}$ to live 1 before (i.e. 6 hours to live 12); now he needs to work only $\frac{1}{4}$ to live 1 (i.e. 3 hours). If he worked a whole day, he could live 2; if he worked 12 hours, 24; if he worked 6, 12 hours. But he now has to work 12 hours to live 12. He would need to work only $\frac{1}{2}$ in order to live 1; but he has to work $2 \times \frac{1}{2} = 1$ to live 1. In the old state of the productive force, he had to work 10 days to live 15, or 12 hours to live 18; or 1 hour to live $1\frac{1}{2}$, or 8 hours to live 12, i.e. $\frac{2}{3}$ of a day to live $\frac{3}{3}$. But he has to work $\frac{2}{3}$ to live $\frac{2}{3}$, i.e. $\frac{1}{3}$ too much. The doubling of the productive force increases the relation of surplus time from $1:1\frac{1}{2}$ (i.e. 50%) to $1:2$ (i.e. 100%). In the earlier labour time relation: he needed 8 to live 12, i.e. $\frac{2}{3}$ of the whole day was necessary labour; he now needs only $\frac{1}{2}$, i.e. 6, to live 12. That is why capital now employs 5 workers instead of 10. If the 10 (cost 50) produced 75 before, then now the 25, 50: i.e. the former only 50%, the second 100. The workers work 12 hours as before; but in the first case capital bought 10 working days, now merely 5; because the force of production doubled, the 5 produce 5 days of surplus labour; because in the first case 10 working days yielded only 5 days of surplus labour; now, with the force of production doubled, i.e. risen from 50% to 100% – 5, 5; in the first case 120 working hours (= 10 working days) produce 180; in the second, 60, 60; i.e. in the first case, the surplus time is $\frac{1}{3}$ of the whole day (50% of necessary labour) (i.e. 4 hours out of 12; necessary time 8); in the second case surplus time is $\frac{1}{2}$ the whole day (100% of necessary labour) (i.e. 6 hours out of 12; necessary time 6); hence the 10 days yielded 5 days of surplus time (surplus labour) in the first case, and in the second the 5 yield 5. Thus relative surplus time has doubled; relative to the first relation it grew by only $\frac{1}{2}$ compared to $\frac{1}{3}$; i.e. by $\frac{1}{6}$, i.e. by 16 $\frac{4}{6}$%.⟩

	constant	variable	
100	60 +	40	(original relation)
100	75 +	25	(+ 25) = 125 (25%)
160	120 +	40	(+ 40) = 200 (25%)

Since surplus labour, or surplus time, is the presupposition of capital, it therefore also rests on the fundamental presupposition that there exists a surplus above the labour time necessary for the maintenance and reproduction of the individual; that the individual e.g. needs to work only 6 hours in order to live one day, or 1 day in order to live 2 etc. With the development of the forces of production, necessary labour time decreases and surplus labour time thereby increases. Or, as well, that one individual can work for 2 etc. (*'Wealth is disposable* time and nothing more. . . . If the whole labour of a country were sufficient only to raise the support of the whole population, there would be no *surplus labour*, consequently nothing that can be allowed to accumulate as capital . . . Truly wealthy a nation, if there is *no interest* or if the working day is 6 hours rather than 12 . . . Whatever may be *due* to the capitalist, he can only receive the *surplus labour* of the labourer; for the labourer must live.' (*The Source and Remedy of the National Difficulties*.)[14]

'*Property*. Origin in the productivity of labour. If one can produce only enough for one, everyone a worker; there can be no property. When one man's labour can maintain five, there will be four idle men for one employed in production. Property grows from the improvement in the mode of production . . . The growth of the property, this greater ability to maintain idle men and improductive industry = capital . . . machinery itself can seldom be applied with success to abridge the labours of an individual: *more time would be lost in its construction than could be saved by*

14. Quotations taken from pp. 4–6 of an anonymous pamphlet published in London in 1821 and entitled *The Source and Remedy of the National Difficulties, deduced from principles of political economy in a letter to Lord John Russell.*

its application. It is only really useful when it acts on great masses, when a single machine can assist the labours of thousands. It is accordingly in the most populous countries where there are most idle men that it is always most abundant. It is not called into action by scarcity of men, but by the facility with which they are brought together . . . Not ¼ of the English population provides everything that is consumed by all. Under William the Conqueror for example the amount of those directly participating in production much greater relative to the idle men.' (Ravenstone, IX, 32.)[15]

Just as capital on one side creates surplus labour, surplus labour is at the same time equally the presupposition of the existence of capital. The whole development of wealth rests on the creation of disposable time. The relation of *necessary* labour time to the *superfluous* (such it is, initially, from the standpoint of necessary labour) changes with the different stages in the development of the productive forces. In the less productive[16] stages of exchange, people exchange nothing more than their *superfluous labour time*; this is the measure of their exchange, which therefore extends only to superfluous products. In production resting on capital, the existence of *necessary* labour time is conditional on the creation of *superfluous* labour time. In the lowest stages of production, firstly, few human needs have yet been produced, and thus few to be satisfied. Necessary labour is therefore restricted, not because labour is productive, but because it is not very necessary; and secondly, in all stages of production there is a certain common quality [*Gemeinsamkeit*] of labour, *social* character of the same, etc. The force of social production develops later etc. (Return to this.)[17]

Increase of surplus labour time. Increase of simultaneous working days (Population). (*Population can increase in proportion as* necessary labour time *becomes smaller, i.e. the time required to produce living labour capacities decreases.*) – *Surplus capital and surplus population.* – *Creation of free time for society*

Surplus time is the excess of the working day above that part of it which we call *necessary* labour time; it exists secondly as the

15. Ravenstone, *Thoughts on the Funding System and its Effects*, pp. 11, 13, 45–6.

16. The original text has 'more productive' here.

17. See below, pp. 459–515.

multiplication of *simultaneous working days*, i.e. of the *labouring population*. (It can also be created – but this is mentioned here only in passing, belongs in the chapter on wage labour – by means of forcible prolongation of the working day beyond its natural limits; by the addition of women and children to the labouring population.) The first relation, that of the surplus time and the necessary time in the day, can be and is modified by the development of the productive forces, so that necessary labour is restricted to a constantly smaller fractional part. The same thing then holds relatively for the population. A labouring population of, say, 6 million can be regarded as one working day of 6×12, i.e. 72 million hours: so that the same laws applicable here.

It is a law of capital, as we saw, to create surplus labour, disposable time; it can do this only by setting *necessary labour* in motion – i.e. entering into exchange with the worker. It is its tendency, therefore, to create as much labour as possible; just as it is equally its tendency to reduce necessary labour to a minimum. It is therefore equally a tendency of capital to increase the labouring population, as well as constantly to posit a part of it as surplus population – population which is useless until such time as capital can utilize it. (Hence the correctness of the theory of surplus population and surplus capital.) It is equally a tendency of capital to make human labour (relatively) superfluous, so as to drive it, as human labour, towards infinity. Value is nothing but objectified labour, and surplus value (realization of capital) is only the excess above that part of objectified labour which is necessary for the reproduction of labouring capacity. But labour as such is and remains the presupposition, and surplus labour exists only in relation with the necessary, hence only in so far as the latter exists. Capital must therefore constantly posit necessary labour in order to posit surplus labour; it has to multiply it (namely the *simultaneous* working days) in order to multiply the surplus; but at the same time it must suspend them as necessary, in order to posit them as surplus labour. As regards the single working day, the process is of course simple: (1) to lengthen it up to the limits of natural possibility; (2) to shorten the necessary part of it more and more (i.e. to increase the productive forces without limit). But the working day, regarded spatially – time itself regarded as space – is *many working days alongside one another*. The more working days capital can enter into exchange with at once, during which it exchanges *objectified for living labour*, the greater its realization *at once*. It can leap over the *natural* limit formed by one individual's living, working day, *at a given stage in the development of the forces of production* (and it does not in itself change anything that this stage is changing) only by positing *another* working day alongside the *first* at the same time – by the spatial addition *of more simultaneous working days*. E.g. I can drive the surplus labour of A no higher than 3 hours; but if I add the days of B, C, D etc., then it becomes 12 hours. In place of a surplus time of 3, I have created one of 12. This is why capital solicits the increase of population; and the very process by means of which necessary labour is reduced makes it possible to put new necessary labour (and hence surplus labour) to work. (I.e. the *production of workers* becomes cheaper, more workers can be produced in the same time, in proportion as *necessary labour time* becomes smaller or the time required for the *production of living labour capacity* becomes relatively smaller. These are identical statements.) (This still without regard to the fact that the increase in population increases the productive force of labour, since it makes possible a greater division and combination of labour etc. The increase of population is a *natural force* of labour, for which nothing is paid. From this standpoint, we use the term *natural force* to refer to the *social force*. All *natural forces of social labour* are themselves historical products.) It is, on the other side, a tendency of capital – just as in the case of the single working day – to reduce the many simultaneous necessary working days (which, as regards their value, can be taken as *one* working day) to the minimum, i.e. to posit as many as possible of them as *not necessary*. Just as in the previous case of the single working day it was a tendency of capital to reduce the necessary working hours, so now the necessary working days are reduced in relation to the total amount of objectified labour time. (If 6 are necessary to produce 12 superfluous working hours, then capital works towards the reduction of these 6 to 4. Or 6 working days can be regarded as one working day of 72 hours; if necessary labour time is reduced by 24 hours, then two days of necessary labour fall away – i.e. 2 workers.) At the same time, the newly created surplus capital can be realized as such only by being again exchanged for living labour. Hence the tendency of capital simultaneously to increase the *labouring population* as well as to reduce constantly its *necessary* part (constantly to posit a part of it as reserve). And the increase of population itself the chief means for reducing the necessary part. *At bottom this is only an application of the relation of the single working day.* Here already lie, then, all the contradictions which modern population theory expresses as such, but does not grasp. Capital, as the positing of surplus labour, is equally and in the same moment the positing and the not-positing of necessary labour; it exists only in so far as necessary labour both exists and does not exist.*

If the relation of the necessary working days to the total number of objectified working days was = 9:12 (hence surplus labour = $\frac{1}{4}$), then the striving of capital is to reduce it to 6:9 (i.e. $\frac{2}{3}$, hence surplus labour = $\frac{1}{3}$). (Develop this more closely later; still, the major basic traits here, where we are dealing with the general concept of capital.)

Transition from the process of the production of capital into the process of circulation. – Devaluation of capital itself owing to increase of productive forces. (Competition.) (Capital *as unity and contradiction of production process and realization process.) Capital as barrier to production. – Overproduction. (Demand by the workers themselves.) –*
Barriers to capitalist production

We have now seen how, in the *realization process*, capital has (1) maintained its value by means of exchange itself (exchange,

---

*It does not belong here, but can already be recalled here, that the creation of surplus labour on the one side corresponds to the creation of minus-labour, relative idleness (or *not-productive* labour at best), on the other. This goes without saying as regards capital itself; but holds then also for the classes with which it shares; hence of the paupers, flunkeys, lickspittles etc. living from the surplus product, in short, the whole train of retainers; the part of the *servant* [*dienenden*] class which lives not from capital but from revenue. Essential difference between this *servant* class and the *working* class. In relation to the whole of society, the creation of *disposable time* is then also creation of time for the production of science, art etc. The course of social development is by no means that because one individual has satisfied his need he then proceeds to create a superfluity for himself; but rather because one individual or class of individuals is forced to work more than required for the satisfaction of its need – because *surplus labour* is on one side, therefore not-labour and surplus wealth are posited on the other. In reality the development of wealth exists only in these opposites [*Gegensätze*]: in potentiality, its development is the possibility of the suspension of these opposites.[18] Or

---

18. Cf. Hegel, *Science of Logic*, pp. 546–7.

that is, with living labour); (2) increased, created a surplus value. There now appears, as the result of this unity of the process of production and the process of realization, the product of the process, i.e. capital itself, emerging as product from the process whose presupposition it was – as a product which is a value, or, *value* itself appears as the product of the process, and specifically a *higher value*, because it contains more objectified labour than the value which formed the point of departure. This value as such is *money*. However, this is the case only *in itself*; it is not posited as such; that which is *posited* at the outset, which is on hand, is a commodity with a certain (ideal) price, i.e. which exists only ideally [*ideell*] as a certain sum of money, and which first has to *realize* itself [*sich realisieren*] as such in the exchange process, hence has to re-enter the process of simple circulation in order to be posited as *money*. We now come therefore to the *third side of the process* in which capital is posited as such.

(3) Looked at precisely, that is, the *realization process* of capital – and money becomes capital only through the realization process – appears at the same time as its *devaluation process* [*Entwertungsprozess*], its demonetization. And this in two respects. First, to the extent that capital does not increase absolute labour time but rather decreases the relative, necessary labour time, by increasing the force of production, to that extent does it reduce the costs of its own production – in so far as it was presupposed as a certain sum of commodities, reduces its exchange value: one part of the capital on hand is constantly devalued owing to a decrease in the costs of production at which it can be *reproduced*; not because of a decrease in the amount of labour objectified in it, but because of a decrease in the amount of living labour which it is henceforth necessary to objectify in this specific product. This constant devaluation of the *existing* capital does not belong here, since it already presupposes capital as completed. It is merely to be noted here in order to indicate how later developments are already contained in the general concept of capital. Belongs in the

---

because an individual can satisfy *his own* need only by simultaneously satisfying the need of and providing a surplus above that for *another* individual. This brutal under slavery. Only under the conditions of wage labour does it lead to *industry, industrial* labour. – Malthus therefore quite consistent when, along with surplus labour and surplus capital, he raises the demand for surplus idlers, consuming without producing, or the necessity of waste, luxury, lavish spending etc.

doctrine of the concentration and competition of capitals. – The *devaluation* being dealt with here is this, that capital has made the transition from the form of money into the form of a *commodity*, of a product, which has a certain price, which is to be *realized*. In its money form it existed as *value*. It now *exists* as product, and only ideally as price; but not as *value as* such. In order to *realize* itself, i.e. to maintain and to multiply itself as value, it would first have to make the transition from the form of money into that of use values (raw material – instrument – wages); but it would thereby lose the *form* of value; and it now has to enter anew into circulation in order to posit this form of general wealth anew. The capitalist now enters the process of circulation not simply as one engaged in exchange, but as *producer*, and the others engaged in exchange are, relative to him, *consumers*. They must exchange money in order to obtain his commodity for their consumption, while he exchanges his product to obtain their money. Suppose that this process breaks down – and the separation by itself implies the possibility of such a miscarriage in the individual case – then the capitalist's money has been transformed into a worthless product, and has not only not gained a new value, but also lost its original value. But whether this is so or not, in any case devaluation forms one moment of the realization process; which is already simply implied in the fact that the product of the process in its immediate form is not *value*, but first has to enter anew into circulation in order to be realized as such. Therefore, while capital is reproduced as value and new value in the production process, it is at the same time posited as *not-value*, as something which first has to be *realized as value by means of exchange*. The three processes of which capital forms the unity are external; they are separate in time and space. As such, the transition from one into the other, i.e. their unity as regards the individual capitalists, is accidental. Despite their *inner unity*, they exist *independently* alongside one another, each as the presupposition of the other. Regarded broadly and as a whole, this inner unity must necessarily maintain itself to the extent that the whole of production rests on capital, and it must therefore realize all the necessary moments of its self-formation, and must contain the determinants necessary to make these moments real. But at the point we have reached so far, capital still does not appear as the determinant of circulation (exchange) itself but merely as one moment of the latter, and it appears to stop being capital just at the point where it enters into circulation. As a *commodity*, capital now shares the fate of commodities in general; it is a matter of accident whether or not it is exchanged for money, whether its *price* is realized or not.

In the production process itself – where capital continued to be presupposed as value – its *realization* appeared totally dependent solely on the relation of itself as objectified labour to living labour; i.e. on the relation of capital to wage labour. But now, as a product, as a commodity, it appears dependent on circulation, which lies outside this process. (In fact, as we have seen, it returns into it as its ground, but also and equally emerges from it again.)[19] As a commodity, it must be (1) a use value and, as such, an object of need, object of consumption; (2) it must be exchanged for its equivalent – in money. The new value can be realized only through a sale.

If it contained objectified labour at a price of 100 thalers before, and now at a price of 110 (the price here merely an expression, in money, of the amount of objectified labour), then this has to be demonstrated through the exchange of the labour objectified in the newly produced commodity for 110 thalers. The product is devalued [*entwertet*] initially in so far as it must be exchanged for money at all, in order to obtain its form as value again. Inside the production process, realization appeared totally identical with the production of surplus labour (the objectification of surplus time), and hence appeared to have no *bounds* other than those partly presupposed and partly posited within this process itself, but which are always posited within it as *barriers* to be forcibly overcome. There now appear barriers to it which lie *outside* it. To begin with, even on an entirely superficial inspection, the commodity is an exchange value only in so far as it is at the same time a *use value*, i.e. an object of consumption (still entirely irrelevant here, what kind of consumption); it ceases to be an exchange value when it ceases to be a use value (since it does not yet exist as money again, but rather still in a specific mode of existence coinciding with its natural quality). Its first barrier, then, is *consumption itself* – the *need for it*. (Given the present presuppositions, there is no basis whatever for speaking of ineffective, *non-paying needs*; i.e. a need which does not itself possess a commodity or money to give in exchange.) Then, secondly, there has to be an equivalent for it, and, since circulation was pre-

19. See p. 255, n. 28.

supposed at the outset as ·a constant magnitude – as having a given volume – but since, on the other hand, capital has created a new value in the production process, it seems indeed as if no equivalent were available for it. Thus, by emerging from the production process and re-entering circulation, capital (a) as *production*, appears to encounter a barrier in the available magnitude of *consumption* – of *consumption capacity*. As a specific use value, its quantity is irrelevant up to a certain point; then, however, at a certain level – since it satisfies only a specific need – it ceases to be required for consumption. As a *specific, one-sided, qualitative* use value, e.g. grain, its quantity itself is irrelevant only up to a certain level; it is required only in a specific quantity; i.e. in a certain *measure*. This measure, however, is given partly in its quality as use value – its *specific* usefulness, applicability – partly in the number of individuals engaged in exchange who have a need for this specific consumption. The number of consumers multiplied by the magnitude of their need for this *specific* product. Use value in itself does not have the boundlessness of value as such. Given objects can be consumed as objects of needs only up to a certain level. For example: No more than a certain amount of grain is consumed etc. Hence, as *use value*, the product contains a barrier – precisely the barrier consisting of the need for it – which, however, is measured not by the need of the producers but by the total need of all those engaged in exchange. Where the need for a certain use value ceases, it ceases to be a use value. It is measured as a use value by the need for it. But as soon as it ceases to be a use value, it ceases to be an object of circulation (in so far as it is not money). (b) As *new value* and as *value* as such, however, it seems to encounter a barrier in the magnitude of *available equivalents*, primarily money, not as medium of circulation but as money. The surplus value (distinct, obviously, from the original value) requires a surplus equivalent. This now appears as a second barrier.

(c) Money – i.e. wealth as such, i.e. wealth existing in and because of the exchange for *alien objectified labour* – originally appeared to collapse into itself [*in sich zusammenzufallen*] to the extent that it did not proceed to the exchange for *alien living labour*, i.e. to the production process. Circulation was incapable of renewing itself from within itself. At the same time, the production process now appears to be in a fix, in as much as it is not able to make the transition into the process of circulation. Capital, as production resting on wage labour, presupposes circulation as the necessary condition and moment of the entire motion. This specific form of production presupposes this specific form of exchange which finds its expression in the circulation of money. In order to renew itself, the entire product has to be transformed into money; not as in earlier stages of production, where exchange is by no means concerned with production in its totality, but only with superfluous production and superfluous products.

These are, then, the contradictions which present themselves of their own accord to a simple, objective, non-partisan view. How they are constantly suspended in the system of production resting on capital, but also constantly created again – and are suspended only by force (although this suspension appears up to a certain point merely as a quiet equilibration) – this is another question. The important thing at present is to take note of the existence of these contradictions. All the contradictions of circulation come to life again in a new form. The product as use value is in contradiction with itself as value; i.e. in as much as it exists in a specific quality, as a specific thing, as a product of specific natural properties, as a substance of need in contradiction with its substance as value, which it possesses exclusively on account of its being *objectified labour*. But this time, this contradiction is posited not merely as it was in circulation, as a *merely formal difference*; rather the quality of being measured by use value is here firmly determined as the quality of being measured by the total requirement for this product by all those engaged in exchange – i.e. by the amount of total consumption. The latter here appears as *measure* for it as use value and hence also as *exchange value*. In simple circulation it had simply to be transposed from the form of a particular use value into the form of exchange value. Its barrier then appeared only in the fact that, [coming] from circulation, it existed in a particular form owing to its *natural composition*, rather than in the value form in which it could be exchanged for all other commodities directly. What is posited now is that the *measure* of its availability is given in its *natural composition* itself. In order to be transposed into the general form, the use value has to be present in a limited and specific quantity; a *quantity* whose *measure* does not lie in the amount of *labour objectified in it*, but arises from its *nature as use value*, in particular, *use value for others*. At the same time, the previous contradiction, that money for-itself [*das für sich seiende Geld*] had to proceed to exchange itself for living labour, now appears even greater, in as much as the surplus money, in order to exist as such, or the surplus value, has to exchange itself for surplus value. Hence, as value, it encounters its barrier in alien production, just as, as use value, its barrier is alien consumption; in the latter, its measure is the amount of need for the specific product, in the former, the amount of *objectified labour* existing in circulation. The indifference of value as such towards use value is thereby brought into just as false a position [*Position*] as are, on the other side, the substance of value and its measure as objectified labour in general.*

The main point here – where we are concerned with the general concept of capital – is that it is this *unity of production and realization*, not *immediately* but only as a *process*, which is linked to certain conditions, and, as it appeared, *external* conditions.†

The creation by capital of *absolute surplus value* – more objectified labour – is conditional upon an expansion, specifically a constant expansion, of the sphere of circulation. The *surplus value* created at one point requires the creation of surplus value at *another* point, for which it may be exchanged; if only, initially, the production of more gold and silver, more money, so that, if surplus value cannot directly become capital again, it may exist in the form of money as the possibility of new capital. A precondition of production based on capital is therefore *the production of a constantly widening sphere of circulation*, whether the sphere itself is directly expanded or whether *more points within it are created as points of production*. While circulation appeared at first as a constant magnitude, it here appears as a moving magnitude, being expanded by production itself. Accordingly, it already appears as a moment of production itself. Hence, just as capital has the

---

*The transition to the relation of supply, demand, prices cannot be made yet, as their development proper presupposes capital. Should not demand and supply, in so far as they are abstract categories and do not yet express any particular economic relations, perhaps be examined already together with simple circulation or production?

† We saw earlier that the capital realization process presupposes the prior development of the *simple production process*.[20] This will be the case with *demand and supply* as well, to the extent that simple exchange presupposes a need for the product. The (direct) producer's *own* need as the need for others' demand. In the course of this development itself it will be seen what has to be presupposed to it, and all this is then to be thrown into the first chapters.

---

20. See above, p. 401.

tendency on one side to create ever more surplus labour, so it has the complementary tendency to create more points of exchange; i.e., here, seen from the standpoint of *absolute* surplus value or surplus labour, to summon up more surplus labour as complement to itself; i.e. at bottom, to propagate production based on capital, or the mode of production corresponding to it. The tendency to create the *world market* is directly given in the concept of capital itself. Every limit appears as a barrier to be overcome. Initially, to subjugate every moment of production itself to exchange and to suspend the production of direct use values not entering into exchange, i.e. precisely to posit production based on capital in place of earlier modes of production, which appear primitive [*naturwüchsig*] from its standpoint. *Commerce* no longer appears here as a function taking place between independent productions for the exchange of their excess, but rather as an essentially all-embracing presupposition and moment of production itself.*

On the other side, the production of *relative surplus value*, i.e. production of surplus value based on the increase and development of the productive forces, requires the production of new consumption; requires that the consuming circle within circulation expands as did the productive circle previously. Firstly quantitative expansion of existing consumption; secondly: creation of new needs by propagating existing ones in a wide circle; *thirdly*: production of *new* needs and discovery and creation of new use values. In other words, so that the surplus labour gained does not remain a merely quantitative surplus, but rather constantly increases the circle of qualitative differences within labour (hence of surplus labour), makes it more diverse, more internally differentiated. For example, if, through a doubling of productive force, a capital of 50 can now do what a capital of 100 did before, so that a capital of 50 and the necessary labour corresponding to it become free, then, for the capital and labour which have been

---

*Of course, all production aimed at direct use value decreases the number of those engaged in exchange, as well as the sum of exchange values thrown into circulation, and above all the production of surplus values. Hence the tendency of capital (1) continually to enlarge the periphery of circulation; (2) to transform it at all points into production spurred on by capital.[21]

---

21. Marx wrote this sentence in English. The word 'spurred' is a suggested emendation in place of the word 'occurred' which appears in the original text.

set free, a new, qualitatively different branch of production must be created, which satisfies and brings forth a new need. The value of the old industry is preserved by the creation of the fund for a new one in which the relation of capital and labour posits itself in a *new* form. Hence exploration of all of nature in order to discover new, useful qualities in things; universal exchange of the products of all alien climates and lands; new (artificial) preparation of natural objects, by which they are given new use values.* The exploration of the earth in all directions, to discover new things of use as well as new useful qualities of the old; such as new qualities of them as raw materials etc.; the development, hence, of the natural sciences to their highest point; likewise the discovery, creation and satisfaction of new needs arising from society itself; the cultivation of all the qualities of the social human being, production of the same in a form as rich as possible in needs, because rich in qualities and relations – production of this being as the most total and universal possible social product, for, in order to take gratification in a many-sided way, he must be capable of many pleasures [*genussfähig*], hence cultured to a high degree – is likewise a condition of production founded on capital. This creation of new branches of production, i.e. of qualitatively new surplus time, is not merely the division of labour, but is rather the creation, separate from a given production, of labour with a new use value; the development of a constantly expanding and more comprehensive system of different kinds of labour, different kinds of production, to which a constantly expanding and constantly enriched system of needs corresponds.

Thus, just as production founded on capital creates universal industriousness on one side – i.e. surplus labour, value-creating labour – so does it create on the other side a system of general exploitation of the natural and human qualities, a system of general utility, utilising science itself just as much as all the physical and mental qualities, while there appears nothing *higher in itself*, nothing legitimate for itself, outside this circle of social production and exchange. Thus capital creates the bourgeois society, and the universal appropriation of nature as well as of the social bond itself by the members of society. Hence the great civilizing influence of capital; its production of a stage of society in comparison to which all earlier ones appear as mere *local*

---

*The role played by *luxury* in antiquity in contrast to its role among the moderns, to be alluded to later.

developments of humanity and as *nature-idolatry*. For the first time, nature becomes purely an object for humankind, purely a matter of utility; ceases to be recognized as a power for itself; and the theoretical discovery of its autonomous laws appears merely as a ruse so as to subjugate it under human needs, whether as an object of consumption or as a means of production. In accord with this tendency, capital drives beyond national barriers and prejudices as much as beyond nature worship, as well as all traditional, confined, complacent, encrusted satisfactions of present needs, and reproductions of old ways of life. It is destructive towards all of this, and constantly revolutionizes it, tearing down all the barriers which hem in the development of the forces of production, the expansion of needs, the all-sided development of production, and the exploitation and exchange of natural and mental forces.

But from the fact that capital posits every such limit as a barrier and hence gets *ideally* beyond it, it does not by any means follow that it has *really* overcome it, and, since every such barrier contradicts its character, its production moves in contradictions which are constantly overcome but just as constantly posited. Furthermore. The universality towards which it irresistibly strives encounters barriers in its own nature, which will, at a certain stage of its development, allow it to be recognized as being itself the greatest barrier to this tendency, and hence will drive towards its own suspension.

Those economists who, like Ricardo, conceived production as directly identical with the self-realization of capital – and hence were heedless of the barriers to consumption or of the existing barriers of circulation itself, to the extent that it must represent counter-values at all points, having in view only the development of the forces of production and the growth of the industrial population – supply without regard to demand – have therefore grasped the positive essence of capital more correctly and deeply than those who, like Sismondi, emphasized the barriers of consumption and of the available circle of counter-values, although the latter has better grasped the limited nature of production based on capital, its negative one-sidedness. The former more its universal tendency, the latter its particular restrictedness. The whole dispute as to whether *overproduction* is possible and necessary in capitalist production revolves around the point whether the process of the realization of capital within production directly posits its realization in circulation; whether its realization posited in the *production process* is its *real* realization. Ricardo himself, of course, has a suspicion that the *exchange value* of a commodity is not a value apart from exchange, and that it proves itself as a value only in exchange; but he regards the barriers which production thereby encounters as accidental, as barriers which are overcome. He therefore conceives the overcoming of such barriers as being in the essence of capital, although he often becomes absurd in the exposition of that view; while Sismondi, by contrast, emphasizes not only the encounter with the barriers, but their creation by capital itself, and has a vague intuition that they must lead to its breakdown. He therefore wants to put up barriers to production, from the outside, through custom, law etc., which of course, as merely external and artificial barriers, would necessarily be demolished by capital. On the other side, Ricardo and his entire school never understood the really *modern crises*, in which this contradiction of capital discharges itself in great thunderstorms which increasingly threaten it as the foundation of society and of production itself.

The attempts made from the orthodox economic standpoint to deny that there is *general overproduction* at any given moment are indeed childish. Either, in order to rescue production *based on capital* (see e.g. MacCulloch),[22] all its specific qualities are ignored and their specific character as forms omitted, and capital is conceived as its inverse, as simple production for *immediate use value*. Totally abstracts away the essential relations. In fact, in order to cleanse it of contradictions, it is virtually dropped and negated.[23] – Or, like e.g. Mill, more perceptively (copied from the dull Say): *supply* and *demand* are allegedly identical, and should therefore necessarily correspond.[24] Supply, namely, is allegedly a demand measured by its own amount. Here a great confusion: (1) This identity of supply, so that it is a demand measured by its own amount, is true only to the extent that it is *exchange value* = to a certain amount of objectified labour. To that extent it is the

22. J. R. MacCulloch (1789–1864), statistician and economist, editor of the *Scotsman* from 1818 to 1828, Professor of Political Economy in London from 1828 to 1832, 'past master in pretentious cretinism', 'at once the vulgarizer of Ricardian economics and the most pitiful image of its dissolution' (Marx).

23. MacCulloch, *The Principles of Political Economy*, Edinburgh, 1825, pp. 166–90.

24. James Mill, *Éléments d'économie politique*, Paris, 1823, pp. 250–60.

measure of its own demand – as far as *value* is concerned. But, as such a value, it first has to be realized through the exchange for *money*, and as object of exchange for money it depends (2) on its *use value*, but as use value it depends on the mass of needs present for it, the demand for it. But as use value it is absolutely not measured by the labour time objectified in it, but rather a measuring rod is applied to it which lies outside its nature as exchange value. Or, it is further said: *Supply itself is demand for a certain product* of a *certain value* (which expresses itself in the demanded amount of the product). Then, if the supplied product is unsaleable, it proves that too much has been produced of the supplied commodity and too little of what the supplier demands. Thus allegedly there is no general overproduction, but merely overproduction of one or a few articles, as against underproduction of others. This again forgets that what the producing capital demands is not a specific use value, but *value* for itself, i.e. money – money not in the role of medium of circulation, but as a general form of wealth, or a form of the realization of capital in one regard, a return to its original dormant state in the other. But the assertion that too little *money* is produced means indeed nothing else than what is being asserted, that production is not identical with realization, i.e. that it is *overproduction*, or, what is the same, that it is production which cannot be transformed into money, into *value*; production which does not pass the test of circulation. Hence the illusion of the money-artists (including Proudhon etc.), that it is a case of lack of *means of circulation* – on account of the high cost of money – and that more money has to be created artificially.[25] (See also the Birminghamites, e.g. the *Gemini*.)[26] Or it is said that *production and consumption* are the same *from the social standpoint*, that hence an excess or disproportion between the two can never take place. Social standpoint here means the abstraction which ignores precisely the specific social structure and relations and hence also the contradictions which emerge from it. Storch, for example, remarked quite correctly against Say that a great part of consumption is not consumption for immediate use, but consumption in the production process,

25. See p. 319, n. 33.

26. A reference to the pamphlet *The Currency Question. The Gemini Letters*, London, 1844, written by two upholders of the currency doctrines of the Birmingham banker Thomas Attwood, T. B. Wright and J. Harlow. See below, pp. 804–5.

e.g. consumption of machines, coal, oil, required buildings etc.[27] This consumption is in no way identical with that at issue here. Malthus and Sismondi have likewise correctly remarked that e.g. the workers' consumption is in no way in itself a *sufficient* consumption for the capitalist.[28] The moment of realization is here simply thrown out entirely, and production and consumption are simply equated, i.e. not production based on capital but production based directly on *use value* is presupposed. Or, expressed *socialistically*[29]: labour and the exchange of labour, i.e. production and its exchange (circulation), are allegedly the entire process; how then could a disproportion arise except by oversight, miscalculation? Labour is here regarded not as wage labour, nor capital as capital. On one side, the consequences of production based on capital are accepted, on the other side the presuppositions and conditions of these consequences are denied – necessary labour as posited by and for surplus labour. Or – e.g. Ricardo – since production is itself regulated by the costs of production, it allegedly regulates itself, and if one branch of production does not realize itself then capital withdraws from it to a certain degree and throws itself on another point where it is needed.[30] But apart from the fact that this necessity of evening-up already *presupposes* the unevenness, the disharmony and hence the contradiction – in a general crisis of overproduction the contradiction is not between the different kinds of productive capital, but between industrial and loanable capital – between capital as directly involved in the production process and capital as money existing (relatively) outside of it. Finally: *proportionate production* (this is already in Ricardo also, etc.) only when it is capital's tendency to distribute itself in correct proportions, but equally its necessary tendency – since it strives limitlessly for surplus labour, surplus productivity, surplus consumption etc. – to drive beyond the proportion. (In *competition* this inner tendency of capital appears as a compulsion exercised over it by *alien capital*, which drives it forward beyond the correct proportion with a constant *march, march!* Free competition, as Mr Wakefield

27. See p. 94, n. 17.
28. Malthus, *Principles*, p. 405; *Definitions*, pp. 258–9. Sismondi, *Études*, Vol. I, p. 61 n.
29. '*Socialistically*': in the manner of the early utopian socialists, in particular John Gray; see above, pp. 153–6.
30. Ricardo, *On the Principles of Political Economy*, pp. 80–85.

correctly sniffs out in his commentary on Smith, has *never yet* been developed by the economists, no matter how much they prattle about it, and [no matter] how much it is the basis of the entirety of bourgeois production, production resting on capital.[31] It has been understood only negatively: i.e. as negation of monopolies, the guild system, legal regulations etc. As negation of feudal production. But it also has to be something *for itself*, after all, since a mere 0 is an empty negation, abstraction, from a barrier which immediately arises again e.g. in the form of monopoly, natural monopolies etc. Conceptually, *competition* is nothing other than the inner *nature of capital*, its essential character, appearing in and realized as the reciprocal interaction of many capitals with one another, the inner tendency as external necessity.) (Capital exists and can only exist as many capitals, and its self-determination therefore appears as their reciprocal interaction with one another.) Capital is just as much the constant positing as the suspension of *proportionate production*. The existing proportion always has to be suspended by the creation of surplus values and the increase of productive forces. But this demand, that production should be expanded *simultaneously* and *at once in the same proportion*, makes external demands upon capital which in no way arise out of it itself; at the same time, the departure from the given proportion in one branch of production drives all of them out of it, and in unequal proportions. So far (for we have not yet reached the aspect of capital in which it is *circulating capital*, and still have circulation on one side and capital on the other, or production as its presupposition, or ground from which it arises), even from the standpoint of production alone, circulation contains the relation to consumption and production – in other words, surplus labour as counter value [*Gegenwert*], and differentiation of labour in an ever richer form.

The simple concept of capital has to contain its civilizing tendencies etc. *in themselves*; they must not, as in the economics books until now, appear merely as external consequences. Likewise the contradictions which are later released, demonstrated as already latent within it.

So far in the realization process, we have only the indifference of the individual moments towards one another; that they determine each other internally and search for each other extern-

31. Adam Smith, *Wealth of Nations*, pp. 244–6.

ally; but that they may or may not find each other, balance each other, correspond to each other. The inner necessity of moments which belong together, and their indifferent, independent existence towards one another, are already a foundation of contradictions.

Still, we are by no means finished. The contradiction between production and realization – of which capital, by its concept, is the unity – has to be grasped more intrinsically than merely as the indifferent, seemingly reciprocally independent appearance of the individual moments of the process, or rather of the totality of processes.

To approach the matter more closely: *First of all, there is a limit, not inherent to production generally, but to production founded on capital*. This limit is double, or rather the same regarded from two directions. It is enough here to demonstrate that capital contains a *particular* restriction of production – which contradicts its general tendency to drive beyond every barrier to production – in order to have uncovered the foundation of *overproduction*, the fundamental contradiction of developed capital; in order to have uncovered, more generally, the fact that capital is not, as the economists believe, the *absolute* form for the development of the forces of production – not the absolute form for that, nor the form of wealth which absolutely coincides with the development of the forces of production. The stages of production which precede capital appear, regarded from its standpoint, as so many fetters upon the productive forces. It itself, however, correctly understood, appears as the condition of the development of the forces of production as long as they require an external spur, which appears at the same time as their bridle. It is a discipline over them, which becomes superfluous and burdensome at a certain level of their development, just like the guilds etc. These inherent limits have to coincide with the nature of capital, with the essential character of its very concept. These necessary limits are:

(1) *Necessary labour* as limit on the exchange value of living labour capacity or of the wages of the industrial population;

(2) *Surplus value* as limit on surplus labour time; and, in regard to relative surplus labour time, as barrier to the development of the forces of production;

(3) What is the same, the *transformation into money*, exchange value as such, as limit of production; or exchange founded on

value, or value founded on exchange, as limit of production. This is:

(4) again the same as *restriction of the production of use values by exchange value*; or that real wealth has to take on a *specific* form distinct from itself, a form not absolutely identical with it, in order to become an object of production at all.

However, these limits come up against the *general tendency of capital* (which showed itself in simple circulation, where money as medium of circulation appeared as merely vanishing, without independent necessity, and hence not as limit and barrier) to forget and abstract from:

(1) necessary labour as limit of the exchange value of living labour capacity; (2) surplus value as the limit of surplus labour and development of the forces of production; (3) money as the limit of production; (4) the restriction of the production of use values by exchange value.

Hence overproduction: i.e. the sudden *recall* of all these necessary moments of production founded on capital; hence general devaluation in consequence of forgetting them. Capital, at the same time, [is] thereby faced with the task of launching its attempt anew from a higher level of the development of productive forces, with each time greater collapse *as capital*. Clear, therefore, that the higher the development of capital, the more it appears as barrier to production – hence also to consumption – besides the other contradictions which make it appear as burdensome barrier to production and intercourse.

⟨The entire *credit system*, and the over-trading, over-speculation etc. connected with it, rests on the necessity of expanding and leaping over the barrier to circulation and the sphere of exchange. This appears more colossally, classically, in the relations between peoples than in the relations between individuals. Thus e.g. the English forced to *lend* to foreign nations, in order to have them as customers. At bottom, the English capitalist exchanges doubly with *productive* English capital, (1) as himself, (2) as Yankee etc. or in whatever other form he has placed his money.⟩

⟨Capital as *barrier to production* is pointed out: e.g. Hodgskin[32]: 'In the present state, every accumulation of capital adds to the

---

32. Thomas Hodgskin (1787–1869) was a socialist journalist and agitator active in the 1820s. In his economic works he developed the socialist implications in Ricardo's theory of value, in particular in *Labour Defended against the Claims of Capital* (1825) and *Popular Political Economy* (1827).

amount of profit demanded from the labourer, and extinguishes all that labour which would only procure the labourer his comfortable existence ... *Profit* the limitation of production.' (H[odgskin, Notebook,] p. 46.)[33] Through foreign trade, the barrier of the sphere of exchange [is] expanded, and [it is] made possible for the capitalist to consume more surplus labour: 'In a series of years the world can take no more from us than we can take from the world. Even the profits made by our merchants in their foreign trade are paid by the consumer of the return goods here. Foreign trade mere barter, and as such exchange for the convenience and enjoyment of the capitalist. But he can consume commodities to a certain degree only. He exchanges cottons etc. for the wines and silks of foreign countries. But these *represent only the surplus labour of our own population* as much as the clothes and cottons, and in this way the *destructive power of the capitalist is increased beyond all bounds*. Thus nature is *outwitted.*' (*Source and Remedy* etc., pp. 27, 28.)[34] How the *glut* is connected with the *barrier* of necessary labour: 'The very meaning of an increased demand by the labourers is, a disposition to take less themselves, and leave a larger share for their employers; and if it be said that this, *by diminishing consumption, increases glut*, I can only say that *glut then is synonymous with high profits.*' (*Enquiry*, London, 1821, p. 12.)[35] Herein the one side of the contradiction completely expressed. 'The practice of stopping labour at that point where it can produce, in addition to the subsistence of the labourer, a profit for the capitalist, opposed to the natural law which regulates production.' (H[odgskin, Notebook,] 41, IX.)[36] 'The more the capital accumulates, the more the *whole amount of profit demanded does so*; so there arises an *artificial check* to production and population.' (H[odgskin, Notebook,] 46.)[37] The contradictions between capital as instrument of production in general and as instrument of production of value, developed as follows by Malthus (X, 40 seq.): 'Profits are invariably measured by *value* and never by *quantity* ... The *wealth* of a

33. Hodgskin, *Popular Political Economy*, pp. 245–6.

34. *The Source and Remedy of the National Difficulties*, London, 1821, pp. 17–18.

35. *An Inquiry into those Principles Respecting the Nature of Demand and the Necessity of Consumption Lately Advocated by Mr Malthus*, anonymous pamphlet, London, 1821, p. 59.

36. Hodgskin, *Popular Political Economy*, p. 238.

37. ibid., p. 246.

country depends partly upon the *quantity of produce* obtained by its labour, and partly upon *such an adaptation of this quantity to the wants and powers of the existing population* as is calculated to give it value. Nothing can be more certain than that it is not determined by either of them alone. But where wealth and value are perhaps the most nearly connected, is in *the necessity of the latter to the production of the former*. The value set upon commodities, that is the sacrifice of labour which people are willing to make in order to sustain them, in the actual state of things may be said to be *almost the sole cause* of the existence of wealth ... The consumptive demand occasioned only by the workmen employed in productive labour can never *alone* furnish a motive to the accumulation and employment of capital ... *the powers of production alone do not secure the creation of a proportionate degree of wealth*, as little as the *increase of population*. What it requires in addition is *such a distribution of produce*, and such an adaptation of this produce to the wants of those who are to consume it, as constantly to increase *the exchangeable value of the whole mass*, i.e. the powers of production are only called fully into motion by the unchecked demand for all that is produced ...[38] This is however brought about on the one hand by constantly new branches of industry (and *reciprocal* expansion of the old), by means of which the old obtain new *markets* etc. Production indeed itself creates demand, in that it employs more workers in the same branch of business, and creates new branches of business, where new capitalists again employ new workers and at the same time alternately become market for the old; but the demand created by the productive labourer himself can never be an *adequate* demand, because it does not go to the full extent of what he produces. If it did, there would be no profit, consequently no motive to employ him. The very existence of a profit upon any commodity presupposes *a demand exterior to that of the labourer who has produced it*.' 'Both labourers and capital may be redundant compared with the means of employing them profitably.'⟩[39]

⟨To be noted for (3), to which we shall soon proceed, that the provisional accumulation, as which capital appears *vis-à-vis* labour, and by means of which it is the command over labour, is

38. Malthus, *Principles of Political Economy*, pp. 266, 301, 302, 315, 372–82, in part paraphrased by Marx.
39. ibid., p. 405, note by the editor, William Otter.

at first nothing else but *surplus labour* itself in the form of *surplus produce*, at the same time *claim on alien co-existing labour.*⟩

The point here, of course, is not yet to develop overproduction specifically, but only the predisposition to it, such as it is posited in primitive form in the capital relation itself. We must also, therefore, omit here any regard for the other possessing and consuming etc. classes, which do not produce but live from their revenue, hence exchange with capital; form centres of exchange for it. We can consider them only partly (but better, along with *accumulation*), in so far as they are most important for the historic formation of capital.

In production based on slavery, as well as in patriarchal agricultural-industrial production, where the greatest part of the population directly satisfies the greatest part of its needs directly by its labour, the sphere of circulation and exchange is still very narrow; and more particularly in the former, the slave does not come into consideration as *engaged in exchange* at all. But in production based on capital, consumption is mediated at all points by exchange, and labour never has a *direct* use value for those who are working. Its entire basis is labour as exchange value and as the creation of exchange value.

Well. First of all

the wage worker as distinct from the slave is himself an independent centre of circulation, someone who exchanges, posits exchange value, and maintains exchange value through exchange. *Firstly*: in the exchange between that part of capital which is specified as wages, and living labour capacity, the *exchange value* of this part of capital is posited immediately, before capital again emerges from the production process to enter into circulation, or this can be conceived as itself still an act of circulation. *Secondly*: To each capitalist, the total mass of all workers, with the exception of his own workers, appear not as workers, but as consumers, possessors of exchange values (wages), money, which they exchange for his commodity. They are so many centres of circulation with whom the act of exchange begins and by whom the exchange value of capital is maintained. They form a proportionally very great part – although not quite so great as is generally imagined, if one focuses on the industrial worker proper – of all consumers. The greater their number – the number of the industrial population – and the mass of money at their disposal, the greater the sphere of exchange for capital. We have seen that it is the tendency of capital to increase the industrial population as much as possible.

Actually, the relation of one capitalist to the workers of *another* capitalist is none of our concern here. It only shows every capitalist's illusion, but alters nothing in the relation of capital in general to labour. Every capitalist knows this about his worker, that he does not relate to him as producer to consumer, and [he therefore] wishes to restrict his consumption, i.e. his ability to exchange, his wage, as much as possible. Of course he would like the workers of *other* capitalists to be the greatest consumers possible of *his own* commodity. But the relation of *every* capitalist to *his own* workers is the *relation as such* of *capital and labour*, the essential relation. But this is just how the illusion arises – true for the individual capitalist as distinct from all the others – that *apart from his* workers the whole remaining working class confronts him as *consumer* and *participant in exchange*, as money-spender, and not as worker. It is forgotten that, as Malthus says, 'the very existence of a profit upon any commodity pre-supposes a *demand exterior to that of the labourer who has produced it*',[40] and hence the *demand of the labourer himself can never be an adequate demand*. Since one production sets the other into motion and hence creates consumers for itself in the *alien* capital's workers, it *seems* to each individual capital that the demand of the working class posited by production itself is an 'adequate demand'. On one side, this demand which production itself posits drives it forward, and must drive it forward beyond the *proportion* in which it would have to produce with regard to the workers; on the other side, if the demand *exterior to the demand of the labourer himself* disappears or shrinks up, then the collapse occurs. Capital itself then regards *demand by the worker* – i.e. the payment of the wages on which this demand rests – not as a gain but as a loss. I.e. the *immanent relation between capital and labour* asserts itself. *Here again it is the competition among capitals*, their indifference to and independence of one another, which brings it about that the individual capital relates to the workers of the entire remaining capital *not as to workers*: hence is driven beyond the right proportion. What precisely distinguishes capital from the master–servant relation is that the *worker* confronts him as consumer and possessor of exchange values, and that in the form of the

40. ibid., p. 414, note by Malthus.

possessor of money, in the form of money he becomes a simple centre of circulation – one of its infinitely many centres, in which his specificity as worker is extinguished.*

To begin with: capital forces the workers beyond necessary labour to surplus labour. Only in this way does it realize itself, and create surplus value. But on the other hand, it posits necessary labour only *to the extent* and *in so far as* it is surplus labour and the latter is *realizable* as *surplus value*. It posits surplus labour, then, as the condition of the necessary, and surplus value as the limit of objectified labour, of value as such. As soon as it cannot posit value, it does not posit necessary labour; and, given its foundation, it cannot be otherwise. It therefore restricts labour and the creation of value – by an artificial check, as the English express it – and it does so on the same grounds as and to the same extent that it posits surplus labour and surplus value. By its nature, therefore, it posits a *barrier* to labour and value-creation, in contradiction to its tendency to expand them boundlessly. And in as much as it both posits a barrier *specific* to itself, and on the other side equally drives over and beyond *every* barrier, it is the living contradiction.†

While capital thus, on one side, makes surplus labour and its *exchange* for *surplus labour* into the precondition of necessary

*It is quite the same with the demand created by production itself for raw material, semi-finished goods, machinery, means of communication, and for the auxiliary materials consumed in production, such as dyes, coal, grease, soap, etc. This effective, exchange-value-positing demand is adequate and sufficient as long as the producers exchange among themselves. Its inadequacy shows itself as soon as the final product encounters its limit in direct and final consumption. This *semblance*, too, which drives beyond the correct proportion, is founded in the essence of capital, which, as will be developed more closely in connection with competition, *is* something which repels itself, *is* many capitals mutually quite indifferent to one another. In so far as one capitalist *buys* from others, buys commodities, or sells, they are within the simple exchange relation; and do not relate to one another as capital. The *correct* (imaginary) proportion in which they must exchange with one another in order to realize themselves at the end as capital lies *outside* their relation to one another.

†Since value forms the foundation of capital, and since it therefore necessarily exists only through exchange for *counter-value*, it thus necessarily repels itself from itself. A *universal capital*, one without alien capitals confronting it, with which it exchanges – and from the present standpoint, nothing confronts it but wage labourers or itself – is therefore a non-thing. The reciprocal repulsion between capitals is already contained in capital as realized exchange value.

labour and hence of the positing of *labour capacity* [*Arbeits-vermögen*] as a centre of exchange – hence already narrows and attaches conditions to the sphere of exchange from this side – it is just as essential to it, on the other side, to restrict the worker's consumption to the amount necessary to reproduce his labour capacity – to make the value which expresses *necessary labour* the barrier to the realization of labour capacity and hence of the worker's *exchange capacity*, and to strive to reduce the relation of this necessary labour to surplus labour to the minimum. [Thus we have] a new barrier to the sphere of exchange, which is, however, at the same time identical, as is the first, with the tendency of capital to relate to every limit on its self-realization as to a barrier. The boundless enlargement of its value – boundless creation of value – therefore absolutely identical here with the positing of barriers to the sphere of exchange, i.e. the possibility of reali-zation – the realization of the value posited in the production process.

The same with the *productive force*. On the one hand, the necessary tendency of capital to raise it to the utmost, in order to increase relative *surplus time*. On the other hand, thereby decreases *necessary labour time*, hence the worker's exchange capacity. Further, as we have seen, relative *surplus value* rises much more slowly than the force of production, and moreover this proportion grows ever smaller as the magnitude reached by the productive forces is greater. *But the mass of products grows in a similar proportion* – if not, then new capital would be set free – as well as labour – which did not enter into circulation. But to the same degree as the mass of products grows, so grows the difficulty of realizing the labour time contained in them – because the demands made on consumption rise. (We are still concerned here only with the way in which the capital *realization process* is its *devalu-ation process*. Out of place here would be the question how, while it has the tendency to *heighten the productive forces boundlessly*, it *also and equally* makes one-sided, limits etc. the *main force of production, the human being himself*, and has the tendency in general to restrict the forces of production.)

Capital, then, posits *necessary labour time* as the barrier to the exchange value of living labour capacity; *surplus labour time* as the barrier to necessary labour time; and *surplus value* as the barrier to surplus labour time; while at the same time it drives over and beyond all these barriers, to the extent that it posits *labour capacity* opposite itself as something simply engaged in exchange, as money, and surplus labour time as the only barrier, because creatrix of surplus value. (Or, from the first aspect, it posits the exchange of surplus values as the barrier to the exchange of the necessary values.)

In one and the same moment, it posits the *values on hand* in circulation – or, what is the same, the proportion of values posited by it to the values contained in it and *presupposed* in circulation – as the barrier, the necessary barrier to its value-creation; on the other hand, its productivity as the only barrier and creatrix of values. It therefore drives constantly on one side towards its own devaluation, on the other side towards the obstruction of the productive forces, and of labour which objectifies itself in values.

Overproduction. – Proudhon (How is it possible that in the price of the commodity which the worker buys, he pays the profit etc. and still obtains his necessary wages). – Price of the commodity and labour time. Surplus etc. (Price and value etc.) – Capitalist does not sell too dear; but still above what the thing costs him. – Price (fractional). Bastiat. Decline of the fractional price. – Price can fall below value without damage to capital. Number and unit (measure) important in the multiplication of prices

⟨This nonsense about the impossibility of overproduction (in other words, the assertion of the immediate identity of capital's process of production and its process of realization) has been expressed in a manner which is at least sophistical, i.e. ingenious, as mentioned above,[41] by James Mill, in the formula that supply = its own demand, that supply and demand therefore balance, which means in other words the same thing as that value is determined by labour time, and hence that *exchange adds nothing to it*, and which forgets only that exchange does have to take place and that this depends (in the final instance) on the *use value*. Mill says, then, that if demand and supply do not balance, this comes about because too much has been produced of one specific product (the supplied product) and too little of the other (the one in demand). This too much and too little concerns not the exchange value, but the use value. More of the supplied product exists than is 'needed'; this is what it boils down to. Hence that

41. See above, p. 411, and note 24.

overproduction comes from use value and therefore from exchange itself. This in stultified form in Say – products are exchanged only for products;[42] therefore, at most, too much has been produced of one and too little of another. Forgetting: (1) that values are exchanged for values, and a product exchanges for another only to the extent that it is value; i.e. that it is or becomes money; (2) it exchanges for labour. The good gentleman adopts the standpoint of *simple exchange*, in which indeed no overproduction is possible, for it is indeed concerned not with exchange value but with use value. Overproduction takes place in connection with realization, not otherwise.[43]⟩

Proudhon, who certainly hears the bells ringing but never knows where, therefore sees the origin of overproduction in the fact 'that the worker cannot buy back his product'.[44] By this he understands that interest and profit are added on to it; or that the price of the product is an overcharge on top of its real value. This demonstrates first of all that he understands nothing about the determination of value, which, generally speaking, can include no overcharge. In practical commerce, capitalist A can screw capitalist B. The one pockets what the other loses. If we add them both together, then the sum of their exchange = the sum of the labour time objectified in it, of which capitalist A has merely pocketed more than his share in relation to B. From all the profits made by capital, i.e. the total mass of capitalists, there is deducted (1) the constant part of capital; (2) the wage, or, the amount of objectified labour time necessary in order to reproduce living labour capacity. They can therefore divide nothing among themselves other than the surplus value. The proportion – just or unjust – in which they distribute this surplus value among themselves alters absolutely nothing about exchange or about the exchange relation between capital and labour.

It might be said that *necessary labour time* (i.e. the wage), which therefore excludes profit, and is rather to be deducted from it, is itself again determined by the *prices* of products which already include profit. Where else could the profit come from which the capitalist who does not directly employ this worker makes in the exchange with him? For example, the spinner's worker exchanges his wages for so many bushels of grain. But in

42. Say, *Traité d'économie politique*, pp. 142–56.
43. Marx wrote 'not else' in English here.
44. Bastiat et Proudhon, *Gratuité du crédit*, pp. 207–8.

the price of each bushel, the profit of the farmer, i.e. of capital, is already included. So that the price of the consumption goods which are bought by necessary labour itself already includes surplus labour time. It is clear, first of all, that the wage paid by the spinner to his workmen must be high enough to buy the necessary bushel of wheat, regardless of what profit for the farmer may be included in the *price* of the bushel of wheat; but that, likewise, on the other side, the wage which the farmer pays his workers must be high enough to procure for them the necessary quantity of clothing, regardless of what profit for the weaver and the spinner may be included in the *price* of these articles of clothing.

The puzzle arises simply because (1) *price* and *value* are being mixed up; (2) relations are brought in which are irrelevant to the determination of value of such. Suppose initially – and this is the conceptual relation – that capitalist A himself produces all the consumption goods which the worker needs, or which represent the sum of use values in which his necessary labour objectifies itself. Then, with the money which he obtains from the capitalist – money appears in this transaction only as medium of circulation – the worker would have to buy back from the capitalist, with that money, a fractional part – the part representing his necessary labour – of his product. The *price* of a fractional part of capitalist A's product is of course the same for the worker as for everyone else engaged in exchange. From the moment he buys from the capitalist, his specific quality as worker is extinguished; the money contains no trace of the relation in which, or of the operation by which, it was obtained; in circulation he confronts the capitalist simply as M, and the capitalist confronts him as C; as realizer of the *price* of C, which is hence presupposed for him just as for every other representative of M, i.e. buyer. Good. But in the price of the fractional part of the commodity which he buys, the profit is included in which the surplus value going to the capitalist appears. If his necessary labour time, therefore, represents 20 thalers = a certain fractional part of the product, it follows that, if the profit is 10%, the capitalist sells him the commodity for 22 thalers.

That is what Proudhon thinks, and concludes from it that the worker cannot buy back his product, i.e. the fractional part of the total product which objectifies his *necessary labour*. (We will come back directly to his other conclusion, that *therefore* capital cannot adequately exchange, *hence* overproduction.) To make the matter tangible, say that the worker's 20 thalers = 4 bushels of grain. Consequently – if 20 thalers is the value of the 4 bushels expressed in money – if the capitalist sells them for 22, then the worker could not buy back the 4 bushels, or rather he could buy only $3\frac{7}{11}$ bushels. In other words, he imagines that the monetary transaction distorts the relation. 20 thalers is the price of necessary labour = 4 bushels; and the capitalist pays this to the worker; but as soon as the latter presents his 20 thalers and asks for the 4 bushels, he gets only $3\frac{7}{11}$. Since he would thereby receive less than the *necessary* wage, he could not live at all, and thus Mr Proudhon proves more than he intends.*

But the presupposition, if you please, is wrong. If 5 thalers expresses the *value* of a bushel, i.e. the labour time objectified in it, and if 4 bushels express the necessary wages of labour, then capitalist A sells these 4 bushels not, as Proudhon thinks, for 22 but for 20 thalers. But the thing is this: let the total product (including necessary and surplus labour time) equal 110 thalers = 22 bushels; let 16 of these bushels = 80 thalers, represent the capital invested in seed, machinery etc.; 4 bushels = 20 thalers for necessary labour time; 2 bushels = 10 thalers, surplus labour time. The capitalist sells each bushel at 5 thalers, the necessary value of the bushel, and nevertheless he makes a gain of 10% on each bushel, or $\frac{5}{10}$ of a thaler, $\frac{1}{2}$ a thaler = 15 silver groschen. How? Because he sells 22×5 instead of 20×5. We can here equate to 0 the additional capital he would have to lay out in order to produce 2 additional bushels, since these can dissolve in pure surplus labour, more thorough ploughing, elimination of weeds, procurement of mineral fertilizer which, say, costs him nothing, etc. The value contained in the 2 surplus bushels has cost *him nothing*, hence makes up a surplus above his expenditures. If he sells 20 of the 22 bushels for what they cost him, for 100 thalers, plus 2, which cost him nothing – but whose value = the labour contained in them – for 10 thalers, then it is the same for

---

*It is beside the point here that capital, in practice as well as in general tendency, directly employs *price*, as e.g. in the truck system, to defraud *necessary labour*, and to reduce it below the standard given by nature as well as by a specific state of society. We must always presuppose here that the wage paid is *economically* just, i.e. that it is determined by the general laws of economics. The contradictions have to follow here from the general relations themselves, and not from fraud by individual capitalists. The further forms which this assumes in reality belong in the doctrine of wages.

him as if he sold all of them, each bushel for 15 silver groschen more than it cost him. (For $\frac{1}{2}$ a thaler or 10% of 5 thalers $= \frac{5}{10}$.) Therefore, although he makes 2 thalers on the 4 bushels he sells to the worker, the worker obtains each bushel at its necessary value. The capitalist makes 2 thalers on them only because, beside these 4 bushels, he sells 18 additional ones at the identical price. If he sold only 16, he would make nothing; for then he would sell a total of: $5 \times 20 = 100$, his invested capital.

Indeed, in manufacturing, too, it is possible that the capital's outlays do not increase, while a surplus value is sold nevertheless; i.e. it is not necessary that the outlay in raw material and machinery should grow. Assume that the same product obtains a higher finish through labour by hand – the mass of required raw material and instrument held constant – and hence its use value, therefore the use value of the product, increases, not in quantity, but in quality, owing to the increased hand labour employed on it. Its exchange value – the labour objectified in it – simply grows in relation to this labour. If the capitalist then sells for 10% more, then the worker gets paid the fractional part of the product, expressed in money, which represents necessary labour; and if the product could be divided, then the worker could buy this fractional part. The capitalist's profit would come not from over-charging the worker for this fractional part, but from the fact that in the whole of the product he sells a fractional part which he has not paid for, and which represents, precisely, *surplus labour time*. The product is always divisible as value; in its natural form, it need not be so. Profit here always comes from the fact that the whole value contains a fractional part which is not paid, and hence a fractional part of surplus labour is paid in each fractional part of the whole. So in the above example. When the capitalist sells 22 bushels, i.e. 2 which represent surplus labour, it is the same as if he sold an extra $\frac{1}{10}$ of a bushel per bushel, i.e. $\frac{1}{10}$ surplus value. If e.g. only one clock has been produced, where the relation of labour, capital and surplus value is the same, then the quality of the clock has been raised $\frac{1}{10}$ in value by $\frac{1}{10}$ labour time which costs the capitalist nothing.

Third case, that the capitalist, as is usual in manufacturing (but not in extractive industry), needs more raw material (let the instrument remain constant; however, nothing is changed if it, too, is variable) in which the surplus labour time objectifies itself. (Actually this does not belong here yet, for capital here can or

must just as well be assumed as having also produced the raw
material, e.g. the cotton, and surplus production at any point
has to reduce itself to *mere* surplus labour, or, what is rather the
reality, presupposes *simultaneous* surplus labour at all points of
circulation.) Assume that he spins up 25 lb. of cotton, which cost
him 50 thalers, and for which he requires machinery (which we
will assume to be entirely consumed in the production process)
at 30 thalers, and wages 20 thalers, for 25 lb. of twist, which he
sells at 110. He sells each pound of twist, then, for $4\frac{2}{5}$ thalers, or
4 thalers 12 silver groschen. The worker thus obtains $4\frac{6}{11}$ lb. of
twist, if he wants to buy it again. If the worker were working
for himself, he would likewise sell the pound for 4 thalers 12
silver groschen and make no profit – presupposing that he
performs only the necessary labour; but he would spin up less
cotton.

As we know, the value of a pound of twist consists exclusively
of the amount of labour time objectified in it. Now suppose that
the value of the pound of twist $= 5$ thalers. Given that $\frac{4}{5}$, i.e.
4 thalers, represent cotton, instrument etc.; then 1 thaler represents the labour realized in the cotton by means of the instrument. If the worker, in order to live from spinning, needs say
20 thalers per month, then – since he earns 1 thaler for spinning 1
lb. of twist, but needs 20 – he would have to spin 20 lb. of twist.
If he himself owned the cotton, material etc., and were working
for himself, hence were his own master, then he would have to
sell 20 lb. of twist; since he would earn only $\frac{1}{5}$ on each, one thaler,
and $1 \times 20 = 20$. If he works for the capitalist, then the labour
which spins up 20 lb. of cotton only represents the necessary
labour; for, by presupposition, of the 20 lb. of twist or $20 \times 5 =$
100 thalers, 80 thalers only represent the already purchased cotton
and instrument, and the newly reproduced value represents
nothing but *necessary labour*. Of the 20 lb. of twist, 4 lb. $= 20$
thalers would represent necessary labour, and 16 nothing more
than the constant part of capital. $16 \times 5 = 80$ thalers. Each
additional pound which the capitalist orders to be produced over
and above the 20 contains $\frac{1}{5}$ surplus labour, surplus value for
him. (Objectified labour which he has sold without having paid
for it.) If he orders 1 more pound spun, he gains 1 thaler; 10 lb.
more, 10 thalers. Out of 10 lb. or 50 thalers, the capitalist would
have 40 thalers to replace his investment and 10 thalers of surplus

labour; or 8 lb. of twist with which to buy the material for 10 (machinery and cotton), and 2 lb. of twist, or their value, which have cost him nothing. If we now summarize the capitalist's accounts, we find that he has invested, in thalers

	Wages	Surplus value
$80 + 40 = 120$ (raw material, instrument etc.)	20	10
120	20	$10 = 150$

Altogether he has produced 30 lb. of twist ($30 \times 5 = 150$); the pound at 5 thalers, the exact *value* of the pound, i.e. purely determined by the labour objectified in it, and deriving value only from the latter. Of this 30 lb., 24 represent constant capital, 4 lb. go for wages, and 2 form *the surplus value*. Calculating it on the basis of his total investment, 140 thalers or 28 lb., as the capitalist himself does, this surplus value forms $\frac{1}{14} = 7\frac{1}{7}\%$ (although, in the example given, the surplus value amounts to 50% on labour).

Now assume that the productivity of labour grows to the extent that he is capable of spinning 40 lb. with the same wage cost. According to our assumption he would sell these 40 lb. at their real value, i.e. the pound at 5 thalers, of which 4 thalers is labour objectified in cotton etc., 1 thaler is newly added labour. He would then sell:

40 lb. – the lb. @ 5 thalers $= 40 \times 5 = 200$; from these 40 lb., deduct

20 lb. for necessary labour $= 100$

100   On the first 20 lb. he would have made not a farthing; of the remaining hundred, take off $\frac{4}{5} = 4 \times 20 = 80$.

80   for material etc.
—— Leaves:
20   thalers

On an investment of 200 thalers the capitalist would have earned 20, or 10%. 10% on total investment; but in fact 20 on the second hundred thalers or second 20 lb., in which he did not pay the objectified labour. Now assume that he is capable of making double that, say

lb.	*Thalers*	
80	400	Of this, take off 20 lb. for [necessary labour]

20 for necessary labour etc. = 100

Leaves: 300 Of these, take off $\frac{4}{5}$ for material
240 etc.

Leaves: 60 A profit of 60 on 400 is = 6 on
40 = 15%.

In fact in the above example the capitalist's investment is only 180; on this he makes 20, or $11\frac{1}{9}$%.

The smaller the part of the outlay becomes which represents necessary labour, the greater the gain, although it stands in no obvious relation to the real surplus value, i.e. surplus labour. For example. In order for the capitalist to gain 10%, he has to spin 40 lb. of twist; the worker needs to spin only 20 = necessary labour. Surplus labour = necessary labour, 100% surplus value. This is our old law. But this is not the matter at issue here.

In the above example with the 40 lb., the *real value* of the pound is 5 thalers, and, like the capitalist, the worker himself, if he conducted his own business *as a worker* (and could advance himself enough funds to be able to realize the raw material etc. to the extent necessary to allow him to live as a worker), would sell the pound at 5 thalers. He would, however, produce only 20 lb., and from its sale he would use $\frac{4}{5}$ to obtain new raw material, and $\frac{1}{5}$ to live. The only thing he would make out of the 100 thalers would be his wages. The capitalist's gain comes not from selling the pound *too dear* – he sells it at its *exact value* – but from selling it above the *costs of production, his* costs (not *the* costs, for the $\frac{1}{5}$ costs the worker surplus labour). If he sold at less than 5 thalers, he would be selling *below* the value, and the buyer would have the $\frac{1}{5}$ of labour contained in every pound of twist above the investment etc., for nothing. But the capitalist calculates in this manner:

Value of 1 pound = 5 thalers
of 40 pounds = 200 thalers; from which take off costs:
180
———
20 Leaves 20.

What he calculates is not that he gains 20 thalers out of the second 100 thalers, but that he gains 20 on his entire investment of ...

180 thalers. This gives him a profit of $11\frac{1}{9}$%, instead of 20. He calculates further that, in order to make this profit, he has to sell 40 lb. 40 lb. at 5 thalers gives him not $\frac{1}{5}$, or 20%, but 20 thalers distributed over 40 lb., or $\frac{1}{2}$ a thaler per pound. At the price for which he sells the pound, he makes $\frac{1}{2}$ a thaler out of 5 thalers; or 1 out of 10 thalers; 10% of the selling price. The price is determined by the price of the fractional unit (1 pound) multiplied by the number to be sold; here 1 pound at 5 thalers $\times$ 40. While this determination of price is correct for the capitalist's pocket, it is equally liable to lead one astray theoretically, in as much as it now seems as if an overcharge above the *real* value took place in each individual pound, and the origin of the surplus value in each individual pound has become invisible. This *determination of price by the multiplication of the value of the unit (measure) of the use value (pound, yard, ton etc.) with the number of these units produced* is important later in the theory of prices. There follows from it among other things that a decline in the price of the unit and an increase in the number of units – brought about by growth of the productive forces – shows that profit increases in relation with labour, or that the proportion [*Verhältnis*] of necessary labour declines in relation [*im Verhältnis*] to surplus labour – and not the opposite, as is the opinion of Mr Bastiat etc.[45] E.g. if labour grew, owing to productivity, to the point where the worker was producing twice as many pounds in the same time as before – presupposing that 1 lb. of twist renders him entirely the same service, regardless of its cost, and that twist, clothing, is all he needs to live – then the value added by labour to 20 lb. of twist would no longer amount to $\frac{1}{5}$ but now only to $\frac{1}{10}$, because he would be transforming the 20 lb. cotton into twist in $\frac{1}{2}$ the time. To the 80 thalers which the raw material cost, there would then be added not 20 thalers but only 10. The 20 lb. would cost 90 thalers and each pound $\frac{90}{20}$ or $4\frac{10}{20}$ thalers. But if the total labour time remained the same, then labour would now transform 80 lb. of cotton into twist, instead of 40. 80 lb. twist, the pound at $4\frac{9}{20}$ thalers, = 356 thalers.[46] The capitalist's account would be –

45. For Bastiat's view, see *Gratuité du crédit*, pp. 127–32.

46. Marx wrote $4\frac{9}{20}$ thalers when he meant to write $4\frac{10}{20}$ thalers. This naturally affects the subsequent calculations, which should be amended as follows: 80 lb. at $4\frac{10}{20}$ thalers a pound = 360 thalers. 360 thalers + 90 = 270. 270 — 216 = 54. 360 — 54 = 306. 54 represents 15% profit on 360 thalers.

Total receipts 356 thalers; deduct for labour

$$90$$

$$\overline{}$$

266   Of which, take off for investment etc.

$239\frac{17}{80}$

$$\overline{}$$

$26\frac{7.8}{80}$ The capitalist's gain thus $26\frac{7.8}{80}$ instead of 20. Say 27 (which a little too high ($\frac{17}{80}$ too high)). His total outlays etc. 330; over 12%, although he would make less on the individual pound.

The capitalist's gain from the value of the measure (unit) of use value – pound, yard, quarter etc. – decreases in proportion as the relation of living labour to raw material etc. – of newly added labour – decreases; i.e. the less labour time is necessary to give the raw material the form which the unit expresses. Yard of cloth etc. But on the other side, – since this identical with the increased productivity of labour, or the growth of surplus labour time – the number of these units grows, units in which surplus labour time is contained, i.e. labour time not paid for.

It further follows from the above that the price can fall *below* the value, and capital can still make a gain; he must sell, however, a number multiplied by the unit large enough to form a surplus over the number multiplied by the unit which forms the necessary price of labour. If the relation of labour to raw material etc. is $\frac{1}{5}$, then he can sell at e.g. only $\frac{1}{10}$ above the constant value, since the surplus labour *costs* him *nothing*. He then makes a present of $\frac{1}{10}$ of the surplus labour to the consumer and realizes only $\frac{1}{10}$ for himself. This very important in competition; overlooked in particular by Ricardo. The determination of prices is founded on the determination of values, but new elements enter in. The price, which originally appeared only as the value expressed in money, becomes further determined as itself a specific magnitude. If 5 thalers is the *value* of a pound of twist, i.e. the same labour time as is contained in 5 thalers is contained in 1 pound of twist, then this remains its value regardless of whether 4 or 4 million lb. of twist are being appraised. The moment of the NUMBER OF POUNDS, because it expresses the relation of surplus labour to necessary labour in another form, becomes decisively important in the *determination of price*. This matter brought to popular awareness in the question of the *ten hours' bill* etc.

Specific accumulation *of capital* (*transformation of surplus labour* (*revenue*) *into capital*). – *Proudhon. Value- and price- determination. In antiquity* (*slaves*) *not overproduction but over-consumption*

It follows further from the above:

If the worker were to restrict himself to *necessary labour*, he would spin no more than 20 lb. of twist, and realize no more raw material, machinery etc. than would have a value of 80 thalers monthly. Apart from the raw material, machinery etc. which are required for the worker's *reproduction*, self-maintenance, the capitalist must *necessarily* lay out capital in raw material (and machinery, even if not in the same proportion) for the objectification of surplus labour. (In agriculture, fishery, in short, the extractive industries, this is not absolutely necessary; it becomes so, however, when they are conducted on a large scale, i.e. *industrially*; it appears then as surplus outlay not in raw material itself, but in the instruments to take it out with.) These surplus outlays – i.e. the tendering of the material for surplus labour – of the objective elements of its realization [*Verwirklichung*] are actually what forms the specific so-called *provisional accumulation* of capital: the accumulation of the stock (let us say for the time being) *specifically* of capital. For it is stupid, as we shall see more closely, to regard it as a quality specific to capital – that the objective conditions of living labour must be present, as such – whether they are furnished by nature or produced in history. These *specific advances* which capital makes signify nothing more than that it *realizes* objectified surplus labour – surplus product – in new living surplus labour, instead of investing (spending) it, like, say, Egyptian kings or Etruscan priest-nobles for pyramids etc.

Into the *determination of prices* (as we shall also see with profit) there also enters – *fraud, reciprocal chicanery*. One party can win in exchange what the other loses; all they can distribute among themselves is the surplus value – capital as a class. But these proportions open a field for individual deception etc. (apart from supply and demand) which has nothing to do with the determination of value as such.

Thus, out the window goes Mr Proudhon's discovery that the worker cannot buy back his product. The basis on which this rests is that he (Proudhon) understands nothing, either about value-determination or about price-determination. But, furthermore and regardless of that, his conclusion that *this is why* there is overproduction is false in this abstraction. In the slave relation, the masters are not troubled by the fact that the workers do not compete with them as consumers. (Nevertheless, *production for luxury* as it presents itself in antiquity is a necessary result of the slave relation. Not overproduction, but *over-consumption* and *insane consumption*, signifying, by its turn towards the monstrous and the bizarre, the downfall of the old system of states.)

After capital steps out of the production process as *product*, it must be transformed into money again. The money which previously appeared merely as realized commodity etc., now appears as *realized capital*, or, realized capital as *money*. This an aspect of *money* (as of capital). The mass of money as medium of circulation has nothing to do with the difficulty of making capital into a reality [*realisieren*], i.e. of realizing it [*verwerten*]. This can already be seen from the above development.

The general rate of profit. – If the capitalist merely sells at his own cost of production, then it is a transfer to another capitalist. Worker gains almost nothing thereby

In the above example, where the capitalist, if he sells the pound of twist at 5 thalers – i.e. 40 lb. at 5 thalers each – hence sells the pound of twist at its *real value* and thereby gains $\frac{1}{2}$ a thaler out of 5 (the selling price), 10% on the selling price, or $\frac{1}{2}$ on $4\frac{1}{2}$, i.e. $11\frac{1}{9}$% of his outlay, if he sells at only 10% – assume now a profit of merely $\frac{9}{20}$ of a thaler on $4\frac{1}{2}$ thalers (this is a $\frac{1}{20}$ difference from $\frac{1}{2}$ on $4\frac{1}{2}$ thalers; a difference of just $1\frac{1}{9}$%). He then sells the pound at $4\frac{1}{2}$ thalers $+ \frac{9}{20}$ of a thaler; i.e. at $4\frac{19}{20}$ thalers or the 40 lb. at 198 thalers. Now various cases are possible. The capitalist with whom he exchanges – to whom he sells his 40 lb. – assume him to be the owner of a silver mine, i.e. silver producer – pays him only 198 thalers – hence gives him 2 thalers too little objectified labour in silver for the labour objectified in 40 lb. of cotton. Posit that with this capitalist B, the proportions of the outlay are exactly the same, etc. If capitalist B also takes only 10 instead of $11\frac{1}{9}$, then for 200 thalers he could not demand 40 lb. twist, but only $39\frac{3}{4}$. It is therefore impossible that both capitalists at the same time sell at $1\frac{1}{9}$% too little, or that the one offered 40 lb. for 198 thalers and the other offered 200 thalers for $39\frac{3}{4}$ lb., a case that cannot occur. In the previously assumed case, capitalist B would have paid $1\frac{1}{9}$% too little in his purchase of 40 lb. twist, i.e. apart from the profit which he does not obtain from exchange, but which exchange merely confirms, i.e. a profit of $11\frac{1}{9}$, he would also have gained the $1\frac{1}{9}\%$ lost by the other capitalist, for a total of $12\frac{2}{9}\%$. From his own workers – the labour set into motion by his own capital – he would have gained $11\frac{1}{9}\%$; the additional $1\frac{1}{9}\%$ are surplus labour by the workers of capitalist A, which he appropriates for himself. The *general rate of profit* can therefore fall in one or another branch of business if competition etc. forces the capitalist to sell below the *value*, i.e. to realize a part of the surplus labour not for himself, but for those who buy from him. But the general rate cannot fall in this way; it can fall only if the proportion of surplus labour to necessary labour falls *relatively*, and this, as we saw earlier, takes place if the proportion is already very large, or, expressed differently, if the proportion of living labour set into motion by capital is very small – if the part of capital which exchanges for living labour is very small compared to that which exchanges for machinery and raw material. The general rate of profit can fall in that case, even though absolute surplus labour rises.

With that, we come to another point. A *general rate of profit* as such is possible only if the rate of profit in one branch of business is too high and in another too low; i.e. that a part of the surplus value – which corresponds to surplus labour – is transferred from one capitalist to the other. If in 5 branches of business, for example, the respective rate of profit is

A   B   C   D   E
15%, 12%, 10%, 8%, 5%

then the average rate is 10%; but, in order for this to exist in reality, capitalist A and B have to give up 7% to D and E – more particularly, 2 to D and 5 to E – while C remains as it was. It is impossible for rates of profit on the same capital of 100 to be equal, since the relations of surplus labour are altogether different, depending on the productivity of labour and on the relation between raw material, machinery and wages, and on the overall volume in which production takes place. But suppose that a given branch of business, E, is necessary, say, the bakery trade, then the average 10% has to be paid to it. But this can happen only if A and B credit E with a part of their surplus labour. The capitalist class thus to a certain extent distributes the total surplus value so that, to a certain degree, it [shares in it] evenly in accordance with the *size* of its capital, instead of in accordance with the surplus values actually created by the capitals in the various branches of business. The larger profit – arising from the real surplus labour within a branch of production, the really created surplus value – is pushed down to the average level by competition, and the deficit of surplus value in the other branch of business raised up to the average level by withdrawal of capitals from it, i.e. a favourable relation of demand and supply. Competition cannot lower this level itself, but merely has the tendency to create such a level. Further developments belong in the section on competition. This is realized [*realisiert*] by means of the relation of prices in the different branches of business, which fall *below* the *value* in some, rise *above* it in others. This makes it seem as if an equal sum of capital in unequal branches of business created *equal surplus labour or surplus value*.

Now in the above example, where capitalist A is forced, say by competition, to sell at a profit of 10% instead of $11\frac{1}{9}\%$, and hence sells the pound of twist at $\frac{1}{20}$ of a thaler too cheaply, the worker would continue to obtain 20 thalers as before, in money, his necessary wages; but in twist, he would obtain $4\frac{4}{90}$ lb. instead of 4 lb. If his wages were in twist, he would have obtained $\frac{4}{20}$ of a thaler $= \frac{1}{5}$ of a thaler or 6 silver groschen, i.e. 1% more than his necessary wages. If the worker works in a branch of business whose product lies entirely outside the sphere of his consumption, then he gains not a farthing in this operation; rather, for him it is a matter of performing a part of his surplus labour indirectly for capitalist B, instead of directly for capitalist A; i.e. through the mediation of capitalist A. He can gain from the fact that capitalist A lets go of a part of the labour objectified in his product for nothing, only if he is himself a consumer of this product, and only to the extent that he is such a consumer. Thus, if his consumption of twist makes up $\frac{1}{10}$ of his expenditure, then he gains exactly $\frac{1}{10}$ of a thaler from the operation ($\frac{1}{100}$ of a thaler out of 2 thalers, $\frac{1}{100}$ of 1, exactly 1% of the 2 thalers), i.e. $\frac{1}{10}\%$ of his total wages of 20 thalers, or, $7\frac{1}{2}$ pfennigs. This would be the proportion – $7\frac{1}{2}$ pfennigs – in which he would participate in his own surplus labour of 20 thalers. Such are the proportions of the surplus wages which the worker makes at best, when the *price* in the branch of business where he is occupied falls below the necessary value. In the *best case* – and this is impossible – the limit (in the instance given) is 6 silver groschen or 1%, i.e. if he could live exclusively on twist; i.e. in the best case his surplus wages are determined by the relation of necessary labour time to surplus labour time. In the luxury-goods industries proper, from whose consumption he is himself excluded, it is always $= 0$.

Now let us assume that capitalists A, B, C exchange among one another; the total product of each $= 200$ thalers. Let A produce twist, B grain and C silver; let the relations of surplus and necessary labour, and of outlays and profit be just the same. A sells 40 lb. twist at 198, instead of at 200 thalers, and loses $1\frac{1}{5}\%$ of his gains; ditto B his, say 40 bushels wheat, at 198 instead of 200; but C exchanges the labour objectified in his 200 thalers in full. Between A and B the relation is such that neither of them loses in the exchange with the other. A would obtain 40 bushels wheat, B 40 lb. twist; but each of them a value of only 198. C obtains 40 lb. twist or 40 bushels wheat for 198 thalers and in both cases pays 2 thalers too little, or obtains $\frac{2}{5}$ lb. twist or $\frac{2}{5}$ bushel wheat too much. But now assume that the relation takes the form that A sells his 40 lb. to the silver man, C, for 200 thalers, but C has to pay 202 to the grain man, B, or 2 thalers above its value. Between twist A and silver C everything is all right; both exchange at value with each other; but because B's price has risen above its value, the 40 lb. twist and the 200 thalers silver, when expressed in grain, have fallen by $1\frac{1}{5}\%$, or, neither of them could in fact any longer buy 40 bushels grain for 200 thalers, but only $39\frac{3}{5}$. $39\frac{3}{5}$ bushels wheat would cost 200 thalers, or the single bushel wheat,[47] instead of 5 thalers, $5\frac{1}{20}$ thalers; 5 thalers $1\frac{1}{4}$ silver groschen. Now, in this last relation, assume that the worker's consumption consists $\frac{1}{2}$ of wheat; his twist consumption was $\frac{1}{10}$ of his income; his wheat consumption $\frac{5}{10}$. On the $\frac{1}{10}$ he had gained $\frac{1}{10}\%$ on his total wages; on the wheat, he loses $\frac{5}{10}$; thus on the whole he loses $\frac{4}{10}\%$ instead of gaining. Although the capitalist would have paid him his necessary labour, his wages would fall beneath the necessary pay as a consequence of grain man B's overcharging. If this continued on, then his necessary *wages* would have to *rise*. Thus if the sale of twist by capitalist A is due to a rise above value in the price of *grain* or of other use values which form the most essential part of the worker's consumption – then capitalist A's worker would lose in the same relation as his consumption of the now more expensive product is greater than the cheaper product he himself produces. But if A had sold twist at $1\frac{1}{5}\%$ above its value, and B sold grain at $1\frac{1}{5}\%$ below,

47. The substitution of 'wheat' for 'grain' here and at subsequent points has no bearing on Marx's argument. He uses the two words interchangeably.

then, in the best case, if the worker consumed nothing but grain, he could gain at most 6 silver groschen, or, since we presupposed half in grain, only 3 silver groschen, or $\frac{1}{2}\%$ on his wages of 20 thalers. Thus the worker may experience all three cases: his gain or loss from the operation = 0; it may depreciate his necessary wages, so that they no longer suffice, hence make him fall below the necessary minimum; it can thirdly bring him a surplus wage, which is resolved into a very small share of his own surplus labour.

We saw above that if the relation of necessary labour to the other conditions of production = $\frac{2}{5}$ (20 out of 100 total outlay) or = 40% of the total value (in 20 lb. twist = 4 lb. twist) (or of 100 thalers, 80 raw material and instrument, 20 labour) and the relation of surplus labour to necessary labour is 100% (i.e. the same quantity), then the capitalist makes $11\frac{1}{9}\%$ on his outlay.

If he took only 10% and made a gift of the $1\frac{1}{9}$ or 2 thalers (transferred surplus value), then the worker, in so far as he is a consumer, would likewise gain, and in the best (impossible) case, if he lived only from the products of his master, it would [be], as we saw:

Suppose the capitalist sold the pound of twist at $4\frac{11}{20}$ ($4\frac{1}{2}$) instead of at 5 thalers, then the worker would gain $\frac{9}{20}$ on the pound, and $\frac{20}{20} = 1$ on 4 lb.; but 1 out of 20 = $\frac{1}{20} = 5\%$ (1 thaler out of 20); the capitalist would sell the 40 lb. at $4\frac{11}{20}$ thalers $= \frac{19}{4}$ of a thaler $\times$ 40 = 190 thalers; his outlays 180, his gain = 10 $= 5\frac{5}{9}[\%]$, his minus-gain = $5\frac{5}{9}$; if he, the capitalist, sold at $4\frac{16}{20}$, then the worker would gain $\frac{4}{20}$ thalers per pound, $\frac{16}{20}$ per 4 lb., 1 thaler $\frac{12}{20}$ or $1\frac{3}{5}$ thalers on his total wages, i.e. $8\frac{44}{116}\%$, while the capitalist would lose 16 thalers of the surplus gain, or would only keep altogether 184 thalers, or 4 thalers gain on 180 = $\frac{4}{45}$ of 180 = $2\frac{2}{9}\%$; would lose $8\frac{8}{9}$; assume finally the capitalist sold the pound of twist at $4\frac{1}{2}$ thalers; the 40 lb. at 180; his profit = 0; he would make the consumer a present of the worker's surplus value or surplus labour time, then the worker's gain = $\frac{1}{2}$ of a thaler per lb., = $\frac{2}{4}$ of a thaler = 2 thalers, or 2 thalers out of 20 = 10%.	$1\frac{1}{9}\%$ loss on the capitalist's side: = $5\frac{5}{9}$; (= 10 thalers) $= 8\frac{8}{9}\%$ (= 16) Gain = 0 (loss $=11\frac{1}{9}\%$)	$1\% = 6$ silver groschen on 20 thalers (= $\frac{1}{3}$ of a thaler out of 20) gain above wages for the worker: = 1 thaler = 5% (1 thaler out of 20) = $8\frac{44}{116}\%$ (1 thaler 18 silver groschen) = 10% (2 thalers) (*less than $\frac{1}{2}$ pound*)

If on the other hand the capitalist had raised wages by 10%
from 20 to 22 thalers, because, say, the demand for labour in his
branch of business had risen above the supply – while he continued
to sell the pound of twist at its value, i.e. at 5 thalers as before,
then his profit would have fallen by only 2 thalers, from 200 to 198,
i.e. by $1\frac{1}{9}$%, and would still have been 10%.

It follows from this that if the capitalist, say, out of consideration for Mr Proudhon, sold his commodities at the production
costs they cost *him*, and if his total profit $= 0$, this would be
merely a transfer of the surplus value or surplus labour time from
capitalist A to B, C, D etc., and as regards his worker, his gain at
best – i.e. his share of his own surplus labour – would be limited to
that part of the wage which he consumed in the depreciated commodity; and if he spent his entire wages on it, the gain could not be
greater than the proportion of necessary labour to the total pro-
duct (in the above example $20:200 = \frac{1}{10}$, $\frac{1}{10}$ of 20 = 2 thalers).
As regards the other workers, the case is entirely the same; they
gain from the depreciated commodity only in relation (1) as they
consume it; (2) relative to the size of their wage, which is determined by necessary labour. If the depreciated commodity were,
e.g. grain – one of the staffs of life – then first its producer, the
farmer, and following him all other capitalists, would make the
discovery that the worker's necessary wage is no longer the
necessary wage; but stands above its level; hence it is brought
down; hence ultimately only the surplus value of capitals A, B,
C etc. is increased, and the surplus labour of those occupied in
them.

Posit 5 capitalists, A. B, C, D and E. Let E produce a commodity which is consumed only by workers. E would then realize
his profit purely in the exchange of his commodity with wages;
but, as always, his profit would originate not in the exchange of his
commodity for the workers' money, but in the exchange of his
capital with living labour. Posit that necessary labour relates in all
5 branches of business at $\frac{1}{3}$; let $\frac{1}{3}$ be surplus labour in all of them;
let constant capital be $= \frac{2}{3}$ in all. Capitalist E exchanges his product
for $\frac{1}{3}$ of capital A, $\frac{1}{3}$ of capital B, $\frac{1}{3}$ of capital C, $\frac{1}{3}$ of capital D, and
$\frac{1}{3}$ constitutes his wages. He would make no profit on this last $\frac{1}{3}$,
as we have seen; or rather his profit would not arise from the fact
that he gives the workers $\frac{1}{3}$ of his capital in money, and that they
buy back the same $\frac{1}{3}$ from him as money – would not originate
from the exchange with them as *consumers*, as centres of circula-

tion. His whole transaction with them as consumers rests on the basis that he gives them his product in the form of money, and they give him back the same money for exactly the same fractional part of the product. With the workers of A, B, C, D, his relation is not that of capitalist to worker, but of C[ommodity] to M[oney], of vendor to buyer. We have presupposed that the workers of A, B, C, D consume no part of their own products; D does, however, exchange for $\frac{1}{3}$ of the product of A, B, C and E, i.e. $\frac{2}{3}$ of their product; but this exchange is only a detour to get to the wages which A, B, C and D pay their own workers. They each give the workers money to the value of $\frac{1}{3}$ of their product, or $\frac{1}{3}$ of their ·product as payment for necessary labour, and with this, with $\frac{2}{3}$ of the value of their product or capital, they then buy E's commodity. But this exchange with E is then only an indirect form of advancing the part of capital which represents necessary labour – i.e. *deduction* from their capital. They cannot therefore gain thereby. The gain comes from the realization of the remaining $\frac{2}{3}$ of capital A, B, C, D, and this realization consists of each of them, through the exchange, getting back the labour objectified in his product, in another form. For each of them, since there is a division of labour, $\frac{2}{3}$ replaces his constant capital, raw material and material of labour. Their gain – the realization of surplus labour time, its positing as surplus value – consists in the reciprocal realization of the last $\frac{1}{3}$. It is not necessary that capitals A, B, C, D exchange the entire $\frac{2}{3}$ with one another. Since they are, as capitalists, at the same time large consumers, and can in no way live on air, but since, as capitalists, they do not live from their labour either, they have nothing to exchange or to consume apart from other peoples' products. That is, for their own consumption they exchange just that $\frac{1}{3}$ which represents surplus labour time, the labour created by means of capital. Posit that each consumes $\frac{1}{5}$ of this $\frac{1}{3}$, i.e. $\frac{1}{25}$, in the form of his own product. There remain $\frac{4}{25}$ to be either realized or to be transformed into use values for their own consumption through exchange. Let A exchange $\frac{2}{25}$ with B, $\frac{1}{25}$ with C, $\frac{1}{25}$ with E, and likewise on the part of B, C, E.

The case we have posited, where capital E realizes the whole of its profit in exchange with wages, is the most favourable – or expresses, rather, the only correct relation in which it is possible for capital to realize the surplus value created in *production* through *exchange* with the workers' consumption. But capitals A, B, C, D can realize their value in this case only through exchange among one another, i.e. through the exchange of capitalists among themselves. Capitalist E consumes nothing of his own commodity, since he has paid $\frac{1}{5}$ of it to his own workers, exchanged $\frac{1}{5}$ for $\frac{1}{5}$ of capital A, $\frac{1}{5}$ for $\frac{1}{5}$ of capital B, $\frac{1}{5}$ for $\frac{1}{5}$ of capital C, $\frac{1}{5}$ for $\frac{1}{5}$ of capital D. A, B, C, D make no profit on this exchange, since it is the respective $\frac{1}{5}$ which they have paid to their own workers.

Given the relation we have assumed, of $\frac{2}{5}$ raw material, $\frac{1}{5}$ machinery, $\frac{1}{5}$ workers' necessaries, and $\frac{1}{5}$ surplus product, from which Messrs the capitalists at the same time live and realize their surplus value, then we need, if the total product of each of A, B, C, D, E $= 100$, a producer E for workers' necessaries, 2 capitalists A and B, who produce raw materials for all the others, 1, C, who produces the machinery, and 1, D, who makes the surplus produce. The accounts would be these (the machinery-maker etc. has to produce every part of his commodity for himself):

	For labour	Raw material	Machinery	Surplus product	
(A) Raw material manufacturer	20	40	20	20	$= 100\ 2\frac{1}{2}$
(B) Ditto	20	40	20	20	$= 100\ 2\frac{1}{2}$
(C) Machinery manufacturer	20	40	20	20	$= 100\ 2\frac{1}{2}$
(E) Workers' necessaries	20	40	20	20	$= 100\ 2\frac{1}{2}$
(D) Surplus producer	20	40	20	20	$= 100$
	10	20	10	10	$= 50$

E therefore exchanges his entire product of 100 for 20 in his own workers' wages, 20 in wages for workers of raw material A, 20 for the workers of raw material B, 20 for the workers of machinery maker C, 20 for the workers of surplus producer D; of this he exchanges 40 for raw material, 20 for machinery, 20 he obtains back for workers' necessaries, and 20 remain for him to buy surplus produce, from which he himself lives. Likewise the others in the relation. What constitutes their surplus value is the $\frac{1}{5}$ or 20, which all of them can exchange for surplus product. If they consumed the entire surplus, then they would have come no further at the end than they were at the beginning, and the surplus value of their capital would not grow. Posit that they eat up only 10; or $\frac{1}{10}$, half of the surplus value; then surplus producer D himself would eat up 10 less; and each of the others 10 less; all in all, then, he would sell only half of his commodity, $= 50$, and could not begin his business anew. Posit therefore that he consumes only 50 in consumables. Likewise, 50 in money, then each of the capitalists A, B, C, D, E, would accumulate 10 thalers in money. These would represent the surplus value not consumed. These 10 thalers, or together 50, could be realized, however, only by being laid out for new labour. In order to produce more raw material, A and B need 4 thalers more of living labour, and, since they have no additional machinery for it, more labour by hand to the amount of 6 thalers. Thus, out of the 400 thalers which exist in raw materials, machines and workers' necessaries, only 50 are there for capitalists' consumables. But each of the capitalists now owns a surplus of 10, out of which 4 are in raw material, 2 in machines, 2 in workers' necessaries, on which he must make a gain of 2 (like 100 from 80, as before); D has gained 10 on his 40 and can therefore increase his production in the same proportion, i.e. by 5. The next year he produces $7\frac{1}{2}\%$ more $= 57\frac{1}{2}$.

This example may or may not be continued later. Does not actually belong here. This much is clear, that realization here takes place in the exchange among the capitalists, for although E produces only for workers' consumption, he exchanges with the others through the form of wages, $\frac{1}{4}$ of A, $\frac{1}{4}$ of B, $\frac{1}{4}$ of C, $\frac{1}{4}$ of D etc. A, B, C, D likewise exchange with E: not directly, but indirectly, in that each of them requires $\frac{1}{4}$ from him as necessaries for his workers. The realization consists of each of them exchanging his own product for fractional parts of the products of the other four, and this in such a way that a part of the surplus product goes for the capitalist's own consumption, and a part is transformed into surplus capital with which to set new labour into motion. The realization consists of the *real possibility* of increased realization – production of new and larger values. It is clear here that D and E, where E represents all commodities consumed by the workers and D all those consumed by the capitalists, would have produced too much – that is, too much relative to the proportion of the part of capital going to the worker, or too much relative to the part of capital consumable by the capitalists (too much relative to the proportion by which they must increase their capital; and this proportion later obtains a minimum limit in the form of interest) – that *general overproduction* would take place, not because relatively *too little* [*sic*] had been produced of the commodities consumed by the workers or too little [*sic*] of those consumed by the capitalists, but because too much *of both* had been produced – *not* too much *for consumption*, but too much to retain *the correct relation between consumption and realization; too much for realization.*

Barrier of capitalist production. – Relation of surplus labour to necessary labour. Proportion of the surplus consumed by capital to that transformed into capital. – Devaluation during crises

In other words: At a given point in the development of the productive forces – for this will determine the relation of necessary labour to surplus labour – a fixed relation becomes established, in which the product is divided into one part – corresponding to raw material, machinery, necessary labour, surplus labour – and finally surplus labour divides into one part which goes to consumption and another which becomes capital again. This inner division, inherent in the concept of capital, appears in exchange in such a way that the exchange of the capitals among one another takes place in specific and restricted proportions – even if these are constantly changing, in the course of production. If the relations are e.g. those of $\frac{2}{5}$ raw material, $\frac{1}{5}$ machinery, $\frac{1}{5}$ wages, $\frac{1}{5}$ surplus product, of which $\frac{1}{10}$ for consumption, $\frac{1}{10}$ for new production – this is the division within capital – this will appear in the exchange process as distribution among, say, 5 capitals. This gives, in any case, both the sum total of the exchange which can take place, and the proportions in which each of these capitals must both exchange and produce. If the relation of necessary labour to the constant part of capital is, as e.g. in the above example, $= \frac{1}{5}:\frac{3}{5}$, then we have seen that the capital which works for the consumption of capitalists and workers combined may not be greater than $\frac{1}{5} + \frac{1}{10}$ of the 5 capitals, each of which represents 1, $= 1\frac{1}{2}$ capitals. Given likewise is the relation in which each capital must exchange with each other one, which represents a specific one of its own moments. Finally, in which each of them must exchange at all. If, for example, the relation of raw material $= \frac{2}{5}$, then the capitals which produce raw material can at any final point exchange no more than $\frac{3}{5}$, while $\frac{2}{5}$ must be regarded as fixed. (E.g. as seed etc. in agriculture.) *Exchange* in and for itself gives these conceptually opposite moments an indifferent being; they exist independently of one another; their inner necessity becomes *manifest* in the crisis, which puts a forcible end to their seeming indifference towards each other.

A revolution in the forces of production further alters these relations, *changes* these relations themselves, whose foundations – from the standpoint of capital and hence also of that of realization through exchange – always remains *the relation of necessary to surplus labour*, or, if you like, of the different moments of objectified to living labour. It is possible, as we have already indicated earlier, that the capital as well as the living labour capacity set free owing to the increase in productive forces must both lie dormant, because they are not present in the proportions in which production must take place on the basis of the newly developed productive forces. If it proceeds regardless of that, then ultimately a minus, a negative magnitude, will come out of the exchange on one side or the other.

The barrier always remains, that exchange – hence production as well – takes place in such a way that the relation of surplus labour to necessary labour remains the same – for this is = to the constancy [*Gleichbleiben*] of the realization of capital. The second relation – the proportion between the part of the surplus product consumed by capital and that part transformed anew into capital – is determined by the first relation. Firstly, *the magnitude of the sum to be divided into these two parts depends on this original relation*; secondly, just as the creation of surplus value by capital depends on the creation of surplus labour, so does the increase of capital as capital (accumulation, and, without accumulation, capital cannot form the foundation of production, since it would remain stagnant, and would not be an element of progress, required already by the mere increase of population etc.) depend on the transformation of a part of this surplus product into new capital. If the surplus value were simply consumed, then capital would *not* have realized itself as capital, and not produced itself as *capital*, i.e. as value which produces value.

We have seen that if 40 lb. of twist of a value of 200 thalers – because they contain labour time objectified in 200 thalers – are exchanged for 198 thalers, then not only does the manufacturer of twist lose $1\frac{1}{9}\%$ gain; but also his product is devalued, has been sold *below* its real value, although it is sold at a *price* which still leaves him a profit of 10%. On the other hand, the producer of silver gains 2 thalers. Keeps 2 thalers as liberated capital. Nevertheless, a devaluation has taken place as regards the total sum. For the sum is 398 thalers instead of 400. For, in the hand of the producer of silver, the 200 thalers of twist are also worth only 198; it is the same for him as if the productive force of his labour had increased to the point where the same objectified labour were contained in 200 thalers as before, but that 2 of these thalers had left the column of necessary outlays in his books and gone over into the column of surplus value, so that he would have paid 2 thalers less for necessary labour. The opposite could be the case only if the silver producer were able to re-sell for 200 thalers the 40 lb. of twist he bought at 198 thalers. Then he would have 202 thalers, and say he sold them to a manufacturer of silk who gave him silk to the value of 200 thalers in exchange for the 40 lb. of twist. The 40 lb. twist would then have been sold at their true value, although not first-hand by their producer, but rather second-hand, by their buyer, and the total accounts would look as follows: Exchanged, 3 products each containing objectified labour of a value of 200 thalers; hence *sum* of the values of the capitals: 600. The manufacturer of twist, A, the manufacturer of silver, B, the manufacturer of silk, C: A 198, B 202 (i.e. 2 extra from the first exchange and 200 in silk), C 200. *Total* 600. In this case the combined value of the capitals remained the same, and all that took place was a displacement, in that B pocketed as an extra the value-fraction which A lost.

If A, the twist maker, could sell only 180 (the cost of the thing for *him*), and absolutely could not find a buyer for 20 twist, then objectified labour in the amount of 20 thalers would have become valueless. The same would be the case if he gave a value of 200 for 180 thalers; for B, the manufacturer of silver – to the extent that this necessity had arisen for A owing to overproduction of twist, so that B, too, could not get rid of the value contained in the 40 lb. twist for more than 180 – 20 thalers of his capital would have been set free. He would have in hand a relative surplus value of 20 thalers, but in absolute values – objectified labour time to the extent that it is exchangeable – he would have only 200 as before – that is, 40 lb. twist at 180 and 20 thalers liberated capital. It would be the same for him as if the production costs of twist had decreased, i.e. as if, owing to increased labour productivity, 40 lb. twist contained 20 thalers less labour time, or as if, with a working day = 4 thalers, 5 working days less were necessary in order to transform x lb. of cotton into 40 lb. twist; so that, then, he would have to exchange less labour time objectified in silver for the labour time objectified in twist. But the combined sum of the values on hand would be 380 instead of 400. Thus a *general depreciation* of 20 thalers would have taken place, or a destruction of capital to the amount of 20 thalers. A *general devaluation* thus takes place despite the fact that the *depreciation* of the twist manufacturer's 40 lb. twist from 200 to 180 necessarily appears as an appreciation on the part of silver, a depreciation of twist relative to silver; and a general depreciation of prices as such always includes an appreciation of money, i.e. of the commodity in which all the others are appraised. Thus, in a crisis – a general depreciation of prices – there occurs up to a certain moment a *general devaluation* or *destruction of capital*. The devaluation, like the *depreciation*, can be absolute and not merely relative, because value expresses not merely a relation between one commodity and another, as does price, but rather the relation between the price of the commodity and the labour objectified in it, or between one amount of objectified labour of the same quality and another. If these amounts are not equal, then *devaluation* takes place, which is not outweighed by appreciation on the other side, for the other side expresses a fixed amount of objectified labour which remains unchanged by exchange. In general crises, this devaluation extends even to living labour capacity itself. In consequence of what has been indicated above, the destruction of value and capital which takes place in a crisis coincides with – or means the same thing as – a general growth of the *productive forces*, which, however, takes place not by means of a real increase of the productive force of labour (the extent to which this happens in consequence of crises is beside the point here), but by means of a decrease of the existing value of raw materials, machines, labour capacity. For example. The cotton manufacturer loses capital on his products (e.g. twist), but he buys the same value of cotton, labour etc. at a lower price. It is the same for him as if the *real value* of labour, of cotton etc., had decreased, i.e. as if they had been produced more cheaply owing to an increase in the productive force of labour. In the same way, on the other hand, a sudden general increase in the forces of production would relatively devalue all the *present values* which labour objectifies at the lower stage of the productive forces, and hence would destroy present capital as well as present labouring capacity. The other side of the crisis resolves itself into a real decrease in production, in living labour – in order to restore the correct relation between necessary and surplus labour, on which, in the last analysis, everything rests.

(Thus it is by no means true, as Lord Overstone thinks – as a true usurer – that crises simply resolve themselves in enormous profits for the one, and tremendous losses for the other.)[48]

Capital coming out of the production process becomes money again

Exchange does not change the inner characteristics of realization; but it projects them to the outside; gives them a reciprocally independent form, and thereby lets their unity exist merely as an inner necessity, which must therefore come forcibly to the surface in crises. Both are therefore posited in the essence of capital: the devaluation [*Entwertung*] of capital in the production process, as well as the suspension of devaluation and the creation of the conditions for the realization [*Verwertung*] of capital. The process by which this takes place in reality can be examined only as soon as *real* capital, i.e. competition etc. – the actual real conditions – have been examined. Does not belong here yet. On the other hand, *without* exchange the production of capital as such would not exist, since *realization* as such cannot exist without exchange. Without exchange, the only question of concern would be the measurement etc. of the *use value* produced, only use value as such.

After capital, in the production process, (1) has realized itself, i.e. created a new value; (2) become devalued, i.e. made the transition from money to the form of a particular commodity, it (3) realizes itself together with its new value, in that the product is thrown into circulation again, and, as C, is exchanged for M. At the point where we stand now, where capital is being examined only in general, the real difficulties of this third process are present only as *possibilities*, and are therefore suspended, again as *possibilities*. Therefore, the product now posited as having been transformed back into money.

Capital is thus now posited as money again, and money therefore posited in the *new* aspect of *realized capital*, not merely as realized price of the commodity. Or, the commodity realized in the price is

48. Samuel Jones Loyd (1796–1883, banker and economist, expert witness before the Parliamentary Commissions of 1833, 1840, 1848, and 1857, author of numerous pamphlets on money and banking, leading theorist of the Currency School in the controversy over Peel's Act of 1844, created Baron Overstone in 1860). The source of this quotation has not been found; it is most probably from the *Evidence Presented to the House of Commons Select Committee of 1857*, ed. J. R. MacCulloch, London, 1858.

now realized capital. We will examine this new aspect of money, or rather of capital as money, later. In accord with the initial nature of money, the only apparent feature by which capital – when transformed into money – may be measured is the new value which it has created; i.e. the first aspect of money as the general measure of commodities repeats itself; now as the measure of surplus value – of the realization of capital. In the form of money, this realization appears as measured by itself; as being its own measure. The capital was originally 100 thalers; because it is now 110, the measure of its realization is posited in its own form – as a proportion of the capital returned (returned to its money form) from the production process and from exchange, relative to the original capital; no longer as a relation between two unequal qualities – objectified and living labour – or necessary labour and surplus labour. When capital is posited as money, it is therefore posited in the first aspect of money, as measure of value. Here, however, this value is its own value, or the measure of its self, negation.[49] We will return to this (under profit).

The second form of money was that of the medium of circulation, and in this regard the money form of capital appeared as a mere vanishing moment for the purpose of exchanging it again, but not, as in the case of money as a medium of circulation in general, an exchange in return for commodities – use values – for final consumption, but rather an exchange in return for those particular use values in which it is able to begin its course as capital anew – raw material and instrument on the one hand, living labour capacity on the other. In this role it is *circulating capital*, about which later. However, the end-product of money in its role as medium of circulation is the beginning of the act of production with *posited* capital as the point of departure, and this is the point which we will here examine before we go further. (In the first aspect, *measure*, the *new value* did appear as measured; but the difference merely formal; instead of surplus labour, money – surplus labour objectified in a specific commodity. But the *qualitative* nature of this new value also undergoes a change – i.e. the magnitude of the measure itself, to be examined only later. Secondly, as medium of circulation the disappearance of the money form is also merely *formal*. It only becomes *essential* after not only the first but also the second circular path has been completed. Thus initially it results only in

49. Cf. Hegel, *Science of Logic*, pp. 344–7.

our standing again at the beginning of the *realization process*. We therefore begin to take up the continuation at *this point*.)

The third form of money, as independent value in a negative relation *vis-à-vis* circulation, is capital which does not step out of the production process into exchange again to become money. Rather, it is capital which becomes a commodity and enters into circulation in the form of self-sufficient value [*sich auf sich selbst beziehenden Werts*]. This third form presupposes capital in the earlier forms and at the same time forms the transition from *capital* to the *particular capitals*, the real capitals; since now, in this last form, capital already in its very concept divides into two capitals with an independent existence. Along with the duality, plurality in general is then given. Such is the march of this development.[50]

⟨Before we go any further, just one remark. *Capital in general*, as distinct from the particular capitals, does indeed appear (1) *only as an abstraction*; not an arbitrary abstraction, but an abstraction which grasps the specific characteristics which distinguish capital from all other forms of wealth – or modes in which (social) production develops. These are the aspects common to every capital as such, or which make every specific sum of values into capital. And the distinctions within this abstraction are likewise abstract particularities which characterize every kind of capital, in that it is their position [*Position*] or negation [*Negation*] (e.g. fixed capital or circulating capital); (2) however, capital in general, as *distinct* from the particular real capitals, is itself a *real* existence. This is recognized by ordinary economics, even if it is not *understood*, and forms a very important moment of its doctrine of equilibrations etc. For example, capital in this *general form*, although belonging to individual capitalists, in its *elemental form* as capital, forms the capital which accumulates in the banks or is distributed through them, and, as Ricardo says, so admirably distributes itself in accordance with the needs of production.[51] Likewise, through loans etc., it forms a level between the different countries. If it is therefore e.g. a law of capital in general that, in order to realize itself, it must posit itself doubly, and must realize itself in this double form, then e.g. the capital of a particular nation which represents capital *par excellence* in antithesis to another will have to lend itself out to a third nation in order to be able to realize itself. This double positing, this relating to self as to an alien, becomes

50. This sentence is in English in the original.
51. Ricardo, *On the Principles of Political Economy*, p. 139.

damn real in this case. While the general is therefore on the one hand only a mental [*gedachte*] mark of distinction [*differentia specifica*], it is at the same time a *particular* real form alongside the form of the particular and individual.[52] (We will return later to this point, which, while having more of a logical than an economic character, will nevertheless have a great importance in the course of our inquiry. The same also in algebra. For example, *a*, *b*, *c* are numbers as such; in general; but then again they are whole numbers as opposed to *a*/*b*, *b*/*c*, *c*/*b*, *c*/*a*, *b*/*a* etc., which latter, however, presuppose the former as their general elements.⟩

Surplus labour or surplus value becomes surplus capital. All determinants of capitalist production now appear as results of (wage) labour itself. The realization process [Verwirklichungsprozess] of labour at the same time its de-realization process [Entwirklichungsprozess]

The new value, then, [is] itself posited as capital again, as objectified labour entering into the process of exchange with living labour, and hence dividing itself into a constant part – the objective conditions of labour, material and instrument – and the conditions for the subjective condition of labour, the existence of living labour capacity, the necessaries, subsistence goods for the worker. With this second entrance by capital in this form, some points appear clarified which were altogether unclear in its first occurrence – as money in transition from its role as value to its role as capital. Now they are solved through the process of realization and production itself. In the first encounter, the *presuppositions* themselves appeared to come in from the outside, out of circulation; as external presuppositions for the arising of capital; hence not emergent from its inner essence, and not explained by it. These *external* presuppositions will now appear as moments of the motion of capital itself, so that it has itself – regardless how they may arise historically – pre-posited them as its own moments.

Within the production process itself, surplus value, the surplus value procured through compulsion by capital, appeared as *surplus labour*, itself in the form of living labour, which, however, since it cannot create something out of nothing, finds its objective conditions laid out before it. Now this *surplus labour* appears in

52. Cf. Hegel, *Science of Logic*, p. 600: 'This universal Notion contains the three moments: universality, particularity, and individuality.'

objectified form as *surplus product*, and, in order to realize itself as capital, this surplus product divides into a double form: as *objective condition of labour* – material and instrument; as subjective – consumption goods for the living labour now to be put to work. The general form as value – objectified labour – and objectified labour coming out of circulation – is of course the general, self-evident presupposition. Further: the surplus product in its totality – which objectifies surplus labour in its totality – now appears as *surplus capital* (in contrast to the original capital, before it had undertaken this cycle), i.e. as independent exchange value, in which living labour capacity encounters its *specific use value*. All moments which confronted living labour capacity, and employed it as *alien, external* powers, and which consumed it under *certain conditions independent of itself*, are now posited as *its own product and result*.

Firstly : *surplus value or the surplus product* are nothing but a specific sum of objectified living labour – the sum of surplus labour. This new *value* which confronts living labour as independent, as engaged in exchange with it, as capital, is the *product of labour*. It is itself nothing other than the *excess of labour as such above necessary labour* – in objective form and hence as *value*.

Secondly: the particular forms which this value must adopt in order to realize itself anew, i.e. to posit itself as capital – on one side as raw material and instrument, on the other as subsistence goods for labour during the act of production – are likewise, therefore, only *particular* forms of surplus labour itself. Raw material and instrument are produced by it in such relations – or, it is itself objectively posited in production as raw material and instrument in such a proportion – that a given sum of necessary labour – i.e. living labour which reproduces (the value of) the consumption goods – can objectify itself in it, and objectify itself in it continuously, i.e. can always begin anew the diremption into the objective and subjective conditions of its self-preservation and self-reproduction. In addition to this, living labour, in the process of reproducing its objective conditions, has at the same time posited raw material and instrument in such proportions that it can realize itself in them as *surplus labour, as labour beyond the necessary*, and can hence make them into material for the creation of *new* values. The objective conditions of *surplus labour* – which are restricted to the proportion of raw material and instrument beyond the requirements of necessary labour, whereas the objective conditions of necessary labour divide within their objectivity into objective and subjective, into objective moments of labour as well as subjective (consumption goods for living labour) – therefore now appear, are therefore now posited, as the product, result, objective form, external existence of surplus labour itself. Originally, by contrast, the fact that instrument and necessaries were on hand in the amounts which made it possible for living labour to realize itself not only as *necessary*, but also as *surplus* labour – this appeared alien to living labour itself, appeared as an act of capital.

Thirdly: The independent, for-itself existence [*Fürsichsein*] of value *vis-à-vis* living labour capacity – hence its existence as capital – the objective, self-sufficient indifference, the *alien quality* [*Fremdheit*] of the objective conditions of labour *vis-à-vis* living labour capacity, which goes so far that these conditions confront the person of the worker in the person of the capitalist – as personification[53] with its own will and interest – this absolute *divorce, separation* of property, i.e. of the objective conditions of labour from living labour capacity – that they confront him as *alien property*, as the reality of other juridical persons, as the absolute realm of *their* will – and that labour therefore, on the other side, appears as *alien labour* opposed to the value personified in the capitalist, or the conditions of labour – this absolute separation between property and labour, between living labour capacity and the conditions of its realization, between objectified and living labour, between value and value-creating activity – hence also the alien quality of the content of labour for the worker himself – this divorce now likewise appears as a product of labour itself, as objectification of its own moments. For, in the new act of production itself – which merely confirmed the exchange between capital and living labour which preceded it – surplus labour, and hence the surplus product, the total product of labour in general (of surplus labour as well as necessary labour), has now been posited as capital, as independent and indifferent towards living labour capacity, or as exchange value which confronts its mere use value. Labour capacity has appropriated for itself only the subjective conditions of necessary labour – the means of subsistence for actively producing labour capacity, i.e. for its reproduction as mere labour capacity separated from the conditions of its realization – and it has posited these conditions themselves as

53. The original text has 'personifications', evidently referring back to 'conditions'.

things, values, which confront it in an alien, commanding personification. The worker emerges not only not richer, but emerges rather poorer from the process than he entered. For not only has he produced the conditions of necessary labour as conditions belonging to capital; but also the value-creating possibility, the realization [*Verwertung*] which lies as a possibility within him, now likewise exists as surplus value, surplus product, in a word as capital, as master over living labour capacity, as value endowed with its own might and will, confronting him in his abstract, objectless, purely subjective poverty. He has produced not only the alien wealth and his own poverty, but also the relation of this wealth as independent, self-sufficient wealth, relative to himself as the poverty which this wealth consumes, and from which wealth thereby draws new vital spirits into itself, and realizes itself anew. All this arose from the act of exchange, in which he exchanged his living labour capacity for an amount of objectified labour, except that this objectified labour – these external conditions of his being, and the independent externality [*Ausserihmsein*] (to him) of these objective conditions – now appear as posited by himself, as *his own product*, as his own self-objectification as well as the objectification of himself as a power independent of himself, which moreover rules over him, rules over him through his own actions.

In *surplus capital*, all moments are products of *alien labour – alien surplus labour* transformed into capital; means of subsistence for necessary labour; the objective conditions – material and instrument – whereby necessary labour can reproduce the value exchanged for it in means of subsistence; finally the amount of material and instrument required so that new surplus labour can realize itself in them, or a new surplus value can be created.

It no longer seems here, as it still did in the first examination of the production process, as if capital, for its part, brought with it any value whatever from circulation. Rather, the objective conditions of labour now appear as labour's product – both to the extent that they are value in general, and as use values for production. But while capital thus appears as the product of labour, so does the product of labour likewise appear as capital – no longer as a simple product, nor as an exchangeable commodity, but as *capital*; objectified labour as mastery, command over living labour. The product of labour appears as *alien property*, as a mode of existence confronting living labour as independent, as *value* in its being for itself; the product of labour, objectified labour, has been endowed by living labour with a soul of its own, and establishes itself opposite living labour as an *alien power*: both these situations are themselves the product of labour. Living labour therefore now appears from its own standpoint as acting within the production process in such a way that, as it realizes itself in the objective conditions, it simultaneously repulses this realization from itself as an alien reality, and hence posits itself as insubstantial, as mere penurious labour capacity in face of this reality alienated [*entfremdet*] from it, belonging not to it but to others; that it posits its own reality not as a being for it, but merely as a being for others, and hence also as mere other-being [*Anderssein*], or being of another opposite itself.[54] This realization process is at the same time the de-realization process of labour. It posits itself objectively, but it posits this, its objectivity, as its own not-being or as the being of its not-being – of capital. It returns back into itself as the mere possibility of value-creation or realization [*Verwertung*]; because the whole of real wealth, the world of real value and likewise the real conditions of its own realization [*Verwirklichung*] are posited opposite it as independent existences. As a consequence of the production process, the possibilities resting in living labour's own womb exist outside it as realities – but as *realities alien* to it, which form wealth in opposition to it.

In so far as the surplus product is realized anew as surplus capital, enters anew into the process of production and self-realization, it divides into (1) means of subsistence for the workers, to be exchanged for living labour capacity; let this part of *capital* be designated as *labour fund*; this labour fund, the part allotted for the maintenance of living labour capacity – and for its progressive maintenance, since surplus capital constantly grows – now likewise appears as the product of *alien* labour, labour alien to *capital*, as well as (2) its other component parts – the material conditions for the reproduction of a value = to these means of subsistence + a surplus value.

Further, if we consider this surplus capital, then the division of capital into a constant part – raw material and instrument with an antediluvian existence before labour – and a variable part, i.e. the necessary goods exchangeable for living labour capacity, appears as purely formal, in so far as both of them are equally

54. See p. 244, n. 21.

posited by labour and are equally posited by it as its own *presuppositions*. Now, however, this internal division of capital appears in such a way that labour's own product – objectified surplus labour – splits into two component parts – the objective conditions for new realization of labour (1), and a labour fund for maintaining the possibility of this living labour, i.e. of living labour capacity as alive (2), but in such a way that labour capacity can only re-appropriate that part of its own result – of its own being in objective form – which is designated as labour fund, can appropriate and extract this part from the form of the alien wealth which confronts it, only by reproducing not merely its own value, but by also realizing that part of the new capital which represents the objective conditions for the realization of new surplus labour and surplus production, or production of surplus values. Labour has itself created a new fund for the employment of new necessary labour, or, what is the same, a fund for the maintenance of new living labour capacities, of workers, but has created at the same time the condition that this fund can be employed only if new surplus labour is employed on the extra part of the surplus capital. Thus, the production by labour of this surplus capital – surplus value – is at the same time the creation of the real necessity of new surplus labour, and thus surplus capital is itself at the same time the real possibility both of new surplus labour and of new surplus capital. It here becomes evident that labour itself progressively extends and gives an ever wider and fuller existence to the objective world of wealth as a power alien to labour, so that, relative to the values created or to the real conditions of value-creation, the penurious subjectivity of living labour capacity forms an ever more glaring contrast. The greater the extent to which labour objectifies itself, the greater becomes the objective world of values, which stands opposite it as alien – alien property. With the creation of surplus capital, labour places itself under the compulsion to create yet further surplus capital etc. etc.

In regard to the original not-surplus capital, the relation has changed, as regards labour capacity, in so far as (1) the part of it which is exchanged for necessary labour has been reproduced by this labour itself, i.e. no longer comes to it out of circulation, but is its own product; and (2) that part of the value which, as raw material and instrument, represents the real conditions for the realization [*Verwertung*] of living labour, has been maintained by it itself in the production process; and, since every use value by its nature consists of transitory material, but since exchange value is present, exists, only in use value, therefore this maintenance = protection from decay and ruin, or negation of the transitory nature of the values owned by the capitalists; hence, this maintenance means to posit them as values for-themselves, as *indestructible wealth*. Hence, this original sum of values has been posited for the first time as capital in the production process, by living labour.

Formation of surplus capital I. – Surplus capital II. –
Inversion of the law of appropriation. – Chief result of the
production and realization process: the reproduction and new
production of the relation of capital and labour itself,
of capitalist and worker

Now, from the standpoint of capital: As regards the *surplus capital*, the capitalist represents value for-itself, money in its third moment, wealth, by means of simple *appropriation of alien labour*; since every moment of surplus capital, material, instrument, necessaries, resolves into *alien labour*, which the capitalist does not appropriate by means of *exchange* for existing values, but has appropriated *without exchange*. True, the exchange of a part of *values belonging to him*, or of *objectified labour* possessed by him, for alien living labour capacity, appears as the *original precondition* for this *surplus capital*. For the formation of *surplus capital I*, if we give that name to the surplus capital emerging from the original production process, i.e. for the *appropriation of alien labour*, of *objectified alien labour*, it appears as a condition that the capitalist should possess *values*, of which he *formally* exchanges one part for living labour capacity. We say formally, because living labour must replace and return to him these *exchanged* values as well. But be this as it may. In any case, it appears as a condition for the formation of surplus capital I, i.e. for the appropriation of alien labour or of the values in which it is objectified, that there must be an exchange of values belonging to the capitalist, thrown into circulation by him, and supplied to living labour capacity by him – of values which do *not* arise from his *exchange* with living labour, or not from his relation as *capital* to *labour*.

But now let us think of this surplus capital as having been thrown back into the production process, as realizing its surplus value anew in exchange, and as appearing anew as new surplus capital at the beginning of a third production process. This, *surplus capital II*, has different presuppositions from surplus capital I. The presupposition of surplus capital I was the existence of values belonging to the capitalist and thrown by him into circulation, or, more exactly, into the exchange with living labour capacity. The presupposition of surplus capital II is nothing more than the existence of surplus capital I; i.e. in other words, the presupposition that the capitalist has already appropriated alien labour without exchange. This puts him into a position where he is able to begin the process again and again. True, in order to create surplus capital II, he had to exchange a part of the value of surplus capital I in the form of means of subsistence for living labour capacity, but the values he gave in that exchange were not values which he originally put into circulation out of his own funds; they were, rather, objectified alien labour which he appropriated without giving any equivalent whatever, and which he now re-exchanges for alien living labour; in the same way, moreover, as the material etc. in which this new labour realizes itself and in which it creates surplus value have come into his hands without exchange, by mere appropriation. *The previous appropriation of alien labour now appears as the simple precondition for the new appropriation of alien labour*; or, his ownership of alien labour in objective (material) form, in the form of existing values, appears as the condition of his ability to appropriate new alien *living* labour capacity, hence surplus labour, labour without equivalent. The fact that he has previously confronted living labour as capital appears as the only condition required in order that he may not only maintain himself as capital, but also, as a growing capital, increasingly *appropriate* alien labour without equivalent; or, that he may extend his power, his existence as capital opposite living labour capacity, and on the other side constantly posit living labour capacity anew in its subjective, insubstantial penury as living labour capacity. Property – previous, or objectified, alien labour – appears as the only condition for further appropriation of present or living alien labour. In so far as surplus capital I was created by means of a simple exchange between objectified labour and living labour capacity – an exchange entirely based on the laws of the exchange of equivalents as measured by the quantity of labour or labour time contained in them – and *in so far as* the legal expression of this exchange presupposed nothing other than everyone's right of property over his own products, and of free disposition over them – but in so far as the relation of surplus capital II to I is therefore a consequence of this first relation – we see that, by a peculiar logic, the right of property undergoes a dialectical inversion [*dialektischer Umschlag*], so that on the side of capital it becomes the right to an alien product, or the right of property over alien labour, the right to appropriate alien labour without an equivalent, and, on the side of labour capacity, it becomes the duty to relate to one's own labour or to one's own product as to *alien property*. The right of property is inverted, to become, on the one side, the right to appropriate alien labour, and, on the other, the duty of respecting the product of one's own labour, and one's own labour itself, as values belonging to others. The exchange of equivalents, however, which appeared as the original operation, an operation to which the right of property gave legal expression, has become turned round in such a way that the exchange by one side is now only illusory, since the part of capital which is exchanged for living labour capacity, firstly, is itself *alien labour*, appropriated without equivalent, and, secondly, *has to be replaced with a surplus by living labour capacity*, is thus in fact not consigned away, but merely changed from one form into another. The relation of exchange has thus dropped away entirely, or is a *mere semblance*. Furthermore, the right of property originally appeared to be based on one's own labour. Property now appears as the right to alien labour, and as the impossibility of labour appropriating its own product. The complete separation between property, and, even more so, wealth, and labour, now appears as a consequence of the law which began with their identity.

Finally, the result of the process of production and realization is, above all, the reproduction and new production of the *relation of capital and labour itself*, of *capitalist and worker*. This social relation, production relation, appears in fact as an even more important result of the process than its material results. And more particularly, within this process the worker produces himself as labour capacity, as well as the capital confronting him, while at the same time the capitalist produces himself as capital as well as the living labour capacity confronting him. Each reproduces itself, by reproducing its other, its negation. The capitalist produces labour as alien; labour produces the product as alien. The capitalist produces the worker, and the worker the capitalist etc.

Original accumulation of capital. (*The real accumulation*). –
*Once developed historically, capital itself creates the conditions
of its existence* (*not as conditions for its arising, but as results
of its being*). – (*Performance of personal services, as opposed to
wage labour.*) – *Inversion of the law of appropriation. Real
alien relation* [Fremdheit] *of the worker to his product.
Division of labour. Machinery etc.*

Once production founded on capital is presupposed – money has
become transformed into capital actually only at the *end of the
first production* process, which resulted in its reproduction and in
the new production of surplus capital I; surplus capital I, however,
is itself *posited*, realized as surplus capital, only when it has produced surplus capital II, i.e. as soon as those presuppositions of
money, while it is in the process of passing over into capital,
which still lie outside the movement of *real* capital have vanished,
and when capital has therefore itself posited, and posited in
accordance with its immanent essence, the conditions which
form its point of departure in production – [then] the condition that the capitalist, in order to posit himself as capital,
must bring values into circulation which he created with his
own labour – or by some other means, excepting only already available, previous wage labour – belongs among the antediluvian conditions of capital, belongs to its *historic presuppositions*, which,
precisely as such *historic* presuppositions, are past and gone, and
hence belong to the *history of its formation*, but in no way to its
contemporary history, i.e. not to the real system of the mode of
production ruled by it. While e.g. the flight of serfs to the cities is
one of the *historic* conditions and presuppositions of urbanism,
it is not a *condition*, not a moment of the reality of developed cities,
but belongs rather to their *past* presuppositions, to the presuppositions of their becoming which are suspended in their being.
The conditions and presuppositions of the *becoming*, of the
arising, of capital presuppose precisely that it is not yet in being
but merely in *becoming*; they therefore disappear as real capital
arises, capital which itself, on the basis of its own reality, posits the
conditions for its realization. Thus e.g. while the process in which
money or value for-itself originally becomes capital presupposes
on the part of the capitalist an accumulation – perhaps by means
of savings garnered from products and values created by his
own labour etc., which he has undertaken as a *not-capitalist*, i.e.
while the presuppositions under which money becomes capital

appear as given, external *presuppositions* for the arising of capital –
[nevertheless,] as soon as capital has become capital as such, it
creates its own presuppositions, i.e. the possession of the real
conditions of the creation of new values *without exchange* – by
means of its own production process. These presuppositions, which
originally appeared as conditions of its becoming – and hence
could not spring from its *action as capital* – now appear as results
of its own realization, reality, as *posited by it* – *not as conditions
of its arising, but as results of its presence.* It no longer proceeds
from presuppositions in order to become, but rather it is itself
presupposed, and proceeds from itself to create the conditions
of its maintenance and growth. Therefore, the conditions which
preceded the creation of surplus capital I, or which express the
becoming of capital, do not fall into the sphere of that mode of
production for which capital serves as the presupposition; as
the historic preludes of its becoming, they lie behind it, just as the
processes by means of which the earth made the transition from a
liquid sea of fire and vapour to its present form now lie beyond its
life as finished earth. That is, individual capitals can continue to
arise e.g. by means of hoarding. But the hoard is transformed into
capital only by means of the exploitation of labour. The bourgeois
economists who regard capital as an eternal and *natural* (not
historical) form of production then attempt at the same time to
legitimize it again by formulating the conditions of its becoming
as the conditions of its contemporary realization; i.e. presenting the
moments in which the capitalist still appropriates as not-capitalist
– because he is still becoming – as the very conditions in which he
appropriates *as capitalist*. These attempts at apologetics demonstrate a guilty conscience, as well as the inability to bring the mode
of appropriation of capital as capital into harmony with the
general laws of property proclaimed by capitalist society itself.
On the other side, much more important for us is that our method
indicates the points where historical investigation must enter in,
or where bourgeois economy as a merely historical form of the
production process points beyond itself to earlier historical modes
of production. In order to develop the laws of bourgeois economy,
therefore, it is not necessary to write the *real history of the
relations of production.* But the correct observation and deduction
of these laws, as having themselves become[55] in history, always

55. Having themselves become = having themselves undergone the process
of becoming, as indicated on pp. 459–60.

leads to primary equations – like the empirical numbers e.g. in natural science – which point towards a past lying behind this system. These indications [*Andeutung*], together with a correct grasp of the present, then also offer the key to the understanding of the past – a work in its own right which, it is to be hoped, we shall be able to undertake as well.[56] This correct view likewise leads at the same time to the points at which the suspension of the present form of production relations gives signs of its becoming – foreshadowings of the future. Just as, on one side the pre-bourgeois phases appear as *merely historical*, i.e. suspended pre-suppositions, so do the contemporary conditions of production likewise appear as engaged in *suspending themselves* and hence in positing the *historic presuppositions* for a new state of society.

Now, if we initially examine the relation such as it has become, value having become capital, and living labour confronting it as mere use value, so that living labour appears as a mere means to realize objectified, dead labour, to penetrate it with an animating soul while losing its own soul to it – and having produced, as the end-product, alien wealth on one side and [, on the other,] the penury which is living labour capacity's sole possession – then the matter is simply this, that the process itself, in and by itself, posits the real objective conditions of living labour (namely, material in which to realize itself, instrument with which to realize itself, and necessaries with which to stoke the flame of living labour capacity, to protect it from being extinguished, to supply its vital processes with the necessary fuels) and posits them as alien, independent existences – or as the mode of existence of an *alien person*, as self-sufficient values for-themselves, and hence as values which form wealth alien to an isolated and subjective labour capacity, wealth of and for the capitalist. The objective conditions of living labour appear as *separated, independent* [*verselbständigte*] values opposite living labour capacity as subjective being, which therefore appears to them only as a value of *another kind* (not as value, but different from them, as use

56. On 22 February 1858, Marx wrote to Lassalle that he was planning three works: (1) a critique of the economic categories or the system of bourgeois economy critically presented, (2) a critique and history of political economy and socialism, and (3) a short historical sketch of the development of economic relations or categories (*Marx-Engels Selected Correspondence*, Moscow n.d., p. 125). Marx referred here to the third work, which he never produced in a completed form. Pages 459–514 of the present edition would no doubt have formed part of it.

value). Once this separation is given, the production process can only produce it anew, reproduce it, and reproduce it on an expanded scale. How it does this, we have seen. The objective conditions of living labour capacity are presupposed as having an existence independent of it, as the objectivity of a subject distinct from living labour capacity and standing independently over against it; the reproduction and *realization* [*Verwertung*], i.e. the expansion of these *objective conditions,* is therefore at the same time their own reproduction and new production as the wealth of an alien subject indifferently and independently standing over against labour capacity. What is reproduced and produced anew [*neuproduziert*] is not only the *presence* of these objective conditions of living labour, *but also their presence as independent values, i.e. values belonging to an alien subject, confronting this living labour capacity.* The objective conditions of labour attain a subjective existence *vis-à-vis* living labour capacity – capital turns into capitalist; on the other side, the merely subjective presence of the labour capacity confronted by its own conditions gives it a merely indifferent, objective form as against them – it is merely a *value* of a particular use value *alongside* the conditions of its own realization [*Verwertung*] as *values* of another use value. Instead of their being realized [*realisiert*] in the production process as the conditions of its realization [*Verwirklichung*], what happens is quite the opposite: it comes out of the process as mere condition for *their* realization [*Verwertung*] and preservation as values for-themselves opposite living labour capacity. The material on which it works is *alien* material; the instrument is likewise an *alien* instrument; its labour appears as a mere accessory to their substance and hence objectifies itself in things not *belonging to it.* Indeed, living labour itself appears as *alien vis-à-vis* living labour capacity, whose labour it is, whose own life's expression [*Lebensäusserung*] it is, for it has been surrendered to capital in exchange for objectified labour, for the product of labour itself. Labour capacity relates to its labour as to an alien, and if capital were willing to pay it *without* making it labour it would enter the bargain with pleasure. Thus labour capacity's own labour is as alien to it – and it really is, as regards its direction etc. – as are material and instrument. Which is why the product then appears to it as a combination of alien material, alien instrument and alien labour – as *alien property,* and why, after production, it has become poorer by the life forces expended, but otherwise begins the drudgery anew, existing as a mere subjective labour capacity separated from the conditions of its life. The recognition [*Erkennung*] of the products as its own, and the judgement that its separation from the conditions of its realization is improper – forcibly imposed – is an enormous [advance in] awareness [*Bewusstsein*], itself the product of the mode of production resting on capital, and as much the knell to its doom as, with the slave's awareness that he *cannot be the property of another*, with his consciousness of himself as a person, the existence of slavery becomes a merely artificial, vegetative existence, and ceases to be able to prevail as the basis of production.

However, if we consider the original relation, before the entry of money into the self-realization process, then various conditions appear which have to have arisen, or been given historically, for money to become capital and labour to become capital-positing, capital-creating labour, wage labour. (*Wage labour*, here, in the strict economic sense in which we use it here, and no other – and we will later have to distinguish it from other forms of labour for day-wages etc. – is capital-positing, capital-producing labour, i.e. living labour which produces both the objective conditions of its realization as an activity, as well as the objective moments of its being as labour *capacity*, and produces them as alien powers opposite itself, as *values for-themselves, independent of it*.) The essential conditions are themselves posited in the relation as it appears originally: (1) on the one side the presence of living labour capacity as a merely *subjective* existence, separated from the *conditions* of living labour as well as from the *means of existence, the necessary goods*, the means of self-preservation of living *labour capacity*; the living possibility of labour, on the one side, in this complete abstraction; (2) the value, or objectified labour, found on the other side, must be an accumulation of use values sufficiently large to furnish the objective conditions not only for the production of the products or values required to reproduce or maintain living labour capacity, but also for the absorption of surplus labour – to supply the objective material for the latter; (3) a free exchange relation – money circulation – between both sides; between the extremes a relation founded on exchange values – not on the master–servant relation – i.e., hence, production which does not directly furnish the producer with his necessaries, but which is mediated through exchange, and which cannot therefore usurp alien labour directly, but must buy it, exchange it, from the worker himself; finally (4) one side – the side representing the objective conditions of labour in the form of independent values for-themselves – must present itself as *value*, and must regard the positing of value, self-realization, money-making, as the ultimate purpose – not direct consumption or the creation of use value.

So long as *both* sides exchange their labour with one another in the form of *objectified* labour, the relation is impossible; it is likewise impossible if *living labour capacity* itself appears as the property of the other side, hence as not engaged in exchange. (The fact that slavery is possible at individual points within the bourgeois system of production does not contradict this. However, slavery is then possible there only because it does not exist at other points; and appears as an anomaly opposite the bourgeois system itself.)

The conditions under which the relation appears at the origin, or which appear as the historic presuppositions of its becoming, reveal at first glance a two-sided character – on one side, dissolution of lower forms of living labour; on the other, dissolution of happier forms of the same.

The first presupposition, to begin with, is that the relation of slavery or serfdom has been suspended. Living labour capacity belongs to itself, and has disposition over the expenditure of its forces, through exchange. Both sides confront each other as persons. *Formally*, their relation has the equality and freedom of exchange as such. As far as concerns the legal relation, the fact that this form is a mere *semblance*, and a *deceptive semblance*, appears as an *external* matter. What the free worker sells is always nothing more than a specific, particular measure of force-expenditure [*Kraftäusserung*]; labour capacity as a totality is greater than every particular expenditure. He sells the particular expenditure of force to a particular capitalist, whom he confronts as an independent *individual*. It is clear that this is not his relation to the existence of capital as capital, i.e. to the capitalist class. Nevertheless, in this way everything touching on the individual, real person leaves him a wide field of choice, of arbitrary will, and hence of formal freedom. In the slave relation, he belongs to the *individual, particular* owner, and is his labouring machine. As a totality of force-expenditure, as labour capacity, he is a thing [*Sache*] belonging to another, and hence does not relate as subject to his particular expenditure of force, nor to the act of living labour. In the serf relation he appears as a moment of property in land itself, is an appendage of the soil, exactly like draught-cattle. In the slave relation the worker is nothing but a living labour-machine, which therefore has a value for others, or rather is a value. The totality of the free worker's labour capacity appears to him as his property, as one of his moments, over which he, as subject, exercises domination, and which he maintains by expending it. This to be developed later under wage labour.

The exchange of objectified labour for living labour does not yet constitute either capital on one side or wage labour on the other. The entire class of so-called *services* from the bootblack up to the king falls into this category. Likewise the free day-labourer, whom we encounter sporadically in all places where either the oriental community [*Gemeinwesen*] or the western commune [*Gemeinde*] consisting of free landowners dissolves into individual elements – as a consequence of increase of population, release of prisoners of war, accidents by which the individual is impoverished and loses the objective conditions of his self-sustaining labour, owing to division of labour etc. If A exchanges a value or money, i.e. objectified labour, in order to obtain a service from B, i.e. living labour, then this can belong:

(1) *within the relation of simple circulation*. Both in fact exchange only use values with one another; one exchanges necessaries, the other labour, a service which the other wants to consume, either directly – personal service – or he furnishes him the material etc. from which, with his labour, with the objectification of his labour, he makes a use value, a use value designed for A's consumption. For example, when the peasant takes a wandering tailor, of the kind that existed in times past, into his house, and gives him the material to make clothes with. Or if I give money to a doctor to patch up my health. What is important in these cases is the service which both do for one another. *Do ut facias* here appears on quite the same level as *facio ut des*, or *do ut des*.[57] The man who takes the cloth I supplied to him and makes me an article of clothing out of it gives me a use value. But instead of giving it directly in objective form, he gives it in the form of activity. I give him a completed use value; he completes another for me. The difference between previous, objectified labour and living, present labour here appears as a merely formal difference

57. *Do ut facias*: I give that you may do; *facio ut des*: I do that you may give; *do ut des*: I give that you may give. (Roman law.)

between the different tenses of labour, at one time in the perfect and at another in the present. It appears in fact as a merely formal difference, a difference mediated by division of labour and by exchange, whether B himself produces the necessaries on which he has to subsist, or whether he obtains them from A and, instead of producing the necessaries himself, produces an article of clothing, in exchange for which he obtains them from A. In both cases he can take possession of the use value possessed by A only by giving him an equivalent for it; which, in the last analysis, always resolves itself into his own living labour, regardless of the objective form it may adopt, whether before the exchange is concluded, or as a consequence of it. Now, the article of clothing not only contains a specific, form-giving labour – a specific form of usefulness imparted to the cloth by the movement of labour – but it contains also a certain quantity of labour – hence not only use value, but *value* generally, *value* as such. But this value does not exist for A, since he consumes the article, and is not a clothes-dealer. He has therefore bought the labour not as *value-positing* labour, but as an activity which creates utility, use value. In the case of personal services, this use value is consumed as such without making the transition from the form of movement [*Bewegung*] into the form of the object [*Sache*]. If, as is frequently the case in simple relations, the performer of the service does not obtain *money*, but direct use values themselves, then it no longer even seems as if *value* were being dealt in on one or the other side; merely use values. But even given that A pays money for the service, this is not a transformation of his money into capital, but rather the positing of his money as mere medium of circulation, in order to obtain an object for consumption, a specific use value. This act is for that reason not an act which produces wealth, but the opposite, one which consumes wealth. The point for A is not the objectification in the cloth of labour as such, of a certain amount of labour time, hence *value*, but rather the satisfaction of a certain need. Here A sees his money not *realized* but *devalued* in its transposition from the form of value into that of use value. Labour is here exchanged not as use value for value, but as itself a particular use value, as value for use. The more frequently A repeats the exchange, the poorer does he become. This exchange is not an *act of wealth-getting* for him, not an act of *value creation*, but of *devaluation* of the values he has in hand, in his possession. The money which A here exchanges for living labour – service in kind, or service objectified in a thing – is not *capital* but revenue, money as a medium of circulation in order to obtain use value, money in which the form of value is posited as merely vanishing, not money which will preserve and realize itself as such through the acquisition of labour. Exchange of *money as revenue*, as a mere medium of circulation, for living labour, can never posit money as capital, nor, therefore, labour as wage labour in the economic sense. A lengthy disquisition is not required to show that to consume (spend) money is not the same as to produce money. In situations in which the greatest part of surplus labour appears as agricultural labour, and where the owner of the land therefore appears as owner both of surplus labour and of the surplus product, it is the revenue of the owner of the land which forms the labour fund for the free worker, for the worker in manufactures (here, hand crafts) as opposed to the agricultural labourers. The exchange with them[58] is a form of the consumption of the owner of the land – he divides another part of his revenue directly – for personal services, often only the illusion of services, with a heap of retainers. In Asiatic societies, where the monarch appears as the exclusive proprietor of the agricultural surplus product, whole cities arise, which are at bottom nothing more than wandering encampments, from the exchange of his revenue with the 'free hands', as Steuart calls them.[59] There is nothing of wage labour in this relation, but it *can* stand in opposition to slavery and serfdom, though *need* not do so, for it always repeats itself under various forms of the overall organization of labour. To the extent that *money* mediates this exchange the determination of prices will become important on both sides, but it will do so for A only in so far as he does not want to pay too much for the *use value* of the labour; not in so far as he is concerned with its *value*. The essence of the relation remains unchanged even if this price, which begins as conventional and traditional, is thereafter increasingly determined economically, first by the relation of demand and supply, finally by the production costs at which the vendors themselves of these living services can be produced; nothing is essentially changed thereby, because the determination of prices remains a merely formal moment for the exchange of mere use values, as before. This determination itself, however, is created by other relations,

58. That is, with the free workers in manufactures (hand crafts).
59. Steuart, *An Inquiry*, Vol. I, p. 40.

by the general laws and the self-determination of the ruling mode of production, acting, as it were, behind the back of this particular act of exchange. One of the forms in which this kind of pay [*Besoldung*] first appears in the old communities is where an *army* is maintained. The pay [*Sold*] of the common soldier is also reduced to a minimum – determined purely by the production costs necessary to procure him. But he exchanges the performance of his services not for *capital*, but for the revenue of the state.

In bourgeois society itself, all exchange of personal services for revenue – including labour for personal consumption, cooking, sewing etc., garden work etc., up to and including all of the unproductive classes, civil servants, physicians, lawyers, scholars etc. – belongs under this rubric, within this category. All menial servants etc. By means of their services – often coerced – all these workers, from the least to the highest, obtain for themselves a share of the surplus product, of the capitalist's *revenue*. But it does not occur to anyone to think that by means of the exchange of his revenue for such services, i.e. through private consumption, the capitalist posits himself as capitalist. Rather, he thereby spends the fruits of his capital. It does not change the nature of the relation that the proportions in which revenue is exchanged for this kind of living labour are themselves determined by the general laws of production.

As we have already mentioned in the section on *money*,[60] it is here rather the performer of the service who actually posits *value*; who transposes a use value – a certain kind of labour, service etc. – into *value, money*. Hence in the Middle Ages, those who are oriented towards the production and accumulation of money proceed partly not from the side of the consuming landed nobility, but quite the opposite, from the side of living labour; they accumulate and thus become capitalists, δυνάμει, for a later period. The emancipated serf becomes, in part, the capitalist.

It thus does not depend on the general relation, but rather on the natural, particular quality of the service performed, whether the recipient of payment receives it as day-wages, or as an honorarium, or as a sinecure – and whether he appears as superior or inferior in rank to the person paying for the service. However, with the presupposition of capital as the dominant power, all these relations become more or less *dishonoured*. But this does not

60. Marx did not in fact mention this in the Chapter on Money but rather on pp. 272–3, in the Chapter on Capital.

belong here yet – this *demystification* [*Entgötterung*] of personal services, regardless of the lofty character with which tradition may have poetically endowed them.

It is not, then, simply the exchange of *objectified labour* for *living* labour – which appear, from this standpoint, as two different aspects, as use values in different forms, the one objective, the other subjective – which constitutes capital and hence wage labour, but rather, the exchange of objectified labour as *value*, as self-sufficient value, for living labour as *its* use value, as use value not for a specific, particular use or consumption, but as use value for *value*.

In the exchange of money for labour or service, with the aim of direct consumption, a real exchange always takes place; the fact that *amounts of labour* are exchanged on both sides is of merely *formal* interest for measuring the *particular* forms of the utility of labour by comparing them with each other. This concerns only the *form* of the exchange; but does not form its *content*. In the exchange of capital for labour, *value* is not a measure for the exchange of two use values, but is rather the *content of the exchange* itself.

(2) In periods of the dissolution of *pre-bourgeois* relations, there sporadically occur free workers whose services are bought for purposes not of consumption, but of *production*; but, *firstly*, even if on a large scale, for the production only of *direct* use values, not of *values*; and *secondly*, if a nobleman e.g. brings the free worker together with his serfs, even if he re-sells a part of the worker's product, and the free worker thus creates *value* for him, then this exchange takes place only for the superfluous [product] and only for the sake of superfluity, for *luxury consumption*; is thus at bottom only a veiled purchase of alien labour for immediate consumption or as use value. Incidentally, wherever these free workers increase in number, and where this relation grows, there the old mode of production – commune, patriarchal, feudal etc. – is in the process of dissolution, and the elements of real wage labour are in preparation. But these free servants [*Knechte*] can also emerge, as e.g. in Poland etc., and vanish again, without a change in the mode of production taking place.

⟨In order to express the relations into which capital and wage labour enter as *property relations* or *laws*, we need do no more than express the conduct of both sides in the *realization process* as an *appropriation process*. For example, the fact that surplus labour is posited as surplus value of capital means that the worker does not appropriate the product of his own labour; that it appears to him as *alien property*; inversely, that *alien labour* appears as the property of capital. This second law of bourgeois property, the inversion of the first – which, through laws of inheritance etc., attains an existence independent of the accidental transitoriness of individual capitalists – becomes just as established in law as the first. The first is the identity of labour with property; the second, labour as negated property, or property as negation of the alien quality of alien labour. In fact, in the production process of capital, as will be seen more closely in its further development, labour is a totality – a combination of labours – whose individual component parts are alien to one another, so that the overall process as a totality is *not* the *work* of the individual worker, and is furthermore the work of the different workers together only to the extent that they are [forcibly] combined, and do not [voluntarily] enter into combination with one another. The combination of this labour appears just as subservient to and led by an alien will and an alien intelligence – having its *animating unity* elsewhere – as its material unity appears subordinate to the *objective unity* of the *machinery*, of fixed capital, which, as *animated monster*, objectifies the scientific idea, and is in fact the coordinator, does not in any way relate to the individual worker as his instrument; but rather he himself exists as an animated individual punctuation mark, as its living isolated accessory. Thus, combined labour is combination *in-itself* in a double way; not combination as a mutual relation among the individuals working together, nor as their predominance either over their particular or individual function or over the instrument of labour. Hence, just as the worker relates to the product of his labour as an alien thing, so does he relate to the combination of labour as an alien combination, as well as to his own labour as an expression of his life, which, although it belongs to him, is alien to him and coerced from him, and which A. Smith etc. therefore conceives as a *burden, sacrifice* etc.[61] Labour itself, like its product, is *negated as the labour of the particular, isolated worker*. This isolated labour, negated, is now indeed communal or combined labour, posited. The *communal or combined labour* posited in this way – as activity and in the passive, objective form – is however at the same time posited as an other towards the really existing individual labour – as an *alien objectivity* (alien property) as well as an *alien subjectivity* (of capital). Capital thus represents both labour and

61. Adam Smith, *Wealth of Nations*, Vol. I, pp. 104–5.

its product as negated individualized labour and hence as the negated property of the individualized worker. Capital therefore is the existence of social labour – the combination of labour as subject as well as object – but this existence as itself existing independently opposite its real moments – hence itself a *particular* existence apart from them. For its part, capital therefore appears as the predominant subject and owner of *alien labour*, and its relation is itself as complete a contradiction as is that of wage labour.⟩

Forms which precede capitalist production. (Concerning the process which precedes the formation of the capital relation or of original accumulation)

A presupposition of wage labour, and one of the historic preconditions for capital, is free labour and the exchange of this free labour for money, in order to reproduce and to realize money, to consume the use value of labour not for individual consumption, but as use value for money. Another presupposition is the separation of free labour from the objective conditions of its realization – from the means of labour and the material for labour. Thus, above all, release of the worker from the soil as his natural workshop – hence dissolution of small, free landed property as well as of communal landownership resting on the oriental commune. In both forms, the worker relates to the objective conditions of his labour as to his property; this is the natural unity of labour with its material [*sachlich*] presuppositions. The worker thus has an objective existence independent of labour. The individual relates to himself as proprietor, as master of the conditions of his reality. He relates to the others in the same way and – depending on whether this *presupposition* is posited as proceeding from the community or from the individual families which constitute the commune – he relates to the others as co-proprietors, as so many incarnations of the common property, or as independent proprietors like himself, independent private proprietors – beside whom the previously all-absorbing and all-predominant communal property is itself posited as a particular *ager publicus*[62] alongside the many private landowners.

In both forms, the individuals relate not as workers but as proprietors – and members of a community, who at the same time work. The aim of this work is not the *creation of value* – although they may do surplus labour in order to obtain *alien*, i.e. surplus

62. State property.

products in exchange – rather, its aim is sustenance of the individual proprietor and of his family, as well as of the total community. The positing of the individual as a *worker*, in this nakedness, is itself a product of *history*.

In the first form of this landed property, an initial, naturally arisen spontaneous [*naturwüchsiges*] community appears as first presupposition. Family, and the family extended as a clan [*Stamm*],[63] or through intermarriage between families, or combination of clans. Since we may assume that *pastoralism*, or more generally a *migratory* form of life, was the first form of the mode of existence, not that the clan settles in a specific site, but that it grazes off what it finds – humankind is not settlement-prone by nature (except possibly in a natural environment so especially fertile that they sit like monkeys on a tree; else roaming like the animals) – then the *clan community*, the natural community, appears not as a *result* of, but as a *presupposition for the communal appropriation* (temporary) *and utilization of the land*. When they finally do settle down, the extent to which this original community is modified will depend on various external, climatic, geographic, physical etc. conditions as well as on their particular natural predisposition – their clan character. This naturally arisen clan community, or, if one will, pastoral society, is the first presupposition – the communality [*Gemeinschaftlichkeit*] of blood, language, customs – for the *appropriation of the objective conditions* of their life, and of their life's reproducing and objectifying activity (activity as herdsmen, hunters, tillers etc.). The earth is the great workshop, the arsenal which furnishes both means and material of labour, as well as the seat, the *base* of the community. They relate naïvely to it as the *property of the community*, of the community producing and reproducing itself in living labour. Each individual conducts himself only as a link, as a member of this community as *proprietor* or *possessor*. The *real appropriation* through the labour process happens under these *presuppositions*, which are not themselves the *product* of labour, but appear as its natural or *divine* presuppositions. This form, with the same land-relation as its foundation, can realize itself in very different ways. E.g. it is not in the least a contradiction to it that, as in most of the *Asiatic* landforms, the *comprehensive unity* standing above all these little communities appears as the higher *proprietor* or as the *sole proprietor*;

63. The word *Stamm* here refers broadly to any extended kinship grouping; e.g. clan, tribe, *gens*, etc.

the real communities hence only as *hereditary* possessors. Because the *unity* is the real proprietor and the real presupposition of communal property, it follows that this unity can appear as a *particular* entity above the many real particular communities, where the individual is then in fact propertyless, or, property – i.e. the relation of the individual to the *natural* conditions of labour and of reproduction as belonging to him, as the objective, nature-given inorganic body of his subjectivity – appears mediated for him through a cession by the total unity – a unity realized in the form of the despot, the father of the many communities – to the individual, through the mediation of the particular commune. The surplus product – which is, incidentally, determined by law in consequence of the real appropriation through labour – thereby automatically belongs to this highest unity. Amidst oriental despotism and the propertylessness which seems legally to exist there, this clan or communal property exists in fact as the founda- tion, created mostly by a combination of manufactures and agri- culture within the small commune, which thus becomes altogether self-sustaining, and contains all the conditions of reproduction and surplus production within itself. A part of their surplus labour belongs to the higher community, which exists ultimately as a *person*, and this surplus labour takes the form of tribute etc., as well as of common labour for the exaltation of the unity, partly of the real despot, partly of the imagined clan-being, the god. Now, in so far as it actually realizes itself in labour, this kind of com- munal property can appear either in the form where the little com- munes vegetate independently alongside one another, and where, inside them, the individual with his family work independently on the lot assigned to them (a certain amount of labour for the *communal reserves, insurance* so to speak, and to *meet the ex- penses of the community as such*, i.e. for war, religion etc.; this is the first occurrence of the lordly *dominium* in the most original sense, e.g. in the Slavonic communes, in the Rumanian etc. There- in lies the transition to villeinage [*Frondienst*] etc.); or the unity may extend to the communality of labour itself, which may be a formal system, as in Mexico, Peru especially, among the early Celts, a few clans of India. The communality can, further, appear within the clan system more in a situation where the unity is re- presented in a chief of the clan-family, or as the relation of the patriarchs among one another. Depending on that, a more despotic or a more democratic form of this community system. The communal conditions of real appropriation through labour, *aqueducts*, very important among the Asiatic peoples; means of communication etc. then appear as the work of the higher unity – of the despotic regime hovering over the little communes. Cities proper here form alongside these villages only at exceptionally good points for external trade; or where the head of the state and his satraps exchange their revenue (surplus product) for labour, spend it as labour-fund.

The second form – and like the first it has essential modifications brought about locally, historically etc. – product of more active, historic life, of the fates and modifications of the original clans – also assumes the *community* as its first presupposition, but not, as in the first case, as the substance of which the individuals are mere accidents, or of which they form purely natural component parts – it presupposes as base not the countryside, but the town as an already created seat (centre) of the rural population (owners of land). The cultivated field here appears as a *territorium* belonging to the town; not the village as mere accessory to the land. The earth in itself – regardless of the obstacles it may place in the way of working it, really appropriating it – offers no resistance to [attempts to] relate to it as the inorganic nature of the living individual, as his workshop, as the means and object of labour and the means of life for the subject. The difficulties which the commune encounters can arise only from other communes, which have either previously occupied the land and soil, or which disturb the commune in its own occupation. War is therefore the great comprehensive task, the great communal labour which is required either to occupy the objective conditions of being there alive, or to protect and perpetuate the occupation. Hence the commune consisting of families initially organized in a warlike way – as a system of war and army, and this is one of the conditions of its being there as proprietor. The concentration of residences in the town, basis of this bellicose organization. The clan system in itself leads to higher and lower ancestral lineages [*Geschlechtern*],[64] a distinction which is still further developed through intermixture with subjugated clans etc. Communal property – as state property, *ager publicus* – here separated from private property. The property [*Eigentum*] of the individual is here not, unlike the first case,

64. *Geschlechter* may also refer to the sexes, linguistic groups, generations, etc. It is not entirely certain which of these distinctions Marx had foremost in mind here.

itself directly communal property; where it is, the individual has no property as distinct from the commune, but rather is merely its possessor [*Besitzer*]. The less it is the case that the individual's property can in fact be realized solely through communal labour – thus e.g. the aqueducts in the Orient – the more the purely naturally arisen, spontaneous character of the clan has been broken by historic movement, migration; the more, further, the clan removes itself from its original seat and occupies *alien* ground, hence enters into essentially new conditions of labour, and develops the energy of the individual more – its common character appearing, necessarily, more as a negative unity towards the outside – the more, therefore, are the conditions given under which the individual can become a *private proprietor* of land and soil – of a particular plot – whose particular cultivation falls to him and his family. The commune – as state – is, on one side, the relation of these free and equal private proprietors to one another, their bond against the outside, and is at the same time their safeguard. The commune here rests as much on the fact that its members consist of working landed proprietors, small-owning peasants, as the peasants' independence rests on their mutual relations as commune members, on protection of the *ager publicus* for communal needs and communal glory etc. Membership in the commune remains the presupposition for the appropriation of land and soil, but, as a member of the commune, the individual is a private proprietor. He relates to his private property as land and soil, but at the same time as to his being as commune member; and his own sustenance as such is likewise the sustenance of the commune, and conversely etc. The commune, although already a *product of history* here, not only in fact but also known as such, and therefore *possessing an origin*, is the presupposition of *property* in land and soil – i.e. of the relation of the working subject to the natural presuppositions of labour as belonging to him – but this belonging [is] mediated by his being a member of the state, by the being of the state – hence by a *presupposition* regarded as divine etc.[65] Concentration in the town, with the land as *territorium*; small agriculture working for direct consumption; manufacture as domestic side occupation of wives and daughters (spinning and weaving) or, independently, in

65. This is one possible reconstruction of the sentence beginning 'The commune', which has a number of grammatical loose ends in the original. Two other possible variants are presented in *Pre-Capitalist Economic Formations*, tr. J. Cohen, London, 1964, p. 73.

individual branches only (*fabri*[66] etc.). The presupposition of the survival of the community is the preservation of equality among its free self-sustaining peasants, and their own labour as the condition of the survival of their property. They relate as proprietors to the natural conditions of labour; but these conditions must also constantly be posited as real conditions and objective elements of the personality of the individual, by means of personal labour. On the other side, the tendency of this small bellicose community system drives beyond these barriers etc. (Rome, Greece, Jews etc.). 'When the auguries', Niebuhr says, 'had assured Numa of the divine sanction of his election, the pious king's first concern was not worship at the temple, but a human one. He divided the lands which Romulus had won in war and given over to occupation: he endowed the order of Terminus. All the law-givers of antiquity, Moses above all, founded their success in commanding virtue, integrity and proper custom on landed property, or at least on secured, hereditary possession of land, for the greatest possible number of citizens.' (Vol. I, 245, 2nd edition. *Röm. Gesch.*)[67] The individual is placed in such conditions of earning his living as to make not the acquiring of wealth his object, but self-sustenance, his own reproduction as a member of the community; the reproduction of himself as proprietor of the parcel of ground, and, in that quality, as a member of the commune. The survival of the commune is the reproduction of all of its members as self-sustaining peasants, whose surplus time belongs precisely to the commune, the work of war etc. The property in one's own labour is mediated by property in the condition of labour – the hide of land, guaranteed in its turn by the existence of the commune, and that in turn by surplus labour in the form of military service etc. by the commune members. It is not cooperation in wealth-producing labour by means of which the commune member reproduces himself, but rather cooperation in labour for the communal interests (imaginary and real), for the upholding of the association inwardly and outwardly. Property is *quiritorium*,[68] of the Roman variety; the private proprietor of land is such only as a Roman, but as a Roman he is a private proprietor of land.

A[nother] form of the property of working individuals, self-

66. Craftsmen, workers.
67. Georg Niebuhr, *Römische Geschichte. Erster Theil. Zweyte, völlig umgearbeitete, Ausgabe*, Berlin, 1827, p. 245.
68. The property of the *quirites*, i.e. the Romans.

sustaining members of the community, in the natural conditions of their labour, is the *Germanic*. Here the commune member is neither, as such, a co-possessor of the communal property, as in the specifically oriental form (wherever property exists *only* as communal property, there the individual member is as such only *possessor* of a particular part, hereditary or not, since any fraction of the property belongs to no member for himself, but to him only as immediate member of the commune, i.e. as in direct unity with it, not in distinction to it. This individual is thus only a possessor. What exists is only *communal* property, and only *private possession*. The mode of this possession in relation to the communal property may be historically, locally etc. modified in quite different ways, depending on whether labour itself is performed by the private possessor in isolation, or is in turn determined by the commune or by the unity hovering above the particular commune); nor is the situation such as obtains in the Roman, Greek form (in short, the form of classical antiquity) – in this case, the land is occupied by the commune, Roman land; a part remains to the commune as such as distinct from the commune members, *ager publicus* in its various forms; the other part is divided up and each parcel of land is Roman by virtue of being the private property, the domain of a Roman, the part of the *laboratorium* belonging to him; but, also, he is a Roman only in so far as he possesses this sovereign right over a part of the Roman earth. ⟨In antiquity, urban occupation and trade little esteemed, agriculture, however, highly; in the Middle Ages the contrary appraisal.⟩ ⟨The right of *using* the communal land through *possession* originally appertained to the patricians, who then granted it to their clients; the *transfer of property* out of the *ager publicus* appertained exclusively to the plebeians; all assignments in favour of the plebeians and compensation for a share of the communal property. *Actual property in land*, excepting the area around the city walls, originally only in the hands of the plebeians (rural communes included later.)⟩ ⟨Basis of the Roman plebs as a totality of agriculturists, as is indicated in their quiritary property. Antiquity unanimously esteemed agriculture as the *proper occupation* of the free man, the soldier's school. In it the ancestral stock of the nation sustains itself; it changes in the cities, where alien merchants and dealers settle, just as the indigenous move where gain entices them. Wherever there is slavery, the freedman seeks his support in such dealings, in which he then often gathers riches: thus these occupations were mostly in their hands in antiquity, and were therefore not proper for a citizen: hence the opinion that admission of the craftsmen to full citizenship rights would be a risky undertaking (among the earlier Greeks they were as a rule excluded). 'οὐδενὶ γὰρ ἐξῆν Ῥωμαίων οὔτε κάπηλον οὔτε χειροτέχνην βίον ἔχειν.'[69] Antiquity had no inkling of a privileged guild-system such as prevailed in the history of medieval cities; and already here the martial spirit declined as the guilds defeated the aristocratic lineages, and was finally extinguished altogether; and consequently, with it, the cities' external respect and freedom.⟩ ⟨The clans of the ancient states were founded on two different principles, either on *ancestry* [*Geschlecht*] or on the *locality*. The *ancestral clans* preceded the locality clans in time and are almost everywhere pushed aside by the latter. Their most extreme, strictest form is the caste-order, in which one is separated from the other, without the right of inter-marriage, quite different in [degree of] privilege; each with an ex-clusive, irrevocable occupation. The *locality clans* originally corre-sponded to a partition of the countryside into districts and villages; so that someone residing in a given village at the time of this partition, in Attica under Cleisthenes, was registered as a *demotes* (villager) of that village, and as a member of the *phylon* (tribe) of the village's region. Now, his descendants, as a rule, re-mained in the same *phylon* and the same *demos* without regard to their residence; whereby this partition also took on an ancestral appearance.⟩ ⟨These Roman *gens* not blood relatives; to the com-munal name, Cicero adds descent from free men as a sign. Com-munal *sacra* (shrines) for the Roman gentiles; later ceased (already in Cicero's time). Practice of co-gentile inheritance, in cases with-out dependents or will, survived longest of all. In the earliest periods, obligation of all members of the *gens* to help those of their own who require this, to carry unaccustomed burdens. (This occurs originally everywhere among the Germans, remains longest among the Dithmarschen.) The *gentes*, corporations [*Innungen*]. There was in the world of antiquity no more general institution than that of kin groups. Thus among the Gaels the noble Camp-bells and their vassals forming one clan.⟩[70] Since the patrician

69. 'No Roman citizen was permitted to earn a livelihood as a tradesman or artisan' (Dionysius of Halicarnassus. *Roman Antiquities*, Bk IV, Ch. 25).

70. The passages in pointed brackets, on pp. 477–8, are taken from Niebuhr's *Römische Geschichte. Erster Theil*, and in this order: (1) p. 148; (2) pp. 435–6; (3) pp. 614–15 and footnotes 1224 and 1225; (4) pp. 317–18; (5) pp. 326–35.

represents the community in a higher degree, he is the *possessor* of the *ager publicus* and uses it through his clients etc. (and also appropriates it little by little). The Germanic commune is not concentrated in the town; by means of such a concentration – the town as centre of rural life, residence of the agricultural workers, likewise the centre of warfare – the commune as such would have a merely outward existence, distinct from that of the individual. The history of classical antiquity is the history of cities, but of cities founded on landed property and on agriculture; Asiatic history is a kind of indifferent unity of town and countryside (the really large cities must be regarded here merely as royal camps, as works of artifice [*Superfötation*] erected over the economic construction proper); the Middle Ages (Germanic period) begins with the land as the seat of history, whose further development then moves forward in the contradiction between town and countryside; the modern [age] is the urbanization of the countryside, not ruralization of the city as in antiquity.

NOTEBOOK V

22 January –
Beginning of February 1858

The Chapter on Capital (continuation)

With its coming-together in the city, the commune possesses an economic existence as such; the city's mere *presence,* as such, distinguishes it from a mere multiplicity of independent houses. The whole, here, consists not merely of its parts. It is a kind of independent organism. Among the Germanic tribes, where the individual family chiefs settled in the forests, long distances apart, the commune exists, already from *outward* observation, only in the periodic gathering-together [*Vereinigung*] of the commune members, although their unity-*in-itself* is posited in their ancestry, language, common past and history, etc. The *commune* thus appears as a *coming-together* [*Vereinigung*], not as a *being-together* [*Verein*]; as a unification made up of independent subjects, landed proprietors, and not as a unity. The commune therefore does not in fact exist as a *state* or *political body*, as in classical antiquity, because it does not exist as a *city*. For the commune to come into real existence, the free landed proprietors have to hold a *meeting*, whereas e.g. in Rome it *exists* even apart from these assemblies in the existence of the *city itself* and of the officials presiding over it etc. True, the *ager publicus,* the communal or people's land, as distinct from individual property, also occurs among the Germanic tribes. It takes the form of hunting land, grazing land, timber land etc., the part of the land which cannot be divided if it is to serve as means of production in this specific form. But this *ager publicus* does not appear, as with the Romans e.g., as the particular economic presence of the state as against the private proprietors, so that these latter are actually *private* proprietors as such, in so far as they are *excluded*, deprived, like the plebeians, from using the *ager publicus*. Among the Germanic tribes, the *ager publicus* appears rather merely as a complement to individual property, and figures as property only to the extent that it is defended militarily as the common property of one tribe against a hostile tribe. Individual property does not appear mediated by the commune; rather, the existence of the commune and of communal property appear as mediated by, i.e. as a relation of, the independent subjects to one another. The economic totality is, at bottom, contained in each individual household, which forms an independent centre of production for itself (manufactures purely as domestic secondary task for women etc.). In the world of antiquity, the city with its territory is the economic totality; in the Germanic world, the totality is the ind vi¹ual residence, which itself appears as only a small dot on the l₎ nd belonging to it, and which is not a concentration of many proprietors, but the family as independent unit. In the Asiatic form (at least, predominantly), the individual has no property but only possession; the real proprietor, proper, is the commune – hence property only as *communal property* in land. In antiquity (Romans as the most classic example, the thing in its purest, most fully developed form), the form of state property in land and that of private property in land [are] antithetical, so that the latter is mediated by the former, or the former itself exists in this double form. The private proprietor of land hence at the same time urban citizen. Urban citizenship resolves itself economically into the simple form that the agriculturist [is a] resident of a city. In the Germanic form, the agriculturist not citizen of a state, i.e. not inhabitant of a city; [the] basis [is] rather the isolated, independent family residence, guaranteed by the bond with other such family residences of the same tribe, and by their occasional coming-together [*Zusammenkommen*] to pledge each others' allegiance in war, religion, adjudication etc. Individual landed property here appears neither as a form antithetical to the commune's landed property, nor as mediated by it, but just the contrary. The commune exists only in the interrelations among these individual landed proprietors as such. Communal property as such appears only as a communal accessory to the individual tribal seats and the land they appropriate. The commune is neither the substance of which the individual appears as a mere accident; nor is it a generality with a *being and unity* as such [*seiende Einheit*] either in the mind and in the existence of the city and of its civic needs as distinct from those of the individual, or in its civic land and soil as its particular presence as distinct from the particular economic presence of the commune member; rather, the commune, on the one side, is presupposed in-itself prior to the individual proprietors as a communality of language, blood etc., but it exists as a presence, on the other hand, only in its *real assembly* for communal purposes; and to the extent that it has a particular economic existence in the hunting and grazing lands for communal use, it is so used by each individual proprietor as such, not as representative of the state (as in Rome); it is really the common property of the individual proprietors, not of the union of these proprietors endowed with an existence separate from themselves, the city itself.

The main point here is this: In all these forms – in which landed property and agriculture form the basis of the economic order, and where the economic aim is hence the production of use values, i.e. the *reproduction of the individual* within the specific relation to the commune in which he is its basis – there is to be found: (1) Appropriation not through labour, but presupposed to labour; appropriation of the natural conditions of labour, of the *earth* as the original instrument of labour as well as its workshop and repository of raw materials. The individual relates simply to the objective conditions of labour as being his; [relates] to them as the inorganic nature of his subjectivity, in which the latter realizes itself; the chief objective condition of labour does not itself appear as a *product* of labour, but is already there as *nature*; on one side the living individual, on the other the earth, as the objective condition of his reproduction; (2) but this *relation* to land and soil, to the earth, as the property of the labouring individual – who thus appears from the outset not merely as labouring individual, in this abstraction, but who has an *objective mode of existence* in his ownership of the land, an existence *presupposed* to his activity, and not merely as a result of it, a presupposition of his activity just like his skin, his sense organs, which of course he also reproduces and develops etc. in the life process, but which are nevertheless presuppositions of this process of his reproduction – is instantly mediated by the naturally arisen, spontaneous, more or less historically developed and modified presence of the individual as *member of a commune* – his naturally arisen presence as member of a tribe etc. An isolated individual could no more have property in land and soil than he could speak. He could, of course, live off it as substance, as do the animals. The relation to the earth as property is always mediated through the occupation of the land and soil, peacefully or violently, by the tribe, the commune, in some more or less naturally arisen or already historically developed form. The individual can never appear here in the dot-like isolation [*Punktualität*] in which he appears as mere free worker. If the objective conditions of his labour are presupposed as belonging to him, then he himself is subjectively presupposed as member of a commune, through which his relation to land and soil is mediated. His relation to the objective conditions of labour is mediated through his presence as member of the commune; at the same time, the real presence of the commune is determined by the specific form of the individual's property in the objective conditions of labour. Whether this property mediated by commune-membership appears as *communal property*, where the individual is merely the possessor and there is no private property in land and soil – or whether property appears in the double form of state and private property alongside one another, but so that the latter appears as posited by the former, so that only the citizen is and must be a private proprietor, while his property as citizen has a separate, particular existence at the same time – or whether, finally, the communal property appears only as a complement to individual property, with the latter as the base, while the commune has no existence for-itself except in the *assembly* of the commune members, their coming-together for common purposes – these different forms of the commune or tribe members' relation to the tribe's land and soil – to the earth where it has settled – depend partly on the natural inclinations of the tribe, and partly on the economic conditions in which it relates as proprietor to the land and soil in reality, i.e. in which it appropriates its fruits through labour, and the latter will itself depend on climate, physical make-up of the land and soil, the physically determined mode of its exploitation, the relation with hostile tribes or neighbour tribes, and the modifications which migrations, historic experiences etc. introduce. The survival of the commune as such in the old mode requires the reproduction of its members in the presupposed objective conditions. Production itself, the advance of population (this too belongs with production), necessarily suspends these conditions little by little; destroys them instead of reproducing them etc., and, with that, the communal system declines and falls, together with the property relations on which it was based. The Asiatic form necessarily hangs on most tenaciously and for the longest time. This is due to its presupposition that the individual does not become independent *vis-à-vis* the commune; that there is a self-sustaining circle of production, unity of agriculture and manufactures, etc. If the individual changes his relation to the commune, he thereby changes and acts destructively upon the commune; as on its economic presupposition; on the other side, the alteration of this economic presupposition brought about by its own dialectic – impoverishment etc. In particular, the influence of warfare and of conquest, which e.g. in Rome belonged to the essential conditions of the commune itself, suspends the real bond on which it rests. In all these forms, the *reproduction of presupposed* relations – more or less naturally arisen or historic as well, but become traditional – of the individual to his commune, together. with a *specific, objective* existence, *predetermined* for the individual, of his relations both to the conditions of labour and to his co-workers, fellow tribesmen etc. – are the foundation of development, which is therefore from the outset *restricted*, but which signifies decay, decline and fall once this barrier is suspended. Thus among the Romans, the development of slavery, the concentration of land possession, exchange, the money system, conquest etc., although all these elements up to a certain point seemed compatible with the foundation, and in part appeared merely as innocent extensions of it, partly grew out of it as mere abuses. Great developments can take place here within a specific sphere. The individuals may appear great. But there can be no conception here of a free and full development either of the individual or of the society, since such development stands in contradiction to the original relation.

Do we never find in antiquity an inquiry into which form of landed property etc. is the most productive, creates the greatest wealth? Wealth does not appear as the aim of production, although Cato may well investigate which manner of cultivating a field brings the greatest rewards, and Brutus may even lend out his money at the best rates of interest.[1] The question is always which mode of property creates the best citizens. Wealth appears as an end in itself only among the few commercial peoples – monopolists of the carrying trade – who live in the pores of the ancient world, like the Jews in medieval society. Now, wealth is on one side a thing, realized in things, material products, which a human being confronts as subject; on the other side, as value, wealth is merely command over alien labour not with the aim of ruling, but with the aim of private consumption etc. It appears in all forms in the shape of a thing, be it an object or be it a relation mediated through the object, which is external and accidental to the individual. Thus the old view, in which the human being appears as the aim of pro-

1. Cicero, *Letters to Atticus*, Vol. V, 21, lines 10–13; Vol. VI, 1, lines 3–7; Vol. VI, 2, lines 7–10.

duction, regardless of his limited national, religious, political character, seems to be very lofty when contrasted to the modern world, where production appears as the aim of mankind and wealth as the aim of production. In fact, however, when the limited bourgeois form is stripped away, what is wealth other than the universality of individual needs, capacities, pleasures, productive forces etc., created through universal exchange? The full development of human mastery over the forces of nature, those of so-called nature as well as of humanity's own nature? The absolute working-out of his creative potentialities, with no presupposition other than the previous historic development, which makes this totality of development, i.e. the development of all human powers as such the end in itself, not as measured on a *predetermined* yardstick? Where he does not reproduce himself in one specificity, but produces his totality? Strives not to remain something he has become, but is in the absolute movement of becoming? In bourgeois economics – and in the epoch of production to which it corresponds – this complete working-out of the human content appears as a complete emptying-out, this universal objectification as total alienation, and the tearing-down of all limited, one-sided aims as sacrifice of the human end-in-itself to an entirely external end. This is why the childish world of antiquity appears on one side as loftier. On the other side, it really is loftier in all matters where closed shapes, forms and given limits are sought for. It is satisfaction from a limited standpoint; while the modern gives no satisfaction; or, where it appears satisfied with itself, it is *vulgar*.

What Mr Proudhon calls the *extra-economic* origin of property, by which he understands just landed property,[2] is the *pre-bourgeois* relation of the individual to the objective conditions of labour, and initially to the *natural* objective conditions of labour – for, just as the working subject appears naturally as an individual, as natural being – so does the first objective condition of his labour appear as nature, earth, as his inorganic body; he himself is not only the organic body, but also the subject of this inorganic nature. This condition is not his product but something he finds to hand – presupposed to him as a natural being apart from him. Before we analyse this further, one more point: the worthy Proudhon would not only be able to, but would have to, accuse *capital* and *wage labour* – as forms of property – of having an *extra-economic* origin. For the encounter with the objective conditions of labour as

2. P.-J. Proudhon, *Système des contradictions économiques*, Vol. II, p. 265.

separate from him, as *capital* from the worker's side, and the encounter with the *worker* as propertyless, as an abstract worker from the capitalist's side – the exchange such as takes place between value and living labour, presupposes a *historic process*, no matter how much capital and labour themselves reproduce this relation and work out its objective scope, as well as its depth – a historic process, which, as we saw, forms the history of the origins of capital and wage labour. In other words: the *extra-economic origin* of property means nothing else than the *historic origin* of the bourgeois economy, of the forms of production which are theoretically or ideally expressed by the categories of political economy. But the fact that pre-bourgeois history, and each of its phases, also has its own *economy* and an *economic foundation* for its movement, is at bottom only the tautology that human life has since time immemorial rested on production, and, in one way or another, on *social* production, whose relations we call, precisely, economic relations.

The original conditions of production (or, what is the same, the reproduction of a growing number of human beings through the natural process between the sexes; for this reproduction, although it appears as appropriation of the objects by the subjects in one respect, appears in another respect also as formation, subjugation of the objects to a subjective purpose; their transformation into results and repositories of subjective activity) *cannot themselves* originally *be products* – results of production. It is not the *unity* of living and active humanity with the natural, inorganic conditions of their metabolic exchange with nature, and hence their appropriation of nature, which requires explanation or is the result of a historic process, but rather the *separation* between these inorganic conditions of human existence and this active existence, a separation which is completely posited only in the relation of wage labour and capital. In the relations of slavery and serfdom this separation does not take place; rather, one part of society is treated by the other as itself merely an *inorganic and natural* condition of its own reproduction. The slave stands in no relation whatsoever to the objective conditions of his labour; rather, *labour* itself, both in the form of the slave and in that of the serf, is classified as *an inorganic condition* of production along with other natural beings, such as cattle, as an accessory of the earth. In other words: the original conditions of production appear as natural presuppositions, *natural conditions of the producer's existence* just as his living body, even though he reproduces and develops it, is originally not posited by himself, but appears as the *presupposition of his self*; his own (bodily) being is a natural presupposition, which he has not posited. These *natural conditions of existence*, to which he relates as to his own inorganic body, are themselves double: (1) of a subjective and (2) of an objective nature. He finds himself a member of a family, clan, tribe etc. – which then, in a historic process of intermixture and antithesis with others, takes on a different shape; and, as such a member, he relates to a specific nature (say, here, still earth, land, soil) as his own inorganic being, as a condition of his production and reproduction. As a natural member of the community he participates in the communal property, and has a particular part of it as his possession; just as, were he a natural Roman citizen, he would have an ideal claim (at least) to the *ager publicus* and a real one to a certain number of *iugera*³ of land etc. His *property*, i.e. the relation to the natural presuppositions of his production as belonging to him, as *his*, is mediated by his being himself the natural member of a community. (The abstraction of a community, in which the members have nothing in common but language etc., and barely that much, is obviously the product of much later historical conditions.) As regards the individual, it is clear e.g. that he relates even to language itself *as his own* only as the natural member of a human community. Language as the product of an individual is an impossibility. But the same holds for property.

Language itself is the product of a community, just as it is in another respect itself the presence [*Dasein*] of the community, a presence which goes without saying. ⟨Communal production and common property as they exist e.g. in Peru are evidently a *secondary* form; introduced by and inherited from conquering tribes, who, at home, had common property and communal production in the older, simpler form such as is found in India and among the Slavs. Likewise the form which we find among the Celts in Wales e.g. appears as a transplanted, *secondary* form, introduced by conquerors among the lesser, conquered tribes. The completion and systematic elaboration of these systems by a *supreme central authority* shows their later origin. Just as the feudalism introduced into England was more perfect in form than that which arose spontaneously in France.⟩ ⟨Among nomadic pastoral tribes – and all pastoral peoples are originally migratory – the earth appears

3. Latin plural of *iugerum*, a Roman measure of land.

like other natural conditions, in its elemental limitlessness, e.g. in the Asiatic steppes and the high plateau. It is grazed etc., consumed by the herds, from which the pastoral peoples in turn live. They relate to it as their property, although they never stabilize this property. This is the case too with the hunting grounds of the wild Indian tribes in America; the tribe regards a certain region as its hunting domain, and asserts it by force against other tribes, or tries to drive others off the domains they assert. Among the nomadic pastoral peoples, the commune is indeed constantly united; the travelling society, the caravan, the horde, and the forms of supremacy and subordination develop out of the conditions of this mode of life. What is in fact *appropriated* and *reproduced* here is not the earth but the herd; but the earth is always used *communally* at each halting place.⟩ The only barrier which the community can encounter in relating to the natural conditions of production – the earth – as to *its own property* (if we jump ahead to the settled peoples) is *another community*, which already claims it as its own inorganic body. *Warfare* is therefore one of the earliest occupations of each of these naturally arisen communities, both for the defence of their property and for obtaining new property. (We can indeed content ourselves here with speaking of land and soil as original property, for among the herding peoples property in natural products of the earth – e.g. sheep – is at the same time property in the pastures they wander through. In general, property in land and soil includes its organic products.) ⟨If human beings themselves are conquered along with the land and soil as its organic accessories, then they are equally conquered as one of the conditions of production, and in this way arises slavery and serfdom, which soon corrupts and modifies the original forms of all communities, and then itself becomes their basis. The simple construction is thereby negatively determined.⟩

Property thus originally means no more than a human being's relation to his natural conditions of production as belonging to him, as his, as *presupposed* along with *his own being*; relations to them as *natural presuppositions* of his self, which only form, so to speak, his extended body. He actually does not relate to his conditions of production, but rather has a double existence, both subjectively as he himself, and objectively in these natural nonorganic conditions of his existence. The forms of these *natural conditions of production* are double: (1) his existence as a member of a community; hence the existence of this community, which in its

original form is a *clan* system, a more or less modified *clan* system;
(2) the relation to *land and soil* mediated by the community, as *its
own*, as communal landed property, at the same time *individual
possession* for the individual, or in such a way that only the fruits
are divided, but the land itself and the labour remain common.
(However, *residences* etc., even if only the Scythians' wagons,
always appear in individual possession.) A natural condition of
production for the living individual is his belonging to a *naturally
arisen, spontaneous society*, clan etc. This is e.g. already a condition
for his language etc. His own productive existence is possible only
on this condition. His subjective existence is thereby conditioned
as such, just as it is conditioned by his relation to the earth as his
workshop. (Property is, it is true, originally *mobile*, for mankind
first seizes hold of the ready-made fruits of the earth, among
whom belong e.g. the animals, and for him especially the ones that
can be tamed. Nevertheless even this situation – hunting, fishing,
herding, gathering fruits from trees etc. – always presupposes appropriation of the earth, whether for a fixed residence, or for
roaming, or for animal pasture etc.)

Property therefore means *belonging to a clan* (community)
(having subjective-objective existence in it); and, by means of the
relation of this community to the land and soil, [relating] to the
earth as the individual's inorganic body; his relation to land and
soil, to the external primary condition of production – since the
earth is raw material, instrument and fruit all in one – as to a presupposition belonging to his individuality, as modes of his presence. *We reduce this property to the relation to the conditions of
production.* Why not to consumption, since the production of the
individual is originally restricted to the reproduction of his own
body through the appropriation of ready objects prepared by
nature itself for consumption? Even where the only task is to *find*
and to *discover*, this soon requires exertion, labour – as in hunting,
fishing, herding – and production (i.e. development) of certain
capacities on the part of the subject. Then also, situations in which
it is possible to seize hold of the things available without any instruments whatever (i.e. products of labour destined for production), without alteration of form (which already takes place for
herding) etc., are themselves transitional and in no case to be
regarded as normal; nor as normal original situations. The original
conditions of production, incidentally, of course include substances consumable directly, without labour; thus the consump-

tion fund appears as a component part of the *original production fund*.

The fundamental condition of property resting on the clan system (into which the community originally resolves itself) – to be a member of the clan – makes the clan conquered by another clan *propertyless* and throws it among the *inorganic conditions* of the conqueror's reproduction, to which the conquering community relates as its own. Slavery and serfdom are thus only further developments of the form of property resting on the clan system. They necessarily modify all of the latter's forms. They can do this least of all in the Asiatic form. In the self-sustaining unity of manufacture and agriculture, on which this form rests, conquest is not so necessary a condition as where *landed property, agriculture* are exclusively predominant. On the other hand, since in this form the individual never becomes a proprietor but only a possessor, he is at bottom himself the property, the slave of him in whom the unity of the commune exists, and slavery here neither suspends the conditions of labour nor modifies the essential relation.

It is now clear, further, that:

Property, in so far as it is only the conscious relation – and posited in regard to the individual by the community, and proclaimed and guaranteed as law – to the conditions of production as *his own*, so that the producer's being appears also in the objective conditions *belonging to him* – is only realized by production itself. The real appropriation takes place not in the mental but in the real, active relation to these conditions – in their real positing as the conditions of his subjective activity.

It is thereby also clear that *these conditions change*. Only when tribes hunt upon it does a region of the earth become a hunting domain; only cultivation of the soil posits the land as the individual's extended body. After the *city of Rome* had been built and the surrounding countryside cultivated by its citizens, the conditions of the community were different from what they had been before. The aim of all these communities is survival; i.e. *reproduction of the individuals who compose it as proprietors, i.e. in the same objective mode of existence as forms the relation among the members and at the same time therefore the commune itself*. This *reproduction, however, is at the same time necessarily new production and destruction of the old form*. For example, where each of the individuals is supposed to possess a given number of acres of land, the advance of population is already under way. If this is to be corrected, then colonization, and that in turn requires wars of conquest. With that, slaves etc. Also, e.g., enlargement of the *ager publicus*, and therewith the patricians who represent the community etc. Thus the preservation of the old community includes the destruction of the conditions on which it rests, turns into its opposite. If it were thought that productivity on the same land could be increased by developing the forces of production etc. (this precisely the slowest of all in traditional agriculture), then the new order would include combinations of labour, a large part of the day spent in agriculture etc., and thereby again suspend the old economic conditions of the community. Not only do the objective conditions change in the act of reproduction, e.g. the village becomes a town, the wilderness a cleared field etc., but the producers change, too, in that they bring out new qualities in themselves, develop themselves in production, transform themselves, develop new powers and ideas, new modes of intercourse, new needs and new language. The older and more traditional the mode of production itself – and this lasts a long time in agriculture; even more in the oriental supplementation of agriculture with manufactures – i.e. the longer the *real process* of appropriation remains constant, the more constant will be the old forms of property and hence the community generally. Where there is already a separation between the commune members as private proprietors [on one side,] and they themselves as the urban commune and proprietors of the commune's *territorium* [on the other], there the conditions already arise in which the individual can *lose* his property, i.e. the double relation which makes him both an equal citizen, a member of the community, and a *proprietor*. In the oriental form this *loss* is hardly possible, except by means of altogether external influences, since the individual member of the commune never enters into the relation of freedom towards it in which he could lose his (objective, economic) bond with it. He is rooted to the spot, ingrown. This also has to do with the combination of manufacture and agriculture, of town (village) and countryside. In classical antiquity, manufacture appears already as a corruption (business for *freedmen*, clients, aliens) etc. This development of productive labour (not bound in pure subordination to agriculture as a domestic task, labour by free men for agriculture or war only, or for religious observances, and manufactures for the community – such as construction of houses, streets, temples), which necessarily develops through intercourse with aliens and slaves, through the desire to exchange the surplus product etc., dissolves the mode of production on which the community rests, and, with it, the *objective individual*, i.e. the individual defined as Roman, Greek, etc. Exchange acts in the same way; indebtedness etc.

The original unity between a particular form of community (clan) and the corresponding property in nature, or relation to the objective conditions of production as a natural being, as an objective being of the individual mediated by the commune – this unity, which appears in one respect as the particular form of property – has its living reality in a specific *mode of production* itself, a mode which appears both as a relation between the individuals, and as their specific active relation to inorganic nature, a specific mode of working (which is always family labour, often communal labour). The community itself appears as the first great force of production; particular kinds of production conditions (e.g. stock-breeding, agriculture), develop particular modes of production and particular forces of production, subjective, appearing as qualities of individuals, as well as objective [ones].

In the last analysis, their community, as well as the property based on it, resolves itself into a specific stage in the development of the productive forces of working subjects – to which correspond their specific relations amongst one another and towards nature. Until a certain point, reproduction. Then turns into dissolution.

Property, then, originally means – in its Asiatic, Slavonic, ancient classical, Germanic form – the relation of the working (producing or self-reproducing) subject to the conditions of his production or reproduction as his own. It will therefore have different forms depending on the conditions of this production. Production itself aims at the reproduction of the producer within and together with these, his objective conditions of existence. This relation as proprietor – not as a result but as a presupposition of labour, i.e. of production – presupposes the individual defined as a member of a clan or community (whose property the individual himself is, up to a certain point). Slavery, bondage etc., where the worker himself appears among the natural conditions of production for a third individual or community (this is *not* the case e.g. with the general slavery of the Orient, *only* from the

European point of view) – i.e. property no longer the relation of the working individual to the objective conditions of labour – is always secondary, derived, never original, although [it is] a necessary and logical result of property founded on the community and labour in the community. It is of course very simple to imagine that some powerful, physically dominant individual, after first having caught the animal, then catches humans in order to have them catch animals; in a word, uses human beings as another naturally occurring condition for his reproduction (whereby his own labour reduces itself to ruling) like any other natural creature. But such a notion is stupid – correct as it may be from the standpoint of some particular given clan or commune – because it proceeds from the development of *isolated individuals*. But human beings become individuals only through the process of history. He appears originally as a *species-being* [*Gattungswesen*], *clan being, herd animal* – although in no way whatever as a ζῶον πολιτικόν[4] in the political sense. Exchange itself is a chief means of this individuation [*Vereinzelung*]. It makes the herd-like existence superfluous and dissolves it. Soon the matter [has] turned in such a way that as an individual he relates himself only to himself, while the means with which he posits himself as individual have become the making of his generality and commonness. In this community, the objective being of the individual as proprietor, say proprietor of land, is presupposed, and presupposed moreover under certain conditions which chain him to the community, or rather form a link in his chain. In bourgeois society, the worker e.g. stands there purely without objectivity, subjectively; but the thing which *stands opposite* him has now become the *true community* [*Gemeinwesen*],[5] which he tries to make a meal of, and which makes a meal of him.

All forms (more or less naturally arisen, spontaneous, all at the same time however results of a historic process) in which the community presupposes its subjects in a specific objective unity with their conditions of production, or in which a specific subjective mode of being presupposes the communities themselves as conditions of production, necessarily correspond to a development of the forces of production which is only limited, and indeed limited in principle. The development of the forces of production dissolves these forms, and their dissolution is itself a development of the human productive forces. Labour begins with a certain

4. Political animal; literally, city-dweller.   5. See p. 223, n. 2.

foundation – naturally arisen, spontaneous, at first – then historic presupposition. Then, however, this foundation or presupposition is itself suspended, or posited as a vanishing presupposition which has become too confining for the unfolding of the progressing human pack.

In so far as classical landed property reappears in modern small-parcel landownership, it itself belongs to political economy and we shall come to it in the section on landed property.

(All this is to be returned to at greater depth and length.)

What we are here concerned with is this: the relation of labour to capital, or to the objective conditions of labour as capital, presupposes a process of history which dissolves the various forms in which the worker is a proprietor, or in which the proprietor works. Thus above all (1) *Dissolution* of the relation to the earth – land and soil – as natural condition of production – to which he relates as to his own inorganic being; the workshop of his forces, and the domain of his will. All forms in which this property appears presuppose a *community*, whose members, although there may be formal distinctions between them, are, as members of it, *proprietors*. The original form of this property is therefore itself *direct common property* (*oriental form*, modified in the Slavonic; developed to the point of antithesis, but still as the secret, if antithetical, foundation in classical and Germanic property). (2) *Dissolution of the relations* in which he appears as *proprietor of the instrument*. Just as the above form of landed property presupposes a *real community*, so does this property of the worker in the instrument presuppose a particular form of the development of manufactures, namely *craft, artisan work*; bound up with it, the guild-corporation system etc. (The manufacture system of the ancient Orient can be examined under (1) already.) Here labour itself still half artistic, half end-in-itself etc. Mastery. Capitalist himself still master-journeyman. Attainment of particular skill in the work also secures possession of instrument etc. etc. Inheritability then to a certain extent of the mode of work together with the organization of work and the instrument of work. Medieval cities. Labour still as his own; definite self-sufficient development of one-sided abilities etc. (3) Included in both is the fact that he has the means of consumption in his possession before production, which are necessary for him to live as producer – i.e. during production, *before* its completion. As proprietor of land he appears as directly provided with the necessary consumption fund. As master in a craft he has inherited it, earned it, saved it up, and as a youth he is first an *apprentice*, where he does not appear as an actual independent worker at all, but shares the master's fare in a partriarchal way. As journeyman (a genuine one) there is a certain communality in the consumption fund possessed by the master. While it is not the journeyman's *property* either, still, through the laws of the guild, tradition etc., at least co-possession etc. (To be gone into further.) (4) *Dissolution* likewise at the same time of the relations in which the *workers themselves*, the *living labour capacities* themselves, still belong *directly among the objective conditions of production*, and are appropriated as such – i.e. are slaves or serfs. For capital, the worker is not a condition of production, only work is. If it can make machines do it, or even water, air, so much the better. And it does not appropriate the worker, but his labour – not directly, but mediated through exchange.

These are, now, on one side, historic presuppositions needed before the worker can be found as a free worker, as objectless, purely subjective labour capacity confronting the objective conditions of production as his *not-property*, as *alien property*, as *value* for-itself, as capital. But the question arises, on the other side, which conditions are required so that he finds himself up against a *capital?*

⟨The formula of capital, where living labour relates to the raw material as well as to the instrument and to the means of subsistence required during labour, as negatives, as not-property, *includes*, first of all, *not-land-ownership*, or, the negation of the situation in which the working individual relates to land and soil, to the earth, as his own, i.e. in which he works, produces, as proprietor of the land and soil. In the best case he relates not only as worker to the land and soil, but also as proprietor of the land and soil to himself as working subject. Ownership of land and soil potentially also includes ownership of the raw material, as well as of the primordial instrument, the earth itself, and of its spontaneous fruits. Posited in the most original form, it means relating to the earth as proprietor, and finding raw material and instrument on hand, as well as the necessaries of life created not by labour but by the earth itself. Once this relation is reproduced, secondary instruments and fruits of the earth created through labour itself appear as included with landed property in its primitive forms. This historic situation is thus first of all negated as a full property relation, in the worker's relation to the conditions of labour as capital. This is historic state No. I, which is negated in this relation or presupposed as historically dissolved. Secondly, however, where there is *ownership of the instrument* on the part of the worker, i.e. the worker relates to the instrument as his own, where the worker works as owner of the instrument (which at the same time presupposes the subsumption of the instrument under his individual work, i.e. a particular, limited developmental stage of the productive force of labour), where this form of the *worker as owner* or of the *working owner* is already posited as an independent form beside and apart from *landed property* – the artisan-like and urban development of labour – not, as in the first case, as accidental to landed property and subsumed under it – hence where the raw material and the necessaries of life are also *mediated* as the craftsman's property, mediated through his craft work, through his property in the instrument – there a second historical stage is already presupposed beside and apart from the first, which must itself already appear significantly modified, through the *achievement of independence by this second sort of property* or by *working owners*. Since the instrument itself is already the product of labour, thus the element which constitutes property already exists as posited by labour, the community can no longer appear here in a naturally arisen, spontaneous form as in the first case – the community on which this form of property founded – but rather as itself already a produced, made, derived and secondary community, produced by the worker himself. It is clear that wherever ownership of the instrument is the relation to the conditions of production as property, there, in the real labour process, the instrument appears *only as a means* of individual labour; the art of really appropriating the instrument, of handling it as an instrument of labour, appears as the worker's particular skill, which posits him as the owner of the instrument. In short, the essential character of the guild-corporation system, of craft work as its subject, constituted by owners – can be resolved into the relation to the instrument of production – the instrument of labour as property – as distinct from the relation to the earth, to land and soil (to the raw material as such) as one's own. That the relation to this one moment of the conditions of production constitutes the working subject as owner, makes him into a working owner, this [is] historic situation No. II, which by its nature can exist only as antithesis to or, if one will, at the same time as complement of a modified form of the first – likewise negated in the first formula of capital. The third *possible form*, in which the worker relates as owner only to the necessaries of life, finding them on hand as the natural condition of the working subject, without relating to the land and soil, or to the instrument, or even (therefore) to labour itself as his own, is at bottom the formula of slavery and bondage, which is likewise negated, posited as a historically dissolved condition, in the relation of the worker to the conditions of production as capital. The original forms of property necessarily dissolve into the relation to the different objective moments which condition production, as one's own; they form the economic foundation of different forms of community, just as they for their part have specific forms of the community as presupposition. These forms are essentially modified by the inclusion of labour itself among the *objective conditions of production* (serfdom and slavery), through which the simply affirmative character of all forms of property included under No. I is lost and modified. They all contain, within themselves, slavery as possibility and hence as their own suspension. As regards No. II, where the particular kind of work – mastery of it, and, consequent upon that, an identity between property in the instrument and property in the conditions of production – while it excludes slavery and bondage, can take on an analogous negative development in the form of the caste system.⟩ ⟨The third form, ownership of the necessaries of life – if it does not reduce itself to slavery and serfdom – cannot contain a relation by the *working* individual to the conditions of production and hence of existence; it can therefore only be the relation of a member of the original community based on land ownership who has lost his landed property and not yet proceeded to variety No. II of property, such as the Roman *plebs* at the time of the bread and circuses.⟩ ⟨The relation of personal servitude, or of the retainers to their lord, is essentially different. For it forms, at bottom, only a mode of existence of the land-proprietor himself, who no longer works, but whose property includes, among the other conditions of production, the workers themselves as bondsmen etc. Here the *master–servant relation* [*Herrschaftsverhältnis*] as essential element of appropriation. Basically the appropriation of animals, land etc. cannot take place in a master–servant relation, although the animal provides service. The presupposition of the master–servant relation is the appropriation of an alien *will*. Whatever has no will, e.g. the animal, may well provide a service, but does not thereby make its owner into a *master*. This much can be seen here, however, that the *master–servant relation* likewise belongs in this formula of the appropriation of the instruments of production; and it forms a necessary ferment for the development and the decline and fall of all original relations of property and of production, just as it also expresses their limited nature. Still, it is reproduced – in mediated form – in capital, and thus likewise forms a ferment of its dissolution and is an emblem of its limitation.⟩

⟨'The power to sell one's self and one's own when in distress was a grievous general right; it prevailed in the North as well as among the Greeks and in Asia: the power of the creditor to take into servitude a debtor who could not make payment, and to obtain payment through sale of the debtor's labour or of his person, was almost equally widespread.' (Niebuhr, I, p. 600.)⟩ ⟨In one passage Niebuhr says that the Greek writers writing in the period of Augustus had great difficulty with, and misunderstood, the relation between patricians and plebeians, confusing this relation with that between patrons and clients, because they 'write at a time when *rich and poor were the only true classes of citizens*; where the needy person, no matter how noble his ancestry, required a patron, and where the millionaire, even if he were a freed slave, was sought out as a patron. They could hardly find a trace of inherited dependency-relations any longer.' (I, 620.)⟩ ⟨'Craftsmen were to be found in both classes' – *Metoikoi*[6] *and freedmen and their descendants* – 'and the plebeian who abandoned agriculture assumed the limited civic rights to which these were restricted. They did not lack the privilege of *legal corporations*; and their guilds were so highly esteemed, that Numa[7] was named as their founder: they were 9: pipers, goldsmiths, carpenters, dyers, harness makers, tanners, coppersmiths, potters, and the ninth guild, the miscellaneous remainder ... Those among them who were independent citizens; isopolites,[8] who belonged to no patron – if there was such a right; and descendants of servitors, whose bondage was dissolved by

6. Aliens who resided in Athens but were not classed as citizens.

7. According to Roman tradition, Numa Pompilius was the second king of Rome.

8. Citizens of one Greek city-state who were granted full citizenship in another.

extinction of their patron's line; all these people without a doubt remained as distant from the wranglings of the patricians and the commune as did the Florentine guilds from the feuds of the Guelphs and the Ghibellines: the servitors probably still stood entirely under the command of the patricians.' (I, 623.)⟩

On one side, historic processes are presupposed which place a mass of individuals in a nation etc. in the position, if not at first of real free workers, nevertheless of such who are so δυνάμει, whose only property is their labour capacity and the possibility of exchanging it for values then present; individuals who confront all objective conditions of production as *alien property*, as their own *not-property*, but at the same time as *values*, as exchangeable, hence appropriable to a certain degree through living labour. Such historic processes of dissolution are also the dissolution of the bondage relations which fetter the worker to land and soil and to the lord of land and soil; but which factually presuppose his ownership of the necessaries of life – this is in truth the process of his release from the earth; dissolution of the landed property relations, which constituted him as a yeoman, as a free, working small landowner or tenant (*colonus*), a free peasant*; dissolution of the guild relations which presuppose his ownership of the instrument of labour, and which presuppose labour itself as a craftsmanlike, specific skill, as property (not merely as the source of property); likewise dissolution of the client-relations in the various forms in which *not-proprietors* appear in the retinue of their lord as co-consumers of the surplus product and wear the livery of their master as an equivalent, participate in his feuds, perform personal services, imaginary or real etc. It will be seen on closer inspection that all these processes of dissolution mean the dissolution of relations of production in which: use value predominates, production for direct consumption; in which exchange value and its production presupposes the predominance of the other form; and hence that, in all these relations, payments in kind and services in kind predominate over payment in money and money-services. But this only by the way. It will likewise be found on closer observation that all the dissolved relations were possible only with a definite degree of development of the material (and hence also the intellectual) forces of production.

What concerns us here for the moment is this: the process of

*The dissolution of the still earlier forms of communal property and real community goes without saying.

dissolution, which transforms a mass of individuals of a nation etc. into free wage labourers δυνάμει – individuals forced solely by their lack of property to labour and to sell their labour – presupposes on the other side *not* that these individuals' previous sources of income and in part conditions of property have *disappeared*, but the reverse, that *only* their utilization has become different, that their mode of existence has changed, has gone over into other hands as a *free fund* or has even in part remained *in the same* hands. But this much is clear: the same process which divorced a mass of individuals from their previous relations to the *objective conditions of labour*, relations which were, in one way or another, affirmative, negated these relations, and thereby transformed these individuals into *free workers*, this same process freed – δυνάμει – these *objective conditions of labour* – land and soil, raw material, necessaries of life, instruments of labour, money or all of these – from their *previous state of attachment* to the individuals now separated from them. They are still *there on hand*, but in another form; as a *free fund*, in which all political etc. relations are obliterated. The objective conditions of labour now confront these unbound, propertyless individuals only in the form of *values*, self-sufficient values. The same process which placed the mass face to face with the *objective conditions of labour* as free workers also placed these conditions, as *capital*, face to face with the free workers. The historic process was the divorce of elements which up until then were bound together; its result is therefore not that one of the elements disappears, but that each of them appears in a negative relation to the other – the (potentially) free worker on the one side, capital (potentially) on the other. The separation of the objective conditions from the classes which have become transformed into free workers necessarily also appears at the same time as the achievement of independence by these same conditions at the opposite pole.

If the relation of capital and wage labour is regarded not as already commanding and predominant over the whole of production,* but as arising historically – i.e. if we regard the original transformation of money into capital, the process of exchange between capital, still only existing δυνάμει on one side and the free workers existing δυνάμει on the other – then of course one

---

*For in that case the capital presupposed as condition of wage labour is wage labour's own product, and is presupposed by it as its own presupposition, created by it as its own presupposition.

cannot help making the simple observation, out of which the economists make a great show,[9] that the side which appears as capital has to possess raw materials, instruments of labour and necessaries of life so that the worker can live during production, before production is completed. This further takes the form that there must have taken place on the part of the capitalist an accumulation – an accumulation prior to labour and not sprung out of it – which enables him to put the worker to work and to maintain his effectiveness, to maintain him as living labour capacity.* This act by capital which is independent of labour, not posited by labour, is then shifted from the prehistory of capital into the present, into a moment of its reality and of its present activity, of its self-formation. From this is ultimately derived the eternal right of capital to the fruits of alien labour, or rather its mode of appropriation is developed out of the simple and 'just' laws of equivalent exchange.[10]

Wealth present in the form of money can be exchanged for the objective conditions of labour only because and if these are separated from labour itself. We saw that money can be piled up in part by way of the sheer exchange of equivalents; but this forms so insignificant a source that it is not worth mentioning historically – if it is presupposed that this money is gained through the exchange of one's own labour. The monetary wealth which becomes transformed into capital in the proper sense, into industrial capital, is rather the mobile wealth piled up through usury – especially that practised against landed property – and through mercantile profits. We shall have occasion

---

*Once capital and wage labour are posited as their own presupposition, as the basis presupposed to production itself, then what appears initially is that the capitalist possesses, in addition to the fund of raw materials and necessaries required for the labourer to reproduce himself, to create the required means of subsistence, i.e. to realize *necessary labour*, a fund of raw material and means of labour in which the worker realizes his surplus labour, i.e. the capitalist's profit. On further analysis this takes the form that the worker constantly creates a double fund for the capitalist, or in the form of capital. One part of this fund constantly fulfils the conditions of his own existence and the other part fulfils the conditions for the existence of capital. As we have seen, in the case of the surplus capital – and surplus capital in relation to its antediluvian relation to labour – all *real, present capital* and each of its elements has equally been *appropriated* without exchange, without an equivalent, as objectified, appropriated *alien labour*.

---

9. See p., 299 n. 5.   10. See p. 319, n. 33.

below to speak further of both of these forms – in so far as they appear not as themselves forms of capital, but as earlier forms of wealth, as presuppositions for capital.

It is inherent in the concept of capital, as we have seen – in its origin – that it begins with *money* and hence with wealth existing in the form of money. It is likewise inherent in it that it appears as coming out of circulation, as the *product* of circulation. The formation of capital thus does not emerge from landed property (here at most from the *tenant* [*Pächter*] in so far as he is a dealer in agricultural products); or from the guild (although there is a possibility at the last point); but rather from merchant's and usurer's wealth. But the latter encounter the conditions where free labour can be purchased only when this labour has been released from its objective conditions of existence through the process of history. Only then does it also encounter the possibility of buying these *conditions* themselves. Under guild conditions, e.g., mere money, if it is not itself guild money, masters' money, cannot buy the looms to make people work with them; how many an individual may operate etc. is prescribed. In short, the instrument itself is still so intertwined with living labour, whose domain it appears, that it does not truly circulate. What enables money-wealth to become capital is the encounter, on one side, with free workers; and on the other side, with the necessaries and materials etc., which previously were in one way or another the *property* of the masses who have now become object-less, and are also *free* and purchasable. The other condition of labour, however – a certain level of skill, instrument as means of labour etc. – is already *available* to it in this preliminary or first period of capital, partly as a result of the urban guild system, partly as a result of domestic industry, or industry which is attached to agriculture as an accessory. This historic process is not the product of capital, but the presupposition for it. And it is through this process that the capitalist inserts himself as (historic) middle-man between landed property, or property generally, and labour. History knows nothing of the congenial fantasies according to which the capitalist and the workers form an association etc., nor is there a trace of them in the conceptual development of capital. *Manufactures* may develop sporadically, locally, in a framework which still belongs to a quite different period, as e.g. in the Italian cities *alongside* the guilds. But as the sole predominant forms of an epoch, the conditions for capital have to be developed not only locally but on a grand scale. (Notwithstanding this, individual guild masters may develop into capitalists with the dissolution of the guilds; but the case is rare, in the nature of the thing as well. As a rule, the whole guild system declines and falls, both master and journeyman, where the capitalist and the worker arise.)

It goes without saying – and shows itself if we go more deeply into the historic epoch under discussion here – that in truth the *period of the dissolution* of the earlier modes of production and modes of the worker's relation to the objective conditions of labour *is at the same time a period* in which *monetary wealth* on the one side *has* already developed to a certain extent, and on the other side grows and expands rapidly through the same circumstances as accelerate the above dissolution. It is itself one of the agencies of that dissolution, while at the same time that dissolution is the condition of its transformation into capital. But the *mere presence of monetary wealth*, and even the achievement of a kind of supremacy on its part, is in no way sufficient for this *dissolution into capital* to happen. Or else ancient Rome, Byzantium etc. would have ended their history with free labour and capital, or rather begun a new history. There, too, the dissolution of the old property relations was bound up with development of monetary wealth – of trade etc. But instead of leading to industry, this dissolution led in fact to the supremacy of the countryside over the city. – The *original formation* of capital does not happen, as is sometimes imagined, with capital *heaping up* necessaries of life and instruments of labour and raw materials, in short, the *objective* conditions of labour which have already been unbound from the soil and animated by human labour.* Capital does not create the objective conditions of labour. Rather, its *original formation* is that, through the historic process of the dissolution of the old mode of production, value existing as money-wealth

---

*The first glance shows what a nonsensical circle it would be if on the one hand the *workers* whom capital has to put to work in order to posit itself as capital had first to be *created*, to be brought to life through its *stockpiling* if they waited for its command, *Let There Be Workers!*; while at the same time it were itself incapable of *stockpiling* without alien labour, could at most stockpile *its own labour*, i.e. could itself exist in the form of *not-capital* and *not-money*; since labour, before the existence of capital, can only realize itself in forms such as craft labour, petty agriculture etc., in short, all forms which can *not stockpile*, or only sparingly; in forms which allow of only a small surplus product and *eat up* most of it. We shall have to examine this notion of *stockpiling* [*Aufhäufung*] still more closely later on.

is enabled, on one side, *to buy* the objective conditions of labour; on the other side, to exchange money for the *living labour* of the workers who have been set free. All these moments are present; their divorce is itself a historic process, a process of dissolution, and it is *the latter* which enables money to transform itself into *capital*. Money itself, to the extent that it also plays an active role, does so only in so far as it intervenes in this process as itself a highly energetic solvent, and to that extent assists in the creation of the *plucked*, object-less *free workers*; but certainly not by *creating* the objective conditions of their existence; rather by helping to speed up their separation from them – their propertyless-ness. When e.g. the great English landowners dismissed their retainers, who had, together with them, consumed the surplus product of the land; when further their tenants chased off the smaller cottagers etc., then, firstly, a mass of living labour powers was thereby thrown onto the *labour market*, a mass which was free in a double sense, free from the old relations of clientship, bondage and servitude, and secondly free of all belongings and possessions, and of every objective, material form of being, *free of all property*; dependent on the sale of its labour capacity or on begging, vagabondage and robbery as its only source of income. It is a matter of historic record that they tried the latter first, but were driven off this road by gallows, stocks and whippings, onto the narrow path to the labour market; owing to this fact, the *governments*, e.g. of Henry VII, VIII etc. appear as conditions of the historic dissolution process and as makers of the conditions for the existence of capital. On the other side, the necessaries of life etc., which the landowners previously ate up together with their retainers, now stood at the disposal of any money which might wish to buy them in order to buy labour through their instrumentality. Money neither *created* nor *stockpiled* these necessaries; they were there and were consumed and reproduced before they were consumed and reproduced through its mediation. What had changed was simply this, that these necessaries were now thrown on to the *exchange market* – were separated from their direct connection with the mouths of the retainers etc. and trans-formed from use values into exchange values, and thus fell into the domain and under the supremacy of money wealth. Likewise with the instruments of labour. Money wealth neither invented nor fabricated the spinning wheel and the loom. But, once un-bound from their land and soil, spinner and weaver with their stools and wheels came under the command of money wealth. *Capital proper does nothing but bring together the mass of hands and instruments which it finds on hand. It agglomerates them under its command.* That is its *real stockpiling*; the stockpiling of workers, along with their instruments, at particular points. This will have to be dealt with more closely in the so-called *stockpiling* of capital. Monetary wealth – as merchant wealth – had admittedly helped to speed up and to dissolve the old relations of production, and made it possible for the proprietor of land for example, as A. Smith already nicely develops,[11] to exchange his grain and cattle etc. for use values brought from afar, instead of squandering the use values he himself produced, along with his retainers, and to locate his wealth in great part in the mass of his co-consuming retainers. It gave the *exchange value* of his revenue a higher significance for him. The same thing took place in regard to his tenants, who were already semi-capitalists, but still very hemmed-in ones. The development of exchange value – favoured by *money* existing in the form of the merchant estate – dissolves production which is more oriented towards direct use value and its corresponding forms of property – the relations of labour to its objective conditions – and thus pushes forward towards the making of the *labour market* (certainly to be distinguished from the slave market). However, even this action of money is only possible given the presupposition of an *urban artisanate* resting *not* on capital but on the organization of labour in guilds etc. Urban labour itself had created means of production for which the guilds became just as confining as were the old relations of landownership to an improved agriculture, which was in part itself a consequence of the larger market for agricultural products in the cities etc. The other circumstances which e.g. in the sixteenth century increased the mass of circulating commodities as well as that of money, which created new needs and thereby raised the exchange value of indigenous products etc., raised prices etc., all of these promoted on one side the dissolution of the old relations of production, sped up the separation of the worker or non-worker but able-bodied individual from the objective conditions of his reproduction, and thus promoted the transformation of money into capital. There can therefore be nothing more ridiculous than to conceive this *original formation* of capital as if capital had stockpiled and created the *objective conditions of production* – necessaries, raw materials, instrument – and then

11. Adam Smith, *Wealth of Nations*, Vol. III, Bk III, Ch. 4.

offered them to the worker, who was *bare* of these possessions.
Rather, monetary wealth in part helped to *strip* the labour
powers of able-bodied individuals from these conditions; and
in part this process of divorce proceeded without it. When the
formation of capital had reached a certain level, monetary wealth
could place itself as mediator between the objective conditions of
life, thus liberated, and the liberated but also *homeless* and *empty-
handed* labour powers, and buy the latter with the former. But now,
as far as the *formation of money-wealth* itself is concerned, this
belongs to the prehistory of the bourgeois economy. Usury, trade,
urbanization and the treasury rising with it play the main roles
here. So, too, *hoarding* by tenants, peasants etc.; although to a
lesser degree. – This shows at the same time that the development
of exchange and of exchange value, which is everywhere mediated
through trade, or whose mediation may be termed trade — money
achieves an independent existence in the merchant estate, as does
circulation in trade – brings with it both the dissolution of *labour's
relations of property in its* conditions of existence, in one respect,
and at the same time the dissolution of *labour* which is itself *classed
as one of the objective conditions of production*; all these are relations which express a predominance of use value and of production directed towards use value, as well as of a real community
which is itself still directly present as a presupposition of production. Production based on exchange value and the community
based on the exchange of these exchange values – even though they
seem, as we saw in the previous chapter on money, to posit property as the outcome of *labour* alone, and to posit private property
over the product of one's own labour as condition – and labour as
general condition of wealth, all presuppose and produce the separation of labour from its objective conditions. This exchange of
equivalents proceeds; it is only the surface layer of a production
which rests on the appropriation of alien labour *without exchange*,
but with the *semblance of exchange*. This system of exchange rests
on *capital* as its foundation, and, when it is regarded in isolation
from capital, as it appears on the surface, as an *independent*
system, then it is a mere *illusion*, but a *necessary illusion*. Thus there
is no longer any ground for astonishment that the system of exchange values – exchange of equivalents measured through labour –
turns into, or rather reveals as its hidden background, the *appropriation of alien labour without exchange*, complete separation
of labour and property. For the domination of exchange value

itself, and of exchange-value-producing production, *presupposes* alien labour capacity itself as an exchange value – i.e. the separation of living labour capacity from its objective conditions; a relation to them – or to its own objectivity – as alien property; a relation to them, in a word, as *capital*. Only in the period of the decline and fall of the feudal system, but where it still struggles internally – as in England in the fourteenth and first half of the fifteenth centuries – is there a golden age for labour in the process of becoming emancipated. In order for labour to relate to its objective conditions as its property again, another system must take the place of the system of private exchange, which, as we saw, posits the exchange of objectified labour for labour capacity, and therefore the appropriation of living labour without exchange. – The way in which money transforms itself into capital often shows itself quite tangibly in history; e.g. when the merchant induces a number of weavers and spinners, who until then wove and spun as a rural, secondary occupation, to work for him, making their secondary into their chief occupation; but then has them in his power and has brought them under his command as wage labourers. To draw them away from their home towns and to concentrate them in a place of work is a further step. In this simple process it is clear that the capitalist has prepared neither the raw material, nor the instrument, nor the means of subsistence for the weaver and the spinner. All that he has done is to restrict them little by little to one kind of work in which they become dependent on selling, on the *buyer*, the *merchant*, and ultimately produce only *for* and *through* him. He bought their labour originally only by buying their product; as soon as they restrict themselves to the production of this exchange value and thus must directly produce *exchange values*, must exchange their labour entirely for money in order to survive, then they come under his command, and at the end even the illusion that they *sold* him products disappears. He buys their labour and takes their property first in the form of the product, and soon after that the instrument as well, or he leaves it to them as *sham property* in order to reduce his own production costs. – The original historic forms in which capital appears at first sporadically or *locally*, *alongside* the old modes of production, while exploding them little by little everywhere, is on one side *manufacture* proper (not yet the factory); this[12] springs up where

12. 'This' refers back to 'manufacture'. See the definition of 'factory' given by Ure, cited by Marx on p. 690.

mass quantities are produced for export, for the external market –
i.e. on the *basis of large-scale overland and maritime commerce*, in
its emporiums like the Italian cities, Constantinople, in the Flemish, Dutch cities, a few Spanish ones, such as Barcelona etc. Manufacture seizes hold initially not of the so-called *urban trades*, but
of the *rural secondary occupations*, spinning and weaving, the two
which least requires guild-level skills, technical training. Apart
from these great emporiums, where the external market is its basis,
where production is thus, so to speak, *naturally* oriented towards
exchange value – i.e. manufactures directly connected with ship-
ping, shipbuilding itself etc. – it takes up its first residence not in
the cities, but on the land, in villages lacking guilds etc. The rural
subsidiary occupations have the broad basis [characteristic] of
manufactures, while the urban trades demand great progress in
production before they can be conducted in factory style. Likewise certain branches of production – such as glassworks, metal
works, sawmills etc., which demand a higher concentration of
labour powers from the outset, apply more natural energy from
the outset, demand mass production, likewise concentration of the
means of labour etc. Likewise paper mills. On the other side the
rise of the tenant and the transformation of the agricultural population into free day-labourers. Although this transformation in the
countryside is the last to push on towards its ultimate consequences
and its purest form, its beginnings there are among the earliest.
Classical antiquity, which could never get beyond the urban
artisanate proper, could therefore never get to large industry. The
first presupposition of the latter is to draw the land in all its expanse into the production not of use values but of exchange
values. Glass factories, paper mills, iron works etc. cannot be
operated on guild principles. They demand mass production; sales
to a general market; *monetary wealth* on the part of their entrepreneur – not that he creates the conditions, neither the subjective
nor the objective ones; but under the old relations of property and
of production these conditions cannot be brought together. – The
dissolution of relations of serfdom, like the rise of manufacture,
then little by little transforms all branches of work into branches
operated by capital. – The cities themselves, it is true, also contain an element for the formation of wage labour proper, in the
non-guild day-labourers, unskilled labourers etc.

While, as we have seen, the transformation of money into capital
presupposes a historic process which divorces the objective con-

ditions of labour from the worker and makes them independent of him, it is at the same time the effect of capital and of its process, once arisen, to conquer all of production and to develop and complete the divorce between labour and property, between labour and the objective conditions of labour, everywhere. It will be seen in the course of the further development how capital destroys craft and artisan labour, working small-landownership etc., together with itself in forms in which it does *not* appear in opposition to labour – in *small capital* and in the intermediate species, the species between the old modes of production (or their renewal on the foundation of capital) and the classical, adequate mode of production of capital itself.

The only stockpiling presupposed at the origin of capital is that of *monetary wealth*, which, regarded in and for itself, is altogether unproductive, as it only springs up out of circulation and belongs exclusively to it. Capital rapidly forms an internal market for itself by destroying all rural secondary occupations, so that it spins, weaves for everyone, clothes everyone etc., in short, brings the commodities previously created as direct use values into the form of exchange values, a process which comes about by itself through the separation of the workers from land and soil and from property (even in the form of serf property) in the conditions of production.

With the urban crafts, although they rest essentially on exchange and on the creation of exchange values, the direct and chief aim of this production is *subsistence as craftsmen*, as *master-journeymen*, hence use value; not *wealth*, not *exchange value as exchange value*. Production is therefore always subordinated to a given consumption, supply to demand, and expands only slowly.

The *production of capitalists and wage labourers is thus a chief product of capital's realization process*. Ordinary economics, which looks only at the things produced, forgets this completely. When objectified labour is, in this process, at the same time posited as the worker's *non-objectivity*, as the objectivity of a subjectivity antithetical to the worker, as *property* of a will alien to him, then capital is necessarily at the same time the *capitalist*, and the idea held by some socialists that we need capital but not the capitalists is altogether wrong. It is posited within the concept of capital that the objective conditions of labour – and these are its own product – take on a *personality* towards it, or, what is the same, that they are posited as the property of a personality alien to the worker. The concept of capital contains the capitalist. Still, this error is in no way greater than that of e.g. all philologists who speak of *capital* in antiquity, of Roman, Greek capitalists. This is only another way of expressing that labour in Rome and Greece was *free*, which these gentlemen would hardly wish to assert. The fact that we now not only call the plantation owners in America capitalists, but that they *are* capitalists, is based on their existence as anomalies within a world market based on free labour. If the concern is the word, capital, which does not occur in antiquity* then the still migrating hordes with their herds on the Asiatic high plateau are the biggest capitalists, since capital originally means cattle, which is why the *métairie* contract still frequently drawn up in southern France, for lack of capital, just as an exception, is called: *Bail de bestes à cheptel*.[14] If one wants to descend to bad Latin, then our capitalists or *Capitales Homines* would be those '*qui debent censum de capite*'.[15]

The conceptual specification of capital encounters difficulties which do not occur with money; capital is essentially *capitalist*; but at the same time again as an element of his existence distinct from him, or production in general, *capital*. We shall likewise find later that many things are subsumed under *capital* which do not seem to belong within it conceptually. E.g. capital is lent out. It is stockpiled etc. In all these designations it appears to be a mere thing, and to coincide entirely with the matter in which it is present. But this and other questions will be cleared up in the course of the development. (Noted incidentally as a joke: the good Adam Müller, who takes all figurative ways of speaking as very mystical, has also heard of *living capital* in ordinary life as opposed to *dead* capital, and now rationalizes this theosophically.[16] King Aethelstan could

*Although ἀρχεῖα among the Greeks, corresponding to the *principalis summa rei creditae*.[13]

---

13. This statement is taken directly from Du Cange, *Glossarium mediae et infimae Latinitatis*, ed. G. A. L. Henschel, Paris, 1842, Vol. 2, p. 139, article entitled '2. Capitale'. However, Du Cange was wrong. The word ἀρχεῖα means 'government buildings', never 'loan' or 'principal sum of money owed' as suggested there; the Greek word for loan, which Du Cange probably had in mind, is χρέος.

14. *métairie*: share-cropping, the modern *métayage*. *Bail de bestes à cheptel*: lease with livestock as capital. Cf. Du Cange, *Glossarium*, Vol. 2, p. 139.

15. 'Those who have to pay a head tax'.

16. Adam H. Müller (1774–1829, leading advocate of the Romantic reaction in history and economics during the early nineteenth century; Austrian state official under Metternich, ennobled for his propagandistic activities), *Die Elemente der Staatskunst, Erster Theil*, Berlin, 1809, pp. 226–41.

teach him a lesson here: *Reddam de meo proprio decimas Deo tam in Vivente Capitale* (livestock), *quam in mortis fructuis terrae* (dead fruits of the earth).)[17] Money always remains the same form in the same substratum; and can thus be more easily conceived as a mere thing. But one and the same commodity, money etc., can represent capital or revenue etc. Thus it is clear even to the economists that money is not something tangible; but that one and the same thing can be subsumed sometimes under the title capital, sometimes under another and contrary one, and correspondingly *is* or *is not* capital. It is then evident that it is a *relation, and can only be a relation of production.*

We have seen that the true nature of capital emerges only at the *end of the second cycle.* What we have to examine now is this cycle itself, or the *circulation of capital.* Production originally appeared to lie beyond circulation, and circulation beyond production. The circulation of capital – circulation posited as the circulation of capital – spans both moments. Production appears in it as the conclusion and the point of departure of circulation, and vice versa. The independence of circulation is here reduced to a mere semblance, as is the otherworldliness of production.

Exchange of labour for labour rests on the worker's propertylessness

⟨But one more remark on the topic above: The exchange of equivalents, which seems to presuppose ownership of the products of one's own labour – hence seems to posit as identical: *appropriation through labour,* the real economic process of making something one's own [*Zueigen-Machen*], and *ownership of objectified* labour; what appeared previously as a real process is here recognized as a legal relation, i.e. as a general condition of production, and therefore recognized by law, posited as an expression of the general will – turns into, reveals itself through a necessary dialectic as absolute divorce of labour and property, and appropriation of alien labour without exchange, without equivalent. Production based on exchange value, on whose surface this free and equal exchange of equivalents proceeds, is at its base the exchange of *objectified labour* as exchange value for living labour as use

---

17. 'I shall grant a tenth part of my own to God both in livestock and in dead fruits of the earth', quoted by Du Cange, *Glossarium,* p. 140, from Athelstan's Ordinance of 925 on tithes.

value, or, to express this in another way, the relating of labour to
its objective conditions – and hence to the objectivity created by
itself – as alien property: *alienation [Entäusserung] of labour*. At
the same time, the condition of exchange value is its measurement by labour time, and hence living labour – not its value – as
measure of values. The notion that production and hence society
depended in all states of production on the *exchange of mere
labour for labour* is a delusion. In the various forms in which
labour relates to the conditions of production as its own property,
the reproduction of the worker is by no means posited through
mere labour, for his property relation is not the result but the
presupposition of his labour. In landed property this is clear; it
must also become clear in the guild system that the particular
kind of property which labour creates does not rest on labour
alone or on the exchange of labour, but on an objective connection between the worker and a community and conditions
which are there before him, which he takes as his basis. These too
are products of labour, of the labour of world history; of the labour
of the community – of its historic development, which does not
proceed from the labour of individuals nor from the exchange of
their labours. Therefore, mere labour is also not the presupposition
of realization [*Verwertung*]. A situation in which labour is merely
exchanged for labour – whether in the direct, living form, or in the
form of the product – presupposes the separation of labour from its
original intertwinement with its objective conditions, which is why
it appears as mere labour on one side, while on the other side its
product, as objectified labour, has an entirely independent existence as value opposite it. *The exchange of labour for labour –
seemingly the condition of the worker's property – rests on the
foundation of the worker's propertylessness.*⟩

(It will be shown later that the *most extreme form of alienation*,
wherein labour appears in the relation of capital and wage labour,
and labour, productive activity appears in relation to its own conditions and its own product, is a necessary point of transition –
and therefore already contains in *itself*, in a still only inverted
form, turned on its head, the dissolution of all *limited presuppositions of production*, and moreover creates and produces the
unconditional presuppositions of production, and therewith the
full material conditions for the total, universal development of
the productive forces of the individual.)

Circulation of capital and circulation of money. – Presupposition
of value within each single capital (instrument etc.). – Production
process and circulation process moments of production. –
The productivity of the different capitals (branches of industry)
determines that of the individual capital. – Circulation period.
Velocity of circulation substitutes for volume of capital.
Mutual dependence of capitals in the velocity of their circulation.
Circulation a moment of production. Production process and its
duration. Transformation of the product into money.
Duration of this operation. Retransformation of money into
the conditions of production. Exchange of part of the capital
with living labour. – Transport costs

The circulation of money began at an infinite number of points
and returned to an infinite number of points. The point of return
was in no way posited as the point of departure. In the circulation
of capital, the point of departure is posited as the terminal point
and the terminal point as the point of departure. The capitalist
himself is the point of departure and of return. He exchanges
money for the conditions of production, produces, realizes the
product, i.e. transforms it into money, and then begins the process
anew. The circulation of money, regarded for itself, necessarily
becomes extinguished in money as a static thing. The circulation of
capital constantly ignites itself anew, divides into its different
moments, and is a *perpetuum mobile*. The positing of prices on the
side of money circulation was purely formal, in so far as *value* is
presupposed independently of money circulation. The circulation
of capital *posits prices*, not only formally but really, in so far as it
posits value. If value itself appears within it as presupposition, this
can only be as *value posited* by another capital. The breadth of the
path for money circulation has been measured in advance, and the
circumstances which accelerate or retard it are external impulses.
In its circulation, capital expands itself and its path, and the speed
or slowness of its circulation itself forms one of its intrinsic
moments. It becomes qualitatively altered in circulation and the
totality of the moments of its circulation are themselves the
moments of its production – its reproduction as well as its new
production.

⟨We saw how at the end of the second cycle, i.e. the second
cycle of surplus value which has been realized as surplus capital,
the illusion disappears that the capitalist exchanges anything at all

with the worker other than a part of the latter's own objectified labour.[18] However, within the mode of production already founded on capital, the part of capital which represents raw materials and instrument appears to the individual capital as a value *presupposed* to it and likewise presupposed to the *living labour* which it buys. These two headings turn out to have been posited by *alien capital*, hence again by *capital*, but another one. One capitalist's raw material is another's product. One's product is the other's raw material. One capitalist's *instrument* is another's product, and may even serve as raw material for the production of another instrument. Thus, what we called the constant value which appeared as a presupposition in the case of the individual capital is nothing but the presupposition of capital by capital, i.e. the fact that the different capitals in the different branches of industry posit one another reciprocally as presupposition and condition. Each of them regarded for itself can be resolved into dead labour which, as *value*, has *become independent vis-à-vis* living labour. None of them in the last analysis contains anything other than labour – apart from the natural material from which value is absent. The introduction of *many* capitals must not interfere with the investigation here. The relation of the *many* will, rather, be explained after what they all have in common, the quality of being capital, has been examined.⟩

The circulation of capital is at the same time its becoming, its growth, its vital process. If anything needed to be compared with the circulation of the blood, it was not the formal circulation of money, but the content-filled circulation of capital.

Since circulation presupposes production at all points – and is the circulation of products, whether money or commodity, while the latter always arise from the production process, which is itself the process of capital – it follows that the circulation of money itself now appears as determined by the circulation of capital, whereas previously it seemed to run *side by side with* the production process. We shall return to this point.

If we now consider circulation, or the circulation of capital as a whole, then the great distinction within it appears to be that between the production process and circulation itself, both as moments of its circulation. How long capital remains within the sphere of the production process depends on the latter's technological conditions, and the time it spends in this phase directly

18. See above, pp. 457–8.

coincides – even though the duration is necessarily different depending on the type of production, its object etc. – with the development of the productive forces. The duration is here nothing but the labour time necessary for the making of the product (false!).[19] The smaller this labour time, the greater, as we have seen, the relative surplus value. If less labour time is required to make a given quantity of products, it is the same thing as if more finished products can be supplied in a given amount of labour time. The abbreviation of the time during which a given amount of capital remains within the production process and is withdrawn from circulation, 'embarked',[20] coincides with the abbreviation of the labour time required to make the product – [therefore coincides] with the development of the forces of production, the utilization of the forces of nature, of machinery, and of the natural powers of social labour – the agglomeration of the workers, the combination and division of labour. Thus no new moment seems to enter in from this side. However, when it is recalled that, as far as the individual capital is concerned, the part of it which constitutes raw material and instrument (means of labour) is itself the product of an alien capital, then it may be seen that the speed with which it can repeat the production process anew is at the same time determined by the development of the productive forces in all other branches of industry. This becomes quite clear if one supposes the same capital to produce its own raw materials, instruments and final products. The length of time during which capital remains in the phase of the production process becomes itself a moment of circulation, if we presuppose *various* capitals. But we are not yet concerned with *many* capitals here. This moment therefore does not belong here.

The second moment is the space of time running from the completed transformation of capital into the product until when it becomes transformed into money. The frequency with which capital can repeat the production process, self-realization, in a given amount of time, evidently depends on the speed with which this space of time is run through, or on its duration. If a capital – say originally a capital of 100 thalers – turns over 4 times in one year; let the gain be 5 % of itself each time, if the new value is not capitalized; this is the same as if a capital 4 times as large, say 400, at the same percentage, were to turn over *once* in one year; each

19. '(false!)' was inserted afterwards, above the line. [MELI note]
20. In English in the original.

time 20%. The velocity of turnover therefore – the remaining conditions of production being held constant – substitutes for the *volume* of capital. Or, if a value 4 times smaller realizes itself as capital 4 times in the same period in which a 4 times greater value realizes itself as capital only once, then the smaller capital's gain – production of surplus value – is *at least as great* as the larger's. We say at least. It can be greater, because the surplus value can itself again be employed as surplus capital. For example, assume that a capital of 100 has a profit (here anticipating *this form* of surplus value for the calculation's sake) of 10% each time, no matter how often it turns over. Then, at the end of the first 3 months, it would be 110, at the end of the second 121, at the end of the third $133\frac{1}{10}$, and at the end of the last turnover $146\frac{41}{100}$, while a capital of 400 with one annual turnover would be only 440. In the first case the gain $= 46\frac{41}{100}$, in the second only $= 40$. (The fact that the presupposition is wrong, in as much as capital does not bring the *same* rate of profit with each increase in its size, is beside the point as far as the example is concerned, for the issue here is not how much more than 40 it brings, but the very fact that in the first case it does – and it does – bring in more than 40.) We have already encountered the law of the substitution of velocity for mass, and mass for velocity, in money circulation. It holds in production just as in mechanics. It is a circumstance to return to when we consider the equalization of the rate of profit, price etc. The question which interests us here is this: Does not a moment of value-determination enter in independently of labour, not arising directly from it, but originating in circulation itself? ⟨The fact that *credit* equalizes the differences in capital turnover does not belong here yet. But the question itself belongs here, because it arises out of the simple concept of capital – regarded in general.⟩ The more frequent turnover of capital in a given period of time resembles the more frequent harvests during the natural year in the southerly countries compared with the northerly. As already stated above, we here abstract entirely from the different amounts of time which capital must spend in the phase of production – in the productive realization process itself. Just as grain when it is put in the soil as seed loses its immediate use value, is *devalued* as immediate use value, so is capital *devalued* from the completion of the production process until its retransformation into money and from there into capital again. ⟨This velocity with which it can transpose itself from the form of money back into the conditions of production – unlike in slavery, it is not the worker himself who appears among these conditions of production, but rather the exchange with him – depends on the production speed and continuity of the remaining capitals, which supply him with raw material and instrument, as well as on the availability of workers, and in this last respect a relative surplus population is the best condition for capital.⟩ ⟨Quite apart from capital A's production process, the speed and continuity of production process B appears as a moment which conditions the retransformation of capital A from the form of money into the form of industrial capital. The duration of the *production process* of capital B thus appears as a moment in the *velocity of the circulation process* of capital A. The duration of one capital's production phase determines the velocity of the other's circulation phase. Their *simultaneity* is a condition required so that A's circulation is not obstructed – the fact that its own elements, for which it has to exchange and be exchanged, are thrown into production and circulation simultaneously. For example. In the final third of the eighteenth century, the hand-spinning system was incapable of supplying the required amounts of raw material for weaving – or, what is the same – spinning could not put the flax or cotton through its production process with the required simultaneity – simultaneous velocity. The consequence was the invention of the spinning machine, which supplied a greater product in the same labour time, or, what is the same thing, required less labour time for the same product – less time delay in the spinning process. All moments of capital which appear involved in it when it is considered from the point of view of its general concept obtain an independent reality, and, further, only show themselves when it appears as real, as many capitals. The inner, living organization, which takes place in this way within and through competition, thus develops all the more extensively.⟩

If we examine the entire turnover of capital, then four moments appear, or, each of the two great moments of the production process and the circulation process appears again in a duality: we can take either circulation or production as the point of departure here. This much has now been said, that circulation is itself a moment of production, since capital becomes capital only through circulation; production is a moment of circulation only in so far as the latter is itself regarded as the totality of the production process. The moments are: (I) The real production process and its duration. (II) Transformation of the product into money. Duration of this operation. (III) Transformation of the money in the proper proportions into raw material, means of labour and labour, in short, into the elements of productive capital. (IV) The exchange of a part of the capital for living labour capacity can be regarded as a particular moment, and must be so regarded, since the labour market is ruled by other laws than the product market etc. Here population is the main thing, not in absolute but in relative terms. Moment I does not come into consideration here, as stated, since it coincides with the conditions of realization generally. Moment III can be considerd only when the theme is not capital generally, but many capitals. Moment IV belongs in the section on wages etc.

We are concerned here only with Moment II. In money circulation there was a merely formal alternation of exchange value as money and as commodity. Here *money, commodity, are conditions of production*, ultimately of the production process. The moments here are different; they are filled with content. The differences in capital turnover as posited in II – since it depends neither on greater difficulty in the exchange with labour, nor on delays resulting from the fact that raw material [*Rohstoff*] and raw material [*Rohmaterial*][21] are not present simultaneously in circulation, nor in the different durations of the production process – could therefore arise only from increased difficulties in realization. This is obviously not an immanent case arising from the relation itself, but rather coincides here, where we are examining capital in general, with what we have said about the way in which realization simultaneously results in devaluation.[22] No business will be founded on the principle that it can sell its products with *greater difficulty* than another. If this resulted from the smaller size of the market, then not a larger – as presupposed – but a smaller capital would be employed there than in the business with a larger market. It could be connected, however, with the *greater distance of the market in space* and hence the delayed return. The longer time required by capital A to realize itself would be due here to the greater spatial distance it has to travel after the production

21. Marx's distinction between *Rohstoff* and *Rohmaterial* has no English equivalent. *Rohstoff* is the raw material in its pristine state, before being subjected to human labour; *Rohmaterial* is the raw material which has been formed by human labour but has yet to enter into the final product. Cf. *Capital*, Vol. I, Moscow, 1954, pp. 178–82.

22. See above, p. 402.

process in order to exchange as C for M. But cannot e.g. the product produced for China be regarded in such a way that the product is completed, its production process completed, only when it has reached the Chinese market? Its realization costs would rise by the costs of transport from England to China. (We cannot yet speak about the compensation for the longer fallow period of capital here, because the secondary and derived forms of surplus value – interest – would already have to have been presupposed.) The costs of production would resolve into the labour time objectified in the direct production process + the labour time contained in transport. Now the question is initially this: Given the basic principles we have so far asserted, can a surplus value be extracted from the transport costs? Let us deduct the constant part of the capital consumed in transport, ship, vehicle etc. and everything which falls under the heading of their application, since this element contributes nothing to the question, and it is irrelevant whether this is posited as $= 0$ or $= x$. Is it possible, then, that there is surplus labour in these transport costs, and that capital can therefore squeeze a surplus value out of them? The question is simple to answer if we ask a further question, where and which is the necessary labour or the value in which it objectifies itself? The product must pay (1) its own exchange value, the labour objectified in itself; (2) the surplus time, which the shipper, carter etc. employs on its transportation. Whether he can or cannot extract the surplus value depends on the wealth of the country into which he brings the product and on its needs etc., on the use value of the product for this land. In direct production, it is clear that all the surplus labour which the manufacturer makes the worker do is surplus value for him, in that it is labour objectified in new use values, which costs him nothing. But he can obviously not employ him during transport for a longer time than is required for the transporting. Otherwise he would throw labour time away instead of realizing it, i.e. he would not objectify it in a use value. If the sailor, the carter etc. require only half a year of labour time to live a full year (if this is generally the proportion of labour necessary for subsistence), then the capitalist employs him for a whole year and pays him a half. By adding a whole year's labour time to the value of the transported products, but paying only $\frac{1}{2}$, he gains a surplus value of 100% on necessary labour. The case is entirely the same as in direct production, and the original surplus value of the transported product can come about only because the workers are *not paid* for a part of the transportation time, because it is surplus time, time *over and above* the labour necessary for them to live. That an individual product might be made so much more expensive, owing to the transport costs, that it could not be sold – on account of the disproportion between the value of the product and its surplus value as a transported product, a quality which becomes extinguished in it as soon as it has arrived at its destination– does not affect the matter. If a manufacturer were to set his entire machinery into motion in order to spin 1 lb. of twist, then the value of this lb. would likewise rise so that it would hardly find a market. The rise in the prices of imported products, as well as the smaller consumption of them in the Middle Ages etc., stem precisely from this cause. Whether I extract metals from mines, or take commodities to the site of their consumption, both movements are equally spatial. The improvement of the means of transport and communication likewise falls into the category of the development of the productive forces generally. The fact that it can depend on the value of the products whether or not they are able to bear transport costs; that, further, commercial traffic in mass quantities is required to reduce transport costs – a ship with a loading capacity of 100 tons can carry 2 or 100 tons with the same transport costs etc. – and in order to make means of communication pay etc., all this does not belong here. (Nevertheless, it will be necessary to devote a special section to the means of communication, since they make up a form of fixed capital which has its own laws of realization.) If one imagines the same capital both producing and transporting, then both acts fall within direct production, and circulation as we have considered it so far, i.e. transformation into money as soon as the product has achieved its final form for consumption, would begin only when the product had been brought to its point of destination. This capitalist's delayed return compared to that of another, who gets rid of his product on the spot, would resolve into another form of greater use of fixed capital, with which we are not yet concerned here. Whether A requires 100 thalers more for instrument, or whether he needs 100 thalers more in order to bring his product to its destination, to market, is the same thing. In both cases more fixed capital is used; more *means* of production, which is consumed in direct production. In this respect, then, no immanent case would be posited here; it would fall under the examination of the difference between fixed capital and circulating capital.

Circulation costs. – Means of communication and transport.
(*Division of the branches of labour.*) (Concentration *of many*
workers. Productive force of this concentration.)
(Mass *production.*) – General as distinct from particular
conditions of production

Still, an additional moment enters here: the *costs of circulation*,
which are not contained in the simple concept of circulation and
do not concern us yet. Only in connection with interest and particularly with credit can we speak of the *costs of circulation* arising
from circulation as an economic act – as a relation of production,
not as a direct moment of production, as was the case with the
means of transport and communication. Circulation as we regard it
here is a process of transformation, a qualitative process of value,
as it appears in the different form of money, production (realization) process, product, retransformation into money and surplus
capital. [We are concerned here] in so far as new aspects are
created within this process of transformation as such – in this
transition from one form to another. The costs of circulation are
not necessarily included e.g. in the transition from product to
money. They can be = 0.

However, in so far as circulation itself creates costs, itself requires surplus labour, it appears as itself included within the production process. In this respect circulation appears as a moment of
the direct production process. Where production is directly oriented towards use, and only the excess product is exchanged, the
costs of circulation appear only for the excess product, not for the
main product.[23] The more production comes to rest on exchange
value, hence on exchange, the more important do the physical
conditions of exchange – the means of communication and transport – become for the costs of circulation. Capital by its nature
drives beyond every spatial barrier. Thus the creation of the physical conditions of exchange – of the means of communication and
transport – the annihilation of space by time – becomes an extraordinary necessity for it. Only in so far as the direct product can
be realized in distant markets in mass quantities in proportion to
reductions in the transport costs, and only in so far as at the same
time the means of communication and transport themselves can
yield spheres of realization for labour, driven by capital; only in so
far as commercial traffic takes place in massive volume – in which
more than necessary labour is replaced – only to that extent is the

23. See above, pp. 256–7.

production of cheap means of communication and transport a condition for production based on capital, and promoted by it *for that reason*. All labour required in order to throw the finished product into circulation – it is in economic circulation only when it is present on the market – is from capital's viewpoint a barrier to be overcome – as is all labour required as a *condition* for the production process (thus e.g. expenses for the security of exchange etc.). The sea route, as the route which moves and is transformed under its own impetus, is that of trading peoples κατ' ἐξοχήν.[24] On the other side, highways originally fall to the community, later for a long period to the governments, as pure deductions from production, deducted from the common surplus product of the country, but do not constitute a source of its wealth, i.e. do not cover their production costs. In the original, self-sustaining communes of Asia, on one side no need for roads; on the other side the lack of them locks them into their closed-off isolation and thus forms an essential moment of their survival without alteration (as in India). Road construction by means of the *corvée*, or through taxes, which is another form, is a forced transformation of a part of a country's surplus labour or surplus product into roads. If an individual capital is to undertake this – i.e. if it is to create the conditions of the production process which are not included in the *production* process directly – then the work must provide a profit.

Presupposing a certain road between A and B (let land cost nothing), then this contains no more than a definite quantity of labour, hence value. Whether the capitalist or the state has it built is the same thing. Does the capitalist make a gain here, then, by creating surplus labour and hence surplus value? First, strip off what is puzzling about the road, which arises from its nature as fixed capital. Imagine that the road could be sold at once, like a coat or a ton of iron. If the production of the road cost say 12 months, then its value = 12 months. If the general standard of labour is such that a worker can live from say 6 months of objectified labour, then, if he built the entire road, he would create surplus value for himself to the amount of 6 months' labour; or if the commune built the road, and the worker wanted to work only the necessary time, then another worker would have to be drawn in to work 6 months. The capitalist, however, forces the one worker to work 12 months, and pays him 6. The part of the value of the road

24. *par excellence*.

which contains his surplus labour forms the capitalist's profit. The material form in which the product appears must absolutely not interfere in laying the foundations of the theory of value through objectified labour time. But the question is precisely: can the capitalist realize the road [*den Weg verwerten*], can he realize [*realisieren*] its value through exchange? This question naturally arises with every product, but it takes a special form with the general conditions of production. Suppose the value of the road is not realized. But it is built anyway, because it is a necessary use value. How does the matter stand then? It has to be built and has to be paid for – in so far as its cost of production must be exchanged for it. It comes into existence only through a certain consumption of labour, means of labour, raw materials etc. Whether it is built by *corvée* or through taxes is the same. But it is built only because it is a necessary use value for the commune, because the commune requires it at any price. This is certainly a surplus labour which the individual must perform, whether in the form of forced labour, or in the indirect form of taxes, over and above the direct labour necessary for his subsistence. But to the extent that it is necessary for the commune, and for each individual as its *member*, what he performs is not surplus labour, but a part of his *necessary* labour, the labour necessary for him to reproduce himself as *commune member* and hence to reproduce the community, which is itself a general condition of his productive activity. If the labour time were entirely consumed in direct production (or, expressed indirectly, if it were impossible to raise surplus tax revenue for this specific purpose), then the road would have to remain unbuilt. If the whole society is regarded as one individual, then necessary labour would consist of the sum of all the particular labour functions which the division of labour separates off. This one individual would have to spend e.g. so much time for agriculture, so much for industry, so much for trade, so much for making instruments, so much, to return to our subject, for road building and means of communication. All these necessities resolve into so much labour time which must be directed towards different aims and expended in particular activities. How much labour time could be employed would depend on the amount of labour capacity (= the mass of individuals capable of labour who constitute the society) and on the development of the productive force of labour (the mass of products (use values) which it can create in a given span of time). Exchange value, which presupposes a more or less developed division of labour, depending on the level of exchange itself, presupposes that, instead of one individual (the society) doing different kinds of labour and employing his labour time in different forms, each and every individual's labour time is devoted exclusively to the necessary particular functions. If we speak of *necessary labour time*, then the particular separate branches of labour appear *as necessary*. Where exchange value is the basis, this reciprocal necessity is mediated through exchange, and shows itself precisely in the fact that every particular [piece of] objectified labour, every particularly specified and materialized [piece of] labour time exchanges for the product and symbol of labour time in general, of objectified labour time pure and simple, for money, and can thus be exchanged again for every particular labour. This necessity is itself subject to changes, because needs are produced just as are products and the different kinds of work skills. Increases and decreases do take place within the limits set by these needs and necessary labours. The greater the extent to which historic needs – needs created by production itself, social needs – needs which are themselves the offspring of social production and intercourse, are posited as *necessary*, the higher the level to which real wealth has become developed. Regarded *materially*, wealth consists only in the manifold variety of needs. The crafts themselves do not appear *necessary* ALONGSIDE self-sustaining agriculture, where spinning, weaving etc. are done as a secondary domestic occupation. But e.g. if agriculture itself rests on scientific activities – if it requires machinery, chemical fertilizer acquired through exchange, seeds from distant countries etc., and if rural, patriarchal manufacture has already vanished – which is already implied in the presupposition – then the machine-making factory, external trade, crafts etc. appear as *needs* for agriculture. Perhaps guano can be procured for it only through the export of silk goods. Then the manufacture of silk no longer appears as a luxury industry, but as a necessary industry for agriculture. It is therefore chiefly and essentially because, in this case, agriculture no longer finds the natural conditions of its own production within itself, naturally, arisen, spontaneous, and ready to hand, but these exist as an independent industry separate from it – and, with this separateness the whole complex set of interconnections in which this industry exists is drawn into the sphere of the conditions of agricultural production – it is because of this, that what previously appeared as a luxury is now necessary, and that so-called luxury needs appear e.g. as a necessity for the most naturally necessary and down-to-earth industry of all. This pulling-away of the natural ground from the foundations of every industry, and this transfer of its conditions of production outside itself, into a general context – hence the transformation of what was previously superfluous into what is necessary, as a historically created necessity – is the tendency of capital. The general foundation of all industries comes to be general exchange itself, the world market, and hence the totality of the activities, intercourse, needs etc. of which it is made up. *Luxury* is the opposite of the *naturally necessary*. Necessary needs are those of the individual himself reduced to a natural subject. The development of industry suspends this natural necessity as well as this former luxury – in bourgeois society, it is true, it does so only in *antithetical form*, in that it itself only posits another specific social standard as necessary, opposite luxury. These questions about the *system of needs* and *system of labours* – at what point is this to be dealt with? Will be seen in due course.

Now back to our road. If it can be built at all, it proves that the society possesses the labour time (living labour and objectified labour) required for its construction.* Why, then, as soon as production based on exchange value and division of labour appears does road building not become the business of individuals? (And it does not so become where it is conducted through taxes by the state.) First of all: the society, the united individuals, may possess the surplus time to build the road, but only in concentration. Concentration is always the addition of the part of labour capacity which each individual can employ on road building, apart from his particular work; but it is *not only* addition. The unification of their forces increases their *force of production*; but this is by no means the same as saying that all of them added together numerically would possess the same labour capacity if they did not *work together*, hence if to the sum of their labour capacities were not added the *surplus* existing only in and through their *united, combined* labour. Hence the violent rounding-up of the people in Egypt, Etruria, India etc. for forced construction and compulsory public works. Capital effects the same concentration in *another*

* It is here presupposed of course that it follows a correct instinct. It could eat up the seed grain, let the field lie fallow, and build roads. But it would thereby not have accomplished the *necessary labour*, because it would not *reproduce* itself, not maintain itself as living labour capacity through this labour. Alternatively the living labour capacities may be directly murdered, as e.g. by Peter I, to build Petersburg. This sort of thing does not belong here.

way, through the manner of its exchange with free labour.*
Secondly: On one side, the population may be developed far
enough, and the support which it finds in the employment of
machinery etc. may be far enough advanced on the other side, so
that the power arising only from the material, *massive concentration*
of labour – and in antiquity it is always this *massive* effect of forcibly concentrated labour – may be superfluous, and a *relatively*
smaller *mass of living labour* may be required.† A special class of
road-workers may form, employed by the state,‡ or a part of the
occasionally unemployed population is used for it, together with a
number of superintendents etc., who do not work as capitalists,
however, but as more highly educated *menials*. (About the relation
of this skilled labour etc. later.) The workers are then wage workers,
but the state employs them not as such, but as menial servants.

Now, for the capitalist to undertake road building as a business, at his expense,§ various conditions are required, which all
amount to this, that the mode of production based on capital is
already developed to its highest stage. *Firstly*: *Large capital* is itself

*That capital has to do not with isolated, individual labour but with com-
bined labour, just as it is in and for itself already a social, combined force, is a
point which should perhaps be treated already in the general history of the rise
of capital.

†The greater the extent to which production still rests on mere manual
labour, on use of muscle power etc., in short on physical exertion by individual
labourers, the more does the increase of the *productive force* consist in their
collaboration *on a mass scale*. The opposite features, particularization and
individualization, are displayed by the semi-artistic crafts; the skilfulness of
individual, but uncombined labour. Capital, in its true development, combines mass labour with skill, but in such a way that the former loses its physical
power, and the skill resides not in the worker but in the machine and in the
scientific combination of both as a whole in the factory. The social spirit of
labour obtains an objective existence separate from the individual workers.

‡*Among the Romans, the army constituted a mass* – but already divorced
from the whole people – which was disciplined to labour, whose surplus time
also belonged to the state; who sold their entire labour time for pay to the
state, exchanged their entire labour capacity for a wage necessary for the
maintenance of their life, just as does the worker with the capitalist. This
holds for the period when the Roman army was no longer a citizen's army but
a mercenary army. This is here likewise a free sale of labour on the part of the
soldier. But the state does not buy it with the production of values as aim.
And thus, although the wage form may seem to occur originally in armies,
this pay system is nevertheless essentially different from wage labour. There is
some similarity in the fact that the state uses up the army in order to gain an
increase in power and wealth.

§If the state lets this sort of matter be conducted through *state-contractors*,
then this still always takes place indirectly through the *corvée* or taxes.

presupposed, a large capital concentrated in his hands, in order that he may be able to undertake work of such dimensions and of such slow turnover, [and hence] realization. Hence mostly *share-capital*, the form in which capital has worked itself up to its final form, in which it is posited, not only *in itself*, in its substance, but is posited also in its *form*, as social power and product. *Secondly*: It must bring *interest*, but not necessarily *profit* (it may bring more than interest, but this is not required). We do not yet need to examine this point any further here. *Thirdly*: As presupposition, such a volume of traffic – commercial, above all – that the road pays for itself, i.e. that the price demanded for the use of the road *is worth* that much exchange value for the producers, or supplies a productive force for which they can pay that much. *Fourthly*: A portion of idle wealth which can lay out its revenue for these articles of locomotion. But these two presuppositions are what remains essential: (1) Capital in the required mass, employable for this object, at attractive interest; (2) it has to be worth it for the productive capitals, for industrial capital, to pay the price of passage. Thus e.g. the first railway between Liverpool and Manchester had become a necessity of production for the Liverpool cotton brokers and even more for the Manchester manufacturers.* Capital as such – its being posited with the necessary scope – will produce roads only when the production of roads has become a necessity for the producers, especially for productive capital itself; a condition for the capitalist's *profit-making*. Then the road will pay for itself. But in this case, a large volume of traffic is already presupposed. It is the same presupposition *doubly*: On one side, the wealth of the country sufficiently concentrated and transformed into the form of capital, to allow it to undertake such works as realization processes for capital; on the other side the volume of traffic sufficient, and the barrier formed by the lack of means of communication sufficiently felt as such, to allow the capitalist to realize the value of the road (in instalments over time) as road (i.e. its use). All *general conditions* of *production*, such as roads, canals, etc., whether they facilitate circulation or even make it possible at all, or whether

Competition is better suited to create the necessity of e.g. the railway in a country where the previous development of its forces of production would not yet push so far. The effect of *competition among nations* belongs in the section on *international intercourse*. The civilizing influences of capital particularly show themselves here.

they increase the force of production (such as irrigation works etc. as in Asia and, incidentally, as still built by governments in Europe), presuppose, in order to be undertaken by capital instead of by the government which represents the community as such, the highest development of production founded on capital. The separation of *public works* from the state, and their migration into the domain of the works undertaken by capital itself, indicates the degree to which the real community has constituted itself in the form of capital. A country, e.g. the United States, may feel the need for railways in connection with production; nevertheless the direct advantage arising from them for production may be too small for the investment to appear as anything but *sunk capital*. Then capital shifts the burden on to the shoulders of the state; or, where the state traditionally still takes up a position superior to capital, it still possesses the authority and the will to force the society of capitalists to put a part of their *revenue*, not of their capital, into such generally useful works, which appear at the same time as *general* conditions of production, and hence not as *particular* conditions for one capitalist or another – and, so long as capital does not adopt the form of the joint-stock company, it always looks out only for its *particular* conditions of realization, and shifts the *communal* conditions off on to the whole country as national requirements. Capital undertakes only *advantageous* undertakings, advantageous in its sense. True, it also speculates unsoundly, and, as we shall see, *must* do so. It then undertakes *investments* which do not pay, and which pay only as soon as they have become to a certain degree *devalued*. Hence the many undertakings where the first *investment* is sunk and lost, the first entrepreneurs go bankrupt – and begin to realize themselves only at second or third hand, where the invested capital has become smaller owing to *devaluation*. Incidentally, the state itself and everything connected with it belongs with these deductions from *revenue*, belongs so to speak to the *consumption costs* for the individual, the production costs for society. A road itself may so increase the force of production that it creates new traffic which then makes the road profitable. There are works and investments which may be necessary without being productive in the capitalist sense, i.e. without the realization of the *surplus labour* contained in them through circulation, through exchange, as *surplus value*. If a worker works e.g. 12 hours per day for a year building a road, and if the generally necessary labour time is = 6 hours on the average, then he works a surplus time of 6 hours. But if the road cannot be sold for 12 hours, perhaps only for 6, then this road construction is not an undertaking for capital, and road building is not productive labour for it. Capital must be able to sell the road (the timing and mode of the sale are beside the point here) in such a way that both the necessary and the surplus labour are realized, or in such a way that it obtains out of the general fund of profits – of surplus values – a sufficiently large share to make it the same as if it had created surplus value. *This relation* is to be examined *later in connection with profit and necessary labour*. The highest development of capital exists when the general conditions of the process of social production are not paid out of *deductions from the social revenue*, the state's taxes – where revenue and not capital appears as the labour fund, and where the worker, although he is a free wage worker like any other, nevertheless stands economically in a different relation – but rather out of *capital as capital*. This shows the degree to which capital has subjugated all conditions of social production to itself, on one side; and, on the other side, hence, the extent to which social reproductive wealth has been *capitalized*, and all needs are satisfied through the exchange form; as well as the extent to which the *socially posited* needs of the individual, i.e. those which he consumes and feels not as a single individual in society, but communally with others – whose mode of consumption is social by the nature of the thing – are likewise not only consumed but also produced through exchange, individual exchange. In the case of the above road, road building must be so advantageous that the transformation of a given amount of labour time into the road must reproduce the worker's labour capacity to the same degree as if he transformed it into cultivated fields. Value is determined by objectified labour time, whatever form it may take. But it does depend now on the use value in which it is realized, whether this *value* is realizable. It is presupposed here that the road is a requirement for the commune, hence the use value is presupposed. For capital, on the other side, if it is to undertake the building of the road, it must be presupposed that not only the *necessary labour time* but also the *surplus labour time* worked by the worker can be paid for – this is where his profit comes from. (The capitalist often compels this payment by means of protective tariffs, monopoly, state coercion; while the individuals engaged in exchange, under conditions of free exchange, would *at most* pay the necessary labour.) It is very possible that surplus labour time is present but not paid for (which can after all happen to every capitalist). *Where capital rules* (just as where there is slavery and bondage or serfdom of any sort), *the worker's absolute labour time is posited for him as condition of being allowed to work the necessary labour time, i.e. of being allowed to realize the labour time necessary for the maintenance of his labour capacity in use values for himself.* Competition then has the result, in every kind of work, that he must work the full time – i.e. surplus labour time. But it may be the case that this surplus labour time, although present in the product, is not exchangeable. For the worker himself – compared with the other wage workers – it is surplus labour. For the employer, it is labour which, while it has a use value for him, like e.g. his cook, has no exchange value, hence the entire distinction between *necessary and surplus labour time* does not exist. Labour may be necessary without being productive. All *general, communal* conditions of production – so long as their production cannot yet be accomplished by capital as such and under its conditions – are therefore paid for out of a part of the country's revenue – out of the government's treasury – and the workers do not appear as productive workers, even though they increase the productive force of capital.

The result of our digression is, incidentally, that the production of the means of communication, of the physical conditions of circulation, is put into the category of the production of fixed capital, and hence does not constitute a special case. Meanwhile, and incidentally, there opened up for us the prospect, which cannot be sharply defined yet at this point, *of a specific relation of capital to the communal, general conditions of social production,* as distinct from the conditions of a *particular capital* and its *particular production* process.

Transport to market (spatial condition of circulation) belongs in the production process. Credit, the temporal moment of circulation. – Capital is circulating capital. – Money circulation a mere illusion. – Sismondi. Cherbuliez. (Capital. Its various component parts)

Circulation proceeds in space and time. Economically considered, the spatial condition, the bringing of the product to the market, belongs to the production process itself. The product is really finished only when it is on the market. The movement through which it gets there belongs still with the cost of making it. It does not form a necessary moment of circulation, regarded as a particular value-process, since a product may be bought and even consumed at the point of its production. But this spatial moment is important in so far as the expansion of the market and the exchangeability of the product are connected with it. The reduction of the costs of this *real* circulation (in space) belongs to the development of the forces of production by capital, the reduction of the costs of its realization. In certain respects, as an external condition for the existence of the economic process of circulation, this moment may also be reckoned as part of the *production costs* of circulation, so that, with respect to this moment, circulation itself appears as a moment not only of the production process in general, but also of the direct production process. In any case, what appears here is the determination of this moment by the general degree of development of the productive forces, and of production based on capital generally. This locational moment – the bringing of the product to market, which is a necessary condition of its circulation, except when the point of production is itself a market – could more precisely be regarded as the transformation of the product *into a commodity*. Only on the market is it a *commodity*. (Whether or not this forms a particular moment is a matter of chance. If capital produces to order, then neither this moment nor the transformation into money exists as a particular moment for it. *Work done to order*, i.e. supply corresponding to a prior demand, as a *general or predominant situation*, is not characteristic of large industry and in no way arises from the nature of capital as a condition.)

Secondly, the temporal moment. This is an essential part of the concept of circulation. Suppose the act of making the transition from commodity to money is fixed by contract, then this still requires time – calculating, weighing, measuring. The abbreviation of this moment is likewise development of productive force. However, this is time still conceived only as an *external* condition for the transition from the state of money into that of commodity; the transition itself is presupposed; the question is the time which *elapses during this presupposed act*. This belongs to the *cost of production*. Quite different is the time which generally passes before the commodity makes its transition into money;

or the time during which it remains a *commodity*, only a potential but not a real value. This is pure loss.

It is clear from everything said above that circulation appears as an essential process of capital. The production process cannot be begun anew before the transformation of the commodity into money. The *constant continuity* of the process, the unobstructed and fluid transition of value from one form into the other, or from one phase of the process into the next, appears as a fundamental condition for production based on capital to a much greater degree than for all earlier forms of production. On another side, while the necessity of this continuity is given, its phases are separate in time and space, and appear as particular, mutually indifferent processes. It thus appears as a matter of chance for production based on capital whether or not its essential condition, the continuity of the different processes which constitute its process as a whole, is actually brought about. The suspension of this chance element by capital itself is *credit*. (It has other aspects as well; but this aspect arises out of the direct nature of the production process and is hence the foundation of the necessity of credit.) Which is why *credit* in any developed form appears in no earlier mode of production. There was borrowing and lending in earlier situations as well, and usury is even the oldest of the antediluvian forms of capital. But borrowing and lending no more constitute *credit* than working constitutes *industrial labour* or *free wage labour*. And credit as an essential, developed relation of production appears *historically* only in circulation based on capital or on wage labour. (*Money* itself is a form for suspending the unevenness of the times required in different branches of production, to the extent that this obstructs exchange.) Although *usury* is itself a form of credit in its *bourgeoisified* form, the form *adapted to capital*, in its pre-bourgeois form it is rather the *expression of lack of credit*.

(The retransformation of money into objective moments or conditions of production presupposes the latters' *availability*. It constitutes the various *markets* where the producer encounters them as commodity – in the hands of a merchant – markets which (alongside the labour market) are essentially distinct from the markets for direct, individual, final consumption.)

Money became transformed into commodity through circulation, and in the exchange of M–C, consumption completed the process; or, the commodity was exchanged for money – and in the exchange C–M, M was either a vanishing moment itself to be exchanged for C again, in which case the process ended with consumption again, or the money withdrew from circulation and transformed itself into dead treasure, merely symbolic wealth. At no point did the process ignite from within, but rather the presuppositions of money circulation lay outside it, and it constantly required a new push from the outside. In so far as both moments were exchanged, their change of form within circulation was merely formal. But in so far as content entered in, it dropped out of the economic process; content did not form a part of it. The commodity did not sustain itself as money, nor the money as commodity; each was either one or the other. Value as such did not sustain itself in and through circulation as predominant over the process of its transformation, its metamorphosis; nor was the *use value* itself (as is the case in the capital production process) produced by the *exchange value*. With capital the consumption of the commodity is itself not final; it falls within the production process; it itself appears as a moment of production, i.e. of *value-positing* [*Wertsetzen*].

Capital is now posited, however, as not merely sustaining itself formally, but as *realizing itself as value*, as value relating to itself as value in every one of the moments of its metamorphosis, in which it appears at one time as money, at another time as commodity, then again as exchange value, then again as use value. The passage from one moment to the other appears as a particular process, but each of these processes is the transition to the other. Capital is thus posited as value-in-process, which is capital in every moment.[25] It is thus posited as *circulating capital*; in every moment capital, and circulating from one form into the next. The point of return is at the same time the point of departure and vice versa – namely the *capitalist*. All capital is originally circulating capital, product of circulation, as well as producing circulation, tracing in this way its own course. From the present standpoint, money circulation now appears as itself merely a moment of the circulation of capital, and its independence is posited as a mere *semblance*. It appears as determined on all sides by the circulation of capital, to which we shall return. In so far as it forms an independent motion alongside that of capital,

25. Cf. Hegel, *System of Philosophy*, I, *Logic*, para. 161: 'The concept remains at home with itself in its process; no new content is posited by the process, only an alteration of form is produced.'

this independence is posited only by the *continuity* of the circulation of capital, so that this one moment may be held constant and regarded for itself.

⟨'Capital a permanent, *self-multiplying* value which never decays. This *value* tears itself loose from the commodity which created it; remains, like a *metaphysical, insubstantial quality*, always in the possession of the same farmer,' (e.g.), 'for whom it cloaks itself in different forms.' (Sism. VI.)[26] 'In the exchange of labour for capital, the worker demands subsistence *in order to live*; the capitalist demands *work in order to make a profit.*' (Sism. loc. cit.) 'The master of the workshop gains, makes a profit from every *increase in the powers of production* which the *division of labour* brings about.' (loc. cit.)[27] 'Sale of labour = renunciation of all fruits of labour.' (Cherbuliez, ch. XXVIII.)[28] 'The three component parts of capital do not grow evenly' (i.e. *matière première*, instrument, *approvisionnement*),[29] 'nor are they in the *same relation* in the different stages of society. The *approvisionnement* remains the same for a certain period, regardless of how quickly the *speed of production* and consequently the *quantity of products* may increase. Thus an increase of *productive capital* does not necessarily entail an increase of the *approvisionnement* which is destined to form the price of labour; it can be accompanied by a reduction of it.' (loc. cit.)[30]⟩

Influence of circulation on the determination of value. – Circulation time = time of devaluation. – Difference between the capitalist mode of production and all earlier ones (universality etc.). Propagandistic nature of capital. – Abbreviation of circulation (credit). – Storch. – What the capitalist advances is labour. (Malthus.) – Barriers to capitalist production. (Thompson)[31]

⟨In as much as the renewal of production depends on the sale of the finished products; transformation of the commodity into money and retransformation of money into the conditions of

---

26. Sismondi, *Nouveaux Principes d'économie politique*, Vol. I, p. 89. See above, p. 261.

27. ibid., Vol. I, pp. 91–2.   28. Cherbuliez, *Richesse ou pauvreté*, p. 64.

29. In Cherbuliez; raw material, instrument of labour, and supply of articles of consumption. See above, p. 299.

30. Cherbuliez, *Richesse ou pauvreté*, pp. 25–6.

31. William Thompson (1783–1833) was an Irish landowner who embraced Owenism, and criticized political economy from a utopian socialist position, but on the basis of Ricardo's doctrines.

production – raw material, instrument, wages; in as much as the circuits which capital travels in order to go from one of these forms into the other constitute sections of circulation, and these sections are travelled in specific *amounts of time* (even spatial distance reduces itself to time; the important thing e.g. is not the market's distance in space, but the speed – the amount of time – with which it can be reached), by that much the velocity of circulation, the *time* in which it is accomplished, is a determinant of how many products can be produced in a given period of time; how often capital can be realized in a given period of time, how often it can *reproduce* and *multiply* its value. Thus a moment enters *into value-determination* which indeed does not come out of the direct relation of labour to capital. The frequency with which the same capital can repeat the production process (creation of new value) in a given period of time is evidently a condition not posited directly by the production process itself. Thus, while circulation does not itself produce a moment of *value-determination,* for that lies exclusively in labour, its speed does determine the speed with which the production process is repeated, values are created – thus, if not *values*, at least to a certain extent the mass of values. Namely, the values and surplus values posited by the production process, multiplied by the number of repetitions of the production process in a given period of time. When we speak of the velocity of the circulation of capital, we postulate that delays in the transition from one phase to the next arise only from *external barriers*, not such as arise from the production process and circulation itself (such as crises, overproduction etc.). Thus, in addition to the labour time realized in production, the *circulation time* of capital enters in as a moment of value creation – of productive labour time itself. While labour time appears as value-positing activity, this circulation time of capital appears as the *time of devaluation*. The difference shows itself simply in this: if the totality of the labour time commanded by capital is set at its maximum, say infinity, ∞, so that necessary labour time forms an infinitely small part and surplus labour time an infinitely large part of this ∞, then this would be the maximum realization of capital, and this is the tendency towards which it strives. On the other side, if the *circulation time of capital* were $= 0$, if the various stages of its transformation proceeded as rapidly in reality as in the mind, then that[32] would likewise be the maximum of the

32. 'That', i.e. 'that situation'.

factor by which the production process could be repeated, i.e. the number of capital realization processes in a given period of time. The repetition of the production process would be restricted only by the amount of time which it lasts, the amount of time which elapses during the transformation of raw material into product. *Circulation time* is therefore not a positive value-creating element; if it were = to 0, then value-creation would be at its maximum. But if either surplus labour time or necessary labour time = 0, i.e. if necessary labour time absorbed all time, or if production could proceed altogether *without* labour, then neither value, nor capital, nor value-creation would exist. *Circulation time* therefore determines value only in so far as it appears as a *natural barrier* to the realization of labour time. It is therefore in fact a deduction from *surplus labour time*, i.e. an increase of *necessary labour time*. It is clear that necessary labour time has to be paid for, whether the circulation process proceeds slowly or quickly. E.g. in trades where specific workers are required, who can, however, only be employed for a part of the year because the products are, say, saleable only in a given season, [in those trades] the workers would have to be paid for the entire year, i.e. surplus labour time is decreased in exact proportion to the reduction in their possibilities of employment during a given period of time, but still they must be paid in one way or another. (For example in the form that their wages for 4 months suffice to maintain them for a year.) If capital could utilize them for 12 months, it would pay them no higher, and would have gained that much surplus labour. *Circulation time thus appears as a barrier to the productivity of labour* = an increase in necessary labour time = a decrease in surplus labour time = a decrease in surplus value = an obstruction, a barrier to the self-realization process [*Selbstverwertungsprozess*] of capital. Thus, while capital must on one side strive to tear down every spatial barrier to intercourse, i.e. to exchange, and conquer the whole earth for its market, it strives on the other side to annihilate this space with time, i.e. to reduce to a minimum the time spent in motion from one place to another. The more developed the capital, therefore, the more extensive the market over which it circulates, which forms the spatial orbit of its circulation, the more does it strive simultaneously for an even greater extension of the market and for greater annihilation of space by time. (If labour time is regarded not as the working day of the individual worker, but as the indefinite working day of an indefinite number of workers, then all *relations of population* come in here; the basic doctrines of population are therefore just as much contained in this first chapter on capital as are those of profit, price, credit etc.) There appears here the universalizing tendency of capital, which distinguishes it from all previous stages of production. Although limited by its very nature, it strives towards the universal development of the forces of production, and thus becomes the presupposition of a new mode of production, which is founded not on the development of the forces of production for the purpose of reproducing or at most expanding a given condition, but where the free, unobstructed, progressive and universal development of the forces of production is itself the presupposition of society and hence of its reproduction; where advance beyond the point of departure is the only presupposition. This tendency – which capital possesses, but which at the same time, since capital is a limited form of production, contradicts it and hence drives it towards dissolution – distinguishes capital from all earlier modes of production, and at the same time contains this element, that capital is posited as a mere point of transition. All previous forms of society – or, what is the same, of the forces of social production – foundered on the development of wealth. Those thinkers of antiquity who were possessed of consciousness therefore directly denounced wealth as the dissolution of the community. The feudal system, for its part, foundered on urban industry, trade, modern agriculture (even as a result of individual inventions like gunpowder and the printing press). With the development of wealth – and hence also new powers and expanded intercourse on the part of individuals – the economic conditions on which the community rested were dissolved, along with the political relations of the various constituents of the community which corresponded to those conditions: religion, in which it was viewed in idealized form (and both [religion and political relations] rested in turn on a given relation to nature, into which all productive force resolves itself); the character, outlook etc. of the individuals. The *development of science alone* – i.e. the most solid form of wealth, both its product and its producer – was sufficient to dissolve these communities. But the *development of science*, this ideal and at the same time practical wealth, is only one aspect, one form in which the *development of the human productive forces*, i.e. of wealth, appears. Considered *ideally*, the dissolution of a given form of conscious-

ness sufficed to kill a whole epoch. In reality, this barrier to consciousness corresponds to a *definite degree of development of the
forces of material production* and hence of wealth. True, there was
not only a development on the old basis, but also a *development
of this basis itself*. The highest development of this *basis* itself
(the flower into which it transforms itself; but it is always *this*
basis, *this* plant as flower; hence wilting *after* the flowering and as
consequence of the flowering) is the point at which it is itself
worked out, developed, into the form in which it is compatible
with the *highest development of the forces of production*, hence
also the richest development of the individuals. As soon as this
point is reached, the further development appears as decay, and
the new development begins from a new basis. We saw earlier
that property in the conditions of production was posited as
identical with a limited, definite form of the community; hence
of the individual with the characteristics – limited characteristics
and limited development of his productive forces – required to
form such a community. This presupposition was itself in turn
the result of a limited historic stage of the development of the
productive forces; of wealth as well as of the mode of creating it.
The purpose of the community, of the individual – as well as the
condition of production – [is] *the reproduction of these specific
conditions of production* and of the individuals, both singly and
in their social groupings and relations – as living carriers of these
conditions. Capital posits the *production of wealth* itself and hence
the universal development of the productive forces, the constant
overthrow of its prevailing presuppositions, as the presupposition
of its reproduction. Value excludes no use value; i.e. includes no
particular kind of consumption etc., of intercourse etc. as absolute
condition; and likewise every degree of the development of the
social forces of production, of intercourse, of knowledge etc.
appears to it only as a barrier which it strives to overpower. Its
own presupposition – value – is posited as product, not as a
loftier presupposition hovering over production. The barrier to
capital is that this entire development proceeds in a contradictory way, and that the working-out of the productive forces, of
general wealth etc., knowledge etc., appears in such a way that
the working individual *alienates* himself [*sich entäussert*]; relates
to the conditions brought out of him by his labour as those not of
his *own* but of an *alien wealth* and of his own poverty. But this
antithetical form is itself fleeting, and produces the real conditions

of its own suspension. The result is: the tendentially and potentially general development of the forces of production – of wealth as such – as a basis; likewise, the universality of intercourse, hence the world market as a basis. The basis as the possibility of the universal development of the individual, and the real development of the individuals from this basis as a constant suspension of its *barrier*, which is recognized as a barrier, not taken for a *sacred limit*. Not an ideal or imagined universality of the individual, but the universality of his real and ideal relations. Hence also the grasping of his own history as a *process*, and the recognition of nature (equally present as practical power over nature) as his real body. The process of development itself posited and known as the presupposition of the same.[33] For this, however, necessary above all that the full development of the forces of production has become the *condition of production*; and not that specific *conditions of production* are posited as a limit to the development of the productive forces. –

If we now return to the *circulation time* of capital, then its abbreviation (except for development of the means of communication and transport required to bring the product to market) [means] in part the *creation* of a continuous and hence an ever more extensive market; and in part the development of *economic* relations, development of forms of capital, by means of which it *artificially* abbreviates the circulation time. (*All forms of credit*.) ⟨It may be further remarked at this point that, since capital alone possesses the conditions of the production of capital, hence satisfies and strives to realize [them], [it is] a general tendency of capital at all points which are presuppositions of circulation, which form its productive centres, to assimilate these points into itself, i.e. to transform them into capitalizing production or production of capital. This propagandistic (civilizing) tendency a property exclusively of capital – as distinct from the earlier conditions of production.⟩ The modes of production where circulation does not form the immanent, dominant condition of production, naturally [do] not [meet] the specific circulation requirements of capital and hence also do not [provide for] the working-out of the economic forms as well as of the real forces of production corresponding to them. – Production based on capital originally came out of circulation; we now see that it posits cir-

33. 'Of the same' (*desselben*) probably refers back to 'recognition of nature ([and] practical power over nature)'. The contraction is ambiguous.

culation as its own condition, and likewise the production process in its immediacy as moment of the circulation process, as well as the circulation process as one phase of the production process in its totality. – In so far as different capitals have different circulation times (e.g. one a more distant market, the other a near one; one a guaranteed transformation into money, the other a risky one; one more fixed capital, the other more circulating capital), this makes for differences among them in realization. But this happens only in the secondary realization process. Circulation time in itself is a *barrier* to realization (*necessary labour time* is of course also a barrier; but at the same time an element, since value and capital would vanish without it); [it is a] deduction from surplus labour time or an increase in *necessary labour time* in relation to *surplus labour time*. The circulation of capital *realizes value*, while living labour *creates value*. Circulation time is only a barrier to this realization of value, and, to that extent, to value creation; a barrier arising not from production generally but specific to production of capital, the suspension of which – or the struggle against which – hence also belongs to the specific economic development of capital and gives the impulse for the development of its forms in credit etc. ⟨Capital itself is the contradiction [, in] that, while it constantly tries to suspend *necessary labour time* (and this is at the same time the reduction of the worker to a minimum, i.e. his existence as mere living labour capacity), *surplus labour time* exists only in antithesis with necessary labour time, so that capital posits necessary labour time as a *necessary* condition of its reproduction and realization. At a certain point, a development of the forces of material production – which is at the same time a development of the forces of the working class – *suspends capital itself.*⟩

⟨'The entrepreneur can resume production only after he has sold the completed product, and has employed the price for the purchase of new materials and wages: thus, the more prompt circulation is in bringing about these two effects, the more is he capable of beginning his production anew, and the more products does the capital supply in a given period of time.' (Storch, 34.)[34]⟩ ⟨'The specific *advances of the capitalist* do not consist of cloth etc., but of labour.' (Malthus, IX, 26.)[35]⟩ ⟨'The accumu-

34. Storch, *Cours d'économie politique*, Vol. I, pp. 411–12.

35. Malthus, *The Measure of Value Stated and Illustrated, with an Application of it to the Alterations in the Value of the English Currency since 1790*, London, 1823, p. 17.

lation of the general capital of the community in other hands
[than] those of the operative labourers, necessarily retards the
progress of all industry save that of the usual remuneration of
capital, which the time and circumstances afford to the holders of
the capital ... In the previous systems, the *force of production
regarded in reference to and subordinate to actual accumulations*,
and to the perpetuating of the existing modes of distribution.
Actual accumulation and distribution are subordinate to the
power of producing.' (Thompson, 3.)[36]⟩

*Circulation and creation of value. (Equalization between
different capitals in the conditions of circulation.) Capital not a
source of value-creation. – Circulation costs. – Continuity of
production presupposes suspension of circulation time*

It follows from the relation of circulation time to the production
process that the sum of values produced, or the total realization
of capital in a given epoch, is determined not simply by the new
value which it creates in the production process, or by the surplus
time realized in the production process, but rather by this surplus
time (surplus value) multiplied by the number which expresses
how often the production process of capital can be repeated
within a given period of time. The number which expresses this
frequency of repetition may be regarded as the coefficient of the
production process or of the surplus value created through it.
However, this coefficient is not positively but negatively determined by the velocity of circulation. I.e. if the velocity of circulation were absolute, i.e. if no interruption in production
resulting from circulation occurred at all, then this coefficient
would be at its maximum. If the real conditions of e.g. wheat
production in a given country permit only one harvest, then no
velocity of circulation can make two harvests out of it. But if an
obstruction in the circulation occurred, if the farmer could not sell
his wheat soon enough e.g. to hire workers again, then production
would be delayed. The maximum of the coefficient of the production process or the realization process in a given period of time is
determined by the absolute time taken up by the production
phase itself. With circulation completed, capital is able to begin its

36. William Thompson, *An Inquiry into the Principles of the Distribution of
Wealth, Most Conducive to Human Happiness, Applied to the Newly Proposed
System of Voluntary Equality of Wealth*, London, 1824, p. 176.

production process anew. Thus if circulation caused no delay at all, if its velocity were absolute and its duration = 0, i.e. if it were accomplished in no time, then this would only be the same as if *capital* had been able to begin its production process anew directly it was finished; i.e. circulation would not have existed as a limiting barrier for production, and the repetition of the production process in a given period of time would be absolutely dependent on, identical with, the duration of the production process. Thus if the development of industry allowed *x* lb. of twist to be produced in 4 months with a capital of 100, then with that capital the production process could be repeated only 3 times per year, and only 3*x* lb. of twist could be produced. No velocity of circulation could increase the reproduction of capital, or rather the repetition of its realization process, beyond that point. That could occur only in consequence of an *increase in the forces of production*. Circulation time in itself is not a *productive force* of capital, but a *barrier to its productive force* arising from its nature as exchange value. The passage through the various phases of circulation here appears as a *barrier to production*, a barrier posited by the specific nature of capital itself. All that can happen through the acceleration and abbreviation of *circulation time* – of the circulation process – is the reduction of the barrier posited by the nature of capital. The natural barriers to the repetition of the production process e.g. in agriculture coincide with the duration of one cycle of the production phase. The barrier posited by capital is the lag not between seeding and harvest, but between harvest and the transformation of the harvest into money, and retransformation of the money into say e.g. purchase of labour. The circulation-artists who imagine that they can do something with the velocity of circulation other than lessen the obstacles to reproduction posited by capital itself are on the wrong track. (Even madder, of course, are those circulation-artists who imagine that credit institutes and inventions which abolish the lag of circulation time will not only do away with the delays and interruptions in production caused by the transformation of the finished product into capital, but will also make the capital, with which productive capital exchanges, itself superfluous; i.e. they want to produce on the basis of exchange value but to remove at the same time, by some witchcraft, the necessary conditions of production on this basis.) The most that credit can do in this respect – as regards *mere* circulation – is maintain the continuity of the production process, *if* all other conditions of this continuity are present, i.e. if the capital to be exchanged with actually exists etc.

It is posited in the circulation process that the transformation of the capital into money is posited as a condition for the realization of capital through production, for the exploitation of labour by capital; or, the exchange of capital for capital* is posited as barrier to the exchange of capital for labour and vice versa.

Capital exists as capital only in so far as it passes through the phases of circulation, the various moments of its transformation, in order to be able to begin the production process anew, and these phases are themselves phases of its realization – but at the same time, as we saw, of its *devaluation*. As long as capital remains frozen in the form of the finished product, it cannot be active as capital, it is *negated* capital. Its realization process is delayed in the same degree, and its value-in-process [*prozessierender Wert*] negated. This thus appears as a loss for capital, as a relative loss of its value, for its value consists precisely in its realization process. This loss of capital means in other words nothing else but that time passes it by unseized, time during which it could have been appropriating alien labour, *surplus labour time* through exchange with living labour, if the deadlock had not occurred. Now let us imagine *many* capitals in particular branches of business, all of which are *necessary* (which would become evident if, in the eventuality of a massive flight of capital from a given branch, supply falling below demand, the market price would therefore rise above the natural price in that branch), and let a single branch of business require e.g. that capital A remain longer in the form of devaluation, i.e. that the time in which it passes through the various phases of circulation is longer than in all other branches of business, in which case this capital A would regard the smaller new value which it could produce as a positive loss, just as if it had so many more outlays to make in order to produce the same value. It would thus charge relatively more exchange value for its products than the other capitals, in order to share the same rate of gain. But this could take place in fact only if the loss were distributed among the other capitals. If A demands more exchange value for the product than there is labour objectified in it, then

* For from the present standpoint we still only have labour or capital at all points of circulation.

it can obtain this *more* only if the others obtain less than the real value of their products. That is, the less favourable conditions under which A has produced would be borne in proportional shares by all the capitalists who exchange with it, and in this way an equal average level would come out. But the sum of the surplus value created by all these capitals together would be lessened exactly by the amount of capital A's lesser realization in relation to the other capitals; only, instead of this reduction falling exclusively on capital A, it is borne as a general loss, as a loss shared proportionally by all the capitals. Nothing can therefore be more ridiculous than the notion (see e.g. Ramsay)[37] that, apart from the exploitation of labour, capital forms an *original* source, separately from labour, of *value-creation*, because the distribution of surplus labour among the capitals takes place not in proportion to the surplus labour time achieved by the individual capital, but in proportion to the *total surplus labour* which the totality of capitals achieved, and hence a higher value-creation can be attributed to the *individual capital* than is directly explicable from its *particular* exploitation of labour power. But this *more* on one side has to be compensated by a *less* on the other. This is what *average* means, if it means anything at all. The question how the relation of capital to alien capital, i.e. the competition of capitals, distributes the surplus value among them obviously has nothing to do with the absolute amount of this surplus value. Nothing more absurd, then, than to conclude that, because one capital obtains a compensation for its *exceptional* circulation time, i.e. puts its relatively lesser realization to account as positively greater realization, now all *capitals* combined, *capital* can make something out of nothing, make a plus out of a minus, make a plus-surplus value out of a minus-surplus value or out of minus-surplus labour time, and that it possesses, therefore, a *mystical* wellspring of value independent of the appropriation of alien labour. The manner in which the capitals among other things compute their proportional share of the *surplus value* – not only according to the surplus labour time which they set in motion, but also *in accordance with the time which their capital has worked as such*, i.e. lain fallow, found itself in the phase of devaluation – does of course not alter in the least the total sum of the surplus value which they have to distribute among themselves. This sum itself cannot grow by being smaller than it would have

37. Ramsay, *An Essay on the Distribution of Wealth*, p. 55.

been if capital A, instead of lying fallow, had created surplus value; i.e. by having created less surplus value in the same time as the other capitalists. And this *lying-fallow* is made good for capital A only in so far as it arises necessarily out of the conditions of the particular branch of production, and hence appears in respect to *capital as such* as a burden on realization, as a *necessary barrier* to its realization generally. The division of labour leaves this barrier as a barrier only as regards the production process of this particular capital. If the production process is regarded as conducted by capital as such, this lying-fallow is a *general barrier* to capital's realization. If one imagines all production carried out by labour alone, then all the larger advances which it requires during its realization appear as what they are – *deductions from surplus value*.

Circulation can *create value* only in so far as it requires fresh employment – of *alien labour* – in addition to that directly consumed in the production process. This is then the same as if more *necessary labour* were used in the direct production process. Only the actual *circulation costs* increase the *value* of the product, but decrease the surplus value.

To the extent that the circulation of capital (the product etc.) does not merely express the phases necessary to begin the production process anew, this circulation (see Storch's example) does not form a moment of production in its totality – is hence not circulation posited by production, and, in so far as it creates expenses, these are *faux frais de production*.[38] The costs of circulation generally, in so far as their merely economic moments, circulation proper, are concerned (bringing the product to market gives it a *new use value*), are to be regarded as deduction from *surplus value*, i.e. as an increase of necessary labour in relation to surplus labour.

The continuity of production presupposes that circulation time has been suspended. If it has not been suspended, then time must pass between the different metamorphoses through which capital must travel; its circulation time *must* appear as deduction from its production time. On the other hand, the nature of capital presupposes that it travels through the different phases of circulation not as it does in the mind, where one concept turns into the next at the speed of thought, in no time, but rather as situations which are separate in time. It must spend some time as a cocoon before it can

38. See p. 310, n. 26.

take off as a butterfly. Thus the conditions of production arising out of the nature of capital itself contradict each other. The contradiction can be suspended and overcome only* in two ways:

Firstly, credit: A pseudo-buyer B – i.e. someone who really *pays* but does not really buy – mediates the transformation of capitalist A's product into money. But B himself is paid only after capitalist C has bought A's product. Whether the money which this credit-man, B, gives to A is used by A to buy labour or to buy raw material and instrument, before A can replace either of them from the sale of his product, does not alter the case. Given our presupposition, he must basically give him both – i.e. all the conditions of production (these represent, however, a greater value than the original ones with which A began the production process). In this case capital B replaces capital A; but they are not realized at the same time. Now B takes the place of A; i.e. his capital lies fallow, until it is exchanged with capital C. It is frozen in the product of A, who has made his product liquid in capital B.

Ramsay. Circulation time. Concludes therefore that capital is its own source of profit. – Ramsay. Confusion about surplus value and profit and law of values. (No surplus value according to Ricardo's law.) – Ricardo. Competition. – Quincey.[39] *Ricardo's theory of value. Wages and profit.* Quincey. – Ricardo. – Wakefield. *Conditions of capitalist production [in] colonies*

The economists' absolute confusion in respect of Ricardo's determination of value through labour time – something which is founded on a basic defect of his own development – emerges very clearly with Mr Ramsay. He says (after having previously drawn, from the influence of the circulation time of capitals on their *relative realization*, i.e. their relative share of the general surplus value, the nonsensical conclusion that: 'This shows how capital

---

*Except if one imagines that all capitals produce to order for each other, and that the product is therefore always immediately money, a notion which contradicts the nature of capital and hence also the practice of large-scale industry.

---

39. Thomas de Quincey (1785–1859), the essayist, author of *Confessions of an Opium Eater*, was also a writer on political economy, and a follower of Ricardo.

may regulate value independently of labour' (IX, 84. R, 43)[40] or that 'capital is a source of value independent of labour'[41]) – he says, literally: 'A circulating capital (*approvisionnement*) will always maintain more labour than that formerly bestowed upon itself. Because, could it employ no more than had been previously bestowed upon itself, *what advantage* could arise to the owner from the use of it *as such*?' (loc. cit. 49.) 'Given two capitals of equal value, each produced through the labour of 100 men operating for a given time, of which the one is entirely circulating, the other entirely fixed, and may perhaps consist of wine kept to improve. Now, this circulating capital, *raised by the labour of 100 men, will set 150 men in motion.* Therefore the product at the end of the coming year will in this case be the result of the labour of 150 men. But still it will be of no more value than the wine at the termination of the same period, although only 100 men employed upon the latter.' (50.) 'Or is it asserted that the quantity of labour which every circulating capital *will employ* is no more than equal to the [quantity] previously bestowed upon it? That would mean, that the *value of the capital expended* = that of the product.' (52.) Great confusion between the labour bestowed upon capital and that which it will employ. The capital which is exchanged for labour capacity, the *approvisionnement* – and this he here calls *circulating capital* – can never employ more labour than has been bestowed upon it. (The reaction of a development of the productive forces on present capital is beside the point here.) But there has been more labour bestowed upon it than it has paid for – *surplus labour*, which is converted into *surplus value and surplus produce*, enabling the capital to renew this profitable bargain, where the mutuality is all on one side, on a more enlarged scale. It is enabled to employ more new living labour, because during the process of production a portion of fresh labour has been bestowed upon it beyond the accumulated labour of which it consisted before entering that process.

Mr Ramsay seems to imagine that, if a capital is the product of 20 working days (necessary and surplus together), this product of 20 working days can employ 30 working days. But this is by no means the case. Say that 10 days of necessary labour and 10 surplus days were employed on the product. Then the surplus value = 10

40. Ramsay, *An Essay on the Distribution of Wealth*, p. 43. The references in pages 550–53 of the text are to the page numbers of Ramsay's book. The quotations themselves are as usual in a mixture of English and German.

41. ibid., p. 55.

surplus days. If the capitalist then exchanges these again for raw material, instrument and labour, then he can set new *necessary labour* into motion with the *surplus product*. The point is not that he employed more labour time than is present in the product, but that he exchanges the surplus labour time, which costs him nothing, for new necessary labour time – in other words, precisely, that he employs the *entire labour time* bestowed upon the product, while he has paid only part of that labour. Mr Ramsay's conclusion, that if the quantity of labour which every circulating capital will employ was no more than equal to that previously bestowed upon it, the value of the capital expended would be equal to that of the produce, i.e. no surplus value would be left, would be correct only if the quantity of labour bestowed upon the capital *were wholly paid for*, i.e. if capital did not appropriate a part of the labour *without equivalent*. These misunderstandings on Ricardo's part[42] obviously arise from the fact that he himself was not clear about the process, nor, as a bourgeois, could he be. Insight into this process is = to the statement that capital is not only, as A. Smith thinks,[43] command over alien labour, in the sense that every exchange value is that, since it gives its possessor *buying power*, but that it is the power to appropriate alien labour *without exchange, without equivalent*, but with the semblance of exchange. Ricardo knows no argument to refute those, like A. Smith and others, who fall into the same error regarding value as determined by labour, and value as determined by the price of labour (wages), other than to say: with the product of the same quantity of labour one can set sometimes more and sometimes less living labour into motion, i.e. he regards the product of labour in respect of the worker only as *use value* – only the part of the product which he needs to be able to live as worker. But how it comes about that the worker suddenly only represents *use value* in the exchange, or only draws use value from the exchange, is by no means clear to him, as is already proved by his arguments against A. Smith, which are never in general terms, but always about particular examples. But why is it, then, that the share of the worker in the value of the product is determined not by the value, but rather by the use value of the product, thus not by the labour time employed on it,

42. Misunderstandings on *Ramsay's* part (cf. Ramsay, *An Essay*, p. 22 n.) in which he followed Ricardo's own misunderstandings (cf. Ricardo, *On the Principles of Political Economy*, pp. 5, 7–8, 9).

43. Adam Smith, *Wealth of Nations*, Vol. I, pp. 101–2, 131–4.

but by its quality of maintaining living labour capacity? If he tries to explain this with, say, competition among the workers, then the answer which would have to be given is the same as that which he gives A. Smith about competition among capitalists, i.e. that competition may well even out, equalize the level of profit, but in no way creates the measure of this level.[44] Likewise, competition among the workers could press down a higher wages level etc., but the general standard of wages, or as Ricardo puts it the natural price of wages, could not be explained by the competition between worker and worker, but only by the original relation between capital and labour. Competition generally, this essential locomotive force of the bourgeois economy, does not establish its laws, but is rather their executor. Unlimited competition is therefore not the presupposition for the truth of the economic laws, but rather the consequence – the form of appearance in which their necessity realizes itself. For the economists to presuppose, as does Ricardo, that unlimited competition exists[45] is to presuppose the full reality and realization of the bourgeois relations of production in their specific and distinct character. Competition therefore does not *explain* these laws; rather, it lets them be *seen*, but does not produce them. Then Ricardo says, too: the production costs of living labour depend on the production costs of making the values required to reproduce it.[46] While he previously regarded the product in relation to the worker only as a use value, he now regards the worker only as an *exchange value* in relation to the product. The historic process through which product and living labour come into this mutual relation is none of his concern. He is just as vague about the way in which this relation is perpetuated. Capital, with him, is the *result of saving*; this already shows that he misunderstands the process of its origins and reproduction. He therefore also imagines that production is impossible without capital, although he can very well imagine capital possible without ground rent. The distinction between *profit* and *surplus value* does not exist for him, proof that he is clear about the nature of neither one. His procedure already shows this from the very beginning. Originally, he makes workers exchange with workers – and their exchange is then determined by the equivalent, by the labour time

44. Ricardo, *On the Principles of Political Economy*, pp. 338–9.
45. ibid., p. 3: 'In speaking of commodities ... we mean commodities ... on the production of which competition operates without restraint.'
46. ibid., p. 86.

reciprocally expended in production. Then comes the real problem of his economics, to demonstrate that this determination of value is not altered by the accumulation of capitals – i.e. by the presence [*Dasein*] of capital. Firstly, he has no inkling that his first spontaneous relation is itself only a relation abstracted from the mode of production resting on capital. Secondly, what he has available is a *definite amount of objective labour time*, which may of course increase, and he asks himself, how is it *distributed*? The question is rather how is it created, and there it is precisely the specific nature of the relation of capital and labour, or the specific and distinct character of capital, which explains this. As Quincey (X, 5) puts it, modern economics (the economics of Ricardo) is in fact concerned only with the dividends, while the total product is regarded as fixed, determined by the quantity of labour employed on it – its value appraised in accordance with that.[47] Accordingly, Ricardo has rightly been accused of not understanding *surplus value*, although his opponents understand it even less. Capital is represented as appropriating a certain part of the ready and available value of labour (of the product); the creation of this value, which it appropriates above and beyond the reproduced capital, is not presented as the *source* of the surplus value. This creation is identical with the appropriation of alien labour *without exchange*, and for that reason the bourgeois economists are never permitted to understand it clearly. Ramsay accuses Ricardo of forgetting that the fixed capital (which consists of capital not included in *approvisionnement*, with Ramsay the *raw material* at the same time along with the *instrument*) is a deduction from the sum total available for distribution among capitalist and worker. 'Ricardo forgets that the whole product is divided not only between wages and profits, but that another part is necessary for replacing fixed capital.' (IX, p. 88. R. 174, note.) Indeed, since Ricardo does not grasp the relation between objectified and living labour in its living movement – [a relation] not to be deduced from the dividends of a given quantity of labour, but from the positing of surplus labour – and does not, therefore, grasp the relation among the different component parts of capital, it therefore seems with him as if the entire product were divided into wages and profits, so that the reproduction of capital is itself counted as part of profit. Quincey (loc. cit. Notebook X, 5) gives this exposition of the Ricardian doctrine: 'If the price is 10s. then wages and profit as a

47. De Quincey, *The Logic of Political Economy*, Edinburgh, 1844, p. 204.

whole cannot exceed 10s. But do not the wages and profits as a whole, themselves, on the contrary, predetermine the price? No, that is the old superannuated doctrine.' (p. 204). 'The new economics has shown that all price is governed by *proportional quantity of the producing labour*, and by that only. Being itself once settled, then ipso facto, *price settles the fund* out of which both wages and profits must derive their *separate dividends*.' (loc. cit. 204.)[48] Capital here appears not as positing surplus value, i.e. surplus labour, but only as making deductions from a given quantity of labour. The fact that instrument and raw material appropriate these *dividends* then has to be explained by their *use value* in production, which then presupposes the absurdity that raw material and instrument create use value through their *separation* from labour. For this *separation* makes them into capital. Considered for themselves, they are themselves labour, accumulated labour. Besides, this clashes with sound common sense, because the capitalist knows very well that he counts wages and profit among the production costs and regulates the *necessary price* accordingly. This contradiction in the determination of the product by relative labour time, and the limitation of the sum of profit and wages by the sum of this labour time, and the *real determination of prices* in practice, comes about only because profit is not grasped as itself a derivative, secondary form of *surplus value*; the same is true of what the capitalist justly regards as *his production costs*. His profit arises simply from the fact that a part of the cost of production costs him nothing, hence does not enter into *his* outlays, *his* production costs.

48. De Quincey, *The Logic of Political Economy*, p. 204.

NOTEBOOK VI

February 1858

The Chapter on Capital (continuation)

'Any change that can disturb the existing relations between wages and profits must originate in wages.' (Quincey. loc. cit. (X, 5) p. 205.) This is true only in so far as any variations in the mass of surplus labour must be derived from a variation in the relation between necessary and surplus labour. But this can likewise come about if necessary labour becomes less productive and hence a greater part of the total labour falls to it, or if the total labour becomes more productive, hence necessary labour time is reduced. It is nonsense to say that this productive force of labour arises from *wages*. The relative reduction of wages is rather its result. But it arises (1) from the appropriation by capital of the growth in the productive forces resulting from division of labour, trade which brings cheaper raw materials, science etc.; (2) but this increase of the productive forces has to be regarded as being initiated by capital in so far as it is realized through the employment of a greater capital etc. Further: profit and wages, although determined by the relation of necessary and surplus labour, do not coincide with it, are only secondary forms of the same. The point, however, is this: the Ricardians presuppose a definite quantity of labour; this determines the price of the product, out of which labour, in wages, and capital, in profits, then draw their dividends; the workers' dividend = the price of the necessaries of life. Hence in the 'existing relations between wages and profits', the rate of profit is at its maximum and that of wages at its minimum. Competition among capitals can change only the relation in which they share the total profit, but cannot alter the relation between total profit and total wages. The general standard of profit is this relation of the total profit to the total wages, and this is not altered through competition. Hence, where does the alteration come from? Certainly not because the profit rate voluntarily declines, and it would have to do so voluntarily since competition does not have this result. Hence it is due to an alteration in wages, whose necessary costs may rise (theory of the progressive deterioration of the soil in agriculture; theory of rent) in consequence of a decrease in the productive force of labour due to natural causes. Carey etc. replies, correctly, to this (but, in the way he explains it, incorrectly again) that the rate of profit falls, as a result not of a decrease but rather of an increase in the productive force.[1] The solution of the whole matter is simply that the rate of profit is not the same as the absolute surplus value, but is rather the surplus value in relation to the capital employed, and that the growth of productive force is accompanied by the decrease of that part of capital which represents *approvisionnement* in relation to that part which represents invariable capital; hence, when the relation between total labour and the capital which employs it falls, then the part of labour which appears as surplus labour or surplus value necessarily falls too. This inability to explain one of the most striking phenomena of modern production is the source of Ricardo's failure to understand his own principle. But the difficulties in which he thereby entangles his disciples may be seen in this quotation among others from Quincey: 'It is the common paralogism, that if upon the same farm you have always kept 5 men, and in 1800 their produce was 25 qrs, but in 1845 50 qrs, you are apt to view the *produce only as variable*, and the *labour as constant*: whereas *virtually* both have varied. In 1800 each qr must have cost $\frac{1}{5}$ part of a man; in 1845 each has cost no more than $\frac{1}{10}$ part of a man.' (loc. cit. 214.) In both cases the absolute labour time was the same, 2 days; but in 1845 the productive force of labour had doubled in comparison with 1800, and therefore the cost of producing necessary labour was less. The labour bestowed upon 1 quarter was less, but the total labour was the same. Mr Quincey should, however, have learned from Ricardo that the productive force of labour does not determine the value of the product – although it determines the surplus value, albeit not in step with the increase of the productive force. These arguments *against* Ricardo, as well as the desperate sophistries of his disciples (e.g. Mr MacCulloch, who cites surplus labour as the source of the surplus value of old wine compared with new wine).[2] Nor is value to be determined by the labour which the unit cost, i.e. the *price* of the single quarter. *Rather, the*

1. Carey, *Principles of Political Economy*, Part I, p. 99.
2. J. R. MacCulloch, *The Principles of Political Economy*, London, 1825, pp. 313–18.

price multiplied by the number constitutes the value. The 50
quarters in 1845 had *the same value* as the 25 in 1800, because they
objectified the same amount of labour. The price of each single
quarter, the unit, *must* have been different, and the *total price* (expressed in money) may have been different, for very different
reasons. (What Quincey says about the machine holds for the
worker: 'A machine, as soon as its secret is known, will not sell for
the labour produced, but for the labour producing . . . it will no
longer be viewed as a *cause equal to certain effects*, but *as an effect
certainly reproducible* by a known cause *at a known cost.*' (84.) De
Quincey says about Malthus: 'Malthus in his Political Economy
refuses to see, nay he positively denies, that if two men produce a
variable result of ten and five, then in one case each unit of the
result has cost double the labour which it has cost in the other.
On the contrary, because there are always two men, Mr Malthus
obstinately insists that the *cost in labour* is constant.' (loc. cit.
215, note.) In fact: *the cost in labour is constant*, because, by presupposition, just as much labour is contained in ten as in five. But
the *cost of labour* is not constant, because in the first case, where
the productive force of labour [is] double, the time belonging to
necessary labour [is] in a certain proportion less. We shall go into
Malthus's view immediately after this. Here, before we go further
in the development of the circulation time of capital and its
relation to labour time, it is proper first to examine Ricardo's
whole doctrine about this matter, in order to establish the difference between our own conception and his more sharply. (The
quotations from Ricardo in Notebook VIII.)[3]

First presupposition with him, '*competition without restriction*',
and unhampered increase of products through industry. (19.
R. 5.)[4] This means in other words nothing other than that the
laws of capital are completely realized only within *unlimited
competition* and *industrial production*. Capital develops adequately
on the latter productive basis and in the former relation of production; i.e. its immanent laws enter completely into reality. Since
this is so, it would have to be shown how this *unlimited competition*
and *industrial production* are conditions of the realization of capital,

3. The extracts from Ricardo appear in a 'Notebook VIII' of an earlier
series of notebooks dated 1851. Excerpts are printed in *Grundrisse* (MELI)
as an appendix, omitted in the present edition.
4. R.5: Ricardo, *On the Principles of Political Economy*, p. 5 (in fact
p. 3).

conditions which it must itself little by little produce (instead of the hypothesis appearing here as merely that of the theoretician, who places free competition and the productive mode of capital's existence externally and arbitrarily into the relation of capital to itself as capital, not as developments of capital itself, but as imaginary presuppositions of capital for the sake of purity.) This by the way the only place in Ricardo where a faint notion of the *historic* nature of the laws of bourgeois economy. With this presupposition, the *relative value* of commodities (this word meaningless, since absolute value is nonsense) is determined by the different quantity which can be produced in the same labour time, or by the quantity of labour relatively realized in different commodities. (p. 4.) (Notebook, 19.) (Henceforth the first number for the page in the notebook; the second for the page in Ricardo.)[5] Now, how one gets from value as equivalent determined by labour to the non-equivalent, i.e. to the value which posits surplus value through exchange, i.e. how one gets from value to capital, from one aspect to its apparent opposite, this does not interest Ricardo. The only question for him: how the *value relation* between the commodities can remain the same and can and must be determined by relative quantities of labour, *although* the owners of accumulated labour ... do not exchange labour *equivalents* in living labour, i.e. despite the relation of capital and labour. It is then a very simple arithmetical proof that commodity A and commodity B can exchange in relation to the labour realized in them, although the producers of A or B *distribute* product A, or the product B exchanged for it, in different ways among themselves. But since all *distribution* here proceeds on the basis of exchange, it appears in fact altogether impossible to explain why one of the exchange values – living labour – is exchanged according to the amount of labour time realized in it, while the other exchange value – accumulated labour, capital – is not exchanged according to the standard of the labour time realized in it. Bray e.g. therefore believes that he is the first to draw the true conclusion from Ricardo with his equal exchange between living and dead labour.[6] That from the standpoint of exchange alone, the *worker's pay* would have to = *the value of the product*, i.e. the amount of labour in objective form which the worker obtains in pay, = the amount of labour in subjective form which he expends in labour, is so

5. The page numbers in Ricardo refer to the third edition (1821).
6. Bray, *Labour's Wrongs*, p. 48.

necessary a conclusion that A. Smith falls into it.[7] Ricardo, by contrast, avoids this fallacy, but how? 'The *value* of labour, and the quantity of commodities which a specific quantity of labour can buy, are not identical.' Why not? '*Because* the worker's product or an equivalent of this product is not = to the worker's pay.' I.e. the identity does not exist, *because* a difference exists. 'Therefore' (because this is not the case) 'it is not the value of labour which is the measure of value, but the quantity of labour bestowed on the commodity.' (19, 3.)[8] Value of labour is not identical with wages of labour. *Because* they are different. *Therefore* they are not identical. This is a strange logic. There is basically no reason for this other than that it is *not* so in practice. But it ought to be so, according to the theory. For the exchange of values [is] determined by the labour time realized in them. Hence equivalents are exchanged. Thus a specific quantity of labour time in living form would have to exchange for the same quantity of labour time in accumulated form. What would have to be demonstrated is precisely that the law of exchange turns into its precise opposite. Not even a faint suspicion that it does so is expressed here. Or the suspicion would have to lie in the frequently repeated admonition against mixing them up; that the distinction between past and living labour cannot do the job either is readily admitted: 'The comparative quantity of commodites which a given quantity of labour will produce determines their past and present value' (19, 9) where living labour thus even determines the value of past labour retroactively. Why then is capital not also exchanged for living labour in proportion to the labour realized in the capital? Why is it that a quantity of living labour is not itself = the quantity of labour in which it has objectified itself? 'Labour is by nature of different quality, and it is difficult to compare different hours of labour in different branches of business. But this scale is very soon established in practice.' (19, 13.) 'For short periods, at least from year to year, the variation in this inequality is insignificant, and is *therefore* left out of account.' (19, 15.) This is nothing. If Ricardo had applied his own principle, the amounts of (simple) labour to which the different *labour capacities* are reducible, then the matter would have been simple. Generally, he is concerned straight away with the hours of labour. What the capitalist

7. Adam Smith, *Wealth of Nations*, Vol. I, pp. 100–102, 130–31.

8. Marx, here as elsewhere, quotes in his own abbreviated German. The text therefore differs slightly from Ricardo's original. Compare Ricardo, *Principles*, p. 5.

acquires through exchange is *labour capacity*: this is the exchange value which he pays for. Living labour is the use value which this exchange value has for him, and out of this use value springs the surplus value and the suspension of exchange as such. Because Ricardo allows exchange with living labour – and thus falls straight into the production process – it remains an insoluble antinomy in his system that a certain quantity of living labour does not = the commodity which it creates, in which it objectifies itself, although the value of the commodity = to the amount of labour contained in it. The value of the commodity 'includes also the labour of bringing the commodity to market'. (19, 18.) We shall see that circulation time, in so far as it appears as determining value with Ricardo, is only the labour required to bring the commodities to market. 'The principle of value-determination by the relative amounts of labour contained in the commodity is considerably modified by the employment of machinery and other fixed and durable capital. A rise or fall in wages differently affects two capitals of which one is almost entirely circulating, the other almost entirely fixed; likewise the unequal duration of the fixed capital employed. Namely, there is added the *profit on fixed capital* (interest), as well as the compensation for the greater length of time which must elapse before the more valuable of the two commodities can be brought to market.' (19, 29, 30.) The latter moment concerns only the duration of the production process, i.e. labour time directly employed, at least in Ricardo's example of the farmer and the baker. (If one farmer's wheat becomes ready for the market later than another's, then this so-called *compensation* already presupposes *interest*; thus already something derivative, not an original aspect.)

'Profit and wages are only *portions* in which the two classes, of capitalists and workers, partake in the original commodity, i.e. also in that exchanged for it.' (p. 31.) The very great extent to which the production of *the original commodity*, its origin, is itself determined by these *portions*, the extent to which, therefore, it *precedes* these portions as basic determinant, proves that the *original commodity* [would] not be produced at all, if it did not contain surplus labour for capital. 'Commodities on which the same quantity of labour has been bestowed vary in relative value if they cannot be brought to market in the same amount of time. With a *greater fixed capital*, too, the higher value of a commodity is due to the greater length of time which must elapse before it can be brought to market . . . The difference arises in both cases from the profits being accumulated as capital, and is only a compensation for the *time during which profits were withheld.*' (34, 35.) This means absolutely nothing other than that capital lying fallow is *reckoned in and up* as if it were not lying fallow, but were being exchanged with surplus labour time. This has nothing to do with the determination of value. It belongs with price. (In the case of fixed capital it [enters] into the determination of value only as *another method* of paying for the objectified labour, abstracted from the profit.)

'There is another principle of labour which nothing points out to the economic inquirer in old countries, but of which every colonial capitalist has been made conscious in his own person. By far the greater part of the operations of industry, and especially those of which the *produce is great in proportion to the capital and labour employed*, require *a considerable time for* [*their*] *completion*. As to most of them, it is not worth while to make a commencement without the certainty of being able to carry them on for several years. A large portion of the capital employed in them is *fixed, inconvertible, durable*. If anything happens to stop the operation, all this capital is lost. *If the harvest cannot be gathered, the whole outlay in making it grow* has been thrown away . . . This shows that *constancy* is a no less important principle than combination of labour. The importance of the principle of constancy is not seen here, because rarely indeed does it happen, that the labour which carries on a business, is stopped against the will of the capitalists . . . But in the *colonies* just the opposite. Here capitalists are so much afraid of it that they avoid its occurrence as much as they can, by avoiding, as much as possible, operations which require much time for their completion.' (Wakefield, 169, XIV, 71.)[9] 'There are numerous *operations of so simple a kind* as not to admit a *division into parts*, which cannot be performed without the cooperation of many pairs of hands. For example, the lifting of a large tree on to a wain, keeping down weeds in a large field of growing crops, shearing a large flock of sheep at the same time, gathering a harvest of corn at the time when it is ripe enough and not too ripe, moving any great weight; everything, in short, which cannot be done unless a good many pairs of hands help together in the same undivided employment, and at the same time.' (168 loc. cit.) '*Combination and constancy*

9. Wakefield, *A View of the Art of Colonization*, p. 169.

of labour are provided for in old countries, without an effort or thought on the part of the capitalist, merely by the *abundance of labourers for hire.* The scarcity of labourers for hire is the universal complaint of colonies.' (170 loc. cit.) 'Only the *cheapest land* in a colony is that whose price affects the *labour market. The price of this land, as of all bare land, and of everything else which it costs nothing to produce,* depends of course on the *relation between the demand and supply.*' (p. 332.) . . . 'In order that *the price of waste land* should accomplish its objects' (namely of making the worker into a *non*-landowner), 'it must be *sufficient* for the purpose. Hitherto the price has been everywhere insufficient.' (338 loc. cit.) This 'sufficient' price: 'In founding a colony the price might be so low as to render the quantity of land appropriated by settlers practically unlimited: it might be high enough to occasion a proportion between land and people similar to that of old countries, in which case, if this very high price did not prevent emigration, the cheapest land in the colony might be as dear, and the superabundance of labourers as deplorable as in England: or it might be a just medium between the two, occasioning neither superabundance of people nor superabundance of land, but so limiting the quantity of land as to give the cheapest land a market value that would have the effect of compelling labourers to work some considerable time for wages before they could become landowners.' (339 loc. cit.) (Notebook XIV, 71.) (These excerpts here quoted from Wakefield's *Art of Colonization* belong with the ones given above about the necessary separation of the worker from the conditions of property.)

Surplus value and profit. Example (*Malthus*). – *Profit and surplus value.* Malthus – *Difference between labour and labour capacity. – The peculiar assertion that the introduction of capital in no way changes the payment of labour. – Carey's theory of the cheapening of capital for the worker. – (Decline of the profit rate.) – Wakefield on the contradiction between Ricardo's theories of wage labour and of value*

(The calculation of profit as distinct from the calculation of the real surplus value which capital posits in the exchange with living labour, made clear e.g. in the following example. It is a statement in the *first Report of the Factory Commissioners.* (Malthus's *Princip. of Polit. Economy*, 1836, 2nd ed. (Notebook X, p. 42).)

Capital sunk in building and machinery £10,000
Floating capital   £7,000
  £500 interest on £10,000 fixed capital
    350   floating capital
    150   Rents, taxes, rates
    650   Sinking fund of $6\frac{1}{2}\%$ for wear and tear of the
                     fixed capital

———
£1,650
£1,100 Contingencies, carriage, coal, oil

———
2,750
2,600 Wages and salaries

———
5,350
10,000 for about 400,000 lb. raw cotton at 6d.

———
15,350
16,000 for 363,000 lb. twist spun. Value £16,000

The capital laid out in labour is 2,600; the surplus value $=$ 1,650 (850 interest $+$ 150 rents etc., makes 1,000 $+$ 650 profit).

But $2,000:1,650 = 100:63\frac{6}{13}$. Thus the rate of surplus value is $63\frac{6}{13}\%$. According to the profit calculation it would have to be 850 interest, 150 rents and 650 profit, or 1,650:15,350; nearly $10\cdot1\%$.

In the above example, the floating capital turns over 167/70 times per year; the fixed capital turns over once in $15\frac{5}{13}$ years; once in 200/13 year.

Profit: 650 or about $4\cdot2^{10}$. The wages of the operatives $\frac{1}{4}$. The profit is indicated here as $4\cdot2$; say it were only 4%. This 4% figured on an outlay of 15,350. But then we also have 5% interest on £10,000 and 5% on 7,000; £850 $= 5\%$ of 17,000. From the actual annual advances made, we must deduct (1) the part of the fixed capital which does not figure in the sinking fund; (2) that which is figured as interest. (It is possible that capitalist A does not pocket the interest, but capitalist B. In any case they are revenue, not capital; surplus value.) From the £15,350 outlays thus deduct 850; leaves: £14,500. Of the £2,600 for wages and

———

10. Should read $4\cdot7\%$, but the error has been taken over from Malthus himself. Cf. Malthus, *Principles of Political Economy*, pp. 269–70. Two other petty errors of arithmetic in these passages have been corrected as indicated by the MELI editors.

salaries there were £183⅓ in the form of salary, since ⅙ of 14,500 is not 2,600 but 2,416⅔, and 14,500 divided by this is 6.

Thus, he sells the 14,500 at 16,000 or a profit of 1,500; makes 10⅔%; but let us ignore these ⅔ and say 10%; ⅙ of 100 is 16⅔. Thus, out of 100, he would give: 83⅓ for advances, 16⅔ wages and 10 profit. In detail:

	Advances	*Wages*	*Sum*	*Reproduces*	*Profit*
£ St.:	83⅓	16⅔	100	110	10

10 of 16⅔ or of $\frac{50}{3}$ is exactly 60%. Thus, in order that, in the capitalist's calculation, an annual profit of 10% (it was slightly more) be made on a capital of £17,000, wherein labour makes up only ⅙ of the annual advances of 14,500, the worker (or capital, as you like) has to create a surplus value of 60%. Or, of the total labour time 40% are for necessary and 60 for surplus labour; they relate as 4:6 or = 2:3 or 1:$\frac{3}{2}$. If, however, the advances on capital had been 50, the advances on wages also 50, then only 20% surplus value would have to be created in order that the capitalist should have 10%; 50 50 10 = 110. But 10 to 50 = 20:100 or 20%. If necessary labour in the second case posited as much surplus labour as in the first, then the capitalist's profit would amount to £30; on the other hand if the rate of real value-creation, the positing of surplus labour, in the first case, were only as great as in the second, then the profit would amount to only £3⅓, and if the capitalist had to pay 5% interest to another capitalist, then he would have to carry an actual loss. This much arises simply from the formula, (1) that, in order to determine the size of the real surplus value, one must calculate the profit on the advance made for wages; the percentage which expresses the proportion between the so-called profit and wages; (2) the relatively smaller percentage made up by the proportion between the outlay in living labour and the total outlay presupposes a greater outlay in fixed capital, machinery etc.; greater division of labour. Thus, although the percentage of labour is smaller than in the capital working with more labour, the mass of labour really set in motion must be significantly greater; i.e. a greater capital generally has to be worked with. The proportional part of labour out of the total advance is smaller; but the absolute sum of labour set in motion is larger for the individual capital; i.e. it must itself be larger. (3) If it is a case not of larger machinery etc., but of an instrument which does not set more labour into motion and itself represents

no greater fixed capital (e.g. manual lithography) but merely replaces labour, then the profit of the capital working with the machine is absolutely smaller than that of the capital working with living labour. (But the latter can make a percentage profit higher than the former, and thus throw him out of the market.) (etc.) The examination of how far the rate of profit can decrease as capital grows, while the gross profit nevertheless increases, belongs to the doctrine of profit (*competition*).

In his *Principles of Political Economy*, 2nd ed., 1836, Malthus has an inkling that profit, i.e. not profit, but *real surplus value*, has to be calculated not in respect of capital advanced, but of living labour advanced, whose value is expressed objectively in wages; but this leads him into playing games which become absurd if they are to serve as a basis for any determination of value, or for reasoning about the relation of labour to the determination of value.

For example, if I take the total value of the finished product, then I can compare every part of the product advanced with the part of the outlay corresponding to it; and the percentage of profit in relation to the whole product is naturally the same percentage for any fractional part of the product. Say e.g. that 100 thalers brought 110; thus 10% the whole product; 75%, say, for the invariable part of capital, 25 for labour, i.e. $\frac{3}{4}$ for the former, $\frac{1}{4}$ for living labour. Now if I take $\frac{1}{4}$ of the total product, i.e. of 110, then I obtain $27\frac{2}{4}$ or $27\frac{1}{2}$. On an outlay of 25 for labour, the capitalist would have a gain of $2\frac{1}{2}$, i.e. 10%. Likewise Malthus could have said that if I take $\frac{3}{4}$ of the total product, i.e. 75, then these $\frac{3}{4}$ are represented in the total product by $82\frac{1}{2}$; then $7\frac{1}{2}$ out of 75 is exactly 10%. This obviously means nothing other than that if I gain 10% on 100 then the gain on every part of 100 amounts to as much as, when added together, will be 10% on the total sum. If I have gained 10 on 100, then on 2×50 I have gained 5 each time etc. The fact that, if I gain 10 on 100, I gain $2\frac{1}{2}$ on $\frac{1}{4}$ of 100 and $7\frac{1}{2}$ on $\frac{3}{4}$ takes us not a single step further. If I have gained 10 on 100, how much have I then won on $\frac{1}{4}$ of 100 or on $\frac{3}{4}$? Malthus's insight can be reduced to this childishness. The advance for labour amounted to $\frac{1}{4}$ of the 100, and the gain on it amounted to 10%. 10% of 25 is $2\frac{1}{2}$. Or the capitalist, if he has gained 10 on 100, has gained $\frac{1}{10}$ on every part of his capital, i.e. 10%. This gives the parts of the capital no qualitative character whatever, and it therefore holds for fixed capital etc. just as well as for the part advanced in labour. Moreover, this only expresses the illusion that each part of the capital is involved to an equal degree in the newly created value. Nor has the $\frac{1}{4}$ of the capital advanced for wages created the surplus value; rather, the unpaid living labour has done so. However, from the relation of the total value – here the 10 thalers – to wages we can see what percentage of labour was not paid, or, how much surplus labour there was. In the above relation, the necessary labour is objectified in 25 thalers, the surplus labour in 10; thus they relate as $25:10 = 100:40$; 40% of the labour was surplus labour, or, what is the same, 40% of the value it produced was surplus value. It is quite true that the capitalist can make this reckoning: if I make 10 on 100, then, on wages, $= 25$, I have made $2\frac{1}{2}$. It is impossible to see what use this calculation is. But what Malthus wants to do with it will be seen shortly when we go into his determination of value. However, it is clear from the following that he indeed believes that his simple arithmetical example contains a real determination:

'Suppose the capital be expended only for wages, £100 expended in immediate labour. The returns at the end of the year 110, 120, or 130; it is evident that in each case the profits will be determinated by the proportion of the *value of the whole produce* which is required to pay the labour employed. If the value of the produce in the market $= 110$, the proportion required to pay the labourers $= \frac{10}{11}$ of the value of the produce, or the profits $= 10\%$.' (Here Mr Malthus does nothing more than to express the original advance, £100, as a relation to the total product. 100 is $\frac{10}{11}$ of 110. Whether I say I gain 10 on 100, i.e. $\frac{1}{10}$ of 100, or I say $\frac{1}{11}$ of the 110 are gain, it is the same.) 'If the value of the product is 120, the proportion for labour $= \frac{10}{12}$ and the gain 20%; if 130, the proportion required to pay the labour $= \frac{10}{13}$ and the gain $= 30\%$.' (Instead of saying: I gain 10 on 100, I can also say that $\frac{10}{11}$ of the 110 were the advances; or, 20 on the 100, the advances amount only to $\frac{10}{12}$ of 120 etc. The character of these advances, whether in labour or otherwise, has absolutely nothing to do with this other arithmetic form of expressing the matter. If a capital of 100 has brought in 110, then either I can start with the capital and say I gained 10 on it, or I can start with the product, with 110, and say that I advanced only $\frac{10}{11}$ on it beforehand. The relation is, of course, the same.) 'Now assume that the capitalist's advances do not consist entirely of labour. The capitalist *expects an equal benefit on all parts of the capital he advances*' (that means simply that he distributes the benefit he has made, and whose origin may be quite obscure to him, among all parts of his outlays equally, entirely abstracting away their qualitative difference). 'Suppose $\frac{1}{4}$ of the advances, for labour' (direct), '$\frac{3}{4}$ consisting of accumulated labour and profits, with any additions which may arise of rents, taxes and other outgoings. *Then strictly true that the profits of the capitalist will vary with the varying value of this $\frac{1}{4}$ of the produce compared with the quantity of labour employed.*' (Not quantity with Mr Malthus, but rather compared with the salary paid.) (Thus strictly true that his profits will vary with the varying value of the $\frac{3}{4}$ of his profits compared with the advances in accumulated labour, i.e. the gain relates to the total capital advanced (10:100) as every part of the total product (110) does to the part of the advance corresponding to it.) 'For example,' Malthus continues, 'a farmer employs £2,000 in cultivation, of which 1,500 in seed, keep of horses, wear and tear of his fixed capital, etc., and £500 on immediate labour, and the returns at the end are 2,400. His profit 400, on 2,000 = 20%. And it is immediately obvious that if we took $\frac{1}{4}$ of the value of the produce, namely £600, and compared it with the amount paid in the wages of the immediate labour, the result would show exactly the same rate of profits.' (loc. cit. 267, 268. Notebook X, 41, 42.) (It is equally obvious that if we took $\frac{3}{4}$ of the value of the produce, namely 1,800, and compared it with the amount paid in the advances on accumulated labour, namely with 1,500, the result would show exactly the same rate of profits. 1,800:1,500 = 18:15 = 6:5. And 6 is $\frac{1}{5}$ more than 5, hence 20%.) (Malthus here has two different arithmetic formulae in mind and gets them mixed up: *firstly*, if I make 10 on 100, then on every part of the 100 my gain is not 10 but 10%: i.e. 5 on 50, $2\frac{1}{2}$ on 25 etc.; to gain 10 on 100 means to gain $\frac{1}{10}$ on each part of the 100, and consequently the profit has to show up also as $\frac{1}{10}$ profit on wages, and if the profit is distributed evenly among all parts of the capital, then I can say that the rate of profit on the total capital varies with the rate of profit on each of its parts, including e.g. the part advanced as wages; *secondly* if I gained 10% on 100, then the total product 110. Now, if wages formed $\frac{1}{4}$ of the advances = 25, then they form only a $4\frac{2}{5}$ part of 110; i.e. they form a fraction that is smaller by $\frac{2}{5}$, and it will form an ever smaller part of the total product in proportion as the latter has risen in comparison with the original. This is again only another way of calculating. 10 is $\frac{1}{10}$ of 100 but only $\frac{1}{11}$ of 110. I can therefore say that as the total product grows larger, each of the fractional parts of the original capital forms a relatively smaller part of it. Tautology.)

In his work *The Measure of Value Stated and Illustrated*, London, 1823 (Notebook IX), Malthus asserts that the '*value of labour*' is '*constant*' and is hence the true Measure of Value generally. 'Any given quantity of labour must be of the *same value* as the wages which command it, or for which it actually exchanges.' (p. 5, loc. cit.) (IX, 29.) He is speaking here, of course, about wage labour. The truth is rather: any given quantity of labour is = the same quantity of labour expressed in a product; or, each product is only a specific quantity of labour, objectified in the value of the product, which is measured with respect to other products by this quantity. Wages, however, express the value of living labour capacity, but in no way the *value* of living labour, which is expressed, rather, in wages + profit. Wages are the price of *necessary labour*. If the worker had to work 6 hours in order to live, and if he produced for himself as mere worker, then he would daily receive the commodity of 6 hours of labour, say 6d. Now the capitalist makes him work 12 hours, and pays him 6d. He pays him $\frac{1}{2}$d. per hour, i.e. a given quantity of 12 hours of labour has the value of 12d., and 12d. is indeed the value for which the product exchanges, when it gets sold. On the other hand, the capitalist commands with this value, if he could re-invest it in mere labour, 24 hours. The wages command, therefore, a much greater quantity of labour than they consist of, and a given quantity of living labour actually exchanges for a much smaller one of accumulated labour. The only thing that is sure is that the price of labour, wages, must always express the quantity of labour which the labourers want in order to keep soul and body together. The wages of any quantity of labour must be equal to the quantity of labour which the labourer must expend upon his own reproduction. In the above instance a man would set to work two men for 12 hours each – together 24 hours – with the quantity of labour afforded by one man. In the case above, the product would be exchanged for another product with a value of 12d., or for 12 hours of labour, and this would be the source of its profit of 6d. (its surplus value for the capitalist). The value of products is determined by the labour contained in them, not by that part of the labour in them which the employer pays for. *The value of the product is constituted by labour done, including that not paid for*; but wages *only* express *paid labour*, never all labour *done*. The measure of this payment itself depends on the productivity of labour, for the latter determines the amount of necessary labour time. And since these wages constitute the *value of labour* (labour itself posited as commodity), this value is constantly variable, and is the opposite of constant. The amount of labour which the worker works is very different from the amount of labour that is worked up into his labour capacity, or which is required to reproduce his labour capacity. But he does not sell as commodity the use made of him, he sells himself not as cause but as effect. Let us listen how Mr Malthus exerts himself to get the matter clear:

'The conditions of the supply of commodities do not require that they should retain always the same relative values, but that each should retain its proper *natural* value, or the means of obtaining those objects which will continue to the producer *the same power of production* AND accumulation ... profits are calculated upon the advances necessary to production . . . *the specific advances of capitalists do not consist of cloth, but of labour;* AND *as no other object whatever can represent a given quantity of labour*, it is clear that it is the *quantity of labour which a commodity will command*, and not the quantity of any other commodity, which can represent the condition of its supply, or its *natural value*.' (17, 18.) (IX, 29.) Already, from the fact that the capitalist's *advances* consist of *labour*, Malthus could have seen that the matter has not become clear. Posit that the necessary labour time is 6 hours; also A, B, two men each of whom works for himself but who exchange with one another. Let A work 6 hours, B 12 hours. Now if A wants to eat up the 6 extra hours worked by B, if he wants to consume the product of B's 6 surplus hours, there is nothing he can give him other than 6 hours of living labour, say the next day. B now has a product of 6 hours of labour more than A. Now posit that under these circumstances he begins to fancy himself a capitalist and stops working altogether. Then on the third day, the only thing he could give in exchange for A's 6 hours is his own accumulated product of 6 hours, and, as soon as this exchange was accomplished, he would have to begin working again himself, or starve. But if he continues to work 12 hours for A, and A continues to work 6 hours for himself and 6 for B, then they exchange exactly 12 hours with one another. The *natural value* of the commodity, says Malthus, consists in its giving back to its possessor through exchange *the same power of production* AND *accumulation*. His commodity consists of 2 quantities of labour, one quantity of accumulated labour + one quantity of immediate labour. Thus if he exchanges his commodity for another which contains exactly the same total quantity of labour, then his power of production and accumulation has remained at least the same, equal. But it grew, because a part of the immediate labour has cost him *nothing*, while he sells it nevertheless. Yet Malthus comes to the conclusion that the quantity of labour of which the product consists is paid labour *only*, hence = to the sum of the wages, or, that *wages* are the measuring rod of the value of the commodity. If every amount of labour contained in the commodity were paid for, then Mr Malthus's doctrine would be correct, but it would be equally true that his capitalist would have no 'advances of labour' to make, and his 'powers of accumulation would become totally forfeited'. Where is the profit to come from, if no unpaid labour is performed? Well, thinks Mr Malthus, [from] the wages for accumulated labour. But since labour *done* has ceased to work, it also ceases to draw wages. True, the product in which it exists could now be again exchanged for living labour, but posit that this product = 6 hours of labour; then the worker would give 6 hours of living labour and would receive the advances, the capitalist's 6 hours of done labour, in return; so that the capitalist would not have budged a single step forward. Living labour would very soon be in possession of his dead labour. The reason Malthus gives, however, is that because 'no other object whatsoever can represent a given quantity of labour', the natural value of a commodity consists of 'the quantity of labour which a commodity will command, and not the quantity of any other commodity'. That means a given quantity of labour can be represented only by a quantity of living (immediate) labour. Not 'no other object whatsoever' but rather 'every object whatsoever' can represent a given quantity of labour, namely every object in which the same quantity of labour is contained. But Malthus wants the quantity of labour contained in the commodity to be measured by, to be equal to, not the *quantity of living labour* which it can set in motion, but the *quantity of paid labour* which it sets in motion. Posit that the commodity contains 24 hours of labour; he thinks, then, that the capitalist can buy 2 working days with it; and if the capitalist paid all of this labour, or if the quantity of labour done = the quantity of paid living labour, then he could buy *only*

24 hours of living labour with his 24 hours of done labour, and his 'powers of accumulation' would have gone to the wall. But the capitalist does not pay the worker the labour time, the amount of labour, but rather pays him only the necessary labour, while forcing him to work the rest free of charge. Thus, with the 24 hours of done labour he may perhaps set 48 hours of living labour into motion. Thus he in fact pays 1 hour of done labour for 2 hours of living labour, and thus gains 100% on the exchange. The value of his commodity now = 48 hours, but is in no way equal to the wages exchanged for them, nor equal to the wages for which it then in turn exchanges. If he continues in the same way, his 48 hours of done labour will buy 96 hours of living labour.

Posit that no capitalists exist at all, but that the independent and mutually exchanging workers worked more than necessary to live, because they want to accumulate too, etc. Call that part of the work which the worker does in order to live, *wages*; and the surplus time he works in order to accumulate, *profit*. Then the value of his commodity would be = to the total amount of labour contained in it, = to the total sum of living labour time; but in no way = to the wages he paid himself, or equal to the part of the commodity which he would have to reproduce in order to live. Because the value of a commodity = a specific quantity of labour, Malthus says it is = to the quantity of necessary labour (i.e. wages) contained in it, and not = to the total sum of labour contained in it; its totality is = to a fraction of it. But the worker's 'powers of accumulation' evidently would arise only because he has worked more than necessary to pay himself his wages. If a specific quantity of living labour time were = to the time required for the worker to live, then a specific quantity of living labour would be = to the wages which he produces, or the wages would be exactly equal to the living labour which they set in motion. If such were the case, capital would of course be impossible. If the worker, in the whole of his working time, can produce not a farthing more than his wages, then with the best of wills he cannot squeeze out a farthing for the capitalist. Property is the offspring of the productivity of labour. 'If one can produce only for one, everyone a worker; there can be no property. If one's man labour can maintain 5, there will be 4 idle men for 1 employed in production.' (Ravenstone.)[11] We saw above how Malthus's fantasiz-

11. Ravenstone, *Thoughts on the Funding System*, p. 11.

ing profundity expressed itself in a purely childish kind of calculation. What lay behind this, by the way, was the doctrine that
the value of labour was constant and that wages constituted price.
Because the rate of profit on a total capital can be expressed as
the same rate on the fraction of the capital made up by wages, he
asserts that this fractional part constitutes and determines the
price. Exactly the same *profundity* as here. If commodity A = an
amount of x commodity, he thinks that this can mean nothing
else than that it $= x$ living labour, for only labour can represent
labour. From this he concludes that commodity A = the amount
of *wage labour* which it can command, and that therefore the
value of labour is constant, because always = to the commodity
by which it is set in motion. The nub of it is simply that the
amount of living labour and the amount of wage labour are
identical for him, and that he believes that every fractional part
of wage labour is really paid for. But x living labour can be (and,
as wage labour, always is) $= x - y$ necessary labour (wages) $+$
y surplus labour. x dead labour can therefore set in motion
$x - y$ necessary labour (wages) $+ y$ surplus labour time; i.e.
it always sets in motion as many additional hours of living
labour time as there are hours of surplus labour time over and
above necessary labour time contained within x hours of
labour.

Wage labour always consists of paid and unpaid labour.

The value of labour is constant, thus means nothing other than
that all labour time is necessary, i.e. wage-producing labour time.
There is no surplus labour time but – nevertheless – there are
'powers of accumulation' and capital. Since wages are always
equal to a given quantity of labour, namely the quantity of living
labour which they set in motion, and since this is the same quantity of labour contained in the wages, therefore the *value of labour* is
constant, for it is always = to the quantity of objectified labour.
The rise and fall in the price of commodities, not of the *value of
labour*. If a worker gets 8s. silver per week or 16, this comes about
only because the price of shillings has risen or fallen, but the value
of labour has remained the same. In both cases he obtains a week
of done labour for a week of living labour. Mr M. proves this as
follows:

'If labour alone, without capital, were employed in procuring
the fruits of the earth, the greater facility of procuring one sort of
them compared with another would not, it is acknowledged, alter

the value of labour, or the exchangeable value of the whole produce obtained by a given quantity of exertion.'[12]

This means nothing but that each of the commodities, regardless of their quantity, would be determined by the labour contained in it, despite the fact that, depending on the degree of its productivity, it would express itself in one case in more, in another in fewer, use values. '*We should, without hesitation, allow that the difference was in the cheapness or dearness of the produce, not of the labour.*'[13] We would say labour is more productive in one branch than in the other, or, alternatively, the product costs more or less labour. We could not speak of cheapness or dearness of labour, since no *wage labour* existed, and hence an hour of immediate labour would always command an hour of objectified labour, which would naturally not prevent one hour from being more productive than another. But still, to the extent that we distinguish the part of labour necessary for subsistence from the part that is surplus labour – and if any hours of the day are at all worked as surplus time, then it is the same as if every fractional part of labour time consisted of a part necessary and a part surplus labour – done by the immediate labourers, it could still not be said that the *value of labour*, i.e. *wages* (the part of the product exchanged for necessary labour, or the part of the total labour which is employed for the necessary product), are *constant*. The fractional part of labour time which reproduces wages would vary with productivity; thus, with the productivity of labour, the *value of labour*, i.e. wages, would constantly vary. Wages would be measured both before and after by a definite *use value*, and since the latter constantly varies in its exchange value depending on the productivity of labour, wages would change, or [in other words] the *value of labour*. *Value of labour* presupposes in principle that living labour is *not* equal to its product, or, what is the same, that it is sold not as an acting cause, but as itself a produced effect. 'The value of labour is constant' means nothing further than that it is constantly measured by the quantity of labour contained in it. A product may contain more or less labour. Therefore sometimes a greater, sometimes a lesser portion of product A may exchange for product B. But the quantity of living labour which the product buys can never be greater or smaller than the done labour which it represents, for a given quantity of labour is always a given quantity

12. Malthus, *The Measure of Value*, p. 33.
13. ibid.

of labour, whether it exists in the form of objectified or in the form of living labour. Thus if more or less of a product is given for a specific quantity of living labour, i.e. if wages rise and fall, then this comes about not because the value of labour rose or fell, for the value of a specific quantity of labour is always equal to the same specific quantity of labour, but rather because the products have cost more or less labour, because a greater or lesser quantity of the products thus represents the same quantity of labour. *Thus the value of labour remains constant. Only the value of the products changes*, i.e. the productivity of labour changes, not its values. This is the pith of the theory of Malthus, if you can call such a shallow fallacy a theory. First of all, a product which has cost only half a working day may suffice for me to live and work a whole day. Whether or not the product possesses this quality depends not on its *value*, i.e. the labour time bestowed on it, but rather on its *use value*, and the exchange which takes place in this regard between living labour and the product of labour is not an exchange between both as use values, but rather their relation lies on the one side in the use value of the product, on the other side in the conditions of the existence of living labour capacity. Now, if objectified labour were exchanged for living labour, then according to the laws of exchange value the product which = half a day of work could only buy half a day of living labour, even though the worker could live from it for a whole day of work; and if his entire working day were to be bought, then he would have to obtain a whole working day in the product, with which, according to the assumption, he could live for two working days. But on the basis of capital, living labour and done labour do not exchange with one another as exchange values, as identical quantities: the same quantity of labour in objectified form as *value* being equivalent to the same quantity of labour in living form. Rather, what is exchanged is a product, and labour capacity, which is itself a product. Labour capacity is not = to the living labour which it can do, = to the quantity of labour which it can get done – this is its *use value*. It is equal to the quantity of labour by means of which *it must itself be produced* and can be reproduced. The product is thus in fact exchanged not for living labour, but for objectified labour, labour objectified in labour capacity. Living labour itself is a use value possessed by the exchange value [, labour capacity,] which the possessor of the product [, the capitalist,] has acquired in trade, and whether he has acquired less or more of this living labour than he has spent in the form of the product [, wages,] for labour capacity depends on the amount of living labour paid to the worker in the product. If an amount of labour were exchanged for an amount of labour, regardless of whether it were living or objectified, then of course every amount of labour would be equal to itself and its value equal to its amount. The product of half a working day thus could buy only half a working day. But then in fact no *wages* would exist, and no *value of labour*. Labour would have no *value distinct* from that of its product or the equivalent of its product, no *specific* value, and it is precisely the latter which constitutes the *value of labour*, wages.

From the fact, therefore, that a specific quantity of labour = a specific quantity of labour, or also that a specific quantity = itself, from the great discovery that a specific quantity is a specific quantity, Mr Malthus concludes that wages are constant, that the value of labour is constant, namely = to the same amount of labour objectified. This *would be* correct if living labour and stored-up labour were exchanged for one another as *exchange values*. But then there would exist neither *value of labour*, nor *wages*, nor *capital*, nor *wage labour*, nor Malthus's inquiries. All of these are based on the fact that living labour appears as a *use value* and living labour capacity as an *exchange value* opposite the labour stored up in capital. Malthus calmly proceeds: '*The same holds* if *capital and profits enter into the computation of value and the demand for labour varies.*'[14] Here we have the whole profundity. As soon as capital and profits are introduced, living labour capacity begins to be bought, and therefore a smaller portion of stored-up labour is exchanged for a larger portion of living labour. It is a general characteristic of this profundity that the entry of capital, which posits wage labour and which for the first time transforms labour into wage labour and labour capacity into a commodity, introduces no *change* whatever, either into the realization of labour or into the realization of stored-up labour. *Capital, a specific form of the relation of labour to its product and to its value, is, according to Malthus, 'entering' without changing anything.* It is just as if he allowed of no change in the constitution of the Roman Republic other than the introduction, the 'entering of emperors'. He continues: 'If an increased reward of the labourers takes place without an increase in the produce, this is possible only with a fall of profits . . . To obtain any given portion of the produce the same

14. Malthus, *The Measure of Value*, p. 29.

quantity of labour is necessary as before, but profit being diminished, the value of the produce is decreased; while this diminution
of profits in reference to the value of wages is just counterbalanced
by the increased quantity of labour necessary to procure the increased produce awarded to the labourer, leaving the value of
labour the same as before.' (p. 33, 34 loc. cit. Notebook IX, 29.)
According to the presupposition, the product contains the same
quantity of labour. But its value is supposed to have diminished
because profits have fallen. However, if the labour time contained
in the product has remained the same, how can profits fall? If
wages rise while total labour time remains the same – not for
momentary causes such as e.g. that competition has become favourable for the workers – then this means nothing other than that
the productivity of labour has fallen, that a greater amount of
time is necessary to reproduce labour capacity; that, therefore, a
larger part of the living labour set in motion by capital falls to
necessary labour and a smaller part to surplus labour. Let us leave
these trivia for later. Only the following final quotation now for the
sake of completeness: 'Inversely in the opposite case. A smaller
quantity of the produce would be awarded to the labourer and
profits would rise. A given quantity of produce, which had been
obtained by the same quantity of labour as before, would rise in
value on account of the rise of profits; while this rise of profits, in
reference to the wages of the labourer, would be balanced by the
smaller quantity of labour necessary to obtain the diminished
produce awarded to the labourer.' (M. p. 35) (loc. cit. IX, 29.)
What he says on this occasion about *money prices in different
countries*, proceeding from his principles, to be looked at later.⟨For
example, commodity A can buy one working day; it pays only a
half (the necessary half), but it exchanges for the whole. The
amount of the total labour purchased by the commodity is then
equal to necessary + surplus time. Thus if I know the price of
necessary labour $= x$, then the price of the whole labour $= 2x$,
and I could in this way appraise the newly created commodity in
terms of wages, and thus establish the prices of all commodities in
wages. But this would indeed be anything but a *constant value*.
Through the confusion that in civilized countries an average time
must indeed be worked for wages, say 12 hours, regardless of the
wages and regardless of how many of these 12 hours are necessary
or surplus labour time, Mr Carey as well – who reduces the amount
of labour to working days (and indeed they can be reduced to

living work days) – is led to make the assertion that, because the same capital costs constantly less labour time to reproduce, a machine of £100 will, for example, cost after a time only £50 owing to the growth of the productive forces, and hence will be the result of half as much labour time, working days or hours, whichever you like. From this Mr Carey concludes that *the worker* can buy, can obtain *this machine*, with half as many working days as before.[15] He commits the little mistake of regarding the growth of surplus labour time as if it had been gained *for* the worker, whereas the whole matter comes down to just the opposite, namely that the worker spends less of his whole working day working for himself, and more for capital, hence that the objective power of capital grows rapidly over against him, in a specific relation with the increase of the productive forces. Mr Carey lets the worker buy or borrow the machine; in short, he transforms him into a capitalist. And he is supposed to achieve this increased power over capital precisely because the reproduction of a specific quantity of capital costs less necessary labour, i.e. less paid labour, thus wages fall in relation to profit. In America, as long as the worker there still appropriates a part of his surplus labour for himself, he may accumulate enough to become e.g. a farmer etc. (although that too is already coming to a halt now). In places where wage labour in America can still get somewhere rapidly, this happens through the reproduction of earlier modes of production and property on the foundation of capital (e.g. the independent peasantry). In short, he regards the working days as working days belonging to the worker, and *instead of concluding that he has to produce more capital in order to be employed for the same labour time, he concludes that he has to work less in order to buy the capital* (to appropriate the conditions of production for himself).[16] If he produced 20 machines and can now produce 40 owing to increased productivity, then indeed the single machine becomes cheaper, but, because a smaller part of the working day is necessary in order to produce a given quantity of it, it does not follow that the product of the working day rose for the worker, but rather the reverse, that less living labour is employed for the production of a given quantity of machinery. By the way, Mr Carey, whose aim is *harmony*, himself finds that if the rate of profit declines, then the gross profit rises, because an ever larger capital is required in proportion to employed living

15. Carey, *Principles of Political Economy*, Part I, pp. 76–8.
16. ibid., p. 99.

labour, and it *therefore* becomes ever more impossible for the worker to appropriate the necessary sum of capital, the minimum of capital required for the productive employment of labour at the new stage of production. A fractional part of the capital requires less labour time for its reproduction, but a larger mass of capital is required in order to realize the lesser labour time. The growth of the productive forces expresses itself in a continuous decline of the part of capital consisting of labour compared with that laid out in advances, machinery etc. Carey's entire bad joke, which was of course grist to Bastiat's mill, rests on his transformation of the labour time or working days necessary for production into labour time *belonging* to the worker, whereas this time belongs in fact to capital, and an ever smaller portion of it remains for the worker in proportion to the growth in the productive force of labour. *The less living labour time a given capital has to buy* — or, the greater the total sum of the capital and the less the living labour employed by it relative to its size – the greater, according to Mr Carey, the chance for the worker to become owner of capital, *because* capital is *reproduced by less living labour*. The greater the capital and the smaller the number of workers it employs, relatively, the greater the chance these workers have of becoming capitalists, for has not capital now been reproduced with fewer working days? Cannot it *therefore* also be bought, gained with fewer working days? Take a capital of £100, employing 50 on advances, 50 on labour, and making 50% profit, for the decline of the rate of profit is Carey's chief hobby horse and belongs with his theory. Let each £ in wages be equal to 1 working day = 1 worker. Now take another capital of £16,000, which uses 14,500 in advances, 1,500 in wages (let this also = 1,500 workers) and makes only 20% profit. In the first case the product = 150; in the second (for convenient calculation's sake let the fixed capital turn over in one year) = 19,200 (3,200 profit). Here we have the most advantageous case for Mr Carey. The rate of profit has declined from 50% to 20, i.e. by $\frac{3}{5}$ or by 60%. In the one case, a product of 50 is the result of 50 living work days. In the other case, a product of 3,200 by 1,500 workers. In the first case the result of 1 working day a product of 1; in the second the result of 1 working day a product of $2\frac{2}{15}$. In the second case less than half the labour time is necessary to produce a value of 1 as in the first. Now, does this mean that in the second case half the worker's day produces $\frac{1}{15}$ for himself, while the other produces only 1 in twice the time, i.e. that he is on the high road to becoming a capitalist? He would first have to acquire a capital of £16,000, and buy alien labour instead of working himself, before this decrease in necessary labour time would aid him in the least. All it has done this way is created an infinite gap between his labour and *the conditions of* its employment, and decreased the rate of *necessary labour*, thus, in proportion to the first relation, thrown more than 6 times as many workers into the street. These workers thrown into the street are now supposed to console themselves with the thought that if they had the conditions to work independently, or rather to work as capitalists, then they themselves would have to hire fewer workers. In the first case the entire capital necessary is £100, and there is more of a chance here for the individual worker in an exceptional case to save up enough, and, with a special combination of luck, himself become a *capitalist* at the same level as capitalist A. The labour time which the worker works is the same with A and B, although the total sum of working days needed by the capitalists is essentially different. For every 6 workers needed by the first capitalist, the second needs not quite 1. The remainder therefore have to work just as much and more surplus time. That capital needs fewer living work days at the stage of production to which it has risen along with the forces of production is the same thing, according to Carey, as that the worker needs fewer working days to appropriate capital for himself; probably with the working·days of the un-'occupied' workers.⟩ Because the capitalist needs fewer workers to realize his immense capital, the worker employed by him can, with less labour, make the greater capital his own. Such is the logic of Mr Carey, the harmonizer.

In connection with Ricardo's theory, Wakefield says (Notebook VII, p. 74) loc. cit. p. 231 note:

'Treating labour as a commodity, and capital, the produce of labour, as another, then, if the value of these two commodities were regulated by equal quantities of labour, a given amount of labour would, under all circumstances, exchange for that quantity of capital which had been produced by the same amount of labour; *antecedent* labour would always exchange for the same amount as *present* labour ... But the value of labour, in relation to other commodities, in so far, at least, as wages depend upon share, is determined, not by equal quantities of labour, but by the proportion between supply and demand.'[17]

17. Adam Smith, *Wealth of Nations*, Vol. I, pp. 230–31, note by Wakefield the editor.

Dormant capital. Increase of production without previous
increase of capital. *Bailey*

⟨Bailey: *Money and its Vicissitudes in Value etc.*, London, 1837
(Notebook V, p. 26 seq.), has remarks about *dormant capital*
which can be set in motion through faster circulation (according to
him, through a greater volume of currency; he should have said
money) and tries to demonstrate that if capital were always fully
employed in a country, then no increase of demand could bring
about an increase of supply. The concept of *dormant capital* belongs within circulation, since capital which is not in circulation is
asleep. The relevant quotations are: 'Much capital and productive
skill may exist in an inert state. Those economists are wrong who
believe that the number of labourers and the quantity of capital
are certain definitive powers who ought inevitably to produce a
determinate result in any country where they exist.' (p. 54.) 'Far
from the amount of commodities which the existing producers
and the existing capital bring to market, being fixed and determined, it is subject to a wide range of variation.' (p. 55.) Thus 'not
essential to an increase of production that new capital or new
labourers should arise' (e.g. in a country where there is a want of
precious metals) . . . 'Some commodities or, what is the same, the
power to produce them, may be in excess at one place, other commodities at another place likewise, and the holder of each wishing
to exchange their articles for those held by the other, but kept in
a state of non-intercourse for want of a common medium of
exchange, and in a state of inaction because they have no motive
for production.' (55, 56.) In the circulation of capital, money appears doubly, as the transformation of capital into money as well
as realization of the price of the commodity; but here this positing
of prices is not a formality. The transformation of the product into
money is here the retransformation of capital into *value* as such,
independently existing value; capital as money or money as
realized capital. Secondly, in the role of mere medium of circulation; this is where it serves merely to retransform capital into
the conditions of production. In this second moment, a definite
amount of money has to be present at once in the form of wages,
as medium of circulation, means of payment. Now the fact that
money plays this double role in the circulation of capital makes it
appear in all crises as if money were lacking as medium of circulation,
whereas capital lacks *value* and hence cannot *monetize* itself. The
mass of circulating money may even increase at the same time. A

particular section must be made for the new aspects of money when posited as moment of the circulation of capital, partly as the medium of its circulation, partly as *capital's realized value*, as itself *capital*; when we speak of interest etc.⟩ ⟨Bailey continues: 'The labour made active by no means depends on a country's available capital alone. It depends on whether food, tools and raw materials are distributed slowly or rapidly to those parts where it is wanted; whether it circulates with difficulty or not, whether it exists for long intervals in inert masses, and so as a result does not furnish sufficient employment to the population.' (56, 57.) (Gallatin's example, loc. cit. 68, of the western counties of Pennsylvania.)[18] 'Political economists are inclined to regard a given quantity of capital and a given number of workers as production instruments of a uniform power or operating with a certain uniform intensity ... The producer who employs a certain capital may have his products on hand a long time or a short, and while he waits for the occasion to exchange them, his power of producing is stopped or retarded, so that in a given period, such as one year e.g., he may produce only half of what he would, had a prompt demand been present. This remark is equally appropriate to the labourer who is his instrument. The adjustment of the various occupations of men in society to each other must, at least imperfectly, be effected. But there is a wide distance between the stages in which it is realized – every expedient that facilitates traffic is a step towards this adjustment. The more unimpeded and easy the interchange of commodities becomes, the shorter will be those unproductive intervals, in which men, eager for work, seem separated by an impassable barrier from the capital ... which, although close at hand, is condemned to barren inertness.' (p. 59–60.) 'General principle, that a new demand will be met by fresh exertions; by the active employment of capital and labour before dormant, and not by the diversion of productive power from other objects. The latter possible only if the employment of capital and labour in a country were capable of no further growth. The exportation of the goods perhaps does not directly set new labour in motion, but it does then absorb commodities on hand as dead stock, and sets at liberty capital tied up in an unproductive state.' (p. 65.) 'Those who assert

18. Albert Gallatin (1761–1849; American public figure of Swiss origin, academic, diplomat, and banker, author of many books on financial questions), *Considerations on the Currency and Banking System of the United States*, Philadelphia, 1831, p. 68.

that an influx of money cannot promote the production of other commodities, since these commodities are the sole agents of production, prove that production cannot be enlarged at all, for it is required for such an enlargement that food, raw materials, and tools should be previously augmented, which in fact is maintaining *that no increase of production can take place without a previous increase'* (but is this not the economic theory of accumulation?) 'or in other words, that an increase is impossible.' (p. 70.) 'Now it is admittedly argued that if the buyer goes to market with an increased quantity of money and if he does not raise the prices of the commodities he finds there, then he gives no additional encouragement to production: if he raises the prices, however, then if prices are proportionally enhanced, the purchasers have no greater power of demand than before.' (73.) 'It is to be denied as a general principle that a purchaser cannot give additional encouragement to production, *unless his demand raise prices* ... Apart from the circumstance that the preparation of a larger quantity admits of a more effective division of labour and the employment of superior machinery, there is in this matter that sort of latitude, arising from a quantity of labour and capital lying unemployed, *and ready to furnish additional commodities at the same rate*. Thus does it happen that a considerable increase of demand often takes place without raising prices.'(73.)⟩

Wade's *explanation of capital*.[19] *Labour as mere agency of capital*. Capital, collective force. *Civilization, together with my remarks about it.* (*All social powers of labour as powers of capital. Manufacture. Industry.* Division of labour. *Formal unification of different branches of labour etc. by capital. Accumulation of capital. Transformation of money into capital. Science. Original accumulation and concentration the same. Free and coerced association. Capital as distinct from earlier forms*)

⟨John Wade: *History of the Middle and Working Classes* etc., 3rd ed., Lond., 1835 (Notebook p. 20) says: 'Labour is the agency

19. John Wade (1788–1875) was a journalist and historian, and parliamentary reformer, who worked for a long time with the *Spectator*, and whose *History of the Middle and Working Classes* was described by Marx as 'theoretically ... original in some parts ... historically ... a shameless plagiarism from Sir F. M. Eden'.

by which capital is made *productive of wages, profit, or revenue.*' (p. 161.) 'Capital is stored up industry, provided to develop itself in new and equivalent forms; it is *collective force.*' (p. 162.) 'Capital is only another name for *civilization.*' (164.) Like all productive powers of labour, i.e. those which determine the degree of its intensity and hence of its extensive realization, the association of the workers – the cooperation and division of labour as fundamental conditions of the productivity of labour – appears as the *productive power of capital*. The collective power of labour, its character as social labour, is therefore the *collective power* of capital. Likewise *science*. Likewise the division of labour, as it appears as division of the occupations and of exchange corresponding to them. All social powers of production are productive powers of capital, and it appears as itself their subject. The association of the workers, as it appears in the factory, is therefore not posited by them but by capital. Their combination is not *their* being, but the *being* [*Dasein*] of capital. *Vis-à-vis* the individual worker, the combination appears accidental. He relates to his own combination and cooperation with other workers as *alien*, as modes of capital's effectiveness. Unless it appears in an inadequate form – e.g. small, self-employed capital – capital already, at a certain greater or lesser stage, presupposes concentration both in objective form, i.e. as concentration in one hand, which here still coincides with accumulation, of the necessaries of life, of raw material and instruments, or, in a word, of money as the general form of wealth; and on the other side, in subjective form, the accumulation of labour powers and their concentration at a single point under the command of the capitalist. There cannot be one capitalist for every worker, but rather there has to be a certain quantity of workers per capitalist, not like one or two journeymen per master. Productive capital, or the mode of production corresponding to capital, can be present in only two forms: manufacture and large-scale industry. In the former, the division of labour is predominant; in the second, the combination of labour powers (with a regular mode of work) and the employment of scientific power, where the combination and, so to speak, the communal spirit of labour is transferred to the machine etc. In the first situation the mass of (accumulated) workers must be large in relation to the amount of capital; in the second the fixed capital must be large in relation to the number of the many cooperating workers. But the concentration of many, and their distribution among the machinery as so many cogs (why it is different in agriculture does not belong here), is, however, already presupposed here. Case II therefore does not need to be specially examined here, but only case I. The development proper to manufacture is the *division of labour*. But this presupposes the (preliminary) gathering-together of many workers under a single command, just as the *process through which money becomes capital presupposes the previous liberation of a certain amount of necessaries of life, raw materials and instruments of labour*. The division of labour is therefore also to be abstracted away here as a later moment. Certain branches of industry, e.g. mining, already presuppose cooperation from the beginning. Thus, so long as capital does not exist, this labour takes place as forced labour (serf or slave labour) under an overseer. Likewise road building etc. In order to take over these works, capital does not create but rather takes over the accumulation and concentration of workers. Nor is this in question. The simplest form, a form independent of the division of labour, is that capital employs different hand weavers, spinners etc. who live independently and are dispersed over the land. (This form still exists alongside industry.) *Here, then, the mode of production is not yet determined by capital, but rather found on hand by it*. The point of unity of all these scattered workers lies only in their mutual relation with capital, which accumulates the product of their production in its hands and, likewise, the surplus values which they created above and beyond their own revenue. The coordination of their work exists only *in itself*, in so far as each of them works for capital – hence possesses a centre in it – without working together. Their unification by capital is thus merely *formal*, and concerns only the product of labour, not labour itself. Instead of exchanging with many, they exchange only with the one capitalist. This is therefore a *concentration of exchanges* by capital. Capital engages in *exchange* not as an individual, but as representing the consumption and the needs of many. It *no longer exchanges* as individual exchanger, but rather, in the act of exchange, represents society. *Collective exchange* and *concentrative exchange* on the part of capital with the scattered working weavers etc., whose products are collected, united through this exchange, and whose labours are thereby also united, although they proceed independently of one another. The unification of their labours appears as a particular act, alongside which the independent fragmentation of their labours continues. This is the *first condition* necessary for *money* to be exchanged as capital for free labour. The second is the suspension of the independent fragmentation of these many workers, so that the *individual capital* no longer appears towards them merely as *social collective power in the act of exchange*, uniting many exchanges, but rather gathers them in one spot under its command, into one manufactory, and no longer leaves them in the *mode of production found already in existence*, establishing its power on that basis, but rather creates a mode of production corresponding to itself, as its basis. It posits the *concentration* of the workers in production, a unification which will occur initially only in a common location, under overseers, *regimentation, greater discipline, regularity and the* POSITED *dependence in production itself on capital*. Certain *faux frais de production* are thereby saved from the outset. (On this whole process compare Gaskell, where special regard is had to the development of large industry in England.)[20] Now capital appears as the collective force of the workers, their social force, as well as that which ties them together, and hence as the unity which creates this force. Afterwards as before, and at every stage of the development of capital, this all continues to be mediated through the many exchanging with it as the one, so that exchange itself is concentrated in it; the social character of exchange; it exchanges socially with the workers, but they individually with it. With craft production, the main concern is the quality of the product and the particular skill of the individual worker; the master, as master, is supposed to have achieved mastery in this skill. His position as master rests not only on his ownership of the conditions of production, but also on his own skill in the particular work. With the production of capital, and from the very outset, the point is not this half-artistic relation to labour – which corresponds generally with the development of the use value of labour, the development of particular abilities of direct manual work, the formation of the human hand etc. The point from the outset is mass, because the point is exchange value and surplus value. The principle of developed capital is precisely to make special skill superfluous, and to make manual work, directly physical labour, generally superfluous both as skill and as muscular exertion; to transfer skill, rather, into the dead forces of nature. Now, with the presupposition of the rise of manufacture as the rise of the mode of production of capital (slaves are combined in themselves, because under a single master), it is presup-

20. Gaskell, *Artisans and Machinery*, pp. 11–114.

posed that the productive force of labour, still to be brought to
life by capital, does not yet exist. It is a presupposition, therefore,
that necessary labour still takes up a great portion of the entire
available labour time in manufacture, hence that surplus labour
per individual worker is still relatively small. Now, this is compensated on one side, and the progress of manufactures is correspondingly accelerated, by the fact that the rate of profit is
higher, hence that capital accumulates more rapidly in relation to
its already existing amount, than it does in big industry. If out of
100 thalers 50 go for labour and surplus time $= \frac{1}{5}$, then the value
created $= 110$ or 10%. If out of 100 only 20 went for labour and
surplus time $= \frac{1}{4}$, then the value created $= 105$ or 5%. On the
other side, manufacture obtains this higher profit rate only through
the employment of many workers at once. The greater surplus
time can be gained only by collecting together the surplus time of
many workers in relation to capital. Absolute, not relative surplus
time predominates in manufacture. This is even more the case
originally where the scattered, independent workers still realize a
part of their own surplus labour for themselves. For capital to
exist as capital, to be able to live off profit, as well as to accumulate, its gain must $=$ the sum of the surplus time of many simultaneous living work days. In agriculture, the soil itself with its
chemical etc. action is already a machine which makes direct
labour more productive, and hence gives a surplus *earlier*, because
work is done here at an *earlier* stage with a machine, namely a
natural one. This the only correct basis of the doctrine of the
Physiocrats, which in this respect considers agriculture in comparison with a still quite undeveloped system of manufacture. If
the capitalist employed one worker in order to live from that one's
surplus time, then he would obviously gain doubly if he himself
also worked, with his own funds, for then he would gain, in addition to the surplus time, the wage paid the worker. He would
lose in the process. I.e. he would not yet be in the situation of
working as a capitalist, or the worker would only be his helper,
and thus he would not stand in relation to him as capital.

Thus, in order that money may become transformed into
capital, it is necessary not only that it should be able to set surplus
labour in motion, but also that there should be a *certain quantity of
surplus labour,* the surplus labour of a given mass of necessary
labour, i.e. of *many workers* at once, so that their combined sum
is sufficient for it not only to lead an existence as *capital,* i.e. to

represent wealth in consumption in contrast to the worker's life, but also to set aside surplus labour for accumulation. From the outset, capital does not produce for use value, for immediate subsistence. Surplus labour must therefore be large enough from the beginning to allow a part of it to be re-employed as capital. Thus, whenever the stage is reached where a certain mass of social wealth is already concentrated in one hand, which is objectively capable of appearing as capital, first as the exchange with many workers, later as production by many workers in combination, and is capable of setting a certain quantity of living labour capacities to work simultaneously, then, at that point, production by capital begins, which thus from the outset appears as the *collective force,* the social force, the suspension of individual isolation, first that of exchange with the workers, then that of the workers themselves. The workers' individual isolation still implies their relative independence. Hence their regroupment around the individual capital as the exclusive base of their subsistence implies full dependence on capital, complete dissolution of the ties between the workers and the conditions of production. The result will be the same – or it is the same in another form – when the point of departure is the particular form of exchange which is presupposed for capital to exchange as capital, where money must already *represent many exchangers* or possess a *buying power* surpassing that of the individual and his individual surplus, one which, while belonging to an individual, is already more than individual, and belongs to him as a social function, in his capacity as representative, within exchange, of the social wealth – and it arises on the other side from the conditions of *free labour*. The detachment of the individual from the production conditions of labour = the regroupment of many around one capital.*⟩

'*This continual progression of knowledge and of experience,*' says Babbage, 'is our great power.'[21] This progression, this social progress belongs [to] and is exploited by capital. All earlier forms of property condemn the greater part of humanity, the slaves, to be pure instruments of labour. Historical development, political development, art, science etc. take place in higher circles over their

---

*Merchant capital also from the outset the concentration of many exchanges in one hand. It already represents a mass of exchangers both as M and as C.

---

21. Babbage, *Traité sur l'économie*, p. 485.

heads. But only capital has subjugated historical progress to the service of wealth.

⟨Before accumulation by capital, there is presupposed an accumulation which constitutes capital, which is a part of its conceptual determination; we can hardly call it *concentration* yet, because this takes place in distinction to many capitals; but if one still speaks only of capital *generally*, then concentration still coincides with accumulation or with the concept of capital. I.e. it does not yet form a particular aspect. However, capital does indeed exist from the outset as One or Unity as opposed to the workers as Many. And it thus appears as the concentration of workers as distinct from that of work, as a unity falling outside them. In this respect, concentration is contained in the concept of capital – the concentration of many living labour capacities for one purpose; a concentration which does not in any way need to have been established in production, or penetrated production, at the origin. Centralizing effect of capital on labour capacities, or positing of itself as the independent and external unity of these many available existences.⟩

⟨Rossi says in his *Cours d'économie politique*[22] (Notebook, p. 26): 'Social progress cannot consist in the dissolution of all association, but in the replacement of the forced and oppressive associations of times past by voluntary and equitable associations. The highest degree of isolation is the condition of the savage; the highest degree of forced, oppressive association is barbarism. Apart from these extremes, history shows us a great diversity of varieties and shadings. Perfection is found in voluntary associations, which by their union multiply the forces, without taking away the energy, the morality and the responsibility of individual authority.' (p. 354.) Under capital, the *association* of workers is not compelled through direct physical force, forced labour, statute labour, slave labour; it is compelled by the fact that the conditions of production are alien property and are themselves present as *objective association*, which is the same as accumulation and concentration of the conditions of production.⟩

22. Pellegrino Rossi (1787–1848; Italian political economist, supporter of Napoleon I, in exile from 1815, first in Geneva then in France, professor of political economy at the Collège de France 1833–40, created a peer in 1844, returned to Italy as French ambassador, became prime minister of the Pope's government in 1848, finally assassinated in the course of a speech in favour of moderation), *Cours d'économie politique*, Brussels, 1843.

Rossi. *What is capital? Is raw material capital? Wages necessary for it?* (*Approvisionnement, capital?*)

⟨The way of conceiving capital in its physical attribute only, as instrument of production, while entirely ignoring the economic form which makes the instrument of production into capital, entangles the economists in all manner of difficulties. Thus Rossi asks, loc. cit. (Notebook, 27): 'Is the raw material truly an instrument of production? Is it not rather the object on which the productive instruments must act?' (p. 367.) Thus capital is entirely identical for him here with the instrument of production in the technological sense, according to which every savage is a capitalist. (Which Mr Torrens in fact asserts in the case of the savage who throws a *stone* at a bird.)[23] Incidentally, even from the standpoint of the purely physical abstraction – i.e. of abstraction from the economic category itself – Rossi's remark is one-sided and shows only that he has not understood his teachers in England. Accumulated labour used as instrument for new production; or produce pure and simple applied to production; the raw material is employed for production, i.e. submitted to transformation, just as well as the instrument, which is also a product. *The finished result of production in turn becomes a moment of the production process.* The statement means nothing more than that. Within the production process it may figure as raw material or as instrument. But it is an instrument of production not in so far as it serves as an instrument within the direct production process, but rather in so far as it is a means of the renewal of the production process itself – one of its presuppositions. More important and more to the point is the question whether the *approvisionnement* forms a part of capital, i.e. wages, and here the entire confusion of the economists is revealed. 'It is said that the worker's payment is capital, because the capitalist advances it him. If all workers' families had enough to live for a year, there would be no wages. The worker could say to the capitalist: you advance the capital for our common project, and I contribute the labour; the product will be divided among us in such-and-such proportions. As soon as it is realized, each will take his share.' (p. 369.) 'Then there would be no advance to the workers. They would nevertheless consume even if the work stood still. What they would consume would belong to the consumption fund, and not at all to capital. Therefore: the advances to the workers

23. R. Torrens, *An Essay on the Production of Wealth*, London, 1821, pp. 70–71.

are not necessary. *Hence wages is not a constituent element of production. It is an accident, a form of our state of society.* Capital, labour, land, by contrast, are necessary in order to produce. *Secondly*: the word wages is used in a double sense: one says that wages are a capital, but what do wages represent? Labour. He who says wages says labour and vice versa. Thus if the wages advanced are a component of capital, then there would be only two instruments of production to speak of: capital and land.' (p. 370.) And further: '*Basically the worker consumes not the capitalist's possessions but his own; what is given to him as reward of labour is his proportional share of the product.*' (p. 370.) 'The capitalist's contract with *the worker is not among the phenomena of production* ... The entrepreneur lends himself to this agreement, since it may facilitate production. But this agreement is nothing but a *second operation*, an operation of a quite different nature, grafted onto a productive operation. *In another organization of labour it may disappear.* Even today there are kinds of production where it has no place. The part of the fund which the entrepreneur devotes to the payment of wages does not make up a part of capital ... It is a separate operation, which undoubtedly may speed the course of production, but which cannot be termed a *direct* instrument of production.' (370.) 'To conceive labour power, while abstracting from the workers' means of subsistence during production, is to conceive a being existing only in the mind. He who says labour, who says labour power, thereby says worker and means of subsistence, labourer and wages ... *the same element reappears under the name of capital; as if the same thing could be simultaneously part of two different instruments of production.*' (370, 371.) Now here there is a great deal of confusion, legitimate because Rossi takes the economists at their word and equates the *instrument of production* as such with capital. First of all he is quite right that wage labour is not an absolute form of labour, but he forgets in the process that capital is not an absolute form of the means and materials of labour either, and that these two forms are two different moments of one and the same form, and hence rise and fall together; that it is nonsensical, therefore, for him to speak of capitalists without wage labourers. [Note] his example of the workers' families who can live for a year without the capitalists, hence are owners of their conditions of production, who perform their necessary labour without the permission of Mr Capitalist. The capitalist whom Rossi has approaching the workers with his proposal thus is no other than a producer of instruments of production – the solicitation means nothing more than a division of labour mediated through exchange with the outside. The two then divide up the common product among themselves even without any agreement – through simple exchange. The exchange is the act of division. A further agreement is not necessary. What these worker families would then exchange would be surplus labour, absolute or relative, made possible for them by the instrument – either new secondary labour in addition to their old labour, from which they could live year after year before the appearance of the c[apitalist], or through the application of the instrument in their old branch of work. Here Mr Rossi makes the worker the owner and vendor of his surplus labour, and has thereby happily extinguished the last trace which might brand him a wage labourer, but has also thereby wiped out the last trace which makes the instrument of production into capital. It is true that the worker 'basically does not consume the capitalist's possessions, but his own', but not exactly as Mr Rossi means, because it is only a *proportional* part of *the* product, but rather because it is a *proportional* part of *his* product, and because, if the semblance of exchange is stripped away, the payment consists of the fact that he works a part of the day for himself and another part for the capitalist, but *only so long as he obtains permission to work at all*, as his work permits this division. The *act of exchange* itself, as we have seen, is not a moment of the direct production process, but rather one of its conditions. Within the total production process of capital, which includes the different moments of its exchanges, its circulation, this exchange is, however, posited as a moment of the total process. But, says Rossi: wages appear twice in the account: once as capital, the other time as labour; thus the wage represents two distinct instruments of production. If the wage represents the instrument of production which is labour, then it cannot represent the instrument of production which is capital. Here another muddle, arising because Rossi takes the orthodox economic distinctions seriously. Wages figure only once in production, as a fund destined to be transformed into wages, as *virtual* wages. As soon as they have become real wages, they are paid out, and then only figure in consumption as the worker's revenue. But what is exchanged for wages is labour capacity, and this does not figure in production at all, but only in the use made of it – *labour*. Labour appears as the instrument of the production of value because it is not paid for, hence not represented by wages. As the activity which creates use values, it likewise has nothing to do with itself as paid labour. In the hand of the worker, the wage is no longer a wage, but a consumption fund. It is wages only in the hand of the capitalist, i.e. the part of capital destined to be exchanged for labour capacity. It has reproduced a saleable labour capacity for the capitalist, so that in this regard even the worker's consumption takes place in the service of the capitalist. He does not pay for labour itself at all, only for labour capacity. This he can do, however, only if this capacity is set to work. If the wage appears twice, it is not because it represents two different instruments of production, but because it appears the first time from the viewpoint of production, the second time from the viewpoint of distribution. This specific form of distribution, however, is not an arbitrary arrangement which could be different; it is, rather, posited by the form of production itself, is only one of its own moments considered from another angle. The value of the machine certainly forms a part of the capital laid out in it; but the machine does not produce, as value, although it brings the manufacturer income. The wage does not represent labour as an instrument of production, any more than value represents the machine as instrument of production. It represents only labour capacity, and, since the latter's value exists separately from it as capital, a part of the capital. In so far as the capitalist appropriates *alien* labour and buys new alien *labour* with it, the wage – i.e. the representative of labour – does, if Mr Rossi wishes to put it this way, appear doubly, (1) as the property of capital, (2) as representative of labour. What actually worries Rossi is that the wage appears as the representative of *two instruments of production*, of *capital* and of *labour*; he forgets that labour as a productive force is incorporated in capital, and that, as *labour in esse*, not *in posse*,[24] it is in no way an *instrument of production* distinct from capital, but is, rather, that without which capital would not be an instrument of production. As for the distinction between wages as forming a part of capital and at the same time the worker's revenue, we will come to that in the section on profit, interest, with which we shall conclude this first chapter on capital.⟩

24. Labour in being, not in potency.

Malthus. Theory of value and of wages. (*Capital to do with proportion, labour only with portion. See my remarks on* surplus value *and* profit.) Ricardo's *theory.* (*Carey contra Ricardo.*) *Malthus: the wage* [*has*] *nothing to* [*do*] *with proportion. Malthus's theory of value*

⟨In connection with the above-mentioned work, *The Measure of Value* etc., Malthus returns to the theme again in his *Definitions in Political Economy* etc., London, 1827. He remarks in the latter: 'No writer that I have met with, anterior to Mr Ricardo, ever used the term *wages* or real wages, as implying *proportions.* Profits, indeed, imply proportions; and the *rate of profits* had always justly been estimated by a *percentage upon the value of the advances.* But wages had uniformly been considered as rising and falling, not *according to any proportion* which they might bear to the whole produce obtained by a certain quantity of labour, but by the greater or smaller quantity of any particular produce received by the labourer, or by the greater or smaller power which such produce would carry of commanding the necessaries and conveniences of life.' (M. 29, 30.) (Notebook X, p. 49.) The only value produced by capital in a given production is that added by the new amount of labour. This value, however, consists of necessary labour, which reproduces wages – the advances made by capital in the form of wages – and of surplus labour, hence surplus value above and beyond the necessary. The advances made in the form of material and machine are merely transposed from one form into another. The instrument passes into the product just as much as does the raw material, and its wearing-out is at the same time the product's formation. If raw material and instrument cost nothing, as in some extractive industries where they are still almost $= 0$ (the *raw material* always, in every extractive industry, metal and coal mining, fishing, hunting, lumbering in virgin forests etc.), then they also add absolutely nothing to the value of the production. Their value is the result of previous production, not of the immediate production in which they serve as instrument and material. *Surplus value* can therefore be estimated only in proportion to necessary labour. *Profits* is only a secondary, derivative and transformed form of the surplus value, the bourgeois form, in which the traces of its origin are extinguished. Ricardo himself never grasped this, because he (1) always speaks only of the division of an available, *ready* amount, not of the original positing of this difference; (2) because this understanding would have forced him to see that there is a relation between capital and labour which is entirely different from that of exchange; and he was not allowed the insight that the bourgeois system of equivalents turns into appropriation without equivalent and is based on that; (3) his statement about proportionate profits and wages means only that [if] a certain total value is divided into two portions, any quantity at all is divided in two, then the magnitude of the two parts is necessarily in inverse relation.[25] And then his school justly reduced the matter to this triviality. His aim in asserting the proportionality of wages and profits was not to get to the bottom of the creation of surplus value – for since he begins with the presupposition that a given value is to be divided between wages and profit, between labour and capital, he thereby presupposes this division as self-evident – but rather, firstly, it was to counter the common determination of prices by asserting the correct one, of value, in that he showed that the limit of value is itself not affected by its distribution, different division among profits and wages; *secondly*: to explain not the merely transitory, but rather the continuing decline in the rate of profit, which was inexplicable to him on the presupposition that a fixed portion of value goes to labour; *thirdly*: in explaining the decline of profit by the rise of wages, and the latter in turn by the rise in *value* of agricultural products, i.e. the rising difficulty of their production, thereby at the same time to explain *ground rent* as not being in conflict with his determination of value. This at the same time furnished a polemical weapon for industrial capital, against the exploitation of the progress of industry by landed property. But at the same time, driven by simple logic, he had thereby proclaimed the contradictory nature of profit, of labour and of capital, despite his efforts to convince the worker afterwards that this contradictory character of profit and wages does not influence his real income, and that a *proportional* (not absolute) rise of wages is *harmful* to him, because it hinders accumulation, and the development of industry then benefits only the lazy landowner. Still, the contradictory form had been proclaimed, and Carey, who does not understand Ricardo, could therefore abuse him as the father of the communists etc., where he

25. Cf. Ricardo, *On the Principles of Political Economy*, pp. 31–2, 'There can be no rise in the value of labour without a fall of profits . . . If cloth . . . be divided between the workman and his employer, the larger the proportion given to the former, the less remains for the latter.'

is again right in a sense he himself does not understand.[26] But the other economists, who, like Malthus, want to have absolutely nothing to do with the proportional (and hence contradictory) nature of wages, *desire* on the one hand to hush up the contradiction; on the other hand they cling to the notion that the worker simply exchanges a specific use value, his labour capacity, for capital, and hence gives up the productive force, the power of labour to create new value, and that he *has nothing to do with the product*, and hence the exchange between capitalists and workers, wages, is concerned, like every simple exchange where economic *equivalents* are presupposed, only with *quantity,* the quantity of use value. As correct as this is in one regard, it also introduces the apparent form of barter, of exchange, so that when competition permits the worker to bargain and to argue with the capitalists, he measures his demands against the capitalists' profit and demands a certain share of the surplus value created by him; so that the *proportion* itself becomes a real moment of economic life itself. Further, in the struggle between the two classes – which necessarily arises with the development of the working class – the measurement of the distance between them, which, precisely, is expressed by wages itself as a proportion, becomes decisively important. The *semblance of exchange* vanishes in the course [*Prozess*] of the mode of production founded on capital. This course itself and its repetition posit what is the case in itself, namely that the worker receives as wages from the capitalist what is only a part of his own labour. This then also enters into the consciousness of the workers as well as of the capitalists. The *question for Ricardo is actually only what proportion of the total value do necessary wages form in the course of development*? It always remains only the *necessary wage*; hence its proportional nature does not interest the worker, who always obtains the same minimum, but only the capitalist, whose deductions from the total income vary, without the workers obtaining a greater amount of use values. But the fact that Ricardo formulated the contradictory nature of profit and wages, even if for quite different purposes, already shows by itself that the mode of production founded on capital had, by his time, taken on a form more and more adequate to its nature. In the cited *Definitions* (Notebook IX, p. 49, 50), Malthus remarks in regard to Ricardo's theory of value: 'Ricardo's assertion, that as the value of wages

26. H. C. Carey, *The Past, the Present, and the Future*, Philadelphia, 1848, pp. 74–5.

rises, profits proportionally fall and vice versa, is true only on the presupposition that commodities in which the same amount of labour is contained, are always of the same value, and this is true in 1 case out of 500, and necessarily so, because with the progress of civilization and improvement, the quantity of fixed capital employed steadily grows, and makes more various and unequal the times of the returns of the circulating capital.' (loc. cit. 31, 32.) (This concerns *prices*, not *value*.) Malthus remarks in connection with his own discovery of the true standard of value: '*Firstly*: I had nowhere seen it stated, that the ordinary *quantity of labour which a commodity will command* must represent and measure the *quantity of labour worked up in it, with the addition of profits* . . . By representing the labour worked up in a commodity, with the addition of profits, labour represents the natural and necessary conditions of its supply, or the elementary costs of its production . . . *Secondly*: I had nowhere seen it stated that, however the fertility of the soil might vary, the elementary costs of producing the wages of a given quantity of labour must always necessarily be the same.' (196, 197.) Means only: wages always equal to the labour time necessary for their production, which varies with the productivity of labour. The quantity of commodities remains the same. 'If one regards value as the general power of purchase of a commodity, then this relates to the purchase of all commodities, of the general mass of commodities. But this is quite unmanageable . . . . Now, if any one [should] object, it cannot for a moment be denied that labour best represents an average of the general mass of productions.' (205.) 'A large class of commodities, like raw produce, rise with the progress of society, compared with labour, while the manufactured articles fall. Thus not far from truth to say that the average mass of commodities which a given quantity of labour will command in the same country, during the course of some century, may not very essentially vary.' (206.) 'Value must always be value in exchange for labour.' (224, note, loc. cit.) In other words, the doctrine is: the value of a commodity, the labour worked up in it, is represented by the living work days which it commands, for which it may be exchanged, and hence by *wages*. Living work days contain both time and surplus time. Let us do for Malthus the biggest favour we can do for him. Let us namely assume that the relation of surplus labour to necessary labour, hence the relation of wages to profit, always remains constant. To begin with, the fact that Mr Malthus speaks of the labour worked up in the commodity *with the addition of profits* already demonstrates his confusion, since these profits can form nothing other than a part of the labour worked up. What he has in mind with this *is profits above and beyond labour worked up, which* are supposed to come *out of fixed capital* etc. This can only affect the distribution of the total profit among the different shareholders, but not its total quantity, for if everyone obtained for his commodity the labour worked up in it + profits, then where would these latter come from, Mr Malthus? If one person obtains the labour worked up in his commodity + profit, then the other has to obtain labour worked up − profit, profit here regarded as the excess quantity of real surplus value. This is therefore null and void. Now posit that the labour worked up = 3 working days, and, if the proportion of surplus labour time is as 1:2, then these have been obtained in payment for 1½ working days. The workers indeed worked 3 days, but each of them was paid only half a day. Or, the commodity which they obtain for their 3 days of labour had only 1½ days worked up in it. Thus, all other relations being the same, the capitalist would obtain 6 working days for the 3 working days worked up in his commodity. (The matter is correct only because surplus labour time is posited as = to necessary labour time, hence in the second case *only* the first is repeated.) (*Relative surplus value obviously restricted not only by the relation cited earlier, but also by the degree to which the product enters into the worker's consumption.* If the capitalist could obtain twice the number of *cashmere shawls*, owing to an increase in the productive forces, and if he sold them at their *value*, then he would have created no relative surplus value because the workers do not consume such shawls, and thus the time necessary for the reproduction of their labour capacity would remain the same as before. But this not so in practice, because in such cases the price rises above the value. At this point in the theory it does not concern us yet because capital is here regarded in itself, not in a particular branch). That means, he will pay the wages of 3 days and get 6 days of work; with each ½ day he buys a day; hence with $\frac{6}{2}$ days, = 3 days, 6 days. To assert, then, that the working days a commodity commands, or the wages it pays, express its value is to understand absolutely nothing of the nature of capital and wage labour. It is the pith of all value-creation and of capital-creation that objectified working days command a greater number of living ones. It would have been correct if Malthus had said that the living labour time a commodity commands expresses the measure of its *realization*, the measure of the *surplus labour* it posits. But this would only be the tautology that it posits more labour to the extent that it posits more, or it would be the expression of the opposite of what Malthus wants, that surplus value arises because the living labour time a commodity commands never represents the labour worked up in it. (Now we have finally done with Malthus.)⟩

Aim of capitalist production value (money), not commodity, use value etc. Chalmers.[27] – *Economic cycle.* – *Circulation process.* Chalmers

⟨We have demonstrated above, in the development of the concept of capital, that it is value as such, *money*, which both preserves itself through circulation and also increases itself through exchange with living labour. That, hence, the aim of producing capital is *never use value*, but rather the general form of wealth as wealth. The cleric Th. Chalmers, in the otherwise in many respects ridiculous and repulsive work: *On Political Economy in Connection with the Moral State and Moral Prospects of Society*, 2nd. ed., Lond., 1832, has correctly struck upon this point, without at the same time falling into the asininity of types like Ferrier etc., who confuse money as the value of capital with the really available metallic money.[28] In crises, capital (as commodity) is not exchangeable, not because *too few* means of circulation are available; but, rather, it does not circulate because it is *not exchangeable*. The importance assumed by cash in times of crisis arises only because, while capital is not exchangeable for its value – and only for that reason does its value appear opposite it in the money form – there are obligations to pay off; alongside the interrupted circulation a *forced circulation* takes place. Chalmers says (Notebook IX, p. 57): 'When a consumer refuses certain commodities, it is not always, as is assumed by the new economists, because he wants to purchase others in preference, but because he wants to reserve entire the general power of purchasing. And when a *merchant* brings commodities to market, it is generally not in quest of other commodities to be given in return for them ... he will extend his *general power of purchase of all commodities*. It is useless to say that

27. The Reverend Thomas Chalmers (1780–1847) was a Scottish Presbyterian minister who taught moral philosophy and divinity, as well as political economy; 'one of the most fanatical Malthusians' (Marx).
28. See p. 214, n. 67.

money is also a *commodity*. The real metallic money for which a merchant has any use does not amount to more than a small *fraction of his capital,* even of *his monied capital*; all of which, though estimated in money, can be made, on the strength of written contracts, to describe its orbit, and be effective for all its purposes, with the aid *of coin amounting to an insignificant proportion of the whole.The great object of the monied capitalist,* in fact, is to add to the *nominal amount of his fortune.* It is that, if expressed pecuniarily this year by £20,000 e.g., it should be expressed pecuniarily next year by £24,000. *To advance his capital, as estimated in money,* is the only way in which he can advance his interest as a merchant. The importance of these objects for him is not affected by fluctuations in the currency or by a change in the real value of money. For example, in one year he comes from 20 to 24,000 pounds; through a fall in the value of money he may not have increased his command over the comforts etc. Nevertheless, this is his interest just as much as if money had not fallen; for else his monied fortune would have remained stationary and his real wealth would have declined in the proportion of 24 to 20 ... *Commodities'* (i.e. use value, real wealth) 'thus not the terminating object of the trading capitalist.' (The illusion of the Monetary System, however, was that it regarded real metallic money (or paper, would change nothing), in short, the *form* of value, as *real money,* as the *general form of wealth* and of self-enrichment, whereas precisely as *money* increases as the accumulation of general power of purchase, it undergoes a relative decline in its specific form as medium of exchange or also as *realized hoard.)* As *assignation* in real wealth or productive power [the capitalist's money] gains a thousand forms, *'quite apart from expenditure of his revenue in purchases for the sake of consumption.* In the *outlay of his capital,* and *when he purchases for the sake of production*, money is his terminating object' (not *coin, notabene*). (164–6.)

'Profit,' says the same Chalmers, 'has the effect of attaching the services of the disposable population to other masters, besides the mere landed proprietors, ... while their expenditure reaches higher than the necessaries of life.' (78. Notebook IX, p. 53.)⟩

In the book just referred to, Chalmers calls the whole *circulation process* the economic cycle: 'The world of trade may be conceived to revolve in what we shall call an economic cycle, which accomplishes one revolution by business coming round again, through its successive transactions, to the point from which it set out. Its commencement may be dated from the point at which the capitalist has obtained those returns by which his capital is replaced to him: whence he proceeds anew to engage his workmen; to distribute among them, in wages, their maintenance, or rather the power of lifting it; to obtain from them in finished work, the articles in which he specially deals; to bring these articles to market, and there terminate the orbit of one set of movements, by effecting a sale, and receiving in its proceeds, a return for the whole outlays of the period. The intervention of money alters nothing in the real character of this operation . . .' (85 loc. cit.) (Notebook, p. 54, 55.)

Difference in return. *Interruption of the production process*
(or rather its failure to coincide with the labour process).
Total duration of the production process. (Agriculture. Hodgskin.)
Unequal periods of production

The difference in the return, in so far as it depends on the phase of the circulation process which coincides with the direct production process, depends not only on the longer or shorter labour time required to complete the article (e.g. canal building etc.), but also, in certain branches of industry – agriculture – on the interruptions of the work which are due to the nature of the work itself, where on the one hand the capital lies fallow, and, on the other, labour stands still. Thus the example given by A. Smith, that wheat is a crop taking 1 year, the ox a crop taking 5 years, etc.[29] Therefore 5 years of labour are employed on the latter, only 1 on the former. Little labour is employed e.g. on cattle raised on pasture. At the same time, in agriculture, the labour applied e.g. during the winter is also little. In agriculture (and to a greater or lesser degree in many another branch of production} there are interruptions given by the conditions of the production process itself, pauses in labour time, which must be begun anew at the given point in order to continue or to complete the process; the constancy of the production process here does not coincide with the continuity of the labour process. This is one moment of the difference. *Secondly*: the product generally requires a longer time to be *completed*, to be put into its finished state; this is the total duration of the production process, regardless of whether interruptions take place in the

29. Adam Smith, *Wealth of Nations*, Vol. II, p. 10.

operations of labour or not; the different duration of the production phase generally. *Thirdly*: after the product is finished, it may be necessary for it to lie idle for some time, during which it needs relatively little labour, in order to be left in the care of natural processes, e.g. wine. (This will be, conceptually, approximately the same case as I.) *Fourthly*: a longer time to be brought to market, because destined for a more distant market. (This coincides conceptually with case II.) *Fifthly*: The shorter or longer period of the total return of a capital (its total reproduction), in so far as it is determined by the relation of fixed capital and circulating capital, is concerned obviously not with the *immediate production process* and its duration, but rather takes its character from circulation. The total capital's period of reproduction is determined by the total process, circulation included.

'Inequality in the periods necessary for production.'[30]

'The *difference of time* required to complete the products of agriculture, and of other species of labour, is the main cause of the great dependence of the agriculturists. They cannot bring their commodities to market in less time than a year. For that whole period they are obliged to borrow from the shoemaker, the tailor, the smith, the wheelwright and the various other labourers, whose products they need and which are completed in a few days or weeks. Owing to this natural circumstance, and owing to the more rapid increase of the wealth produced by other labour than that of agriculture, the monopolizers of all the land, although they have also monopolized the legislation, are unable to save themselves and their servants, the farmers, from being the most dependent class in the community.' (Thomas Hodgskin, *Popular Polit. Econ.* Four lectures etc. London, 1827, p. 147 note.) (Notebook IX, p. 44.) 'The natural circumstance of all commodities being produced in unequal periods, while the wants of the labourer must be supplied daily . . . This inequality in the time necessary to complete different commodities, would in the savage state cause the hunter etc. to have a surplus of game etc., before the maker of bows and arrows etc. had any commodity completed to give for the surplus game. No exchange could be made; the bow-maker must be also a hunter and division of labour impossible. This difficulty contributed to the invention of money.' (179, 180.) (loc. cit.)

30. Hodgskin, *Popular Political Economy*, p. 140.

The concept of the free labourer contains the pauper.
Population and overpopulation etc.

⟨It is already contained in the concept of the *free labourer*, that he is a *pauper*: virtual pauper. According to his economic conditions he is merely a *living labour capacity*, hence equipped with the necessaries of life. Necessity on all sides, without the objectivities necessary to realize himself as labour capacity. If the capitalist has no use for his surplus labour, then the worker may not perform his necessary labour; not produce his necessaries. Then he cannot obtain them through exchange; rather, if he does obtain them, it is only because alms are thrown to him from revenue. He can live as a worker only in so far as he exchanges his labour capacity for that part of capital which forms the labour fund. This exchange is tied to conditions which are accidental *for him*, and indifferent to his *organic* presence. He is thus a virtual pauper. Since it is further the condition of production based on capital that he produces ever more surplus labour, it follows that ever more *necessary labour* is set free. Thus the chances of his pauperism increase. To the development of surplus labour corresponds that of the surplus population. In different modes of social production there are different laws of the increase of population and of overpopulation; the latter identical with pauperism. These different laws can simply be reduced to the different modes of relating to the conditions of production, or, in respect to the living individual, the conditions of his reproduction as a member of society, since he labours and appropriates only in society. The dissolution of these relations in regard to the single individual, or to part of the population, places them outside the reproductive conditions of this specific basis, and hence posits them as overpopulation, and not only lacking in means but incapable of appropriating the necessaries through labour, hence as paupers. Only in the mode of production based on capital does pauperism appear as the result of labour itself, of the development of the productive force of labour. Thus, what may be overpopulation in one stage of social production may not be so in another, and their effects may be different. E.g. the colonies sent out in antiquity were overpopulation, i.e. their members could not continue to live in the same space with the material basis of property, i.e. conditions of production. The number may appear very small compared with the modern conditions of production. They were, nevertheless, very far from being paupers. Such was, however, the

Roman plebs with its bread and circuses. The overpopulation which leads to the great migrations presupposes different conditions again. Since in all previous forms of production the development of the forces of production is not the basis of appropriation, but a specific relation to the conditions of production (forms of property) appears as *presupposed barrier* to the forces of production, and is merely to be reproduced, it follows that the development of population, in which the development of all productive forces is summarized, must even more strongly encounter an *external barrier* and thus appear as something to be restricted. The conditions of the community [were] consistent only with a specific amount of population. On the other side, if the barriers to population posited by the elasticity of the specific form of the conditions of production *change in consequence of the latter, if they contract or expand* – thus overpopulation among hunting peoples was different from that among the Athenians, in turn different among the latter from that among the Germanic tribes – then so does the absolute rate of population increase, and hence the rate of overpopulation and population. The amount of overpopulation posited on the basis of a specific production is thus just as determinate as the adequate population. Overpopulation and population, taken together, are *the* population which a specific production basis can create. The extent to which it goes beyond its barrier is given by the barrier itself, or rather by the same base which posits the barrier. Just as necessary labour and surplus labour together [are] the whole of labour on a given base.

Malthus's theory, which incidentally not his invention, but whose fame he appropriated through the clerical fanaticism with which he propounded it – actually only through the weight he placed on it – is significant in two respects: (1) because he gives brutal expression to the brutal viewpoint of capital; (2) because he *asserted* the fact of overpopulation in all forms of society. Proved it he has not, for there is nothing more uncritical than his motley compilations from historians and travellers' descriptions. His conception is altogether false and childish (1) because he regards *overpopulation* as being *of the same kind* in all the different historic phases of economic development; does not understand their specific difference, and hence stupidly reduces these very complicated and varying relations to a single relation, two equations, in which the natural reproduction of humanity appears on the one side, and the natural reproduction of edible plants (or means of subsistence) on the other, as two natural series, the former geometric and the latter arithmetic in progression. In this way he transforms the historically distinct relations into an abstract numerical relation, which he has fished purely out of thin air, and which rests neither on natural nor on historical laws. There is allegedly a natural difference between the reproduction of mankind and e.g. grain. This baboon thereby implies that the *increase of humanity* is a purely natural process, which requires *external restraints*, *checks*, to prevent it from proceeding in geometrical progression. This *geometrical reproduction* is the natural reproduction process of mankind. He would find in history that population proceeds in very different relations, and that overpopulation is likewise a historically determined relation, in no way determined by abstract numbers or by the absolute limit of the productivity of the necessaries of life, but by limits posited rather by *specific conditions of production*. As well as restricted numerically. How small do the numbers which meant overpopulation for the Athenians appear to us! Secondly, restricted according to character. An overpopulation of free Athenians who become transformed into colonists is significantly different from an overpopulation of workers who become transformed into workhouse inmates. Similarly the begging overpopulation which consumes the surplus produce of a monastery is different from that which forms in a factory. It is Malthus who abstracts from these specific historic laws of the movement of population, which are indeed the history of the nature of humanity, the *natural* laws, but natural laws of humanity only at a specific historic development, with a development of the forces of production determined by humanity's own process of history. Malthusian man, abstracted from historically determined man, exists only in his brain; hence also the geometric method of reproduction corresponding to this natural Malthusian man. Real history thus appears to him in such a way that the reproduction of his natural humanity is not an abstraction from the historic process of real reproduction, but just the contrary, that real reproduction is an application of the Malthusian theory. Hence the inherent conditions of population as well as of overpopulation at every stage of history appear to him as a series of *external checks* which have *prevented* the population from developing in the Malthusian form. The conditions in which mankind historically produces and reproduces itself appear as *barriers* to the reproduction of the Malthusian natural man, who is a Malthusian creature. On the other hand, the production of the necessaries of life – as it is checked, determined by human action – appears as a *check* which it posits to itself. The ferns would cover the entire earth. Their reproduction would stop only where space for them ceased. They would obey no arithmetic proportion. It is hard to say where Malthus has discovered that the reproduction of voluntary natural products would stop for intrinsic reasons, without *external checks*. He transforms the immanent, historically changing limits of the human reproduction process into *outer barriers*; and the *outer barriers* to natural reproduction into *immanent limits* or *natural laws* of reproduction.

(2) He stupidly relates a specific quantity of people to a specific quantity of necessaries.[31] Ricardo immediately and correctly confronted him with the fact that the quantity of grain available is completely irrelevant to the worker if he has no *employment*; that it is therefore the means of employment and not of subsistence which put him into the category of surplus population.[32] But this should be conceived more generally, and relates to the *social mediation* as such, through which the individual gains access to the means of his reproduction and creates them; hence it relates to the *conditions of production* and his relation to them. There was no barrier to the reproduction of the Athenian slave other than the producible necessaries. And we never hear that there were *surplus slaves* in antiquity. The call for them increased, rather. There was, however, a surplus population of non-workers (in the immediate sense), who were not too many in relation to the necessaries available, but who had lost the conditions under which they could appropriate them. The invention of surplus labourers, i.e. of propertyless people who work, belongs to the period of capital. The beggars who fastened themselves to the monasteries and helped them eat up their surplus product are in the same class as the feudal retainers, and this shows that the surplus produce could not be eaten up by the small number of its owners. It is only another form of the retainers of old, or of the menial servants of today. The overpopulation e.g. among hunting peoples, which shows itself in the warfare between the tribes, proves not that the earth could not support their small numbers, but rather that the condition of their reproduction required a great amount of territory for few people. Never a relation to a *non-existent* absolute

31. T. R. Malthus, *An Inquiry into the Nature and Progress of Rent*, London, 1815, p. 7.

32. Ricardo, *On the Principles of Political Economy*, p. 493.

mass of means of subsistence, but rather relation to the conditions
of reproduction, of the production of these means, including likewise the *conditions of reproduction of human beings*, of the total
population, of relative surplus population. This surplus purely
relative: in no way related to the *means of subsistence as* such, but
rather to the mode of producing them. Hence also only a *surplus*
at this state of development.

(3) What is not actually proper to Malthus at all, the introduction of the theory of rent – at bottom only a formula for saying
that in the stage of industry familiar to Ricardo etc., agriculture remained behind industry, which incidentally inherent in bourgeois
production although in varying relations – does not belong here.⟩

Necessary labour. Surplus labour. Surplus population.
Surplus capital

⟨As to production founded on capital, the greatest absolute mass
of necessary labour together with the greatest relative mass of surplus labour appears as a condition, regarded absolutely. Hence, as
a fundamental condition, maximum growth of population – of
living labour capacities. If we further examine the conditions of the
development of the productive forces as well as of exchange, division of labour, cooperation, all-sided observation, which can
only proceed from many heads, science, as many centres of exchange
as possible – all of it identical with growth of population. On
another side, it is also inherent in the condition of the appropriation of alien surplus labour that, in addition to the necessary
population – i.e. that which represents necessary labour, labour
necessary for production – there should be a *surplus population*,
which does not work. The further development of capital shows
that besides the industrial part of this surplus population – the
industrial capitalist – a purely consuming part branches off: idlers,
whose business it is to consume alien products and who, since
crude consumption has its limits, must have the products furnished
to them partly in refined form, as luxury products. This idle surplus population is not what the economists have in mind when they
speak of surplus population. On the contrary, it – and its business
of consuming – is treated by the population fanatics as precisely
the necessary population, and justly (logically) so. The expression,
surplus population, concerns exclusively labour capacities, i.e. the
necessary population; surplus of *labour capacities*. But this arises

simply from the nature of capital. Labour capacity can perform its necessary labour only if its surplus labour has value for capital, if it can be realized by capital. Thus, if this realizability is blocked by one or another barrier, then (1) *labour capacity* itself appears *outside the conditions of the reproduction of its existence*; it exists without the *conditions of its existence*, and is therefore a mere encumbrance; needs without the means to satisfy them; (2) necessary labour appears as superfluous, because the superfluous is not necessary. It is necessary only to the extent that it is the condition for the realization of capital. Thus the relation of necessary and surplus labour, as it is posited by capital, turns into its opposite, so that a part of necessary labour – i.e. of the labour reproducing labour capacity – is superfluous, and this labour capacity itself is therefore used as a *surplus* of the necessary working population, i.e. of the portion of the working population whose necessary labour is not superfluous but necessary for capital. Since the necessary development of the productive forces as posited by capital consists in increasing the relation of surplus labour to necessary labour, or in decreasing the portion of necessary labour required for a given amount of surplus labour, then, if a definite amount of labour capacity is given, the relation of *necessary* labour needed by capital must necessarily continuously decline, i.e. part of these labour capacities must become superfluous, since a portion of them suffices to perform the quantity of surplus labour for which the whole amount was required previously. The positing of a specific portion of labour capacities as superfluous, i.e. of the labour required for their reproduction as superfluous, is therefore a necessary consequence of the growth of surplus labour relative to necessary. The decrease of relatively necessary labour appears as increase of the relatively superfluous labouring capacities – i.e. as the positing of surplus population. If the latter is supported, then this comes not out of the labour fund but out of the revenue of all classes. It takes place not through the labour of the labour capacity itself – no longer through its normal reproduction as worker, but rather the worker is maintained as a living being through the mercy of others; hence becomes a tramp and a pauper; because he no longer sustains himself through his necessary labour; hence, through the exchange with a part of capital; he has fallen out of the conditions of the relation of apparent exchange and apparent independence; secondly: society in its fractional parts undertakes for Mr Capitalist the business of keeping his virtual instrument of labour – its wear and tear – intact as reserve for later use. He shifts a part of the reproduction costs of the working class off his own shoulders and thus pauperizes a part of the remaining population for his own profit. At the same time, capital has the tendency both to posit and equally to suspend this pauperism, because it constantly reproduces itself as surplus capital. It acts in opposite directions, so that sometimes one, sometimes the other is predominant. Finally, the positing of surplus capital contains a double moment: (1) It requires a growing population in order to be set into motion; if the relative population it requires has become smaller, then it has itself become correspondingly larger; (2) it requires a part of the population which is unemployed (at least relatively); i.e. a relative surplus population, in order to find the readily available population for the growth of surplus capital; (3) at a given stage of the productive forces, the surplus value may be present, but not yet in the proportions sufficient to be employed as capital. Not only a minimum of the stage of production, but posited for its expansion. In this case surplus capital and surplus population. Likewise, a surplus population may be present, but not enough, not in the proportions required for more production. In all these investigations, the variations in sales, contraction of the market etc., in short, everything which presupposes the *process of many capitals*, has been intentionally abstracted away.⟩

A. Smith. *Work as sacrifice.* (*Senior's theory of the capitalist's sacrifice.*) (*Proudhon's surplus.*) – A. Smith. Origin of profit. *Original accumulation.* Wakefield. – *Slave and free labour.* – Atkinson. – *Profit.* – *Origin of* profit. MacCulloch.

⟨A. Smith's view, [is] that *labour never changes its value*, in the sense that a *definite amount of labour* is always a definite *amount of labour for the worker*, i.e., with A. Smith, a sacrifice of the *same quantitative magnitude*. Whether I obtain much or little for an hour of work – which depends on its productivity and other circumstances – I have *worked* one hour. What I have had to pay for the result of my work, my wages, is always the same *hour of work*, let the result vary as it may. 'Equal quantities of labour must at all times and in all places have the same value for the worker. In his normal state of health, strength and activity, and with the common degree of skill and facility which he may possess, he must always give up the *identical portion of his tranquillity, his freedom,* and his *happiness.* Whatever may be the quantity or composition of the commodities he obtains in reward of his work, the *price he pays* is always the same. Of course, this price may buy sometimes a lesser, sometimes a greater quantity of these commodities, but only because their value changes, not the value of the labour which buys them. Labour alone, therefore, never changes its own value. It is therefore the *real price* of commodities, money is only their nominal value.' (ed. by Garnier, Vol. I, pp. 64–6.) (Notebook, p. 7.)[33] In the sweat of thy brow shalt thou labour! was Jehovah's curse on Adam.[34] And this is labour for Smith, a curse. 'Tranquillity' appears as the adequate state, as identical with 'freedom' and 'happiness'. It seems quite far from Smith's mind that the individual, 'in his normal state of health, strength, activity, skill, facility', also needs a normal portion of work, and of the suspension of tranquillity. Certainly, labour obtains its measure from the outside, through the aim to be attained and the obstacles to be overcome in attaining it. But Smith has no inkling whatever that this overcoming of obstacles is in itself a liberating activity – and that, further, the external aims become stripped of the semblance of merely external natural urgencies, and become posited as aims which the individual himself posits – hence as self-realization, objectification of the subject, hence real freedom, whose action is, precisely, labour. He is right, of course, that, in its historic forms as slave-labour, serf-labour, and wage-labour, labour always appears as repulsive, always as *external forced labour*; and not-labour, by contrast, as 'freedom, and happiness'. This holds doubly: for this contradictory labour; and, relatedly, for labour which has not yet created the subjective and objective conditions for itself (or also, in contrast to the pastoral etc. state, which it has lost), in which labour becomes attractive work, the individual's self-realization, which in no way means that it becomes mere fun, mere amusement, as Fourier, with *grisette*-like[35] naïveté, conceives it.[36] Really free working, e.g. composing, is at the same time precisely the most damned seriousness, the most intense exertion. The work of material production can

33. *Recherches sur la nature et les causes de la richesse des nations*; traduction nouvelle, avec des notes et observations; par Germain Garnier, Paris, 1802, 2 volumes. The French edition of Adam Smith, excerpted by Marx already in 1844; see *MEGA*, 1/3, pp. 457–93.

34. Genesis iii, 19.   35. *grisette*: young shop-girl.

36. Fourier, *Le Nouveau Monde industriel et sociétaire*, in *Œuvres complets*, Paris, 1848, Vol. VI, pp. 245–52.

achieve this character only (1) when its social character is posited, (2) when it is of a scientific and at the same time general character, not merely human exertion as a specifically harnessed natural force, but exertion as subject, which appears in the production process not in a merely natural, spontaneous form, but as an activity regulating all the forces of nature. A. Smith, by the way, has only the slaves of capital in mind. For example, even the semi-artistic worker of the Middle Ages does not fit into his definition. *But* what *we* want *here initially* is not to go into his view on labour, his philosophical view, but into the economic moment. Labour regarded merely as a *sacrifice*, and hence value-positing, as a *price* paid for things and hence giving them price depending on whether they cost more or less labour, is a purely *negative* characterization. This is why Mr Senior, for example, was able to make capital into a source of production in the same sense as labour, a source *sui generis* of the production of *value*, because the capitalist too brings a *sacrifice*, the sacrifice of *abstinence*, in that he grows wealthy instead of eating up his product directly.[37] Something that is merely negative creates nothing. If the worker should, e.g. enjoy his work – as the miser certainly enjoys Senior's *abstinence* – then the product does not lose any of its value. Labour *alone* produces; it is the only *substance* of products as *values*.* Its measure, labour time – presupposing equal intensity – is therefore the measure of values. The qualitative difference between workers, in so far as it is not natural, posited by sex, age, physical strength etc. – and thus basically expresses not the qualitative value of labour, but rather the division and differentia-

---

*Proudhon's lack of understanding of this matter is evident from his axiom that every labour leaves a surplus.[38] What he denies for capital, he transforms into a natural property of labour. The point is, rather, that the labour time necessary to meet absolute needs leaves *free* time (different at the different stages of the development of the productive forces), and that therefore a surplus product can be created if *surplus labour* is worked. The aim is to suspend the relation itself, so that the surplus product itself appears as necessary. Ultimately, material production leaves everyone surplus time for other activity. There is no longer anything mystical in this. Originally, the free gifts of nature abundant, or at least merely to be appropriated. From the outset, naturally arisen association (family) and the division of labour and co-operation corresponding to it. For needs are themselves scant at the beginning. They too develop only with the forces of production.

---

37. Nassau Senior, *Principes fondamentaux*, pp. 309–35.
38. Bastiat et Proudhon, *Gratuité du crédit*, p. 200.

tion of labour – is itself only a product of history, and is in turn suspended for the great mass of labour, in that the latter is itself simple; while the qualitatively higher takes its economic measure from the simple. The statement that *labour time*, or the amount of labour, is the measure of values means nothing other than that the measure of labour is the measure of values. Two things are only commensurable if they are of the *same nature*. Products can be measured with the measure of labour – labour time – only because they are, by their nature, *labour*. They are objectified labour. As objects they assume forms in which their being as labour may certainly be apparent in their form (as a purposiveness posited in them from outside; however, this is not at all apparent with e.g. the ox, or with reproduced natural products generally), but in which this being has, apart from itself, no other features in common. They exist as equals as long as they exist as activity. The latter is measured by time, which therefore also becomes the measure of objectified labour. We will examine elsewhere to what extent this *measurement* is linked with exchange, not with organized social labour – a definite stage of the social production process. Use value is not concerned with human activity as the source of the product, with its having been posited by human activity, but with its being for mankind. In so far as the product has a measure for itself, it is its natural measure as natural object, mass, weight, length, volume etc. Measure of utility etc. But as effect, or as static presence of the force which created it, it is measured only by the measure of this force itself. The measure of labour is time. Only because products ARE labour can they be measured by the measure of labour, by labour time, the amount of labour consumed in them. The negation of tranquillity, as mere negation, ascetic sacrifice, creates nothing. *Someone may castigate and flagellate himself all day long like the monks etc., and this quantity of sacrifice he contributes will remain totally worthless.* The *natural price* of things is not the sacrifice made for them. This recalls, rather, the pre-industrial view which wants to achieve wealth by sacrificing to the gods. There has to be something besides sacrifice. The sacrifice of tranquillity can also be called the sacrifice of laziness, unfreedom, unhappiness, i.e. negation of a negative state. A. Smith considers labour psychologically, as to the fun or displeasure it holds for the individual. But it is something else, too, in addition to this *emotional* relation with his activity – firstly, for others, since A's mere sacrifice would be of no use for B; secondly, a definite relation by his own self to the thing he works on, and to his own working capabilities. It is a *positive, creative activity*. The measure of labour – time – of course does not depend on labour's productivity; its measure is precisely nothing but a unit of which the proportional parts of labour express a certain multiple. It certainly does not follow from this that the *value* of labour is constant; or, follows only in so far as equal quantities of labour are of the same measured magnitude. It is then found upon further examination that the values of products are measured not by the labour employed in them, but by the labour necessary for their production. Hence not sacrifice, but labour as a condition of production. The equivalent expresses the condition of the products' reproduction, as given to them through exchange, i.e. the possibility of repeating productive activity anew, as posited by its own product.⟩ ⟨By the way, Smith's view of labour as a *sacrifice*, which incidentally correctly expresses the *subjective relation of the wage worker to his own activity*, still does not lead to what he wants – namely the determination of value by labour time. An hour of work may always be an equal sacrifice for the worker. But the value of commodities in no way depends on his feelings; nor does the value of his hour of work. Since A. Smith admits that one can buy this sacrifice sometimes more cheaply, sometimes more dearly, it becomes distinctly peculiar that it is supposed always to be *sold* for the same price. And he is indeed inconsistent. Later he makes *wages* the measure of value, not the amount of labour. *The slaughter of the ox is always the same sacrifice, for the ox. But this does not mean that the value of beef is constant.*⟩ ⟨'Now, although equal quantities of labour always have the same value as regards the worker, they appear sometimes of smaller, sometimes of larger value for him who employs the worker. He purchases them sometimes with a smaller, sometimes a larger quantity of commodities. For him, therefore, the price of labour varies like that of any other thing, although in reality it is only the commodities which are sometimes dearer, sometimes cheaper.' (p. 66 A. Smith, loc. cit. Vol. I.) (Notebook, p. 8.)⟩

⟨The way in which A. Smith lets profit arise is very naïve. 'In the primitive state, the product of labour belongs wholly to the worker. The quantity' (including also the greater difficulty etc.) 'of labour employed to obtain or to produce an exchangeable object is the *only circumstance* which governs the quantity of labour which this object can on the average buy, command or obtain in exchange ... BUT *as soon as a stock* accumulates in the hands of *private persons, the value which the workers add to the object dissolves into two parts,* of which one pays their wages, the other the profit which the entrepreneur makes on the sum of the stock which has served him to advance these wages and the materials of labour. He would have *no interest* in employing these workers if he did not expect from the sale of their works something more than is necessary to replace this fund, and he would have no interest in employing a larger in preference over a small amount of funds if his profit did not stand in some proportion to the volume of the funds employed.' (loc. cit. p. 96, 97.) (N., p. 9.) (See A. Smith's peculiar view that *before the division of labour,* 'where every one produced everything necessary, no stock was necessary'. As if, in this state, while he finds no stock in nature, he would not have to find the objective conditions of life, in order to work. Even the savage, even animals, set aside a reserve. Smith can at most have in mind a situation in which the impulse to labour is still a direct, momentary instinct, and then a *stock* still has to be present in nature in one way or another *without labour*. (Notebook, p. 19.) (Smith is confused here. *Concentration of the stock* in a single hand then not necessary.)⟩

⟨In Vol. III of his edition of A. Smith, Wakefield remarks: 'The labour of slaves being combined, is more productive than the much divided labour of freemen. The labour of freemen is more productive than that of slaves, only when it comes to be combined *by means of greater dearness of land, and the system of hiring for wages.*' (Note to p. 18.) (Notebook VIII, p. 1.) 'In countries where land remains very cheap, either all the people are in a state of barbarism, or some of them are in a state of slavery.' (Note to p. 20.)⟩

⟨'*Profit* is a term signifying the increase of capital or wealth; so, failing to find the laws which govern the rate of profit, is failing to find the laws of the formation of capital.' (p. 55. Atkinson (W.), *Principles of Political Economy,* London, 1840.) (Notebook, p. 2.)⟩

⟨'Man is as much the *produce of labour* as any of the machines constructed by his agency; and it appears to us that in all economical investigations he ought to be considered in precisely the same point of view. Every individual who has arrived at maturity ... may, with perfect propriety, be viewed as a machine which it has cost 20 years of assiduous attention and the expenditure of a considerable capital to construct. And if a further sum is laid out for his education or qualification for the exercise of a business etc., his value is proportionally increased, just as a machine is made more valuable through the expenditure of additional capital or labour in its construction, in order to give it new powers.' (McCulloch, *The Principles of Pol. Econ.*, London, 1825, p. 115.) (Notebook, p. 9.)⟩ ⟨'In point of fact, a commodity will always exchange for more' labour (than it was produced by): 'and it *is this excess that constitutes profits.*' (p. 221, McCulloch loc. cit.) (Notebook, p. 13.) The same gentle McCulloch, about whom Malthus rightly says that he sees it as the proper task of science to equate everything with everything else,[39] says: '*the profits of capital* are only another name for the wages of *accumulated labour*' (p. 291) (loc. cit. Notebook, 14) and hence no doubt the wages of labour are only another name for the profits of living capital. 'Wages ... really consist of a *part of the produce of the industry of the labourer*; consequently, they have a high real value if the labourer receives a comparatively high share of the product of his industry, and vice versa.' (295 loc. cit.) (Notebook, p. 15.)⟩

Surplus labour. Profit. Wages. *Economists. Ramsay. Wade*

The positing of *surplus labour* through capital has on the whole been so little understood by the economists that they present striking phenomena of its occurrence as something *special*, as a curiosity. Thus Ramsay, with night work. Likewise John Wade e.g., in *History of the Middle and Working Classes*, 3rd ed., London, 1835 (p. 241) (Notebook, p. 21) says: 'The standard of wages is *also* connected with the hours of work and rest periods. It was the policy of the masters in recent years' (before 1835) 'to usurp on operatives in this respect, by cutting or abridging holidays and mealtimes and gradually stretching the hours of work; knowing that an increase of $\frac{1}{4}$ in the time of work is equivalent to a reduction in wages by the same amount.'

Immovable capital. *Return of capital. Fixed capital.* John St. Mill

John St. Mill: *Essays on Some Unsettled Questions of Political Economy*, London, 1844. (The few original ideas of Mill Junior are contained in this narrow little volume, not in his fat, pedantic *magnum opus*.)

'Whatever is destined to be employed reproductively, be it in

39. Malthus, *Definitions in Political Economy*, pp. 69–70.

its existing form, or indirectly by a previous (or even subsequent) exchange, is *capital*. Suppose I have laid out all my money in wages and machinery, and the article I produce is just finished: in the interval, before I can sell these articles, realize the gain, and lay it out again in wages and tools, will it be said that I have *no capital*? Certainly not: I have the same capital as before, perhaps a larger one, but it is tied down, and is not disposable.' (p. 55.) (Notebook, p. 36.) 'At all times a very large part of the capital in a country lies idle. The annual product of a country never achieves in height what it could, if all resources were devoted to reproduction, if, in short, all the country's capital were in full employment. *If every commodity on the average remained unsold for a length of time equal to that required for its production, then it is clear that at any one time not more than a half of the productive capital of the country would in reality perform the function of capital. The employed half is a fluctuating portion*, composed of various elements; but the result would be that every producer would be capable of producing each year only half the supply of commodities which he could produce if he were sure of selling them at the moment of their completion.' (loc. cit. p. 55, 56.) 'This, or something similar, is, however, the usual state of a very great part of all capitalists in the world.' (p. 56.) 'The number of producers or vendors who turn over their capital in the very shortest time is very small. Few have so rapid a sale of their commodities that all goods which their own or borrowed capital can supply them can be *cleared out* as quickly as supplied. The majority do not have an *extent of business* at all adequate to the amount of capital they dispose of. It is true that in communities where industry and trade are practised with the greatest success, the contrivances of banking enable the owner of a capital greater than he can himself employ, to apply it productively and to derive a revenue from it. Still, even then, there is a great quantity of capital which remains *fixed* in the form of implements, machinery, buildings etc., whether only half employed or in complete employment: and every dealer keeps a *stock in trade*, to be ready for a possible sudden demand, although he may not be able to dispose of it for an indefinite period.' (p. 56.) '*This constant non-employment of a large part of capital* is the *price we pay for the division of labour. The purchase is worth what it costs; but the price is considerable.*' (56.) If I have 1,500 thalers in the shop and take in 10%, while 500 lie idle to ornament the shop, it is the same as if I invest 1,000 thalers at $7\frac{1}{2}\%$ ....'In many trades there are a few dealers who sell articles of equal quality at a lower price than other dealers. This is not a voluntary sacrifice of profits; from the consequent overflow of customers they expect to turn over their capital more rapidly, and to be the winners by keeping the whole of their capital in more constant employment, although on a given operation their gains are smaller.' (p. 56, 57.) 'It is question-able whether there are any dealers for whom one additional buyer is of no use; and for the great majority, this hypothesis altogether inapplicable. An additional customer is for most dealers equiva-lent to a growth of their productive capital. It enables them to transform a part of their capital, which lay idle (and perhaps would never have become productive in their hands until a customer had been found), into wages and instruments of production ... A country's aggregate product for the following year is hence increased; not through pure exchange, but by *calling into activity* a portion of the national capital which, had it not been for the exchange, would have remained unemployed for some time longer.' (57, 58.) 'The advantages gained from a *new customer* are, for the producer or dealer: (1) say, a part of his capital lies in the form of unsold goods, producing (during a longer or shorter time) nothing at all; then a part thereof is *called into greater activity* and *becomes more constantly productive.* (2) If the additional demand exceeds what can be supplied through liberation of capital existing as unsold goods, and if the dealer has additional resources (e.g. in government bonds), but not in his own trade, then he is enabled to obtain on a portion of these, no longer interest, but profit, and thus to gain the difference between the rate of interest and of profits. (3) If all his capital is employed in his own business and no part stored up as unsold goods, then he can conduct a surplus business with borrowed capital and gain the difference between interest and profit.' (59.)

Turnover of capital. *Circulation process. Production process. Turnover. Capital circulates. Likewise fixed capital. Circulation costs. Circulation time and labour time. (Capitalist's free time.) (Transport costs)*

Now back to our subject.

The phases through which capital travels, which form one turnover of capital, begin conceptually with the transformation of money into the conditions of production. Now, however, that we begin not with capital in the process of becoming, but capital which has become, [we can see that] it travels through the following phases: (1) Creation of surplus value, or immediate production process. Its result, the product. (2) Bringing the product to market. Transformation of product into commodity. (3) (α) Entry of the commodity into ordinary circulation. Circulation of the commodity. Its result: transformation into money. This appears as the first moment of ordinary circulation. (β) Retransformation of money into the conditions of production: money circulation; in ordinary circulation, the circulation of commodities and the circulation of money always appear distributed among two different subjects. Capital circulates first as a commodity, then as money, and vice versa. (4) Renewal of the production process, which appears here as reproduction of the original capital, and production process of surplus capital.

The costs of circulation break down into costs of movement; costs to bring the product to market; the labour time required to effect the transformation from one state to the other; all of which actually come down to accounting operations and the time they cost (this is the foundation of a special, technical money trade). (Whether the latter costs are to be considered deductions from the surplus value or not will be seen later.)

If we examine this movement, we find that the circulation of capital, through the operation of exchanges, opens up at one point to release the product into general circulation, and to constitute itself out of the latter as equivalent in money. What happens to this product, which has in this way fallen out of the circulation of capital and into ordinary circulation, is here beside the point. On the other side, capital throws its form as money out of its circulation process again (partially, that is, in so far as it is not wages), or, after having realized itself as value in ordinary circulation and at the same time posited itself as the measure of its own realization, it then moves in the money form only as medium of circulation, and thus sucks into itself out of general circulation the commodities necessary for production (conditions of production). As commodity, capital throws itself out of its own circulation into general circulation; and, again as commodity, capital leaves general circulation and enters its own course, issuing into the production process. The circulation of capital thus contains a relation to general circulation, of which its own circulation forms a moment, while the latter likewise appears as posited by capital. This to be examined later.

The total production process of capital includes both the circulation process proper and the actual production process. These form the two great sections of its movement, which appears as the totality of these two processes. On one side, labour time, on the other, circulation time. And the whole of the movement appears as unity of labour time and circulation time, as unity of production and circulation. This unity itself is motion, process. Capital appears as this unity-in-process of production and circulation, a unity which can be regarded both as the totality of the process of its production, as well as the specific completion of *one* turnover of the capital, *one* movement returning into itself.

The condition, for capital, of circulation time is – besides labour time – only the same as the condition of production based on division of labour and exchange, in adequate form, in the highest form. The costs of circulation are costs of the division of labour and of exchange, which are necessarily found in every previous, pre-capitalist form of production resting on this basis.

As the subject predominant [*übergreifend*] over the different phases of this movement, as value sustaining and multiplying itself in it, as the subject of these metamorphoses proceeding in a circular course – as a spiral, as an expanding circle – capital is *circulating capital*. Circulating capital is therefore initially not a *particular* form of capital, but is rather *capital* itself, in a further developed aspect, as subject of the movement just described, which it, itself, is as its own realization process. In this respect, therefore, every capital is *circulating capital*. In simple circulation, circulation itself appears as the subject. One commodity is thrown out of it, another enters into it. But the same commodity is within it only fleetingly. Money itself, in so far as it ceases to be a medium of circulation and posits itself as independent value, withdraws from circulation. Capital, however, exists as the subject of circulation; circulation is posited as its own life's course. But while capital thus, as the whole of circulation, is *circulating capital*, is the process of going from one phase into the other, it is at the same time, within each phase, posited in a specific aspect, restricted to a particular form, which is the negation of itself as the subject of the whole movement. Therefore, capital in each of its particular phases is the negation of itself as the subject of all the various metamorphoses. Not-circulating capital. *Fixed capital*, actually *fixated* capital, fixated in one of the different particular aspects, phases, through which it must move. As long as it persists in one of these phases – [as long as] the phase itself does not appear as fluid transition – and each of them has its duration, [then] it is not circulating, [but] fixated. As long as it remains in the production process it is not capable of circulating; and it is virtually devalued. As long as it remains in circulation, it is not capable of producing, not capable of positing surplus value, not capable of engaging in the process as capital. As long as it cannot be brought to market, it is fixated as product. As long as it has to remain on the market, it is fixated as commodity. As long as it cannot be exchanged for conditions of production, it is fixated as money. Finally, if the conditions of production remain in their form as conditions and do not enter into the production process, it is again fixated and devalued. As the subject moving through all phases, as the moving unity, the unity-in-process of circulation and production, capital is *circulating* capital; capital as restricted into any of these phases, as posited in its *divisions*, is *fixated* capital, *tied-down* capital. As circulating capital it fixates itself, and as fixated capital it circulates. The distinction between *circulating capital* and *fixed capital* thus appears initially as a formal characteristic of capital, depending on whether it appears as the unity of the process or as one of its specific moments. The concept of *dormant capital*, capital lying fallow, can refer only to its barren existence in one of these aspects, and it is a condition of capital that part of it always lies fallow. This takes the visible form that a part of the national capital is always stuck in one of the phases through which capital has to move. *Money* itself, to the extent that it forms a particular part of the nation's capital, but always remains in the form of medium of circulation, i.e. never goes through the other phases, is therefore regarded by A. Smith as a subordinate form of fixed capital.[40] Capital can likewise lie fallow, be fixated in the form of money, of value withdrawn from circulation. During crises – *after* the moment of panic – during the standstill of industry, money is immobilized in the hands of bankers, billbrokers etc.; and, just as the stag cries out for fresh water, money cries out for a field of employment where it may be realized as capital.

Much confusion in political economy has been caused by this, that the aspects of circulating and fixed are initially nothing more

40. Adam Smith, *Wealth of Nations*, Vol. II, Bk II, Ch. 2, pp. 270–77.

than capital itself posited in the two aspects, first as the unity of the process, then as a particular one of its phases, itself in *distinction* to itself as unity – not as two particular kinds of capital, not capital of two particular kinds, but rather as different *characteristic forms of the same capital*. While some held fast to the aspect of a material product in which it was supposed to be circulating capital, others had no difficulty in pointing out the opposite aspect, and vice versa. Capital as the unity of circulation and production is at the same time the division between them, and a division whose aspects are separated in space and time, at that. In each moment it has an indifferent form towards the other. For the individual capital, the transition from one into the other appears as chance, as dependent on external, uncontrollable circumstances. *One and the same* capital therefore always appears in both states; this is expressed by the appearance of one part of it in one [phase], another in another; one part tied down, another part circulating; circulating, here, not in the sense that it is in the *circulatory phase proper* as opposed to the *production phase*, but rather in the sense that in the phase in which it finds itself it is in a *fluid* phase, a phase in-process, a phase in transition to the next phase; not stuck in one of them as such and hence delayed in its total process. For example: the industrialist uses only a part of the capital at his disposal (whether borrowed or owned is beside the point here, nor, if we consider capital as a whole, does it affect the economic process) in production, because another part requires a certain amount of time before it comes back out of circulation. The part moving [*prozessierend*] within production is then the circulating part; the part in circulation is the immobilized part. His total productivity is thereby restricted; the reproduced part restricted, hence also the part thrown on to the market restricted. Thus the merchant; a part of his capital is tied down as *stock in trade*, the other part moves. To be sure, sometimes one and sometimes another part is in this phase, as with the industrialist, but his total capital is always posited in both aspects. Then again, since this limit arising out of the nature of the realization process itself is not fixed, but changes with circumstances, and since capital can approach its adequate character as that which circulates, to a greater or lesser degree; since the decomposition into these two aspects, in which the realization process appears at the same time as the devaluation process, contradicts the tendency of capital towards maximum realization, it therefore invents contrivances to abbreviate the phase of fixity; and at the same time also, instead of the simultaneous coexistence of both states, *they alternate*. In one period the process appears as altogether fluid – the period of the maximum realization of capital; in another, a reaction to the first, the other moment asserts itself all the more forcibly – the period of the maximum devaluation of capital and congestion of the production process. The moments in which both aspects appear alongside one another themselves only form interludes between these violent transitions and turnings-over. It is extremely important to grasp these aspects of circulating and fixated capital as *specific characteristic forms* of capital generally, since a great many phenomena of the bourgeois economy – the period of the economic cycle, which is essentially different from the single turnover period of capital; the effect of new demand; even the effect of new gold- and silver-producing countries on general production – [would otherwise be] incomprehensible. It is futile to speak of the stimulus given by Australian gold or a newly discovered market. If it were not in the nature of capital to be never completely occupied, i.e. always partially *fixated*, devalued, unproductive, then no stimuli could drive it to greater production. At the same time, [note] the senseless contradictions into which the economists stray – even Ricardo – when they presuppose that capital is always fully occupied; hence explain an increase of production by referring exclusively to the creation of new capital. Every increase would then presuppose an earlier increase or growth of the productive forces.

These barriers to production based on capital are even more strongly inherent in the earlier modes of production, in so far as they rest on exchange. But they do not form a law of production pure and simple; [and,] as soon as exchange value no longer forms a barrier to material production, as soon as its barrier is rather posited by the total development of the individual, the whole story with its spasms and convulsions is left behind. As we saw earlier that money suspends the barriers of barter only by generalizing them – i.e. separating purchase and sale entirely – so shall we see later that *credit* likewise suspends these barriers to the realization of capital only by raising them to their most general form, positing one period of overproduction and one of underproduction as two periods.

The value which capital posits in one cycle, one revolution, one

turnover, is = to the value posited in the production process, i.e.
= to the value reproduced + the new value. Whether we regard
the turnover as completed at the point where the commodity is
transformed into money, or at the point where the money is
transformed back into conditions of production, the result,
whether expressed in money or in conditions of production, is
always absolutely equal to the value posited in the production
process. We count the physical bringing of the product to market
as = to 0; or, rather, we include it in the direct production process.
The economic circulation of the product begins only when it is
on the market as a commodity – only then does it circulate. We
are dealing here only with the economic differences, aspects,
moments of circulation; not with the physical conditions for
bringing the finished product into the second phase, that of
circulation as commodity; nor are we concerned with the technological process by which the raw material is transformed into
product. The greater or lesser distance of the market from the
producer etc. does not concern us here yet. What we want to
determine here first of all is that the costs arising from the
motion through the different economic moments as such, the
costs of circulation as such, do not add anything to the value of
the product, are not value-positing costs, regardless of how much
labour they may involve. They are merely *deductions from the
created* value. If, of two individuals, each one were the producer
of his own product, but their labour rested on division of labour,
so that they exchanged with each other, and the realization of
their product depended on the satisfaction of their needs through
this exchange, then obviously the time which this exchange would
cost them, e.g. the mutual bargaining, calculating before closing
the deal, would make not the slightest addition either to their
products or to the latter's exchange values. If A were to argue
that the exchange takes up so much time, then B would respond in
kind. Each of them loses just as much time in the exchange as the
other. The exchange time is their common time. If A demanded
10 thalers for the product – its equivalent – and 10 thalers for the
time it costs him to get the 10 thalers from B, then the latter
would declare him a candidate for the madhouse. This loss of
time arises from the division of labour and the necessity of
exchange. If A produced everything himself, then he would lose
no part of his time in exchanging with B, or in transforming his
product into money and the money into product again. The *costs*

of circulation proper (and they achieve a significant independent development in the money trade) are not reducible to productive labour time. But they are also by nature restricted to the time it necessarily costs to transform the commodity into money and the money back into commodity; i.e. to the time it costs to transpose capital from one form into the other. B and A might now find that they could save time by inserting a third person C as middleman between them, who consumed his time in this *circulation process* – circumstances which would arise e.g. if there were enough exchangers, enough subjects of the circulation processes, so that the time needed by each pair of them alternately over a year = one year; each individual, say, had to spend $\frac{1}{50}$ of a year alternately in circulation, and there are 50 of them, then 1 individual could spend his entire time in this occupation. For this individual, if only his necessary labour time were paid him, i.e. if he had to give up his entire time in exchange for the necessaries of life, then the reward which he would obtain would be wages. But if it amounted to his entire time, then the wage he would obtain would be an equivalent, objectified labour time. This individual then, would have added nothing to the value, but would, rather, have obtained a share of the surplus value belonging to capitalists A, B, etc. They would have gained, since, according to the presupposition, a lesser deduction from their surplus value would have taken place. (Capital is not a quantity simply, nor an operation simply; but both at the same time.) *Money* itself, to the extent that it consists of precious metals, or its production generally – e.g. in paper circulation – creates expense, to the extent that it also costs labour time, adds no value to the exchanged objects – to the exchange values; rather, its costs are a deduction from these values, a deduction which must be borne in proportional parts by the exchangers. The preciousness of the instrument of circulation, of the instrument of exchange, expresses only the *costs of exchange*. Instead of adding to value, they subtract from it. Gold money and silver money, e.g., are themselves values, *like others* (not in the sense of money), in so far as labour is objectified in them. But that these values serve as *medium of circulation* is a deduction from disposable wealth. The same relation holds for the production costs of the circulation of capital. This adds nothing to the values. The *costs of circulation* as such *do not posit value*, they are *costs of the realization of values* – deductions from them. *Circulation as a series of transformations*, in which capital posits itself; but, as regards value, circulation does not add to it, but posits it, rather, in the *form* of value. The potential value which is transformed into money through circulation is presupposed as a result of the production process. In so far as this series of processes takes place in time and involves costs, costs labour time, or objectified labour time, these *circulation costs* are deductions from the sum of value. When circulation costs are posited = 0, then the result of *one* turnover of capital, as regards value, = the value posited in the production process. That is, the value presupposed to circulation is the same as emerges from it. The most that can happen is that – owing to the circulation costs – a smaller value can come out than went in. In this respect, circulation time adds nothing to value; circulation time does not appear as value-positing time, the same as labour time. If production has created a commodity = to the value of £10, then circulation is necessary in order to equate this commodity to the £10, its value, which exists as money. The costs involved in this process, caused by this change of form, are a deduction from the value of the commodity. *The circulation of capital is the change of forms by means of which value passes through different phases.* The *time* which this process lasts or costs to bring about belongs among the *production costs of circulation, of the division of labour, of production based on exchange.*

This holds for *one turnover of capital*, i.e. for the single course of capital through this, its different moments. The process of capital as value has its point of departure in money and ends in money, but in a greater quantity of money. The difference is only quantitative. M–C–C–M has thus obtained a content. If we examine the cycle up to this point, we stand at the point of departure again. Capital has become money again. But it is now at the same time posited, it has now become a condition for this money that it becomes capital again, money which preserves and multiplies itself through the purchase of labour, by passing through the production process. Its form as money is posited as mere form; one of the many forms through which it moves in its metamorphosis. If we regard this point now not as a terminal point, but rather – as we must now regard it – as transition point, or new point of departure, itself posited by the production process as a vanishing terminal point and only a seeming point of departure, then it is clear that the retransformation of value, posited as money, into value-in-process, into value entering into the production process, can only proceed – that the *renewal of the production process* can only take place – when the part of the circulation process which is distinct from the production process has been completed. The *second turnover* of capital – the retransformation of money into capital as such, or the renewal of the production process – depends on the time capital requires to complete its circulation; i.e. on its *circulation time*, the latter here as distinct from production time. But since we have seen that the total value created by capital (reproduced value as well as newly created), which is realized in circulation as such, is exclusively determined by the production process, it follows that the sum of values which can be created in a given period of time depends on the number of repetitions of the production process within this period. The repetition of the production process, however, is determined by circulation time, which is equal to the velocity of circulation. The more rapid the circulation, the shorter the circulation time, the more often can the same capital repeat the production process. Hence, in a specific cycle of turnovers of capital, the sum of values created by it (hence surplus values as well, for it posits necessary labour always merely as labour necessary for surplus labour) is *directly proportional to the labour time and inversely proportional to the circulation time*. In a given cycle, the total value (consequently also the sum of newly posited surplus values) = labour time multiplied by the number of turnovers of the capital. Or, the surplus value posited by capital now no longer appears as simply determined by the surplus labour appropriated by it in the production process, but rather [it is determined] by the coefficient of the production process; i.e. the number which expresses how often it is repeated in a given period of time. This coefficient, in turn, is determined by the circulation time required by the capital for one turnover. The sum of values (surplus values) is thus determined by the value posited in one turnover multiplied by the number of turnovers in a given period of time. One turnover of capital is = to the production time + the circulation time. If circulation time is presupposed as given, then the total time required for one turnover depends on the production time. If production time is given, the duration of the turnover depends on the circulation time. Hence, to the extent that circulation time determines the total mass of production time in a given period of time, and to the extent that the repetition of the production process, its renewal in a given period depends on the circulation time, to that extent is it itself a moment of production, or rather appears as a limit of production. This is the nature of capital, of production founded on capital, that circulation time becomes a determinant moment for labour time, for the creation of value. The independence of labour time is thereby negated, and the production process is itself posited as determined by exchange, so that immediate production is socially linked to it and dependent on this link – not only as a material moment, but also as an *economic* moment, a determinant, characteristic form. The maximum of circulation – the limit of the renewal of the production process through it – is obviously determined by the duration of production time during one turnover. Suppose the production process of a specific capital, i.e. the time it needs to reproduce its value and to posit surplus value, lasts 3 months. (Or, the time required to complete a quantity of product = to the total value of the producing capital + the surplus value.) Then this capital could under no circumstances renew the production or realization process more often than 4 times a year. The maximum turnover of this capital would be 4 turnovers per year; i.e. if no interruptions took place between the completion of one production phase and the renewal. The maximum number of turnovers would be = to the continuity of the production process, so that, as soon as the product was finished, new raw material would be worked up into product again. This continuity would extend not only to the continuity within a single production phase, but to the *continuity of these phases themselves*. But supposing now that this capital required one month of circulation time at the end of each phase – time to return to the form of conditions of production – then it could effect only 3 turnovers. In the first case the number of turnovers was = 1 phase × 4; or 12 months divided by 3. The maximum value-creation by capital in a given space of time is this space of time divided by the duration of the production process (by production time). In the second case, the capital would effect only 3 turnovers a year; it would repeat the realization process only 3 times. The sum of its realization process would be, then, = $\frac{12}{4} = 3$. The divisor here is the total circulation time it requires: 4 months; or the circulation time required for one circulation phase, multiplied by the number of times this circulation time is contained in a year. In the first case, the number of turnovers = 12 months, a year, a given time, divided by the time of one production phase, or by the duration of production time itself; in the second case, it equals the same time divided by circulation time. The maximum realization of capital, as also the maximum continuity of the production process, is circulation time posited as $= 0$; i.e. then, the conditions under which capital produces, its restriction by circulation time, the necessity of going through the different phases of its metamorphosis, are suspended. It is the necessary tendency of capital to strive to equate circulation time to 0; i.e. to suspend itself, since it is capital itself alone which posits circulation time as a determinant moment of production time. It is the same as to suspend the necessity of exchange, of money, and of the division of labour resting on them, hence capital itself. If we ignore for a moment the transformation of surplus value into surplus capital, then a capital of 100 thalers, which produced a surplus value of 4% on the total capital in the production process, would, in the first case, reproduce itself 4 times and would at the end of the year have posited a surplus value of 16. At the end of the year, the capital would be $= 116$. It would be the same as if a capital of 400 had turned over once a year, likewise with a surplus value of 4%. As regards the total production of commodities and values, these would have quadrupled. In the other case, a capital of 100 thalers only created a surplus value of 12; the total capital at the end of the year $= 112$. As regards total production – in respect of either values or use values – the difference still more significant. In the first case e.g. a capital of 100 transformed 400 thalers of leather into boots, in the second only 300 thalers of leather.

The total realization of capital is hence determined by the duration of the production phase – which we posit as identical with labour time, for the moment – multiplied by the number of turnovers, or renewals of this production phase in a given period of time. If the turnovers were determined only by the duration of one production phase, then the total realization would be simply determined by the number of production phases contained in a given period of time; or, the turnovers would be absolutely determined by production time itself. This would be the *maximum of realization*. It is clear, therefore, that circulation time, regarded absolutely, is a deduction from the maximum of realization, is $<$ absolute realization. It is therefore impossible for any velocity of circulation or any abbreviation of circulation to create a realization $>$ that posited by the production phase itself. The maximum that the velocity of circulation could effect, if it rose to ∞, would be to posit circulation time $= 0$, i.e. to abolish itself. It can therefore not be a positive, value-creating moment, since its abolition – circulation without circulation time – would be the maximum of realization; its negation = to the highest position of the productivity of capital.* The total productivity of capital is = the duration of one production phase multiplied by the number of times it is repeated in a certain period of time. But this number is determined by circulation time.

Let us assume a capital of 100 turned over 4 times a year; posited the production process 4 times; then, if the surplus value = 5% each time, at the end of the year the surplus value created by the capital of 100 would = 20; then, for a capital of 400, which turned over once a year at the same percentage, would likewise = 20. So that a capital of 100, circulating 4 times, would give a gain of 20% a year, while a 4 times greater capital with a single turnover would give a profit of only 5%. (We shall see shortly, in more detail, that the surplus value is exactly the same.) It seems, therefore, that the magnitude of the capital can be replaced by the velocity of turnover, and the velocity of turnover by the magnitude of the capital. This is how it comes to appear as though circulation time were in itself productive. We must therefore clarify the matter by discussing this case.

Another question which arises: If the turnover of 100 thalers 4 times a year brings 5% each time, say, then at the beginning of the second turnover, the production process could be begun with 105 thalers, and the product would be $110\frac{1}{4}$; at the beginning of the third *turnover*, $110\frac{1}{4}$, of which the product would be $115\frac{61}{80}$; at the beginning of the fourth turnover, $115\frac{61}{80}$, and at its end, $121\frac{881}{1600}$. The number itself here is beside the point. The point is that, in the case of a capital of 400 which turns over once a year at 5%, the total gain can only be 20; while, by contrast, a 4 times smaller capital turning over 4 times at the same percentage makes a gain of $1 + \frac{881}{1600}$ more. In this way it appears as if the mere moment of turnover – repetition – i.e. a moment determined by circulation time, or rather a moment determined by *circulation*, not only realized value, but brought about an absolute growth of value. This also to be examined.

Circulation time only expresses the velocity of circulation; the velocity of circulation only the barrier to circulation. *Circulation*

*The productivity of capital as capital is not the productive force which increases use values; but rather its capacity to create value; the degree to which it produces value.

without circulation time – i.e. the transition of capital from one phase to the next at the speed of thought – would be the maximum, i.e. the identity of the renewal of the production process with its termination.

The act of exchange – and the economic operations through which circulation proceeds are reducible to a succession of acts of exchange – up to the point at which capital does not relate as commodity to money or as money to commodity, but as value to its specific use value, labour – the act of the exchange of value in one form for value in the other, money for commodity, commodity for money (and these are the moments of simple circulation), posits the value of one commodity in the other, and thus realizes it as exchange; or, also, posits the commodities as equivalents. The act of exchange is thus *value-positing* in so far as values are pre-supposed to it; it realizes the value-*character* of the subjects of exchange.[41] But an act which posits a commodity as *value*, or, what is the same, which posits another commodity as its *equivalent* – or, again the same, posits the *equivalence* of both commodities, obviously for its part adds nothing to value, as little as the sign $\pm$ increases or decreases the number coming after it. If I posit 4 as plus or as minus – through this operation, 4, independently of the sign, remains equal to itself, 4, becomes neither 3 nor 5. Likewise, if I exchange a lb. of cotton with an exchange value of 6d. for 6d., then it is posited as value; and it can equally be said that the 6d. are posited as value in the lb. of cotton; i.e. the labour time contained in the 6d. (here 6d. regarded as *value*) is now expressed in another materialization of the same amount of labour time. But, since through this act of exchange the lb. of cotton as well as the 6d. of copper are each posited at = to their value, it is impossible that through this exchange the value either of the cotton, or of the 6d. or of the sum of both values should increase quantitatively. As the positing of equivalents, exchange only changes the form; realizes the potentially existing values; realizes the prices, if you like. To posit equivalents, e.g. A and B as equivalents, cannot raise the value of A, for it is the act in which A is posited as = to its own value, hence not as unequal to it; unequal only where the form is concerned, in so far as it was previously not posited as value; it is at the same time the act by means of which the value of A is posited as = to the value of B, and the value of B

41. 'Subjects of exchange' should clearly read 'objects of exchange'. [MELI note]

as = the value of A. The sum of the values transposed in the exchange = value A + value B. Each remains = to its own value;
hence their sum remains equal to the sum of their values. Exchange as the *positing of equivalents* cannot therefore by its nature
increase the sum of values, nor the value of the commodities exchanged. (The fact that it is different with the exchange with labour
arises because the use value of labour is itself *value-positing,* but is
not directly connected with its exchange value.) And if a single
operation of exchange cannot increase the value of the thing exchanged, neither can a sum of exchanges do it.* Whether I repeat
an act which creates no value once or an infinite number of times,
the repetition cannot change its nature. The repetition of a non-
value-creating act can never become an act of value-creation. E.g.
¼ expresses a specific proportion. If I transform this ¼ into a decimal
fraction, i.e. posit it = 0·25, then its form has been changed. This
transformation leaves the value the same. Similarly, when I transform a commodity into the form of money, or money into the form
of the commodity, then the value remains the same, but the form
is changed. It is clear, therefore, that circulation – since it consists
of a series of exchange operations with equivalents – cannot increase
the value of circulating commodities. Therefore, if labour time is
required to undertake this operation, i.e. if values have to be consumed, for all consumption of values reduces itself to the consumption of labour time or of objectified labour time, products;
i.e. if circulation entails costs, and if circulation time costs labour
time, then this is a deduction from, a relative suspension of the
circulating values; their devaluation by the amount of the circulation costs. If one imagines two workers who exchange with
each other, a fisherman and a hunter; then the time which both
lose in exchanging would create neither fish nor game, but would
be rather a deduction from the time in which both of them can
create values, the one fish, the other hunt, objectify their labour
time in a use value. If the fisherman wanted to get compensation for
this loss from the hunter: demand more game, or give him fewer
fish, then the latter would have the same right to compensation.
The loss would be common to both of them. These costs of cir-

---

*It is altogether necessary to make this clear; because the distribution of
the surplus value among the capitals, the *calculation* of the total surplus value
among the individual capitals – this *secondary* economic operation – gives
rise to phenomena which are confused, in the ordinary economics books, with
the primary ones.

culation, costs of exchange, could appear only as a deduction from the total production and value-creation of both of them. If they commissioned a third, C, with these exchanges, and thus lost no labour time directly, then each of them would have to cede a proportional share of his product to C. What they could gain thereby would only be a greater or lesser loss. But if they worked as joint proprietors, then no exchange would take place, only communal consumption. The costs of exchange would therefore vanish. Not the division of labour; but the division of labour founded on exchange. It is wrong, therefore, for J. St. Mill to regard the cost of circulation as *necessary price of the division of labour*.[42] It is the cost only of the [not-] spontaneous division of labour resting not on community of property, but on private property.

Circulation costs as such, i.e. the consumption of labour time or of objectified labour time, of values, in connection with the operation of exchange and a series of exchange operations, are therefore a deduction either from the time employed on production, or from the values posited by production. They can never increase the value. They belong among the *faux frais de production*, and these *faux frais de production* belong to the inherent costs of production resting on capital. The merchant's trade and still more the money trade proper – in so far as they do nothing but carry on the operations of circulation as such, e.g. the determination of prices (measurement of values and their calculation), these exchange operations generally, as a function which has gained independence through the division of labour, in so far as they represent this function of the total process of capital – represent merely the *faux frais de production* of capital. In so far as they reduce these *faux frais*, they add to production, not by creating value, but by reducing the negation of created values. If they operate purely as such a function, then they would always only represent the minimum of *faux frais de production*. If they enable the producers to create more values than they could without this division of labour, and, more precisely, so much more that a surplus remains after the payment of this function, then they have in fact increased production. Values are then increased, however, not because the operations of circulation have created value, but because they have absorbed less value than they would have done otherwise. But they are a necessary condition for capital's production.

42 See above, p. 617.

The time a capitalist loses during exchange is as such not a deduction from labour time. He is a capitalist – i.e. representative of capital, personified capital, only by virtue of the fact that he relates to labour as alien labour, and appropriates and posits alien labour for himself. The costs of circulation therefore do not exist in so far as they *take away the capitalist's time*. His time is posited as *superfluous time: not-labour time, not-value-creating time*, although it is capital which realizes the created value. The fact that the worker must work surplus labour time is identical with the fact that the capitalist does not need to work, and his time is thus posited as not-labour time; that he does not work the *necessary* time, either. The worker must work surplus time in order to be allowed to objectify, to realize the labour time necessary for his reproduction. On the other side, therefore, the *capitalist's necessary labour time* is *free* time, not time required for direct subsistence. Since all *free time* is time for free development, the capitalist usurps the *free time* created by the workers for society, i.e. civilization, and Wade is again correct in this sense, in so far as he posits capital = civilization.[43]

Circulation time – to the extent that it takes up the time of the capitalist as such – concerns us here exactly as much as the time he spends with his mistress. If time is money, then from the standpoint of capital it is only alien labour time, which is of course in the most literal sense the capitalist's money. In regard to capital as such, circulation time can coincide with labour time only in so far as it interrupts the time during which capital can appropriate alien labour time, and it is clear that this relative devaluation of capital cannot add to its realization, but can only detract from it; or, in so far as circulation costs capital objectified alien labour time, values. (For example because it has to pay someone who takes over this function.) In both cases, circulation time is of interest only in so far as it is the suspension, the negation of alien labour time; either because it interrupts capital in the process of its appropriation; or because it forces it to consume a part of the created value, to consume it in order to accomplish the operations of circulation, i.e. to posit itself as capital. (Very much to be distinguished from the private consumption of the capitalist.) Circulation time is of interest only in its relation – as barrier, negation – to the production time of capital; this production time, however, is the time during which it appropriates alien labour, the

43. See above, p. 585.

alien labour time posited by it. To regard the time the capitalist spends in circulation as value-creating time or even surplus-value-creating time is to fall into the greatest confusion. Capital as such has no labour time apart from its production time. The capitalist absolutely does not concern us here except as capital. And he functions as such only in the total process we are examining. Otherwise, it could still be imagined that the *capitalist draws compensation for the time during which he does not earn money as another capitalist's wage labourer* – or that he *loses this time*. [Or] that it belongs together with the costs of production. The time which he employs or loses as capitalist is *lost time* altogether, sunk and unrecoverable from this standpoint. We will later look at the *capitalist's* so-called *labour time* as distinct from the worker's labour time, which former is alleged to form the basis of his *profits*, as a wage of its own type.

Nothing is more common than to bring transport etc., to the extent that they are connected with trade, into the pure circulation costs. In so far as trade brings a product to market, it gives it a new form. True, all it does is change the location. But the mode of the transformation does not concern us. It gives the product a new use value (and this holds right down to and including the retail grocer, who weighs, measures, wraps the product and thus gives it a form for consumption), and this new use value costs labour time, is therefore at the same time exchange value. Bringing to market is part of the production process itself. The product is a commodity, is in circulation only when it is on the market.

Circulation. Storch. – Metamorphosis of capital and metamorphosis of the commodity. – Capital's change of form and of substance. Different forms of capital. – Turnover in a given period. – Circulating capital as general character of capital. – Year *the measure of turnovers of circulating capital.* Day *the measure of labour time*

⟨'In every species of industry, the entrepreneurs become sellers of products, while the entire remainder of the nation and often even other nations are the buyers of these products . . . the constant and incessantly repeated path which *circulating capital* describes in order to take leave of the entrepreneur and in order to return to him in the first form is comparable to a circle; hence the name *circulant* given to this capital, and the use of the word circulation for its movement.' (p. [404,] 405.) (Storch. *Cours d'économie politique*, Paris, 1823, Vol. I, p. 405, Notebook, p. 34.) 'In the broad sense, circulation includes the motion of every commodity exchanged.' (p. 405, loc. cit.) 'Circulation proceeds by exchanges . . . from the instant of [the introduction of] currency, they [the commodities] are no longer exchanged but sold.' (p. 406, loc. cit.) 'For a commodity to be in circulation, it is sufficient that it be in supply . . . Wealth in circulation: *commodity*.' (p. 407, loc. cit.) 'Commerce only a part of circulation; the former includes only merchants' purchases and sales; the latter, those of all entrepreneurs and even of all . . . inhabitants.' (p. 408, loc. cit.) 'Only so long as the *costs* of circulation are indispensable to allow the *commodities to reach the consumers* is circulation real, and does *its value* increase the annual product. From the instant when it exceeds this degree, circulation is artificial and no longer contributes anything to the wealth of the nation.' (p. 409.) 'In recent years we saw examples of artificial circulation in St Petersburg in Russia. The slack state of foreign trade had led the merchants to realize their unemployed capitals in another way; no longer being able to employ them to bring in foreign commodities and to export domestic ones, they decided to take advantage of this by buying and reselling the commodities on hand. Monstrous quantities of sugar, coffee, hemp, iron etc. rapidly passed from one hand to the other, and a commodity often changed proprietors twenty times, without leaving the warehouse. This kind of circulation offers the dealers all manner of speculative opportunities; but while it enriches some, it ruins the others, and the nation's wealth gains nothing thereby. Likewise with the circulation of money . . . This kind of artificial circulation, based simply on a variation of prices, is termed *agiotage*.' (p. 410, 411.) 'Circulation brings no profit for society except in so far as it is indispensable to bring the commodity to the consumer. Every detour, delay, intermediate exchange which is not absolutely necessary for this purpose, or which does not contribute *to diminishing the circulation costs*, harms the national wealth, by uselessly raising the prices of commodities.' (p. 411.) 'Circulation is the more productive the more rapid it is; i.e. the less time it requires to relieve the entrepreneur of the finished product and bring it to market, and to bring the capital back to him in its first form.' (p. 411.) 'The entrepreneur can begin production again only after he has sold the completed product and has employed the price in purchasing new materials and new wages:

hence, the more promptly circulation acts to bring about these two effects, the sooner is he in a position to begin his production anew, and the more profits does his capital bring in a given period of time.' (p. 412.) 'The nation whose capital circulates with a proper speed, so as to return several times a year to him who set it into motion, is in the same situation as the labourer of the happy climates who can raise three or four harvests in succession from the same soil in one year.' (p. 412, 413.) 'A slow circulation makes the objects of consumption more expensive (1) indirectly, through diminution of the mass of commodities which can exist; (2) directly because, as long as a product is in circulation, *its value progressively* increases by the interest of capital employed on its production; the slower the production, the more do these interest charges accumulate, which uselessly elevates the price of commodities.' 'Means for the abbreviation and acceleration of circulation: (1) the separating-out of a class of workers occupied exclusively with trade; (2) ease of transport; (3) currency; (4) credit.' (p. 413.)⟩

Simple circulation consisted of a great number of simultaneous or successive exchanges. Their unity, regarded as circulation, was actually present only from the observer's standpoint. (The exchange can be accidental, and it more or less has this character where it is restricted to the exchange of the excess product, and has not seized upon the totality of the production process.) In the circulation of capital we have a series of exchange operations, acts of exchange, each of which represents a qualitatively different moment towards the other, a moment in the reproduction and growth of capital. A system of exchanges, changes of substance, from the standpoint of value as such. Changes of form, from the standpoint of use value. The product relates to the commodity as use value to exchange value; thus the commodity to money. Here one series attains its peak. Money relates to the commodity into which it is retransformed as exchange value to use value; even more so, money to labour.

In so far as capital in every moment of the process is itself the possibility of going over into its other, next phase, and is thus the possibility of the whole process, which expresses capital's act of life, to that extent each of the moments appears potentially as capital – hence commodity capital, money capital – along with the value positing itself in the production process as capital. The commodity can represent money as long as it can transform itself into money, i.e. can buy wage labour (surplus labour); this in respect of the *formal side*, which emerges from the circulation of capital. On the material, physical side, it remains capital as long as it consists of raw material (proper or semi-fabricated), instrument, or necessaries for the workers. Each of these forms is potential capital. Money is in one respect the realized capital, capital as realized value. In this respect (regarded as a terminal point of circulation, where it then has to be regarded as a point of departure as well), it is capital, κατ᾽ ἐξοχήν. It is then especially capital again in regard to the part of the production process in which it exchanges itself for living labour. By contrast, in its exchange for the commodity (new purchase of raw material etc.) by the capitalist, it appears not as capital, but as medium of circulation; merely a vanishing mediation, through which the capitalist exchanges his product for the latter's original elements.

Circulation is not merely an external operation for capital. Just as it only becomes capital through the production process, in that value immortalizes and increases itself through that process, so does it become retransformed into the pure *form* of value – in which the traces of its becoming, as well as its specific presence in use value, have been extinguished – only through the first act of circulation; while the repetition of this act, i.e. the life process [of capital] is made possible only through the second act of circulation, which consists of the exchange of money for the conditions of production and forms the introduction to the act of production. Circulation therefore belongs *within* the concept of capital. Just as, originally, money or stockpiled labour appeared as presupposition *before* the exchange with free labour; the seeming independence of the objective moment of capital towards labour, however, was suspended, and objectified labour, become independent as value, appeared on all sides as the *product of alien labour*, the *alienated product* of labour itself; so does capital only now appear as presupposed to its circulation (capital as money was presupposed to its becoming capital; but capital as the result of value which has absorbed and assimilated living labour appeared as the point of departure not of circulation generally, but of the *circulation* of capital), so that it would exist independently and indifferently, even *without* this process. *However, the movement of the metamorphoses through which it must pass now appears as a condition of the production process* itself; just as much as its result. Capital, in its reality, therefore appears as a series of turnovers in a given *period*. It is no longer merely *one turnover*, one circulation; but rather the positing of turnovers; positing of the whole process. Its value-positing therefore appears as conditioned (and value is capital only as self-immortalizing and self-multiplying value) (1) *qualitatively*; in that it cannot renew the production phase without passing through the phases of circulation; (2)*quantitatively*; in that the mass of the values it posits depends on the number of its turnovers in a given period; (3) in that circulation time appears in both respects as limiting principle, as barrier of production time, and vice versa. Capital is therefore essentially *circulating capital.* While in the workshop of the production process capital appears as proprietor and master, in respect of circulation it appears as dependent and determined by social connections, which, from our present standpoint, make it enter into and figure in simple circulation alternately as C towards M and M towards C. But this circulation is a haze under which yet another whole world conceals itself, the world of the interconnections of capital, which binds this quality originating in circulation – in social intercourse – to itself, and robs it of the independence of self-sustaining property, as well as of its character. Two vistas into this presently still distant world have already opened up, at the two points at which the circulation of capital pushes the value posited and circulated by it in the form of the product out of its path, and, secondly, the point at which it pulls another product out of circulation into its own orbit; transforms this product itself into one of the moments of its presence [*Dasein*]. At the second point it presupposes production; not its own immediate production; at the first point it may presuppose production, if its product is itself raw material for other production; or consumption if it has obtained the final form for consumption. This much is clear, that consumption need not enter into its circle *directly*. The actual circulation of capital, as we shall see later, is still circulation between dealers and dealers. The circulation between dealers and consumers, identical with the retail trade, is a second circle which does not fall within the immediate circulation sphere of capital. An orbit which it describes after the first is described, and simultaneously alongside it. *The simultaneity of the different orbits of capital*, like that of its different aspects, becomes clear only after many capitals are presupposed. Likewise, the course of human life consists of passing through different ages. But at the same time all ages exist side by side, distributed among different individuals.

Considering that the production process of capital is at the same time a technological process – production process absolutely – namely [the process] of the production of specific use values through specific labour, in short, in a manner determined by this aim itself; considering that the most fundamental of these production processes is that through which the body reproduces its necessary metabolism, i.e. creates the necessaries of life in the physiological sense; considering that this production process coincides with agriculture; and the latter also at the same time directly (as with cotton, flax etc.) or indirectly, through the animals it feeds (silk, wool, etc.), furnishes a large part of the raw materials for industry (actually all except those belonging to the extractive industries); considering that reproduction in agriculture in the temperate zone (the home of capital) is bound up with general terrestrial circulation; i.e. harvests are mostly *annual*; it follows that the *year* (except that it is figured differently for various productions) has been adopted as the general period of time by which the sum of the turnovers of capital is calculated and measured; just as the *natural working day* provided such a natural unit as measure of labour time. In the calculation of profit, and even more of interest, we consequently see the unity of circulation time and production time – capital – posited as such, and as its own measure. Capital itself as *in process* – hence, as accomplishing one turnover – is regarded as *working capital*, and the fruits, which it is supposed to yield, are calculated according to its working time – the total circulation time of one turnover. The mystification which thereby takes place lies in the nature of capital.

Fixed (*tied down*) *capital and circulating capital.* – (*Surplus. Proudhon. Bastiat.*) – *Mill. Anderson. Say. Quincey. Ramsay.* – *Difficulty with interest on interest.* – *Creating market through trade.* – Fixed and circulating capital. Ricardo. Money and capital. *Eternity of value.* – *Necessity of rapid or less rapid reproduction.* Sismondi. *Cherbuliez. Storch.* – *Capital's advance to labour*

Now, before we go more closely into the above-mentioned considerations, we want to see what distinctions the economists draw between *fixed capital* and *circulating capital*. We have already found, above, a new moment which enters with the calculation of profit as distinct from surplus value. Likewise already at this point a new moment has to arise between profit and interest.

Surplus value in connection with *circulating capital* obviously appears as profit, in distinction to *interest* as the surplus value in connection with *fixed capital*. Profit and interest are both forms of the surplus value. Profit contained in the *price*. Hence, profit comes to an end and is realized as soon as capital has come to the point of its circulation where it is retransformed into money or passes from its form as commodity into the form of money. The striking ignorance on which Proudhon's polemic against interest rests, later. (Here one more time, so as not to forget, in regard to Proudhon: the surplus value which causes all Ricardians and anti-Ricardians so much worry is solved by this fearless thinker simply by mystifying it, 'all work leaves a surplus', 'I posit it as an axiom' . . .[44] The actual formulation to be looked up in the notebook. The fact that *work goes on beyond* necessary labour is transformed by Proudhon into a mystical quality of labour. This not to be explained by the mere growth of the productive force of labour; this may increase the products of a given labour time; but it cannot give a surplus value. It enters only in so far as it liberates surplus time, time for labour beyond the necessary. The only *extra-economic* fact in this is that the human being does not need his entire time for the production of the necessaries, that he has free time at his disposal above and beyond the labour time necessary for subsistence, and hence can also employ it for surplus labour. But this is in no way something mystical, since his necessaries are small to the same degree that his labour power is in a primitive state. But wage labour as such enters only where the development of the productive force has already advanced so far that a significant amount of time has become free; this liberation is here already a historic product. Proudhon's ignorance only equalled by Bastiat's decreasing rate of profit which is supposed to be the equivalent of a rising rate of wages.[45] Bastiat expresses this nonsense, borrowed from Carey, in a double way: first, the *rate* of profit falls (i.e. the proportion of surplus value in relation to the employed capital); secondly: prices decline, but value, i.e. the total sum of prices, rises, which is only another way of saying that the gross profit rises, not the rate of profit.)

Firstly, in the sense used by us above, of *fixated* capital, John St. Mill (*Essays on some Unsettled Questions of Political Econ.*, Lond., 1844, p. 55), [speaks of it] as tied-down, not disposable, not available capital. Stuck in one phase of its total circulation process. In

44. Bastiat and Proudhon, *Gratuité du crédit*, p. 200.   45. ibid., p. 288.

this sense he says correctly, like Bailey in the above quotations, that a great part of the capital of a nation always lies idle.

'The difference between fixed and circulating capital is more apparent than real; e.g. gold is fixed capital; floating only in so far as it is consumed for gilding etc. Ships are fixed capital, although literally floating. Foreign railway shares are articles of commerce in our markets; so may our railways be in the markets of the world; and so far they are floating capital, on a par with gold.' (Anderson, *The Recent Commercial Distress etc.*, London, 1847, p. 4.) (Notebook I, 27.)[46]

According to Say: capital 'so much involved in one *kind of production* that it can no longer be diverted from it to be devoted to *another kind of production*'.[47] The identification of capital with a specific use value, use value for the production process. This quality of capital, *being tied down* as value to a particular use value – use value within production – is, however, an important aspect. This expresses more than the inability to circulate, which actually only says that fixed capital is the opposite of circulating capital.

In his *Logic of Political Economy* (p. 114) (Notebook X, 4), de Quincey says: '*Circulating capital*, in its normal idea, means *any agent whatever*' (beautiful logician) 'used productively which perishes in the very act of being used.' (According to this, coal would be *circulating capital*, and *oil*, but not cotton etc. It cannot be said that cotton perishes by being transformed into twist or calico, and such transformation certainly means using it productively); 'capital is *fixed* when the thing serves repeatedly always for the same operation, and by how much larger has been the range of iterations, by so much more intensely is the *tool, engine,* or *machinery* entitled to the denomination of fixed.' (p. 114.) (Notebook X, 4.) According to this, the circulating capital would die out, be consumed in the act of production; the fixed capital – which, for greater clarity, is characterized as *tool, engine,* or *machinery* (thus improvements incorporated in the soil are, for instance, excluded) – would serve repeatedly, always for the same operation. The distinction here concerns only technological differ-

46. A. Anderson (Scottish chemical manufacturer, not to be confused with James Anderson, Scottish farmer, and eighteenth-century originator of the theory of ground rent), *The Recent Commercial Distress*; *or, the Panic, Analysed: Showing the Cause and Cure*, London, 1847.

47. Say, *Traité d'économie politique*, Vol. II, p. 430.

ences in the act of production, not in the least the form-relation; circulating and fixed capital, in the differences here indicated, do have distinguishing features by means of which one particular agent is fixed and the other circulating, but neither of them any qualification which would entitle it to the '*denomination*' of *capital*.

According to Ramsay (IX, 84)[48] only 'the *approvisionnement* is *circulating capital*, because the capitalist must part with it immediately, and it *does not enter into the reproduction process at all*, but is rather exchanged directly for living labour, for consumption. All other capital (including raw material) remains in the possession of its owner or employer until the *produce is completed*.' (loc. cit. p. 21.) '*Circulating capital* consists only of subsistence and other necessaries advanced to the workman, previous to the completion of the produce of his labour.' (loc. cit. p. 23.) In regard to *approvisionnement* he is correct in so far as it is the only part of capital which circulates during the production phase itself, and which is in this respect circulating capital *par excellence*. In another respect it is false to say that fixed capital remains in the possession of its owner or employer 'until the produce is completed' and no longer than that. He consequently also later explains fixed capital as 'any portion of that labour (bestowed upon any commodity) *in a form* in which, though assisting to raise the future commodity, it does not *maintain labour*'. (But how many commodities do not maintain labour! I.e. do not belong among the workers' articles of consumption. These, according to Ramsay, are all *fixed capital*.)

(If the interest on £100 at the end of the first year or of the first 3 months is £5, then the capital at the end of the first year 105 or $100(1 + 0.05)$; at the end of the 4th year $= 100(1 + 0.05)^4 =$ £121. $£\frac{55}{100}$ and $£\frac{1}{1600} = $ £121 11s. $\frac{3}{20}$ farthing or £121 11s. 0·15 farthing. Hence £1 11s. $\frac{3}{20}$ farthing more than 20.)

(In the question posed above, assume that a first capital of 400 turns over only once a year, a second [capital of 100,] 4 times, both at 5%. In the first case the capital would make 5% once a year, $=$ 20 on 400; in the second case $4 \times 5\%$, likewise $= 20$ per year on 100. The velocity of turnover would substitute for the size of the capital; just as in simple money circulation 100,000 thalers which circulate 3 times a year $= 300,000$, while 3,000 which circulate 100 times $= 300,000$ also. But if the capital circulates 4 times a year, then it is *possible* that the surplus gain itself is ploughed into

48. Ramsay, *An Essay on the Distribution of Wealth*

the capital for the second turnover, and turned over with it, producing thereby the difference of £1 11s. 0·15 farthing. But this difference in no way follows from the presupposition. All that is there is the *abstract* possibility. What would follow, rather, from the presupposition is that 3 months are required for the turnover of a capital of £100. E.g. therefore, if the month = 30 days, then for £105 – with the same turnover relation, with the same relation between the turnover time and the size of the capital – not 3 months are required,* but rather $105:x = 100:90; x = \dfrac{90 \times 105}{100}$ $= \dfrac{9450}{100} = 94\frac{5}{10}$ days = 3 months, $4\frac{1}{2}$ days. With that, the first difficulty is completely solved.)

(From the fact that a larger capital with a slower turnover does not create more surplus value than a smaller with a relatively more rapid turnover, it does not in the least automatically follow that a smaller capital turns over more rapidly than a larger. This is indeed the case in so far as the larger capital consists of more fixed capital and in so far as it has to search out more distant markets. The size of the market and the velocity of turnover are not necessarily inversely related. This occurs only as soon as the present, physical market is not the economic market; i.e. as the economic market becomes more and more distant from the place of production. To the extent, by the way, that [this relation] does not arise purely from the distinction between fixed and circulating capital, the moments which determine the circulation of different capitals cannot be at all developed yet here. An incidental remark: to the extent that trade posits new points of circulation, i.e. brings different countries into intercourse, discovers new markets etc., this is something entirely different from the mere costs of circulation required to carry out a given mass of exchange operations; it is the positing not of the operations of exchange, but of the exchange itself. Creation of markets. This point will have to be examined in particular before we have done with circulation.)

Now let us continue with our review of the opinions about 'fixed' and 'circulating capital'. 'Depending on whether *capital* is more or less *transitory*, hence *must be more or less frequently reproduced in a given time*, it is called *circulating or fixed capital*.

*Otherwise it could also be assumed, alternatively, that, if the production process is continuous, the obtained surplus is re-transformed into capital every 3 months.

Furthermore, capital circulates or returns to its employer in *very* unequal times; e.g. wheat which the farmer buys to sow is *relatively fixed* capital compared to the wheat a baker buys to make bread.' (Ricardo VIII, 19.) Then he remarks also: 'Different *proportions of fixed capital and circulating capital* in different trades; different *durability of fixed capital* itself.' (Ricardo, loc. cit.)[49] 'Two kinds of commerce can employ a capital of equal value, but which may be divided in a very different way as regards the fixed part and the circulating part. They may even employ an equal value of fixed capital and circulating capital, but the durability of the fixed capital may be very unequal. For example, one a steam engine of £10,000, the other, ships.' (This out of Say's translation of Ricardo, Vol. I, p. 29, 30.) The error from the outset is that, according to Ricardo, capital is supposed to be *'more or less transitory'*. Capital as capital – *value* – is not transitory. But the use value in which the value is fixated, in which it exists, is 'more or less transitory', and must therefore be *'more or less frequently reproduced in a given time'*. The difference between fixed capital and circulating capital is therefore reduced here to the *greater or lesser necessity for reproducing the given capital in a given time*. This is one distinction made by Ricardo. The other distinction concerns the different *degrees of durability*, or *different degrees of fixed capital*, i.e. *different degrees, relative durability of the relatively fixed*. So that fixed capital is itself more or less fixed. *The same capital* appears in the same business in the two different forms, the *particular modes of existence* of *fixed and circulating*, hence exists doubly. To be fixed or circulating appears as a *particular* aspect of capital apart from that of being capital. It must, however, proceed to this particularization. Finally, as for the third distinction, 'that capital circulates or returns in very *unequal times'*, what Ricardo means by this, as his example of the baker and the farmer shows, is nothing more than the difference in the time during which capital is *fixed, tied up* in the *production phase* as distinct from the circulation phase, in different branches of business. Hence, *fixed capital* occurs here in the same way as we had it previously, as being fixated in each phase; except that the specifically longer or shorter fixation in the production phase, this phase in particular, is regarded as a peculiarity, particularity of

49. Ricardo, *On the Principles of Political Economy*, pp. 26–7. The passage is sometimes compressed, sometimes expanded, in the quoting, in line with Marx's usual method in the notebooks.

capital [as value-] positing. Money attempted to posit itself as *imperishable value*, as eternal value, by relating negatively towards circulation, i.e. towards the exchange with real wealth, with transitory commodities, which, as Petty describes very prettily and very naïvely, dissolve in fleeting pleasures.[50] Capital posits the permanence of value (to a certain degree) by incarnating itself in fleeting commodities and taking on their form, but at the same time changing them just as constantly; alternates between its eternal form in money and its passing form in commodities; permanence is posited as the only thing it can be, a passing passage – process – life. But capital obtains this ability only by constantly sucking in living labour as its soul, vampire-like. The permanence – the duration of value in its form as capital – is posited only through reproduction, which is itself double, reproduction as commodity, reproduction as money, and unity of both these reproduction processes. In its reproduction as commodity, capital is fixated in a particular form of use value, and is thus not *general exchange value*, even less realized *value*, as it is supposed to be. The fact that it has posited itself as such in the act of reproduction, the production phase, is proved only through circulation. The greater or lesser perishability of the commodity in which value exists requires a slower or faster reproduction; i.e. repetition of the labour process. The *particular nature of use value*, in which the value exists, or which now appears as capital's body, here appears as itself a *determinant* of the *form* and of the action of capital; as giving one capital a particular property as against another; as particularizing it. As we have already seen in several instances, nothing is therefore more erroneous than to assert[51] that the distinction between use value and exchange value, which falls outside the characteristic economic form in simple circulation, to the extent that it is *realized* there, falls outside it in general. We found, rather, that in the different stages of the development of economic relations, exchange value and use value were determined in different relations, and that this determination itself appeared as a different determination of value as such. Use value itself plays a role as an economic category. Where it plays this role is given by the development itself. Ricardo, e.g., who believes that the bourgeois economy deals only with exchange value, and is concerned with use value only

50. Petty, *Political Arithmetic*, pp. 178–9.

51. 'Assert' is a suggested emendation for 'overlook' as found in the original text.

exoterically, derives the most important determinations of exchange value precisely from use value, from the relation between the two of them: for instance, *ground rent, wage minimum, distinction between fixed capital and circulating capital*, to which he imputes precisely the most significant influence on the determination of prices (through the different reaction produced upon them by a rise or fall in the rate of wages); likewise in the relation of demand and supply etc. One and the same relation appears sometimes in the form of use value and sometimes in that of exchange value, but at different stages and with a different meaning. To use is to consume, whether for production or consumption. Exchange is the mediation of this act through a social process. Use can be posited as, and be, a mere consequence of exchange; then again, exchange can appear as merely a moment of use, etc. From the standpoint of capital (in circulation), exchange appears as the positing of its use value, while on the other side its use (in the act of production) appears as positing for exchange, as positing its exchange value. Likewise with production and consumption. In the bourgeois economy (as in every economy), they are posited in specific distinctions and specific unities. The point is to understand precisely these specific, distinguishing characteristics. Nothing is accomplished by the [assertions of] Mr Proudhon or of the social sentimentalists that they are *the same*.

The good thing in Ricardo's explanation is that it begins by emphasizing the moment of the necessity of *quicker or slower reproduction*; hence that the greater or lesser durability – consumption (in the sense of self-consumption), slower or more rapid – is regarded in connection with *capital* itself. Hence a relation of use value for *capital* itself. Sismondi by contrast immediately introduces a determinant initially exoteric to capital; *direct or indirect human consumption*: whether the article is a direct or an indirect necessary of life for the human consumer; he thereby joins this with the *quicker or slower consumption of the object itself*. The objects which serve directly as necessaries of life are more perishable, because designed to perish, than those which help to produce the necessaries of life. With the latter, their duration is their character; their transitoriness – fate. He says: 'Fixed, indirect capital is *slowly consumed*, in order to assist in consuming that which man destines for his use; circulating capital does not cease to be directly applied to the use of man ... Whenever a thing is consumed, it *never returns* for him who consumes it; while a thing consumed

for reproduction is there for him at the same time.' (Sismondi VI.)
He also presents the relation in such a way that: 'the *first transformation* of annual consumption into durable foundations, suitable for *increasing the productive powers of future labour – fixed
capital*; this first labour always accomplished by labour, represented by a wage, exchanged for necessaries which the worker
consumes during labour. *Fixed capital is consumed slowly*' (i.e.
is slowly worn out). *Second transformation:* '*Circulating capital*
consists of *labour-seeds* (raw material) and of the *worker's consumption.*' (loc. cit.)[52] This is more concerned with the origin.
Firstly the *transformation*, that fixed capital is itself only circulating capital which has assumed a stationary form, *fixated*
circulating capital; second, the *destination*: the one destined to be
consumed as means of production, the other as product; or the
different mode of its *consumption*, determined by its role among the
conditions of production in the production process. Cherbuliez
simplifies the matter to the point where circulating capital is the
consumable, fixed capital the not consumable part of capital.[53]
(One you can eat, the other not. A very easy method of taking the
thing.) In a quotation already given above[54] (29 in the Notebook),
Storch vindicates for circulating capital generally the circulating
nature of capital. He contradicts himself by saying: 'all fixed
capital comes originally from a circulating capital, and needs
continually to be maintained at the latter's expense' (hence comes
out of circulation, or is itself circulating in its first moment and
constantly renews itself *through* circulation; thus although *it* does
not go *into circulation*, circulation goes into *it*). As for what
Storch adds further: 'NO *fixed capital can give a revenue* EXCEPT
by means of a circulating capital' (26a. Notebook),[55] we shall
return to that later.

⟨'Reproductive consumption is not properly an expense, but
only an *advance*, because it is reimbursed to its agent'; p. 54 in
Storch's polemic against Say[56] (p. 5b. *Second* notebook on
Storch). (The capitalist gives the worker a part of the latter's own
surplus labour in the form of *advance*, as something for which he

---

52. Sismondi, *Nouveaux Principes d'économie politique*, Vol. I, pp. 94–8.

53. Cherbuliez, *Richesse ou pauvreté*, pp. 16–19.

54. The number 29 refers to Notebook V, p. 29. See above, p. 543, and
Storch, *Cours d'économie politique*, Vol. I, pp. 411–12.

55. Storch, *Cours d'économie politique*, Vol. I, p. 246. The number 26a
refers to an excerpt-book.

56. Storch, *Considérations sur la nature du revenu national*, Paris, 1824.

must reimburse the capitalist not merely with an equivalent, but with surplus labour as well.)⟩

(The formula for *computing compound interest* is: $S = c(1 + i)^n$. (S, the total magnitude of capital c after n years at an interest rate i.)

The formula for *computing an annuity* is:

$$x \text{ (the annuity)} = \frac{c(1 + i)^n}{1 + (1 + i) + (1 + i)^2 + (1 + i)^{n-1}}.)$$

Constant and variable capital

We divided capital above into *constant* and *variable value*; this is always correct as regards capital within the production phase, i.e. in its immediate realization process. How it is that capital itself, as presupposed value, can change its value as its reproduction costs rise or fall, or as a consequence of a decline in profits also etc., evidently belongs to the section where capital is regarded as real capital, as the interaction of many capitals on one another, not here in its general concept.

Competition

⟨Because competition appears historically as the dissolution of compulsory guild membership, government regulation, internal tariffs and the like within a country, as the lifting of blockades, prohibitions, protection on the world market – because it appears historically, in short, as the negation of the limits and barriers peculiar to the stages of production preceding capital; because it was quite correctly, from the historical standpoint, designated and promoted by the Physiocrats as *laissez faire, laissez passer*; it has [therefore] never been examined even for this merely negative side, this, its merely historical side, and this has led at the same time to the even greater absurdity of regarding it as the collision of unfettered individuals who are determined only by their own interests – as the mutual repulsion and attraction of free individuals, and hence as the absolute mode of existence of free individuality in the sphere of consumption and of exchange. Nothing can be more mistaken. While free competition has dissolved the barriers of earlier relations and modes of production, it is necessary to observe first of all that the things which were a barrier to it were the inherent limits of earlier modes of production, within which they spontaneously developed and moved. These limits became barriers only after the forces of production and the relations of intercourse had developed sufficiently to enable capital as such to emerge as the dominant principle of production. The limits which it tore down were barriers to its motion, its development and realization. It is by no means the case that it thereby suspended all limits, nor all barriers, but rather only the limits not corresponding to it, which were barriers to it. Within its own limits – however much they may appear as barriers from a higher standpoint, and are posited as such by its own historic development – it feels free, and free of barriers, i.e. as limited only by itself, only by its own conditions of life. Exactly as guild industry, in its heyday, found in the guild organization all the fullness of freedom it required, i.e. the relations of production corresponding to it. After all, it posited these out of itself, and developed them as *its* inherent conditions, and hence in no way as external and constricting barriers. The historical side of the negation of the guild system etc. by capital through free competition signifies nothing more than that capital, having become sufficiently strong, by means of the mode of intercourse adequate to itself, tore down the historic barriers which hindered and blocked the movement adequate to it. But competition is very far from having only this historic significance, or merely being *this negative* force. *Free competition* is the relation of capital to itself as another capital, i.e. the real conduct of capital as capital. The inner laws of capital – which appear merely as tendencies in the preliminary historic stages of its development – are for the first time posited as laws; production founded on capital for the first time posits itself in the forms adequate to it only in so far as and to the extent that free competition develops, for it is the free development of the mode of production founded on capital; the free development of its conditions and of itself as the process which constantly reproduces these conditions. It is not individuals who are set free by free competition; it is, rather, capital which is set free. As long as production resting on capital is the necessary, hence the fittest form for the development of the force of social production, the movement of individuals within the pure conditions of capital appears as their freedom; which is then also again dogmatically propounded as such through constant reflection back on the barriers torn down by free competition. Free competition is the real development of capital. By its means, what corresponds to the nature of capital is posited as external necessity for the individual capital; what corresponds to the concept of capital, is posited as external necessity for the mode of production founded on capital. The reciprocal compulsion which the capitals within it practise upon one another, on labour etc. (the competition among workers is only another form of the competition among capitals), is the *free*, at the same time the *real* development of wealth as capital. So much is this the case that the most profound economic thinkers, such as e.g. Ricardo, *presuppose* the absolute predominance of free competition[57] in order to be able to study and to formulate the adequate laws of capital – which appear at the same time as the vital tendencies governing over it. But free competition is the adequate form of the productive process of capital. The further it is developed, the purer the forms in which its motion appear. What Ricardo has thereby admitted, despite himself, is the *historic nature* of capital, and the limited character of free competition, which is just the free movement of capitals and nothing else, i.e. their movement within conditions which belong to no previous, dissolved stages, but are its own conditions. The predominance of capital is the presupposition of free competition, just as the despotism of the Roman Caesars was the presupposition of the free Roman 'private law'. As long as capital is weak, it still itself relies on the crutches of past modes of production, or of those which will pass with its rise. As soon as it feels strong, it throws away the crutches, and moves in accordance with its own laws. As soon as it begins to sense itself and become conscious of itself as a barrier to development, it seeks refuge in forms which, by restricting free competition, seem to make the rule of capital more perfect, but are at the same time the heralds of its dissolution and of the dissolution of the mode of production resting on it. Competition merely *expresses* as real, posits as an external necessity, that which lies within the nature of capital; competition is nothing more than the way in which the many capitals force the inherent determinants of capital upon one another and upon themselves. Hence not a single category of the bourgeois economy, not even the most basic, e.g. the determination of value, becomes real through free competition alone; i.e. through the real process of capital, which appears as the interaction of capitals and of all other relations of production and intercourse determined by capital. Hence, on the other side, the

57. Ricardo, *On the Principles of Political Economy*, p. 3.

insipidity of the view that free competition is the ultimate development of human freedom; and that the negation of free competition = negation of individual freedom and of social production founded on individual freedom. It is nothing more than free development on a limited basis – the basis of the rule of capital. This kind of individual freedom is therefore at the same time the most complete suspension of all individual freedom, and the most complete subjugation of individuality under social conditions which assume the form of objective powers, even of overpowering objects – of things independent of the relations among individuals themselves. The analysis of what free competition really is, is the only rational reply to the middle-class[58] prophets who laud it to the skies or to the socialists who damn it to hell. The statement that, within free competition, the individuals, in following purely their private interest, realize the communal or rather the *general* interest means nothing other than that they collide with one another under the conditions of capitalist production, and hence that the impact between them is itself nothing more than the re-creation of the conditions under which this interaction takes place. By the way, when the illusion about competition as the so-called absolute form of free individuality vanishes, this is evidence that the conditions of competition, i.e. of production founded on capital, are already felt and thought of as *barriers*, and hence already *are* such, and more and more become such. The assertion that free competition = the ultimate form of the development of the forces of production and hence of human freedom means nothing other than that middle-class rule is the culmination of world history – certainly an agreeable thought for the parvenus of the day before yesterday.⟩

Surplus value. Production time. Circulation time.
Turnover *time*

⟨Before we go further with the review of opinions about fixed capital and circulating capital, we return for a moment to something developed earlier.

We assume for the time being that production time and labour time coincide. The case where interruptions take place within the production phase itself, owing to the technological process, will be looked at later.

58. 'Middle-class': in English in the original text.

Suppose the production phase of a capital equal to 60 working days; of which 40 are necessary labour time. Then, according to the law developed earlier, the surplus value, or the value newly posited by capital, i.e. appropriated alien labour time = 60 − 40; = 20. Let us call this surplus value (=20) S; the production phase – or the labour time employed in production – p. In a period of time which we shall call T – e.g. 360 days – the total value can never be greater than the number of production phases contained in, say, 360. The highest coefficient of S – i.e. the maximum of surplus value which capital can create on the given presuppositions – equals the number of times the creation of S is repeated in 360 days. The outer limit of this reproduction – the reproduction of capital, or rather, now, the reproduction of its production process – is determined by the relation of the production period to the total period of time in which the former can be repeated. If the given period = 360 days, and the duration of production = 60 days, then $\frac{360}{60}$ or $\frac{T}{p}$, i.e. 6, is the coefficient indicating how many times p is contained in T, or how often, given its own inherent limits, the reproduction process of the capital can be repeated within 360 days. It goes without saying that the maximum of the creation of S, i.e. the positing of surplus value, is given by the number of processes in which S can be produced, in a given period of time. This relation is expressed by $\frac{T}{p}$. The quotient of $\frac{T}{p}$, or q, is the highest coefficient of S in the period of 360 days, in T generally. $\frac{ST}{p}$ or Sq is the maximum of value. If $\frac{T}{p} = q$, then $T = pq$; i.e. the entire duration of T would be production time; the production phase, p, would be repeated as often as it is contained in T. The total value created by capital in a certain time would be = to the surplus labour it appropriates in one production phase, multiplied by the number of times this production phase is contained in the given time. Thus in the above example, = $20 \times \frac{360}{60} = 20 \times 6 = 120$ days. q, i.e. $\frac{T}{p}$, would express the number of *turnovers* of the capital; but since $T = pq$, therefore $p = \frac{T}{q}$; i.e. the duration of one production phase would be equal to the total time divided by the number of turn-overs. Thus one production phase of capital would be equal to one of its turnovers. Turnover time and production time would be completely identical; the number of turnovers therefore [would be] exclusively determined by the relation of one production phase to the total time.

However, on this assumption, circulation time is posited as $= 0$. Yet circulation time has a definite magnitude, which can never become $= 0$. Now assume additionally that there are 30 days for circulation for every 60 days of production time; call this circulation time added to p, c. In this case, one turnover of capital, i.e. the total time it requires before it can repeat the realization process – the positing of surplus value – would be $= 30 + 60 = 90$ days $(= p + c)$ $(1R$ (turnover) $= p + c)$. One turnover of 90 days can be repeated in 360 days only $\frac{360}{90}$ times, i.e. 4 times. The surplus value of 20 could therefore be posited only 4 times; $20 \times 4 = 80$. In 60 days the capital produces 20 surplus days; but it has to circulate for 30 days; i.e. during these 30 days it can posit no surplus labour, no surplus value. This is the same for it (as regards the result) as if it had posited a surplus value of only 20 in the period of 90 days. While previously the number of turnovers was determined by $\dfrac{T}{p}$, it is now determined by $\dfrac{T}{p + c}$ or $\dfrac{T}{R}$; the maximum of value was $\dfrac{ST}{p + c}$; $(20 \dfrac{300}{60 + 30} = 20\dfrac{360}{90} = 20 \times 4 = 80)$. The number of turnovers hence $=$ the total time divided by the sum of production time and circulation time, and the total value $= S$ multiplied by the number of turnovers. But this formulation does not yet suffice for us to express the relations of surplus value, production time and circulation time.

The maximum of value creation contained in the formula $\dfrac{ST}{p}$; value creation restricted by circulation, $\dfrac{ST}{p + c}\left(\text{or } \dfrac{ST}{R}\right)$; when we subtract the second amount from the first, then $\dfrac{ST}{p} - \dfrac{ST}{p + c} = \dfrac{ST(p + c) - STp}{p(p + c)} = \dfrac{STp + STc - STp}{p(p + c)} = \dfrac{STc}{p(p + c)}$.

As difference we then obtain $\dfrac{STc}{p(p+c)}$ or $\dfrac{ST}{p} \times \dfrac{c}{p+c}$; $\dfrac{ST}{p+c}$ or S', as we may call this value in the second form, $S' = \dfrac{ST}{p} - \left(\dfrac{ST}{p} \times \dfrac{c}{p+c}\right)$. But before we develop this formula further, there are still others to be introduced.

If we call the quotient of $\dfrac{T}{p+c}$ q', then q' expresses the number of times $R = (p+c)$ is contained in T, the number of turnovers. $\dfrac{T}{p+c} = q'$; hence $T = pq' + cq'$. pq' then expresses the total production time and cq' the total circulation time.

Let us call total circulation time C (hence $cq' = C$). ($T(360) = 4 \times 60\,(240) + 4 \times 30\,(120)$.) With our presupposition, $q' = 4$. $C = cq' = 4c$; 4 being $=$ to the number of turnovers. We saw previously that the maximum of value-creation $= \dfrac{ST}{p}$; but in this case T was posited as $=$ to production time. But the real production time is now $T - q$; as indeed follows from the equation. $T = pq'$ (total production time) $+ cq'$ (total circulation time, or C). Hence $T - C = cq'$. Hence $S\,\dfrac{T-C}{p}$ the maximum value creation. Because production time not 360 days, but $360 - cq'$, i.e. $- 4 \times 30\,[=]\,120$; hence $20\left(\dfrac{360-120}{60}\right)$; $\dfrac{20 \times 240}{60} = 80$.

Now, finally, as regards the formula
$$S' = \dfrac{ST}{p} - \left(\dfrac{ST}{p} \times \dfrac{c}{c+p}\right) = \dfrac{360 \times 20}{60} - 20\left(\dfrac{360}{60} \times \dfrac{30}{30+60}\right)$$
$$= 120 - (120 \times \tfrac{30}{90}) = 6 \times 20 - (6 \times 20 \times \tfrac{3}{9})$$
$$= 20 \times 6 - (20 \times 6 \times \tfrac{1}{3}) \quad \text{or}$$
$$= 120 - (120 \times \tfrac{1}{3}) = 120 - 40 = 80,$$
it signifies that value is equal to the maximum of value, i.e. to value determined only by the relation of production time to total time, minus the number which expresses how often the circulation time is contained in this maximum, plus $\dfrac{c}{c+p} = \dfrac{c}{R}$; $\dfrac{c}{R}$ expresses the relation of circulation time to one turnover of

capital. If we multiply numerator and denominator by q', then $\dfrac{cq'}{(c+p)q'} = \dfrac{C}{T}$; $\dfrac{c}{c+p} = \dfrac{30}{30+60} = \frac{1}{3}$. $\dfrac{c}{c+p}$ or $\frac{1}{3}$ expresses the relation of circulation time to total time, for $\frac{360}{3} = 120$. The turnover $(c+p)$ is contained in C, $\dfrac{c}{c+p}$ or $\frac{1}{3}$ times (or $\dfrac{c}{T}$ times), and this number is the maximum itself multiplied by the number of times a turnover is contained in c, in the circulation time added to one turnover, or divided by the number which expresses how often c is contained in $c+p$ or C in T. If $c = 0$, then S' would be $= \dfrac{ST}{p}$ and would be at its maximum. S' becomes smaller in the same degree as C grows, is inversely related to it, for the factor $\dfrac{c}{c+p}$ and $\dfrac{ST}{p}$ grows to the same degree. The number to be subtracted [from] the maximum value, $\dfrac{ST}{p} \times \dfrac{c}{c+p}$ or $\dfrac{ST}{p} \times \dfrac{c}{R}$.

We have, then, the three equations: (1) $S' = \dfrac{ST}{p+c} = \dfrac{ST}{R}$; (2) $S' = \dfrac{S(T-C)}{p}$; (3) $S' = \dfrac{ST}{p} - \left(\dfrac{ST}{p} \times \dfrac{c}{c+p}\right) = S\left[\dfrac{T}{p} - \left(\dfrac{T}{p} \times \dfrac{c}{c+p}\right)\right]$.

Hence: $S:S' = \dfrac{ST}{p} : \dfrac{S(T-C)}{p}$; or $S:S' = T:(T-C)$. The maximum of value is to the real value as a given period of time is to this period of time minus total circulation time. Or, as well, $S:S' = pq':(pq' - q'c)$, i.e. $= p:(p-c)$.

On (3) $S' = \dfrac{ST}{p} - \left(\dfrac{ST}{p} \times \dfrac{c}{c+p}\right) = S\left[\dfrac{T}{p} - \left(\dfrac{T}{p} \times \dfrac{c}{c+p}\right)\right]$ or, since $\dfrac{T}{p} = q$,

$S' = S\left(q - q \cdot \dfrac{c}{c+p}\right) = S\left(q - q\dfrac{c}{R}\right)$. The total surplus value, therefore, $=$ to the surplus value posited in one production phase, whose coefficient is the number of times the production time is contained in the total time minus the number of times the circulation time of one turnover is contained in this latter number.

$$S\left(q - q\frac{c}{R}\right) = Sq\left(1 - \frac{1c}{R}\right) = Sq\left(\frac{R-c}{R}\right) = \frac{Sqp}{R} = \frac{ST}{p+c}, \text{which}$$

is the first equation. Thus equation 3 means ... *equation* 1: the total surplus value equals the surplus value of one production phase multiplied by total time, divided by turnover time or multiplied by the number of times the sum of production time and circulation time is contained in total time.

Equation 2: The total value equals surplus value multiplied by total time minus the total circulation time, divided by the duration of one production phase.⟩

Competition

⟨The fundamental law in competition, as distinct from that advanced about value and surplus value, is that it is determined not by the labour contained in it, or by the labour time in which it is produced, but rather by the labour time in which it can be produced, or, the labour time necessary for reproduction. By this means, the individual capital is in reality only placed within the conditions of capital as such, although it seems as if the original law were overturned. *Necessary* labour time as determined by the movement of capital itself; but only in this way is it posited. This is the fundamental law of competition. Demand, supply, price (production costs) are further specific forms; price as market price; or general price. Then the positing of a general rate of profit. As a consequence of the market price, the capitals then distribute themselves among different branches. Reduction of production costs etc. In short, here all determinants appear in a position which is the *inverse* of their position in capital in general. There price determined by labour. here labour determined by price etc. etc. The influence of individual capitals on one another has the effect precisely that they must conduct themselves as *capital*; the seemingly independent influence of the individuals, and their chaotic collisions, are precisely the positing of their general law. Market here obtains yet another significance. The influence of capitals as individuals on each other thus becomes precisely their positing as general beings, and the suspension of the seeming independence and independent survival of the individuals. This suspension takes place even more in credit. And the most extreme form to which the suspension proceeds, which is however at the same time the *ultimate positing* of capital in the form adequate to it – is joint-stock capital.) (Demand, supply, price, production costs, contradiction of profit and interest, different relations of exchange value and use value, consumption and production.)

Surplus value. Production time. Circulation time. Turnover time. *Part of capital in production time, part in circulation time. – Circulation time. – Surplus value and production phase. Number of reproductions of capital = number of turnovers. – Total surplus value etc.*

We have seen, then, that the surplus value a capital can posit in a given period of time is determined by the number of times the realization process can be repeated, or the capital can be reproduced in a given period of time; and that the number of these reproductions is determined by the relation of the duration of the production phase not to the total period of time, but rather to this total time minus circulation time. Circulation time thus appears as time during which the ability of capital to reproduce itself, and hence to reproduce surplus value, is suspended. Its productivity – i.e. its creation of surplus values – is therefore inversely related to circulation time, and would reach its maximum if the latter declined to 0. Circulation is an inescapable condition for capital, a condition posited by its own nature, since circulation is the passing of capital through the various conceptually determined moments of its necessary metamorphosis – its life process. In so far as it costs time for capital to run through this course, in this time capital cannot *increase* its value, because it is *not*-production time, time in which it does *not* appropriate living labour. Hence this circulation time can never increase the value created by capital, but can only posit *not-value-positing* time, hence appear as barrier to the increase of value, in the same relation as it stands towards labour time. This circulation time cannot be counted as part of value-creating time, for the latter is labour time which objectifies itself in value, and nothing else. It does not belong to the production costs of value, nor to the production costs of capital; but it is a condition which makes its self-reproduction more difficult. The obstacles which capital encounters in the path of its realization – i.e. its appropriation of living labour – do not, of course, form a moment of its realization, of its value-creation. Hence it is ridiculous to take *production costs* here in the original sense. Or we have to distinguish production costs as a particular form from the labour time which objectifies itself in value (as we must distinguish profit from surplus value). But even then, circulation time does not belong among capital's production costs in the same sense as wages etc.; but rather it is an item which comes into consideration as part of the capitalists' settling of accounts with one another, because they distribute the surplus value among themselves according to certain general proportions. Circulation time is not time during which capital creates value, but rather during which it realizes the value created in the production process. It does not increase its quantity, but rather transposes it into another form, from the form of product into that of commodity, from commodity to that of money etc.; the fact that the price which previously existed ideally in the commodity is now really posited, that it is now really exchanged for its price – money – does not, of course, increase this price. Thus circulation time appears as time which does not determine the price; and the number of turnovers, in so far as it is determined by circulation time, appears not in such a way that capital brings in a new value-determining element, an element proper to it, *sui generis*, as distinct from labour; but rather as a limiting, negative principle. The necessary tendency of capital is therefore *circulation without circulation time*, and this tendency is the fundamental determinant of credit and of capital's credit contrivances. At the same time, credit is then also a form in which capital tries to posit itself as distinct from the individual capitals, or the individual capital [tries to posit] itself as capital as distinct from its quantitative barrier. But the highest result it achieves in this line is, on one side, *fictitious capital*; on the other side, credit only appears as a new element of *concentration*, of the destruction of capitals by individual, centralizing capitals. Circulation time is in one respect objectified in *money*. Attempt by credit to posit money as a merely formal moment; so that it mediates the formal transformation without itself being *capital*, i.e. value. This is one form of circulation *without circulation time*. Money is itself a product of circulation. It will be shown how capital, in credit, creates new products of circulation. But if the striving of capital in one direction is *circulation without circulation time*, it strives in the other direction to give *circulation time value*, the value of *production time*, in the various organs which mediate the process of circulation time and of circulation; to posit them all as money, and, more broadly, as capital. This is another side of credit. All this springs from the same source. All the requirements of circulation, money, transformation of commodity into money, transformation of money into commodity etc. – although they take on different and seemingly quite heterogeneous forms, are all derived from *circulation time*. The machinery for abbreviating it is itself a part of it. *Circulation time* is that part of capital which may be regarded as the time it takes to perform its specific motion as capital, as distinct from production time, in which it reproduces itself; and in which it lives not as finished capital which must merely pass through formal metamorphoses, but as capital-in-process, creative capital, sucking its living soul out of labour.

The contradiction of labour time and circulation time contains the entire doctrine of credit, to the extent, namely, that the history of currency etc. enters here. Now, of course, later, where circulation time is not the only deduction from possible production time, there also appear real costs of circulation, i.e. values which have already been really posited must be spent on circulation. But these are all in fact only costs – deductions from already created surplus values – which capital undertakes in order to increase the sum of surplus values possible e.g. in a year, i.e. to increase the proportion of production time out of a given total time – i.e. to abbreviate circulation time. Of course, in practice, production time does not really appear interrupted by circulation time (except in crises and depressions of trade). But this is only because every capital is divided into parts, one part in the production phase, the other in the circulation phase. Thus, for example, it is not the entire capital that is active (depending on the relation of circulation time to production time), but only $\frac{1}{3}$, $1/x$ of it; the other is engaged in circulation. Or the matter can further take the form that a given capital doubles (through credit, e.g.). For this capital – the original capital – it is then the same as if circulation time did not exist at all. But then the capital borrowed by it is in this plight. And if ownership is disregarded, again exactly the same as if one capital were divided in two. Instead of *a* dividing into two and *b* dividing into two, *a* absorbs *b* and divides into *a* and *b*. Illusions about this process frequent among credit-mystics[59] (who are rarely creditors, but rather debtors).

We already pointed out above that the double and contra-

59. See p. 412, n. 26.

dictory condition of capital, the continuity of production and the necessity of circulation time, and also the continuity of circulation (not circulation time) and the necessity of production time, can be mediated only by capital dividing itself into parts, of which one *circulates as finished* product, and the other *reproduces itself in the production process*. These parts alternate; when one part returns into phase *P* (production process), the other departs. This process takes place daily, as well as at longer intervals (dimensions of time). The whole capital and the total value are reproduced as soon as both parts have passed through the production process and circulation process, or as soon as the second part enters anew into circulation. The point of departure is thereby the terminal point. The turnover therefore depends on the size of the capital, or rather, here, still on the *total sum* of these two parts. Only when the total sum is reproduced has the entire *turnover* been completed; otherwise only $\frac{1}{2}$, $\frac{1}{3}$, $1/x$, depending on the relation of the constantly circulating part.

It has further been emphasized that each part can be regarded as fixed or as circulating in contrast to the other, and that they really relate to each other in this alternating way. The simultaneity of the process of capital in different phases of the process is possible only through its division and break-up into parts, each of which is capital, but capital in a different aspect. This change of form and matter is like that in the organic body. If one says e.g. the body reproduces itself in 24 hours, this does not mean it does it all at once, but rather the shedding in one form and renewal in the other is distributed, takes place simultaneously. Incidentally, in the body the skeleton is the fixed capital; it does not renew itself in the same period of time as flesh, blood. There are different degrees of speed of consumption (self-consumption) and hence of reproduction. (Here, then, already *transition to* many capitals.) The important thing here above all is to examine capital as such for itself first of all; since the aspects being developed here are those which make value in general into capital; which constitute the specific distinguishing characteristics of capital as such.

Before we go further, let us call attention once more to the important point that circulation time – i.e. the time during which capital is separated from the process in which it absorbs labour, i.e. the labour time of capital as capital – is only the transposition of *previously created* value from one form into the other, but not a *value-creating*, value-*increasing* element. The transformation of a value of 4 working days existing in the form of twist into the form of 4 working days existing as money, or of a symbol recognized as the representative of 4 working days as such, 4 working days in general, transposes the *previously created* and *measured* value from one form into another, but that value is not increased. The exchange of equivalents leaves the working days *after* the exchange just as they were *before*, *qua* amounts of value. If one thinks of one capital, or one thinks of the various capitals of a country as one capital (national capital) as distinct from that of other countries, then it is clear that the time during which this capital does not act as productive capital, i.e. posits no surplus value, is a deduction from the realization time available to this capital. In this abstract conception, still without any regard to the costs of circulation itself, it appears as the negation not of the really posited realization time, but of the *possible* realization time, i.e. possible if circulation time $= 0$. It is clear, now, that the national capital cannot regard the time during which it does not multiply itself as time in which it does multiply itself, no more than e.g. an isolated peasant can regard the time during which he can neither harvest nor sow, during which his labour generally is interrupted, as time which makes him rich. The fact that capital regards itself, and necessarily so, as productive and fruit-bearing independently of labour, of the absorption of labour, assumes itself as fertile at all times, and calculates its circulation time as value-creating time – as production cost – is quite another thing. In this way one can see what is wrong when e.g. Ramsay says: 'the use of fixed capital modifies to a considerable extent the principle that value depends on quantity of labour. For some commodities on which the same quantity of labour has been expended require very different periods before they are fit for consumption. But as during this time the capital brings no return, *in order that the employment in question should not be less lucrative than others in which the produce is sooner ready for use*, it is necessary that the commodity, when at last brought to market, should be increased in value *by all the amount of profit withheld*.' (This already assumes that capital as such regularly brings profit, like a healthy tree brings fruit.) '*This shews . . . how capital may regulate value independently of labour.*'[60] E.g. wine in the cellar. (Ramsay, IX,

60. Ramsay, *An Essay on the Distribution of Wealth*, p. 43.

84.) Here as if circulation time as well as labour time – or on the same level with it – produced *value*. Capital, of course, contains both moments in itself. (1) *Labour time* as a value-creating moment. (2) *Circulation time* as a moment which restricts labour time and thus restricts the total value creation of capital; as necessary, because value, or capital, as an immediate result of the production process, is indeed *value*, but value not posited in its adequate form. The time which is required for these changes of form – i.e. which elapses between production and reproduction – is time which devalues capital. Thus, like *continuity*, so is the *interruption* of continuity contained in the character of capital as circulating, in process.

The economists who correctly characterize circulation, the revolution which capital must go through to fire itself up for new production, as a series of exchanges thereby admit that this circulation time is not time which increases the quantity of values – hence it cannot be time which posits new values – because a series of exchanges, no matter how many exchanges it may include, and how much time the completion of these operations may cost, is merely the exchange of equivalents. The positing of values – the extremes of the mediation – as equivalents naturally cannot posit them as non-equivalents. Regarded quantitatively, they can have neither increased nor diminished through the exchange.

The surplus value of a production phase is determined by the surplus labour set in motion (appropriated) by capital during it; the sum of the surplus values a capital can create in a given period of time is determined by the repetition of the production phase in this period of time; or by the *turnover* of capital. The turnover, however, equals the duration of the production phase plus the duration of circulation, equals the sum of circulation time and production time. The turnover approaches production time as circulation time diminishes, i.e. the time which elapses between capital's departure from production and its return to it.

Surplus value is in fact determined by the labour time objectified during one production phase. The more frequent the reproduction of capital, the more often does the production of surplus value take place. The number of reproductions = the number of turnovers. Hence the total surplus value = $S \times nR$ (if n is the number of turnovers). $S' = S \times nR$; hence $S = \dfrac{S'}{nR}$. If the pro-

duction time required by a capital of £100 in a certain branch of
industry equals 3 months, then it could turn over 4 times a year,
and if the *S*-value created each time = 5, then the total surplus
value = 5 (the *S* created in one production phase) × 4 (the
number of turnovers, determined by the relation of production
time to the year) = 20. But if circulation time = e.g. $\frac{1}{4}$ of production time, then 1 turnover would = 3 + 1 months, equals 4
months, and the capital of 100 could turn over only 3 times a
year = 15. Hence, although the capital posits an *S*-value of £5 in 3
months, it is the same for it as if it posited a value of 5 in only
4 months, because it can only posit 5 × 3 per year. It is the same
for it as if it produced an *S* of 5 every 4 months; hence produced
only $\frac{15}{4}$ or $3\frac{3}{4}$ in 3 months, and in the one circulation month,
$1\frac{1}{4}$. In so far as turnover is distinct from the duration posited by
the conditions of production, it is = to circulation time. The
latter, however, is not determined by labour time. In this way the
sum of surplus values which capital posits in a given period of
time appears determined not simply by labour time, but by
labour time as well as circulation time, in the relations indicated
above. But, as shown above, the determination which capital
here brings into the positing of value is *negative, limiting*.

If e.g. a capital of £100 needs 3 months for production, say 90
days, then, if circulation time = 0, the capital could turn over 4
times a year; and it would be *entirely* active as capital the whole
time, i.e. positing surplus labour, multiplying its value. If 80 of
the 90 days represented necessary labour, then 10, surplus labour.
Now posit that circulation time amounts to $33\frac{1}{3}\%$ of production
time, or $\frac{1}{3}$ of it. Hence 1 month for every 3. Circulation time then

$$= \tfrac{90}{3}; \text{ a third of production time} = 30 \text{ days}, c = \tfrac{1}{3}\,p;\ (c = \frac{p}{3}).$$

Well. The question is, what part of the capital can now continuously be occupied in production (during the whole year)? If the
capital of 100 had worked 90 days, and then circulated as a
product of 105 for one month, then during this month it could
employ no labour at all. (The 90 working days can of course
equal 3, 4, 5, *x* times 90, depending on the number of workers
employed during the 90 days. These would be = to only 90 days
if only 1 worker were employed. But this is beside the point for
now.) (In all these calculations it is presupposed that the surplus
value is not in turn capitalized, but that capital rather continues
to work with the same number of workers; but at the same time

as the surplus is realized, the entire capital is only then realized as money.) That is, during one month the capital could not be employed at all. (The capital of 100 employs e.g. 5 workers continuously; this contains their surplus labour, and the product which is circulated is never the original capital, but rather that which has absorbed this surplus labour and hence has a surplus value. Hence the circulation of a capital of 100 actually means e.g. circulation of the capital of 105; i.e. of capital together with the profit posited in one act of production. But this error irrelevant here, particularly in the above question.)

(Posit that at the end of 3 months £100 worth of twist have been produced.) Now it will be 1 month before the money comes in and I can begin production again. Now, in order to set the same number of workers to work during the 1 month while the capital is circulating, I would have to have a surplus capital of £33⅓; for if £100 set a given quantity of labour in motion for 3 months, then ⅓ of £100 would set it in motion for 1 month. At the end of the fourth month, the capital of 100 would return to the production phase, and that of 33⅓ would enter the circulation phase. The latter would require ⅓ of a month for circulation, given the same relations; would hence return into production after 10 days. The first capital could enter into circulation again only at the end of the seventh month. The second, which entered into circulation at the beginning of the fifth month, would have returned say on the 10th of the fifth month, would re-enter circulation on the 10th of the sixth month and would return on the 20th of the sixth month, to re-enter circulation on the 20th of the seventh month; at the end of the seventh month it would be back again, at which time the first capital would just be beginning its course again at the same moment when the second was returning. Beginning of the eighth month, and return on the etc. Beginning of the ninth etc. In a word: if the capital were ⅓ larger – just the amount the circulation time adds up to – then it could continuously employ the same number of workers. Or, alternately, it could continuously remain in the production phase if it continuously employed ⅓ less labour. If the capitalist began with a capital of only 75, then production would finish at the end of the third month; then the capital would circulate for one month; but during this month he could continue production because he would have retained a capital of 25, and, if he needs 75 to set a given mass of labour in motion during 3 months, he needs 25 to set the same in motion for 1 month. He would continuously have the same number of workers at work. Each of his commodities requires $\frac{1}{12}$ of a year before it is sold.

If he always needs $\frac{1}{3}$ of the production time to sell his commodities, then etc. This matter must be reducible to a very simple equation, to which we shall return later. It does not actually belong here. But the question is important because of the credit questions later. This much is clear, however. Call production time *pt*, circulation time *ct*. Capital, *C*. *C* cannot be in its production phase and its circulation phase at the same time. If it is to continue to produce while it circulates, then it must break into two parts, of which one in the production phase, while the other in the circulation phase, and the continuity of the process is maintained by part *a* being posited in the former aspect, part *b* in the latter. Let the portion which is always in production be *x*; then $x = C - b$ (let *b* be the part of the capital always in circulation). $C = b + x$. If *ct*, circulation time, were $= 0$, then *b* likewise would be $= 0$, and $x = C$. *b* (the part of the capital in circulation) : *C* (the total capital) $= ct$ (circulation time) : *pt* (production time); $b : C = ct : pt$; i.e. the relation of circulation time to production time is the relation of the part of capital in circulation to the total capital.

If a capital of 100 at a profit of 5% turns over every 4 months, so that there is 1 month of circulation time for every 3 months of production time, then the total surplus value, as we saw, will be $= \dfrac{5 \times 12}{4}$ *M* (month) $= 5 \times 3 = 15$; instead of 20 as when $c = 0$; for then $S' = \dfrac{5 \times 12}{3} = 20$. But now 15 is the gain on a capital of 75 at 5% whose circulation time $= 0$; which turned over 4 times a year; was continuously occupied. At the end of the first quarter $3\frac{3}{4}$; at the end of the year 15. (But only a total capital of 300 would turn over; while one of 400 if in the above case $ct = 0$.) Hence a capital of 100, with respect to which circulation time amounts to 1 month on every 3 *M* production time, can constantly employ productively a capital of 75; a capital of 25 is constantly circulating and unproductive. $75 : 25 = 3 \ M : 1 \ M$, or, if we call the part of the capital occupied in production *p*, the part in circulation *c*, and the corresponding times *c'* and *p'*, then $p : c = p' : c'$ ($p : c = 1 : \frac{1}{3}$). The part of the *C* in production constantly relates to the part in circulation as $1 : \frac{1}{3}$; this $\frac{1}{3}$ constantly

represented by changing component parts. But $p:C = 75:100$
$= \frac{3}{4}; \ c = \frac{1}{4}; \ p:C = 1:\frac{4}{3}$ and $c:C = 1:4$. The total turnover
$= 4 \ M, p:R = 3 \ M:4 \ M = 1:\frac{4}{3}$.

Change of form and of matter in the circulation of capital. –
C – M – C. M – C – M.

A change of form [*Formwechsel*] and a change of matter [*Stoff-wechsel*] take place simultaneously in the circulation of capital.
We must begin here not with the presupposition of M, but with
the production process. In production, as regards the material
side, the instrument is used up and the raw material is worked up.
The result is the product – a newly created use value, different
from its elemental presuppositions. As regards the material
side, a product is created only in the production process. This is
the first and essential material change. On the market, in the
exchange for money, the product is expelled from the circulation
of capital and falls prey to consumption, becomes object of consumption, whether for the final satisfaction of an individual need
or as raw material for another capital. In the exchange of the
commodity for money, the material and the formal changes
coincide; for, in money, precisely the content itself is part of the
economic form. The retransformation of money into commodity
is here, however, at the same time present in the retransformation
of capital into the material conditions of production. The reproduction of a specific use value takes place, just as well as of value
as such. But, just as the material element here was posited, from
the outset, at its entry into circulation, as a product, so the commodity in turn was posited as a condition of production at the
end of it. To the extent that money figures here as medium of
circulation, it does so indeed only as mediation of production,
on one side with consumption, in the exchange where capital
discharges value in the form of the product, and as mediation,
on the other side, between production and production, where
capital discharges itself in the form of money and draws the
commodity in the form of the condition of production into its
circulation. Regarded from the material side of capital, money
appears merely as a medium of circulation; from the formal side,
as the nominal measure of its realization, and, for a specific phase,
as value-for-itself; capital is therefore $C – M – M – C$ just as
much as it is $M – C – C – M$, and this in such a way, specific-

ally, that both forms of simple circulation here continue to be determinants, since M – M is money, which creates money, and C – C a commodity whose use value is both reproduced and increased. In regard to money circulation, which appears here as being absorbed into and determined by the circulation of capital, we want only to remark in passing – for the matter can be thoroughly treated only after the many capitals have been examined in their action and reaction upon one another – that money is obviously posited in different aspects here.

Difference between production time and labour time. – Storch. Money. Mercantile estate. Credit. Circulation

Until now it has been assumed that production time coincides with labour time. But now there take place, e.g. in agriculture, interruptions of work within the production process itself, before the product is finished. The same labour time may be applied and the duration of the production phase may differ, because work is interrupted. If the difference is only that the product in one case requires a longer working time in order to be finished than in another case, then no case at all is constituted, because it is then clear according to the general law that the product in which a greater quantity of labour is contained is of that much greater value, and if the reproduction is less frequent in a given period of time, then the reproduced value is all the greater. And 2 × 100 is just as much as 4 × 50. As with the total value, then, so with the surplus value. The question is constituted by the unequal duration required by different products, although the same amount of labour time (namely stored-up and living labour together) is employed upon them. The fixed capital here allegedly acts quite by itself, without human labour, like e.g. the seed entrusted to the earth's womb. In so far as additional labour is required, this is to be deducted. The question to be posed in pure form. If circulation time here the same, then the turnover is less frequent because the production phase longer. Hence production time + turnover time = 1R, larger than in the case where production time coincides with labour time. The time required here for the product to reach maturity, the interruptions of work, here constitute conditions of production. Not-labour time constitutes a condition for labour time, in order to turn the latter really into production time. The question obviously belongs only with the equalization of the rate of profit. Still, the ground must be cleared here. The slower return – this is the essential part – here arises not from circulation time, but rather from the conditions themselves in which labour becomes productive; it belongs with the technological conditions of the production process. It must absolutely be denied, it is downright nonsensical to claim, that a natural circumstance which hinders a capital in a specific branch of production from exchanging with the same amount of labour time in the same amount of time as another capital in another branch of production can in any way contribute to *increasing* the former's value. Value, hence also surplus value, is not = to the time which the production phase lasts, but rather to the labour time, objectified and living, employed during this production phase. The living labour time alone – and, indeed, in the proportion in which it is employed relative to objectified labour time – can create surplus value, because [it creates] surplus labour time.* It has therefore correctly been asserted that in this regard agriculture for instance is less productive (productivity is concerned here with the production of values) than other industries. Just as in another respect – *in so far as a growth of productivity in it* DIRECTLY *reduces necessary labour time – it is more productive than all the others.* But this circumstance can accrue to its advantage only where *capital* already rules, together with the general form of production corresponding to it. This interruption in the production phase already signifies that agriculture can never be the sphere in which capital starts; the sphere in which it takes up its original residence. This contradicts the primary fundamental conditions of industrial labour. Hence agriculture is claimed for capital and becomes industrial only retroactively. Requires a high development of competition on one side, on the other a great development of chemistry, mechanics etc., i.e. of manufacturing industry. History shows, consequently, that agriculture never *appears in pure form* in the modes of production preceding capital, or which correspond to its own undeveloped stages. A rural secondary industry, such as spinning, weaving etc. must make up for the limit on the employment of labour time posited here – and located in these interruptions. The non-

---

*It is clear that other aspects also enter in with the equalization of the rate of profit. Here, however, the issue is not the distribution of surplus value but its creation.

identity of production time with labour time can be due generally only to natural conditions, which stand directly in the path of the realization of labour, i.e. the appropriation of surplus labour by capital. These obstacles in its path do not of course constitute advantages, but rather, from its point of view, losses. The whole case is worth mentioning here actually only as an example of fixated capital, capital fixated in one phase. The point to remember here is only that capital creates no surplus value as long as it employs no living labour. The reproduction of the employed fixed capital itself is of course not the positing of surplus value.

(In the human body, as with capital, the different elements are not exchanged at the same rate of reproduction, blood renews itself more rapidly than muscle, muscle than bone, which in this respect may be regarded as the fixed capital of the human body.)

As means of speeding up circulation, Storch lists: (1) formation of a class of 'workers' who busy themselves only with trade; (2) easy means of transport; (3) money; (4) credit. (See above.)[61]

This motley combination reveals the whole confusion of the political economists. Money and money circulation – what we called simple circulation – is the presupposition, condition, of capital itself, as well as of the circulation of capital. Money as it exists, hence, as a relation of intercourse belonging to a stage of production preceding capital, money as money, in its immediate form, can therefore not be said to speed up the circulation of capital, but is rather its presupposition. When we speak of capital and of its circulation, we stand on a stage of social development where the introduction of money does not enter as a discovery etc., but is rather a *presupposition*. To the extent that money in its immediate form itself has value, and is not merely the value of other commodities, the symbol of their value – for, if something which is itself immediate is supposed to be something else which is also immediate, then it can only *represent* the latter, in one way or another, as symbol – but rather, itself has value, is itself objectified labour in a specific use value, to that extent, money, so far from speeding up the circulation of capital, rather delays it. Regarded in both of the aspects in which it occurs in the circulation of capital, both as medium of circulation and as the realized value of capital, money belongs among the costs of circulation in so far as it is itself labour time employed to abbrevi-

61. The quotation from Storch is on p. 637.

ate circulation time on the one hand, and, on the other hand, to represent a qualitative moment of circulation – the retransformation of capital into itself as value-for-itself. In neither aspect does it increase the value. In one aspect it is a precious form of representing value, i.e. a costly form, costing labour time, hence representing a deduction from surplus value. In the other aspect it can be regarded as a machine which saves circulation time, and hence frees time for production. But, in so far as it itself, as such a machine, costs labour and is a product of labour, it represents for capital *faux frais de production*. It figures among the costs of circulation. The original cost of circulation is circulation time itself as opposed to labour time. The real costs of circulation are themselves objectified labour time – machinery for the purpose of abbreviating the original costs of circulation. Money in its immediate form, as it belongs to a historic stage of production preceding capital, thus appears to capital as a cost of circulation, and the efforts of capital hence tend in the direction of transforming it into a form adequate for its own ends; hence attempting to make it into a representative of one moment of circulation which does not itself cost labour, and has itself no value. Capital hence tends in the direction of suspending money in its inherited, immediate reality, and transforming it into something merely *posited* and at the same time suspended by capital, into something purely *ideal*. It cannot be said, therefore, as does Storch, that money as such is a means of speeding up the circulation of capital; it must rather be said to the contrary that capital attempts to transform money into a merely *ideal* moment of its circulation, and first to raise it into the adequate form corresponding to it. Suspension of money in its immediate form appears as a demand made by money circulation once it has become a moment of the circulation of capital; because in its immediate, presupposed form it is a *barrier* to the circulation of capital. The tendency of capital is *circulation without circulation time*; hence also the positing of the instruments which merely serve to abbreviate circulation time as mere *formal aspects* posited by it, just as the different moments through which capital passes in its circulation are qualitative aspects of its own metamorphosis.

As regards the formation of a special mercantile estate – i.e. a development of the division of labour which has transformed the business of exchanging into a particular kind of work – for which, of course, the sum of exchange operations must already have reached a certain height – (if the exchange among 100 people occupied the 100th part of their labour time, then each man is $\frac{1}{100}$ of an exchanger; $\frac{100}{100}$ exchangers would represent one single man. Then one merchant could arise per 100. The separation of commerce from production itself, or the development of exchange itself as a representation opposite the exchangers, requires as such that exchange and intercourse have developed to a certain degree. The merchant represents all buyers to the seller, all sellers to the buyer and vice versa, hence he is not an extreme, but rather the middle of the exchange itself; appears hence as mediator, middleman) – the formation of the merchant estate, which presupposes that of money, even if not developed in all its moments, is likewise a presupposition for capital, and hence cannot be listed as being a mediator of its specific circulation. Since commerce is both historically as well as conceptually a presupposition for the rise of capital, we shall have to return to it before concluding this chapter, since it belongs before or in the section on the origin of capital.

The facilitation of the means of transport, to the extent that it means facilitation of the physical circulation of commodities, does not belong here, where we are examining merely the characteristic forms of the circulation of capital. The product becomes a commodity, leaves the production phase, only when it is on the *market*. On the other side, the means of transportation do belong here in so far as the *returns* of capital – i.e. circulation time – must grow with the distance of the market from the point of production. Its abbreviation by means of transport thus appears as belonging directly, in this respect directly, to the examination of the circulation of capital. But this actually belongs to the doctrine of the market, which itself belongs to the section on capital.

Finally, *credit*. This form of circulation etc. directly posited by capital – which arises, hence, specifically from the nature of capital, this specific characteristic of capital – is mixed up here by Storch etc. together with money, mercantile estate, etc., which belong generally with the development of exchange and of the production more or less founded on it. The presentation of the specific, distinguishing characteristics is here both the *logical* development and the key to the understanding of the *historical* development. Thus we find in history, too, e.g. in England (likewise in France), [attempts] to replace money by paper; then also to give capital, in so far as it exists in the form of *value*, a form purely posited by itself; finally attempts to found credit directly with the rise of capital. (E.g. Petty, Boisguillebert.)

Small-scale circulation. The process of exchange between capital and labour capacity generally. Capital in the reproduction of labour capacities

Within circulation as the total process, we can distinguish between large-scale and small-scale circulation. The former spans the entire period from the moment when capital exits from the production process until it enters it again. The second is continuous and constantly proceeds simultaneously with the production process. It is the part of capital which is paid out as wages, exchanged for labouring capacity. The circulation process of capital, which is posited in the form of an exchange of equivalents, but is in fact suspended as such, and posited as such only formally (the transition from value to capital, where the exchange of equivalents turns into its opposite, and where, on the basis of exchange, exchange becomes purely formal, and the mutuality is all on one side), is to be developed in this way: Values which become exchanged are always objectified labour time, an objectively available, *reciprocally* presupposed quantity of labour (present in a use value). Value as such is always an effect, never a cause. It expresses the amount of labour by which an object is produced, hence – presupposing the same stage of the productive forces – the amount of labour by which it can be reproduced. The capitalist does not exchange capital directly for labour or labour time; but rather time contained, worked up in commodities, for time contained, worked up in living labour capacity. The living labour time he gets in exchange is not the exchange value, but the use value of labour capacity. Just as a machine is not exchanged, paid for as cause of effects, but as itself an effect; not according to its use value in the production process, but rather as product – definite amount of objectified labour. The labour time contained in labour capacity, i.e. the time required to produce living labour capacity, is the same as is required – presupposing the same stage of the productive forces – to reproduce it, i.e. to maintain it. Hence, the exchange which proceeds between capitalist and worker thus corresponds completely to the laws of exchange; it not only corresponds to them, but also is their highest development. For, as long as labour capacity does not itself exchange itself, the foundation of production does not yet rest on exchange, but exchange is rather merely a narrow circle resting on a foundation of non-exchange, as in all stages preceding bourgeois production. But the use value of the value the capitalist has acquired through exchange is itself the element of realization and its measure, living labour and labour time, and, specifically, more labour time than is objectified in labour capacity, i.e. more labour time than the reproduction of the living worker costs. Hence, by virtue of having acquired labour capacity in exchange as an equivalent, capital has acquired labour time – to the extent that it exceeds the labour time contained in labour capacity – in exchange *without equivalent*; it has appropriated alien labour time *without exchange* by means of the *form* of exchange. This is why exchange becomes merely formal, and, as we saw, in the further development of capital even the semblance is suspended that capital exchanges for labour capacity anything other than the latter's own objectified labour; i.e. that it exchanges anything at all for it. The turn into its opposite [*Umschlag*] therefore comes about because the ultimate stage of free exchange is the exchange of labour capacity as a commodity, as value, for a commodity, for value; because it is given in exchange as objectified labour, while its use value, by contrast, consists of living labour, i.e. of the positing of exchange value. The turn into its opposite arises from the fact that the use value of labour capacity, as value, is itself the value-creating force; the substance of value, and the value-increasing substance. In this exchange, then, the worker receives the equivalent of the labour time objectified in him, and gives his value-creating, value-increasing living labour time. He sells himself as an effect. He is absorbed into the body of capital as a cause, as activity. Thus the exchange turns into its opposite, and the laws of private property – liberty, equality, property – property in one's own labour, and free disposition over it – turn into the worker's propertylessness, and the dispossession [*Entäusserung*] of his labour, [i.e.] the fact that he relates to it as alien property and vice versa.

The circulation of the part of capital which is posited as wages accompanies the production process, appears as an economic form-relation alongside it, and is simultaneous and interwoven with it. This circulation alone posits capital as such; is the condition of its realization process, and posits not only the latter's characteristic form, but also its substance. This is the constantly circulating part of capital, which at no time enters into the production process itself, [but] constantly accompanies it. It is the part of capital which does not even for a single instant enter into its reproduction process, which is not the case with raw material. The worker's *approvisionnement* arises out of the production process, as product, as result; but it never enters as such into the production process, because it is a finished product for individual consumption, enters directly into the worker's consumption, and is directly exchanged for it. This, therefore, as distinct from raw material as well as instrument, is the circulating capital κατ᾽ ἐξοχήν. Here is the only moment in the circulation of capital where consumption enters directly. At the point where the commodity becomes exchanged for money, it may be acquired by another capital as raw material for new production. Further, given the presuppositions, capital encounters not the individual consumer but rather the merchant; someone who buys the commodity itself in order to sell it for money. (This presupposition is to be developed in connection with the merchant estate in general. The circulation among dealers thereby different from that between dealers and consumers.) Thus the circulating capital here appears directly as that which is specified for the workers' individual consumption; specified for direct consumption generally, and hence existing in the form of finished product. Thus, while in one respect capital appears as the presupposition of the product, the finished product also at the same time appears as the presupposition of capital – which means, historically, that capital did not begin the world from the beginning, but rather encountered production and products already present, before it subjugated them beneath its process. Once in motion, proceeding from itself as basis, it constantly posits itself ahead of itself in its various forms as consumable product, raw material and instrument of labour, in order constantly to reproduce itself in these forms. They appear initially as the conditions presupposed by it, and then as its result. In its reproduction it produces its own conditions. Here, then – through the relation of capital to living labour capacity and to the natural conditions of the latter's maintenance – we find circulating capital specified in respect of its use value as well, as that which enters directly into individual consumption, to be directly used up by the latter. It is a mistake to conclude from this, as has been done,[62] that circulating capital is therefore *consumable* capital generally, as if coal, oil, dye etc., instruments etc., improvements of the land etc. factories etc. were not all consumed likewise, if by consumption is meant the suspension of their use value and of their form; however, one could just as well say that none of them is consumed, if this is taken to mean individual consumption, i.e. consumption in the proper sense. In this circulation, capital constantly expels itself as objectified labour, in order to assimilate living labour power, its life's breath. Now, as regards the worker's consumption, this reproduces one thing – namely himself, as living labour capacity. *Because this, his reproduction, is itself a condition for capital, therefore the worker's consumption also appears as the reproduction not of capital directly, but of the relations under which alone it is capital. Living labour capacity belongs just as much among capital's conditions of existence as do raw material and instrument. Thus it reproduces itself doubly, in its own form, [and] in the worker's consumption, but only to the extent that it reproduces him as living labour capacity.* Capital therefore calls this consumption productive consumption – productive not in so far as it reproduces the individual, but rather individuals as labour capacities. If Rossi is offended that wages are allegedly counted twice, first as the worker's revenue, then as reproductive consumption of capital,[63] then the objection holds only against those who let wages enter directly into the production process of capital as value. For the payment of wages is an act of circulation which proceeds simultaneously with and alongside the act of production. Or, as Sismondi says from this perspective – the worker consumes his wages unreproductively; but the capitalist consumes them productively, since he gets labour in the exchange, which reproduces the wages and more than the wages. This concerns capital itself regarded merely as an object. But in so far as capital is a relation, and, specifically, a relation to living labour capacity, [to that extent] the worker's consumption reproduces this relation; or, capital reproduces itself doubly, as value through purchase of labour – as a possibility of beginning the realization process anew, of acting as capital anew – and as a relation through the worker's

62. By de Quincey and Ramsay; see above, pp. 642–3.
63. See above, p. 592, and Rossi, *Cours d'économie politique*, p. 370.

consumption, which reproduces him as labour capacity exchange-able for capital – wages as part of capital.

This circulation between capital and labour, then, yields the characterization of one part of capital as constantly circulating, the *approvisionnement*; constantly consumed; constantly to re-produce. This circulation strikingly reveals the difference be-tween capital and money; the circulation of capital and the circulation of money. Capital pays wages e.g. weekly; the worker takes his wages to the grocer etc.; the latter directly or indirectly deposits them with the banker; and the following week the manufacturer takes them from the banker again, in order to distribute them among the same workers again, etc. and so forth. The same sum of money constantly circulates new portions of capital. The sum of money itself, however, does not determine the portions of capital which are thus circulated. If the money value of wages rises, then the circulating medium will increase, but the mass of the medium does not determine the rise. If the production costs of money did not fall, then no increase of money would exercise an influence on the portion of it entering into this circu-lation. Here money appears as mere medium of circulation. Since many workers are to be paid at the same time, a certain sum of money is required at one time, which grows with the number of workers. Then, however, the velocity of the circulation of the money makes a lesser sum necessary than in situations where there are fewer workers but the machinery of monetary circu-lation is not so arranged. This circulation is a condition of the production process and thereby of the circulation process as well. On the other hand, if capital does not return from circulation, then this circulation between worker and capital could not begin anew; hence it is itself conditional upon capital passing through the various moments of its metamorphosis *outside* the production process. If this did not happen, it would be not because there was not enough *money* as *medium of circulation*, but rather either because capital was not available in the form of products, because this part of *circulating* capital was lacking, or because capital did not posit itself in the *form of money*, i.e. did not realize itself as capital, which in turn, however, would arise not from the quantity of the medium of circulation, but because capital did not posit itself in the *qualitative aspect* of money, which in no way requires that it posit itself in the form of hard cash, in the immediate money form; and whether or not it posited itself in that form would again depend not on the quantity of money circulating as medium of circulation, but rather on the exchange of capital for value as such; again a qualitative, not a quantitative, moment, as we shall point out in more detail when we speak of capital as money. (Interest etc.)

Threefold character, or mode, of circulation. – *Fixed capital and circulating capital. – Turnover time of the total capital divided into circulating and fixed capital. – Average turnover time of such a capital. – Influence of fixed capital on the total turnover time of capital. – Circulating fixed capital.* Say. Smith. Lauderdale. (*Lauderdale on the origin of* profit)

Regarded as a whole, circulation thus appears threefold: (1) the total process – the course of capital through its different moments; accordingly, it is posited as being in flow; as circulating; in so far as the continuity is virtually interrupted, and may resist the passage into the next phase, capital here likewise appears as fixated in different relations, and the various modes of this fixation constitute different capitals, commodity capital, money capital, capital as conditions of pioduction.

(2) Small-scale circulation between capital and labour capacity. This accompanies the production process and appears as contract, exchange, form of intercourse; these things are presupposed before the production process can be set going. The part of capital entering into this circulation – the approvisionnement – is circulating capital κατ' ἐξοχήν. It is specified not only in respect to its form; in addition to this, its use value, i.e. its material character as a consumable product entering directly into individual consumption, itself constitutes a part of its form.

(3) Large-scale circulation; the movement of capital outside the production phase, where its time appears in antithesis to labour time, as circulation time. The distinction between *fluid* and *fixed capital* is the product of this opposition between the capital engaged in the production phase and the capital which issues from it. Fixed is that which is fixated in the production process and is consumed within it; comes out of large-scale circulation, certainly, but does not return into it, and, in so far as it circulates, circulates only in order to be consumed in, confined to, the consumption process.

The three different distinctions in the circulation of capital yield the three distinctions between circulating and fixated capital; they posit one part of capital as circulating κατ' ἐξοχήν, because it never enters into the production process, but constantly accompanies it; and thirdly, [they yield] the distinction between *fluid* and *fixed* capital. Circulating capital in form No. 3 also includes No. 2, since the latter is also in antithesis to the fixed; but No. 2 does not include No. 3. The part of capital which belongs as such to the production process is the part of it which serves, materially, only as *means of production*; forms the link between living labour and the material to be worked on. A part of the liquid capital, such as coal, oil etc., also serves merely as means of production. Everything which serves merely as a means to keep the machine, or the engine, running. This distinction will have to be examined yet more closely. First of all, this does not contradict aspect 1, since the fixed capital as *value* also circulates in proportion as it is worn out. Precisely in this aspect as *fixed* capital – i.e. in the character in which capital has lost its fluidity and become identified with a *specific* use value, which robs it of its ability to transform itself – does *developed capital* – to the extent we know it so far, as productive capital – most strikingly manifest itself, and it is precisely in this seemingly inadequate form, and in the latter's increasing relation to the form of circulating capital in No. 2, that the development of capital as capital is measured. This contradiction pretty. To be developed.

The different kinds of capital, which, in economics, fall out of the sky, here appear as so many precipitates of the movements arising out of the nature of capital itself, or rather of this movement itself in its different moments.

Circulating capital constantly 'parts' from the capitalist, in order to return to him in the first form. *Fixed capital* does not (Storch).[64] '*Circulating capital* is that portion of the capital which does not yield profit *till it is parted with*; fixed etc. yields such profit, *while it remains in the possession of the owner.*' (Malthus.)[65] 'Circulating capital gives its master no revenue or profit, *so long as it remains in his possession*; *fixed capital* gives this profit without changing masters, and without requiring circulation.' (A. Smith.)[66]

64. Storch, *Cours d'économie politique*, Vol. I, p. 405.

65. Malthus, *Definitions in Political Economy*, pp. 237–8.

66. Adam Smith, *Recherches sur la nature et les causes de la richesse des nations*, Vol. II, pp. 197–8.

In this respect, since capital's departure on a voyage away from its owner ('*partir de son possesseur*')[67] means nothing more than the *sale* of property or possessions which takes place in the act of exchange, and since it is the nature of all exchange value, hence all capital, to become value for its owner by means of sale, the definition in its above formulation cannot be correct. If fixed capital were [capital] for its owner without the mediation of exchange and of the use value[68] included in it, then, in fact, fixed capital would be a mere use value, hence not capital. But the basis of the above definition is this: fixed capital circulates as *value* (even if only in portions, successively, as we shall see). It does not circulate as *use value*. As far as its material aspect is concerned, as a moment of the production process, *fixed capital* never leaves its boundaries; is not sold by its possessor; remains in his hand. It circulates as capital only in its *formal aspect*, as self-eternalizing value. This distinction between form and content, use value and exchange value, does not take place in circulating capital. In order to circulate, to exist, as the latter, it has to step into circulation as the former, must be sold. Use value for *capital* as such is only value itself. Circulating capital realizes itself as value for capital as such only when it is sold. As long as it remains in its hand, it only has value *in itself*; but it is not *posited*; only in potency – but not in act. Fixed capital, by contrast, realizes itself as value only as long as it remains in the capitalist's hand as a use value, or, expressed as an objective relation, as long as it remains in the production process, which may be regarded as the inner organic movement of capital, its relation to itself, as opposed to its animal movement, its presence for another. Hence, since *fixed capital*, once it has entered the production process, remains in it, it also passes away in it, is consumed in it. The duration of this consumption does not yet concern us here. In this respect, then, *fixed capital* also includes what Cherbuliez calls the *matières instrumentales*,[69] such as coal, oil, wood, grease etc., which are completely destroyed in the production process, which only have a *use value* for the process of production itself. The same materials, however, also have a use value outside production, and can also be consumed in another way, just as buildings, houses, etc. are

67. '*partir de son possesseur*'. Storch, *Cours d'économie politique*, Vol. I, p. 405.

68. 'Use value': this ought to read 'exchange value'.

69. Cherbuliez, *Richesse ou pauvreté*, pp. 14–15.

not necessarily specified for production. They are *fixed capital* not because of the specific mode of their being, but rather because of their use. They become fixed capital as soon as they step into the production process. They are *fixed capital*, as soon as they are posited as moments of the production process of capital; because they then lose their property of being potentially circulating capital.

Therefore, just as the part of capital entering into the small-scale circulation of capital – or capital, in so far as it enters into this movement – circulation between capital and labour capacity, the part of capital circulating as wages – *never leaves the circulation process and never enters into the production process of capital*, as regards its material aspect, as use value, but rather is always ejected from a previous production process as its product, result, so, inversely, does the part of capital specified as *fixed capital*, as a use value, as regards its material presence, never leave the *production process* and *never go back into circulation*. While the latter only enters into circulation as *value* (as part of the value of the finished product), the former only enters into the production process as *value*, in that necessary labour is the reproduction of wages, of the part of the capital's value which circulates as wages. This, then, is the *first* characteristic of fixed capital, and in this respect it also includes the *matières instrumentales*.

Secondly: Fixed capital can enter into circulation as value, however, only to the extent that it passes away as use value in the production process. It passes, as value, into the product – i.e. as labour time worked up or stored up in it – in so far as it passes away in its independent form as use value. In being used, it is used up, but in such a way that its value is carried over from its form into the form of the product. If it is not used, not consumed in the production process itself – if the machinery stands still, the iron rusts, the wood rots – then of course its value passes away together with its transitory presence as use value. Its circulation as value corresponds to its consumption in the production process as use value. Its total value is completely reproduced, i.e. is fully returned via circulation only when it has been completely consumed as use value in the production process. As soon as it is completely dissolved into value, and hence completely absorbed into circulation, it has completely passed away as use value and hence must be replaced, as a necessary moment of production, by a new use value of the same kind, i.e. must be reproduced. The necessity of reproducing it, i.e. its reproduction time, is determined by the time in which it is used up, consumed within the production process. With circulating capital, reproduction is determined by circulation time; with fixed capital, circulation is determined by the time in which it is consumed as use value, in its material presence, within the act of production, i.e. by the period of time within which it must be reproduced. A thousand pounds of twist can be reproduced as soon as they are sold and the money obtained for them is again exchanged for cotton, in short, for the elements of the production of twist. Their reproduction is determined, hence, by circulation time. A machine of a value of £1,000 which lasts 5 years, which is used up in 5 years and then becomes nothing more than scrap iron, is used up, say, by $\frac{1}{5}$ per year, if we take the average consumption in the production process. Hence every year only $\frac{1}{5}$ of its value enters into circulation, and only with the passing of the 5 years has it completely gone into circulation and returned from it. Its entry into circulation is thus purely determined by the time of its wearing out; and the time which its value needs to enter totally into circulation and to return from it is determined by its total reproduction time, the time in which it must be reproduced. Fixed capital enters into the product only as value; while the use value of circulating capital has remained in the product as the latter's substance, and has merely obtained another form. This distinction essentially modifies the *turnover time* of a total capital divided into circulating and fixed capital. Let total capital $= S$; its circulating part $= c$; its fixed part $= f$; let the fixed capital form $\frac{1}{x}S$; the circulating capital $\frac{S}{y}$. Let the circulating capital turn over 3 times a year, the fixed capital only twice every 10 years. In 10 years, f or $\frac{S}{x}$ will turn over twice; while in the same 10 years $\frac{S}{y}$ will turn over $3 \times 10 = 30$ times. If S were $= \frac{S}{y}$, i.e. circulating capital only, then R, its turnover, would be $= 30$; and the total capital turned over $= 30 \times \frac{S}{y}$; the total capital turned over in 10 years. But the fixed capital turns over only twice in 10 years. Its $R' = 2$; and the total fixed capital turned over $= \frac{2S}{x}$. But $S = \frac{S}{y} + \frac{S}{x}$ and its total turnover time = the total turnover time of both these parts. If the fixed capital turns over twice in 10 years, then in one year $\frac{2}{10}$ or $\frac{1}{5}$ of it turns over; while in one year the circulating capital turns over 3 times. $\frac{S}{5x}$ turns over once a year.

The question simply this: if a capital of 1,000 thalers = 600 circulating capital and 400 fixed capital; thus $\frac{3}{5}$ circulating and $\frac{2}{5}$ fixed capital; if the fixed capital lasts 5 years, hence turns over once in 5 years and the circulating turns over 3 times a year, then what is the average turnover or turnover time of the total capital? If it were circulating capital only, then it would turn over 5 × 3, 15 times; the total capital turned over in the 5 years would be 15,000. But $\frac{2}{5}$ of it turn over only once in 5 years. Hence, of the 400 thalers, $\frac{400}{5} = 80$ thalers turn over in one year. Of the 1,000 thalers, 600 annually turn over 3 times, 80 once; or, in one year, only 1,880 would turn over; hence in 5 years 5 × 1,880 = 9,400 turn over; i.e. 5,600 less than if the total capital consisted only of circulating capital. If the entire capital consisted only of circulating capital, then it would turn over once in $\frac{1}{3}$ of a year.

If the capital = 1,000; $c = 600$, turns over twice a year; $f = 400$, turns over once a year; then 600 ($\frac{3}{5}S$) turns over in half a year; $\frac{400}{2}$ or $\left(\frac{2S}{5 \times 2}\right)$ likewise in half a year. Hence in half a year, 600 + 200 = 800 (i.e. $c + f/2$) turns over. IN A WHOLE YEAR, hence, 2 × 800 or 1,600 turn over; 1,600 thalers in 1 year; hence 100 in $\frac{12}{16}$ months, hence 1,000 in $\frac{120}{16}$ months = $7\frac{1}{2}$ months. The total capital of 1,000 thus turns over in $7\frac{1}{2}$ months, while it would turn over in 6 months if it consisted of circulating capital only. $7\frac{1}{2}:6 = 1:1\frac{1}{4}$ or as $1:\frac{5}{4}$. If the capital = 100, circulating = 50, fixed = 50; the former turns over twice a year, the latter once; then $\frac{1}{2}$ 100 turns over once in 6 months; and $\frac{1}{4}$ 100 likewise once in 6 months; hence in 6 months $\frac{3}{4}$ of the capital turns over, $\frac{3}{4}$ 100 in 6 months; or 75 in 6 months, and 100 in 8 months. If $\frac{2}{4}$ 100 turn over in 6 months, and in the same 6 months $\frac{1}{4}$ 100 ($\frac{1}{2}$ of the fixed capital), then $\frac{3}{4}$ 100 turn over in 6 months. Hence $\frac{1}{4}$ in $\frac{6}{3} = 2$ [months]; hence $\frac{4}{4}$ 100 or 100 in 6 + 2, in 8 months. The total turnover time of the capital = 6 (the turnover time of the entire circulating capital and $\frac{1}{2}$ of the fixed capital or $\frac{1}{4}$ of the total capital) + $\frac{6}{3}$, i.e. + this turnover time divided by the number expressing the ratio of the remaining fixed capital to the capital turned over in the turnover time of circulating capital. Thus in the above example: $\frac{2}{3}$ 100 turns over in 6 months; ditto $\frac{1}{3}$ 100; hence $\frac{2}{3}$ 100 in 6 months; hence the remaining $\frac{1}{3}$ 100 in $\frac{6}{4}$ months; hence the total capital in $6 + \frac{6}{4}$ months $= 6 + 1\frac{1}{2}$ or $7\frac{1}{2}$ months. Thus, expressed in general terms:

Average turnover time $=$ the turnover time of circulating capital $+$ this turnover time divided by the number which expresses how often the remaining part of the fixed capital is contained in the total sum of the capital which was circulated in this turnover time.

If there are two capitals of 100 thalers, one of them entirely composed of circulating capital, the other half fixed capital, each at 5% profit, the one turning over twice a year, and in the other the circulating capital likewise twice, but the fixed capital only once; then the total capital turning over would be $= 200$ in the first case, and the profit $= 10$; in the second $= 3$ turnovers in 8 months, $1\frac{1}{2}$ in 4; or 150 would turn over in 12 months; profit then $= 7\frac{1}{2}$. This kind of calculation has strengthened the common prejudice that circulating capital or fixed capital through some mysterious innate power brings a gain, as even in Malthus's phrase 'the circulating capital brings a gain when its possessors part with it etc.'[70]; likewise, in the above-quoted lines from his *Measure of Value* etc., the way in which he makes fixed capital accumulate profits.[71] The greatest confusion and mystification has arisen because the doctrine of surplus profit has not been examined in its pure form by previous economists, but rather mixed in together with the doctrine of real profit, which leads up to distribution, where the various capitals participate in the general rate of profit. The profit of the capitalists as a class, or the profit of *capital* as such, has to exist before it can be distributed, and it is extremely absurd to try to explain its origin by its distribution. According to the above, profit declines because the turnover time of capital increases* in proportion as the component

* Its size posited as permanent – this does not concern us here at all, since the statement is true for a capital of any size. Capitals have different sizes. But the size of each individual capital *is equal to itself*, hence, in so far as only its quality as capital is concerned, any size. But if we examine two capitals in comparison to each other, then the difference in their size introduces a relation of a qualitative characters. Size becomes itself a distinguishing quality.

70. Màlthus, *Definitions in Political Economy*, pp. 237–8.
71. See above, p. 574, and Malthus, *The Measure of Value*, p. 33.

part of it which is called fixed capital increases. A capital of the same size, 100 in the above case, would turn over entirely twice a year if it consisted only of a circulating capital. But it turns over only twice in 16 months, or only 150 thalers are turned over in one year, because half of it consists of fixed capital. As the number of its reproductions in a given period declines, or the amount of it reproduced in this given time declines, so does the production of surplus time or surplus value decline, since capital posits value at all only in so far as it posits surplus value. (This at least is its tendency, its adequate action.)

Fixed capital, as we saw, circulates as value only to the degree that it is used up or consumed as use value in the production process. But the time in which it is consumed and in which it must be reproduced in its form as use value depends on its relative durability. Hence its durability, or its greater or lesser perishability – the greater or smaller amount of time during which it can continue to perform its function within the repeated production processes of capital – this aspect of its use value here becomes a form-determining moment, i.e. a determinant for capital as regards its form, not as regards its matter. The necessary reproduction time of fixed capital, together with the proportion of the total capital consisting of it, here modify, therefore, the turnover time of the total capital, and thereby its realization. The greater durability of capital (the diminution (duration) of its necessary reproduction time) and the proportion of fixed capital to the total capital, then, here influence realization just as does a slower turnover due either to a greater distance in space of the market from which the capital returns as money, so that a longer time is required to complete the path of circulation (as e.g. capitals working in England for the East India market return more slowly than those working for nearer foreign markets or for the domestic market), or to the production phase being itself interrupted by natural conditions, as in agriculture. Ricardo, who was the first to emphasize the influence of fixed capital on the realization process, throws all these aspects into one motley heap, as one can see from the excerpts quoted above.[72]

This is an essential aspect, of which size is only one single instance, of how the study of capital as such differs from the study of one capital in relation to another capital, or the study of capital in its reality.

72. See above, pp. 644–5.

In the first case (fixed capital), the turnover of capital is reduced because the fixed capital is consumed slowly within the production process; or the cause lies in the duration of the time required for its reproduction. In the second case the reduced turnover arises from the prolongation of *circulation time* (in the first case the fixed capital necessarily always circulates as rapidly as the product, *in so far as* it circulates, enters circulation at all, because it circulates not in its material existence, but only as value, i.e. as an ideal component part of the total value of the product) and, specifically, from the circulation time of the second half of the circulation process proper, the retransformation into money; in the third case the reduced turnover arises from the longer time the capital requires, not, as in the first case, to pass away in the production process, but rather to emerge from it as product. The first case is peculiar specifically to fixed capital; the other belongs to the category of capital which is not liquid, but fixated, fixated in one or another phase of the total circulation process (fixed capital of a considerable degree of durability, *or* circulating capital returnable at distant periods. McCulloch, *Principles of Political Economy*. Notebook, p. 15.)[73]

Thirdly: We have regarded fixed capital so far only from the aspect in which its particular relation, its specific relation, distinguishes it from the circulation process proper. Still further distinctions will arise in this respect. Firstly, the return of its value in successive parts, whereas each part of circulating capital is exchanged in its entirety; this because in the former, the existence of the value coincides with that of the use value. Secondly, not merely [because of] its influence on the average turnover time of a given capital, as we have indicated up to now, but also [because of] its own turnover time. The latter circumstance becomes important where the fixed capital appears not as a mere instrument of production within the production process, but rather as an independent form of capital, e.g. in the form of railways, canals, roads, aqueducts, improvements of the land, etc. This latter aspect becomes notably important for the proportion in which the total capital of a country is divided into these two forms. Then, the way in which it is renewed and maintained; which the economists formulate in the form that it can bring revenue only by means of circulating capital etc. This last is basically nothing but the examination of the moment where it appears, not as a particular

73. MacCulloch, *The Principles of Political Economy*, p. 300.

independent existence *alongside* and *outside* circulating capital, but rather as circulating capital transformed into fixed capital. But what we want to examine here first of all is the relation of fixed capital not towards the outside, but rather the extent to which the relation is given through its continued enclosure within the production process. It is thereby posited that it is a definite moment of the production process itself.

⟨It is not necessarily the case that *fixed capital* is capital which in all its aspects serves not for individual consumption, but only for production. A house can serve for production as well as for consumption; likewise all vehicles, a ship and a wagon, for pleasure outings as well as a means of transport; a street as a means of communication for production proper, as well as for taking walks etc. *Fixed capital* in this second aspect does not concern us here at all, since we regard capital here only as process of realization and process of production. The second aspect will enter when we study interest. Ricardo can have only this aspect in mind when he says: 'Depending on whether the capital is more or less perishable, hence must be more or less frequently reproduced in a given time, it is called circulating or fixed capital.' (Ricardo, VIII, 19.)[74] According to this, a coffee-pot would be fixed capital, but coffee circulating capital. The crude materialism of the economists who regard as the *natural properties* of things what are social relations of production among people, and qualities which things obtain because they are subsumed under these relations, is at the same time just as crude an idealism, even fetishism, since it imputes social relations to things as inherent characteristics, and thus mystifies them. (The difficulty of defining a thing as fixed capital or circulating capital on the basis of its natural qualities has here, by way of exception, led the economists to the discovery that things in themselves are neither fixed nor circulating, hence not capital at all, any more than it is a natural quality of gold to be money.⟩

(Also included in the points listed above, so that it is not forgotten, is the circulation of fixed capital as circulating capital, i.e. transactions through which it changes its owners.)

'Fixed capital – *tied up*: capital so *tied up in one kind of production* that it can no longer be diverted to *another kind of production.*' (Say, 24.)[75] 'Fixed capital is consumed in order to help

74. Ricardo, *On the Principles of Political Economy*, p. 26.
75. J.-B. Say, *Traité d'économie politique*, Vol. II, p. 430.

produce the things useful to man . . . it consists of *durable founda-tions which increase the productive powers of future labour.*' (Sismondi, VI.) [76] '*Fixed capital* the capital necessary to main-tain the instruments, machines etc. of labour.' (Smith, Vol. II, p. 226.) 'Floating capital is consumed, fixed capital merely used in the great work of production.' (*Economist*. Notebook VI, p. 1.)[77] 'We shall show that the first stick or the first stone which he took in his hand to assist him in the pursuit of these objects, by accomplishing a part of his labour, performed precisely the function of the capitals presently employed by the commercial nations.' (Lauderdale, p. 120. Notebook, 8a.) 'It is one of the characteristic and distinguishing traits of the human species to *replace labour in this way* with a capital transformed into ma-chines.' (p. 120.) (p. 9, Notebook Lauderdale.) 'It may now be seen that the profit of capitals always arises either because they replace a portion of the work which man must do by hand, or because they accomplish a portion of work which is beyond the personal effort of man, and which he could not perform by him-self.' (p. 119 loc. cit.) Lauderdale polemicizes against Smith and Locke, whose view that labour is the creator of profit, has the following result, according to him: 'if this idea of capital's benefits were rigorously correct, then it would follow that it would not be an *original source* of wealth, but rather a derived one; and one could not consider capital as one of the principles of wealth, its *profit being nothing more than a transfer from the worker's pocket to that of the capitalist.*' (loc. cit. 116, 117.) 'The profit of capitals always arises either because they *replace* a portion of the work which man must do by hand, or because they accomplish a portion of work which is beyond the personal effort of man, and which he could not perform by himself.' (p. 119, loc. cit., p. 9b.) 'It is well to remark that while the capitalist, with the use he makes of his money, saves the class of consumers a certain amount of labour, *he does not substitute for it an equal portion of his own*; which proves that *his capital* performs it, and not he himself.' (10, Notebook, loc. cit., p. 132.) 'If Adam Smith, instead of imagining that the effect of a machine is to facilitate labour, or, as he expresses it, to increase the productive power of labour (it is only through a strange confusion of ideas that Mr Smith has been able to assert that the effect of capital is to increase the productive

76. Sismondi, *Nouveaux Principes d'économie politique*, Vol. I, pp. 94–8.
77. *The Economist*, Vol. V, No. 219, 6 November 1847, p. 1271.

power of labour. With the same logic one could very well claim that *to shorten by half a roundabout path between two points is to double the walker's speed*) had perceived that the money spent on machinery brings a profit by replacing labour, he would have attributed the origin of profit to the same circumstance.' (p. 11, p. 137.) 'Capitals in domestic commerce, whether fixed or circulating, far from serving to set labour in motion, far from increasing its productive power, are, on the contrary, useful and profitable only in two circumstances, either when they obviate the necessity of a portion of the work which man would otherwise have to do with his hands; or when they perform a particular piece of work which man does not have the power to do unaided.' This, says Lauderdale, is not merely a semantic difference. 'The idea that capital sets labour into action, and adds to its productive power, gives rise to the opinion that labour is everywhere proportional to the quantity of existing capitals; that a country's industry is always in proportion to the funds employed: from which it would follow that the increase of capital is the sovereign and unlimited means of increasing wealth. Instead of that, if one admits that capital can have no profitable or useful employment other than to replace a certain work, or to perform it, then one will draw the natural conclusion that the State would gain no benefit whatever from the possession of more capitals than it can employ in doing the work or in substituting for it in the production and fabrication of the things the consumer demands.' (p. 151, 152, pp. 11, 12.) To prove his view that capital is a source *sui generis* of profit and hence of wealth, independently of labour, he points to the surplus profits which the owner of a newly invented machine has before his patent runs out and competition presses down the prices, and concludes then with the words: 'This change of rule for the price does not prevent the benefit' (as regards use value) 'of the machine from coming from a fund of the same nature as that from which it came before the expiration of the patent: *this fund is always that part of a country's revenues which was formerly destined to pay the wages of the labour which the new invention replaces.*' (loc. cit. 125, p. 10b.) By contrast, Ravenstone (IX, 32): 'Machinery can seldom be applied with success to abridge the labours of an individual; more time would be lost in its construction than could be saved by its application. It is only really useful when it acts on great masses, when a single machine can assist the labours of thousands. It is accordingly in the most populous countries where there are most idle men that it is always most abundant. It is not called into action by a scarcity of men, but by the facility with which they are brought together.' (loc. cit.)[78]

'Division of machines into (1) machines employed to produce power; (2) machines whose purpose is simply to transmit power and to perform the work.' (Babbage, *Notebook*, p. 10.)[79] '*Factory* signifies the cooperation of several classes of workers, adults and non-adults, watching attentively and assiduously over a system of productive mechanisms, continually kept in action by a central force ... excludes any workshop whose mechanism does not form a continuous system, or which does not depend on a single source of power. Examples of this latter class among textile factories, copper foundries etc. ... In its most rigorous sense, this term conveys the idea of a vast automaton, composed of numerous *mechanical and intellectual organs* operating in concert and without interruption, towards one and the same aim, all these organs being subordinated to a motive force which moves itself.' (Ure, 13.)[80]

The labour process. – Fixed capital. Means of labour. Machine. –
*Fixed capital. Transposition of powers of labour into powers of
capital both in fixed and in circulating capital. – To what
extent* fixed capital (machine) *creates* value. – *Lauderdale.
Machine presupposes a mass of workers.*

Capital which consumes itself in the production process, or fixed capital, is the *means of production* in the strict sense. In a broader sense the entire production process and each of its moments, such as circulation – as regards its material side – is only a means of production for capital, for which value alone is the end in itself. Regarded as a physical substance, the raw material itself is a means of production for the product etc.

But the determination that the use value of fixed capital is that which eats itself up in the production process is identical to the

78. Ravenstone, *Thoughts on the Funding System*, p. 45.

79. Babbage, *Traité sur l'économie des machines et des manufactures*, pp. 20–21.

80. Andrew Ure (1778–1857; Scottish doctor, chemist, astronomer, apologist for the factory system of the early nineteenth century and opponent of the Factory Acts), *Philosophie des manufactures*, Brussels, 1836 (French translation of the 2nd edition, London, 1835), Vol. I, pp. 18–19.

proposition that it is used in this process only as a means, and itself exists merely as an agency for the transformation of the raw material into the product. As such a means of production, its use value can be that it is merely the technological condition for the occurrence of the process (the site where the production process proceeds), as with buildings etc., or that it is a direct condition of the action of the means of production proper, like all *matières instrumentales*. Both are in turn only the material presuppositions for the production process generally, or for the employment and maintenance of the means of labour. The latter, however, in the proper sense, serves only within production and for production, and has no other use value.

Originally, when we examined the development of value into capital, the labour process was simply included within capital, and, as regards its physical conditions, its material presence, capital appeared as the totality of the conditions of this process, and correspondingly sorted itself out into certain qualitatively different parts, *material of labour* (this, not raw material, is the correct expression of the concept), *means of labour* and *living labour*. On one side, capital was divided into these three elements in accordance with its material composition; on the other, the *labour process* (or the merging of these elements into each other within the process) was their moving unity, the product their static unity. In this form, the material elements – material of labour, means of labour and living labour – appeared merely as the essential moments of the labour process itself, which capital appropriates. But this material side – or, its character as use value and as real process – did not at all coincide with its formal side. In the latter,

(1) the three elements in which it appears before the exchange with labour capacity, before the real process, appeared merely as quantitatively different portions of itself, as quantities of value of which it, itself, as sum, forms the unity. The physical form, the use value, in which these different portions existed did not in any way alter their formal identity from this side. As far as their formal side was concerned, they appeared only as quantitative subdivisions of capital;

(2) within the process itself, as regards the form, the elements of labour and the two others were distinct only in so far as the latter were specified as constant values, and the former as value-positing. But as far as their distinctness as use values, their

material side was concerned, this fell entirely outside the capital's specific character as form. Now, however, with the distinction between circulating capital (raw material and product) and *fixed capital* (means of labour), the distinctness of the elements as use values is posited simultaneously as a distinction within capital as capital, on its formal side. The relation between the factors, which had been merely quantitative, now appears as a qualitative division within capital itself, and as a determinant of its total movement (turnover). Likewise, the material of labour and the product of labour, this neutral precipitate of the labour process, are already, as *raw material* and *product*, materially specified no longer as material and product of labour, but rather as the use value of capital itself in different phases.

As long as the means of labour remains a means of labour in the proper sense of the term, such as it is directly, historically, adopted by capital and included in its realization process, it undergoes a merely formal modification, by appearing now as a means of labour not only in regard to its material side, but also at the same time as a particular mode of the presence of capital, determined by its total process – as *fixed capital*. But, once adopted into the production process of capital, the means of labour passes through different metamorphoses, whose culmination is the *machine*, or rather, an *automatic system of machinery* (system of machinery: the *automatic* one is merely its most complete, most adequate form, and alone transforms machinery into a system), set in motion by an automaton, a moving power that moves itself; this automaton consisting of numerous mechanical and intellectual organs, so that the workers themselves are cast merely as its conscious linkages. In the machine, and even more in machinery as an automatic system, the use value, i.e. the material quality of the means of labour, is transformed into an existence adequate to fixed capital and to capital as such; and the form in which it was adopted into the production process of capital, the direct means of labour, is superseded by a form posited by capital itself and corresponding to it. In no way does the machine appear as the individual worker's means of labour. Its distinguishing characteristic is not in the least, as with the means of labour, to transmit the worker's activity to the object; this activity, rather, is posited in such a way that it merely transmits the machine's work, the machine's action, on to the raw material – supervises it and guards against interruptions. Not as with the instrument, which the worker animates and makes into his organ with his skill and strength, and whose handling therefore depends on his virtuosity. Rather, it is the machine which possesses skill and strength in place of the worker, is itself the virtuoso, with a soul of its own in the mechanical laws acting through it; and it consumes coal, oil etc. (*matières instrumentales*), just as the worker consumes food, to keep up its perpetual motion. The worker's activity, reduced to a mere abstraction of activity, is determined and regulated on all sides by the movement of the machinery, and not the opposite. The science which compels the inanimate limbs of the machinery, by their construction, to act purposefully, as an automaton, does not exist in the worker's consciousness, but rather acts upon him through the machine as an alien power, as the power of the machine itself. The appropriation of living labour by objectified labour – of the power or activity which creates value by value existing for-itself – which lies in the concept of capital, is posited, in production resting on machinery, as the character of the production process itself, including its material elements and its material motion. The production process has ceased to be a labour process in the sense of a process dominated by labour as its governing unity. Labour appears, rather, merely as a conscious organ, scattered among the individual living workers at numerous points of the mechanical system; subsumed under the total process of the machinery itself, as itself only a link of the system, whose unity exists not in the living workers, but rather in the living (active) machinery, which confronts his individual, insignificant doings as a mighty organism. In machinery, objectified labour confronts living labour within the labour process itself as the power which rules it; a power which, as the appropriation of living labour, is the form of capital. The transformation of the means of labour into machinery, and of living labour into a mere living accessory of this machinery, as the means of its action, also posits the absorption of the labour process in its material character as a mere moment of the realization process of capital. The increase of the productive force of labour and the greatest possible negation of necessary labour is the necessary tendency of capital, as we have seen. The transformation of the means of labour into machinery is the realization of this tendency. In machinery, objectified labour materially confronts living labour as a ruling power and as an active subsumption of the latter under itself, not only by appropriating it, but in the real production process itself; the relation of capital as value which appropriates value-creating activity is, in fixed capital existing as machinery, posited at the same time as the relation of the use value of capital to the use value of labour capacity; further, the value objectified in machinery appears as a pre-supposition against which the value-creating power of the individual labour capacity is an infinitesimal, vanishing magnitude; the production in enormous mass quantities which is posited with machinery destroys every connection of the product with the direct need of the producer, and hence with direct use value; it is already posited in the form of the product's production and in the relations in which it is produced that it is produced only as a conveyor of value, and its use value only as condition to that end. In machinery, objectified labour itself appears not only in the form of product or of the product employed as means of labour, but in the form of the force of production itself. The development of the means of labour into machinery is not an accidental moment of capital, but is rather the historical reshaping of the traditional, inherited means of labour into a form adequate to capital. The accumulation of knowledge and of skill, of the general productive forces of the social brain, is thus absorbed into capital, as opposed to labour, and hence appears as an attribute of capital, and more specifically of *fixed capital*, in so far as it enters into the production process as a means of production proper. *Machinery* appears, then, as the most adequate form of *fixed capital*, and fixed capital, in so far as capital's relations with itself are concerned, appears as *the most adequate form of capital* as such. In another respect, however, in so far as fixed capital is condemned to an existence within the confines of a specific use value, it does not correspond to the concept of capital, which, as value, is indifferent to every specific form of use value, and can adopt or shed any of them as equivalent incarnations. In this respect, as regards capital's external relations, it is *circulating capital* which appears as the adequate form of capital, and not fixed capital.

Further, in so far as machinery develops with the accumulation of society's science, of productive force generally, general social labour presents itself not in labour but in capital. The productive force of society is measured in *fixed capital*, exists there in its objective form; and, inversely, the productive force of capital grows with this general progress, which capital appropriates free of charge. This is not the place to go into the development of machinery in detail; rather only in its general aspect; in so far as the *means of labour*, as a physical thing, loses its direct form, becomes *fixed capital*, and confronts the worker physically as *capital*. In machinery, knowledge appears as alien, external to him; and living labour [as] subsumed under self-activating objectified labour. The worker appears as superfluous to the extent that his action is not determined by [capital's] requirements.

NOTEBOOK VII

End of February. March.
End of May –
Beginning of June 1858

The Chapter on Capital (continuation)

The full development of capital, therefore, takes place – or capital has posited the mode of production corresponding to it – only when the means of labour has not only taken the economic form of *fixed capital*, but has also been suspended in its immediate form, and when *fixed capital* appears as a machine within the production process, opposite labour; and the entire production process appears as not subsumed under the direct skilfulness of the worker, but rather as the technological application of science. [It is,] hence, the tendency of capital to give production a scientific character; direct labour [is] reduced to a mere moment of this process. As with the transformation of value into capital, so does it appear in the further development of capital, that it presupposes a certain given historical development of the productive forces on one side – science too [is] among these productive forces – and, on the other, drives and forces them further onwards.

Thus the quantitative extent and the effectiveness (intensity) to which capital is developed as fixed capital indicate the general degree to which capital is developed as capital, as power over living labour, and to which it has conquered the production process as such. Also, in the sense that it expresses the accumulation of objectified productive forces, and likewise of objectified labour. However, while capital gives itself its adequate form as use value within the production process only in the form of machinery and other material manifestations of fixed capital, such as railways etc. (to which we shall return later), this in no way means that this use value – machinery as such – is capital, or that its existence as machinery is identical with its existence as capital; any more than gold would cease to have use value as gold if it were no longer *money*. Machinery does not lose its use value as soon as it ceases to be capital. While machinery is the most appropriate form of the use value of fixed capital, it does not at all follow that therefore subsumption under the social relation of capital is the most appropriate and ultimate social relation of production for the application of machinery.

To the degree that labour time – the mere quantity of labour – is posited by capital as the sole determinant element, to that degree does direct labour and its quantity disappear as the determinant principle of production – of the creation of use values – and is reduced both quantitatively, to a smaller proportion, and qualitatively, as an, of course, indispensable but subordinate moment, compared to general scientific labour, technological application of natural sciences, on one side, and to the general productive force arising from social combination [*Gliederung*] in total production on the other side – a combination which appears as a natural fruit of social labour (although it is a historic product). Capital thus works towards its own dissolution as the form dominating production.

While, then, in one respect the transformation of the production process from the simple labour process into a scientific process, which subjugates the forces of nature and compels them to work in the service of human needs, appears as a quality of *fixed capital* in contrast to living labour; while individual labour as such has ceased altogether to appear as productive, is productive, rather, only in these common labours which subordinate the forces of nature to themselves, and while this elevation of direct labour into social labour appears as a reduction of individual labour to the level of helplessness in face of the communality [*Gemeinsamkeit*] represented by and concentrated in capital; so does it now appear, in another respect, as a quality of *circulating capital*, to maintain labour in one branch of production by means of *co-existing labour* in another. In small-scale circulation, capital advances the worker the wages which the latter exchanges for products necessary for his consumption. The money he obtains has this power only because others are working alongside him at the same time; and capital can give him claims on alien labour, in the form of money, only because it has appropriated his own labour. This exchange of one's own labour with alien labour appears here not as mediated and determined by the simultaneous existence of the labour of others, but rather by the advance which capital makes. The worker's ability to engage in the exchange of substances necessary for his consumption during production appears as due to an attribute of the part of *circulating capital* which is paid to the worker, and of circulating capital generally. It appears not as an exchange of substances between the simultaneous labour powers, but as the metabolism [*Stoffwechsel*] of capital; as the existence of circulating capital. Thus all powers of labour are transposed into powers of capital; the productive power of labour into fixed capital (posited as external to labour and as existing independently of it (as object [*sachlich*])); and, in circulating capital, the fact that the worker himself has created the conditions for the repetition of his labour, and that the exchange of this, his labour, is mediated by the co-existing labour of others, appears in such a way that capital gives him an advance and posits the simultaneity of the branches of labour. (These last two aspects actually belong to accumulation.) Capital in the form of circulating capital posits itself as mediator between the different workers.

Fixed capital, in its character as means of production, whose most adequate form [is] machinery, produces value, i.e. increases the value of the product, in only two respects: (1) in so far as it *has* value; i.e. is itself the product of labour, a certain quantity of labour in objectified form; (2) in so far as it increases the relation of surplus labour to necessary labour, by enabling labour, through an increase of its productive power, to create a greater mass of the products required for the maintenance of living labour capacity in a shorter time. It is therefore a highly absurd bourgeois assertion that the worker shares with the capitalist, because the latter, with fixed capital (which is, as far as that goes, itself a product of labour, and of *alien labour* merely appropriated by capital) makes labour easier for him (rather, he robs it of all independence and attractive character, by means of the machine), or makes his labour shorter. Capital employs machinery, rather, only to the extent that it enables the worker to work a larger part of his time for capital, to relate to a larger part of his time as time which does not belong to him, to work longer for another. Through this process, the amount of labour necessary for the production of a given object is indeed reduced to a minimum, but only in order to realize a maximum of labour in the maximum number of such objects. The first aspect is important, because capital here – quite unintentionally – reduces human labour, expenditure of energy, to a minimum. This will redound to the benefit of emancipated labour, and is the condition of its emancipation. From what has been said, it is clear how absurd Lauderdale is when he wants to make fixed capital into an independent source of value, independent of labour time. It is such a source only in so far as it is itself objectified labour time, and in so far as it posits surplus labour time. The employment of machinery itself historically presupposes – see above, Ravenstone – superfluous hands. Machinery inserts itself to replace labour only where there is an overflow of labour powers. Only in the imagination of economists does it leap to the aid of the individual worker. It can be effective only with masses of workers, whose concentration relative to capital is one of its historic presuppositions, as we have seen. It enters not in order to replace labour power where this is lacking, but rather in order to reduce massively available labour power to its necessary measure. Machinery enters only where labour capacity is on hand in masses. (Return to this.)

Lauderdale believes himself to have made the great discovery that machinery does not increase the productive power of labour, because it rather replaces the latter, or does what labour cannot do with its own power. It belongs to the concept of capital that the increased productive force of labour is posited rather as the increase of a force [*Kraft*] outside itself, and as labour's own debilitation [*Entkräftung*]. The hand tool makes the worker independent – posits him as proprietor. Machinery – as fixed capital – posits him as dependent, posits him as appropriated. This effect of machinery holds only in so far as it is cast into the role of fixed capital, and this it is only because the worker relates to it as wage-worker, and the active individual generally, as mere worker.

Fixed capital and circulating capital *as two particular kinds of capital. Fixed capital and continuity of the production process. – Machinery and living labour. (Business of inventing)*

While, up to now, fixed capital and circulating capital appeared merely as different passing aspects of capital, they have now hardened into two particular modes of its existence, and fixed capital appears separately alongside circulating capital. They are now two particular kinds of capital. In so far as a capital is examined in a particular branch of production, it appears as divided into these two portions, or splits into these two kinds of capital in certain p[rop]ortions.

The division within the production process, originally between means of labour and material of labour, and finally product of labour, now appears as circulating capital (the last two) and fixed capital [the first].[1] The split within capital as regards its merely physical aspect has now entered into its form itself, and appears as differentiating it.

From a viewpoint such as Lauderdale's etc., who would like to have capital as such, separately from labour, create *value* and hence also *surplus value* (or profit), fixed capital – namely that whose physical presence or use value is machinery – is the form which gives their superficial fallacies still the greatest semblance of validity. The answer to them, e.g. in *Labour Defended*, [is] that the road-builder may share [profits] with the road-user, but the 'road' itself cannot do so.[2]

Circulating capital – presupposing that it really passes through its different phases – brings about the decrease or increase, the brevity or length of circulation time, the easier or more troublesome completion of the different stages of circulation, a decrease of the surplus value which could be created in a given period of time without these interruptions – either *because the number of reproductions grows smaller*, or because the quantity of *capital continuously engaged in the production process* is reduced. In both cases this is not a reduction of the initial value, but rather a reduction of the rate of its growth. From the moment, however, when fixed capital has developed to a certain extent – and this extent, as we indicated, is the measure of the development of large industry generally – hence fixed capital increases in proportion to the development of large industry's productive forces – it is itself the objectification of these productive forces, as presupposed product – from this instant on, every interruption of the production process acts as a direct reduction of capital itself, of its initial value. The value of fixed capital is reproduced only in so far as it is used up in the production process. Through disuse it loses its use value without its value passing on to the product. Hence, the greater the scale on which fixed capital develops, in the sense in which we regard it here, the more does the *continuity of the production process* or the constant flow of reproduction become an externally compelling condition for the mode of production founded on capital.

In machinery, the appropriation of living labour by capital

1. The manuscript has: '. . . now appears as circulating capital (the first two) and fixed capital'.
2. Hodgskin, *Labour Defended*, p. 16.

achieves a direct reality in this respect as well: It is, firstly, the analysis and application of mechanical and chemical laws, arising directly out of science, which enables the machine to perform the same labour as that previously performed by the worker. However, the development of machinery along this path occurs only when large industry has already reached a higher stage, and all the sciences have been pressed into the service of capital; and when, secondly, the available machinery itself already provides great capabilities. Invention then becomes a business, and the application of science to direct production itself becomes a prospect which determines and solicits it. But this is not the road along which machinery, by and large, arose, and even less the road on which it progresses in detail. This road is, rather, dissection [*Analyse*] – through the division of labour, which gradually transforms the workers' operations into more and more mechanical ones, so that at a certain point a mechanism can step into their places. (*See under economy of power*.) Thus, the specific mode of working here appears directly as becoming transferred from the worker to capital in the form of the machine, and his own labour capacity devalued thereby. Hence the workers' struggle against machinery. What was the living worker's activity becomes the activity of the machine. Thus the appropriation of labour by capital confronts the worker in a coarsely sensuous form; capital absorbs labour into itself – 'as though its body were by love possessed'.[3]

Contradiction between the foundation of bourgeois production (value as measure) *and its development. Machines etc.*

The exchange of living labour for objectified labour – i.e. the positing of social labour in the form of the contradiction of capital and wage labour – is the ultimate development of the *value-relation* and of production resting on value. Its presupposition is – and remains – the mass of direct labour time, the quantity of labour employed, as the determinant factor in the production of wealth. But to the degree that large industry develops, the creation of real wealth comes to depend less on labour time and on the amount of labour employed than on the power of the agencies set in motion during labour time, whose 'powerful effectiveness' is

3. '*als hätt' es Lieb im Leibe*', Goethe, *Faust*, Pt I, Act 5, Auerbach's Cellar in Leipzig.

itself in turn out of all proportion to the direct labour time spent on their production, but depends rather on the general state of science and on the progress of technology, or the application of this science to production. (The development of this science, especially natural science, and all others with the latter, is itself in turn related to the development of material production.) Agriculture, e.g., becomes merely the application of the science of material metabolism, its regulation for the greatest advantage of the entire body of society. Real wealth manifests itself, rather – and large industry reveals this – in the monstrous disproportion between the labour time applied, and its product, as well as in the qualitative imbalance between labour, reduced to a pure abstraction, and the power of the production process it superintends. Labour no longer appears so much to be included within the production process; rather, the human being comes to relate more as watchman and regulator to the production process itself. (What holds for machinery holds likewise for the combination of human activities and the development of human intercourse.) No longer does the worker insert a modified natural thing [*Naturgegenstand*] as middle link between the object [*Objekt*] and himself; rather, he inserts the process of nature, transformed into an industrial process, as a means between himself and inorganic nature, mastering it. He steps to the side of the production process instead of being its chief actor. In this transformation, it is neither the direct human labour he himself performs, nor the time during which he works, but rather the appropriation of his own general productive power, his understanding of nature and his mastery over it by virtue of his presence as a social body – it is, in a word, the development of the social individual which appears as the great foundation-stone of production and of wealth. The *theft of alien labour time, on which the present wealth is based*, appears a miserable foundation in face of this new one, created by large-scale industry itself. As soon as labour in the direct form has ceased to be the great well-spring of wealth, labour time ceases and must cease to be its measure, and hence exchange value [must cease to be the measure] of use value. The *surplus labour of the mass* has ceased to be the condition for the development of general wealth, just as the *non-labour of the few*, for the development of the general powers of the human head. With that, production based on exchange value breaks down, and the direct, material production process is stripped of the form of penury and antithesis. The free development of individualities, and hence not the reduction of necessary labour time so as to posit surplus labour, but rather the general reduction of the necessary labour of society to a minimum, which then corresponds to the artistic, scientific etc. development of the individuals in the time set free, and with the means created, for all of them. Capital itself is the moving contradiction, [in] that it presses to reduce labour time to a minimum, while it posits labour time, on the other side, as sole measure and source of wealth. Hence it diminishes labour time in the necessary form so as to increase it in the super-fluous form; hence posits the superfluous in growing measure as a condition – question of life or death – for the necessary. On the one side, then, it calls to life all the powers of science and of nature, as of social combination and of social intercourse, in order to make the creation of wealth independent (relatively) of the labour time employed on it. On the other side, it wants to use labour time as the measuring rod for the giant social forces thereby created, and to confine them within the limits required to main-tain the already created value as value. Forces of production and social relations – two different sides of the development of the social individual – appear to capital as mere means, and are merely means for it to produce on its limited foundation. In fact, however, they are the material conditions to blow this foundation sky-high. 'Truly wealthy a nation, when the working day is 6 rather than 12 hours. *Wealth* is not command over surplus labour time' (real wealth), 'but rather, *disposable time* outside that needed in direct production, for *every individual* and the whole society.' (*The Source and Remedy* etc. 1821, p. 6.)

Nature builds no machines, no locomotives, railways, electric telegraphs, self-acting mules etc. These are products of human industry; natural material transformed into organs of the human will over nature, or of human participation in nature. They are *organs of the human brain, created by the human hand*; the power of knowledge, objectified. The development of fixed capital indicates to what degree general social knowledge has become a *direct force of production*, and to what degree, hence, the condi-tions of the process of social life itself have come under the control of the general intellect and been transformed in accor-dance with it. To what degree the powers of social production have been produced, not only in the form of knowledge, but also as immediate organs of social practice, of the real life process.

Significance of the development of fixed capital (*for the development of capital generally*). *Relation between the creation of fixed capital and circulating capital. Disposable time.*
To create it, chief role of capital. Contradictory form of the same in capital. – Productivity of labour and production of fixed capital. (The Source and Remedy.) – *Use and consume:* Economist. *Durability of fixed capital*

The development of fixed capital indicates in still another respect the degree of development of wealth generally, or of capital. The aim of production oriented directly towards use value, as well as of that directly oriented towards exchange value, is the product itself, destined for consumption. The part of production which is oriented towards the production of fixed capital does not produce direct objects of individual gratification, nor direct exchange values; at least not directly realizable exchange values. *Hence, only when a certain degree of productivity has already been reached – so that a part of production time is sufficient for immediate production – can an increasingly large part be applied to the production of the means of production.* This requires that society be able to wait; that a large part of the wealth already created can be withdrawn both from immediate consumption and from production for immediate consumption, in order to employ this part for labour which is *not immediately productive* (within the material production process itself). This requires a certain level of productivity and of relative overabundance, and, more specifically, a level directly related to the transformation of circulating capital into fixed capital. As the *magnitude of relative surplus labour depends on the productivity of necessary labour, so does the magnitude of labour time* – living as well as objectified – *employed on the production of fixed capital depend on the productivity of the labour time spent in the direct production of products. Surplus population* (from this standpoint), as well as *surplus production*, is a condition for this. That is, the output of the time employed in direct production must be larger, relatively, than is directly required for the reproduction of the capital employed in these branches of industry. The *smaller* the direct fruits borne by *fixed capital*, the less it intervenes in the *direct production process*, the greater must be this relative *surplus population and surplus production*; thus, more to build railways, canals, aqueducts, telegraphs etc. than to build the machinery directly active in the direct production process. Hence – a subject to which we will return later – in the constant under- and over-production of modern industry – constant fluctuations and convulsions arise from the disproportion, when sometimes too little, then again too much circulating capital is transformed into fixed capital.

⟨*The creation of a large quantity of disposable time* apart from necessary labour time for society generally and each of its members (i.e. room for the development of the individuals' full productive forces, hence those of society also), this creation of not-labour time appears in the stage of capital, as of all earlier ones, as not-labour time, free time, for a few. What capital adds is that it increases the surplus labour time of the mass by all the means of art and science, because its wealth consists directly in the appropriation of surplus labour time; since *value directly its purpose*, not use value. It is thus, despite itself, instrumental in creating the means of social disposable time, in order to reduce labour time for the whole society to a diminishing minimum, and thus to free everyone's time for their own development. But its tendency always, on the one side, *to create disposable time, on the other, to convert it into surplus labour*. If it succeeds too well at the first, then it suffers from surplus production, and then necessary labour is interrupted, because *no surplus labour can be realized by capital*. The more this contradiction develops, the more does it become evident that the growth of the forces of production can no longer be bound up with the appropriation of alien labour, but that the mass of workers must themselves appropriate their own surplus labour. Once they have done so – and *disposable time* thereby ceases to have an *antithetical* existence – then, on one side, necessary labour time will be measured by the needs of the social individual, and, on the other, the development of the power of social production will grow so rapidly that, even though production is now calculated for the wealth of all, *disposable time* will grow for all. For real wealth is the developed productive power of all individuals. The measure of wealth is then not any longer, in any way, labour time, but rather disposable time. *Labour time as the measure of value* posits wealth itself as founded on poverty, and disposable time as existing *in and because of the antithesis to surplus labour time*; or, the positing of an individual's entire time as labour time, and his degradation therefore to mere worker, subsumption under labour. *The most developed machinery thus forces the worker to work longer than the savage does, or than he himself did with the simplest, crudest tools.*⟩

'If the entire labour of a country were sufficient only to raise the support of the whole population, there would be no *surplus labour*, consequently nothing that could be allowed to accumulate as capital. If in one year the people raises enough for the support of two years, one year's consumption must perish, or for one year men must cease from productive labour. But the *possessors of* [*the*] *surplus produce or capital* . . . employ people upon *something not directly and immediately productive*, e.g. in the erection of machinery. So it goes on.' (*The Source and Remedy of the National Difficulties*, p. 4.)

⟨As the basis on which large industry rests, the appropriation of alien labour time, ceases, with its development, to make up or to create wealth, so does *direct labour* as such cease to be the basis of production, since, in one respect, it is transformed more into a supervisory and regulatory activity; but then also because the product ceases to be the product of isolated direct labour, and the *combination* of social activity appears, rather, as the producer. 'As soon as the division of labour is developed, almost every piece of work done by a single individual is a part of a whole, *having no value or utility of itself. There is nothing on which the labourer can seize: this is my produce, this I will keep to myself.*' (*Labour Defended*, p. 25, 1, 2, XI.) In direct exchange, individual direct labour appears as realized in a particular product or part of the product, and its communal, social character – its character as objectification of general labour and satisfaction of the general need – as posited through exchange alone. In the production process of large-scale industry, by contrast, just as the conquest of the forces of nature by the social intellect is the precondition of the productive power of the means of labour as developed into the automatic process, on one side, so, on the other, is *the labour of the individual in its direct presence posited as suspended individual, i.e. 'as social, labour. Thus the other basis of this mode of production falls away.*⟩

The labour time employed in the production of fixed capital relates to that employed in the production of circulating capital, within the production process of capital itself, as does *surplus labour time to necessary* labour time. To the degree that production aimed at the satisfaction of immediate need becomes more productive, a greater part of production can be directed towards the need of production itself, or the production of means of production. In so far as the production of *fixed capital*, even in its physical aspect, is directed immediately not towards the production of direct use values, or towards the production of values required for the direct reproduction of capital – i.e. those which themselves in turn represent use value in the value-creation process – but rather towards the production of the means of value creation, that is, not towards value as an immediate object, but rather towards value creation, towards the means of realization, as an immediate object of production – the production of value posited physically in the object of production itself, as the aim of production, the objectification of productive force, the value-producing power of capital – to that extent, it is in the production of *fixed capital that capital posits itself as end-in-itself* and appears active as capital, *to a higher power than it does in the production of circulating capital*. Hence, in this respect as well, the dimension already possessed by fixed capital, which its production occupies within total production, is the measuring rod *of the development* of wealth founded on the mode of production of capital.

'The number of workers depends as much on *circulating capital* as it depends on the quantity *of products of co-existing labour*, which labourers are allowed to consume.' (*Labour Defended*, p. 20.)

In all the excerpts cited above from various economists fixed capital is regarded as the part of capital which is locked into the production process. 'Floating capital is consumed; fixed capital is merely used in the great process of production.' (*Economist*, VI, 1.)[4] This wrong, and holds only for the part of circulating capital which is itself consumed by the fixed capital, the *matières instrumentales*. The only thing consumed 'in the great process of production', if this means the immediate production process, is *fixed capital*. Consumption within the production process is, however, in fact *use, wearing-out*. Furthermore, the *greater durability of fixed capital* must not be conceived as a purely physical quality. The iron and the wood which make up the bed I sleep in, or the stones making up the house I live in, or the marble statue which decorates a palace, are just as durable as iron and wood etc. used for machinery. But *durability* is a condition for the instrument, the means of production, not only on the technical ground that metals etc. are the chief material of all

4. See p. 688, n. 77.

machinery, but rather because the instrument is destined to play the same role constantly in repeated processes of production. Its durability as means of production is a required quality of its use value. The more often it must be replaced, the costlier it is; the larger the part of capital which would have to be spent on it uselessly. Its durability is its existence as means of production. Its duration is an increase of its productive force. With circulating capital, by contrast, in so far as it is not transformed into fixed capital, durability is in no way connected with the act of production itself and is therefore not a conceptually posited moment. The fact that among the articles thrown into the consumption fund there are some which are in turn characterized as *fixed capital* because they are consumed slowly, and can be consumed by many individuals in series, is connected with further determinations (renting rather than buying, interest etc.) with which we are not yet here concerned.

'Since the general introduction of soulless mechanism in British manufactures, people have with rare exceptions been treated as a secondary and subordinate machine, and far more attention has been given to the perfection of the raw materials of wood and metals than to those of body and spirit.' (p. 31. Robert Owen: *Essays on the Formation of the Human Character*, 1840, London.)

Real saving – economy – = saving of labour time = development of productive force. Suspension of the contradiction between free time and labour time. – True conception of the process of social production

⟨Real economy – saving – consists of the saving of labour time (minimum (and minimization) of production costs); but this saving identical with development of the productive force. Hence in no way *abstinence from consumption*, but rather the development of power, of capabilities of production, and hence both of the capabilities as well as the means of consumption. The capability to consume is a condition of consumption, hence its primary means, and this capability is the development of an individual potential, a force of production. The saving of labour time [is] equal to an increase of free time, i.e. time for the full development of the individual, which in turn reacts back upon the productive power of labour as itself the greatest productive power. From the standpoint of the direct production process it can be regarded as the production of *fixed capital*, this fixed capital being man himself. It goes without saying, by the way, that direct labour time itself cannot remain in the abstract antithesis to free time in which it appears from the perspective of bourgeois economy. Labour cannot become play, as Fourier would like,[5] although it remains his great contribution to have expressed the suspension not of distribution, but of the mode of production itself, in a higher form, as the ultimate object. Free time – which is both idle time and time for higher activity – has naturally transformed its possessor into a different subject, and he then enters into the direct production process as this different subject. This process is then both discipline, as regards the human being in the process of becoming; and, at the same time, practice [*Ausübung*], experimental science, materially creative and objectifying science, as regards the human being who has become, in whose head exists the accumulated knowledge of society. For both, in so far as labour requires practical use of the hands and free bodily movement, as in agriculture, at the same time exercise.

As the system of bourgeois economy has developed for us only by degrees, so too its negation, which is its ultimate result. We are still concerned now with the direct production process. When we consider bourgeois society in the long view and as a whole, then the final result of the process of social production always appears as the society itself, i.e. the human being itself in its social relations. Everything that has a fixed form, such as the product etc., appears as merely a moment, a vanishing moment, in this movement. The direct production process itself here appears only as a moment. The conditions and objectifications of the process are themselves equally moments of it, and its only subjects are the individuals, but individuals in mutual relationships, which they equally reproduce and produce anew. The constant process of their own movement, in which they renew themselves even as they renew the world of wealth they create.⟩

Owen's *historical conception of industrial* (capitalist) *production*

(In his *Six Lectures Delivered at Manchester*, 1837, Owen speaks about the difference which capital, by its very growth (and wide-

5. Fourier, *Le Nouveau Monde industriel et sociétaire*, Vol. VI, pp. 242–52.

spread appearance, and it obtains the latter only with large-scale industry, which is connected with the development of fixed capital), creates between workers and capitalists; but formulates the development of capital as a *necessary condition* for the recreation of society, and recounts about himself: 'It was by being gradually trained to create and conduct some of these large' (manufacturing) 'establishments, that your lecturer' (Owen himself) 'was taught to understand the great errors and disadvantages of the past and present attempts to ameliorate the character and situation of his fellow beings.' (p. 58.) We here put down the entire excerpt, to be used on another occasion.

'The producers of developed wealth can be divided into workers in soft and workers in hard materials, under the immediate direction generally of masters whose object it is to make money through the labour of those they employ. Before the introduction of the chemical and mechanical manufacturing system, operations were carried out on a limited scale; there were many small masters, each with a few day-labourers, who expected in due time to become small masters themselves. They usually ate at the same table and lived together; a spirit and feeling of equality reigned among them. Since the period when scientific power began by and large to be employed in the business of manufacturing, a gradual change has taken place in this regard. Almost all manufactures, to be successful, must now be carried out extensively and with a great capital; small masters with small capitals have only little chance of success, particularly in the manufactures of soft materials, such as cotton, wool, flax etc.; and it is indeed evident now, that so long as the present classification of society and the mode of directing business life should endure, the small masters will be increasingly displaced by those who possess great capitals, and that the former relatively happier equality among the producers must give way to the greatest inequality between master and worker, such as has never before occurred in the history of mankind. The large capitalist is now elevated to the position of a commanding lord, treating the health, the life and death, indirectly, of his slaves, as he likes. He obtains this power through combination with other great capitalists, engaged in the same interest with himself, and thus effectively bends to his purpose those he employs. The large capitalist now swims in wealth, whose proper use he has not been taught and does not know. Through his wealth, he has gained power. His wealth and his power blind his reason; and when he oppresses altogether grievously, he believes he is bestowing favours ... His servants, as they are called, his slaves in fact, are reduced to the most hopeless degradation; the majority robbed of health, of domestic comfort, of the leisure and healthy open-air pleasures of earlier days. Through excessive exhaustion of their powers, brought about by lengthy, drawn-out monotonous occupations, they are seduced into habits of intemperance, and made unfit for thinking or reflection. They can have no physical, intellectual or moral amusements other than of the worst sort; all real pleasures of life are far distant from them. The life which a very large part of the workers lead under the present system is, in a word, not worth having. But the individuals are not to blame for the changes of which these are the result; *they proceed in the regular order of nature and are preparatory and necessary stages towards the great and important social revolution* now in progress. Without great capitals no great establishments can be founded; men cannot be brought to understand the practicability of effecting new combinations, in order to ensure a superior character to all and the production of more annual wealth than can be consumed by all; and that wealth, too, should be of a higher kind than that hitherto generally produced.' (loc. cit. 56, 57.) 'It is this new chemical and mechanical manufacturing system which now expands human abilities, and prepares men to understand and to adopt other principles and practices, and thus to effect the most beneficial change in affairs which the world has yet known. And it is this new manufacturing system which now creates the necessity for another and higher classification of society.' (loc. cit. 58.))

Capital and value of natural agencies. – Scope of fixed capital indicates the level of capitalist production. – Determination of raw material, product, instrument of production, consumption. – Is money fixed capital or circulating capital? – Fixed capital and circulating capital in regard to individual consumption

We remarked earlier that the force of production (fixed capital) only has value, hence only imparts value, in so far as it is itself produced, itself a given quantity of objectified labour time. But now natural agencies enter in, such as water, land (this notably), mines etc., which are appropriated, hence possess exchange value, and hence come as values into the calculation of production costs. This is, in a word, the entry of landed property (which includes earth, mines, water). The value of means of production which are not the product of labour does not belong here yet, since it does not arise out of the examination of capital itself. They appear for capital, initially, as given, historic presupposition. And we leave them as such, here. Only the form of landed property – or of natural agencies as value-determining magnitudes – modified to correspond to capital belongs within the examination of the system of bourgeois economy. It does not affect the examination of capital at the point we have so far reached, to regard land etc. as a form of fixed capital.

Since *fixed capital*, in the sense of a produced production force, as agency of production, increases the mass of use values created in a given time, it cannot grow without the raw material it works on also growing (in manufacturing industry. In the extractive industries, such as fishery, mining, labour merely consists in overpowering the obstacles in the way of the seizure and appropriation of the raw products or primary products. There is no raw material to be worked up for production; rather, the existing raw product is appropriated. By contrast, in agriculture the raw material is the earth itself; seed the circulating capital etc.). Its employment on a larger scale thus presupposes expansion of the part of circulating capital consisting of raw materials; hence growth of capital generally. It likewise presupposes (relative) decrease of the portion of capital exchanged for living labour.

In *fixed capital*, capital exists materially, too, not only as objectified labour, destined to serve as the means of new labour, but rather as value, whose use value is to create new values. The existence of fixed capital is therefore κατ' ἐξοχήν its existence as productive capital. Hence the stage of development reached by the mode of production based on capital – or the extent to which capital itself is already presupposed as the condition of its own production, has presupposed itself – is measured by the existing scope of fixed capital; not only by its quantity, but just as much by its quality.

Finally: in *fixed capital*, the social productivity of labour [is] posited as a property inherent in capital; *including the scientific power as well as the combination of social powers within the production process, and finally, the skill transposed from direct labour into the machine, into the dead productive force. In circulating capital*, by contrast, it is the exchange of labours, of the different branches of labour, their interlacing and system-forming quality, the co-existence of productive labour, which appear as *property of capital*.*

Fourthly:

We have now to examine the other relations of fixed capital and circulating capital.

We said above that the social relation between different labours is posited as a property of capital in *circulating capital*, as the social productive power of labour in fixed capital.

'The circulating capital of a nation is: money, necessaries of life, raw materials, and finished products.' (Adam Smith, tome II, p. 218.) Smith is in a quandary whether he should call money circulating or fixed capital. In so far as it always serves merely as instrument of circulation, which is itself a moment of the total reproduction process, it is *fixed capital* – as instrument of circulation. But its use value itself is only to circulate and never to be absorbed either into the production process proper nor into individual consumption. It is the part of capital constantly fixed in the circulation phase, and in this respect it is the most perfect form of circulating capital; in the other respect, because it is fixed as an instrument, it is *fixed capital*.

In so far as a distinction between *fixed capital and circulating capital* enters in from the perspective of individual consumption, this is already given in the fact that *fixed capital* does not enter into circulation as use value. (A part of the seed in agriculture does enter into circulation as use value, because it multiplies itself.) This non-entry-into-circulation supposes that it does not become the object of individual consumption.

*The determinations of raw material, product, instrument of production, change according to the role which the use values play in the production process itself. What may be regarded as a mere raw material (certainly not agricultural products, which are all reproduced, and not only reproduced in their original form, but also modified in their natural being itself to correspond to human needs. Quote from Hodges etc.[6] The products of purely extractive industry such as e.g. coal, metals, are themselves the result of labour, not only to bring them to light, but also in order to give them the form, as with metals, in which they can serve as raw materials for industry. But they are not reproduced, since we do not yet know how to create metals) is itself the pro-

6. The author referred to here may be J. F. Hodges, who wrote *Lessons on Agricultural Chemistry* (1849), and *First Steps to Practical Chemistry for Agricultural Students* (1857); or Marx may have intended to write 'Hodgskin'.

*Turnover time of capital consisting of fixed capital and
circulating capital. Reproduction time of fixed capital. With
circulating capital, the only requirement is that the interruption
should be not so great as to ruin its use value. With fixed
capital, continuity of production absolutely necessary etc. –
Unit of labour time the day; for circulating capital, the year.
Longer total period as unit with the entry of fixed capital. –
Industrial cycle. – Circulation of fixed capital. – The so-called
risk. – All parts of capital yield an equal profit – false.*
Ricardo *etc. – The same commodity sometimes fixed capital,
sometimes circulating capital. – Sale of capital as capital. –
Fixed capital which enters into circulation as use value. –*
Every moment which a presupposition of production, at the
same time its result. Reproduction of its own conditions.
Reproduction of capital as fixed capital and circulating capital

'Fixed capital' serves over and over again for the same operation,
'and by how much larger has been the range of these iterations,
by so much [the] more intensely is the tool, engine, or machinery,
entitled to the denomination of fixed'. (De Quincey, X, 4.)[7] If a

---

duct of labour. The product of one industry is the raw material for another
and vice versa. The instrument of production itself is the product of one
industry, and serves as instrument of production only in the other. One
industry's waste is the raw material of the other. In agriculture, a part of the
product (seed, cattle etc.) itself appears as raw material for the same industry;
hence, like fixed capital, it never leaves the production process; the portion of
the agricultural products destined for animal feed can be regarded as *matière
instrumentale*; but seed is reproduced in the production process, while the
instrument as such is consumed in it. Could not seed, considering that it
always remains within the production process, like draught animals, be
regarded as fixed capital, like draught animals? No; otherwise all raw materials
would have to be so regarded. As raw material it is always comprised within
the production process. Finally, products entering into direct consumption
in turn come out of consumption as raw materials for production, fertilizer in
the process of nature etc., paper out of rags etc.; but secondly, their consumption reproduces the individual himself in a specific mode of being, not only in
his immediate quality of being alive, and in specific social relations. So that
the ultimate appropriation by individuals taking place in the consumption
process reproduces them in the original relations in which they move within
the production process and towards each other; reproduces them in their
social being, and hence reproduces their social being – society – which appears
as much the subject as the result of this great total process.

---

7. De Quincey, *The Logic of Political Economy*, p. 114.

capital consists of £10,000, of which 5,000 is fixed and 5,000 circulating; the latter turns over 1 time in 1 year, the former 1 time in 5 years; then 5,000 turn over, or $\frac{1}{2}$ of the total capital, 1 time in one year. During the same year, $\frac{1}{5}$ of the fixed capital or £1,000 turn over; hence in 1 year £6,000 or $\frac{3}{5}$ of the total capital turn over. Hence $\frac{1}{5}$ of the total capital turns over in $\frac{12}{3}$ months and the total capital, in $\frac{12 \times 5}{3}$ months, in $\frac{60}{3} = 20$ months $= 1$ year and 8 months. In 20 months the total capital of £10,000 is turned over, although the fixed capital is replaced only in 5 years. This turnover time holds, however, only for the repetition of the production process and thus for the creation of surplus value; not for the reproduction of the capital itself. If the capital begins the process anew less frequently – returns from circulation into the form of fixed capital – then it returns all the more often into the form of circulating capital. But the capital itself is not replaced thereby. So with the circulating capital itself. If a capital of 100 returns 4 times a year and hence brings in 20%, like a capital of 400 which circulates only once, then the capital remains 100 at the end of the year as at the beginning, and the other capital remains 400, although it has effected a production of use values and a positing of surplus value equal to a 4 times larger capital. The fact that the velocity of turnover here substitutes for the magnitude of the capital shows strikingly that it is only the amount of surplus labour set into motion, and of labour generally, which determines the creation of value as well as the creation of surplus value, and not the magnitude of the capital for itself. The capital of 100 has, during the year, set in motion successively as much labour as one of 400, and hence created the same surplus value.

But the issue here is this. In the above example, the circulating capital of 5,000 first returns in the middle of the first year; then at the end of the second half; in the middle of the second; in the second half of the second (in the first 4 months) £3,333$\frac{2}{6}$ of it have returned and the rest will have come back at the end of this half year.

But, of the fixed capital, only $\frac{1}{5}$ was returned in the first year, $\frac{1}{5}$ in the second. At the end of the first year, the owner has on hand £6,000; at the end of the second, 7,000; the third, 8,000; the fourth, 9,000; the fifth, 10,000. Only at the end of the fifth is he again in possession of his total capital, with which he began the production process; although *in the creation of surplus value his capital acted as if it had wholly turned over in 20 months; thus the total capital itself is only reproduced in 5 years. The former aspect of turnover important for the relation of its realization*; the latter, however, brings in a new relation which does not take place with circulating capital at all. *Since circulating capital is completely absorbed into circulation and returns from it as a whole, it follows that it is reproduced as capital as many times as it is realized as surplus value* or as surplus capital. But since fixed capital never enters circulation as a use value, and enters it as value only to the extent that it is consumed as a use value, it follows that it is by no means reproduced as soon as the *surplus value determined by the average turnover time of the total capital is posited.* The turnover of the circulating capital must take place 10 times in the 5 years before the fixed capital is reproduced; i.e. the period of the revulsions of circulating capital must be repeated 10 times while that of fixed capital is repeated once, and the *total average turnover of the capital – 20 months – has to be repeated 3 times before the fixed capital is reproduced.* Hence, the larger is the part of the capital consisting of fixed capital – i.e. the more capital acts in the mode of production corresponding to it, with great employment of produced productive force – and the more durable the fixed capital is, i.e. the longer its reproduction time, the more its use value corresponds to its specific economic role – the more often must the part of capital which is determined as circulating *repeat the period of its turnover, and the longer is the total time the capital requires for the achievement of its total circulation.* Hence the *continuity* of production becomes an external necessity for capital with the development of that portion of it which is determined as fixed capital. For circulating capital, *an interruption, if it does not last so long as to ruin its use value, is only an interruption in the creation of surplus value. But with fixed capital, the interruption,* in so far as in the meantime its use value is necessarily destroyed relatively unproductively, i.e. without replacing itself as value, is the destruction of its original value itself. Hence the continuity of the production process which corresponds to the concept of capital is posited as *conditio sine qua [non]* for its maintenance only with the development of fixed capital; hence likewise the continuity and the constant growth of consumption.

This is No. I. But No. II, the formal side, even more important.

The total time in which we measured the return of capital was the year, while the time unit in which we measure labour is the day. We did [so] firstly because the year is more or less the natural reproduction time, or duration of the production phase, for the reproduction of the largest part of the vegetable raw materials used in industry. The turnover of circulating capital was determined, therefore, by the number of turnovers in the total time of a year. In fact, the circulating capital begins its reproduction at the end of each turnover, and while the number of turnovers during the year affects the total value, and the fate it encounters during each turnover appears as a determinant of the conditions under which it begins reproduction anew, yet each of them for itself is a complete lifespan for the circulating capital. As soon as capital is transformed back into money, it can transform itself e.g. into conditions of production other than the original ones, throw itself from one branch of production into another one, so that *reproduction, regarded materially, is not repeated in the same form.*

The introduction of fixed capital changes this; and neither the turnover time of capital, nor the unit in which their number is measured, the year, henceforth appear as the measure of time for the motion of capital. This unit is now determined, rather, by the *reproduction time* required for fixed capital, and hence the total circulation time it needs to enter into circulation as value, and to come back from it in the totality of its value. The reproduction of the circulating capital must *also proceed in the same material form* during this whole time, and the number of its necessary turnovers, i.e. *the turnovers necessary for the reproduction of the original capital, is distributed over a longer or shorter series of years.* Hence a longer *total period* is posited as the unit in which its turnovers are measured, and their *repetition* is now not merely externally, but rather necessarily connected with this unit. According to Babbage, the average reproduction of machinery in England 5 years;[8] the real one hence perhaps 10 years. There can be no doubt whatever that the cycle which industry has passed through since the development of fixed capital on a large scale, at more or less 10-yearly intervals, is connected with this *total reproduction phase of capital.* We shall find other determinant causes as well. But this is one of them. There were good and bad times for industry before, too, as well as for harvests (agriculture). But the

8. Babbage, *Traité sur l'économie des machines et des manufactures,* pp. 375–6.

industrial cycle of a number of years, divided into characteristic periods, epochs, is peculiar to large-scale industry.

Now the new distinction, No. III, appears.

Circulating capital was ejected from the production process in the form of the product, of the newly created use value, and thrown wholly into circulation; when transformed back into money, the entire value of the product (the entire labour time objectified in it, necessary and surplus labour time) was realized, and thereby the surplus value realized and all conditions of reproduction fulfilled. With the realization of the price of the commodity, all these conditions were fulfilled, and the process could begin anew. This holds, however, only for that part of the circulating capital which entered into large-scale circulation. As to the other portion of it, which continuously accompanies the process of production itself, the circulation of that part of it which is transformed into wages, it naturally depends on whether the labour is used for the production of fixed capital or of circulating capital whether these wages themselves are replaced by a use value entering into circulation or not.

Fixed capital, by contrast, does not itself circulate as a use value, but rather enters as value into the manufactured raw material (in manufactures and agriculture) or into the directly extracted raw material (mining industry etc.) only to the extent that it is used up as use value in the production process. Fixed capital in its developed form hence only returns in a cycle of years which embraces a series of turnovers of circulating capital. It is not at once exchanged as product for money, in such a way that its reproduction process might coincide with the turnovers of circulating capital. It enters into the price of the product only in successive bits, and hence returns as value only successively. *It returns fragmentarily over longer periods, while circulating capital circulates wholly in shorter periods.* To the extent that fixed capital remains as such, [it] does not return, because it does not enter into circulation; to the extent that it enters into circulation, it no longer remains as fixed capital, but rather forms an ideal value-component of the circulating capital. It returns in principle only to the extent that it *transposes itself directly or indirectly into the product, hence into circulating capital.* Because it is not a direct use value for consumption, it does not enter into circulation as use value.

This different kind of return of fixed and circulating capital will appear significant later as the difference between selling and renting, annuity, interest and profit, rent in its different forms, and profit; and the incomprehension of this *merely formal* distinction has led Proudhon and his gang to the most confused conclusions; as we shall see.[9] In its observations on the last crisis, the *Economist* reduces the whole difference between fixed capital and circulating capital to the 'resale of articles within *a short period and at a profit*' (*Economist* No. 754, 6 Feb. 1858) and 'production of a revenue large enough to provide for *expenses*, risk, *wear and tear*, and the market rate of interest'.* The shorter return through the sale of the whole article, and the merely annual return of a part of the fixed capital, analysed above. As to profit – merchant's profit does not concern us here – each part of the circulating capital which leaves and returns to the production process, i.e. contains objectified labour (the value of the advances), necessary labour (the value of wages) and surplus labour – brings profit as soon as it passes fully through circulation, because the surplus labour which the product contains is realized with it. But it is neither the circulating capital nor the fixed capital which create the profit, but rather the appropriation of alien labour which both of them mediate, hence at bottom only the part of circulating capital which enters into small-scale circulation. This profit is

---

*Risk, which plays a role for the economists in the determination of profit – it can obviously play none in the surplus gain, because the creation of surplus value is not increased thereby, and possible that capital incurs risk in the *realization* of this surplus value – is the danger that the capital does not pass through the different phases of circulation, or remains fixated in one of them. We have seen that the surplus gain is part of the production costs, not of the capital, but of the product. The necessity for capital to realize this surplus gain or a part of it confronts it as a double external compulsion. As soon as profit and interest become separated, so that the industrial capitalist must pay interest, a portion of the surplus gain is *cost of production* from capital's viewpoint, i.e. belongs itself among his outlays. In another respect, it is the average assecurance which it gives itself in order to cover the risk of devaluation which it runs in the metamorphoses of the total process. A part of the surplus gain appears to the capitalist only as a compensation for the risk he runs so as to make more money; a risk which can lead to the loss of the presupposed value itself. In this form, the necessity of realizing the surplus gain appears to him as means to ensure its reproduction. Both relations, of course, do not determine the surplus value, but rather make its positing appear as an external necessity for capital, and not only as the satisfaction of its tendency to seek riches.

---

9. See below, pp. 843–5.

realized in practice, however, only through the entry of capital into circulation, hence only in its form as circulating capital, never in its form as fixed capital. But what the economist here understands by fixed capital is – as far as revenues from it are concerned – the form of fixed capital in which it does not directly enter into the production process as machinery, but rather in railways, buildings, agricultural improvements, drainings etc.,* where, hence, the realization of the value and surplus value contained in it appears in the form of an annuity, where interest represents the surplus value and the annuity the successive return of the value advanced. This is therefore not in fact a case (although it is the case with agricultural improvements) of fixed capital entering into circulation as value by forming a part of the product, but rather of the sale of fixed capital in the form of its use value. It is here sold not all at once, but as an annuity. Now, it is clear, firstly, that some forms of fixed capital figure initially as circulating capital, and become fixed capital only when they become fixed in the production process; e.g. the circulating products of a machine-maker are machines just as those of a cotton-weaver are calico, and they enter into circulation in just the same way, for him. For him they are circulating capital; for the manufacturer who uses them in the production process, fixed capital; because product for the former, and instrument of production only for the latter. Likewise even houses, despite their immovability, are circulating capital for the building-trade; for him who buys them to rent them out again, or to use them as buildings for production, they are fixed capital. Now(in so far as fixed capital itself circulates as use value, i.e. is sold, changes hands, we shall speak of it further, below.

But the viewpoint that capital is sold as capital – whether as money or in the form of fixed capital – is obviously not relevant here, where we are considering circulation as the movement of capital in which it posits itself in its various conceptually specific

---

* We are not concerned here with the illusion that *all parts of capital equally bring a profit*, an illusion arising out of the division of the surplus value into average portions, independently of the relations of the component parts of capital as circulating and fixed, and the part of it transformed into living labour. Because Ricardo half shares this illusion, he considers the influence of the proportions of fixed and circulating capital from the start of his determination of value as such, and the reverend parson Malthus stupidly and simple-mindedly speaks of the profits accruing to fixed capital, as if capital grew organically by some power of nature.

moments. Productive capital becomes product, commodity, money, and is transformed back into the conditions of production. It remains capital in each of these forms, and it becomes capital only by realizing itself as such. So long as it remains in one of these phases, it is fixed as commodity capital, money capital, or industrial capital. But each of these phases forms only one moment of its movement, and in the form from which it must propel itself to pass over into another phase it ceases to be capital. If it rejects itself as commodity and becomes money, or vice versa, then it does not exist as capital in the rejected form, but rather in the newly reached one. Of course, the rejected form can in turn become the form of another capital, or it can be the direct form of the consumable product. But this does not concern us and does not concern capital as far as the course it traces out in its internal circulation is concerned. Rather, it rejects each of the forms as its not-capital-being, so as to assume them again later. But if capital is lent out as money, as land and soil, house etc., then it becomes a commodity *as capital*, or, the commodity put into circulation is *capital as capital*. This to be further pursued in the next section.

What is paid for in the transposition of the commodity into money, as far as the part of the price which is the value of part of the fixed capital is concerned, is the part required for its partial reproduction, the part worn out and used up in the production process. What the buyer pays, then, is the use or wear of the fixed capital, in so far as it is itself value, objectified labour. Since this wear takes place successively, he pays it in portions in the product, whereas in the price he pays for the product he replaces the whole value of the fractional part of the raw material contained in the product. The worn-out, used-up fractional part of fixed capital is paid for not only successively, but also by a mass of buyers simultaneously, in relation as they buy products. Since capital appears in the first half of its circulation as C and the buyer as M, since its aim is value while the buyer's is use (whether in turn productive, no matter here, where we are examining only the formal aspect such as it appears towards capital in its circulation), it follows that the relation of the buyer to the product is that of the consumer generally. Indirectly, then, in all commodities the buyer successively and bit by bit pays for the wear and use of fixed capital, even though the latter does not enter into circulation as use value. But there are forms of fixed capital where he pays directly for its use value – as with means of communication, transport etc. In all these cases the fixed capital in fact never leaves the production process, as with railways etc. But while it serves for some as means of communication within the production process itself, to bring the product to market, and for the producers themselves [as] means of circulation, it can serve others as means of consumption, as use value, for holiday travel, etc. Regarded as a means of production, it distinguishes itself from machinery etc. here in that it is used up by various capitals at the same time, as a common condition for their production and circulation. (We are not yet concerned with consumption as such here.) It does not appear as locked within a particular production process, but rather as the connecting artery of a mass of such production processes of particular capitals, who use it up only in portions. In contrast to all these particular capitals and their particular production processes, then, fixed capital is here cast as the product of a particular branch of production separate from them, in which, however, it is not sold by one producer as circulating capital and bought by another as fixed capital, as with machinery, but, rather, in which it can be sold only in the form of fixed capital itself. Then its successive return, hidden in the commodity, becomes apparent. But this fixed capital then also includes the surplus value, since it is itself a sold product (for the industrialist, the machine he uses is not a product), hence the return of interest and profit, if any. Since it can be consumed in the same common and successive form, can be use value for direct consumption, it follows that its sale – not as an instrument of production but as a commodity generally – also appears in the same form. But in so far as it is sold as an instrument of production – a machine is *sold* as a mere commodity and only becomes an instrument of production in the industrial process – i.e. as its sale directly coincides with its use in the general social production process, this is a determination which has no place within the examination of the simple circulation of capital. In the latter, fixed capital, in so far as it enters as an agency of production, appears as a presupposition of the production process, not as its result. It can therefore only be a matter of the replacement of its value, in which no surplus value for the user is included. What is rather the case is that *he* has paid this surplus value to the machine-maker. Railways, however, or buildings rented for production, are *simultaneously* instruments of production, and are simultaneously realized by their seller as product, as capital.

Since each moment which appears as presupposition of production is at the same time its result – in that it reproduces its own conditions – the original division of the capital within the production process now appears in such a way that the production process divides into three production processes, in which different portions of the capital – which now also appear as particular capitals – are at work. (Here we can still assume a form in which one capital is at work, because we are examining capital *as such*, and this way of looking at it simplifies what needs to be said about the proportion of these different kinds.) The capital is annually reproduced in different and changing portions as raw material, as product, and as means of production; in a word, as fixed capital and as circulating capital. The minimum presupposition which appears in all of these production processes is the part of circulating capital destined for exchange with labouring capacity and for the maintenance and consumption of the machinery or the instrument, and the means of production. In purely extractive industries, e.g. mining, the mine itself exists as the material of labour, but not as raw material passing over into product, which latter must, in the manufacturing industry, by contrast, have a particular existence in all forms. In agriculture, seed, fertilizer, cattle etc., may be regarded as raw material as well as *matières instrumentales*. Agriculture forms a mode of production *sui generis*, because the organic process is involved, in addition to the mechanical and chemical process, and the natural reproduction process is merely controlled and guided; extractive industry (mining the most important) is likewise an industry *sui generis*, because no reproduction process whatever takes place in it, at least not one under our control or known to us. (Fishery, hunting etc. can involve a reproduction process; likewise forestry; this is therefore not necessarily purely extractive industry.) Now, in so far as the means of production, fixed capital as the product of capital and hence containing objectified surplus time, is itself constituted in such a way that it can be ejected by its producer as circulating capital, e.g. like machinery by the machine builder, before it becomes fixed capital, i.e. first enters into circulation as use value, [to that extent] its circulation contains no new aspect whatever. But in so far as it can never be sold while it serves at the same time as instrument of production, as e.g. railways, or in proportion as it is used up as such, it shares with fixed capital generally the quality that its value returns only successively; but there is also the addition that this return of its value includes the return of its surplus value, of the surplus labour objectified in it. It then has a special form of return.

The important thing now is that the production of capital thus appears as the production in definite portions of circulating capital and fixed capital, so that capital itself produces its double way of circulating as fixed capital and circulating capital.

Fixed capital and circulating capital. Economist. Smith.
Counter-value of circulating capital must be produced within the
year. Not so for fixed capital. It engages the production of
subsequent years

Before we settle the last point, first a few secondary matters. 'Floating capital is consumed, fixed capital merely used, in the great work of production.' (*Economist*, VI, p. 1.) The distinction between *consume* and *use* dissolves into gradual or rapid destruction. We need dwell on this point no further.

'Floating capital assumes an *infinite variety of forms*, fixed capital *has only one*.' (*Economist*, VI, p. 1.)[10] This 'infinite variety of forms', as regards the production process of capital itself, is much more correctly reduced by Adam Smith to a mere change of form. Fixed capital is of use to its master 'so long as it continues to remain in the same form'. That means it remains within the production process as use value, in a specific material presence. Circulating capital, by contrast (A. Smith, tome II, p. 197, 198) 'constantly passes out of his hands in a specific form' (as product) 'to return in another' (as condition of production) 'and brings profit only by means of this circulation and successive changes'. Smith does not speak here of the 'infinite variety of forms' in which circulating capital appears. Regarded materially, 'fixed capital' also assumes 'an infinite variety of forms'; but this proceeds from the metamorphoses which circulating capital passes through as itself a use value, and the 'infinite variety of forms' reduces itself, therefore, to the qualitative differences of the various phases of circulation. Regarded within a specific production process, circulating capital always returns in the same form of raw materials and money for wages. The material presence is the same at the end of the process as at the beginning. Incidentally, elsewhere the *Economist* itself reduces the 'infinite variety of

10. *The Economist*, Vol. V, No. 219, 6 November 1847, p. 1271.

forms' to the conceptually determined change of forms in circulation. 'The commodity is wholly consumed in the shape in which it is produced' (i.e. enters into circulation as use value and is ejected from it) 'and replaced in his hands in *a new shape*' (as raw material and wages), 'ready to repeat a *similar* operation' (rather, the same operation). (loc. cit. VI, p. 1.)[11] Smith also says explicitly that fixed capital 'requires no circulation'. (tome II, 197, 198.) With *fixed capital*, the value is imprisoned within a specific use value; with circulating capital, value takes the form of various different use values, likewise assumes as well as rejects the independent form distinct from every particular use value (as money); hence constant change of matter and form goes on.

'Circulating capital supplies him' (the entrepreneur) 'with the materials and wages of the workers, and sets industry into activity.' (A. Smith, tome II, p. 226.) '*Every fixed capital comes originally from a circulating capital*, and needs to be continually maintained *by means of a circulating capital*.' (loc. cit. p. 207.) 'Since so great a part of the circulating capital is being withdrawn continuously to be spent in the other two branches of the general social fund, this capital needs in turn to be renewed by continual replenishment, otherwise it would soon be reduced to nothing. These replenishments are drawn from three principal sources: the produce of the soil, of mines, and of fisheries.' (loc. cit. p. 208.)

⟨We have already developed one distinction emphasized by the *Economist*: 'Every production the whole cost of which is returned to the producer out of the *current income* of the country is *floating capital*; but every production, in respect of which only an *annual sum is paid for the use, is – fixed capital*.' (Notebook VI, p. 1.)[12] 'In the first case, the producer is entirely dependent on the country's current income.' (loc. cit.) We have seen that only part of the fixed capital returns in the time determined by circulating capital, which serves as the unit of its turnovers because it is the natural unit for the reproduction of the greatest part of food products and raw materials, just as, and because, it appears as the natural epoch in the life process (cosmic process) of the earth. This unit is the year, whose bourgeois calculation deviates more or less, but insignificantly, from its natural magnitude. The more the material presence of fixed capital corresponds to its concept, the more adequate its material mode of existence is, the more does its turnover time span a cycle of years. Since circulating capital is

11. *The Economist,* Vol. V, No. 219, 6 November 1847, p. 1271.   12. ibid

wholly exchanged first for money, secondly for its elements, it presupposes that a *countervalue has been produced* equal to its whole value (including the surplus value). It cannot be said that it enters or can enter into consumption entirely; since it must also in part serve in turn as raw material, or as an element for fixed capital; in short itself, in turn, as an element of production – a counter-production. A part of the use value ejected by capital as the product, as the result of the production process, becomes an object of consumption and thus drops out of the circulation of capital altogether; another part enters into another capital as a condition of production. This is itself posited in the circulation of capital *as such*, since it ejects itself from itself in the first half of circulation, as commodity, i.e. as use value; i.e. dismisses itself *with respect to itself* in this form from its own circulation as use value, article of consumption; but exchanges itself as money for commodity as condition of production, in the second half of its circulation. Thus, as circulating use value itself, it posits its material presence both as an article of consumption and as a new element of production, or rather an element of reproduction. But in both cases the whole of its countervalue must be on hand; i.e. it must have been wholly produced during the year. For example, the sum of manufactured products which can be exchanged during a year for agricultural products is determined by the mass of the raw products produced in a year, counted from harvest to harvest. Since we speak here of capital *as such*, capital in the process of becoming, we are not yet concerned with anything else in addition – in that the many capitals are not yet present for us – nothing but it itself and simple circulation, out of which it absorbs value in the double form of money and commodity and into which it throws it in the double form of money and commodity. When an industrial people producing on the foundation of capital, such as the English, e.g., exchange with the Chinese, and absorb value in the form of money and commodity from out of their production process, or rather absorb value by drawing the latter within the sphere of the circulation of their capital, then one sees right away that the Chinese do not therefore need to produce as capitalists. Within a single society, such as the English, the mode of production of capital develops in one branch of industry, while in another, e.g. agriculture, modes of production predominate which more or less antedate capital. Nevertheless, it is (1) its necessary tendency to conquer the mode of production in all respects, to bring them under the rule of capital. Within a given national society this already necessarily arises from the transformation, by this means, of all labour into wage labour; (2) as to external markets, capital imposes this propagation of its mode of production through international competition. Competition is the mode generally in which capital secures the victory of its mode of production. Still, this much is clear: quite regardless of whether it is another capital or whether it is capital itself as another which stands on both sides of the successive exchanges, each time in the opposite aspect, both aspects are already posited before we proceed to examine this double movement from the circulation of capital *as such* itself. In the first phase it ejects itself out of the movement of capital as use value, as commodity, and exchanges itself for money. The commodity expelled from the circulation of capital is no longer the commodity as a moment of self-perpetuating value, as the presence of value. It is, thus, its presence as use value, its being for consumption. Capital is transposed out of the form of commodity into the form of money only because an exchanger appears *opposite it* in ordinary circulation as consumer, who transposes M into C; [completes] this transposition in its material aspect, so that he relates to the use value as use value, as consumer, and only in this way is the use value replaced for capital as *value*. Thus, capital creates articles of consumption, but ejects them from itself in this form, ejects them from its circulation. On the basis of the aspect developed so far, no other relations exist. The commodity which is ejected as such from the circulation of capital loses its character as value and fulfils the role of use value for consumption, as distinct from fulfilling it for production. But in the second phase of circulation, capital exchanges money for commodity, and its transformation into commodity now itself appears as a moment of value-positing, because the commodity is accepted as such into the circulation process of capital. While it presupposes consumption in the first phase, in the second it presupposes production, production for production; for value in the form of the commodity is here taken into the circulation of capital from the outside, or, the inverse process is undertaken in the first phase. The commodity, as use value for capital itself, can only be the commodity as an element, use value, for its production process. In its double form, the process presents itself in this way: capital *a* exchanges its product as C for capital *b*'s M in the first phase; in the second, capital *b* as

C exchanges for capital *a*'s M. Or, in the first phase, capital *b* as M exchanges for capital *a*'s C, in the second, *a* as M for capital *b*'s C. That is, capital is simultaneously posited in each of the two circulation phases as M and C; but in two different capitals, which are always in the opposite phase of their circulation process. In the simple circulation process, the acts of exchange, C—M or M—C appear either as directly coinciding or as directly divided. Circulation is not only the succession of both forms of exchange, but it is at the same time each of them distributed to two different sides. But we are not yet concerned here with exchange among many capitals. This belongs to the theory of competition or to that of the circulation of capitals (of credit). What concerns us here is the presupposition of consumption on one side – of the commodity ejected from the movement of value as use value – and the presupposition of production for production – of value, posited as use value, as a condition of its reproduction posited externally to the circulation of capital on the other side – so that these two sides arise out of the examination of the simple form of the circulation of capital. This much is clear: Since the entire circulating capital exchanges as C for M in the first phase, and as M for C in the second, then, if we regard the year as the unit of time of its evolutions, its transformations are limited both by the annual reproduction of raw materials etc. (the commodity for which it exchanges as money must have been produced, a simultaneous production must correspond to it), and by the constant creation of an annual revenue (the part of M which exchanges for commodity as use value) to consume the product of capital which is ejected as use value. Since further-developed relations are not present yet, such revenues are only those of the capitalists themselves and those of the workers. The examination of the exchange of capital and revenue, by the way, another form of the relation of production and consumption, does not belong here yet. In another respect, since fixed capital is exchanged only to the extent it enters as value into circulating capital, since it is, thus, realized only in part during the year, it presupposes only a *partial counter-value*, i.e. only the partial production of this counter-value during the course of the year. It is paid for only in proportion to its wear. This much clear, then, which already follows from the difference introduced by fixed capital into the industrial cycle, namely that *it engages the production of subsequent years*, and, just as it contributes to the creation of a large revenue, it anticipates further labour as a counter-value. The anticipation of future fruits of labour is therefore in no way a consequence of the state debt etc., in short, not an invention of the credit system. It has *its roots in the specific mode of realization, mode of turnover, mode of reproduction of fixed capital.*⟩

Since we are essentially concerned here with grasping the pure, specific economic forms, hence with not joining together things that do not belong, it has thus become clear from the above that the different forms in which circulating capital and fixed capital bring revenue – as well as the examination of revenue generally – do not yet belong here at all; but only the different ways in which they return and affect the total turnover of capital, the movement of its reproduction generally. Nevertheless, the incidental points made here are important – in that they reject the economists' motley compilations, which have no place yet in the examination of the simple distinction between fixed capital and circulating capital – and because they showed us that the differences in revenue etc. have their basis in the difference of form between the reproduction of fixed and circulating capital. The issue here is still only the simple return of the value. Only later will it be found how the latter becomes the return of revenue, and that in turn becomes the difference in the determination of revenue.

Maintenance costs

We have said nothing so far about the *maintenance costs*, the *frais d'entretien* of fixed capital. These are partly the *matières instrumentales* it consumes in its action. They make up fixed capital in the first sense, as we have regarded it within the production process. These are circulating capital and may just as well serve for consumption. They become fixed capital only in so far as they are consumed in the production process, but do not have, like fixed capital proper, a material substance determined purely by their formal presence. The second part of these maintenance costs consists of the labour necessary for repairs.

Revenue of fixed capital and circulating capital

A. Smith's determination that every fixed capital comes originally from a circulating capital and must be constantly maintained by a circulating capital: 'Every fixed capital originally comes from a circulating capital and must be continually kept up at the latter's expense. *No fixed capital can yield revenue except at the expense of a circulating capital.*' (Storch, 26a.)[13] As to Storch's remark about revenue–an aspect which does not belong here–it is clear: fixed capital returns as value only in proportion as it becomes extinguished as use value, as fixed capital, and enters into circulating capital as value. Hence it can return in the form of a circulating capital only in so far as its *value* is concerned. But it does not circulate at all as use value. Further, since it has a use value only for production, it can return for individual use, for consumption, also only in the form of circulating capital. Improvements of the soil can directly enter chemically into the reproduction process and in this way be directly transformed into use values. But then they are consumed in their form as fixed capital. *A capital can bring revenue at all only in the form in which it enters into and returns from circulation, because the production of revenue in direct use values, use values not mediated through circulation, contradicts the nature of capital. Hence, since fixed capital returns as value only in the form of circulating capital, it can bring revenue only in this form.* Revenue is nothing whatsoever other than the part of the surplus value destined for immediate consumption. Its returns thus depend on the mode of return of value itself. Hence the different forms in which fixed capital and circulating capital bring revenue. Likewise, since fixed capital as such never enters circulation as use value, hence is never thrown out of the realization process as use value, it never serves for immediate consumption.

Now as to Smith, his view becomes clearer for us when he says that circulating capital must be annually replaced and constantly renewed by constantly drawing it from the sea, the soil, and from mines. Here, then, circulating capital becomes purely material for him; it is fished out by the hairs, chipped out, harvested; they are the movable primary products which are released from their connection with the earth, isolated, made movable thereby, or separated from their element in their ready-made individuality, like fish etc. Still regarded as pure material, it is further certain that, if Smith presupposes the production of capital and does not

13. The first part of this quotation is taken over by Storch from the French edition of Adam Smith, Vol. II, p. 207 (see above, p. 728); the whole quotation, with the addition of Storch's remark about revenue, is to be found in Storch, *Cours d'économie politique*, Vol. I, p. 246.

suppose himself at the beginning of the world, then every circulating capital likewise comes originally from a fixed capital. Without nets he can catch no fish; without a plough, till no fields; and without a hammer, etc., drive no mines. If he uses even so little as a stone for a hammer etc., then this stone is certainly no circulating capital, no capital of any sort, but rather a means of labour. As soon as he has to produce, man possesses the resolve to use a part of the available natural objects directly as means of labour, and, as Hegel correctly said it, subsumes them under his activity without further process of mediation.[14] The place where all capital, circulating as well as fixed, not only originally but continually comes from is the appropriation of alien labour. But this process presupposes, as we have seen, a continuous small-scale circulation, the exchange of wages for labour capacity, or *approvisionnement*. Assuming the production process of capital: *All capital returns only in the form of a circulating capital*; hence fixed capital can be renewed only by a process in which a part of circulating capital becomes fixed; hence, by the employment of part of the raw materials produced, and a part of labour consumed (hence also a part of the *approvisionnement* exchanged for living labour) for the production of fixed capital. In agriculture, e.g., part of the product is consumed by labour to build irrigation systems or a part of the grain is exchanged for guano, chemical substances etc., which are incorporated into the earth, but also in fact have no use value except in so far as they are surrendered to the chemical process of the soil. A part of the circulating capital has a use value only for the reproduction of the fixed capital, and is produced (even if its production consisted only of the labour time spent in changing its location) only for fixed capital. But fixed capital itself can be renewed as capital only by becoming a value-component of circulating capital, and its *elements are thus reproduced through the transformation of circulating capital* into fixed capital. *Fixed capital is as much a presupposition for the production of circulating capital as circulating capital is for the production of fixed capital*. Or, the reproduction of fixed capital requires: (1) the return of its value in the form of a circulating capital, for only in this way can it in turn be exchanged for the

14. Cf. Hegel, *Science of Logic*, p. 746: 'The relation of the activity of the end through the means to the external object is . . . an immediate relation of the middle term to the other extreme. It is immediate because the middle term has an external object in it and the other extreme is another such object.'

conditions of its production; (2) that a part of living labour and of the raw material be used to produce instruments of production, direct or indirect ones, instead of producing exchangeable products. Circulating capital enters as use value into fixed capital, just as does labour, while fixed capital enters as value into circulating capital; and, as movement (where it is direct machinery), as static motion, as form, into the use value.

Free labour = latent pauperism. Eden[15]

⟨In connection with our statements developed above, that pauperism latent in free labour, the following statements by Sir Fr. Morton Eden, Bt: *The State of the Poor, or an History of the Labouring Classes in England from the Conquest etc.*, 3 vols., 4°, London, 1797. (The quotations from Vol. I, bk I.) (In book I, chapter I, it says: 'Our zone requires labour for the satisfaction of needs, and *therefore* at least *one part* of society must *always tirelessly* labour; others labour in the arts etc., and some, who do not work, still have the products of diligence at their disposal. For this, these proprietors have only *civilization and order* to thank; they are purely the creatures of *civilized institutions.* For these have recognized that one can also obtain the fruits of labour through ways other than labour; the men of independent fortune owe their *wealth almost entirely to the labour of others*, not to their own ability, which is not at all better. What divides the rich from the poorer is not the ownership of land or of money, but rather the command of labour.' *Poverty* as such begins with the tiller's freedom – the feudal fetters to the soil, or at least the locality, had until then spared the legislature the task of occupying itself with the vagrants, poor etc. Eden believes that the various commercial guilds etc. also fed their own poor. He said: 'Without the most distant idea, then, of disparaging the numberless benefits derived for the country from manufactures and commerce, the result of this investigation seems to lead *to this inevitable conclusion that manufactures and commerce*' (i.e. the first sphere of production in which capital became predominant) 'are *the true parents of our national poor.*' In the same place: Beginning with

15. Sir Frederick Morton Eden, Bt (1766–1809) was inspired by the high prices of 1794 and 1795 to make the first ever investigation into working-class history. 'The only disciple of Adam Smith throughout the eighteenth century who produced anything of importance' (Marx).

Henry VII (where at the same time there began the clearing of the land of superfluous mouths through transformation of the tilled fields into pasture, continuing for more than 150 years, at least the litigation and legislative interference; hence the number of hands made available for industry grew), wages in industry were no longer fixed, only in agriculture. 11, Henry VII. (With free labour, wage labour is not yet completely posited. The labourers still have support in the feudal relations; their supply is still too small; capital hence still unable to reduce them to the minimum. Hence statutory determination of wages. So long as wages are still regulated by statute, it cannot yet be said either that capital has subsumed production under itself as capital, or that wage labour has attained the mode of existence adequate to it.) The act cited also mentions linen weavers, building craftsmen, shipwrights. The same act also fixes the hours of labour: 'Because many day labourers waste half the day, arrive late, leave early, take a long afternoon nap, spend a long time at breakfast, lunch and dinner, etc. etc.,' it ordains the following hours: 'from 15 March to 15 September, from 5 a.m., $\frac{1}{2}$ hour breakfast, $1\frac{1}{2}$ dinner and siesta, $\frac{1}{2}$ hour for noon meal, and work until between 7 and 8 p.m. In winter, however, no siesta during daylight; this permitted only from 15 May to 15 August.'⟩

⟨Wages again regulated in 1514, almost like the previous time. Hours of work again fixed. Whoever will not work upon application, arrested. Hence still *compulsory labour* by free workers at the given wages. They must first be *forced* to work within the conditions posited by capital. The propertyless are more inclined to become vagabonds and robbers and beggars than workers. The last becomes normal only in the developed mode of capital's production. In the prehistory of capital, state coercion to transform the propertyless into *workers* at conditions advantageous for capital, which are not yet here forced upon the workers by competition among one another.⟩ (Very bloody means of coercion of this sort employed under Henry VIII et. al.) (Suppression of the *monasteries* under Henry VIII likewise frees many hands.) (Under Edward VI still sharper laws against able-bodied labourers who do not want to work. '1 Edw. VI, 3: Who is able to work, refuses to labour, and lives idle for 3 days, shall be branded with redhot iron on the breast with the letter V – and shall be adjudged the slave for two years of the person who should inform against such idler etc.' 'If he runs away from his master for 14 days he shall become his slave for life and be branded on forehead or cheek with letter S, and if he runs away a second time and shall be convicted thereof by two sufficient witnesses, he shall be taken as a felon and suffer pains of death.' (1376 first mention of the vagrants, sturdy rogues, 1388 the paupers.) (Similar cruel statute 1572 under Elizabeth.)[16]

The smaller the value of fixed capital in relation to its product, the more useful. – Movable, immovable, fixed and circulating. – Connection of circulation and reproduction. Necessity of reproducing use value in definite *time*

Circulating capital and fixed capital, which appeared earlier as changing forms of the same capital in the different phases of its turnover, are now, when fixed capital is developed to its highest form, posited at the same time as two different modes of the existence of capital. They become such through the difference in kind of their return. Circulating capital which returns slowly has a quality in common with fixed capital. But it distinguishes itself from it because its use value itself – its material presence – enters into circulation and is at the same time shed by it, thrown beyond the bounds of the turnover process; while fixed capital – to the extent that it has been developed at this point – enters into circulation only as value, and, as long as it is still in circulation as a use value, such as e.g. the machine in circulation, it is fixed capital only δυνάμει. However, this distinction between fixed capital and circulating capital, resting initially on the relation of the material presence of the capital, or of its presence as use value, towards circulation, must, with reproduction, be posited at the same time as the reproduction of the capital in the double form of fixed capital and circulating capital. In so far as the reproduction of capital in every form is the positing not only of objectified labour time, but rather of surplus labour time, not only reproduction of its value but of a surplus value, the production of fixed capital cannot therefore be different in this regard from the production of circulating capital. Hence, in the manufacture of instruments or machines – in all the forms where fixed capital appears first as circulating capital in its material presence, in its presence as use

16. The passages from Eden's book (Vol. I, Bk 1) are as follows, beginning with the passage on p. 735 of the present edition: pp. 1–2; pp. 57–61; pp. 75–6; p. 100; p. 101.

value before becoming fixed as fixed capital, i.e. before it is consumed, for it is precisely its consumption which binds it to the production phase and distinguishes it as fixed capital – there is no difference at all, as to the realization of capital, whether it reproduces itself in the form of fixed or of circulating capital. Hence no new economic determination enters here, either. But where fixed capital as such is thrown into circulation by its producer – and not as circulating capital – hence where *its proportionate use is sold, either for production* or for consumption – for in the transformation of C into M, which takes place in the first section of the circulation of capital, it is irrelevant to the latter whether the commodity in turn enters into the circulation sphere of another productive capital, or whether it serves the purpose of direct consumption; for the first capital, it is rather *always determined as a use value* whenever it ejects it from itself, exchanges it for M – there the mode of return must be different for the producer of fixed capital from that for the producer of circulating capital. The surplus value created by him can return only proportionately and successively with the value itself. This to be looked at in the next section. Finally, although circulating capital and fixed capital now appear as two different kinds, circulating capital is still posited through the consumption, the wear of fixed capital; while fixed capital, for its part, exists only as a circulating capital transformed into this specific form. All capital transformed into objectified productive power – all fixed capital – is a use value fixated in this form, and hence a use value snatched away from consumption as well as from circulation. The transformation of wood, iron, coal and living labour (hence also indirectly that of the products consumed by the worker) into the specific use values of a machine or a railway would not by itself turn them into fixed capital if the other determinants developed above were absent. When circulating capital is transformed into fixed capital, then a part of the use values in whose form capital circulated, as well as indirectly the part of the capital which exchanges for living labour, are transformed into capital whose counter-value is created only over a longer cycle; which enters into circulation as value only proportionately and successively; and which can be realized as value only through being used up in production. The transformation of circulating capital into fixed capital presupposes relative surplus capital, since it is capital employed not for direct production but rather for new means of production. Fixed capital itself can in turn serve as a direct instrument of production – as a means within the immediate production process. In this case its value enters into the product and is replaced by the successive return of the products. Or it does not enter into the immediate production process – appears rather as a general condition for production processes, such as buildings, railways etc., and its value can be replaced only through circulating capital, to whose creation it indirectly contributed. Questions of greater detail about the proportion in the production of fixed capital and circulating capital belong to the following section. If valuable machinery were employed to supply a small quantity of products, then it would not act as a force of production, but rather make the product infinitely more expensive than if the work had been done without machinery. It creates value not in so far as it has value – for the latter is simply replaced – but rather only in so far as it increases relative surplus time, or decreases necessary labour time. In the same proportion, then, as that in which its scope grows, the mass of products must increase, and the living labour employed relatively decrease. *The less the value of the fixed capital in relation to its effectiveness, the more does it correspond to its purpose.* All unnecessary fixed capital appears as *faux frais de production*, like all unnecessary circulation costs. If capital could possess the machinery without employing labour for the purpose, then it would raise the productive power of labour and diminish necessary labour without having to buy labour. The value of the fixed capital is therefore never an end in itself in the production of capital.

Circulating capital, then, is transformed into fixed capital, and fixed capital reproduces itself in circulating capital; both, only in so far as capital appropriates living labour.

'Every saving in fixed capital is an increase in the net revenue of society.' (A. Smith.)[17]

The final and last distinction cited by economists is that between *movable and immovable*; not in the sense that the former enters into the movement of circulation, the latter does not; rather in the sense that the former is physically fixed, immovable, in the same way as movable and immovable property is distinguished. For example, improvements sunk in the soil, aqueducts, buildings; and machinery itself in great part, since it must be physically

17. Adam Smith, *Recherches sur la nature et les causes de la richesse des nations*, Vol. II, p. 226.

fixed, to act; railways; in short, every form in which the product of industry is welded fast to the surface of the earth. This basically adds nothing to the determination of fixed capital; but it is indeed part of this character that it becomes fixed capital in a more eminent sense the more its use value, its material presence, corresponds to its specific economic form. The immovable use value, such as house, railway etc., is therefore the most tangible form of fixed capital. Of course, it can then still circulate in the same sense as immovable property generally – as title; but not as use value; it cannot circulate in the physical sense. Originally, the growth of movable property, its increase as against immovable, indicates the ascendant movement of capital as against landed property. But once the mode of production of capital is presupposed, the level to which it has conquered the conditions of production is indicated in the transformation of capital into immovable property. It thereby establishes its residence on the land itself, and the seemingly solid presuppositions given by nature, themselves [appear], in landed property, as merely posited by industry.

(Originally, life in the community and, through its mediation, the relationship to the earth as property, are basic presuppositions of the reproduction both of the individual and of the community. Among pastoral peoples, land and soil appear merely as precondition of the migratory life, hence appropriation does not take place. Fixed settlements with soil cultivation follow – thus landed property is initially held in common, and even where it advances to private property the individuals' connection to it appears as posited by his relation to the community. It appears as a mere fief of the community; etc. etc. The transformation of the latter into mere exchangeable value – its mobilization – is the product of capital and of the complete subordination of the state organism to it. Land and soil, even where they have become private property, are therefore exchange value only in a restricted sense. Exchange value begins in the isolated natural product, separated from the earth and individualized through industry (or mere appropriation). Individual labour first arises here too. Exchange as such does not begin within the original communes, but on their boundaries, where they cease to be. Of course, to exchange the land, their residence, to pawn it to alien communes, would be treason. Exchange can expand only little by little from its original realm, movable property, to immovable property. Only through expansion of the former does it little by little gain control over the latter. Money is the chief agent in this process.)

A. Smith at first distinguishes circulating capital and fixed capital by their role in the *production process*. Only later does he adopt the expression: 'One can gainfully lay out a capital in different ways, (1) as circulating capital, (2) as fixed capital.'[18] This second expression obviously does not belong to the examination of this distinction as such, since fixed capital and circulating capital first have to be presupposed as two kinds of capital before we can speak about how to lay out capital gainfully in both forms.

'The total capital of each entrepreneur is necessarily divided into his fixed capital and his circulating capital. If the sum is equal, then the one becomes larger as the other diminishes.' (A. Smith, tome II, p. 226.)

Since capitals are (1) divided into fixed and circulating capital in unequal portions; (2) [have] an interrupted or uninterrupted production phase and return from more distant or nearer markets, hence, unequal circulation time; it follows that the determination of the surplus value created in a given time, e.g. annually, must be unequal because the number of reproduction processes in the given period is unequal. The amount of value created appears determined not simply by the labour employed during the immediate production process, but by the degree to which this exploitation of labour can be repeated within a given period of time.

Finally, then: While, in the examination of the simple production process, capital appeared to realize itself as value only in connection with wage labour, and circulation lay alongside, without connection to it, here, in its reproduction process, circulation is included in it in both the moments of circulation, C–M–M–C (as a system of exchanges through which it must pass, and to which the same number of qualitative changes within it correspond). In so far as its form as money is the point of departure and hence of return, circulation appears included in it as M–C–C–M. It contains both circular courses, and not merely as either change of form or change of substance, but rather as both of them included within the determination of value itself. The production process, as containing within itself the conditions of its renewal, is a reproduction process whose speed is determined by various relations developed above, which all arise from dif-

18. Adam Smith, *Recherches sur la nature et les causes de la richesse des nations*, Vol. II, pp. 197–8.

ferences of circulation. The reproduction of capital also contains
the reproduction of the use values in which it is realized – or the
constant renewal and reproduction by human labour of the use
values which enter human consumption and are themselves
perishable. The change of substance and of form subordinated to
human need through human labour appears from the viewpoint
of capital as its own reproduction. It is at bottom the constant
reproduction of labour itself. 'Capital values perpetuate themselves by reproduction: the products which compose a capital
are consumed just like any others; but their value, at the same
time as it is destroyed by consumption, is reproduced in other
materials or in the same one.' (Say, 14.)[19] Exchange and a system
of exchanges, and, included in that, the transformation into
money as independent value, appears as condition and barrier
for the reproduction of capital. With capital, production itself
is on all sides subordinate to exchange. These exchange operations,
circulation as such, produce no surplus value, but are conditions
for its realization. They are conditions of the *production of capital
itself*, in so far as its *form as capital* is posited only to the extent
that it passes through them. The reproduction of capital is at the
same time the production of specific formal conditions; of
specific modes of relationship in which personified objectified
labour is posited. Circulation is thus not merely the exchange of
the product for the conditions of production – i.e. of produced
wheat, e.g., for seed, new labour etc. The worker must exchange
his product for the conditions of production, so as to begin anew,
in every form of production. The peasant producing for immediate
consumption also transforms part of the product into seed, instrument of labour, beasts of burden, fertilizer etc., and begins his
labour anew. The transformation into money is necessary for the
reproduction of capital as such, and its reproduction is necessarily
the production of surplus value.* Although labour must merely

* In regard to the reproduction phase (especially circulation time), note that
use value itself places limits upon it. Wheat must be reproduced in a year.
Perishable things like milk etc. must be reproduced more often. Meat on the
hoof does not need to be reproduced quite so often, since the animal is alive
and hence resists time; but slaughtered meat on the market has to be reproduced in the form of money in the very short term, or it rots. The reproduction of value and of use value partly coincide, partly not.

19. Say, *Traité d'économie politique*, Vol. II, p. 185.

maintain the value of what we earlier called constant capital in one production process, it must constantly reproduce it in another, since what appears as presupposition of material and instrument in one production process is product in the other, and this renewal, reproduction, must constantly proceed simultaneously.

Capital as Fructiferous. Transformation of Surplus Value into Profit

We now come to the

THIRD SECTION. CAPITAL AS FRUCTIFEROUS. INTEREST. PROFIT. (PRODUCTION COSTS ETC.)

Rate of profit. – Fall of the rate of profit. – Rate of profit. – Sum of profit. – Atkinson. A. Smith. Ramsay. Ricardo. – Surplus value as profit *always expresses a lesser proportion. – Wakefield. Carey. Bastiat*

Capital is now posited as the unity of production and circulation; and the surplus value it creates in a given period of time, e.g. in one year, is $= \dfrac{ST}{p+c} = \dfrac{ST}{R}$ or $= S\left(\dfrac{T}{p} - \dfrac{T}{p} \times \dfrac{c}{c+p}\right)$. Capital is now realized not only as value which reproduces itself and is hence perennial, but also as value which posits value. Through the absorption of living labour time and through the movement of its own circulation (in which the movement of exchange is posited as its own, as the inherent process of objectified labour), it relates to itself as positing new value, as producer of value. It relates as the foundation to surplus value as that which it founded. Its movement consists of relating to itself, while it produces itself, at the same time as the foundation of what it has founded, as value presupposed to itself as surplus value, or to the surplus value as posited by it. In a definite period of time which is posited as the unit measure of its turnovers because it is the natural measure of its reproduction in agriculture, capital produces a definite surplus value, which is determined not only by the surplus value it posits in one production process, but rather by the number of repetitions of the production process, or of its reproductions in a specified period of time. Because of the inclusion of circulation, of its movement outside the immediate production process, within the reproduction process, surplus value *appears* no longer to be posited by its simple, direct relation to living labour; this relation appears, rather, as merely a moment of its total movement. Proceeding from itself as the active subject, the subject of the process – and, in the turnover, the direct production process indeed appears determined by its movement as capital, independent of its relation to labour – capital relates to itself as self-increasing value; i.e. it relates to surplus value as something posited and founded by it; it relates as well-spring of production, to itself as product; it relates as producing value to itself as produced value. It therefore no longer measures the newly produced value by its real measure, the relation of surplus labour to necessary labour, but rather by itself as its presupposition. A capital of a certain value produces in a certain period of time a certain surplus value. Surplus value thus measured by the value of the presupposed capital, capital thus posited as self-realizing value – is *profit*; regarded not *sub specie aeternitatis*, but *sub specie – capitalis*, the surplus value is profit; and capital as capital, the producing and reproducing value, distinguishes itself within itself from itself as profit, the newly produced value. The product of capital is *profit*. The magnitude, surplus value, is therefore measured by the value-magnitude of the capital, and the *rate of profit* is therefore determined by the proportion between its value and the value of capital. A very large part of what belongs here has been developed above.[20] But the anticipated material is to be put here. In so far as the newly posited value, which is of the same nature as the capital, is itself in turn taken up into the production process, itself in turn maintains itself as capital, to that extent the capital itself has grown, and now acts as a capital of greater value. After it has distinguished the profit, as newly reproduced value, from itself as presupposed, self-realizing value, and has posited profit as the measure of its realization, it suspends the separation again, and posits it in its identity to itself as capital which, grown by the amount of the profit, now begins the same process anew in larger dimensions. By describing its circle it expands itself as the subject of the circle and thus describes a self-expanding circle, a spiral.

The general laws developed previously here briefly summarized thus: The real surplus value is determined by the relation of

20. See above, pp. 333–53.

surplus labour to necessary labour, or by the portion of the capital, the portion of objectified labour, which exchanges for living labour, relative to the portion of objectified labour by which it is replaced. But surplus value in the form of profit is measured by the total value of the capital presupposed to the production process. Presupposing the same surplus value, *the same surplus labour in proportion to necessary labour*, then, the *rate of profit* depends on the relation between the part of capital exchanged for living labour and the part existing in the form of raw material and means of production. Hence, the smaller the portion exchanged for living labour becomes, the smaller becomes the rate of profit. Thus, in the same proportion as capital takes up a larger place as capital in the production process relative to immediate labour, i.e. the more the relative surplus value grows – the value-creating power of capital – the more *does the rate of profit fall*. We have seen that the magnitude of the capital already presupposed, presupposed to reproduction, is specifically expressed in the growth of fixed capital, as the produced productive force, objectified labour endowed with apparent life. The total value of the producing capital will express itself in each of its portions as a diminished proportion of the capital exchanged for living labour relative to the part of capital existing as constant value. Take e.g. manufacturing industry. In the same proportion as fixed capital grows here, machinery etc., the part of capital existing in raw materials must grow, while the part exchanged for living labour decreases. Hence, the rate of profit falls relative to the total value of the capital presupposed to production – and of the part of capital acting as capital in production. The wider the existence already achieved by capital, the narrower the relation of newly created value to presupposed value (reproduced value). *Presupposing equal surplus value, i.e. equal relation of surplus labour and necessary labour*, there can therefore be an unequal profit, and it must be unequal relative to the size of the capitals. The rate of profit can rise although real surplus value falls. Indeed, the capital can grow and the rate of profit can grow in the same relation if the relation of the part of capital presupposed as value and existing in the form of raw materials and fixed capital rises at an equal rate relative to the part of the capital exchanged for living labour. But this equality of rates presupposes growth of the capital without growth and development of the productive power of labour. One presupposition suspends the other. This contradicts the law of the development of capital, and especially of the development of fixed capital. Such a progression can take place only at stages where the mode of production of capital is not yet adequate to it, or in spheres of production where it has assumed predominance only formally, e.g. in agriculture. Here, natural fertility of the soil can act like an increase of fixed capital – i.e. relative surplus labour can grow – without the amount of necessary labour diminishing. (E.g. in the *United States*.) The *gross profit*, i.e. the surplus value, regarded apart from its formal relation, not as a proportion but rather as a simple magnitude of value without connection with any other, will grow on the average *not as does the rate of profit, but as does the size of the capital*. Thus, while the rate of profit will be inversely related to the value of the capital, the *sum of profit* will be directly related to it. However, even this statement is true only for a restricted stage of the development of the productive power of capital or of labour. A capital of 100 with a profit of 10% yields a smaller sum of profit than a capital of 1,000 with a profit of 2%. In the first case the sum is 10, in the second 20, i.e. the gross profit of the larger capital is twice as large as that of the 10 times smaller capital, although the rate of the smaller capital's profit is 5 times greater than that of the larger. But if the larger capital's profit were only 1%, then the sum of its profit would be 10, like that for the 10 times smaller capital, because the rate of profit would have declined in the same relation as its size. If the rate of profit of the capital of 1,000 were only $\frac{1}{2}$%, then the sum of its profit would be only half as large as that of the smaller capital, only 5, because the rate of profit would be 20 times smaller. Thus, expressed in general terms: if the rate of profit declines for the larger capital, but not in relation with its size, then the gross profit rises although the rate of profit declines. If the profit rate declines relative to its size, then the gross profit remains the same as that of the smaller capital; remains stationary. If the profit rate declines more than its size increases, then the gross profit of the larger capital decreases relative to the smaller one in proportion as its rate of profit declines. This is in every respect the most important law of modern political economy, and the most essential for understanding the most difficult relations. It is the most important law from the historical standpoint. It is a law which, despite its simplicity, has never before been grasped and, even less, consciously articulated. Since this decline in the rate of profit is identical in meaning (1) with the productive power already produced, and the foundation formed by it for new production; this simultaneously presupposing an enormous development of scientific powers; (2) with the decline of the part of the capital already produced which must be exchanged for immediate labour, i.e. with the decline in the immediate labour required for the reproduction of an immense value, expressing itself in a great mass of products, great mass of products with low prices, because the total sum of prices is = to the reproduced capital + profit; (3) [with] the dimension of capital generally, including the portion of it which is not fixed capital; hence intercourse on a magnificent scale, immense sum of exchange operations, large size of the market and all-sidedness of simultaneous labour; means of communication etc., presence of the necessary consumption fund to undertake this gigantic process (workers' food, housing etc.); hence it is evident that the material productive power already present, already worked out, existing in the form of fixed capital, together with the population etc., in short all conditions of wealth, that the greatest conditions for the reproduction of wealth, i.e. the abundant development of the social individual – that the development of the productive forces brought about by the historical development of capital itself, when it reaches a certain point, suspends the self-realization of capital, instead of positing it. Beyond a certain point, the development of the powers of production becomes a barrier for capital; hence the capital relation a barrier for the development of the productive powers of labour. When it has reached this point, capital, i.e. wage labour, enters into the same relation towards the development of social wealth and of the forces of production as the guild system, serfdom, slavery, and is necessarily stripped off as a fetter. The last form of servitude assumed by human activity, that of wage labour on one side, capital on the other, is thereby cast off like a skin, and this casting-off itself is the result of the mode of production corresponding to capital; the material and mental conditions of the negation of wage labour and of capital, themselves already the negation of earlier forms of unfree social production, are themselves results of its production process. The growing incompatibility between the productive development of society and its hitherto existing relations of production expresses itself in bitter contradictions, crises, spasms. The violent destruction of capital not by relations external to it, but rather as a condition of its self-preservation, is the most striking form in which advice is given it to be gone and to give room to a higher state of social production. It is not only the growth of scientific power, but the measure in which it is already posited as fixed capital, the scope and width in which it is realized and has conquered the totality of production. It is, likewise, the development of the population etc., in short, of all moments of production; in that the productive power of labour, like the application of machinery, is related to the population; whose growth in and for itself already the presupposition as well as the result of the growth of the use values to be reproduced and hence also to be consumed. Since this decline of profit signifies the same as the decrease of immediate labour relative to the size of the objectified labour which it reproduces and newly posits, capital will attempt every means of checking the smallness of the relation of living labour to the size of the capital generally, hence also of the surplus value, if expressed as profit, relative to the presupposed capital, by reducing the allotment made to necessary labour and by still more expanding the quantity of surplus labour with regard to the whole labour employed. Hence the highest development of productive power together with the greatest expansion of existing wealth will coincide with depreciation of capital, degradation of the labourer, and a most straitened exhaustion of his vital powers. These contradictions lead to explosions, cataclysms, crises, in which by momentaneous suspension of labour and annihilation of a great portion of capital the latter is violently reduced to the point where it can go on. These contradictions, of course, lead to explosions, crises, in which momentary suspension of all labour and annihilation of a great part of the capital violently lead it back to the point where it is enabled [to go on] fully employing its productive powers without committing suicide.[21] Yet, these regularly recurring catastrophes lead to their repetition on a higher scale, and finally to its violent overthrow. There are moments in the developed movement of capital which delay this movement other than by crises; such as e.g. the constant devaluation of a part of the existing capital: the transformation of a great part of capital into fixed capital which does not serve as agency of direct production; unproductive waste of a great portion of capital etc. (Pro-

21. The sentence preceding this one was inserted by Marx, above the line, *in English*; thus the apparent virtual repetition. (The sentence following also appears in English in the original.)

ductively employed capital is always replaced doubly, as we have seen, in that the positing of value by a productive capital presupposes a counter-value. The unproductive consumption of capital replaces it on one side, annihilates it on the other.* That the fall of the rate of profit can further be delayed by the omission of existing deductions from profit, e.g. by a lowering of taxes, reduction of ground rent etc., is actually not our concern here, although of importance in practice, for these are themselves portions of the profit under another name, and are appropriated by persons other than the capitalists themselves.† The fall [in the rate of profit] likewise delayed by creation of new branches of production in which more direct labour in relation to capital is needed, or where the productive power of labour is not yet developed, i.e. the productive power of capital.) (Likewise, monopolies.) 'Profit is a term signifying the increase of capital or wealth; so failing to find the laws which govern the rate of profit, is failing to find the laws of the formation of capital.' (William Atkinson, *Principles of Political Economy etc.*, London, 1840, p. 55.) He has however failed to understand even what the rate of profit is. A. Smith explained the fall of the rate of profit, as capital grows, by the competition among capitals.[22] To which Ricardo replied that competition can indeed reduce profits in the various branches of business to an average level, can equalize the rate, but cannot depress this average rate itself.[23] A. Smith's phrase is correct to the extent that only in competition – the action of capital upon capital – are the inherent laws of capital, its tendencies, realized. But it is false in the sense in which he under-

*The same law expresses itself simply – but this expression to be looked at later in the theory of population – as the relation of the growth of population – namely its labouring part – to the capital already presupposed.

†The other way in which this same law also expresses itself, in the relation among many capitals, i.e. in competition, likewise belongs in another section. It can also be formulated as a law of the accumulation of capitals; as e.g. by Fullarton. We shall come to this in the next section. It is important to call attention to the point that this law deals not simply with the development of productive power δυνάμει, but at the same time with the scope in which this productive power acts as capital, and is realized as fixed capital above all in one respect, and as population in the other.

22. Adam Smith, *Recherches sur la nature et les causes de la richesse des nations*, Vol. I, p. 193.

23. Ricardo, *On the Principles of Political Economy*, pp. 338–9.

stands it, as if competition imposed laws on capital from the outside, laws not its own. Competition can permanently depress the rate of profit in all branches of industry, i.e. the average rate of profit, only if and in so far as a general and permanent fall of the rate of profit, having the force of a law, is conceivable *prior to* competition and regardless of competition. Competition executes the inner laws of capital; makes them into compulsory laws towards the individual capital, but it does not invent them. It realizes them. To try to explain them simply as results of competition therefore means to concede that one does not understand them. Ricardo, for his part, says: 'No accumulation of capitals can *permanently* reduce profits unless an equally permanent cause raises wages.' (p. 92, tome II, Paris 1835, translated by Constancio.) He finds this cause in the growing, relatively growing unproductivity of agriculture, 'the growing difficulty of increasing the quantity of subsistence', i.e. in the growth of proportionate wages, so that labour's real wage is no greater, but the product obtains more labour; in a word, a greater portion of necessary labour is required for the production of agricultural products. The falling rate of profit hence corresponds, with him, to the nominal growth of wages and real growth of ground rent. His one-sided mode of conceiving it, which seizes on only one single case, just as the rate of profit can fall because wages momentarily rise etc., and which elevates a historical relation holding for a period of 50 years and reversed in the following 50 years to the level of a general law, and rests generally on the historical disproportion between the developments of industry and agriculture – in and for itself it was strange that Ricardo, Malthus, etc. constructed general and eternal laws about physiological chemistry at a time where the latter hardly existed – this method that Ricardo has of conceiving the matter has therefore been attacked from all sides, partly because of an instinct that it is wrong and unsatisfactory; but mostly for its true rather than for its false aspects.

'A. Smith thought that accumulation or increase of stock in general lowered the rate of profits in general, on the same principle which makes the increase of stock in any particular trade lower the profits of that trade. But such increase of stock in a particular trade *means* an increase in a greater *proportion* than stock is at the same time increased in other trades. It is relative.' (p. 9, *An Inquiry into those Principles respecting the Nature of Demand and the Necessity of Consumption, lately advocated by Mr Malthus.* London, 1821.)

'The competition among the industrial capitalists can level profits which rise particularly above the level, but cannot lower this ordinary level.' (Ramsay, IX, 88.)[24] (Ramsay and other economists correctly distinguish between whether productivity grows in the branches of industry which make fixed capital, and naturally wages, or in other industries, e.g. luxury-goods industries. The latter cannot diminish necessary labour time. This they can do only through exchange for agricultural products of other countries, which is then the same as if productivity had increased in agriculture. Hence the importance of free trade in grain for the industrial capitalists.) Ricardo says (English edition *On the Principles of Political Economy and Taxation.* 3rd edition, London, 1821): 'The farmer and manufacturer can no more live without profits, than the labourer without wages.' (p. 23 loc. cit.) 'There is a natural tendency for profits to fall, because in the progress of society and of wealth, the additional food requires more and more labour. This tendency, this gravitation of profits, is delayed in repeated intervals by improvement of the machinery involved in the production of necessaries, as well as by discoveries in the science of agriculture, which reduce the costs of production.' (loc. cit. p. 121.) Ricardo at once identifies profit directly with surplus value; he did not make this distinction at all. *But whereas the rate of surplus value is determined by the relation of surplus labour employed by the capital to necessary labour, the rate of profit is nothing but the relation of the surplus value to the total value of the capital presupposed to production.* Its proportion falls and rises, hence, in relation with the part of the capital exchanged for living labour relative to the part existing as material and fixed capital. *Under* ALL *circumstances, the surplus value regarded as profit must express a smaller proportion of the gain than the real proportion of the surplus value.* For, under all circumstances, it is measured by the total capital, which is always larger than that employed for wages and exchanged for living labour. Since Ricardo simply mixes surplus value and profit together in this way, and since the surplus value can constantly decline, can *tendentially* decline only if the relation of surplus labour to necessary labour, i.e. to the labour required for the reproduction of labouring capacity, declines, but since the latter is possible only if the productive force of labour declines, Ricardo assumes that the productive force of labour decreases in agriculture, although it grows in industry, with the accumulation

24. Ramsay, *An Essay*, pp. 179–80.

of capital. He flees from economics to seek refuge in organic chemistry. We have demonstrated the necessity of this tendency without any reference to ground rent, nor did we have to refer e.g. to rising demand for labour etc. The connection between ground rent and profit is to be treated only in the examination of ground rent itself, does not belong here. But modern chemistry has demonstrated that Ricardo's physiological postulate, expressed as a general law, is false.[25] As for Ricardo's disciples, in so far as they are more than his pious echos, they have quietly let drop whatever is unpleasant to them in their master's principles, as has the newer economics generally. To drop the problem is their general method of solving it. Other economists, such as e.g. Wakefield, seek refuge in the examination of the *field of employment* for the growing capital. This belongs in the examination of competition, and is rather the *difficulty for capital to realize the growing profit, hence denial of the inherent tendency towards the fall of the rate of profit*. But the need for capital to seek a constantly more extensive field of employment is itself again a consequence. One cannot count Wakefield and similar people among those who have posed the question itself. (Is in certain respects a reproduction of A. Smith's view.) Finally, the harmonists among the most modern economists, at their head the American, Carey, whose most obnoxious adherent was the Frenchman Bastiat (by the way, it is the nicest irony of history that the Continental free-traders worship Mr Bastiat, who, for his part, gets his wisdom from the protectionist, Carey), accept the fact of the tendency of the rate of profit to fall in measure as productive capital grows. But they explain it simply and entirely as due to growth in the value of labour's share; growth of the proportion of the total product obtained by the worker, while the capital is allegedly compensated for this by the growth of gross profits. The unpleasant contradictions, antagonisms within which classical economics moves, and which Ricardo emphasizes with scientific ruthlessness, are thus watered down into well-to-do harmonies. In Carey's development, it sometimes seems as if he still had a mind of his own. This concerns a law which we need look at only in the doctrine of competition, where we will then settle ac-

25. Marx made extracts from these works on organic chemistry: J. von Liebig, *Die organische Chemie*, 4th edn, Brunswick, 1842; J. F. W. Johnston, *Lectures on Agricultural Chemistry and Geology*, 2nd edn, London, 1847; and J. F. W. Johnston, *Catechism of Agricultural Chemistry and Geology*, Edinburgh, 1849.

counts with him. We can finish up here with the witlessness of Bastiat, who expresses commonplaces in a paradoxical way, grinds and polishes them into facets, and hides an utter poverty of ideas under a cover of formal logic.* In the *Gratuité du Crédit*. Discussion entre M. Fr. Bastiat et M. Proudhon, Paris, 1850 (Proudhon, by the way, cuts a highly ridiculous figure in this polemic, where he hides his dialectical feebleness under a great show of rhetoric), it says in Bastiat's letter No. VIII (where this noble spirit, by the way, simply transforms, with his conciliatory dialectic, the gain resulting from the simple division of labour both for the road-builder and for the road-user into a gain owed to the 'road' (i.e. to capital) itself): 'To the degree that capitals increase (and the products with them), the absolute part returning to capital increases, and its proportional part diminishes. To the degree that capitals increase (and the products with them), labour's proportional part and its absolute part increase . . . Since capital's absolute part grows even while it successively obtains only $\frac{1}{2}, \frac{1}{3}, \frac{1}{4}, \frac{1}{5}$ of the total product, it follows that labour, which successively obtains $\frac{1}{2}, \frac{2}{3}, \frac{3}{4}, \frac{4}{5}$, evidently receives a progressively increasing share of the whole, both in the proportional and in the absolute sense.' He gives as *illustration*:

Total product		Capital's share	Labour's share
1st period	1,000	$\frac{1}{2}$ or 500	$\frac{1}{2}$ or 500
2nd	1,800	$\frac{1}{3}$ or 600	$\frac{2}{3}$ or 1,200
3rd	2,800	$\frac{1}{4}$ or 700	$\frac{3}{4}$ or 2,100
4th	4,000	$\frac{1}{5}$ or 800	$\frac{4}{5}$ or 3,200
			(p. 130, 131.)

The same joke is repeated (p. 288) in the form of increasing gross profit with declining rate of profit, but increasing mass of products sold at lower prices, and weighty words are spoken on that occasion about 'the law of unlimited decline which never reaches zero, a law well known to mathematicians'. (p. 288.) 'Here we have' (hawking his wares) 'an endlessly decreasing multiplier, because the multiplicand is ever growing.' (p. 288 loc. cit.)

Ricardo had anticipated his Bastiat. Emphasizing that the sum of

---

*Some things from Notebook III about the antithesis of Carey and Bastiat can be included at this point.[26]

26. See the section on Bastiat and Carey, pp. 883–93.

profit grows as capital grows despite the decline of the rate of profit – thus anticipating Bastiat's whole profundity – he does not fail to note that this progression 'is true only for a certain time'. He says, word for word: 'Regardless of how the rate of profit on stock may decline in consequence of the accumulation of capital on the land and of a rise of wages' (by which Ricardo understands, N.B., the rise of the cost of production of the agricultural products necessary for the maintenance of labour capacity), 'the aggregate amount of profits must nevertheless grow. Supposing, then, that in repeated accumulations of £100,000 the rate of profits fell from 20 to 19, 18, 17%, we should expect that the whole amount of profits received by the successive owners of capital would be always progressive; that it would be greater with the capital of £200,000 than with that of 100,000; yet greater with 300,000; and so on, increasing, although at a decreasing rate, with every increase of capital. *However, this progress is true only for a certain time*: thus 19% on £200,000 is more than 20 on 100,000; 18% on 300,000 more than 19% on 200,000; but after capital has accumulated to a large amount and profits have fallen, further accumulation diminishes the sum of profits. Thus, supposing the accumulation of 1,000,000 and profits of 7%, then the total amount of profit will be £70,000; now if an addition of 100,000 is made to the million, and profits fall to 6%, then £66,000 or a decrease of £4,000 will be received by the owners of the stock, although the amount of capital will be increased from 1,000,000 to 1,100,000.' (loc. cit. p. 124, 125.) Of course this does not prevent Mr Bastiat from undertaking the operation of making a growing multiplicand grow in such a way that, with the declining multiplier, it produces a growing product, in true elementary-school pupil style, just as the laws of production did not prevent Dr Price from constructing his compound interest calculations. Because the rate of profit declines, it declines relative to wages, which must consequently grow proportionally and absolutely. So reasons Bastiat. (Ricardo observed this tendency towards the decline of the profit rate with the growth of capital; and since he confuses profit with surplus value, he was forced to make wages rise in order to let profits fall. But since he saw at the same time that wages really declined more than they rose, he let the value of wages grow, i.e. the quantity of necessary labour, without letting its use value grow. Thus in fact he only let ground rent increase. The harmonic Mr Bastiat discovers, however, that, with the accumulation of capitals, wages rise proportionally and absolutely.) He assumes what he has to prove, that the decline of the profit rate is identical with the increase in the rate of wages, and then 'illustrates' his presupposition with an arithmetical example which appears to have amused him greatly. If the decline of the profit rate expresses nothing more than the decline of the relation in which the total capital requires living labour for its reproduction, then it is another matter. Mr Bastiat overlooks the trifling circumstance that, in his presupposition, while the profit rate on capital declines, the capital itself increases, the capital presupposed to production. Now even Mr Bastiat ought to have had an inkling that the value of the capital cannot grow without appropriating surplus labour. The misery of agricultural overproduction, recorded in French history, could have shown him that the mere increase of products does not increase their value. The question would then revolve simply around an investigation of whether the fall of the profit rate is identical with the growth of the rate of surplus labour relative to necessary labour, or, instead, with the fall of the total rate of living labour employed relative to the reproduced capital. Mr Bastiat also therefore divides the product simply between capitalist and worker, instead of dividing it into raw material, instrument of production and labour, and asking himself in what proportional parts its value in exchange is applied against these different portions. The part of the product exchanged for raw material and instrument of production is obviously none of the workers' business. What they divide with capital, as wages and profit, is nothing other than the newly added living labour itself. But what particularly worries Bastiat is who, after all, is to eat up the increased product? Since the capitalist eats up a relatively small part, does not the worker have to eat up a relatively large one? Particularly in France, whose total production is sufficient only in Bastiat's fantasy to give anyone at all very much to eat, Mr Bastiat could have found convincing testimony that a mass of parasitic bodies come to cluster around capital, and, under one or another title, they lay hands on so much of the total production as to leave little danger of the workers being overwhelmed by abundance. It is clear, of course, that with large-scale production the total mass of labour employed can increase although the proportion of labour employed relative to capital decreases, and that there is no obstacle, therefore, which prevents an increasing working population from requiring a greater mass of products as capital increases. Incidentally, Bastiat

– in whose harmonic brain all cows are grey – (see above, wages),[27] confuses the decline of interest with the increase of wages, since this is rather an increase of industrial profit, which concerns the workers not at all, but concerns only the relation in which different species of capitalists divide up the total profit among themselves.

Capital and revenue (profit). Production and distribution.
Sismondi. – Production costs from capital's viewpoint.
Profit, ditto. – Inequality of profits. Equalization and communal rate
of profit. – Transformation of surplus value into profit. – Laws

Back to our topic. The product of capital, then, is profit. By relating to itself as profit, it relates to itself as the *source of the production of value, and the rate of profit expresses the proportion to which it has increased its own value.* But the capitalist is not merely capital. He has to live, and since he does not live by working he must live from profit, i.e. from the alien labour he appropriates. Thus capital is posited as the source of wealth. Since capital has incorporated productivity into itself as its inherent quality, capital relates to profit as *revenue.* It can consume a part of it (seemingly all of it, but this will prove to be false) without ceasing to be capital. After consumption of this fruit it can bear new fruit. It can represent consumption wealth without ceasing to represent the general form of wealth, something which money in simple circulation could not possibly do. The latter had to *abstain in order to remain the general form* of wealth; or, if it exchanged for real wealth, for consumer gratifications, it ceased to be the general form of wealth. Thus profit appears as a *form of distribution,* like wages. But since capital can grow only through the retransformation of profit into capital – into surplus capital – profit is at the same time a *form of production for capital*; just exactly as wages are a mere *relation of production* from the standpoint of capital, a relation of distribution from the worker's standpoint. This shows that the relations of distribution are themselves produced by the relations of production, and represent the latter themselves from another point of view. It shows further that the relation of production to consumption is posited by production itself. Note the fatuitousness of all bourgeois economists, including e.g. J. St. Mill, who considers the bourgeois relations of production as eternal, but

27. In fact, see below, pp. 889–90.

their forms of distribution as historical, and thereby shows that he understands neither the one nor the other.[28] As to simple exchange, Sismondi correctly remarks: 'An exchange always presupposes two values; each may have a different share; but the *quality of capital and revenue* does not follow from the object exchanged; it attaches to the person who is its owner.' (Sismondi, VI.)[29] Hence the simple exchange relation provides no basis for the explanation of revenue. The quality of a value obtained in exchange, whether it represents capital or revenue, is determined by relations lying outside simple exchange. Absurd, therefore, to want to reduce these more complex forms to the earlier, simpler exchange relations, as do the harmonic freetraders. From the standpoint of simple exchange, and considering accumulation as the mere accumulation of money (exchange value), capital's profit and revenue are impossible. 'If the rich spend the accumulated wealth for luxury products – and they can obtain commodities only through exchange – then their funds would soon be exhausted ... But, in the social order, wealth has achieved the quality of reproducing itself through *alien labour*. Wealth, like labour, and *through labour*, yields an annual fruit which may be *destroyed* each year without the rich man thereby becoming poorer. This fruit is the revenue springing from capital.' (Sismondi, IV.)[30] While profit thus appears in one respect as the result of capital, it appears in the other as the *presupposition of capital formation*. Thus is posited anew the circular movement in which the result appears as presupposition. 'Thus a part of the revenue became transformed into capital, into a permanent, self-multiplying value, which did not perish; this value tore itself free from the commodity which created it; like a metaphysical, insubstantial quality it always remained in possession of the same *cultivateur*' (capitalist), 'assuming various forms for him.' (Sismondi, VI)[31]

When capital is posited as profit-creating, as a source of wealth independently of labour, each part of the capital is thereby assumed to be equally productive. Just as surplus value in the form of profit is measured against the total value of the capital, so does it appear to be created by its different components to an equal degree. Thus its circulating part (the part consisting of raw materials and *approvisionnement*) brings no more profit than the component

28. See p. 86, n. 7.
29. Sismondi, *Nouveaux Principes*, Vol. I, p. 90.
30. op. cit., Vol. I, p. 82.   31. op. cit., Vol. I, p. 89.

which consists of the fixed capital, and, more particularly, profit accrues to these component parts in proportion to their magnitude.

Since the profit of capital is realized only in the price which is paid for it, for the use value created by it, profit is determined by the *excess of the price obtained over the price which covers outlays*. Since, furthermore, this realization proceeds only through *exchange*, the individual capital's *profit is not necessarily restricted by its surplus value*, by the surplus labour contained in it; but is relative, rather, to the excess of price obtained in exchange. It can exchange more than its *equivalent, and then its profit is greater than its surplus value*. This can be the case only to the extent that the other party to the exchange does not obtain an equivalent. The total surplus value, as well as the *total profit*, which is only *surplus value itself, computed differently*, can neither grow nor decrease through this operation, ever; what is *modified thereby* is not it, but only *its distribution among the different capitals*. However, this examination belongs only with that of the many capitals, it does not yet belong here. In relation to profit, the value of the capital presupposed in production appears as *advances – production costs* which must be replaced in the product. After deduction of the part of the price which replaces them, the excess forms the profit. Since surplus labour – of which profit and interest are, both, only portions – costs capital nothing, hence does not figure as part of the value advanced by it – not as part of the value which it possessed before the production process and the realization of the product – it follows that this surplus labour, which is included in the production costs of the product and forms the source of surplus value and hence of profit as well, does not figure as part of the production costs of capital. The latter are equal only to the values actually advanced by it, not including the surplus value appropriated in production and realized in circulation. The production costs from the standpoint of capital are therefore not the real production costs, precisely because surplus labour does not cost *it* anything. The excess of the price of the product over the price of the production costs gives it its profit. Thus profit can exist for capital even without the realization of the real production costs – i.e. the whole surplus labour set to work by capital. Profit – the excess over the advances made by capital – may be smaller than surplus value – the surplus of living labour gained in exchange by capital in excess of the objectified labour it has given in exchange for labour capacity. However, through the separation of interest from profit – which we will look at immediately – a part of the surplus value is posited as production cost even for productive capital itself. The confusion of *production costs* from the standpoint of capital with the amount of labour objectified in capital's product, surplus labour included, has given rise to statements such as that 'profit is not included in the natural price'. It is allegedly 'absurd to call the excess, or profit, a part of the expenditure'. (Torrens, IX, 30.)[32] This then leads to a mass of confusion; either by having profit not realized in, but rather arising from, exchange (which can always be the case only relatively, if one of the parties to the exchange does not obtain his equivalent), or by ascribing to capital some magic power which makes something out of nothing. Since the value posited in the production process realizes its price through exchange, the price of the product appears in fact determined by the sum of money which expresses an equivalent for the total quantity of labour contained in raw material, machinery, wages and in unpaid surplus labour. Thus price still appears here merely as a formal modification of value; as value expressed in money; but the magnitude of this price is presupposed in the production process of capital. Capital thereby appears as a determinant of price, so that price is determined by the advances made by capital + the surplus labour realized by it in the product. We shall see later that price, on the contrary, appears as determining profit. And, while here the total *real* production costs appear as determining price, price appears later as determining the production costs. So as to impose the inherent laws of capital upon it as external necessity, competition seemingly turns all of them over. *Inverts them.*

To repeat once more: the profit of capital does not depend on its magnitude; but rather, given an equal magnitude, on the relation between its component parts (the constant and the variable part); and then on the productivity of labour (which is expressed, however, in the above proportion, since, with diminished productivity, the same capital could not work up the same material with the same portion of living labour); on the turnover time, which is determined by the different proportions between fixed and circulating capital, different durability of fixed capital, etc. etc. (see above). The inequality of profit in different branches of industry with capitals of equal magnitudes is the condition and presupposition for their equalization through competition.

32. Torrens, *An Essay on the Production of Wealth*, p. 52.

In so far as capital obtains raw material, instrument, labour, through exchange, buys them, its elements are themselves already present in the form of prices; already posited as prices; presupposed to it. The comparison of the market price of its product with the prices of its elements then becomes decisive for it. But this belongs only in the chapter on competition.

Thus the surplus value which capital posits in a given turnover period obtains the form of *profit* in so far as it is measured against the total value of the capital presupposed to production. While surplus value is measured directly by the surplus labour time which capital gains in the exchange with living labour. Profit is nothing but another form of surplus value, a form developed further in the sense of capital. Surplus value no longer regarded here as exchanged for capital itself in the production process; not for labour. Hence capital appears as capital, as presupposed value relating to itself, through the mediation of its own process, as posited, produced value, and the value posited by it is called *profit*.

The two immediate laws which this transformation of surplus value into the shape of profit yields for us are these: (1) *Surplus value expressed as profit always appears as a smaller proportion than surplus value in its immediate reality actually amounts to.* For, instead of being measured by a part of the capital, the part exchanged for living labour (a relation which turns out to be that of necessary to surplus labour), it is measured against the whole. Whatever may be the surplus value which a capital A posits, and whatever may be the proportion within A of c and v, the constant and the variable part of the capital, the surplus value s must appear smaller when measured against $c + v$ than when measured against its real measure, v. Profit, or – if it is regarded not as an absolute sum but rather, as is usually done, as a *proportion* (the rate of profit is profit expressed as the *relation in which* capital has posited surplus value) – the rate of profit never expresses the real rate at which capital exploits labour, but always a much smaller relation, and the larger the capital, the more false is the relation it expresses. The rate of profit could express the real rate of surplus value only if the entire capital were transformed solely into wages; if the entire capital were exchanged for living labour, i.e. if the *approvisionnement* alone existed, and if it not only existed not in the form of already produced raw material (which has happened in extractive industry), hence if not only the raw material were $= 0$, but if the means of production, also, whether in the form of instruments or in the form of developed fixed capital, were $= 0$. The latter case cannot occur on the basis of the mode of production corresponding to capital. If $A = c + v$, whatever the numerical value of s, then

$$\frac{s}{c + v} < \frac{s}{v}.^{33}$$

(2) The second great law is that the rate of profit declines to the degree that capital has already appropriated living labour in the form of objectified labour, hence to the degree that labour is already capitalized and hence also acts increasingly in the form of fixed capital in the production process, or to the degree that the productive power of labour grows. The growth of the productive power of labour is identical in meaning with (a) the growth of relative surplus value or of the relative surplus labour time which the worker gives to capital; (b) the decline of the labour time necessary for the reproduction of labour capacity; (c) the decline of the part of capital which exchanges at all for living labour relative to the parts of it which participate in the production process as objectified labour and as presupposed value. The profit rate is therefore inversely related to the growth of relative surplus value or of relative surplus labour, to the development of the powers of production, and to the magnitude of the capital employed as [constant] capital within production. In other words, the second law is the *tendency of the profit rate to decline* with the development of capital, both of its productive power and of the extent in which it has already posited itself as objectified value; of the extent within which labour as well as productive power is capitalized.

Other causes which additionally act upon the rate of profit, which can depress it for longer or shorter periods, do not yet belong here. It is quite correct, as regards the production process as a whole, that the capital acting as material and as fixed capital not only is objectified labour, but must also be reproduced, and continuously reproduced, by new labour. Its presence assumes, therefore – the extent which its presence has attained assumes, therefore, the extent of the labouring population, population on a large scale, which in and for itself is the condition of all productive power – but this reproduction everywhere proceeds on the presupposition

33. $\dfrac{s}{c + v} < \dfrac{s}{v}$ is the correct expression; but the manuscript has: $\dfrac{c + v}{s} < \dfrac{v}{s}$, struck out but not replaced by anything else. [MELI note]

of the action of fixed capital and of raw material and of scientific power, both as such, and as appropriated within production and already realized within it. This point is to be developed in more detail only in the examination of accumulation.

It is clear, further, that although the part of capital exchanged for living labour declines in relation to the total capital, the total mass of living labour employed can increase or remain the same if capital grows in the same or a larger relation. Hence a constant growth in the population may accompany a relative decline in necessary labour. If capital A lays out $\frac{1}{2}$ in c and $\frac{1}{2}$ in v, while capital A' lays out $\frac{3}{4}$ in c and $\frac{1}{4}$ in v, then capital A' could employ $\frac{2}{4}$ v for $\frac{6}{4}$ c. But if it was originally $= \frac{3}{4} c + \frac{1}{4} v$, then it is now $= \frac{6}{4} c + \frac{2}{4} v$, or it grew by $\frac{4}{4}$; i.e. it doubled. However, this relation also is to be examined more closely only in connection with the theory of accumulation and population. All in all we must not at this point be sidetracked by drawing the consequences which follow from the laws, and by turning them over in the mind from one angle or another.

The rate of profit is determined, then, not only by the relation of surplus labour to necessary labour, or by the relation in which objectified labour is exchanged for living labour, but by the overall relation of living labour employed to objective labour; by the portion of capital exchanged for living labour relative to the part which participates in the production process as objectified labour. This portion, however, declines in the same relation as surplus labour increases in relation to necessary labour.

Surplus value = *relation of surplus labour to necessary labour*

(Since the worker must reproduce the part of the capital which is exchanged for his labour capacity just as much as he must reproduce the other parts of the capital, the relation in which the capitalist gains from the exchange with labour capacity appears as determined by the relation of surplus labour to necessary labour. Originally this appears in such a way that the necessary labour only replaces his outlay. But since he lays out nothing other than labour itself – as is shown in reproduction – the relation can be expressed simply in this way – the relation of surplus value as the relation of surplus labour to necessary labour.)

Value of fixed capital *and its* productive power. *Durability of fixed capital, ditto. – The powers of society, division of labour etc.* cost *capital nothing. – Distinction between this and machinery* (*capitalist's* economy *in the employment of machinery*). – *Profit and surplus value*

⟨We have still to note in regard to fixed capital – and its durability, as one of its conditions which does not enter in from the outside: To the extent that the instrument of production is itself a value, objectified labour, *it does not contribute as a productive force.* If a machine which cost 100 working days to make replaced only 100 working days, then it would in no way increase the productive power of labour and in no way decrease the cost of the product. The more durable the machine, the more often can the same quantity of product be created with it, or the more often can the circulating capital be renewed, its reproduction be repeated, and the smaller is the value-share (that required to replace the depreciation, the wear and tear of the machine); i.e. the more is the price of the product and its unit production cost decreased. However, we may not introduce the price relation at this point in the development. The reduction of the price as condition for conquest of the market belongs only to competition. It must therefore be developed in a different way. If capital could obtain the instrument of production at no cost, for 0, what would be the consequence? The same as if the cost of circulation = 0. That is, the labour necessary for the maintenance of labour capacity would be diminished, and thus surplus labour, i.e. surplus value, [increased], without the slightest cost to capital. Such an increase of the force of production, a piece of machinery which costs capital nothing, is the division of labour and the combination of labour within the production process. This assumes, however, work proceeding on a large scale, i.e. development of capital and wage labour. Another productive force which costs it nothing is scientific power. (It goes without saying that it must always pay a certain contribution for parsons, schoolmasters and scholars, whether the scientific power they develop is great or small.) But it can appropriate the latter only through the employment of machinery (and in part through the chemical process). The growth of population is a productive force of this kind, and it costs it nothing. In short, all the social powers developing with the growth of population and with the historic development of society cost it nothing. To the extent, however, that a substratum which itself exists in the form of objectified labour, i.e. is itself produced by labour, is required to employ them within the direct production process, hence to the extent that they are themselves values, it can appropriate them only through equivalents. Well. Fixed capital whose employment required more labour for its production or maintenance than it replaced would be a nuisance. The kind that would cost nothing, but merely needed to be appropriated by capital, would have the maximum value for capital. It follows from the simple proposition that machinery is most valuable for capital when its value $= 0$, that every reduction of its cost is a gain for capital. *While it is the tendency of capital, on one side, to increase the total value of the fixed capital,* [so], *at the same time,* [is its tendency] *to decrease the value of each of its fractional parts.* To the extent that fixed capital enters into circulation as value, it ceases to act as use value within the production process. Its use value is precisely that it increases the productive power of labour, decreases necessary labour, and increases relative surplus labour and hence surplus value. To the extent that it enters into circulation, its value is merely replaced, not increased. By contrast, the product, the circulating capital, is the vehicle of the surplus value, which is realized only when it steps outside the production process and into circulation. If machinery lasted for ever, if it did not itself consist of transitory material which must be reproduced (quite apart from the invention of more perfect machines which would rob it of the character of being a machine), if it were a *perpetuum mobile*, then it would most completely correspond to its concept. Its value would not need to be replaced because it would continue to last in an indestructible materiality. Since fixed capital is employed only to the extent that its value is smaller than the value it posits, it follows that, even if it never itself entered into circulation as value, the surplus value realized in the circulating capital would nevertheless soon replace the advances, and it would thus act to posit value after its costs for the capitalist, as well as the cost of the surplus labour he appropriates, were $= 0$. It would continue to act as a productive power of labour and at the same time be money in the third sense, constant value for-itself. Take a capital of £1,000. Let one-fourth be machinery; the sum of surplus value $= 50$. The value of the machinery then equal to 200. After 4 turnovers the machinery would be paid for. And, in addition, since the capital would continue to possess, in the machine, objectified labour to the amount of 200, then, beginning with the fifth turnover, it would be the same as if it made 50 on a capital which only costs it 800; hence $6\frac{1}{4}\%$ instead of 5%. As soon as fixed capital enters into circulation as value, its use value for the capital realization process ceases, or, it enters into it only as soon as the latter ceases. Hence, the more durable, the less it requires repair, total or partial reproduction, the longer its circulation time, the more does it act as productive power of labour, as capital; i.e. as objectified labour, which posits living surplus labour. The durability of fixed capital, which is identical with the circulation time of its value, or with the time required for its reproduction, arises from its concept itself, as its value-moment. (That in and for itself, as regards its *material* side only, it lies in the concept of the means of production is something which needs no elucidation.) The rate of surplus value is determined simply by the relation of surplus labour to necessary labour; the rate of profit is determined not only by the relation of surplus to necessary labour, but by the relation of the part of capital exchanged for living labour to the total capital entering into production.⟩

Profit as we still regard it here, i.e. as the profit of capital *as such*, not of an individual capital at the expense of another, but rather as the *profit of the capitalist class*, concretely expressed, *can never be greater than the sum of the surplus value*. As a sum, it is the sum of the surplus value, but it is this same sum of values as a proportion relative to the total value of the capital, instead of to that part of it whose value really grows, i.e. is exchanged for living labour. *In its immediate form, profit is nothing but the sum of the surplus value expressed as a proportion of the total value of the capital.*

Machinery and surplus labour. Recapitulation of the doctrine of surplus value generally

The transformation of surplus value into the form of profit, this method by which capital calculates surplus value, is necessary from the standpoint of capital, regardless of how much it rests on an illusion about the nature of surplus value, or rather veils this nature.*

---

*It is easy to form the notion that machinery as such posits value, because it acts as a productive power of labour. But if machinery required no labour, then it would be able to increase the use value; but the exchange value which it would create would never be greater than its own costs of production, its own value, the labour objectified in it. It creates value not because it replaces

If we look at a single worker's day, then the decrease of necessary labour relative to surplus labour expresses itself in the appropriation of a larger part of the working day by capital. The living labour employed here remains the same. Suppose that an increase of the force of production, e.g. employment of machinery, made 3 workers superfluous out of 6, each of whom worked 6 days a week. If these 6 workers themselves possessed the machinery, then each of them would thereafter work only half a day. Now, instead, 3 continue to work a whole day every day of the week. If capital were to continue to employ the 6, then each of them would work only half a day, but perform no surplus labour. Suppose that necessary labour amounted to 10 hours previously, the surplus labour to 2 hours per day, then the total surplus labour of the 6 workers was 2×6 daily, equal to a whole day, and was equal to 6 days a week $= 72$ hours. Each one worked one day a week for nothing. Or it would be the same as if the sixth worker had worked the whole week long for nothing. The 5 workers represent necessary labour, and if they could be reduced to 4, and if the one worker worked for nothing as before – then the relative surplus value would have grown. Its relation previously was $= 1:6$, and would now be $1:5$. *The previous law, of an increase in the number of hours of surplus labour, thus now obtains the form of a reduction in the number of necessary workers.* If it were possible for this same capital to employ the 6 workers at this new rate, then the surplus value would have increased not only relatively, but absolutely as well. Surplus labour time would amount to $14\frac{2}{5}$ hours. $2\frac{2}{5}$ hours [each] performed by 6 workers is of course more than $2\frac{2}{5}$ performed by 5.

If we look at absolute surplus value, it appears determined by the absolute lengthening of the working day above and beyond necessary labour time. Necessary labour time works for mere use value, for subsistence. Surplus labour time is work for exchange value, for wealth. It is the first moment of industrial labour. The natural limit is posited – presupposing that the conditions of labour are on hand, raw material and instrument of labour, or one of them, depending on whether the work is merely extractive or formative, whether it merely isolates the use value from nature or

labour; rather, only in so far as it is a means to increase surplus labour, and only the latter itself is both the measure and the substance of the surplus value posited with the aid of the machine; hence of labour generally.

whether it shapes it – the natural limit is posited by the number of simultaneous work days or of living labour capacities, i.e. by the labouring population. At this stage the difference between the production of capital and earlier stages of production is still merely formal. With kidnapping, slavery, the slave trade and forced labour, the increase of these labouring machines, machines producing surplus product, is posited directly by force; with capital, it is mediated through exchange.

Use values grow here in the same simple relation as exchange values, and for that reason this form of surplus labour appears in the slave and serf modes of production etc., where use value is the chief and predominant concern, as well as in the mode of production of capital, which is oriented directly towards exchange value, and only indirectly towards use value. This use value may be purely imaginary, as e.g. with the Egyptian pyramids, in short, with the works of religious ostentation which the mass of the nation in Egypt, India etc. was forced [to undertake]; or may be directed at immediate utility as e.g. with the ancient Etruscans.

In the second form of surplus value, however, as relative surplus value, which appears as the development of the workers' productive power, *as the reduction of necessary labour time relative to the working day*, and *as the reduction of the necessary labouring population* relative to the population (this is the antithetical form), in this form there directly appears the industrial and the distinguishing historic character of the mode of production founded on capital.

The forcible transformation of the greater part of the population into wage labourers, and the discipline which transforms their existence into that of mere labourers, correspond to the first form. Throughout a period of 150 years, e.g. from Henry VII on, the annals of English legislation contain the bloody handwriting of coercive measures employed to transform the mass of the population, after they had become propertyless and free, into free wage labourers. The dissolution of the monastic orders, the confiscation of church lands, the abolition of the guilds and confiscation of their property, the forcible ejection of the population from the land through the transformation of tillage into pasture, enclosures of commons etc., had posited the labourers as mere labour capacities. But they now of course preferred vagabondage, beggary etc. to wage labour, and had still to be accustomed forcibly to the latter. This is repeated in a similar fashion with the introduction of large industry, of factories operating with machines. Cf. Owen.[34]

Only at a certain stage of the development of capital does *the exchange of capital and labour become in fact formally free.* One can say that wage labour is completely realized in form in England only at the end of the eighteenth century, with the repeal of the law of apprenticeship.

The tendency of capital is, of course, to link up absolute with relative surplus value; hence *greatest stretching of the working day with greatest number of simultaneous working days, together with reduction of necessary labour time to the minimum, on one side, and of the number of necessary workers to the minimum, on the other*. This contradictory requirement, whose development will show itself in different forms as overproduction, over-population etc., asserts itself in the form of a process in which the contradictory aspects follow closely upon each other in time. A necessary consequence of them is the *greatest possible diversification of the use value of labour – or of the branches of production –* so that the production of capital constantly and necessarily creates, on one side, the *development of the intensity of the productive power of labour*, on the other side, the *unlimited diversity of the branches of labour*, i.e. thus the most universal wealth, in form and content, of production, bringing all sides of nature under its domination.

Capital pays nothing for the increase of the productive force arising by itself, in large-scale production, from division and combination of labour, from savings on certain expenses – conditions for the labour process – which *remain the same or diminish when labour is done in common, such as heating* etc., *industrial buildings* etc.; it obtains this increased productive power of labour free of charge. If the force of production increased simultaneously in the production of the different conditions of production, raw material, means of production and means of subsistence, and in the [branches of production] determined [by them], then their growth would bring about no change in the relation between the different component parts of the capital. If e.g. the productive force of labour grows simultaneously in the production of flax and of looms and of weaving itself (by division of labour), then a greater quantity of raw material etc. would correspond to the greater quantity woven in a day. In extractive work, e.g. the mining industry, it is not necessary for raw materials to increase when

34. Robert Owen, *Six Lectures Delivered in Manchester*, Manchester, 1837, p. 58; see above, pp. 712–14.

labour becomes more productive, since no raw material is used. To make harvests more productive, it is not even necessary for the number of instruments to have grown, but rather merely for them to be *concentrated* and for the work, *previously done fragmentarily by hundreds*, to be done *communally*. However, what is required for all forms of surplus labour is *growth of population*; of the labouring population for the first form; of population generally for the second, since it requires the development of science etc. Population, however, appears here as the basic source of wealth.

Relation between the objective conditions of production. Change in the proportion of the component parts of capital

But as we regard capital originally, raw material and instrument appear to come out of circulation, not to be produced by capital itself; just as, in reality, the individual capital obtains the condition of its production from circulation, although they are in turn produced by capital, but by another capital. From this follows, on one side, capital's necessary tendency to subjugate production to itself on all sides; its tendency to posit the production of labour materials and of raw materials, as well as instruments, as likewise produced by capital, even if it is a different capital; the propagandistic tendency of capital. Secondly, however, it is clear that if *the objective conditions of production which it obtains from circulation remain unchanged in value*, i.e. if the same amount of labour objectifies itself in the same amount of use value, then a lesser part of the capital can be laid out for living labour, or, there is a *change in the proportion of the component parts of capital*. If the capital amounts to e.g. 100, raw material $\frac{2}{5}$, the instrument $\frac{1}{5}$, labour $\frac{2}{5}$, and if, owing to a doubling of the productive force (division of labour), the same labour using the same instrument could work up double the raw material, then the capital would have to grow by 40; hence a capital of 140 would have to work; of which 80 in raw material, 20 in instrument, 40 for labour. Labour would now relate 40:140 (previously = 40:100); labour previously related as 4:10; now only as 4:14. Or, of the same capital of 100, now $\frac{3}{5}$ would go for raw material, $\frac{1}{5}$ for the instrument, and $\frac{1}{5}$ for labour. The gain would be 20, as before. But surplus labour would be 60%, whereas it was 50 earlier. It now only takes 20 in labour for 60 in raw material and 20 in instrument. 80/20/100. A capital of 80 gives the capitalist a profit of 20. Now if the capital were to employ all the labour at this stage of production, it would have to grow to 160; namely 80 for raw material, instrument 40, and 40 for labour. This would give a surplus value of 40. At the earlier stage, where the capital of 100 gives a surplus value of only 20, a capital of 160 would give a surplus value of only 32, i.e. 8 less, and the capital would have to grow to 200 in order to produce the same surplus value of 40.

The following distinctions must be drawn: (1) Labour, increasing (or *intensity, speed of labour*), requires no greater advance in material or instrument of labour. E.g. the same 100 workers with instruments of the same value catch more fish, or till the soil better, or draw more ores from the mines or coal from the pits, or beat more leaf from the same amount of gold as a result of greater skill, better combination and division of labour etc., or waste less raw material, hence get further with the same value of raw materials. In this case then, if we assume either that their products enter into their own consumption, then their necessary labour time diminishes; they perform a greater amount of work at the same maintenance costs. Or, a smaller part of their labour is necessary for the reproduction of labour capacity. The necessary part of labour time diminishes relative to surplus labour time, and, although the value of the product remains the same 100 working days, the part going to capital, the surplus value, increases. If the total surplus worker was $= \frac{1}{10}$, i.e. $= 10$ working days, and if it is now $\frac{1}{5}$, then surplus labour time has grown by 10 days. The workers work 80 days for themselves and 20 for the capitalists, whereas in the first case 90 for themselves and only 10 for the capitalist. (This calculation by working days, and labour time as the only substance of value, shows itself in this open way where relations of bondage exist. With capital, covered up by money.) Of the newly created value, a greater portion accrues to capital. But the relations between the various component parts of the invariable capital remain the same, on this presupposition. That is, although the capitalist employs a greater mass of surplus labour, because he pays less wages, he does not employ more capital in raw materials and instruments. He gives a smaller part of objectified labour in exchange for the same amount of living labour, or the same amount of objectified for a greater amount of living labour. This possible only in extractive industry; in manufacturing, only in so far as there is greater economy in use of raw materials; further, where chemical processes increase the material, in agriculture; in the transporting industry.

(2) Productivity increases at the same time not only in the given branch of production, but also in its conditions; in the case, namely, where raw material or instrument or both must be increased along with an increase in the intensity of labour, the increase of the number of products produced by labour in the same time. (The raw material need not cost anything, e.g. reeds for basket-making; free wood etc.) In this case the relation of capital remains the same. That is, with the growing productivity of labour the capital need not lay out a greater value in raw material and instruments.

(3) The increased productivity of labour requires a greater outlay of capital for raw material and instrument. If an unchanged number of workers has become more productive merely through division of labour etc., then the instrument remains the same; the raw material alone must grow; since the same labour time processes a greater amount of it in the same time; and, according to the presupposition, the productivity arose only from greater skill on the part of the workers, division and combination of labour etc. In this case the part of the capital exchanged for living labour not only diminishes (it remains the same if absolute labour time alone increases; decreases, if relative time grows) relative to the other component parts of capital, which remain the same, by an amount equal to its own decline, but likewise by an amount equal to their growth.

If it was

	Raw material:	Instrument:	Labour:	Surplus:
Working days:	180	90	80	10
	411$\frac{3}{7}$	90	70	20

in the first case: so that out of 90 working days, 10 are surplus working days; surplus labour 12$\frac{1}{2}$%. In the second case, the relation of the raw material rose in the same proportion as the relation of surplus labour rose, compared to the first case.

While the growth of the surplus value in all cases presupposes growth of the population, in this case [it presupposes] additionally accumulation, or a greater capital entering into production. (This ultimately comes down to a larger population of workers occupied in the production of raw material.) In the first case the total part of the capital employed for labour forms $\frac{1}{4}$ of the total capital, and relates to the constant part of the capital as $= 1:3$; in the second case capital employed for labour forms less than $\frac{1}{6}$ of the total capital, and the total part of the capital employed for labour relates as less than $1:5$ to the constant part of the capital. Hence, although *the increase of productive power resting on division and combination of labour rests on absolute increase of the labour power employed, it is necessarily linked with a decrease of the latter, relative to the capital which sets it in motion.* And while, in the first form, the form of *absolute surplus labour, the mass of labour employed must grow in the same relation as the capital employed*, in the *second case it grows in a lesser relation*, and, more precisely, *in inverse relation to the growth of the force of production.*

If the productivity of the soil doubled owing to employment of the latter method of agricultural labour, if the same amount of labour yielded 1 quarter of wheat instead of $\frac{1}{2}$, then necessary labour would fall by $\frac{1}{2}$, and capital could employ twice the number for the same wages. (This, if expressed in grain only.) But the capitalist would not need additional workers to work his land. Hence he will employ the same labour with half the previous wages; a part of his capital, the part earlier laid out in money, becomes free; the labour time employed has remained the same relative to the capital employed, but its surplus part has risen relative to the necessary part. If the relation of necessary labour to the total working day was $= \frac{3}{4}$ of the working day or 9 hours, before, then it will now be equal to $\frac{3}{8}$ or $= 4\frac{1}{2}$ hours. In the first case the surplus value was 3 hours; in the second $= 7\frac{1}{2}$.

The course of the process is this: With a given population of workers and length of the working day, i.e. length of the working day multiplied by the number of simultaneous working days, surplus labour can be increased only relatively, by means of greater productive power of labour, the possibility of which is already posited in the presupposed growth of the population and [its] training for labour (including thereby also a certain amount of free time for non-labouring, not directly labouring population, hence development of mental capacities etc.; mental appropriation of nature). Given a certain stage of the development of the productive forces, surplus labour can be absolutely increased only through transformation of a greater part of the population into workers, and increase of the number of simultaneous working days. The first process is *decrease of the relative working popu-*

lation, although it remains the same in absolute terms; the second is *its increase*. Both tendencies necessary tendencies of capital. The unity of these contradictory tendencies, hence the living contradiction, only with machinery, which we will discuss in a moment. The first form obviously allows only a *small non-labouring population relative to the labouring one*. The second, since the quota of living labour required in it increases more slowly than the quota of capital employed, allows *a larger non-labouring population relative to the labouring one*.

During the formative stages of capital, where it obtains raw material and instrument, the conditions of the product, from circulation, it relates to these component parts and to their relations as given presuppositions. Although this appearance vanishes on closer examination, since all these moments appear as equally the products of capital, and since it would otherwise not have conquered the total conditions of its production, they nevertheless remain always in the same relation for the individual capital. Hence, one part of it can always be regarded as constant value, and only the part laid out in labour varies. These component parts do not develop evenly, but, as will be seen in competition, [it is] the tendency of capital to distribute the force of production evenly.

Since the growing productivity of labour would lead capital to encounter a barrier in the not-growing mass of raw material and machinery, industrial development takes the following course: the introduction of labour on a large scale, as well as the employment of machinery, begins in the branches which are closest to being production of raw materials for industry, raw material both for the material of labour and [for the] instrument, where the material of labour most closely approaches mere raw material. Thus, in spinning before in weaving, in weaving before printing etc. First of all in the production of metals, which are the chief raw material for the instruments of labour themselves. If the actual raw product which makes up the raw material for industry at the lowest stage cannot itself be rapidly increased – then refuge is sought in more rapidly increasable substitutes. (*Cotton* for linen, wool and silk.) The same happens for the necessaries of life in the substitution of potatoes for grain. The higher productivity in the latter case through production of a worse article containing fewer nourishing substances and hence cheaper organic conditions of the worker's reproduction. The latter belongs in the examination of wages. In the discussion of the minimum wage, not to forget Rumford.[35]

Now we come to the third case of relative surplus labour as it presents itself in the employment of machinery.

⟨It has become apparent in the course of our presentation that value, which appeared as an abstraction, is possible only as such an abstraction, as soon as money is posited; this circulation of money in turn leads to capital, hence can be fully developed only on the foundation of capital, just as, generally, only on this foundation can circulation seize hold of all moments of production. This development, therefore, not only makes visible the historic character of forms, such as capital, which belong to a specific epoch of history; but also, [in its course] categories such as value, which appear as purely abstract, show the historic foundation from which they are abstracted, and on whose basis alone they can appear, therefore, in this abstraction; and categories which belong more or less to all epochs, such as e.g. money, show the historic modifications which they undergo. The economic concept of value does not occur in antiquity. Value distinguished only juridically from *pretium*, against fraud etc. The concept of value is entirely peculiar to the most modern economy, since it is the most abstract expression of capital itself and of the production resting on it. In the concept of value, its secret betrayed.⟩

What distinguishes surplus labour founded on machinery is the reduction of necessary labour time, which takes the form that fewer simultaneous working days are employed, fewer workers. The second moment, that the increase in productive power must be paid for by capital itself, is not free of charge. The means by which this increase in the force of production is set to work is itself objectified direct labour time, value, and, in order to lay hands upon it, capital must exchange a part of its value for it. It is easy to develop the introduction of machinery out of competition and out of the law of the reduction of production costs which is triggered[36] by competition. We are concerned here with

35. Benjamin Thompson (1753–1814), American adventurer, who entered the service of George III, was created Count of Rumford in 1784, issued *Essays, Political, Economical, and Philosophical,* in London, 1796–1802, in which he recommended various inferior forms of food for labourers; discussed by Marx in *Capital,* Vol. I, Moscow 1954, p. 601.

36. The MELI edition gives *aufgelöst* (dissolved) rather than *ausgelöst* (triggered, released). This is in all probability a misreading of the handwritten manuscript. (The *f* and one form of the *s* are virtually indistinguishable in the old-style German script Marx used at that time.)

developing it out of the relation of capital to living labour, without reference to other capitals.

If a capitalist annually employed 100 workers at spinning cotton, which annually cost him £2,400, and if he replaced 50 workers with a machine costing £1,200, but in such a way that the machine would likewise be worn out within the year and have to be replaced again at the beginning of the second year, then he would obviously have gained nothing; nor could he sell his product more cheaply. The remaining 50 workers would do the same work as 100 did earlier; each individual worker's surplus labour would have increased in the same relation as their number had diminished, hence would have remained the same. If previously it was = 200 hours of work daily, i.e. 2 hours for each of the 100 working days, then it would now likewise be = 200 hours of work, i.e. = 4 for each of the 50 working days. Relative to the worker, his surplus time would have increased; for capital the matter would be unchanged, since it would now have to exchange 50 working days (necessary and surplus time together) for the machine. The 50 days of objectified labour which it exchanged for machinery would only give him an equivalent, hence no surplus time, as if it had exchanged 50 days of objectified labour for 50 living ones. This would be replaced, however, by the surplus labour time of the remaining 50 workers. If the form of exchange is stripped off, the matter would be the same as if the capitalist employed 50 workers whose entire working day were necessary labour only, and 50 additional ones whose working day made good this 'loss'. But posit now that the machine cost only £960, i.e. only 40 working days, and that the remaining workers produce 4 hours of surplus labour time each, as before, i.e. 200 hours or 16 days, 4 hours ($16\frac{1}{3}$ days), then the capitalist would have saved £240 on outlays. While he gained only 16 days 4 hours with his previous outlay of 2,400, he would now likewise gain 200 hours of work on an outlay of 960. 200 is to 2,400 as 1:12; while $200:2,160 = 20:216 = 1:10\frac{4}{5}$. Expressed in days of work, in the first case he would gain 16 days 4 hours per 100 working days, in the second, the same amount on 90; in the first, on 1,200 hours of work daily, 200; in the second, on 1,080. $200:1,200 = 1:6$, $200:1,080 = 1:5\frac{2}{5}$. In the first case the individual worker's surplus time $= \frac{1}{6}$ working day $= 2$ hours. In the second case $= 2\frac{6}{27}$ hours per worker. Furthermore, with the employment of machinery, the part of the capital which was previously employed in instruments must be deducted from the additional cost caused by the machinery.

Money and fixed capital: *presupposes certain amount of wealth.* (Economist.) – *Relation of fixed capital and circulating capital. Cotton-spinner* (Economist)

⟨The money circulating in a country is a *certain portion of the capital* of the country, absolutely withdrawn from productive purposes, in order to facilitate *or increase the productiveness of the remainder*. A certain amount of wealth is, therefore, as necessary, in order to adopt gold as a circulating medium, *as it is to make a machine, in order to facilitate any other production.*' (*Economist*, Vol. V, p. 520.)⟩ ⟨'What is the practice? A manufacturer obtains £500 from his banker on Saturday, for wages; he distributes these among his workers. On the same day the majority of money is brought to the shopkeepers, and through them returned to their various bankers.' (loc. cit. p. 575.)⟩

⟨'A cotton spinner, with a capital of £100,000, who laid out £95,000 for his mill and machinery, would soon find he wanted means to buy cotton and pay wages. His trade would be hampered and his finances deranged. And yet men expect that a nation, which has recklessly sunk the bulk of its available means in railways, should nevertheless be able to conduct the infinite operations of manufacture and commerce.' (loc. cit. p. 1271.)⟩

Slavery and wage labour (Steuart). – Profit upon alienation. *Steuart*

'Money . . . *an adequate equivalent for any thing alienable.*' (J. Steuart.) (p. 13) (Vol. I, p. 32, ed. Dublin, 1770.)

⟨'In the old times to make mankind labour beyond their wants, to make one part of a state work, to maintain the other gratuitously, to be brought about only through slavery . . . If mankind be not forced to labour, they will only labour for themselves; and if they have few wants, there will be few [who] labour. But when states come to be formed and have occasion for idle hands to defend them against the violence of their enemies, food at any rate must be procured for those who do not labour; and as, by the supposition, the wants of the labourers are small, a method must be found to increase their labour above the proportion of their wants. For this purpose slavery was calculated . . . Here then was a violent method of making men laborious in raising food; . . . men were then forced to labour because they were slaves of others; men are now forced to labour because they are slaves to their own wants.' (Steuart, Vol. I, p. 38–40.) 'It is the *infinite variety of wants*, and of the *kinds of commodities* necessary to their gratification, which alone renders the passion for wealth indefinite and insatiable.' (Wakefield *on* A. Smith, p. 64 note.)⟩[37]

'*Machines* I consider as a method of augmenting (virtually) the number of industrious, without the expense of feeding an additional number.' (Steuart, Vol. I, p. 123.) 'When manufacturers get together in bodies, they depend not directly upon *consumers*, but upon *merchants*.' (Steuart, Vol. I, p. 154.) 'The abusive agriculture is no *trade*, because it applies no *alienation*, but is purely a method of subsisting.' (loc. cit. p. 156.) '*Trade* is an operation, by which the wealth, or work, either of individuals, or of societies, may be exchanged, by a set of men called *merchants*, for an equivalent, proper for supplying every want, without any interruption to industry, or any check upon consumption.' (Steuart, I, p. 166.) 'While wants continue simple and few, a workman finds time enough to distribute all his work; when wants become more multiplied, men must work harder: *time becomes precious*; hence trade is introduced. The merchant as mediator between the workman and consumer.' (loc. cit. p. 171.) 'Money the *common* price of all things.' (loc. cit. p. 177.) 'Money represented by the merchant. To the consumers, the merchant represents the totality of manufacturers, towards the latter, the totality of consumers, and to both classes his credit supplies the use of money. He represents wants, manufacturers and money by turns.' (loc. cit. p. 177, 178.) (Steuart, see Vol. I, p. 181–3, regards profit as distinct from *real value*, which he defines very confusedly (has production costs in mind) as the amount of objectified labour (what a workman can perform in a day etc.), necessary expense of the workmen, price of the raw material, as *profit upon alienation* fluctuating with demand.) (With Steuart the categories still vary greatly; they have not yet become fixed, as with A. Smith. We just saw that *real value* identical with production costs, in which, besides the labour of the workmen and the value of the material, wages, also, confusingly, figure as a separate component part. At another

37. Wakefield's note on p. 64 of Vol. I of his edition of Adam Smith (London, 1835–9).

point he takes the *intrinsic value* of a commodity to mean the value of its raw material or the raw material itself, while, by *useful value*, he understands the labour time employed on it. 'The first is something real in itself; e.g. the silver in a silver lattice-work. The *intrinsic worth* of a silk, woollen or linen manufacture is less than the primitive value employed, because it is rendered almost unserviceable for any other use but that for which the manufacture is intended; the *useful value by contrast must be estimated according to the labour it has cost to produce it. The labour employed in the modification represents a portion of a man's time*, which having been usefully employed, *has given a form to some substance* which has rendered it useful, ornamental, or in short, fit for man, mediately or immediately.' (p. 361, 362, Vol. I loc. cit.) (The real use value is the form given to the substance. But this form itself is only static labour.) 'When we suppose a common standard on the price of any thing, we must suppose the alienation of it to be frequent and familiar. In countries where simplicity reigns, ... it is hardly possible to determine any standard for the price of articles of first necessity ... in such states of society the articles of food and necessaries are hardly found in commerce: no person purchases them; because the principal occupation of everybody is to procure them for himself ... Sale alone can determine prices, and frequent sale can only fix a standard. Now the frequent sale of articles of the first necessity marks a distribution of inhabitants in labourers and free hands' etc. (Vol. I, p. 395 seq. loc. cit.) (The doctrine of the determination of prices by the mass of the circulating medium first advanced by Locke, repeated in the *Spectator*, 19 October 1711, developed and elegantly formulated by Hume and Montesquieu, its basis raised to its formal peak by Ricardo, and with all its absurdities in practical application to the banking system, by Loyd, Colonel Torrens etc.). Steuart polemicizes against it, and his development materially anticipates more or less everything later advanced by Bosanquet, Tooke, Wilson. (Notebook, p. 26.)[38] (He says among other things as historic illustration: 'It is a fact that at the time when Greece and Rome abounded in wealth, when every rarity and the work of choicest artists was carried to an excessive price, an ox was bought for a mere trifle and grain was cheaper perhaps than ever it was in Scotland ...

38. Steuart, *An Inquiry into the Principles of Political Economy*, Vol. I, p. 399.

The demand is proportioned, not to the number of those who consume, but of those who buy; now those who consume are all the inhabitants, but those who buy are only the few industrious who are free ... In Greece and Rome, slavery: Those who were fed by the labour of their own slaves, the slaves of the state, or by grain distributed free of charge among the people, had no occasion to go to the market: they did not enter into competition with the buyers ... The few manufacturers then known made wants in general less extensive; consequently, the number of the industrious free was small, and *they* were the only persons who *could* have occasion to purchase food and necessaries: consequently, the competition of the buyers must have been small in proportion, and prices low; further the markets were supplied partly from the surplus produced on the lands of the great men, laboured by slaves; who being fed from the lands, the surplus cost in a manner nothing to the proprietors; and since the number of those who had occasion to buy, very small, this surplus was sold cheap. Also, the grain distributed to the people free of charge must necessarily have held the market down, etc. By contrast, for a fine mullet or an artist, etc. great competition and hence prices rising extraordinarily. The luxury of those times, though excessive, was confined to a few, and as money, in general, circulated but slowly through the hands of the multitude, it was constantly stagnating in those of the rich who found no measure, but their own caprice, in regulating the prices of what they wished to possess.') (26, 27, Notebook. Steuart.)[39] '*Money of account* is nothing but an arbitrary scale of equal parts, invented for measuring the respective value of things vendible. Money of account quite different from *money-coin*, which is price, and could exist, even if there were no substance in the world which was the proportional equivalent for all commodities.' (Vol. II, p. 102.) 'Money of account does the same service for value as things like minutes, seconds etc. do for angles, or scales for geographical maps etc. In all these inventions some denomination is always taken for the unit.' (loc. cit.) 'The usefulness of all those inventions being solely confined to the marking of *proportion*. Just so, the unit in money can have no invariable determinate proportion to any part of value, i.e. it cannot be fixed to any particular quantity of gold, silver or any other commodity whatsoever. The unit once fixed, we can, by multiplying it, ascend to

39. ibid., pp. 403–5.

the greatest value' etc. (p. 103.) 'So money a scale for measuring value.' (p. 102.) 'The value of commodities, therefore, depending upon a general combination of circumstances relative to themselves and to the fancies of men, their value ought to be considered as changing only with respect to one another; consequently, any thing which troubles or perplexes the ascertaining those *changes of proportion by the means of a general, determinate and invariable scale*, must be hurtful to trade and a clog upon alienation.' (loc. cit.) 'It is absolutely necessary to distinguish between *price* (i.e. coin) considered as a measure and *price* considered as an equivalent for value. The metals do not perform both functions equally well ... *Money is an ideal scale of equal parts*. If it be demanded what ought to be the standard of value of one part? I answer by putting another question: What is the standard length of a degree, a minute, a second? It has none – but so soon as one part becomes determined, by the nature of a scale, all the rest must follow in proportion.' (p. 105.) 'Examples of this ideal money are the bank money of Amsterdam and the Angola money on the African coast. – The bank money stands invariable like a rock in the sea. According to this ideal standard are the prices of all things regulated.' (p. 106, 107 seq.)

In Custodi's anthology of the Italian economists, *Parte Antica, Tomo III*: Montanari (Geminiano), *Della moneta*, written about 1683,[40] says of the 'invention' of money: 'Intercourse between nations spans the whole globe to such an extent that one may almost say all the world is but a single city in which a permanent fair comprising all commodities is held, so that by means of money all the things produced by the land, the animals and human industry can be acquired and enjoyed by any person in his own home. A wonderful invention!' (p. 40.) 'But, since it is another peculiarity of measures that they enter into such a relation with the things measured that in a certain manner the thing measured becomes the measure of the measuring unit, it follows that, just as motion is the measure of time, time may be the measure of the motion itself; hence it occurs that not only are the coins measures of our wants, but also our wants are, reciprocally, the measure of the coins themselves and of value.' (p. 41, 42.) 'It is quite clear that the greater the number of coins circulating in

40. Geminiano Montanari, *Della moneta, trattato mercantile*, in Custodi (ed.), Scrittori Classici Italiani di Economia Politica, Parte Antica, Tomo III, Milan, 1804.

commerce within the confines of a given district, in proportion to the marketable goods there are in that place, the more expensive will they be. Can a thing be said to be expensive because it is worth a large quantity of gold in countries where gold is abundant? Should not the gold itself, which is estimated as of the same quantity as another thing which comes to be considered elsewhere as cheap, be rather described as cheap in that case?' (p. 48.)

'100 years earlier the chief feature in the commercial policy of nations was the *amassing* of gold and silver, as a kind of wealth par excellence.' (p. 67.) (Gouge, Wm. *A Short History of Paper Money and Banking in the United States. Philadelphia,* 1833.) (*Barter in United States* (*see* Gouge Notebook VIII, p. 81 seq.): 'In Pennsylvania as in the other colonies, significant traffic was carried on by barter ... as late as 1723 in Maryland, an act was passed making tobacco a legal tender at one penny a pound, and Indian corn at 20d. a bushel.' (p. 5.) (Part II.) Soon however, 'their trade with the West-Indies and a clandestine commerce with the Spanish made silver so plentiful, that in 1652 a mint was established in New England for coining shillings, sixpences and threepenny pieces.' (p. 5.) (loc. cit.) 'Virginia in 1645 forbade dealings by barter, and established the Spanish piece of 8 to 6s. as the standard currency of the colony (the Spanish dollar) ... The other colonies affixed different denominations to the dollar ... The money in account was everywhere nominally the same as in England. The coin of the realm was especially Spanish and Portuguese' etc. cf. p. 81 Notebook VIII). (p. 6. By an act of Queen Anne an attempt was made to put an end to this confusion.)

Wool industry in England since Elizabeth (Tuckett). – *Silk-manufacture* (*Same*). *Ditto Iron. Cotton*

Tuckett: *A History of the Past and Present State of the Labouring Population* etc., 2 vols., London, 1846.

'*Wool manufactures*: During Elizabeth's time the *clothier* occupied the place of the *mill-owner or manufacturer*; he was the capitalist who brought the wool, and delivered it to the weaver, in portions of about 12 pounds, to be made into cloth. At the beginning, manufacture was *confined to cities* and *corporate and market-towns*, the inhabitants of the villages making little more than [sufficed] for the use of their families. Later, in non-corporate towns favoured by local advantages, and also in country places by farmers, graziers and husbandmen, who commenced making cloth for sale, as well as for domestic use.' (The cruder sorts.) 'In 1551 a statute was passed, restricting the number of looms and apprentices which might be held by clothiers and weavers residing out of cities; and that no country weaver should have a tucking mill, nor any tucker a loom. By a law of the same year, all weavers of broad cloth had to undergo an apprenticeship of 7 years. Nevertheless, *village manufacture*, as an *object of mercantile profit*, took firm root. 5 and 6 *Edward VI*, c. 22, a statute, prohibits the use of *machinery* . . . The Flemish and Dutch thus maintained superiority in this manufacture until the end of the seventeenth century . . . In 1668 the Dutch loom was introduced from Holland.' (p. 138–41.) '*Owing to the introduction of machinery, in 1800 one person could do as much work as 46 in the year 1785.* In the year 1800 the capital invested in mills, machinery etc. appropriate for the woollen trade was not less than *6 million pounds sterling and the total number of persons of all ages occupied in England in this branch was 1,500,000.*' (p. 142–3.) Thus the productive power of labour grew 4,600%. But, firstly, this number only about $\frac{1}{6}$ of the fixed capital alone; relative to the total capital (raw material etc.) perhaps only $\frac{1}{20}$. 'Hardly any manufacture had such an advantage from the improvements in science as the art of dyeing cloth through the application of the *laws of chemistry*.' (loc. cit. p. 144.)

Silk manufacture. Until the beginning of the eighteenth century, 'the art of *silk throwing* most successful in Italy, where machinery of a particular description adopted to this purpose. In 1715 John Lombe, one of three brothers who had a business as throwers and silk-merchants, travelled to Italy and was able to obtain a model in one of the mills . . . A silk mill, with the improved machinery, erected in 1719 in Derby by Lombe and his brothers. This mill contained 26,586 wheels, all turned by one water wheel . . . Parliament gave him £14,000 for throwing open the secret to the trade. This mill came nearer to the idea of a modern factory than any previous establishment of the kind. The machine had 97,746 wheels, movements, and individual parts working day and night, all of which were moved by one large water wheel and were governed by one regulator: and it employed 300 persons to attend and supply it with work.' (133–4.) (No spirit of invention showed itself in the English silk trade; first introduced by the weavers of Antwerp, who fled after the sacking of the town by the Duke of Parma; then different branches by the French refugees 1685–92.)

In 1740, 1,700 tons of iron were produced by 59 high furnaces; 1827: 690,000 by 284. Furnaces thus increased $= 1:4\frac{48}{49}$; less than quintupled; the tons $= 1:405\frac{15}{17}$. (Comp. on the relation over a series of years loc. cit. Notebook p. 12.)[41]

Glass manufacturing, among other things, best shows how dependent [is] the progress of science on manufactures. On the other side e.g. the invention of quadrants arose from the needs of navigation, parliament offered a prize for inventions.

8 cotton machines, which cost £5,000 in 1825, were sold in 1833 for £300. (On cotton spinning, see loc. cit. p. 13, Notebook.)[42]

'A first rate cotton spinning factory cannot be built, filled with machinery, and fitted with gas work and steam engine, under £100,000. A steam engine of one hundred horse power will turn 50,000 spindles, which will produce 62,500 miles of fine cotton-thread per day. In such a factory, 1,000 persons will spin as much thread as 250,000 persons could without machinery. McCulloch estimates the number in Britain at 130,000.' (p. 218, loc. cit.)

Origin of free wage labour. *Vagabondage.* Tuckett

'Where there are no regular roads, there can hardly be said to be a community; the people could have nothing in common.' (p. 270. Tuckett loc. cit.)

'Of the produce of the earth, useful to men, $\frac{99}{100}$ are the produce of men.' (loc. cit. p. 348.)

'When slavery or life-apprenticeship was abolished, the labourer became his own master and was left to his own resources. But if without sufficient employment etc., men will not starve whilst they can beg or steal; consequently the first character the poor assumed was that of thieves and mendicants.' (p. 637 note, Vol. II, loc. cit.) 'One remarkable distinction of the present state of society, since Elizabeth, is that her poor law was especially a law for the enforcement of industry, intended to meet the mass of vagrancy that grew out of the suppression of the monasteries and the transition from slavery to free labour. As example, the 5th act of Elizabeth, directing households using half a plough of land in tillage, to require any person they might find unemployed,

41. Tuckett, *A History*, Vol. I, p. 157 n.   42. ibid., p. 204.

to become their apprentice in husbandry, or in any art or mystery; and, if unwilling, to bring him before a justice, who was almost compelled to commit him to ward until he consented to be bound. Under Elizabeth, out of every 100 people, 85 were required for the production of food. At present, not a lack of industry, but a profitable employment ... *The great difficulty then was* to overcome the propensity of idleness and vagabondage, not to procure them remunerative occupation. During this reign there were several acts of the legislature to enforce the idle to labour.' (p. 643, 644. Vol. II, loc. cit.)

'*Fixed capital*, when once formed, ceases to affect the demand for labour, but during its formation it gives employment to just as many hands as an equal amount would employ, either of circulating capital, or of revenue.' (p. 56. John Barton, *Observations on the Circumstances which Influence the Condition of the Labouring Classes of Society*, London, 1817.)

Blake *on accumulation and rate of profit.* (*Shows that prices etc. not indifferent because a class of mere consumers does not at the same time consume and reproduce.*) – *Dormant capital*

'The community consists *of two classes of persons*, one, which consumes and reproduces, the other, which consumes without reproduction. If the entire society consisted of producers, then of little consequence at what price they exchanged their commodities among one another; but those who are only consumers form too numerous a class to be overlooked. Their power of demanding arises from seats, mortgages, annuities, professions and services of various descriptions rendered to the community. The higher the price at which the class of consumers can be made to buy, the greater will be the profit of the producers upon the mass of commodities which they sell to them. Among these purely consuming classes, the government takes up the most prominent station.' (W. Blake, *Observations on the Effects Produced by the Expenditure of Government during the Restriction of Cash Payments*, London, 1823, p. 42, 43.) In order to show that the capital lent to the state is not necessarily such as was previously employed productively – and we are concerned here only with the admission that a part of capital is always dormant – Blake says: 'The error lies in the supposition (1) that the whole capital of the country is fully employed; (2) *that there is immediate employment for succes-*

sive accumulations of capital as it accrues from saving. I believe
there are at all times some portions of capital devoted to undertakings that yield very slow returns and slender profits, and some
portions lying wholly dormant in the form of goods, for which
there is no sufficient demand . . . Now, if these dormant portions
and savings could be transferred into the hands of government in
exchange for its annuities, they would become sources of new
demand, without encroaching upon existing capital.' (p. 54, 55
loc. cit.) '*Whatever amount of produce is withdrawn from market
by the demand of the saving capitalist, is poured back again, with
addition, in the goods that he reproduces*. The government, by
contrast, takes it away from consumption without reproduction
. . . Where savings are made from revenue, it is clear that the
person entitled to enjoy the portion saved is satisfied without
consuming it. It proves that the industry of the country is capable
of raising more produce than the wants of the community require.
If the quantity saved is employed as capital in reproducing a
value equivalent to itself, together with a profit, this new creation,
when added to the general fund, can be drawn out by that person
alone who made the savings, i.e. by the very person who has
already shown his disinclination to consume . . . If everyone consumes what he has a right to consume, there must of necessity be a
market. Whoever saves from his revenues, foregoes this right, and
his share remains undisposed of. Should this spirit of economy be
general, the market is necessarily overstocked, and it must
depend on the degree, to which this surplus accumulates, whether
it can find new employments as capital.' (56, 57.) (Cf. this work
generally in the section on *accumulation*.) (Cf. Notebook p. 68
and p. 70, where it is shown that the rate of profits and wages
rose owing to *prices*, caused by war demand, without any respect
'to the quantity of land taken last into cultivation'.) 'During the
revolutionary war the market rate of interest rose to 7, 8, 9 and
even 10%, although during the whole time lands of the lowest
quality were cultivated.' (loc. cit. p. 64–6.) 'The rise of interest to
6, 8, 10 and even 12% proves the rise of profit. The depreciation
of money, supposing it to exist, could not change the relation of
capital and interest. If £200 are worth only £100; £10 interest
worth only £5, whatever affected the value of the principal would
equally affect the value of profits. It could not alter the relation
between the two.' (p. 73.) 'Ricardo's reasoning, that the price of
wages cannot make the prices of commodities rise, does not apply

to a society *where a large class are not producers.*' (loc. cit.) 'More
than the just share is obtained by the producers at the expense of
that portion, which of right belongs to the class who are only
consumers.' (74.) This of course important, since capital exchanges
not only for capital, but also for revenue, and each capital can
itself be eaten up as revenue. Still, this does not affect the determination of profit in general. Under the various forms of profit,
interest, rent, pensions, taxes etc., it may be distributed (like a part
of wages even) under different titles among different classes of
the population. They can never divide up among them more than
the total surplus value of the total surplus product. The ratio in
which they distribute it is of course economically important;
[but] does not affect the question before us.

'If the circulation of commodities of 400 million required a
currency of 40 million, and this proportion of $\frac{1}{10}$ were the due
level, then, if the value of the commodities to be circulated grows
to 450 million, from natural causes, the currency, in order to
continue at its level, would have to grow to 45 million, or the 40
million must be made to circulate with such increased rapidity, by
banking or other improvements, as to perform the functions of 45
million ... such an augmentation, or such rapidity, the consequence and not the cause of the increase of prices.' (W. Blake.
loc. cit., p. 80 seq. cf. Notebook p. 70.)

'The upper and middle class of Rome gained great wealth by
Asiatic conquest, but not being created by commerce or manufactures, it resembled that obtained by Spain from her American
colonies.' (p. 66 Vol. I, Mackinnon, *History of Civilisation,*
London, 1846, Vol. I.)

Domestic agriculture at the beginning of the sixteenth century.
Tuckett

'In the fifteenth century, Harrison asserts' (see also Eden),[43]
'that the farmers are barely able to pay their rents without selling
a cow, or a horse, or some of their produce, although they paid at
the most £4 for a farm ... The farmer in these times consumed
the chief party of the produce to be raised, his servants taking their
seats with him at his table ... *The principal materials for clothing
were not bought, but were obtained by the industry of each family.
The instruments of husbandry* were so simple that many of them

43. Eden, *The State of the Poor*, Vol. I, pp. 119–20.

were made, or at least kept in repair, by the farmer himself. Every yeoman was expected to know how to make yokes or bows, and plough gear; *such work* employed their winter evenings.' (p. 324, 325 loc. cit. Tuckett, Vol. II.)

Profit. Interest. Influence of machinery on the wage fund.
Westminster Review

Interest and Profit: 'Where an individual employs his own savings productively, the remuneration of his time and skill – *agency for superintendence* (*profit* further includes the risk to which his capital may have been exposed in his particular business); and the remuneration for the productive employment of his savings, *Interest*. The whole of this remuneration, *Gross Profit*; where an individual employs the savings of another, he obtains the agency only. Where one individual lends his savings to another, only the *interest* or the *net profit*.' (*Westminster Review*, January 1826, p. 107, 108.) Thus here interest = *net profit* = *remuneration for the productive employments of savings*; the actual profit the remuneration for the *agency for superintendence* during his productive employment. The same philistine says: 'Every improvement in the arts of production, that does not disturb the proportion between the portions devoted to capital and not devoted to the payment for wages, is attended with an increase of employment to the labouring classes: every fresh application of machinery and horse labour is *attended with an increase of produce and consequently of capital*; to whatever extent it may diminish the *ratio* which that part of the national capital forming the fund for the payment of wages bears to that which is otherwise employed, its tendency is not to diminish but to increase the *absolute amount of that fund* and hence to increase the quantity of employment.' (loc. cit. p. 123.)

[*Money as measure of values and yardstick of prices. Critique of theories of the standard measure of money.*]

The role of money as *measure*, as well as, secondly, the fundamental law that the mass of the circulating medium, at a definite velocity of circulation, is determined by the prices of the commodities and by the mass of commodities circulating at definite prices, or by the total price, the aggregate amount of commodities, which is itself in turn determined by two circumstances: (1) the level of the commodity price; (2) the mass of circulating commodities at definite prices; further, (3) the law that money as medium of circulation becomes coin, mere vanishing moment, mere *symbol* of the values it exchanges – all this leads to more particular aspects which we shall develop only when and in so far as they coincide with more complicated economic relations, credit circulation, exchange rate etc. It is necessary to avoid all detail, and where detail must be brought in, it is to be brought in only at the point where it loses the elementary character.

First of all, money circulation, as the most superficial (in the sense of: driven out onto the surface) and the most abstract form of the entire production process, is in itself quite without content, except in so far as its own formal distinctions, precisely the simple aspects developed in section II, make up its content. It is clear that simple money circulation, regarded in itself, is not bent back into itself, [but] consists of an infinite number of indifferent and accidentally adjacent movements. The coin, e.g., may be regarded as the point of departure of money circulation, but there is no law of any reflux back to the coin except for depreciation through wear and tear, which necessitates melting-down and new issue of coins. This concerns only the material side and does not at all form a moment of circulation itself. Within circulation itself, the point of return may be different from the point of departure; in so far as it bends back into itself, money circulation appears as the mere appearance of a circulation going on behind it and determining it, e.g. when we look at the money circulation between manufacturer, worker, shopkeeper and banker. Furthermore, the factors which affect the mass of commodities thrown into circulation, the rise and fall of prices, the velocity of circulation, the amount of simultaneous payments etc., are all circumstances which lie *outside* simple money circulation itself. They are relations which express themselves in it; it provides the names for them, as it were; but they are not to be explained by its own differentiation. Different metals serve as money, and they have a different and changing value relation to one another. Thus the question of the double standard etc. enters, which takes on world-historical forms. But it takes them on, and the double standard itself enters, only through external trade, hence, to be usefully examined, supposes the development of much higher relations than that of the simple money relation.

Money as the *measure* of value is not expressed in amounts of bullion, but rather in accounting money, arbitrary names for fractional parts of a specific amount of the money-substance. These names can be changed, the relation of the coin to its metallic substance can be changed, while the name remains the same. Hence counterfeiting, which plays a great role in the history of states. Further, the different kinds of money in various countries. This question [is of] interest only in exchange rate.[44]

Money is a *measure* only because it is labour time materialized in a specific substance, hence itself *value*, and, more particularly, because this specific materiality counts as its general objective one [*allgemeingegenständliche*], as the materiality of labour time as such, as distinct from its merely particular incarnations; hence because it is an *equivalent*. But since, in its function as *measure*, money is only an imagined point of comparison, only needs to exist ideally – only the ideal transposition of commodities into their general value-presence takes place –; since, further, in this quality as measure it figures first as accounting coin, and I say a commodity is worth so many shillings, francs etc., when I transpose it into money; this has given rise to the confused notion of an *ideal measure*, developed by Steuart and refurbished at various periods, even recently, in England, as a profound discovery. Namely in this sense, that the names, pound, shillings, guinea, dollar etc., which count as accounting units are not specific names for specific quantities of gold, silver etc., but merely arbitrary points of comparison which do not themselves express value, no definite quantity of objectified labour time. Hence the whole nonsense about fixing the price of gold and silver – price understood here as the name by which fractional parts are called. An ounce of gold now divided into £3 17s. 10d. This is called fixing the price; it is, as Locke correctly remarks, only fixing the name of fractional parts of gold and silver etc. Expressed in itself, gold, silver is naturally equal to itself. An ounce is an ounce, whether I call it £3 or £20. In short, this *ideal measure* in Steuart's sense means this: if I say commodity A is worth £12, commodity B 6, commodity C 3, then their relation to one another $= 12 : 6 : 3$. Prices express only the relations in which they are exchanged for one another. 2B are exchanged for 1A and $1\frac{1}{2}$B for 3C. Now, instead of expressing the relation of A, B, C in

44. Marx collected and annotated an immense amount of material on the various theories of the exchange rate: he included this in a draft of 1854–5 entitled 'Money System, Credit System, and Crises'. This manuscript remains unpublished. See Foreword, p. 12.

real money, money which itself has value, is value, could I not, instead of the £ which expresses a specific mass of gold, just as well take any name you like, without content (this means, here, *ideally*), e.g. mackerels? A = 12 mackerels; B = 6M, C = 3M. This word M is here only a name, without any relation to a content belonging to itself. Steuart's example with a degree, line, second, proves nothing; for although degree, line, second have changing magnitudes, they are not merely names, but rather always express the fractional part of a specific magnitude of space or of time. They thus have in fact a substance. The fact that money in the role of measure functions only as something *imagined* is here transformed into it supposedly being any imagined thing you like, a mere *name*, namely a name for the numerical value-relation. In that case, however, it would be correct to express no names at all, but merely a numerical relation, for the whole affair comes down to this: I obtain 6B for 12A, 3C for 6B; this relation can also be expressed in this way, $A = 12x$, $B = 6x$, $C = 3x$, where the x is itself only a name for the relation of A:B and B:C. The mere, unnamed numerical relation would not do. For A:B = 12:6 = 2:1, and B:C = 6:3 = 2:1. Hence $C = \frac{1}{2}$. Hence $B = \frac{1}{2}$, hence B = C. Hence A = 2 and B = 2; hence A = B.

Let me take any price list, e.g. potash, 35s. the ton; cocoa, lb., 60s.; iron (bars) (p. ton) 145s. etc. In order to have the relation of these commodities to one another, not only can I forget the silver in the shilling; the numbers alone, 35, 60, 145 suffice to define the reciprocal value relations of potash, cocoa, iron bars. Undenominated numbers now suffice; and not only can I give their unit, 1, any name, regardless of any value; I need not give it any name at all. Steuart insists that I must give it one or another name, but that this name then, as mere arbitrary name of the unit, as mere *marking of proportion* itself, cannot be fixed to any portion of the quantity of gold, silver or any other commodity.

With every measure, as soon as it serves as point of comparison, i.e. as soon as the different entities to be compared are put into a numerical relation to the measure as unit, and are now related to one another, the nature of the measure becomes irrelevant and vanishes in the act of comparison itself; the unit of measure has become a mere unit of numbers; the quality of this unit has vanished, e.g. that it is itself a specific magnitude of length or of time or of an angle. But is it only when the different entities are already presupposed as measured that the unit of measure *marks only pro-*

portion between them, thus e.g. in our case the proportion of their values. The accounting unit not only has different names in different countries; but is the name for different fractional parts of an ounce of gold, e.g. But the exchange rate reduces all of them to the same unit of weight of gold or silver. Thus if I presuppose the various magnitudes of commodities, e.g. as above, = 35s., 60s., 145s., then, to compare them, since the 1 is presupposed as equal in all of them, since they have been made commensurable, it is wholly superfluous to bring in the observation that s. is a specific quantity of silver, the name for a specific amount of silver. But, as mere numerical magnitudes, as amounts of any unit of the same name, they only become comparable to one another, and only express proportions towards one another, when each individual commodity is measured with the one which serves as unit, as measure. But I can only measure them against one another, only make them commensurable, if they have a unit – the latter is the labour time contained in both. The measuring unit must therefore [be] a certain quantity of a commodity in which a quantity of labour is objectified. Since the same quantity of labour is not always expressed in the same quantity of e.g. gold, it follows that the value of this measuring unit itself variable. But, in so far as money is regarded only as measure, this variability is no obstacle. Even in barter, to the extent that it is somewhat developed as barter, i.e. is a repeated, normal operation, not merely an isolated act of exchange, some other commodity appears as measuring unit, e.g. cattle with Homer. Among the savage Papuans of the coast, who, in order 'to obtain a foreign article, barter 1 or 2 of their children, and if they are not to hand, borrow those of their neighbours, promising to give their own in exchange, when they come to hand, this request being rarely refused', there exists no measure for exchange. The only side of exchange which exists for the Papuan is that he can obtain the alien thing only by dispossessing himself of something he possesses. This dispossession [*Entäusserung*] itself is regulated for him by nothing but his fancy on one side, and the scope of his movable possessions on the other. In the *Economist* of 13 March 1858, we read, in a letter addressed to the editor: 'As the substitution in France of gold for silver in the coinage (which has been the principal means hitherto of absorbing the new discoveries of gold) must be approaching its completion, particularly as less coinage will be wanted for a stagnant trade and reduced prices, we may expect ere long that our fixed price of £3 17s. 10½d. an ounce will attract the gold here.'[45] Now what does this, our 'fixed price of an ounce' of gold, mean? Nothing other than that a certain aliquot part of an ounce is called pence, a certain multiple of this penny-weight of gold a shilling, and a certain multiple of this shilling-weight of gold a pound? Does the gentleman imagine that in other countries the golden Guilder, the Louis d'or etc. do not likewise signify a specific quantity of gold, i.e. that a specific quantity has a fixed name? and that this is an English privilege? or a speciality? That, in England, a monetary coin expressed in gold is more than a monetary coin, and in other countries, less? It would be interesting to know what this noble spirit imagines the exchange rate to be.

What leads Steuart astray is this: the prices of commodities express nothing but the relations in which they are exchangeable for one another, the *proportions* in which they exchange for one another. These proportions given, I can call the unit any name whatever, because the undenominated abstract number would suffice, and instead of saying that this commodity = 6 stivers, the other = 3 etc., I could say this one = 6 ones, the other = 3; I would not have to give the unit any name at all. Since the numerical relation is all that matters at that point, I can give it any name whatever. But it is already presupposed here that these proportions are *given,* that the commodities have previously become commensurable magnitudes. As soon as magnitudes have once been posited as commensurable, their relations become simple numerical relations. Money appears as measure, and a specific quantity of the commodity in which it represents itself appears as measuring unit, precisely in order to find the *proportions*, and to articulate and to handle commodities as commensurable ones. This real unit is the labour time relatively objectified in them. However, it is labour time itself posited as general. The process by which values within the money system are determined by labour time does not belong in the examination of money itself, and falls outside circulation; proceeds behind it as its effective base and presupposition. The question here could only be this: instead of saying this commodity is = to one ounce of gold, why does one not say directly it is = to x labour time, objectified in the ounce of gold? Why is labour time, the substance and measure of value, not at the same time the measure of prices, or, in other words, why are price and value

45. *The Economist*, Vol. XVI, No. 759, 13 March 1858, p. 290, article entitled 'Will the Low Rate of Interest Last?'.

different at all? Proudhon's school believe it a great deed to demand that this identity be posited and that the price of commodities be expressed in labour time. The coincidence of price and value presupposes the equality of demand and supply, exchange solely of equivalents (hence not of capital for labour) etc.; in short, formulated economically, it reveals at once that this demand is the negation of the entire foundation of the relations of production based on exchange value. But if we suppose this basis suspended, then on the other side the problem disappears again, which exists only on it and with it. That the commodity in its unmediated presence as use value is not value, is not the adequate form of value = that it is [the adequate form of value] as an objective other, or that it is this as equated to another object; or, that value possesses its adequate form in a specific object as distinct from another. Commodities, as values, are objectified labour; the adequate value must therefore itself appear in the form of a specific thing, as a specific form of objectified labour.

Steuart illustrates this drivel about an ideal standard with two historic examples, of which the first, the bank money of Amsterdam, shows just the opposite, since it is nothing but the reduction of circulating coins to their bullion content (metal content); the second one has been repeated after him by all the moderns who follow the same tendency. For example, Urquhart cites the example of the Barbary Coast, where an ideal bar, an iron bar, a merely imaginary iron bar, counts as standard which neither rises nor falls. If e.g. the real iron bar falls, say by 100%, then the bar is worth 2 iron bars; if it rises again by 100%, then only one. Mr Urquhart claims to have observed at the same time that the Barbary Coast knows neither commercial nor industrial crises, but least of all monetary crises, and ascribes this to the magical effects of this ideal standard of value.[46] This 'ideal' imaginary standard is nothing but an imagined real value; an imagined notion, however, which, because the monetary system has not developed its further determinants – a development depending on quite different relations – achieves no objective reality. It is the same as if, in mythology, one were to consider as the higher religions those whose god-figures are not worked out in visible form but remain stuck in the imagination, i.e. where they obtain at most an oral, but not a graphic presence. The bar rests on a real iron bar, which

46. David Urquhart, *Familiar Words as Affecting England and the English* London, 1856, p. 112.

was later transformed into a fantasy-creature and fixated as such. An ounce of gold, expressed in English accounting money, = £3 17s. 10½d. Well. Well. Say a pound of silk had had exactly this price; but that it had later fallen to where Milanese raw silk stood on 12 March '58 in London, the lb. at £1 8s. It is the imaginary conception of an amount of iron, an iron bar, which keeps the same value (1) relative to all other commodities, (2) relative to the labour contained in it. This iron bar is of course purely imaginary, but it is not so fixed and 'standing like a rock in the sea'[47] as Steuart, and nearly a 100 years later Urquhart, believes. The only thing fixed in the iron bar is the name; in one case the real iron bar contains 2 ideal ones, in the other, only 1. This is expressed in such a way that the same, unchangeable ideal one is first = 2, then = 1 real bar. Thus, this posited, only the relation of the real iron bar has changed, not the ideal one. But in fact the ideal iron bar is twice as long in one case as in the other, and only its name is un-changed. In one case 100 lb. of iron are called e.g. a bar, in the other, 200 a bar. Suppose money were issued which represented labour time, e.g. time-chits; this time-chit itself could be baptized any name one wished, e.g. one pound, a twentieth of an hour 1s., $\frac{1}{240}$th of an hour 1d. Gold and silver, like all other commodities, depending on the production time they cost, would express differ-ent multiples or fractional parts of pounds, shillings,[48] pence etc., and an ounce of gold could just as well be = £8 6s. 3d. as = £3 17s. 10½d. These numbers would always be the expression of the proportion in which a specific quantity of labour is contained in the ounce. Instead of saying that £3 17s. 10½d. = one ounce of gold, now cost only ½ lb. of silk, one can imagine that the ounce is now = £7 15s. 9d. or that £3 17s. 10½d. are now only equal to half an ounce, because they are now only half the value. If we com-pare prices in England in e.g. the fifteenth century with those of the eighteenth, then we may find that two commodities had e.g. entirely the same nominal money value, e.g. 1 pound sterling. In this case the pound sterling is the standard, but expresses four or five times as much value in the first case as in the second, and we could say that, if the value of this commodity is = 1 ounce in the fifteenth century, then it was = ¼ ounce of gold in the eighteenth; because in the eighteenth, 1 ounce of gold expresses the same labour time as ¼ ounce in the fifteenth century. It could be said,

47. See above, p. 782, quotation from Steuart.
48. 'Sterlings' in the original text.

therefore, that the measure, the pound, had remained the same, but in one case = four times as much gold as in the other. This is the *ideal standard*. The comparison we make here could have been made by the people of the fifteenth century themselves, if they had lived on into the eighteenth; they would say that 1 ounce of gold, which is now worth £1, was only worth ¼ before. 4 pounds of gold now worth no more than 1 in the fifteenth century. If this pound previously had the name of *livre*, then I can imagine that one *livre* had been = 4 pounds at that time, and is now = to only 1; the value of gold had changed but that the standard, the *livre*, had remained the same. In fact, one *livre* in France and England originally meant 1 pound of silver, and now only $1/x$. It can be said, therefore, that the name, *livre*, the standard, had remained nominally the same always, but that silver had changed its value in comparison to it. A Frenchman who had lived from the time of Charlemagne until today could say that the *livre* of silver had always remained the standard of value, unchanged; it had once been worth 1 pound of silver, but, owing to a variety of misfortunes, had finished up being worth only $\dfrac{1}{x}$ of a pennyweight. The ell is the same; only its length is different in different countries. It is in fact the same as if the product of one working day, the gold brought to light in one day of work, were given the name *livre*; this *livre* would always remain the same, although it would express very different amounts of gold in different periods.

What do we do in fact when we compare £1 of the fifteenth century with £1 of the eighteenth? Both are the same mass of metal (each = 20s.), but of a different value; since the metal was then worth 4 times as much as now. We say therefore that, compared with today, the *livre* was = 4 times the mass of metal it contains today. And one could imagine that the *livre* had remained unchanged, but had been = 4 real *livres* of gold then, only = 1 today. The matter would be correctly comparable not in regard to the quantity of metal contained in a *livre*, but rather in regard to its value; this value, however, in turn expresses itself quantitatively in such a way that ¼ *livre* gold, then, = 1 *livre* gold today. Well; the *livre* identical, but at that time = 4 real *livres* of gold (by today's value) and now only = 1. If gold falls in value, and its relative fall or rise as regards other articles is expressed in their price, then, instead of saying that an object which cost £1 of gold before now costs 2, it could be said that it still costs 1 pound, but 1 pound is now worth 2 real *livres* of gold etc.; i.e. 1 *livre* of 2 real gold *livres* etc. Instead of saying: I sold this commodity yesterday at £1, today I sell it at £4, I might say that I sell it at £1, but yesterday at 1 pound of 1 real pound, today at 1 pound of 4 real pounds. The remaining prices all follow by themselves as soon as the relation of the real bar to the imaginary one is established; but this simply the comparison between the past value of the bar and its present one. The same as if we calculated everything in the £ of the fifteenth century for instance. This Berber or Negro does the same thing that every historian must do who pursues one kind of coin, one accounting name for a coin of the same metallic content, from one century to the next; if he computes it in contemporary money, he must equate it to more or less gold depending on its changing value in different centuries.[49] It is semi-civilized man's effort to establish an unchanging value for the unit of money, for the mass of metal which counts as measure; to fix this value, also, as a constant measure. But at the same time, the cleverness to know that the bar has changed its real value. With the small number of commodities which this Berber has to measure, and with the vigour of tradition among the uncivilized, this complicated method of calculating is not as difficult as it looks.

1 ounce is = £3 17s. 10½d., i.e. not quite = £4. But for convenience's sake let us assume it to be exactly = £4. Then ¼ of an ounce of gold therefore obtains the name pound, and serves under this name as accounting coin. But this pound changes its value, partly relative to the value of other commodities which change their value, partly in so far as it is itself the product of more or less labour time. The only firm thing about it is the name, and the quantity, the fractional part of the ounce, of the weight-unit of gold, whose baptismal name it is; which is contained, thus, in one piece of money, called one pound.

The savage wants to hold it constant as unchangeable value, and thus the quantity of metal it contains changes for him. If the value of gold falls by 100%, then the pound is the measure of value for

49. Marx's English in the above sentence has been altered to conform to modern usage. His use, in these and other passages, of terms which today have an offensive ring (e.g. 'semi-civilized', 'uncivilized', 'savage', 'semi-savage', where what is meant is simply 'pre-capitalist') reflects the general blindness of European scholarship towards non-European civilizations, and indicates the relative weakness of anti-colonial political movements at the time. This did not prevent Marx from being an enemy of colonialism and of great-power chauvinism in every form.

him as before; but a pound of $\frac{2}{4}$ ounces of gold etc. The pound for him always equals a mass of gold (iron) which has the same value. But since this value changes, it sometimes equals a greater, sometimes a smaller quantity of real gold or iron, depending on whether more or less of them must be given in exchange for other commodities. He compares the contemporary value with the past value, which latter counts as standard for him, and survives only in his imagination. Thus, instead of calculating in $\frac{1}{4}$ ounce of gold, whose value changes, he calculates in the value which $\frac{1}{4}$ ounce of gold previously had, hence in an imaginary unchanged $\frac{1}{4}$ ounce-value, which expresses itself, however, in varying quantities. On one side the effort to establish a fixed value for the value-standard; on the other side, the cleverness of nevertheless avoiding trouble by making a detour. But it is altogether absurd to take this accidental displacement, this way in which semi-savages have assimilated the measurement of values in money, forced on them from the outside, by first displacing it and then getting themselves straight again in the displacement, and to regard this as an organic historical form, or even to erect it as a higher form compared to more developed relations. These savages also take a quantity, the iron bar, as point of departure; but they hold fast to the value which this traditionally had, as accounting unit etc.

This question achieved significance in the modern economy chiefly owing to two circumstances: (1) It has been experienced at various times, e.g. in England during the Revolutionary War[50] that the price of raw gold rose above the price of minted gold. This historic phenomenon thus seemed irrefutably to prove that the names which are given to certain fractional weight-parts of gold (precious metal), pound, shilling, pence etc., by some inexplicable process act in an independent way towards the substance of which they are the name. How else could an ounce of gold be worth more than the same ounce of gold minted in £3 17s. $10\frac{1}{2}$d.? Or how could an ounce of gold be worth more than 4 *livres* of gold, if *livre* is merely the name for $\frac{1}{4}$ ounce? On closer inspection it was found, however, that the coins which circulated under the name pound in fact no longer contained the normal metallic content, so that, for instance, 5 circulating pounds in fact weighed only 1 ounce of gold (of the same refinement). Since a coin which allegedly represented $\frac{1}{4}$ ounce of gold (thereabouts) in fact represented only $\frac{1}{5}$, it was very simple that the ounce $= 5$ of this kind of circulating

50. The wars of the Revolutionary and Napoleonic periods, 1793–1815.

£; hence that the value of the bullion price rose above the mint price, in that in fact no longer ¼ but merely ⅕ of an ounce of gold was called pound, represented money, had that name; was merely the name, now, for ⅕ of an ounce. The same phenomenon took place when, although the metal content of the circulating coins had not fallen below their normal measure, they circulated at the same time as depreciated paper money, while to melt them down and to export them was prohibited. In that case, the ¼ ounce of gold circulating in the form of £ shared in the depreciation of the notes; a fate from which gold in bars was exempt.* The fact was again the same; the accounting name, pound, had ceased to be the name for ¼ ounce, became the name for a lesser amount. Thus the ounce equalled e.g. 5 of such pounds. This means, then, that the bullion price rose above the mint price. These or analogous historical phenomena, all capable of equally simple solution and all belonging to the same series, led therefore to the notion of the *ideal measure*, or, that money as measure was only a point of comparison, not a specific quantity. Hundreds of volumes have been written about this case in England in the past 150 years.

That a specific sort of coin should rise above its bullion content is not in itself something strange, since new labour (to give it form) is added to the coin. But regardless of that, it happens that the value of a specific sort of coin rises above its bullion content. This is of no economic interest whatever, and has as yet led to no economic studies. It means nothing more than that, for certain purposes, gold and silver was requisite in precisely this form, say of British pounds or of Spanish dollars. The directors of the Bank had, of course, a particular interest in proving that the value of notes had not fallen, but rather that of gold had risen. As to the last question, this can be treated only later.

(2) But the theory of the *ideal measure* was first brought up at the beginning of the eighteenth century and again in the second decade of the nineteenth, where questions were at issue in which money figures not as measure, nor as medium of exchange, but rather as constantly self-identical equivalent, as value for-itself (in the third aspect) and hence as the universal material of contracts. The issue both times was whether or not debts of state, and other debts, contracted in a depreciated money, should be acknowledged and paid back in full-valued money. It was a question simply between the

* The mint price can also be raised above the bullion price within a country by the mintage.

creditors of the state and the mass of the nation. This question itself does not concern us here. Those who demanded a readjustment of claims on the one side, and of payments (obligations) on the other, chose the wrong battlefield in asking whether or not the *standard of money* ought to be changed. On this occasion, then, crude theories of this type were brought forward about the standard of money, fixing of the price of money, etc. ('Altering the standard like altering the national measures or weights.' Steuart. It is clear at the first glance that the mass of grain in a nation does not change by the unit measure of e.g. the bushel being doubled or halved. But the change would be very important for e.g. farmers who had to pay grain rent in a specific number of bushels, if, were the measure doubled, they then had to supply the same number of bushels as before.) In this case, it was the creditors of the state who clung to the name 'pound', regardless of the fractional weight-unit of gold which it expressed, i.e. to the 'ideal standard' – for the latter is in fact only the accounting name for the weight-unit of metal which serves as measure. Strangely enough, however, it was precisely their opponents who advanced this theory of the 'ideal standard', and they themselves who combated it. Instead of simply demanding a readjustment, or that the creditors of the state ought to be paid back only the amount, in gold, which they had in fact advanced, they demanded that the standard be reduced in accordance with depreciation; thus e.g. if the pound sterling had fallen to $\frac{1}{3}$ of an ounce of gold, that this $\frac{1}{3}$ ounce should henceforth carry the name pound, or that the pound ought perhaps to be minted in 21 shillings instead of in 20. This reduction of the *standard* was called raising the value of money; in that the ounce now = £5 instead of = 4 as previously. Thus, they did not say that those who had advanced e.g. 1 ounce of gold in 5 depreciated pounds now ought to get 4 full-valued pounds back; they said, rather, that they should be repaid 5 pounds, but that the pound ought henceforth to express $\frac{1}{20}$ of an ounce less than before. When they raised this demand in England after the resumption of cash-payment, the accounting coin had regained its old metal value. On this occasion yet further crude theories about money as the measure of value were constructed, and, on the pretence of refuting these theories, whose falsity was simple to prove, the interests of the creditors of the state were smuggled through. The first battle of this sort between Locke and Lowndes. From 1688 to 1695 the state contracted debts in depreciated money – depreciated owing to all full-weighted money having been melted down, and only the light-weight being in circulation. The guinea had risen to 30s. Lowndes (mintmaster?) (secretary to the treasury) wanted to have the £ reduced by 20%; Locke stood by the old standard of Elizabeth. In 1695 the general recoinage. Locke won the day. Debts contracted at 10 and 14s. the guinea, paid back at the rate of 20s. This equally advantageous for the state and for the landed proprietors. 'Lowndes posed the question on the wrong basis. First he asserted that his scheme was not a debasement of the old standard. Then he ascribed the rise of the bullion price to the inherent value of silver and not to the lightness of the coin with which it was bought. He always supposed that it was the stamp and not the substance which made the currency ... For his part, Locke only asked himself whether or not Lowndes's scheme included a debasement, but never inquired into the interests of those who are engaged by permanent contracts. Mr Lowndes's great argument for reducing the standard was that silver bullion was risen to 6s. 5d. per ounce (i.e. that it might have been bought with 77 pence of shillings of $\frac{1}{77}$ part of a pound troy) and was therefore of the opinion that the pound troy should be coined into 77s., which was a diminution of the value of the £ by 20% or $\frac{1}{5}$. Locke replied to him that the 77s. were paid in clipped money and that they were not more than 62 pence standard coin, by weight ... But ought a man who had borrowed £1,000 in this clipped money to be obliged to pay back £1,000 in standard weight? Both Lowndes and Locke developed only quite superficially the influence of a change of standard on the relation of debtors and creditors, ... the credit system then still little developed in England ... the landed interest and the interest of the crown, were only attended to. Trade at that time was almost at a stop, and had been raised at a piratical war ... Restoring the standard was the most favourable, both for the landed interest and the exchequer; and so it was gone in for.' (Steuart loc. cit. Vol. II. p. 178, 179.) Steuart ironically remarks on the whole transaction: 'By this raising of the standard the government gained significantly as regards taxes, and creditors on their capital and interest; and the nation, which was the principal loser, was satisfied (pleased) (quite joyful) because *its* standard' (i.e. the measure of its own value) 'was not debased; so were all the three parties satisfied.' (loc. cit. Vol. II, p. 156.) Compare John Locke. *Works*. 4 vols. 7th ed., London, 1768; as well as the essay 'Some Considerations on the Lowering of Interest and Raising the Value of Money' (1691); and also: 'Further Considerations Concerning Raising the Value of Money, wherein Mr Lowndes's arguments for it, in his late Report concerning "An Essay for the amendment of the silver coins", are particularly examined', both in Vol. II. In the first monograph it says, among other things:

'The *raising of money*, about which so much nonsense is now being uttered, is either *raising value of our money*, and that you cannot do; or *raising the denomination of our coin*.' (p. 53.) 'For example, term a crown what previously was called $\frac{1}{2}$ a crown. The value remains determined by the metal content. If the abating $\frac{1}{20}$ of the quantity of the silver of any coin, does not lessen its value, the abating $\frac{19}{20}$ of the quantity of the silver of any coin, will not abate its value. Thus, according to this theory, a single three pence or a single farthing, being called a crown, will buy as much spice or silk, or any other commodity, as a crown-piece which contains 20 or 60 times as much silver.' (p. 54.) 'The raising of money is thus nothing but giving a less quantity of silver the stamp and denomination of a greater.' (loc. cit.) 'The stamp of the coin a guarantee to the public; it must contain so much silver under such a denomination.' (57.) 'It is silver, and not names, that pays debts and purchases commodities.' (p. 58.) 'The mint stamp suffices as guarantee for the weight and the fineness of the piece of money, but lets the thus-coined gold money find its own rate, like other commodities.' (p. 66.) In general one can do nothing with the raising of money but make 'more money in tale', but not more 'money in weight and worth'. (p. 73.) 'Silver is altogether a different standard from the others. The ell or the quart with which people measure may remain in the hands of the seller, of the buyer or of a third person: it matters not whose it is. But silver is not only the measure of bargains, it is the thing bargained for, and passes in trade from the buyer to the seller, as being in such a quantity equivalent to the thing sold: and so it not only *reassumes* the value of the commodity it is applied to, but is given in exchange for it, as of equal value. But this it does only by its quantity, and nothing else.' (p. 92.) 'The raising being but giving of names at pleasure to aliquot parts of any piece, viz. that now the sixtieth part of an ounce still be called a penny, may be done with what increaze you please.' (118.) 'The privilege that bullion has, to be exported freely, will give it a little advance above our coin, let the denomination of that be raised, or fall as you pleaze, whilst there is need of its exportation, and the exportation of our coin is prohibited by law.' (p. 119, 120.)

The same position adopted by Lowndes against Locke, in that the former believed the rise of the bullion price to be due to a rise in the value of bullion, as a result of which the value of the accounting coin had declined (i.e. because the value of bullion rose, the value of a fractional part of it, called £, fell), was adopted by the little-shilling-men – Attwood and the others of the Birmingham school 1819 seq. (Cobbett had posed the question on the correct ground: non-adjustments of national debts, rents etc.; but spoiled it all by his false theory which condemned paper money as such.[51] (Strangely enough, he came to this conclusion by beginning, like Ricardo, who comes to the opposite conclusion, from the same false premise, the determination of price by the quantity of the medium of circulation).) Their entire wisdom in the following phrases: 'In his dispute with the Birmingham Chamber of Commerce, Sir R. Peel asks: "What will *your* pound note represent" ' (p. 266. 'The Currency Question', *The Gemini Letters*, London, 1844) (namely, the pound note if not paid in gold). 'Now what is meant by the present standard of value? . . . £3 17s. 10½d., do they signify one *ounce of gold* or its *value*? If the ounce itself, why not call things by their names and say, instead of pound, shilling, pence, ounces, pennyweights and grains? Then we go back to *a direct system of barter*.' (p. 269. Not quite. But what would Mr Attwood have gained if people said ounce instead of £3 17s. 10½d., and so many pennyweight instead of shillings? That, for convenience in calculating, the fractional parts are given names – which apart from that, also indicates that the metal is here given a social quality alien to itself – what witness does it bear either for or against Attwood's doctrine?) 'Or the *value*? If an ounce = £3 17s. 10½d., why at different periods money £5 4s., and then again 3,17, 9? . . . the expression pound has reference to *value*, but not *a fixed standard value* . . . *Labour* is the parent of cost, and gives the relative value to gold or iron.' (And that is in fact why the value of one ounce and of £3 17s. 10½d. changes.) ' *Whatever denomination or words are used to express the daily or weekly labour of a man*, such words express the cost of commodity produced.' (p. 270.) The word 'one pound is the *ideal* unit'. (p. 272.) The last sentence important because it shows how this doctrine of the 'ideal unit' dissolves into the demand for a money which is supposed directly to represent labour. Pound then e.g. the expression for 12 days' work. The demand is this, that the determination of value should

51. Cobbett, *Paper against Gold*, London, 1828, p. 2.

not lead to that of money as a distinct quality, or that labour as the measure of values should not compel the labour objectified in a specific commodity to be made the measure of the other values. The important thing is that this demand is here made from the standpoint of the bourgeois economy (thus also by Gray, who actually works out this matter to perfection, and of whom we will speak in a moment), not from the standpoint of the negation of the bourgeois economy, as e.g. with Bray. The Proudhonists (see e.g. Mr Darimon) have indeed succeeded in raising this demand both as one corresponding to the present relations of production and also as a demand which totally revolutionizes them, and a great innovation, since, as *crapauds*,[52] they are of course not required to know anything of what has been written or thought on the other side of the Channel. At all events, already the simple fact that this demand was raised more than 50 years ago in England by a fraction of bourgeois economists shows to what extent the socialists who pretend thereby to advance something new and anti-bourgeois are on the wrong track. About the demand itself, see above. (Only a few things from Gray can be added here. As to the rest, the matter can be gone into in detail only in the banking system.)

[More on the critique of theories about medium of circulation and money. – *Transformation of the medium of circulation into money. – Formation of treasures. – Means of payment. – Prices of commodities and quantity of circulating money. – Value of money*]

As regards money as constantly self-identical equivalent, i.e. as *value* as such, and thus as the material of all contracts, it is clear that the changes in the value of the material in which it represents itself (directly, as in gold, silver, or indirectly, as claims, in notes, on specific quantity of gold, silver etc.) must bring about great revolutions between the different classes of a state. This not to be examined here, since these relations presuppose knowledge of the various economic relations. Only something by way of illustration. In the sixteenth and seventeenth centuries, it is well known that the depreciation of gold and silver, due to the discovery of America, depreciated the labouring class and that of the landed proprietors; raised that of the capitalists (specially of the industrial capitalists).

52. Literally, 'toads'. A French term of abuse.

In the Roman republic, the appreciation of copper turned the plebeians into the slaves of the patricians. 'Since one was forced to pay the largest sums in copper, one had to hold this money in masses or in stamped fragments which were tendered and received by weight. Copper in this state was *aes grave*. Metal money weighed.[53] ⟨Originally copper without stamp among the Romans; then stamping of external coins. *Servius rex ovium boumque effigie primus aes signavit.*[54] (Pliny, *Historia naturalis* I. 18, c. 3.)⟩ After the patricians had stockpiled a mass of this dark and ugly metal ... they tried to free themselves from it, either by buying from the plebeians all the land which the latter would sell, or by lending at long term. This value had cost them nothing to acquire, and was a hindrance to them, so they were forced to rid themselves of it unsparingly. The competition of all who had the same desire of getting rid of it necessarily brought about, in a short time, a considerable reduction of the price of copper in Rome. At the beginning of the fourth century after the foundation of Rome, as one may see from the Lex Menenia (302 A.U.C.), the relation of copper to silver = 1:960 ... This metal, so depreciated in Rome, at the same time one of the most sought-after articles of trade (since the Greeks made their works of art out of bronze etc.) ... The precious metals came to be exchanged in Rome for copper, with enormous profits, and so lucrative a commerce stimulated new imports each day ... Little by little the patricians exchanged their treasure for ingots of gold and of silver, *aurum infectum, argentum infectum*,[55] in place of these piles of old copper, so troublesome to dispose of and so disagreeable to look at. After the defeat of Pyrrhus and particularly after the conquests in Asia ... the *aes grave* had already quite vanished, and the requirements of circulation had necessitated the introduction of the Greek victoria, and the name *victoriatus* ... of a weight of $1\frac{1}{2}$ scruples of silver, like the Attic coin, the drachma; in the *seventh century* A.U.C. the lex Clodia made Roman coin of it. It was usually exchanged for the pound of copper or the *as of 12 ounces*. Thus between silver and copper the relation of 192:1, i.e. a 5 times weaker relation than during the time of the greatest depreciation of copper due to export; still, copper cheaper in Rome than in Greece and Asia. This great revolution in the exchange value of the monetary

53. Garnier, *Histoire de la monnaie*, Vol. II, p. 11.
54. 'King Servius first stamped money with the image of sheep and oxen.'
55. 'Unwrought gold, unwrought silver'.

substance, to the measure it proceeded, most cruelly worsened the lot of the unfortunate plebeians, who had obtained the depreciated copper as a loan, and, having spent or used it at the rate it then had, now owed, by the letter of their contracts, a five times greater sum than they had borrowed in reality. They had no means to buy their way out of servitude ... Whoever had borrowed 3,000 *as* during the time when this sum = 300 oxen or 900 *scruples* of silver, could then obtain these only for 4,500 *scruples* of silver, when the *as* was represented by $1\frac{1}{2}$ *scruples* of this metal ... If the plebeian gave back $\frac{1}{5}$ of the copper he had obtained, then he had in reality paid off his debt, for $\frac{1}{5}$ now the same value as 1 at the time the contract was made. Copper had risen 5 times in value compared to silver ... The plebeians demanded a revision of the debt, a new appraisal of the sum due, and a change in the title of their original obligation ... While the creditors did not demand the restitution of the capital, the payment of interest was itself unbearable, because the interest, originally stipulated as 12%, had, owing to the excessive rise in cost of the specie, become as onerous as if it had been fixed at 60% of the principal. By way of concession, the debtors obtained a law that deducted the accumulated interest from the capital ... The senators resisted letting go of the means by which they held the people in the most abject dependence. The masters of nearly all landed property, armed with legal titles which authorized them to throw their debtors into irons and to sentence them to corporal punishment, suppressed the uprisings and persecuted the most mutinous. Every patrician's home was a prison. Finally wars were got up which gave the debtor some payment, with a suspension of obligations, and which opened to the creditor new sources of wealth and of power. This the internal situation in Rome at the time of the defeat of Pyrrhus, the capture of Taranto and important victories over the Samnians, Lucanians and other South-Italian peoples etc. ... 483 or 485 the first Roman silver coin, the *libella*; ... was called *libella* because of small weight = *libra* of 12 ounces of copper.' (Garnier, Germain, *Histoire de la Monnaie* etc., 2 vols., Paris, 1819. Vol. II. p. 14–24.)

⟨*Assignats*. '*National Property. Assignat of* 100 *frs*.' legal tender ... They are distinguished from all other notes in not *even professing to represent any specified thing*. The words 'national property' meant that their value could be obtained by buying confiscated properties with them at the continuous auctions of the latter. But no reason why this value called 100 fr. It depended on the comparative quality of the property so purchasable and the number of assignats issued.' (78, 79, Nassau W. Senior, *Three Lectures on the Cost of Obtaining Money*' etc., London, 1830.)

'The *livre de compte*, introduced by Charlemagne, almost never represented by a real equivalent coin, retained its name, as well as its divisions into *sous* and *deniers*, until the end of the eighteenth century, while real coins have varied infinitely in form, size, value, not only with every change of government, but even under the same reign. The value of the *livre de compte* nevertheless underwent enormous diminutions ... but this always an act of force.' (p. 76, Vol. I. Garnier, loc. cit.) All coins in antiquity originally weights. (loc. cit. p. 125.)

'Money is in the first place the universally marketable commodity, or that in which every one deals for the purpose of procuring other commodities.' (Bailey: '*Money and its Vicissitudes*' etc., London, 1837, p. 1.) 'It is the great *medial* commodity.' (loc. cit. p. 2.) It is the *general commodity of contracts*, or that in which the majority of bargains about property, to be completed at a future time, are made. (p. 3.) Finally, it is the '*measure of value* ... Now, as all articles are exchanged for money, the mutual values of A and B are necessarily shown by their values in money or their prices ... as the comparative weight of substances are seen by their weight in relation to water, or their specific gravities.' (p. 4.) 'The first essential requisite is that money should be uniform in its physical qualities, so that equal quantities should be so far identical as to present no ground for preferring one to the other ... For example, grain and cattle already for this reason not useful, because an equal quantity of grain and equal numbers of cattle are not always alike in the qualities for which they are preferred.' (p. 5, 6.) 'The *steadiness of value* is so desirable in money as medial commodity and a commodity of contract; it is quite unessential to it in its capacity of the measure of value.' (p. 9.) 'Money may continually vary in value, and yet be as good a measure of value as if it remained perfectly stationary. Suppose e.g., it is reduced in value and the reduction in value implies a reduction of value in relation to some one or more commodities, suppose it is reduced in value in relation to corn and labour. Before the reduction, a guinea would purchase three bushels of wheat, or six days' labour; subsequently, it would purchase only two bushels of wheat or four days' labour. In both cases, the relations of wheat and labour to money being given, their mutual relations can be inferred; in other words, we can ascertain that a bushel of wheat is worth two days' labour. This, which is all that measuring value implies, is as readily done after the reduction as before. The excellence of any thing as a measure of value is altogether independent of its own variableness in value . . . One confuses invariableness of value with invariableness in fineness and weight ... The command of *quantity* being that which constitutes value, a *definite quantity* of a substance of some uniform commodity must be used as a unit to measure value; and it is this definite *quantity* of a substance of uniform quality which must be invariable.' (p. 11.) In all money contracts the issue at stake is the *quantity* of the gold and silver to be lent, not its value. (p. 103.) 'If someone were to insist that it be a contract for a specified *value*, he is bound to show in relation to what commodity: thus, he would be maintaining that a pecuniary contract does not relate to a quantity of money as expressed on the face of it, but to a quantity of some commodity of which no mention is made.' (p. 104.) 'It is not necessary to restrict this to contracts where actual *money* is lent. It holds for all obligations for the future payment of money, whether for articles of any kind sold on credit, or for services, or as rent of land or houses; they are precisely in the same condition as pure loans of the medial commodity. If A sells a ton of iron to B for ten pounds, at twelve months' credit, it is just the same in effect as lending the ten pounds for a year and the interests of both contracting parties will in the same way be affected by changes in currency.' (p. 110, 111.)

The confusion of giving names to specified and unchangeable fractional parts of the money substance which is to serve as unit of measure – confusing the denomination of it with fixing the *price* of money – is also displayed, among others, by the high-flown romanticist of political economy, Mr Adam Müller. He says, among other things: 'Every one can see how much depends on the true *determination* of the *mint price*, above all in a country like England, where the government, with generous liberality' (i.e. at the country's expense and the profit of the Bank of England bullion dealers) 'mints without charge, collects no mintage etc., and thus, if it set the mint price significantly higher than the market price, if, instead of paying an ounce of gold at £3 17s. 10½d., as now, it set £3 19s. as the mint price of one ounce of gold, then all gold would flow towards the mint, all the silver there would be changed into the cheap gold here, and thus be brought to the mint anew, and the currency system would become disordered.' (p. 280, 281, Vol. II. *Die Elemente der Staatskunst*, Berlin, 1809.) Herr Müller does not know, then, that pence and shillings here are only names for fractional parts of a gold ounce. Because silver and copper coins – which, notabene, are not minted according to the proportion of silver and copper to gold, but are issued as markers for the equivalent parts of gold, and hence need be accepted in payment only in very small amounts – circulate under the names of shillings and pence, he imagines that an ounce of gold is divided into pieces of gold, of silver, and of copper (thus triple standard of value). A couple of steps later he suddenly remembers again that there is no double standard in England, hence even less a triple one. Herr Müller's lack of clarity about the 'common' economic relations is the real foundation of his 'higher' conception.

From the general law that the total price of commodities in circulation determines the mass of the circulating medium at a given stage of the velocity of circulation, it follows that at a given stage of growth of the values thrown into circulation, the more precious metal – the metal of greater specific value, i.e. which contains more labour time in a smaller amount – takes the place of the less precious as the predominant medium of circulation; hence, copper, silver, gold, each one replacing the previous one as the predominant medium of circulation. The same aggregate sum of prices can be circulated e.g. with 14 times as few gold coins as silver coins. Copper or even iron coin as predominant medium of circulation supposes weak circulation. Just as the more powerful but more valuable means of transport and means of circulation takes the place of the less valuable to the degree that the mass of circulating commodities, and circulation generally, grows.

On the other side it is clear that the small retail traffic of everyday life requires exchange on a very diminutive scale – the smaller, the poorer the country and the weaker is circulation as such. It is in this retail traffic, where very small amounts of commodities on the one side, hence also very small values circulate, that money appears in the most proper sense of the word merely as vanishing medium of circulation, and does not congeal as realized price. Consequently, a subsidiary medium of circulation enters for this traffic, which is merely the symbol of the fractional parts of the predominant media of circulation. These are silver and copper markers, which are therefore not minted in the relation of the value of their substance to the value of e.g. gold. Here money appears still only as symbol, even if itself still in a relatively valuable substance. Gold e.g. would have to be divided into excessively small fractions to serve as equivalent of the division of commodities required by this retail traffic.

This is why these subsidiary media of circulation need be accepted in payment, by law, in only very small amounts, so that they can never solidify as realization of price. For example, in England, copper in the amount of 6d., silver in the amount of 20s. The more developed circulation is generally, the greater the mass of prices of the commodities entering into circulation, the more does their wholesale exchange separate off from their retail exchange, and they require different sorts of coin for their circulation. The velocity of the circulation of these markers is inversely related to the magnitude of their value.

'In the early stage of society, when nations are poor, and their payments trifling, copper has frequently been known to answer all the purposes of currency and it is coined into pieces of very low denominations in order to facilitate the inconsiderable exchanges which then take place. So in the early age of the Roman Republic and of Scotland.' (p. 3.) (David Buchanan, *Observations on the Subjects, treated of in Dr Smith's Inquiry*' etc., Edinburgh, 1814.) 'The general wealth of a country is very accurately measured by the nature of its payments and the state of its coin; and the decided prevalence of a coarse metal in its currency, joined to the use of coins of very low denomination, marks a rude state of society.' (p. 4.) Later 'the business of currency becomes divided into two distinct departments; the duty of effecting the main payments ... for the more precious metals; the inferior metals by contrast retained for some trivial exchanges, and thus purely subservient to the main currency. Between the first introduction of a precious metal into the currency of a country, and its exclusive use in the main payments, a wide interval; and the payments of the retail trade must in the interval have become so considerable, owing to the increase of wealth, that at least in part they could be conveniently managed by the new and more valuable coin; since no coin can be used for the main payments' (this is false, as the notes show) 'which is not suited, at the same time, to the transactions of the retail trade, since every trade ultimately obtains from the consumer ... the return of its capital ... Silver has maintained itself everywhere on the continent in the main payments ... In Britain the quantity of silver in circulation does not exceed what is necessary for the smaller payments . . . in fact few payments to the amount of 20s. made in silver . . . Before the reign of William III silver was brought in large bags to the treasury in payment of the national revenue. At this period the great change took place . . . The exclusive introduction of gold in the main payments of England was a clear proof that the *returns of the retail trade at this time were made mainly in gold*; this possible without a single payment ever exceeding or even equalling any of the gold coins; because, in the general abundance of gold, and scarcity of silver, gold coins naturally offered for small sums and a balance of silver demanded in return; so that gold, by thus assisting in the retail trade and in economizing the use of silver, even for the small payments, would prevent its *accumulation* by the retail trader . . . At the same time, as in England gold was sub-stituted for silver' (1695) 'for the main payments, silver for copper in Sweden . . . *Clear, that the coin used for the larger payments can only pass current at its intrinsic worth* . . . But intrinsic worth *not necessary for a subsidiary currency* . . . In Rome, so long as copper the prevailing coin, current only for its intrinsic value . . . 5 years before the beginning of the first Punic war, silver introduced, little by little displaced copper in the main payments . . . 62 years after the silver, gold, but it never seems to have excluded silver from the main payments . . . In India, copper not a subsidiary currency; passes therefore for its intrinsic worth. The rupee, a silver coin of 2s. 3d., is the money of account; in relation to which the mohour, a gold coin, and the pice, a copper coin, are allowed to find their value in the market; the number of pice currently exchanged for a rupee constantly varies with the weight and value of the coin, while here 24 halfpence always = 1s. without reference to their weight. In India the retail dealer must still take considerable quantities of copper for his goods, and he cannot afford to take it therefore but for its intrinsic value . . . In the currencies of Europe, copper passes for whatever value is fixed upon it, without examination of its weight and fineness.' (p. 4–18.) In England 'an excess of copper spent 1798 by private traders; and although copper only legal payment for 6d., found its way (the surplus) to the retail traders; they sought to put it in circulation again; but ultimately returned to them. When this currency was stopped, copper accumulated with the retail traders in sums of £20, £30, even £50, which they finally had to sell at their intrinsic value.' (p. 31.)

In the subsidiary currency, the medium of circulation takes on a particular form as such, as a merely vanishing medium, alongside the medium of circulation which is at the same time equivalent, which realizes prices, and accumulates as independent value. Thus, here, pure symbol. Thus it may be issued only in the quantity absolutely required for the small retail trade, so that it can never thereby accumulate. The quantity must be determined by the mass of prices which it circulates, divided by its velocity. Because the mass of the circulating medium, of a certain value, is determined by prices, it follows automatically that if a greater quantity than required by circulation itself were artificially thrown into it and could not run off (which is not the case here, because, as medium of circulation, it is above its intrinsic worth), then it would be depreciated; not because the quantity determines prices, but because prices determine the quantity, and hence only a specific amount can remain in circulation at a specific value. Thus, if there are no openings by which circulation can throw out the superfluous quantity, if the circulating medium cannot change from that form into the form of value for itself, then the value of the medium of circulation must fall. But this can only take place, apart from artificial hindrances, prohibition of melting-down, of export etc., if the circulating medium is merely a symbol, and does not itself possess a real value corresponding to its nominal value, hence cannot make the transition from the form of circulating medium into that of the commodity in general, and shed its stamp; if it is imprisoned in its existence as coin. It follows on the other side that the symbol, the money marker, can circulate at the nominal value of the gold it represents – without possessing any value whatever of its own – in so far as it represents the medium of circulation only in that quantity in which it would itself circulate. But then [it becomes] at the same time a condition either that it is itself then on hand only in such a small quantity that it circulates only in the subsidiary form, hence does not cease for an instant to be a medium of circulation (where it constantly serves partly in the exchange with small amounts of commodities, partly merely to make exchange for the real medium of circulation), hence can never accumulate; or it must possess no value whatever, so that its nominal value can never be compared with its intrinsic value. In the latter case it is posited as mere *symbol*, which, by means of itself, points to value as something existing outside itself. In the other case it never comes to a comparison between its intrinsic value and its nominal value.

Which is why counterfeits of money show an effect immediately; while total destruction of its value does not damage it. It might otherwise appear paradoxical that money can be replaced by worthless paper; but that the slightest alloying of its metallic content depreciates it.

The double function of money in circulation contradicts itself as such; to serve as mere medium of circulation, where it is a vanishing mediation; and at the same time as realization of prices, in which form it accumulates and turns into its third character as money. As medium of circulation it is worn out; thus does not contain the metal content which makes it into objectified labour in a fixed amount. Its correspondence to its value hence always more or less illusory. One example to be presented.

It is important to bring in the determination of quantity already at this point in the chapter on money, but deduced in just the opposite way to the usual doctrine. Money can be replaced because its quantity is determined by the prices it circulates. In so far as it, itself, has value – as in the subsidiary medium of circulation – its quantity must be so determined that it can never accumulate as an equivalent, and in fact always figures as an auxiliary cog of the medium of circulation proper. In so far, however, as it is to replace the latter, it must have no value whatsoever, i.e. its value must exist apart from itself. The variations in circulation determined by the amount and number of transactions. (*Economist*.) Circulation may rise, prices remaining equal, by increase in the amount of commodities; if the amount remains constant, by increase of their prices; by both together.

With the proposition that prices regulate the quantity of currency and not the quantity of currency prices, or in other words that trade regulates currency (the quantity of the medium of circulation), and currency does not regulate trade, [it] is, of course, as our deduction has shown, supposed that price is only value translated into another language. Value, and value determined by labour time, is the presupposition. It is clear, therefore, that this law is not equally applicable to the fluctuations of prices in all epochs; e.g. in antiquity, e.g. in Rome, where the circulating medium does not itself arise from circulation, from exchange, but from pillage, plunder etc.

'No country may consequently have more than one standard;

more than one standard for the *measure of value*; for this standard must be uniform and unchanging. No article has a uniform and unchanging value relative to others: it only has such with itself. A piece of gold is constantly of the same value as the other, of exactly the same fineness, the same weight and in the same place; but this cannot be said of gold *and* any other article, e.g. silver.' (*Econ.* Vol. I p. 771.)[56] '*Pound* is nothing but a denomination in account, which has reference to a given and fixed quantity of gold of standard quality.' (loc. cit.) 'To speak of making one ounce of gold worth £5 instead of £3 17s. 10½d. is to say only that it ought henceforth to be minted in 5 sovereigns instead of in 3 $\frac{420}{480}$ sovereigns. We would not thereby alter the *value of the gold*, but only the *weight* and hence the *value of* the *pound* or *sovereign*. An ounce of gold would have the same value relative to wheat and all other commodities as before, but since a pound, although bearing the same name as before, would represent a smaller part of an ounce of gold, it would represent a correspondingly smaller quantity of wheat and other commodities. Just as if we had said that a *quarter of wheat* should *no longer be divided into 8, but rather into 12 bushels*; we could not thereby change the value of wheat, but merely diminish the quantity contained in a bushel, and hence the latter's value.' (p. 772 loc. cit.) 'Whatever temporary or permanent change might take place, its *price* is always expressed in the same amount of money; an ounce of gold will remain £3 17s. 10½d. of our money. The change in its value indicated by the greater or lesser quantity of the commodities it can purchase.' (loc. cit. p. 890.)[57]

The ideal bar to be compared e.g. with the *ideal milrea* in Buenos Aires (likewise the pound in England during the depreciation of notes etc.). What is fixed here is the name *milrea*; what fluctuates is the quantity of gold or silver it expresses. In Buenos Aires the currency is inconvertible paper money (paper dollars); these dollars originally = 4s. 6d. each; now approximately 3¾d. and has been as low as 1½d. An ell of cloth formerly worth 2 dollars, now *nominally* 28 dollars in consequence of the depreciated paper.

'In Scotland, the *medium of exchange*, not to be confused with the standard of value, in the amount of £1 and upwards may be

56. *The Economist*, Vol. I, No. 37, 11 May 1844, p. 771, article entitled 'The First Step in the Currency Question – Sir Robert Peel'.

57. *The Economist*, Vol. I, No. 42, 15 June 1844, p. 890, article entitled 'The Action of Money on Prices'.

said to be exclusively paper, and gold does not circulate at all; yet gold is as much the standard of value as if nothing else circulated, because the paper is convertible into the *same fixed quantity* of that metal; and it circulates only on the faith of being so convertible.' (p. 1275.)[58]

'Guineas are *hoarded* in times of distrust.' (Thornton, p. 48.)[59] The *hoarding principle*, in which money functions as independent value, is, apart from the striking forms in which it appears, necessary as *one moment* of exchange resting on money circulation; since everyone, as A. Smith says, needs, beside his own commodity, the medial quantity, a certain proportion of the 'general commodity'. '*The man in trade has property in trade.*' (loc. cit. p. 21.)⟩

Capital, not labour, *determines the value of the commodity. Torrens*

'Equal capitals or in other words equal quantities of accumulated labour will often put in motion different quantities of immediate labour, but that does not alter the matter.' (p. 31. Torrens, 'An Essay on the Production of Wealth', London, 1821.) 'In the early period of society ... it is the total quantity of labour, accumulated and immediate, expended on production ... which *determines the relative value of commodities*. But as soon as stock is accumulated and a class of capitalists distinguishes itself from another class, of workers, when the person who undertakes any branch of industry does not perform his own work, but advances subsistence and materials to others, then it is the amount of capital, or the quantity of accumulated labour expended in production, which determines the exchangeable power of commodities.' (p. 33, 34.) 'So long as two capitals are equal ... their products are of *equal value*, however we may vary the quantity of immediate labour which they put in motion, or which their products may require. If they are unequal, ... their products are of unequal value, though the total quantity of labour expended upon each should be precisely equal.' (p. 39.) Thus 'after this separation of capitalists and labourers, it is the amount of capital, the quantity of accumulated labour, and not, as before this

58. *The Economist*, Vol. I, No. 58, 5 October 1844, p. 1,275.

59. H. Thornton, *An Enquiry into the Nature and Effects of the Paper Credit of Great Britain*, London, 1802, p. 48.

separation, the sum of accumulated *and* immediate labour, expended on production, which determines the exchange value.' (loc. cit.) Mr Torrens's confusion correct compared to the abstract way of the Ricardians. In itself, fundamentally wrong. Firstly, the determination of value by pure labour time takes place only on the foundation of the production of capital, hence the separation of the two classes. The positing of *prices* as equal, in consequence of the same average rate of profit – and even this with a grain of salt – has *nothing* to do with the determination of value, rather *supposes* the latter. This point important so as to show the Ricardians' confusion.

The minimum of wages

The rate of surplus value as profit is determined (1) by the magnitude of the surplus value itself; (2) by the relation of living labour to accumulated (the ratio of the capital expended as wages to the capital employed as such). Both the causes which determine (1) and (2), to be examined separately. The law of rent, e.g., belongs to (1). For the time being, necessary labour supposed as such; i.e. that the worker always obtains only the minimum of wages. This supposition is necessary, of course, so as to establish the laws of profit in so far as they are not determined by the rise and fall of wages or by the influence of landed property. All of these fixed suppositions themselves become fluid in the further course of development. But only by holding them fast at the beginning is their development possible without confounding everything. Besides it is practically sure that, for instance, however the standard of necessary labour may differ at various epochs and in various countries, or how much, in consequence of the demand and supply of labour, its amount and ratio may change, at any given epoch the standard is to be considered and acted upon as a fixed one by capital. To consider those changes themselves belongs altogether to the chapter treating of wage labour.

'Exchangeable value is determined not by the absolute, but by the relative cost of production. If the cost of producing gold remained the same, while the cost of producing all other things doubled, then would gold have a less power of purchasing all other things than before; and its exchangeable value would fall one half; and this diminution in its exchange value precisely the same in effect as if the cost of producing all other things remained unaltered, while that of producing gold had been reduced one half.' (p. 56, 57. Torrens, loc. cit.) This important for prices. For determination of value, absolutely not; mere tautology. The value of a commodity is determined by the amount of labour it contains; this means that it exchanges for the same quantity of labour in every other form of use value. It is therefore clear that, if the labour time necessary for the production of object A doubles, then now only $\frac{1}{2}$ of it = its earlier equivalent, B. Since equivalence is determined by the equality of labour time or of the amount of labour, the difference of value is of course determined by the inequality of labour time, or, labour time is the measure of value.

1826 cotton machinery and workmen. Hodgskin

'In 1826, the various machinery used in manufacturing cotton employed 1 man to perform the work of 150. Now suppose that only 280,000 men are employed in it at present; then, half a century earlier, 42,000,000 would have had to be in it.' (p. 72.) (Hodgskin.) 'The relative value of the precious metals to other commodities determines how much of them must be given for other things; and the number of sales to be made, within a given period, determines, as far as money is the instrument for effecting sales, the quantity of money required.' (loc. cit. p. 188.)

'Abundant reason to believe that the practice of coining originated with individuals and carried on by them before it was seized on and monopolized by governments. Such long the case in Russia.' (See Storch.) (loc. cit. p. 195 note.)

Hodgskin is of a different opinion from the romantic Müller: 'The mint stamps only what individuals bring, most injudiciously charging them nothing for the labour of coining; and taxing the nation for the benefit of those who deal in money.' (p. 194. *Popular Polit. Econ.* etc., London, 1827.)

How the machine creates raw material. Linen industry.
Tow yarn. Economist

After all these digressions about money – and we will occasionally have to take them up again, before ending this chapter – we return to the point of departure (see p. 25 [pp. 776–8]). As example of how, in manufacturing industry also, the improvement of machinery and the consequent increase of the force of production creates (relatively) *raw material*, instead of demanding an absolute increase of it: 'The factory system in the linen trade is very recent. Before 1828 the great mass of linen yarn in Ireland and England spun by hand. About this time the flax spinning machine so much improved, especially through the persistence of Mr Peter Fairbairn in Leeds, that it came into very general use. From this time on, spinning mills erected very intensively at Belfast and other parts of Northern Ireland, as in different parts of Yorkshire, Lancashire and Scotland, for spinning fine yarns, and in a few years, spinning by hand given up ... Fine tow yarn now manufactured from what, 20 years earlier, was thrown away as waste.' (*Economist*, 31 Aug. 1850.)

Machinery and surplus labour

With all application of machinery – let us initially look at the case such as it arises directly, that a capitalist puts a part of his capital into machinery rather than into immediate labour – a part of the capital is taken away from its variable and self-multiplying portion, i.e. that which exchanges for living labour, so as to add it to the constant part, whose value is merely reproduced or maintained in the product. But the purpose of this is to make the remaining portion more productive. *First case: the value of the machinery equal to the value of the labour capacity it replaces.* In this case the newly produced value would be diminished, not increased, if the surplus labour time of the remaining part of labour capacity did not grow at the same rate as its amount is diminished. If 50 out of 100 workers are let go and replaced by machinery, then the remaining 50 have to accomplish as much surplus labour time as the 100 did before. If the 100 worked 200 hours' surplus labour time every day out of 1,200 hours' work, then the 50 must now create the same quantity of surplus labour time; hence 4 hours per day, if the former only 2. In that case the surplus labour time remains $50 \times 4 = 200$, the same as before, $100 \times 2 = 200$, although the absolute labour time has decreased. In this case, the situation for capital is the same; it is concerned only with the production of surplus labour. In this case, the raw material worked up would remain the same; hence the outlay for it; that for instrument of labour would have increased; that for labour decreased. The value of the total product would be the same, because = to the same sum of objectified and surplus labour time. Such a case would be altogether no incentive for capital. What it would gain in surplus labour time on one side, it would lose on the part of capital which would enter production as objectified labour, i.e. as invariable value. It is also to be kept in mind that the machinery takes the place of more imperfect instruments of production, which possessed a specific value; i.e. had been exchanged for a definite sum of money. The part of the capital employed at a less-developed stage of the productive force is deducted from the cost of the machinery for the capitalist who sets up a new business, although not for the capitalist who is already in business.

Thus e.g. if, as soon as the machine is introduced for £1,200 (50 labour capacities), an earlier expenditure of, say, 240 pounds for instruments of production ceases to be necessary, then the additional expenditure of capital amounts to only £960; the price of 40 workers a year. In this case then, if the remaining 50 workers together produce exactly as much surplus labour as did the 100 previously, then now 200 hours of surplus labour are produced with a capital of £2,160; before, with a capital of £2,400. The number of workers has decreased by half, absolute surplus labour has remained the same, 200 hours of labour as before; the capital invested in material of labour is also the same; but the relation of surplus labour to the invariable part of the capital has increased absolutely. Altogether £9,240. The relationship is this:

Since the capital laid out in raw material has remained the same, and that laid out in machinery increased, but not in the same relation as that laid out in labour diminished; it follows that the *total outlay of capital diminished*; surplus labour remained the same, hence grown relative to the capital, not only at the rate at which surplus labour time must grow to remain the same with half as many workers, but by more than that; namely by the rate at which the [outlay] for the old means of production is deducted from the costs of the new.

The introduction of machinery or a general increase in the force of production has objectified labour as its substratum, hence costs something; therefore, if a part of the capital previously laid out for labour is laid out as a component part of the part of the capital which enters into the production process as constant value, then the introduction of machinery can take place only if the rate of surplus labour time does not merely remain the same, i.e. grow relative to the living labour employed, but if it grows at a greater rate than the relation between the value of the machinery and the value of the dismissed workers. This can happen either because the entire expenditure incurred for the previous instrument of production must be deducted. In this case the *total sum of the capital laid out diminishes*, and, although the relation of the total sum of employed labour relative to the constant part of the capital has diminished, the surplus labour time has remained the same, and has hence grown not only relative to the capital laid out for labour, for necessary labour time, but also relative to the total capital, to the total value of the capital, because the latter has diminished. Or, the value for machinery may be as great as that previously laid out for living labour, which has now become superfluous; but the rate of surplus labour of the remaining capital has increased so that the 50 workers supply not only as much surplus labour as the 100 did before, but a greater amount. Say, e.g. instead of 4 hours each, 4¼ hours. But in this case a greater part of the capital is required for raw materials etc., in short, a greater total capital is required. If a capitalist who previously employed 100 workers for £2,400 annually, lets 50 go, and puts a machine costing £1,200 in their place, then this machine – although it costs him as much as 50 workers did before – is the product of fewer workers, because he pays the capitalist from whom he buys the machine not only the necessary labour, but also the surplus labour. Or, if he had his own workers build the machine, he would have used a part of them for necessary labour only. In the case of machinery, thus, increase of surplus labour with absolute decrease of necessary labour time. It may be accompanied both by absolute diminution of the employed capital, and by its growth.

Capital and profit. *Value makes the product.* – Relation of the worker to the conditions of labour in *capitalist production.* – *All parts of capital bring a profit.* – *Relation of fixed and circulating capital in the cotton mill. Senior's surplus labour and profit. Tendency of the machine to prolong labour.* – *Influence of transport on circulation etc.* – *Transport increasingly suspends hoarding.* – Absolute surplus labour and machinery. Senior

Surplus value, as posited by capital itself and measured by its quantitative relation to the total value of the capital, is *profit*. Living labour, as appropriated and absorbed by capital, appears as capital's own vital power; its self-reproducing power, additionally modified by its own movement, by circulation, and by the time belonging to its own movement, circulation time. Only by distinguishing itself as presupposed value from itself as posited value is capital posited as self-perenniating and multiplying value. Since capital enters wholly into production, and since, as capital, its various component parts are only formally distinct from one another, are equally sums of value, it follows that the positing of value appears to be equally inherent in them. Furthermore, since the part of the capital which exchanges for labour acts productively *only in so far as the other parts of capital are posited together with it* – and since the relation of this productivity is conditioned by the magnitude of the value etc., the various relations of these parts to one another (as fixed capital etc.) – it follows that the positing of surplus value, of profit, appears to be determined by all parts of capital equally. Because on one side the conditions of labour are posited as objective component parts of the capital, on the other side labour itself is posited as activity incorporated in it, the entire labour process appears as capital's own process and the positing of surplus value as its own product, whose magnitude is therefore also not measured by the surplus labour which it compels the worker to do, but rather as a magnified productivity which it lends to labour. The product proper of capital is profit. To that extent, it is now posited as the source of wealth. But in so far as it creates use values, it produces use values, but *use values determined by value*: 'Value makes the product.' (Say.)[60] Accordingly, it produces for consumption. In so far as it eternalizes itself through the constant renewal of labour, it appears as permanent value, a presupposition for production, which latter depends on its preservation. To the extent that it constantly exchanges itself anew for labour, it appears as labour fund. The worker can naturally not produce without the objective conditions of labour. Now, in capital, the latter are separated from him, confront him as independent. He can relate to them as conditions of labour only in so far as his labour itself has previously been appropriated by capital. From the standpoint of capital, the objective conditions of labour do not appear as necessary for the worker; what rather appears as necessary is that they *exist independently opposite him – his separation from them, their ownership by the capitalist* – and that the suspension of this separation takes place only when he cedes his producing power to capital, in exchange for which the latter maintains him as abstract labour capacity, i.e. precisely as the mere capacity of reproducing wealth opposite himself as capital, as the power which rules him.

Thus all parts of the capital bear profit simultaneously, both the circulating part (laid out in wages and raw material etc.) and the part laid out in fixed capital. The capital can now reproduce itself either in the form of circulating capital or in the form of fixed capital. Since we saw earlier, in the examination of circulation, that its value returns in a different form depending on in which of these two forms it is presupposed, and since, from the standpoint of profit-producing capital, what returns is not simply the value, but rather the value of the capital plus the profit, value as itself and value as self-realizing, it follows that the capital will be posited as profit-bearing in a different form corresponding to each of these two forms. The circulating capital enters wholly into circulation, with its use value as vehicle of its exchange value; and thus exchanges for money. I.e. then, it is sold, entirely, although each time only a part of it enters into circulation. In one turnover, however, it has entirely gone over into consumption (whether this be merely individual, or in turn productive) as product, and has completely reproduced itself as value. This value includes the surplus value, which now appears as profit. It is sold as use value, in order to be realized as exchange value. This, then, is *sale at a profit*. On the other side, we have seen that the fixed capital returns only in portions over the course of several years, of several cycles of the circulating capital, and, more specifically, enters into circulation as exchange value and returns as such only to the degree that it is used up (at that time, in the immediate act of production). However, the entry as well as the return of the exchange value is now posited as the entry and return not only of the value of the capital, but also at the same time of the profit, so that a fractional part of profit corresponds to the fractional part of capital.

'The capitalist expects an equal benefit from all parts of the capital he advances.' (Malthus, *Principles of Political Economy*, 2nd ed. Lond., 1836, p. 267.)

'Where Wealth and Value are perhaps the most nearly connected, is in the necessity of the latter to the production of the former.' (loc. cit. p. 301.)

⟨'The *fixed capital*' (in the cotton factories) 'usually $= 1:4$ to the circulating, so that if a manufacturer has £50,000, he spends £40,000 in erecting his mill and filling it with machinery, and only £10,000 in the purchase of raw material (cotton, coals etc.) and the payment of wages.' (Nassau W. Senior, *Letters on the Factory Act* etc., 1837, p. 12.) 'The fixed capital is subject to incessant deterioration, not only through wear and tear, but also through constant mechanical improvements . . .' (loc. cit.) 'Under present laws, no mill in which persons under 18 years of age are employed can be worked more than $11\frac{1}{2}$ hours by day, i.e. 12 hours for 5 days and 9 on Saturday. Now, the following analysis shows that, in a mill so worked, the whole *net profit* is derived from the *last hour*. Let a manufacturer invest £100,000 – 80,000 in his mill and machinery, and 20,000 in raw material and wages. As to the annual return of the mill, supposing the capital to be turned once a year, and gross profits to be 15%, his goods must be worth £115,000, produced by the constant conversion and reconversion of the £20,000 circulating capital, from money into goods and from goods into money' (in fact the conversion and reconversion of surplus labour first into commodity and then again into necessary labour etc.) 'in periods of rather more than two months. Of these £115,000, each of the 23 half hours of work produces $\frac{5}{115}$th or $\frac{1}{23}$rd. Of the $\frac{22}{23}$, constituting the whole 115,000, $\frac{20}{23}$, i.e. £100,000 out of the 115,000, only replace the capital; $\frac{1}{23}$ (or 5,000 out of the 115,000) makes up for deterioration of the mill and machinery. The remaining $\frac{2}{23}$, i.e. the last 2 of the 23 half hours of every day, produce the net profit of 10%. If, therefore (prices remaining the same), the factory could be kept at work for 13 hours instead of $11\frac{1}{2}$, by an addition of about £2,600 to the circulating capital, the net profit would be more than doubled.' (I.e. 2,600 would be worked up, without requiring relatively more fixed capital, and without payment to *labour at all*. The gross and net profit is $=$ to the material which is worked up for the capitalist *free of charge*, and then of course one hour is $= 100\%$ more, if the surplus labour, as Mr Shit[61] falsely presupposes, is only $= \frac{1}{12}$ day or only $\frac{2}{23}$, as Senior says. 'On the other side, if the daily hours of work were reduced by 1 hour per day (prices remaining the same), *net* profit would be destroyed; if reduced by $1\frac{1}{2}$ hours, gross profit as well. The circulating capital would be replaced, but there would be no fund to compensate

61. *sic*.

the progressive deterioration of the fixed capital.' (12, 13.) (As false as Mr Senior's data, so important his illustration for our theory.) 'The relation of fixed capital to circulating grows constantly for two reasons: (1) the tendency of mechanical improvement to throw on machinery more and more the work of production ... (2) the improvement of the means of transport and the consequent diminution of the stock of raw material in the manufacturer's hands waiting for use. Formerly, when coals and cotton came by water, the incertainty and irregularity of supply forced him to keep on hand 2 or 3 months' consumption. Now, a railway brings it to him week by week, or rather day by day, from the port or the mine. Under such circumstances, I fully anticipate that, in a very few years, the fixed capital, instead of its present proportion, will be as 6 or 7 or even 10 to 1 to the circulating; and, *consequently, that the motives to long hours of work will become greater, as the only means by which a large proportion of fixed capital can be made profitable.* "When a labourer", said Mr Ashworth to me, "lays down his spade, he renders useless, for that period, a capital worth 18d. When one of our people leaves the mill, he renders useless a capital that has cost £100."' (13, 14.)⟩ ⟨This a very nice proof that, under the rule of capital, the application of machinery does not shorten labour; but rather prolongs it. What it abbreviates is necessary labour, not the labour necessary for the capitalist. Since fixed capital becomes devalued to the extent it is not used in production, its growth is linked with the tendency to make labour *perpetual*. As for the other point raised by Senior, the diminution of the circulating capital relative to the fixed capital would be as great as he assumes if prices remained constant. But if e.g. cotton, on the average, has fallen below its average price, then the manufacturer will purchase as great a supply as his floating capital permits, and vice versa. With coal, however, where production regular and no special circumstances give grounds for anticipating an extraordinary rise in demand, Senior's remark correct. We have seen that transport (and hence means of communication) do not determine circulation, in so far as they concern bringing the product to market or its transformation into commodity. For in this respect they are themselves included as part of the production phase. But they determine circulation in so far as they determine (1) the return; (2) the retransformation of the capital from the money form into that of the conditions of production. The more rapid and uninterrupted the supply of material and *matières instrumentales*, the smaller a supply does the capitalist need to buy. He can therefore all the more often turn over or reproduce the same circulating capital in this form, instead of having it lie around as dormant capital. On the other side, as Sismondi already noted, this also has the effect that the retail merchant, the shopkeeper, can all the more rapidly restore his stock, thus also has less need to keep commodities in stock, because he can renew the supply at any instant. All this shows how with the development of production there is a relative decline of accumulation in the sense of hoarding; increases only in the form of fixed capital, while however continuous simultaneous labour (production) increases in regularity, in intensity, and in scope. The speed of the means of transport, together with their all-sidedness, increasingly transforms (with the exception of agriculture) the necessity of antecedent labour, as far as circulating capital is concerned, into that of simultaneous, mutually dependent, differentiated production. This observation important for the section on accumulation.⟩ '*Our cotton factories, at their commencement, were kept going the whole 24 hours*. The difficulty of cleaning and repairing the machinery, and the divided responsibility, arising from the necessity of employing a double staff of overlookers, book-keepers etc. have nearly put an end to this practice, but until Hobhouse's Act reduced them to 69, our factories generally worked from 70 to 80 hours per week.' (p. 15, loc cit.)

*Cotton factories in England. Workers. Example for machinery
and surplus labour.* – Example from Symons.[62] *Glasgow.
Power-loom factory etc.* (These examples for the rate of profit.) –
Different ways in which machinery *diminishes necessary labour.
Gaskell. – Labour the immediate market for capital*

'According to Baines a first-rate cotton-spinning factory cannot be built, filled with machinery, and fitted with steam engines and gas works, under £100,000. A steam-engine of 100 horse-power will turn 50,000 spindles, which will produce 62,500 miles of fine cotton thread per day. In such a factory 1,000 persons will spin as much thread as 250,000 persons could without machinery.' (p. 75. S. Laing, *National Distress etc.*, London, 1844.)

62. Jelinger Cookson Symons (1809–60) was a lawyer who was appointed in 1835 by the government to draw up a report on the situation of the hand-loom weavers; later he reported on the miners, and the educational system in Wales; author of many books on economic and educational questions.

'When *profits fall,* circulating capital is disposed to become to some extent *fixed capital.* When interest 5%, capital not used in making new roads, canals or railways, until these works yield a corresponding large percentage; but when interest only 4 or 3%, capital would be advanced for such improvements, if it obtained but a proportional lower percentage. *Joint-stock companies,* to accomplish great improvements, are the natural offspring of a falling rate of profit. It also induces individuals to *fix* their capital in the form of buildings and machinery.' (p. 232. Hopkins (Th.), *Great Britain for the last 40 Years* etc., London, 1834.) ' McCulloch thus estimates the numbers and incomes of those engaged in the cotton manufacture:

833,000 weavers, spinners, blackers etc. at £24 each a year	£20,000,000
111,000 joiners, engineers, machine makers etc. at £30 each	£3,330,000
Profits, superintendence, coal and materials of machines	£6,670,000
944,000	£30,000,000

'Of the 6⅔ millions, 2 millions are supposed to go for coal, iron and other materials, for machinery and other outgoings, which would give employment at £30 a year each, to 666,666, making a total population employed of 1,010,666; add to these ½ the number of children, aged etc., dependent on those who work, or an additional 505,330; so a total, supported on wages, of 1,515,996 persons. Added to these, those who are supported, directly or indirectly, by the 4⅔ millions of profit etc.' (Hopkins loc. cit. 336, 337.) According to this calculation, then, 833,000 directly engaged in production; 176,666 in the production of the machinery and the *matières instrumentales* which are required only because of the employment of machinery. The latter are reckoned, however, at £30 per head; thus, so as to resolve their labour into labour of the same quality as that of the 833,000, this must be calculated at £24 per head; thereby, £5,333,000 would give about 222,208 workers; this would give about 1 occupied in the production of machinery and *matières instrumentales* per 3¾ occupied in the production of the cotton fabric. Less than 1 to 4, but say 1 to 4. Now, if the 4 remaining workers worked only as much as 5 did earlier, thus each of them ¼ more surplus labour time, then no profit for capital. The remaining 4 have to supply more surplus labour than the 5 did before; or the number of workers employed for machinery must be smaller than the number of workers displaced by the machinery. Machinery profitable for capital only in relation as it increases the surplus labour time of the workers employed in machinery (not in so far as it reduces it; only in so far as it reduces the relation of surplus labour time to necessary, so that the latter has not only relatively declined, while the number of simultaneous working days has remained the same, but has diminished absolutely).

The increase of absolute labour time supposes the same or an increasing number of simultaneous working days; ditto the increase of the force of production by division of labour etc. In both cases the aggregate labour time remains the same or grows. With the employment of machinery, relative surplus labour time grows not only relative to necessary labour time and hence correlative with aggregate labour time; but rather the relation to necessary labour time grows while aggregate labour diminishes, i.e. the number of simultaneous working days diminishes (relative to surplus labour time).

A Glasgow manufacturer gave Symons (J. C.), author of *Arts and Artisans at Home and Abroad,* Edinb., 1839, the following pieces of information (we cite several of them here in order to have examples for the relation of fixed capital, circulating, the part of the capital laid out in wages, etc.):

Glasgow: 'Expense of *erecting a power-loom factory* of 500 looms, calculated to weave a good fabric of calico, or shirting, such as is generally made in Glasgow, would be about

Glasgow: 'Expense of *erecting a power-loom factory* of 500 looms, calculated to weave a good fabric of calico, or shirting, such as is generally made in Glasgow, would be about	£18,000
Annual produce, say 150,000 pieces of 24 yards, at 6s.	£45,000
Which cost as under:	
Interest on sunk capital, and for depreciation of value of the machinery	1,800
Steam power, oil, tallow, etc. keeping up machinery, utensils etc.	2,000
Yarns and flax	32,000
Wages to workmen	7,500
Suppose profit	1,700
	£45,000'
	(p. 233)

Thus if we take 5% interest on machinery, then the gross profit 1,700 + 900 = 2,600. The capital laid out in wages amounts, however, to only 7,500. Thus profit relates to wages = 26:75 = $5\frac{1}{5}$:15, hence = $34\frac{2}{3}$%.

'Probable expense of erecting a [spinning] *cotton-mill* with hand mules, calculated to produce No. 40 of [a] fair average quality £23,000

If patent self-actors, £2,000 additional.

Produce annually to the present prices of cottons and the rates at which yarns could be sold	25,000
Cost of which as follows:	
Interest of sunk capital, allowance for depreciation of value of the machinery 10%	2,300
Cotton	14,000
Steam power, oil, tallow, gas, and general expense of keeping up utensils and machinery in repair	1,800
Wages to workers	5,400
Profit	1,500
	£25,000'
	(p. 234)

(Thus assuming floating capital of £7,000, since 1,500 5% on 30,000.)

'The produce of the mill taken at 10,000 lb. weekly.' (234 loc. cit.) Here, then, profit = 1,150 + 1,500 = 2,650; 2,650:5,400 (wages) = $1:2\frac{2}{53}$, = $49\frac{8}{108}$%.

'Cost of a *cotton spinning mill of 10,000 throstles*, calculated to produce a fair quality of No. 24 £20,000

Taking present value of produce, the amount would annually be costing	£23,000
Interest on sunk capital, depreciation of value of machinery at 10%	2,000
Cotton	13,300
Steam power, tallow, oil, gas, keeping machinery in repair etc.	2,500
Wages to workers	3,800
Profit	1,400
	£23,000'
	(p. 235)

Hence gross profit = 2,400; wages 3,800; 2,400:3,800 = 24:38 = 12:19 = $63\frac{3}{19}$%.

In the first case $34\frac{2}{3}\%$; in the second $49\frac{8}{108}\%$ and in the last $63\frac{3}{19}\%$. In the first case, wages $\frac{1}{6}$ of the total price of the product; in the second more than $\frac{1}{4}$; in the last, more than $\frac{1}{6}$. But in the first case wages related to the value of the capital as $= 1:4\frac{8}{15}$; in the second case $= 1:5\frac{5}{27}$; in the third $= 1:7\frac{2}{19}$. At the same rate as the total ratio of the part of the capital laid out in wages declines relative to the part laid out in machinery and circulating capital (this, together, 34,000 in the first case; 30,000 in the second; 28,000 in the third), the profit on the part laid out in wages must naturally rise, to allow the percentage of profit to remain the same.

The absolute decrease of aggregate labour, i.e. of the working day multiplied by the number of simultaneous working days, can appear doubly. In the first-cited form, that one part of the hitherto employed workers is dismissed in consequence of the use of fixed capital (machinery). Or, that the introduction of machinery will diminish the *increase* of the working days employed, even though productivity grows and, indeed, at a greater rate (of course) than it diminishes in consequence of the '*value*' of the newly introduced machinery. In so far as the fixed capital has *value*, it does not magnify, but rather diminishes the productivity of labour. 'The surplus hands would enable the manufacturers to lessen the rate of wages; but the certainty that any considerable reduction would be followed by immediate immense losses from turnouts, extended stoppages, and various other impediments which would be thrown in their way, makes them prefer the slower process of mechanical improvement, by which, though they may triple production, they require no new men.' (Gaskell, *Artisans and Machinery*, London, 1836.) (p. 314.) 'When the improvements not quite displace the workmen, they will render one man capable of producing, or rather superintending, the production of quantity now requiring ten or twenty labourers.' (315, loc. cit.) 'Machines have been invented which enable 1 man to produce as much yarn as 250, or 300 even, could have produced 70 years ago: which enable 1 man and 1 boy to print as many goods as a 100 men and a 100 boys could have printed formerly. The 150,000 workmen in the spinning mills produce as much yarn as 40 millions with the one-thread wheel could have produced.' (316, loc. cit.)

'*The immediate market for capital, or field for capital, may be said to be labour*. The amount of capital which can be invested at a given moment, in a given country, or the world, so as to return not less than a given rate of profits, seems principally to depend on the quantity of labour, which it is possible, by laying out that capital, to induce the then existing number of human beings to perform.' (p. 20. *An Inquiry into those Principles respecting the Nature of Demand* etc., London, 1821.) (By a Ricardian against Malthus's *Principles* etc.)

Alienation of the conditions of labour with the development of capital. (Inversion.) The inversion is the foundation of the capitalist mode of production, not only of its distribution.

The fact that in the development of the productive powers of labour the objective conditions of labour, objectified labour, must grow relative to living labour – this is actually a tautological statement, for what else does growing productive power of labour mean than that less immediate labour is required to create a greater product, and that therefore social wealth expresses itself more and more in the conditions of labour created by labour itself? – this fact appears from the standpoint of capital not in such a way that one of the moments of social activity – objective labour – becomes the ever more powerful body of the other moment, of subjective, living labour, but rather – and this is important for wage labour – that the objective conditions of labour assume an ever more colossal independence, represented by its very extent, opposite living labour, and that social wealth confronts labour in more powerful portions as an alien and dominant power. The emphasis comes to be placed not on the state of being *objectified*, but on the state of being *alienated*, dispossessed, sold [Der Ton wird gelegt nicht auf das *Vergegenständlichtsein*, sondern das *Entfremdet-*, Entäussert-, Veräussertsein]; on the condition that the monstrous objective power which social labour itself erected opposite itself as one of its moments belongs not to the worker, but to the personified conditions of production, i.e. to capital. To the extent that, from the standpoint of capital and wage labour, the creation of the objective body of activity happens in antithesis to the immediate labour capacity – that this process of objectification in fact appears as a process of dispossession from the standpoint of labour or as appropriation of alien labour from the standpoint of capital – to that extent, this twisting and inversion [*Verdrehung und Verkehrung*] is a *real* [*phenomenon*], not a merely *supposed one* existing merely in the imagination of the workers and the capitalists. But obviously this process of inversion is a merely *historical* necessity, a necessity for the development of the forces of production solely from a specific historic point of departure, or basis, but in no way an *absolute* necessity of production; rather, a vanishing one, and the result and the inherent purpose of this process is to suspend this basis itself, together with this form of the process. The bourgeois economists are so much cooped up within the notions belonging to a specific historic stage of social development that the necessity of the *objectification* of the powers of social labour appears to them as inseparable from the necessity of their *alienation vis-à-vis* living labour. But with the suspension of the *immediate* character of living labour, as merely *individual*, or as general merely internally or merely externally, with the positing of the activity of individuals as immediately general or *social* activity, the objective moments of production are stripped of this form of alienation; they are thereby posited as property, as the organic social body within which the individuals reproduce themselves as individuals, but as social individuals. The conditions which allow them to exist in this way in the reproduction of their life, in their productive life's process, have been posited only by the historic economic process itself; both the objective and the subjective conditions, which are only the two distinct forms of the same conditions.

The worker's propertylessness, and the ownership of living labour by objectified labour, or the appropriation of alien labour by capital – both merely expressions of the same relation from opposite poles – are fundamental conditions of the bourgeois mode of production, in no way accidents irrelevant to it. These modes of distribution are the relations of production themselves, but *sub specie distributionis*. It is therefore highly absurd when e.g. J. St. Mill says (*Principles of Political Economy*, 2nd ed., London, 1849, Vol. I, p. 240): 'The laws and conditions of the production of wealth partake of the character of physical truths . . . It is not so with the distribution of wealth. That is a matter of human institutions solely.' (p. 239, 240.) The 'laws and conditions' of the production of wealth and the laws of the 'distribution of wealth' are the same laws under different forms, and both change, undergo the same historic process; are as such only moments of a historic process.

It requires no great penetration to grasp that, where e.g. free labour or wage labour arising out of the dissolution of bondage is the point of departure, there machines can only *arise* in antithesis to living labour, as property alien to it, and as power hostile to it;

i.e. that they must confront it as capital. But it is just as easy to perceive that machines will not cease to be agencies of social production when they become e.g. property of the associated workers. In the first case, however, their distribution, i.e. that they *do not belong* to the worker, is just as much a condition of the mode of production founded on wage labour. In the second case the changed distribution would start from a *changed* foundation of production, a new foundation first created by the process of history.

Merivale. *Natural dependence of the worker in colonies to be replaced by* artificial *restrictions*

Gold, in the figurative language of the Peruvians, 'the tears wept by the sun'. (Prescott.) 'Without the use of the tools or the machinery familiar to the European, each individual' (in Peru) 'could have done but little; but acting in large masses and under a common direction, they were enabled by indefatigable perseverance to achieve results etc.' (loc. cit.)[63]

⟨The money prevalent among the Mexicans (more with barter and oriental landed property), 'a regulated currency of different values. This consisted of transparent quills of gold dust; of bits of tin, cut in the form of a T; and of bags of cocoa, containing a specified number of grains. "*O felicem monetam*", says Peter Martyr (*de Orbe novo*), "*quae suavem utilemque praebet humano generi potum, et a tartarea peste avaritiae suos immunes servat possessores, quod suffodi aut diu servari nequeat*".' (Prescott.)[64] 'Eschwege (1823) estimates the total value of the diamond workings in 80 years at a sum hardly exceeding 18 months' produce of sugar or coffee in Brazil.' (Merivale.)[65] 'The first' (British) 'settlers' (in North America) 'cultivated the cleared ground about their villages in common . . . this custom prevails until 1619 in Virginia' etc. (Merivale, Vol. I. p. 91.) (Notebook, p. 52.) ('In 1593 the Cortes made the following representation to Philip II: "The Cortes of

63. W. H. Prescott, *History of the Conquest of Peru*, 4th edn, London, 1850, Vol. I. p. 127.

64. 'O blessed money, which furnishes mankind with a sweet and nutritious beverage, and protects its innocent possessors from the infernal disease of avarice, because it cannot be long hoarded, nor hidden underground!', quoted in ibid., p. 123 n.

65. H. A. M. Merivale, *Lectures on Colonization*, London, 1841, Vol. I, p. 52 n.

Valladolid of the year '48 begged Your Majesty to cease to permit the entry into the kingdom of candles, mirrors, jewellery, knives and similar things from the exterior, these articles, so useless to human life, being exchanged *for gold, as if Spaniards were Indians*".' (Sempéré.))[66]

'In densely peopled colonies the labourer, although free, is naturally dependent on the capitalist; in thinly peopled ones the want of this natural dependence must be supplied by artificial restrictions.' (Merivale, 314, Vol. II. *Lectures on Colonization* etc., London, 1841, 1842.)⟩

How the machine etc. saves material.[67] Bread.
Dureau de la Malle

Roman money: *aes grave* pound copper (*emere per aes et libram*). This the *as*.* 485 A.U.C., *deniers d'argent* = 10 *as* (these *denarii* 40 per pound: in 510, 75 *deniers* per pound; each *denarius* still = 10 *as*, but 10 *as* of 4 ounces each). In 513, the *as* reduced to 2 ounces; the denarius still = 10 *as*, but only $\frac{1}{84}$ of the pound of silver. The latter figure, $\frac{1}{84}$, held firm until the end of the Republic, but in 537 the denier was 16 *as* to the ounce, and in 665 only 16 *as* the half ounce ... The silver *denarius anno* 485 of the Republic = 1 franc 63; 510 = 87 *centimes*; 513 — 707 = 78 *centimes*. From Galba to the Antonines, 1 franc. (Dureau de la Malle, Vol. 1.) At the time of the first silver *denarius*, 1 pound silver to 1 pound copper = 400:1. Beginning of the second Punic war = 112:1. (loc. cit., Vol. I, pp. 82–4.) 'The Greek colonies in the south of Italy drew the silver from which they had fabricated coins since the sixth and fifth century B.C. from Greece and Asia, directly or by way of Tyre and Carthage. Despite this proximity, for political reasons the Romans prohibited the use of gold and silver. The People and the Senate felt that so *easy a medium of circulation* would lead to *concentration*, to decay of the old mores and of agriculture.' (loc. cit. p. 64, 65.) 'According to Varro, the slave an *instrumentum vocale*, the animal *instrumentum semi-mutum*, the plough *instrumentum mutum*.' (loc.

---

* *as* or *libra* = 12 ounces; 1 ounce = 24 *scrupula*; 288 *scrupula* per pound.

---

66. J. Sempéré y Guarinos, *Considérations sur les causes de la grandeur et de la décadence de la monarchie espagnole*, Paris, 1826, Vol. I, pp. 275–6.

67. This heading, though taken from Marx's own index to his notebooks ⟨*Grundrisse* (MELI), p. 966), seems to be out of place here.

cit. p. 253, 254.) (A Roman city-dweller's daily consumption some-what more than 2 French *livres*; of a countryman, more than 3 *livres*. A Parisian eats 0·93 of bread; a countryman in the 20 departments where wheat the chief staple, 1·70. (loc. cit.) In Italy (today) 1 lb. 8 ounces, where wheat the main food. Why did the Romans eat relatively more? Originally they ate wheat raw or just softened in water; afterwards they decided to roast it ... Later they discovered the art of milling, and at first the paste made with this flour was eaten raw. To mill the grain, they used a pestle, or two stones beaten and turned against one another ... The Roman soldier prepared a several days' supply of this raw paste, *puls*. Then they invented the winnowing-basket, to clean the grain, and a means was found to separate the bran from the flour; finally they added yeast, and at first they ate the bread raw, until an accident taught them that, by cooking it, one could prevent it from going sour and one could store it much longer. Only after the war against Perseus, 580, did Rome have bakers. (p. 279 loc. cit.) 'In pre-Christian times, the Romans were unacquainted with windmills.' (280 loc. cit.)) 'Parmentier has demonstrated that the art of milling has made great progress in France since Louis XIV, and that the difference between the old and the new millage amounts to $\frac{1}{2}$ the bread supplied by the same grain. At first 4, then 3, then 2, then finally $1\frac{1}{3}$ *setiers* of wheat were allotted for the annual consumption of an inhabitant of Paris ... Thus the enormous disproportion between the daily consumption of wheat among the Romans and among us is easily explained by the imperfections of the processes of milling and baking.' (p. 281 loc. cit.) 'The agrarian law was a limitation of landed property among active citizens. The limitation of property formed the foundation of the existence and prosperity of the old republics.' (loc. cit. p. 256, 257.) 'The state's revenue consisted of the estates, of contributions in kind, of forced labour, and of some taxes in silver payable at the entry and exit of mer-chandise, or levied on the sale of certain goods. This mode ... still exists almost without change in the Ottoman Empire ... At the time of Sulla's dictatorship and even at the end of the seventh century A.U.C., the Roman Republic took in only 40 million francs annually, *anno* 697 ... In 1780, the revenue of the Turkish Sultan, in coined piastres, only 35,000,000 piastres or 70 million francs .. The Romans and the Turks levied the bulk of their revenue in kind. Among the Romans ... $\frac{1}{10}$ of the grain, $\frac{1}{5}$ of the fruit, among the Turks, varying from $\frac{1}{2}$ to $\frac{1}{10}$ of the product ... Since the Roman

Empire was only an immense agglomeration of independent municipalities, the greater part of the costs and expenditures remained communal.' (pp. 402–7.) (The Rome of Augustus and Nero, without the suburbs, only 266,684 inhabitants. Assumes that in the fourth century of the Christian era the suburbs had 120,000 inhabitants, the Aurelian belt 382,695, altogether 502,695, 30,000 soldiers, 30,000 aliens; altogether 562,000 heads, in round numbers. *Madrid,* during a period of 1½ centuries after Charles V, capital of a part of Europe and of half the new world, many resemblances to Rome. Its population also did not grow in proportion to its political importance. (405, 406, loc. cit.)) 'The social condition of the Romans at the time resembled much more that of Russia or of the Ottoman Empire than that of France or of England: little commerce or industry; immense fortunes side by side with extreme misery.' (p. 214, loc. cit.) (Luxury only in the capital and in the residences of the Roman satraps.) 'From the destruction of Carthage to the foundation of Constantinople, Roman Italy had existed in the same condition, *vis-à-vis* Greece and the Orient, as was Spain during the eighteenth century *vis-à-vis* the rest of Europe. Alberoni said: "Spain is to Europe what the mouth is to the body: everything enters, nothing stays".' (loc. cit. p. 385 seq.)

Usury originally unrestricted in Rome. The law of the 12 tables (303 A.U.C.) had fixed the interest on money at 1 % per year (Niebuhr says 10).[68] These laws promptly violated. Duilius (398 A.U.C.) again reduced the interest on money to 1%, *unciario faenore.*[69] Reduced to ½% in 408; in 413, lending at interest was absolutely forbidden by a plebiscite engineered by the tribune, Genucius. It is not surprising that, in a republic where industry, where commerce either wholesale or retail were prohibited to citizens, there was also a prohibition against *commerce in money.* (p. 260, 261 Vol. II, loc. cit.) This situation lasted 3 years, until the capture of Carthage. 12%, then: 6% the average annual rate of interest. (261 loc. cit.) Justinian fixed interest at 4%; ... *usura quincunx*[70] under Trajan the legal interest is 5%. Commercial interest in Egypt, 146 years B.C., was 12%. (loc. cit. p. 263.)

The involuntary alienation of feudal landed property develops with usury and with money: 'The introduction of money which buys all things, and hence the advantage for the creditor, who

68. Niebuhr, *Römische Geschichte, Erster Theil,* p. 608.
69. At an interest of one-twelfth.
70. At an interest of five-twelfths.

lends money to the land owner, brings in the necessity of legal alienation for the advance.' (124. John Dalrymple, *An Essay towards a General History of Feudal Property in Great Britain*, 4th ed., Lond., 1759.)

In medieval Europe: 'Payments in *gold* customary with only a few articles of commerce, mostly with precious goods. Most prevalent outside the mercantile sphere, with gifts by the great, certain high obligations, heavy fines, purchase of landed estates. *Unminted* gold was not infrequently measured to suit in pounds or marks (half pounds) . . . 8 ounces = 1 mark; one [ounce] hence = 2 pennyweight or 3 carats. Of *minted gold* until the Crusades, familiar only with the Byzantine *solidus*, the Italian *Tari* and the Arabian *maurabotini*' (afterwards *maravedi*). (Hüllmann, *Städtewesen des Mittelalters*, 1st Part, Bonn, 1826.) (p. 402–4.) 'In Frankish laws, the *solidus* also as *mere money of account*, in which the value of agricultural products to be paid as fines was expressed. E.g. among the Saxons, a *solidus* a yearling ox in usual autumn condition . . . In Ripuarian law, a healthy cow represented one *solidus* . . . 12 *denars* = 1 gold *solidus*.' (405, 406.) 4 *Tari* = 1 Byzantine *solidus* . . . Since the thirteenth century, various gold coins minted in Europe. *Augustales* (of the emperor *Frederick II* in Sicily: Brundisium and Messina); *florentini* or *floreni* (Florence 1252); . . . *ducats* or *zecchini* (Venice since 1285). (409–11, loc. cit.) 'Larger gold coins minted also in Hungary, Germany and the Netherlands since the fourteenth century; in Germany, were simply called *Gulden*.' (loc. cit. 413.) '*With payments in silver*, the prevailing custom in all larger payments was weighing, usually in marks . . . Even minted silver weighed for such payments, since the coin still of almost wholly pure silver, hence weight the only question. Hence the name *pound* (*livre, lire*)* and mark, partly the name of imaginary or accounting coins, partly passed over to real silver coins. *Silver coins: denari* or *kreuzer* . . . In Germany these denari were called *Pfennige* (Penig, Penning, Phennig) . . . since as early as the ninth century. Originally Pending, Penthing, Pfentini . . . from pfündig, in the old form pfünding . . . the same as full-weighted: hence pfündige denari, abbreviated pfündinge . . . Another name for the denari, from the beginning of the twelfth century in France, Germany, Netherlands, England, from the star pictured on them in place of the cross: *sternlinge, sterlinge*,

---

* *Notabene*: In Mexico we found money but no weights; in Peru weights but no money.

starlinge ... Denari sterlings = pfennig sterlings ... In the fourteenth century, 320 of the Netherlands sterlings made a pound, 20 to the ounce ... *In the earlier Middle Ages, silver solidi not real coins, but rather inclusive name for 12 denari* ... 1 gold solidus = 12 sterling denari, for this was the median relation of gold and silver ... Oboli, half pfennigs, halflings circulated as *small change* ... With the increasing spread of petty trade, more and more of the small commercial cities and petty princes obtained the right to strike their own local coin, thus for the most part small change. Alloyed it with copper, in increasing proportions ... Thick pennies, gros deniers, grossi, groschen, groten, first minted in Tours before the middle of the thirteenth century. These groschen originally double pfennigs.' (415–33.)

'The ecclesiastical assessments levied by the popes on nearly all Catholic countries contributed in no small measure, firstly, to the development of the entire money system in commercially active Europe, and then, as a consequence, to the rise of a variety of efforts to circumvent the ecclesiastical prohibition (of interest). The pope made use of the Lombards in the collection of official dues and other obligations from the archbishoprics. These, the chief usurers and pawnbrokers, under papal protection. Already generally known since the middle of the twelfth century. Especially from Siena. "Public *usurarii*". In England they called themselves "Roman Pontifical Money-Dealers". Some bishops in Basle and elsewhere pawned the episcopal ring, silken robes, all the ecclesiastical vessels at low rates with Jews, and paid interest. But bishops, abbots, priests themselves also practised usury with the church vessels by lending them for a share of the gain to Tuscan money dealers from Florence, Siena and other cities.' etc. (see loc. cit. Notebook, p. 39.)[71]

Because money is the *general equivalent, the general power of purchasing*, everything can be bought, everything may be transformed into money. But it can be transformed into money only by being alienated [*alieniert*], by its owner divesting himself of it. Everything is therefore alienable, or indifferent for the individual, external to him. Thus the so-called *inalienable, eternal* possessions, and the immovable, solid property relations corresponding to them, break down in the face of money. Furthermore, since money itself exists only in circulation, and exchanges in turn for articles of consumption etc. – for values which may all ultimately be re-

71. Hüllmann, op. cit., Teil II, pp. 36–45.

duced to purely individual pleasures, it follows that everything is valuable only in so far as it exists for the individual. With that, the independent value of things, except in so far as it consists in their mere being for others, in their relativity, exchangeability, the absolute value of all things and relations, is dissolved. Everything sacrificed to egotistic pleasure. For, just as everything is alienable for money, everything is also obtainable by money. Everything is to be had for 'hard cash', which, as itself something existing external to the individual, is to be catched [sic] by fraud, violence etc. Thus everything is appropriable by everyone, and it depends on chance what the individual can appropriate and what not, since it depends on the money in his possession. With that, the individual is posited, as such, as lord of all things. There are no absolute values, since, for money, value as such is relative. There is nothing inalienable, since everything alienable for money. There is no higher or holier, since everything appropriable by money. The '*res sacrae*' and '*religiosae*', which may be '*in nullius bonis*', '*nec aestimationem recipere, nec obligari alienarique posse*', which are exempt from the '*commercio hominum*',[72] do not exist for money – just as all men are equal before God. Beautiful that the Roman church in the Middle Ages itself the chief propagandist of money.

'Since the ecclesiastical law against usury had long lost all significance, in 1425 Martin formally annulled it.' (Hüllmann, part II, loc. cit. Bonn, 1827, p. 55.) 'No country in the Middle Ages a general rate of interest. Firstly, the priests strict. Uncertainty of the juridical arrangements for securing the loan. Accordingly higher rates in individual cases. The small circulation of money, the necessity to make most payments in cash, since the brokerage business still undeveloped. Hence great variety of views about interest and concepts of usury. In Charlemagne's time it was considered usurious only when 100% was taken. At Lindau on Lake Constance, in 1344, local citizens took $216\frac{2}{3}$%. In Zurich the Council fixed the legal interest at $43\frac{1}{3}$% ... In Italy, 40% had to be paid during some periods, although from the twelfth to the fourteenth century the usual rate does not exceed 20% ... Frederick II in his decree ... 10%, but this only for Jews. He did not wish to speak for the Christians ... 10% was already usual in the thirteenth century in the Rhineland of Germany.' (55–7 loc. cit.)

72. 'Things sacred and religious, which cannot be in the possession of anyone, and cannot either receive a valuation or be mortgaged or alienated, which are exempt from the commerce of men' (Justinian, *Institutes*, II, 1).

Productive consumption. Newman. – Transformations of
capital. Economic cycle. (*Newman*)

'*Productive consumption*, where the consumption of a commodity
is *a part of the process of production.*' (Newman etc. Notebook
XVII, 10.)[73] 'It will be noticed, that in these instances *there is no
consumption of value*, the same value existing under a new form.'
(loc. cit.) 'Further *consumption* . . . the appropriation of individual
revenue to its different uses.' (p. 297.) (loc. cit.)

'*To sell for money* shall at all times be made so easy as it is now
to buy with money, and production would become the uniform and
never failing cause of demand.' (John Gray, *The Social System*
etc., Edinburgh, 1831.) (p. 16.) 'After land, capital, labour, the
fourth necessary condition of production is: *instant power of exchanging.*' (loc. cit. 18.) 'To be able to *exchange* is' for the man in
society 'as important as it was to Robinson Crusoe to be able to
produce.' (loc. cit. 21.)

'According to Say, credit only transfers capital, but does not
create any. This true only in the one case of a loan to an industrialist by a capitalist . . . but not of credit between producers in their
mutual advances. What one producer advances to another is not
capital; it is products, commodities. These products, these commodities, can and undoubtedly will become active capital in the
hands of the borrower, i.e. instruments of labour, but at the time
they are nothing but products for sale in the hands of their owner,
and everywhere inactive . . . One must distinguish . . . between
product and commodity . . . and instrument of labour and productive capital . . . As long as a product remains in the hands of its
producer, it is only a commodity, or, if you like, inactive, inert
capital. Far from being of benefit for the industrialist who holds it,
it is a burden for him, a ceaseless cause of trouble, of *faux frais* and
of losses: storage costs, maintenance costs, protection costs, interest on capital etc., without counting the waste and spoiling
which nearly all commodities suffer when they are inactive for
long . . . Thus, if he sells this, his commodity, on credit, to another
industrialist who can use the commodities for the kind of work for
which they are fit, then, from having been inert commodities, they
have become, for the latter, active capital. In this case, therefore,
there will be an increase of productive capital on one side without

73. S. P. Newman, *Elements of Political Economy*, Andover and New York,
1835, p. 296.

any diminution on the other. Even more: if one takes note that the seller, while furnishing his commodity on credit, has received in exchange a bill which he has the right to negotiate on the spot, is it not clear that by that very fact he too has obtained the means to renew his raw materials and his instruments of labour so as to begin work again? Thus there is here a double growth of productive capital, in other words, a power acquired on both sides.' (Charles Coquelin, 'Du Crédit et des Banques dans l'Industrie', *Revue des deux mondes,* Vol. 31, 1842, p. 799 *seq.*) 'Let the whole mass of commodities for sale pass rapidly from the state of inert product into that of active capital, without delays and obstacles: the country will be filled with so much new activity! ... this rapid transformation is precisely the advantage which credit allows to be realized ... This is the *activity of circulation* ... Thus credit may increase the industrialists' business tenfold ... In a given period of time, the dealer or producer renews his materials and his products ten times instead of once ... Credit brings this about by increasing everyone's purchasing power. Instead of reserving this power to those who presently have the ability to pay, it gives it to all those people ... whose position and whose morality provide the guarantee of a future payment; it gives it to any person who is capable of utilizing these products through labour ... Hence the first benefit of credit is to increase, if not the sum of values a country possesses, yet at least the sum of active values. This is the immediate effect. Flowing out of it ... is the increase of the productive powers, hence also of the sum of values etc.' (loc. cit.)

Letting is a conditional sale, or sale of the use of a thing for a limited time. (Corbet, Th., '*An Inquiry into the Causes and Modes of the Wealth of Individuals*' etc., Lond., 1841, p. 81.)

'Transformations to which capital is subjected in the work of production. Capital, to become productive, must be consumed.' (p. 80. S. P. Newman, *Elements of Political Economy,* Andover and New York, 1835.) '*Economic cycle* ... the whole course of production, from the time that outlays are made, till returns are received. In agriculture, seed time is its commencement, and harvesting its ending'. (81). *The basis of the difference between fixed and circulating* capital is that during every economic cycle, a part is partially, and another part totally consumed. (loc. cit.) *Capital as directed to different employments.* (loc. cit.) Belongs in the doctrine of competition. '*A Medium of Exchange*: In undeveloped nations, whatever commodity constitutes the larger share of the wealth of the community, or from any cause becomes more frequently than others an object of exchange, is wont to be used as a circulating medium. So cattle a medium of exchange among pastoral tribes, dried fish in Newfoundland, sugar in the West Indies, tobacco in Virginia. *Precious metals* ... advantage ... : (a) sameness of quality in all parts of the world ... (b) admit of minute division and exact apportionment; (c) rarity and difficulty of attainment, (d) they admit of coinage.' (100 loc. cit.)

Dr Price. *Innate power of capital*

The notion of capital as a self-reproducing being – as a value perenniating and increasing by virtue of an innate quality – has led to the marvellous inventions of Dr Price, which leaves the fantasies of the alchemists far behind, and which Pitt earnestly believed and made into the pillars of his financial sagacity in his sinking fund laws (see Lauderdale).[74] The following, a few striking excerpts from the man:

'Money bearing compound interest increases at first slowly. But, the rate of increase being continually accelerated, it becomes in some time so rapid, as to mock all the powers of the imagination. One penny, put out at our Saviour's birth to 5% compound interest, would, before this time, have increased to a greater sum than would be obtained in a 150 millions of Earths, all solid gold. But if put out to simple interest, it would, in the same time, have amounted to no more than 7 shillings 4½d. Our government has hitherto chosen to improve money in the *last*, rather than the first of these ways.' (18, 19. Price, Richard, *An Appeal to the Public on the Subject of the National Debt*, London, 1772, 2nd ed.) (His secret: the government should borrow at simple interest, and lend out the borrowed money at compound interest.) In his *Observations on Reversionary Payments* etc., London, 1772, he flies even higher: 'A shilling put out to 6% compound interest at our Saviour's birth would ... have increased to a greater sum than the whole solar system could hold, supposing it a sphere equal in diameter to the diameter of Saturn's orbit.' (loc. cit. XIII, note.) 'A state need never, therefore, be under any difficulties; for, with the *smallest* savings, it may, in as little time as its interest can require, pay off the largest debts.' (p. xiv.) The good Price was simply dazzled by the enormous quantities resulting from geometrical progression of

74. Lauderdale, *Recherches*, pp. 173–82.

numbers. Since he regards capital as a self-acting thing, without any regard to the conditions of reproduction of labour, as a mere self-increasing number, he was able to believe that he had found the laws of its growth in that formula (see below). Pitt, 1792, in a speech where he proposed to increase the sum devoted to the sinking fund, takes Dr Price's mystification quite seriously. $(S = C (1 + i)^n.)$

McCulloch, in his *Dictionary of Commerce*, 1847, cites, as properties of metallic money: 'The material must be: (1) divisible into the smallest portions; (2) capable of being stored for an indefinite period without deterioration; (3) easily transportable from place to place owing to great value in small bulk; (4) a piece of money, of a certain denomination, always equal in size and quality to every other piece of the same denomination; (5) its value comparatively steady.' (581.)[75]

Proudhon. Capital and simple exchange. Surplus. –
Necessity of workers' propertylessness. Townsend. Galiani. –
The infinito *in process.* Galiani

In the whole polemic by Mr Proudhon against Bastiat in *Gratuité du crédit. Discussion entre M. Fr. Bastiat et M. Proudhon*, Paris, 1850, Proudhon's argument revolves around the fact that lending appears as something quite different to him from selling. To lend at interest 'is the ability of selling the same object again and again, and always receiving its price anew, without ever giving up ownership of what one sells'. (9, in the first letter [to] Chevé, one of the editors of *La Voix du Peuple*.)[76] The different form in which the reproduction of capital appears here deceives him into thinking that this constant reproduction of the capital – whose price is always obtained back again, and which is always exchanged anew for labour at a profit, a profit which is realized again and again in purchase and sale – constitutes its concept. What leads him astray is that the 'object' does not change owners, as with purchase and sale; thus basically only the form of capital lent at interest with the form of reproduction peculiar to fixed capital. With house rent, about which Chevé speaks, it is directly the form of fixed capital. If

75. J. R. MacCulloch, *A Dictionary, Practical, Theoretical, and Historical, of Commerce and Commercial Navigation*, London, 1847, p. 836.

76. C.-F. Chevé (1813–75) was a Catholic socialist, who supported Proudhon between 1848 and 1850, and edited the Proudhonist journal *La Voix du Peuple*, in which the discussion between Bastiat and Proudhon first appeared (1849).

the circulating capital is regarded in its whole process, then it may be seen that, although *the same object* (this specific pound of sugar, e.g.) is not always sold anew, the same value does always reproduce itself anew, and the sale concerns only the form, not the substance. People who are capable of making such objections are obviously still unclear about the first elementary concepts of political economy. Proudhon grasps neither how profit, nor, therefore, how interest, arises from the laws of the exchange of values. 'House', money etc. should therefore not be exchanged as 'capital', but rather as 'commodity . . . at cost price'. (44.) (The good fellow does not understand that the whole point is that value is exchanged for labour, according to the law of values; that, hence, to abolish interest, he would have to abolish *capital* itself, the mode of production founded on exchange value, hence wage labour as well. Mr Proudhon's inability to find even one difference between loan and sale: 'In effect, the hatter who sells hats . . . obtains their value in return, neither more nor less. But the lending capitalist . . . not only gets back the whole of his capital; he receives more than the capital, more than he brings into the exchange; he receives an interest above the capital.' (69.) Thus Mr Proudhon's hatters reckon neither profit nor interest as part of their cost price. He does not grasp that, precisely by receiving the *value* of their hats, they obtain more than these cost them, because a part of this value is appropriated in the exchange, without equivalent, with labour. Here also his great thesis mentioned above: 'Since in commerce, the interest on capital is added to the worker's wages to make up the price of the commodity, it is impossible for the worker to buy back what he has himself produced. To live by working is a principle which, under the reign of interest, implies a contradiction.' (105.) In letter IX (p. 144–52), the good Proudhon confuses money as medium of circulation with capital, and therefore concludes that the 'capital' existing in France bears 160% (namely 1,600 millions annual interest in the state debt, mortgage etc. for a capital of a thousand millions, . . . the sum of currency . . . circulating in France). How little he understands about capital in general and its continual reproduction [is shown by] the following, which he imputes as specific to money-capital, i.e. to money lent out as capital: 'Since, with the accumulation of interest, money-capital, exchange after exchange, always comes back to its source, it follows that this re-lending, always done by the same hand, always profits the same person.' (154.) '*All labour must leave a surplus.*' (Everything ought to be *sold*, nothing *lent*. This the simple secret. Inability to see how the exchange of commodities rests on the exchange between capital and labour, and profit and interest in the latter. Proudhon wants to cling to the simplest, most abstract form of exchange.)

The following pretty demonstration by Mr Proudhon: 'Since value is nothing more than a proportion, and since all products are necessarily proportional to one another, it follows that from the social viewpoint products are always values and produced values: for society, the difference between capital and product does not exist. This difference is entirely subjective to individuals.' (250.)

The antithetical nature of capital, and the necessity for it of the propertyless worker, is naïvely expressed in some earlier English economists, e.g. the Reverend Mr J. Townsend,[77] the father of population theory, by the fraudulent appropriation of which Malthus (a shameless plagiarist generally; thus e.g. his theory of rent is borrowed from the farmer, Anderson) made himself into a great man. Townsend says: 'It seems to be a *law of nature* that the poor should be to a certain degree improvident, that there may be always some to fulfil the most servile, the most sordid, and the most ignoble offices in the community. The stock of human happiness is thereby much increased. The more delicate ones are thereby freed from drudgery, and can pursue higher callings etc. undisturbed.' (*A Dissertation on the Poor-laws*, edition of 1817, p. 39.) 'Legal constraint to labour is attended with too much trouble, violence, and noise, creates ill will etc., whereas hunger is not only a peaceable, silent, unremitted pressure, but, as the most natural motive to industry and labour, it calls forth the most powerful exertions.' (15.) (This the answer to what labour is in fact more productive, the slave's or the free worker's. A. Smith could not raise the question, since the mode of production of capital presupposes free labour. On the other side, the developed relation of capital and labour confirms A. Smith in his distinction between productive and unproductive labours. Lord Brougham's stale jokes against it, and the objections, supposed to be serious, by Say, Storch, MacCulloch and *tutti quanti* do not make any impact on it.

77. The Reverend Joseph Townsend (1739–1816) was a Methodist clergyman who originally studied medicine; he opposed the Poor Law legislation, and (among others) invented the theory of population later taken over by Malthus; he issued the pamphlet *A Dissertation on the Poor Laws, By a Well-Wisher to Mankind* anonymously in 1786.

A. Smith misses the mark only by somewhat too crudely conceiving the objectification of labour as labour which fixates itself in a tangible [*handgreiflich*] object. But this is a secondary thing with him, a clumsiness in expression.)

With Galiani, too, the workmen are supplied by a law of nature. Galiani published the book in 1750. 'God makes sure that the men who exercise occupations of primary utility are born in abundant numbers.' (78. *Della Moneta*, Vol. III, Scrittori Classici Italiani di Economia Politica. Parte Moderna. Milano, 1803.) But he already has the correct concept of value: 'It is only toil which gives value to things.' (74.) Of course, labour is distinct qualitatively as well, not only in so far as it [is performed] in different branches of production, but also more or less intensive etc. The way in which the equalization of these differences takes place, and all labour is reduced to unskilled simple labour, cannot of course be examined yet at this point. Suffice it that this reduction is in fact *accomplished* with the positing of products of all kinds of labour as values. As values, they are equivalents in certain proportions; the higher kinds of labour are themselves appraised in simple labour. This becomes clear at once if one considers that e.g. Californian gold is a product of simple labour. Nevertheless, every sort of labour is paid with it. Hence the qualitative difference is suspended, and the product of a higher sort of labour is in fact reduced to an amount of simple labour. Hence these computations of the different qualities of labour are completely a matter of indifference here, and do not violate the principle. 'Metals . . . are used for money because they are valuable, . . . they are not valuable because they are used for money.' (loc. cit. 95.) 'It is the velocity of circulation of money, and not the quantity of metal, which makes more or less money appear.' (99.) 'Money is of two kinds, *ideal and real*; and is adapted to two uses, to *evaluate* things and to *purchase* them. Ideal money is as good as, sometimes better than, real money for evaluating things . . . the other use of money is to buy those things to which its value may be equal . . . prices and contracts are valued in ideal money and executed in real.' (p. 112 seq.) '*The metals have the peculiar and singular quality that in them alone all relations reduce themselves to one only, which is their quantity; nature did not endow them with a varying quality either in their internal constitution or in their external form and shape.*' (126, 127.) This is very important observation. Value supposes a common substance, and all differences, proportions etc. reduced to merely quantitative ones. This the case with precious metals, which thus appear as the natural substance of value. 'Money . . . like a law which reduces all things to their necessary proportions is that which articulates all things in a single voice: *price*.' (152.) 'Only this same ideal money is *of account*, which is to say, all things are stipulated, contracted and evaluated in it; which came about for the same reason that the moneys which are ideal today are the most ancient moneys of a nation, and all of them were once real, and, because they were real, they were used in accounting.' (152.) (This also the formal clarification of Urquhart's ideal money etc. For the blacks etc. the iron bar was originally real money, then changed into ideal; but they tried at the same time to hold onto its previous value. Now, since the value of iron, as becomes apparent to them in commerce, fluctuates relative to gold etc., therefore the ideal bar, so as to preserve its original value, expresses varying proportions of real amounts of iron, a laborious calculation which does honour to these gentlemen's power of abstraction.) (In the debates caused by the Bullion Committee 1810, Castlereagh advanced similar confused notions.) A beautiful statement by Galiani: 'The infinity which' (things) 'lack in progression, they find in circulation.' (156.)

About use value, Galiani nicely says: 'Price is a relation . . . the price of things is their proportion relative to our need, which has as yet no fixed measure. But this will be found. I myself believe it to be *man himself*.' ([159,] 162.) 'Spain, during the same period when it was the greatest as well as the richest power, counted in reales and in the tiniest maravedis.' (172, 173.) 'It is, rather, he' (man) 'who is the sole and true wealth.' (188.) '*Wealth is a relation between two persons*.' (221.) 'When the price of a thing, or rather its proportion relative to others, changes proportionately to all of them, it is a clear sign that it is its value alone, and not that of all the others, which has changed.' (154.) (The costs of preserving the capital, of repairing it, also have to be taken into account.)

'The *positive limitation of quantity in paper* money would accomplish the only useful purpose that cost of production does in the other.' (Opdyke.)[78] The merely quantitative difference in the material of money: 'Money is returned *in kind only*' (with loans); 'which fact distinguishes this agent from all other machinery . . . indicates the nature of its service . . . clearly proves the singleness of its office.' (267.) 'With money in possession, we have but one exchange to make in order to secure the object of desire, while with

78. G. Opdyke, *A Treatise on Political Economy*, New York, 1851, p. 300.

other surplus products we have two, the first of which (securing the money) is infinitely more difficult than the second.' (287, 288.)

'*Banker* ... differs from the old *usurer* ... that he lends to the rich and seldom or never to the poor. Hence he lends with less risk, and can afford to do it on cheaper terms; and for both reasons, he avoids the popular odium which attended the usurer.' (44.) (Newman, F. W., *Lectures on Political Economy*, London, 1851.)

Advances. *Storch*. – Theory of savings. *Storch*. –
MacCulloch. *Surplus*. – *Profit*. – Periodical destruction of capital. *Fullarton*. – Arnd. *Natural interest*

Everyone hides and buries his money quite secretly and deeply, but especially the *Gentiles*, who are the almost exclusive masters of commerce and of money, and who are infatuated with this belief that the gold and silver they hide during their lifetime will be of use to them after death. (314.) (François Bernier, Vol. I, *Voyages contenant la description des états du Grand Mogol* etc., Paris, 1830.)

Matter in its natural state ... is always *without value* ... Only through labour does it obtain exchange value, become element of wealth. (MacCulloch, *Discours sur l'origine de l'économie politique* etc. transl. by Prévost. Geneva and Paris, 1825. p. 57.)

Commodities in exchange are each other's *measure*. (Storch. *Cours d'Économie Politique* avec des notes etc. par J. B. Say, Paris, 1823, Vol. I, p. 81.) 'In the trade between Russia and China, silver is used to evaluate all commodities; nevertheless, this commerce is carried on by barter.' (p. 88.) 'Just as labour is not the *source* ... of wealth, so is it not its *measure*.' (p. 123 loc. cit.) 'Smith ... let himself be misled into the opinion that the same cause which made material things *exist* was also the source and the measure of value.' (p. 124.) 'Interest the price one pays for the use of a capital.' (p. 336.) Currency must have a direct value, but be founded on an artificial need. Its material must not be indispensable for human existence; because the whole amount of it which is used for currency cannot be used individually, and must always circulate. (Vol. II, p. 113, 114.) 'Money takes the place of anything.' (p. 133.) T.V.[79] *Considérations sur la nature du revenu national*, Paris, 1824:

79. Volume 5, which Storch issued separately, under the title mentioned, as a counter-blast to the four-volume edition of his *Cours d'économie politique*, produced and annotated by J.-B. Say.

'Reproductive consumption is not properly an expense, but only an *advance*, because it is reimbursed to him who makes it.' (p. 54.) 'Is there not a manifest contradiction in this proposition that a people grows wealthy by its savings, or its *privations*, that is to say, by voluntarily condemning itself to poverty?' (p. 176.) 'At the time when hides and pelts served as money in Russia, the inconvenience involved in circulating so voluminous and perishable a currency gave rise to the idea of replacing them by small pieces of stamped leather, which thereby became symbols payable in hides and pelts . . . They kept up this usage until 1700' (namely, later, of representing the fractions of silver kopecks), 'at least in the city of Kaluga and its environs, until Peter I' (1700) 'ordered them to be turned in and exchanged for small copper coins.' (Vol. IV, p. 79.)

An indication of the marvels of compound interest is already found in the great seventeenth-century champion of the fight against usury: in Jos. Child. *Traités sur le commerce* etc. trad. de l'anglois (English publication 1669, Amsterdam and Berlin, 1754.) (pp. 115–17.)

'In point of fact a commodity will always exchange for more labour than has produced it; *and it is this excess that constitutes profits.*' (p. 221. McCulloch, *The Principles of Political Economy*, London, 1830.) Shows how well Mr McCulloch has understood the Ricardian principle. He distinguishes between *exchange value* and *real value*; the former (1) quantity of labour expended in its appropriation or production; (2) the second, *buying power* of certain quantities of labour of the other commodities. (p. 211.) Man is as much the *produce of labour* as any [of] the machines constructed by his agency; and it appears to us that in all economical investigations he ought to be considered in precisely the same point of view. (115 loc. cit.) Wages . . . really consist of a part of the produce of the industry of the labourer. (p. 295.) The profits of capital are only another name for the wages of accumulated labour. (p. 291.)

'A periodical destruction of capital has become a necessary condition of any market rate of interest at all, and, considered in that point of view, these awful visitations, to which we are accustomed to look forward with so much disquiet and apprehension and which we are so anxious to avert, may be nothing more than the natural and necessary corrective of an overgrown and bloated opulence, the *vis medicatrix* by which our social system, as at present constituted, is enabled to relieve itself from time to time of an ever-recurring plethora which menaces its existence, and to regain a sound and wholesome state.' (p. 165. Fullarton (John): *On the Regulation of Currency* etc. Lond., 1844.)

Money – *General Power of Purchasing.* (Chalmers.)[80]

'*Capital* ... services and commodities used in production. *Money*: the measure of value, the medium of exchange, and the universal equivalent; more practically: the *means of obtaining capital; the only means of paying for capital* previously obtained for credit; virtually – security for obtaining its equivalent value in capital: *Commerce* is the exchange of capital for capital through the medium of money, and the contract being for the medium, money alone can satisfy the contract and discharge the debt. In selling, one kind of capital is disposed for money for obtaining its equivalent value in any kind of capital. *Interest* – the consideration given for the loan of money. If the money is borrowed for the purpose of *procuring capital*, then the consideration given is a remuneration for the use of capital (raw materials, labour, merchandise etc.), which it obtains. If borrowed for the purpose of discharging a debt, for paying for capital previously obtained and used (contracted to be paid for in money), then the consideration given is for the use of money itself, and in this respect interest and discount are similar. *Discount* solely the remuneration for money itself, for converting credit money into real money. A good bill gives the same command over capital as bank notes, minus the charge for discount; and bills are discounted for the purpose of obtaining money of a more convenient denomination for wages and small cash payments, or to meet larger engagements falling due; and also for the advantage to be gained when ready money can be had by discounting at a lower rate than 5%, the usual allowance made for cash. The main object, however, in discounting depends fundamentally upon the supply and demand of legal tender money ... The rate of interest depends mainly on the demand and supply of capital, and the rate of discount entirely on the supply and demand of money.' (13 March '58, *Economist*, letter to the editor.)

Mr K. Arnd, quite in his proper place where he reasons about the 'dog tax',[81] has made the following interesting discovery:

80. See above, pp. 600–602.

81. Karl Arnd (1788–1877) was a state official in the small German principality of Electoral Hesse, as well as a prolific compiler of economics textbooks; hence his familiarity with the dog tax.

'In the natural course of the production of goods, there is only *one* phenomenon, which – in wholly settled and cultivated countries – seems destined to regulate the rate of interest to some extent; – this is the rate at which the amount of timber in the European forests increases with their annual new growth – this growth proceeds, quite independently of its exchange value, at the rate of 3 to 4 per cent.' (p. 124, 125. *Die naturgemässe Volkswirtschaft* etc., Hanau, 1845.) This deserves to be called the forest-primeval [*waldursprüngliche*] rate of interest.

Interest and profit. – Carey. *Pawning in England*

'The remaining value or overplus will in each trade be in proportion to the value of the capital employed.' (Ricardo.)[82]

In regard to *interest*, two things are to be examined: *Firstly*, the division of *profit* into interest and profit. (As the unity of both of these the English call it *gross profit*.) The difference becomes perceptible, tangible as soon as a class of monied capitalists comes to confront a class of industrial capitalists. *Secondly*: *Capital* itself becomes a commodity, or the commodity (money) is sold as capital. Thus it is said e.g. that capital, like any other commodity, varies in price according to demand and supply. These then determine the rate of interest. Thus here capital as such enters into circulation.

Monied capitalists and industrial capitalists can form two particular classes only because profit is capable of separating off into two branches of revenue. The two kinds of capitalists only express this fact; but the split has to be there, the separation of profit into two particular forms of revenue, for two particular classes of capitalists to be able to grow up on it.

The form of interest is older than that of profit. The level of interest in India for communal agriculturists in no way indicates the level of profit. But rather that profit as well as part of wages itself is appropriated in the form of interest by the usurer. It requires a sense of history like that of Mr Carey to compare this interest with that prevailing on the English money market, which the English capitalist pays, and to conclude therefrom how much higher the 'labour share' (the share of labour in the product) is in England than in India. He ought to have compared the interest which English handloom-weavers, e.g. in Derbyshire, pay, whose

82. Ricardo, *On the Principles of Political Economy*, p. 84.

material and instrument is advanced (lent) by the capitalist. He would have found that the interest is here so high that, after settlement of all items, the worker ends up being the debtor, after not only having made restitution of the capitalist's advance, but also having added his own labour to it free of charge. Historically, the form of industrial profit arises only after capital no longer appears alongside the independent worker. Profit thus appears originally determined by interest. But in the bourgeois economy, interest determined by profit, and only one of the latter's parts. Hence profit must be large enough to allow of a part of it branching off as interest. Historically, the inverse. Interest must have become so depressed that a part of the surplus gain could achieve independence as profit. There is a natural relation between wages and profit – necessary labour and surplus labour; but is there any between profit and interest, same [as] that which is determined by the competition between these two classes arranged under these different forms of revenues? But in order that this competition exist, the [existence of the] two classes, the division of the surplus value into profits and interest, is already presupposed. To examine capital in general is not a mere abstraction. If I regard the total capital of e.g. a nation as distinct from total wage labour (or, as distinct from landed property), or if I regard capital as the general economic basis of a class as distinct from another class, then I regard it in general. Just as if I regard man e.g. as physiologically distinct from the animals. The real difference between profit and interest exists as the difference between a moneyed class of capitalists and an industrial class of capitalists. But in order that two such classes may come to confront one another, their double existence presupposes a divergence within the surplus value posited by capital.

(Political economy has to do with the specific social forms of wealth or rather of the production of wealth. The material of wealth, whether subjective, like labour, or objective, like objects for the satisfaction of natural or historical needs, initially appears as common to all epochs of production. This material therefore appears initially as mere presupposition, lying quite outside the scope of political economy, and falls within its purview only when it is modified by the formal relations, or appears as modifying them. What it is customary to say about this in general terms is restricted to abstractions which had a historic value in the first tentative steps of political economy, when the forms still had to be laboriously peeled out of the material, and were, at the cost of great effort, fixed upon as a proper object of study. Later, they become leathery commonplaces, the more nauseating, the more they parade their scientific pretentions. This holds for everything which the German economists are in the habit of rattling off under the category 'goods'.)

The important thing is that both interest and profit express relations of *capital*. As a particular form, interest-bearing capital stands opposite, not labour, but rather opposite profit-bearing capital. The relation in which on one side the worker still appears as independent, i.e. not as wage labourer, but on the other side his objective conditions already possess an independent existence alongside him, forming the property of a particular class of usurers, this relation necessarily develops in all modes of production resting more or less on exchange – with the development of merchant wealth or money wealth in antithesis to the particular and restricted forms of agricultural or handicraft wealth. The development of this mercantile wealth may itself be regarded as the development of exchange value and hence of circulation and of money relations in the former spheres. Of course, this relation shows us, on one side, the growing independence, the unbinding of the conditions of labour – which more and more come out of circulation and depend on it – from the worker's economic being. On the other side, the latter is not yet subsumed into the process of capital. The mode of production therefore does not yet undergo essential change. Where this relation repeats itself within the bourgeois economy, it does so in the backward branches of industry, or in such branches as still struggle against their extinction and absorption into the modern mode of production The most odious exploitation of labour still takes place in them, without the relation of capital and labour here carrying within itself any basis whatever for the development of new forces of production, and the germ of newer historic forms. In the mode of production itself, capital still here appears materially subsumed under the individual workers or the family of workers – whether in a handicraft business or in small-scale agriculture. What takes place is exploitation by capital without the mode of production of capital. The rate of interest appears very high, because it includes profit and even a part of wages. This form of usury, in which capital does not seize possession of production, hence is capital only formally, presupposes the predominance of pre-bourgeois forms of production; but reproduces itself again in subordinate spheres within the bourgeois economy itself.

Second historic form of interest: Lending of capital to wealth which is engaged in consumption. Appears historically important here as itself a moment in the original rise of capital, in that the income (and often the land, too) of the landed proprietors accumulates and becomes capitalized in the pockets of the usurer. This is one of the processes by which circulating capital or capital in the form of money comes to be concentrated in a class independent of the landed proprietors.

The form of realized capital as well as of its realized surplus value is money. Profit (not only interest) thus expresses itself in money; because in that value is realized and measured.

The necessity of payments in money – not only of money for the purchase of commodities etc. – develops wherever exchange relations and money circulation take place. It is by no means necessary that exchange should be simultaneous. With money, the possibility is present that one party cedes his commodity and the other makes his payment only later. The need for money for this purpose (later developed in loans and discounts) a chief historic source of interest. This source does not concern us at all yet at this point; is to be looked at only along with credit relations.

Difference between *buying* (M–C) and *selling* (C–M): 'when I sell, I have (1) added the profit to the commodity and obtained it; (2) an article universally representative or convertible, money, for which, money being always saleable, I can always command every other commodity; the superior saleableness of money being the exact effect or natural consequence of the less saleableness of commodities ... With buying, different. If he buys to sell again or supply customers, whatever may be the probability, there is no absolute certainty of his selling at a remunerative price ... But not all buy so as to sell again, but rather for their own use or consumption' etc. (p. 117 seq. Corbet, Th. *An Inquiry into the Causes and Modes of the Wealth of Individuals*, London, 1841.)

Economist, 10 April [1858]: 'A parliamentary return moved for by Mr James Wilson, shows that the mint coined in 1857 gold to the value of £4,859,000, of which £364,000 was in half sovereigns. The silver coinage of the year amounted to £373,000, the cost of the metal used being £363,000 ... The total amount coined in the ten years ending the 31st of December, 1857, was £55,239,000 in gold, and 2,434,000 in silver ... The copper coinage last year amounted in value to £6,720 – the value of the copper being £3,492; of this 3,163 was in pence, 2,464 in half-pence, and 1,120 in farthings ... The total value of the copper coinage of the last ten years was £141,477, the copper of which it was composed being purchased for £73,503.'

'According to Thomas Culpeper (1641), Josiah Child (1670), Paterson (1694), Locke (1700), wealth depends on the self-enforced reduction of the interest rate of gold and silver. Accepted in England during nearly two centuries.' (Ganilh.)[83] When Hume, in antithesis to Locke, developed the determination of the interest rate by the rate of profit, he already had before his eyes a far greater development of capital; even more so Bentham when, towards the end of the eighteenth century, he wrote his defence of usury. (From Henry VIII to Anne, statutory reduction of interest.)

'In every country: (1) a producing class and (2) a monied class, which lives from the interest on its capital.' (p. 110.) (J. St. Mill, *Some Unsettled Questions of Political Economy,* London, 1844.)

'It is by frequent fluctuation in a month, and by pawning one article to relieve another, where a small sum is obtained, that the premium for money becomes so excessive. 240 licensed pawnbrokers in London and about 1450 in the country ... The capital employed is estimated at about 1 million. Turned over at least three times annually ... Each time on the average for $33\frac{1}{3}\%$ profit; so that the inferior orders of England pay 1 million annually for a temporary loan of one million, exclusive of what they lose by goods being forfeited.' (p. 114.) (Vol. I. J. D. Tuckett, *A History of the Past and Present State of the Labouring Population* etc., London, 1846.)

How merchant takes the place of master

'Some works cannot be operated on other than a large scale, e.g. porcelain making, glass making etc. Hence are never handicrafts. Already in the thirteenth and fourteenth centuries, some works, like weaving, were carried on on a large scale.' (Poppe, p. 32.)

'In earlier times all factories belonged to the crafts, and the *merchant* remained merely the distributor and promoter of the handicrafts. This was still most strictly observed in the manu-

83. Charles Ganilh, *Des systèmes d'économie politique*, Paris, 1809, Vol. I, pp. 76–7.

facture of cloth and textiles. But, by and by, in many localities the merchants began to set themselves up as masters' (of course without the old masters' guild prejudices, traditions, relations to the journeymen), 'and to take journeymen into their employ for day-wages.' (Poppe. p. 92, Vol. 1. *Geschichte der Technologie*, Göttingen, 1807–11.) This was a chief reason why, in England, industry proper struck root and arose in non-incorporated cities.

Merchant wealth

Mercantile capital, or money as it presents itself as merchant wealth, is the first form of capital, i.e. of value which comes exclusively from circulation (from exchange), maintains, reproduces and increases itself within it, and thus the exclusive aim of this movement and activity is exchange value. There are two movements, to buy so as to sell, and to sell so as to buy; but the form M–C–C–M predominates. Money and its increase appear as the exclusive purpose of the operation. The merchant neither buys the commodity for his own needs, for the sake of its use value, nor does he sell it so as to e.g. pay off contracts written in money, or so as to obtain another commodity for his own needs. His direct aim is increase of value, and namely in its direct form as money. Mercantile wealth is, firstly, money as medium of exchange; money as the mediating movement of circulation; it exchanges commodity for money, money for commodity and vice versa. Money likewise appears here as an end-in-itself, but without therefore existing in its metallic existence. It is here the living transformation of value into the two forms of commodity and money: the indifference of value towards the particular form of use value which it assumes, and at the same time its metamorphosis into all of these forms, which appear, however, merely as disguises. Thus, while the action of commerce concentrates the movements of circulation, hence money as merchant wealth is in one respect the first existence of capital, still appears as such historically, this form appears on the other side as directly contradictory to the *concept of value*. To buy cheap and sell dear is the law of trade. *Hence not the exchange of equivalents, with which trade, rather, would be impossible as a particular way of gaining wealth.*

Nevertheless, money as trading wealth – as it appears in the most various forms of society and at the most various stages of the development of the forces of social production – is merely the mediating movement between two extremes, which it does not dominate, and presuppositions which it does not create.

A. Smith, Vol. II (ed. Garnier): 'The great *trade* of every civilized society is that which is established between the inhabitants of the town and those of the countryside . . . it consists in the *exchange of the raw product* for the *manufactured product* . . . either directly, or by the intervention of money.' (p. 403.) Trade always concentrates; production originally on a small scale. 'The town is a continual fair or marketplace where the inhabitants of the countryside go to exchange their raw product for manufactured products. It is this trade which supplies the inhabitants of the town both with the material of their labour and with the means of their subsistence. The quantity of *manufactured goods* which they šell to the inhabitants of the countryside necessarily determines the quantity of materials and subsistence they buy.' (p. 408 [409].)

So long as 'means of subsistence and of pleasure' the chief aim, use value predominates.

It is part of the concept of value that it maintains itself and increases only through exchange. But the existing value, initially, money.

'This industry, whose aim was something beyond absolute necessity, established itself in the towns long before it could be commonly practised by the cultivators of the countryside.' (p. 452.)

'Although the inhabitants of a town ultimately draw their subsistence and all the means and materials of their industry from the countryside, yet those of a town lying near the shores of the sea or of a navigable river may draw them also from the farthest corners of the world, either in exchange for the manufactured product of their own industry, or by performing the service of carriers alternately between distant countries and exchanging the products of these countries among them. Thus a city may become very wealthy, while not only the land in its immediate environs, but also all lands where it trades, are poor. Each of these countries, taken separately, can offer it only a very small part of subsistence and for business; but all of these countries, taken collectively, can supply it with a great quantity of subsistence and a great variety of employment.' (p. [452,] 453.) (Italian cities were the first in Europe to rise by trade; during the crusades – Venice, Genoa, Pisa – partly by the transport of people and always by that of the supplies which had to be delivered to them. These republics were, in a manner of speaking, the supply commissaries of these armies.) (loc. cit.)

Merchant wealth, as constantly engaged in exchange and exchanging for the sake of exchange value, is in fact living money.

'The inhabitants of mercantile towns imported refined objects and luxury articles from wealthier countries at a high price, thus furnishing new food for the vanity of the great landed proprietors, who bought them with alacrity, by paying great quantities of the raw produce of their estates for them. Thus the commerce of a great part of Europe at this time consisted in exchange of the raw produce of one country for the manufactured produce of a country more advanced in industry.' (p. [454,] 455.) 'When this taste had become sufficiently general to create a considerable demand, the merchants sought, so as to save the costs of transport, to establish similar manufactures in their own country. This the origin of the first manufactures for distant markets.' Luxury manufactures, arisen out of foreign commerce, established by merchants (p. [456–] 458) (worked up foreign materials). Ad. Smith speaks of a second sort, which 'arose naturally and by itself through successive refinement of the crude and domestic employments'. Worked up home-grown materials. (p. 459.)

The trading peoples of antiquity like the gods of Epicurus in the spaces between the worlds, or rather like the Jews in the pores of Polish society. Most of the independent trading peoples or cities attained the magnificent development of their independence through the *carrying trade*, which rested on the barbarity of the producing peoples, between whom they played the role of money (the mediators).

In the preliminary stages of bourgeois society, trade dominates industry; in modern society, the opposite.

Trade will naturally react back to varying degrees upon the communities between which it is carried on. It will subjugate production more and more to exchange value; push direct use value more and more into the background; in that it makes subsistence more dependent on the sale than on the immediate use of the product. Dissolves the old relations. Thereby increases money circulation. First seizes hold of the overflow of production; little by little lays hands on the latter itself. However, the dissolving effect depends very much on the nature of the producing communities between which it operates. For example, hardly shook the old

Indian communities and Asiatic relations generally. Fraud in exchange is the basis of trade such as it appears independently.

But capital arises only where trade has seized possession of production itself, and where the merchant becomes producer, or the producer mere merchant. Opposed to this, the medieval guild system, the caste system etc. But the rise of capital in its adequate form presupposes it as commercial capital, so that production is no longer for use, more or less mediated by money, but for wholesale trade.

Commercial wealth as an independent economic form and as the foundation of commercial cities and commercial peoples exists and has existed between peoples on the most diverse stages of economic development, and within the commercial city itself (e.g. the old Asian, the Greek, and the Italian etc. of the Middle Ages) production can continue on in the form of guilds etc.

Steuart. 'Trade is an operation, by which the wealth, or work, either of individuals, or of societies, may be exchanged by a set of men called merchants, for an equivalent, proper for supplying every want, without any interruption to industry, or any check to consumption. *Industry* is the application to ingenious labour in a free man, in order to procure, by the *means of trade*, an equivalent, fit for supplying every want.' (Vol. I, p. 166.)

'While wants continue simple and few, a workman finds time enough to distribute all his work; when wants become more multiplied, men must work harder; *time becomes precious*; hence trade is introduced . . . The merchant as mediator between workmen and consumers.' (p. 171.)

The collection (of products) into a few hands is the introduction of trade. (loc. cit.) The consumer does not buy so as to sell again. The merchant buys and sells solely with a view to a gain (p. 174) (i.e. for value). 'The simplest of all trades is that which is executed by *bartering of the most necessary means of subsistence*' (between the surplus food of the farmers and the free hands). 'Progress chiefly to be ascribed to the introduction of money.' (p. 176.) As long as mutual needs are supplied by barter, there is not the least occasion for money. This the simplest combination. When needs have multiplied, bartering becomes more difficult: upon this, *money* is introduced. This is the common price of all things. A proper equivalent in the hands of those who want. This operation of buying and selling is somewhat more complex than the first.

Thus (1) *barter*; (2) *sale*; (3) *commerce*. The merchant must intervene. What was earlier called wants is now represented by the consumer; industry by the manufacturer, money by the merchant. The merchant represents money by substituting credit in its place; and as money invented for the facilitation of barter, so the merchant, with credit, a new refinement upon the use of money. This operation of buying and selling is now trade; it relieves both parts of the whole trouble of transportation and adjusting wants to needs, or wants to money; the merchant represents by turns the consumer, the manufacturer, and money. Towards the consumer he represents the totality of manufacturers, to the latter the totality of consumers, and to both classes his credit supplies the use of money. (p. 177, 178.) *Merchants are supposed to buy and sell not out of necessity, but rather with a view to profit.* (p. 203.)

' First the industrialist produces for others' not for his own use; these goods begin to be of use to him only from the moment he exchanges them away. They thus make trade and the art of exchange necessary. They are only appraised by their exchangeable value.' (p. 161.) (Sismondi, *Études sur l'économie politique*, Vol. II, Brussels, 1837.) Trade has robbed things, pieces of wealth, of their primitive character of usefulness: *it is the antithesis between their use value and their exchangeable value to which commerce has reduced all things.* (p. 162.) At the beginning, utility is the true measure of values; . . . trade exists then, in the patriarchal state of society; but it has not entirely absorbed the society; it is practised only upon the surplus of each one's production, and not on what constitutes its existence. (p. 162, 163.) By contrast, the character of our economic progress is that *trade* has taken on the burden of the *distribution* of the totality of the annually produced wealth and it has consequently suppressed absolutely its character of use value, letting only that of exchangeable value remain. (163.) Before the introduction of trade . . . the increase in the quantity of the product was a direct increase of wealth. Less significant at that time was the quantity of labour by means of which this useful thing was obtained . . . And really, the thing demanded loses none of its usefulness even if no labour at all were needed to obtain it; grain and linen would not be less necessary to their owners . . . even if they fell to them from heaven. This is without a doubt the true estimate of wealth, enjoyment, and usefulness. But from the moment when men . . . made their subsistence dependent on the exchanges they could make, or on commerce, they were forced to adhere to a different estimation, to exchange value, to value which results not from usefulness but rather from *the relation between the needs of the whole society and the quantity of labour which was sufficient to satisfy this need*, or as well the quantity of labour which might satisfy it in the future. (p. 266, loc. cit.) In the estimation of values, which people endeavoured to measure with the introduction of currency, the concept of usefulness is quite displaced. It is *labour*, the exertion necessary to procure oneself the two things exchanged for one another, which has alone been regarded. (p. 267.)

Gilbart (J. W.): *The History and Principles of Banking,* London, 1834, has this to say about interest:

'That a man who borrows money with *the intention of making a profit on it*, should give a portion of the profit to the lender, is a self-evident principle of natural justice. A man makes a profit usually by means of traffic. But in the Middle Ages the population purely agricultural. And there, like under the feudal government, there can be only little traffic and hence little profit ... Hence the usury laws in the Middle Ages justified ... Furthermore: in an agricultural country a person seldom wants to borrow money except he be reduced to poverty or distress by misery.' (p. 163.) Henry VIII limited interest to 10%, James I to 8, Charles II to 6, Anne to 5. (164, 165.) In those days, the lenders were, if not legal, still actual monopolists, and thus it was necessary to place them under restraint like other monopolists. (p. 165.) In our time the rate of profit governs the rate of interest; in those days the rate of interest governed the rate of profit. If the money-lender burdened the merchant with a higher rate of interest, then the merchant had to put a higher rate of profit on his goods, hence a greater sum of money taken out of the pockets of the buyers so as to bring it into the pockets of the money-lenders. This additional price put on the goods made capital less able and less inclined to buy them. (p. 165.) (loc. cit.)

Commerce with equivalents impossible. Opdyke

'Under the rule of invariable equivalents *commerce* etc. would be impossible.' (G. Opdyke, *A Treatise on Political Economy,* New York, 1851, p. 67.)

'The positive limitation of quantity on this instrument' (i.e. paper money) 'would accomplish the only useful purpose that cost of production does in the other' (metal money). (loc. cit. 300.)

Principal and interest

Interest. 'If a fixed sum of precious metal falls, then this no reason that a smaller quantity of money should be taken for its use, for if the principal worth less for the borrower, so the interest in the same measure less difficult for him to pay . . . In California 3 % per month, 36% per annum because of the unsettled state . . . In Hindustan, where borrowing by Indian princes for *unproductive expenses*, in order to balance the losses of capital on the average, very high interest, 30%, *having no relation to profit* which might be gained in industrial operations.' (*Economist*, 22 January 1853.) (The lender 'here charges interest so high as to be sufficient to re-place the principal in a short time, or at least as on the average of all his lending transactions, might serve to counterbalance his losses in particular instances, by the apparently exorbitant gains acquired in others.' (loc. cit.))

The rate of interest depends: (1) on the rate of profit; (2) on the proportion in which the entire profit divided between lender and borrower. (loc. cit.)

Abundance or scarcity of the precious metals, the high or low scale of general prices prevailing, determines only whether a greater or less amount of money will be required in effecting the exchanges between borrowers and lenders, as well as every other species of exchange . . . Difference only, that a greater sum of money would be needed to represent and transfer capital lent . . . the relation between the sum paid for the use of capital and the capital ex-presses the rate of interest as measured in money. (loc. cit.)

Double Standard. Previously, in countries where gold and silver legal standard, silver circulated almost exclusively, because from 1800 to 1850 the tendency was for gold to become dearer than silver . . . The gold was somewhat risen against silver, bore a premium in France on its relation to silver as fixed in 1802 . . . so in the United States; . . . in India. (In the latter now silver standard, as in Holland etc.) . . . The circulation of the United States the first affected. Great import of gold from California, premium on silver in Europe . . . extensive shipment of silver coins and replace-ment by gold. The United States government struck silver coins as low as 1 dollar . . . Substitution of silver for gold in France. (*Economist*, 15 November 1851.) Let the 'standard of value' be what it will, 'and let the current money represent *any* fixed portion of that standard, that may be determined upon, the two can only have a fixed and permanent value in relation to each other, by being convertible at the will of the holder.' (*Economist*.)[84]

The only way in which any class of coins can command a premium is that no one is obliged to pay them, while every one is obliged to take them as a legal tender. (*Economist*.)[85]

No country may consequently have more than one standard (more than *one* standard of the measure of value); for this standard must be uniform and unchanging. No article has a uniform, unchanging value relative to another; it only has such with itself. A gold piece is always of the same value as another, of exactly the same fineness, the same weight, and the same value in the same place; but this cannot be said of gold *and* any other article, e.g. silver. (*Economist*, 1844.)[86]

The English £ somewhat less than $\frac{1}{3}$ of its original value, the German florin $= \frac{1}{6}$, Scotland before the union [reduced] its pound to $\frac{1}{36}$, the French *livre* $= \frac{1}{74}$, the Spanish *maravedi* $=$ less than 1/1,000, the Portuguese *re* still lower. (p. 13, Morrison.)[87]

Before the law of 1819, causes in existence in determinating the bullion price apart from the circulation of bank notes: (1) the more or less perfect condition of the coin. If the circulating metallic coin is debased below its standard weight, then the slightest turn of exchange causing a demand for exportation must raise the price of the uncoined bullion by at least the degradation of the coin. (2) penal laws which forbade the melting and exporting of coin, and permitted the traffic in bullion. With intensive demand for export, this gave latitude for variation of bullion price against coin even at times when paper completely convertible. In 1783, 1792, 1795, 1796 ... 1816, the bullion price rose above the mint price, because the bank-creditors, in their anxiety to prepare for the resumption of cash payment, accepted gold considerably above the mint price. (Fullarton.)[88]

The standard may be for gold, without one ounce of gold circulating. (*Economist*.)

Under George III (1774) silver legal tender only for £25. And

84. *The Economist*, Vol. V, No. 215, 9 October 1847, p. 1158.

85. *The Economist*, Vol. IX, No. 386, 18 January 1851, p. 59.

86. *The Economist*, Vol. I, No. 37, 11 May 1844, p. 771.

87. William Hampson Morrison, *Observations on the System of Metallic Currency Adopted in this Country,* London, 1837, p. 13.

88. John Fullarton, *On the Regulation of Currencies*, 2nd edn, London, 1845, pp. 7–10.

the bank, by statute, now paid only in gold. (Morrison.) Lord Liverpool (beginning of the nineteenth century) made silver and copper into purely representative coins. (loc. cit.)[89]

Dissolving effect of money. *Money a means of cutting up property*

Urquhart's nonsense about the standard of money: 'The value of gold is to be measured by itself; how can any substance be the measure of its own worth in other things? The worth of gold is to be established by its own *weight*, under a false denomination of that weight – and an *ounce* is to be worth so many *pounds* and fractions of pounds. This is – falsifying a *measure*, not establishing a *standard*!' (*Familiar Words*.)[90]

Ad. Smith calls labour the *real* and money the *nominal measure of value*; presents the former as the original.[91]

Value of money. J. St. Mill. 'If the quantity of goods sold is given, and the number of sales and resales of these goods, then the value of money depends on its quantity, together with the number of times that each piece of money changes hands in this process.' 'The quantity of money in circulation = the money value of all commodities sold, divided by the number which expresses the velocity of circulation.' 'If the amount of commodities and transactions be given, then the value of money is the inverse of its quantity multiplied by its velocity of circulation.' But all these statements to be understood only in the sense 'that we speak only of the quantity of money which really circulates and is factually exchanged for commodities'. 'The necessary quantity of money determined partly by its production costs, partly by the velocity of its circulation. If the velocity of circulation is given, then the costs of production are determinant; if the production costs are given, then the quantity of money depends on the velocity of circulation.'[92]

89. Morrison, *Observations*, pp. 21–5.
90. Urquhart, *Familiar Words*, pp. 104–5.
91. Adam Smith, *Wealth of Nations*, Vol. I, pp. 100–101.
92. J. S. Mill, *On the Principles of Political Economy*, London, 1848, Vol. II, pp. 17–30.

Money has no equivalent other than itself or commodities. Hence degrades everything. At the beginning of the fifteenth century in France even the sacred vessels of the church (chalices) etc. pawned to the Jews. (Augier.)[93]

Money not a direct object of consumption: the currency never becomes an object of consumption, always remains a commodity, never becomes a good. Has a direct intrinsic value only for society; an exchangeable one for each individual. Its material must therefore have value, but founded on an artificial need, must not be indispensable for human existence; for the whole quantity of it which is used as currency can never be employed individually; it must always circulate. (Storch.)[94]

John Gray: *The Social System. A Treatise on the Principle of Exchange,* Edinburgh, 1831.

'To sell for money ought at all times to be made as easy as to buy with money; production would then become the uniform and never failing cause of demand.' (16.) It is the quantity that can be sold at a profit, not the quantity that can be made, that is the present limit to production. (59.)

Money should be merely a *receipt*, an evidence that the holder of it has either contributed a certain value to the national stock of wealth, or that he has acquired a right to the said value from some one who has contributed to it ... Money should be nothing more or less than portable, transferable, divisible, and inimitable evidences of the existence of wealth in store. (63, 64.) *An estimated value being previously put upon produce*, let it be lodged in a bank, and drawn out again whenever it is required; merely stipulating, by common consent, that he who lodges any kind of property in the proposed National Bank may take out of it an equal value of whatever it may contain, instead of being obliged to draw out the selfsame thing that he put in ... The proposed national banker should receive and take charge of *every* description of valuable, and give back *any* description of valuable again. (loc. cit. 68.)

'If money,' says Gray, 'be of *equal value* with that which it represents, it ceases to be a *representative* at all. It is one of the chief desideratums in money, that the holder of it should be

93. M. Augier, *Du crédit public*, Paris, 1842, pp. 95, 101.
94. Storch, *Cours d'économie politique*, Vol. II, pp. 109–14.

compelled at one time or other to present it for payment at the place from whence he received it. But if money be of the same *intrinsic value* as that which is given for it, no such necessity exists.' (74.)

'*Depreciation of stock* ... should form an item of national charge.' (p. [115,] 116.) 'The business of every country is to be conducted ... on a national capital.' (171.) 'All land to be transformed into national property.' (298.)

Gray (John), *Lectures on the nature and use of Money* (Edinburgh, 1848): 'Man collectively *should* know no limit to his physical means of enjoyment, save those of the exhaustion either of *his industry or* [of] *his productive powers*: whilst we, by the adoption of a monetary system, false in principle, and destructive in practice, have consented to restrict the amount of our physical means of *enjoyment to that precise quantity which can be profitably exchanged for a commodity, one of the least capable of multiplication by the exercise of human industry* of any upon the face of the earth.' (29.) What will be required for a good system, is (1) a bank system through whose operations the *national* relationship of supply and demand would be restored; (2) a *true* standard of value, instead of the existing fiction. (108.) (In this book the idea of the exchange-bank developed in still more detail and with preservation of the present mode of production.) 'There must be a minimum price of labour payable in standard money.' (p. 160.) Let us call e.g. the lowest rate of wages per week for 60–72 hours that may by law be given, 20s. or £1 standard. (161.) 'Shall we retain our *fictitious* standard of value, *gold*, and thus keep the productive resources of the country in bondage, or shall we resort to the *natural* standard of value, *labour*, and thereby set our productive resources free?' (p. 169.) The amount of this minimum wage being once fixed ... it should remain the same for ever. (174.) 'Merely let gold and silver take their proper place in the market beside butter and eggs and cloth and calico, and then the value of the precious metals will interest us no more than that of the diamond' etc. (182 [, 183].) No objection to make to gold and silver used *as instruments of exchange*, ... but only as *measures of value* ... In a short time one would see how many ounces of gold or silver were obtainable in London, Edinburgh or Dublin in exchange for a hundred pound standard note. (p. 188.)

Interest. As the class of rentiers increases, so also does that of lenders of capital, for they are one and the same. From this cause alone, interest must have had a tendency to fall in old countries. (201, 202 Ramsay.) 'It is probable that in all ages the precious metals cost more in their production than their value ever repaid.' (101, II. Jacob, W. *An Historical Enquiry into the Production and Consumption of Precious Metals*, London, 1831.)

Value of money. The value of all things, divided by the number of transactions of which they were the object, from product[ion] to the produc[er], = the value of the *écus* used to buy them, divided by the number of times that these thalers have been transferred in the same space of time. (Sismondi, *Nouveaux Principes d'Économie Politique*, etc.)

The most formal development of the false theory of prices is by James Mill (quoted from the translation by J. T. Parisot, Paris, 1823. *Éléments d'Économie Politique*).

The chief passages in Mill are:

'*Value* of money = the proportion in which one exchanges it for other articles, or the quantity of money which one gives in exchange for a specific quantity of other things.' (p. 128.) This relation is determined by the *total quantity* of money existing in a country. If one supposes all the commodities of a country brought together on one side, and all the money on the other, then it is evident that in the exchange between both sides, the value of money, i.e. the quantity of the commodities for which it has been exchanged, entirely depends on its own quantity. (loc. cit.) The case is wholly the same in the actual state of things. The total mass of the commodities of a country is *not* exchanged *at once* for the total mass of the money, but rather the commodities are exchanged in portions, and often very small portions, at various periods in the course of the year. The same piece of money which has served today for one exchange may serve tomorrow for another. A part of the money is used for a very great number of exchanges, another part for a very small number, a third is stockpiled and serves for no exchange. Among these variations there will be a median rate, based on the number of exchanges for which each piece of money would be used if all had effected an equal number of exchanges. Let this rate be fixed at some convenient number, e.g. 10. If every piece of money in the country has served for 10 purchases, then it is the same as if the total number of pieces of money had increased tenfold, and each had served for only a single exchange. In this case the value of all commodities is equal to 10 times the value of the money etc. (p. 129, 130.) If, instead of each coin serving for 10 purchases a year, the total mass of money had increased tenfold, and the coin served for only one exchange, then it is evident that every increase of this mass would cause a relative diminution in the value of each of these coins taken separately. Since *it is supposed* that the mass of all commodities for which the money may exchange remains *the same*, therefore the value of the total mass of the money has become no greater after the increase of its quantity than before. If *one supposes* an increase of one-tenth, then the value of each of its parts, e.g. an ounce, must have diminished by one-tenth. (p. 130, 131.) 'Thus, whatever may be the degree of the increase or decrease of the total mass of money, if the quantity of the other things remains the same, then this total mass and each of its parts experiences inversely a relative diminution or increase. It is clear that this thesis is of absolute truth. Whenever the *value of money* has experienced a rise or fall, and whenever the quantity of the commodities for which it could be exchanged, and the movement of circulation, remained the same, this change must have had as cause a relative increase or diminution of money, and can be ascribed to no other cause. If the mass of commodities decreases while the quantity of money remains the same, then it is as if the totality of money had increased, and vice versa. Similar changes are the result of every alteration in the *movement of circulation*. Every increase of the number of purchases produces the same effect as a total increase of money; a decrease of this number produces directly the *opposite* effect.' (p. 131, 132.) If a portion of the annual product has not been exchanged at all, like that which the producers consume, or is not exchanged for money, then this portion must not be put on the account, because whatever does not exchange for money is in the same situation relative to money as if it did not exist. (p. 131, 132.) Whenever the increase or diminution of money can proceed freely, this quantity is governed by the value of the metal . . . Gold and silver, however, are commodities, products . . . The *costs of production* govern the value of gold and silver, like that of all other products. (p. 136.)

The insipidness of this reasoning is quite evident.

(1) *If one supposes* that the mass of commodities remains the same, and the velocity of circulation as well, but that nevertheless a great mass of gold or silver exchanges for this same mass of commodities (without the value, i.e. the amount of labour contained in gold and silver, having changed), then one supposes exactly what one wanted to prove, namely that the prices of commodities are determined by the quantity of the circulating medium and not vice versa.

(2) Mill concedes that the commodities not thrown into circulation do not exist for money. It is equally clear that the money not thrown into circulation does not exist for the commodities. Thereby there exists no fixed relation between the value of money generally and the mass of it which enters into circulation. That the mass actually in circulation, divided by the number of its turnovers, is equal to the value of money is merely a tautological circumlocution for saying that the value of the commodity expressed in money is its price; since the money in circulation expresses the value of the commodities it circulates – it follows that the value of these commodities is determined by the *mass* of the circulating money.

(3) The confusion of Mill's view is clearly shown in his thesis that the value of money diminishes or increases with 'every alteration in the movement of circulation'. Whether one pound sterling circulates 1 time or 10 times a day, in each exchange it expresses an equivalent for the commodity, exchanges for the same value in commodities. Its own value remains the same in every exchange, and is hence altered neither by slower nor by rapid circulation. The mass of the circulating money is altered; but neither the value of the commodity, nor the value of the money. 'If it is said: a piece of cloth is worth £5, then it means: it possesses the value of 616,370 grains of standard gold. The reason assigned above may be paraphrased thus: "prices must fall because commodities are estimated as being worth so many ounces of gold; and the amount of gold in this country is diminished".' (Hubbard, J. G., *The Currency and the Country*, London, 1843, p. 44.)

(4) Mill at first supposes, in theory, that the whole mass of the money in a country is exchanged *at once* for the whole mass of the commodities which are to be found in it. Says, then, that this is so in reality, namely for the main reason that in practice just the opposite takes place, and only portions of money are ex-

changed for portions of commodities, the fewest payments arranged by payment on the spot – time bargains. Follows, therefore, that the total amount of transactions or purchases, made in a day, is entirely independent of the money circulating on this day, and that the mass of money circulating on any given day is not the cause but the effect of a mass of previous transactions, each of them wholly independent of the money supply at the time.

(5) Finally, Mill himself admits that with free circulation of money, and this is our only concern, the value of money is determined by its cost of production, i.e., according to his own admission, by the labour time contained in it.

Monetary affairs. In Ricardo's pamphlet: *Proposals for an Economical and Secure Currency with Observations on the Profits of the Bank of England,* London, 1816, there is a passage where he makes a shambles of his whole viewpoint. It says, namely: 'The amount of notes in circulation depends ... on the amount required for the circulation of the country, and this is governed by the *value* of the standard, the amount of payments, and the economy applied to accomplish them'. (p. 8 loc. cit.)

Under Louis XIV, XV, XVI France still had, for its state taxes, taxes in kind levied on the rural people. (Augier.)[95]

Prices and mass of the circulating medium. Mere rise of prices not sufficient to create demand for additional currency. This only the case if production and consumption rise simultaneously. E.g. the price of grain rises, but its supply declines. Can thus be governed with the same quantity of currency ... but if rise of prices due to rising demand, new markets, enlarged scale of production, in a word, *rise of prices and of the general sum of transactions*, then it is necessary for the intervention of money to be multiplied in number and enlarged in magnitude. (Fullarton.)[96]

Trade governs money, not money trade. The servant of trade must follow the variations (in the prices) of the other commodities. (D'Avenant.)[97]

95. Augier, *Du crédit public*, p. 128.
96. Fullarton, *On the Regulation of Currencies*, pp. 102–4.
97. D'Avenant, *Discourses on the Publick Revenues, and on the Trade of England*, Pt II, London, 1698, p. 16.

(Under the feudal kings, the few articles bought in mass quantities by the people fell so much that no gold or silver coin small enough to correspond to the daily requirement of the labourer . . . current money thus like in ancient Rome only the inferior metals, copper, tin, iron.) (Jacob.)[98]

Jacob assumes that in this century, $\frac{2}{3}$ of the gold and silver in Europe in other articles, utensils and ornament, not in coin. (In another passage he calculates the precious metal so used in Europe and America at £400 million.)[99]

Prices and mass of the circulating medium. Locke, *Spectator* (19 Oct. 1711), Hume, Montesquieu – their doctrine rests on three theses:

(1) Prices of commodities proportionate to the mass of money in the country; (2) the coin and current money of a country representative of all its labour and commodities, so that the more or less representation, the more or less quantity of the thing represented goes to the same quantity of it; (3) increase commodities, they become cheaper; increase money, they rise in their value. (Steuart.)

Markers (small copper money or silver money, *counters*) in antithesis to money of intrinsic worth. (loc. cit.)

Dissolving effect of money. Money a means of cutting up property (houses, other capital) into countless fragments and consuming it piece by piece through exchange. (Bray.)[100] (Without money, a mass of inexchangeable, inalienable objects.) 'As immobile and immutable things came into human commerce just as well as movable things made for exchange, money came into use as rule and measure (square), by which these things obtained appraisal and value.' (*Free Trade*, London, 1622.)[101]

Coin. The silver and copper markers are *representatives* of fractional parts of the pound sterling. (*Thus in a recent answer of the Lord of the Treasury.*)

98. Jacob, *An Historical Inquiry*, Vol. I, p. 302.

99. ibid., Vol. II, pp. 214–15.

100. Bray, *Labour's Wrongs*, pp. 140–41.

101. *Free Trade, or the Meanes to Make Trade Flourish*, anonymously published in London (1622) by Edward Misselden, p. 21.

Exchange value. F. Vidal says (likewise, Lauderdale) (and in certain respects Ricardo): 'The true social value is use or consumption value; exchangeable value serves only to characterize the *relative wealth* of each of the members of a society in comparison to the others.' (70. *De la Répartition des Richesses* etc., Paris, 1846.) On the other side, exchange value expresses the *social form* of value, while use value no economic form of it whatever, rather, merely. the being of the product, etc. for mankind generally.

Two nations may exchange according to the law of profit in such a way that both gain, but one is always defrauded

⟨From the possibility that profit may be *less than* surplus value, hence that capital [may] exchange profitably without realizing itself in the strict sense, it follows that not only individual capitalists, but also nations may continually exchange with one another, may even continually repeat the exchange on an ever-expanding scale, without for that reason necessarily gaining in equal degrees. One of the nations may continually appropriate for itself a part of the surplus labour of the other, giving back nothing for it in the exchange, except that the measure here [is] not as in the exchange between capitalist and worker.⟩

Money in the third role, as money. (Value for-itself, equivalent etc.) How important a role money still plays in this role – even in its immediate form – is revealed in time of crises, harvest failures etc., in short, whenever one nation must *suddenly* liquidate its account with another. Money in its immediate, metallic form then appears as the sole absolute *means of payment*, i.e. as the sole *counter-value*, acceptable equivalent. And consequently it pursues a moving course which directly contradicts that of all other commodities. Commodities are transported as means of payment etc. from the country where they are cheapest to the country where they are most expensive. Money, the opposite; in all periods where it brings out its specific inner nature, where, hence, money is called for, in antithesis to all other commodities, as value for-itself, as absolute equivalent, as general form of wealth, in the specific form of gold and silver – and such moments are always more or less moments of crisis, whether a general one, or a grain crisis – then gold and silver are always transmitted from the country where they are most expensive – i.e. where all commodity prices have fallen by the relatively greatest amount – to the country where they are cheapest, i.e. where the prices of commodities are relatively higher. 'It is a singular anomaly in the economy of the exchanges, and one particularly deserving of remark, that ... the course of transit (of gold between two nations equally employing gold as a circulating medium) is always *from* the country where for the moment the metal is *dearest*, to the country where it is *cheapest*, a rise of the market price of the metal to its highest limit in the home market, and a fall of the premium in the foreign market, being the certain results of that tendency to an efflux of gold which follows a depression of the exchanges.' (J. Fullarton, *On the Regulation of Currencies* etc. 2nd ed., London, 1845, p. 119.)

Just as exchange as such begins where the communities end, and as money, as the measure, medium of exchange and general equivalent created by exchange itself, arose not in internal traffic but rather in that between different communities, peoples, etc., and there obtains its specific importance, so it was also κατ' ἐξοχήν as medium of international payments – for the liquidation of international debts – that money cast its spell, in the sixteenth century, the period of bourgeois society's infancy, holding the exclusive interest of states and of incipient political economy. The important role which money (gold and silver) in this third form still plays in international traffic has only become fully clear and been again recognized by the economists since the regular succession of money crises in 1825, 1839, 1847 and 1857. The economists try to extricate themselves by pointing out that money is called for here not as medium of circulation, but as *capital*. This is correct. Only it should not be forgotten that capital is being called for in the specific form of gold and silver, and not in that of any other commodity. Gold and silver appear in the role of absolute medium of international payments, because they are money as value-for-itself, as independent equivalent. 'This, in fact, is not a question of *currency* but of *capital*.' (It is rather a question of money, not of currency, nor of capital, because it is not *capital* which is indifferent to the special form in which it exists, but value in the specific form of money which is requested) '... all those various causes which, in the existing condition of monetary affairs, are capable ... of directing the stream of bullion from one country to another' (i.e. giving origin to a *drain of*

bullion), 'resolve themselves under a single head, namely the state
of the balance of foreign payments, and the continually recurring
necessity of transferring *capital*' (but *notabene*! capital in the
form of money) 'from one country to another to discharge it.
For example failure of crops ... Whether that capital is *transmitted in merchandise or in specie* is a point which in no way affects
the nature of the transaction' (*affects it very materially!*). Further,
war-expenditure. (The case of transmission of capital in order to
place it out to greater advantage at interest does not concern us
here; nor does that of a surplus quantity of foreign goods imported, which Mr Fullarton cites, although this case certainly
belongs here if this surplus importation coincides with crises.)
(Fullarton, loc. cit. 130, 131.) 'Gold is preferred for this transmission of capital' (but in cases of violent drains of bullion it is
absolutely not a question of preference) 'only in those cases where
it is likely to effect the payment more conveniently, promptly,
or profitably, *than any other description of stock or capital.*' (Mr
Fullarton falsely treats the transmission of gold or another form
of capital as a matter of preference, whereas the question is
precisely those cases when *gold* must be transmitted in the international trade, just as at the same time bills in the domestic trade
must be acquitted in the legal money, and not in any substitute.)
'Gold and silver ... can always be conveyed to the spot where
it is wanted with precision and celerity, and may be counted
upon to realize on its arrival nearly the exact sum required to be
provided, rather than incur the hasard of sending it in tea, coffee,
sugar, or indigo. *Gold and silver possess an infinite advantage over
all other descriptions of merchandise for such occasions*, from the
circumstance of their being universally in use as money. It is not
in tea, coffee, sugar, or indigo that debts, whether foreign or
domestic, are *usually contracted to be paid, but in coin*; and a
remittance, therefore, either in the identical coin designated, or
in bullion which can be promptly turned into that coin through
the Mint or Market of the country to which it is sent, must always
afford to the remitter the most certain, immediate, and accurate
means of effecting this object, without risk of disappointment
from the failure of demand or fluctuation of price.' (132, 133.)
Thus he cites precisely its property of being money, general
commodity of contracts, standard of values, and with the possibility of being immediately converted at liberty in medium of
circulation. The English have the apt expression *currency* for

money as medium of circulation (*Münze*, coin, does not correspond to this, because it is itself the medium of circulation in a particular form again) and *money* for it in its third attribute. But since they have not particularly developed the latter, they declare this money to be *capital*, although they are then in practice forced to distinguish again between this particular form of capital, and capital generally.

'Ricardo appears to have entertained very peculiar and extreme opinions as to the limited extent of the offices performed by gold and silver in the adjustment of foreign balances. Mr Ricardo had passed his life amid the controversies which grew out of the Restriction Act,[102] and had accustomed himself so long to consider all the great fluctuations of exchange and of the price of gold as the result of the excessive issues of the Bank of England, that at one time he seemed scarcely willing to allow that such a thing could exist as an adverse balance of commercial payments ... And so slight an account did he set on the functions performed by gold in such adjustments, as to have even anticipated that *drains* for *exportation* would cease altogether so soon as cash payments should be resumed, and the currency restored to the metallic level ... (See *Ricardo's Evidence before the Lords' Committee of 1819 on the Bank of England*, p. 186.) ... But since 1800, when paper quite displaced gold in England, our merchants did not really want it; for, owing to the unsettled state of continental Europe, and the increased consumption there of imported manufactures, in consequence of the interruption given to industry and to all domestic improvement by the incessant movement of invading armies, together with the complete monopoly of the colonial trade which England had obtained through her naval superiority, the export of commodities from Great Britain to the Continent continued greatly to exceed her imports from thence, so long as the intercourse remained open; and after that intercourse was interrupted by the Berlin and Milan decrees, the transactions of trade became much too insignificant to affect exchanges in one way or the other. It was the foreign military expenditures and the subsidies, and not the necessities of commerce, that contributed in so extraordinary a manner to derange the exchanges and enhance the price of bullion in the latter years of the war. The distinguished economists of that period, therefore, had

102. The Bank Restriction Act of 1797, under which the Bank of England was allowed to suspend cash payments.

few or no real opportunities of practically estimating the range of which foreign *commercial* balances are susceptible.' (Believed that with war and over-issue, the international transmission of bullion would cease.) 'Had Mr Ricardo lived to witness the drains of 1825 and 1839, he would no doubt have seen reason to alter his views.' (loc. cit. 133–6.)

Price is the *money value* of commodities. (Hubbard.)[103] Money has the quality of being always exchangeable for what it measures, and the quantity required for the purposes of exchange must vary, of course, according to the quantity of property to be exchanged. (100. J. W. Bosanquet. *Metallic, Paper, and Credit Currency* etc., London, 1842.) 'I am ready to admit that gold is a commodity in such general demand that it may always command a market, that it can always buy [all] other commodities; whereas, other commodities cannot always buy gold. The markets of the world are open to it as merchandise at less sacrifice upon an emergency than would attend an export of any other article, which might in quantity or kind be beyond the usual demand in the country to which it is sent.' (Th. Tooke. *An Enquiry into the Currency Principle* etc., 2nd ed., London, 1844, p. 10.) 'There must be a very considerable amount of the precious metals applicable and applied as the most convenient mode of adjustment of international balances, being a commodity more generally in demand, and less liable to fluctuations in market value than any other.' (p. 12, 13.)

(Causes, according to Fullarton, of the rise of bullion price above the mint price: 'Coin debased by wear to the extent of 3 or 4% below its standard weight; ... penal laws which prohibited the melting and exportation of the coin, while the traffic in the metal of which that coin was composed remained perfectly free. These causes themselves, however, acted only during periods of unfavourable rate of exchange ... [The market price of money] fell, however, from 1816 to 1821 always to the *bank price* of bullion, when the exchange in favour of England; never rose higher, when the exchange unfavourable, than to such a rate as would indemnify the melters of the coin for its degradation by wear and for the penal consequences of melting it, but rose no higher.' (Fullarton, see his book, p. 8, 9.) 'From 1819 to the present time, amid all the vicissitudes which the money has undergone during that eventful period, the market-price of gold has on no occasion

103. J. G. Hubbard, *The Currency and the Country*, London, 1843, p. 33.

risen above 78s. per oz., nor fallen below 77s. 6d., an extreme range of only 6 in the ounce. Nor would even that extent of fluctuation be now possible; for it was solely owing to the renewed deterioration of the coin that even so trivial a rise occurred as $1\frac{1}{2}$d. in the ounce, or about $\frac{1}{6}$% above the Mint-price; and the fall to 77s. 6d. is entirely accounted for by the circumstance of the Bank having at one time thought proper to establish that rate as the limit for its purchases. Those circumstances, however, exist no longer. For many years the Bank has been in the practice of allowing 77s. 9d. for all the gold brought to it for coinage' (i.e. the bank pockets $1\frac{1}{2}$d. mintage, which the coin gives it free of charge); 'and as soon as the recoinage of sovereigns now in progress shall be completed, there will be an effectual bar, until the coin shall again become deteriorated, to any future fluctuation of the price of gold bullion in our market beyond the small fractional difference between 77s. 9d. allowed by the Bank, and the Mint-price of 77s. $10\frac{1}{2}$d.' (loc. cit. p. 9, 10.)

Contradiction between money as measure and equivalent on one side and as medium of circulation. In the latter, abrasion, loss of metallic weight. Garnier already remarks that 'if a somewhat worn *écu* were taken as being worth somewhat less than a quite new one, then circulation would be constantly hampered, and every payment would give rise to disputes.'[104]

(The material designed for accumulation naturally sought for and chosen from the realm of *minerals.* Garnier.)[105]

'It being obvious that the coinage, in the very nature of things, must be forever, unit by unit, falling under depreciation by the mere action of ordinary and unavoidable abrasion (to say nothing of the inducement which a very restoration of the coinage holds out to the whole legion of "players" and "sweaters"), it is a physical impossibility at any time, even for a single day, utterly to exterminate light coins from circulation.' (*The Currency Theory reviewed* etc. By a Banker in England. Edinburgh, 1845, p. 69.) This written December 1844 commenting upon the operation of the then recent proclamations respecting the light gold in

104. Garnier, *Histoire de la monnaie*, Vol. I, p. 24.
105. ibid., p. 7.

circulation in a letter to *The Times*. (Hence difficulty: If the light money is refused, then all standards insecure. If it is accepted, then door is opened to fraud and the same result.) That is why he says, in regard to the above-cited proclamations: 'The effect ... has virtually been to denounce the whole of the current gold coin as an unsafe and illegal medium for monetary transactions.' (p. 68, 69, loc. cit.) 'In English law, when a gold sovereign is more than 0·774 grains deficient in weight, it may no longer pass as current. No such law for silver money.' (54. Wm H. Morrison, *Observations on the System of Metallic Currency Adopted in this Country,* London, 1837.)

Assertion by the currency people that the value of a currency depends on its quantity. (Fullarton, p. 13.) If the value of the currency is given, and prices and the mass of transactions likewise (as well as the velocity of circulation), then of course only a *specific quantity* can circulate. Given prices and the mass of transactions as well as the velocity of circulation, then this quantity depends exclusively on the *value* of the currency. Given this value and the velocity of circulation, it depends exclusively on prices and on the mass of transactions. In this way is the quantity determined. If, however, the money in circulation is representative money – mere value-symbols – then it depends on the standard they represent what quantity of them can circulate. From this it has been wrongly concluded that quantity alone determines its value. For example, paper chits representing pounds cannot circulate in the same quantity as those which represent shillings.

Profit-bearing capital is the real capital, value posited as simultaneously self-reproducing and multiplying, and as constantly self-equivalent presupposition, distinguished from itself as surplus value posited by itself. Interest-bearing capital is in turn the purely abstract form of profit-bearing capital.

Since capital is posited as profit-bearing, in accordance with its value (presupposing a specific stage of the force of production), the commodity – or the commodity posited in its form as money (in its corresponding form as independent value, or, as we may now say, as realized capital) – may enter into circulation as *capital*; it may become a commodity, *as capital*. In this case, it is capital lent out at interest. The form of its circulation – or of the exchange it undergoes – then appears as specifically distinct from that examined hitherto. We have seen that capital posits itself both in the role of the commodity and in the role of money; but this happens only in so far as both appear as moments of the circulation of capital, in which it alternately realizes itself. These are only its vanishing and constantly re-created modes of existence, moments of its life's process. But capital as capital, capital itself as commodity, has not itself become a moment of circulation. The commodity has not been sold as capital; nor money as capital. In a word, neither commodity nor money – and we need actually regard only the latter as the adequate form – have entered into circulation as *profit-bearing values*.

Maclaren says:

' "Mr Tooke, Mr Fullarton, and Mr Wilson consider money as possessing intrinsic value as a commodity, and exchanging with goods according to that value, and not merely in accordance with the supply of pieces at the time; and they suppose with Dr Smith that exports of bullion are made quite irrespective of the state of the currency, to discharge balances of international debt, and to pay for commodities such as corn, for which there is a sudden demand, and that they are taken from a fund which forms no part of the internal circulation, nor affects prices, but is set apart for these purposes ... Difficulty in explaining in what manner the bullion they say is set apart for this purpose, and has no effect on prices, can escape the laws of supply and demand, and though existing in the shape of money lying unemployed and known for the making of purchases, is neither applied for that purpose nor affects prices by the possibility of its being so applied." The reply to this is, that the stock of bullion in question represents surplus-capital, not surplus-income, and is not available, therefore, merely to increase the demand for commodities, except on condition of increasing also the supply. Capital in search of employment is not a pure addition to the demanding power of the community. It cannot be lost in the currency. If it tends to raise prices by a demand, it tends to lower them by a corresponding supply. Money, as the security for capital, is not a mere purchasing power – it purchases only in order to sell, and finally goes abroad in exchange for foreign commodities rather than disburse itself in merely adding to the currency at home. Money, as the security for capital, never comes into the market so as to be set off against commodities, because its purpose is to produce commodities; it is only the money which represents *consumption* that can finally affect prices.' (*Economist*, 15 May '58.)[106]

'Mr Ricardo maintained that prices depend on the relative amount of the circulating medium and of commodities respectively, and that prices rise only through a depreciation of the currency, that is, from a too great abundance of it in proportion to commodities, that they fall either from a reduction in the amount of the currency, or from a relative increase in the stock of general commodities which it circulates. *All* the bullion and gold coin in the country is, according to Mr Ricardo, to be reckoned currency, and if this increases without a corresponding increase in commodities, the currency is depreciated, and it becomes profitable to export bullion rather than commodities. On the other hand, if a bad harvest or any other calamity cause a great destruction of commodities, without any corresponding change in the amount of the circulation, the currency, whose amount was proportioned to the estimated rather than to the suddenly reduced market of commodities, again becomes redundant or "depreciated", and must be diminished by exportation before its value can be restored. According to this view of the circulation, which is at the root of Lord Overstone's theory, the supply of circulating medium or currency is always capable of being indefinitely increased in amount, and diminishes in value according to that increase; and can be restored to its proper value only by exportation of the superabundant portion. Any issue, therefore, of paper money which might supply the gap caused by the exportation of the bullion, and so prevent the "natural" fall of prices otherwise certain to ensue, is held by Mr Ricardo's school to be an interference with the economical laws of price, and a departure from the principles which would necessarily regulate a purely metallic currency.' (loc. cit.)

106. *The Economist*, Vol. XVI, No. 768, 15 May 1858, pp. 536–7, article by James Maclaren, entitled 'Literature. A Sketch of the *History of the Currency, comprising a Brief Review of the Opinions of the Most Eminent Writers on the Subject*'.

(1) Value

This section to be brought forward.

The first category in which bourgeois wealth presents itself is that of the *commodity*. The commodity itself appears as unity of two aspects. It is *use value*, i.e. object of the satisfaction of any system whatever of human needs. This is its material side, which the most disparate epochs of production may have in common, and whose examination therefore lies beyond political economy. Use value falls within the realm of political economy as soon as it becomes modified by the modern relations of production, or as it, in turn, intervenes to modify them. What it is customary to say about it in general terms, for the sake of good form, is confined to commonplaces which had a historic value in the first beginnings of the science, when the social forms of bourgeois production had still laboriously to be peeled out of the material, and, at great effort, to be established as independent objects of study. In fact, however, the use value of the commodity is a given presupposition – the material basis in which a specific economic relation presents itself. It is only this specific relation which stamps the use value as a commodity. Wheat, e.g., possesses the same use value, whether cultivated by slaves, serfs or free labourers. It would not lose its use value if it fell from the sky like snow. Now how does use value become transformed into commodity? Vehicle of *exchange value*. Although directly united in the commodity, use value and exchange value just as directly split apart. Not only does the exchange value not appear as determined by the use value, but rather, furthermore, the commodity only becomes a commodity, only realizes itself as exchange value, in so far as its owner does not relate to it as use value. He appropriates use values only through their sale [*Entäusserung*], their exchange for other commodities. Appropriation through sale is the fundamental form of the social system of production, of which exchange value appears as the simplest, most abstract expression. The use value of the commodity is presupposed, not for its owner, but rather for the society generally. (Just as a Manchester family of factory workers, where the children stand in the exchange relation towards their parents and pay them room and board, does not represent the traditional economic organization of the family, so is the system of modern private exchange not the spontaneous economy of societies. Exchange begins not between the individuals within a community, but rather at the point where the communities end – at their boundary, at the point of contact between different communities. Communal property has recently been rediscovered as a special Slavonic curiosity. But, in fact, India offers us a sample chart of the most diverse forms of such economic communities, more or less dissolved, but still completely recognizable; and a more thorough research into history uncovers it as the point of departure of all cultured peoples. The system of production founded on private exchange is, to begin with, the historic dissolution of this naturally arisen communism. However, a whole series of economic systems lies in turn between the modern world, where exchange value dominates production to its whole depth and extent, and the social formations whose foundation is already formed by the dissolution of communal property, without

[Here the manuscript breaks off.]

[BASTIAT AND CAREY][107]

Bastiat. Harmonies économiques. *2 édition Paris, 1851*

Foreword

The history of modern political economy ends with Ricardo and Sismondi: antitheses, one speaking English, the other French – just as it begins at the end of the seventeenth century with Petty and Boisguillebert. Subsequent political-economic literature loses its way, moving either towards eclectic, syncretistic compendia, such as e.g. the work of J. St. Mill, or into deeper elaboration of individual branches, such as e.g. Tooke's *History of Prices* and, in general, the newer English writings about circulation – the only branch in which real new discoveries have been made, since the works about colonization, landed property (in its various forms), population etc. actually differ from the older ones only in the greater completeness of their material – or the reproduction of old economic disputes for a wider public, and the practical solution of questions of the day, such as the writings on free trade and protection – or, finally, into tendentious exaggerations of the classical tendencies, a relation which e.g. Chalmers occupies toward Malthus and Gülich to Sismondi, as well as in certain respects the older writings of MacCulloch and Senior to Ricardo. It is altogether a literature of epigones; reproduction, greater elaboration of form, wider appropriation of material, exaggeration, popularization, synopsis, elaboration of details; lack of decisive leaps in the phases of development, incorporation of the inventory on one side, new growth at individual points on the other. The only exceptions seem to be the writings of Carey, the Yankee, and Bastiat,

---

107. This is the earliest part of the manuscript of 1857–8; it was written in July 1857. It occupies the first seven pages of a notebook which, when it became part of the *Grundrisse* manuscript, obtained the designation 'Notebook III'. (See p. 293, n. 1.)

the Frenchman, the latter of whom confesses that he leans on the former.[108] Both grasp that the antithesis to political economy – namely socialism and communism – finds its theoretical presupposition in the works of classical political economy itself, especially in Ricardo, who must be regarded as its complete and final expression. Both of them therefore find it necessary to attack, as a misunderstanding, the theoretical expression which the bourgeois economy has achieved historically in modern economics, and to demonstrate the harmony of the relations of production at the points where the classical economists naïvely described this antagonism. Notwithstanding the altogether different, even contradictory national environment from within which each of them writes, they are driven to identical endeavours. Carey is the only original economist among the North Americans. Belongs to a country where bourgeois society did not develop on the foundation of the feudal system, but developed rather from itself; where this society appears not as the surviving result of a centuries-old movement, but rather as the starting-point of a new movement; where the state, in contrast to all earlier national formations, was from the beginning subordinate to bourgeois society, to its production, and never could make the pretence of being an end-in-itself; where, finally, bourgeois society itself, linking up the productive forces of an old world with the enormous natural terrain of a new one, has developed to hitherto unheard-of dimensions and with unheard-of freedom of movement, has far outstripped all previous work in the conquest of the forces of nature, and where, finally, even the antitheses of bourgeois society itself appear only as vanishing moments. That the relations of production within which this enormous new world has developed so quickly, so surprisingly and so happily should be regarded by Carey as the eternal, normal relations of social production and intercourse, that these should seem to him as hampered and damaged by the inherited barriers of the feudal period, in Europe, especially England, which actually represents Europe to him, and that the English economists should appear to him to give a distorted, falsified reflection, generalization of these relations, that they should seem to him to confuse accidental distortions of the latter with their intrinsic character – what could be more natural? American relations against English ones: to this his critique of the English theory of landed property, wages, population, class anti-

108. Bastiat, *Harmonies économiques*, p. 364 n.

theses etc. may be reduced. In England, bourgeois society does not exist in pure form, not corresponding to its concept, not adequate to itself. How then could the English economists' concepts of bourgeois society be the true, undimmed expression of a reality, since that reality was unknown to them? In the last analysis, the disturbing effect which traditional influences, influences not arising from the womb of bourgeois society itself, exercise upon its *natural* relations reduces itself for Carey to the influence, to the excesses and interferences of the state in bourgeois society. It is in the nature of wages, e.g., to rise with the productivity of labour. If we find that reality contradicts this law, then, whether in Hindustan or in England, we have only to abstract from the influence of the government, taxes, monopolies etc. If the bourgeois relations are regarded in themselves, i.e. after deduction of state influences, they will indeed always confirm the harmonic laws of the bourgeois economy. The question to what extent these state influences, public debt, taxes etc., grow out of the bourgeois relations themselves – and hence, e.g. in England, in no way appear as results of feudalism, but rather as results of its dissolution and defeat, and in North America itself the power of the central government grows with the centralization of capital – is one which Carey naturally does not raise. While Carey thus brings the higher power to which bourgeois society is developed in North America to bear against the English economists, Bastiat brings to bear the lower power of bourgeois society in France, against the French socialists. You believe yourselves to be rebelling against the laws of bourgeois society, in a land where these laws were never allowed to realize themselves! You only know them in the stunted French form, and regard as their inherent form what is merely its French national distortion. Look across, at England. Here, in our own country, the task is to free bourgeois society from the fetters which the state imposes on it. You want to multiply these fetters. First work out the bourgeois relations in their pure form, and then we may talk again. (Bastiat has a point, in so far as in France, owing to its peculiar social formation, many a thing is considered socialism that counts in England as political economy.)

Carey, however, whose point of departure is the American emancipation of bourgeois society from the state, ends with the call for state intervention, so that the pure development of bourgeois relations is not disturbed by external forces, as in fact happened in America. He is a protectionist, while Bastiat is a freetrader. All over the world, the harmony of economic laws appears as disharmony, and even Carey himself is struck by the beginnings of this disharmony in the United States. What is the source of this strange phenomenon? Carey explains it with the destructive influence of England, with its striving for industrial monopoly, upon the world market. Originally, the English relations were distorted by the false theories of her economists, internally. Now, externally, as the commanding power of the world market, England distorts the harmony of economic relations in all the countries of the world. This disharmony is a real one, not one merely based on the subjective conceptions of the economists. What Russia is, politically, for Urquhart, England is, economically, for Carey. The harmony of economic relations rests, according to Carey, on the harmonious cooperation of town and countryside, industry and agriculture. Having dissolved this fundamental harmony in its own interior, England, by its competition, proceeds to destroy it throughout the world market, and is thus the destructive element of the general harmony. The only defence lies in protective tariffs – the forcible, national barricade against the destructive power of large-scale English industry. Hence, the state, which was at first branded the sole disturber of these '*harmonies économiques*', is now these harmonies' last refuge. On the one side, Carey here again articulates the specific national development of the United States, their antithesis to and competition with England. This takes place in the naïve form of suggesting to the United States that they destroy the industrialism propagated by England, so as, by protective tariffs, to develop the same more rapidly themselves. This naïveté apart, with Carey the harmony of the bourgeois relations of production ends with the most complete disharmony of these relations on the grandest terrain where they appear, the world market, and in their grandest development, as the relations of producing nations. All the relations which appear harmonious to him within specific national boundaries or, in addition, in the abstract form of general relations of bourgeois society – e.g. concentration of capital, division of labour, wage labour etc. – appear as disharmonious to him where they appear in their most developed form – in their world market form – as the internal relations which produce English domination on the world market, and which, as destructive influences, are the consequence of this domination. If patriarchal gives way to industrial production within a country, this is harmonious, and the process of dissolution which accompanies this development is conceived in its positive aspect alone. But it becomes disharmonious when large-scale English industry dissolves the patriarchal or petty-bourgeois or other lower stages of production in a foreign country. The concentration of capital within a country and the dissolving effect of this concentration present nothing but positive sides to him. But the monopoly of concentrated English capital and its dissolving effect on the smaller national capitals of other countries is disharmonious. What Carey has not grasped is that these world-market disharmonies are merely the ultimate adequate expressions of the disharmonies which have become fixed as abstract relations within the economic categories or which have a local existence on the smallest scale. No wonder, then, that he in turn forgets the positive content of these processes of dissolution – the only side he recognizes in the economic categories in their abstract form, or in the real relations within the specific countries from which they are abstracted – when he comes to their full appearance, the world market. Hence, where the economic relations confront him in their truth, i.e. in their universal reality, his principled optimism turns into a denunciatory, irritated pessimism. This contradiction forms the originality of his writings and gives them their significance. He is equally an American in his assertion of the harmony within bourgeois society, as in his assertion of the disharmony of the same relations in their world-market form. In Bastiat, none of this. The harmony of these relations is a world beyond, which begins just at the point where the boundaries of France end; which exists in England and America. This is merely the imaginary, ideal form of the un-French, the Anglo-American relations, not the real form such as he confronts it on his own land and soil. Hence, as with him the harmony in no way arises out of the abundance of living observation, but is rather the *flat*, stilted product of a thin, drawn, antithetical reflection, hence the only moment of reality with him is the demand that the French state should give up its economic boundaries. Carey sees the contradictions in the economic relations as soon as they appear on the world market as *English* relations. Bastiat, who merely imagines the harmony, begins to see its realization only at the point where France ceases, and where all nationally separate component parts of bourgeois society compete among one another liberated from the supervision of the state. This ultimate among his harmonies – and the presupposition of all his earlier, imaginary ones – is however itself in turn merely a postulate, which is supposed to be realized through free-trade legislation. Thus, while Carey, quite apart from the scientific value of his researches, has at least the merit of articulating in abstract form the large-scale American relations, and, what is more, of doing so in antithesis to the old world, the only real background in Bastiat would be the small scale of the French relations, which everywhere poke their long ears through his harmonies. Still, this meritorious contribution is superfluous, because the relations of so old a country are sufficiently known and least of all require to become known by so negative a detour. Carey is rich, therefore, in, so to speak, *bonafide* research in economic science, such as about credit, rent, etc. Bastiat is preoccupied merely with pacifying paraphrases of researches ending in contrasts; hypocrisy of contentment. Carey's generality is Yankee universality. France and China are equally close to him. Always the man who lives on the Pacific and the Atlantic. Bastiat's generality is to ignore all countries. As a genuine Yankee, Carey absorbs from all directions the massive material furnished him by the old world, not so as to recognize the inherent soul of this material, and thus to concede to it the right to its peculiar life, but rather so as to work it up for his purposes, as indifferent raw material, as inanimate documentation for his theses, abstracted from his Yankee standpoint. Hence his strayings and wanderings through all countries, massive and uncritical use of statistics, a catalogue-like erudition. Bastiat, by contrast, presents fantasy history, his abstractions sometimes in the form of arguments, another time in the form of supposed events, which however have never and nowhere happened, just as a theologian treats sin sometimes as the law of human existence, then at other times as the story of the fall from grace. Hence both are equally unhistorical and anti-historical. But the unhistoric moment in Carey is the contemporary historic principle of North America, while the unhistoric element in Bastiat is a mere reminiscence of the French eighteenth-century manner of generalizing. Hence Carey is formless and diffuse, Bastiat affected and formally-logical. The most he achieves is commonplaces, expressed paradoxically, ground and polished into facets. With Carey, a couple of general theses, advanced in schoolmasterly form. Following them, a shapeless material, compendium, as documentation – the substance of his theses in no way digested. With Bastiat, the only material – abstracting from a few local examples, or whimsically refashioned English trivia – consists in the general theses of the economists.

Carey's chief antithesis, Ricardo, in short, the modern English economists; Bastiat's, the French socialists.

XIV. On Wages

The following are Bastiat's main theses: All men strive for constancy of income, *fixed revenue*. ⟨Truly French example: (1) All men want to be civil servants or make their sons civil servants. (p. 371.)⟩ Wages are a fixed form of remuneration (p. 376) and hence a very perfect form of association, in whose original form 'the aleatory' predominates, in so far as 'all the associated' are subject to 'all the risks of the enterprise'. ⟨If capital takes the risk on its own account, the remuneration of labour becomes established under the name *wages*. If labour wants to take the consequences, good and bad, then the remuneration of capital splits off and establishes itself under the name *interest* (382).⟩ (On this juxtaposition, see further p. 382, 383.) However, while the aleatory originally predominates in the worker's condition, the stability of wage labour is not yet sufficiently secured. There is an 'intermediate degree which separates the aleatory from stability'. This last stage is reached by 'saving, during days of work, the means to provide for the needs of days of old age and illness'. (p. 388.) The final stage develops by means of 'mutual aid societies' (loc. cit.) and in the final instance by means of the 'workers' *retirement fund*'. (p. 393.) (As man began with the need to become a civil servant, so he ends with the satisfaction of drawing a pension.)

As to 1. Suppose everything Bastiat says about the fixity of wages to be correct. Then we would still not know the *proper character* of wages, its characteristic specificity, simply because wages are subsumed under the fixed revenues. One of its relations – which it has in common with other sources of income – would be emphasized. Nothing more. This would already be something, admittedly, for the advocate who wishes to plead the advantages of wage labour. It would still be nothing for the economist who wishes to understand the peculiarity of this relation in its entire scope. A one-sided characterization of a relation, of an economic form, so as to make it the object of panegyrics in contrast to the opposite form; this cheap practice of lawyers and apologists is what distinguishes the logician, Bastiat. Thus, in place of wages, put: fixed income. Is a fixed income not a good thing? Does not everyone love to count on a sure thing? Especially every petty-bourgeois, narrow-minded Frenchman? the 'ever-needy' man? Human bondage has been defended in the same way, perhaps on better grounds. The opposite could also be asserted, and has been asserted. Equate wages to non-fixedness, i.e. progression past a certain point. Who does not love to get ahead, instead of standing still? Can a relation be bad which makes possible an infinite bourgeois progress? Naturally, Bastiat himself in another passage asserts wages as non-fixedness. How else, apart from non-fixedness, would it be possible for the worker to stop working, to become a capitalist, as Bastiat wishes? Thus wage labour is good because it is fixedness; it is good because it is non-fixedness; it is good because it is neither one nor the other, but both at the same time. What relation is not good, if it is reduced to a one-sided characterization and the latter is regarded as position, not as negation? All opportunist chattering, all apologetics, all philistine sophistry rests on this sort of abstraction.

After this general preface, we come to Bastiat's actual construction. Only, be it noted in passing that his rural sharecropper,[109] this type who combines in himself the misfortune of the wage labourer with the bad luck of the small capitalist, might indeed consider himself fortunate if he were put on fixed wages. Proudhon's 'descriptive and philosophical history' hardly holds a candle to that of his opponent Bastiat. The original form of association, wherein all the associates share all the risks of chance, is followed, as a higher stage of association entered into voluntarily by both sides, by a form in which the worker's remuneration is fixed. We will not call attention here to the genius of a procedure which begins by presupposing a capitalist on one side and a worker on the other, so as then, afterwards, to let the relation of capital and wage labour arise between them by their mutual agreement.

The form of association in which the worker is exposed to all the chance risks of the business – in which all producers are equally exposed to these risks – and which immediately precedes the form of wages, where the remuneration of labour gains fixity, becomes stable, as thesis precedes antithesis – is, as Bastiat tells us, the state in which fishing, hunting and herding form the dominant forms of production and society. First the wandering fisherman, hunter, herdsman – and then the wage labourer. Where and when has this *historic* transition from the semi-savage state into the modern taken place? If at all, then only in the burlesque. In real history,

109. Bastiat, *Harmonies économiques*, p. 388.

wage labour arises out of the dissolution of slavery and serfdom – or of the decay of communal property, as with oriental and Slavonic peoples – and, in its adequate, epoch-making form, the form which takes possession of the entire social being of labour, out of the decline and fall of the guild economy, of the system of Estates, of labour and income in kind, of industry carried on as rural subsidiary occupation, of small-scale feudal agriculture etc. In all these real historic transitions, wage labour appears as the dissolution, the annihilation of relations in which labour was fixed on all sides, in its income, its content, its location, its scope etc. *Hence as negation of the stability of labour and of its remuneration.* The direct transition from the African's fetish to Voltaire's supreme being, or from the hunting gear of a North American savage to the capital of the Bank of England, is not so absurdly contrary to history as is the transition from Bastiat's fisherman to the wage labourer. (Furthermore, in all these developments there is no sign of voluntary changes arising from mutual agreement.) This construction – in which Bastiat dishonestly conjures up his flat abstraction in the form of a historic event – is quite of the same rank as the synthesis in which the English friendly societies and the savings banks appear as the last word of wage labour and as the suspension of all social antinomies.

Thus the historic character of wage labour is non-fixity: the opposite of Bastiat's construction. But how did he come at all to construe fixity as the all-compensating aspect of wage labour? What led him to the wish to present wage labour in this form historically in other forms of society and of association, as a higher form of the remuneration of labour?

All economists, when they come to discuss the prevailing relation of capital and wage labour, of profit and wages, and when they demonstrate to the worker that he has no legitimate claim to share in the risks of gain, when they wish to pacify him generally about his subordinate role *vis-à-vis* the capitalist, lay stress on pointing out to him that, in contrast to the capitalist, he possesses a certain fixity of income more or less independent of the great adventures of capital. Just as Don Quixote consoles Sancho Panza with the thought that, although of course he takes all the beatings, at least he is not required to be brave. Thus an attribute which the economists attach to wage labour in antithesis to profit is transformed by Bastiat into an attribute of wage labour in antithesis to earlier forms of labour, and as progress relative to the remuneration of labour in these earlier relationships. A commonplace which takes up the standpoint of the prevailing relation, which consoles one of its sides towards the other, is taken out of this relation by Mr Bastiat and turned into the historic foundation of this relation's origin. In the relation of wages to profit, wage labour to capital, say the economists, wages have the advantage of fixity. Mr Bastiat says this fixity, i.e. one of the aspects of the relation of wages to profit, is the historical foundation on which wage labour arose (or, is an attribute of wages in antithesis not to profit, but rather to the earlier forms of the remuneration of labour), hence on which profit, hence the whole relation arose likewise. Thus a truism about one facet of the relation of wages and profit is surreptitiously transformed for him into the historic basis of this whole relation. This happens because he is constantly preoccupied by reflections upon socialism, which latter is then dreamed to be everywhere the first form of association. This an example of the importance assumed in Bastiat's hands by the apologetic commonplaces which accompany the course of development in the economists' writings.

To return to the economists. Of what does this fixity of wages consist? Are wages immutably fixed? This would altogether contradict the law of demand and supply, the basis of the determination of wages. No economist denies the fluctuations, the rise and fall of wages. Or are wages independent of crises? Or of machines which make wage labour redundant? Or of divisions of labour, which displace it? To assert any of this would be heterodox, and it is not asserted. What is meant is that in a certain average, wages realize a fair average level, i.e. the minimum wage for the whole class, a concept so hateful to Bastiat, and that a certain average continuity of labour takes place, e.g. that wages may continue on even in cases where profit falls or momentarily disappears entirely. Now, what does this mean other than that, if wage labour is presupposed as the dominant form of labour, as the foundation of production, then the working class exists from wages, and that labour individually possesses, on the average, the fixity of working for wages? In other words, a tautology. Where capital and wage labour is the dominant relation of production, there exists an average continuity of wage labour, and, to that extent, a fixity of wages for the worker. Where wage labour exists, it exists. And this is regarded by Bastiat as its all-compensating attribute. Furthermore, that in the state of society where capital is developed, social production as a whole is more regular, continuous, all-sided – hence, also, the income of the elements employed in it 'more fixed' – than where capital, i.e. production, is not yet developed to this stage, is yet another tautology which is given with the concept of capital itself and of production resting on it. In other words: that the general presence of wage labour presupposes a higher development of the productive forces than in the stages preceding wage labour, who denies this? And what would lead the socialists to the idea of raising higher demands if they did not presuppose this higher development of the forces of social production, brought about by wage labour? The latter is rather the presupposition of their demands.

Note. The first form in which wages make their general appearance – military pay [*Sold*], which arises with the decline and fall of national armies and of citizens' militias. First, the citizens themselves are paid as soldiers. Soon after that, their place is taken by mercenaries who have ceased to be citizens.

(2) (*It is impossible to pursue this nonsense any further. We, therefore, drop Mr Bastiat.*)

Note on Previous Editions of the
Works of Marx and Engels

Until recently there existed no complete edition of the works of Marx and Engels in any language. The Marx-Engels Institute, under its director D. Ryazanov, began to produce such an edition in the late 1920s; the collapse of the project in 1935 was no doubt connected with Ryazanov's dismissal and subsequent disappearance. However, eleven indispensable volumes did emerge between 1927 and 1935, under the title *Karl Marx – Friedrich Engels: Historisch-Kritische Gesamtausgabe*, commonly referred to as the *MEGA* edition. The *MEGA* contains the works of both men down to 1848, and their correspondence, but nothing more. For the next thirty years, the field was held by the almost inaccessible Russian edition, the Marx-Engels *Sochineniya* (twenty-five volumes, 1928–46).

Only in 1968 did the East Germans complete the first German definitive edition, the forty-one volume *Marx-Engels Werke* (*MEW*). Until then, the works of Marx and Engels existed only in separate editions and smaller collections on specific themes. For this reason, the translations into English have followed the same pattern – innumerable pamphlets and brochures issued individually by Lawrence and Wishart on one side; the three volumes of *Capital* and the two volumes of the *Marx-Engels Selected Works* (*MESW*) on the other. Now things are beginning to change: the *MESW* have been expanded to three volumes, and Lawrence and Wishart have produced a complete translation of the three-volume work *Theories of Surplus Value*. They also plan to issue a complete English-language edition based on the *MEW* (which will inevitably take time). Finally, there is the present edition, the Pelican Marx Library. This occupies an intermediate position between the *MESW* and the projected complete edition. It brings together the majority of Marx's larger works, including the *Grundrisse*, a number of previously unavailable minor works, and the well-known classic texts of Marxism, such as the *Manifesto*.

Chronology of the Works of Marx and Engels

Date[1]	Author[2]	Title	English edition[3]
1843	M	*Critique of Hegel's Doctrine of the State*	P *EW*
1843	M	*On the Jewish Question*	P *EW*
1843–4	M	*A Contribution to the Critique of Hegel's Philosophy of Right: Introduction*	P *EW*
1844	M	*Excerpts from James Mill's* Elements of Political Economy	P *EW*
1844	E	*Outlines of a Critique of Political Economy*	*EPM* App.
1844	M	*Economic and Philosophical Manuscripts*	P *EW*
1844	M	*Critical Notes on the Article 'The King of Prussia and Social Reform. By a Prussian'*	P *EW*
1844	M & E	*The Holy Family, or a Critique of Critical Critique*	LW 1957
1844–5	E	*Condition of the Working Class in England*	Blackwell 1958
1845	M	*Theses on Feuerbach*	*MESW I*
1845–6	M & E	*The German Ideology*	LW 1964

---

1. Date of composition, except for *Capital*, where the date of first publication is given.

2. M = Marx, E = Engels.

3. The following abbreviations are used:

EPM App.: Appendix to Marx, *Economic and Philosophical Manuscripts of 1844,* Lawrence and Wishart, 1959.

LW: Lawrence and Wishart.

MESW: *Karl Marx and Frederick Engels, Selected Works in Three Volumes,* Progress Publishers, 1969.

P: Pelican Marx Library.

P *EW*: *Early Writings* (Pelican Marx Library).

P *FI*: *The First International and After* (Pelican Marx Library).

P *R1848*: *The Revolutions of 1848* (Pelican Marx Library).

P *SE*: *Surveys from Exile* (Pelican Marx Library).

Date	Author	Title	English edition
1846–7	M	*The Poverty of Philosophy*	LW 1956
1847	M & E	*Speeches on Poland*	P *R1848*
1847	M	*Wage-Labour and Capital*	MESW 1
1847–8	M & E	*Manifesto of the Communist Party*	P *R1848*
1848	M & E	*Speeches on Poland*	P *R1848*
1848	M & E	*Demands of the Communist Party in Germany*	P *R1848*
1848–9	M & E	*Articles in the* Neue Rheinische Zeitung	P *R1848* (selection)
1850 (March)	M & E	*Address of the Central Committee to the Communist League*	P *R1848*
1850 (June)	M & E	*Address of the Central Committee to the Communist League*	P *R1848*
1850	M & E	*Reviews from the* Neue Rheinische Zeitung. Revue	P *R1848*
1850	M	*The Class Struggle in France, 1848 to 1850*	P *SE*
1850	E	*The Peasants' War in Germany*	LW 1956
1851–2	E	*Revolution and Counter-Revolution in Germany*	MESW I
1852	M	*The Eighteenth Brumaire of Louis Bonaparte*	P *SE*
1852	M	*Revelations on the Cologne Communist Trial*	LW 1970
1856	M	*Speech at the Anniversary of the* People's Paper	P *SE*
1857–8	M	*Grundrisse*	P
1859	M	*A Contribution to the Critique of Political Economy*	LW 1971
1852–61	M & E	*Articles in the* New York Daily Tribune	P *SE* (selections)
1861	M	*Articles in* Die Presse *on the Civil War in the United States*	P *SE* (selections)
1861–3	M	*Theories of Surplus Value*, Vol. 1	LW 1967
		Vol. 2	LW 1970
		Vol. 3	LW 1972
1863	M	*Proclamation on Poland*	P *SE*
1864	M	*Inaugural Address of the International Working Men's Association*	P *FI*
1864	M	*Provisional Rules of the International Working Men's Association*	P *FI*
1865	E	*The Prussian Military Question and the German Workers' Party*	P *FI*

Date	Author	Title	English edition
1865	M	*Wages, Prices, and Profit*	*MESW II*
1866	E	*What Have the Working Classes to Do with Poland?*	P *FI*
1867	M	*Capital*, Vol. 1	P
1867	M	*Instructions for Delegates to the Geneva Congress*	P *FI*
1868	M	*Report to the Brussels Congress*	P *FI*
1869	M	*Report to the Basel Congress*	P *FI*
1870	M	*The General Council to the Federal Council of French Switzerland (a circular letter)*	P *FI*
1870	M	*First Address of the General Council on Franco-Prussian War*	P *FI*
1870	M	*Second Address of the General Council on the Franco-Prussian War*	P *FI*
1871	M	First draft of *The Civil War in France*	P *FI*
1871	M	*The Civil War in France*	P *FI*
1871	M & E	*Resolution of the London Conference on Working-Class Political Action*	P *FI*
1872	M & E	*The Alleged Splits in the International*	P *FI*
1872	M	*Report to the Hague Congress*	P *FI*
1872–3	E	*The Housing Question*	*MESW II*
1874	M	*Political Indifferentism*	P *FI*
1874	E	*On Authority*	*MESW II*
1874–5	M	*Conspectus of Bakunin's Book* Statism and Anarchy	P *FI*
1875	M & E	*For Poland*	P *FI*
1875	M	*A Critique of the Gotha Programme*	P *FI*
1876–8	E	*Anti-Dühring*	LW 1955
1879	M & E	*Circular Letter to Bebel, Liebknecht, Bracke, et al.*	P *FI*
1879–80	M	*Marginal Notes on Adolph Wagner's* Lehrbuch der politischen Ökonomie	P
1880	E	*Socialism: Utopian and Scientific*	*MESW III*
1880	M	*Introduction to the Programme of the French Workers' Party*	P *FI*
1873–83	E	*Dialectics of Nature*	LW 1954
1884	E	*The Origin of the Family, Private Property, and the State*	*MESW III*
1885	M	*Capital*, Vol. 2	P
1886	E	*Ludwig Feuerbach and the End of Classical German Philosophy*	*MESW III*
1894	M	*Capital*, Vol. 3	P

Index